Garage Sale & Flea Market

Annual

THIRD EDITION

NOSTALGIA PUBLISHING
C·O·M·P·A·N·Y

The current values in this book should be used only as a guide. They are not intended to set prices, which vary from one section of the country to another. Auction prices as well as dealer prices vary greatly and are affected by condition as well as demand. Nostalgia Publishing Co., Inc. does not assume responsibility for any losses that might be incurred as a result of consulting this guide.

On the cover top to bottom, left to right:

Bracelet, link, Bakelite, circa 1930, $75.00. Courtesy of Lisa Stroup.

Early plastic brooch, $25.00. Courtesy of Lisa Stroup.

Ohio Art child's toy drum, tin, 9½"x9". $40.00.

Roseville pottery, 3", marked #663. $35.00. Courtesy of Lisa Stroup.

Cat handle clothes brush, marked Made in Japan, 8" long. $25.00. Courtesy of Beth Summers.

Hancock Co. Creamery 1 qt. milk container, waxed cardboard. $15.00. Courtesy of B.J. Summers.

Georgian Love Bird Depression Glass creamer. $13.00. Courtesy of Lisa Stroup.

Mickey Mouse cookbook, 1975. $18.00.

· · · ● · · · ● · · ● · · · ● · · · ● · · · ● · · · ● · · · ● · · ·

Nostalgia Publishing Co. Inc.
P.O. Box 277
La Center, Kentucky 42056

· · · ● · · · ● · · ● · · · ● · · · ● · · · ● · · · ● · · ·

A Word from the Editor

If baseball is America's favorite pastime, then garage sales have to be the second. Personally, I'm skeptical of that order. And I'm assuming, since you were interested enough to pick up a book with a title like *The Garage Sale and Flea Market Annual* in the first place, that you yourself are either already addicted or at the very least you're wondering what the rest of us are up to, whether you want to admit it or not. Whatever our motives were when we began to make the garage sale rounds — furnishing our first little apartment, picking up some inexpensive items for the nursery, or just to get out for some fresh air — very few of us have remained oblivious to the fact that in addition to useable everyday items, many times you can find some good antiques and collectibles as well, and more likely than not, they can be had for a song. Even if you're not familiar with antiques, chances are you may have bought a few of the nice older pieces that especially appealed to you. Now you'd like to know a little about their history, and you're probably curious about their worth. That's just what this book is about. Though most price guides cover 18th- and 19th-century antiques and some of the 20th-century collectibles that are already well established, for the most part we've concentrated on items that have been made since the 1930s — the very things you'll be finding on your garage sale rounds.

Let's imagine a typical garage sale: maybe some lamps, an old rocking chair, a bookcase full of old books, and a huge box of old Christmas ornaments line one side of the driveway. On the opposite side there's a box of assorted odds and ends with a cardboard sign taped to one end that reads 'Choice, 50¢.' Next to that there may be a clothes rack with some old hat boxes on the shelf above it — maybe a purse or two.

Once inside the garage you spot a pile of jewelry sealed up in plastic sandwich bags, odds and ends of glassware and china, a stack of old games and puzzles, kid's toys and dolls on the floor under the table, old records next to that, and off in the corner, several old tools thrown in a heap. If you're really into this scene, your mind is spinning. If you're not, you probably glance over the merchandise and leave empty handed, unless you see something you think you might find use for.

But let's go back and start up that drive again. Is that just any old lamp? Or is it an Aladdin? Every one is after their kerosene lamps, but during the 1930s to the 1950s, they were also a leading manufacturer of electric lamps. Many are collectible, but this isn't common knowledge. Someone — you, if you're sharp enough to take notice — could leave with a beautiful electric Aladdin in tow. And the rocker . . . Mission style? Check for a maker's mark. A Stickley Brothers' rocker is worth a minimum of $400.00. There may be a first edition in that bookcase. And don't neglect to check through the Christmas decorations very thoroughly. Blown glass ornaments and fragile Dresden candy containers may be few and far between, but a boxed string of bubble lights that still work are valued at about $50.00 and that old Santa tree topper circa 1950 at $15.00 or so. You might pick up an advertising letter opener, a deck of cards (is that Santa on the back holding a Coke?) or an unusual cigarette lighter, if you take the time to check the 50¢ box; and even if there's no vintage fur on the clothes rack, there might be vintage denims! Look for Levi products with a capital 'E' on a red tab or back pocket. Jeans with the big 'E' in good condition sell at funky fashion boutiques for $30.00 and up. And if they also have visible rivets, the price will double. Not so fast! Don't overlook the handbag — plastic purses are hot. A Lucite bag is hard to find for less than $40.00 (when you buy from a savvy dealer), and that's just for one in a plain, basic style. If it has a good Deco shape, a rhinestone handle, or is obviously a quality purse, its value would go up substantially. Look in the hat boxes. You might find a hatpin or two — or maybe some white kid gloves from the fifties. Now let's go on inside.

I'd start with the costume jewelry. The bigger, gaudier pieces first! Look for a maker's mark. With the market what it is today, if you find one and the piece is in good condition, at garage sale prices you can't go wrong. Even unmarked jewelry can be very collectible and very worthy of your attention if it is well made and has a good design. Next, unless you spot glassware or a piece of pottery you suspect might be valuable, I'd suggest you turn your attention *under* the table to those toys and games. Toys are the hot collectibles of the nineties, especially toys from the fifties through the seventies. And this is just the place to find them! Barbie dolls and GI Joe's, TV show character-related items, Transformers, robots, play sets, Hot Wheels, and model kits are just a very few of the many types of collectible toys you're very likely to run across. And Star Trek and Star Wars stuff is a shoo-in. The records — don't forget those. And check for picture sleeves on those 45s. They're usually worth more than the records!

OK, now back to the table top. Figural salt and pepper shakers bear checking out — even if they're plastic. Look for marks on the bases of any vases. McCoy advertised their success by claiming that every household in the country contained at least one piece of their pottery. I think they were right. And these days, even the most unassuming McCoy vase seems to find a ready buyer. What about that partial dinnerware set. Homer Laughlin, you say? Wonderful. It doesn't have to be Fiesta anymore; just about anything from HLC is very collectible. Times are changing!

You men shoppers would probably have hit the tools well before this point, and when you did you may have found a good old plane with a rosewood handle initialed by the maker. Or one made by Stanley, or Keen Kutter, or Winchester – any one of which could be worth well over $100.00.

Wow! What a sale! Now obviously not every one will be as exciting as our fantasy sale — we all know that. But the undisputable fact is, that armed with the knowledge this book contains, every sale you do attend will have that potential.

It's always fun to hear about those really wonderful garage sale finds. This season (here in the Midwest from spring thaw until Thanksgiving), some of my best buys were: a 'bandit raccoon' cookie jar by Metlox for 75¢ (I see them for sale at $135.00, and I bought it to sell but fell in love with it instead), a Fostoria Coin Glass fruit bowl in amber, also 75¢ (it books for $65.00), a pair of Rosemeade buffalo salt and pepper shakers for $3.00 ($75.00), a necklace with matching earrings signed Miriam Haskell also for $3.00 (it's an early set, so I'm guessing it's worth $100.00 minimum), and a San Ildefonso black-on-black bowl vase signed 'Marie and Julian' for 40¢. (I never let go of that one until I got it home — $400.00 would be a realistic value.) Among our office staff, some of the better buys were twenty pieces of Indiana Custard (Depression glass) for $6.00 (it books for $400.00), three Breyer horses at $5.00 for the lot (about a $60.00 value), a $40.00 Brush Onyx vase for 50¢, Schiaparelli earrings for 50¢, and a coral and turquoise Indian silver ring for a nickel. A friend of mine found a tall Moon and Stars candy dish in blue for $1.00 and a Shawnee Bo Peep planter for 25¢, either one of which is worth $40.00, and I know a lady who paid 50¢ for a $450.00 Fiesta vase. None of these are made up; they're all genuine garage-sale finds.

So we've made a good argument for going to garage sales. But what, you say, will I do with all that 'good stuff' once I buy it? Obviously you'll be finding bargains too good to pass up even though they're not the type of thing you personally collect or even like, for that matter. Our answer — buy and sell. Turn a profit. Not only do antiques and collectibles have sound investment potential should you decide to hold on to them and enjoy them for awhile, but by becoming a dealer, you'll find a wonderful opportunity to increase your income, perhaps by a substantial amount, depending on how involved you are willing to get. At the very least, you can certainly support your own 'habit.'

Almost everyone collects something. Antique malls are everywhere, flea markets ranging in size from a few dealers to thousands spring up at just about any fairgrounds or wide spot in the road, especially during festivals and holidays, and there are literally thousands of tradepapers, some general, some very specialized, chock full of both 'for sale' and 'wanted to buy' ads placed by dealers and collectors ranging from normal (a few) to fanatic (the majority). It's our intention herein to offer you a plan to help you enter the buying and selling market, if that is your goal, or at least to make you a more knowledgeable and perceptive collector. We'll tell you how to have your own garage sale if you first need to raise a little capitol, what's hot and what's not so you'll know what is selling, and then suggest several ways you might want to market your merchandise for the best profit margin. The antiques and collectibles industry is thriving, and there has never been a better time for you to get involved.

Preparing Yourself to Know a Bargain When You See It

It would do you little good to go bear hunting if you'd never seen a bear, never took time to learn the things a good hunter should know and were generally unprepared. Barring more than your share of dumb luck, chances of your being successful would be slim. When applied to hunting for antiques and collectibles, the same principles hold true. You need to be mentally prepared.

Books are an absolute necessity. Because we deal with such a wide variety of subjects, this book can only begin to scratch the surface of any one in particular. But in most of our category narratives, we've listed other reading material that will broaden your knowledge in just about any field you have taken a special interest in. The books we refer you to are written by many of today's experts and leading authorities. They contain a wealth of information that will help beginners as well as seasoned collectors and dealers develop a keen understanding of today's market. Self-published books or those published by other companies can be ordered from the authors themselves; their addresses are given in the Buyers section. You'll find your money well spent if you'll begin immediately to build a substantial library on a broad range of subjects.

In addition to books, tradepapers are a good source of information. Study the ads. Note the prices dealers are putting on their merchandise. Many papers not only feature special articles on timely subjects but report on prices realized at auction as well. And more and more quality magazines designed especially for collectors appear on today's newsstands and supermarket checkout aisles. One of the features of this book is the section called *Clubs, Newsletters and Other Publications*. If you're not already familiar with a good tradepaper, refer to this section. We've also listed hundreds of clubs and newsletters that cater to collectors in virtually every field of interest from 'a' to 'z.'

Attend collector shows in your area. Go to antique malls. You'll have thousands of mental images to draw upon when you're out shopping at garage sales. This learning process is gradual. But I've always found that it doesn't take long to be able to recognize garage-sale bargains having first seen similar merchandise on flea market tables or in show booths. And you'll find that just about any dealer will be glad to answer your questions, providing they aren't busy dealing with customers at the moment.

If you're a novice, it will probably be best at first to choose a few areas that you find most interesting and learn just what particular examples or types of items are most in demand within that field. Obviously no one can be an expert in everything, but gradually you can begin to broaden your knowledge. I recommend that within each of these fields you concentrate on the better items. These things are always sure sellers. Most market activity centers around harder-to-find, high-quality merchandise, and that is where you'll find the most satisfaction as a dealer. Common, run-of-the-mill items seldom bring book price, simply because most collectors would rather seek out bargains, knowing that because they are plentiful, there's a good chance not much 'leg work' will be required. Supply and demand dictate prices, and when an item is in good supply, prices become very competitive.

How to Hold Your Own Garage Sale

Let's suppose now that you've followed my advice so far, you've done your legwork and your homework, and the idea of supplementing you income (or subsidising your collecting habit) sounds better all the time. You're ready to try your hand at discovering those bargains. How about having your own garage sale first, so you'll have a little capital of your own to begin with? Having a garage sale can be fun as well as profitable. Everyone has items they no longer use, and you can turn yours into that extra cash you need. Here's how.

Get Organized. Gather up your merchandise. Though there's not a lot of money in selling clothing, this is the perfect time to unload things you're not using. Kids' clothing does best, since it's usually outgrown before it's worn out, and there's lots of budget-minded parents who realize this and think it makes good sense to invest as little as possible in their own children's wardrobes. Everything should of course be clean and relatively unwrinkled to sell at all, and try to get the better items on hangers. Leave no stone unturned. Clean out the attic, the basement, the garage — then your parent's attic, basement, and garage. If you're really into it, bake cookies, make some crafts. Divide your house plants; pot the starts in attractive little containers — ladies love 'em. Discarded and outgrown toys sell well. Framed prints and silk flower arrangements you no longer use, recipe books and paperbacks, tapes, records, and that kitchen appliance that's more trouble to store than it's worth can be turned into cash to get you off an running!

After you've gathered up your merchandise, you'll need to price it. Realistically, clothing will bring about 25% of what you had to pay for it, if it's still in good, ready-to-wear shape. There's tons of used clothing out there, and no one is going to buy much of anything with buttons missing or otherwise showing signs of wear. If you have good brand-name clothing that has been worn very little, you would probably do better by taking it to a resale or consignment shop. They normally price things at about one-third of retail, with their cut being 30% of that. Not much difference money-wise, but the garage-sale shopper that passes up that $150.00 suit you're asking $35.00 for will probably give $50.00 for it at the consignment shop, simply because like department stores, many have dressing rooms with mirrors so you can try things on and check them for fit before you buy. Even at $35.00, the suit is no bargain if you can't use it when you get it home.

Remember that garage-sale buyers expect to find low prices. Depending on how long you plan on staying open, you'll have one day, possibly two to move everything. If you start out too high, you'll probably be stuck with lots of leftover merchandise, most of which you've already decided is worthless to you. The majority of your better buyers will hit early on; make prices attractive to them and you'll do alright. If you come up with some 'low-end' collectibles — fast-food toys, character glasses, played-with action figures, etc. — don't expect to get much out of them at a garage sale. Your competition down the block may underprice you. But if you have a few things you think have good resale potential, offer them at about half of 'book' price. If they don't sell at your garage sale, take them to a flea market or a consignment shop. You'll probably find they sell better on that level, since people expect to find prices higher there than at garage sales.

You can use pressure-sensitive labels or masking tape for price tags on many items. But *please* do not use either of these on things where damage is likely to occur when they are removed. For instance, (as one reader pointed out) on boxes containing toys, board games, puzzles, etc.; on record labels or album covers; or on ceramics or glass with gold trim or unfired, painted decoration. Unless a friend or a neighbor is going in on the sale with you, price tags won't have to be removed; the profit will all be yours. Of course, you'll have to keep tabs if others are involved. You can use a sheet of paper divided into columns, one for each of you, and write the amount of each sale down under the appropriate person's name, or remove the tags and restick them on a piece of poster board, one for each seller. I've even seen people use straight pins to attach small squares of paper which they remove and separate into plastic butter tubs. When several go together to have a sale, the extra help is nice, but don't let things get out of hand. Your sale can get *too* big. Things become too conjested, and it's hard to display so much to good advantage.

Advertise. Place your ad in your local paper or on your town's cable TV information channel. It's important to make your ad interesting and upbeat. Though most sales usually start early on Friday or Saturday mornings, some people are now holding their sales in the early evening, and they seem to be having good crowds. This gives people with day jobs an opportunity to attend. You *might* want to hold your sale for two days, but you'll do 90% of your selling during the first two or three hours, and a two-day sale can really drag on. Make signs — smaller ones for street corners near your home to help direct passers-by, and a large one for your yard. You might even want to make another saying 'Clothing ½-Price after 12:00.' (It'll cut way down on leftovers that you'll otherwise have to dispose of yourself.) Be sure that you use a wide-tipped felt marker and print in letters big enough that the signs can be read from the street. Put the smaller signs up a few days in advance unless you're expecting rain. (If you are, you might want to include a rain date in your advertising unless your sale will be held under roof.) Make sure you have lots of boxes and bags, and plenty of change. If you price your items in increments of 25¢, you won't need anything but a few rolls of quarters, maybe ten or fifteen ones, and a few five-dollar bills. Then on the day of the sale, put the large sign up in a prominent place out front with some balloons to attract the crowd. Take a deep breath, brace yourself, and raise the garage door!

What To Do With What's Left. After the sale, pack up any good collectibles that didn't sell. Think about that consignment shop or setting up at a flea market. (We'll talk about that later on.) Sort out the better items of clothing for Goodwill or a similar charity, unless your city has someone who will take your left-overs and sell them on consignment. This is a fairly new concept, but some of the larger cities have such 'bargain centers.'

Learning to Become a Successful Bargain Hunter

Let me assure you, anyone who takes the time to become an informed, experienced bargain hunter will be successful. There is enough good merchandise out there to make it well worthwhile, at all levels. Once you learn what to look for, what has good resale potential, and what price these items will probably bring for you, you'll be equipped and ready for any hunting trip. You'll be the one to find treasures like those I described to you earlier.

Garage sales are absolutely wonderful for finding bargains. But you'll have to get up early! Even non-collectors can spot quality merchandise, and at those low, low garage sale prices (unless held by an owner who's done his homework) those items will be the first to move.

In order for you to be a successful garage sale shopper, you have to learn how to get yourself organized. It's important to conserve your time. The sales you hit during the first early-morning hour will prove to be the best nine times out of ten, so you must have a plan before you ever leave home. Plot your course. Your local paper will have a section on garage sale ads and local cable TV channels may also carry garage sale advertising. Most people hold their sales on the weekend, but some may start earlier in the week, so be sure to turn to the 'Garage Sales' ads daily. Write them down and try to organize them by areas — northwest, northeast, etc. At first, you'll probably need your city map, but you'll be surprised at how quickly the streets will become familiar to you. Upper middle-class neighborhoods generally have the best sales and the best merchandise, so concentrate on those areas. When you've decided where you want to start, go early! If the ad says 8:00, be there at 7:00. This may seem rude and pushy, but if you can bring yourself to do it, it will pay off. And chances are when you get there an hour early, you'll not be their first customer. If they're obviously not ready for business, just politely inquire if you may look. If you're charming and their nerves aren't completely frayed from trying to get things ready, chances are they won't mind.

Competition can be fierce during those important early-morning hours. Learn to scan the tables quickly, then move to the area that looks the most promising. Don't be afraid to ask for a better price if you feel it's too high, but most people have already priced garage sale merchandise so that it will sell. Keep a notebook to jot down items you didn't buy the first time around but think you might be interested in if the price were reduced later on. After going through dozens of sales (I've done as many as thirty or so in one morning), you won't remember where you saw what! Often by noon, at least by mid-afternoon, veteran garage sale buyers are finished with their rounds and attendance becomes very thin. Owners are usually much more receptive to the idea of lowering their prices, so it may pay you to make a second pass. In fact some people find it advantageous to go to the better sales on the last day as well as the first. They'll make an offer for everything that's left, and since most of the time the owner is about ready to *pay* someone to take it at that point, they can usually name their price. Although most of the collectibles will normally be gone at this point, there are nearly always some useable household items and several pieces of good, serviceable clothing left. The household items will sell at flea markets or consignment shops, and if there are worthwhile clothing items, take them to a resale boutique. They'll either charge the 30% commission fee or buy the items outright for about half of the amount they feel they can ask, a new practice some resale shops are beginning to follow. Because they want only clothing that is in style, in season, and like new, their prices may be a little higher than others shops, so half of that asking price is a good deal.

Tag sales are common in the larger cities. They are normally held in lieu of an auction, when estates are being dispersed, or when families are moving. Sometimes only a few buyers are admitted at one time, and as one leaves another is allowed to take his place. So just as is true with garage sales, the early bird gets the goodies. Really serious shoppers begin to arrive as much as an hour or two before the scheduled opening time. I know of one who will spend the night in his van and camp on the 'doorstep' if he thinks the sale is especially promising. And he can tell you fantastic success stories! But since it's customary to have tag sale items appraised before values are set, be prepared to pay higher prices. That's not to say, though, that you won't find bargains here. If you think an item is overpriced, leave a bid. Just don't forget to follow through on it, since if it doesn't sell at their asking price, they may end up holding it for you. It's a good idea to check back on the last day of the sale. Often the prices on unsold items may have been drastically reduced.

Auctions can go either way. Depending on the crowd and what items are for sale, you can sometimes spend all day and never be able to buy anything anywhere near 'book' price. On the other hand, there are often 'sleepers' that can be bought cheaply enough to resell at a good profit. Toys, dolls, Hummels, Royal Doultons, banks, cut glass, and other 'high-profile' collectibles usually go high, but white ironstone, dinnerware sets from the '20s through the '50s, silverplated hollowware, books, records, and linens, for instance, often pass relatively unnoticed by the majority of the buyers.

If there is a consignment auction house in your area, check it out. These are usually operated by local auctioneers, and the sales they hold in-house often involve low-income estates. You won't find something every time, so try to investigate the merchandise ahead of schedule to see if it's going to be worth your time to attend. Competition is probably less at one of these than in any of the other types of sales we've mentioned, and wonderful buys have been made from time to time.

Flea markets, I would have to say, are my favorite places to find bargains. I don't like the small ones — not that I don't find anything there, but I've learned to move through them so fast (to beat the crowd), I don't get my 'fix'; I just leave wanting more. If you've never been to a large flea market, you don't know what you're missing. Even if you're not a born-again collector, I guarantee you will love it. And they're excellent places to study the market. You'll be able to see where the buying activity is, you can check and compare prices, talk with dealers and collectors, and do hands-on inspections. I've found that if I first study a particular subject by reading a book or a magazine article, this type of exposure to that collectible really 'locks in' what I have learned.

Because there are many types of flea market dealers, there are plenty of bargains. The casual, once-in-a-while dealer may not always keep up with changing market values. Some of them simply price their items by what they themselves had to pay for it. Just as being early at garage sales is important, here it's a must. If you've ever been in line waiting for a flea market to open, you know that cars are often backed up for several blocks, and people will be standing in line waiting to be admitted hours before the gate opens. Browsers? Window shoppers? Not likely. Competition. So if you're going to have a chance at all, you'd better be in line yourself. Take a partner and split up on the first pass so that you can cover the grounds more quickly. It's a common sight to see the serious buyers conversing with their partners via walkie-talkies, and if you like to discuss possible purchases with each other before you actually buy, this is a good way to do it.

Learn to bargain with dealers. Their prices are usually negotiable, and most will come down by 10% to 20%. Be polite and fair, and you can expect the same treatment in return. Unpriced items are harder to deal for. I have no problem offering to give $8.00 if an item is marked $10.00, but it's difficult for me to have to ask the price and then make a counter offer. So I'll just say 'This isn't marked. Will you take...?' I'm not an aggressive barterer, so this works for me.

There are so many reproductions on the flea market level (and at malls and co-ops), that you need to be suspicious of anything that looks too new! Some fields of collecting have been especially hard hit. Whenever a collectible becomes so much in demand that prices are high, reproductions are bound to make an appearance. For instance, Black Americana, banks, toys of all types, teddy bears, lamps, glassware, doorstops, cookie jars, prints, advertising items, and many other fields have been especially vulnerable. Learn to check for telltale signs — paint that is too bright, joints that don't fit, variations in sizes or colors, creases in paper that you can see but not feel, and so on. Remember that zip codes have been used only since 1963, and this can sometimes help you date an item in question. Check glassware for areas of wavy irregularities often seen in new glass. A publication we would highly recommend to you is called *Antique and Collector Reproduction News*, a monthly report of 'Fakes, Frauds, and Facts.' To subscribe, call 1-800-227-5531. Rates are very reasonable compared to the money you may save by learning to recognize reproductions.

Antique malls and co-ops should be visited on a regular basis. Many mall dealers restock day after day, and traffic and buying competition is usually fierce. As a rule, you won't often find great bargains here; what you do save on is time. And if time is what you're short of, you'll be able to see lots of good merchanise under one roof, on display by people who've already done the leg work and invested *their* time, hence the higher prices. But there are always underpriced items as well, and if you've taken the time to do your homework, you'll be able to spot them right away. This past year in just one of Pennsylvania's largest co-ops I bought a Laughlin Art China vase that books at $185.00 for $25.00, a Weller jardiniere and pedestal for $200.00 ($350.00 would have been very reasonable), and a Kay Finch owl at $35.00 that could easily have been $75.00.

Unless the dealer who rents the booth happens to be there, though, mall and co-op prices are usually firm. But often times they'll run sales — '20% off everything in booth #101.' if you have a dealer's license, and you really should get one, most will give you a courtesy 10% discount on items over $10.00, unless you want to pay with a credit card.

Antique shows are exciting to visit, but obviously if a dealer is paying several hundred dollars to set up for a three-day show, he's going to be asking top price to offset expenses. So even though bargains will be few, the merchandise is usually superior, and you may be able to find that special item you've been looking for.

Mail order buying is not only very easy, but most of the time economical as well. Many people will place an ad in 'For Sale' sections of tradepapers. Some will describe and price their merchandise in their ad, while others offer lists of items they have in exchange for a SASE (stamped, self-addressed envelope). You're out no gas or food expenses, their overhead is minimal so their prices are usually very reasonable, so it works out great for both buyer and seller. I've made lots of good buys this way, and I've always been fairly and honestly dealt with. You may want to send a money order or cashier's check to save time, otherwise (especially on transactions involving larger sums of money) the seller might want to wait until your personal check clears.

Goodwill stores and re-sale shops are usually listed in the teleponeo book. When you travel, it will pay you to check them out. This past summer I found a Chalaine blue refrigerator jar for $1.00 (worth $100.00), several well-underpriced pieces of Moon and Star (a line of glassware that's really catching on fast), some character-related games, record albums, and a few pieces of jewelry. If there's one in your area, visit it often. You never know what may turn up there.

Insider Tips on Today's Market — What's Hot!

The antiques and collectibles market place is so vast and varied that anyone you talk with will have his or her own ideas of where the most concentrated interest seems to be. Certainly that overview will reflect that person's own personal preference and experience. There are broad, general categories that have a huge following — for instance, toys, cookie jars, Depression glass, dolls, and salt and pepper shakers. They're well established and have been for years. There are may 'fringe areas' to each category, some that have a substantial amount of interest, others where there is relatively little. But in each line of glassware, any type of pottery or toys, or any other collectible I could mention, there are examples that are more desirable than others, and these are the ones you need to be able to recognize. Concentrate on the top 25%. This is where you'll do 75% of your business. Do your homework. Quality sells. Check the back of this book for information on clubs and newsletters, always a wonderful source of up-to-date information on any subject.

Toys are probably the biggest news of the nineties. Though antique toys are wonderful investments, the most activity centers around toys from the forties on, particularly toys that the Baby Boomer generation remembers from childhood. GI Joes and Barbies were bringing high prices last year, and their values continue to climb. Character toys are very strong, especially Western heroes, characters from kids' TV shows, Disney, and advertising characters. Action figures, articulated 'boy dolls' like Masters of the Universe, Power Rangers, and X-Men and their accessories are very big news! Model kits, banks, vehicles — especially replicas of the muscle cars of the '50s through the '70s, battery-operated toys from Japan, vintage bicycles, marbles, toy guns, lunch boxes, Liddle Kiddles and other plastic dolls, robots, and space toys of all types are sure sellers.

Anytime you can buy figural pottery at bargain prices, buy it. It goes without saying that cookie jars are selling. It's not news; they've been hot for years. Though the influx of so many reproductions may have caused some leveling off, they continue to be at the top of any list of today's hot collectibles. Salt and pepper shakers are good sellers, as any dealer will tell you — so are figural banks and planters, especially if they happen to be marked or character related. Toothbrush holders are very popular. Condiment sets are picking up steam. Wall pockets are a newer area of interest in figural pottery collecting, and dealers report that kitchen items such as Enesco's Prayer Lady and Holt Howard's pixies are moving well for them. So are Lefton's kitchenware lines, Blue Bird, Young Lady, and Cat, in particular. The popularity of head vases continues to be strong as are all types of figural items made by the mid-century California artists such as Kay Finch, Max Weil, Howard Pierce, Will George, Hedi Schoop, Florence, and Brayton. Royal Copley and Ceramic Art Company's figurines are climbing in value, and Josef Originals are coming on strong with the publication of a new book on the subject.

In glassware, Depression and elegant glassware continue to be strong sellers, and some of the more recently produced Fenton is already very collectible. Eyewinker, some of Imperial's and Westmoreland's reproductions, Avon's Cape Cod, and the carnival glass made by Indiana Glass during the 1980s are noticeably harder to find than they were this time last year — a sure sign of collector activity. Moon and Star is another line that has become extremely popular lately. It was made in a variety of colors and in a good range of shapes, and some dealers tell us it moves better than their Depression glass. Kitchen glassware — especially reamers; items made of jadite, opaque blue, aquamarine, or other unusual colors; rolling pins; refrigerator dishes; canisters; butter dishes; and measuring cups — continues to be a strong area of interest.

In pottery, nearly any marked example is good, as long as it is not totally uninteresting. Roseville is generally of high quality, and there are collectors who love it but are unable to buy top-of-the-line examples, so instead concentrate on the 6" vases or the 3" jardinieres, for instance. (Generally I don't see this trend in other lines of pottery.) McCoy collectors seem to be a very dedicated group. Just about anything with the McCoy mark will sell. Lately we've noticed that even the simple, pastel-glazed flower vases are selling well. From California, Sascha Brastoff and Marc Bellaire are good. (We've already mentioned several other artists from California that are best known for their figural pieces.)

You'll find some background information as well as suggested values for nearly all of these collectibles in this book. The few we haven't included are just now beginning to come on, and even though we don't have enough information for this edition, we will next year. In the meantime, you heard it here first! Now's your chance to grab up those goodies well before everyone else.

In addition to the newer collectibles, there are many more areas with major amounts of activity. All are covered in the following pages. The thousands of current values found in this book will increase your awareness of today's wonderful world of buying, selling, and collecting antiques and collectibles. Use it to educate yourself to the point that you'll be the one with the foresight to know what and how to buy as well as where and how to turn those sleepers into cold, hard cash.

How to Evaluate Your Holdings

In addition to this one, there are several other very fine price guides on the market. One of the best is *Schroeder's Antiques Price Guide*, another is *The Flea Market Trader*. Both are published by Collector Books. *The Antique Trader Antiques and Collectibles Price Guide*, *Warman's Antiques and Their Prices*, and *Kovel's Antiques and Collectibles Price List* are others. You may want to invest in a copy of each. Where you decide to sell will have a direct bearing on how you price your merchandise, and nothing will affect an item's worth more than condition.

If you're not comfortable with using a price guide, here's a few tips that may help you. When convenient and reasonable, antiques will be sorted by manufacturer. This is especially true of pottery and most glassware. If you don't find the item you're looking for under manufacturer, look under a broader heading, for instance, carnival glass, cookie jars, etc. *And don't forget to use the index.* Most guides of this type have very comprehensive indexes — a real boon to the novice collector. If you don't find the exact item you're trying to price, look for something similar. For instance, if it's a McCoy rabbit planter you're researching, go through the McCoy section and see what price range other animal planters are in. Or if you have a frame-tray puzzle with Snow White and the Seven Dwarfs, see what other Disney frame-trays are priced at. Just be careful not to compare apples to oranges.

Once you've found 'book' price, decide how much less you can take for it. 'Book' price represents a high average. A collectible will often change hands many times, and obviously it will not always be sold at book price. How quickly do you want to realize a profit? Will you be patient enough to hold out for top dollar, or would you rather price your merchandise lower so it will turn over more quickly? Just as there are both types of dealers, there are two types of collectors. Many are bargain hunters. They shop around . . . do the leg work themselves. On the other hand, there are those who are willing to pay whatever the asking price is to avoid spending precious time searching out pieces they especially want, but they represent the minority. You'll often see tradepaper ads listing good merchandise (from that top 25% we mentioned before) at prices well above book value. This is a good example of a dealer who knows that his merchandise is good enough to entice the second type of buyer we mentioned and doesn't mind waiting for him (or her) to come along, and that's his prerogative.

Once you have a price range in mind, the next step is to assess condition. Most people, especially inexperienced buyers and sellers, have a tendency to overlook some flaws and to overrate merchandise. Mint condition means that an item is complete and undamaged, in effect, just as it looked the day it was made. Glassware, china, and pottery may often be found in mint condition, though signs of wear will downgrade anything. Unless a toy is still in its original box and has never been played with, you seldom see a toy in mint condition. Paper collectibles are almost never found without deterioration or damage. Most price guides will list values that apply to glass and ceramics that are mint (unless another condition is specifically indicated within some descriptions). Other items are usually evaluated on the assumption that they are in the best as-found condition common to that area of collecting. Grade your merchandise as though you were the buyer, not the seller. You'll be building a reputation that will go a long way toward contributing to your success. If it's glassware or pottery you're assessing, an item in less than excellent condition will be mighty hard to sell at any price. Just as a guideline (a basis to begin your evaluation, though other things will factor in), use a scale of one to five with Good being a one, Excellent being a three, and Mint being a five. As an example, a beer tray worth $250.00 in mint condition would then be worth $150.00 if excellent and $50.00 if only good. Remember, the first rule of buying (for resale or investment) is 'Don't put your money in damaged goods.' And the second rule should be be, 'If you do sell damaged items, indicate 'as is' on the price tag, and don't price the item as though it were mint.' The Golden Rule applies just as well to us as antique dealers as it does in any other phase of interaction. Some shops and co-ops have poor lighting — your honesty will be greatly appreciated. If you include identification on your tags as well, be sure it's accurate. If you're not positive, it's better to let the buyer decide.

Deciding Where to Best Sell Your Merchandise

Personal Transactions are just one of many options. Overhead and expenses will vary with each and must be factored into your final pricing. If you have some especially nice items and can contact a collector willing to pay top dollar, that's obviously the best of the lot. Or you may decide to sell to a dealer who may be willing to pay you only half of book. Either way, your expenses won't amount to much more than a little gas or a phone call.

Classified Ads are another way to get a good price for your more valuable merchandise without investing much money or time. Place a 'For Sale' ad or run a mail bid in one of the collector magazines or newsletters, several of which are listed in the back of this book. Many people have had excellent results this way. One of the best to reach collectors in general is *The Antique Trader Weekly* (P.O. Box 1050, Dubuque, Iowa 52004). It covers virtually any and all types of antiques and collectibles and has a very large circulation. If you have glassware, china, or pottery from the Depression era, you should have good results through *The Depression Glass Daze* (Box 57, Otisville, Michigan 48463). If you have several items and the cost of listing them all is prohibitive, simply place an ad saying (for instance) 'Several pieces of Royal Copley (or whatever) for sale, send SASE for list.' Be sure to give your correct address and phone number.

When you're making out your list or talking with a prospective buyer by phone, try to draw a picture with words. Describe any damage in full; it's much better than having a disgruntled customer to deal with later, and you'll be on your way to establishing yourself as a reputable dealer. Sometimes it's wise to send out photographs. Seeing the item exactly as it is will often help the prospective buyer make up his or her mind. Send a SASE along and ask that your photos be returned to you, so that you can send them out again, if need be. A less expensive alternative is to have your item photocopied. This works great for many smaller items, not just flat shapes but things with some dimension as well. It's wonderful for hard-to-describe dinnerware patterns or for showing their trademarks.

If you've made that 'buy of a lifetime' or an item you've hung onto for a few years has turned out to be a scarce, highly sought collectible, a mail bid is often the best way to get top dollar for your prize. This is how you'll want your ad to read. 'Mail Bid. Popeye cookie jar by American Bisque, slight wear (or 'mint' — briefly indicate condition), closing 6/31/95, right to refuse' (standard self-protection clause meaning you will refuse ridiculously low bids), and give your phone number. Don't commit the sale to any bidder until after the closing date, since some may wait until the last minute to try to place the winning bid.

Be sure to let your buyer know what form of payment you prefer. Some dealers will not ship merchandise until personal checks have cleared. This delay may make the buyer a bit unhappy. So you may want to request a money order or a cashier's check.

Be very careful about how you pack your merchandise for shipment. Breakables need to be well protected. There are several things you can use. Plastic bubble wrap is excellent, or scraps of foam rubber such as carpet padding (check with a carpet-laying service or confiscate some from family and friends who're getting new carpet installed). I've received items wrapped in pieces of egg-crate type mattress pads (watch for these at garage sales!). If there is a computer business near you, check their dumpsters for discarded foam wrapping and other protective packaging. It's best not to let newspaper come in direct contact with your merchandise, since the newsprint may stain certain types of items. After you've wrapped them well, you'll need boxes. Find smaller boxes (one or several, whatever best fits your needs) that you can fit into a larger one with several inches of space between them. First pack your well-wrapped items snuggly into the smaller box, using crushed newspaper to keep them from shifting. Place it into the larger box, using more crushed paper underneath and along the sides, so that it will not move during transit. Remember, if it arrives broken, it's still your merchandise, even though you have received payment. You may want to insure the shipment; check with your carrier. Some have automatic insurance up to a specified amount.

After you've mailed it out, it's good to follow it up with a phone call after a few days. Make sure the box arrived in good condition and that your customer is pleased with the merchandise. Most people who sell by mail allow a 10-day return privilege, providing their original price tag is still intact. You can simply initial a gummed label or use one of those pre-printed return address labels that most of us have around the house.

For very large or heavy items such as furniture or slot machines, ask your buyer for his preferred method of shipment. If the distance involved is not too great, he may even want to pick it up himself.

Flea Market Selling can either be lots of fun, or it can turn out to be one of the worst experiences of your life. Obviously you will have to deal with whatever weather conditions prevail, so be sure to listen to weather reports so that you can dress accordingly. You'll see some inventive shelters you might want to copy. Even a simple patio umbrella will offer respite from the blazing sun or a sudden downpour. I've recently been seeing stands catering just to the needs of the flea market dealer — how's that for being enterprising! Not only do they carry specific items the dealers might want, but they've even had framework and tarpaulins for shelters they'll erect right on the spot!

Be sure to have plastic table covering in case of rain and some large clips to hold it down if there's much wind. The type of clip you'll need depends on how your table is made, so be sure to try them out before you actually have need for them. Otherwise your career as a flea market dealer may be cut short for lack of merchandise!

Price your things, allowing yourself a little bargaining room. Unless you want to collect tax separately on each sale (for this you'd need lots of small change), mentally calculate the amount and add this on as well. Sell the item 'tax included.' Everybody does.

Take snacks, drinks, paper bags, plenty of change, and somebody who can relieve you occasionally. Collectors are some of the nicest people around. I guarantee that you'll enjoy this chance to meet and talk them, and often you can make valuable contacts that may help you locate items you're especially looking for yourself.

Auction Houses are listed in the back of this book. If you have an item you feel might be worth selling at auction, be sure to contact one of them. Many have appraisal services; some are free while others charge a fee, dependent on number of items and time spent. We suggest you first make a telephone inquiry before you send in a formal request.

In Summation

Whatever the reason you've become interested in the antiques and collectibles field, whether to supplement your income part-time, go into it on a full-time basis, simply because you want to be a wise collector/investor, I'm confident that you will achieve your goals. Aside from monetary gain, it's a wonderful hobby, a real adventure. There's never been a better time to become involved. With study comes knowledge, and knowledge is the key to success. The time you invest in reading, attending shows, talking with experienced collectors, and pursuing understanding of the field in every way you can devise will pay off handsomely as you enjoy the hunt for today's collectibles, tomorrow's antiques.

Abbreviations

MIB – mint in (original) box
M – mint condition
MIP – mint in package
MOC – mint on card
NM – near mint
EX – excellent
VG – very good
G – good
lg – large
med – medium
sm – small
oz – ounce
pt – pint
qt – quart
gal – gallon
pr – pair
dia – diameter
w/ – with
pc – piece

Abingdon Pottery

You may find smaller pieces of Abingdon around, but it's not common to find many larger items. This company operated in Abingdon, Illinois, from 1934 until 1950, making not only nice vases and figural pieces but some kitchen items as well. Their cookie jars are very well done and popular with collectors. They sometimes used floral decals and gold to decorate their wares, and a highly decorated item is worth about 25% more than the same shape with no decoration. Some of their glazes also add extra value. If you find a piece in black, bronze, or red, you can add 25% to those as well.

If you talk by phone about Abingdon to a collector, be sure to mention the mold number on the base. To learn more about Abingdon cookie jars, we recommend *The Collector's Encyclopedia of Cookie Jars* by Joyce and Fred Roerig and *Illustrated Guide to Cookie Jars* by Ermagene Westfall.

Vase, Laurel, blue, #442, 6", $33.00

Ashtray, box shape, turquoise, 1936-38, #488	$45.00
Ashtray, donkey, black, scarce, #510, 5½" dia	$95.00
Bookends, colts, #363, 5¾", pr	$65.00
Bowl, flared, #540	$30.00
Bowl, leaf shape, beige, 1937, #408, 6½"	$65.00
Bowl, Panel, #460, 8"	$40.00
Bowl, Ti Leaf, #529, 16"	$30.00
Candle holder/vase, Fern Leaf, #429, 8"	$25.00
Candle holders, Classic, white, #126, 2", pr	$38.00
Console bowl, star, chartreuse, #713	$25.00
Cookie jar, Daisy, 1949, #677	$45.00
Cookie jar, Hobby Horse, #602	$185.00
Cookie jar, Humpty Dumpty, #663	$250.00
Cookie jar, Little Girl, #693	$60.00
Cookie jar, Miss Muffet, #622	$205.00
Cookie jar, Pineapple, #664	$60.00
Cookie jar, Three Bears, #696	$90.00
Cookie jar, Windmill, #678	$185.00
Creamer & sugar bowl, Daisy, #681 & #682	$27.50
Figurine, goose, white, #571, 5"	$25.00
Figurine, heron, #574	$28.00
Figurine, shepherdess & fawn, yellow w/gold traces, #3906, 11½"	$95.00
Jar, Ming, turquoise, #301	$80.00
Mint compote, pink, footed, 1942-47, #568, 6"	$28.00
Pitcher, Fern Leaf, white, 1937-38, #430, 8"	$135.00
Pitcher, ice lip, #200, 2-qt	$30.00
Planter, daffodil, #668, 5¼"	$20.00
Salad plate, dark blue, square, #339, 7½"	$32.00
Tea tile, coolie, white matte glaze, paper label, #401	$70.00
Tea tile, geisha, square, #400, 5"	$80.00
Vase, Arden, green, 1934-50, #517, 7"	$24.00
Vase, Beta, blue, #110, 10"	$35.00
Vase, Beta, maroon, #102, 10"	$58.00
Vase, Classic, #116, 10"	$20.00
Vase, Delta Classic, 10", #104	$28.00
Vase, medallion, #464, 8"	$30.00
Wall pocket, carriage, charteuse, #711	$35.00
Wall pocket, double morning-glory, white, #375, 7¾"	$45.00
Window box, Han, #498, lg, 14½" long	$25.00

Advertising Collectibles

If you're a beginning advertising collector, you have probably been drawn into this field because of a special attraction you have for a particular advertising character, or maybe you have a certain product in mind. But were you to attempt to be more generalized in your collecting, you'd want to keep some of these things in mind:

Graphics are very important. Watch for bright colors, well placed subjects, and good details. There are some products that are generally considered more collectible than others — tobacco, talcum powders, beer, peanut butter, and many soft drinks, for instance. Items with character logos are always good. There's Reddy Kilowatt, Poppin' Fresh, the Campbell Kids, and Elsie, just to name a few. Anything that depicts sports, famous people, modes of transportation, or might have a patriotic, Western or Black Americana theme will be very desirable to collectors. Watch for condition, it's very important. A mint condition item may bring twice what the same item in only very good condition will, and often (unless they're rare or especially sought after) things that are damaged are very slow to sell.

You'll find ashtrays, dolls, pin-back buttons, and tons of other small items from the past few decades that have a market value of $50.00 or less, and these are the types of things that make up a good percentage of today's sales.

There are several books we recommend: *Huxford's Collectible Advertising* by Sharon and Bob Huxford; *Advertising Memorabilia Value Guide* by B.J. Summers; *Advertising Character Collectibles* by Warren Dotz; *Antique Advertising Encyclopedia, Vols 1 and Vol 2* and *Antique Advertising Handbook*, both by Ray Klug; *Advertising Dolls Identification and Value Guide* by Joleen Ashman Robinson and Kay Sellers; *Pepsi-Cola Collectibles* by Bill Vehling and Michael Hunt; and *The Collector's Guide to Key-Wind Coffee Tins* by James H. Stahl.

See also Airline Memorabilia; Ashtrays; Automobilia; Avon; Beer Cans; Breweriana; Bubble Bath Containers; Cereal Boxes; Character and Promotional Drinking Glasses; Coca-Cola Collectibles; Cookbooks; Cracker Jack Collectibles; Dairy

Bottles; Decanters; Fast-Food Collectibles; Gas Station Collectibles; Keen Kutter; Labels; Pez Candy Containers; Pin-Back Buttons; Planters Peanuts; Playing Cards; Pepsi-Cola; Posters; Salt and Pepper Shakers; Soda Bottles; Soda Pop Memorabilia; Vending Machines; Watch Fobs.

Bank, A&P, red vinyl pig w/logo on each side, 2x3x5", VG..$20.00

Bank, Kool-Aid, pitcher standing on yellow base, coin placed in pitcher's hand falls into suitcase, plastic, 1970s, VG...$24.00

Bank, Poll-Parrot Shoes, plastic shoe form, G $20.00

Bank, Prudential Life Insurance Co, glow-in-the-dark Rock of Gibralter, plastic, 1950s, 2x4x5", EX...................$20.00

Bank, Southern Comfort, mechanical, hunter shoots coin into lg bottle, painted white metal, 6", NM $70.00

Bank, Tootsie Roll, lg canister shaped like a Tootsie Roll, cardboard w/metal top & bottom, EX $15.00

Bank, Van Dyke Teas, Lincoln's cabin, ceramic, 2⅜"..$18.00

Bathroom scale, Bacardi Rum, metal, working, 12½x10½", EX..$20.00

Bowl, Cheerios, bright yellow w/You Made Cheerios Number One around rim, You Did It lettered in bowl, 6" dia, EX..$20.00

Bowl, Post Sugar Crisp, yellow plastic w/embossed Indians, M..$35.00

Calendar, Doe-Wah-Jack, 1925, pictures Indian trading good-luck belt with pioneer woman, 20¾x10¾", EX, $225.00

Calendar, Hills Cascara Quinine Bromide, 1903, pictures little girl, framed, 5x10", EX.....................................$50.00

Calendar, National Life Insurance Co, 1958, pictures bears, EX..$10.00

Can, Braq's Root Beer, steel, EX $5.00

Can, Daufuski Oysters, Indian in profile w/product name above & below, no lid, 1-gal...............................$30.00

Can, Daufuski Oysters, Indian in profile w/product name above & below, no bottom, 1-pt..........................$16.00

Can, Snow Crest Syrup, white bear w/product lettering on label, full, 1-pt, EX...$25.00

Candy jar, Baby Ruth, clear glass barrel shape, red & white tin w/Curtiss Candy Co lettered over Baby Ruth, 3¾"..$15.00

Cheese box, Borden's Process Cheese Food, red & green logo & lettering on wood, 1950s, 4x12x4", EX+ ...$20.00

Child's tea set, Dunkin' Donuts, plastic, 1970s, MIB ...$90.00

Clock, Alka-Seltzer, shaped like Alka-Seltzer tablet, MIB .$50.00

Clock, DuPont Paint, round w/#12 & dots surrounding product name, metal frame w/glass lens, 15" dia, EX...$80.00

Clock, Hartford Time Tested Insurance, blue numbers surround yellow logo, round light-up w/glass lens & metal frame, EX+..$165.00

Clock, Pure Milk Co All Star Dairy & Ice Cream, Milk, round w/glass lens & metal frame, 10" dia, EX+ $90.00

Clock, S&H Green Stamps, round white face on dark green, We Give... below, electric, wood frame, 23x15", EX+..$75.00

Clock, Sunkist, pictures boy & girl, Good Vibrations, plastic, G $65.00

Coloring book, Peter Pan Peanut Butter, unused, EX .$15.00

Coloring book, Poll-Parrot Shoes, features Howdy Doody, 1950s, M...$45.00

Cookie jar, Famous Amos Cookies, brown paper-bag shape w/Famous Amos in script above lg cookie, ceramic, NM..$50.00

Cookie jar, Nabisco, tan barrel-shaped jar w/red trim, Nabisco embossed in white across front, McCoy 78, pottery, EX+...$85.00

Display, Seagram's Golden Cooler, light-up, EX..........$18.00

Display, Sherwin-Williams Products, painter dips brush in paint can, Use Sherwin-Williams Products..., 22½x30", EX..$25.00

Display bottle, Wild Turkey Bourbon, inflatable, 24", EX...$8.00

Display box, Wrigley's Spearmint Gum, folds open to display gum, Wrigley man promoting product, 1x6x4", VG+..$45.00

Display rack, Kellogg's Cereals, for sm restaurant boxes, 1950, VG...$85.00

Frisbee, Kraft Macaroni & Cheese, white w/logo, EX....$5.00

Frisbee, Oreo Cookies, black soft plastic, no date, NM.$14.00

Grocer's want book, Clabber Girl Baking Powder, pictures can of product, lined pages inside, 8x3¾", EX+ ...$12.00

Growth chart, Brach's Candies, shows Bugs Bunny holding a carrot, 1989, VG+ $8.00

Ledger marker, Aetna Insurance Co, horizontal image of Mt Vesuvious erupting, Insure With..., 12½x3", G ...$100.00

Ledger marker, Comic Opera Co, tin, pictures Mr Thomas Q Seabrooke & actors from his opera company, 12¼x3¼", G+..$175.00

Ledger marker, State Mutual Life Assurance Co, image of building w/lettering above & below, 12½x3", G+ ..$75.00

Letter opener, De Laval Cream Separator Co, brass, 1878-1928, EX..$40.00

Lunch box w/thermos, Crest Toothpaste, plastic, M ...$35.00

Lunch box w/thermos, Tropicana, plastic, NM...........$15.00

Magazine ad, California Perfume Co, pictures dental products, matted & framed, horizontal, ca 1915, EX....$85.00

Mirror, Old Bushmill Irish Whiskey, wood frame, 16x17", EX $15.00

Mirror, Old Grandad Whiskey, wood frame, 22½x18", EX+ **$25.00**

Mug, Post Toasties, for car, ceramic, EX+ **$8.00**

Mug, Raid, 30th Anniversary, 1986, NM **$10.00**

Mug, Royal Beer, transfer print w/motto on reverse, stoneware, 3¾", G..**$25.00**

Necklace, Bubble Yum Bubble Gum, yellow fruit gum pack on plastic cord, EX.....................................**$4.00**

Necktie, Wheaties, repeated logo on blue, 1970s, EX.**$15.00**

Paperweight, Northwestern National Life Insurance Co, pictures building, glass, G **$22.00**

Pet toy, Ralston Purina Meow Mix, yellow & white vinyl cat standing w/arms down, Meow Mix on belly, 1976, 5", NM **$25.00**

Pitcher, Canadian Lord Calvert, EX...........................**$12.00**

Pitcher, Nestle Quick, brown plastic w/original paper label, Free When You Buy One 2 Lb Can (Any Flavor)..., 9¾", M **$15.00**

Pitcher, Seagram's Crown Royal, shaped like a Crown Royal bottle, brown pottery, EX..............**$15.00**

Pitcher, Seagram's 7, white pottery w/Seagram's embossed on red background, 7 embossed on each side, EX......**$10.00**

Pocket mirror, Boston Herald/Sunday Herald, shows boy hawking newspaper, lettering around rim, 1¾" dia, EX..**$80.00**

Pocket mirror, Boston Varnish Co, reversible head image of man who did & didn't use product, 2⅛" dia, VG+...**$25.00**

Pocket mirror, Bromo-Seltzer, bottle of product w/product name & Cures All Headaches lettered on rim, 2¼" dia, G...**$50.00**

Pocket mirror, Campbell's Soup, 6 plates & 10 Cents flank soup can, lettering below, 1¾" dia, VG+...............**$80.00**

Pocket mirror, Carmen Complexion Powder, lettering above lady in oval before draped curtain, 1¾" dia, EX ...**$20.00**

Pocket mirror, Cooper Underwear Co, Buy White Cat Union Suits above smiling white cat, oval, 2¾", VG+......**$35.00**

Pocket mirror, Garrett's Rye, celluloid, draped nude w/transparent veil shooting bow & arrow, Oldest Brand..., oval, G+ **$35.00**

Pocket mirror, Gillett's Lye Eats Dirt lettered on sign straddled by Black man in straw hat, 1¼" dia, EX......**$120.00**

Pocket mirror, John C Roth Packing Co, pictures dressed wolf w/pig, oval in embossed tin frame w/handle, 4", EX...**$50.00**

Pocket mirror, Little Imps, 5¢ & Devil's image, For All Who Breathe, 1½" dia, EX...................................**$50.00**

Pocket mirror, Monarch Typewriter Co, Monarch on banner above early typewriter, Is Visable below, 2⅛" dia, EX..**$60.00**

Pocket mirror, Nature's Remedy, close-up of eyes, nose & mouth w/lettering over nose, lettering on rim, 2⅛" dia, VG+...**$15.00**

Pocket mirror, Ponciana Chewing Gum, pack of gum w/WJ White above, America's Favorite, horizontal oval, 2¾", EX **$100.00**

Pocket mirror, The Allies lettered below stand of 6 flags of the allied countries, oval, 2¾", VG+ **$15.00**

Pocketknife, Red Rose Feeds, 3 blades, 3⅜" long, VG, $25.00

Push bar, Colonial Bread, embossed & painted metal, Colonial Is Good Bread lettered on bar, 31½" long, EX.......**$110.00**

Push bar, Colonial Bread, red, white & blue w/chrome handle, 30" long, VG.....................................**$75.00**

Push bar, Schmudt's Blue Ribbon Bread, multicolored die-cut loaf attached to bar, 26½" long, G...................**$20.00**

Push bar, Sunbeam Bread, Reach For in red script left of Sunbeam Bread in white script on dark blue, metal, VG...**$55.00**

Ruler, Clark's Teaberry Gum, ca 1937, EX.....................**$4.00**

Ruler, Tums, wood, 12", EX **$5.00**

Sign, Borden's Ice Cream, Enjoy Borden's... in gold letters on simulated wood ground, It's Real Food on red, 13x22", EX..**$140.00**

Sign, Carter's Overalls, tin, blue & red w/white lettering, depicts train in center, Union Made, lg chip, 6x15", VG **$150.00**

Sign, Champion Coal, It's The Best, Subway Coal & Ice Co, rust around nail holes, logoed center, horizontal, VG...**$60.00**

Sign, Cliquot Club Beverages, tin, 12x30", EX **$50.00**

Sign, De Laval Cream Separators, embossed tin, milkmaid w/cow surrounded by vignettes, ornate frame, 40½x29½", G **$450.00**

Sign, De Laval Milker, tin, black letters on bright yellow, We Use The De Laval Milker, 12x16", EX...................**$40.00**

Sign, Ivory Soap, cardboard, features little girl washing doll clothes, illustrated by Maud Humphrey, 24½x17", VG, $450.00

Sign, Red Jacket Coal, painted embossed tin, Indian standing left of lettering on black & yellow background, 12x24", EX **$230.00**

Sign, Red Rose Tea, white Red Rose Tea Is Good Tea on red, white outline, tin, 4x23½", NM **$65.00**

Sign, Yoo-Hoo Chocolate, features cartoon image of Yogi Berra & a modern-day rock band, 1970s, 17x11", M **$35.00**

Store box, CD Boss & Son Biscuits, wood w/paper labels, w/lid, 11x20x13", G **$50.00**

Store jar, Dr King's New Liver Pills, glass w/reverse-painted label, 4-sided w/stopper-type lid, 13x5¼x5½", G ..**$150.00**

Swizzle stick, Jack Daniel's Whiskey, full-figure image of Jack Daniel on top of stick, white plastic, 1960s, 6½", EX **$12.00**

Tape measure, Prudential Life Insurance Co, metal, EX ..**$4.00**

Thermometer, Calumet Baking Powder, painted & stenciled wood, blue & red on yellow, rounded corners, 22", G+ **$310.00**

Thermometer, Donovan's Red Diamond Coffee, painted & stenciled tin, coffee bag & can left of bulb, arched top, 15", G+ **$85.00**

Thermometer, Hills Bros Coffee, porcelain, man in robe & turban lifts cup, red ground, round top, 1930-40, NM **$275.00**

Thermometer, Ken-L Ration, painted & stenciled tin, For Best results! Feed Your Dog..., rounded corners, 26½", G+ **$50.00**

Thermometer, Lister's Jellies, painted wood, red & green on white, arched top, straight bottom, 24", VG **$70.00**

Thermometer, Ramon's Brownie & Pink Pills, yellow metal w/the doctor right of bulb, arched top, straight bottom, 21", EX **$325.00**

Thermometer, Sweet Heart Flour, porcelain steel, red & white on blue, white border, arched top, straight bottom, 27", VG **$260.00**

Thermometer, Tums, white, yellow & blue lettering on blue, Tums For The Tummy, lettering below, aluminum, 9", VG **$20.00**

Thermometer, White House Coffee, painted & stenciled wood, black lettering on white, arched top, raised rim, 21", G **$20.00**

Tin, Benjamin's Horehound #5 Coughdrops, 4-sided w/sm round top, shows 3 different scenes, VG+ **$85.00**

Tin, Bravo Coffee, round, 1-lb, VG **$95.00**

Tin, Bridal Brand Coffee, lettering above & below man w/donkeys & harbor scene, slip lid, oval, 5¾x4¾x3½", VG **$250.00**

Tin, Brown Betty Coffee, key-wind lid, 1-lb, EX **$85.00**

Tin, Canton Ginger, 5x3x1½", EX **$16.50**

Tin, Cashmere Bouquet Talcum, sample, NM **$40.00**

Tin, Crescent Salted Peanuts, product lettering above & below logo, pry lid, 10-lb, VG **$175.00**

Tin, Dr Koch's Velvet Talcum, NM **$35.00**

Tin, Golden Bear Cookies, Bridge Assortment, bear logo, no lid, 1-lb, VG **$20.00**

Tin, Herald Square Typewriter Ribbon, square w/rounded corners, EX **$12.00**

Tin, Loving Cup Coffee, key-wind lid, 1-lb, NM **$40.00**

Tin, Luzianne Coffee & Chicory, red paper label w/ Black lady serving hot coffee, Wm B Reily & Company, Inc, 1-lb, EX, $125.00

Tin, Mennen Baby Powder, product name above baby's face emerging from rose petals, EX **$15.00**

Tin, Milky Way, pictures hearts & cupids, 1991, 6¼x4", EX **$8.00**

Tin, Monarch Mocha Rich Coffee, key-wind lid, 2-lb, EX+ **$40.00**

Tin, Old Master Coffee, bearded man in oval flanked by flowering vines, paper label, 1930-40, 1-lb, EX ..**$130.00**

Tin, Quaker Oats, 1992, 7x5" dia, EX **$15.00**

Tin, Ritz Crackers, 1986, 6¾x4¼", EX **$7.00**

Tin, Squirrel Peanut Butter, yellow pail w/squirrel logo, red lettering above & below, slip lid & bail, 1-lb, G .**$120.00**

Tin, Surefine Coffee, product name on split bands above cup of coffee in circular inset, key-wind lid, 10-lb, EX+..**$30.00**

Tin, Towle's Log Cabin Syrup, pictures pancakes, EX ...**$12.00**

Tin, United Coffee, blue & white w/gold seal over patriotic bow tie, product name above & below, 1-lb, EX ..**$115.00**

Tin, White Rose Coffee, 1-lb, 4", EX **$40.00**

Tin, William's Baby Talc, blue & yellow w/blue accents, image of baby on both sides, shaker top, 5", G ...**$80.00**

Tip tray, Bromo-Seltzer, bottle featured in center w/lettering on rim, Cures All Headaches, 4¼" dia, EX **$130.00**

Tip tray, Cheon Tea, features Japanese lady w/tray of drinks, For Iced Tea Use Cheon lettered on rim, 4¼" dia, EX **$230.00**

Tip tray, Prudential Life Insurance Co, features The Rock logo w/advertising, plain rim, vertical, oval, EX...**$15.00**

Toy figure, Hershey's, Milk Chocolate bar, brown w/white accents & lettering, tan shoes, PVC, 1980s, 4½", M ..**$8.00**

Tray, Hulls Beer, woodgrain w/logo, 1940s, EX.........**$25.00**

Tray, Stokley's Finest Foods, rectangular w/Stokley's logo in center, products lettered on rim, 10½x13", VG **$30.00**

Trolley sign, Wrigley's on scrolled banner above king & Wrigley's boys flanked by packs of gum, framed, 11x21", G **$110.00**

Weinermobile, Oscar Mayer, new version of original, no Oscar figure, black-walled tires, plastic, 1991, 10" long, EX .**$30.00**

Wristwatch, Hershey's, Jordache, 1980s, MIB **$25.00**

Advertising Character Collectibles

Atlas Annie, Allied Van Lines, doll, cloth, 15", EX.......**$20.00**

Aunt Jemima, dolls, Aunt Jemima, Uncle Moses, Wade & Diana, stuffed cloth, 12½" to 8¾", set of 4, EX ...**$625.00**

Aunt Jemima, mask, her head wrapped in scarf, die-cut cardboard, cutouts for eyes & nose, 13x12", M ..**$200.00**

Aunt Jemima, puzzle, 2 products on string attached to her image, die-cut cardboard, 4x5", EX **$125.00**

Big Boy, bank, vinyl figure, 1970s, EX, $20.00

Big Boy, pillow doll, 1978, MIP **$75.00**

Big Boy in car, figure, PVC, 3", M.................................**$6.00**

Big Boy on surfboard, figure, PVC, 3", NM **$5.00**

Buster Brown, bank, No Parents Allowed, vinyl, 11"..**$40.00**

Buster Brown, color transfer kit, Time Machine – 68..**$10.00**

Buster Brown, mask, upper portion of Buster's head in red hat, stiff die-cut paper, 1905, 8x10", VG **$75.00**

Buster Brown & Tige, Buster Brown Bread, pin-back button, Buster & Tige displaying sign, product name on rim, 1¼", NM **$40.00**

Buster Brown & Tige, Buster Brown Shoes, shoe tree, figures of Buster & Tige at top, 4½", NM.....................**$35.00**

Buster Brown & Tige, game, Pin the Tie & Tail on Buster & Tige, 1967 ....**$25.00**

Camel Joe, Camel Cigarettes, can cooler, Camel Joe's head in sunglasses w/dangling cigarette, vinyl, 1991, 4", M **$12.00**

Camel Joe, Camel Cigarettes, cap, corduroy w/embroidered Camel Joe & insignia, EX.................................**$12.00**

Campbell Kid, Campbell's Soup, child's electric mixer, Mirro, Kids on sides, 1960s, rare, MIB.................**$225.00**

Campbell Kids, Campbell's Alphabet Soup, word game w/plastic letters in cardboard canister w/tin lid, EX.............**$25.00**

Campbell Kids, Campbell's Soup, child's fork, Kid's head engraved above M-m-m Good on handle, EX **$5.00**

Campbell Kids, Campbell's Soup, coloring book, A Story of Soup, 1976, 14x11", M **$20.00**

Campbell Kids, Campbell's Soup, doll, stuffed girl, blue bibs w/red & white checked shirt, 1973, 15½", EX.......**$65.00**

Campbell Kids, Campbell's Soup, dolls, as Paul Revere & Betsy Ross, vinyl, 1974, 10", MIB..................**$200.00**

Campbell Kids, Campbell's Soup, jigsaw puzzle, All Aboard, #319, 1986, 28-pc, VG **$30.00**

Campbell Kids, Campbell's Soup, salt & pepper shakers, plastic, figures of Kids as chefs, 1950s, 4½", pr, $40.00

Campbell Kids, Campbell's Soup, squeeze toys, vinyl Kids, pr..**$30.00**

Campbell Kids, Campbell's Soup, storybook, features Kids on front, Rand McNally, 1954, 8x6½", VG.............**$25.00**

Campbell Kids, Campbell's Soup, tea set, cups, tray, dish & utensils, features Campbell Kids, 1982, MIB **$70.00**

Campbell Kids, Campbell's Soup, word game, cardboard canister w/tin lid, Kids pictured, contains red plastic letters, EX **$22.00**

Cap'n Crunch, bank, plastic figural.............................**$25.00**

Cap'n Crunch, booklet, Scratch 'n Sniff, 1975, NM......**$15.00**

Cap'n Crunch, Cap'n Crunch Cereal, kaleidoscope, cardboard, paper label w/6 different characters, 1970s, 7x2" dia, NM **$12.00**

Cap'n Crunch, puzzle, cardboard frame-tray type, M..**$25.00**

Charlie the Tuna, Starkist, bank, Charlie surrounded by stacks of coins on tuna-can base, ceramic, 1988, 9½", M **$20.00**

Charlie the Tuna, Starkist, doll, M................................**$15.00**

Charlie the Tuna, Starkist, radio, MIB.........................**$30.00**

Charlie the Tuna, Starkist, squeeze toy, soft vinyl, 1973, 8", MIB **$80.00**

Chester Cheeta, Cheetos, tumbler, plastic, features Chester, NM...**$6.00**

Chocks Man, Chocks Vitamins, doll, stuffed cloth, 20", EX $25.00

Chuck E Cheese, bank, plastic, M.............................$20.00

Chuck E Cheese, figure, PVC, 2½", M.......................$6.00

Count Chocula, General Mills, doll, vinyl, 8" $35.00

Curad Kid, doll, 7", M $25.00

Dino the Dinosaur, Sinclair Oil, bank, Dino figure, green plastic, 1960s, 4", NM.....................................$25.00

Dino the Dinosaur, Sinclair Oil, inflatable vinyl figure, 1960s, 12", M $20.00

Dino the Dinosaur, Sinclair Oil, red wax figure, NM ..$42.00

Dino the Dinosaur, Sinclair Oil, soap figure, 1950s, MIB .$18.50

Dutch Boy, Dutch Boy Paints, puppet, good likeness of the Dutch Boy, soft vinyl w/cloth body, 1960s, 12x8½", EX $25.00

Dutch Girl, Blue Bonnet Margarine, doll, hard plastic, 8", MIB..$8.50

Elsie the Cow, Borden, bendee, 3¾", M.....................$20.00

Elsie the Cow, Borden, book, Elsie & the Looking Club, hardbound, 1946 ....$25.00

Elsie the Cow, Borden, book Adventures w/Elsie the Famous Cow, her travels from 1939-64 World's Fairs.........$65.00

Elsie the Cow, Borden, bowl, Elsie dancing in flowers, Cambridge, M...$180.00

Elsie the Cow, Borden, chalkboard, tin, features Elsie, VG $110.00

Elsie the Cow, Borden, coloring book, My Family & Friends, 6 pages, 7x5", EX $10.00

Elsie the Cow, Borden, cookie cutter, image of Elsie's head in center of flower, yellow plastic, 2½" dia, M......$20.00

Elsie the Cow, Borden, creamer, lg, EX $45.00

Elsie the Cow, Borden, doll, stuffed plush w/rubber head, 12", VG, $70.00

Elsie the Cow, Borden, drinking glass, tapered clear glass w/image of Elsie's head, 1950s, 6x3" dia, M $20.00

Elsie the Cow, Borden, Elsie's Good Food Line Train, punch-out cardboard, orig mailer, 1940s, M.......$245.00

Elsie the Cow, Borden, Elsie's Milkman Game, 1963, EX $85.00

Elsie the Cow, Borden, figure in apron, rubber, 4", EX..**$15.00**

Elsie the Cow, Borden, lapel pin, metal, white or blue w/yellow daisy & Elsie's face, EX **$4.50**

Elsie the Cow, Borden, mug, pointed handle, EX.......**$65.00**

Elsie the Cow, Borden, place mat, full-color image of Elsie, 11x17", M...**$12.00**

Elsie the Cow, Borden, tumbler, w/windmill & bouquet of flowers, EX **$45.00**

Elsie the Cow, Borden, wristwatch, white border & numbers around raised head of Elsie, missing link bands, 1950s, EX...**$18.00**

Energizer Bunny, Eveready Batteries, Energizer Bunny beating on drum, squeeze & he lights up, vinyl 4½", M.......**$12.00**

Frankenberry, General Mills Frankenberry Cereal, figure, 1983, MIP **$3.00**

Frankenberry, General Mills Frankenberry Cereal, pencil sharpener, figural, on original card, M **$6.00**

Gerber baby, doll, Sun Rubber, sculpted hair, w/bib, 1955, 12" **$45.00**

Hawaiian girl, S&H Sugar, doll, stuffed cloth, 15", MIP.**$5.00**

Hersheykin, Hershey's Mr Goodbar, figure, PVC, 1980s, 2", M..**$6.00**

Humble Tiger, Humble Oil, bank, tiger sitting on haunches w/1 paw up & 1 on knee, plastic, 1960s, 8½", NM...**$25.00**

ICEE Bear, bank, vinyl, EX......................................**$25.00**

Jack Frost, Jack Frost Sugar Co, doll, stuffed cloth, blue & white w/yellow hair, 17", EX **$35.00**

Jolly Green Giant, doll, vinyl **$75.00**

Jolly Green Giant, Halloween costume, Kuskan, 1960s, MIB **$50.00**

Jolly Green Giant, jigsaw puzzle, 204 pcs, 24x36", EX ..**$15.00**

Jolly Green Giant, kite, in original mailer envelope, M ..**$15.00**

Jolly Green Giant, squeeze toy, w/arms folded, green vinyl, 1975, 9½", EX **$55.00**

Keebler Elf, radio, EX **$45.00**

Keebler Elf, squeeze toy, rubber, 7", NM **$20.00**

Keebler Elf, telephone, 1980s, EX+.............................**$75.00**

Kitten, Lime-Away, doll, soft plush, 10", M **$10.00**

Little Caeser's Pizza Man, figure, 6", M.....................**$10.00**

Little Debbie, Little Debbie Snack Cakes, doll, bisque w/brunette hair & blue gingham dress, 30th anniversary, 15", MIB **$60.00**

Little Miss Sunbeam, Sunbeam Bread, doll, plastic w/vinyl head, eyes move, 1968, 17", VG **$35.00**

Little Sprout, Green Giant, doll, vinyl, 1980s, EX.........**$15.00**

Little Sprout, Green Giant, jump rope, plastic w/figural handles, 1979, M **$5.00**

Little Sprout, Green Giant, radio, 1970s, MIB **$65.00**

Little Sprout, Green Giant, squeeze toy, green vinyl, 1975, 6½", EX **$5.00**

Marky Maypo, Maypo Cereal, bank, Marky figure seated w/legs spread, red, blue & brown vinyl, name on hat, 1960s, 9", NM **$35.00**

Mermaid, Chicken of the Sea, doll, cloth, 1992, NM ...**$15.00**

Mohawk Tommy, Mohawk Carpet, doll, cloth, EX......**$20.00**

Montgomery Moose, Bounce Fabric Softener, doll, brown plush, knit shirt & corduroy pants, 1985, 15", EX.**$15.00**

Morton Salt Girl, mugs, pictures Salt Girl, 1968, set of 4, MIB...$25.00

Morton Salt Girl, pocket mirror, When It Rains It Pours lettered below image, 3x2", EX..................................$50.00

Mother Nature, Chiffon Margarine, doll, cloth, in original package, M..$20.00

Mr Bubble, bank, pink figural plastic w/blue lettering, 9½", M..$75.00

Mr Magoo, General Electric, doll, vinyl head on stuffed body, 14", EX+..$100.00

Mr Salty, Nabisco Pretzels, doll, stuffed cloth, 11", EX.$10.00

Nestle Bunny, Nestle Quick Chocolate Syrup, bendee, 6".$12.00

Otto the Orkin Man, bank, Otto standing on wood-tone base w/Orkin logo, gold-tone metal, 1960s, 4", EX........$75.00

Panadol Bear, figure, plastic, 2"..................................$10.00

Penguin, Munsingwear, doll, vinyl, 1970s, 7", EX.......$18.00

Pineapple man, Del Monte, doll, stuffed, 1983, M......$12.00

Poppie Fresh, Pillsbury, finger puppet, vinyl, 3½", EX..$15.00

Poppin' Fresh, Pillsbury, bank, ceramic, 1987, 7½", MIB....$25.00

Poppin' Fresh, Pillsbury, doll, stuffed cloth, 1970s, 14½", VG $9.00

Poppin' Fresh, Pillsbury, squeeze toy, white vinyl w/blue eyes & dot on hat, 1970s, 6½", EX........................$12.00

Poppin' Fresh, Pillsbury, utensil holder, ceramic, 1983, 8"...$16.00

Poppin' Fresh & Poppie, Pillsbury, magnets, white & blue molded plastic, 1970s, 4x2" & 3½x2½", EX+, pr ...$20.00

Punchy, Hawaiian Punch, beach raft, yellow canvas w/white rope, Punchy image, Let's Get Together..., 1970s, 34x19", EX...$15.00

Purina Dog, key ring, PVC figure, 2½"..........................$8.00

Quaker Man, Quaker Oats, doll, stuffed cloth, 1965, scarce, 10", NM...$60.00

Quaker Man, Quaker Oats, jigsaw puzzle, man feeding little girl, 5x6½", EX..$45.00

Raid Bug, beach bag, Bug Out To The Beach, canvas, 1980s, 11x17", M..$30.00

Raid Bug, telephone, MIB, minimum value...............$150.00

Raid Bug, windup, working, rare, EX+.....................$200.00

Red Goose, Red Goose Shoes, bank, goose on red base w/embossed lettering, plastic, 1960s, 5", M..........$15.00

Red Goose, Red Goose Shoes, display figure, plaster of Paris, name embossed on chest, 11", EX, $100.00

Red Goose, Red Goose Shoes, sign, Red Goose image on yellow background, porcelain, 17¼x12", EX $170.00

Reddy Kilowatt, ashtray, glass w/his face in red, 3x3", EX.$8.00

Reddy Kilowatt, bank, Reddy against background of blue & white clouds, plastic, rare, 1960s, 5x6½", VG ..$1,600.00

Reddy Kilowatt, decal, full figure, 2½x1¼", M $7.50

Reddy Kilowatt, egg separator, yellow plastic w/blue lettering, shows Reddy's face, Do It Electrically..., EX....$7.00

Reddy Kilowatt, magnetic pot holder, Reddy's face on front, 5½x5½", EX..$15.00

Reddy Kilowatt, necklace charm, full figure, red w/gold head, hands & feet, The Mighty Atom, MOC........$15.00

Reddy Kilowatt, stickpin, full figure, red w/gold accents, Your Favorite Pinup, MOC..................................$12.00

Reddy Tomato, Del Monte, doll, red plush, Country Yumpkin, 1984, 11", M...$8.00

Scrubbing Bubble, Dow Bathroom Cleaner, squeeze toy, molded vinyl, 1989, 3½", M....................................$1.00

Smokey Bear, US Dept of Agriculture, badge, Junior Forest Ranger, 1950s, VG...$12.00

Smokey Bear, US Dept of Agriculture, Smokey figure holding Prevent Forest Fires sign & shovel, plastic, 1972, 14", NM...$40.00

Snap!, Crackle! & Pop!, Kellogg's Rice Krispies, canteen, w/assembly instructions, 4½" $5.00

Snap!, Crackle! & Pop!, Kellogg's Rice Krispies, coloring book, 50 Years w/Snap!, Crackle! & Pop!, uncolored, 1978, M..$25.00

Snap!, Crackle! & Pop!, Kellogg's Rice Krispies, push-button puppet on base w/paper label, plastic, 1984, 4", EX, each..$15.00

Snap!, Kellogg's Rice Krispies, doll, plastic w/jointed arms & legs, red hair, 1984, 4½", MIP..................................$15.00

Speedy Alka-Seltzer, figure, molded vinyl, 8"............$500.00

Speedy Alka-Seltzer, squeeze toy, molded vinyl, 1960s, 5½", NM...$250.00

Sta Puf Man, figure, vinyl, 7", EX...............................$10.00

Sugar Bear, Post Wheat Puffs, doll, stuffed cloth, MIB..$30.00

Sweet Pea, Del Monte, doll, 1991, M............................$9.00

Tang Lips, figure, PVC, 1980s, 3", M.............................$2.00

Tony the Tiger, Kellogg's Frosted Flakes, bank, figural, EX...$60.00

Tony the Tiger, Kellogg's Frosted Flakes, bicycle horn, Tony graphics, MIB $45.00

Tony the Tiger, Kellogg's Frosted Flakes, bowl & spoon, w/USA Olympic logos, 1992, NM $9.00

Tony the Tiger, Kellogg's Frosted Flakes, doll, stuffed cloth, orange w/black & white, red accents, 1972, 14", NM...$40.00

Tony the Tiger, Kellogg's Frosted Flakes, frisbee, 1988, 3¾", NM..$3.00

Tony the Tiger, Kellogg's Frosted Flakes, game, Astronaut Breakfast, complete $12.00

Toucan Sam, Kellogg's Fruit Loops, push-button puppet, Toucan Sam on red base w/paper label, plastic, 1984, 4", EX, each $15.00

Trix Rabbit, Trix cereal, squeeze toy, white vinyl w/rosy cheeks, 1977, 9", EX...$25.00

Wile E Coyote, Brach's, doll, brown plush body w/beige head & chest, 1989, 16½", M **$15.00**

Wizard of O's, Franco American Spaghetti-O's, squeeze toy, red & yellow vinyl, O's on hat & tie, 1978, 7½", EX **$10.00**

24-Hour Bug, Pepto Bismol, bank, bug figure in green vinyl, 1970s, 7", M **$35.00**

7-Up Spot, figure, Spot wearing sunglasses, PVC, 1980s, 4", NM **$3.00**

Tony the Tiger, Kellogg's Frosted Flakes, bank, figural, EX, $60.00

Advertising Trade Cards

During the last decade of the 19th century, these trade cards became a popular way to advertise merchandise of all types. They were collectible even then. They were often packed inside containers of the products they advertised, and many were available directly from the corner grocery store and other places of business. Children as well as adults delighted in pasting the colorful cards in albums, so when you buy today, be sure they've not been damaged by having once been pasted down. Many people collect cards from a specific category — cats, transportation, children, or a favorite product, for instance.

Ad cards range in size from 2" x 3" up to 4" x 6", though some may be larger. Many common examples may be bought for under $5.00. Metamorphics (mechanicals), diecuts, and hold-to-lights will be more pricey. Those listed here are among the more expensive and serve to illustrate the features that contribute to the value of more desirable trade cards.

Acorn Stoves & Ranges, folder, leaf & acorn logo on front, 1881 calendar inside, VG **$16.00**

Ayer's Pills, The Little Fairies, group of girls holding banner, Ayer's Pills, Sugar Coated, EX **$15.00**

Ball's Hip Skating Corset, corset inset, shows girls skating, EX **$35.00**

Bradley's Fertilizers, interior scene w/farmer sleeping in chair, insets of various crops above, EX **$48.00**

Buckeye Lawn Mowers, surreal image of little boy riding an insect, prices on reverse, EX **$16.00**

Buttermilk Toilet Soap, wallet-shaped card folds down into 4-panel colorful 4-part story of Jack & Jill, EX **$20.00**

Candee Rubbers, puppy in a shoe, advertising on reverse, sepia tones, EX **$18.00**

Cashmere Bouquet Perfume, young lady w/tray of flowers, die-cut bird at top, Colgate & Co, EX **$5.00**

Continental Insurance Co, beach scene on front, fire insurance advertising on reverse, VG **$16.00**

Cure-All Malt Bitters, The House That Jack Built, shows colorful bottle, EX **$4.00**

Dixon's Carburet of Iron Stove Polish, Black woman cleaning child, EX **$20.00**

Dr D Jayne's Sanative Pills, Little Red Riding Hood, EX . **$12.00**

Dr Seth Arnold's Cough Killer, little girl holding puppy, It Works Like Magic, Price 25 Cents, EX **$20.00**

Eagle Pencil Co's Colored Crayons, crayon over floral design & paint palette, ...Made In Over Fifty Shades, EX... **$22.00**

EH Barney Skates, ice skate surrounded by text, blue & white, VG **$25.00**

Estey Organ Co, parlor scene w/2 women dancing to organ music, EX **$8.00**

Fairbank's Cottolene, Black woman picking cotton, recipes for making donuts on reverse, EX **$18.00**

Franco American Food, boys painting sign, ...French Soups, Game & Chicken Pates..., EX **$32.00**

Gem Freezer, little girl feeding her doll ice cream, EX.. **$16.00**

Gold Medal Cotton Netting, die-cut of Gold Metal Kid holding fish & hat, coins below, EX **$20.00**

Greer's California Perfume, lady carrying fruit, scenic background, EX **$22.00**

Heckers Flour, little girl & boy carrying lg box of flour overhead, If You Want Muffins, Fritters, Waffles..., EX.. **$12.00**

Heinz Peanut Butter, girl leaning on park bench w/basket, EX **$18.00**

Hires Root Beer, lady seated in black dress, EX **$15.00**

Hoods Liver Pills, features little girl w/hands on cheeks, concave sides w/gold filigree border, 3⅛x3⅛", EX, $6.00

Huyler's Vanilla Chocolate, little girl in rocking chair, If You Only Knew How Nice It Is!, EX **$16.00**

James Pyle's Pearline Cleanser, 3 little girls in elegant dresses & bonnets individually die-cut to fold, EX **$12.00**

Jos Yund & Son Furniture, black & white lettering superimposed over insets of furniture in pink, EX **$45.00**

Libby, McNeill & Libby Corned Beef, man & dog traveling through mountains,...Is Valuable For Explorers..., EX .**$25.00**

Lily White Flour, children playing w/kittens, EX **$4.00**

Maid's Sure Cure, Palmer Cox Brownies moving a pumpkin, EX...**$12.00**

MM Corsets, corset shape w/protruding angel on front, GT Haley, Gardiner ME, EX.............................**$15.00**

Nestle's Milk Food, Little Miss Muffet & lg can of product, nursery rhyme at top, EX **$15.00**

New Process Starch, double image of Chinese man having problems ironing & woman doing perfect job, EX.**$25.00**

Newsboy Cut Plug Tobacco, Where Is Mother, shows group of puppies, VG **$7.50**

Page Woven Fence Co, mother & children watching buffalo fight through fence, Don't Be Afraid Darling..., EX .**$22.00**

Palmer's Perfumes, die-cut vase of flowers, Solon Palmer NY, Estb 1847 on foot of vase, EX.........................**$15.00**

Parker's Cutaneous Charm for Skin, insets showing various uses, blue, brown & white, EX **$25.00**

Quilted Side Corsets, portrait of a woman, advertising on reverse, black & white, EX **$10.00**

Rex Brand Extract of Beef, die-cut folder, labeled jar, Cudahy Packing Co, advertising inside, EX **$20.00**

Runkel Brothers Cocoa & Chocolate, girl looking through curtain w/cup of cocoa, EX...............................**$35.00**

Santa Wood's Boston Coffee, Santa in balloon w/lots of toys, EX...**$15.00**

Shilling's Blossom Tea, romantic couple, Ah! Augustus, How Too Is Blossom Tea, EX **$7.50**

T Kingsford & Son Starch, starch exhibit on front, factory scene on reverse, EX **$18.00**

Tarrant's Seltzer Aperient, sickly man opens up to healthy man, scarce, EX...**$28.00**

Universal Clothes Wringer, Black woman being reprimanded for torn clothing opens to Black woman being praised, EX **$22.00**

Van Houten's Cocoa, unhappy man w/cup labeled Imitation opens to man drinking Van Houten's, EX.............**$35.00**

Woolson Spice Co's Midsummer Greetings, embossed image of hunters shooting at game birds, EX **$24.00**

Airline Memorabilia

Items from commercial airlines such as dinnerware, flatware, playing cards, and pins and buttons worn by the flight crew represent a relatively new field of collector interest. Anything from before the war is rare and commands a high price. Advertising material such as signs, models of airplanes from travel agencies, and timetables are included in this area of collecting as well.

See also Playing Cards.

Ashtray, Air France, 2½" **$5.00**

Belt buckle, Delta, EX...**$5.00**

Book, Flight for Life, Charles Lindbergh **$14.00**

Bowl, Piedmont Airlines, oval w/logo, 6", EX **$12.00**

Cake plate, Eastern Airlines, Rosenthal, EX..................**$5.00**

Candy dish, Air France, olive green w/logo in bottom, 3" dia, EX **$8.00**

Coasters, Continental Airlines, red plastic, set of 6......**$20.00**

Coin, Lucky Linde **$35.00**

Cup, Eastern Airlines, white china w/worn gold trim, 3" .**$6.00**

Cup & saucer, Air Atlanta, EX **$4.00**

Cup & snack plate, American Airlines, white china w/blue logo & trim, EX, $10.00

Dish, Piedmont logo, oval, 6" **$12.00**

Dish, United Airlines, light gray, 1½x6x4½" **$5.00**

Flatware, fork, Braniff **$5.00**

Flatware, fork, Pan American, marked Exclusive...........**$6.00**

Flatware, knife, Eastern Airlines, corkscrew type, EX .**$10.00**

Flatware, knife, fork & spoon set, Air France, wooden handles...**$12.00**

Flatware, knife, Pan American, marked Exclusive **$6.00**

Flatware, spoon, Braniff **$4.00**

Flatware, teaspoon, Braniff...**$5.00**

Menu, Air France, dated 5/21/62, Scandinavia cover, EX.**$4.00**

Money clip, w/file & knife, Capital Airlines **$65.00**

Pin, United Airlines, 100,000 miles, gold-tone lapel w/spinner back, ⅞", EX **$12.00**

Playing cards, Western Airlines, complete w/box, EX...**$6.00**

Salt & pepper shakers, Eastern Airlines, EX, pr **$3.00**

Serving set, American Airlines, 6" dia silver tray w/coffee holder **$35.00**

Shot glass, Eastern Airlines, EX **$2.00**

Shot glass, Southern Air Lines, 10th Anniversary, gold, 1959 ....**$35.00**

Skycap's hat pin, Eastern Airlines, EX **$25.00**

Toy captain's wings, Delta Jr, gold-tone metal pin-back, 2¼", EX..**$5.00**

Toy flight bag, Western Airlines, EX............................**$20.00**

Toy stewardess wings, American Airlines Jr, adjustable, EX........................$6.00

Tray, American Airlines, silver w/coffee holder, shows old logo, 6" dia, EX........................$35.00

Wine glass, Frontier........................$5.00

Wings, American Airlines, metal pin-back, AA symbol w/eagle, EX........................$10.00

Akro Agate

Everybody remembers the 'Aggie' marbles from their childhood; this is the company that made them. They operated in West Virginia from 1914 until 1951, and in addition to their famous marbles they made children's dishes as well as many types of novelties — flowerpots, powder jars with scotty dogs on top, candlesticks, and ashtrays, for instance — in many colors and patterns. Though some of their glassware was made in solid colors, their most popular products were made of the same swirled colors as their marbles. Nearly everything they made is marked with their logo: a crow flying through the letter 'A' holding an Aggie in its beak and one in each claw. Some children's dishes may be marked 'JP,' and the novelty items may instead carry one of these trademarks: 'JV Co, Inc,' 'Braun & Corwin,' 'NYC Vogue Merc Co USA,' 'Hamilton Match Co,' and 'Mexicali Pickwick Cosmetic Corp.'

In the children's dinnerware listings below, you'll notice that color is an important worth-assessing factor. As a general rule, an item in green or white opaque is worth only about one-third as much when compared to the same item in any other opaque color. Marbleized pieces are about three times higher than solid opaques, and of the marbleized colors, blue is the most valuable. It's followed closely by red, with green about 25% under red. Lemonade and oxblood is a good color combination, and it's generally three times higher item for item than the transparent colors of green or topaz.

For further study we recommend *The Collector's Encyclopedia of Akro Agate Glassware* by Gene Florence and *The Collector's Encyclopedia of Children's Dishes* by Margaret and Kenn Whitmyer.

Chiquita, creamer, baked-on colors, 1½", $8.00; sugar bowl (open), opaque green, 1½", $8.00; teapot (open), baked-on colors, 2¾", $12.00

Children's Dishes

Chiquita, saucer, opaque green, 3⅛"........................$2.00

Chiquita, 12-piece boxed set, transparent cobalt........................$90.00

Concentric Rib, creamer, opaque colors other than green or white, 1¼"........................$14.00

Concentric Rib, saucer, opaque green or white, 2¾"........................$2.00

Concentric Rib, 10-pc boxed set, opaque green or white........................$50.00

Concentric Ring, cereal bowl, marbleized blue, 3⅜"........................$45.00

Concentric Ring, creamer, solid opaque colors, 1¼"........................$18.00

Concentric Ring, creamer, solid opaque colors, 1⅜"........................$15.00

Concentric Ring, cup, pumpkin, 1⅜" (larger of 2 sizes).........................$15.00

Concentric Ring, plate, azure blue, 3¼"........................$6.00

Concentric Ring, plate, marbleized blue, 3¼"........................$22.00

Concentric Ring, saucer, transparent cobalt, 3⅛"........................$10.00

Concentric Ring, saucer, yellow, 2¾"........................$4.50

Concentric Ring, sugar bowl, transparent cobalt, 1¼".$35.00

Concentric Ring, teapot, transparent cobalt, 3¾"........................$60.00

Interior Panel, cereal bowl, marbleized blue & white, 3⅜"........................$30.00

Interior Panel, cereal bowl, transparent green, 3⅜".....$12.50

Interior Panel, creamer, azure blue or yellow, 1¼" $32.00

Interior Panel, creamer, marbleized red & white, 1¼"..$32.00

Interior Panel, cup, azure blue or opaque yellow, 1⅜".$32.00

Interior Panel, pitcher, green lustre, 2⅞"........................$14.00

Interior Panel, plate, transparent topaz, 4¼"........................$5.00

Interior Panel, saucer, lemonade or oxblood, 3⅛" $10.00

Interior Panel, saucer, marbleized green & white, 3⅛" .$6.50

Interior Panel, saucer, pink lustre, 2⅜"........................$4.00

Interior Panel, teapot, marbleized green & white, 3⅜".$32.00

Interior Panel, teapot, transparent green, 3¾"........................$35.00

Interior Panel, 8-pc boxed set, sm-size $125.00

JP, cup, baked-on colors, 1½"........................$7.50

JP, plate, transparent red or brown, 4¼"........................$14.50

JP, saucer, transparent cobalt w/ribs, 3¼"........................$2.50

JP, teapot, light blue or crystal, 2¾"........................$38.00

Miss America, creamer, white, 1¼"........................$45.00

Miss America, cup, forest green, 1⅝"........................$45.00

Miss America, saucer, white w/decal, 3⅝"........................$14.00

Miss America, teapot, white, 3¼"........................$70.00

Miss America, teapot, white w/decal, 3¼"........................$115.00

Octagonal, cereal bowl, beige, pumpkin or light blue, 3⅜"........................$20.00

Octagonal, creamer, lemonade or oxblood, tab handle, 1½"........................$26.00

Octagonal, cup, pumpkin, yellow or lime green, 1¼".$22.00

Octagonal, pitcher, dark green, blue or white, 2¾".....$18.00

Octagonal, plate, green, white or dark blue, 4¼"........................$4.00

Octagonal, sugar bowl, green, white or dark blue, tab handle, 1½"........................$12.50

Octagonal, sugar bowl, lemonade or oxblood, tab handle, 1½"........................$45.00

Octagonal, teapot, dark green, blue or white, 3⅜"......$18.00

Octagonal, tumbler, pumpkin, yellow or lime green, 2" .$16.00

Octagonal, 21-pc boxed set, green, white or dark blue, lg-size........................$125.00

Raised Daisy, creamer, yellow, 1¾"........................$44.00

Raised Daisy, plate, blue, 3".................................$14.00
Raised Daisy, teapot, blue, 2⅜".......................$34.00
Raised Daisy, tumbler, yellow, 2" $25.00
Stacked Disc, creamer, opaque green or white, 1¼"...$14.00
Stacked Disc, cup, opaque colors other than green or white, 1¼" $12.00
Stacked Disc, pitcher, opaque green or white, 2⅞"...$12.00
Stacked Disc, tumbler, opaque green or white, 2" $7.50
Stacked Disc, 21-pc boxed set, opaque green or white, sm- size..$110.00
Stacked Disc & Interior Panel, cereal bowl, solid opaque colors, 3⅜"....................................$25.00
Stacked Disc & Interior Panel, creamer, transparent cobalt, 1⅜"...$30.00
Stacked Disc & Interior Panel, creamer, transparent cobalt, 1¼" $35.00
Stacked Disc & Interior Panel, plate, marbleized blue, 4¾"...$20.00
Stacked Disc & Interior Panel, plate, solid opaque colors, 3¼"...$6.50
Stacked Disc & Interior Panel, saucer, marbleized blue, 3¼" $12.00
Stacked Disc & Interior Panel, saucer, solid opaque colors, 3¼".......................................$6.00
Stacked Disc & Interior Panel, saucer, transparent green, 2¾"...$6.50
Stacked Disc & Interior Panel, sugar bowl, transparent green, 1¾".....................................$40.00
Stacked Disc & Interior Panel, teapot, marbleized blue, 3¾" $105.00
Stacked Disc & Interior Panel, tumbler, transparent cobalt, 2"..$14.50
Stippled Band, cup, transparent azure, 1½" $25.00
Stippled Band, cup, transparent green, 1¼" $6.50
Stippled Band, saucer, transparent amber, 2¾".............$2.50
Stippled Band, saucer, transparent green, 3¼"...............$2.50
Stippled Band, sugar bowl, transparent amber, 1¾"....$25.00
Stippled Band, teapot, transparent green, 3⅜"............$18.00
Stippled Band, tumbler, transparent amber, 1¾" $8.50

Other Lines of Production

Ashtray, Hotel Edison $45.00
Ashtray, Hotel Lincoln, green...............................$50.00
Ashtray, oxblood & white, square, 3"..................$10.00
Ashtray, Scallop Shell, green & white.....................$6.00
Bowl, #321, orange, tab handles............................$25.00
Bowl, Graduated Darts, #320, black.....................$35.00
Bowl, Stacked Disc, blue & white $85.00
Candlesticks, royal blue, 3¼", pr $250.00
Candlesticks, Westite, orange & beige, 8¼", pr $45.00
Cup & saucer, demitasse; yellow $25.00
Flowerpot, Banded Dart, #302, yellow...................$50.00
Flowerpot, Braun & Corwin, #290, 1¼".................$25.00
Flowerpot, Graduated Darts, signed, 3" $28.00
Flowerpot, Plain Band, #298, blue, 1⅞"................$18.00
Flowerpot, Ribs & Flutes, #296, ivory...................$12.00
Flowerpot, Ribs & Flutes, #305, yellow $18.00

Jardiniere, bell shape, yellow, 4¾" $38.50
Knife, #739, grid style, pink.................................$65.00
Lamp, crystal, wall hanging.................................$15.00
Marbles, Chinese Checkers, MIB...........................$25.00
Marbles, 100 #1 moss agates, MIB......................$250.00
Planter, #656, blue & white, rectangular $10.00
Planter, Westite, Japanese style, brown & white $100.00
Powder box, J Vivaudou, orange & white, rare........$250.00
Powder jar, apple form, ivory.................................$400.00
Powder jar, Mexicali, orange & white $25.00
Vase, #317, royal blue, tab handles $30.00
Vase, embossed wheat on trumpet form, rare, 5" $750.00
Vase, Graduated Dart, #312, blue, 8¾".....................$65.00

Basket, 2-handled, marbleized colors, $28.00

Aladdin Lamps

Aladdin lamps have been made continually since 1908 by the Mantle Lamp Company of America, now Aladdin Industries Inc. in Nashville, Tennessee. Their famous kerosene lamps are highly collectible, and some are quite valuable. Most were relegated to the storage shelf or thrown away after electric lines came through the country. Today many people keep them on hand for emergency light.

Few know that Aladdin was one of the largest manufacturers of electric lamps from 1930 to 1956. They created new designs, colorful glass, and unique paper shades. These are not only collectible but are still used in many homes today. Many Aladdin lamps, kerosene as well as electric, can be found at garage sales, antique shops, and flea markets. You can learn more about them in the book *Aladdin Electric Lamps* written by J.W. Courter, who also periodically issues updated price guides for both kerosene and electric Aladdins.

Electric Aladdins

G-184, amber table lamp...$200.00

G-193, Alacite table lamp w/night light......................$60.00
G-229, Alacite table lamp, double shades.................$150.00
G-236, Alacite table lamp $65.00
G-24, Alacite Cupid boudoir lamp..........................$125.00
G-30, Alacite boudoir lamp $60.00
G-33, white moonstone boudoir lamp $50.00
G-351, Alacite pinup..$60.00
G-355C, Hopalong Cassidy Gun-in-Holster..............$275.00
G-375, Alacite Dancing Ladies Urn.......................$700.00
G-41, Alacite boudoir lamp $45.00
M-175, metal table lamp $45.00
P-146, ceramic table lamp $35.00
2080, bridge floor lamp $150.00
3967, floor lamp w/night light $225.00
4567, torchier floor lamp $225.00

Kerosene Aladdins (with good burners)

B-101, amber Corinthian, EX...................................$100.00
B-111, green moonstone Cathedral, EX $225.00
B-116, rose moonstone Corinthian, EX $175.00
B-28, rose Simplicity, EX.....................................$125.00
B-53, clear Washington Drape, EX $70.00
B-75, Alacite Tall Lincoln Drape, EX $100.00
B-80, clear Beehive, EX..$90.00
B-92, green Vertique, EX......................................$225.00
Model C, caboose lamp w/shade, aluminum..............$75.00
Model 11, nickel table lamp, EX.............................$85.00
Model 12, green Venetian Vase lamp #1243, EX.......$150.00
Model 12, nickel table lamp, EX.............................$80.00
Model 12, 4-post hanging lamp, #616 shade $350.00
Model 23, amber Short Lincoln Drape, 1974..............$75.00
Model 23, cobalt Short Lincoln Drape, 1989.............$100.00
Model 6, nickel table lamp, EX...............................$90.00

Aluminum

This is an exciting, relatively new field of collecting, and your yard-sale outings will often yield up some nice examples at very little expense. You'll find all types of serving pieces and kitchenware, most of which will be embossed with fruit or flowers. Some will have a hand-hammered texture; these pieces are generally thought to be from the fifties, though aluminum ware was popular from the late 1930s on. The best buys are those with a backstamp. A good one to watch for is Wendell August Forge. Russel Wright and Royal Hickman were two highly renowned designers of dinnerware and ceramics that used this medium for some of their work; items signed by either are very collectible. For more information we recommend the newsletter *The Aluminist* published by Dannie Woodard, author of *Hammered Aluminum, Hand Wrought Collectibles*. Another book on the subject is titled *Collectible Aluminum, An Identification and Value Guide*, by Everett Grist (Collector Books).

Bar tray, rectangular w/anchor, rope & sea gulls motif, rounded corners, applied handles, Everlast, 9x15".$60.00

Basket, hexagon shape w/round flower & fruit decor, upturned serrated edges, inside double-looped handle, 6x10" dia..$18.00
Basket, oblong w/pine cone pattern, double twisted handle, Hand Forged, 9x7"............................$15.00
Bowl, round & footed w/chrysanthemum design, serrated rim & foot, unmarked, 4x9" dia $40.00
Bowl, round w/allover dogwood pattern, fluted & crimped rim, Wendell August Forge, 2x7" dia...................$30.00
Bowl, round w/allover hammered pattern, unevenly scalloped rim, McClelland & Barclay, 1½x6" dia.........$20.00
Bread tray, oval shape w/wild rose pattern on hammered background, serrated rim, self-handles, Continental, 6x13"...$15.00
Bread tray, oval w/acorns & grapes in leafy chain pattern around fluted rim, Wendell August Forge, 7x11"..$45.00
Bun warmer, plain w/ribbed edge, S-shaped legs w/tulip decor, C-shaped finial w/2 beads on dome lid, unmarked, 8x9" dia..................................$40.00
Butter dish, oblong w/bamboo pattern & bamboo finial, tray has plain flat edge w/rounded corners, Everlast, 4x4x7" long $20.00
Candelabra, square hammered base w/looped center rod holding 3 cups, Art Nouveau look, Langbein, 13x6", pr..$125.00
Candlesticks, hammered design w/scalloped base & fluted bobeche, Everlast, 3x4" dia, pr....................$30.00
Candy dish, center handle attached to 2 fluted bowls w/scrolled daisy design, serrated rim, unmarked, 12x6"...$10.00
Candy dish, stylized leaf shape w/twisted loop handle, Buenilum, 5x15" long................................$20.00
Casserole, round w/hammered effect, lid w/scalloped edge overlaps bowl, tulip & ribbon finial, Rodney Kent, 6x8" dia $20.00
Casserole, round w/plain bottom, lid w/plain edge & hammered effect in center, ring handles, Neocraft, 6x9"..$15.00
Child's cup, patriotic shield & St Louis engraved between ribbed bands, rolled lip, applied handle, unmarked, 2x2" dia..$18.00
Child's plate, alphabet embossed around edge, unmarked, 7" dia..$30.00
Cigar holder, shaped to hold 3 cigars, floral engraving on hinged & locking lid, unmarked, 2½x5⅛"............$25.00
Cigarette box, rectangular w/pine cone pattern on hinged lid, hammered background, Town, 3⅜x5⅜" $75.00
Coasters, round w/concentric spiral design & serrated rim, dish-rack type holder, Everlast, 3" dia, set of 8.....$20.00
Compote, fluted dish w/stylized floral design & serrated rim, curlicue stem w/cone-shaped base, unmarked, 5x8" dia..$15.00
Creamer & sugar bowl (open), urn-shaped w/allover hammered effect & fluted rims, ear-shaped handles, unmarked $15.00
Crumb brush & tray, grapevine pattern in center of tray, Lucite brush w/hammered handle, Everlast.........$20.00
Fondue pot, plain w/beaded edges on pot, Sterno cup & base, wooden handle, Buenilum, 3x11x5¼" dia ...$20.00

Fruit bowl w/knives, round w/fruit & flower pattern, serrated rim & pedestal foot, double-loop handles, unmarked, 4x11" **$25.00**

Ice bucket (open), round & tapered w/allover hammered effect, fluted rim, 'barbell' handles, w/tongs, Everlast, 5x10" **$25.00**

Lazy Susan, round w/flat serrated rim & foot, embossed tulip design w/2 applied tulip & ribbon accents, 18" dia..**$20.00**

Meat server, stylized oval w/plain flat rim, flying ducks & cattail pattern in center, Serve-It, 13x18" **$30.00**

Mint dish, pansy shape w/single chrysanthemum design & fork-type fluting on rim, open flower finial, unmarked, 10" dia..**$30.00**

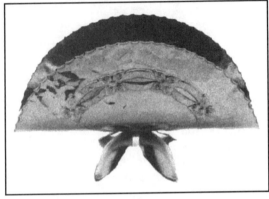

Napkin holder, fan shape w/floral & ribbon pattern & fluted rim on 4 leaf-shaped legs, unmarked, 3½x2x6",$15.00

Nut bowl, flower & leaf pattern on ruffled bowl w/serrated rim, low pedestal foot, w/6 picks & cracker, Wilson, 4x7" **$20.00**

Pitcher, hammered pattern w/flared & rolled rim & lip, applied ice lip, lg ear-shaped handle, Gailstyn, 8x6" dia...**$15.00**

Powder box, ribbed glass dish w/poppy pattern on round aluminum lid, black plastic finial, unmarked, 3x5" dia **$15.00**

Relish tray, rectangular w/flying geese pattern repeated in 4 compartments, self-handled, Arthur Armour, 5x16".**$75.00**

Salad bowl, round w/stylized wheat design, plain rim, Palmer-Smith, 4x14" dia....................................**$90.00**

Sandwich tray, serrated rim w/4 8-petal daisy designs, applied handles, Buenilum, 12" dia.....................**$15.00**

Servant's bell, plain w/beaded edge, figure-8 handle, Arthur Armour, 5¾" **$20.00**

Serving tray, rectangular w/goldfish pattern on hammered background, applied walnut handles, unmarked, 10x14" **$45.00**

Serving tray, round & w/morning-glory design on hammered ground, fluted rim, 'folded' loop handles, Farberware, 14" dia **$15.00**

Serving tray, round dish-type w/flat rim, pheasant pattern, marked Westbend, 18" dia **$25.00**

Silent butler, wheat design on hammered background, serrated edge, Kraftware **$28.00**

Tidbit, single plate w/finely fluted rim & T-shaped handle, pine cone pattern, marked Made in Canada, 12" dia **$10.00**

Tidbit, 2-tiered w/grapevine pattern, circular handle, Everlast, 11x10" dia **$30.00**

Tumbler, hammered effect w/single band top & bottom, plain flared rim, Gailstyn **$4.00**

Vase, cylinder shape tapering slightly at bottom, serrated rim & base, chrysanthemum design, Continental, 10x5" dia.**$85.00**

Animal Dishes

Glass dishes with animal and bird figures on the lids are a common sight at flea markets today, but you'll need to study the subject thoroughly to be able to tell the old ones from the new. Many were made in the latter 1800s and the early years of this century. Some of the smaller ones were sold to food processors who filled them with products such as mustard or baking powder. Several companies have recently made reproductions. In the 1960s, Kemple made a cat, duck, dove, fox, hen, lamb, lion, rabbit, rooster, and turkey; Westmoreland was making some in the 1980s, and some you'll see were made yesterday! Beware. *Covered Animal Dishes* by Everett Grist will help you in your study. If no color is given in the descriptions, assume that the following examples are clear.

Atterberry duck, reproduced by Imperial, dated & marked IG, all colors...**$40.00**

Bird on basket-weave base w/braided edge, milk glass, Vallerysthal...**$95.00**

Bird w/berry, milk glass, transparent, clear or colored..**$300.00**

Camel (resting), milk glass, attributed to Westmoreland, early **$120.00**

Cat on oval wide-ribbed base, milk glass..................**$40.00**

Chick atop vertical egg, milk glass w/gold accents.....**$65.00**

Chicks on round 2-handled basket, milk glass **$175.00**

Dog on oval wide-ribbed base, amber, Westmoreland..**$65.00**

Dog on oval wide-ribbed base, milk glass head w/opaque blue body & base..**$65.00**

Donkey powder jar, clear, probably Jeannette Glass ..**$15.00**

Elephant (standing), clear, Co-operative Flint Glass or Indiana Glass, 9" long **$25.00**

Elephant w/rider, clear frosted, Vallerysthal, 7" long ..**$200.00**

Fish lying on base, transparent green..........................**$75.00**

Fish on collared base, clear frosted, Central Glass Co.**$150.00**

Fox on ribbed base, milk glass, dated........................**$175.00**

Hand & dove on lacy rectangular base, dated...........**$125.00**

Hen on diamond-weave basket, milk glass w/blue head..**$65.00**

Lamb on oval split-ribbed base, amber **$45.00**

Lamb on rectangular picket base w/concave corners, milk glass **$45.00**

Lion on rectangular picket base w/concave corners, milk glass **$95.00**

Lovebirds powder jar (new), clear w/cross-hatched design, may be Westmoreland **$7.00**

Pintail duck on oval split-ribbed base (reproduction), milk glass, Kemple **$65.00**

Poodle powder jar, carnival glass, Jeannette Glass, 1950s.**$20.00**

Rabbit on clear 8" oval basket-weave nest, US Glass, $85.00

Rooster (standing), clear w/painted comb & waddle, attributed to LE Smith..**$45.00**

Rooster on oval wide-ribbed base, dark opaque blue ..**$90.00**

Setter on footed rectangular base featuring gun & hunting bag w/leaf design, milk glass, attributed to Vallerysthal **$225.00**

Snail on strawberry, milk glass w/paint traces, Vallerysthal, lg **$120.00**

Swan, clear frosted, Vallerysthal, 5½" long **$65.00**

Swan creamer & sugar bowl, milk glass w/paint traces, Westmorland, reproduced by Summit Art Glass ...**$45.00**

Swimming Duck, yellow, Vallerysthal, paper label, marked PV France **$120.00**

Turtle, amber, originally by Vallerystal, this one reproduced by LG Wright & Co **$45.00**

Art Deco Collectibles

During the period from about 1925 until 1950, popular taste and fashions favored architecture, home furnishings and decorations, jewelry, appliances, and even automobiles with sleek aerodynamic lines, cubist forms, or sweeping curves. Lightning bolts, slender nudes, sleek grayhounds, and geometrics were preferred decorative motifs. Chrome, vinyl, and plastic was high style, though at the other end of the spectrum, lush fabrics and exotic woods were used as well. When Art Deco furnishings began showing up in some of our leading home decorating magazines a few years back, collector demand for authentic pieces ran high. Many moderately priced items are around today, but signed pieces often carry high-dollar price tags.

For further study we recommend *The Collector's Guide to Art Deco* by Mary Frank Gaston.

See also Chase Brass and Copper Company.

Belt buckle, red plastic square w/canted corners, oval cutout w/diagonal bar in center............................**$10.00**

Bracelet, 3 rows of yellow Bakelite half-circles connected by gold-tone rods w/ball-shaped ends....................**$100.00**

Candle holders, chrome, round w/ribbed edges on cup & base, stylized fish handles, 1x4" dia, pr.................**$60.00**

Candle holders & nut dish, chrome balls on blue mirrored bases, Chase, 3-pc set..**$200.00**

Centerpiece bowl, hand-painted ceramic diamond shape w/stepped sides tapering down to 2-step base, Myott & Son, 11" dia, $80.00

Centerpiece bowl, transparent green glass diamond shape tapering down to square base, molded fan designs at corners, 4"..**$75.00**

Cheese board, chrome dome lid w/yellow celluloid handle on round wooden base, Chase, 6½" dia **$100.00**

Cheese dish, chrome dome lid w/black finial on flat chrome dish w/circular bands **$125.00**

Clock, bronze, rectangular w/rounded corners on lg rectangular base, digital, Silvercrest, mid-1930s, 19" long **$225.00**

Clock, bronze desk type w/tall arched case on rectangular base, sterling silver Deco trim, round numbered face, Lux..**$175.00**

Clock, mantle type w/gold-painted dog lying atop green ceramic base, round chrome-trimmed face, stepped ends **$125.00**

Desk accessories, bronze calendar & envelope holders, rectangular, Silvercrest, set......................................**$100.00**

Figurine, dancer w/fan, porcelain on metal base, floral design around hem of dress, attributed to Goldscheider, 12"..**$225.00**

Figurine, pr of ceramic Russian wolfhounds in running pose on long base w/rounded corners, German, signed B Kopecki, 13"..**$250.00**

Frame, plain brass rectangular table-type w/single ball & tab on each side, 2 ball feet at bottom, 6x4".............**$80.00**

Hairbrush, mottled brown plastic step design w/long tapered handle **$20.00**

Handbag, white plastic beads form pentagon body w/loop handles **$35.00**

Incense burner, cast iron, round top w/cut-out floral design on geometric pedestal base, marked Made in France, 6½"...**$150.00**

Inkwell, hammered copper & cast brass, round w/glass insert & hinged lid **$125.00**

Mannequin head, plaster w/gold finish, short molded hair parted in middle, 10".............................**$175.00**

Necklace, orange & clear plastic beads alternating w/black beads...**$15.00**

Perfume bottle, black glass, tall flat rectangular shape w/silver lattice band around beveled shoulder, French **$100.00**

Perfume tray, blue glass rectangle w/chrome-trimmed 'wand'-shaped handles, silver-painted cameo of lady & dog, 9x12"...**$25.00**

Powder box, chrome 'top' shape on round base w/3 shades of green bands on lid, center rod w/ball finial, glass insert **$60.00**

Powder box, chrome round shape w/Bakelite hearts surrounding ebony heart finial, glass insert, Chase ...**$60.00**

Serving bowl, porcelain w/lustre finish, oval w/scalloped rim & cut-out self-handles, leaf & berry decor, 10½" long...**$30.00**

Silent bulter, chrome 'book' shape w/hinged lid, line design, loop handle, 9" long **$55.00**

Sugar bowl, porcelain w/lustre finish, round shape tapering down to slightly flared bottom, zigzag design, 5¼".**$35.00**

Vase, black glass 'trumpet' shape, 12"..............**$55.00**

Vase, blue, cream & orange lustre, bulbous w/slighly flared rim, 6¼" **$50.00**

Vase, honey-tan glaze, rectangular shape w/embossed flying duck duck on 1 side w/cactus on reverse, Frankoma, 7x6" **$25.00**

Vase, multicolored flowers on tan & blue lustre, bulbous w/slightly flared rim, 9", minimum value **$60.00**

Vase, transparent green glass 'rocket' shape w/silver trim on legs & rim, 9"...**$90.00**

Vases, dark green glaze, stylized lily shapes, paper labels marked marked Camden Art & Tile Pottery, 11", pr.**$35.00**

Wall pocket, white glaze, woman's head w/lg hat......**$75.00**

Ashtrays

Ashtray collecting is just hitting its stride, so don't pass over them without first giving them the attention they deserve. Those we've listed illustrate the features that contribute to their values. Quality is easy to spot. Marked items are usually good, especially when combined with distinctive styling such as embossed or intaglio designs, applied decorations, added figures of animals or people, Art Deco lines, interesting advertising messages, etc. Some people particularly like souvenir ashtrays.

Manufacturers of tires issued miniature versions containing ashtray inserts that were usually embossed with an advertising message. Some were sold as souvenirs from World's Fairs. The inserts were often made of clear glass, but a few were colored, and once in awhile you'll find a tin one. The tires themselves were usually black, though other colors turn up once in awhile too. For ladies and non-smokers, some miniature tires contained a pin tray.

Aluminum, embossed bamboo pattern, single holder, Everlast, 5" dia **$30.00**

Bellhop w/attached holder, ceramic w/multicolored matte finish, Japan, 5¾" **$135.00**

Boston Red Sox, plaster, 1930s **$30.00**

Brass, bull's head in relief, 4½x5".....................**$60.00**

Camel figure, ceramic w/green glossy finish, Japan, 3¼".**$15.00**

Cat on canoe, ceramic w/blue & tan lustre finish, Japan, 1½" **$12.50**

Clown seated in heart shape, ceramic w/tan lustre & blue glossy finish, Japan, 2½"........................**$35.00**

Chrome, round dish w/double rests extending out from side, black enamel trim, Art Deco styling, 7" long..........**$10.00**

Cowboy hat shape, ceramic w/tan lustre finish, Japan, 3¾" long...**$8.50**

Dog on heart shape, ceramic w/black & orange glossy finish, Japan, 1¾".......................................**$12.50**

Elf figure, ceramic w/tan lustre finish, blue collar & green hat, Japan, 2½" **$12.50**

Frog w/mouth open wide, ceramic w/green glossy finish, white lustre belly, Japan, 3"........................**$15.00**

Hand shape, ceramic w/white glossy finish & gold highlights, Japan, 5½"..**$18.00**

Knight w/shield, green & white w/gold highlights, marked HP Ardalt, Lenwile China #6332....................**$8.00**

Leaf shape, metal, Occupied Japan, 6" **$7.50**

Leaf shape w/embossed grapes, metal, Occupied Japan, sm **$4.00**

Metal, embossed sailboat in center, floral border, Occupied Japan...**$4.00**

Metal, floral design in center w/cut-out floral design around edge, Occupied Japan, 5½" dia **$6.00**

Metal, football shape w/embossed figure in center, Occupied Japan **$6.00**

Mexican siesta figure, ceramic w/orange, blue & yellow glossy finish, Japan, 3"............................**$12.50**

Peacock figure, ceramic w/white lustre finish, red & blue features, Japan, 3¼" **$18.00**

Pig playing violin beside card suit of spades, ceramic w/tan lustre finish & black trim, multicolored pig, Japan, 2½"...**$12.50**

Reclining clown balancing bowl on his feet, ceramic w/orange & green lustre finish, Japan, 2½" **$18.00**

Snufferette, ceramic w/cobalt blue glaze, Ekstrand Mfg Co, The Executive, 4⅛" dia, $35.00

Snufferette, round light-green ceramic dish, marked, National Porcelain Co, Art Deco styling, 4" dia **$30.00**

Wolf beside card suit of clubs, ceramic w/tan lustre finish, brown glossy wolf, Japan, 2¼".............................**$12.50**

Advertising

Bacardi Rum, porcelain, made in Ireland, 1960...........**$15.00**

Big Boy Hamburgers, glass, 4½" dia............................**$25.00**

Ceresota Flour, ceramic, brown image of Ceresota boy in center of round dish, gold trim, 4 rests, 7" dia, NM.**$5.00**

Graham Motor Cars, aluminum w/embossed helmet logo **$50.00**

Newport Cigarettes, white china, pictures 3 packs of cigarettes, 3¾" dia, EX..**$12.00**

Player's Navy Cut Tobacco, ceramic, pictures sailor in center, ca 1940, 6" dia, EX, $25.00

Player's Navy Mixture, embossed ships on brass **$145.00**

Ralston Purina, shaped like dog's feeding dish w/colorful graphic on white background, 5⅞" dia, EX...........**$35.00**

Sheridan Stoves, stamped metal, ...Quincy Ill.............**$25.00**

Smirnoff Vodka, clear glass w/red & black lettering on white bottom, 3¾x3¾" **$4.00**

Waldorf-Astoria Hotel, NY, glass, 1930s.......................**$20.00**

White Owl Cigars, blue, white & brown, pictures an owl atop burning cigar, 1930s, 3½x3½", EX **$8.00**

Souvenir

Alaska, metal w/embossed husky dog in center, Occupied Japan, round..**$12.50**

California International Pacific, 2 pelicans on edge, ceramic, w/blue & white lustre finish, Occupied Japan, 3" ..**$18.00**

Georgia, ceramic state shape w/colorful graphics, gold trim, Occupied Japan..**$14.00**

Montreal, metal heart shape, scenic w/floral border, Occupied Japan **$6.50**

New Orleans, metal heart shape, city scene, Occupied Japan **$6.50**

New York City, metal w/embossed Statue of Liberty, decorative border, Japan, oval **$12.50**

Washington DC, metal w/embossed image of the White House, decorative border, Japan, oval **$4.00**

Tire Ashtrays

BF Goodrich Life Saver Radial, 100th Anniversary, 1970, M **$35.00**

Brunswick Tires, 1920s, glass chipped, tire EX...........**$20.00**

Firestone Great Lakes Exposition, Cleveland Ohio, 1936, Depression Glass, M **$50.00**

Firestone Safety Lock Cord Champion, tire only **$15.00**

Goodrich Silvertown Heavy Duty Cord, EX................**$45.00**

Goodyear Aqua Tread **$12.00**

Goodyear Inflatible Goodyear Blimp............................**$7.50**

Goodyear Polysteel...**$10.00**

Goodyear Tower Torque..**$12.00**

Goodyear Vector...**$10.00**

Goodyear Wrangler **$12.00**

Hood Tires, arrow logo on glass insert, M..................**$60.00**

Kelly Springfield Super Armor Track, M.....................**$25.00**

Autographs

'Philography' is an extremely popular hobby, one that is very diversified. Autographs of sports figures, movie stars, entertainers, and politicians from our lifetime may bring several hundred dollars, depending on rarity and application, while John Adams' simple signature on a document from 1800, for instance, might bring thousands. A signature on a card or photograph is the least valuable type of autograph. A handwritten letter is the most valuable, since in addition to the signature you get the message as well. Depending upon what it reveals about the personality who penned it, content can be very important and can make a major difference in value.

Many times a polite request accompanied by an SASE to a famous person will result in receipt of a signed photo or a short handwritten note that might in several years be worth a tidy sum!

Obviously as new collectors enter the field, the law of supply and demand will drive the prices for autographs upward, especially when the personality is deceased. There are forgeries around, so before you decide to invest in expensive autographs, get to know your dealers.

Aaron, Hank; inscribed color photo of 715th home run, 11x14" **$55.00**

Allen, Tim; signed card, 3x5" **$10.00**

Allen, Tim; signed color photo, 8x10" **$75.00**

Allen, Woody; signed card, 3x5"...................................**$30.00**

Allison, Davey; signed color photo, 8x10" **$75.00**

Anderson, Harry; signed card, 3x5" **$5.00**

Andretti, Mario; signed card, 3x5"...............................**$3.00**

Andretti, Mario; signed color photo, 8x10" **$20.00**

Andy Griffith Show, TV still photo signed by Don Knotts & Jim Nabors.................................**$125.00**

Archer, Ann; signed card, 3x5".................................**$9.00**

Baker, Buddy; signed color photo, 8x10" **$12.00**

Bancroft, Dave; signed card, 3x5"...........................**$75.00**

Beatty, Warren; signed movie still from *Bugsy*, 8x10".**$95.00**

Becker, Boris; inscribed color photo, 8x10"................**$25.00**

Bennett, Tony; signed black & white photo, 8x10".....**$30.00**

Berman, Shelley; inscribed black & white photo, 8x10".**$12.00**

Bernstein, Kenny; signed color photo, 8x10"..............**$10.00**

Bird, Larry; inscribed autobiography, dust jacket **$75.00**

Black, Clint; signed black & white photo, 8x10" **$85.00**

Blake, Robert; signed black & white photo, 8x10"......**$12.00**

Bolton, Michael; signed-in-person black & white photo, scarce, 8x10"...**$125.00**

Bonet, Lisa; signed black & white photo, 8x10" **$35.00**

Bonnett, Neil; signed gum/trading card **$25.00**

Boone, Pat; signed black & white photo, 8x10" **$15.00**

Borge, Victor; signed black & white photo, 8x10".......**$17.00**

Borgnine, Ernest; signed movie still from the original 1974 *Law & Disorder*, 8x10" **$25.00**

Bowie, David; signed color photo, 8x10"....................**$50.00**

Boy George, signed black & white photo, 8x10" **$40.00**

Brooks, Garth; signed-in-person black & white photo, 8x10"...**$85.00**

Burke, Billie; signed black & white photo, 8x10"......**$165.00**

Caesar, Sid; signed black & white photo, 8x10" **$15.00**

Campanella, Roy; signed pre-accident card **$215.00**

Cannon, Dyan; signed black & white photo, 8x10".....**$25.00**

Carlisle, Kitty; signed black & white photo, 8x10".......**$12.00**

Carney, Art; early black & white photo, 8x10".............**$20.00**

Cass, Peggy; signed black & white photo, 8x10" **$15.00**

Chamberlain, Wilt; inscribed photo, 8x10".................**$15.00**

Como, Perry; early black & white photo, 8x10" **$15.00**

Costner, Kevin; color movie still from *Robin Hood*, 8x10"...**$100.00**

Crenshaw, Ben; signed card, 3x5" **$5.00**

Cruise, Tom; black & white movie still from *Far & Away*, 8x10" **$85.00**

Crystal, Billy; black & white movie still from *Throw Mama from the Train*, 8x10"..........................**$50.00**

Cunningham, Randall; signed color photo, 8x10"........**$17.50**

Curtis, Jamie Lee; signed color photo, 8x10" **$45.00**

Curtis, Tony; signed color photo, 8x10" **$10.00**

Dafoe, Willem; signed color portrait, matted..............**$17.50**

Davis, Bette; signed black & white movie still from *Dead Image*, matted, 8x10" **$55.00**

Davis, Bette; signed black & white photo, 8x10" **$125.00**

Davis, Sammy Jr; signed black & white photo, 8x10" ..**$150.00**

Dee, Sandra; inscribed black & white photo, 8x10"....**$23.50**

DeNiro, Robert; signed movie still from *Cape Fear*, 8x10"...**$80.00**

Depp, Johnny; signed black & white photo, 8x10" **$37.50**

Devito, Danny; signed black & white photo, 8x10"....**$27.50**

Dey, Susan; signed color photo, 8x10".......................**$45.00**

Dickerson, Eric; inscribed color photo as Colt, 8x10".**$10.00**

Douglas, Donna; as Elly Mae, signed color photo, 8x10".**$30.00**

Douglas, Kirk; signed black & white photo, 8x10"......**$30.00**

Drysdale, Don; signed card, 3x5" **$15.00**

Eastwood, Clint; signed black & white photo, 8x10" ..**$65.00**

Elvira, signed black & white photo, 8x10" **$20.00**

Feliciano, Jose; signed black & white photo, 8x10" **$30.00**

Field, Sally; signed card, 3x5" **$10.00**

Flutie, Doug; signed card, 3x5"..................................**$12.00**

Ford, Tennessee Ernie; signed black & white photo, 8x10" **$65.00**

Foster, Jodie; signed black & white photo, 8x10"......**$100.00**

Foyt, AJ; signed color photo, 8x10" **$15.00**

Frazier, Joe; early signed photo, 8x10" **$12.00**

Garcia, Andy; signed color photo, 8x10" **$38.00**

Glenn, John; inscribed black & white photo, 8x10" **$12.00**

Goldberg, Whoopi; signed color photo, 8x10" **$12.00**

Gooden, Dwight; inscribed color poster, 20x24".........**$35.00**

Goodman, John; as Babe Ruth, color movie still, 8x10".**$150.00**

Griffith, Melanie; signed color photo, 8x10" **$65.00**

Grodin, Charles; signed black & white photo, 8x10".....**$6.00**

Hanks, Tom; signed color movie still from *Philadelphia*, 8x10"...**$85.00**

Harry, Debbie; signed color photo, 8x10"...................**$75.00**

Hodges, Gil; signed card, 3x5".................................**$40.00**

Hoover, Herbert; 31st President, typed letter declining invitation, signed & dated 1935, w/print & button, framed **$150.00**

Howe, Gordie; signed card, 3x5"...............................**$10.00**

Hutton, Laura; signed color photo, 8x10" **$55.00**

January, Don; signed color photo, 8x10" **$10.00**

Jimmy the Greek, signed card, 3x5" **$15.00**

Joel, Billy; signed-in-person color photo, 8x10" **$85.00**

Jones, Tom; signed color photo, 8x10" **$25.00**

Lithgow, John; signed color photo, 8x10" **$50.00**

Lawrence, Steve; & Eydie Gorme, signed black & white photo, framed, 5x7", $30.00

Mathis, Johnny; signed black & white photo, 8x10"....**$30.00**

Melton, Sid; signed black & white photo, 8x10".........**$15.00**

Midler, Bette; signed-in-person color movie still from *The Boys*, 8x10" **$75.00**

Morgan, Henry; black & white photo signed in blue, 8x10" **$15.00**

Page, Patti; signed black & white photo, 8x10" **$25.00**

Parton, Dolly; signed color glossy, 8x10" **$65.00**

Poston, Tom; signed black & white photo, 8x10" **$15.00**

Quaid, Dennis; signed color photo, 8x10" **$25.00**

Quaid, Randy; signed black & white photo, 8x10"......**$15.00**

Reeves, Keanu; signed color photo, 8x10" **$34.00**

Reiner, Rob; inscribed black & white photo, 8x10".......**$5.00**

Rogers, Roy; signed black & white photo, matted & framed, 16x12", $70.00

Roosevelt, Franklin D; clipped signature from letter, VG .**$175.00**

Ryan, Meg; signed color photo, 8x10".........................**$100.00**

Sales, Soupy; signed black & white photo, 8x10"........**$15.00**

Savalas, Telly; color movie still from 'Kojak,' 8x10" **$35.00**

Snipes, Wesley; signed black & white photo, 8x10"....**$35.00**

Stallone, Sylvester; signed color movie still from *Rambo*, 8x10" **$90.00**

Stoltz, Eric; signed color portrait, matted **$15.00**

Stone, Sharon; signed color photo, 8x10" **$50.00**

Storch, Larry; signed black & white photo, 8x10".......**$18.00**

Sutherland, Kiefer; signed color photo, 8x10" **$40.00**

Swayze, Patrick; signed color photo, 8x10" **$50.00**

Thomas, Clarence; official calling card, 3x5" **$25.00**

Tompkins, Daniel; Monroe's VP & Govenor of New York, clipped signature..**$85.00**

Travis, Randy; signed portrait, matted.........................**$12.00**

Travolta, John; signed black & white photo, 8x10".......**$8.00**

Turner, Tina; signed color photo, 8x10".......................**$45.00**

Van Halen, Eddie; signed color photo, 8x10" **$40.00**

Vinton, Bobby; signed black & white photo, 8x10" **$30.00**

Walker, Nancy; signed black & white portrait, 8x10" ..**$17.00**

Washington, Denzel; signed color photo, 8x10"..........**$40.00**

White, Vanna; inscribed black & white photo, 8x10"....**$3.00**

Automobilia

A specialized field that attracts both advertising buyers and vintage car buffs alike, 'automobilia' is a term collectors use when referring to auto-related items and accessories such as hood ornaments, gear shift and steering wheel knobs, owner's manuals, license plates, brochures, and catalogs. Many figural hood ornaments bring from $75 to $200 — some even higher. Things from the thirties through the fifties are especially popular right now.

Almanac, Chevrolet, 32 pages, 1945, EX **$10.00**

Banner, '53 Dodge Beauty-Action Styling, red on yellow w/black fringe, rod hanger, minor wear, 37x55", VG..**$35.00**

Banner, Ford, shows colored & lettered circle connected by lines, silk w/fringed bottom, hanger top, 1953, 48x39", VG+ **$35.00**

Blotter, Ford Trucks Last Longer lettered on logs protruding from back of truck, unused, 6x3", EX....................**$4.00**

Booklet, Cadillac Engine, 20 pages, 1949, NM..............**$8.00**

Booklet, Dodge, dealer stamp center front, 24 pages, 1967, EX **$5.00**

Booklet, Ford at the Fair, 28 pages, 1934, EX.............**$20.00**

Booklet, Nash, sepia tones, 4 pages, 1950, NM **$6.00**

Booklet, Plymouth, black, blue & white, 8 pages, 1953, NM...**$6.00**

Booklet, Pontiac, 16 pages, 1964, NM **$6.00**

Calendar, Federal Trucks, 1946, girl in stream posed w/fish in net, trucks behind, company name below full pad, EX+ **$75.00**

Coin, Corvette, Motorama commemorative, gold color, 1954, EX **$15.00**

Coloring book, Buick, 1958, G **$10.00**

Compass, Union 76, orange, blue & white, suction-cup mount, EX...**$14.00**

Display, Buick, light-up, wood w/glass front, 1960 Buick pictured on front, hinged lid, VG+ **$50.00**

Display, Ford emblem, composition, blue, orange, cream, red & gray, 20¼x17", G+, $85.00

Display, Ford logo atop light bulb on black base, ...See the Light lettered on top of base, plastic, 1960s, 26x11", NM...**$110.00**

Display, 1947 Ford giveaway advertising above image of sedan, neon tubing around heavy metal frame, 19x16x6", VG..**$225.00**

Emblem, Plymouth, cast-metal plate attachment, round ship logo above name, minor tarnishing & discoloring, 3½x5¼" **$35.00**

Flag holder, straps to radiator cap, Pat 1927, EX **$35.00**

Grille cover, Nash, metal, 1920s, 19x33", EX **$50.00**

Handout, features Winston #1 1974 Dodge Charger built by Petty Enterprises, fact sheet on reverse, postcard-size, EX **$5.00**

Hat visor, Chevrolet, blue & white logo, 20 Years Sales Leadership, EX **$5.00**

Key chain, Chevrolet, 50th Anniversary, 1962, EX **$15.00**

Key chain, Dodge, enameled leather background, EX ..**$12.00**

Key chain, Ford, tubular, blue & white w/oval script logo, EX **$20.00**

License plate attachment, Missouri, 1965, plastic, EX **$4.00**

License plate topper, Chrysler-Plymouth Sales & Service, blue & white w/both logos, EX **$25.00**

Lighter, table type, Dodge/Plymouth, oil drum shape, M **$25.00**

Lighter, Zippo pocket type, Ford 300-500 Club, in original box, EX **$35.00**

Magazine, Buick, May 1951, EX **$5.00**

Matchbook, Plymouth, 1940, EX **$5.00**

Matchbook cover, Chevrolet, 1965, EX **$3.00**

Mechanical pencil, Ford, script logo in black oval, EX ..**$20.00**

Money clip, Ford, green & black, heavy metal, 2¼x2½", EX **$15.00**

Pen & pencil set, Chevrolet, The Heartbeat of America, Parker, in original box, EX **$15.00**

Plaque, Cadillac Seville, molded plastic car emblem above name on textured background, metal frame, 22¼x18¼", VG+ **$15.00**

Plaque, Ford emblem, blue, orange, cream, red & gray painted composition, some chipping & soiling, 20¼x17" **$85.00**

Plate, 1982 Collector Series featuring the Indianapolis 500, 6", EX **$25.00**

Playing cards, Nash Auto, pictures automobiles, double deck, in original box, G **$50.00**

Pocket mirror, Studebaker Vehicle Works, aerial view of factory w/lettering below, horizontal oval, 2¾", EX **$50.00**

Postcard, Dodge Trucks, 1951, 7½x4", EX **$4.00**

Postcard, Plymouth Belvedere Sport Coupe, glossy, 1955, 5½x3½", NM **$6.00**

Poster, 1929 Ford Coupe w/scene, EX **$120.00**

Poster, 1937 Ford Convertible Sedan, EX, lg **$265.00**

Print, Oldsmobile Six 4-Door Sedan, mother & daughter being picked up by friend in early Olds, black frame, 13x25", EX **$115.00**

Print, 1958 Impala Convertible, family scene at car w/badminton game in background, black frame, 18½x32", EX **$100.00**

Puzzle, Buick, Best Buy & Buick lettered on sm white & black plastic tiles that move about in square frame, EX **$25.00**

Showroom brochure, Harley-Davidson, trifold featuring the 1936 #45 Twin, #73 Twin & #80 Twin, EX **$75.00**

Showroom brochure, Studebaker, dealer stamp upper left front, foldout, 8 pages, 1950, 8x6", NM **$10.00**

Showroom catalog, Oldsmobile, Rocket Engine Cars lettered lower right, Earth logo above left, hard-bound, 10x13¾", VG **$60.00**

Sign, '56 Clipper Custom 4-Door, celluloid, lettering above car image w/lettered band below, self-border, 12x16", NM, $80.00

Sign, Cadillac, tin, crown & shield encircled by leaf design above Cadillac 1977, gold ground, wood frame, 24x19", NM **$60.00**

Sign, Chevrolet, embossed lettering on cardboard, To Be First In Service..., logo below, 9x12", VG **$25.00**

Sign, Dodge/Plymouth, neon, Dodge on blue band above Plymouth on white band, 35x65", G **$1,200.00**

Sign, Fordor Sedan, car in center & lower left, 60 Horsepower... upper right, framed cardboard, 1940s, 25x37", EX+ ..**$75.00**

Soup cup, Ford, single green band w/script logo, Shenango China, M **$20.00**

Spoon, Ford, script logo on handle, Royal Stainless, 1930s, EX **$8.00**

Telephone index, Ford, Bates Dialist Model, Ford logo & dealer's name & address in center of rotary dial, 6½x4", VG+ **$20.00**

Thermometer, Studebaker, lettering on red & white checked ground, Have You Seen The New..., stenciled wood, 11¾", G+ **$200.00**

Trunk emblem, Dodge Brothers, 6-point star logo, black, gold & silver, 8" wide, EX **$40.00**

Visor mirror, decorative brown & tan plastic case, place to write service record **$15.00**

Windshield scraper, Pontiac, 1957, EX **$5.00**

Autumn Leaf Dinnerware

A familiar dinnerware pattern to just about all of us, Autumn Leaf was designed by Hall China for the Jewel Tea Company who offered it to their customers as premiums. In fact, some people refer to the pattern as 'Jewel Tea.' First made in 1933, it continued in production until 1978. Pieces with this date in the backstamp are from the overstock that was in the company's warehouse when production was suspended. There are matching pitchers, tumblers, and stemware all made by the Libbey Glass Company, and a set of enameled cookware that came out in 1979. You'll find blankets, tablecloths, metal canisters, clocks, playing cards, and many other items designed around the Autumn Leaf pattern. All are collectible.

Since 1984 Hall Company has been making items for the National Autumn Leaf Collectors Club. So far, these pieces have been issued: a teapot (their New York style); a restyled vase; candlesticks; a (Philadelphia) teapot, sugar bowl and creamer set; a sugar packet holder; a tea-for-two set; a Solo tea set; a donut jug; a punch bowl with 12 cups; a Donut teapot; and a large oval casserole. All are plainly marked and dated. These are often found at malls and flea markets, so we've included current market values for them in our listings — the description lines contain the letters 'NALCC' and the date they were released.

Limited edition items (by Hall) are being sold by China Specialties, a company in Ohio; but once you become familiar with the old pieces, these are easy to identify, since the molds have been redesigned or were not previously used for Autumn Leaf production. So far, these are the pieces I'm aware of: the Airflow teapot, the Norris refrigerator pitcher, a square-handled beverage mug, a restyled Irish mug, 'teardrop' salt and pepper shakers, a mustard jar, a set of covered onion soup bowls, sherbets, an ashtray, the automobile teapot, a tankard-shaped beer pitcher, fluted salt and pepper shakers, an oval handled relish, a reamer, a round butterdish, a hurricane lamp with a glass shade, a collector's prayer wall plaque, a Hook Cover teapot, a Fort Pitt baker (6" x 4½" x 1¼"), and a 1-handle (2½-pint) bean pot. In glassware they have made cruets, water and wine goblets, juice tumblers, shot glasses, dessert plates, and beer pilsners. These are crystal (not frosted) and are dated '92 at the base of one of the leaves. Their accessory items include playing cards that are dated in the lower right-hand corner.

For further study, we recommend *The Collector's Encyclopedia of Hall China* by Margaret and Kenn Whitmyer.

Afghan, 60th Anniversary, 50x70"	**$145.00**
Baker, Fort Pitt, oval	**$90.00**
Bean pot, 1 handle	**$500.00**
Blanket, twin	**$150.00**
Bowl, cereal; 6"	**$10.00**
Bowl, cream soup; 2 handles	**$30.00**
Bowl, fruit; 5½"	**$5.50**
Bowl, Royal Glas-Bake, set of 4	**$45.00**
Bowl, vegetable; oval, w/lid, 10"	**$35.00**
Bowl cover set, plastic, 7 assorted covers in pouch	**$50.00**
Bread box, metal	**$225.00**
Butter dish, ¼-lb, 8" long	**$150.00**
Cake plate, 9½"	**$12.00**
Cake safe, metal, motif on top & sides, 5"	**$35.00**
Candle holder, Christmas; NALCC, 1991	**$100.00**
Candle holders, NALCC, 1989, pr	**$235.00**
Candy dish, ceramic, ruffled edge, square	**$30.00**
Canister, metal w/ivory plastic lid, round	**$10.00**

Canister, tall round shape, copper-color lid	**$75.00**
Canister, tea or coffee; square, 4", each	**$20.00**
Casserole, Royal Glas-Bake, shallow, clear glass lid	**$20.00**
Casserole, w/lid, NALCC, 1991	**$95.00**
Casserole/souffle, 10-oz	**$10.00**
Coaster, rubber, truck shape	**$10.00**
Coffee maker, metal dripper, 9-cup, 8"	**$35.00**
Coffee percolator, china, electric	**$225.00**
Cookbook, Mary Dunbar #2	**$15.00**
Cookie jar, Rayed	**$130.00**
Cookie jar, Tootsie	**$165.00**
Creamer, Old Style, 4¼"	**$15.00**
Cup & saucer, Melmac	**$8.00**
Cup & saucer, St Denis	**$22.00**
Decanter, Jim Beam truck, full	**$150.00**
Egg cup, ceramic	**$12.50**
Enamelware set: Dutch oven w/lid, 2-qt pan w/lid, 1½-qt pan w/lid, & skillet, 7-piece	**$425.00**
Fondue set, wooden lid knob & handle, complete	**$55.00**
Fruit cake tin	**$10.00**

Gravy boat, $18.00

Jug, Baby Ball, NALCC, 1992	**$75.00**
Malted milk mixer	**$150.00**
Marmalade jar, 3-pc	**$55.00**
Mug, chocolate; NALCC, 1992	**$25.00**
Mustard jar, 3½"	**$55.00**
Napkin holder, ceramic	**$12.50**
Paper towel holder, oak	**$45.00**
Pickle dish or gravy liner, oval, 9"	**$18.00**
Pitcher, utility; 2½-pt, 6"	**$15.00**
Place mat, paper, scalloped	**$25.00**
Plate, 6"	**$5.00**
Plate, 8"	**$10.00**
Platter, Melmac, 14"	**$12.50**
Platter, oval, 9"	**$20.00**
Punch bowl, w/12 cups, NALCC	**$250.00**
Reamer, ceramic, 2-part	**$30.00**
Sauce dish, serving; Douglas, Bakelite handle	**$125.00**
Shaker, regular, ruffled	**$10.00**
Shelf paper, single sheet	**$25.00**
Spoon rest, ceramic	**$8.50**
Sugar bowl, Rayed	**$20.00**
Sugar bowl, Ruffled-D	**$13.50**
Sugar packet holder, NALCC, 1990	**$100.00**
Tablecloth, ecru muslin, 56x81"	**$150.00**

Tea for Two, NALCC, 1900..........................$185.00
Tea set, Philadelphia $265.00
Tea set, Philadelphia, NALCC, 1990...........$225.00
Teakettle, metal enamelware $150.00
Teapot, French, NALCC, 1992....................$100.00
Teapot, long spout, 7" $45.00
Teapot, New York, NALCC, 1984 ....$500.00
Teapot, Newport, dated 1978.....................$125.00
Teapot, Solo, NALCC, 1991 ....$85.00
Thermos, NM $275.00
Tidbit, 2-tier...$35.00

Tidbit, 3-tier, $55.00

Toaster cover, plastic, fits 2-slice toaster $25.00
Towel, kitchen; Startex $60.00
Trash can, metal, red................................$100.00
Tray, glass w/wood handle, 19½x11¼"........................$95.00
Tumbler, Brockway, 16-oz..........................$20.00
Tumbler, etched gold frost design, footed, 6½-oz.......$45.00
Tumbler, frosted, 9-oz, 3¾"........................$18.00
Tumbler, Libbey, 10-oz...............................$32.00
Vase, Edgewater, NALCC, 1987..................$250.00
Warmer base, oval.....................................$150.00
Warmer base, round, w/4 original candles, original box .$125.00
Water jug, Donut, NALCC, 1991 ....$100.00

Avon

You'll find Avon bottles everywhere you go! But it's not just the bottles that are collectible — so are jewelry, awards, magazine ads, catalogs, and product samples. Of course, the better items are the older ones (they've been called Avon since 1939 — California Perfume Company before that), and if you can find them mint in box (MIB), all the better.

See also Cape Cod.

Aladdin's Lamp, green glass w/gold cap, holds bath oil in 5 fragrances, 1971-73, 6-oz, 7½" long, MIB $10.00

Alka-Seltzer soaps, blue, white & red box w/2 bars of soap shaped like tablets, 1978-79, MIB $7.00
Aqua Car, red & white plastic bubble-bath container, 1964-65, 8-oz $10.00
Baby Talc, blue & white metal container w/ribbon design at top, 1951-55......................$12.50
Bay Rum Aftershave, green & white jug form w/black cap, 1962-65, 8-oz....................$10.50
Blue Blazer Deluxe set, blue & red box holds aftershave, deodorant & silver tie tac, 1965, MIB $68.00
Bright Night Cologne, clear glass pear-shape w/gold-speckled cap, gold neck cord w/paper label, 1954-61, 4-oz, MIB $14.50
Brocade Cream Sachet, brown ribbed glass jar w/paisley design & paper label on lid, 1967-68, .66-oz, MIB..$3.25
Brocade Perfume Rollette, brown frosted glass w/horizontal ribs, gold cap, 1967-72, MIB......................$3.00
Buttons 'n Bows Cologne, clear glass bottle w/pink lettering, white cap, 1960-63, 2-oz $9.50

California Perfume Co, Trailing Arbutus Perfumed Talc, original box, NM, $12.00

Cameo set, white, gold & green box holds compact, lipstick & brooch, 1965, MIB.............................$30.00
Charisma Cologne Silk, frosted glass w/red cap, 1969, 3-oz, MIB...........................$4.50
Cornucopia, milk glass w/gold cap, holds Skin-So-Soft, 1971-76, 6-oz, 5½", MIB.....................$7.00
Cotillion Bath Oil, clear bottle w/pink-painted label, pink cap, 1954-59, 4½-oz $8.50
Country Peaches Soaps, decorative blue glass canning jar w/wire wire bail, holds 6 yellow soaps, M $8.00
Daisies Won't Tell Beauty Dust, blue, white & yellow box w/elegant girl on lid, 1957, MIB $20.00
Double Dip Bubble Bath, orange & white plastic figural ice-cream cone, red cap, 1968-70, 5-oz, MIB $4.50
Excalibur Soap on a Rope, blue, 1969-71, MIB...........$10.00

Forever Spring Powder Sachet, clear w/green-painted label, yellow cap, 1953-56, 1¼-oz....................**$9.50**

Freddie the Frog, white glass mug w/red or orange top & white ball-shaped cap, holds bubble bath, 1970, 5-oz, MIB .**$7.00**

French Telephone, milk-glass base holds bath oil, frosted glass receiver holds cologne, 1971 ....**$25.00**

Golden Promise Perfume, clear square-shaped bottle w/gold & white label, flat glass stopper, 1954-56, ½-oz....**$85.00**

Honey Bun set, pink & white octagon-shaped box holds Young Hearts Toilet Water & Pomade Lipstick, 1952, MIB **$50.00**

Hooper the Hound Soap Holder & Soap, white & black plastic head w/pink, green & yellow hoops, yellow bar soap, 1974, MIB..................**$8.00**

Imp the Chimp Bath Brush, brown figural plastic chimp w/yellow, black & pink trim, curled tail, 1980, 10" long, MIB **$4.00**

Jasmine Powder Sachet, clear glass bottle w/black cap & label, 1946-50, 1¼-oz..................**$14.50**

Little Missy Rolling Pin, pink plastic rolling pin w/orange ends, for children's shampoo, 1966-67, 12" long **$8.50**

Marionette Sachet, clear glass w/vertical ribs, paper label, turquoise metal cap, 1938, 1¼-oz **$24.00**

Miss Lollipop Cologne Boot, glass boot w/red tassel & gold cap, 1967-69, 2-oz..................**$5.50**

One Two Lace My Shoe, pink plastic shoe w/orange tie holds bubble bath, 1968-69, 8-oz..................**$8.50**

Persian Wood Beauty Dust, red glass jar w/red & gold tin lid, 1957-60, M..................**$10.00**

Persian Wood Mist, red plastic-coated glass w/gold crown-style cap, 1959-64, 3-oz, MIB **$5.50**

Pick a Daisy set, pink & blue box holds Daisies Won't Tell cream sachet & soap on a rope, 1963-64, MIB **$32.00**

Picture-Frame Cologne Bottle, gold-painted glass w/gold plastic cap, holds 4 fragrances, 1970-71, 4-oz, M..**$15.00**

Pink Panther Sponge Mitt & Soap set, pink face mitt w/yellow eyes, blue, green & pink wrapped soap, 1977-80, MIB..................**$8.00**

Pretty Peach Cologne, clear glass bottle w/painted label, peach-shaped cap, 1964-67, 2-oz..................**$5.00**

Quaintance Body Powder, white container w/red rose & lettering, shaker top, 1948-56, 5-oz..................**$12.50**

Rapture Beauty Dust, light blue plastic container w/2 white doves on lid, 1964-70, MIB..................**$5.00**

Royal Apple Cologne Bottle, red frosted glass apple shape w/gold leaf-shaped cap, holds 4 fragrances, 1972-73, 3-oz **$7.00**

Royal Fountain Cream Sachet, blue glass base w/silver & gold fountain top, 1970, MIB **$4.50**

Silver Fawn Cologne Bottle, fawn figure in silver-coated glass, Sweet Honesty or Charisma, 1978-79, .5-oz, MIB **$4.00**

Somewhere Perfume Mist, pink bottle w/gold band around top, white cap, 1964-66 ....**$6.50**

Spray of Roses set, pink & white box w/pink satin lining holds Wild Rose beauty dust & cologne, 1961, MIB...........**$30.00**

Strawberries & Cream Bath Foam, milk-glass pitcher form w/strawberry design, red cap, 1970, 4-oz **$6.50**

Strawberry Bubble Bath Gellee, clear glass decanter & lid w/stainless-steel spoon, 1980-81, 5.5-oz, MIB.........**$6.00**

Stylish Lady Decanter, milk-glass pig figure w/pink hat & pump, choice of cleanser or hand lotion, 1982-83, 8-oz, MIB..................**$9.00**

Sweethearts set, blue & white heart-shaped box w/white satin lining holds cologne mist & cream sachet, 1958, MIB **$45.00**

Tea Time Powder Sachet, frosted white teapot w/floral design, gold cap, came in 3 fragrances, 1.25-oz, MIB **$7.00**

To a Wild Rose Talc, blue metal container w/pink flowers around bottom, 1954-55..................**$8.50**

Topaz Perfume Oil, clear glass bottle w/canted corners, painted label, gold cap, 1963-69, ½-oz..................**$4.50**

Tot 'n Tyke Baby Shampoo, white plastic bottle w/blue cap, 1959-64, 6-oz..................**$6.25**

Wishing Perfumed Skin Softener, white glass jar w/gold & white lid, 1964-69, 5-oz **$3.00**

Miscellaneous

Bell, Birthday, clear crystal w/flowers, 1986, 5¾", MIB .**$12.00**

Bell, Giving Thanks, painted porcelain pumpkin w/pilgrim boy atop, 1990, 4½", MIB **$15.00**

Bell, Treasured Moments, Fostoria, embossed vertical heart-shape designs w/heart-shape finial, 1984, 5", MIB ..**$11.00**

Candle, Bunny Patch, colored wax rabbit figure, 1988, 6", MIB..................**$5.00**

Candle, Christmas Teddy, colored wax bear on wreath, 3", MIB..................**$5.00**

Candle, Mr & Mrs Santa (hugging), colored wax figures, 1987, MIB..................**$4.00**

Candle, turtle, white glass body w/green glass shell embossed w/flower design, 1972, MIB **$12.00**

Candle holder, Snug 'n Cozy Cat, clear-glass sleeping cat figure w/fragrance candle, 1980-82, MIB..................**$10.00**

Candle holder, Ultra Shimmer, crystal octagon shape w/'zigzag' ribbing, 1981-82, 2½", gold box, MIB **$9.00**

Candle holders, Floral Medley, tulip-shaped, 1 yellow, 1 purple frosted glass, holds perfumed candles, 1971-72, pr, MIB..................**$10.00**

Candy dish, crystal w/etched hummingbird design, short pedestal foot, 1989, 5" dia, MIB **$30.00**

Christmas bell, white porcelain w/kids in winter scene, wreath finial w/gold bow, dated 1986, 5", MIB **$15.00**

Christmas ornament, crystal teardrop shape w/etched hummingbird design & dated 1986, 3½", 10" **$10.00**

Christmas ornament, crystal tree, angel or village, Fostoria, 1985, MIB, each........................**$7.00**

Christmas ornament, Dashing Through the Snow, silver-plated deer in circle, w/red flannel pouch, 1992, 3⅝" dia, M..................**$10.00**

Christmas ornament, The Holy Family, white porcelain, 1985, MIB..................**$8.00**

Christmas-tree topper, Snow Angel, porcelain head & hands, blue lace dress, 1986, 10½", MIB **$12.00**

Cup & saucer, white china w/pink roses & green leaves, gold trim, made by Stoke-on-Trent, England, 1974-76, MIB **$12.00**

Doll, Little Blossom, Daisy Dreamer or Scamper Lily, stuffed cloth, 1986, 11" & 10½", ea.....................................**$10.00**

Doll, Southern Bell, porcelain head & arms w/pink & blue dress & hat, w/metal stand, 1988, 8¼", MIB **$30.00**

Doll, Victorian style w/porcelain head, arms & legs, w/metal stand, 1983-84, 8", MIB...**$25.00**

Egg, Butterfly Fantasy, white porcelain w/butterfly & floral decal, horizontal w/flat bottom, 1974 issue, 5½", MIB............**$25.00**

Egg, Winter's Treasure, white porcelain w/poinsettia decal, 3" vertical on 1" wooden base, 1987, MIB **$15.00**

Mug, Honey Bear 'Sweetheart,' white ceramic w/decals, curved handle, 1988, MIB, each..............................**$7.00**

Mug, Sweet Sentiments, white ceramic w/wraparound heart design, double-heart handle, 1986, MIB.................**$6.00**

Mug w/puzzle, With All My Heart, ceramic, windowpane squares w/speckled heart design, holds 11-pc puzzle, 1989, MIB...**$8.00**

Nativity figurine, Heavenly Blessing Angel, porcelain, 1986, 3", MIB **$8.00**

Nativity figurine, Heavenly Blessing Donkey, porcelain in pastel colors, 1986, 3½" long, MIB.........................**$8.00**

Plate, Christmas 1978, turquoise rim w/gold edge around tree-trimming scene in snow, Wedgewood, 8⅝" dia, MIB **$20.00**

Plate, Freedom, ceramic w/blue & gold trim around patriotic decal, Wedgewood, 1974-77, 9", MIB....................**$20.00**

Plate, I Baked It With Love, porcelain w/lettering & floral decor around rim plain center, 1982, 9", MIB.......**$20.00**

Plate, Mother's Day 1981, Cherished Moments, porcelain w/gold rim around decaled center, w/stand, 5" dia, MIB **$10.00**

Plate, School Is Beginning, porcelain w/gold rim, 1986, 5", MIB...**$8.00**

Azalea Dinnerware

Although this line of dinnerware was made earlier than most of the collectibles we're dealing with, it was produced in huge quantities, and you're likely to find a piece or two now and then. It was manufactured by the Noritake Company from 1916 until about 1935 and was offered through the catalogs of the Larkin Company who gave it away as premiums to club members and home agents.

Collectors use the catalog order numbers assigned by Larkin to designate each piece. There were more than seventy items in the dinnerware line as well as six pieces of matching, hand-painted crystal.

Bowl, #101, vegetable (open); 10½".............................**$62.00**
Bowl, fruit; 5¼" **$10.00**
Bowl, grapefruit or candy; #185, rare.....................**$198.00**
Bowl, oatmeal; #55, 5¾"..**$30.00**
Bowl, soup; #19, 7⅛"...**$26.00**
Casserole, #16 ....**$128.00**

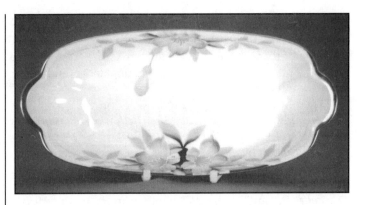

Celery/roll tray, #444, $380.00

Cheese or butter dish, #314 ....**$138.00**
Creamer & sugar bowl, #401, gold finial, rare **$160.00**
Creamer & sugar bowl, #7..**$45.00**
Creamer & sugar bowl, demitasse; #123 ....**$142.00**
Cup & saucer, #2...**$18.00**
Cup & saucer, bouillon; #124.......................................**$26.00**
Cup & saucer, demitasse; #183 ....**$150.00**
Egg cup, #120, rare **$62.00**
Jam or honey jar, #125 ....**$158.00**
Jug, #100, 1-qt..**$200.00**
Match or toothpick holder, #192, rare **$130.00**
Mustard jar, #191, w/spoon...**$62.00**
Plate, dinner; #13, 9¾"...**$28.50**
Plate, grill; #338, 3 compartments, rare, 10¼"............**$170.00**
Platter, #17, 14" **$62.00**
Relish, #171, divided..**$60.00**
Relish, #18, oval, w/spoon holder, 8¼".......................**$20.00**
Salt & pepper shakers, #11, bell **$32.00**
Whipped cream set, #3..**$40.00**

Banks

There are several types of collectible banks: mechanical (these are the ones with parts that move when the coin is inserted), still, advertising, and registering (those that tabulate the amount of money as you deposit it). This is a very diverse field, with literally thousands of shapes and variations available. If you find yourself drawn toward collecting banks, careful study and observation of the market is a must. Reproductions, though not very good ones, abound at flea markets allover the country. Since many of these banks were produced from the 1870s until about 1940, pass right on by any bank with paint that looks new and is too bright. Examine their construction; parts fit together well in the old banks. If the parts fit loosely and the designing is crude, they're new.

Prices for old banks continue to accelerate rapidly. Several of the auction houses we list in the back, especially those that specialize in toys, will often hold large, cataloged bank auctions. Condition is of the utmost importance; good paint can mean the difference of hundreds of dollars. And they must be complete and original to bring top price. Repaired banks or those with replaced parts are worth much less.

Although the mechanicals are at the top of the price structure, still banks are widely collected as well. Cast iron examples are preferred, but lead banks are coming on, and tin and pottery banks are attracting more and more collector interest.

There are a number of good books on the market for further study; among them are: *The Dictionary of Still Banks* by Long and Pitman, *The Penny Bank Book* by Moore, *The Still Bank Book* by Norman, *Penny Lane* by Davidson, *The History of Antique Mechanical Toy Banks* by Al Davidson, and *The Collector's Encyclopedia of Toys and Banks* by Don Cranmer. In our listings, 'M' numbers refer to the Moore book, 'L' to the book by Long and Pitman, 'N' to the Norman book, and 'D' to Davidson's.

See also Advertising Collectibles; Disney; Character Collectibles; World's Fair.

Mechanical Banks

Atomic Bank, white metal, 3¾", NM..............................**$35.00**
Birdhouse Bank, tin, original box, 5¼", NM **$130.00**
Birdie Putt Bank, painted cast iron, golfer & caddie on rectangular base, 7", NM **$210.00**

Bulldog, cast iron, brown version, J&E Stevens, 1880s, EX, $2,200.00

Butting Goat, D-91, cast iron, goat springs forward & butts coin into tree trunk, HL Judd, ca 1887, 4¾" long, VG **$385.00**
Clown, N-1870, tin, bust figure w/no hat, Chein, 5", NM .**$110.00**
Dog on Turntable, D-159, cast iron, copper finish, HL Judd, 4¾", G...**$200.00**
Eagle & Eaglets, eaglets chirp for food, Book of Knowledge reproduction, NM....................................**$275.00**
Elephant Howdah, D-173, painted cast iron w/wood figure, man pops out of howdah, Enterprise, replaced tunic, 6", VG..**$250.00**
Home Bank (no dormer windows), N-243, painted cast iron, cashier takes coin, J&E Stevens, 5", G................**$250.00**

I Always Did 'Spise a Mule, N-250, painted cast iron, boy seated on bench facing mule, J&E Stevens, 9¾" long, G..**$450.00**
Joe Socko, D-262, tin, 2 boxers on base, drop coin into slot & 1 turns to knock out the other, Straits, 3½" base, EX **$450.00**
Jonah & the Whale, Book of Knowledge reproduction, NM **$325.00**
Light of the World Bank, aluminum, lighthouse on round base w/embossed lettering, 10", NM **$80.00**
Milking Cow, Book of Knowledge reproduction, 9⅝", NM **$260.00**
Monkey, N-3990, tin, monkey on round base marked Thank You, Chein, 5½", NM...**$170.00**
Rocket Bank (horizontal), white metal, original box, EX **$100.00**
Rocket Bank (vertical), white metal & vinyl, 13", NM .**$40.00**
Speaking Dog, D-448, painted cast iron, girl & dog on marked base, Harper, repainted, VG...................**$250.00**
Standing Bulldog, D-66, painted cast iron, place coin on tongue, HL Judd, recast tail, 7", VG.....................**$100.00**
Strato Bank, white metal, globe & horizontal rocket on arched base w/label, original box, EX.................**$75.00**
Strike Bank, painted cast iron, bowler on alley, 6½", NM..**$300.00**
Trick Pony, Book of Knowledge reproduction, EX+.**$215.00**
Uncle Sam, Book of Knowledge reproduction, VG ..**$195.00**
Weedens Plantation Darky Saving Bank, D-562, tin windup, jigger & banjo player on stag, 5½", G..................**$400.00**
Wild West Bank, painted white metal, gun shoots coin into bank, original box, NM...**$60.00**

Registering Banks

B&R Mfg, NY, 10¢ register, VG....................................**$15.00**
Bean Pot, M-951, 5¢ register, painted cast iron w/nickel-plated top, 4", EX..**$175.00**
Cannon, tin & wood, Save For Victory, 4¾", EX **$200.00**
Daily Dime Clown, EX..**$20.00**
Elves Rolling Coins, EX **$65.00**
Five-Coin Security Bank, tin, cash register w/center front lever, 7" **$120.00**

Get Rich Quick, tin litho, Marx, 3⅝", EX, $60.00

Honeycomb, C-105, 5¼", EX..................$110.00
Lucky Savings Bank, tin, cash register w/center lever,
    5" $160.00
Popeye, 10¢ register, EX..........................$35.00
TV Bank, W Germany, tin, various denominations, 4", EX..$22.00
Wee Folks Money Bank, tin, English, square, 5" $60.00

Still Banks

Amish Boy, M-193, painted cast iron, J Wright, 1970, 5",
    M..$75.00
Atlas, L-631, pot metal, figure w/world on shoulders, 4½",
    EX $265.00
Billiken on Throne, M-73, painted cast iron, Williams, 6½",
    VG $100.00
Black Boy, M-83, painted cast iron, 2-faced, 4⅛", G.$100.00
Buffalo, M-560, gold-painted cast iron, Williams, 3⅛x4¾",
    EX $195.00
Bulldog, M-372, painted cast iron, J Wright, 1960s, 6",
    M..$85.00
Cat on Tub, M-358, bronze-painted cast iron, 4⅛", NM.$285.00
Charlie McCarthy, M-209, papier-mache, 9¼", EX.....$225.00
County Bank, M-1110, brass, 4¼", EX......................$135.00
Dog on Tub, M-359, bronze-painted cast iron, 4⅛", EX..$225.00
Dog on Tub, M-359, painted cast iron, worn, 4⅛", VG ...$145.00
Duck, M-624, painted cast iron, Hubley, 4¾", EX $295.00
Flatiron Building, M-1160, dark japanning w/gold on cast
    iron, 3", EX..$105.00
Frog, ceramic, in standing position looking up, 4⅛", M.$25.00
German Helmet, M-1405, painted tin, worn, 4⅞", VG..$175.00
Globe on Wire Arc, M-83, painted cast iron, Arcade, 4⅝",
    NM $300.00
Golliwog, M-85, painted cast iron, 6¼", VG $300.00

**Graf Zeppelin, Moore #1428, painted cast iron, 7", EX,
$250.00**

Grenadier Bank, wood & tin, soldier standing behind
    labeled barrel, 6", EX..........................$18.00
Grizzly Bear, M-703, copper-painted lead, 2¾", EX.....$50.00
I Hear a Call, M-438, black-painted cast iron, dated July 20,
    1900, 5¼", VG $185.00
Indian Bust, M-221, lead, full headdress, 3½", VG $55.00
Japanese Helmet, M1404, tin, missing medallion, 1½",
    EX $105.00
Jewel Safe, M-896, cast iron, J&E Stevens, 5⅜", VG ..$185.00
Kewpie, M-301, painted glass w/tin lid, paint traces,
    3¼" $60.00

Lamb, M-600, painted cast iron, J Wright, 1970, 3¼", EX..$65.00
Lincoln Bank, painted white metal, ax stuck in white log cut
    diagonally at ends on legged base, 6½", NM........$80.00
Mailbox on Legs, M-841, painted cast iron, Hubley, 5¼",
    EX $250.00
Mammy w/Basket, M-175, white metal, 5¼", EX.......$275.00
Mammy w/Hands on Hips, M-176A, painted cast iron,
    EX $115.00
Marshall Stove, M-1362, painted cast iron, 3⅞", EX...$250.00
Masonic Temple, M-1061, brass, 5" $525.00

**National Safe Deposit,
cast iron & tin, 5⅞", EX.
$185.00**

National Security Bank, composition, bust of Uncle Sam,
    6¾", EX $95.00
Out Kitchener, M-1313, cast iron, 6½", EX................$165.00
Parrot, M-554, painted lead, w/white wings, worn, 5½",
    G $230.00
Possum, M-561, painted cast iron, 2⅜", G.................$400.00
Prancing Horse, M-520, painted cast iron, old repaint, 7¼",
    EX $95.00
Presto, M-1168, silver- & gold-painted cast iron, Williams,
    3⅝", EX $200.00
Reindeer, M-737, bronze-painted cast iron, Williams, 9½",
    EX $265.00
Rhino, M-721, painted cast iron, 2⅝", VG $300.00
Roof Bank, M-1124, painted cast iron, Grey Iron, 5¼",
    G $135.00
Scottie Dog, M-432, nickel-plated lead, Deco style, 4½",
    EX $165.00
Soldier, M-45, painted cast iron, light wear, 6", EX...$165.00
Stag, M-737, nickel-plated cast iron, worn, 9½", EX....$75.00
Stagecoach Bank, multicolored tin & plastic, w/2 horses,
    original box, 3⅛", NM..........................$105.00
Sunbonnet Sue, M-257, painted cast iron, 1970, 7½",
    NM $215.00
Tank Bank, chalkware, Save For Victory, 5¾", EX+ $80.00
Templeton Radio, M-826, painted cast iron, Kenton, 4¼",
    EX $360.00
Treasure Chest, M-928, painted cast iron, red & gold, worn,
    2¾", EX $200.00
Trunk Bank, tin w/painted accents, 2", EX $35.00
Turkey, M-587, painted cast iron, 3⅜", EX................$160.00
Ulysses S Grant Bust, M-166, painted cast iron, 1976, 5½",
    EX $265.00

Uncle Sam Bank, M-1383, tin patriotic top hat, 3⅛", VG+ **$35.00**

Urn w/Beehive Finial, multicolored wood, Pat May 11, 1875, missing label, 7½" **$105.00**

V Shell, ceramic, embossed V on upright bullet-shaped shell, 6", EX+ **$105.00**

Victory V Bank, ceramic, letter V atop rectangular base w/label, 5½", EX+ **$80.00**

Washington Monument, M-1049, painted cast iron, 7½" VG...**$280.00**

West Point Mule, M-501, painted lead, 4⅞", EX **$230.00**

Wirehaired Terrier, M-422, painted cast iron, 4⅝", EX..**$150.00**

Wireless Bank, N-5980, cast iron, light rust, 6⅝" **$80.00**

WWII Bubble Bank, glass dome on wood base, You Can Bank on America, 6½", EX **$90.00**

Barbie and Her Friends

Barbie dolls are some of the 'hottest' collectible toys on the market today. There are auctions devoted entirely to selling vintage Barbies and accessory items. The first Barbie, issued in 1959, books at a minimum of $3,500.00 (mint in the box). If she happens to be a brunette instead of a blond, tack on another $500.00. Even dolls made more recently can be pricey! For instance, the Empress Barbie, a Bob Mackie original from 1992 already books at $225.00 (mint in the box).

Barbie was first introduced in 1959, and soon Mattel found themselves producing not only dolls but tiny garments, fashion accessories, houses, cars, horses, books, and games as well. Today's Barbie collectors want them all. Though the early Barbies are very hard to find, there are many of her successors still around; don't overlook Ken, Skipper, or any of her other friends.

You'll need to do lots of studying and comparisons to learn to distinguish one Barbie from another, but this is the key to making sound buys and good investments. Some of our values are given for dolls that are nude but still in good condition, like you'll probably be finding many of them; but in parentheses we've described original clothing and accessories that these dolls came out with, just for your information. Collectors are sticklers concerning condition; compared to a doll mint in box, they'll often give an additional 20% if that box has never been opened! If you want a good source for study, refer to one of these fine books: *The Wonder of Barbie* and *The World of Barbie Dolls* by Paris and Susan Manos; or *The Collector's Encyclopedia of Barbie Dolls and Collectibles* by Sibyl DeWein and Joan Ashabraner.

In the section on accessories, values are for mint condition items; worn examples are generally worth at least 50% less.

Dolls

Allan, original blue swim trunks & striped jacket, molded red hair, straight legs, 1964, original box, EX **$65.00**

Barbie, American Girl, brunette, bendable legs, 1965, MIB..**$1,250.00**

Barbie, Benefit Performance 1967, porcelain, limited edition, 1988, MIB...........................**$275.00**

Barbie, Bubble-Cut, 1-pc red nylon swimsuit, blond hair, straight legs, 1961-62, VG **$60.00**

Barbie, Color Magic, 1966 (MIB, $750.00) nude in good condition, $100.00

Barbie, Cool Times, 1988, MIB **$20.00**

Barbie, Dramatic Living (gold & silver swimsuit w/orange net jacket), red hair, bendable joints, 1970, nude, G **$65.00**

Barbie, Empress, Bob Mackie original, 1992, MIB.....**$225.00**

Barbie, Fashion Jeans, 1981, MIB **$25.00**

Barbie, Fashion Queen, 1-pc gold & white swimsuit & turban, 3 wigs & stand, molded brunette hair, 1964.**$60.00**

Barbie, Feelin' Groovy, 1986, MIB.............................**$165.00**

Barbie, Happy Holidays, 1991, MIB **$55.00**

Barbie, Live Action, fringed outfit & headband, Touch 'n Go stand), blond hair, rooted lashes, bendable legs, 1971, VG...**$25.00**

Barbie, Neptune Fantasy, Bob Mackie original, 1992, MIB...**$175.00**

Barbie, Oriental, International Series, 1980, MIB........**$70.00**

Barbie, Ponytail #4, 1-pc striped swimsuit & pearl earrings, brunette hair, 1960, EX.......................**$200.00**

Barbie, Spanish, International Series, 1982, MIB..........**$40.00**

Barbie, Stars 'n Stripes US Navy, Black, #9694, Special Edition, MIB..**$25.00**

Barbie, Swirl Ponytail, 1-pc red swimsuit & pearl earrings, black wire stand included, blond hair, 1964, NMIB..........**$250.00**

Barbie, Winter Fantasy, FAO Schwarz, 1990, MIB.....**$130.00**

Brad, Talking (bright colored shorts & shirt), black skin, molded hair, 1970, nude, G **$35.00**

Christie, Pink 'n Pretty, 1981, MIB **$25.00**

Barbie, Quick Curl Miss America, 1974 (MIB, $50.00) nude in good condition, $15.00

Courtney, Baby-Sitter, 1990, MIB.................................$20.00
Jamie, Walking (checked mini dress & head scarf), blond hair, rooted eyelashes, bendable legs, 1970, nude, G $100.00
Ken, (swim trunks & sandals), brown flocked hair, 1961 ....$35.00
Ken, Day 'n Night, Black, 1984, MIB...........................$15.00
Ken, green pants & short-sleeve shirt, molded brown hair, straight legs, 1961, VG...........................$30.00
Ken, Roller Skating, 1980, MIB $25.00
Ken, Sun Valley, 1973, MIB..$45.00
Ken, Sunsational Malibu, Black w/red Afro, 1981, MIB..$45.00

Ken, Talking, 1969 (MIB, $75.00) nude in good condition, $20.00

Midge, Sea Holiday, 1992, MIB $25.00
Midge, 1-pc striped swimsuit, red hair w/ribbon headband, bendable legs, 1965, NMIB $425.00

Midge (2-pc multicolored swimsuit), rooted Saran hair, straight legs, 1963, nude, G.....................................$50.00

PJ, Free Moving, 1975 (MIB, $75.00) nude in good condition, $15.00

PJ, Gold Medal Gymnast (US Olympic-styled outfit & gear w/doll-size medal), 1975, nude, G......................$15.00
PJ, Twist 'n Turn, MIB $195.00
Scott (Skipper's boyfriend), 1979, MIB $35.00
Skipper, Baton Twirling, 1992, MIB............................$16.50
Skipper, Beach Blast, 1989, MIB.................................$10.00

Skipper, Growing Up, 1975 (MIB, $40.00) nude in good condition, $12.00

Skipper, Quick Curl (long blue & white checked dress), blond hair/freckles, bendable knees & twist waist, 1973, nude, G **$15.00**

Skipper (red, white & blue nautical-style swimsuit), brown hair, bendable legs, 1965, nude **$35.00**

Skooter (blue shorts w/red & white polka dot shirt), blond hair, bendable legs, 1966, nude, G **$50.00**

Stacey, Talking, 1968, MIB **$300.00**

Stacey, Talking (1-pc multicolored swimsuit), red hair, rooted eyelashes, bendable knees, 1969, nude, G **$30.00**

Steffie, Walk Lively (black & white jumpsuit), brunette hair w/flipped-up ends, 1972, nude, G **$25.00**

Todd, 1973, MIB **$70.00**

Whitney, Jewel Secrets, 1986, MIB **$30.00**

Accessories

Book, Barbie Goes to a Party, Wonder, 1964 ....**$5.00**

Booklet, Living Barbie as Full of Life as Your Are **$6.50**

Case, Barbie & Midge Travel Pals, white, square, 1963.**$50.00**

Case, blue w/picture of Barbie in Party Date dress & Ken in Friday Night Date, 1964 ....**$35.00**

Case, white w/picture of Tutti in Swing-a-Ling outfit, 1965, rare **$45.00**

Coloring book, Barbie & Skipper dressed in Masquerade outfit on cover, Whitman, 1973....................................**$25.00**

Coloring book, Quick Curl Barbie, 1975 ....**$20.00**

Drawing set, Dramatic New Living Barbie, #8279, electric, 1970 ....**$25.00**

Dream Bed, Barbie, #5641, 1982 ....**$10.00**

Game, Barbie Miss Lively Livin', 1971 ....**$35.00**

Game, Barbie Queen of the Prom, 1960 ....**$45.00**

Gift set, Barbie & Francie Color Magic Fashion Designer, #4040, 1965 ....**$365.00**

Gift set, Barbie & Friends, Disney, 1991 ....**$40.00**

Gift set, Barbie Dressing Fun, 1993 ....**$30.00**

Gift set, Barbie Secret Hearts, 1993..............................**$35.00**

Gift set, Barbie Twinkle Town, 1968.........................**$500.00**

Gift set, Cool City Blues, 1989 ....**$45.00**

Gift set, Pink & Pretty Barbie, 1981 ....**$85.00**

Gift set, Skooter Cut 'n Button, 1967 ....**$500.00**

Gift set, Tropical Barbie Deluxe, 1985........................**$45.00**

Gift set, Wedding Party Midge, 1990 ....**$125.00**

Magazine, Barbie Bazaar, Sept-Oct, 1989 ....**$25.00**

Mercedes, green, 1963...**$150.00**

Outfit, Barbie, American Airlines Stewardess, #984.....**$70.00**

Outfit, Barbie, Bouncy Flouncy, #1805 ....**$135.00**

Outfit, Barbie, Crisp 'n Cool, #1604 ....**$50.00**

Outfit, Barbie, Golden Girl, #911 ....**$55.00**

Outfit, Francie, First Things First.................................**$35.00**

Outfit, Ken, Campus Corduroys, #1410 ....**$70.00**

Outfit, Ken, Rally Dally, #788, 1961 ....**$40.00**

Outfit, Skipper, Ballet Class, #1905, 1963..................**$55.00**

Outfit, Skipper, Dreamtime, #1909 ....**$70.00**

Outfit, Skipper, School Girl **$20.00**

Paper dolls, Barbie & Ken, Whitman, uncut, 1970 ......**$30.00**

Pencil case, black, 1961..**$75.00**

Puzzle, Barbie's Keys to Fame, 1963 ....**$55.00**

Room-Fulls, Barbie's Firelight Living Room, #7406, 1974.**$50.00**

Starcycle, #2149, 1978..**$10.00**

Suzy Goose Jeweled Wardrobe, #418, 1965...............**$125.00**

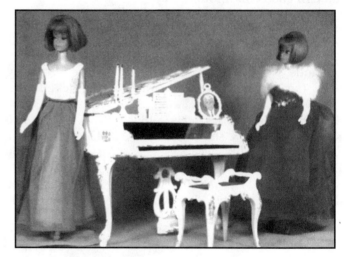

Suzy Goose Music Box, plays I Love You Truly, MIB, $300.00. (Shown between dolls.)

Tea set, Barbie, 25th Anniversary, 1984 ....**$80.00**

Trading cards, Barbie, Deluxe First Edition, 1990........**$25.00**

Watch, Barbie, Bradley, 1973 ....**$75.00**

1957 Belair Chevy, aqua, 1st edition, 1989 ....**$50.00**

Barware

This field covers cocktail shakers, decanters, ice buckets, and the like that were designed to use in mixing and serving drinks. These items are diverse enough that they appeal to a variety of tastes and collecting interests. Some examples are from the Depression era, some carry avertising messages, and others are very Deco or ultramodern, made of chrome, Bakelite, and aluminum.

Gift set, Barbie's Sparkling Pink, #1011, MIB, $500.00

Cocktail shakers come in many forms. The lady's leg was a popular design, and you may find some modeled as penguins, roosters, golf bags, zeppelins, and airplanes. You'll find that *Kitchen Glassware of the Depression Years* and *The Collector's Encyclopedia of Depression Glass,* both by Gene Florence, show several examples of glass decanters as well as ice buckets.

Cocktail picks, miniature wood bar w/chrome trim featuring plastic 'bottle' & 'shaker' picks, 4½x5"..................**$45.00**
Cocktail set, chrome cylinder shaker w/black bands top & bottom, 4 bow-shaped footed tumblers, w/tray, unmarked, 12"..................**$175.00**

Cocktail shaker, chrome, tall footed 'coffeepot' style w/handle & spout, grapes & leaves border, unmarked, 12", $60.00

Cocktail shaker, chrome bell shape w/wooden handle, side pour spout, 11x5½"..................**$35.00**
Cocktail shaker, cobalt blue glass w/white windmill design, chrome top, Hazel Atlas, 10"..................**$30.00**
Cocktail shaker, glass & chrome hourglass form, Maxwell Phillip, 9x5"..................**$75.00**
Cocktail shaker, transparent green glass cylinder w/horizontal ribs, chrome top, Imperial..................**$35.00**
Cocktail shaker, transparent green glass w/etched grape cluster design, chrome top..................**$30.00**
Corkscrew, figural waiter in black suit & apron holding bar towel & bottle, head removes to reveal corkscrew, 8"..................**$40.00**

Gyroscopic rack w/4 glasses, chrome, 20", 8½" dia rings..................**$225.00**
Ice bucket, hammered aluminum 'beehive' shape w/slip handle, 'mushroom' finial, unmarked, 8x8" dia **$15.00**
Ice bucket, hammered aluminum w/black knob finial & handles, Kromax, 12x8" dia..................**$10.00**
Ice bucket, transparent pink glass w/allover design, wrapped handle, knob finial, Fry..................**$200.00**
Ice bucket (open), glass w/window-pane design, decorative gold-tone chrome handle, 6"..................**$50.00**
Jigger, chrome, double, 2½"..................**$12.00**
Soda dispenser, bulbous chrome body w/spigot atop, round base, marked Soda King, 9½"..................**$40.00**
Stirrer, spoon w/red plastic bead attached to end of long twisted handle, 11"..................**$12.00**
Stirrer & jigger combination, silverplate, spoon w/jigger attached to long handle, 9"..................**$15.00**
Tray, 'Here's How!,' features 4 comical flappers & cocktail recipes, J Held Jr..................**$110.00**

Baseball Cards

How do we see the baseball card market? Perhaps softening, but certainly not dead. Since 1987 the new-card market has been literally flooded, and obviously with such an influx, the investment potential of these more current cards may be slim. But many of the older examples continue to climb in value. For instance, Hank Aaron (#128) 1954 Topps card continues to hold at $1,800.00 to $2,000.00 for one in mint condition. But hundreds of cards have been printed, and many are worth less than 20¢; so as you can see, if you're going to collect, you must stay on top of the market by study and observation.

A good card can often represent a significant investment. It wouldn't be unusual to have to pay as much as $50.00 for a early Topps or Bowman superstar, and a 1952 Topps Jackie Robinson books today at $1,300.00, though this is probably a minimum value. Some of the more valuable cards have been reproduced, so beware. Except for only a few, the entire 1952 Topps set was reissued in the early 1980s, but these are clearly marked. You'll need a good price guide before you start to collect, one of the best is *Gene Florence's Standard Baseball Cards Price Guide.*

If you are totally unfamiliar with cards, you'll need to know how to determine the various manufacturers. 1) Bowman: All are coprighted Bowman or B.G.H.L.I., except a few from the fifties that are marked '. . . in the series of Baseball Picture Cards.' 2) Donruss: All are marked with the Donruss logo on the front. 3) Fleer: From 1981 to 1984 the Fleer name is on the backs of the cards; after 1985 it was also on the front. 4) Score & Sportflics: Score written on front, Sportflics on back of each year. 5) Tops: 1951 cards are baseball game pieces with red or blue backs (no other identification). After that either Topps or T.G.C. appears somewhere on the card. 6) Upper Deck: Marked front and back with Upper Deck logo and hologram.

Learn to judge the condition of your card, since its

condition is a very important factor when it comes to making an accurate evaluation. Our values are for excellent-to-mint condition cards. One that is judged to be in only good condition may be worth only one-tenth as much. Superstars' and Hall of Famers' cards are most likely to appreciate, and the colored photo cards from the thirties are a good investment as well. Buy modern cards by the set while they're inexpensive, who knows what they may be worth in years to come. Any of today's rookies may be the next Babe Ruth!

Al Abner, 1953, #233, Topps, M.......................**$90.00**
Al Heist, 1962, #373, Topps, M **$5.00**
Al Kozar, 1950, #15, NM...................................**$50.00**
Al Luplow, 1962, #598, Topps, VG...................**$17.50**
Alan Trammell, 1984, #91, Fleer, M.................**$1.25**
Amos Otis, 1971, #610, Topps, M **$4.00**
Andujar Cedeno, 1991, #20, Donruss, NM **$2.00**
Andy Messersmith, 1969, #296, Topps, M **$3.00**
Aurelio Monteagudo, 1966, #532, Topps, M **$28.00**
Babe Ruth, 1961, #401, Topps, VG...................**$7.00**

Bob Hooper, 1952, #10, Bowman, M, $18.00

Bench & Seaver, 1982, #634, Fleer, M, $1.50

Barry Bonds, 1986, #11, Donruss, M **$16.00**
Bennie Daniels, 1963, #497, Topps, M **$12.00**
Bernie Allen, 1962, #596, Topps, M..............**$60.00**
Bernie Carbo, 1971, #478, Topps, M.............**$2.00**
Bill Bryan, 1967, #601, Topps, M..................**$16.00**
Bill Davis, 1965, #546, Topps, M...................**$5.60**
Bill Heath, 1966, #539, Topps, M..................**$20.00**
Bill Howerton, 1952, #167, Topps, M............**$28.00**
Bill Madlock, 1977, #1, Topps, M..................**$4.00**
Bill McDonald, 1952, #138, Topps, VG..........**$7.00**
Bill Swift, 1989, #623, Upper Deck, M...........**$1.00**
Billy Hatcher, 1985, #649, Fleer, M...............**$1.50**
Billy Klaus, 1957, #292, Topps, M.................**$20.00**
Billy Martin, 1956, #181, Topps, VG.............**$25.00**
Billy Meyer, 1952, #387, Topps, VG **$43.75**
Billy Williams, 1961, #141, Topps, VG **$22.50**
Bo Jackson, 1990, #697, Score, M **$2.00**

Bob Humphreys, 1967, #478, Topps, M **$6.00**
Bob Keegan, 1953, #196, Topps, M............................**$18.00**
Bob Keely, 1954, #176, Topps, M................................**$15.00**
Bob Kelly, 1952, #348, Topps, VG...............................**$43.75**
Bob McClure, 1976, #599, Topps, M **$8.00**
Bob Uecker, 1962, #594, Topps, M..............................**$80.00**
Bobby Bonilla, 1986, #30, Donruss, NM.......................**$5.00**
Bobby Knoop, 1964, #502, Topps, M **$4.00**
Bobby Thompson, 1948, #47, Bowman, NM **$80.00**
Boog Powell, 1963, #398, Topps, M............................**$22.00**
Brady Anderson, 1988, #14, Donruss, NM....................**$1.50**
Brock Davis, 1963, #553, Topps, VG...........................**$60.00**
Brooks Robinson, 1957, #328, Topps, VG **$100.00**
Cal Eldred, 1992, #380, Fleer, M................................**$1.50**
Cal Ripken Jr, 1989, #4676, Upper Deck, M.................**$2.00**
Carl Eldred, 1993, #34, Donruss, M............................**$1.00**
Carl Yastrzemski, 1960, #148, Topps, M....................**$260.00**
Casey Cox, 1966, #549, Topps, M...............................**$15.00**
Chico Cardenas, 1962, #381, Topps, M.......................**$5.00**
Clarence Gaston, 1969, #304, Topps, M **$7.00**
Clarence Marshall, 1952, #174, Topps, M...................**$28.00**
Craig Biggio, 1991, #4, Donruss, M.............................**$2.00**
Dale Mitchell, 1953 (color), #119, Bowman, M............**$50.00**
Dale Murphy, 1982, #299, Donruss, M **$1.00**
Dalton Jones, 1970, #682, Topps, M...........................**$5.00**
Dan Quisenberry, 1980, #667, Topps, M **$2.00**
Danny Ainge, 1981, #727, Topps, M...........................**$6.00**
Danny Tartabull, 1985, #647, Fleer, M.........................**$8.00**
Darrell Porter, 1973, #582, Topps, M..........................**$3.00**
Darryl Strawberry, 1983, #108, Topps, M **$70.00**
Darryl Strawberry, 1989, #260, Upper Deck, M...........**$1.00**
Dave Campbell, 1971, #46, Topps, M...........................**$6.00**
Dave Justice, 1990, #711, Upper Deck, M....................**$4.00**
Dave Koslo, 1950, #65, Bowman, NM.........................**$50.00**
Dave Melton, 1958, #391, Topps, M............................**$4.00**
Dave Nied, 1993, #27, Upper Deck, M.........................**$3.00**
Dave Oliver, 1978, #704, Topps, M **$18.00**
Dave Palmer, 1984, #750, Topps, M...........................**$1.00**

Dave Parker, 1975, #29, Topps, M $7.00
Dave Stewart, 1982, #213, Topps, M..................$6.00
Dave Stewart, 1982, #410, Donruss, M $3.00
Dave Winfield, 1974, #456, Topps, VG..................$40.00
Dave Winfield, 1984, #143, Fleer, M..................$5.00
Dean Palmer, 1990, #74, Upper Deck, M $2.00
Dean Palmer, 1991, #56, Fleer, M..................$4.00
Deion Sanders, 1992, #3, Upper Deck, M $8.00
Dennis Eckersley, 1981, #96, Donruss, M..................$2.00
Dennis Menke, 1967, #518, Topps, M $6.00
Denny Doyle, 1972, #768, Topps, M $5.00
Denny Martinez, 1977, #491, Topps, M..................$7.00
Dick Brown, 1962, #438, Topps, M..................$5.00
Dick Drago, 1971, #752, Topps, M $9.00
Dick Hall, 1957, #308, Topps, M..................$20.00
Dick Kokos, 1953, #232, Topps, VG..................$22.50
Dodgers Team, 1956, #166, Topps, VG..................$40.00
Don Buddin, 1960, #520, Topps, M..................$11.00
Don Buford, 1966, #465, Topps, M..................$6.00
Don Money, 1970, #645, Topps, M..................$5.00
Don Sutton, 1966, #288, Topps, M $140.00
Doug Drabek, 1991, #15, Donruss, M..................$2.00
Doug Rader, 1967, #412, Topps, M..................$4.00
Duke Maas, 1956, #57, Topps, M..................$8.00
Dusty Baker, 1971, #709, Topps, M..................$60.00
Ed McGhee, 1955, #32, Topps, M..................$9.00
Eddie Murry, 1981, #112, Donruss, M..................$2.75
Eddie Robinson, 1955, #153, Bowman, NM $7.00
Elliot Maddox, 1973, #658, Topps, M $2.40
Eric Anthony, 1990, #82, Donruss, NM..................$3.00
Eric Davis, 1985, #627, Topps, M..................$4.00
Eric Karos, 1993, #14, Score, M..................$1.00
Ernie Banks, 1969, #20, Topps, M $20.00
Ferguson Jenkins, 1966, #254, Topps, VG..................$32.50
Frank Kellert, 1956, #291, Topps, M..................$10.00
Frank Robinson, 1957, #35, Topps, VG..................$65.00
Frank Thomas, 1990, #86, Score, M..................$6.00
Frank Thomas, 1992, #4, Upper Deck, M..................$10.00
Freddie Marsh, 1953, #240, Topps, M..................$90.00
Gair Allie, 1954, #179, Topps, M..................$15.00
Gary Dotter, 1965, #421, Topps, M..................$4.00
Gary Pettis, 1991, #9, Donruss, M $2.00
Gary Sheffield, 1989, #13, Upper Deck, M..................$10.00
Gaylord Perry, 1966, #598, Topps, VG..................$65.00
Gaylord Perry, 1991, #2, Upper Deck, M..................$14.00
George (Jorge) Bell, 1982, #609, Fleer, M..................$6.00
George Brett, 1984, #344, Fleer, M..................$5.00
George Brett, 1993, #5, Upper Deck, M..................$10.00
George Foster, 1971, #276, Topps, M..................$8.00
George Kell, 1952, #246, Topps, VG..................$20.00
George Medich, 1973, #608, Topps, M..................$4.00
George Metkovich, 1952, #310, Topps, M..................$50.00
Giants Team, 1956, #226, Topps, VG..................$18.00
Gil Hodges, 1955, #158, Bowman, M..................$40.00
Gil McDougald, 1953, #43, Topps, M..................$48.00
Glenn Davis, 1985, #652, Fleer, M..................$3.00
Goose Gossage, 1984, #44, Fleer, M..................$1.00
Gordon Jones, 1955, #78, Topps, M $9.00

Greg Maddux, 1987, #70, Topps, M..................$3.00
Greg Maddux, 1990, #25, Donruss, M..................$5.00
Greg Swindell, 1992, #23, Donruss, M..................$1.00
Gregg Jefferies, 1988, #137, Fleer, M..................$2.50
Gregg Olson, 1989, #723, Upper Deck, M..................$1.50
Hal Jeffcoat, 1952, #341, Topps, VG..................$43.75
Hank Aaron, 1960, #566, Topps, VG..................$30.00
Hank Aguire, 1957, #96, Topps, M..................$8.00
Hank Allen, 1967, #569, Topps, VG..................$125.00
Harmon Killabrew, 1991, #1, Upper Deck, M..................$14.00
Harry Craft, 1963, #491, Topps, M..................$12.00
Howard Johnson, 1983, #328, Donruss, M..................$5.00
Howie Fox, 1952, #209, Topps, VG..................$7.00
Ivan Rodriguez, 1991, #55, Upper Deck, M..................$1.50
Ivan Rodriguez, 1991, #82, Score, M..................$1.00

Ivan Rodriguez, 1992, #415, Topps Stadium Club, M, $1.50

Jack Dittmer, 1954, #53, Topps, M..................$30.00
Jack Hamilton, 1962, #593, Topps, M..................$21.00
Jack McClure, 1965, #553, Topps, M..................$5.60
Jack Merson, 1952, #375, Topps, VG..................$43.75
Jack Morris, 1984, #415, Donruss, M..................$3.00
Jamie Navarro, 1990, #85, Donruss, M..................$2.00
JC Martin, 1963, #499, Topps, M..................$12.00
Jeff Bagwell, 1991, #79, Fleer, M..................$8.00
Jeff Reardon, 1981, #819, Topps, M..................$14.00
Jerry Koosman, 1968, #177, Topps, VG..................$375.00
Jesse Jefferson, 1973, #604, Topps, M..................$3.00
Jim Abbott, 1990, #31, Donruss, NM..................$5.00
Jim Davenport, 1958, #413, Topps, M..................$6.00
Jim Heard, 1952, #337, Topps, VG..................$43.75
Jim Hegan, 1952, #17, Topps, VG..................$13.75
Jim Hunter, 1967, #369, Topps, M..................$20.00
Jim Palmer, 1966, #126, Topps, VG..................$45.00
Jim Palmer, 1984, #576, Donruss, M..................$4.00
Jim Perry, 1961, #584, Topps, M..................$32.00
Jimmie Hall, 1965, #580, Topps, M..................$10.00
Joe Carter, 1984, #41, Donruss, M..................$48.00
Joe Dobson, 1951, #36, Bowman, M $20.00

Joe Dobson, 1952, #254, Topps, VG............................$12.50
Joe Garagiola, 1951, #122, M $140.00
Joe Haynes, 1952, #145, Topps, M............................$28.00
Joe Jay, 1954, #141, Topps, M................................$18.00

Joe Moeller, 1964, #549, Topps, M, $9.00

Joe Torre, 1962, #218, Topps, M...............................$22.00
John Knox, 1974, #604, Topps, M...............................$5.00
John Smoltz, 1989, #17, Upper Deck, M.......................$4.00
Johnny Kline, 1955, #173, Topps, M...........................$25.00
Jose Canseco, 1986, #39, Donruss, EX........................$50.00
JT Snow, 1993, #23, Upper Deck, M............................$3.00
Julio Franco, 1983, #525, Donruss, M.........................$6.00
Ken Griffey Jr, 1990, #245, Donruss, M......................$25.00
Ken Hamlin, 1960, #542, Topps, M $11.00
Ken Hubbs, 1962, #461, Topps, M..............................$22.00
Ken Hunt, 1960, #522, Topps, M...............................$11.00
Ken Johnson, 1960, #135, Topps, M.............................$3.00
Ken Singleton, 1971, #16, Topps, M............................$3.00
Kevin Maas, 1990, #446, Donruss, M...........................$1.00
Kevin McReynolds, 1984, #307, Fleer, M......................$2.00
Kevin Pasley, 1977, #476, Topps, M...........................$30.00
Kevin Seitzer, 1991, #5, Donruss, M $2.00
Kirby Puckett, 1985, #536, Topps, M..........................$20.00
Kirby Puckett, 1989, #376, Upper Deck, M $1.50
Lance Parrish, 1978, #708, Topps, M $15.00
Larry Jansen, 1954, #200, Topps, M...........................$15.00
Larry Walker, 1990, #466, Upper Deck, M $2.00
Larry Walker, 1990, #631, Score, M...........................$1.00
Lee Smith, 1982, #603, Fleer, M...............................$7.00
Lenny Dykstra, 1986, #482, Donruss, NM......................$2.00
Lou Johnson, 1960, #476, Topps, M............................$5.00
Manny Ramirez, 1992, #63, Upper Deck, M...................$1.00
Mark Grace, 1990, #137, Donruss, M..........................$2.00
Mark Knudson, 1974, #605, Topps, M..........................$5.00
Mark McGwire, 1989, #300, Upper Deck, M $1.50
Marquis Grissom, 1990, #107, Donruss, M $5.00
Matt Williams, 1988, #118, Score, M $1.75
Maurice (Mo) Vaughn, 1990, #675, Score, M.................$1.50
Mickey Harris, 1952, #135, Bowman, NM $15.00

Mickey Mantle, 1953, #44, Bowman, VG $112.50
Mike Andrews, 1967, #314, Topps, M..........................$7.00
Mike Blyzka, 1954, #152, Topps, M............................$15.00
Mike Corkins, 1970, #573, Topps, M............................$2.00
Mike Garman, 1972, #79, Topps, VG...........................$25.00
Mike Hedlund, 1965, #546, Topps, M...........................$5.00
Mike Maddux, 1952, #366, Topps, VG $43.75
Mike Marshall, 1982, #681, Topps, M $5.00
Mike McCormick, 1960, #530, Topps, M $11.00
Mike Mussina, 1991, #12, Donruss, M.........................$12.00
Mike Mussina, 1991, #4, Fleer, M..............................$10.00
Mike Plazza, 1993, #252, Score, M..............................$2.00
Mike Schmidt, 1973, #615, Topps, VG.........................$120.00
Mike Schmidt, 1989, #406, Upper Deck, M $1.50
Minnie Minoso, 1959, #80, Topps, M..........................$10.00
Monte Kennedy, 1952, #124, Topps, M........................$28.00
Morrie Martin, 1953, #227, Topps, VG........................$22.50
Nigel Wilson, 1993, #9, Upper Deck, M........................$2.00
Nippy Jones, 1952, #213, Topps, M............................$28.00
Nolan Ryan, 1973, #220, Topps, VG...........................$20.00
Nolan Ryan, 1989, #145, Upper Deck, M $4.00
Norman McRae, 1971, #93, Topps, M...........................$1.00
Orestes Destrade, 1988, #110, Score, M........................$2.00
Orioles Team, 1965, #572, Topps, M...........................$28.00
Orlando (Marty) Martinez, 1967, #504, Topps, M $6.00
Orlando McFarlane, 1966, #569, Topps, M....................$28.00
Ozzie Smith, 1979, #116, Topps, M $70.00
Ozzie Smith, 1984, #59, Donruss, M...........................$5.00
Pat Borders, 1988, #99, Score, M..............................$2.50
Pat Jarvis, 1972, #675, Topps, M $5.00
Pat Listach, 1993, #29, Donruss, M............................$4.00
Paul Foytack, 1957, #282, Topps, M...........................$8.00
Paul Jaeckel, 1965, #386, Topps, M............................$4.00
Paul Minner, 1953, #92, Topps, M.............................$16.00
Paul O'Neill, 1986, #646, Fleer, M.............................$3.00
Paul Penson, 1954, #236, Topps, M............................$15.00
Pete Rose, 1964, #125, Topps, VG.............................$40.00
Pete Rose, 1984, #61, Donruss, M..............................$4.00
Pete Smith, 1988, #84, Score, M................................$2.50
Phil Niekro, 1964, #541, Topps, VG...........................$55.00
Phillies Team, 1959, #8, Topps, VG...........................$10.00
Ralph Hamner, 1949, #212, Bowman, M......................$75.00
Ramon Martinez, 1989, #18, Upper Deck, M................$2.00
Randy Gumpert, 1951, #59, Bowman, VG......................$3.50
Randy Hundley, 1966, #392, Topps, M.........................$5.00
Randy Jones, 1976, #201, Topps, M............................$1.00
Ray Barker, 1967, #583, Topps, M.............................$18.00
Ray Fosse, 1969, #244, Topps, M...............................$3.00
Reggie Jackson, 1984, #57, Donruss, M........................$7.00
Rick Kester, 1970, #621, Topps, M............................$24.00
Rick Monday, 1967, #542, Topps, M...........................$12.00
Rickey Henderson, 1980, #482, Topps, VG...................$22.50
Rickey Henderson, 1984, #54, Donruss, M....................$12.00
Rickey Henderson, 1991, #4, Score, M.........................$2.00
Ritchie Ashburn, 1951, #3, Topps, M........................$175.00
RJ Reynolds, 1984, #97, Fleer, M..............................$1.00
Rob Dibble, 1988, #86, Score, M...............................$3.00
Rob Gardner, 1966, #534, Topps, M...........................$15.00

Roberto Alomar, 1988, #35, Donruss, VG......................**$3.00**
Roberto Kelly, 1988, #212, Fleer, M...........................**$2.00**
Robin Yount, 1993, #5, Upper Deck, M **$10.00**
Rod Carew, 1971, #210, Topps, M............................**$45.00**
Rod Carew, 1984, #352, Donruss, NM **$5.00**
Roger Clemens, 1989, #195, Topps, M........................**$2.00**
Roger Craig, 1966, #543, Topps, M..........................**$40.00**
Roger Maris, 1964, #331, Topps, VG **$30.00**
Roger Metzger, 1971, #404, Topps, M.........................**$2.00**
Rollie Hemsley, 1954, #143, Topps, M **$15.00**
Ron Gant, 1988, #538, Fleer, M................................**$4.00**
Ron Hunt, 1963, #558, Topps, M.............................**$12.00**
Ron Jackson, 1956, #186, Topps, M..........................**$15.00**
Ron Santo, 1961, #35, Topps, M..............................**$50.00**
Roy Campanella, 1955, #70, Bowman, M..................**$100.00**
Royals Team, 1971, #742, Topps, M **$10.00**
Ruppert Jones, 1977, #488, Topps, M........................**$10.00**
Russ Meyer, 1952, #220, Bowman, NM **$28.00**
Rusty Staub, 1963, #544, Topps, M..........................**$40.00**
Ryne Sandberg, 1983, #83, Topps, M **$55.00**
Ryne Sandberg, 1989, #120, Upper Deck, M.................**$1.50**
Ryne Sandberg, 1992, #181, Fleer, M..........................**$1.00**
Sam Jones, 1952, #382, Topps, VG **$50.00**
Sam McDowell, 1962, #591, Topps, VG **$12.50**
Scott Erickson, 1992, #21, Donruss, M........................**$2.00**
Scott Sanderson, 1992, #10, Donruss, M......................**$1.00**
Shane Mack, 1985, #398, Topps, M............................**$3.00**
Shane Mack, 1987, #42, Donruss, M **$1.00**
Sheldon Jones, 1952, #130, Topps, M.........................**$28.00**
Sid Hudson, 1953, #251, Topps, VG **$22.50**
Solly Hermus, 1952, #212, Bowman, NM **$15.00**
Sparky Lyle, 1969, #311, Topps, M...........................**$12.00**
Spook Jacobs, 1956, #151, Topps, M **$10.00**
Steve Barber, 1960, #514, Topps, M..........................**$16.00**
Steve Carlton, 1984, #111, Donruss, M **$4.00**
Steve Hamilton, 1972, #766, Topps, M........................**$5.00**
Steve Sax, 1982, #103, Topps, M...............................**$7.00**
Ted Abernathy, 1967, #597, Topps, M........................**$16.00**
Ted Gray, 1952, #86, Topps, VG...............................**$7.00**
Ted Gray, 1953 (color), #72, Bowman, NM **$30.00**
Ted Simmons, 1971, #117, Topps, M.........................**$20.00**
Ted Williams, 1954, #1, Topps, VG **$158.00**
Ted Williams, 1992, #2, Upper Deck, M......................**$4.00**
Terry Hughes, 1974, #604, Topps, M..........................**$5.00**
Tigers Team, 1956, #213, Topps, M..........................**$55.00**
Tim Jones, 1978, #703, Topps, M.............................**$14.00**
Tim Raines, 1982, #202, Fleer, M..............................**$2.00**
Tim Salmon, 1993, #25, Upper Deck, M......................**$3.00**
Tom Foley, 1991, #13, Donruss, M **$2.00**
Tom Haller, 1962, #356, Topps, M.............................**$4.00**
Tom Henke, 1984, #134, Donruss, M **$2.00**
Tom Hurd, 1956, #256, Topps, M.............................**$15.00**
Tom Johnson, 1975, #618, Topps, M...........................**$1.00**
Tom Seaver, 1967, #581, Topps, VG **$300.00**
Tom Seaver, 1984, #106, Fleer, M............................**$25.00**
Tommy Helms, 1965, #243, Topps, M **$3.00**
Tony Gwynn, 1983, #482, Topps, VG **$8.75**
Tony Perez, 1965, #581, Topps, VG **$37.50**

Tony Perez, 1970, #380, Topps, M.............................**$8.00**
Travis Fryman, 1991, #149, Donruss, M.......................**$3.00**
Vern Bickford, 1951, #42, Bowman, M.......................**$14.00**
Vic Albury, 1972, #778, Topps, M............................**$15.00**
Vic Power, 1954, #52, Topps, M..............................**$32.00**
Vida Blue, 1970, #21, Topps, M................................**$6.00**
Wade Boggs, 1983, #586, Donruss, NM **$24.00**
Wally Post, 1952, #151, Topps, M............................**$32.00**
Wes Covington, 1957, #283, Topps, M.......................**$20.00**
Wes Parker, 1964, #456, Topps, M.............................**$6.00**
Whitney Ford, 1953, #207, Topps, VG **$40.00**
Willie Crawford, 1965, #453, Topps, M.......................**$5.00**
Willie Mays, 1954, #89, Bowman, VG **$100.00**
Willie McCovey, 1960, #316, Topps, VG **$56.25**
Willie McGee, 1983, #49, Topps, M............................**$4.00**
Willie Miranda, 1953, #278, Topps, VG **$22.50**
Willie Stargell, 1963, #553, Topps, VG **$60.00**
Woody Held, 1963, #435, Topps, M............................**$4.00**
Wynn Hawkins, 1960, #536, Topps, M.......................**$11.00**

Bauer Pottery

Undoubtedly the most easily recognized product of the Bauer Pottery Company who operated from 1909 until 1962 in Los Angeles, California, was their colorful 'Ring' dinnerware (made from 1932 until sometime in the early sixties). You'll recognize it by its bright solid colors: Jade Green, Chinese Yellow, Royal Blue, Light Blue, Orange-Red, Black and White, and by its pattern of closely aligned ribs. They made other lines of dinnerware as well. They're collectible, too, although by no means as easily found.

Bauer also made a line of Gardenware vases and flowerpots for the florist trade. To give you an idea of their values, a 12" vase from this line would bring about $75.00.

To further your knowledge of Bauer, we recommend *The Collector's Encyclopedia of California Pottery* by Jack Chipman.

Al Fresco, bowl, cereal; speckled greens & gray, 5½"...**$5.00**
Al Fresco, bowl, salad; coffee brown or Dubonnet, 13".**$27.50**
Al Fresco, cookie jar, speckled greens or gray **$30.00**
Comtempo, coffee server, all colors, 8-cup.................**$25.00**
Contempo, bowl, fruit; all colors, 5"..........................**$6.00**
Contempo, bowl, vegetable; divided, oval, 7½" **$12.00**
Contempo, cup & saucer, all colors............................**$10.00**
La Linda, bowl, batter; all matte colors, 2-qt...............**$36.00**
La Linda, casserole, burgundy or dark brown, 1-qt.....**$55.00**
La Linda, creamer, old shape, all matte colors.............**$11.00**
La Linda, custard cup, burgundy or dark brown **$10.00**
La Linda, plate, bread & butter; all matte colors, 6".......**$5.50**
La Linda, tumbler, burgundy or dark brown, 8-oz **$20.00**
Monterey, bowl, fruit; all colors but white, 6" **$13.50**
Monterey, plate, relish; all colors but white, 10½".......**$40.00**
Monterey, teapot, all colors but white, 6-cup.............**$55.00**
Monterey Moderne, pitcher, all colors but black, 2½-qt..**$42.50**
Monterey Moderne, plate, grill; round.........................**$20.00**

Ring, beer pitcher & mugs, ca 1932, 5-pc set, $200.00

Ring, bowl, mixing; yellow, light blue or olive, #12, ½-gal **$50.00**
Ring, coffeepot, drip type, chartreuse, gray or red-brown, 9½" **$145.00**
Ring, honey jar, yellow or light blue, rare **$300.00**
Ring, refrigerator jars, yellow, light blue or olive, complete set..**$72.50**
Ring Art & Gardenware, jardiniere, dark blue or white, 8" **$80.00**
Ring Art & Gardenware, vase, ruffled rim, black, 7" ...**$50.00**
Ring Art & Gardenware, vase, turquoise or jade, ruffled rim, 7"...**$25.00**

Beatles Collectibles

Possibly triggered by John Lennon's death in 1980, Beatles fans, recognizing that their dreams of the band ever reuniting were gone along with him, began to collect memorabilia of all types. Recently some of the original Beatles material has sold at auction with high-dollar results. Handwritten song lyrics, Lennon's autographed high school textbook, and even the legal agreement that was drafted at the time the group disbanded are among the one-of-a-kind multi-thousand dollar sales recorded.

Unless you plan on attending sales of this caliber, you'll be more apt to find the commercially produced memorabilia that literally flooded the market during the sixties when the Fab Four from Liverpool made their unprecedented impact on the entertainment world. A word about their records: they sold in such mass quantities that unless the record is a 'promotional,' made to send to radio stations or for jukebox distribution, they have very little value. Once a record has lost much of its originial gloss due to wear and handling, becomes scratched, or has writing on the label, its value is minimal. Even in near-mint condition, $4.00 to $6.00 is plenty to pay for a 45 rpm (much less if its worn) unless the original picture sleeve is present. The exception to this is the white-labeled Swan recording of 'She Loves You/I'll Get You,' which in great condition may go as high

as $50.00. The picture sleeves are usually valued at $30.00 to $40.00, except for the rare 'Can't Buy Me Love,' which is worth ten times that amount. Beware of reproductions!

Beach hat, blue & white printed w/black faces & autographs, NM...**$125.00**
Beach towel, Cannon, 1964, VG **$95.00**
Belt buckle, Beatles in stylized & reflective letters on black, silver edge, 1980s, slightly oval, 2½x3½", EX........**$16.50**
Birthday card, color photo of group on orange background, EX...**$25.00**
Birthday card, unfolds to 21x28" poster, G **$30.00**
Blanket, United Kingdom, tan w/red & black photos, instruments & names, Whitney, VG.................................**$290.00**
Book, All About the Beatles, DeBlasio, paperback, 1964, EX..**$9.50**
Book, Beatles Up To Date, Bill Adler, hard-bound, 1966, EX **$20.00**
Bracelet, ceramic-type group photo on scalloped brass mounting, Yeh, Yeh, Yeh on back, thick chain, MOC **$135.00**
Button, black & white photo of John Lennon, 1964, 2½", EX **$7.50**
Button, color photo of Beatles w/cat-like faces, foreign, 1¼" dia, EX **$3.50**
Button, New England Beatles Convention 1979, color photo, 2½" dia, EX **$6.50**
Calendar, paper, photo of Beatles standing in a doorway, glossy, March sheet, 20x11", EX..........................**$155.00**
Calendar cards, group or individual pictures on front, specific month on back, plastic, Louis F Dow Company, EX.**$40.00**
Candy dish, Washington Pottery, blue fired-on decal of Paul on inside, gold scalloped edges, 4½" dia, EX **$165.00**
Ceramic tile, features Ringo, United Kingdom, 1964, 6x6", VG...**$135.00**
Coin purse, faces of all 4, vinyl, various colors, EX **$35.00**
Coloring book, 1964, few pages colored, VG **$40.00**
Concert book, 1966, VG **$45.00**
Doll, Paul or Ringo w/instrument, Remco, VG, each..**$80.00**
Figurines, United Kingdom, Subuteo, 1964, original box, EX, set of 4...**$190.00**
Gum card, color photo on waxed paper, EX..............**$25.00**
Key chains, Yellow Submarine, color photo of each member, 6x2½", VG, set of 4..**$60.00**

Lunch box, metal, w/thermos, VG, $300.00

Model, Yellow Submarine, plastic w/figures, Model Products Corp, EX $275.00

Mug, United Kingdom, Washington Pottery, fired-on blue, black & gray group photo & names, EX $125.00

Necklace, gold-plated record disk w/black & white group photo on gold chain, EX $75.00

Notebook, Westab, Beatles standing in doorway on cover, spiral-bound, unused, 8½".............................$60.00

Overnight bag, black vinyl w/zipper & strap, white photos & autographs, 13" $500.00

Pencil case, group picture w/signatures, vinyl, variety of colors, Standard Plastic Products, EX $140.00

Pin, plastic guitar shape, 1964, 4", MOC, $45.00

Playing cards, 2 varieties, EX, each deck $275.00

Poster, Dell #1, 1964, 18x52", VG $40.00

Purse, colorful image of John w/guitar on silky material, metal clasp, Canadian, 1970s, EX.....................$40.00

Scarf, Scammonden Woolen Company of England, original package & tag, EX $350.00

Scrapbook, 8 pages of United Kingdom articles, VG ..$55.00

Shirt, knit, label inside states 'The Only Authentic Beatles Shirt,' EX $170.00

Stationery, Flying Horseman or Snapping Turtle Turk, sealed box of 20 sheets w/envelopes, each $45.00

Sunglasses, Solarex, black plastic wrap-around style w/green lenses, paper sticker of 2 Beatles in each corner, NM $325.00

Switch plate, heavy cardboard, Dal Manufacturing Corp, EX $75.00

Tumbler, white plastic w/color photo sealed under clear coating, We Loved the Beatles, Australian, EX ..$225.00

Wall paper, group shots & signatures, 21x21", EX $225.00

Bedroom and Bathroom Glassware

This type of glassware was produced in large quantities during the Depression era by many glasshouses who were simply trying to stay in business. They made puff jars, trays, lamps, and vanity sets for the bedroom; towel bars, soap dishes, and bottles of all types for the bath. These items came in much the same color assortment as the Depression glass dinnerware that has been so popular with collectors for more than twenty years. For the most part, it's not terribly expensive, though prices for items that can be traced to some of the more prestigious companies such as Heisey, Cambridge, Fostoria, or Akro Agate are climbing.

For more information we recommend *Bedroom and Bathroom Glassware of the Depression Years* by Margaret and Kenn Whitmyer.

Atomizer, ivory w/4 panels outlined in black, Cambridge, 4¼" $55.00

Atomizer, jade w/allover sponged gold design, Cambridge, 6" $125.00

Barber bottle, satin amethyst w/hand-painted flowers, made by Fenton for LG Wright, 1960 ....$65.00

Bathroom set, crystal w/embossed lettering, Astringent, Mouthwash, Witch Hazel & Lotion, set of 4 in wooden tray $80.00

Clock, black w/etched design, round face, Fostoria, 5¼" $145.00

Clock, round w/pressed glass body $35.00

Cologne, clear w/pressed quilted pattern, Duncan & Miller...$45.00

Cologne, white horizontal ribbed base, black fan-shaped stopper, footed, Imperial Glass Co, 4½"................$50.00

Comb & brush tray, milk glass, beaded oval surrounded by flowers, open scroll design on handles, Fostoria, 11½" long...$45.00

Cotton ball dispenser, frosted pink bunny rabbit w/ears up, Paden City, rare.......................................$175.00

Doorknob, crystal w/cut design, oval $55.00

Doorknob, topaz w/cut design in center, hexagonal..$110.00

Guest set, cobalt, Fenton #401, water service for bed-side table $85.00

Guest set, green, pink or amber, etched hunt scene, Cambridge #489, water service for bed-side table $125.00

Hair receiver, frosted topaz, Tiffin $40.00

Lamp, fired-on pink, Spanish Dancing Couple, embossed cameo design on ruffled shade $50.00

Lamp, fired-on pink or blue, Prima Donna w/flared glass shade...$50.00

Lamp, fired-on pink or blue, Scotty dog w/ball, flared shade...$135.00

Lamp, frosted crystal, cathedral on black base $70.00

Lamp, frosted crystal, sailboat & cylinder....................$60.00

Lamp, frosted green, Southern Belle figure w/clip-on shade...$110.00

Manicure set, black, heart shape w/7 compartments, 6" long..$85.00

Night light, frosted crystal, covered wagon...............$145.00

Pin tray, emerald w/winged scroll pattern, Heisey ...**$100.00**

Pin tray, transparent pink, seated German Shepherd in center..**$45.00**

Powder jar, crystal, reclining draped nude (Cleopatra I) finial on lid, various sporting scenes on base, 6½" long..**$85.00**

Powder jar, frosted green, lady (Babs I) torso as lid finial, 3-footed, label: Dermay — Fifth Ave NY..., 4½" dia ..**$60.00**

Powder jar, frosted green, 3 embossed figures (Flappers) around base form feet, plain lid w/ball knob, 4x4¼" dia..**$50.00**

Powder jar, frosted lavender, lady (Lillian II) torso finial on lid, allover ripples, Hazel Atlas **$45.00**

Powder jar, frosted pink, Dancing Girl, US Glass, 4½" dia **$75.00**

Powder jar, frosted pink, lady (Southern Belle) torso finial on lid w/hoop skirt to form base, 5" dia.............**$90.00**

Powder jar, frosted pink, reclining nude lady (Godiva) finial on lid, 8-sided diamond-shaped base, 4¾" long...**$85.00**

Powder jar, frosted pink w/black lid, Cinderella's Coach, marked 452, LE Smith Glass Co **$90.00**

Powder jar, frosted yellow, court jester head finial on lid, round base w/12 tab-like feet, 5¼" dia **$75.00**

Powder jar, opaque yellow, vertical ribbed base & lid, footed, Akro Agate..**$35.00**

Powder jar, transparent green or pink, Art Deco Pleated Fan, high dome lid w/fan-like finial & crimped edge..**$45.00**

Puff box, crystal base w/concentric ribs, beehive finial on Jadite lid, New Martinsville..........................**$16.00**

Puff box, opaque cobalt or green, Colonial Lady, Akro Agate, 3½" dia **$195.00**

Puff box, opaque pink, embossed Scotties on base, Scottie finial on lid, Akro Agate, 6½x3½" dia, $55.00

Puff box, peachblow w/etched medallion, Cambridge #584-4 ....**$45.00**

Puff box, transparent colors, embossed Scotties on base, Scottie finial on lid, 6½x3½" dia **$250.00**

Torchiere, frosted green w/black decoration, pull cord..**$35.00**

Towel bar, transparent pink, twisted design, clip holders **$35.00**

Towel bar holder, transparent pink, Westite, pr.........**$55.00**

Travel set, amber w/vertical ribs, gold screw-on lids, 7-pc **$65.00**

Vanity box, coral, cased, Wave Crest **$110.00**

Vanity box, cranberry w/enameled flowers, hinged lid .**$140.00**

Vanity set, crystal w/black star-shaped lids, 3-pc set, $195.00

Beer Cans

In the mid-1930s, beer came in flat-top cans that often carried instructions on how to use the triangular punch-type opener. The 'cone-top' can was patented about 1935, and in the 1960s both types were replaced by the aluminum beer can with the pull-tab opener. There are hundreds of brands and variations available to the collector today. Most are worth very little, but we've tried to list a few of the better ones to help you get a feel for the market.

Condition is very, very important! Collectors grade them as follows: 1) rust-free, in 'new' condition; 2) still no rust, but a few scratches or tiny dents are acceptable; 3) a little faded, minor scratching, maybe a little rusting; 4) all of the above only more pronounced. Our prices are for cans in Grade 1 condition.

Kessler, cone top, blue & black, light rust, 12-oz, $60.00

ABC Ale, pull top, 12-oz..**$1.25**

Black Horse Ale, pull top, white, gold & black, 12-oz..**$2.50**

Bonanza, pull top, red, white & blue, 12-oz...............**$17.50**

Brown Derby, flat top, white & gold, 12-oz.................**$15.00**

Busch Bavarian, flat top, blue & white, 12-oz **$12.50**

Canadian Ice, 1974, 16-oz..**$3.00**

Cincinnati Reds, 1975......................................$1.25
Colt 45 Malt Liquor, pull top, 10-oz.....................$10.00
Deer Brand Export II, pull top, 12-oz.....................$2.00
Drewyr's Extra Dry, flat top, white, 12-oz...............$7.50
Falls City, pull top, 16-oz................................$1.25
Falstaff Light, pull top, 12-oz............................$1.25
Fox DeLuxe, flat top, white & gold, 12-oz...............$8.50
GB Bock Dark, Grace Bros Brewing Co, flat top, goats head
    motif, 1955-60, 12-oz, NM $50.00
Goebel Luxury, flat top, red, black & gold, 12-oz.......$30.00
Grain Belt Premium, pull top, 12-oz......................$1.25
Grand Prize, flat top, silver & blue, 12-oz.............$35.00
Leinenkugel Bock, 1979, 12-oz $1.50
Miller Malt Liquor, red, pull top, 16-oz.................$5.00
Milwaukee's Best, flat top, white, red & gold, 12-oz.....$5.00
O'Keefe Ale, pull top, 12-oz.............................$1.00
Old Chicago, pull top, 16-oz.............................$5.00
Old Frothingslosh, pull top, brown, 12-oz................$5.00
Pioneer, flat top, brown & white, 12-oz.................$35.00
Pittsburg Steelers, 1976 Super Bowl, 12-oz.............$1.50
Point Bicentennial, 12-oz.................................$3.00
Rolling Rock, pull top, 12-oz............................$1.25
Schell's Deer Brand, pull top, 12-oz $1.25
Schlitz Malt Liquor, pull top, 12-oz.....................$1.00

Steinbrau, pull top, white & red, 12-oz, $15.00

Tudor Ale, flat top, green & white, 12-oz $16.00
Valley Brew Pale Premium, El Dorado Brewing Co, flat top,
    1950-55, 12-oz $60.00
Whale's White Ale, pull top, black & white, 12-oz......$22.00
Wiedemann Draft, pull top, 12-oz $1.50
World's Fair, green & white, pull top, 12-oz.............$2.00

Big Little Books

The Whitman Publishing Company started it all in 1933 when they published a book whose format was entirely dif-ferent than any other's. It was very small, easily held in a child's hand, but over an inch in thickness. There was a car-toon-like drawing on the right hand page, and the text was printed on the left. The idea was so well accepted that very soon other publishers — Saalfield, Van Wiseman, Lynn, World Syndicate, and Goldsmith — cashed in on the idea as well. The first Big Little Book hero was Dick Tracy, but soon every radio cowboy, cartoon character, lawman, and space explorer was importalized in his own adventure series.

When it became apparent that the pre-teen of the fifties preferred the comic book format, Big Little Books were finally phased out; but many were saved in boxes and stored in attics, so there's still a wonderful supply of them around. You need to watch condition carefully when you're buying or selling.

Little Orphan Annie & Chizzler, Whitman #748, 1933, VG, $38.00

Andy Panda & Pirate Ghosts, Whitman #1459, 1949, EX..$22.50
Andy Panda & the Mad Dog Mystery, Whitman #1431, 1947,
    NM $40.00
Aquaman Scourge of the Sea, Whitman #2017, 1968, VG .$3.00
Black Silver & His Pirate Crew, Whitman #1414, 1937,
    VG...$20.00
Blondie & Dagwood in Hot Water, Whitman #1410, 1946,
    NM $40.00
Boss of the Chisholm Trail, #1153, NM+ $34.00
Bronc Peeler Lone Cowboy, Whitman #1417, 1937, EX..$25.00
Buck Jones in the Roaring West, Whitman #1174, 1935,
    EX...$28.00
Buckskin & Bullets, Saalfield #1135, 1938, EX.............$30.00
Bugs Bunny & the Secret Storm Island, Dell, 1942, VG..$50.00
Chandu the Magician, Saalfield #1093, 1935, G+.........$25.00
Chitty Chitty Bang Bang, Whitman #2025, 1968, NM $8.00
Danger Trails in Africa, #1151, EX.........................$18.00
Dick Tracy & the Boris Arson Gang, #1163, EX+ $45.00
Dick Tracy & the Mad Killer, Whitman #1436D, 1947,
    EX...$40.00
Erick Noble & the Forty-Niners, #722, EX..................$15.00
Flash Gordon & the Planet Mongo, 1934, EX $60.00
G-Man in Action, Saalfield #1173, 1940, NM..............$35.00
Ghost Avenger Strikes, Whitman #1462A, 1943, VG ...$25.00
In the Name of the Law, 1937, EX..........................$28.00
Invaders Alien Missile Threat, Whitman #12, 1967, VG.$4.50

Invisible Scarlet O'Neil Vs King of Slums, Whitman, 1946, VG **$25.00**

Just Kids, Whitman #1401A, 1937, VG **$32.00**

Li'l Abner in New York, #1198, VG+ **$18.00**

Lone Ranger Outwits Crazy Cougar, Whitman #2013, 1968, VG **$8.00**

Mac of the Marines in Africa, #1189, EX **$25.00**

Major Matt Mason, Moon Mission, Whitman #22, 1968, VG **$5.00**

Mandrake the Magician, Whitman #1167, 1935, G **$12.50**

Mickey Mouse & the Magic Lamp, 1942, G **$15.00**

Mickey Mouse & the Seven Ghosts, Whitman #1475, 1940, EX **$75.00**

Mickey Rooney & Judy Garland, #1493, VG **$15.00**

Nancy & Sluggo, Whitman #1400A, 1946, EX **$45.00**

Phantom of the Sky Pirates, Whitman #1468, 1948, VG+ **$12.00**

Pilot Pete Dive Bomber, Whitman #1466, 1941, VG **$24.00**

Radio Patrol Trailing Safeblowers, Whitman #1173, 1937, EX **$22.50**

Red Barry Undercover Man, Whitman #1426A, 1939, EX ... **$22.50**

Red Ryder in War on Range, Whitman #1473A, 1945, VG . **$22.50**

Return of Tarzan, Whitman #1102A, 1936, NM **$80.00**

Riders of Lone Trails, Whitman #1425A, 1937, EX **$30.00**

Shadow & Living Death, Whitman #1430C, 1940, VG . **$65.00**

Skeezix in Africa, #1112, EX **$210.00**

Smilin' Jack & the Jungle Pipe Line, Whitman #1419, 1947, EX **$50.00**

Snow White & the Seven Dwarfs, Whitman, 1938, VG, $45.00

Sombrero Pete, Whitman #1136, 1936, EX **$20.00**

Spiderman Zaps Mr Zodiac, Whitman, 1976, VG **$4.00**

Tailspin Tommy & Sky Bandits, Whitman #1494, 1936, VG **$36.00**

Tarzan the Fearless, Whitman #769, movie edition, 1934, G **$17.50**

Terry & the Pirates in the Mountain Stronghold, Whitman #149A, 1941, G **$16.50**

Tim Tyler, Saalfield #1053, 1934, VG **$30.00**

Tom & Jerry Meet Mr Fingers, Whitman #2006, 1967, M .. **$6.50**

Tom Swift & His Giant Telescope, Whitman #1485C, 1936, EX **$55.00**

Treasure Island, Jackie Cooper, #1141, VG **$10.00**

Treasure Island, Whitman #720, 1933, VG **$35.00**

Wash Tubbs in Pandemonia, Whitman #751, 1934, VG . **$27.50**

Will Rogers, Saalfield #1096, photo cover, 1935, VG ... **$25.00**

Woody Woodpecker & the Sinister Signal, Whitman #2028, 1969, EX **$8.50**

Wyatt Earp, Whitman #1644, TV edition, 1958, EX **$12.50**

Zane Grey's Tex Thorne Comes Out of the West, Whitman #1440A, 1937, NM **$45.00**

Black Americana

There are many avenues one might pursue in the broad field of Black Americana and many reasons that might entice one to become a collector. For the more serious, there are documents such as bills of sales for slaves, broadsides, and other historical artifacts. But by and far, most collectors enjoy attractive advertising pieces, novelties and kitchenware items, toys and dolls, and Black celebrity memorabilia.

It's estimated that there are at least 50,000 collectors around the country today. There are large auctions devoted entirely to the sale of Black Americana. The items they feature may be as common as a homemade potholder or a magazine or as rare as a Lux Dixie Boy clock or a Mammy cookie jar that might go for several thousand dollars. In fact, many of the cookie jars have become so valuable that they're being reproduced; so are salt and pepper shakers, so beware.

For further study, we recommend *Black Collectibles Sold in America* by P.J. Gibbs, and *Black Dolls, An Identification and Value Guide 1820 - 1991,* by Myla Perkins.

See also Sheet Music; Postcards; Valentines; String Holders.

Ad, Cream of Wheat, That's It — The Breakfast Food of the Nation, by Edward Brewer, in color, framed, 1920, 9x13", EX **$165.00**

Bell doll, Mammy w/metal bell under red polka-dot dress w/white apron, yarn face, 5½", EX **$30.00**

Birthday card, animated pop-up, Don't Be Melon-Cholic Honey..., boy at fence looking at watermelons, full color, EX **$22.00**

Blotter, features 2 comical golliwogs promoting English jellies, 1930s, 3½x5½", M **$10.00**

Book, Little Brown Koko's Pets & Playmates, by Blanche Seale hunt, 1957, 10x8", M **$35.00**

Book, Nicodemus & Petunia, by Inez Hogen, EP Dutton, 7th printing, pair pays a visit to 'de Witch Woman,' 1946, EX **$70.00**

Book, The Story of Little Black Bobtail, written & illustrated by Helen Bannerman, Frederick Stokes Publishing, EX **$125.00**

Book, Topsy Turvy's Pigtails, by Bernice G Anderson, illustrated by Esther Friend, Rand McNally, 1st edition, 1930, EX **$50.00**

Bookmark, hand-painted leather Deco-style bellhop figure in red suit, 10", EX **$70.00**

Bottle opener, man w/guitar, w/magnet, EX **$30.00**

Broom label, paper, features man sitting on fence playing banjo, Dixie lettered above, 1920s, 5x3½", EX......**$12.00**

Cigar box label, Little African/A Dainty Morsel, baby being stalked by alligator, black & red w/gold trim, 6x10", EX.................**$85.00**

Condiment set, ceramic, natives cooking man in pot, lg, EX.................**$175.00**

Condiment set, ceramic, 2 dark brown-skinned natives reclining on yellow & green dish w/lg native's head, 3-pc, EX.................**$160.00**

Condiment set, ceramic, 3 attached black-skinned chefs in 3 sizes, 2 smaller heads remove for shakers, 3-pc, NM.................**$175.00**

Cookie jar, Dottie, a reproduction of the Gilner Mammy, underglazed head w/brown skin tones, head scarf, Berry, NM.................**$100.00**

Cookie jar, Help Yo Self, hand-painted Mammy on bulbous cylinder shape, marked Bauer USA Los Angeles, some wear, VG.................**$350.00**

Cookie jar, Mammy, F&F Mold, NM.................**$400.00**

Cookie jar, Quilting Mammy, Mammy w/colorful quilt on lap, Rick Wisecarver.................**$175.00**

Cookie jar, Watermelon Boy, New Rose Collection, 1 of 100.................**$130.00**

Creamer & sugar bowl, footed black-faced clown heads w/yellow 'straw' hats, coiled bail handles, EX......**$30.00**

Creamer & sugar bowl, Mammy & Uncle Mose, F&F Mold, w/lid.................**$140.00**

Decanter, brown-skinned clown dressed in black suit, some paint wear, VG.................**$70.00**

Doll, Golliwog, black stuffed cloth w/plush hair, orange shirt & red pants, hard plastic eyes, 12", EX.........**$45.00**

Doll, gray-brown stuffed cloth w/no detail on hands & feet, stitched features, original sunsuit, 1930-50, 6½", EX.**$75.00**

Dolls, brown-skinned Raggedy Ann & Andy w/stitched & applied features, 1950-65, 16", pr.................**$175.00**

Dolls, cloth, brown-skinned couple w/stitched features, black hair, overalls & plain dress, 1935-45, 18", EX, pr....**$175.00**

Dolls, stuffed cotton w/stitched features, black yarn hair, 1930s-50s, 6½", pr, $125.00

Dolls, wire, Jamaican dancers, pr.................**$35.00**

Doorstop, painted cast-iron Mammy, paint missing, 8¾".................**$145.00**

Egg timer, lithographed tin showing Mammy in checked dress & white apron cooking at stove, 1930s, 7x5", EX..**$150.00**

Figurine, bisque, Mammy going into outhouse, 3¾", EX..**$50.00**

Figurine, cast iron, brown-skinned Mammy w/hands on hips wearing red dress, white neckerchief & bandanna, 2½", EX+.................**$90.00**

Figurine, ceramic, brown-skinned boxer w/knees bent & head back looking up, 5", EX.................**$30.00**

Figurine, ceramic, brown-skinned gent in turquoise hat & long yellow jacket w/dark tan pants, 1960-70, 10⅜", EX.................**$90.00**

Figurine, painted bisque, black-skinned boy on bale of cotton, 2½", EX.................**$45.00**

Figurine, painted chalkware, brown-skinned boy w/legs crossed eating watermelon on green base, Way Down South, 4", EX.................**$60.00**

Figurines, ceramic, 4 dapper brown-skinned minstrels in top hats playing various instruments, 1930s, 4¾", EX, set.................**$225.00**

Fruit label, paper, features Mammy lettered at left of Mammy's head & hand holding half-peeled orange, 1910-40, 4x9", EX.................**$15.00**

Game, Little Black Sambo (Who Gets the Most Pancakes?), features clawing tigers & Sambo, 1934, 12½x12½", VG+.................**$175.00**

Game, Watch on de Rind, features 3 boys eating watermelon, All-Fair, Churchville NY, 1931, 11½x11½", EX.................**$300.00**

Hot pad, black-skinned pickaninny in yellow sun bonnet w/blue stitching, 1930s, 6x5½", M.................**$60.00**

Mug, ceramic, off-white 'cooking pot' cup w/blue rim, black-skinned native handle in yellow collar & blue skirt, EX.................**$65.00**

Needlework Kit (Bucilla), Sambo doll, stamped fabrics for body & clothes, unopened package, 1950s, M.....**$65.00**

Note holder, plastic black-skinned Mammy in white dress holding 'pencil' broom & wearing 'note paper' apron, 10½", EX.................**$70.00**

Pancake shaker, plastic, yellow & white w/Aunt Jemima logo on lid, EX.................**$75.00**

Paper holder, metal, bust of 'Johnny Griffin,' 4¾", EX..**$250.00**

Pin, black-skinned Nubian bust w/gold-tone turban, earrings, & collar, 2½", EX.................**$25.00**

Pin-back button, celluloid, features 'Slim Timblin' promoting Horton's Melorol Ice Cream, 1" dia, M.................**$100.00**

Pincushion, Mammy doll, marked New Orleans on white aporn, EX.................**$35.00**

Pipe rack, polychromed cast iron w/head of young Black man wearing hat attached to top center of rack, EX.....**$200.00**

Planter, ceramic, black-skinned Mammy in white dress & red bandanna seated on yellow 4-footed 'flour' scoop, McCoy, EX.................**$150.00**

Planter, ceramic, brown-skinned native in boat, EX....**$40.00**

Plate, china w/gold-trimmed scalloped rim, features Famous & Dandy w/dog, 6" dia, VG.................**$150.00**

Playing cards, 2 kittens surprised by Golliwog Jack-in-the-box, double deck in hinged box, NM $135.00

Postcard, Mammy giving boy a bath, Shut Yo' Mouth & Mammy Will Have You White As Snow..., 1930s-50s, 3½x5½", EX $12.00

Postcard, photo image of man seated playing guitar, semigloss finish, no postmark, 1915-40, scarce, 5½x3½", G $35.00

Poster, Harlin Tarbell illustration of vaudeville act w/cartoon images of 2 sorrowful men in derbies, framed, 27x20", G $170.00

Potholder wall plaque, wooden Mammy shape w/yellow printed material, holds 2 potholders, EX.............$35.00

Potholders & caddy, 3-pc hand-embroidered folk-art set featuring pickaninny girls, Hide Your Pot Holders Here, EX $70.00

Record, LP, Music From 'Torching' With Billy Holiday, features illustrated sultry image of Miss Holiday (?), 1956, EX $125.00

Record, LP, The Best of Sam Cooke, pictures smiling Sam Cooke looking forward w/songs listed above, 1962, 12x12", EX $35.00

Salt & pepper shakers, brown Mammy & chef heads, she in red & he in white w/white collar, marked 7859, 3½", NM, pr..$85.00

Salt & pepper shakers, brown-skinned boy on tan elephant sitting upright, pours from top of head, 6", NM, pr......$70.00

Salt & pepper shakers, ceramic, black-skinned bald man's head & slice of watermelon, EX, pr......................$40.00

Salt & pepper shakers, ceramic, black-skinned boy & girl in yellow w/green trim, 2½", NM, pr $55.00

Salt & pepper shakers, ceramic, black-skinned Mammy & chef in pink aprons & hats holding red spoons, NM, pr...$40.00

Salt & pepper shakers, ceramic, brown-skinned native boys in animated poses, 1 holding up shorts, 5½", EX, pr...$35.00

Salt & pepper shakers, ceramic, grass hut & brown-skinned native in red toga, white hat & gold earrings, NM..$40.00

Salt & pepper shakers, ceramic, native mother & baby nesters w/reddish brown skin, gray eyes & yellow lips, EX...$35.00

Salt & pepper shakers, ceramic, palm tree & reddish brown-skinned native boy seated wearing yellow grass skirt, EX, pr......................................$30.00

Salt & pepper shakers, chalkware, dapper brown-skinned gents in gray derbies & green jackets w/hands in pockets, EX, pr....................................$45.00

Salt & pepper shakers, cut-out wood Rastus & Liza figures w/black-painted faces & details, EX, pr $25.00

Scouring-pad holder, heavy pottery, brown-skinned Mammy's head in green neckerchief & bandanna, Coventry, 1940s, 5", EX..$110.00

Shopping list, pegboard type featuring puzzled Mammy above 2 rows of listed items, Reckon Ah Needs?, 8¼x6", EX...$90.00

Shot glass, dancing native couple, gold rim, 2¼", EX .$20.00

Spice jars, Aunt Jemima figures, Allspice, Paprika, Nutmeg, Cloves, Ginger & Cinnamon, F&F Mold, EX, each from $50 to $65.00

Spoon rest, ceramic chef in black plaid jacket w/body as spoon rest, neck & head in upright position, 1920s-40s, EX...$100.00

Spoon rest, heavy pottery, tan-skinned Mammy in yellow dress w/green trim, 6½", EX................................$70.00

String holder, wood coffeepot shape in blue w/black handle, lid & spout, chef's head painted on front, ca 1930s, EX $135.00

Sugar sprinkler, ceramic, brown-skinned Mammy figure in pale blue dress & white bandanna, neckerchief & apron, VG+......................................$65.00

Syrup pitcher, Aunt Jemima premium, F&F Mold Co, 5", EX $70.00

Toaster doll, black-skinned Mammy w/button eyes & red checked bandanna, flowered dress, metal earrings, 1940s, EX......................................$30.00

Toothpick holder, ceramic, black-skinned cello player w/tree trunk holder attached to back, Japan, 1930-40, 4x3¼", EX......................................$65.00

Toy, Bobbin' Sam, black celluloid, applied features, It Floats, It Rattles, It Rocks, 1930s, 4x2½", MIB.......$95.00

Utensil holder, ceramic, black-skinned Mammy in green dress w/pink apron holding 2 barrels, California, 1940s, 7", VG $130.00

Valentine, musician blowing trumpet on heart shape, Jest Horning in on Valentines Day..., EX....................$20.00

Wall pocket, ceramic, dark brown-skinned boy eating slice of watermelon w/'watermelon' planter between legs, EX $70.00

Black Cats

Kitchenware, bookends, vases, and many other items designed as black cats were made in Japan during the 1950s and exported to the United States where they were sold by various distributors who often specified certain characteris-

Salt & pepper shakers, ceramic, Mammy & chef, 4¾", NM, pr, $40.00

tics they wanted in their own line of cats. Common to all these lines were the red clay used in their production and the medium used in their decoration — their features were applied over the glaze with 'cold (unfired) paint.' The most collectible is a line marked (or labeled) Shafford. Shafford cats are plump and pleasant looking. They have green eyes with black pupils; white eyeliner, eyelashes, and whiskers; and red bow ties. The same design with yellow eyes was marketed by Royal, and another fairly easy-to-find 'breed' is a line by Wales with yellow eyes and gold whiskers. You'll find various other labels as well. Some collectors buy only Shafford, while others like them all.

When you evaluate your black cats, be critical of their paint. Even though no chips or cracks are present, if half of the paint is missing, you have a half-price item. Remember this when using the following values which are given for cats with near-mint to mint paint.

Ashtray, flattened full figure, 'Ashes' in body, 2½x3¾" .**$7.50**

Bank, seated cat, green eyes, blue whiskers & eyelashes, Shafford, rare, 6", $125.00

Cigarette lighter, sm cat standing by lamp w/shade, book as base..**$50.00**
Cigarette lighter, upright cat, green eyes, Shafford, rare, 3" **$150.00**
Condiment set, 2 joined heads, 'M' bow on lid for marmalade, 'J' bow on jelly lid, lids have attached spoons, Shafford **$55.00**
Cookie jar, lg head of cat, green eyes, Shafford..........**$85.00**
Creamer & sugar bowl, heads are shakers, yellow eyes, gold whiskers, Regal **$50.00**
Cruet, very slender, gold collar & tie, tail handle **$12.00**
Cruets, oil & vinegar, he has 'O' eyes for oil, she has 'V' eyes, Shafford, pr **$50.00**
Demitasse pot, upright cat, tail handle, flat lid w/bow tie, spout as his right ear, rare, 7½" **$95.00**
Desk caddy, pen forms tail, spring body holds letters, 6½" **$8.00**

Egg cup, footed, green eyes, Shafford..........................**$25.00**
Fork, embossed cat face, green eyes, from wall-handing utensil set, Shafford..**$60.00**
Measuring set, 4 cups on wood rack w/cat's face, rare, Shafford **$150.00**
Mug, face embossed on side, cat handle, green eyes, Shafford, 3½" **$30.00**
Planter, upright cat, green eyes, Shafford **$30.00**
Salt & pepper, long cat, salt in 1 end, pepper in other, green eyes, white whiskers, Shafford, rare **$100.00**
Salt & pepper shakers, round-bodied 'teapot'-type cats, green eyes, Shafford, pr..**$35.00**
Salt & pepper shakers, seated, 1 has head tilted, green eyes, Shafford, 5", pr **$50.00**
Salt & pepper shakers, seated, 1 has head tilted, green eyes, Shafford, 3¾", pr **$25.00**
Salt & pepper shakers, seated (3") & recumbent (1¾"), lg heads, pr..**$12.00**
Sewing cat, pincushion on back, tongue is measure (not Shafford) **$22.50**
Spice set, 3 tiers of shakers w/embossed cat faces in triangular wooden rack, Shafford, rare, minimum **$250.00**
Spice set, 6 square shakers w/embossed cat faces in rectangular wooden rack, Shafford..............................**$125.00**
Stacking tea set, 'mamma' pot, 'kitty' creamer & sugar, tiny cat as finial, yellow eyes..**$50.00**
Teapot, ball-shaped body, green eyes, Shafford, 5¾" .**$45.00**
Teapot, panther-type face, squinty eyes, gold trim, 5" ..**$20.00**

Teapot, upright cat, paw forms spout, tail forms handle, green eyes, Shafford, very rare, 7¼", $150.00

Wall pocket, flattened 'teapot' cat, green eyes, Shafford, rare **$85.00**

Black Glass

Although black glass was made as early as the 1600s, the glass you'll find today is almost certain to be of this century, possibly from the Depression era, when it was made by many companies. It was sometimes molded in relief, etched, or enameled.

To learn more about this subject, we recommend *The Collector's Guide to Black Glass* by Marlena Toohey.

Bookend, rearing horse, LE Smith, 1950s, each...........**$72.00**
Candlesticks, crimped foot, unknown maker, ca 1925-1935, pr..**$42.00**
Celery dish, oblong w/rounded ends, 'cane' handle, Greensburg, #681, ca 1930...**$36.00**
Cigarette box, w/dog finial, rectangular, Greensburg, #1, 2½x3½"..**$42.00**
Compote, paneled bowl & pedestal foot w/flared scalloped rim, 1915-30, 6x8¾" dia **$50.00**
Console bowl, 6 lg flared scallops around rim, low foot, Fenton, #1234, ca 1928-36......................................**$46.00**
Figurine, Scolding Bird, marked Virginia B Evans, Imperial, 1982 ....**$102.00**
Flower cart, Viking, #772, 1940s **$52.00**
Place-card holder, shell-shaped back on square nut dish or ashtray, Fostoria, #2538, 1936, 2½" **$35.00**
Powder box, round hobnail tapering to flat bottom, ball finial, unknown maker, ca 1930-35, 4½" **$35.00**
Relish, 2-part round dish w/scalloped rim, 2-handled, Cambridge, #3400/90, 1931-49, 6" dia........................**$32.00**
Shaving mug, concave sides w/low foot, handled, Fenton, 3½"..**$42.00**
Tray, 2-handled 4-leaf clover shape w/straight-sided rim, Cambridge, #973, 1928-32, 5½".............................**$30.00**
Vase, bulbous w/scalloped rim, flat base, Greensburg, #1018, 1925-35, 6"..**$20.00**
Vase, bulbous urn shape w/angled handles, low foot, plain flared rim, Fostoria, #2360, ca 1926-31, 10"...........**$65.00**

Vase, crimped rim w/square pedestal foot, handled, LE Smith, #432/5, 1930-35, 7", $45.00

Blair Dinnerware

The Blair company operated in Ozark, Missouri, only briefly, opening in 1946 and closing sometime during the fifties. Blair himself was a modernistic painter-turned-potter, and his dinnerware designs reflect his approach to art. He favored square shapes over round, straight-sided hollowware pieces, and simple color combinations and patterns. His work was sold through some of the country's leading department stores, Neiman-Marcus and Marshall Field's among them.

His most popular pattern and the one most easily found today is Gay Plaid. The concept was very simple: intersecting vertical and horizontal brush strokes in brown, dark green, and chartreuse on white. He used twisted rope-like handles and applied leaves as knobs on lids. Yellow Plaid was similar; the same colors were used with yellow added. Rick-Rack featured hand-painted zigzags and diagonals. Bamboo was a bit more artistic with a stalk of bamboo and a few large leaves, and Autumn featured leaves as well. A departure from his earlier lines and the hardest to find today, Bird (except for still using the colors he obviously preferred — browns, white, and green) is different in that he used red clay for the body of the ware and the primitive bird designs were carved in the clay (a process called sgraffito) rather than hand painted. You'll have no problem identifying this dinnerware, since it is clearly marked 'Blair, Decorated by Hand.'

For further study, we recommend *The Collector's Encyclopedia of American Dinnerware* by Jo Cunningham.

Autumn Leaf, bowl **$12.00**
Bamboo, dinner plate, square.................................**$14.00**
Bamboo, onion soup, w/lid.....................................**$22.00**
Bamboo, plate, square, 8" **$10.00**
Bird, dinner plate..**$15.00**
Bird, plate, 6" **$16.00**
Bird, saucer (plain) **$6.50**
Bird, vegetable bowl, divided.................................**$32.00**
Gay Plaid, bowl, triangular, handled.....................**$16.00**
Gay Plaid, cup & saucer, closed handle.................**$16.00**

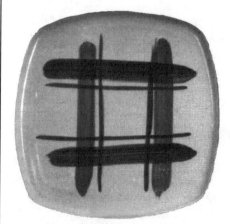

Gay Plaid, dinner plate, $14.00

Gay Plaid, mug..**$20.00**
Gay Plaid, onion soup, w/lid.....................................**$20.00**
Gay Plaid, sugar bowl **$16.00**

Rick-Rack, bowl $14.00
Rick-Rack, cup & saucer....................................$22.00
Rick-Rack, sugar bowl $16.00

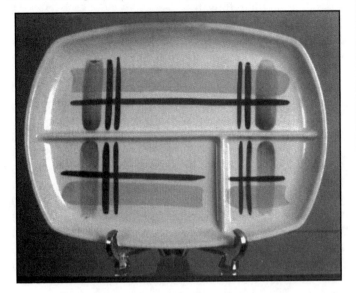

Yellow Plaid, divided serving plate, $26.00

Blue and White Stoneware

Though it hasn't been made since the 1930s, blue and white stoneware is a popular collectible today and carries price tags hefty enough that reproductions are everywhere, so we wanted to forewarn you. Beware of too bright colors, sloppy workmanship, and anything that looks unused. This was strictly utilitarian pottery, and it would be a rare piece indeed that showed no signs of wear. It was made as early as the turn of the century by many of the well-known potters of the era, among them Roseville, Brush McCoy, and Uhl.

For further study, we recommend *Blue and White Stoneware* by Kathryn McNerney.

Butter crock, Eagle, 6x6", M, $450.00

Berry crock, Flying Bird, 2x4" dia................................$90.00
Bowl, cereal or berry; Pale Blue Band, 2x4" dia..........$55.00
Bowl, Currants & Diamonds, fluted rim, 5x9" dia $105.00
Bowl, mixing; Flying Bird, 4x7½" dia........................$210.00
Bowl, Random Dashes, blue rim, spongeware, 2½x5½"
    dia...$105.00
Butter crock, Butterfly, restored bail, handle missing, 5-lb,
    6x10" dia..$100.00
Butter crock, Daisy & Trellis, restored bail & handle, 6¾x7"
    dia...$150.00
Butter crock, Diffused Blue, 1-lb, 4x4½" dia................$80.00
Butter crock, Grapes & Leaves, unglazed rim, marked
    Robinson Clay Pottery Co, Akron, Ohio, 3x6½" dia, min-
    imum value $175.00
Canister, Sugar, Snowflake pattern, maple lids w/china
    knobs, 6¼x5¾" dia...$150.00
Chamber, Open Rose & Spear Point Panels, heavy color on
    low relief flower, sm ring handle, 6x9½" dia......$120.00
Chamber, Wildflower on scalloped design, blue-daubed rim
    & ear-type handle, 6x11" dia................................$185.00
Chamber pot, Fleur-de-Lis & Scrolls, original bail & handle,
    13x10" dia...$220.00
Cookie jar, Turkey Eye color drip, diffused color bands, ball
    form, acorn finial, sm ring handle, 9x8" dia........$225.00
Cooler, Maxwell House Iced Tea, Blue Bands, wooden lid,
    push spigot, 15x13" dia..$210.00
Creamer, Arc & Leaf Panel, 4½x4" dia........................$105.00
Crock, advertising Hirsch's Goodies, 9½x8½" dia $110.00
Crock, spongeware, 6x5¼" dia $130.00
Cup, Bow Tie w/bird transfer, ear-type handle, 3¾x3½"
    dia...$85.00
Cup, Wildflower w/embossed ribbon & bow, 4½x2½", mini-
    mum value...$85.00
Custard cup, Fishscale, rare, 5x2½" dia $75.00
Dispenser, Ice Water, Blue Bands, push spigot, 17x13"
    dia...$200.00
Jug, Diffused Blue, ball form, cork stopper, 7x7" dia..$195.00
Milk crock, Lovebirds, restored bail & handle, 5½x9"
    dia...$145.00
Mug, Basket Weave & Flower, bulbous bottom, rolled rim,
    rope handle w/squared top, 5x3" dia..................$115.00
Mustard jar, Strawberry, marked Robinson Clay Pottery Co,
    Akron, Ohio, original lid, 4x3" dia.......................$135.00
Pickle crock, Blue Band, advertising Dodson & Braun's Fine
    Pickles, St Louis, original bail & handle, 12x9" dia.$175.00
Pitcher, Avenue of Trees, pale blue, long rectangular han-
    dle, 8x7¾" dia $140.00
Pitcher, Barrel Staves, 7x6" dia $120.00
Pitcher, Cherry Cluster on allover beaded squares, flared rim &
    base, applied blue-daubed handle, 7½x6¼" dia $190.00
Pitcher, Dutch Children & Windmill, embossed tulip petals
    above incised lines around base, 9x6" dia..........$200.00
Pitcher, Grape Cluster & Trellis, ear-type handle, Uhl Pottery
    Co, 7x7" dia..$185.00
Pitcher, Grooved Bands, spongeware, squared handle
    w/knobs, 9x7" dia...$275.00
Pitcher, Old-Fashioned Garden Rose, cylinder form, ear-type
    handle, 10x7" dia $190.00

Pitcher, Stag & Pine Trees, spurred handle w/square top, 9x6½" dia...$295.00

Roaster, Heart & Drapery, original lid, 5x12" dia $185.00

Rolling pin, Wildflower, 15" long $250.00

Salt crock, Apricots in medallions, cobalt, 5x5" dia...$145.00

Salt crock, Flying Bird, crisscross design on lid w/mushroom finial, 6x6½" dia, minimum value $350.00

Soap dish, Flower Cluster w/Fishscale $140.00

Soap dish, spongeware, plain clay center w/raised bars, 6" long..$100.00

Spittoon, Lilies & Plumes, fluted rim, 9x9¾" dia........$155.00

Pitcher, Butterfly in medallion, butterflies between raised rope bands top & bottom, 9x7" dia, $250.00

Blue Ridge Dinnerware

Blue Ridge has long been popular with collectors, and prices are already well established; but that's not to say there aren't a few good buys left around. There are! It was made by a company called Southern Potteries, who operated in Erwin, Tennessee, from sometime in the latter thirties until the mid-fifties. They made literally hundreds of patterns, all hand decorated. Some collectors prefer to match up patterns, while some like to mix them together for a more eclectic table setting.

One of the patterns most popular with collectors (and the most costly) is called French Peasant. It's very much like Quimper with simple depictions of a little peasant fellow with his staff. They made many lovely floral patterns, and it's around these where most of the buying and selling activity is centered. You'll also find roosters, plaids, and simple textured designs, and in addition to the dinnerware, some vases and novelty items as well.

Nearly every piece is marked 'Blue Ridge,' though occasionally you'll find one that isn't. Watch for a similar type of ware often confused with Blue Ridge that is sometimes (though not always) marked Italy.

The values suggested below are for the better patterns. To evaluate the French Peasant line, double these figures; for the simple plaids and textures, deduct 25% to 50%, depending on their appeal.

If you'd like to learn more, we recommend *The Collector's Encyclopedia of Blue Ridge Dinnerware, Identification and Values,* by Betty and Bill Newbound.

Ashtray, Mallard, box shape, 3½x2½".........................$28.00
Baking dish, plain, 8x13"...$22.00
Basket, aluminum edge, 7"...$14.00
Batter jug, w/lid...$65.00
Bonbon, Charm House, china.....................................$80.00
Bowl, fruit; 5¼"...$5.50
Bowl, salad; 10½x11½"...$48.00
Bowl, soup or cereal; Premium, 6"...........................$14.00
Bowl, vegetable; oval, 9"...$20.00
Bowl, vegetable; w/lid...$60.00
Box, Rose Step, pearlized...$65.00
Box, Seaside, china...$95.00
Butter dish, Woodcrest...$55.00
Cake lifter..$22.00
Candy dish, china, 6" dia...$110.00
Creamer, Charm House, china...................................$50.00
Creamer, demitasse; earthenware.............................$32.00
Creamer (open), Colonial, no handle........................$12.00
Cup & saucer, demitasse; Premium...........................$42.00
Cup & saucer, Turkey & Acorn..................................$42.00
Egg cup, double...$25.00
Gravy boat, Premium...$30.00
Pie baker...$28.00
Pitcher, Abby, earthenware..$70.00

Pitcher, Betsy, earthenware, 9", $85.00

Pitcher, Helen, china..$85.00
Pitcher, Sculptured Fruit, china..................................$75.00
Pitcher, Virginia, china, 4¼"......................................$80.00
Plate, dinner; Premium, 10½".....................................$40.00

Plate, divided..$18.00
Plate, novelty patterns, square, 6"...................$48.00
Plate, Square Dancers, square, 14" $80.00
Plate, Square Dancers, square or round, 8"........$42.00
Platter, regular patterns, 15", each..................$25.00
Platter, Turkey patterns, each $200.00
Ramekin, w/lid, 5" $28.00
Relish, china, loop handle.................................$70.00
Relish, Mod Leaf, china $60.00
Salad fork, earthenware, lg $32.00
Salt & pepper shakers, Apple, 2¼", pr $14.00

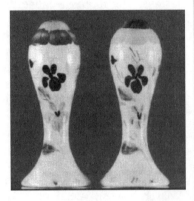

Salt & pepper shakers, Blossom Top, pr, $32.00

Salt & pepper shakers, Good Housekeeping, pr $60.00
Sugar bowl, Waffle $20.00
Sugar bowl (open), Colonial...............................$14.00
Tea tile, round or square, 3" $25.00
Teapot, Charm House, china $125.00
Teapot, Fine Panel, china...................................$110.00
Teapot, Woodcrest..$120.00
Tidbit, 2-tier...$25.00
Vase, bud..$80.00
Vase, china, ruffled top, 9½" $85.00

Blue Willow Dinnerware

Blue Willow dinnerware has been made since the 1700s, first by English potters, then Japanese, and finally American companies as well. Tinware, glassware, even paper 'go-withs' have been produced over the years — some fairly recently, due to on-going demand. It was originally copied from the early blue and white wares made in Nanking and Canton in China. Once in awhile you'll see some pieces in black, pink, red, or even multicolor.

Obviously the most expensive will be the early English wares, easily identified by their backstamps. You'll be most likely to find pieces made by Royal or Homer Laughlin, and even though comparatively recent, they're still collectible, and their prices are very affordable.

For further study we recommend *Blue Willow Identification and Value Guide* by Mary Frank Gaston.

Baking dish, flared rim, oven proof, marked Japan, 2½x5"
    dia $35.00
Biscuit jar, octagonal, cane handle, English, Gibson & Sons
    Ltd, 6½"...$225.00

Biscuit jar, Two Temples II pattern w/Traditional border,
    cane handle, Adderley mark, 4½"......................$150.00
Bowl, berry; Homer Laughlin, sm....................$8.00
Bowl, pedestal base, Holland mark, 4x7½" dia $125.00
Bowl, Royal China, 5½".....................................$4.50
Bowl, soup or cereal; scalloped edge, English, Doulton
    mark, 7½" dia $75.00
Bowl, soup; flat, Royal China............................$10.00
Bowl, unmarked, 5½"...$3.50

Bowl, vegetable; beaded rim, English, Aynsley & Co, 9¼" dia, $60.00

Bowl, vegetable; ring handles & lid finial, marked Japan, 9"
    dia $100.00
Bowl, vegetable; Royal China, 9"....................$15.00
Bowl, vegetable; scalloped edge, Buffalo Pottery mark,
    5½x9"...$200.00
Bowl, vegetable; tab handles, footed, English, unmarked,
    9½x12¼"...$125.00
Bowl, vegetable; Variant pattern w/pictorial border,
    unmarked, 10" dia..$25.00
Butter dish, marked Japan, 1-lb, 6" long $60.00
Cake plate, tab handles, Royal China, 10"....................$12.00
Casserole, w/lid, Royal China $35.00
Cheese dish, Burleigh pattern w/scroll & flower border,
    Burgess & Leigh, Burleigh Ware mark $165.00
Coffee jar, marked Instant Coffee, knob lid, unmarked
    Japan $60.00
Compote, American, Shenango China mark, 3x6" dia.$50.00
Compote, earthenware, Mandarin pattern w/dagger border,
    impressed Copeland mark, 8" dia $175.00
Creamer, ear-type handle, pedestal base, marked Made in
    Japan, 3½"...$18.50
Creamer, individual; scalloped edge, ear-type handle,
    marked England, 2"..$35.00
Creamer, Royal China $5.00

Creamer, Two Temples II pattern w/butterfly border, footed, unmarked, 4x6" long **$75.00**

Creamer & sugar bowl, Canton pattern, GL Ashworth mark, 5" **$75.00**

Cup, Two Temples II pattern, scalloped edge, ear-type handle, English, unmarked, 2½" **$60.00**

Cup, Two Temples II pattern w/line border, ring handle, Sebring Pottery mark, 3½" **$15.00**

Cup & saucer, angular handle, Royal China **$7.50**

Cup & saucer, demitasse; marked Japan **$16.00**

Egg cup, unmarked **$10.00**

Gravy boat & ladle, unmarked **$30.00**

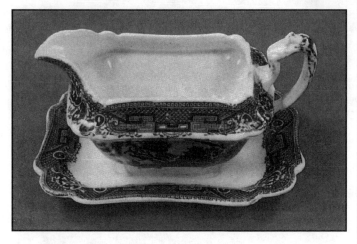

Gravy boat & underplate, scalloped edge, ear-type handle, Allerton mark, 7½" long, $125.00

Honey dish, WR Midwinter mark, 4" dia **$35.00**

Mug, Japan **$10.00**

Mustard pot, flared neck, ear-type handle, unmarked, 2½" **$75.00**

Pitcher, triangular shape w/ear-type handle, Doulton mark, 6" **$175.00**

Plate, advertising Ye Olde Cheshire Cheese, Traditional pattern, 7¾" **$55.00**

Plate, Booths Variant pattern w/bow-knot border, gold trim, octagonal, 8¾" **$55.00**

Plate, cake; Traditional pattern, marked American Royal China Co, 12¼" **$35.00**

Plate, dinner; Royal China, 10" **$10.00**

Plate, grill; Traditional pattern, marked Made in Japan, 10½" **$20.00**

Plate, Japan, 6" **$5.00**

Plate, plain w/pictorial border, Allerton mark w/Pavilion, 7" **$20.00**

Plate, Traditional pattern, scalloped edge, Buffalo Pottery mark, 9½" **$45.00**

Plate, Turner pattern w/scroll & flower border, marked Ideal, 11" **$25.00**

Plate, Two Temples I pattern w/butterfly border, unmarked, 10" **$85.00**

Plate, unmarked, 9" **$5.00**

Plate, Variant pattern w/pictorial border, unmarked, 6" .**$15.00**

Platter, plain w/pictorial border, marked National China Co **$45.00**

Platter, Traditional pattern, marked Made in Occupied Japan, 9½x12¾" **$45.00**

Platter, Traditional pattern, scalloped edge, Buffalo Pottery mark, 11¾" long **$140.00**

Salt & pepper shakers, Royal China, pr **$13.50**

Wall pocket, pitcher form, unmarked **$40.00**

Bookends

You'll find bookends in various types of material and designs. The more inventive their modeling, the higher the price. Also consider the material. Normally bronze and brass examples are higher than cast iron, though elements of design may override the factor of materials. If they are signed by the designer or marked by the manufacturer, you can about triple the price. Those with a decidedly Art Deco appearance are often good sellers, so are cast iron figurals in good paint.

Abraham Lincoln bust, bronze-painted pot metal, 3¼x2¾", pr **$16.00**

Amish man & woman seated, cast iron, 4¾x4¾", pr .**$125.00**

Aviator, bronzed metal, pr **$50.00**

Baseball batter in action, plated white metal, marked WB, 6½", pr **$195.00**

Cherub, cast metal w/dark bronze finish, 6¼", pr **$350.00**

Cocker spaniel, gilt metal, white onyx base, pr **$65.00**

Daffodil silhouette, bronze, G Thew, 1928, 6", pr **$200.00**

Dancing nudes, stylized, bronze w/green finish, on flat bases w/floral design, marked Schroedin, 5", pr **$225.00**

Dog figure, chalkware, pr **$45.00**

Dutch boy & girl, brass, Frankart, pr, $125.00

End of Trail, man & horse, bronze finish on metal, pr ..**$45.00**

Fish, nickle-plated w/bright & satin finish, Deco style, 6", pr **$100.00**

Horse rearing, emerald green glass, 8", pr **$75.00**

Lindbergh bust, pr **$125.00**

Nude, cast iron, Art Nouveau style, pr **$75.00**

Nude in shell, painted chalkware, EX, pr **$40.00**

Pointer dog, bronze-painted cast iron, 8", pr.............**$75.00**
Poodle, ceramic, pr..**$15.00**
Scottie dog, Bradley & Hubbard, paper label, pr **$75.00**
Scottie dog sitting upright on hind legs on 2-step square base, metal w/brass finish, Frankart, 7".............**$150.00**
Sunbonnet Girl, painted cast iron, pr **$125.00**

Books

Books have always fueled the mind's imagination. Before television lured us out of the library into the TV room, everyone enjoyed reading the latest novels. Western, horror, and science fiction themes are still popular to this day — especially those by such authors as Louis L'Amour, Steven King, and Ray Bradbury, to name but a few. Edgar Rice Burrough's Tarzan series and Frank L. Baum's Wizard of Oz books are regarded as classics among today's collectors. A first edition of a popular author's first book (especially if it's signed) is especially sought after, so is a book that 'ties in' with a movie or television program.

On the whole, ex-library copies and book club issues (unless they are limited editions) have very low resale values.

For further information we recommend *Huxford's Old Book Value Guide* by Sharon and Bob Huxford. This book is designed to help the owners of old books evaluate their holdings, and it also lists the names of prospective buyers.

See also Children's Books; Paperback Books; Cookbooks.

Abrams, Louis Enard; Rabbits by the Acre, McBride, 1st edition, 1954, 208 pages, w/dust jacket, VG **$15.00**
Aiken, Conrad; Seizure of Limericks, Holt Rinehart Winston, 1st edition, 1954, 57 pages, w/dust jacket, EX......**$35.00**
Anderson, Dave; Yankees, Random House, 1st edition, 1979, w/dust jacket, VG **$16.50**
Anglund, Joan Walsh; Christmas Is a Time of Giving, Harcourt Brace World, 1st edition, 1961, w/dust jacket, VG **$20.00**
Anthony, Katharine; Lambs, Knopf, 1st edition, 1945, w/dust jacket, VG **$10.00**
Barber, Red; Broadcasters, Dial, 1st edition, 1970, w/dust jacket, EX...**$25.00**
Barth, John; Letters, Putnam, 1st trade edition, signed/dated, 1979, w/dust jacket, VG **$30.00**
Baum, Frank L, Land of Oz, Reilly Lee, Neill illustrated, ca 1940, VG **$60.00**
Bishop, Elizabeth; Complete Poems, Farrar, Straus & Giroux, 1st edition, 1969, w/dust jacket, VG **$20.00**
Burgess, Anthony; End of the World News, Hutchinson, 1982, w/dust jacket, EX **$20.00**
Burgess, Thornton; Little Pete's Adventure, McLoughlin, Harrison Cady illustrator, 1941, scarce, VG.................**$25.00**
Burke, Richard; Murder on High Heels, Gateway, 1945, VG...**$10.00**
Burroughs, Edgar Rice; Tarzan & the Golden Lion, Grosset & Dunlap, EX **$50.00**
Bush, Christopher; Case of the Russian Cross, Macmillan, 1st edition, 1958, G...**$5.00**

Cain, James M; Past All Dishonor, Knopf, 1st edition, 1946, w/dust jacket, VG **$60.00**
Caldwell, Steven; Star Quest, Crescent, 1979, G **$7.50**
Campbell, Bruce; Clue of the Marked Claw, Grosset & Dunlap, VG...**$10.00**
Carmichael, Harry; Most Deadly Hate, Dutton, 1st edition, 1974, w/dust jacket, VG **$17.50**
Carpozi, George Jr; John Wayne Story, Arlington House, review edition, 1979, w/dust jacket, EX **$25.00**
Carr, John Dickson; Death Turns the Tables, Collier, VG.**$10.00**
Carter, Angela; Nights at the Circus, Hogarth, 1984, w/dust jacket, VG **$20.00**
Caudwell, Sarah; Sirens Sang of Murder, London, Collins, 1st edition, 1989, w/dust jacket, EX **$25.00**
Charteris, Leslie; Juan Belmonte Killer of Bulls, Book League, VG...**$15.00**
Chesterton, GK; Father Brown Book, Cassell, 2nd printing, 1959, VG...**$10.00**
Christie, Agatha; Caribbean Mystery, Dodd Mead, 1st edition, 1965, G...**$6.00**
Christie, Agatha; Miss Marples, Final Class, Collins, 1979, VG...**$15.00**
Christie, Agatha; Pocket Full of Rye, Collins, 2nd printing, 1954, w/dust jacket, VG **$35.00**
Christopher, John; When the Tripods Came, Dutton, 3rd printing, w/dust jacket, VG **$15.00**
Clarke, Donald Henderson; Murderer's Holiday, 1948, w/dust jacket, VG **$15.00**
Cole, Burt; Blue Climate, Harper & Row, 1st edition, 1977, w/dust jacket, VG **$12.50**
Collins, Max Allan; Million-Dollar Wound, St Martin, 1st edition, inscribed, 1986, w/dust jacket, EX **$30.00**
Condon, Richard; Money Is Love, Dial Press, 1st edition, 1975, w/dust jacket, VG **$20.00**
Coppel, Alfred; Gate of Hell, Harcourt, Brace & World, 1st edition, 1967, w/dust jacket, VG...........................**$12.50**
Coxe, George Hamilton; Dangerous Legacy, Knopf, 1946, w/dust jacket, VG **$15.00**
Cozzens, James Gould; Guard of Honor, Harcourt Brace, w/dust jacket, G...**$12.50**
Creasey, John; Clutch of Coppers, Holt Rinehart Winston, 2nd printing, 1969, w/dust jacket, VG..................**$12.00**
Creasey, John; Killing Strike, Scribners, 1st edition, 1961, w/dust jacket, VG **$15.00**
Crichton, Michael; Eaters of the Dead, Knopf, 1st edition, 1976, w/dust jacket, EX **$25.00**
Cunningham, EV; Case of the Russian Diplomat, Holt Rinehart, 1978, w/dust jacket, G **$6.00**
Curtiss, Ursula; Forbidden Garden, Book Club, w/dust jacket, G...**$5.00**
Daly, Elizabeth; House Without the Door, Hammond Hammond, 2nd printing, 1950, VG **$17.50**
Davidson, Avram; Redward Edward Papers, Doubleday, 1st edition, 1978, w/dust jacket, VG..........................**$20.00**
Davis, Berrie; Fourth Day of Fear, Putnam, 1st edition, 1973, w/dust jacket, VG **$12.50**
Davis, HL; Proud Riders & Other Poems, Harper, 1st edition, 1942, w/dust jacket, VG **$30.00**

De Camp, L Sprague; Castle of Iron, Gnome Press, 1st edition, 1950, w/dust jacket, VG $75.00

Dean, Amber; Call Me Pandora, Crime Club, 1946, VG .$15.00

Deighton, Len; Billion Dollar Brain, Jonathan Cape, 1st edition, 1966, w/dust jacket, VG $20.00

Dexter, Colin; Dead of Jericho, St Martin, 1st US edition, 1981, w/dust jacket, EX.............................$45.00

Dunbar, Willis F; All Aboard!, Grand Rapids, 2nd printing, 1969, 308 pages, w/slipcase, VG.............................$15.00

Edgar, Ken; As If, Prentice Hall, 1st edition, 1973, w/dust jacket, EX.............................$50.00

Ellroy, James; Suicide Hill, Mysterious, 1st edition, signed, 1986, w/dust jacket, EX.............................$50.00

Evans, Herbert; Silent Call, New York, 1st edition, 1930, w/dust jacket, EX.............................$90.00

Ferber, Edna; Ice Palace, Doubleday, 1st edition, 1958, w/dust jacket, VG $10.00

Francis, Dick; Blood Sport, Harper, 1st edition, 1967, w/dust jacket, EX.............................$100.00

Goldman, William; Colour of Light, Granada, 1st edition, 1984, w/dust jacket, VG $22.00

Goldman, William; Temple of Gold, Knopf, 1st edition, 1957, w/dust jacket, EX.............................$75.00

Gordon, Allison; Night Game, McClelland & Stewart, 1st edition, 1992, w/dust jacket, EX.............................$25.00

Gordon, Caroline; Glory of Hera, Doubleday, 1st edition, 1972, w/dust jacket, VG $20.00

Goudge, Elizabeth; Pilgrim's Inn, Book Club, w/dust jacket, VG $7.50

Greene, Graham; Brighton Rock & the End of the Affair, Peerage Books, 1987, w/dust jacket, EX $15.00

Grey, Zane; Light of Western Stars, Grosset & Dunlap, w/dust jacket, VG $20.00

Grey, Zane; Young Lion Hunter, Grosset & Dunlap, VG $10.00

Grisham, John; Pelican Brief, Book Club, w/dust jacket, EX.............................$10.00

Haggard, H Rider; Child of Storm, MacDonald, 1952, w/dust jacket, VG $30.00

Haggard, H Rider; Way of the Spirit, Musson, 1st Canadian edition, VG $35.00

Hall, Manly Palmer; Way of Heaven, Philosophical Research, 1st edition, 1946, VG $15.00

Halliday, Brett; Dividend on Death, Sun Dial, 1942, VG .$10.00

Hamilton, Edmond; Battle for the Stars, Torquil, 1st edition, 1961, w/dust jacket, VG $10.00

Hardwick, Mollie; Malice Domestic, Century, 1st edition, 1986, w/dust jacket, EX $20.00

Harris, Thomas; Red Dragon, Putnam, 1st edition, 1981, w/dust jacket, VG $95.00

Harrison, Jim; Sundog, Dutton/Lawrence, 1st edition, 1984, w/dust jacket, EX.............................$12.50

Harvester, Simon; Shadows in a Hidden Land, Walker, 1st edition, 1966, w/dust jacket, VG $20.00

Hawk, John; House of Sudden Sleep, Mystery League, 1st edition, 1930, w/dust jacket, VG $25.00

Heinlein, Robert A; Door Into Summer, Book Club, w/dust jacket, VG $10.00

Herbert, Frank; Dragon in the Sea, Doubleday, 1st edition, 1956, w/dust jacket, VG $175.00

Heyer, Georgette; Lady of Quality, Bodley Head, 1st edition, 1972, w/dust jacket, EX $20.00

Hill, Reginald; Clubbable Woman, Foul Play Press, 1984, w/dust jacket, EX $20.00

Hitchcock, Alfred; Ghostly Gallery, Random House, 1962, in decorated boards, VG.............................$15.00

Hoffman, Lee; Loco, Doubleday, 1st edition, 1969, w/dust jacket, VG $17.50

Holme, Timothy; At the Lake of Sudden Death, Detective Book Club, 1987, VG $8.00

Horler, Sydney; Tiger Standish, Crime Club, 1933, VG...$15.00

Hubbard, L Ron; Death Quest, Bridge, 1st edition, 1986, w/dust jacket, EX $25.00

Huxley, Aldous; After Many a Summer Dies the Swan, Vanguard, 1953, VG $10.00

Innes, Michael; Appleby & Honeybath, Gollancz, 1st edition, 1983, w/dust jacket, VG $16.50

Jacobi, Carl; Portraits in Moonlight, Arkham House, 1st edition, 1964, 213 pages, w/dust jacket, EX.............................$55.00

Jeffers, Robinson; Double Axe & Other Poems, Random House, 1st edition, inscribed, 1948, w/dust jacket, EX.........$175.00

Judd, Frances K; Mansions of Secrets, Cupples Leon, 1942, VG.............................$10.00

Kaminsky, Stuart; Exercise in Terror, St Martin, 1st edition, 1985, w/dust jacket, EX $27.50

Keene, Carolyn; Clue in the Cobweb, Grosset Dunlap, 1st edition, 1939, w/dust jacket, VG.............................$90.00

Knight, Kathleen Moore; Intrigue for Empire, Crime Club, 1st edition, 1944, VG $15.00

Lavin, Mary; Collected Stories, Houghton Mifflin, 1st US edition, 1971, w/dust jacket, VG $10.00

Lovesey, Peter; Wobble to Death, Dodd Mead, 1st US edition, 1970, w/dust jacket, VG.............................$40.00

Marquand, JP; Point of No Return, Little Brown, 1st trade edition, 1949, w/dust jacket, VG.............................$22.00

Merrill, James; Seraglio, Knopf, 1st edition, 1957, w/dust jacket, VG $35.00

Moyes, Patricia; Angel Death, Book Club, w/dust jacket, VG $8.00

Muller, Marcia; Edwin of the Iron Shoes, Book Club, w/dust jacket, VG $8.00

Nash, Anne; Cabbages & Crime, Crime Club, 1945, VG.$15.00

Naylor, Gloria; Linden Hills, Ticknor Fields, 2nd printing, 1985, w/dust jacket, EX $6.00

Niven, Larry; Magic Goes Away, Grosset & Dunlap, 1st edition, signed, 1978, w/dust jacket, EX.............................$30.00

Nolan, William F; Death Is for Losers, Sherbourne Press, 1st edition, 1968, w/dust jacket, EX $25.00

Norman, Barry; Matter of Mandrake, Walker, 1st edition, 1968, w/dust jacket, VG $12.50

Norton, Andre; Opal-Eyed Fan, Dutton, 1st edition, 1977, w/dust jacket, VG $20.00

Oliver, Chad; Shadows in the Sun, Crown, 1st edition, 1985, w/dust jacket, EX $14.00

Oppenheim, E Phillips; Gallows of Chance, McClelland & Stewart, 1934, VG.............................$15.00

Orwell, George; Animal Farm, Harcourt Brace, 1st US edition, 1946, w/dust jacket, VG $50.00

Ottum, Bob; See the Kid Run, Simon & Schuster, 1st edition, 1978, w/dust jacket, EX $15.00

Palmer, William J; Dectective & Mr Dickens, Quality Book Club, w/dust jacket, VG $10.00

Pentecost, Hugh; Beautiful Dead, Dodd Mead, 1st edition, 1973, w/dust jacket, VG $24.00

Pentecost, Hugh; Price of Silence, Detective Book Club, 1984, VG $8.00

Perker, T Jefferson; Laguna Heat, Book Club, w/dust jacket, VG $8.00

Peters, Ellis; Hermit of Eyton Forest, Stoddart, 1st edition, 1987, w/dust jacket, EX $20.00

Peters, Ellis; Sanctuary Sparrow, Morrow, 1st US edition, 1983, w/dust jacket, EX $35.00

Petievich, Gerald; Earth Angels, New American Library, 1st edition, 1989, w/dust jacket, VG $18.00

Pickering, James Sayre; Stars Are Yours, Macmillan, 1st edition, 1948, signed, VG $20.00

Pohl, Frederik; Drunkard's Walk, Gnome Press, 1st edition, 1960, w/dust jacket, EX $14.00

Porter, Gene Stratton; Keeper of the Bees, Doubleday Page, 1st edition, 1925, in decorated boards, VG $25.00

Pratt, Fletcher; Invaders from Rigel, Avalon, 1960, w/dust jacket, VG $30.00

Priestley, JR; Festival at Farbridge, Heinemann, 1st edition, 1951, VG $30.00

Proysen, Alf; Mrs Pepperpot Again, Ivan Obolenski, 1st US edition, 1961, VG $12.00

Queen, Ellery; Chinese Orange Mystery, Triangle, 1945, VG $10.00

Queen, Ellery; Sporting Blood, Little Brown, 1st edition, 1942, VG $35.00

Quentin, Patrick; Follower, Simon & Schuster, 1st edition, 1950, w/dust jacket, VG $15.00

Quest, Rodney; Cerberus Murders, McCall, 1st edition, 1970, w/dust jacket, VG $18.00

Raine, William Macleod; Gunsight Pass, Triangle, 1946, VG $8.00

Rathbone, Julian; Base Case, Pantheon, 1st US edition, 1981, w/dust jacket, EX $20.00

Reeve, Arthur B; Stars Scream Murder, Appleton-Century, 1st edition, 1936, VG $30.00

Rendell, Ruth; Sleeping Life, Doubleday, 1st US edition, 1978, w/dust jacket, VG $35.00

Romer, John; Valley of the Kings, Morrow, 1st US edition, 1981, 293 pages, w/dust jacket, VG $20.00

Ryder, Stephanie; Blind Jack, Houghton Mifflin, 1st edition, 1961, 145 pages, EX $12.50

Sawyer, Charles Winthrop; Our Rifles, Boston, 1st edition, 1944, EX $20.00

Shimer, RH; Squaw Point, Harper & Row, 1st edition, 1972, EX $35.00

Smith, H Allen; Lost in the Horse Latitudes, Doubleday Doran, 1st edition, 1944, w/dust jacket, VG $10.00

Snow, CP; Time of Hope, Macmillan, 1st US edition, 1950, w/dust jacket, VG $20.00

Southern, Terry; Magic Christian, Random House, 1st edition, 1960, w/dust jacket, VG $25.00

Stone, Robert; Children of Light, Knopf, 1st US edition, signed, 1986, w/dust jacket, EX $65.00

Sutton, Margaret; Ghost Parade, Grosset Dunlap, VG ...$8.00

Swanwick, Michael; Vacuum Flowers, Simon & Schuster, 1st edition, 1988, w/dust jacket, EX $30.00

Talbot, Michael; Night Things, Book Club, w/dust jacket, VG $8.00

Tapply, William G; Death at Charity's Point, Scribner, 1st edition, 1984, w/dust jacket, EX $125.00

Tate, Peter; Faces in the Flames, Doubleday, 1st edition, 1976, w/dust jacket, VG $12.50

Taylor, P Walker; Murder in the Game Reserve, Thornton Butterworth, 1st edition, 1947, VG $35.00

Tessier, Thomas; Nightwalker, Macmillan, 1st edition, 1979, w/dust jacket, VG $20.00

Theroux, Paul; Half Moon Street, Houghton Mifflin, 1st edition, 1984, w/dust jacket, VG $7.50

Thomson, June; Dying Fall, Crime Club, 1st edition, 1986, w/dust jacket, VG $18.00

Thorp, Roderick; Nothing Lasts Forever, Norton, 1979, w/dust jacket, EX $15.00

Tidyman, Ernest; Line of Duty, WH Allen, 1974, w/dust jacket, EX $20.00

Tolkien, JRR; Lord of the Rings, Houghton Mifflin, 1991, w/dust jacket, EX $60.00

Tresunngar, Hugo; Dark Justice, Sutton House, 1st edition, 1938, 255 pages, w/dust jacket, VG $20.00

Truss, Seldon; Doctor Was a Dame, Crime Club, 1st edition, 1953, w/dust jacket, VG $20.00

Uhnak, Dorothy; False Witness, Simon & Schuster, 1st edition, 1981, w/dust jacket, VG $10.00

Updike, John; Rabbit at Rest, Knopf, 1st trade edition, 1990, w/dust jacket, EX $30.00

Updike, John; Witches of Eastwick, Knopf, 1st edition, 1984, w/dust jacket, VG $20.00

Upfield, Arthur W; Mountains Have a Secret, Crime Club, 1st edition, 1948, w/dust jacket, VG $45.00

Vachss, Andrew; Blossom, Knopf, 1st edition, 1990, w/dust jacket, VG $18.00

Van Der Post, Laurens; Heart of the Hunter, Morrow, 1st edition, 1961, inscribed, 268 pages, w/dust jacket, VG $40.00

Van Dine, SS; Kidnap Murder Case, Scribner, 1st edition, 1936, VG $35.00

Van Vogt, AE; House That Stood Still, Greenberg, 2nd printing, 1950, w/dust jacket, VG $25.00

Vance, Jack; Big Planet, Underwood Miller, 1st edition, 1978, w/dust jacket, VG $40.00

Verne, Jules; Round the World in Eighty Days, Collins, w/dust jacket, VG $15.00

Vinge, Joan D; Phoenix in the Ashes, Bluejay, 1st edition, 1985, w/dust jacket, VG $20.00

Vonnegut, Kurt; Jailbird, Delacorte, 1st edition, 1979, w/dust jacket, VG $30.00

Wainwright, John; Big Tickle, Macmillan, 1st edition, 1969, w/dust jacket, VG $22.00

Walker, Alice; You Can't Keep a Good Woman Down, Harcourt, 1st edition, 1983, w/dust jacket, EX..........**$100.00**

Walker, Ira; Man in the Driver's Seat, Abelard-Schuman, 1st edition, 1964, w/dust jacket **$15.00**

Wallace, Edgar; Frightened Lady, Musson, 1st Canadian edition, 1933, VG **$20.00**

Wallace, Edgar; White Face, Hodder & Stroughton, 1952, VG **$8.00**

Wallace, Marilyn; Sisters in Crime, Book Club, w/dust jacket, VG **$10.00**

Wandrei, Donald; Strange Harvest, Arkham House, 1st edition, 1965, w/dust jacket, EX....................**$45.00**

Waring, Barbara; Heckle & Jeckle Visit the Farm, Wonder Books, 1958, VG **$15.00**

Waugh, Hillary; Eighth Mrs Bluebeard, Book Club, w/dust jacket, VG **$8.00**

Wellman, Manly Wade; Voice of the Mountain, Doubleday, 1st edition, 1984, w/dust jacket, VG **$35.00**

Wells, HG; Thirty Strange Stories, Causeway, 1974, w/dust jacket, VG **$15.00**

West, Wallace; Outposts in Space, Avalon, 1st edition, 1962, w/dust jacket, VG **$30.00**

Wheatley, Dennis; Haunting of Toby Jugg, Hutchinson, 3rd printing, 1951, w/dust jacket, VG **$25.00**

Whitfield, Shelby; Kiss It Goodbye, Abelard Schuman, 1st edition, 1973, w/dust jacket, VG....................**$17.50**

Whitney, Phyllis A; Glass Flame, Book Club, w/dust jacket, VG **$8.00**

Wilhelm, Kate; Somerset Dreams, Harper & Row, 1st edition, 1978, w/dust jacket, EX....................**$20.00**

Williams, Valentine; Mystery of the Gold Box, Collier, VG **$10.00**

Wilson, Colin; Schoolgirl Murder Case, Rupert Hart-Davis, 2nd printing, 1975, w/dust jacket, VG....................**$15.00**

Wilson, Edmund; American Earthquake, Doubleday Anchor, 1st edition, 1958, w/dust jacket, VG **$25.00**

Winterbotham, Russ; Joyce of the Secret Squadron, Whitman, 1942, VG....................**$12.00**

Wodehouse, PG; Jill the Reckless, Herbert Jenkins, 1958, w/dust jacket, VG **$20.00**

Wodehouse, PG; White Feather, Souvenir Press, 1972, w/dust jacket, EX **$14.00**

Wolff, Miles Jr; Season of the Owl, Stein Day, 1st edition, 1980, w/dust jacket, G **$8.00**

Wright, Eric; Death in the Old Country, Collins Crime Club, 1st edition, 1985, w/dust jacket, VG....................**$18.00**

York, Andrew; Captivator, Crime Club, 1974, VG **$10.00**

Zahn, Timothy; Coming of Age, Bluejay, 1st edition, 1984, w/dust jacket, EX....................**$20.00**

Zelazny, Roger; Hand of Oberon, Faber, 1st edition, 1978, w/dust jacket, VG **$45.00**

Bottle Openers

A figural bottle opener is one where the cap lifter is an actual feature of the model being portrayed — for instance, the bill of a pelican or the mouth of a 4-eyed man. Most are made of painted cast iron or aluminum; others were chrome or brass plated. Some of the major bottle opener producers were Wilton, John Wright, L&L, and Gadzik. They have been reproduced, so beware of any examples with 'new' paint. Condition of the paint is an important consideration when it comes to evaluating an opener.

For more information, read *Figural Bottle Openers, Identification Guide*, by the Figural Bottle Opener Collectors. They're listed in the Directory under Clubs, Newsletters, and Catalogs.

All American, F-38, painted cast iron, football player w/blue helmet & yellow pants, 1950s, 4¼x2⅛"..............**$625.00**

Amish man, F-422, cast iron, wall mount, 1953, 4⅛x3⅝"....................**$950.00**

Anchor chain, F-228, steel, 6⅞" long **$60.00**

Buffalo, N-523, bronze, wall mount, 1984, 5⅜x2¾" ...**$80.00**

Buffalo Bill, N-509, bronze, wall mount, 1984, 5½x4½".**$80.00**

Canada Goose, F-105, painted cast iron, feeding position, 1947, 1¾x3⅝"....................**$65.00**

Cowboy sign post, F-14, painted cast iron, 1 leg up, 1950, 4⅛x2¾"....................**$125.00**

Dachshund, F-84, brass, 5⅞" long....................**$30.00**

Dragon, F-145, cast iron, 2½x5"....................**$550.00**

Elephant standing on base, F-58, brass, 2⅛x3"............**$45.00**

Eskimo, F-194, aluminum, on snowshoe, 1956-61 ....**$450.00**

Father Christmas, N-558, painted aluminum, 1988, 4½x2⅛"....................**$95.00**

Four-eyed man, F-413, painted cast iron, wall mount, 1950, 4", $55.00

Goat, F-72, painted cast iron, sitting on green base, 4x2½"....................**$30.00**

Happy Hooligan, F-32, bronze, 5" **$200.00**

Indian brave, N-506, bronze, wall mount, 1984, 4¼x3⅞".**$80.00**

King Tut, N-538, brass, wall mount, 1987, 6¼x5⅜" **$65.00**

Lady w/harp, F-170, cast iron w/patina finish, 6¼"...**$650.00**

Lobster, F-169, painted cast iron, red, 4⅛" long **$32.50**

Lock, F-214, brass, 1961, 2½x1⅝" **$40.00**

Mexican Cactus, F-24, painted cast iron, Mexican sitting w/head down leaning on cactus, 1954, 2⅞x2⅜" ..**$450.00**

Monkey, F-89, aluminum, 1976, 2⅝" **$12.00**

Nude atop globe, F-179, chrome, 4½"........................**$65.00**

Pheasant, F-104, painted cast iron, multicolored, 1950, 2¼x3⅞", EX **$125.00**

Scaled fish, F-160, brass, 4⅛" long..............................**$50.00**

Seahorse, F-142, brass, 3¼x1⅜" **$95.00**

Signpost drunk, F-11, painted cast iron, 1 leg out, 1954, 3⅞x2½" **$7.50**

Skull & cross tools, N-536, painted cast iron, wall mount, 1987, 5x4¼" **$125.00**

Snake, F-144, steel, 1988, 5¼" long............................**$20.00**

Squirrel, F-92, painted cast iron, brown on green base, 1950, 2x2⅞" **$170.00**

Wagon wheel, N-532, bronze, wall mount, 1987, 3¼x2½"..**$80.00**

Bottles

You could spend thousands of dollars and come home with very few bottles to show for your money. As you can see in our listings, certain types of old bottles (many bitters, historical flasks, and the better antique figurals, for instance) are very expensive, and unless you're attending one of the big bottle auctions in the East, you're not too likely to see these around. But flea markets are full of bottles, and it's very difficult to know how to start buying.

Mold seams are a good indicator of age. Bottles from ca 1800 normally will have seams that stop at the shoulder. From about 1875 until approximately 1890 the seam ended between the shoulder and the top of the neck. The line crept gradually on up until about 1910, when it finally reached the top of the neck. Bottles have been reproduced, but 'dug' bottles with these characteristics are most certainly collectible.

Color is an important consideration when collecting old bottles. Aqua, amethyst, yellow, and pink tints are desirable, and deep tones are better yet. When old clear glass is exposed to the sun, it will often turn amethyst (because of its manganese content), so this can also be an indiator of age as well.

Unlike many antiques and collectibles, bottles with imperfections are appreciated for flaws such as crooked necks, bubbles in the glass, or whittle marks (caused from blowing glass into molds that were too cold for the molten glass to properly expand in.) But glass that is stained, cloudy, or sick (having signs of deterioration) is another matter entirely.

Check for mold marks. Three-mold bottles were made in one piece below the shoulder, while the top was made in two. This type of bottle is very old (from the first half of the 19th century) and expensive. Colored examples command premium prices!

There are several types of old bottles — some will have an applied lip (a laid-on-ring), while others are simply 'sheared' (snapped off the blow pipe, reheated, and hand tooled). Pushed-up bottoms (called 'kick-ups' by collectors) were made that way so that they could be packed in a more space-efficient manner. The necks of the bottom layer of bottles would easily fit into the pushed-up bottoms of the layer on top. A 'blob seal' is a blob of applied glass that has a die-stamped product or company name.

If you find yourself interested in collecting bottles, you'll need to study. Go to bottle shows, talk to dealers, and read all you can. There are several books available on this subject: *Collecting Barber Bottles* by Richard Holiner, *The Standard Old Bottle Price Guide* by Carlo and Dorothy Sellari, and *Bottle Pricing Guide* by Hugh Cleveland.

See also Avon; Coca-Cola; Dairy Bottles; Decanters; Pepsi-Cola; Perfume Bottles; and Soda Bottles.

Bitters, Atwood's Jaundice Bitters, aqua, 12-sided, 6¼".**$5.50**

Bitters, Atwood's Quinine Tonic Bitters, light green, rectangular, 8", minimum value **$60.00**

Bitters, Baxter's Mandrake Bitters, Lord Bros, aqua, 12-sided, 6½" **$25.00**

Bitters, Berry Bitters, aqua & clear, rectangular, 8"......**$35.00**

Bitters, Doyles Hop Bitters, amber, 11¼" **$25.00**

Bitters, Drake's Plantation Bitters, dark amber, Pat 1862, 10", $125.00

Bitters, EJB, brown, 9⅛" **$7.50**

Bitters, Flander's Bitters, amber, square, 8¾"..............**$35.00**

Bitters, Golf's Bitters, clear, rectangular, 5½" **$12.50**

Bitters, Hibernia Bitters, amber, square, 10" **$80.00**

Bitters, Langley's Morning Star Bitters, amber, 3-sided, 12¾"...**$90.00**

Bitters, Mile's Tonic Bitters, aqua, rectangular, 7½".....**$12.50**

Bitters, Oxygenated Bitters, aqua, rectangular, 7½".....**$65.00**

Bitters, Romany Wine Bitters, aqua, rectangular, 6½".**$40.00**

Bitters, Royce's Sherry Wine Bitters, aqua, rectangular, 8" **$50.00**

Bitters, Sarasina Stomach Bitters, amber, square, 9⅛".**$70.00**

Bitters, Star Kidney & Liver Bitters, amber, square, 9¼".**$70.00**

Bitters, Sunny Castle Stomach Bitters, amber, 1890-1910, 9¼", $65.00

Bitters, Wakefield's Strengthening Bitters, aqua, rectangular, 8⅜" $35.00

Bitters, Wilson Herbine Bitters, aqua, oval, 6" $35.00

Bitters, Yerba Buena Bitters, amber, flask shape, 8¼".$80.00

Food, Amour's Top Notch Brand, amethyst, 11¼"........$5.00

Food, Burnham's Clam Bouillon, amethyst, 4"..............$4.00

Food, Carnation Fresh Milk, amber, 1-qt......................$5.00

Food, Columbia Catsup Extra Quality, clear, 8"............$2.00

Food, Gebhardt Eagle Chili Powder, amethyst, 5½"......$4.00

Food, Hunt's Pickles, clear, 6"....................................$2.00

Food, McCormick & Co, cobalt, 2⅝" $12.00

Food, Pepper Sauce, amethyst, ribbed, 8½"..................$7.50

Food, Primrose Registered Brand Western Meat Co, clear, 11½"..$4.00

Food, Queen Olives, clear w/paper label, 5½"..............$8.50

Food, Red Snapper Sauce, amethyst, 7¾" $3.00

Food, Rose & Co, aqua, 8" $5.00

Food, San Juan Brand Olive Oil, wax sealer, 6½" $7.50

Food, Souder's Flavoring Extracts, amethyst, 6¼"..........$4.00

Food, Sylmar Brand Olive Oil, clear, 3¼"....................$2.50

Food, Warner & Co's Catsup, clear, 8¼"......................$5.00

Household, Bachelor's Liquid Hair Dye No 1, aqua, 3" .$5.00

Household, Benton Holladay & Co Shoe Polish, aqua, 4⅞"..$5.00

Household, Buckingham Whisker Dye, amber, 4¾"......$4.00

Household, Caulk's Petroid Cement, clear, 2¼"............$2.00

Household, Chamberlain's Hand Lotion, clear, 2½" $7.50

Household, Clark, Woodward & Co, cobalt, 4¼"..........$8.50

Household, Damschinsky Liquid Hair Dye, green, 4⅛".$7.50

Household, Espey's Fragrant Cream Lotion, clear, 4½".$3.50

Household, French Gloss Shoe Polish, blue, 4⅝".........$2.00

Household, Frostilla Fragrant Lotion, clear, 4½" $5.00

Household, Haber's Magic Hair Coloring, cobalt, 6" ...$35.00

Household, Ingram's Milkweed Cream, milk glass, 2¼".$4.00

Household, Jergen's Hand Lotion, clear w/black lid, 5½" .$4.00

Household, Lyon's Powder, amber, 4¼"........................$3.50

Household, Milkweed Cream, milk glass, 2½" $6.50

Household, Putnam Dry Cleaner (embossed on shoulder), sun-colored amethyst, 5¾"....................................$3.50

Household, Rubifoam for the Teeth, amethyst, 4".........$5.00

Household, Scott's Four Roses, clear, 4½"....................$6.50

Household, Whittmore Shoe Polish, green, 5¼" $6.00

Household, William's Brillontine, clear, 3½" $4.00

Ink, Bertinquiot, amber, sheared top, 2x2¼" $25.00

Ink, Carter's, blown-in mold, sun-colored amethyst, applied lip, 2x1½" $5.00

Ink, Challenge, light green, 2¾".................................$8.50

Ink, Diamond Ink Co, clear, 1½" $5.00

Ink, Hooker's, aqua, sheared top, 2" $14.50

Ink, Johnson Ink Co, dark green, sheared top, 5⅞" $25.00

Ink, National Surety Ink, clear, 9" $8.50

Ink, Peerless, amethyst, sheared top, 3" $12.50

Ink, Sanford's, sun-colored amethyst, 2½"....................$4.00

Ink, Stafford's Inks, Made in USA, cobalt, pour spout, 6"..$25.00

Medicine, Absorbine Jr, sun-colored amethyst, 5" $3.00

Medicine, Allen's Dyspeptic Medicine, aqua, rectangular, 6"..$8.50

Medicine, Angier's Petroleum Emulsion, aqua, oval, 7" ..$3.00

Medicine, Ayer's Concentrated Compound Extract of Sarsaparilla, aqua, rectangular, 7¾"...........................$8.50

Medicine, Bauer's Instant Cough Cure, aqua, rectangular, 7" $18.50

Medicine, Brigg's Tonic Pills, aqua, 2½"......................$4.00

Medicine, Caldwell's Syrup Pepsin, aqua, 3"................$5.00

Medicine, California Fig Syrup, clear, rectangular, 7" $2.00

Medicine, Coblentz Cure, cobalt, round, 7½"..............$10.00

Medicine, Crane's Extract Co, clear, round, 6" $7.50

Medicine, Daniel's Colic Cure, clear, square, 3½"..........$8.50

Medicine, Dewitt & Co One Minute Cough Cure, aqua, rectangular, 5½"..$8.50

Medicine, Dr Townsend's Sarsaparilla, olive green, 1840-1855, 9½", $125.00

Medicine, Eno's Fruit Salt, clear, rectangular.................$4.00

Medicine, Fenner's Kidney & Backache Cure, amber, oval, 10¼" $30.00

Medicine, Foley's Kidney & Bladder Cure, amber, rectangular, 7½" $25.00

Medicine, Globe Flower Cough Syrup, aqua, rectangular, 7" $2.00

Medicine, Groder's Botanic Dyspepsia Syrup, aqua, rectangular, 9" $10.00

Medicine, Hays Hair Health, amber, rectangular, 6¾" ...$7.50

Medicine, Heimstreet & Co, cobalt, 8-sided, 6⅞" $18.00

Medicine, Hostetters Essence of Jamaica Ginger, aqua, oval, 6" $8.50

Medicine, Jayne's Exporant, light green, 6¼" $6.00

Medicine, Jones' Liniment, aqua, rectangular, 5" $2.00

Medicine, Kennedy's Rheumatic Liniment, aqua, 6⅝" ...$4.00

Medicine, Laxol, dark blue, 7⅜" $10.00

Medicine, McLean's Liver & Kidney Balm, aqua, 6¼"..$10.00

Medicine, Merrell's Milk of Magnesia, blue, 8" $8.50

Medicine, Mohr & Sons Pharmacists, clear, 4" $3.00

Medicine, Munyon's Germicide Solution, green, rectangular, 3½" $4.00

Medicine, Pain Killing Magic Oil, aqua, rectangular, 6"...$4.00

Medicine, Peptogenic Milk Powder, amber, round, 8" ..$3.00

Medicine, Pinkham's Herb Medicine, clear, 8¼" $6.00

Medicine, Rabell Emulsion, rectangular, 9½" $5.00

Medicine, Rhodes' Fever & Ague Cure, aqua, rectangular, 8¼" $16.00

Medicine, Rumford Chemical Works, aqua, 6½" $7.50

Medicine, Scott & Browne Preventia, green, oval, 4" $8.50

Medicine, Slocum's Coltsfoote Expectorant, aqua, oval, 2¼" $3.50

Medicine, Sylmar Brand Olive Oil, clear, round, 3½" $4.00

Medicine, Thacher's Liver & Blood Syrup, amber, rectangular, 8¼" $8.50

Medicine, Townsend's Sarsaparilla, olive green, 9" $55.00

Medicine, United States Medicine Co, aqua, rectangular, 6" $4.00

Medicine, Vapo Cresolene Co, aqua, square, 3⅞" $3.50

Medicine, Well's Neuralgia Cure, clear, rectangular, 6¾" $15.00

Medicine, Wood's Great Cure for Coughs & Colds, aqua, rectangular, 7" $20.00

Mineral water, Adam's Springs Mineral Water, aqua, blob top cylinder, 11½" $8.50

Mineral water, Aetna Mineral Water, aqua, round, 11½" ..$5.00

Mineral water, Arizona Bottling Works, Phoenix, AZ, aqua, applied top, 8" $8.50

Mineral water, Bartlett Spring Mineral Water California (on paper label), aqua, 12" $5.00

Mineral water, Boley & Co, Sac City, CA, cobalt, applied top, round, 7½" $25.00

Mineral water, Buffalo Mineral Springs Water, aqua, 10" $15.00

Mineral water, Burt, WH, San Francisco, dark green, applied top, round, 7½" $12.50

Mineral water, Bythinia Water, amber, 10" $4.00

Mineral water, Crystal Bottling Co, aqua, intertwined CB in diamond, applied top, 9" $7.50

Mineral water, Farrel & Co, blue, cylinder form, 7½" ..$30.00

Mineral water, Geyser Soda Spring Natural Mineral Water, light green, applied top, round, 7½" $8.50

Mineral water, Humboldt Artesian Mineral Water, aqua, applied top, 7½" $5.00

Mineral water, Lynde & Putnam Mineral Water, San Francisco, CA, cobalt, applied top, round, 7½" $25.00

Mineral water, Oak Orchard Acid Springs, amber, applied top, 10" $8.00

Mineral water, Pioneer Soda Water Co SF, light green w/buffalo in center, applied top, 7½" $10.00

Mineral water, Weddle, JT Jr Celebrated Mineral Water, light green, applied top, 7½" $10.00

Poison, Dick's Ant Destroyer, embossed Dick's & Co Distributors New Orleans, LA, clear, 6" $20.00

Poison, embossed lettering & symbols, cobalt, triangular, 3¼" $75.00

Poison, embossed rat on front, clear, rectangular, 6½" .$6.50

Poison, embossed skull & crossbones, blue, rectangular, 3" $65.00

Poison, Tinct Iodine, embossed skull & crossbones, amber, 2½" $12.50

Snuff, amber, 2¾" $6.50

Snuff, ceramic, brown, 8" $15.00

Snuff, dark amber, 7½" $15.00

Snuff, Garret Snuff Co..$3.00

Spirits, BB Extra Superior, amber, 10½" $12.50

Spirits, Binswanger, Simon & Bros, clear, 6¾" $7.50

Spirits, Case Gine, olive green, applied top, 6½"........$15.00

Spirits, Finest Old Windmill Gin, clear, 10½" $25.00

Spirits, Hock Wine, red & teal blue, 12" $5.00

Spirits, King George IV Whiskey Proprietors, green, 10¾" $7.50

Spirits, Loweirstein & Co Old Harvest Corn Whiskey, amethyst, 6" $5.00

Spirits, Old Fiddle Kentucky Straight Bourbon Whiskey, amber, 10", $35.00

Spirits, Old Kentucky Bourbon, Distilled in 1848, amber, 7¾" $20.00

Spirits, Seagram's Extra Dry Gin, clear, screw-on lid, 10½" $3.00

Boy Scout Collectibles

The Boy Scouts of America was organized in 1910. It was originated in England by General Baden-Powell and inspired by his observations during the Boer War. He believed boys wanted and needed to learn about outdoor-related activities. The first Boy Scout Jamboree was held in Washington DC in 1937. Today people who are or have been active in Scouting are interested in all types of items that relate to its history; for example: patches, uniforms, pins, medals, books and magazines, Jamboree items, Explorer items, pictures, and paper items.

For more information, refer to *Guide to Scouting Collectibles* by R.J. Sayers. See the Buyers section in the back of the book for his address.

Badge, merit; Public Health, khaki, crimped, NM $6.50
Badge, Senior Crew Leader, silver & gold, 1948-58, 3" dia, EX..$8.50
Belt buckle, National Jamboree, pewter, 1985, VG $8.50
Book, African Adventures, Pearson, 1937, EX $25.00
Book, Games & Recreational Methods, Smith, 1949, EX .$14.50
Book, Scouting for Boys, Baden-Powell, red, hard-bound, 1963, 34th printing, EX $16.00
Calendar, A Great Moment, Rockwell cover, 1965, 32x16", EX..$30.00
Handbook, Official Boy Scout, 1979, 1st ed, includes 18 signatures, EX $25.00
Handbook, Onward for God & My Country, 1956-60, EX $7.50
Hatpin, National Jamboree, official logo, 1989, M.........$3.50
Haversack, #573, National Council seal, khaki, EX $14.50
Magazine, Boy's Life, 1928-34, EX, each $12.50
Neckerchief, National Jamboree, red, 1937, VG $85.00
Pamphlet, Insignia Control Guide for Boy Scouts of America, 1986, VG $3.50
Pamphlet, merit badge; National Jamboree Wildlife Management, 1953, VG...$8.00

Paperweight, Be Prepared, emblem form w/eagle, brass & silver finish, 4", $18.00

Paperweight, emblem shape, metal w/gold & silver finish, 4" $18.00

Paperweight, Official Boy Scout, #1744, wood composition, 1937-45, EX...$6.50
Patch, National Order of the Arrow Conference, 1967, EX $15.00
Pennant, National Jamboree, maroon w/logo, 1937, EX .$40.00
Picture book, National Jamboree, 1960, EX $20.00
Pillowcase, National Jamboree, silk, w/logo, 1967, EX .$12.00
Pin, lapel; Onward For God & My Country, clutch-back, M $6.50
Pin, National Jamboree, I'm Going, celluloid, 1953, EX ..$4.50
Pin, World Jamboree, red, 1983, 1" dia, M $4.00
Plate, Our Heritage, Norman Rockwell illus, Gorham, MIB...$50.00
Postcard, Baden-Powell pictured w/Canadian Scout Staff, 1960, EX $6.00
Sheet music, Mafeking Grand March, portrait of Baden-Powell on front, EX $20.00
Song book, World Jamboree, 1967, VG........................$4.50
Stationery, National Jamboree, 1969, in original wrappers...$6.50

Boyd Crystal Art Glass

After the Degenhart glass studio closed (see the Degenhart section for information), it was bought out by the Boyd family, who added many of their own designs to the molds they acquired from the Degenharts and other defunct glasshouses. They are located in Cambridge, Ohio, and the glass they've been pressing in the more than 225 colors they've developed since they opened in 1978 is marked with their 'B in diamond' logo. Since 1988, a line has been added under the diamond. All the work is done by hand, and each piece is made in a selected color in limited amounts — a production run lasts only about six weeks or less. Items in satin glass or an exceptional slag are expecially collectible, so are those with hand-painted details.

Bernie the Eagle, Cardinal Red Carnival.........................$9.50
Bingo the Fawn, Sky Blue..$10.00
Bird Salt, Cardinal Red...$8.00
Bow Slipper, Classic Black Slag $8.50
Bowling Pin Ashtray, Heliotrope Slag............................$6.50
Buzz Saw Wine, Robin Egg Blue $8.50
Chick Salt, Marigold...$20.00
Chick Salt, Mulberry Mist...$8.50
Chick Salt, Platinum Carnival or Winter Swirl..............$10.00
Chuckles the Clown, Ebony $10.00
Colonial Doll, Leona, Indian Orange...........................$20.00
Doberman Paperweight, Rubina $12.50
Elephant Head Toothpick, Candy Swirl $12.50
Forget-Me-Not Toothpick, Avocado Red.....................$10.00
Forget-Me-Not Toothpick, Tropical Green...................$10.00
Freddie the Clown, Cobalt $10.00
Hambone Ashtray, Custard Slag..................................$16.00
Heart Jewel Box, Jungle Green $12.00
Hen on Nest Covered Dish, Lemon Ice.......................$12.50

Hen on Nest Covered Dish, Blue Carnival, $10.00

Joey the Horse, Vaseline Carnival.................................$15.00
Laced Heart Bonbon, Heliotrope..................................$12.50
Lamb on Nest Covered Dish, Purple Variant $16.50
Louise Doll, Candy Swirl..$22.00
Lucky the Unicorn, Lemonade $16.50
Owl Bell, crystal...$12.50
Roller Skate, Golden Delight...$8.50
Santa Bell, Cobalt..$25.00
Teardrop Wine, Willow Blue $8.00

Brass

Because it has become so costly to produce things from brass (due to the inflated price of copper, one of its components), manufacturers have largely turned to plastics and other less-expensive materials. As a result, nearly anything made of brass is becoming collectible.

If you'd like a source for further study, we recommend *Antique Brass and Copper Identification and Value Guide* by Mary Frank Gaston.

Candle holders, inverted baluster stem, English, mid-1800s, 8", pr...$225.00

Candelabrum, 4-light, engraved floral design on center stem, torch flame finial, marked 'P' in triangle, early 1900s, $185.00

Candelabrum, 5-light, Art-Deco style w/embossed floral designs on base & drip pans, 1930s, 16"...............$75.00
Chisel, red brass, marked Beryl Co, S 108 & BE Co, 7½" long...$60.00
Coal bucket, hand-hammered, wrought-iron handle, 18"...$150.00
Colander, 4 circular punched designs, iron handle...$125.00
Creamer & sugar bowl (open), pewter handles, pr...$150.00
Curtain tie-backs, pineapple design, pr......................$25.00
Door knocker, Art-Deco style, 6½" long $50.00
Fire back, masted ship in relief w/ornate border, 1930s-50s...$75.00
Kettle, American, iron bail, late 1800s, 7x13" dia $240.00
Ladle, 19th century, 13" long, 4½" dia bowl $75.00
Letter opener, pierced work on blade, gargoyle design on handle, 10¼" long...$35.00
Mailbox, envelope style w/lion's head opener, mid 1900s..$45.00
Planter, Art-Deco style Egyptian motif on front & back, 1920s, 4½"...$55.00
Playing card case, marked Smoleroff Kard Pack Pat Pend, monogramed EJC, 1920s, 3½x2⅜"........................$25.00
Scale, iron ring & hook, marked Landers Improved Spring Balance Warranted, 150 lbs, 23" long.................$125.00
Scoop, sugar or grain; marked Patented Dec 8, 1868 on handle...$70.00
Shotgun shell crimper, wooden handles....................$150.00
Spittoon, marked Farris Mfg Co, Decatur, Illinois, 3¼x7¼" dia $55.00
Tea caddy, marked Tea, Fine Sinagar on copper label, 8" $175.00
Toasting fork, pierced design w/figural cat handle, 20" long..$40.00
Tray, deep-dish, embossed scroll & floral design on border, 10" dia...$65.00

Tray, horseshoe shape, footed, mid-1900s, 7x10½", $75.00

Trivet, fox & tree design, 7¼" long............................$150.00
Trivet, repousse design w/hand-stippled background, late 1800s-early 1900s, 7x7"...$75.00

Voltage meter, marked British Made, 3½" dia.............**$20.00**
Wine cooler, applied lion-head handles w/rings through noses, pedestal base, mid-1900s, 10x8" dia...........**$75.00**

Brastoff, Sascha

California has always been a big producer of dinnerware and decorative pottery items, and those from the thirties, forties, and fifties are attracting lots of collector interest right now. Designer wares such as those by Sascha Brastoff, Marc Bellaire, and their contemporaries are especially in demand. Brastoff's career was diversified, to say the least. Although he is best-known in our circles for his high-style ceramic, enamelware, and resin pieces which even then (1940s-50s) were expensive, he was also a dancer, costume designer, sculptor, painter, and jeweler.

Brastoff's wares are signed in two ways. If the item was signed with his full signature, it was personally crafted by Brastoff himself. These are much more valuable than items simply stamped 'Sascha B,' a mark used on production pieces that were made by his staff under his supervision. Unless our listings contain the phrase 'full signature,' values that follow are for pieces with the 'Sascha B' stamp.

Jack Chipman has written a book on California potteries in which he devotes a chapter to Brastoff. It is entitled *The Collector's Encyclopedia of California Pottery*; we highly recommend it for further study.

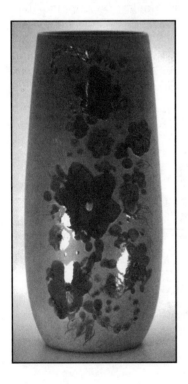

Vase, multicolored flowers on blue, gold highlights, 12⅛", $140.00

Ashtray, blue & gold decor on white, 5".....................**$26.00**
Ashtray, hooded, leaf decor on green.........................**$30.00**
Bowl, ballerina, 3-footed, 2¼x10"................................**$75.00**
Candle holder, yellow, resin, 7¼"................................**$27.00**

Charger, thin wispy figure on platinum, 17".............**$210.00**
Cigarette holder w/matching tray, stylized bird on pipe shape **$72.50**
Dish, Alaska, polar bear, 3½x3½" **$25.00**
Figurine, poodle, satin-matt crackle, 7x9"..................**$155.00**
Figurines, elephants, platinum on light blue matt glaze, 7½" & 8" **$300.00**
Mug, prancing horse handle **$120.00**
Obelisk, striped, w/lid, full signature, 22"..................**$350.00**
Plaque, native mask, gold & black, 9½".....................**$155.00**
Plate, enamel on copper, grape cluster on green, 11" dia..**$75.00**
Plate, Star Steed, horse design, full signature, ca 1959, 10½" **$295.00**
Salt & pepper shakers, horse, white w/stars, hard to find, pr **$155.00**
Vase, cylinder w/abstract design, 12" **$95.00**

Brayton, Laguna

Brayton was the potter, Laguna Beach, California, his residence. Durlin Brayton began making dinnerware in the 1920s and is credited for being the one to introduce the concept of the mixed, solid-color dinnerware lines made later by Bauer and Homer Laughlin (the manufacturer of Fiesta). His pieces were rather crudely designed, and it is said that he simply erected stands and sold the ware in his front yard or carried it in the trunk of his car to wherever people were apt to congregate.

When he married in 1936, his wife helped him develop his business into a larger, more lucrative enterprise. They started producing quality figurines, some of them licensed by Walt Disney Studios. They also made vases, cookie jars, various household items, and larger figurines that they referred to as sculptures. Some of their decorating was done by hand, some by the airbrush-painting method. Finishes varied and included a white crackle as well as a woodtone (stained) bisque among their more standard glazes.

All of their marks include either the word 'Brayton,' 'Laguna,' or both, except for the stamp used on their Pinocchio series. These pieces were marked 'Geppetto Pottery' in an oval. Not everything they made was marked, though, simply because very often there wasn't enough room. But there will be an incised or painted decorator's initial to clue you, and as you see and handle more of the ware, you'll be able to recognize Brayton's unique appearance.

The company did quite well until after WWII, when vast amounts of Japanese imports spelled doom for many small American potteries. They closed in 1968.

For further study, read *The Collector's Encyclopedia of California Pottery* by Jack Chipman.

Box or sm canister, Provincial, wood-tone, w/lid, EX.....**$10.00**
Bud vase, entwined snake, incised marks, 8" **$80.00**

Chess piece, Castle, in-mold mark, 1946, 10½"............$45.00
Cookie jar, Grandma (must be marked to be original)..$500.00
Cookie jar, Grandma w/Wedding Band, reproduction..$125.00
Cookie jar, Granny, white embossed floral apron, yellow
    bodice, EX...$325.00
Cookie jar, Provincial Lady, minimum value $350.00
Figurine, abstract man w/cat, black satin-matt, ca 1957,
    21"...$215.00
Figurine, bear seated, 3½"...$18.00
Figurine, Gay Nineties, Honeymoon, couple in bathing
    suits $100.00
Figurine, peacock, 17"..$90.00
Figurine, purple bull...$125.00
Figurine, purple calf $65.00
Figurine, purple cow $95.00

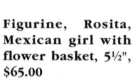

Figurine, Rosita, Mexican girl with flower basket, 5½", $65.00

Figurine, Sambo, 7½"..$160.00
Figurines, dice players, black, without dice, 3½", 4¾" long,
    pr $100.00
Figurines, dice players & dice, black, 3½"x4¾", w/dice,
    pr $225.00
Figurines, dice players & dice, black, 3½"x4¾", no dice,
    pr $195.00
Flower holder, Francis...$20.00
Planter, Mandy $45.00
Planter, Provincial wheelbarrow $20.00
Salt & pepper shakers, honey-toned cylinders w/brown
    embossed gingerbread boy & girl, pr.....................$40.00
Salt & pepper shakers, Provincial boy & girl figures, pr..$40.00
Tile, decorated, 6½"...$105.00

Breweriana

'Breweriana' is simply a term used by collectors to refer to items (usually freebies) given away by breweries to advertise their products. Some people prefer pre-prohibition era bottles, pocket mirrors, foam scrapers, etched and enameled glasses, mugs, steins, playing cards, postcards, pin-back buttons, and the like; but many collectors like the more available items from the past few decades as well. Some specialize either in breweries from a particular state, specific items such as foam scrapers (used to clean the foam off the top of glasses or pitchers of beer), or they might limit their buying to just one brewery.

The books we recommend for this area of collecting are *Back Bar Breweriana* by George J. Baley and *Huxford's Collectible Advertising* (Collector Books).

Bar caddy, Piel Bros Beer, full-color figures of Bert & Harry,
    2 yellow plastic inserts, 8½x8x3⅜", EX.................$90.00
Bottle, olive glass, Blatz, 9¼" $5.00
Bottle, York Brewing Co, embossed eagle & logo, crown
    top, 12-oz, EX..$12.00
Bottle crate, wood w/Schlitz logos on sides, dated 5-33,
    18¼x12x10" $45.00

Calendar, Lykens Brewing Co, 1912, full pad, matted & framed, 23x16½", EX, $300.00

Bottle label, Royal Bock Beer, 1933-50, 12-oz, VG......$10.00
Calendar, Pabst Extract, features an Indian, 1905, NM.$150.00
Clock, Arrow Beer, white lettering on red circle, black
    numbers, wood case w/stenciled tin face, 15½x15½",
    VG+ $80.00
Clock, Ballantine Beer, square w/12-3-6-9 & dots around
    logo, Ask the Man For..., metal frame, 15x15", VG.$60.00
Clock, Cincinnati Burger Brau, numbers surround oval logo
    w/German man holding mug, rectangle w/wood frame,
    19x15x3", VG..$130.00
Clock, Olympia Light, electric, M................................$40.00
Clock, Piel Bros Beer, pictures Bert & Harry, glass lens
    w/metal frame, electric, 13x13", EX....................$125.00
Coaster, Ruppert Beer & Ale, pictures 2 hands holding lg
    mugs of beer, cardboard, 4½" dia, NM...................$6.00
Cookbook, Schmidt & Sons Brewing Co, 'Dainty Home
    Lunches,' G...$8.50

Corkscrew, Anheuser-Busch, nickel-plated brass bottle shape, 23", EX $40.00

Decal, Trommer's Beer, pictures glass & horseshoes, peel & stick, 1952, 9x5", EX.................................$4.00

Display, Anteek Beer, figural waiter holding beer, embossed product name on apron, round base, painted composition, EX...$300.00

Display, Black Label Beer, wall light-up, winter scene with man carrying 2 beer boxes, plastic, 22½x10½", EX .$45.00

Display, Blatz Beer, chalk & plaster figure of dancing barmaid holding mugs of beer, 19x9x6", G..............$175.00

Display, Blatz Beer, metal figure of Blatz man playing banjo on stage beside bottle, felt back drop, 18x10x7", EX+ $95.00

Display, Budweiser, die-cut beer glass, tall footed tapered glass labeled Budweiser, 1940s, 8x15", NM.............$8.00

Display, Budweiser, 8 Clydesdale horses w/elaborate reins pulling wagon w/2 drivers, painted plastic, 6½x35½", EX..$75.00

Display, Budweiser Bottled Beer, reverse-painted glass plate w/gold foil lettering, gold-painted metal base, 17", EX..$130.00

Display, Coors, die-cut stand-up of Elvira w/tray of Coors & black bat featuring advertising, 1992, 71", NM........$35.00

Display, Falls City Beer, nodder, beer bottle w/arms & legs on gold base, painted composition, 1950s, 13½x4½", EX.$65.00

Display, Miller High Life Beer, Miller girl on base w/logo, metallic-gold plastic, 2", EX.....................................$90.00

Display, Schaefer Beer, woman's gloved arm extended to hold bottle or glass, marked F&M Schaefer Brewing Co #455, EX..$45.00

Display, Schmidt's Beer, bronzed bartender figure w/2 mugs standing before half barrel on trapezoid base, 7¾", NM..$150.00

Drinking glass, Jax Beer, straight-sided, EX.................$28.00

Drinking glass, Kiewel's Beer, flared top, heavy flared bottom, EX..$26.00

Drinking glass, Schlitz, 8-oz, EX.................................$4.00

Drinking glass, Schmidt's Beer, flared top, heavy flared bottom, EX..$44.00

Foam scraper, celluloid, Rheingold, M $26.00

Match safe, Bowler Bros Brewers, orange leaf design on both sides, celluloid over metal, 2¾x1½", G.........$35.00

Match striker, American Brewing Co, incised logo of eagle & emblem on stoneware, 3x3¾" dia, VG...............$170.00

Matchbook cover, Anheuser-Busch, features horses & wagon on front, front strike, NM $7.00

Plaque, Schlitz Light Beer, logo & lettering, plastic, 1976, 12" dia, EX $5.00

Plate, Budweiser, Winter Day, 24k-gold trim, 1989, 8½" dia, M $75.00

Pocket mirror, Anthracite Brewing Co, bust-length portrait of a girl, lettering above, 2¾x1¾", VG...................$65.00

Poster, Budweiser Bud Man, shows the Bud Man, Dauntless Defender of Quality, 1970s, 30x20", NM $8.00

Pretzel holder, Anheuser-Busch, eagle logo, 1940s, EX..$90.00

Print, Budweiser, Custer's Last Fight, Home of Budweiser & other lettering below, framed, 36x46", EX $275.00

Puzzle, Blatz Old Heidelberg Beer, shows Cliff Thompson, world's tallest salesman standing at 8' 7" tall, 7x10", EX $30.00

Sign, Bruck's Beer, logo above Bruck's Beer in script, red, cream, black & blue, tin, 6x14", EX...................$50.00

Sign, Budweiser, eagle logo & ornate graphics in red, black & gold, tin, 1960s, 26x17", EX...............................$25.00

Sign, Budweiser, light-up, horse looks out over water, ...King of Beers emblem below, plastic, glass front, 13x20", VG..$35.00

Sign, Lone Star Beer, red, white & gold product emblem above 3 connected circles, framed tin, 1950s, 18x14", NM..$20.00

Sign, Rainer Beer, tin w/rolled corners, stock image of girl leaning on roaring bear in circle inset, 14½x14½", EX..$250.00

Sign, Schlitz Beer, self-framed tin, bird singing Never a Bitter Note next to lg bottle, lettering below, 16x11", VG+ $50.00

Stein, Falstaff, w/lid, 1971, 10½", M...........................$125.00

Thermometer, Bud Lite, pictures Spuds McKenzie, the Original Party Animal, 12" dia, EX $12.00

Tip tray, Adam Scheidt Brewing Co, Standard Beer lettered across gent w/glass of brew, Healthful..., 4⅜" dia, VG+ $130.00

Tip tray, Arnholt & Schaefer Brewing Co, Imperial Malt Extract in Bottles arched above bottle, 4½" dia, VG+ $160.00

Tip tray, German American Brewing Co, Maltosia logo in center w/lettered rim, 5" dia, EX+ $55.00

Tip tray, Miller High Life Beer, pictures mansion, carriage & figures, G $20.00

Tip tray, tin, Indianapolis Brewing Co, 5" dia, EX.......$45.00

Tray, Bartholomy Beers & Ales, deep-dish type w/girl on winged wheel among clouds, 12" dia, G+ $125.00

Tray, Clinton Brewing Co, half-length pose of lady w/hand on hip holding up glass, square w/rounded corners, 13x13", EX $175.00

Tray, Fehr's Famous FFXL Beers, colorful image of classical figures in romantic embrace, 13½" dia, VG, $200.00

Tray, Olympia Beer, pictures lady on bottle, Capitol Brewing Co, rim chips, 13", VG.....................$20.00

Tray, Pabst Blue Ribbon Beer, blue embossed plastic, 13¼" dia, NM $8.00

Tray, Pabst Blue Ribbon Beer, 2 gnomes carrying oversized flagons & signs, decorative rim, oval, 15¼x8½", G.$90.00

Tray, Pickwick Ale, deep-dish type w/2 horses pulling wagon w/3 barrels of ale, 12" dia, EX.................$95.00

Tray, Schaefer Beer, red w/white lettering, 12" dia, G.$10.00

Tray, Schlitz, Real Gusto, yellow & white, 13" dia, EX.$25.00

Tray, Seitz Brewing Co, features standing bulldog w/lettering on rim, square w/rounded corners, 13x13", EX....$195.00

Tumbler, enamel on crystal featuring Bartholomy Rochester logo, 4x2" dia, EX $24.00

Breyer Horses

Breyer horses have been popular children's playthings since they were introduced in 1952, and you'll see several at any large flea market. Garage sales are good sources as well. The earlier horses had a glossy finish, but after 1968 a matt finish came into use. You'll find smaller domestic animals too. They are evaluated by condition, rarity, and desirability; some of the better examples may be worth a minimum of $150.00.

American Indian Pony, #710, 1989, MIB $35.00

Appaloosa Scratching Foal, #168, black & white, EX ..$20.00

Arabian Foal, dapple gray, unmarked $15.00

Arabian Foal, white glossy finish, EX $20.00

Arabian Stallion, Family series, white w/gray points, EX .$12.00

Balking Mule, dark brown w/halter, EX $100.00

Bay horse, grazing, NM, $35.00

Bay Nursing Foal, light brown w/dark brown points, EX.....................$15.00

Bay Stallion, #300, jumping over wall, EX $30.00

Black Angus Bull, EX.....................$26.00

Black Beauty Stallion, #89, running, right front sock, EX .**$16.00**

Black Tennessee Walker Stallion, #60, EX **$24.00**

Buckskin Foal, #166, lying down, EX.....................**$24.00**

Buffalo, EX **$20.00**

Clydesdale Dapple Gray Stallion, #85, glossy, EX **$60.00**

Clydesdale Foal, #84, EX.....................**$10.00**

Colt, running, brown, EX.....................**$5.00**

Deer, doe, ears worn, VG **$10.00**

Fighting Stallion, woodgrain, NM **$75.00**

Five Gaiter Sorrell Stallion, #52, VG **$15.00**

Legionario III Famous Andalusian, #68, MIB **$30.00**

Little Bits Quarter Horse Buckskin Stallion, saddle, EX..**$5.00**

Man 'O War Stallion, #47, EX.....................**$16.00**

Marguerite Henry's Misty, EX **$10.00**

Palomino Mare, #5, Family series, light, glossy, EX.....**$12.00**

Palomino Mare, grazing, light to med color, pink muzzle & ears, EX.....................**$30.00**

Poodle, silver, EX.....................**$35.00**

Red Roan Running Stallion, EX.....................**$75.00**

Shetland Pony, tan & white spotted, glossy, EX **$8.00**

Smokey the Cow Horse, #69, EX **$36.00**

Spanish Fighting Bull, EX.....................**$65.00**

Texas Longhorn Steer, EX **$40.00**

Western Palomino, glossy orange, chain reins, snap-on saddle, EX **$20.00**

Yellow Mount Stallion, no spot on leg, glossy face, light pink nose, EX.....................**$18.00**

British Royal Commemoratives

While seasoned collectors may prefer the older pieces using circa 1840 (Queen Victoria's reign) as their starting point, even present-day souvenirs make a good inexpensive beginning collection. Ceramic items, glassware, metalware, and paper goods have been issued on the occasion of weddings, royal tours, birthdays, christenings, and many other celebrations. Food tins are fairly easy to find, and range in price from about $30.00 to around $75.00 for those made since the 1950s.

For more information, we recommend *British Royal Commemoratives* by Audrey Zeder.

Bell, Elizabeth II's Silver Jubilee, wooden handle, $35.00

Ale bottle, Victoria's 1897 jubilee, green glass...........**$100.00**

Bank, Elizabeth's coronation, iron crown shape **$65.00**

Beaker, Charles & Diana's betrothal, color portrait, Caverswal...**$125.00**

Beaker, Edward VII's coronation, King's Dinner, Royal Doulton..**$130.00**

Bell, Charles & Diana's wedding, multicolored portrait, Royal Grafton, 7"...**$50.00**

Bookmark, Elizabeth II's 1977 jubilee, black leather...**$15.00**

Bust, Queen Mother, Royal Staffordshire, limited edition of 500, 4½"...**$75.00**

Busts, Charles & Diana, Royal Staffordshire, limited edition of 500, 4½", pr...**$150.00**

Calendar, perpetual, Elizabeth II, free standing, plastic.**$25.00**

Compact, Elizabeth II's 1953 coronation, portrait on gold tone...**$50.00**

Covered dish, Elizabeth's coronation, relief portrait on cobalt, Wedgwood...**$75.00**

Cup & saucer, Elizabeth II's 60th birthday, multicolored portrait, Coalport **$65.00**

Cup & saucer, Elizabeth's 1951 Canada visit, Paragon.**$55.00**

Cup & saucer, Elizabeth's 1953 coronation, multicolored portrait on mint green **$55.00**

Dolls, Charles & Diana in wedding attire, Goldberger, 11", pr **$100.00**

Egg cup, Elizabeth II & Philip, multicolored portrait, Bavarian style **$25.00**

Jewel box, Diana's 30th birthday, hinged lid, 2x4x4"..**$80.00**

Matchbook label, Victoria, unused, 2¼x1⅝" **$20.00**

Matchbooks, Charles & Diana's wedding, unused, set of 6...**$10.00**

Medal, George III's 1809 jubilee, 1"...........................**$50.00**

Medal, Prince of Wales 1886 exhibition, bronze, 2" **$75.00**

Medal, Princess Charlotte's 1820 memorial, ¾"...........**$50.00**

Medal, Victoria's 1897 jubilee, sterling silver, Royal Mint, 1" **$60.00**

Mug, Charles & Diana's 1992 separation, color portraits **$30.00**

Mug, cider; Diana's 30th birthday, sepia portrait, limited edition of 250 ....**$40.00**

Mug, Elizabeth's 1992 Annus Horribulus, multicolored portrait & events **$25.00**

Newspaper, headline of Charles & Diana's separation..**$5.00**

Paperweight, Diana's 30th birthday, domed round crystal, 3½" **$45.00**

Photograph, Elizabeth II, blue coat & hat, 1990s, 5x7"..**$20.00**

Pin-back button, George VI's coronation, family group picture, 1¼"..**$40.00**

Pin-back button, George VI's coronation, multicolored portraits of king & queen, 1¼"...................................**$30.00**

Pitcher, Edward VII's 1902 coronation, glass w/etched portrait, 4½"...**$150.00**

Pitcher, Elizabeth's 1953 coronation, relief profile on pink, Johnson **$130.00**

Place mat, Charles & Diana's wedding, luncheon size..**$5.00**

Plaque, portrait of Elizabeth, Queen Mother, Diana & Sara on black background, 6x8" **$25.00**

Plaque, Victoria 1889, bronze w/relief portrait, 7x10".**$375.00**

Plate, Andrew & Sarah's wedding, multicolored portrait, blue rim, 7"..**$30.00**

Plate, Charles & Diana's wedding, filigree border, Minton, 10½"..**$195.00**

Plate, Elizabeth II's 1953 coronation, gold trim, 9", $40.00

Plate, Elizabeth's 60th birthday, multicolored portrait, Coalport, 4½" **$45.00**

Plate, George VI's 1939 Canada visit, relief portrait, Wedgwood...**$150.00**

Plate, Prince Henry's 1984 christening, multicolored portrait, 6¼"..**$35.00**

Postcard, Diana Quits Royal Stage, black & white, limited edition, 1993 ....**$6.00**

Postcard, George VI's 1937 coronation, black & white, Tuck, set of 4..**$20.00**

Postcard, Opening of Buckingham Palace, multicolor, 1993...**$4.00**

Postcard, Princess Anne's wedding, black & white, 1992...**$10.00**

Postcard, Royal Family at Sandringham, multicolored, 1990...**$10.00**

Print, Elizabeth II's 1953 coronation, original matt, 11x14" **$35.00**

Print, Victoria as young lady, 19th-century engraving, 5x7"...**$25.00**

Program, George VI's coronation, official program.....**$35.00**

Puzzle, Charles & Diana wedding scene, original box..**$40.00**

Puzzle, collage of Elizabeth II's coronation tins, 11x14" **$25.00**

Scarf, Charles & Diana's wedding, silhouettes & multicolored design on silk...**$40.00**

Spoon, Charles & Diana's wedding, multicolored portrait on finial, silverplated...**$15.00**

Spoon, Diana, relief portrait & design, silverplated.....**$15.00**

Spoon, Elizabeth II's coronation, relief portrait, silverplated **$25.00**

Spoon, George VI's 1939 Canada visit, silverplated, International...**$45.00**
Stamps, Diana's 21st birthday, 3 stamps & souvenir sheet .**$20.00**
Sticker album, Royal family as of 1984, completed.....**$50.00**
Teapot, Edward VII's 1901 coronation, multicolored portrait on pink lustre, 2-cup...**$225.00**
Teapot, Elizabeth II's 1953 coronation, crown shape, chrome, 2-cup..**$75.00**
Teapot stand, Elizabeth II's jubilee, relief portrait, chrome..**$25.00**
Thimble, Charles & Diana's wedding, multicolored portrait in wedding clothes..**$15.00**
Thimbles, Royal family members, china, 1983, set of 8.**$60.00**
Tin, Charles & Diana's wedding, multicolored portrait on plaid background, Walkers **$30.00**
Tin, Charles & Diana's wedding, multicolored portraits on royal blue, octagonal...**$35.00**
Tin, Princess Elizabeth on horse, Trooping the Colours, Huntley & Palmer...**$75.00**
Toby mug, Diana, hand-painted, limited edition, Kevin Francis...**$275.00**
Toby mug, Elizabeth II on throne w/Corgi, hand-painted, limited edition, K Francis **$275.00**
Trading card album, holds 110 Press Pass cards **$15.00**
Tray, Elizabeth's coronation, portrait w/Philip, faux wood sides, 13"...**$45.00**
Tray, George V's 1935 jubilee, impressed portrait & design on silverplate, 12" dia **$75.00**
Tray, Victoria 1887, relief portrait & design, brass, 12" .**$175.00**
Vehicle, Elizabeth's II 40th wedding anniversary, double-decker bus, LLEDO **$50.00**

Bubble Bath Containers

By now, you're probably past the state of being incredulous at the sight of these plastic figurals on flea market tables with price tags twenty time higher than they carried when new and full. (There's no hotter area of collecting today than items from the fifties through the seventies that are reminiscent of early kids' TV shows and hit movies.) Most of these were made in the 1960s. The Colgate-Palmolive Company produced the majority of them — they're the ones marked 'Soaky' — and these seem to be the most collectible. Each character's name is right on the bottle. Other companies followed suit; Purex also made a line, so did Avon.

Unless noted otherwise, the prices below are for bottles in excellent to near-mint condition. Be sure to check for paint loss, and look carefully for cracks in the brittle plastic heads of the Soakies.

Atom Ant, 1960s...**$40.00**
Baba Looie, w/original sleeve, M **$25.00**
Bullwinkle, brown w/red & yellow striped turtleneck, 1960s **$35.00**
Bullwinkle, Fuller Brush, yellow antlers & feet, red & white bathing suit, 1970, scarce **$70.00**
Droop Along Coyote, 1960s.....................................**$35.00**

Batman, Kid Care, 1991, 10-oz, $5.00

Dick Tracy, Chicago Tribune, 1965, 11-oz, from $30.00 to $40.00

Dum Dum, Purex..**$28.00**
Elmer Fudd, red & black hunting outfit **$25.00**
ET, Avon, 1983...**$15.00**
Felix the Cat, blue w/trick bag, 1960s.........................**$35.00**
Flintstones Fun Bath, Roclar, features all characters, 1971 ....**$90.00**
Frankenstein, Colgate-Palmolive, 1960s **$65.00**
Godzilla **$50.00**
Gumby, Perma Toy, No Tears Shampoo, 1987.............**$6.00**
Hulk Hogan..**$12.50**
Lippy the Lion, Colgate-Palmolive **$32.50**
Lucy, from Charlie Brown, Avon **$5.00**
Mad Hatter, Avon...**$30.00**

Mighty Mouse, 1960s	$25.00
Mushmouse, Colgate-Palmolive, MIB	$35.00
Peter Potamus, w/original sleeve	$30.00
Popeye, 1960s	$35.00
Princess Leia, from Star Wars, full	$20.00
Punkin' Puss, Colgate-Palmolive	$30.00
Robin, 1960s	$85.00
Silverhawks, 1960s	$10.00
Snow White, Colgate-Palmolive, movable arms	$18.00
Spouty Whale, w/original sleeve	$25.00
Sylvester	$15.00
Tennessee Tuxedo, Colgate-Palmolive, 1960s	$25.00
Theodore Chipmunk, Colgate-Palmolive	$15.00
Top Cat, 1960s	$35.00
Tweety Bird on Cage, 1960s	$15.00
Wolfman, 1960s	$85.00
Yakky Doodle, w/original sleeve	$25.00

Butter Pats

Tiny plates made to hold individual pats of butter were popular in Victorian times. As late as the 1970s, some were still being used by hotels, railroads, and steamship lines. They're becoming a popular item of collector interest because they are so diversified (you'll find them in china, silverplate, pewter, and glass), their small size makes them easy to display, and right now, at least, their prices are relatively low.

The new collector might choose to concentrate on pats made of a particular material or those from only one manufacturer or country. Don't confuse them with children's toy dishes, coasters, or small plates intended for other uses; and don't buy them if they're at all damaged.

Blue Willow, Japan	$10.00
Cliff House, San Francisco, vitrified china	$12.00
Daisy & Button, early American pattern glass	$4.50
Flow blue, Argyle, Grindley, ca 1880	$24.00
Flow blue, Touraine, Henry Alcock, ca 1880	$25.00
Germany, pink roses, scalloped edge	$6.00
Heisey, Diamond Point	$12.50
Ironstone, green floral transfer, unmarked English	$5.00
Ironstone, hand-painted scene, England, square	$9.00
Limoges, pink roses, shadow leaves	$8.50
Milk glass, hand-painted roses, square	$6.00
Nippon, pink roses w/gold rim, open handles	$12.00
San Diego Hotel, china	$7.00
Shelley, Rose, Pansy & Forget-Me-Not	$28.00
Spode, Buttercup	$9.00
Sterling, beaded edge, w/monogram	$10.00
Tea Leaf, ironstone	$11.00
Vernon Kilns, Gingham	$4.00

Buttons

Collectors refer to buttons made before 1918 as 'old,' those from 1918 on they call 'modern.' Age is an important consideration, but some modern buttons are very collectible too. You might find some still in your Grandmother's button jar, and nearly any flea market around will have some interesting examples.

Some things you'll want to look for to determine the age of a button is the material it is made of, the quality of its workmanship, the type of its decoration, and how it was constructed. Early metal buttons were usually made in one piece of steel, copper, and brass. Old glass buttons will have irregularities on the back, while the newer ones will be very smooth. 'Picture' buttons with animals and people as their subjects were popular in the last quarter of the 19th century. Many were quite large and very fancy. As a rule, these are the most valuable to collectors.

Black glass, pressed (many resemble lacy glass), from 50¢ to	$2.00
China, calico or stencil, from 25¢ to	$30.00
Clear & colored glass, blown ball of transparent glass lined w/wax	$1.00
Clear & colored glass 'Modern since 1918,' various sizes, from 50¢ to	$7.00
Clear & colored glass paperweights, from $4 to	$80.00
Clear & colored glass Victorians, from $1 to	$5.00
Gilt copper, late 1700s to 1850s (rare examples sell at $300), from $15 to	$65.00
Horn, molded or pressed picture, D'Artagnan	$30.00
Horn, molded or pressed picture, Bird on a Wall	$5.00
Inlay, veneer, or inset, minimum value	$1.00
Kate Greenaway, brass, Sitting on the Rail	$5.00
Kate Greenaway, pewter, See-Saw Jack	$40.00
Pearl, cameo-carved floral design	$5.00
Pipestone, carved by Sioux Indians, ca late 1940s, from $1 to	$5.00
Vegetable ivory, various sizes & designs, from 50¢ to	$3.00
Wooden, may be pictorial or trimmed w/other material, 25¢ to	$22.50

California Raisins

Since they starred in their first TV commercial in 1986, the California Raisins have attained stardom through movies, tapes, videos, and magazine ads. Today we see them everywhere on the secondary market — PVC figures, radios, banks, posters — and they're very collectible. The PVC figures were introduced in 1987. Originally there were four, all issued for retail sales — a singer, two conga dancers, and a saxaphone player. Before the year was out, Hardee's, the fast-food chain, came out with the same characters, though on a slightly smaller scale. A fifth character, Blue Surfboard (horizontal), was created, and three 5½" Bendees with flat pancake-style bodies appeared.

In 1988 the ranks had grown to twenty-one: Blue Surfboard (vertical), Red Guitar, Lady Dancer, Blue/Green Sunglasses, Guy Winking, Candy Cane, Santa Raisin, Bass Player, Drummer, Tamourine Lady (there were two styles), Lady Valentine, Boy Singer, Girl Singer, Hip Guitar Player,

Sax Player with Beret, and four Graduates (styled like the original four, but on yellow pedestals and wearing graduation caps). And Hardee's issued an additional six: Blue Guitar, Trumpet Player, Roller Skater, Skateboard, Boom Box, and Yellow Surfboard.

Still eight more characters came out in 1989: Male in Beach Chair, Green Trunks with Surfboard, Hula Skirt, Girl Sitting on Sand, Piano Player, AC, Mom, and Michael Raisin. They made two movies and thereafter were joined by their fruit and vegetable friends Rudy Bagaman, Lick Broccoli, Banana White, Leonard Limabean, and Cecil Thyme. Hardee's added four more characters in 1991: Anita Break, Alotta Style, Buster, and Benny.

All Raisins are dated with these exceptions: in 1989, only the Beach Scene characters are dated (and they're actually dated 1988); those issued by Hardee's in 1991 are not.

Anita Break, w/boom box & pink boots, Hardee's, marked 1992 CALRAB-Applause, MIP $12.00
Bass Player, 2nd commercial issue, marked 1988 CALRAB-Applause, MIP $25.00
Beach Theme Edition, marked 1988 CALRAB-Applause, set of 4, M $40.00
Buster, w/skateboard, black & yellow sneakers, Hardee's, marked 1992 CALRAB-Applause, MIP $12.00
Captain Toonz, w/blue boom box, yellow sunglasses & sneakers, Hardee's, marked Mfg Applause, sm size, M...$5.00
Cecil Thyme, carrot figure in suit & tie, Meet the Raisins 2nd edition, marked Claymation-Applause, M $50.00

Conga Dancer, orange sunglasses & shoes, Hardee's, CALRAB, 1987, sm size, $4.00

Drummer, black hat w/yellow feather, 2nd commercial issue, marked 1988 CALRAB-Applause, MIP.........$25.00
FF Strings, guitar player w/orange sneakers, Hardee's, marked MFG Applause Inc 1988, sm size, M..........$5.00
Graduate Microphone, key chain, marked 1988 CALRAB 'Lic Applause Lic,' M...$25.00
Graduate Singer, marked 1988 CALRAB w/Claymation on yellow plastic base, M $40.00
Guitar player, 1st commercial issue, marked 1988 CALRAB, M $8.00
Hands, key chain, both hands up, thumbs touch head, marked 1987 CALRAB, M $8.00

Hands, left hand points up, right hand down, Post Raisin Bran, marked 1987 CALRAB, M...............................$4.00
Hands, sandwich music box, marked 1987 CALRAB, M..$15.00

Lick Broccoli, red & orange guitar, Meet the Raisins 1st edition, marked CALRAB-Applause, M, $15.00

Microphone, right hand up, microphone in left hand, Hardee's, CALRAB, 1987, sm size, M $4.00
Mom, yellow hair & pink apron, Meet the Raisins 2nd edition, marked CALRAB-Applause, M $50.00
Ms Delicious, girl w/tambourine, 2nd commercial issue, marked 1988 CALRAB-Applause, M......................$16.00
Ms Sweet, girl singer, hot pink shoes & bracelet, 2nd commercial issue, marked 1988 CALRAB, M...............$16.00
Rudy Bagaman, vegetable w/cigar, purple shirt & flipflops, Meet the Raisins 1st edition, marked Claymation-Applause, M $15.00
Santa, red cap, green sneakers, marked 1988 CALRAB, M.$18.00
Saxaphone Player, Post Raisin Bran, marked 1987 CALRAB, M..$4.00
Saxophone Player, gold sax, no hat, Hardee's, marked 1987 CALRAB, sm size $4.00
Saxophone Player, key chain, gold sax, no hat, marked 1987 CALRAB, M..$8.00
Singer, microphone in left hand, 1st commercial issue, marked 1988 CALRAB, M..$8.00

Sunglasses, Christmas issue, holding candy cane, green glasses & red sneakers, marked 1988 CALRAB, M, $18.00

Sunglasses, key chain, orange glasses, index fingers touch face, marked 1987 CALRAB, M...............**$8.00**

Sunglasses, sandwich music box, both hands out, marked 1987 CALRAB, M...............**$15.00**

Sunglasses 2, aqua sunglasses glued on, eyes can't be seen, 1st commercial issue, marked 1988 CALRAB, M.....**$8.00**

Trumpy Trunote, w/trumpet & blue sneakers, Hardee's, marked Mfg Applause Inc 1988, sm size, M............**$5.00**

Waves Weaver, w/yellow surfboard, Hardee's, marked Mfg Applause Inc 1988, sm size, M...............**$5.00**

Winky, right hand in hitchhike position, 1st commercial issue, marked 1988 CALRAB, M **$8.00**

Camark Pottery

You may occasionally find a piece of pottery marked 'Camark,' though it's fairly scarce. This was an Arkansas company based in the city of Camden, from whence came its name — 'Cam' from the city, 'ark' from the state. They operated from the mid-twenties until they closed in the early 1960s, mainly producing commercial wares such as figurines, vases, and novelty items, though artware was attempted for the first few years they were in existence. This early artware, marked 'Lessell' (for John Lessell, the decorator) or 'Le-Camark,' is very similar to lines by Weller and Owens, and when a piece comes up for sale, it is usually tagged at somewhere between $300.00 to $500.00, depending on its size and decoration.

Vase, urn shape w/pink & plum landscape scene, signed Le-Camark, 8½", $550.00

Basket, embossed flowers on cream, 5x3".................**$14.00**
Cotton dispenser, orange rabbit, 3" **$12.00**
Figurine, cat beside fishbowl, white gloss, 8".............**$30.00**
Figurine, climbing cat, black gloss, 12" **$35.00**
Jug, orange & green ball form, clay stopper, 6½".........**$38.00**
Pitcher, parrot handle, blue gloss, 6½".........**$65.00**
Planter, black swans, double neck, 8"...............**$15.00**

Salt & pepper shakers, blue S&P shapes, pr...............**$10.00**
Salt & pepper shakers, red, white & blue steamships, pr...............**$30.00**
Teapot, bulbous w/deep swirls, matching warmer, 8".**$24.00**
Vase, Deco style w/3 joined cylinders, 8" **$25.00**
Vase, fish form, orange & brown mottling, 8" **$45.00**
Vase, Old English, plum & cream, signed Le-Camark, 8½"...............**$350.00**
Vase, orange & green, fluted, 5"...............**$25.00**
Vase, white w/crackle finish, gold mark, 8" **$125.00**
Wall pocket, pink flour scoop, 8"...............**$12.00**

Cambridge Glassware

If you're looking for a 'safe' place to put your investment dollars, Cambridge glass is one of your better options. But as with any commodity, in order to make a good investment, knowledge of the product and its market is required. There are two books we would recommend for your study, *Colors in Cambridge Glass,* put out by the National Cambridge Collectors Club, and *The Collector's Encyclopedia of Elegant Glass* by Gene Florence.

The Cambridge Glass Company (located in Cambridge, Ohio) made fine quality glassware from just after the turn of the century until 1958. They made thousands of different items in hundreds of various patterns and colors. Values hinge on rarity of shape and color. Of the various marks they used, the 'C in triangle' is the most common. In addition to their tableware, they also produced flower frogs representing ladies and children and models of animals and birds that are very valuable today. To learn more about them, you'll want to read *Glass Animals and Figural Flower Frogs from the Depression Era* by Lee Garmon and Dick Spencer. (See also Glass Animals.)

Apple Blossom, amber, green, pink or yellow; bowl, console; 12½" **$50.00**
Apple Blossom, amber, green, pink or yellow; bowl, fruit; 5½"...............**$13.50**
Apple Blossom, amber, green, pink or yellow; bowl, pickle; 9"...............**$35.00**
Apple Blossom, amber, green, pink or yellow; butter dish, 5½"...............**$200.00**
Apple Blossom, amber, green, pink or yellow; candelabrum, keyhole, 3-light **$47.50**
Apple Blossom, amber, green, pink or yellow; cocktail, fruit/oyster; #3025, 4½"...............**$20.00**
Apple Blossom, amber, green, pink or yellow; comport, fruit cocktail; 4"...............**$20.00**
Apple Blossom, amber, green, pink or yellow; plate, bread & butter; 6" **$7.00**
Apple Blossom, amber, green, pink or yellow; stem, low sherbet; fancy, footed, 7-oz, #3025 ....**$16.00**
Apple Blossom, amber, green, pink or yellow; stem, tall sherbet; #3130, 6-oz...............**$18.00**
Apple Blossom, amber, green, pink or yellow; stem, tall sherbet; #3135, 6-oz...............**$20.00**

Apple Blossom, amber, green, pink or yellow; tumbler, #3025, 4-oz **$17.00**

Apple Blossom, amber, green, pink or yellow; tumbler, #3135, footed, 10-oz **$27.50**

Apple Blossom, amber, green, pink or yellow; tumbler, #3400, footed, 9-oz **$25.00**

Apple Blossom, clear, bowl, finger; #3025, w/plate, footed **$30.00**

Apple Blossom, clear, bowl, flat, 12" **$32.50**

Apple Blossom, clear, bowl, 2-handled, 10" **$25.00**

Apple Blossom, clear, cup **$15.00**

Apple Blossom, clear, pitcher, 76-oz **$125.00**

Apple Blossom, clear, plate, grill; 10" **$20.00**

Apple Blossom, clear, saucer **$3.00**

Apple Blossom, clear, stem, low sherbet; #3130, 6-oz ..**$10.00**

Apple Blossom, clear, sugar bowl, footed **$11.00**

Apple Blossom, clear, tumbler, #3135, footed, 5-oz....**$10.00**

Apple Blossom, clear, tumbler, 6" **$15.00**

Candlelight, clear, bowl, #3900/130, footed, 2-handled, 7" **$30.00**

Candlelight, clear, bowl, #3900/54, 4-toed, flared, 10" .**$55.00**

Candlelight, clear, bowl, #3900/65, 4-toed, handle, 12"..**$85.00**

Candlelight, clear, cake plate, #3900/35, 2-handled, 13½" **$55.00**

Candlelight, clear, candy dish, #3900/165, w/lid, round..**$95.00**

Candlelight, clear, cruet, #3900/100, w/stopper, 6-oz.**$95.00**

Candlelight, clear, lamp, hurricane; #1613, w/bobeche.**$250.00**

Candlelight, clear, lamp, hurricane; #1617 ....**$120.00**

Candlelight, clear, pitcher, Doulton, #3400/141........**$275.00**

Candlelight, clear, plate, #3900/20, 6½" **$12.50**

Candlelight, clear, plate, #3900/26, 4-toed, 12"...........**$55.00**

Candlelight, clear, plate, torte; #3900/33, 4-toed, 13"..**$55.00**

Candlelight, clear, relish, #3900/124, divided, 2-handled, 7" **$35.00**

Candlelight, clear, relish, #3900/126, 3-part, 12".........**$52.50**

Candlelight, clear, stem, cocktail; #3111, 3-oz **$27.50**

Candlelight, clear, stem, oyster cocktail; #3776, 4½" ...**$22.50**

Candlelight, clear, stem, tall sherbet; #3111, 7-oz........**$22.50**

Candlelight, clear, sugar bowl, individual; #3900/40...**$17.50**

Candlelight, clear, tumbler, iced-tea; #3111, footed, 12-oz **$25.00**

Candlelight, clear, tumbler, juice; #3776, 5-oz **$18.00**

Candlelight, clear, vase, #1238, footed, keyhole, 12" ..**$87.50**

Candlelight, clear, vase, globe; #1309, 5" **$52.50**

Candlelight, clear, vase, pedestal; #1299, 11"............**$100.00**

Caprice, blue or pink, ashtray, #214, 3" **$12.00**

Caprice, blue or pink, bowl, #53, crimped, 4-footed, 10½" **$100.00**

Caprice, blue or pink, bowl, #61, crimped, 4-footed, 12½" **$75.00**

Caprice, blue or pink, bowl, relish; #124, 3-part, 8"....**$32.50**

Caprice, blue or pink, candlestick, #70, w/prism, 7", each...**$50.00**

Caprice, blue or pink, comport, #130, low footed, 7" .**$65.00**

Caprice, blue or pink, mayonnaise, #106, 3-pc set, 8" **$110.00**

Caprice, clear, bonbon, #155, oval, footed, 6" **$20.00**

Caprice, clear, bowl, almond; #95, 4-footed, 2"..........**$15.00**

Caprice, clear, bowl, finger; #16, w/liner **$30.00**

Caprice, clear, bowl, relish; #126, 3-part, rectangular, 12"..**$40.00**

Caprice, clear, cake plate, #36, footed, 13", $140.00

Caprice, clear, bowl, salad; #57, 4-footed, 10" **$32.50**

Caprice, clear, candlestick, #67, 2½", each..................**$13.00**

Caprice, clear, celery & relish, #124, 3-part, 8½" **$20.00**

Caprice, clear, cigarette holder, #205, triangular, 2x2¼"..**$13.00**

Caprice, clear, coaster, #13, 3½" **$13.00**

Caprice, clear, creamer, individual; #40 ....**$10.00**

Caprice, clear, mayonnaise, #106, 3-pc set, 8" **$110.00**

Caprice, clear, pitcher, #179, ball shape, 32-oz............**$75.00**

Chantilly, clear, bottle, salad dressing **$75.00**

Chantilly, clear, bowl, relish/pickle; 2-part, 7" **$18.00**

Chantilly, clear, bowl, tab handles, 11" **$30.00**

Chantilly, clear, butter dish, round **$125.00**

Chantilly, clear, cake plate, tab handles, 13½"..............**$32.50**

Chantilly, clear, comport, 5½" **$30.00**

Chantilly, clear, hat, sm **$150.00**

Chantilly, clear, ice bucket, chrome handle **$65.00**

Chantilly, clear, mustard jar...**$45.00**

Chantilly, clear, plate, 4-footed, 13" **$30.00**

Chantilly, clear, salt & pepper shakers, flat, pr **$27.50**

Chantilly, clear, salt & pepper shakers, handled, pr....**$30.00**

Chantilly, clear, saucer...**$2.50**

Chantilly, clear, stem, low sherbet; #3625, 7-oz...........**$16.00**

Chantilly, clear, stem, tall sherbet; #3775, 6-oz............**$15.00**

Chantilly, clear, tumbler, iced-tea; #3775, footed, 12-oz..**$20.00**

Chantilly, clear, tumbler, iced-tea; 12-oz, #3775, footed ..**$20.00**

Chantilly, clear, tumbler, juice; #3625, footed, 5-oz.....**$15.00**

Chantilly, clear, vase, flower; footed, 11" **$40.00**

Chantilly, clear, vase, flower; footed, 13" **$65.00**

Cleo, amber, green, pink or yellow; bowl, cranberry; 6½" **$25.00**

Cleo, amber, green, pink or yellow; bowl, individual almond; 2½" $65.00

Cleo, amber, green, pink or yellow; ice tub $45.00

Cleo, amber, green, pink or yellow; plate, 7" $12.00

Cleo, amber, green, pink or yellow; salt dip, 1½" $65.00

Cleo, amber, green, pink or yellow; tumbler, #3077, footed, 2½" $55.00

Cleo, amber, green, pink or yellow; tumbler, #3077, footed, 8-oz $25.00

Cleo, amber, green, pink or yellow; tumbler, #3115, footed, 2½-oz $45.00

Cleo, amber, green, pink or yellow; tumbler, #3115, footed, ...$37.50

Cleo, blue, bowl, comport; 4-footed, 6" $35.00

Cleo, blue, bowl, 8½" $60.00

Cleo, blue, cup, bouillon; Decagon shape, w/saucer, 2-handled $40.00

Cleo, blue, platter, 12" $150.00

Cleo, blue, stem, cocktail; #3077, 2½-oz $42.50

Cleo, clear, bowl, oval, 11½" $35.00

Cleo, clear, candy box $75.00

Cleo, clear, cup, Decagon shape $25.00

Cleo, clear, stem, #3115, 9-oz $30.00

Cleo, clear, vase, 11" $125.00

Crown Tuscan, ball jug, #3400/114, 64-oz $310.00

Crown Tuscan, flower block, #2899, 3" $35.00

Crown Tuscan, vase, cornucopia; #3900/575, 10" $75.00

Decagon, pastel colors, bowl, bonbon; 2-handled, 5½" ..$10.00

Decagon, pastel colors, bowl, bouillon; w/liner............$7.50

Decagon, pastel colors, bowl, cranberry; flat rim, 3¾" ..$12.00

Decagon, pastel colors, bowl, fruit; flat rim, 5¾" $6.00

Decagon, pastel colors, bowl, relish; 2-part, 9" $9.00

Decagon, pastel colors, bowl, vegetable; oval, 10½" ..$16.00

Decagon, pastel colors, comport, low footed, 6½" $15.00

Decagon, pastel colors, plate, salad; 8½" $6.00

Decagon, pastel colors, plate, 7½" $4.00

Decagon, pastel colors, saucer...................................$1.00

Decagon, pastel colors, stem, water; 9-oz.................$15.00

Decagon, pastel colors, sugar bowl, footed $9.00

Decagon, pastel colors, tray, service; oval, 11" $8.00

Decagon, pastel colors, tumbler, footed, 5-oz $10.00

Decagon, red or blue, bowl, cereal; flat rim, 6" $15.00

Decagon, red or blue, bowl, fruit; 5½" $10.00

Decagon, red or blue, bowl, individual almond; 2½" ..$30.00

Decagon, red or blue, bowl, relish; 2-part, 11" $17.50

Decagon, red or blue, bowl, soup; flat rim, 8½" $25.00

Decagon, red or blue, creamer, scalloped edge $18.00

Decagon, red or blue, cup $10.00

Decagon, red or blue, mayonnaise, w/liner & ladle ...$30.00

Decagon, red or blue, plate, bread & butter; 6¼" $5.00

Decagon, red or blue, salt dip, footed, 1½" $20.00

Decagon, red or blue, stem, cocktail; 3½-oz...............$12.00

Decagon, red or blue, sugar bowl, tall, footed, lg.......$18.00

Decagon, red or blue, tray, service; 2-handled, 13" $30.00

Decagon, red or blue, tumbler, footed, 12-oz.............$25.00

Diane, clear, bowl, bonbon; 2-handled, 5¼" $18.00

Diane, clear, bowl, cream soup; #3400, w/liner $27.50

Diane, clear, bowl, relish/pickle; 7".........................$22.00

Diane, clear, bowl, 2-handled, 11"............................$35.00

Diane, clear, bowl, 4-footed, flared, 10"....................$40.00

Diane, clear, candy box, round $75.00

Diane, clear, cocktail shaker, metal top $90.00

Diane, clear, comport, blown, 5⅜" $35.00

Diane, clear, creamer, #3400, scroll handled $15.00

Diane, clear, cruet, oil; w/stopper, 6-oz....................$110.00

Diane, clear, ice bucket, chrome handle.....................$65.00

Diane, clear, plate, bread & butter; square, 6" $5.00

Diane, clear, plate, service; 4-footed, 12" $35.00

Diane, clear, stem, cocktail; #1066, 3-oz $16.00

Diane, clear, stem, cordial; #3122, 1-oz $55.00

Diane, clear, sugar, individual; #3900, scalloped edge.$13.00

Diane, clear, tumbler, #1066, 3-oz $18.00

Diane, clear, tumbler, #3135, footed, 10-oz $14.00

Diane, clear, tumbler, iced-tea; #3122, footed, 10-oz ..$17.00

Diane, clear, tumbler, juice; #1066, 5-oz $12.50

Diane, clear, tumbler, sham bottom, 5-oz $30.00

Diane, clear, vase, flower, pedestal foot, 11" $60.00

Elaine, clear, basket, favor; 6½", $200.00

Elaine, clear, bowl, bonbon; 2-handled, 5¼" $13.00

Elaine, clear, bowl, relish/pickle; 2-part, 7" $16.00

Elaine, clear, bowl, 4-footed, flared, 12" $35.00

Elaine, clear, cocktail icer, 2-pc $50.00

Elaine, clear, hurricane lamp, candlestick base $110.00

Elaine, clear, ice bucket, chrome handle $60.00

Elaine, clear, plate, service; 4-footed, 12" $25.00

Elaine, clear, stem, brandy; #3104, tall, ¾" $120.00

Elaine, clear, stem, claret; #1402, 5-oz......................$27.50

Elaine, clear, stem, cocktail; #3121, 3-oz $22.00

Elaine, clear, stem, oyster cocktail; #3121, 4½" $15.00

Elaine, clear, stem, sherry; #3104, 2-oz $90.00

Elaine, clear, stem, wine; #3104, 3-oz $85.00

Elaine, clear, sugar bowl, individual..........................$12.00

Elaine, clear, tumbler, iced-tea; #1402, 12-oz.............$25.00

Elaine, clear, tumbler, juice; #3500, footed, 5-oz $17.00

Elaine, clear, vase, footed, 6" $30.00

Elaine, stem, cordial; #1402, 1-oz $55.00

Flower frog, clear, Bashful Charlotte, 6½" **$70.00**

Flower frog, clear, Draped Lady, 8½" **$97.00**

Flower frog, clear, Mandolin Lady **$195.00**

Flower frog, clear, Rose Lady, tall base, 9½" **$155.00**

Gloria, clear, bowl, bonbon; crimped edge, footed, 5" .**$14.00**

Gloria, clear, bowl, console; 4-footed, 12" **$25.00**

Gloria, clear, bowl, fruit; square, 5" **$16.00**

Gloria, clear, bowl, 2-handled, 10" **$32.00**

Gloria, clear, butter dish, 2-handled.....................**$110.00**

Gloria, clear, comport, 2-handled, footed, 9½" **$65.00**

Gloria, clear, icer, w/insert.....................**$55.00**

Gloria, clear, pitcher, w/lid, 64-oz.....................**$150.00**

Gloria, clear, plate, 2-handled, 6" **$8.00**

Gloria, clear, plate, 8½" **$9.00**

Gloria, clear, platter, 11½".....................**$45.00**

Gloria, clear, saucer, after dinner; round.....................**$5.00**

Gloria, clear, stem, cordial; #3135, 1-oz **$55.00**

Gloria, clear, stem, goblet; #3115, 9-oz **$13.00**

Gloria, clear, stem, tall sherbet; #3120, 6-oz **$11.00**

Gloria, clear, stem, water; #3130, 8-oz **$15.00**

Gloria, clear, stem, wine; 2½-oz, #3035 ....**$20.00**

Gloria, clear, vase, squared top, 12" **$50.00**

Gloria, green, pink or yellow; bowl, cream soup; w/round
liner.....................**$35.00**

Gloria, green, pink or yellow; bowl, fruit; 5½" **$7.50**

Gloria, green, pink or yellow; comport, 4-footed, 5" ..**$37.50**

Gloria, green, pink or yellow; mayonnaise, w/liner & ladle,
4-footed **$60.00**

Gloria, green, pink or yellow; plate, 2-handled, 11" ...**$25.00**

Gloria, green, pink or yellow; saucer, round.................**$4.00**

Gloria, green, pink or yellow; sugar shaker, w/glass
top.....................**$250.00**

Gloria, green, pink or yellow; tumbler, #3035, high footed,
10-oz **$12.00**

Gloria, green, pink or yellow; tumbler, #3130, footed, 5-
oz **$20.00**

Gloria, green, pink or yellow; tumbler, 5-oz, #3120,
footed.....................**$12.00**

Gloria, yellow, stem, low sherbet; #3035, 6-oz **$15.00**

**Imperial Hunt Scene,
black, ice bucket,
$120.00**

Imperial Hunt Scene, clear, bowl, 3-part, 8½" **$25.00**

Imperial Hunt Scene, clear, creamer, footed...............**$15.00**

Imperial Hunt Scene, clear, ice bucket.....................**$40.00**

Imperial Hunt Scene, clear, plate, 8" **$12.00**

Imperial Hunt Scene, clear, stem, water; #1402, 10-oz..**$40.00**

Imperial Hunt Scene, clear, stem, wine; #1402, 2½"....**$45.00**

Imperial Hunt Scene, clear, sugar bowl, footed..........**$15.00**

Imperial Hunt Scene, clear, tumbler, #3085, footed, 12-
oz **$35.00**

Imperial Hunt Scene, clear, tumbler, #3085, footed, 2½-
oz **$35.00**

Imperial Hunt Scene, colors, bowl, finger; #3085,
w/plate **$35.00**

Imperial Hunt Scene, colors, bowl, 8".....................**$60.00**

Imperial Hunt Scene, colors, mayonnaise, w/liner......**$50.00**

Imperial Hunt Scene, colors, stem, claret; #3085, 4½-
oz **$55.00**

Imperial Hunt Scene, colors, stem, low sherbet; #3085,
6-oz **$22.50**

Mt Vernon, amber & clear, ashtray, #63, 3½" **$8.00**

Mt Vernon, amber & clear, bonbon, #10, footed, 7" .**$12.50**

Mt Vernon, amber & clear, bowl, #121, flared, 12½"...**$32.00**

Mt Vernon, amber & clear, bowl, #128, 11½" **$30.00**

Mt Vernon, amber & clear, bowl, #39, 2-handled, 10" ..**$20.00**

Mt Vernon, amber & clear, bowl, fruit; #6, 5¼" **$10.00**

Mt Vernon, amber & clear, bowl, preserve; #76, 6".....**$12.00**

Mt Vernon, amber & clear, box, #17, square, 4"..........**$30.00**

Mt Vernon, amber & clear, candelabrum, #38, 13½" ..**$45.00**

Mt Vernon, amber & clear, celery, #79, 10½".............**$15.00**

Mt Vernon, amber & clear, coaster, #60, plain, 3" **$5.00**

Mt Vernon, amber & clear, comport, #11, 7½".............**$25.00**

Mt Vernon, amber & clear, comport, #33, 4½".............**$12.00**

Mt Vernon, amber & clear, comport, #99, 9½".............**$27.50**

Mt vernon, amber & clear, decanter, #47, 11-oz..........**$50.00**

Mt Vernon, amber & clear, mayonnaise, #107, divided, 2
spoons **$25.00**

Mt Vernon, amber & clear, mustard, #28 ....**$22.00**

Mt Vernon, amber & clear, pitcher, #95, ball shape, 80-
oz **$90.00**

Mt Vernon, amber & clear, plate, bread & butter; #19,
6⅜".....................**$4.00**

Mt Vernon, amber & clear, relish, #103, 3-part, 3-han-
dled, 8" **$20.00**

Mt Vernon, amber & clear, relish, #104, 5-part, 12".....**$30.00**

Mt Vernon, amber & clear, salt & pepper shakers, #28,
pr **$22.50**

Mt Vernon, amber & clear, sauce boat, #30-445, w/ladle, tab
handled.....................**$60.00**

Mt Vernon, amber & clear, stem, claret; #25, 4½"........**$13.50**

Mt Vernon, amber & clear, sugar bowl, #8, footed **$10.00**

Mt Vernon, amber & clear, tumbler, #56, 5-oz............**$12.00**

Mt Vernon, amber & clear, tumbler, iced-tea; #20, footed,
12-oz **$17.00**

Mt Vernon, amber & clear, tumbler, water; #3, footed, 10-
oz **$15.00**

Mt Vernon, amber & clear, tumbler, whiskey; #55, 2-oz.**$10.00**

Mt Vernon, amber & clear, vase, #119, crimped, 6" **$20.00**

Mt Vernon, amber & clear, vase, #58, 7" **$30.00**

Nude stem, amber, cocktail.....................**$90.00**

Nude stem, carmen, brandy................................**$120.00**
Nude stem, Crown Tuscan, candlestick **$135.00**
Nude stem, dark green, claret.........................**$100.00**
Portia, clear, bowl, bonbon; tab handled, footed, 7"...**$22.00**
Portia, clear, bowl, bonbon; 2-handled, 5¼".....**$15.00**
Portia, clear, bowl, celery/relish; 5-part, 12"....**$37.50**
Portia, clear, bowl, ear handles, oval, 4-footed, 12"....**$45.00**
Portia, clear, bowl, grapefruit/oyster; 6"..........**$17.00**
Portia, clear, bowl, pickle; footed, 9½"............**$22.00**
Portia, clear, bowl, relish, 2-part, handled, 11"...........**$27.50**
Portia, clear, bowl, seafood...........................**$40.00**
Portia, clear, candlestick, 2-light, 6".............**$35.00**
Portia, clear, cigarette holder, urn shape.............**$55.00**
Portia, clear, cocktail shaker, w/stopper **$90.00**
Rosalie, amber, bottle, French dressing.............**$75.00**
Rosalie, amber, bowl, finger; w/liner.............**$25.00**
Rosalie, amber, bowl, fruit; 5½"......................**$10.00**
Rosalie, amber, bowl, 2-handled, 10" **$27.00**
Rosalie, amber, bowl, 2-handled, 7" **$15.00**
Rosalie, amber, bowl, 2-handled, 8½" **$15.00**
Rosalie, amber, candlestick, keyhole, 5" **$20.00**
Rosalie, amber, candlestick, 3-light, keyhole, 6".........**$25.00**
Rosalie, amber, comport, 5¾" **$15.00**
Rosalie, amber, ice bucket or pail **$45.00**
Rosalie, amber, mayonnaise, footed, w/liner.............**$25.00**
Rosalie, amber, nut dish, footed, 2½".............**$45.00**
Rosalie, amber, plate, 2-handled, 11" **$20.00**
Rosalie, amber, plate, 8¾".............................**$10.00**
Rosalie, amber, relish, 2-part, 9" **$15.00**
Rosalie, amber, sugar bowl, footed **$13.00**
Rosalie, blue, pink or green; bowl, bouillon; 2-handled..**$25.00**
Rosalie, blue, pink or green; comport, 2-handled, 5½"..**$30.00**
Rosalie, blue, pink or green; creamer, footed.............**$17.00**
Rosalie, blue, pink or green; plate, bread & butter; 6¾"..**$7.00**
Rosalie, blue, pink or green; saucer **$5.00**
Rosalie, blue, pink or green; stem, high sherbet, #3077, 6-oz..............................**$18.00**
Rosalie, blue, pink or green; tray for sugar & creamer, center handled **$20.00**
Rosalie, blue, pink or green; tumbler, #3077, footed, 12-oz **$35.00**
Rosalie, blue, pink or green; tumbler, #3077, footed, 8-oz.**$25.00**
Rosalie, blue, pink or green; vase, footed, 5½" **$27.50**
Rose Point, clear, ashtray, #3500/125, 3½"..................**$35.00**
Rose Point, clear, ashtray, #3500/127, 4¼"..................**$45.00**
Rose Point, clear, basket, #3400/1182, 2-handled, 6" ..**$35.00**
Rose Point, clear, bowl, #1402/89, 2-handled, 6" **$40.00**
Rose Point, clear, bowl, #3400/168, flared, 10½".........**$65.00**
Rose Point, clear, bowl, #3400/34, 2-handled, 9½"......**$67.50**
Rose Point, clear, bowl, #3400/49, handled, 5"............**$35.00**
Rose Point, clear, bowl, #3900/62, 4 tab handles, flared, 12" **$67.50**
Rose Point, clear, bowl, bonbon; #3400/1180, handled .**$30.00**
Rose Point, clear, bowl, finger; #3106, w/liner............**$75.00**
Rose Point, clear, bowl, fruit; #3400/56, 5¼"..............**$42.50**
Rose Point, clear, bowl, nut; #3400/71, 4-footed, 3"....**$67.50**
Rose Point, clear, bowl, pickle; #477, 9½" **$50.00**
Rose Point, clear, candelabrum, #1338, 3-light **$55.00**

Rose Point, clear, candlestick, #3400/647, 2-light, keyhole, 6"......................**$37.50**
Rose Point, clear, candlestick, #3500/108, 2½" **$30.00**
Rose Point, clear, candy box, #3500/57, 3-part, 8" **$72.50**
Rose Point, clear, cocktail icer, #3600, 2-pc.................**$70.00**
Rose Point, clear, creamer, #3400/68........................**$20.00**
Rose Point, clear, cup, 3-styles: #3400/54, 3500/1, 3900/17 each......................**$30.00**
Rose Point, clear, mayonnaise, #19 ....**$52.50**
Rose Point, clear, mustard jar, #3500/59, 3-oz...........**$130.00**
Rose Point, clear, plate, #3500/4, 7½".....................**$15.00**
Rose Point, clear, plate, bread & butter; #3400/60, 6"..**$13.50**
Rose Point, clear, plate, salad; #3900/22, 8"................**$20.00**
Rose Point, clear, relish, #3500/60, 2-part, handled, 5½".**$30.00**
Rose Point, clear, relish, #3500/70, 4-part, 7½"...........**$37.50**
Rose Point, clear, stem, low sherbet; #3106, 7-oz........**$25.00**
Rose Point, clear, stem, water; 10-oz, #3500.............**$30.00**
Rose Point, clear, sugar bowl, #137, flat **$105.00**
Rose Point, clear, tray, celery & relish; #3900/125, 3-part, 9" **$47.50**
Rose Point, clear, tray for sugar & creamer, #3900/37...**$25.00**
Rose Point, clear, tumbler, #3106, footed, 3-oz **$25.00**
Rose Point, clear, tumbler, #3900/117, 5-oz................**$45.00**
Rose Point, clear, vase, #1234, footed, keyhole, 12" ...**$85.00**
Rose Point, clear, vase, #3400/103, 6½"....................**$80.00**
Valencia, clear, ashtray, #3500/126, round, 4" **$14.00**
Valencia, clear, bowl, #1402/89, 2-handled, 6" **$18.00**
Valencia, clear, celery, #1402/94, 12" **$30.00**
Valencia, clear, creamer, individual; #3500/15.............**$17.50**
Valencia, clear, mayonnaise, #3500/59, 3-pc **$40.00**
Valencia, clear, plate, breakfast; #3500/5, 8½".............**$12.00**
Valencia, clear, plate, torte; #3500/38, 13" **$25.00**
Valencia, clear, relish, #3500/112, 3-part, 2-handled, 15".**$75.00**
Valencia, clear, stem, low sherbet; #1402....................**$12.50**
Valencia, clear, stem, tall sherbet; #3500, 7-oz **$15.00**
Valencia, clear, stem, wine; #1402...........................**$30.00**
Valencia, clear, sugar bowl, individual; #3500/15........**$17.50**
Valencia, clear, tumbler, #3500, footed, 3-oz..............**$14.00**
Wildflower, clear, bowl, #3900/54, 4-footed, flared, 10".**$35.00**
Wildflower, clear, bowl, relish; #3900/123, 7" **$18.00**
Wildflower, clear, candy box, #3900/165 ....**$60.00**
Wildflower, clear, comport, #3900/136, 5½" **$30.00**
Wildflower, clear, creamer, individual; #3900/40 ....**$17.50**
Wildflower, clear, ice bucket, #3900/671, chrome handle.**$65.00**
Wildflower, clear, mayonnaise set, #3900/129, 3-pc....**$30.00**
Wildflower, clear, plate, #340/176, 7½" **$9.00**

Wildflower, clear, salt & pepper shakers, pr, $70.00

Wildflower, clear, saucer, #3900/17 or #3400/54 .... **$3.50**

Wildflower, clear, stem, low oyster cocktail; #3121, 4½-oz **$18.00**

Wildflower, clear, sugar bowl, individual; #3900/40 ... **$17.50**

Wildflower, clear, tumbler, #3900/115, 13-oz **$25.00**

Wildflower, clear, vase, #1299, pedestal foot, 11" **$45.00**

Cameras

To make good investments when buying cameras, several criteria are involved. Those that hold their values best and have a better resale potential are usually the more unusual, more obscure models in fine condition. Most camera buffs build their collections around either a particular type of camera (those with the same sort of shutter, for instance), or they might limit their buying to cameras made by only one company. But even if you can afford to buy only inexpensive, mass-produced cameras, you'll find it to be a very interesting hobby. You can (many do) add viewers, photography supplies and advertising, projectors, and accessories of all types to round out your collection.

Kodak Hawk-Eye 2A Model BA, ca 1926-34, EX, $35.00

Adams Adlake Repeater, box style, side crank, EX **$55.00**

Adox Blitz, Bakelite box-type, ca 1950, NM **$25.00**

Agfa Billy-Clack, folding, 120 film **$25.00**

Agfa Speedy Compur, Compur shutter, 1934-42, EX ... **$45.00**

Aires, 35-V, 35mm **$80.00**

Balda Glorina, folding type, ca 1936, EX **$42.00**

Bear Photo Special, color-covered Art Deco box style. **$75.00**

Bolsey C, 35mm **$70.00**

Canon Seiki S-11, metal body, 1946-47, NM **$400.00**

Coke, novelty **$50.00**

Conley Snap #2, folding strut type, EX........................ **$22.50**

Coronet Consul, Art Deco box type w/colored cover. **$20.00**

Coronet Eclair Lux, Art Deco box type w/colored cover.. **$30.00**

Genos Special, black Bakelite, box type, 1953, NM **$30.00**

Kodak Autographic Jr #1, folding, 120 film **$10.00**

Kodak Brownie Cresta, black plastic eye-level box type, ca 1955-58 .... **$12.50**

Kodak Brownie Flash IV, Art Deco box type, colored cover **$20.00**

Kodak Brownie 2A Model C, VG **$8.50**

Kodak Duoflex, w/cover, 1930, EX **$15.00**

Kodak Monitor Six-16, Anastigmat Special lens, Supermatic shutter, 1940s, EX **$15.00**

Kodak Signet, 35mm **$20.00**

Kodak Six-16, Art Deco box type w/colored cover **$5.00**

Kodak Six-20, Anastigmat 100mm lens, EX **$15.00**

Kodak Target Hawkeye XIX-16, NM **$18.00**

Kodak 35, 35mm **$15.00**

Nikon S2, chrome w/black dials, 1954-58, EX **$225.00**

Olympus Wide II, lever advance, folding crank, 1958-61, NM **$55.00**

Polaroid Big Shot, fixed focus lens, 1971-75, M **$15.00**

Polaroid 95A, aluminum body, folding bed style, 1950s, EX **$20.00**

Universal Uniflash, plastic, 1940, w/original flash & box, NM **$22.50**

Voigtlander Vito, folding type, yellow hinged filter, 1939-48, NM **$48.00**

Candlewick Glassware

This is a beautifully simple, very diverse line of glassware made by the Imperial Glass Company (a division of Lenox Inc., Bellaire, Ohio) from 1936 until the company closed in 1982. It was named Candlewick because it's design suggested the tufted needlework called Candlewicking done by the Colonial ladies in early America. Rows of small crystal balls surround rims of bowls and plates, foot rings of tumblers, and decorate the handles of pitchers. Some pieces have stems of stacked balls. Though most was made in crystal, a few pieces were made in color as well, while others had a gold wash. Imperial made two etched lines, Floral and Valley Lily, that utilized the Candlewick shapes. Both are very scarce.

Among the hardest-to-find items are the desk calendars that were made as gifts for company employees and customers, the chip and dip set, and the dresser set containing a cologne bottle, powder jar, clock, and mirror.

There were more than 740 items in all, and collectors often use the company's mold numbers to help identify all those variations and sizes. Gene Florence's *Collector's Encyclopedia of Elegant Glassware* has a chapter that gives this line of glassware very good coverage.

From the 1940s through the sixties, Hazel Atlas produced sherbets, cocktail glasses, wines, and water goblets that are being mistaken for Candlewick, so beware. You'll find these in malls and antique shops, priced and labeled as Candlewick. They were made with a crystal, green, amber, or ruby top on a crystal foot ringed with small glass balls. But the flared part of the foot is ribbed, unlike any Candlewick foot, so you can tell the difference. These are becoming very collectible in their own right, but they're certainly not worth Candlewick prices, and you won't want them in your collection. Gene Florence calls them 'Boopie' and indicates values in the $3.00 to $7.00 range for crystal and in the $7.00 to $17.00 range for colors.

Ashtray, #400/172, heart shape, 4½" $9.00
Ashtray, #400/19, round, 2¾" $8.00
Ashtray, #400/653, square, 5¾" $35.00
Bell, #400/108, 5" $75.00
Bowl, #400/106B, 12" $85.00
Bowl, #400/128B, bell shape, 10" $50.00
Bowl, #400/17F, shallow, 12" $45.00
Bowl, #400/5F, round, 7" $20.00
Bowl, #400/52, divided, 2-handled, round, 6" $22.00
Bowl, #400/63B, 10½" $60.00
Bowl, #400/74SC, fancy crimped edge, 4-footed, square, 9" $60.00
Bowl, cream soup; #400/50, 5" $40.00
Bowl, jelly; #400/59, w/lid, 5½" $55.00
Bowl, pickle/celery; #400/58, 8½" $20.00
Bowl, relish; #400/217, oval 2-handled, 10" $40.00
Bowl, relish; #400/268, 2-part, 8" $20.00

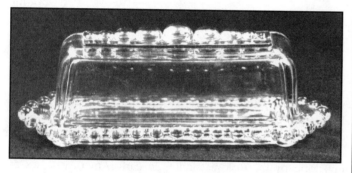

Butter dish, #400/161, beaded lid, ¼-lb, $30.00

Candle holder, #400/207, 3-toed, 4½" $37.50
Candle holder, #400/280, flat, 3½" $20.00
Candy box, #400/59, round, 5½" $42.50
Coaster, #400/78, 4" $6.00
Compote, #400/45, beaded stem, 5½" $22.00
Compote, #400/48F, beaded stem, 8" $70.00
Creamer, #400/30, beaded handle, 6-oz $7.50
Cup, coffee; #400/37 ....$7.50
Egg cup, #400/19, beaded foot $45.00
Ice tub, #400/63, 5½x8" dia $80.00
Mustard jar, #400/156 ....$30.00
Party set, oval plate w/indent for cup, #400/98 ....$30.00
Pitcher, #400/16, plain, 20-oz $40.00
Pitcher, #400/424, plain, 80-oz $55.00
Plate, #400/34, 4½" $6.00
Plate, #400/72D, 2-handled, 10" $17.50
Plate, #400/98, w/indent, oval, 9" $15.00
Plate, bread & butter; #400/1D, 8" $8.00
Plate, salad; #400/5D, 8" $9.00
Plate, serving; 13½", #400/92V, cupped edge $37.50
Plate, torte; #400/113D, 2-handled, 14" $30.00
Punch ladle, #400/91 ....$22.50

Salt & pepper shakers, #400/247, beaded foot, straight-sided, chrome top $16.00
Salt & pepper shakers, individual; #400/109, pr $10.00
Salt dip, #400/19, 2¼" $9.00
Saucer, after dinner; #400/77...$5.00
Stem, brandy; #3800 ....$25.00
Stem, champagne; #3400, 6-oz....................................$17.50
Stem, champagne/sherbet; #3800, 6-oz......................$25.00
Stem, cocktail; #3400, 4-oz..$14.00
Stem, cocktail; #4000 ....$22.00
Stem, goblet; #4000, 11-oz...$18.00
Stem, tall sherbet; #400/190, 5-oz...............................$15.00
Stem, wine; #3400, 4-oz...$24.00
Sugar bowl, #44/122, footed $6.00
Tray, #400/113E, handled, 14" $40.00
Tray, #400/29, 6½" $15.00
Tray, wafer; #400/51T, handle bent to center of dish, 6" ..$22.00
Tumbler, #3400, footed, 9-oz $14.00
Tumbler, cocktail; #400/19, footed, 3-oz.....................$15.00
Tumbler, juice; #400/19, 5-oz......................................$10.00
Tumbler, old-fashioned; #400/18, 7-oz.......................$30.00
Vase, #400/138B, flared rim, footed, 6" $80.00
Vase, #400/25, ball shape, sm neck, beaded foot, 4" ..$40.00

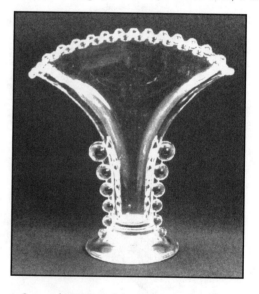

Vase, fan; #400/87F, beaded handle, 8", $35.00

Vase, ivy bowl; #400/74J, 7" $50.00

Candy Containers

Most of us can recall buying these glass toys as a child, since they were made well into the 1960s. We were fascinated by the variety of their shapes then, just as collectors are today. Looking back, it couldn't have been we were buying them for the candy, though perhaps as a child those tiny sugary balls flavored more with the coloring agent than anything else were enough to satisfy our 'sweet tooth.'

Glass candy containers have been around since our country's centennial celebration in 1876 when the first two, the Liberty Bell and the Independence Hall, were introduced. Since then they have been made in hundreds of styles, and some of them have become very expensive. The leading manufacturers were in the East — Westmoreland, Victory Glass, J.H. Millstein, Crosetti, L.E. Smith, Jack Stough, T.H. Stough, and West Bros. made perhaps 90% of them — and collectors report finding many in the Pennsylvania area. Most are clear, but you'll find them in various other colors as well.

If you're going to deal in candy containers, you need a book that will show you all the variations available. *The Compleat American Glass Candy Containers Handbook* by Eikelberner and Agadjaninian (recently revised by Adele Bowden) uses a numbering system that has become universal among collectors. Numbers in our listings refer to this book.

Because of their popularity and considerable worth, many of the original containers have been reproduced. Beware of any questionable glassware that has a slick or oily touch. Among those that have been produced are: Amber Pistol (#283), Auto (#48 and #33), Carpet Sweeper (#132 and #133), Chicken on Nest (#149), Display Case (#177), Dog (#179), Drum Mug (#543), Fire Engine (#213), Independence Hall (#342), Jackie Coogan (#345), Kewpie (#539), Mail Box (#521), Mantel Clock (#164), Mule and Waterwagon (#539), Peter Rabbit (#618), Piano (#577), Rabbit Pushing Wheelbarrow (#601), Rocking Horse (#651), Safe (#661), Santa (#674), Santa's Boot (#111), Station Wagon (#567), Uncle Sam's Hat (#303). Others are possible.

Our values are given for candy containers that are undamaged, in good original paint, and complete (with all original parts and closure). Repaired or repainted containers are worth much less.

See also Christmas; Easter; Halloween.

Gas Pump, green plastic, Millstein, $75.00

Baseball, #76, frosted, no decals	**$25.00**
Bureau, #112	**$200.00**
Candlestick, #119-1	**$400.00**
Chicken in Sagging Basket, #148	**$75.00**
Decorettes	**$125.00**

Dog, Kiddies' Breakfast Bell, #192	**$40.00**
Dog w/Top Hat, #194-2	**$32.00**
Fairy Pups, #193	**$75.00**
Fanny Farmer (Uncle Sam)	**$125.00**
Fire Engine, Little Boiler, #218	**$75.00**
Gas Pump, #240	**$250.00**
Gun, #251, cork closure	**$25.00**
Lamp, #365, Hobnail w/shade	**$350.00**
Lantern, oval panels, light green, 3⅜"	**$35.00**
Limousine, #45, Westmoreland Specialty	**$175.00**
Lynn Doll Nurser, #550	**$32.00**
Mailbox, #521, silver paint	**$150.00**
Mule Pulling Barrel, #539	**$100.00**
Naked Child, #546, Victory Glass	**$65.00**
Passenger Airplane, 3 windows, glass disk wheels, no mark, 2¼x4⅝x5"	**$325.00**
Pencil, #567	**$58.00**
Peter Rabbit, #618	**$25.00**
Rabbit, aluminum ears, 4"	**$350.00**
Rabbit in Egg Shell, #608, gold paint	**$95.00**

Suitcase, #707, $45.00

Telephone, Victory Glass #1, 7½"	**$400.00**
Wagon or Stagecoach, #882	**$125.00**
Wheelbarrow, #832, w/closure	**$80.00**
Windmill, #842, shaker top, original blades	**$375.00**

Canes

If you want to collect canes your collection could certainly be diversified. There are canes that are simple and primitive, while others have hidden compartments that house a collapsible umbrella, a portable bar, or even a weapon. Some had complicated patented mechanisms of one sort or another. Materials used in cane-making are just as varied. Glassblowers made canes of glass that were carried in parades and proudly displayed as evidence of their artistic abilities. Natural formations of tree branches and roots, precious metals, and man-made compositions were also used.

Bamboo, floral-carved bone handle w/bird, pewter band, 34"...**$135.00**

Bamboo, metal tip unscrews for telescoping fly rod, root handle..**$100.00**

Bamboo, silver-gilded white metal smiling head as knob, 35"...**$30.00**

Bamboo, sterling plate on handle, sterling scrolls on shaft..**$40.00**

Birch, intarsia floral & leaf inlay on handle, 36".........**$35.00**

Blown glass, aqua spatter w/spiral twist at handle & end, 31"...**$200.00**

Blown glass, clear w/white, yellow & mahogany looping, 59"...**$150.00**

Blown glass, cranberry & white twists on clear, 50" .**$150.00**

Curly maple, stag horn handle, 35" **$65.00**

Ebony, ivory sphinx handle, ivory tip, 37½"............**$425.00**

Gutta percha, dolphin handle, ebony shaft, horn tip, 36"...**$110.00**

Hardwood, screw-off brass ice chipper tip & screw end, 37" **$85.00**

Malacca, carved lady's leg handle, 35" **$85.00**

Thornwood, repousse floral on silver handle, metal tip, 35"...**$250.00**

Tin, white cast metal knob w/bust of McKinley & 1896, 33"...**$140.00**

Wood, alligator handle, brass tip **$90.00**

Wood, bird handle, dragon on shaft highlighted in black, 37"...**$185.00**

Wood, carved parrot's head handle w/polychrome, Brazil, 36"...**$135.00**

Wood, 2 snakes carved in relief twist along shaft, 1890s, 36"...**$225.00**

Cape Cod

You can't walk through any flea market or mall now without seeing volumes of this ruby red glassware. It has been issued by Avon since the seventies, the small cruet and tall candlesticks, for instance, filled originally with one or the other of their fragrances, the wine and water goblets filled with scented candlewax, and the dessert bowl with guest soap. Many 'campaigns' since then have featured accessory tableware items such as plates, cake stands, and a water pitcher, and obviously the line has been a very good seller for them, judging from the sheer volume of it around and the fact that they still feature some pieces in their catalogs.

I've found some nice pieces at garage sales, so I've bought it with an eye to the future, since it was so cheap. The dealers I've talked with about it tell me that it moves sporadically. I expect it to come into its own. The glassware is of good quality, there's a nice assortment of items in the line, and it's readily available. Even at mall prices, it's not expensive. That's about all it takes to make a collectible.

Bell, marked Christmas 1979 on bottom, 6½" **$20.00**

Bowl, dessert; 1978-80, 5", MIB **$10.00**

Bowl, serving; 1986, 8¾" dia.......................................**$19.00**

Bowl, soup/cereal; 1991, 7½" dia **$13.00**

Butter dish, holds ¼-lb stick, 1983-84, 7" long...........**$17.50**

Cake plate, footed, 1991, 3¼x10¾" dia, MIB **$50.00**

Candle holder, hurricane type w/clear chimney, 1985.**$20.00**

Candle holder, squat form, 1983-84, 3¾" dia, each **$6.50**

Candlestick, holds 3 different cologne fragrances, 1975-80, 5-oz...**$9.00**

Candy dish, footed, 1987, 3½x6" dia **$12.00**

Christmas ornament, w/plaid bow, hexagonal, 1990, 3¼"...**$10.00**

Condiment dish, divided, rectangular, 1985.................**$12.00**

Creamer, footed, 1981-84, 4", MIB **$9.00**

Cruet, 1975-80, 5-oz, $10.00

Cup, 1990, 3½", MIB **$9.00**

Decanter, w/stopper, 1977-80, 16-oz............................**$15.00**

Dessert server, wedge-shaped stainless steel w/red plastic handle, 1981-84, 8" long....................................**$12.00**

Goblet, champagne; 1991, 5¼" **$12.50**

Goblet, water; 1976-80, 6" **$9.00**

Goblet, wine; 1992, 5¼"..**$6.00**

Heart box, 1989, 4" wide, MIB **$13.00**

Mug, pedestal foot, 1982-84, 5"...................................**$10.00**

Napkin rings, set of 4, 1989 ....**$20.00**

Pie plate server, 1992, 11" dia **$30.00**

Pitcher, water; footed, 1984, 8¼" **$30.00**

Plate, bread & butter; 1992, 5¾" dia, MIB **$8.50**

Plate, dessert; 1980, 7½" **$6.50**

Plate, dinner; 1982-83, 11"..**$14.00**

Platter, 1986, 10¾x13½", MIB.....................................**$24.00**

Salt & pepper shakers, marked May 1978 on bottom, pr...**$12.00**

Sauce boat, footed, 1988, 8" long, MIB **$25.00**

Sugar bowl, footed, 1980-83, 3½" **$10.00**

Tidbit tray, 2-tier, brass handle, 1987, 9¾", MIB **$30.00**

Tumbler, footed, 1988, 3¾" **$7.50**

Tumbler, straight-sided, 1990, 5½"................................**$8.50**

Vase, footed, 1985, 8" $15.00
Wine glass, footed, 5" $7.50

Carnival Chalkware

From about 1910 until in the fifties, winners of carnival games everywhere in the United States were awarded chalkware figures of Kewpie dolls, the Lone Ranger, Hula girls, comic characters, etc. The assortment was vast and varied. The earliest were made of plaster with a pink cast. They ranged in size from about 5" up to 16".

They were easily chipped, so when it came time for the carnival to pick up and move on, they had to be carefully wrapped and packed away, a time consuming, tedious chore. When stuffed animals became available, concessionists found that they could simply throw them into a box without fear of damage, and so ended an era.

Today the most valuable of these statues are those modeled after Disney characters, movie stars, and comic book heroes.

Chalkware figures are featured in *The Carnival Chalk Prize, Vols I and II,* written by Thomas G. Morris, who has also included a fascinating history of carnival life in America.

Bathing Beauty, tank-type suit, arms up as if ready to dive, ca 1920s, 12" $95.00
Bellhop, ca 1946, marked Jenkins, 13" $45.00
Bugs Bunny, ca 1945, flat-backed, 9" $55.00
Chinese lady, 'Declaration Day' & 'Tin Toy' on base, ca 1920, 14" $165.00

Donald Duck, ca 1934-50, 14", $75.00

Donald Duck's Uncle Scrooge w/money bag, ca 1940-50, 8" $35.00
Girl sitting in a flower, feet crossed, lg eyes, ca 1920, 11" $120.00
Hula girl, nude, sitting w/feet tucked under her, ca 1935-45, 5½" $35.00
Kewpie Vamp, hand-painted with jointed arms, flapper-type hairdo, side-glancing eyes, wearing veil, ca 1920s, 11" $125.00
Lady in evening dress, ca 1935-45, 13½" $55.00
Lone Ranger & Silver, ca 1938-1950, 10½" $75.00
Pirate girl, marked Capt Kiddo by Jenkins & Real Art Co, ca 1925, 13½" $135.00
Popeye, ca 1930-50, 13½" or 15½", each.....................$95.00
Sailor girl, ca 1930-40, 12¾" $45.00
Sailor girl, marked Copyright 1934, 14" $65.00
Sitting lady, hand-painted with original head scarf, 'Splash Me' marked on back, 6" $60.00

Sugar, marked JY Jenkins, ca 1948, 13", $120.00

Superman, ca 1940-50, 15" $185.00

Carnival Glass

From 1905 until late in the twenties, many companies (Northwood, Fenton, Imperial, Millersburg, Dugan, and others) produced huge quantities of this type of press-molded iridescent glassware. Because it was so inexpensive, lots of it was given away at carnivals, and that's where it got its name. Even today you're apt to find a piece stuck away in Grandma's cabinet or at a tag sale, so we want you to be at least a little familiar with it. It's been widely reproduced over the past twenty-five years, and even the new glass is collectible. A few of the companies that have reproduced it are Indiana Glass, Westmoreland, and Imperial. Just be sure you know what you're buying. It's one thing to buy 'new' glass if you like it, but if you have your heart set on the genuine article, you certainly don't want to make mistakes.

To educate yourself so that this doesn't happen, attend antique shows, go to the better shops in your area, and get to know reputable dealers. Read and study *The Standard Encyclopedia of Carnival Glass* by Bill Edwards. You'll soon find yourself confident and able to recognize old carnival glass as well as the newer reproductions.

See also Indiana Carnival; Westmoreland; Imperial.

Acanthus (Imperial), plate, marigold, 10".................**$200.00**
Acorn (Fenton), bowl, green, 8½" **$85.00**
Acorn Burrs (Northwood), bowl, flat, amethyst, 5" **$40.00**
Acorn Burrs (Northwood), punch cup, aqua opalescent **$575.00**
Apothecary, jar, marigold, sm **$60.00**
Apple Blossom Twigs (Dugan), plate, green............**$300.00**
Apple Panels (English), creamer, marigold **$35.00**
Apple Tree (Fenton), tumbler, blue........................**$65.00**
April Showers (Fenton), vase, green **$150.00**
Arched Panels, tumbler, marigold..........................**$85.00**
Arcs (Imperial), bowl, amethyst, 8½"......................**$60.00**
Asters, bowl, marigold.....................................**$60.00**
August Flowers, shade, marigold..........................**$42.00**
Autumn Acorns (Fenton), bowl, green, 8¼" **$80.00**
Aztec (McKee), creamer, clambroth **$250.00**
Aztec (McKee), rose bowl, clambroth **$400.00**
Baby's Bouquet, child's plate, marigold, scarce.........**$115.00**
Baker's Rosette, ornament, amethyst......................**$90.00**
Ballons (Imperial), compote, smoke **$90.00**
Ballons (Imperial), vase, smoke, 3 sizes...................**$75.00**
Banded Diamonds (Crystal), bowl, marigold, 5" **$50.00**
Banded Diamonds (Crystal), tumbler, amethyst, rare..**$400.00**
Banded Diamonds & Bars, decanter, marigold, complete **$175.00**
Banded Diamonds & Bars (Finland), tumbler, marigold, tall, 4" **$550.00**
Banded Grape (Fenton), tumbler, white **$95.00**
Banded Grape & Leaf (English), water pitcher, marigold, rare...**$650.00**
Banded Panels (Crystal), sugar bowl (open), marigold.**$45.00**
Banded Rose, vase, marigold, sm..........................**$175.00**
Beaded Bull's-Eye (Imperial), vase, amethyst, 14".....**$125.00**
Beaded Hearts (Northwood), bowl, marigold............**$50.00**
Beaded Panels (Westmoreland), compote, amethyst ..**$55.00**
Beaded Shell (Dugan), creamer or spooner, amethyst..**$90.00**
Beaded Shell (Dugan), tumbler, blue.....................**$180.00**
Beaded Spears (Crystal), pitcher, marigold, rare **$490.00**
Beaded Stars (Fenton), bowl, marigold....................**$40.00**
Beads (Northwood), bowl, green, 8½" **$70.00**
Beauty Bud (Dugan), vase, amethyst, regular size **$85.00**
Beetle (Argentina), ashtray, blue, one size, rare........**$350.00**
Bells & Beads (Dugan), bowl, blue, 7½"..................**$120.00**
Bells & Beads (Dugan), compote, amethyst **$75.00**
Bird of Paridise (Northwood), plate, advertising, amethyst...**$450.00**
Birds & Cherries (Fenton), bonbon, marigold **$45.00**

Birds & Cherries (Fenton), compote, green **$65.00**
Blossoms & Band (Imperial), bowl, marigold, 10" **$38.00**
Bull's-Eye & Leaves (Northwood), bowl, green, 8½" ..**$50.00**
Bumblebees, hatpin, amethyst...........................**$70.00**
Butterfly & Berry (Fenton), bowl, marigold, 10".........**$35.00**
Butterfly & Ferns (Fenton), tumbler, green...............**$85.00**
Cane (Imperial), pickle dish, marigold....................**$32.00**
Capitol (Westmoreland), mug, amethyst, sm **$70.00**
Cartwheel #411 (Heisey), compote, marigold............**$50.00**
Cattails, hatpin, amethyst.................................**$50.00**
Cherry (Millersburg), bowl, green, 4"......................**$90.00**
Cherry Blossoms, tumbler, blue...........................**$40.00**
Cherry Chain (Fenton), bowl, green, 10" **$90.00**
Chippendale Souvenir, creamer or sugar bowl, amethyst...**$80.00**
Circle Scroll (Dugan), bowl, marigold, 10".................**$65.00**
Cobblestones (Imperial), bowl, green, 5".................**$50.00**
Coin Spot (Dugan), compote, blue.........................**$65.00**
Concave Flute (Westmoreland), rose bowl, green.......**$65.00**
Cosmos & Cane, bowl, white, 5".............................**$45.00**
Cosmos VT (Fenton), bowl, blue, 10" **$75.00**
Crab Claw (Imperial), bowl, green, 5"......................**$40.00**
Crackle (Imperial), bowl, green, 9".........................**$30.00**
Crocus VT, tumbler, marigold...............................**$45.00**
Cut Arcs (Fenton), bowl, marigold, 10"....................**$40.00**
Daisy Dear (Dugan), bowl, white...........................**$70.00**
Diamond & Sunburst (Imperial), bowl, green, 8".........**$55.00**
Diamond Band (Crystal), sugar bowl (open), marigold ..**$45.00**
Diamond Flutes (US Glass), creamer, marigold..........**$45.00**
Diamond Point Columns (Imperial), compote, pastel colors **$40.00**
Double Scroll (Imperial), bowl, green......................**$55.00**
Double Stem Rose (Dugan), bowl, dome base, amethyst, 8½" **$90.00**
Drapery (Northwood), candy dish, blue **$110.00**
Dutch Mill, plate, marigold, 8"..............................**$50.00**
English Hob & Button (English), bowl, blue, 10" **$70.00**
Engraved Grapes (Fenton), vase, pastel colors, 8" **$65.00**
Estate (Westmoreland), creamer or sugar bowl, marigold...**$55.00**
Fanciful (Dugan), bowl, marigold, 8½" **$90.00**
Fashion (Imperial), creamer or sugar bowl, pastel colors...**$50.00**
Feathered Arrow (English), bowl, marigold, 8½".........**$50.00**
Fern (Fenton), compote, green **$85.00**
File (Imperial & English), creamer or spooner, marigold .**$100.00**
Fine Cut Flowers & VT (Fenton), goblet, green...........**$75.00**
Fine Cut Rings (English), tray, celery; marigold..........**$60.00**
Fine Rib (Northwood, Fenton & Dugan), bowl, green, 5"...**$40.00**
Fishscale & Beads (Dugan), plate, marigold, 7"..........**$50.00**
Flora (English), float bowl, blue **$90.00**
Floral & Grape (Dugan), tumbler, white...................**$50.00**
Floral Fan, vase, etched, marigold.........................**$57.00**
Floral Oval (Hig-Bee), plate, marigold, 7".................**$90.00**
Flowering Dill (Fenton), hat, green **$45.00**
Flowers & Spades (Dugan), bowl, peach opalescent, 10"...**$210.00**

Floral & Wheat (Dugan), compote, amethyst, $45.00

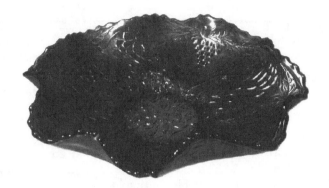

Lotus & Grape, bowl, flat, green, $50.00

Flute (Northwood), bowl, amethyst, 5" $30.00
Footed Drape (Westmoreland), vase, marigold $50.00
Four Flowers, bowl, blue, 6¼" $70.00
French Knots (Fenton), hat, blue....................................$45.00
Frosted Block (Imperial), rose bowl, marigold...........$50.00
Fruit Lustre, tumbler, marigold.......................................$40.00
Garden Path (Dugan), bowl, peach opalescent, 5" $60.00
Georgia Belle (Dugan), compote, peach opal, ftd $140.00
Golden Grapes (Dugan), bowl, pastel colors, 7".........$50.00
Golden Honeycomb (Imperial), compote, marigold ...$50.00
Gooseberry Spray, bowl, blue, 5"...............................$125.00
Grape (Imperial), bowl, green, 5"..................................$30.00
Grape (Imperial), cup, green $35.00
Grape (Northwood's Grape & Cable), creamer or spooner,
    green...$75.00
Grape & Gothic Arches (Northwood), tumbler, blue ..$50.00
Grape Heavy (Imperial), custard cup, marigold $35.00
Headdress, compote, blue...$60.00
Heavy Diamond (Imperial), vase, smoke.....................$85.00
Heisey Cartwheel, compote, pastel colors $85.00
Hex-Optic (Jeannette), tumbler, clear...........................$50.00
Hobnail Soda Gold (Imperial), spittoon, green, lg $75.00
Hobstar & Cut Triangles (English), plate, green $110.00
Hobstar Reversed (English), spooner, marigold $45.00
Holly (Fenton), goblet, blue..$60.00
Holly Panelled (Northwood), spooner, marigold $50.00
Honeycomb & Clover (Fenton), spooner, marigold $95.00
Hourglass, bud vase, marigold...$50.00
Illinois Daisy (English), bowl, marigold, 8".................$40.00
Intaglio Ovals (US Glass), bowl, aqua opalescent, 7" .$70.00
Interior Swirl, vase, footed, marigold, 9"......................$40.00
Inverted Coin Drop (Northwood-Fenton), bowl, green.$70.00
Inverted Strawberry, bowl, amethyst, 5".......................$55.00
Iris (Fenton), buttermilk goblet, green $65.00
Jacob's Ladder, perfume bottle, marigold......................$60.00
Kangaroo (Australian), bowl, amethyst, 5"...................$60.00
Kokomo (English), rose bowl, footed, blue...................$50.00
Lattice & Spears, vase, marigold, 10½" $50.00
Lattice Heart (English), compote, blue..........................$85.00
Lea & Vt (English), creamer, footed, amethyst.............$50.00
Leaf Rays (Dugan), nappy, white....................................$60.00
Lined Lattice (Dugan), vase, green, 14"......................$110.00
Little Beads, bowl, marigold, 8" $22.00
Little Flowers (Fenton), bowl, green, 5½" $70.00
Long Thumbprint (Dugan), vase, blue, 11"..................$40.00

Lustre & Clear (Imperial), tumbler, marigold $40.00
Lustre Flute (Northwood), cup, green............................$20.00
Maple Leaf (Dugan), sugar bowl, blue..........................$75.00
Mayflower, compote, pastel colors $60.00
Maypole, vase, amethyst, 6¼"..$55.00
Melon Rib (Imperial), candy jar, w/lid, marigold $30.00
Mirrored Lotus (Fenton), bonbon, green.....................$100.00
Moonprint (English), creamer, marigold $45.00
Mystic (Cambridge), vase, footed, marigold $165.00
Northern Star (Fenton), bowl, marigold, 7"..................$30.00
Number 270 (Westmoreland), compote, peach opales-
    cent $115.00
Octagon (Imperial), creamer or spooner, marigold.....$55.00
Open Rose (Imperial), fruit bowl, amethyst, 10" $65.00
Optic Flute (Imperial), compote, marigold $55.00
Orange Tree (Fenton), cup, blue.....................................$32.00
Orange Tree Orchard (Fenton), tumbler, green $55.00
Painted Castle, shade, marigold......................................$65.00
Painted Pansy, fan vase, marigold $50.00
Panelled Smocking, sugar bowl, marigold $50.00
Parlor Panels, vase, blue $200.00
Peacock, Fluffy (Fenton), tumbler, green.....................$60.00
Peacock & Urn (Fenton), goblet, blue...........................$85.00
Peacock at the Fountain (Northwood), tumbler,
    amethyst $50.00
Peacock Tail (Fenton), compote, green $60.00
Petals (Dugan), bowl, amethyst, 8¾".............................$55.00
Pillar & Flute (Imperial), celery vase, marigold $60.00
Plain Jane (Imperial), basket, marigold.........................$60.00
Plume Panels, vase, blue, 12"..$65.00
Pond Lily (Fenton), bonbon, blue $65.00
Premium (Imperial), underplate, red, 14" $150.00
Prism, shakers, marigold, pr..$60.00
Prism & Daisy Band (Imperial), creamer or sugar bowl,
    marigold..$35.00
Pulled Loop (Dugan), vase, blue $110.00
Question Marks (Dugan), compote, white.....................$70.00
Raindrops (Dugan), bowl, peach opalescent, 9" $100.00
Ranger (Mexican), nappy, marigold $90.00
Ribbed Holly (Fenton), goblet, amethyst $100.00
Rococo (Imperial), bowl, smoke, 5" $90.00
Rose Bouquet, creamer, marigold...................................$60.00
Rosetime, vase, marigold..$100.00
Sailboats (Fenton), bowl, blue, 6"..................................$70.00
Sawtooth Prisms, jelly jar, marigold..............................$60.00

Scottie, powder jar, w/lid, marigold **$35.00**

Serrated Ribs, shaker, marigold, each........................**$60.00**

Shell, shade, pastel colors **$75.00**

Ship & Stars, plate, marigold, 8" **$40.00**

Singing Birds (Northwood), creamer, green, each **$125.00**

Six Petals (Dugan), hat, amethyst **$60.00**

Small Blackberry (Northwood), compote, marigold....**$50.00**

Smooth Rays (Imperial), pitcher, marigold..................**$90.00**

Snow Fancy (McKee), creamer or sugar bowl, marigold..**$50.00**

Soda Gold (Imperial), tumbler, marigold **$40.00**

Southern Ivy, wine, marigold, 2 sizes........................**$45.00**

Springtime (Northwood), bowl, green, 5" **$75.00**

Star (English), bowl, marigold, 8" **$50.00**

Star & File (Imperial), pickle dish, marigold **$40.00**

Star Medallion (Imperial), tumbler, pastel colors........**$55.00**

Stippled Rambler Rose (Dugan), nut bowl, footed, blue...**$90.00**

Stippled Rays (Fenton), bonbon, green......................**$55.00**

Stippled Strawberry (Jenkins), creamer or sugar bowl, marigold...**$35.00**

Stork & Rushes (Dugan), hat, blue **$30.00**

Studs (Imperial), juice tumbler, marigold...................**$40.00**

Sunken Daisy (English), sugar bowl, marigold...........**$30.00**

Swirl (Imperial), candlestick, marigold, each..............**$35.00**

Swirl (Imperial), cake plate, clear..............................**$85.00**

Texas Headdress (Westmoreland), punch cup, marigold..**$45.00**

Thistle (Fenton), compote, blue..................................**$70.00**

Thumbprint & Spears, creamer, marigold **$50.00**

Tiger Lily (Imperial), pitcher, green, $300.00; tumbler, green, $40.00

Towers (English), hat vase, marigold **$65.00**

Treebark Vt, planter, marigold....................................**$60.00**

Triands (English), butter dish, marigold **$65.00**

Triplets (Dugan), hat, green..**$38.00**

Tulip & Cane (Imperial), goblet, marigold, 8-oz..........**$75.00**

Twins (Imperial), fruit bowl, w/base, marigold...........**$60.00**

Umbrella Prisms, hatpin, amethyst, sm......................**$45.00**

Vining Twigs (Dugan), bowl, amethyst, 7½"...............**$45.00**

Vintage (Fenton), compote, green...............................**$55.00**

Waffle Block (Imperial), creamer or sugar bowl, marigold..**$60.00**

Water Lily & Cattails (Fenton), tumbler, marigold **$95.00**

Whirling Star (Imperial), compote, green....................**$85.00**

Windflower (Dugan), nappy, handled, marigold.........**$85.00**

474 (Imperial), goblet, amethyst **$90.00**

Cat Collectibles

I have no doubt that every cat-lover in America is in some small way a 'cat' collector. More than any other genus, cats have enjoyed tremendous popularity over the years. They were revered in Ancient Egypt and the Orient, and from Biblical times up to the present day they have been modeled in bronze, marble, pottery, and porcelain. They have been immortalized in paintings and prints and used extensively in advertising.

There are several 'cat' books available on today's market; if you want to see great photos representing various aspects of 'cat' collecting, you'll enjoy *Collectible Cats, An Identification and Value Guide,* by Marbena Fyke.

Book, Kitty Cucumber, by James E Lillemore, Merrimack Publishing Corporation, die-cut cat w/color illus, 1983 ..**$7.50**

Book, Little Sally Mandy & the Shiny Penny, by Helen R Van Derveer, Henry Altemus Publishing, 1926.....**$15.00**

Candy dish, milk glass w/reclining cat finial, fluted edge, Westmoreland, 1950s, 5½" long............................**$90.00**

Christmas ornament, Little Drummer Cat, Danbury Mint..**$20.00**

Cigarette holder & ashtray, green cast-metal cat figure w/attached holder & ashtray, 1940s, 4¾" **$40.00**

Creamer & sugar bowl, white ceramic w/green & pink accents, Japan, 4½", $18.00

Doll, porcelain cat in matching overalls & hat w/plaid shirt, 1970s, 13"..**$25.00**

Figurine, Easy Chair, Danbury Mint Cute Cat Series, 3 cats reclining in chair, bisque, 1989, 5½"......................**$30.00**

Figurine, Golden Cat, bronze cat on black marble base, signed Dewitt, 1989, 8½" **$125.00**

Figurine, green Venetian glass cat w/arched back, Celleni, 1950s, 11½"...**$150.00**

Figurine, Patches, Danbury Mint Kitten Series, calico w/blue ball of yarn, stone bisque w/glass eyes, 1988, 9" long...**$75.00**

Figurine, red glass cat, Viking, 1960, 6½".....................**$45.00**

Figurine, Stalking, Danbury Mint Cats of Character Series, black cat in stalking position, bone china, 1987, 4½" long...**$15.00**

Figurine, Suns Up, Danbury Mint Cute Cat Series, black cat in front of door waiting to be let in, bisque, 1989, 6".**$30.00**

Figurine, white ceramic cat w/blue hand-painted flowers, marked Artistic Cats Hand-Painted, 1990, 6½".........**$7.50**

Fishbowl hanger, ceramic Siamese cat, 6½" long.........**$10.00**

Match holder, wood, black w/white & green facial features, handmade folk art, 1940s, 11¾".............................**$18.50**

Miniature, bone china Siamese cat in prowling position, 1½" long..**$8.50**

Miniature, cast-iron cat in prowling position, 1950s, 2" long..**$10.00**

Miniature, flocked kitten w/movable paws, 1950s, 1½".**$10.00**

Miniature, Franklin Mint Curio Cat, arched back, American Pewter..**$30.00**

Miniature, pewter cat in prowling position, ¾" long.....**$4.00**

Miniature, 2 bone-china kittens in wicker basket, new, 1½"..**$8.00**

Napkin rings, 4 white ceramic rings w/cat heads & embossed paws, rush holder, 1950s.....................**$20.00**

Necklace, sterling silver w/2" hollow cat.....................**$25.00**

Nodder, striped flocked kitten in prowling position, blue glass eyes, 1940s, 4½x6" long.............................**$22.00**

Note holder, Siamese cat on red ball of yarn w/clip, plaster of Paris, 1940s...**$15.00**

Painting, cat pawing at bouquet of roses, watercolor on paper, signed AV, 1972.......................................**$45.00**

Paperweight, black glass cat in sleeping position, Langham Glass House, England on paper label, 4¾" long..**$85.00**

Photograph, kitten in basket surrounded by flowers, black & white, 1910, 10¾x8¾".......................................**$35.00**

Pin, 22¢ US Postal stamp featuring cats.....................**$7.50**

Planter, Siamese kitten w/shoe, Royal Copley, 1940s, 9x8"...**$10.00**

Plate, Danbury Mint Diary Series, features Garfield, ...Today I Found Out Why God Created Leaves, 1991, 8½" dia..**$25.00**

Plate, Playmates, Velvet Paw Series, kittens playing in wagon full of hay, Bradford Exchange, 1991, 9½" dia..**$30.00**

Pot holder rack w/thermometer, die-cut wood teapot w/2 reclining cats, 1940s...**$15.00**

Print, Distrust, 2 kittens pawing at spider, signed L Singer, matted & framed, image: 13¼x16½".....................**$65.00**

Print, That's My Baby, winking mama cat beside kitten, by Walter Chandora, matted & framed, 24x20".........**$60.00**

Puzzle, 2 die-cut wood calico kittens, 1940, 5-pc, 7x5½".**$10.00**

Sachet jar, Avon, kitten on pillow decorated w/peach bows..**$4.50**

Salt & pepper shakers, ceramic, Siamese kittens w/heads tilted, pr..**$8.00**

Salt & pepper shakers, ceramic cats shaped like teapots, red & yellow bow ties, ear-type handles, 1950s, pr....**$12.50**

Salt & pepper shakers, pearlized ceramic cats w/heads tilted & eyes closed, pr..**$8.50**

Shelf sitter, stone-bisque kitten w/glass eyes & red neck ribbon, 1977, 6"...**$16.00**

Sponge holder, black & white reclining kitten w/open back for sponge, ceramic, 3" long..............................**$12.50**

Teapot, black & white kitten seated w/right paw up for spout, ceramic, 8"...**$12.50**

Toy, yellow & red cat w/ball, tin windup, celluloid head & tail, late 1940s, 5" long...**$38.00**

Wall tile, cat reaching in fishbowl above In a Cat's Eye All Things Belong To Cats, plaster, new, oval...........**$10.00**

Cat-Tail Dinnerware

Cat-Tail was a dinnerware pattern popular during the late twenties until sometime in the forties. So popular, in fact, that ovenware, glassware, tinware, even a kitchen table was made to coordinate with it. The dinnerware was made primarily by Universal Potteries of Cambridge, Ohio, though even a catalog from Hall China circa 1927 shows a 3-piece coffee service, and there may have been others. It was sold for years by Sears Roebuck and Company, and some items bear a mark with their name.

The pattern is unmistakable: a cluster of red cattails (usually six, sometimes one or two) with black stems on creamy white. Shapes certainly vary; Universal used a minimum of three of their standard mold designs, possibly more. If you're trying to decorate a forties vintage kitchen, no other design could afford you more to work with. To see many of the pieces that are available and to learn more about the line, read *The Collector's Encyclopedia of American Dinnerware* by Jo Cunningham.

Teapot, $30.00

Bowl, deep, 6"..**$10.00**
Bowl, salad; 9½" dia...**$32.00**
Bowl, soup; tab handle, 6"....................................**$10.00**
Bowl, vegetable; oval, 9".......................................**$12.00**
Bowls, refrigerator; set of 3, lids missing...............**$20.00**
Cookie jar, 9"..**$50.00**
Creamer, Laurella shape...**$16.00**
Cup & saucer...**$10.00**
Grease jar..**$15.00**
Jug, batter...**$72.00**
Jug, refrigerator; square shape w/angled handle........**$28.00**
Pitcher, 1-qt, 6"...**$22.00**

Plate, dessert or salad **$5.00**
Plate, dinner; Laurella shape **$12.00**
Plate, sherbet; 6" **$5.00**
Platter, oval...**$20.00**
Platter, tab handles, 11½" **$15.00**
Salad fork & spoon, set **$40.00**
Salt & pepper shakers, 3 different shapes, pr **$14.00**
Saucer, Old Holland shape, marked Wheelock **$5.00**
Shaker set, glass w/red lids on red metal rack, 4-pc set
    marked Salt, Pepper, Flour & Sugar.....................**$32.00**
Sugar bowl (open) **$8.00**
Tumbler, ceramic...**$40.00**
Tumbler, iced-tea; clear glass w/decal **$32.00**

Catalin Napkin Rings

Plastic (Catalin) napkin rings topped with heads of cartoon characters, animals, and birds are very collectible, especially examples in red and orange; blue is also good, and other colors can be found as well.

Rabbit, inlaid eye rod, $35.00. Elephant, no ball on head; inlaid eye rod, $25.00

Band, lathe-turned, amber, red or green, 1¾", each......**$8.00**
Camel, inlaid eye rod **$35.00**
Chicken, no inlaid eyes **$25.00**
Donald Duck, w/decal **$58.00**
Elephant, w/ball on head...............................**$35.00**
Mickey Mouse, w/decal..................................**$58.00**
Schnauzer dog...**$25.00**

Catalina Island

Located on the island of the same name some twenty-five miles off the Los Angeles coastline, this pottery operated for only ten years after it was founded in 1927. The island was owned by William Wrigley, Jr., (the chewing gum tycoon) who with his partner David Renton established the pottery with the purpose in mind of providing year-round employment for residents while at the same time manufacturing brick and tile to use in the island's development. Using the native red clay, they went on to produce garden ware, vases, decorative accessories, and eventually dinnerware. They made a line of hand-painted plates featuring island motifs such as birds, flying fish, and Spanish galleons that are today highly collectible. They developed some remarkable glazes using only oxides available on the island. Even though the red clay proved to be brittle and easily chipped, at Mr. Wriggley's insistence, they continued to use it until after he died in 1932. To make a better product, they began importing a tougher white-burning clay from the mainland; ironically the added expense was a major contributing factor to their downfall. In 1937 the company was sold to Gladding McBean.

Various types of marks were used over the years, but without enough consistency to indicate a production date. Marks are 'Catalina' or 'Catalina Island.' Paper labels were also used. Pieces marked 'Catalina Pottery' were produced by Gladding McBean.

If you'd like to learn more about this pottery, refer to *The Collector's Encyclopedia of California Pottery* by Jack Chipman.

Ashtray, goat figure, blue, souvenir, 4" **$225.00**
Bowl, berry; Catalina Island line.................................**$25.00**
Bowl, Indian design, rare...**$375.00**
Bowl, ruffled rim, ink stamp, 2½x9".............................**$60.00**
Bowl, vegetable; Catalina Island line, 8½" dia **$65.00**
Candle holder, Catalina Island line, low **$75.00**
Candleabrum, 3-tier...**$225.00**
Casserole, Rope Edge line...**$50.00**
Creamer, Rope Edge line...**$35.00**
Mug, Catalina Island line, 6"......................................**$45.00**
Pitcher, Catalina Island line, squat base **$85.00**
Plate, Catalina Island line, rolled rim, 12½"..................**$75.00**
Plate, chop; Rope Edge line, 13½"..............................**$60.00**
Plate, dinner; Catalina Island line, wide rim, 10½" **$25.00**
Plate, salad; Rope Edge line, 8½"...............................**$15.00**
Salt & pepper shakers, cactus, pr...............................**$60.00**
Salt & pepper shakers, tulip, pr **$70.00**
Sugar bowl, Rope Edge line.......................................**$45.00**
Teapot, Catalina Island line, traditional English style.**$250.00**
Teapot, Rope Edge line, 4-cup **$150.00**
Tray, turquoise, rolled edge, forged iron handle, 14½".**$125.00**
Vase, bud; 5"...**$65.00**
Vase, flowerpot shape, Monterey brown, old mark, 5½"..**$60.00**
Wall pocket, basketweave, 9" **$200.00**

Wall pocket, seashell form, turquoise, incised mark, $150.00

Catalogs

Right now, some of the most collectible catalogs are those from the the fifties, sixties, and seventies, especially those Christmas 'wish books.' They're full of the toys that are so sought after by today's collectors — battery-ops, Tonkas, and of course, GI Joes and Barbies. No matter what year the catalog was printed, its value will hinge on several factors: subject, illustrations and the amount of color used, collector demand, size, rarity, and condition. Generally, manufacturer's catalogs are more valuable than those put out by a jobber.

Ala Samaritaine, 1930s, French clothing accessories, housewares & gifts, EX...$25.00
Aldens, 1958, Spring/Summer, general merchandise, 554 pages, EX...$45.00
Allied Radio, 1938, electronics, 160 pages, EX............$40.00
Allied Radio, 1965, Christmas, electronics, 82 pages, EX..$20.00
Arnold Constable & Co, 1928, Spring, children's & infants' clothing, EX..$25.00
Arnold Constable & Co, 1930, Christmas, features several pages of perfumes, EX.................................$45.00
Avon, 1955, Christmas, 42 pages, EX............................$75.00
Bates & Zephyr for Warner's Dept Store, 1930s, features 21 samples for gingham uses, chart of colors & patterns, EX..$15.00
Bennett Bros, 1953, general merchandise, over 600 pages, EX..$70.00
Bennett Bros, 1971, jewelry, silver, toys & general merchandise, 762 pages, EX..................................$45.00
Chicago Mail Order, 1912, Fall/Winter, ladies', men's & children's fashions, 208 pages, EX.................$100.00
Corgi Toys, 1960, 20 pages, EX.....................................$25.00
David Cook, 1937, Sunday school & holiday supplies, 152 pages, EX..$60.00
Decorative Linens & Needlework, 1939, some color illustrations, 31 pages, EX..............................$18.00
Florida Fashions, 1961, Summer, 100 pages, EX.........$15.00
Fuller Brush, 1950, #69A, housewares, EX...................$20.00
Goldworthy's, 1950s, Christmas, 15 pages of toys, EX .$35.00
Hustler, 1933, general merchandise including dolls & toys, fully illustrated, 475 pages, EX.........................$75.00
JC Penney, 1965, Christmas, EX...................................$100.00
JC Penney, 1967, Fall/Winter, 1054 pages, VG $40.00
JC Penney, 1983, Spring/Summer, EX $10.00
John Wanamaker, 1939, Christmas, general plus toys, EX...$45.00
Johnson Smith Co, 1950s, novelties, toys, etc, 496 pages, EX $75.00
Lana La Bell, 1965, Summer, ladies' fashions, 80 pages .$15.00
Lane Bryant, 1938, for the fuller figure, some color illustrations, rare, EX.......................................$45.00
Lee Wards, 1964, Spring/Summer, crafts & supplies, 64 pages, EX...$18.00
Marshall Fields, 1968, Christmas, Fashion of the Hour, EX $25.00
Matchbox, 1979, 78 pages, EX $25.00

McClug's, 1961, giftware & novelty, 216 pages, EX.....$20.00
Miles Kimball, 1952, Christmas, general merchandise, 96 pages, EX...$25.00

Montgomery Ward, 1920s, Plumbing, 11x8½", VG+, $40.00

Montgomery Ward, 1924, February, 124 pages, EX.....$35.00
Montgomery Ward, 1950, wallpaper samples, 82 pages, EX...$75.00
Montgomery Ward, 1959, fishing & hunting, EX.........$35.00
Montgomery Ward, 1963, cameras, EX.........................$25.00
National Bella Hess, 1950s, general merchandise & fashions, 234 pages, w/order blanks, EX.............$18.00
Neiman Marcus, 1975, Christmas, EX..........................$30.00
Nelson Enterprises, 1956, magic tricks & supplies, 146 pages, EX..$40.00
Ovington's, 1938, Spring, gifts, includes order sheets, EX $35.00
Pittsburg Plate Glass Co, 1940, paints, varnishes & supplies, 112 pages, EX..$40.00
Prang Crayons, 1930s, die-cut, color illustrations, EX..$15.00
S&H Green Stamps, 1959, general merchandise, 80 pages, EX...$15.00
Scotty dog, inlaid eye rod $38.00
Sears, 1921, complete line of children's & babies' needs, color illustrations, EX......................................$35.00
Sears, 1922, hard cloth, illustrated shoe fashions, 11x8", EX...$55.00
Sears, 1932, features electrical power tools, 32 pages.$35.00
Sears, 1938, photo illustrations of model homes w/some interiors, rare, EX..$65.00
Sears, 1968, Spring/Summer, Men's Tailored To Order Clothes, includes swatches, 12 pages, EX.............$20.00
Top Value Stamps, 1960, general merchandise, 100 pages, EX...$15.00
Woolworths, 1956, Christmas, 64 pages, EX................$30.00
Wrights Bisa Fold Tape, 1924, features uses w/2 sample packages plus consumer's price list of other items, 23 pages, EX...$35.00

Ceramic Arts Studio

American-made figurines are very popular now, and these are certainly among the best. They have a distinctive look you'll soon learn to identify with confidence, even if you happen to pick up an unmarked piece. They were first designed in the forties and sold well until the company closed in 1955. (After that, the new owner took the molds to Japan and produced them over there for a short time.) The company's principal designer was Betty Harrington, who modeled the figures and knicknacks that so many have grown to love. In addition to the company's mark, 'Ceramic Arts Studios, Madison Wisconsin,' many of the character pieces she designed also carry their assigned names on the bottom.

The company also produced a line of metal items to accessorize the figurines; these were designed by Liberace's mother, Zona.

Though prices continue to climb, once in awhile there's an unmarked bargain to be found, but first you must familiarize yourself with your subject! BA Wellman has compiled *The Ceramic Arts Studio Price Guide* as well as an accompanying video tape that we're sure you'll enjoy if you'd like to learn more.

Bank, Mr Blankety Blank, 4½"	**$65.00**
Bell, Summer Belle, 5¼"	**$60.00**
Bowl, Bonita, 3¾"	**$35.00**

Candle holders, angels, 'See No Evil' & 'Hear No Evil,' 4¾", pr, $90.00

Candle holders, bedtime boy & girl, 4¾", pr	**$64.00**
Figurine, angel singing, 3½"	**$35.00**
Figurine, baby mermaid sitting, 3"	**$28.00**
Figurine, Bali-Gong, 5½"	**$48.00**
Figurine, Balky & Frisky (horses), 3¾", pr	**$65.00**
Figurine, birdbath (for St Francis), 4½"	**$49.00**
Figurine, Bruce & Beth, 6½", 5", pr	**$75.00**
Figurine, bunny, 1¾"	**$24.00**
Figurine, Burmese man, 5"	**$35.00**
Figurine, camel standing (single), 5½"	**$65.00**
Figurine, cellist man sitting, 6½"	**$95.00**
Figurine, colonial man & woman, 6¾", 6½", pr	**$65.00**

Figurine, Daisy (donkey), 4¾"	**$48.00**
Figurine, drum girl, 4¼"	**$45.00**
Figurine, flute girl, 4¾"	**$65.00**
Figurine, French-horn man sitting, 6½"	**$95.00**
Figurine, frog, 2"	**$16.00**
Figurine, Gremlin boy & girl, 4", 2½", pr	**$165.00**
Figurine, gypsy dancers, 6½", 7", pr	**$85.00**
Figurine, harmonica boy, 4"	**$45.00**
Figurine, Inkey (girl baby skunk), 2"	**$22.00**
Figurine, Jim & June, 4¾", 4", pr	**$38.00**
Figurine, lamb (nothing on neck), 3¾"	**$22.00**
Figurine, Little Miss Muffett, 4½"	**$38.00**
Figurine, Mary & lamb (w/bow), 6¼", 3¾", pr	**$38.00**
Figurine, Minnehaha, 6½"	**$95.00**
Figurine, Mrs Monk (monkey), 3½"	**$35.00**
Figurine, Mrs Skunky, 3"	**$32.00**
Figurine, Muff & Puff (kittens), 3", pr	**$55.00**

Figurine, Oriental minstrel couple, cream w/green trim, 6½" each, pr, $65.00

Figurine, Peter Rabbit, 3¾"	**$28.00**
Figurine, Petrov & Petrushka, 5¼", 5", pr	**$48.00**
Figurine, Pied Piper, 6¼"	**$65.00**
Figurine, Piper girl singing, 3"	**$38.00**
Figurine, pixie boy sitting, 2½"	**$22.00**
Figurine, pup sleeping, 2¼"	**$15.00**
Figurine, red-devil imp sitting	**$85.00**
Figurine, Rose standing, 4¾"	**$60.00**
Figurine, Sonny & Honey (spaniels), 5¾" each, pr	**$65.00**
Figurine, spaniel lying, 1¾"	**$38.00**
Figurine, Spring Sue, 5"	**$38.00**
Figurine, Squeaky (squirrel), 3¼"	**$20.00**
Figurine, St Francis w/2 birds, 9½"	**$65.00**
Figurine, sultan, 4½"	**$45.00**
Figurine, Swish & Swirl (fish), 2½", 3", pr	**$48.00**

Figurine, Toby (horse), 2¾" **$32.00**
Figurine, violin lady standing, 8½" **$95.00**
Figurine, zebra, 5" **$40.00**
Honey pot, w/bee knob................................**$95.00**
Jug, Aladdin, 2" **$32.00**
Jug, Buddha ewer, 3½" **$28.00**
Jug, Miss Forward, 4" **$42.00**
Lamp, Fire Man on base...............................**$295.00**
Lamp, Lutist on base...................................**$295.00**
Planter, bamboo, 2" **$25.00**
Planter, Barbie head, 7" **$75.00**
Planter, ivy pot, rectangle, 4x2½" **$18.00**
Planter, Svea head, 6" **$68.00**
Plaque, Comedy & Tragedy masks, 5¼", pr **$75.00**
Plaque, Grace & Greg, 9½", 9", pr **$85.00**
Plaque, water sprite (fish up), 4¼" **$60.00**
Plaque, Zor & Zorina, 9", pr.........................**$95.00**
Salt & pepper shakers, bear, mom & baby, black, 4¼", pr..**$110.00**
Salt & pepper shakers, bunnies, running, 4½", 3½", pr .**$48.00**
Salt & pepper shakers, calico cat & gingham dog, pr .**$45.00**
Salt & pepper shakers, chick in nest, 2¾", pr **$65.00**
Salt & pepper shakers, deer & fawn, stylized in recumbent pose, 4", 2", pr.........................**$68.00**
Salt & pepper shakers, Dem & Rep (donkey & elephant), pr **$135.00**
Salt & pepper shakers, Dokie on fall leaf, 3", pr **$65.00**
Salt & pepper shakers, donkeys, 3¼", 2⅞", pr **$55.00**
Salt & pepper shakers, Fifi & Fufu (poodles), 3", 2½", pr...**$95.00**
Salt & pepper shakers, fox & goose, animated, pr **$95.00**
Salt & pepper shakers, giraffes, 6½", 5½", pr.............**$145.00**
Salt & pepper shakers, kitten & cream pitcher, 2½", pr.**$75.00**
Salt & pepper shakers, leopards, pr **$195.00**
Salt & pepper shakers, Mr & Mrs Skunky, 3x3", pr **$72.00**

Salt & pepper shakers, penguin couple, black & white w/light blue & yellow accents, 3½", each, pr, $68.00

Salt & pepper shakers, Santa & evergreen, 2½", 2¼", pr .**$125.00**

Salt & pepper shakers, spaniel dogs, mom & pup, 2¼", 1¾", pr...**$65.00**
Salt & pepper shakers, stylized ram & ewe, pr...........**$48.00**
Salt & pepper shakers, Suzette, poodle on pillow, 2-pc set..**$85.00**
Salt & pepper shakers, Tembo & Tembino (elephants), 6½", 2½", pr.......................................**$145.00**
Salt & pepper shakers, Thai & Thai Thai, 4¾", 5", pr..**$85.00**
Salt & pepper shakers, zebras, 5" (same mold), pr ...**$150.00**
Shelf sitter, Bali boy & girl, 5½" each, pr **$125.00**
Shelf sitter, En Pos & En Repos, 4¾" each, pr **$75.00**
Shelf sitter, Fluffy (cat family #1), white, 4¾" **$45.00**
Shelf sitter, Jack & Jill, 4¾", 5", pr..........................**$48.00**
Shelf sitter, Little Jack Horner, 4½" **$45.00**
Shelf sitter, Pete & Polly (parrots), 7½", pr...............**$85.00**
Shelf sitter, Tuffy (cat family #2), black, 5¼"............**$65.00**
Shelf sitter, Tuffy (cat family #2), white, 5¼"...........**$45.00**
Shelf sitter, Willy, ball down (white), 4½"..................**$85.00**
Shelf sitters, Maurice & Michele, 7" each, pr..............**$68.00**
Vase, Chinese, square, 2" **$18.00**
Vase, duck motif, round, 2"......................................**$22.00**

Cereal Boxes

Yes, cereal boxes — your eyes aren't deceiving you. But think about it. Cereal boxes from even the sixties have to be extremely scarce. The ones that are bringing the big bucks today are those with a well-known character emblazoned across the front. Am I starting to make more sense to you? Good. Now, say the experts, is the time to look ahead into the future of your cereal box collection. They recommend going to your neighborhood supermarket to inspect the shelves in the cereal aisle today! Choose the ones with Batman, Quisp, Ninja Turtles, or some other nineties' phenomenon. Take them home and (unless you have mice) display them unopened, or empty them out and fold them up along the seam lines. If you want only the old boxes, you'll probably have to find an old long-abandoned grocery store or pay prices somewhere around those in our listings when one comes up for sale.

Store displays and advertising posters, in-box prizes or 'send-a-ways,' coupons with pictures of boxes, and shelf signs and cards are also part of this field of interest.

The prices given below are for mint-condition boxes, either still full or folded flat.

If you want to learn more about this field of collecting, we recommend *Toys of the Sixties* by Bill Bruegman.

C-3PO's, 13-oz..**$35.00**
Cap'n Crunch, Halloween Cereal, 1990......................**$12.50**
Cheerios, San Diego Chicken on front, 1982 ....**$65.00**
Frankenberry, General Mills, 1971 ....**$35.00**
GI Joe, Ralston Purina **$35.00**
Gremlins, Gizmo, 1985 ....**$40.00**
Honey-Nut Cheerios, Star Trek stickers, 1987.........**$25.00**
Kellogg's Corn Flakes, Dennis the Menace cereal bowl offer, 1962 ....**$55.00**

Kellogg's Corn Flakes, Hanna-Barbera cartoon character spoon offer, 1962......................................**$35.00**

Kellogg's Corn Flakes, Huckleberry Hound on front, 1961..**$50.00**

Kellogg's Corn Flakes, Miss America on front, 1973....**$25.00**

Kellogg's Corn Flakes, pictures Jerry Mathers & Tony Dow w/inset of them as the Beaver & Wally, $12.00

Kellogg's Corn Flakes, 85th Anniversary, 1990 ....**$8.50**

King Vitaman, Quaker Oats, 1972 ....**$40.00**

Lucky Charms, Christmas 1990......................................**$8.00**

Pebbles, mirror offer, 1970s **$65.00**

Rice Krispies, Back to the Future cards, 1990...............**$15.00**

Rice Krispies, bracelet offer on back, 1950s.................**$15.00**

Rice Krispies, Roger Rabbit on front, 1987...................**$45.00**

Rice Krispies, 60th Anniversary, 1991..........................**$10.00**

Rice Krispies, 75th Anniversary, 1981..........................**$10.00**

Shredded Wheat, Jane Fonda workout offer, 1988......**$10.00**

Smores Crunch, General Mills, 1988.............................**$12.50**

Sugar Pops, cowboys on front, 1970s...........................**$25.00**

Super Sugar Crisp, Post, Sugar Bear & the Archies, 1969 ....**$28.00**

Wheaties, Dallas Cowboys Championship, 1992.........**$10.00**

Wheaties, Michael Jordan on front, full-color photo inside, 1990 ....**$12.00**

Character and Promotional Drinking Glasses

In any household, especially those with children, I would venture to say, you should find a few of these glasses. Put out by fast-food restaurant chains or by a company promoting a product, they have for years been commonplace. But now, instead of glass, the giveaways are nearly always plastic. If a glass is offered at all, you'll usually have to pay 99¢ for it.

You can find glasses like these for small change at garage sales, and at those prices, pick up any that are still bright and unfaded. They will move well on your flea market table. Some are worth more than others. Among the common ones are Camp Snoopy, B.C. Ice Age, Garfield, McDonald's, Smurfs, and Coca-Cola. The better glasses are those with super heroes, characters from Star Trek and thirties movies such as 'Wizard of Oz,' sports personalities, and cartoon characters by Walter Lantz and Walt Disney. Some of these carry a copyright date, and that's all it is. It's not the date of manufacture.

Many collectors are having a good time looking for these glasses; if you want to learn more about them, we recommend *The Collector's Guide to Cartoon and Promotional Drinking Glasses* by John Hervey.

There are some terms used in the descriptions that my be confusing. 'Brockway' style refers to a thick, heavy glass that tapers in from top to bottom. 'Federal' style, on the other hand, is thinner, and the top and bottom diameters are the same.

Alvin & the Chipmunks, Simon, 1985, EX.....................**$3.00**

Aquaman, Pepsi, 1973 ....**$10.00**

Archie Bunker for President, green goblet, lg................**$7.00**

Archies, Betty & Veronica Give a Party, 1973 ....**$3.00**

Archies, Having a Jam Session, 1971 ....**$3.00**

Archies, Jughead Wins the Pie Eating Contest, green & red on clear..**$3.00**

Archies, Sabrina Calls the Play, 1973 ....**$3.00**

Baby Huey, Harvey Cartoons, 12-oz, NM.....................**$12.00**

Batgirl, Pepsi, 1973 ....**$15.00**

Batman or Superman, Super Heroes Series, 1978, Brockway, 16-oz **$7.00**

Boris & Natasha, PAT Ward/Pepsi, white letters, 16-oz..**$19.00**

Bullwinkle, w/fishing pole, Pizza Hut, CB lingo, 1977..**$65.00**

Cinderella, leaving at midnight, WDP, 1950s...............**$15.00**

Cleveland Browns, 1986 AFC Central Division Champions..**$5.00**

Creature of the Black Lagoon, Anchor Hocking, green & yellow wraparound scene, 1963, 7".......................**$63.00**

Davy Crockett, Crockett in Canoe..., 1950s, lg............**$12.50**

Davy Crockett, fighting bear or Indian, yellow on clear, 1950s...**$10.00**

Domino's Pizza, $1,000 in Savings, champagne size, 1985 ....**$10.00**

Dudley Do-Right, Pepsi, white on black letters, no action, 16-oz...**$10.00**

Elmer Fudd, Pepsi, 1973...**$5.00**

Endangered Species, Panda, Burger Chef **$4.00**

Flash, DC Comics Moon Series, 1976, 6¼" **$12.00**

Flintstones, Bedrock Pet Show, Fred on bottom, 1964..**$6.00**

Flintstones, Fred & His Pals at Work, Welch's, Barney on bottom..**$6.00**

Flintstones, Fred Builds a Doll Cave, Welch's, Wilma on bottom..**$6.00**

Flintstones, Fred's Sports Car, Welch's, Pebbles on bottom..**$6.00**

Flintstones, Pebbles Babysitter, Welch's, Fred on bottom..**$6.00**

Flintstones, 30th Anniversary, Hardee's, 1991, set of 4..**$12.00**

Foghorn Leghorn, Pepsi, 1973, $6.00

Gloria, from Little Lulu comic strip **$50.00**

Goonies, Data on Waterslide, Godfather's Pizza/Coca-Cola, 1985, 5⅝" **$5.00**

Granny, Silvester & Tweety; Warner Bros/Pepsi, action series, 1976, 6¼"..**$46.00**

Happy Birthday Mickey, 50 years **$13.00**

Happy Days, Ralph or Richie, Dr Pepper/Paramount, 1977, 6⅛" **$12.00**

Holly Hobbie, marked #1 of 4, Christmas 1977 ....**$5.00**

Hopalong Cassidy, black Hoppy & lasso on milk glass, EX...**$20.00**

Hot Stuff, Harvey Cartoons/Pepsi, shows action, 12-oz .**$10.00**

Howdy Doody, at circus, Welch's, Professer on bottom, 1950s, minimum value **$10.00**

Howdy Doody, Hip Hip Hooray, Welch's Lead the Parade Each Day, 1963, 4⅛" **$10.00**

Howdy Doody, on train, Welch's, Howdy on bottom, 1950s, minimum value **$10.00**

Howdy Doody, weight lifter, Welch's, Dilly Dally on bottom, 1950s, from $10 to...**$12.00**

Huckleberry Hound & Yogi Bear, Hanna-Barbera/Pepsi, 1977, 6¼" **$18.00**

Indianapolis 500, 1951...**$16.00**

Joker, Pepsi, 1973 ....**$20.00**

Jungle Book, Rama, 1977, 6¼"....................................**$30.00**

Li'l Abner, w/2 shmoos, 1949.......................................**$20.00**

Love Is, 1980s **$1.00**

Mickey's Christmas Carol, 1982, 6⅛", set of 3 ....**$15.00**

Mr Munch, Pizza Time Theatre **$21.00**

Mummy, Anchor Hocking, green, black & white wraparound scene in tomb, 1963, 7" **$55.00**

National Flag Foundation, Coca-Cola, 1976, set of 12 glasses w/pitcher..**$145.00**

Ohio Indians, Blue Jacket...**$6.00**

Olive Oyl, Popeye's Chicken, 1970s **$15.00**

Penguin, Pepsi, DC Comics Moon Series, 1976, 6¼", $17.00

Petunia Pig, Warner Bros/Pepsi, Federal shape, white letters, 1973, 16-oz **$5.00**

Popeye's 10th Anniversary, Olive Oyl, Popeye's Chicken/Pepsi, 1982, 5⅝" **$10.00**

Porky Pig & Daffy Duck, w/pot & ladle, Warner Bros/Pepsi, shows action, 1976, 6¼" **$29.00**

Psych Out, Sports Collector Series **$5.00**

Rescuers, Bernard, 1977, WDP/Pepsi, 6¼" **$10.00**

Rescuers, Penny or Brutus & Nero, WDP/Pepsi, 1977, 6¼" **$10.00**

Return of the Jedi, Coca-Cola/Burger King, 1983 ....**$5.00**

Ringling Bros, Felix & 99 Clowns, Federal, 1975, 6¼".**$12.00**

Robin, Pepsi, DC Comics Moon Series, 1976, 6¼", minimum value **$10.00**

Shazam, Pepsi, DC Comics Moon Series, no action, 1976, 6¼" **$10.00**

Slow Poke, Warner Bros/Pepsi, Brockway shape, black letters, 1973, 16-oz **$38.00**

Sonic, girl on skates, Pepsi..**$20.00**

Spock Lives, Star Trek III; Taco Bell/Paramount Pictures, 1984, 5⅝" **$5.00**

Star Wars Empire Strikes Back, Burger King, 1980, set of 4 ....**$25.00**

Sunday Funnies, Terry & the Pirates, 1976, 5⅝" **$12.00**

Super Girl, Pepsi, Super Heroes Series, 1976..............**$12.00**

Superman, Pepsi, DC Comics Moon Series, 1976, 6¼", $15.00

Superman the Movie, round bottom, 1978, 5⅝"............**$7.00**

Tasmanian Devil, Warner Bros/Pepsi, Brockway shape, black letters, 16-oz...**$12.00**

Tweety Bird, Warner Bros/Pepsi, Brockway shape, no action, 1973, 6¼"...**$5.00**

USA Moonshot Apollo, tall pedestal base, rocket shape, 1969, 6"...**$10.00**

Wile E Coyote, Warner Bros/Pepsi, Federal shape, black letters...**$7.00**

Winnie the Pooh, Winnie & friends, Sears.................**$4.00**

Wizard of Oz, 1950s..**$15.00**

Wonder Woman, Pepsi, Super Hero Series, 1976........**$12.00**

Woody Woodpecker, w/butterfly, Pepsi, 1970s...........**$15.00**

Yosemite Sam, Pepsi, 1973..**$5.00**

Ziggy, Smile, Pizza Hut, 1989..**$2.00**

Plastic Cups

Batman Returns, McDonald's, complete set.................**$12.00**

Black Bolt, 7-Eleven, 1975..**$6.00**

Cosmic Boy, 7-Eleven, 1973...**$5.00**

Doc Savage, 7-Eleven, 1973...**$5.00**

Dr Strange, 7-Eleven, 1977..**$8.00**

Dracula, 7-Eleven, 1977...**$8.00**

Galactus & the Fantastic Four, 7-Eleven, 1977..............**$8.00**

Inhumans, 7-Eleven, 1977..**$8.00**

Iron Fist, 7-Eleven, 1977...**$5.00**

Master of Kung Fu, 7-Eleven, 1977...................................**$5.00**

Medusa, 7-Eleven, 1975...**$6.00**

Odin, 7-Eleven, 1975...**$6.00**

Red Sonya, 7-Eleven, 1977...**$5.00**

Shazam, 7-Eleven, 1973...**$5.00**

Triton, 7-Eleven, 1975...**$6.00**

Valkyrie, 7-Eleven, 1973..**$5.00**

Mugs

Amazing Spiderman, multicolored illustration, 1977 .....**$4.00**

Batman and Robin, milk glass, 1966, minimum value, each, $15.00

Brutus, painted ceramic, MIB...**$5.00**

Darkseid, Burger King..**$5.00**

Dennis the Menace..**$15.00**

Dukes of Hazard, plastic w/photos, 1981 ....**$4.50**

Garfield, I Like Mornings Better...,...................................**$4.00**

Hopalong Cassidy, milk glass, Hoppy w/Topper on front, lunch verse on back, 1950s, 5"...........................**$50.00**

Howdy Doody, Bob Smith & Ovaltine w/Howdy on red plastic, chip on bottom...**$25.00**

Jiminy Cricket, milk glass...**$6.00**

Josie & the Pussycats, plastic, w/handle, 1971............**$12.00**

Lum & Abner, milk glass..**$65.00**

Minnie Mouse, milk glass, Pepsi, $9.00

Peanuts, Christmas 1976..**$20.00**

Peanuts, Snoopy, trainer type **$10.00**

Rainbow Brite, on parade, 1983...**$4.00**

Roy Rogers, F&F Mold & Die, plastic, 1950s...............**$35.00**

Smokey Bear, milk glass..**$10.00**

Super Scout, w/Batman & Superman, 1979 ....**$15.00**

Winnie the Pooh & Tigger, figural, Japan **$32.00**

Woody Woodpecker, molded figures all around, plastic, 1965...**$6.00**

Ziggy, milk glass, 1979 ....**$6.00**

Character Clocks and Watches

There is growing interest in the comic character watches and clocks produced from about 1930 into the fifties and beyond. They're in rather short supply simply because they were made for children to wear (and play with). They were cheaply made with pin-lever movements, not worth an expensive repair job, so many were simply thrown away. The original packaging that today may be worth more than the watch itself was usually ripped apart by an excited child and promptly relegated to the wastebasket.

Condition is very important in assessing value. Unless a watch is in like-new condition, it is not mint. Rust, fading, scratching, or wear of any kind will sharply lessen its value, and the same is true of the box itself. Good, excellent, and mint watches can be evaluated on a scale of one to five, with excellent being a three, good a one, and mint a five. In other words, a watch worth $25.00 in good condition would be worth five times that amount if it were mint ($125.00). Beware of dealers who substitute a generic watch box for the original. Remember that these too were designed to appeal to children as and (99% of the time) were printed with colorful graphics.

Some of these watches have been reproduced, so be on guard. When the description includes the term 'die-debossed (die-stamped) back,' make sure the watch you're trying to evaluate has this design. Otherwise, it's probably not authentic. For more information, we recommend *Comic Character Clocks and Watches* by Howard S. Brenner.

Clocks

Andy Panda, w/alarm, 1972, EX $500.00

Bugs Bunny, w/alarm, Warner Bros, 1970, 4½", EX, $65.00

Donald Duck, LCD desk type, Bradley, 1980, MIB $20.00
Elvis Presley, wall type, hips swing, MIB.....................$35.00
Ernie the Keebler Elf, EX...$40.00
Hamburger Helper's Helping Hand, NM......................$40.00
Land Before Time, battery-operated, M.......................$35.00
Max Headroom/Coke, wall wristwatch, Coca-Cola/Chrysalis Visual, battery-operated, 1987, 57", MIB $45.00
Mickey Mouse, General Electric Youth Electronics, w/alarm radio, 1960s, EX $50.00
Mickey Mouse, w/alarm, metal, Bradley, EX $50.00
Mickey Mouse, w/red plastic schoolhouse, w/alarm, electric..$35.00
Minnie Mouse, w/alarm & 2 bells, Bradley, 1970s, 3", MIB...$75.00
Monkees, w/alarm, multicolored group photo on face, EX $50.00
Peanuts, w/alarm, Allergic to Mornings, NM $40.00
Pinocchio, w/alarm, reproduction of 1930s model, Bayard/France, 1960s, 4½x5", MIB $250.00
Raggedy Ann & Andy, talking, w/alarm, ca 1975, EX .$25.00
Raid Bug, digital, NM..$30.00
R2-D2 & C-3PO, figures standing by round clock face on rectangular base w/decal, Bradley, 1980, MIB......$65.00
Star Trek Next Generation, w/alarm, 1991.................$38.00

Thundercats, talking, w/alarm, quartz, M....................$35.00

Pocket Watches

Bozo, plastic, tin & paper, toy only, Larry Harman/Japan, 1960s, MIP $6.00
Buck Rogers, lightning bolt arms, 1-eyed monster on back, Ingraham, VG...$210.00
Buck Rogers, multicolored dial w/rocket-ship 2nd hand, working, VG+..$260.00
Dan Dare, double animation, Ingersoll, 1953, VG.......$16.50
Hopalong Cassidy, US Time, VG $105.00
Lone Ranger, New Haven, w/fob, 1939, VG..............$120.00
Marilyn Monroe, portrait on black ground, 2", M........$60.00
Mickey Mouse, Bicentennial, Bradley, 1976, MIB........$50.00
Popeye, full-figure Popeye w/hands for time, Wimpy as second hand, New Haven/KFS, 1935, 2", EX...........$400.00
Roy Rogers, w/chain-attached coin, Ingraham, 1959, MIB...$175.00
Tom Mix, second hand features head of Longhorn steer, face has Tom on rearing horse, Ingersoll, 1934, rare, VG $350.00

Wristwatches

Howdy Doody, Ideal, original display box w/Howdy cutout, EX, $325.00

Alice in Wonderland, Alice in flower, leather band, Timex, 1958, VG $35.00
American Tale w/Fievel, Armitron, 1986, MIP $30.00
Barnabus Collins, Abbelare, M....................................$65.00
Bart Simpson, LCD 5-function, Don't Have a Cow Man!, plastic, Nelsonics, man's or woman's $12.00

Batman, Marx, working, original band, 1974, NM **$48.00**
Betty Boop, Bright Ideas, MIB **$35.00**
Black Cauldron, Frito-Lay premium, 1985, MIB..........**$45.00**
Captain America, Nasta, 1984......................................**$25.00**
Charlie Chaplin, Oldies Series, analog, Little Tramp on face, black plastic case & band, Bradley, 1985, M........**$20.00**
Cinderella, Cinderella in foreground, castle at 12 o'clock, replaced leather band, Timex, 1958, VG **$45.00**
Clara Peller, Armitron, 1984, NM **$12.50**
Dark Horse Comics, Image, M **$40.00**
Donald Duck, 1934, VG **$200.00**
Dr Doom, quartz, Masta, 1984, MOC.........................**$22.00**
Duck Tales, 1988, NMIB...**$12.50**
ET, Nelsonic, 1982, MIB **$25.00**
Ghostbusters, purple plastic case w/logo, Columbia Pictures/unknown maker, 1988, MIP........................**$10.00**
Goofy, Pedre, MIB..**$125.00**
Incredible Hulk, Hulk on yellow w/black numbers, round gold-tone case, black band w/yellow stitching, 1976, EX+ **$43.00**
Knight Rider, Larami, 1986, MOC **$17.50**
Mickey Mouse, lg chrome case, stainless back, red vinyl band, WDP/Timex, 1960s, VG **$65.00**
Minnie Mouse, standing Minnie faces left, flower between 12 & 1, denim & leather band, Bradley, 1975, M..**$60.00**
Miss Piggy, 7 jewels, 2nd hand, purple-striped band, plastic case, Picco/Hannson 1979, M **$40.00**
Pee Wee Herman, LCD, MIP **$35.00**
Pokey, quartz, 5-function, Prema/Lewco, Hong Kong, MIB **$15.00**
Red Ryder, commemorative issue, MIB.......................**$75.00**
Robocop, 1989, Fada, MOC, minimum value **$15.00**
Rocketeer, 5-function LCD, gold case, blue vinyl band, WDP/Hope, 1991, MOC **$35.00**
Roger Rabbit, silhouette style, Swiss quartz, gold case, black leather band, Disney/Amblin, 1987, MIB **$60.00**
Ronald McDonald, 1984, MOC.....................................**$12.50**
Roy Rogers w/Dale & Trigger, Bradley LCD, 1985, MOC **$30.00**
Simpsons Family Dancing, 5-function, LCD, plastic, Nelsonics, man's or woman's **$12.00**
Spuds McKenzie, original Budweiser band, EX..........**$40.00**

Character Collectibles

Any popular personality, whether factual or fictional, has been promoted through the retail market to some degree. Depending on the extent of their success, we may be deluged with this merchandise for weeks, months, even years. It's no wonder, then, that the secondary market abounds with these items or that there is such wide-spread collector demand for them today. There are rarities in any field, but for the beginning collector, many nice items are readily available at prices most can afford. Western heroes, TV and movie personalities, super heroes, comic book characters, and sports greats are the most sought after.

For more information, we recommend *Character Toys*

and Collectibles by David Longest and *Toys of the Sixties* by Bill Bruegman. *Schroeder's Collectible Toys, Antique to Modern,* published by Collector Books, contains about 4,000 lines of character collectibles with current market values.

See also Beatles Collectibles; Bubble Bath Containers; California Raisins; Character and Promotional Drinking Glasses; Character Watches; Disney Collectibles; Elvis Presley Memorabilia; Movie Stars; Paper Dolls; Peanuts Collectibles; Pez Candy Containers; Premiums; Puzzles; Rock 'n Roll Memorabilia; Shirley Temple; Star Trek Memorabilia; Star Wars Trilogy; Toys; TV and Movie Characters; Western Heroes; Pin-Back Buttons.

Batman & Robin, bookends, colorful figures on bases embossed w/names, 1960s, 7", pr, $70.00

Alfred E Neuman (MAD), bendee, Concepts Plus, 1988, 9", M **$8.00**
Alfred E Neuman (MAD), postcard, plastic, Plan Ahead, 1958, 6x4", M..**$25.00**
Alvin (Chipmunks), figural soap dispenser, 1978 ....**$8.00**
Andy Gump, doll, jointed wood, mk Sidney Smith, ca 1936, 6", EX+...**$120.00**
Archie, figure, tin, pull string & eyes sparkle, Ronson, 1920s, VG...**$225.00**
Baby Huey, squeeze toy, Harvey................................**$65.00**
Bamm Bamm (Flintstones), doll, Ideal, 1963, 15", NM.**$85.00**
Barney & Betty Rubble (Flintstones), ashtray, VG+.....**$75.00**
Barney Rubble (Flintstones), bank, Barney w/bowling ball, 1973, EX+ **$20.00**
Barney Rubble (Flintstones), doll, green hair, Knickerbocker, MIB...**$90.00**
Barney Rubble (Flintstones), figure, 1960, 10", EX......**$45.00**
Barney Rubble (Flintstones), finger puppet, 1972, MOC.**$12.00**
Batman, activity book, 128 pages, 1966, VG.................**$7.00**
Batman, bendee, Mego, 6", EX **$15.00**
Batman, buckle, unmarked, gold & silver on brass, 3", M **$15.00**
Batman, Colorforms, 1976, MIB **$31.00**
Batman, coloring book, unused, Whitman, 1967, 8x11", NM **$30.00**
Batman, die-cut cardboard hanger, Batman figure, DC Comics, 1977, 36", MIP **$15.00**

Batman, Electric Pinball Game, 1989, 20x12" box, NM .**$100.00**

Batman, fork, stainless steel, 1960s, 6¼", EX+ **$25.00**

Batman, mask, Wilton/DC Comics, 1977, 4½" **$2.00**

Batman, paint-by-number set, no paints, Hasbro, 1966, VG **$35.00**

Batman, pencil sharpener, DC Comics/Hong Kong, 1981, 5", M **$8.00**

Batman, pin, unmarked, foil, 2¼x1¼", M **$2.50**

Batman & Robin, coloring book, Whitman, 1966, M...**$30.00**

Batman & Robin, mask, cardboard, double-sided, 1966, NM **$15.00**

Batman & Robin, pins, figural metal, enamel w/brass finish, 1966, 3", each **$26.00**

Batman & Superman, cake pan set, 1977, VG in VG box..**$35.00**

Beany & Cecil, guitar, wind up to play, 1961, EX **$40.00**

Beany & Cecil, tea set, service for 4, 1950s, MOC......**$70.00**

Beany & Cecil, travel bag, vinyl, 1961, 8", VG+..........**$40.00**

Beetle Bailey, bendee, 1960s, 2½", EX **$7.00**

Betty Boop, bank, tin truck, 1988, MIB......................**$17.50**

Betty Boop, bendee, NJ Croce, 1988, 7½", M **$10.00**

Betty Boop, doll, jointed wood, USA, ca 1932, 4½", EX.**$120.00**

Blabber Mouse, doll, Knickerbocker, 1959, EX **$30.00**

Blondie & Dagwood, interchangeable blocks, w/box, King Features, 1950s, MIB........................**$175.00**

Bluto (Popeye), wall hanging, embossed tile, 4⅛x3", M **$35.00**

Boo-Boo (Huckleberry Hound), hand puppet, original sticker, German, 13", NM.................................**$15.00**

Bozo the Clown, doll, no voice box, Mattel, 1973, VG ..**$15.00**

Bozo the Clown, doll, vinyl head, Knickerbocker, EX ..**$45.00**

Bozo the Clown, membership card & patch, sew-on cloth, bottom of package is membership card, 1970s, MOC **$6.00**

Bozo the Clown, punch-out book, Circus, Whitman, 1966, 8x12", EX+ **$18.00**

Bozo the Clown, straws, figural, MOC, set of 2 ....**$5.00**

Buck Rogers, card & sticker set, Topps, 1979, NMOC .**$15.00**

Buck Rogers, Colorforms Adventure Set, 1979, MIB ...**$18.00**

Buck Rogers, magazine ad, 1952, M................................**$20.00**

Buck Rogers, paint book, Whitman, 1935, VG+........**$120.00**

Buck Rogers, school box, w/original contents, NM ..**$125.00**

Bugs Bunny, bank, figure w/cane & wearing straw hat, 1979, EX...**$28.00**

Bugs Bunny, Cartoon-O-Graph, NM in VG box **$15.00**

Bugs Bunny, doll, talking, Mattel, 1971, 24", EX+ **$50.00**

Bugs Bunny, drawing board, Cartoon-O-Graph, 1940s, MIB **$25.00**

Bugs Bunny, gumball machine, figural, 1972, MIB **$20.00**

Bugs Bunny, napkin, Happy Birthday, 24-count, 1972, MIP...**$5.00**

Bugs Bunny, photo frame, mirrored, 1976, EX...........**$25.00**

Bugs Bunny, squeeze toy, Dell, EX...............................**$45.00**

Bugs Bunny, tablecloth, paper, 1972, 52x96", MIP **$5.00**

Bullwinkle, Brain Twisters, Laramie, 1970s, MOC.......**$18.00**

Bullwinkle, Bumper Tops, Laramie, 1970s, MOC........**$20.00**

Bullwinkle, castanets, wood, Laramie/Ward, 1973, MOC..**$8.00**

Bullwinkle, periscope, Laramie, 1970s, MOC...............**$18.00**

Bullwinkle, plate, NM..**$14.00**

Bullwinkle, spelling & counting board, Laramie, 1969, NM in EX box **$8.00**

Cabbage Patch Kids, crayons, 1983, MOC.....................**$5.00**

Captain America, bike plate, lithographed tin, Marx, 1967, 2x4", M...**$24.00**

Captain America, finger puppet, Imperial, 1978, NM **$5.00**

Captain America, kite, Pressman, 1966, MIP...............**$35.00**

Casper the Friendly Ghost, coloring book, Ghostly Trio, 1968, EX...**$2.00**

Casper the Friendly Ghost, Glo-Whistle, 1987, M on NM card **$5.00**

Casper the Friendly Ghost, sleeping bag, various scenes w/comic-strip background, 1960s-70s, EX **$25.00**

Casper the Friendly Ghost, squeeze toy, Knickerbocker, EX..**$30.00**

Charlie McCarthy, decanter, Jim Beam, 1976, EX+ **$40.00**

Charlie McCarthy, pencil sharpener, Bakelite w/decal, M...**$75.00**

Charlie McCarthy, spoon, Dutchess silverplate, EX+ ...**$25.00**

Chilly Willy, coloring book, Whitman, 1957, NM **$32.00**

Cindy Bear, doll, Knickerbocker, 1959, EX..................**$20.00**

Clarabell (Howdy Doody), push-button puppet, painted wood w/plush hair, Kohner, 5¾", G+ **$60.00**

Daddy Warbucks, canvas bag, NY Newspaper item, 1930s, EX+ **$45.00**

Daffy Duck, color-in poster, 1969, M **$15.00**

Daffy Duck, coloring book, unused, Whitman, 1971, NM **$18.00**

Dennis the Menace, doll, 13", MIB **$30.00**

Dennis the Menace, napkins, 1954, NMIB **$20.00**

Dick Tracy, figure, Breathless Mahoney, PVC, 3", M **$3.00**

Dick Tracy, magnifying glass, Laramie, 1979, MOC.....**$19.00**

Dick Tracy, pop-up book, 1935, 8x9½", VG **$75.00**

Elmer Fudd, coloring book, Watkins, 1962, NM..........**$25.00**

Elvira, belt, MOC..**$20.00**

Felix the Cat, bendee, Applause, 1988, 6", M................**$6.00**

Felix the Cat, coloring book, 1950s, M.........................**$30.00**

Flash Gordon, coloring book, few pages colored, 1952, EX+ **$28.00**

Flash Gordon, coloring book, Flash Gordon & His Adventures in Space, #9545, M, $45.00

Flash Gordon, pencil case, yellow w/red graphics, Eagle Pencil Co/King Features Syndicate, 1951, 4½x8", NM...**$45.00**

Flash Gordon, serving tray, shows Flash fighting lizard, 1979, 17½x13", EX..............................**$12.00**

Fred Flintstone, ashtray, ceramic, Fred playing golf, early 1960s, M...**$45.00**

Fred Flintstone, doll, vinyl, 13", 1960, VG...................**$45.00**

Fred Flintstone, earring tree, painted metal figure of Fred in running pose, holes for pierced earrings, 1970s, 6", EX+...**$10.00**

Fred Flintstone, yo-yo, figural face, Justen, 1976, MOC..**$25.00**

Garfield, gum card set, 100 cards, complete, Skybox, 1992, NM..**$18.00**

Green Hornet, wallet w/photo, 1966, M **$95.00**

Gumby, air freshener, cardboard, oval, 1986, 4", M **$2.00**

Gumby, bendee, Applause, 1989, 5"..............................**$4.00**

Gumby, pin, cloisonne, M...**$5.00**

Gumby, playset, Granny's Porch, house front w/Granny sitting on porch, EX.......................................**$20.00**

Gumby, playset, Sheriff's Office, complete w/horse & carriage, EX..**$18.00**

Honey West, doll, Gilbert, 1965, MIB........................**$65.00**

Howdy Doody, fun book, 1951, EX **$25.00**

Howdy Doody, hand puppet, 1950s, EX......................**$30.00**

Howdy Doody, marionette, composition head, feet & hands, VG..**$75.00**

Howdy Doody, nodder, Howdy as cowboy, composition, Japan, 1950s, VG...**$35.00**

Howdy Doody, salt & pepper shakers, MIB **$75.00**

Howdy Doody, slippers, figural, 1980s, M **$15.00**

Howdy Doody & Clarabell, Christmas stencils, unused, M **$30.00**

Huckleberry Hound, bank, plastic, VG **$20.00**

Huckleberry Hound, camera set, MIB **$35.00**

Huckleberry Hound, cereal bowl, plastic, F&F, VG **$18.00**

Huckleberry Hound, doll, Knickerbocker, 1959, 18", EX **$60.00**

Huckleberry Hound, flasher cards, 3 colorful scenes on ea 1" square card that shows movement when tilted, M **$15.00**

Huckleberry Hound, flashlight, MIP **$20.00**

Huckleberry Hound, hand puppet, German, 1961, 13", NM **$20.00**

Inspector Gadget, serving tray, M..............................**$10.00**

Kukla & Ollie, puppet set, w/stage setup & backdrop, features 6 puppets, complete, Parker Brothers, 1962, EX+...**$50.00**

Lambchop, hand puppet, 1960s.................................**$22.00**

Li'l Abner, balloons, in illustrated bag, 1950s, NM.......**$35.00**

Little Audrey, coloring book, unused, 1960s, M **$20.00**

Little Audrey, doll, Gund, 1960s, EX..........................**$30.00**

Little Lulu, bag & jewelry, M on NM card **$10.00**

Little Lulu, coloring book, reprint of 1959 book, some coloring, Whitman, 1970s, EX..**$5.00**

Little Orphan Annie, coloring & activity book, over 80 pages, Artcraft, 1974, 8x11", NM..............................**$10.00**

Little Orphan Annie, motion lamp, 1982, MIB.............**$40.00**

Little Orphan Annie, shake-up mug, Beetleware, M ...**$65.00**

Magilla Gorilla, doll, plush, Ideal, 1964, 11", NM......**$120.00**

Magilla Gorilla, hand puppet, Ideal, 1960s, VG..........**$40.00**

Magilla Gorilla, push-button puppet, Kohner, EX.......**$30.00**

Mammy Yokum, doll, stuffed w/vinyl head, hands & feet, corn-cob pipe, 1950s, EX **$125.00**

Man From UNCLE, Secret Code Wheel Pin Ball Game, MGM, 1966, EX in EX box, $375.00

Max Headroom, doorknob hanger, Don't Lose Your Head..., w/color photo, 1987, NM **$5.00**

Mighty Mouse, bendee, Jesco, 4½" **$5.00**

Mighty Mouse, book, Scared Scarecrow, Treasure Books, 1954, EX..**$25.00**

Mighty Mouse, wallet, Laramie, 1978, MOC................**$10.00**

Miss Piggy, bank, porcelain figure in lavender dress, Sigma...**$30.00**

Miss Piggy, hand puppet, NM **$5.00**

Mother Goose, drinking straws, M in NM box.............**$18.00**

Mr Magoo, bank, yellow, 1960, lg, VG.......................**$45.00**

Mr Magoo, book, Mr Magoo's Christmas Carol, 1977, EX..**$8.00**

Mr Magoo, tattoos, set of 6 different packages, Fleer, EX..**$35.00**

Odie as Dunce (Garfield), doll, plush, w/original Dakin tag, #31-0096, EX..**$15.00**

Olive Oyl, squeeze toy, in long stride, Rempel, marked King Features, late 1940s, 8x6", EX...............................**$75.00**

Pac-Man, TV tray, 1983, VG **$9.00**

Pink Panther, cake pan, 1977......................................**$20.00**

Popeye, bubble gum machine, Hasbro, 1963, EX+ **$27.00**

Popeye, crayon set, tin, complete, 1950s, EX **$45.00**

Popeye, doll, cloth w/vinyl head, sealed, Uneeda, 1979, 16", MIB..**$125.00**

Popeye, figural toothbrush, MIB.................................**$45.00**

Popeye, float toy, rubber, 1950s, MIP.........................**$40.00**

Popeye, Freeze Sticks, 1950s, MIP **$50.00**

Popeye, hand puppet, Gund, NM.................................**$40.00**

Popeye, mechanical pencil (oversized), Eagle Pencil Co, 1930s, MIB, $175.00

Sarge (Beetle Baily), hand puppet, EX $30.00
Scooby Doo, pendant, 3" figure on chain, 1970s, MOC .$15.00
Sgt Snorkel (Beetle Bailey), nodder, VG $85.00
Smokey Bear, doll, talking, Ideal, 1969, VG+ $50.00
Smurfs, barrettes, set of 2, 1982, MIP...........................$3.00
Smurfs, toothbrush & cup set, MIB.............................$25.00
Smurfs, tote bag, w/Smurfette, MIP $5.00
Spiderman, bike plate, lithographed tin, Marx, 1967, 2x4",
    M...$24.00
Spiderman, gumball dispenser, plastic, lift arm to dispense
    gum, Superior Toy, ca 1984, MIP..........................$10.00
Superman, candle holder for birthday cake, figure w/build-
    ing, Wilton, any from set of 5, MIP.........................$5.00
Superman, necklace, 1990, MOC $5.00
Superman, pop-up book, Random House, 1979, EX.....$5.00
Superman, stencil sheet, 10x8", VG+ $30.00
Sylvester, figure w/sand pail, ceramic, 1977, EX $35.00
Tarzan, Colorforms, 1966, NM in EX box....................$38.00

Popeye, pencil sharpener, M $75.00
Popeye, pin, hard plastic, EX.......................................$25.00
Popeye, pop-up book, 1981, EX....................................$4.00

Popeye, Roly Poly Popeye Target Game, Knickerbocker #686, lithographed paper & plastic, 20" long, VG, $135.00

Tom & Jerry, dolls, stuffed cloth w/molded faces, w/original tag, Georgene, 1949, M, $850.00

Popeye, trinket box, ceramic, figural, 1980, M $45.00
Quick Draw McGraw, doll, gray, white & beige plush,
    Hanna-Barbera/Wonderland, Australia, 15" $50.00
Quick Draw McGraw, lap tray, w/friends, NM $40.00
Rageggy Ann & Andy, lamp, figures on seesaw, musical,
    EX $35.00
Raggedy Ann, cake pan, M $12.50
Raggedy Ann, night light, EX.......................................$40.00
Rainbow Brite, TV tray, 1983, VG $9.00
Ricochet Rabbit, coloring book, Whitman, 1965, NM..$25.00
Ricochet Rabbit, hand puppet, 1960s, EX $40.00
Road Runner, hand puppet, VG $10.00
Rocky & Bullwinkle, wallet, M......................................$20.00
Rocky Squirrel, coloring book, partially colored, 1960, EX..$15.00
Rootie Kazootie, hand puppet, VG+.............................$65.00

Tom & Jerry, tracing book, 1971, EX............................$12.00
Topo Gigio, doll, 1963, 12", VG...................................$45.00
Underdog, doll, plush, PMI Toys, 1991, M...................$35.00
Underdog, sleeping bag, EX $35.00
Wilma Flintstone, push-button puppet, NM.................$35.00
Wimpy, figural soap, EX...$25.00
Woodsy Owl, doll, cloth, Knickerbocker, 1972, MIB ..$20.00
Woody Woodpecker, bubble maker, plastic, figural, 1970s,
    VG $15.00
Woody Woodpecker, toothbrush, MOB......................$12.00
Yogi Bear, book, Bubble Gum Lions, 1974, EX.............$8.00
Yogi Bear, camera, figural, 1976, MOC $25.00
Yogi Bear, doll, original box, Knickerbocker, 1959, NM.$55.00
Yogi Bear, slippers, 1960s, NM $65.00
Yosemite Sam, transfer, Vogart, 1971, MIP $20.00

Chase Brass and Copper Company

In the thirties, this company began to produce quality products styled in the new 'modernist' style that had become so dominate on the European market. They turned to some of the country's leading designers, Russel Wright and Rockwell Kent among them, and developed a wonderful assortment of serving pieces, smoking accessories, and various other items for the home which they marketed at prices the public could afford. They favored chromium over more expensive materials such as silver, copper, brass, and nickel plate (though these continued to be used in limited amounts). Handles were made of Bakelite or some other type of plastic, and many pieces had glass inserts.

Many newlyweds received Chase products as wedding gifts, and now sadly they've reached the time in their lives where they're beginning to unload some of the nice things they've held on to for years. So it's not uncommon to find some very good examples on the market today. Many show little or no sign of use. Most are marked. If you don't find it right away, look on the screws and rivets. Sets may contain only one marked piece. Unmarked items should be carefully evaluated to see if they meet the high Chase standards of quality. It's best to compare them with pictures of verified pieces or similar items that are marked to be sure. Many items are shown in *The Chase Era,* and *Art Deco Chrome, Book 2, A Collector's Guide, Industrial Design in the Chase Era,* both by Richard J. Kilbride.

Ash receiver, #805, black enamel ball shape w/polished nickel trim, 2 rests on rim w/revolving ash disk, ball feet **$80.00**

Ashtray, #28009, Autumn Leaf, polished copper, elongated leaf shape w/step forming cigarette rest, 5" **$16.00**

Ashtrays, #17040, satin chromium finish w/flat fluted rims, set of 4, 4" dia **$60.00**

Bonbon dish, #28016, Delta, satin copper w/white lid, round w/ribbed rim, 3¼x7" dia **$100.00**

Bowl, #17007, polished chromium, beaded rim, sides taper to sm round foot, Von Nessen, 3x9½" dia **$125.00**

Box, #90002, Occasional, blue w/polished nickel trim, frosted glass liner, ball finial, 3⅛x4½" dia **$90.00**

Box, #90074, Iris, vertically ribbed round green base, satin-brass lid w/petal design **$45.00**

Candlestick, #NS-635, Diabolo, satin brass w/sm round cup flaring out to larger 4½" base, each.....................**$125.00**

Candlesticks, #24002, Sunday Supper, polished copper w/round ribbed cup flaring to round ribbed base, set of 4, 1¾" **$60.00**

Candy jar, #NS-316, polished chromium, round curving up to straight side, flat lid w/brass ball finial, 1¾x4" dia **$125.00**

Cigarette server, #853, ball shape, polished chromium top w/black knob, black base, 3⅝" dia........................**$60.00**

Coasters, #08002, polished chromium w/embossed jungle motif, set of 4 ....**$85.00**

Compote, #15002, Octagonal, satin copper finish, 3-step design around rim & pedestal base, 3⅛x6½" dia..**$85.00**

Condiment server, #26006, round divided glass dish w/hinged chromium lid, sides & round tray, 2 blue glass spoons, 2".....................**$50.00**

Creamer & sugar bowl on tray, #26008, Savoy, 2¼" w/5x11" long tray, $125.00

Dessert dish, #17059, Olympia, polished chromium, scrolled handle w/ivory composition ends, 1¼x3⅞" dia....**$70.00**

Flower bowl, #NS-319, round polished copper bowl w/straight side & flat bottom, Von Nessen **$130.00**

Flowerpot, #04003, satin copper, vertical ribbing w/flat bottom flaring at rim, 5⅜" **$65.00**

Flowerpot, #04013B, Cordova, copper, tapers to flat base, 4½" dia......................**$35.00**

Fruit basket, #27028, intertwined copper wire design tapers to round solid bottom w/ball feet, Lurell Gold, 12½" dia......................**$130.00**

Goblet, #90032, Bacchus, copper w/indented circles, flared pedestal foot, 6x3" dia.............................**$52.00**

Humidor, #533, round brass canister w/red enamel middle, lined w/Cuban cedar, lg round flat knob on lid, holds 25 cigars **$130.00**

Jam set, #90018, glass w/hobnail design, chromium dome lid w/ball finial, round chromium tray, 5½"..........**$70.00**

Marmalade & jam globes, #90068, 2 tilted chromium globes on single base w/loop handle, frosted glass dome lids, 4¾" **$70.00**

Mug, #90031, Chesire, polished chromium, rolled rim & curved bottom, half-circle handle, 18-oz, 4x3½" dia......................**$70.00**

Napkin clip, #90105, polished chromium in rectangular form w/embossed squirrel **$30.00**

Pitcher, #90001, Salem, polished copper w/white tin lining, Gerth & Gerth, 2-qt, 9¾" **$130.00**

Plate, #09007, Federal, polished chromium or satin copper, raised rim, eagles form handles, 9" dia **$125.00**

Serving dish, #17058, Olympia, polished chromium boat shape, scrolled handles wrapped around ivory composition ends, 13" **$115.00**

Serving set, #09020, Valentine, polished copper heart-shaped tray & scoop, 10½"................................**$150.00**

Table bell, #13002, Brittany, polished brass girl figure..**$85.00**

Tray, #09023, Target, white lustre round base w/ribbed chromium rim, scrolled handles, 12½" dia **$80.00**

Tray, #17027, Tiffin, rectangular polished copper w/black uplifted angled handles, Von Nessen, 18"..........**$200.00**

Tray, #17074, Four-in-Hand, polished chromium w/plastic ribbed handle, 4-tier, 2 middle trays swing out, 10¼" **$95.00**

Vase, #17039, chromium w/4 black enamel rings on cylinder w/straight bottom, Von Nessen, 9½x4" dia **$110.00**

Vase, #3008, Calyx, polished chromium, trumpet shape w/flat bottom, 6½" **$55.00**

Children's Books

There's lots of interest in children's books; some collectors limit themselves to specific authors or subject matter while others prefer to concentrate on the illustrators. Series books from the twenties and the thirties such as The Rover Boys, The Bobbsey Twins, and Nancy Drew have their own aficionados. They were produced by the Stratemeyer Syndicate and penned under the name Carolyn Keene. As with any book, first editions are the most valuable, and condition is extrememly important.

A Christmas Book, 1983, John Walsh Anglund, color illustrations by author, 1st printing, Random House, 44 pages, VG **$25.00**

A Daughter of the Land, 1949, Gene Stratton-Porter, EX.**$12.50**

A Dog for Joey, 1967, Nan Gilbert, 1st edition, Harper & Row, EX **$4.00**

A Doll Shop of Your Own, 1941, Edith F Ackley, Telka Ackley illustrator, 2nd printing, Lippincott, 114 pgs, VG.....**$18.00**

A Fun Filled Visit to Walt Disney World w/Mickey Mouse, 1972, Hallmark pop-up, VG **$20.00**

A Golden Pear, 1967, Betty McKay, Dewdrop Series, 1st edition, EX **$4.50**

A New Idea for Tony, 1947, Prescott, G **$3.00**

A Time To Dance, 1963, Regina Woody, Chilton Books, EX **$4.00**

Adventures of Plum Tucker, Jo Mendel, Whitman #2302, VG **$3.50**

Adventures of Reddy Fox, 1943, Thornton Burgess, McClelland & Stewart, VG **$6.50**

Adventures of the Wishing Chair, 1971, E Blyton, Dean & Son, EX **$3.50**

Alice in Wonderland-Through the Looking Glass, 1969, L Carroll, B Bryan illustrator, Classic Press, G **$3.50**

Animal Friends Story Book, 1942, Platt & Munk #100F, G **$6.50**

Anne of the Island, 1966, LM Montgomery, w/dust jacket, EX.................**$18.00**

Around & About Buttercup Farm, Whitman Tip Top Tales #2463, G.................**$2.00**

At the Foot of the Rainbow, Gene Stratton Porter, Triangle Books, VG **$7.50**

Baby's Day, Wonder Books #663, VG **$3.50**

Bambi, 1942, Grosset & Dunlap, VG **$22.00**

Barbie Goes to a Party, Wonder Book Easy Reader, VG...**$6.50**

Barbie's New York Summer, 1962, Random House, EX..**$25.00**

Barney & Betty, 1974, Charlton Press, G **$3.00**

Bevis, The Story of a Boy, 1932, R Jefferies, EH Shepherd illustrator, EX.................**$20.00**

Bible Stories, 1952, Mary A Jones, Manning de V Lee illustrator, Rand McNally, G.................**$4.50**

Biggles & the Golden Bird, 1978, Johns, Bjorn Karlstrum illustrator, 1st edition, Hodder & Stroughton, VG.**$15.00**

Biggles Delivers the Goods, 1952, Johns, Hampton Library series, 5th edition, EX **$8.50**

Billy & His Steam Roller, Wonder Books #557, EX........**$2.00**

Billy Whiskers at the Fair, Montgomery, DeBebian illustrator, SPC Popular Edition, VG **$16.00**

Birds in Our Garden, Mary Kerr, Truth in a Tale Series, VG.................**$5.00**

Bobbsey Twins at Meadow Brook, Laura Lee Hope, Grosset & Dunlap, EX **$6.50**

Bobbsey Twins on a Houseboat, Laura Lee Hope, Grosset & Dunlap, EX **$6.50**

Bonanza, 1961, George Anderson, photo cover, Purnel, EX.................**$24.00**

Brains Benton Case of the Waltzing Mouse, Whitman #1564, VG **$3.50**

Brother Dusty-Feet, 1961 reprint, R Sutcliff, Oxford Children's Library, VG **$3.00**

Brownies & Their Animal Friends, 1969, Verily Anderson, 1st edition, Brockhampton Press, EX.................**$6.50**

Buffalo Bill's Life Story, 1966, Wyeth illustrator, VG......**$8.00**

Bug's Bunny's Treasure Hunt, 1949, Golden Story Book #10, VG **$16.50**

Bullard of the Space Patrol, M Jameson, World Junior Library, VG **$10.00**

Bunny Brown & His Sister on Jack Frost Island, Laura Lee Hope, Grosset & Dunlap, VG.................**$3.50**

Candy Does It Again, 1960, Maud Reed, 1st edition, Epworth Press, VG **$4.50**

Captain Cook Explores the South Seas, Random House World Landmark Books, 3rd printing, VG.............**$3.00**

Charlotte's Webb, TH White, Harper & Row, G **$3.75**

Child's Garden of Verse, 1930, Robert Louis Stevenson, Clara M Burd illustrator, Saalfield, VG **$45.00**

Children's Stories of the Bible, 1972, Playmore Deluxe Edition, EX.................**$5.50**

Cinnabar the One O'Clock Fox, 1956, M Henry, W Dennis illustrator, Rand McNally, G.................**$4.00**

Circus of Adventure, 1966, E Blyton, Tresilian illustrator, Macmillan, VG.................**$15.00**

Cocky the Lazy Rooster, Barr, Ladybird Book Series #497, NM.................**$3.50**

Come to Tea w/Me, 1947, Montague Goodman, Pasternoster Press, G.................**$5.00**

Cowboy Eddie, 1970, Rand McNally Tip Top Elf Books #8645, VG.................**$2.00**

Cowboy Sam & the Fair, 1953, Chandler, Merryweather illustrator, Benefic Press, VG.................**$5.00**

Cricket & the Ants, Treasure Hour, London, VG **$2.00**

Curtain Call for Connie, 1954, Betty Baxter-Anderson, 2nd printing, VG.................**$7.50**

Daisy in the Field, Susan Warner, Nisbet Pilgrim Series, gilted, EX.................**$10.00**

Daniel Boone Wilderness Scout, Junior Deluxe Editions, VG.................**$3.50**

Dave Porter & His Classmates, Lothrop, Lee & Shepherd Special Edition, EX.................**$16.50**

Davy Crockett, Rourke, Harcourt-Brace, NM **$10.00**

Dennis the Menace Rides Again, Hank Ketcham, 1956, Pocket Books #1125, 2nd printing, VG..................**$5.00**

Disney's America on Parade, 1975, Abrams, EX..........**$16.50**

Doctor Dolittle's Circus, Hugh Lofting, Lippincott, VG..**$5.00**

Dr Suess, McElligot's Pool, 1975 reprint, Random House, G...**$4.50**

Dreamboats for Trudy, 1954, Mildred Lawrence, Harcourt-Brace, 1st edition, EX...**$3.00**

Drina Dances in Italy, 1974, Estoril, 1st in series, Collins Ballet Library, EX...**$3.50**

Elsie's Friends at Woodburn, Finlay, EX......................**$7.50**

Enter Uncle Henrik, 1958, Eleanor Tompkin, Sunshine Series #20, EX...**$4.50**

Famous Fairy Tales, 1947 reprint, Samuel Lowe Sturdibuilt Book, EX...**$4.00**

Favorite Psalms for Children, 1942, Marie Sterns illustrator, Grosset & Dunlap, VG **$3.50**

Felix on Television, Wonder Books #716, EX...............**$4.00**

Fireside Book of Folk Songs, 1947, Margaret B Boni, Alice & Martin Provensen illustrated, S&S 2nd printing, 323 pages, G..**$12.00**

Five Little Peppers & How They Grew, Sidney, Whitman #2123, G...**$3.50**

Flight of the Silver Ship, Hugh McAlister, Saalfield, VG ..**$3.00**

Flintstones Take a Vacation, 1972, Durabook, Authorized Edition, EX...**$4.50**

Flying the Coast Skyways, Goldsmith Sky Detective Series, EX..**$12.50**

Footprints of the Dragon, 1951, Oakes, Winston Land of the Free series, 2nd printing, VG......................................**$3.00**

Four Little Blossoms & Their Winter Fun, Hawley, Saalfield, VG...**$5.00**

Freddy the Detective, 1954, Walter R Brooks, Kurt Wiese illustrator, 13th printing, worn dust jacket, 264 pages, G **$18.00**

Friendly Monkey, 1972, PL Travers, 1st edition, VG....**$12.50**

Ginny Gordon & the Disappearing Candlestick, Whitman #2336, EX...**$3.50**

Go Ahead Boys & the Treasure Cave, 1931, Goldsmith, EX...**$6.50**

Grizzly Adams, Frontiers of America Series, Children's Press, VG..**$3.50**

Hagar the Horrible, 1977, Target Book #14634, VG **$3.00**

Hamish Meets Bumpy Mackenzie, 1970, Frances Bowen, Collins Seagull Library, G **$3.50**

Hansel & Gretel, 1969, 2nd printing, Golden Press, VG.**$16.00**

Happy Birthday Dear Beany, Lenora Weber, Crowell, 5th printing, EX..**$10.00**

Happy Days, Ready To Go Steady, 1974, photo cover, Tempo Books #5794, VG..**$2.50**

Happy Hollisters on a River Trip, West, Doubleday, VG..**$4.00**

Hardy Boys, Mystery of Cabin Island, 1958, Franklin Dixon, Grosset & Dunlap, EX..**$12.50**

Hardy Boys, Secret of the Lost Tunnel, 1959, Franklin Dixon, Grosset & Dunlap, VG **$12.00**

Hardy Boys, What Happened at Midnight, 1952, Franklin Dixon, Grosset & Dunlap, EX...............................**$16.50**

Hardy Boys & Nancy Drew Mysteries Annual, 1980, Grandreams, VG..**$25.00**

Hector Crosses the River w/George Washington, Wonder Books #769, VG **$5.00**

Heidi Grows Up, 1974, Tritten, G **$3.00**

Helen's Babies, John Habberton, Barse Hopkins, Pleasant Hour Series, $25.00

Here Comes Somebody, 1935, Ben Hur Lampman, Mahlon Blaine illustrator, artist signed, 1st edition, 275 pages, EX..**$30.00**

Hiawatha, 1956, Elf Book #565, VG...............................**$2.75**

Honey Bunch, Her First Trip to the Big Woods, Helen Thorndyke, 1st edition, Grosset & Dunlap, VG **$8.00**

Honey Bunch & Her First Little Garden, Helen Thorndyke, Grosset & Dunlap, VG......................................**$6.00**

Honk the Moose, 1966, Stong, Kurt Weise illustrator, Dodd Mead, VG..**$3.50**

House at Pooh Corner, 1960, AA Milne, McClelland & Stewart, VG...**$5.00**

In a Mirror, Mary Stolz, Harper & Row, EX..................**$4.25**

Invisible Island, 1963, D Marshall, Dutton, 7th printing, VG **$3.00**

Jack & Jill, 1974, Fleetway, VG.....................................**$4.50**

Jacob Two-Two Meets the Hooded Fang, 1975, M Richler, McClelland & Stewart, VG **$4.00**

Julie's Bicycle, 1959, E May Hooton, Pickering & Inglis, 1st edition, VG **$3.50**

Juneau the Sleigh Dog, Lathrop, Grosset & Dunlap Famous Dog Stories, G **$5.50**

Juniper Farm, 1944 reprint, Bazin, Macmillan, G..........**$2.00**

Kazan, The Wolf Dog, Curwood, Grosset & Dunlap Famous Dog Stories, EX **$8.00**

Ken Ward in the Jungle, Zane Grey, Grosset & Dunlap, VG **$6.00**

King Smurf, 1974, Dupuis, EX.......................................**$7.50**

Land of the Giants, Leinster, 1968, 1st printing, Pyramid #X-1846, VG **$3.00**

Lassie & the Secret of the Summer, Whitman #1500, G...**$3.50**

Last of the Great Picnics, 1965, Leslie McFarlane, EX..**$12.50**

Life Story of a Little Monkey, 1930, Ossendowsky, 1st edition, Dutton, VG......**$3.00**

Little Black Sambo, 1928, Saalfield #117, EX......**$70.00**

Little Mexican Donkey Boy, 1931, Madeline Brandeis, photographic illustrations, Grosset & Dunlap, EX **$6.50**

Little Peter Cottontail, Thorton Burgess, Wonder Books #641, G......**$3.75**

Little Tony of Italy, 1934, Madeline Brandeis, photographic illustrations, Grosset & Dunlap, VG......**$6.50**

Little Wooden Duck, CC Cole, 1st Canadian edition, Musson, G......**$2.00**

Littlest Snowman, 1976, Wonder Books #720, VG......**$2.00**

Lost Princess of Oz, Frank Baum, Neill illustrator, Reilly & Lee, w/dust jacket, VG......**$60.00**

Magic Slippers, 1917, Mabel F Blodgett, illustrated by author, 1st edition, 91 pages, G......**$30.00**

Meet the Bobbsey Twins, Wonder Books #623, EX....**$10.00**

Merry Ever After, 1976, Lasker, 1st edition, Viking Press, G......**$5.00**

Miss Boo Is Sixteen, 1941, Margaret L Runbeck, Houghton Miflin, EX......**$9.00**

Moby Dick, H Melville, Saalfield Everyman's Library #3018, NM......**$5.00**

Mod Squad, The Sock It to 'Em Murders, 1968, Pyramid, 1st printing, G......**$3.00**

Moon in the Cloud, 1968, Ray Harris, Faber & Faber, EX......**$2.50**

Moon in the Pocket, 1967, Jenkins, Oliver & Boyd, 1st edition, EX......**$3.50**

Moonbeam Finds a Moon Stone, Wasserman, Benefic Press, EX......**$4.00**

Mother Goose Nursery Rhymes, 1953, Eulalie, illustrated by author, 40 pages, G......**$30.00**

Mother Goose Rhymes, 1953, Platt & Munk #114, G.....**$6.50**

Mr Sims' Argosy, 1958, Eleanor R Wilcox, 1st edition, Dodd Mead, VG......**$6.50**

Mrs Piggle-Wiggle, Betty MacDonald, Bennett illustrator, Lippincott, EX......**$4.00**

My Book of Elves & Fairies, 1960, 3 stories by Jane Shaw, VG......**$7.50**

Mystery at Mill House, 1952, David Morris, Sunshine Series #18, VG......**$4.50**

Mystery of the Golden Horn, 1962, P Whitney, Westminster, G......**$2.50**

Mystery of the Iron Box, 1963, Bruce Campbell, Grosset & Dunlap, EX......**$15.00**

Mystery of the Pilgrim Trading Post, 1964, Molloy, Hasting House Young America Book Club, VG......**$2.50**

Nancy Drew, Mystery of the Moss Covered Mansion, Carolyn Keene, w/dust jacket, EX......**$10.00**

Nancy Drew, Secret of the Wooden Lady, Carolyn Lee, w/dust jacket, EX+......**$12.00**

Night Before Christmas, 1975, Clement C Moore, Tasha Tudor illustrator, 1st printing, McNally, VG......**$30.00**

Noddy & Tessie Bear, E Blyton, Saalfield #612, 1st American edition, EX......**$22.00**

Noddy's Busy Day, 1974, E Blyton, Purnell, hand dated 1975, EX......**$5.00**

Onion John, 1959, Krumgold, 1st printing, VG......**$2.50**

Paddington at Work, 1966, M Bond, 1st edition, Collins, EX......**$10.00**

Paramount Newsreel Men W/Admiral Byrd in Little America, Whitman, 1934, EX, $50.00

Paddy-Paws, 1937, Coolidge, Carr illustrator, Rand McNally, EX......**$6.50**

Partridge Family, Fat & Skinny Murder Mystery, 1972, Curtis Books #6180, VG......**$5.00**

Patty Duke & Mystery Mansion, Whitman #1514, VG ...**$5.00**

Patty Lou & the White Gold Ranch, 1943, Miller, 2nd edition, EX......**$6.50**

Penny Says Good-bye, 1961, A Stephen Tring, Penny Series #8 , Oxford University Press, 1st edition, EX......**$16.00**

Peter Pan & Wendy, 1953, JM Barrie, Edmund Blampied illustrator, worn dust jacket, 216 pages, VG......**$50.00**

Picture Story Book, Thornton Burgess, Nino Carbe illustrator, Garden City Books, EX......**$16.50**

Pippi Goes on Board, 1967, A Lindgren, Viking Press, 9th printing, VG......**$3.00**

Polly & Eleanor, Lillian Roy, Whitman #2319, VG **$3.50**

Polly's Christmas Present, 1978, Wonder Books #819, EX......**$1.50**

Popeye Annual, 1987, Grandreams, EX......**$4.50**

Princess of the Chalet School, 1958, Brent-Dyer, EX...**$15.00**

Raggedy Ann & Marcella's First Day of School, Wonder Books #588, G......**$2.00**

Real Book About Spies, 1953, Epstein & Williams, Garden City, VG......**$3.50**

Rebecca of Sunnybrook Farm, Kate D Wiggin, Whitman Classics #1634, EX......**$5.50**

Red Ryder & the Secret of Lucky Mine, Whitman #2334, Authorized Edition, EX $22.00

River of Adventure, 1955, E Blyton, Tresilian illustrator, Macmillan, 1st edition, VG $35.00

Road to Oz, Frank Baum, Neill illustrator, EX $30.00

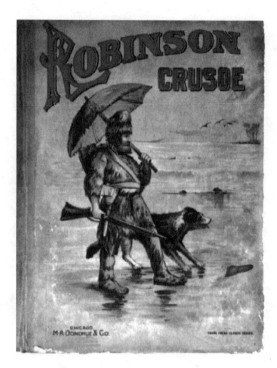

Robinson Crusoe, MA Donahue, Young Folks Classic, VG, $20.00

Sandra Takes Command, 1960, Constance M White, VG .$4.00

Scarecrow of Oz, Frank Baum, Rand McNally, G $6.00

Scouting on Mystery Trail, 1950, Smith, Macmillan, 8th printing, VG......................$2.50

Secret of the Clan, A Story for Girls, 1912, Alice Brown, Sarah Smith illustrator, 1st edition, Macmillan, 314 pages, VG $25.00

Secret of the Lost Planet, 1961 reprint, Angus MacVicar, Burke Falcon Library, VG $6.50

Secret of the Musical Tree, Judy Bolton, Grosset & Dunlap, VG $4.00

Secret of the Rocking Stones, 1967, Dorothy Joy, 1st edition, Epworth Press, Crescent Library Series #3, EX........$5.00

Secret Seven & the Bonfire Adventure, E Blyton, Children's Press, revised American edition, EX $10.00

Sergeant Silk the Prairie Scout, 1931, Saalfield Boys Adventure Series #830, EX $12.50

Shaggy Man of Oz, 1949, Jack Snow, Frank Kramer illustrator, Reilly & Lee, 1st edition, NM $12.00

Silk & Satin Lane, 1948, Esther Wood, Kurt Weise illustrator, Longmans Green, EX $4.50

Silver Chief to the Rescue, 1937, O'Brien, Kurt Weise illustrator, Winston, G......................$6.50

Simba of the White Mane, Arundel, 8th printing, Whittlesey House, VG $4.00

Snoopy & the Red Baron, Schulz, 1967, 6th printing, Holt Reinhart, VG......................$5.00

Space Winners, Gordon R Dickson, Children's Book Club, VG $5.00

Spike of Swift River, O'Brien, Grosset & Dunlap Famous Dog Stories, EX $3.50

Spirit of the Border, Zane Grey, Saalfield #3273, VG $5.00

Squiffy the Skunk, 1954, Elf Real Life Animal Book #476, G......................$2.00

Squinty the Comical Pig, R Barnum, H Tooker illustrator, Barse Kneetime Animal Stories, G $4.00

Stand by for Adventure, 1967, Whitman Classics #1632, VG......................$3.50

Starsky & Hutch, 1978, 1st edition, Ballantine #27340, EX $5.00

Stories from Dickens, Thorndike, Crowe illustrator, Tuck Book, VG $3.00

Stowaways in the Abbey, 1959, Elsie J Oxenham, Collins Abbey School Series, VG $7.50

Susan's Helping Hand, 1968, Jane Shaw, Children's Press, EX......................$3.50

Talking Drums, 1946 reprint, Fleming, Doubleday Young Moderns, VG $3.50

Tarzan & the Jewel of Rah, 1977, Superscope Story Teller, EX......................$4.00

Tarzan the Terrible, E Blyton, St John illustrator, 1st Canadian edition, VG......................$25.00

Teddy & the Mystery Dog, HR Garis, Books Inc, EX $4.50

The Automobile Girls at Palm Beach, Laura Dent Crane, 1 of 5 adventure stories for girls relating to autos, 1910-16, EX......................$80.00

The Motor Boys Overland, Clarence Young, 1 of 15 in Motor Boys Series, embossed cover, illustrated 1906-20, EX, ...$130.00

The Yearling, 1938, Marjorie Kinnan Rawlings, Shenton illustrator, Charles Scribner's Sons, 1st edition, VG $28.00

They Found an Elephant, 1950, Vera Barclay, 1st edition, VG $5.00

Three Bad Puppies & Other Stories, Blackie Easy To Read Storybook #4, EX......................$3.00

Three Little Puppies, 1954, Elf Real Life Animal Book #447, G......................$2.50

Tim & Tip, James Otis, Harper's Young People series, VG $6.00

Told by the Sandman, Abbie Walker, RC Chase illustrator, Harpers, EX $7.25

Tom Swift & His Outpost in Space, Victor Appleton, 1st edition, EX......................$14.50

Tommy & Grizel, 1900, JM Barrie, Bernard Partridge illustrator, 1st edition, 509 pages, VG......................$30.00

Top of the Mountain, 1953, Knight, Doubleday, VG.....$2.50

Tornado Boy, Hinkle, Grosset & Dunlap, VG...............$6.00

Treasure Island, hand dated 1955, Stevenson, Goldsmith, VG $3.50

Trixie Beldon & the Mysterious Visitor, Whitman #1560, EX $5.00

Tugboat, 1937 reprint, Henry Lent, Winslow illustrator, Macmillan, VG......................$2.50

Tune in the Tree, 1950, Maud Hart-Lovelace, Eloise Wilkin illustrator, Crowell, NM...**$35.00**
Two Little Gardeners, Mrs Herbert Strang editor, Little Giant Books, EX...**$3.50**
Uncle Arthur's Bedtime Stories, Volume One, 1964 display copy, Pacific Press, EX...**$6.00**
Uncle Wiggly & the Littletails, 1942, Howard R Garris, Elmer Rache illustrator, 186 pages, VG **$25.00**
Uncle Wiggly & the Sleds, 1939, Platt & Monk #3600F, VG...**$22.50**
Uncle Wiggly's Fortune, 1942, Garis, Rache illustrator, Platt & Munk, VG **$15.00**
Uncle Wiggly's Fortune, 1942, Howard R Garis, Elmer Rache illustrator, 186 pages, EX...**$30.00**
Valley of the Vanishing Birds, 1963, Braithwaite, Little Brown Secret Circle Series #8, EX...........................**$6.50**
Volksy the Little Yellow Car, Elf Book #8695, NM **$4.00**
Walt Disney's Mary Poppins, Whitman #2317, Authorized Edition, EX...**$6.00**
Walt Disney's Vanishing Prairie, 1955, Simon & Schuster, G **$15.00**
Waltons, The Accident, Whitman #1510, VG **$5.50**
We Fell in Love w/the Circus, 1949, Fawcett, 1st edition, EX **$12.50**
Welcome Back Kotter, The Sweat Hog Sit-In, 1977, Tempo #12944, VG **$4.00**
What Happened to Kitty, Theodora Wilson, Blackie's Imperial Library, VG **$5.00**
What Katy Did, 1972, Coolidge, Abbey Classics, VG.....**$3.00**
When Sara Smiled, Kathleen Robinson, Whitman #2309, G.**$3.50**
Why the Bear Has a Short Tail, Wonder Books #508, NM .**$5.00**
Windy Island, Adventure in New Zealand, 1946, Harper, Doubleday Young Moderns, VG...........................**$3.50**
Winnie the Pooh, 1977 reprint, AA Milne, Shepard illustrator, Methuen, G **$5.00**
Wonderful World of Tom & Jerry, 1974, World Dist, EX..**$14.00**
Zippy the Chimp, 1955, Elf Real Life Animal Book #487, VG **$2.50**
100 Animal Stories, 1941, V Cunningham, Dorothea Snow illustrator, Whitman, VG **$6.50**
365 Bedtime Bible Stories, Whitman #5050, Robson illustrator, G **$6.00**

Children's Dinnerware

Little girls have always enjoyed playing house, and glassware and chinaware manufacturers alike have seen to it that they're not lacking in the dinnerware department. Glassware 'just like Mother's' was pressed from late in the 19th century until well into the 20th, and much of it has somehow managed to survive to the present. China was made in England, Japan, and the United States in patterns that ranged from nursery-rhyme themes to traditional designs such as Blue Willow and Tea Leaf. All are very collectible today.

For further study, we recommend *The Collector's Encyclopedia of Children's Dishes* by Margaret and Kenn Whitmyer and *Children's Glass Dishes, China, and Furniture, Vols. 1 and 2,* by Doris Anderson Lechler.

See also Akro Agate.

China

Bowl, Blue Banded Ironstone, 8-sided, 4" **$20.00**
Bowl, Blue Willow, 2" **$35.00**
Bowl, Calico, brown on white, oval, 4"...........................**$25.00**
Bowl, soup; Flow Blue Dogwood, Minton, 4⅛" **$35.00**
Bowl, soup; Gaudy Floral, 4" **$20.00**
Bowl, soup; Kite Fliers, blue on white, 3½"................**$55.00**
Casserole, Blue Acorn, impressed RSR on back, 5" **$30.00**
Casserole, Blue Willow, vertical ribs, oval, 2" **$45.00**
Casserole, Twin Flower, Flow Blue, 4"...................**$90.00**
Compote, Blue Banded Ironstone, 3¼"...................**$35.00**
Creamer, Barnyard Animals, white w/gold trim, 3⅜" ..**$10.00**
Creamer, By the Mill, brown on white **$25.00**
Creamer, Father Christmas & the Children, various scenes on white w/gold trim, Germany, 3½" **$35.00**
Creamer, Lady Standing by Urn, purple on white w/stippled border **$45.00**
Creamer, Merry Christmas, pink & white lustre w/gold highlights, Germany, 2⅞"...**$25.00**
Creamer, Roman Chariots, blue on white, 2"...............**$35.00**
Creamer, Saint Nicholas, pink & white lustre, Germany, 3" **$30.00**
Cup, Punch & Judy, blue on white, 1⅞" **$30.00**
Gravy boat, Blue Marble, 1½" **$50.00**
Gravy boat, Fishers, green fishing scene on white, marked CE&M (Staffordshire Pottery of Cork, Edge & Malkin), 3" **$25.00**
Plate, Amherst Japan, blue & orange Oriental design on white, 4½"...**$18.00**
Plate, Angel w/Shining Star, lustreware w/gold trim...**$16.00**
Plate, Father Christmas & the Children, various scenes on white w/gold trim, Germany, 5" **$12.00**
Plate, Fishers, green fishing scene on white, marked CE&M (Staffordshire Pottery of Cork, Edge & Malkin), 4" .**$7.50**
Plate, Forget-Me-Not, blue on white, 3⅛" **$25.00**
Plate, Gaudy Floral, 4" **$10.00**
Plate, Playful Cats, pink & white lustreware, 5¼"........**$14.00**
Plate, Punch & Judy, blue on white, 5¾" **$25.00**
Platter, Bluebird & Floral, ruffled edge, 5" **$30.00**
Platter, Flow Blue Dogwood, canted corners, Minton, 6¾" **$48.00**
Platter, Gaudy Ironstone, blue & orange on white, 6" .**$40.00**
Platter, Humphrey's Clock, blue on white, Ridgway, 7" ...**$35.00**
Platter, Twin Flower, Flow Blue, 4½" **$70.00**
Saucer, Punch & Judy, blue on white, 4¼" **$12.00**
Saucer, Water Hen, blue on white, 4⅜"...........................**$5.00**
Server, Forget-Me-Not, blue on white, 2¾" **$40.00**
Sugar bowl, Amherst Japan, blue & orange Oriental design on white, 2½" **$50.00**
Sugar bowl, Lady Standing by Urn, purple on white w/stippled border, 3½" **$50.00**
Sugar bowl, Merry Christmas, pink & white lustre w/gold highlights, Germany, 2⅞" **$30.00**

Sugar bowl (open), Pink Open Rose, marked Made in England, 1¾"...**$10.00**

Teapot, Humphrey's Clock, blue on white, Ridgway, 4½", $65.00

Teapot, Mary Had a Little Lamb, Brentleigh Ware Staffordshire, 3½"...**$35.00**

Tray, Bluebird & Floral, ruffled edge, 2 closed handles, 4¾" **$40.00**

Tray, Pink Open Rose, marked Made in England, 4¼" .**$30.00**

Tureen, Blue Acorn, impressed RSR on back, 4"........**$25.00**

Glassware

Banana stand, Daisy & Star, crystal **$45.00**

Bowl, berry; Inverted Strawberry, crystal, Cambridge Glass Co, ½"..**$20.00**

Bowl, berry; Oval Star #300, crystal, Indiana Glass Co, 1"..**$8.50**

Bowl, berry; Wheat Sheaf #500, crystal, Cambridge Glass Co, 1" **$8.00**

Bowl, Circus Scenes, Hazel Atlas Co, 5".....................**$10.00**

Bowl, Kittens, marigold, ruffled, Fenton Glass Co, 4½"..**$110.00**

Bowl, master berry; Wheat Sheaf #500, crystal, 2¼"....**$40.00**

Butter dish, Clear & Diamond Panel, crystal, 4" **$62.00**

Butter dish, Colonial #2630, cobalt, Cambridge Glass Co, 2½" **$55.00**

Butter dish, Fernland #2635, emerald green, Cambridge Glass Co, 2⅝" **$52.00**

Butter dish, Hobnail w/Thumbprint Base #150, crystal, Doyle & Co, 2" **$70.00**

Butter dish, Sawtooth, crystal, 3" **$50.00**

Butter dish, Sawtooth Variation, crystal, 4" **$68.00**

Butter dish, Twist #137, opalescent blue, Albany Glass Co, 3⅝" **$180.00**

Cake stand, Buttons & Loops, crystal, 3⅝"..................**$45.00**

Cake stand, Roses, crystal, 3⅜" **$35.00**

Creamer, Bead & Scroll, crystal, US Glass Co, 3"........**$65.00**

Creamer, Beaded Swirl, crystal, Westmoreland Glass Co, 2¾" **$30.00**

Creamer, Braided Belt, white w/floral decor, 2⅝".....**$100.00**

Creamer, Chimo, crystal, 2" **$45.00**

Creamer, clambroth yellow, Houze Glass Co, 1¾"......**$35.00**

Creamer, Dewdrop, crystal, Columbia Glass Co, 2¾"..**$55.00**

Creamer, Doric & Pansy, pink, Jeannette Glass Co, 1937-38, 2¾"...**$30.00**

Creamer, Fine Cut Star & Fan, crystal, Higbee, 2¼".....**$24.00**

Creamer, Flattened Diamond & Sunburst Thumbelina, crystal, Westmoreland Glass Co, 2¼" **$20.00**

Creamer, Liberty Bell, crystal, 2½" **$85.00**

Creamer, Little Tots Tea Set, transparent green, horizontal lines, 1⅜" **$10.00**

Creamer, Moderntone, beige, aqua or rose, Hazel Atlas, 1940s-early 50s, 1¾" **$7.50**

Creamer, Nursery Rhyme, crystal, US Glass Co, 2½"...**$50.00**

Creamer, Plain Pattern #13, milk glass, King Glass Co, 2¼" **$75.00**

Creamer, Pointed Jewel Long Diamond #15006, crystal, US Glass Co, 2⅞" **$65.00**

Creamer, Rex or Fancy Cut, crystal, Co-operative Flint Glass Co, 2½" **$25.00**

Creamer, Sandwich Ivy, amethyst, 2⅜" **$115.00**

Creamer, Stippled Diamond, crystal, 2¼" **$65.00**

Creamer, Stippled Raindrop & Dewdrop, crystal, 2¼" .**$60.00**

Cup, Laurel, French ivory, McKee Glass Co, 1930s, 1½" .**$22.00**

Cup, Lion, crystal, Gillinder & Sons, 1½" **$40.00**

Cup & saucer, Cat & Dog, amber **$85.00**

Mug, Banded Block, amber...**$35.00**

Mug, Bead & Shield, blue milk glass...........................**$40.00**

Mug, Begging Dog, crystal **$55.00**

Mug, Pointing Dog Scenes, crystal w/square beaded handle, 2⅝", $75.00

Mug, Pups & Chicks, vaseline......................................**$65.00**

Mug, Space Scenes, Hazel Atlas Co, 3⅛".....................**$15.00**

Mug, Three Little Pigs, Hazel Atlas Co, 3⅛" **$7.50**

Pitcher, Arched Panel, crystal, Westmoreland Glass Co, 3¾" **$32.00**

Pitcher, Colonial Flute, crystal, 3¼" **$22.00**

Pitcher, Dutch Boudoir, blue milk glass, 2¼" $120.00
Pitcher, Frances Ware #323, frosted crystal w/amber trim, Hobbs, Brockunier & Co, 4¾".............................$140.00
Pitcher, Oval Star #300, crystal, Indiana Glass Co, 4" ..$60.00
Plate, divided; Circus Scenes, Hazel Atlas Co $12.00
Plate, grill; Kidibake, amber, Fry Glass Co, 1922, 8½"..$24.00
Plate, Homespun, pink, vertical ribs, Jeannette Glass Co, 4½" $8.50
Plate, Laurel, jade green, McKee Glass Co, 1930s, 5⅞" .$8.00
Plate, Three Little Pigs, Hazel Atlas Co, 7" $10.00
Saucer, Doric & Pansy, pink, Jeannette Glass Co, 4½"..$4.50
Saucer, Homespun, crystal, vertical ribs, Jeannette Glass Co, 3¼" $3.00
Saucer, Kittens, marigold, Fenton Glass Co, 4½" $48.00
Saucer, Lion, crystal, Gillinder & Sons, 3¼" $18.00
Saucer, Moderntone, white, Hazel Atlas, 1940s-early 50s, 3⅞" $4.50
Spooner, Braided Belt, crystal, 2⅝"......................$80.00
Spooner, Buzz Saw #2697, crystal, Cambridge Glass Co, 2⅛" $25.00
Spooner, Clear & Diamond Panel, blue, 2¼" $35.00
Spooner, Dewdrop, amber, Columbia Glass Co, 2¾"..$75.00
Spooner, Grapevine w/Ovals, crystal, McKee, 1⅞" $65.00
Spooner, Hawaiian Lei, crystal, JB Higbee Glass Co, 2¼".$25.00
Spooner, Oval Star #300, crystal, Indiana Glass Co, 2½"...$22.00
Spooner, Sawtooth Band #1225, crystal, AH Heisey & Co, 2¼" $70.00
Spooner, Stippled Diamond, amber, 2⅛" $100.00
Spooner, Stippled Vines & Beads, sapphire blue, 2⅛".$100.00
Spooner, Twist #137, opalescent vaseline, Albany Glass Co, 2⅜" $100.00
Sugar bowl, Beaded Swirl, amber or cobalt, Westmoreland Glass Co, 3¾" $40.00
Sugar bowl, Cloud Band, milk glass w/floral decor, Gillinder & Son Inc, 4" $100.00
Sugar bowl, Colonial #2630, cobalt, Cambridge Glass Co, 3" $48.00
Sugar bowl, Flattened Diamond & Sunburst Thumbelina, crystal, Westmoreland Glass Co, 3" $25.00
Sugar bowl, Sawtooth, crystal, 4⅞"...........................$45.00
Sugar bowl, Sweetheart, crystal, Cambridge Glass Co, 3" $18.00
Sugar bowl (open), Cherry Blossom, pink, 2 ear-type handles, Jeannette Glass Co, 2⅝" $30.00
Teapot, clambroth green, Houze Glass Co, 3⅜" $80.00
Teapot, Moderntone, pink w/black lid, Hazel Atlas, 1940s-early 50s, 3½" $80.00
Teapot, Moderntone, turquoise, Hazel Atlas, 1940s-early 50s, 3½" $60.00
Tray, Oval Star #300, crystal, Indiana Glass Co, 7¼" ...$85.00
Tumbler, Frances Ware #323, vaseline, Hobbs, Brockunier & Co, 2¼" $50.00
Tumbler, Little Boy Blue, Hazel Atlas.........................$18.00
Tumbler, Little Red Riding Hood, Hazel Atlas $18.00
Tumbler, Nearcut, crystal, Cambridge Glass Co, 2" $6.00
Tumbler, Rex or Fancy Cut, crystal, Co-operative Flint Glass Co, 1⅝" $18.00
Water set, Pattee Cross, crystal, US Glass Co, 7-pc ...$140.00

Children's Kitchenware

Just as plentiful as their dinnerware, children's kitchenware items such as those we've listed here are fairly easy to find and seem to bring good prices. Because of their small scale, they're easy to display in very little space, and miniature collectors as well as collectors of children's things snap these goodies right up!

All the books mentioned in the Children's Dinnerware narrative above show wonderful examples such as those given here.

Baker, Betty Jane #075, crystal, Glasbake, McKee Glass Co, oval, 4¼x6⅜" $10.00
Bean pot, stoneware, brown glaze, 2¾".....................$45.00
Bowl, white stoneware w/vertical ribs, blue interior, 1¾" $20.00
Bread baker, Kidibake #1928, clear opalescent, 1922, Fry Glass Co, 5" $55.00
Canister set, Jadite, Jeannette Glass Co, 5-pc, 3" $95.00
Casserole, Betty Jane #209, crystal, McKee Glass Co...$30.00
Chamber pot, Dutch Boudoir, milk glass, 2⅛"...........$120.00
Cookie sheet, tinware...$25.00

Cookware set, Wear-Ever 'Hallite Junior,' #250, Wolverine, M in NM box, $75.00

Crock, brown stoneware, Boston Baked Beans, 1¾" ..$22.00
Cup & saucer, blue speckled graniteware....................$35.00
Grater, gray speckled graniteware, 4½"......................$85.00
Ladle, blue speckled graniteware, 4¼" $45.00
Mold, aluminum, spiral..$6.50
Muffin pan, aluminum $12.00
Pie plate, Betty Jane, crystal w/red trim, McKee Glass Co...$16.00
Pie plate, Kidibake #1916, clear opalescent, Fry Glass Co, 1922, 5" $28.00

Pot, 'hammered' aluminum, 2 handles, 2".....................$14.00
Ramekin, Betty Jane #294, crystal w/red trim, McKee Glass
    Co...$7.50
Reamer, frosted crystal w/baby chicks........................$70.00
Reamer, white milk glass w/rabbit, 2 ear-type handles.$90.00
Rolling pin, china, elephant on roller skates, 9".......$140.00
Skillet, light blue speckled graniteware, 4¼" $40.00
Strainer, blue graniteware......................................$35.00
Sugar bowl (open), blue graniteware.......................$25.00
Teapot, copper, 2¾"...$80.00
Teapot, graniteware, white w/blue center band.........$65.00

Chocolate Molds

Molds used to shape chocolate are usually tin, though copper and occasionally even pewter molds were made as well. They are quite often very detailed (on the inside, of course), and variations are endless. Some are as simple as an Easter egg, others as complex as a rabbit hunter equipped with his gun and pouch or a completely decorated Christmas tree.

These seem to be regional; if you live in the East, you're bound to see them.

Rabbit sitting, 5x5", $40.00

Basset hound, #24347, 6" $85.00
Bear, #3607, 2-pc w/clamp, 5¾x2⅞" $80.00
Bride or Groom, #23344/#23343, 10", each $140.00
Chick w/band, #217278, 6½".................................$68.00
Dog, 8½"...$58.00
Donkey w/cart, Holland, 7" $45.00
Duck in water, 5x5½"...$60.00
Easter egg, Randle & Smith, 6½".............................$70.00
Father Christmas, 8" $70.00
Fish, marked GMT Co Germany, 10".........................$50.00
Fruit, wire loop hanger, oval, 4¼x6".......................$35.00
Girl w/veil & robe, #28106, 7" $85.00
Horn of plenty, marked Germany, 7" $20.00
Horse w/cart, 4x7"..$80.00
Jack-o'-lantern, marked USA, 3¼".............................$60.00
Lamb, lying down, 6½x9".......................................$60.00
Pig, 2-pc w/clamp, 6½x3".......................................$90.00
Puppy, #17884, 5½"...$55.00
Rabbit in car, 6½x5½"...$55.00

Rabbit on hind legs, 11½" $95.00
Rabbit pulling cart, 5½x3"......................................$45.00
Rabbit pulling egg cart, 7½x3½".............................$68.00
Rabbit smoking pipe, #8189, 7"...............................$65.00
Rooster, #256, 5"...$40.00
Rooster, #6184, 10½"...$165.00
Rooster, 7"..$60.00
Santa, #8049, 4"...$95.00
Scottie dog, 4½"...$50.00
Soccer player, 2-pc, w/clip.......................................$65.00
Spaceman, 1950s, 4½"..$45.00
Squirrel, tin, 9½"...$85.00
Squirrel, 4½"..$45.00
Train, #4053, 3x6" $85.00

Christmas Collectibles

Christmas is nearly everybody's favorite holiday, and it's a season when we all seem to want to get back to time-honored traditions. The stuffing and fruit cakes are made like Grandma always made them, we go caroling and sing the old songs that were written two hundred years ago, and the same Santa that brought gifts to the children in a time long forgotten still comes to our house and yours every Christmas Eve.

So for reasons of nostalgia, there are thousands of collectors interested in Christmas memorabilia. Some early Santa figures are rare and may be very expensive, especially when dressed in a color other than red. Blown glass ornaments and Christmas tree bulbs were made in shapes of fruits and vegetables, houses, Disney characters, animals, and birds. There are Dresden ornaments and candy containers from Germany, some of which were made prior to the 1870s, that have been lovingly preserved and handed down to our generation. They were made of cardboard that sparkled with gold and silver trim.

Artificial trees made of feathers were produced as early as 1850 and as late as 1950. Some were white, others blue, though most were green, and some had red berries or clips to hold candles. There were little bottle brush trees, trees with cellophane needles, and trees from the sixties made of aluminum.

Collectible Christmas items are not necessarily old, expensive, or hard to find. Things produced in your lifetime have value as well. To learn more about this field, we recommend *Christmas Collectibles* by Margaret and Kenn Whitmyer, and *Christmas Ornaments, Lights, and Decorations* by George Johnson.

Advertising trade card, Star Soap, Santa w/bag of toys in
    front of fireplace, early 1900s, 7x5", EX $20.00
Book, Holly & Mistletoe, Belford Clark & Co, EX $25.00
Book, The Night Before Christmas & Other Happy Rhymes
    from Childhood, WE Skull, 1911, EX....................$20.00
Cake mold, Santa in chimney, aluminum, marked Santa
    Claus Cake Mold, Nordic-Ware, 11½", NM............$25.00
Candle clip, angel on star shape, early 1900s, 2", EX..$50.00
Candle clip, butterfly, enameled, early 1900s, 1", EX..$20.00

Candy container, goose feather tree w/spring-type clips on ends, holly-decorated flowerpot base, 6", EX.....**$100.00**

Candy container, guitar shape, Dresden, 4", EX..........**$85.00**

Candy container, papier-mache Santa w/mesh bag, EX.**$45.00**

Candy container, Santa holding bell, papier-mache w/cotton flannel suit & rabbit fur beard, Germany, 7", $45.00

Candy container, Santa in red cotton-flannel coat & blue bloomers, Japan, 1930s, 7½", EX............................**$65.00**

Candy container, Santa on sled, cardboard w/mica coating, Japan, 4", EX **$45.00**

Candy container, Santa w/net mesh body, celluloid face w/clay hands & feet, Japan, 6", VG **$95.00**

Decoration, plaster-of-Paris Santa head illuminated w/cone-shaped Mazda lamps, 19", EX.............................**$150.00**

Decoration, plastic Santa light between 2 bottle-brush trees, white base, Noma, NM **$15.00**

Decoration, Santa carrying lg bag, ceramic, gold highlights, marked Japan, 1960s, 6½", NM **$20.00**

Fence, white wood on raised platform, pointed dowels, 3x22" square, EX..**$55.00**

Fence, wood w/green paint, 12 sections, each section: 7x22", 44x66" overall, EX..**$85.00**

Figure, bisque snow baby on skis, Japan, 3¼", EX......**$25.00**

Figure, bisque snow baby on wooden sled, Germany, 2½", EX..**$50.00**

Figure, Santa, celluloid, marked Irwin, Made in USA, 1950s, 4", EX **$30.00**

Figure, Santa in sleigh, cotton Santa & reindeer w/cardboard sleigh, Japan, 1930s, 2¾", EX **$50.00**

Figure, Santa on skis, cardboard body w/wire arms, red felt coat & blue cotton bloomers, Occupied Japan, 1950s, 6", EX **$65.00**

Greeting card, die-cut Santa w/poinsettia, Best Christmas Wishes, 1940s-50s, EX..**$8.00**

Greeting card, die-cut teddy atop gift box, Teddy w/His Big Black Eyes Hopes This Will Be a Big Surprise, EX **$18.00**

Lamp, Christmas tree decorated w/moon & stars on square base, cast iron, 11", EX....................................**$175.00**

Lamp, plastic Santa holding bubble light, 1950s, 8", EX ..**$40.00**

Light bulb, beach ball, red & blue, Japan, 1930s-50s, miniature, EX...**$25.00**

Light bulb, clown head w/yellow ruffled collar, EX....**$25.00**

Light bulb, cuckoo clock, red-painted milk glass, EX .**$25.00**

Light bulb, Humpty Dumpty bust, EX **$40.00**

Light bulb, jester pointing to playing card, EX **$85.00**

Light bulb, Little Orphan Annie, 1930s-50s, EX **$85.00**

Light bulb, pink snowman, 1930s-50s, miniature, EX..**$20.00**

Light bulb, Santa face on green chimney, EX **$20.00**

Light bulb, snowman on skis, EX **$40.00**

Light set, Mickey Mouse Lights by Noma, illuminated w/C-6 Mazda lamps, 1939, w/original box, EX, $125.00

Mantel-sitter, Santa holding holly, plaster, 1950s, 7½", EX **$30.00**

Nativity scene, plaster figures w/wood stable, EX.......**$65.00**

Night light, Rudolph w/light-up nose, EMC Art, 12", NM **$65.00**

Ornament, baby buggy, coated cardboard, red & silver, 2¼", EX...**$14.00**

Ornament, bell w/bow reading Wishing You a Merry Christmas, red crepe paper, marked Doubl-Glo, Made in USA, 5", EX **$15.00**

Ornament, bird on a ring, celluloid, Japan, 6", EX......**$45.00**

Ornament, birdcage, silver-plated metal, 2½", EX **$30.00**

Ornament, candy cane, chenille, 5", EX **$6.00**

Ornament, champagne bottle, pressed cotton, red, 3", EX **$35.00**

Ornament, chromo angel on red & gold wire-wrapped glass ball, EX **$35.00**

Ornament, crescent-shaped man in the moon, mold-blown glass, 1920s-30s, 3½", VG **$80.00**

Ornament, cupid on horseshoe, scrap & tinsel, 7", EX..**$55.00**

Ornament, deer, blown milk glass, w/clip, 2½", EX....**$45.00**

Ornament, dog on ball, mold-blown glass, 1930s, 3½", EX **$40.00**

Ornament, ear of corn, mold-blown glass, pre-1940, 5",
EX...$48.00

Ornament, Goldilocks, mold-blown glass, 1930s, 3½",
EX...$80.00

Ornament, icicle, pressed cotton, 6", EX...................$22.00

Ornament, Italian clown, blown glass, 1950s-70s, 6",
NM...$30.00

Ornament, Japanese snow figure on skis, cotton, 4¾",
EX $30.00

Ornament, kugel, cobalt, oval, late 1800s, 6", EX........$80.00

Ornament, mandolin shape, scrap & tinsel, 9", EX......$35.00

Ornament, moth, blown glass body w/spun glass wings,
pre-1940, 2¼", EX $130.00

Ornament, old man in pine cone, mold-blown glass, 1930s,
3½", EX...$70.00

Ornament, Santa, chenille w/clay face, 8", EX.............$25.00

Ornament, Santa scrap encased in bulb atop red glass ball,
5½", EX...$45.00

Ornament, Santa w/gold bag, mold-blown glass, pre-1940,
3⅜", EX $40.00

Ornament, scrap & tinsel featuring Santa w/basket of toys & tree in heart shape, 6", EX, $25.00

Ornament, snowman, cotton batting wrapped around cardboard cylinder, black top hat, 6", EX.....................$50.00

Ornament, snowman in chimney, mold-blown glass, pre-
1940, 4", EX..$95.00

Ornament, sour-faced grape head, mold-blown glass, pre-
1940, 3½", EX..$65.00

Ornament, spun glass & Dresden sunburst w/wax baby in
center, w/clip, 5", EX..$55.00

Ornament, strawberry, blown glass, silver w/red leaves, pre-
1940, 2", EX..$25.00

Ornament, trumpet flower, mold-blown glass, red, yellow &
blue, w/clip, pre-1940, 4", EX $75.00

Ornament, wire-wrapped swan, 4", EX......................$30.00

Pin, gold reindeer w/blue rhinestone eyes in center of holly
wreath, EX...$20.00

Pin, praying angel holding candle, gold w/rhinestones,
EX...$25.00

Postcard, A Bright & Merry Christmas, back view of 2 children
waiting for Santa to come down chimney, EX........$12.50

Postcard, A Merry Christmas, little girl holding new doll,
signed Frances Brundage, EX..................................$25.00

Print, little girl in red bonnet holding snowballs, by Maud
Humphrey, 10x8", NM...$80.00

Ring holder, bisque Santa figure w/round holder, 3½", EX.$18.00

Tin, Huntley & Palmer, Santa w/bag of toys on slip lid, blue
background, round, VG..$30.00

Tin, Jacob's Biscuits, Santa w/cake surrounded by children
on slip lid, octagon, EX $40.00

Tin, Madison Mixed Hard Candy, holly decoration & snowmen on red background, 2 handles, oval, EX.......$20.00

Toy, plastic Santa on tin wind-up motorcycle, marked Made
in Japan, 1950s, 3½" long, EX $85.00

Toy, Santa figure, tin litho windup by Chein, 1920s-30, 5½",
EX...$95.00

Tree, bottle-brush type w/snow-covered bristles, white center post on round base, 10", EX.............................$20.00

Tree, green goose-feather w/candle clips & red composition
berries, round wooden base, early 1900s, 19", EX..$70.00

Tree, tinsel-type wire decorated w/candles & ornaments,
7½", EX...$25.00

Tree, vinyl needles decorated w/candles & miniature bulbs,
round wooden base, 1950s & later, 8", EX............$30.00

Tree, white goose-feather w/red composition berry-tipped
branches, round wooden base, 1930s, 25", EX...$165.00

Tree stand, cast iron, scenes of children watching clown,
house on hillside, children w/Santa, etc, on base,
11x11", EX $45.00

Tree stand, concrete Santa head, red & white, 11½", EX.$200.00

Cigarette Lighters

Collectors of tobacciana tell us that cigarette lighters are definitely hot! Look for novel designs (figurals, Deco styling, and so forth), unusual mechanisms (flint and fuel, flint and gas, battery, etc.), those made by companies now defunct, those with advertising, and quality lighters made by Ronson, Dunhill, Evans, Colibri, Zippo, and Ronson.

For more information we recommend *Collector's Guide to Cigarette Lighters* by James Flanagan.

Advertising, Lucky Strike, chromium & red-painted table lighter, Japan, 1950s, 4¾x3", EX, $15.00

Advertising, Johnnie Walker Old Scotch Whiskey, bottle form, 2⅜", EX **$8.50**
Advertising, Kool Cigarettes, Willie the Penguin figure w/Light Up a Cool on chest, painted metal, 1930s, 4", VG **$85.00**
Advertising, Salem, chromium, Salem Fresh Choices, Zippo, 1991, 2¼x1½", MIB **$20.00**
Advertising, Winston Cigarettes, red & cream, Filter Tipped..., 1¾x2", EX **$8.00**
Advertising, 7-Up, enameled logo over design on metal, NM **$18.00**
Miniature, chromium lift-arm & key chain w/red leather band, Occupied Japan, ca 1948, ⅞x¾", EX **$30.00**
Miniature, chromium lift-arm w/mother-of-pearl band, Aladdin of New York, w/original box, ⅞x¾", EX. **$35.00**
Miniature, chromium lift-arm w/white leather band, Japan, 1950s, ⅞x¾", EX **$25.00**
Miniature, chromium w/mesh band, Japan, ca 1949, 1½x1⅛", EX **$30.00**
Novelty, black & red-painted metal Model T Ford, lighter behind seat, ca 1960, 1¼x3⅛" long, VG **$15.00**
Novelty, brass lamp w/enameled shade, push button on base for light, 1950s, 3½x1¾" dia, EX **$25.00**
Novelty, plastic eight-ball, 1960s, EX **$15.00**
Novelty, plastic ice-cream cone, marked Eat-It-All, 1960s, 3⅝x2½", NM **$10.00**
Novelty, plastic jukebox, lights up & plays music when lit, Germany, 1990, 2¾x1⅜", EX **$15.00**
Pocket, blue enamel w/ivory cherubs, Ronson, ca 1954, 1¾x2⅛", EX **$20.00**
Pocket, brass w/ivory-colored band of flowers, Pigeon, 1960s, 1⅜x1¾", NM **$15.00**
Pocket, brass w/leather band, Elgin American, 1960s, 1¾x1⅜", NM **$25.00**
Pocket, brass w/reddish brown leather band, Japan, 1950s, 1½x2⅛", NM **$15.00**
Pocket, brushed chromium, pictures old concrete mixer truck, Zippo, ca 1986, 2¼x1½" **$15.00**
Pocket, chromium & brown leather, w/flashlight, Aurora, 1960, 2x2½", EX **$20.00**
Pocket, chromium heart shape w/plastic insert to simulate mother-of-pearl, Continental, 1950s, 2x2", NM **$20.00**
Pocket, chromium w/pinup girl, Supreme, 1950s, 2x1⅝", EX **$25.00**
Pocket, chromium w/red leather band, Continental, 1950s, 1¼x1¼", NM **$15.00**
Pocket lighter, gold-plated w/'rocket' design on checked background, marked Royal **$120.00**
Table, brass, knight's helmet, push down on visor for light, 1950s, 5x4", EX **$15.00**
Table, brass cannon shape, Japan, 1938, 2½x5½" long, EX **$25.00**
Table, brass horse head, pull back reins for light, 1940s, 4¾x3¾", EX **$50.00**
Table, bronze dachshund figure, tail is striker, Ronson, ca 1940, 4x9" long, NM **$150.00**
Table, chromium & painted metal kerosene heater shape, battery-operated, 1960s, 5¾x3⅞", M **$40.00**
Table, chromium & white plastic piano, push down on keyboard to light, Occupied Japan, ca 1948, 3¼x2⅝", NM **$95.00**
Table, chromium dinosaur figure, Japan, ca 1988, 4¾x4", NM **$20.00**
Table, chromium rocket ship, squeeze fins together for light, Occupied Japan, ca 1949, 2x5⅛" long, EX **$65.00**
Table, chromium rose shape, lighter under flower, 1960s, 2½", EX **$25.00**
Table, chromium swan figure, Japan, early 1960s, 3x3¾", NM **$15.00**
Table, gold & silver-plated metal penguin figure, 1960s, 2x⅞" dia, EX, minimum value **$40.00**
Table, gold-toned brass apple, opens to reveal lighter, 1950s, 3x2¼" dia, EX **$30.00**
Table, green Wedgwood style, Ronson, 1962, 2¾x2⅛", NM **$40.00**
Table, horse & jockey on green glass base, electric, 1930s, 3½x2⅜" dia, EX **$45.00**
Table, metal elephant figure, ca 1935, 2¼x2½" **$35.00**
Table, plastic book form, Winterreise By Schubert, books separate to reveal lighter, battery-operated, 1950s, 5½", EX **$15.00**
Table, silver-plated barrel shape, Occupied Japan, ca 1948, 3x1¾" dia, EX **$50.00**

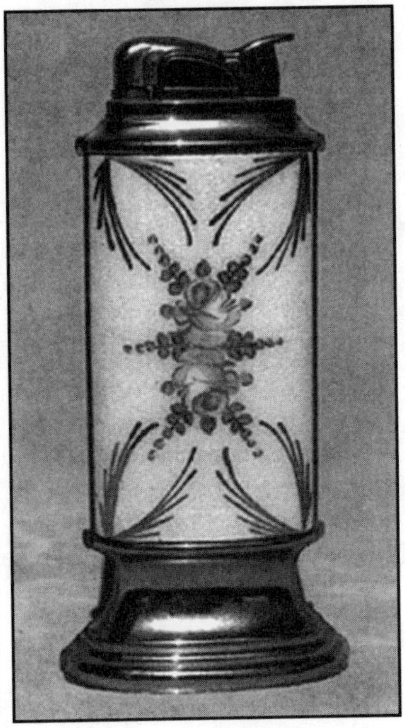

Table, brass w/floral & gold trim, Evans, ca late 1940s, 4⅞x2¼", NM, $40.00

Cleminson Pottery

One of the several small potteries that operated in California during the middle of the century, Cleminson was a family-operated enterprise that made kitchenware, decorative items, and novelties that are beginning to attract a considerable amount of interest. At the height of their productivity, they employed 150 workers, so as you make your 'rounds,' you'll be very likely to see a piece or two offered for sale just about anywhere you go. Prices are not high; this may be a 'sleeper.'

They marked their ware fairly consistently with a circular ink stamp that contains the name 'Cleminson.' But even if you find an unmarked piece, with just a little experience you'll easily be able to recognize their very distinctive glaze colors. They're all strong, yet grayed-down, dusty tones. They made a line of bird-shaped tableware items that they marketed as 'Distlefink' and several plaques and wall pockets that are decorated with mottoes and Pennsylvania Dutch-type hearts and flowers.

In Jack Chipman's *The Collector's Encyclopedia of California Pottery*, you'll find a chapter devoted to Cleminson Pottery. Roerig's *The Collector's Encyclopedia of Cookie Jars* has some more information.

Ashtray, fish, 7½" $25.00
Cleanser shaker, girl figure, 5 holes, w/card explaining how to use it, 6½" $30.00

Cleanser shaker, girl figure, 5 holes, without card, $25.00

Cookie jar, The Way to a Man's Heart, heart form....$125.00
Cookie jar, 6-sided, tulip finial.................................$95.00
Creamer & sugar bowl, Distlefink...............................$24.00
Egg cup, figure of lady in apron, early $35.00
Gravy boat, Distlefink, brown & green $25.00
Hair receiver, girl w/folded hands, 2-pc $28.00
Mug, Morning After, w/lid...$26.00
Pie bird, multicolor on white, 4½"..............................$22.00
Pitcher, Gala Gray, 7" $25.00
Plaque, pastel floral decor, 5¾", pr............................$28.00
Plate (hanging), fruit cluster, 4" $14.00
Salt & pepper shakers, Distlefink, lg, pr.....................$16.00
Spoon rest, cherries $18.00
Spoon rest, 3-lobed, floral decor, 8½" $15.00

String holder, You'll Always Have Pull w/Me, heart form...$35.00
Wall pocket, chef's smiling face, blue eyes, 7¼" $65.00
Wall pocket, coffeepot $20.00

Clothes Sprinkler Bottles

In the days before perma-press, the process of getting wrinkles out of laundered clothing involved first sprinkling each piece with water, rolling it tightly to distribute the moisture, and packing it all down in a laundry basket until ironing day. Thank goodness those days are over!

To sprinkle the water, you could simply dip your fingers in a basin and 'fling' the water around, or you could take a plain old bottle with a screw-on cap, pierce the cap a few times and be in business. Maybe these figural bottles were made to add a little cheer to this dreary job. Anyway, since no one does all this any more, they represent a little bit of history, and collectors now take an interest in them. Prices are already fairly high, but there still may be a bargain or two out there!

See also Pfaltzgraff.

Cat, marble eyes, curled tail, 8" $80.00
Chinese man, pink & green, Sprinkle Plenty, Cleminson.$40.00
Chinese man, red flowers w/black trim, Sprinkle Plenty..$45.00
Chinese man, yellow & green, Cardinal China $28.00
Clothespin, 8" $45.00
Dog, white w/black spots $60.00
Dutch boy or girl, 8", each..$75.00

Elephant, gray w/pink highlights, $50.00

Elephant, red plastic $18.00
Iron, 1950s scene of woman ironing, from $35 to.......$45.00

Mandarin, flowing pink robe **$70.00**
Merry Maid, girl w/hands on her hips, plastic, Made in
    USA **$15.00**
Rooster, 10" **$65.00**
Siamese cat...**$85.00**
Victorian lady w/purse **$120.00**

Clothing and Accessories

Vintage clothing shops are everywhere. Have you
noticed? And what's especially fascinating to buyers today
are fashion items from the fifties, sixties, and even the seventies. Hawaiian shirts have been hot for some time, and
when padded shoulders became fashionable for women,
thirties and forties clothing became very 'trendy.'

While some collectors buy with the intent of preserving
their clothing and simply enjoy having and looking at it,
many buy it to wear. If you do wear it, be very careful how
you clean it. Many fabrics become fragile with age.

Bathing suit, printed jersey, skirted style, 1940s **$20.00**
Bed jacket, rayon w/lace trim, 1940s............................**$20.00**
Cap, baby's, Irish crochet..**$20.00**
Cap, leather, Harley-Davidson, 1950s..........................**$50.00**
Coat, black velvet evening type, 1930s **$95.00**
Coat, black velvet w/wide fox cuffs, 1950s, three-quarter
    length **$40.00**
Coat, turquoise velvet, silk lining, 1930s, EX.............**$135.00**
Dress, black chiffon w/lace overlay & pink tucks, long,
    1930s...**$65.00**
Dress, black crepe, stand-up collar, slit to waist, 1930s .**$55.00**
Dress, chintz, rhinestone trim, short sleeves, 1950s **$30.00**
Dress, chocolate panne velvet, beaded silk, long sleeves,
    1930s...**$65.00**
Dress, faille, fitted bodice, full skirt, short sleeves,
    1940s **$55.00**
Dress, peach silk net, short sleeves, velvet belt w/rhine-
    stones, 1930s **$65.00**
Dress, taffeta, full skirt, short jacket, late 1940s.........**$100.00**
Evening dress, black French lace tent style w/beige
    slip **$50.00**
Evening dress, black velvet, gold stripe flared skirt,
    1950s **$40.00**
Evening dress, pink taffeta, strapless, full skirt, 1950s.**$45.00**
Evening dress, pink w/gold threadwork, short sleeves,
    1950s...**$40.00**
Evening dress, white satin, Jean Harlow style, 1935 ...**$90.00**
Gloves, child's, white wool, 1930s, pr........................**$14.00**
Hat, beaver, gold brushed w/leather banding, Christian
    Dior **$125.00**
Hat, floral brim, lg taffeta bow, 1930s **$45.00**
Hat, man's, white & gray straw, 1950s **$30.00**
Hat, wine velvet w/fuchsia feathers **$40.00**
Jacket, black lace, peplum, long sleeves, 1930s **$35.00**
Jacket, leather, black police type, 1950s **$300.00**
Levi jeans, bell-bottom legs, 1970s **$30.00**
Muff, fake leopard, 1940s..**$25.00**

Muff, monkey fur, 1930s, 12x14" **$35.00**
Nightgown, peach rayon, bias cut, long......................**$40.00**
Nightgown, 6" handmade lace bodice w/ribbons, long,
    1930s...**$35.00**
Petticoat, white cotton w/lace & embroidery.............**$35.00**
Shawl, silk, lavender, green & gold embroidered design on
    cream, long fringe...**$165.00**
Shoes, child's, black oxfords, Red Goose....................**$30.00**
Shoes, child's, black pumps, Poll Parrot....................**$20.00**
Shoes, lady's, black fabric w/leather overlay, 1930s....**$40.00**
Shoes, lady's, black rubber boots, Chatham **$16.50**
Shoes, lady's, brown suede & leather, tie over instep,
    1940..**$35.00**
Shoes, lady's, sling-back heels, Lucite w/seashell design,
    1950s **$40.00**
Shoes, man's, brown, spectator toes...........................**$55.00**
Shorts, flared skort-type w/belt, mid-1940s................**$22.50**
Skirt, circle-type w/applied poodle & embroidery,
    1950s **$25.00**
Skirt, circle-type w/red wool, Pendleton, 1950s **$25.00**
Slip, peach rayon **$12.50**
Stockings, brown cotton, Anna **$7.50**
Stockings, brown silk & cotton, Paramount **$8.50**
Stole, light brown fox fur w/collar **$165.00**
Teddy, champagne silk & georgette w/lace...............**$35.00**
Teddy, rayon w/lace trim..**$40.00**
Wedding dress, lace, hooped skirt, bolero jacket, 1950s .**$250.00**

Coca-Cola Collectibles

Coca-Cola was introduced to the public in 1886. Immediately an advertising campaign began that over the years
and to the present day has literally saturated our lives with a
never-ending variety of items. Some of the earlier calendars
and trays have been known to bring prices well into the four
figures. Because of these heady prices and the extremely
wide-spread collector demand for good Coke items, reproductions are everywhere, so beware! Some of the items that
have been reproduced are pocket mirrors (from 1905, 1906,
1908-11, 1916, and 1920), trays (from 1899, 1910, 1913-14,
1917, 1920, 1923, 1926, 1934, and 1937), tip trays (from 1907,
1909, 1910, 1913-14, 1917, and 1920), knives, cartons, bottles, clocks, and trade cards. Currently being produced and
marketed are an 18" brass 'button,' a 24" brass bottle-shaped
thermometer, cast-iron toys and bottle-shaped door pulls,
Yes Girl posters, a 12" 'button' sign (with one round hole), a
rectangular paperweight, a 1949-style cooler radio, and there
are others. Look for a date line.

In addition to reproductions, 'fantasy' items have also
been made, the difference being that a 'fantasy' never
existed as an original. Don't be deceived. Belt buckles are
'fantasies.' So are glass doorknobs with an etched trademark, bottle-shaped knives, pocketknives, (supposedly from
the 1933 World's Fair), a metal letter opener stamped 'Coca-
Cola 5¢,' a cardboard sign with the 1911 lady with fur (9" x
11"), and celluloid vanity pieces (a mirror, brush, etc.).

When the company celebrated its 100th anniversary in

1986, many 'centennial' items were issued. They all carry the '100th Anniversary' logo. Many of them are collectible in their own right, and some are already high priced.

If you'd really like to study this subject, we recommend these books: *Goldstein's Coca-Cola Collectibles* by Sheldon Goldstein, *Huxford's Collectible Advertising* by Sharon and Bob Huxford, and *Collector's Guide to Coca-Cola Items, Vols. I and II*, by Al Wilson.

Ashtray, 1950s, ceramic, oval w/round metal Drink Coca-Cola insert, NM..$25.00
Ashtray, 1960, red metal, Enjoy That Refreshing New Feeling, EX $12.50
Ashtray, 1970s, metal, Coke Adds Life To Everything Nice, 5x4", EX $8.00
Backpack, 1960s-70s, canvas, Enjoy Coca-Cola, NM $7.50
Backpack, 1984 Olympics, EX.....................................$8.50
Ball, 1980s, rubber, Enjoy Coca-Cola..., It's The Real Thing, red & black on white, 2½" dia, EX $20.00
Bank, cardboard & tin, Drink Coca-Cola, Delicious & Refreshing, In Bottles 5¢ in white on red, 3", EX .$32.00
Bank, plastic, upright vending machine, flat top, Play Refreshed, 5¢, EX...$25.00
Bank, 1980, plastic, shaped as a dispenser, original box, NM $90.00
Banner, 1960s, features Cokes, food & fishtail logo, Coke Brightens Every Bite, 20x14", NM $20.00
Banner, 1972, Santa beside tree w/gifts, 56x35", EX ...$15.00
Banner, 1976 Olympics, Getting People Together, 13x32", EX..$16.50
Banner, 1986, heavy cardboard, Celebration of the Century, 26x72", EX $7.50
Beach bag, mesh w/plastic lining, Can't Beat The Feeling, 21x14", EX $5.00
Bingo game, 1940s, original box, complete, EX.........$75.00

Blotter, 1935, train engineer drinking from bottle on green background, logo upper right, EX, $20.00

Blotter, 1938, hand holding bottle flanked by Drink...Delicious... disk logo & Drink Everybody Loves on green, NM $35.00
Blotter, 1950, Boy Scout offering bottle from cooler, Be Prepared, Be Refreshed, NM....................................$40.00
Blotter, 1957, bottle & altitude records as of 1957, 7½x3½", EX..$10.00
Book, 1960s, Comprehensive Advertising Price Lists of Items from the Early 60s, complete w/pictures, EX......$120.00
Book, 1986, Coca-Cola the First 100 Years, many color plates, hard-bound, original jacket, NM $25.00

Booklet, 1941, Coolers for Coca-Cola, pictures coolers & Mills vending machines inside, EX $75.00
Bottle, green glass, straight-sided, embossed Salem NH, EX..$45.00
Bottle, 1977, Huntsville 75th anniversary, salutes 3rd Cola Clan Convention, EX..$25.00
Bottle, 1980 Olympics, Women's Speed Skating, M $7.50
Bottle, 1981, Iowa Hawkeyes Rose Bowl Bottle, EX.....$6.50
Bottle, 1984 Kentucky Derby, 110th Run For The Roses, EX...$6.50
Bottle, 1986, Washington Redskins 50th anniversary, EX $10.00
Bottle carrier, 1930s-40s, wood, winged logo on ends, Drink Coca-Cola In Bottles on sides, pull-up handle, NM.$85.00
Bottle carrier, 1950s, aluminum, rectangular w/rounded corners, pull-up handle, holds 6 bottles, EX $45.00
Bottle opener, 1950, bottle cap shape w/protruding opener, commemorates 50th anniversary, original box, NM $65.00
Box of straws, 1940s, shows tilted bottle, 8¾x3¾", G.$50.00
Bumper sticker, America — You're The Real Thing, EX.$2.50
Calendar, 1938, girl in lavender seated in front of Venetian blinds w/bottle resting on lap, complete, VG.....$100.00
Calendar, 1941, ice skater resting on log w/bottle, round logo at right, full 2-month pad, VG $75.00
Calendar, 1953, smiling Santa holding up bottle, Talk About Being Good!, 22¼x12¼", complete, NM............$110.00
Calendar, 1980 Olympics, EX.....................................$5.00
Calendar holder, 1970s, tin, It's The Real Thing above contour logo, space for calendar below, vertical, NM.$18.00
Can, 1980s, Play It! Tops contest can, EX....................$3.50
Cassette player w/headphones, 1980s, shaped as vending machine, EX...$30.00
Checkers, 1950s-60s, NMIB $30.00
Christmas tree dangler, 1976, 3-D, 24x14", EX............$12.50
Clock, 1960s, light-up, fishtail logo in center, green numbers, 15" dia, EX..$170.00
Clock, 1960s, plastic, red fishtail logo w/green numbers & hands, 16x16", NM..$110.00
Clock, 1970s, light-up, modern pendulum w/simulated wood case, light-up base w/Coca-Cola logo, NM.$55.00
Clock, 1974, plastic, features Betty, NM $55.00
Clock, 1975, plastic, giant pocket watch complete w/hanging chain, MIB..$45.00
Coaster, 1940s, metallic, image of Golden Gate bridge, 4x4", EX...$5.00
Coaster, 1970s, plastic, Coke Adds Life To..., 3½" dia, EX...$7.50
Coasters, 1980s, metal, features various images of Santa, set of 6, EX...$15.00
Cooler, 1950s, vinyl, red w/Drink...In Bottles in white, zipper top w/2 handles & white piping, 9x14x5", EX.......$85.00
Cup holder, 1950s, plastic, white beveled base w/Coca-Cola, Always Refreshing in red, holds 2 stacks of cups, EX $45.00
Cup/can holder, 1950s, folding aluminum, NM..........$35.00
Decal, 1960s, Things Go Better With Coke in white on red, 9¼x10½", M...$14.50

Dish, 1967, smoked glass, button logo in center over world map, ruffled rim w/various scenes, 7¼" dia, NM, $35.00

Display bottle, 1960s, w/plastic cap, NM $75.00

Doll, 1950s-60s, Santa holding bottle, stuffed cloth, red suit w/black boots & white mittens, EX $50.00

Domino set, Coke Is It, NMIB....................................$25.00

Drinking glass, 1929-40, bell shape w/etched Coca-Cola logo, Trade Mark on tail of C, NM.........................$20.00

Drinking glass, 1960s, Around The World set of 8, NM .$50.00

Fan, 1950, cardboard w/wood handle, hand holding bottle, 8x8", EX $45.00

Fan pull, 1957, 2-sided, Santa shape, Family Size, Serve Coca-Cola, EX...$15.00

Festoon, 1960s, Birthstones & Find Yours on ribbon, girl's head in center, full glasses & fishtail logo, 5-pc, 3-D, NM $350.00

Fly swatter, 1940s, advertising on wood handle, EX $8.00

Game, 1930s, table tennis, original box, NM $60.00

Game, 1957, Shanghai, NMIB $10.00

Hat, soda jerk's, 1970s, paper, red/black on white, It's The Real Thing, adjustable, EX...$4.00

Jacket, 1986, 100th anniversary, size lg, M..................$50.00

Lighter, 1950s, bottle shape, EX..................................$25.00

Lighter, 1960s, can shape w/Enjoy Coca-Cola diamond logo on red, 1½", EX..$25.00

Matchbook, 1960s, Santa w/elves, Promote Coca-Cola, EX..$15.00

Menu board, 1962, tin, fishtail logo above Good With Food, menu area on either side, 8' long, EX $50.00

Miniature music box, 1950s, w/original instruction sheet, NM $200.00

Miniature picnic cooler, 1950s, plastic, red box w/squared wire handle, Drink...In Bottles logo, 6" long, EX..$80.00

Music box, 1950s, plays Let Me Call You Sweetheart, red chest-type cooler shape, white lettering, NM......$145.00

Napkin holder, 1988, cooler shape, Italy, 5x5½x3½", EX.$20.00

Paddle & ball, 1940s-50s, rubber band attached, In Bottles, NM $55.00

Paperweight, 1930s, Coke Is Coca-Cola, has been reproduced, 3½x2½", EX..$40.00

Paperweight, 1960, bronze w/bottle & emblem, given for plant production, EX...$10.00

Pencil, 1970s, Welcome! Production School For Bottlers Of Coca-Cola, M $3.50

Pencil clip, 1960s, red disk, Drink Coca-Cola In Bottles, EX..$6.50

Pencil sharpener, 1933, red metal, bottle shape, EX ...$40.00

Pin-back button, 1950s, Enjoy Coca-Cola, red & white, ¾" dia, EX..$6.00

Pin-back button, 1985, Great New Taste-Better Than Ever, 3" dia, EX..$3.00

Playing cards, 1939, blue w/Drink Coca-Cola In Bottles, vertical stripes & design on left edge, original box, NM $100.00

Playing cards, 1951, close-up of cowgirl holding bottle, original box, complete, M.....................................$80.00

Playing cards, 1976, Coca-Cola Adds Life To Everything Nice, sealed box, NM...$16.00

Playing cards, 1980, 1940s scenes, double deck, original box, complete, M..$35.00

Pocket mirror, 1920, garden girl in yellow dress & floppy wide-brimmed hat holding glass, oval, 2¾x1¾", EX.........$200.00

Pocket mirror, 1936, Coca-Cola memos, 50th anniversary, rectangular, EX..$190.00

Pop gun, Santa airborne in white sleigh w/Coca-Cola logo on back, 4½x7½", NM...$15.00

Pretzel bowl, 1930s, aluminum, 3 bottles attached to bowl, VG...$185.00

Radio, 1970s-80s, bottle shape, NMIB $30.00

Rain hat, 1970s, Coke Adds Life To...Rainy Days, EX....$6.50

Record, 1971, Buy The World A Coke, It's The Real Thing & Little Bit Of Sunshine, 45 rpm, EX $7.50

Record album, 1971, Lone Ranger, EX $20.00

Ruler, 1970s, plastic, It's The Real Thing, 12", EX..........$5.00

Scarf, 1940s-50s, cloth, features bottles & bottle caps w/couple at table & couple dancing, 36x36", NM..........$80.00

Seltzer bottle, 1950s, glass w/metal top, ...Bottling Works, Alliance Ohio, Content 26 Fl Oz, 11½", EX.........$135.00

Shot glass, 1986, Merry Christmas, EX $4.00

Sign, 1940, cardboard, Ice Cold on posted sign beside snowman opening lg bottle, Canadian, 27x16", NM..$270.00

Sign, 1940s, cardboard, girl in purple sweater & yellow skirt on stomach by 6-pack, I Think It's Swell, 29x56", EX $185.00

Sign, 1947, die-cut cardboard, 3 wood-handled 6-packs w/green dot reading Easy To Carry, 33x42", EX.$210.00

Sign, 1948, tin, tilted bottle in circle at right of Drink Coca-Cola, red, white & yellow, 11x34", M..................$275.00

Sign, 1950s, button, white w/decaled hand holding bottle, 16" dia, EX..$235.00

Sign, 1950s, cardboard, features hamburgers, hot dogs & Cokes, Family Favorites, 18x24", EX.....................$55.00

Sign, 1940, cardboard, ice skater sitting on snowy log enjoying a bottle of Coke, gold frame, vertical, EX+, $550.00

Thermometer, 1938, embossed tin w/gold bottle on red background, raised rolled rim, 16x7", NM, $250.00

Sign, 1950s, cardboard, house beyond lady w/bottle standing by party table, Almost Everywhere..., 50x30", VG **$95.00**

Sign, 1950s, porcelain, Drink... on red field pointing to Fountain Service divided by 3 wavy lines, 12x28", VG...**$130.00**

Sign, 1954, cardboard, bottle w/snacks, 3-D, Stock Up Now, Take Some Home, 33x35", NM **$125.00**

Sign, 1954, tin, die-cut in shape of 12-bottle carton, Chill Until Cold, Serve In Bottles, 13x20", NM, A........**$795.00**

Sign, 1958, embossed tin, bottle at right of fishtail logo, green raised rim, 12x32", NM..............................**$200.00**

Sign, 1960, tin, bottle & Ice Cold at right of fishtail logo, Sign Of Good Taste, 18x54", NM........................**$175.00**

Sign, 1960s, cardboard, Pause That Refreshes & bottle above couple w/bottles seated in S-shaped chair, 27x16", EX **$55.00**

Sign, 1960s, tin, Sign Of Good Taste & fishtail logo on white, green raised rim, 24x60", EX **$120.00**

Sign, 1970s, cardboard stand-up, Raquel Welch offers Groovy Accessories, Love Racquel on CBS-TV April 26, 27x19", NM **$70.00**

Sign, 1970s, paper, Santa w/dog, Keep Up The Tradition, 24x18", EX **$15.00**

Sign, 1980s, light-up, Coke w/Ice in neon, M...........**$375.00**

Sign, 1985, metal, made for 11th Cola Clan Convention in Dallas, pictures a cowgirl, 13½x17½", EX **$10.00**

Snack bowl, plastic, features Holly Hobbie, 8½" dia, EX...**$6.50**

Sun visor, red cloth, Enjoy Coca-Cola, adjustable, EX...**$7.50**

Syrup dispenser, 1978, ceramic urn shape, reproduction by MarvArt of 1896 dispenser, NM **$450.00**

Telephone, 10-oz bottle shape, exact size, MIB **$40.00**

Thermometer, 1941, tin, 2 Coke bottles flank thermometer atop Drink Coca-Cola logo, 16x7", NM **$375.00**

Thermometer, 1958, tin, bottle shape, 17", VG............**$50.00**

Thermometer, 1964, dial-type w/glass lens, Things Go Better w/Coke in red, lg-numbered border, 18", EX......**$135.00**

Thermometer, 1970s, plastic, black desktop-type, Piqua Coca-Cola Bottling Co, Piqua Ohio, 5x5", NMIB ..**$10.00**

Tin, 1984, pictures early girls & bottles, 3½x3" dia, EX.**$6.50**

Tip tray, 1920, garden girl in yellow dress & floppy wide-brimmed hat holding glass, oval, 6x4", NM **$350.00**

Toy dishes, 1950s, My Dolly Loves A Party set, original box, NM **$90.00**

Toy train, 1980s, Thunderbolt Express, by Mehano, EX..**$85.00**

Toy van, 1960, metal, friction, yellow w/red trim, disk logo & bottle image on top, 1 of 12 in a series, NM.....**$95.00**

Travel clock, 1950s, brass, Be Really Refreshed, 3x3", EX.**$225.00**

Tray, 1934, Maureen O'Sullivan & Johnny Weismuller posing w/bottles, has been reproduced, 10½x13¼", NM..**$975.00**

Tray, 1937, girl in yellow swimsuit & white cape running on beach w/2 bottles, 13¼x10½", EX, $275.00

Tray, 1940, fishing girl on dock enjoying a bottle of Coke, 13¼x10½", NM......................................**$225.00**

Tray, 1957, sandwiches & bottles on individual trays w/floral centerpiece, 10½x13¼", EX....................**$80.00**

Tray, 1968, deep-dish, center features bottle on ice, Mexican, NM..**$55.00**

Tray, 1973, Santa at fireplace, EX **$15.00**

Tray, 1976, features Bobby Knight & the Indiana Hoosiers, 1976 NCAA Champions, M.....................**$10.00**

Tray, 1976 Olympics, Getting People Together, NM...**$95.00**

Tray, 1980s, Houston Coca-Cola Bottling Co, factory scene, EX...**$10.00**

Tray, 1988, Calgary Winter Olympic Games, EX **$20.00**

Waste basket, 1990, red metal, circus scene, EX **$10.00**

Whistle, 1950s, plastic, Merry Christmas, Coca-Cola Bottling Memphis Tenn, EX...**$15.00**

Writing tablet, pictures flags of the United Nations, bottle & logo in lower left, NM..**$6.00**

Yo-Yo, 1920s-30s, multicolored inlay, NM **$45.00**

Yo-Yo, 1960s, bottle-cap shape, EX............................**$20.00**

Comic Books

Though just about everyone can remember having stacks and stacks of comic books as a child, few of us ever saved them for more than a few months. At 10¢ a copy, new ones quickly replaced the old, well-read stacks. We'd trade them to our friends, but very soon, out they went. If we didn't throw them away, Mother did. So even though they were printed in huge amounts, few survive. Today they're a very desirable collectible.

Factors that make a comic book valuable are condition (as with all paper collectibles, extremely important), content, and rarity, but not necessarily age. In fact, comics printed between 1950 and the late 1970s are most in demand by collectors who prefer those they had as children to the earlier comics. They look for issues where the hero is first introduced, and they insist on quality. Condition is first and foremost when it comes to assessing worth. Compared to a book in excellent condition, a mint issue might be worth six to eight times as much, while one in only good condition should be priced at less than half the price of the excellent example. We've listed some of the more collectible (and expensive) comics, but many are worth very little. You'll really need to check your bookstore for a good reference book before you actively get involved in the comic book market.

Adventure Comics, #440, DC Comics, NM **$3.00**

Adventures of Mighty Mouse, #2, St John Publishing, EX **$35.00**

Alpha Flight, #1, Marvel Comics, NM **$6.00**

Amazing Spiderman, #200, Marvel Comics, NM **$10.50**

Animal Man, #1, DC Comics, NM...............................**$7.50**

Astonishing Tales, #26, Marvel Comics, NM................**$10.50**

Avengers, Annual #7, Marvel Comics, NM **$13.50**

Batgirl #1 Special, DC Comics, 1988, NM....................**$5.00**

Batman, #18, DC Comics, EX...................................**$300.00**

Batman, #366, DC Comics, NM.................................**$15.00**

Batman, Shadow of the Bat, Annual #1, DC Comics, NM..**$3.00**

Battlefront, #44, Atlas, VG **$2.50**

Black Lightning, #1, DC Comics, NM..........................**$2.50**

Black Panther, #1, Marvel Comics, NM.......................**$5.00**

Bloodshot, #6, Image, NM..**$3.50**

Blue Beetle, #1, DC Comics, 1986, NM **$2.00**

Brigade, #1, volume #1, Image, NM **$3.50**

Buccaneers, #19, Quality Comics, G..........................**$36.00**

Bugs Bunny Beach Party, #32, Dell Giant, M **$17.50**

Buster Bear, #8, Quality Comics, NM **$7.50**

Captain America, #332, Marvel Comics, EX+................**$6.00**

Captain Marvel Adventures, #54, Fawcett, EX............**$50.00**

Catwoman #1, DC Comics, 1989, NM..........................**$6.00**

Champions, #1, Marvel Comics, NM.............................**$7.50**

Charlie Chan, #2, Dell, NM..**$8.50**

Cinderella Love, #11, St John Publishing, EX..............**$12.00**

Classic X-Men, #10, Marvel Comics, NM.......................**$3.50**

Contest of Champions, #1, Marvel Comics, EX+ **$5.50**

Daredevil, #158, Marvel Comics, EX+.........................**$30.00**

Darkhawk, #1, Marvel Comics, EX+ **$7.25**

Davy Crockett King of the Wild Frontier, Gold Key Classic, Walt Disney Productions, 1955, NM, $25.00

DC Comics Presents, #26, DC Comics, NM **$15.00**

DC 100 Page Super Spectacular, #DC-15, Superboy, DC Comics, NM **$5.50**

Dear Lonely Heart, #4, Artful, EX...............................**$8.50**

Deathblow, #1, Image, NM..**$2.25**

Deathlock (mini-series), #1, Marvel Comics, NM...........**$5.50**

Defenders, #28, Marvel Comics, NM...........................**$7.25**

Demon, #1, DC Comics, 1972, NM **$7.50**

Detective Comics, #481, DC Comics, NM **$6.50**

Dick Tracy, #4, lg feature, Dell, EX...........................**$150.00**

Doctor Strange, #1, Marvel Comics, NM.....................**$15.00**

Excaliber, #1, Marvel Comics, 1988, NM......................**$4.50**

Fantastic Four, #200, Marvel Comics, NM.....................**$6.75**

Fantastic Four, #236, Marvel Comics, EX+ **$12.50**

Fear, #23, Marvel Comics, NM...................................**$6.00**

Felix the Cat, #2, Dell, EX **$27.50**

Flash, #1, DC Comics, 1987, NM.................................**$7.50**

Geronimo, #2, Avon, EX..........................$17.50
Ghost Rider, #1, Marvel Comics, 1990, EX+.............$15.00
Ghost Rider, #19, Marvel Comics, NM $3.00
GI Joe, #1, Marvel Comics, 1982, NM $18.00
Godzilla, #1, Marvel Comics, 1977, EX+ $5.00
Green Hornet Comics, #33, Harvey, EX+ $52.00
Green Lantern, #195, DC Comics, NM $6.00
Green Lantern Emerald Dawn, #2, DC Comics, NM.....$5.50
Hard Corp, #1, Valiant, NM $3.50
Hollywood Secrets, #5, Quality Comics, NM...........$12.50
Howard the Duck, #1, Marvel Comics, NM.............$8.00
Incredible Hulk, #177, Marvel Comics, NM............$15.00
Incredible Hulk, Annual #3, Marvel Comics, NM.........$4.50
Inhumans, #1, Marvel Comics, NM $5.50
Invaders, Giant #1, Marvel Comics, NM $4.50
Iron Fist, #1, Marvel Comics, NM..........................$15.00
It Really Happened, #1, Kit Carson, EX............$20.00
Joker, #2, DC Comics, 1975, NM..........................$6.50
Josie & the Pussycats, #46, Archie, NM $3.50
Jumbo Comics, #77, Friction House, VG...............$20.00
Justice League of America, #1, DC Comics, 1987, NM...$7.50
King Louie & Mowgli, #1, Gold Key, EX............$6.50
Legion of Super Heroes, #259, DC Comics, 1980, NM ..$4.50
Little Lulu, #146, 4-Color, Dell, VG.....................$50.00
Logans Run, #6, Marvel Comics, NM $10.50
Longshot, #2, Marvel Comics, NM $10.00
Machine Man, #19, Marvel Comics, NM............$13.50
Magnus Robot Warrior, #15, Valiant, NM............$3.50
Marc Spencer, Moon Knight, #1, Marvel Comics, NM...$4.00
Marvel Chillers, #3, Marvel Comics, NM............$3.50
Marvel Comics Presents, #1, Marvel Comics, NM.........$5.00
Marvel Fanfare, #2, Marvel Comics, NM............$6.00
Marvel Premier, #50, Marvel Comics, NM............$7.50
Marvel Spotlight, #12, Marvel Comics, NM............$15.00
Marvel Team Up Annual, #2, Marvel Comics, NM.......$13.50

Mickey Mouse & the House of Many Mysteries, #116, Dell, Walt Disney Productions, 1946, EX, $40.00

Mickey Mouse in Outer Space, #43, Dell Giant, EX $50.00
Ms Marvel, #16, Marvel Comics, NM..........................$4.00

Nam, #1, Marvel Comics, NM.................................$4.50
Namor, #26, Marvel Comics, NM...........................$6.75
New Mutants, #87, Marvel Comics, NM.....................$36.00
New Teen Titans, #1, DC Comics, 1980, NM $13.50
New Terrytoons, #10, Dell, M $7.50
New Warriors, #1, Marvel Comics, NM.....................$10.50
Nick Fury Vs Shield, #2, Marvel Comics, NM.............$12.00
Nova, #1, Marvel Comics, EX+ $8.50
Omego Man, Annual #3, DC Comics, 1982, NM...........$6.75
Patty Powers, #7, Atlas Comics, EX.......................$7.50
Peter Parker the Spectacular Spiderman, #1, Marvel Comics, NM..........................$35.00
Power Pack, #27, Marvel Comics, NM $5.50
Powerman, #84, Marvel Comics, NM.......................$9.00
Punisher, #1, Marvel Comics, NM $22.50
Punisher War Journal, #1, Marvel Comics, NM...........$12.00
Rangers Comics, #5, Fiction House, VG $45.00
Richie Rich Billions, #7, Harvey Comics, NM...........$2.50
Sandman, #3, DC Comics, NM...........................$15.00
Secret Origins, #1, DC Comics, NM.......................$4.50
Secret Wars I, #6, Marvel Comics, NM $6.00
Shadowhawk II, #1, Image, NM..........................$3.00
Silver Surfer, #1, Marvel Comics, NM $7.50
Solar Man of the Atom, #12, Image, NM $3.50
Son of Satan, #7, Marvel Comics, NM $5.50
Spawn, #1, Image, NM...........................$6.00
Spiderman, #1, silver bag, Marvel Comics, M $30.00

Spiderman, Marvel Comics, January 1956, EX, $20.00

Stumbo the Giant, #63, Harvey, M...............$16.00
Tarzan's Jungle World, #25, Dell Giant, NM $95.00
Terry & the Pirates, #44, 4-Color, Dell, EX...............$88.00
Thor, #337, Marvel Comics, NM...............$6.00
Treasury of Comics, #5, St John Publishing, NM $42.50
Warlock, #11, Marvel Comics, NM...............$12.00
Warlord, #1, DC Comics, 1976, NM...............$10.50
Werewolf by Night, #32, Marvel Comics, 1972, NM $30.00
Whiz Comics, #45, Fawcett, EX...............$37.00
Wild Boy of the Congo, #11, Approved Comics, EX...$12.50

Wildstar, Sky Zero; #1, Image, NM **$2.25**
Wolverine, #1, Marvel Comics, 1982, NM.............**$16.00**
Wonder Woman, #267, Marvel Comics, EX............**$7.50**
X-Factor, #1, Marvel Comics, NM......................**$6.00**
X-Men (Uncanny), #201, Marvel Comics, NM.............**$13.50**
X-Men (Uncanny), #266, Marvel Comics, NM.............**$17.50**
X-Men & the New Teen Titans, #1, Marvel Comics, NM ..**$7.50**
X-Men Unlimited, #1, Marvel Comics, NM **$3.50**
2099 Unlimited, #1, Marvel Comics, NM.......................**$3.50**

Compacts and Carryalls

Very new to the collectibles scene, compacts are already making an impact. When 'liberated' women entered the workforce after WWI, cosmetics, previously frowned upon, became more acceptable, and as as result the market was engulfed with compacts of all types and designs. Some went so far as to incorporate timepieces, cigarette compartments, coin holders, and money clips. All types of materials were used, mother-of-pearl, petit point, cloisonne, celluloid, and leather among them. There were figural compacts, those with wonderful Art Deco designs, souvenir compacts, and compacts with advertising messages.

Carryalls were popular from the 1930s to the 1950s. They were made by compact manufacturers and were usually carried with evening wear. They contained compartments for powder, rouge and lipstick, often held a comb and mirror, and some were fitted out with a space for cigarettes and a lighter. Other features might have included a timepiece, a tissue holder, a place for coins or stamps, and some even had music boxes.

For further study, we recommend *Ladies' Compacts of the 19th and 20th Centuries* by Roselyn Gerson.

Lucite, textured blue square center w/gold-tone trim on light blue backgound w/gold-tone frame, Dorset, 3¼x3¼", $40.00

Beaded, multicolored flowers on white, square, minimum value **$75.00**
Brass, embossed lady in profile on lid, Rigaud Mary Garden, round **$70.00**
Chrome, cookie shape w/loop for chain **$40.00**

Gold-tone, black & white enameled dice motif on lid, oblong **$125.00**
Gold-tone, poodle motif set w/red cabochon stones, lipstick fitted in black grosgrain case, Zell Fifth Avenue...**$95.00**
Gold-tone w/brown enamel, compact & cigarette lighter combination, Ronson....................................**$125.00**
Gold-tone w/green enameled scale-work design on lid, R&G NuWhite, octagonal **$80.00**
Gold-tone w/red enamel, bolster shape, miniature.....**$25.00**
Plastic, blue w/silver dancers on metal lid, Terri, square, miniature...**$40.00**
Silver-plated repousse w/finger-ring chain, Jonteel, octagon..**$70.00**
Sterling silver, blue cloisonne decoration on lid w/finger-ring chain, Vermeil, oval **$125.00**

Carryalls

Alligator skin, reddish brown, dome shape, Elgin, 4½" long **$135.00**
Brushed & polished gold-tone w/geometric design, clutch-type, Evans, 5½" long **$135.00**
Brushed gold-tone, black faille carrying case w/handle, Volupte, 6" long..**$140.00**
Chrome & copper, embossed copper rose on lid, Volupte, 6" long...**$125.00**
Cloisonne, yellow w/hand-painted roses, snake chain handle, 3¾" long...**$135.00**
Enamel, black w/gilt flowers, chain handle, dual opening, Zell, 3" long...**$50.00**
Gold electroplated necessaire in original presentation box w/attached lipstick, opens at top & bottom, La Mode **$150.00**
Gold-tone w/basket-weave pattern, mesh carrying chain, dual opening, Evans, 5½" long **$135.00**
Lucite, black w/colorful sparkles, chain handle, dual opening, Zell, 4" long..**$70.00**
Mother-of-pearl, mesh carrying chain, dual opening, 5½" long..**$135.00**
Padded leather w/Persian design, snake chain handle, 5¼" long...**$135.00**
Plastic, mahogany colored w/gold-tone knobs & chain, 6¼" long..**$90.00**
Suede, black w/gold leather handles, Elgin, 4½" long.**$110.00**

Condiment Sets

Whimsical styling make these sets lots of fun to collect. Any specie of animal, plant, bird or mammal that ever existed and many that never did or ever will are represented, so an extensive collection is possible, and prices are still reasonable. These sets are usually comprised of a pair of salt and pepper shakers and a small mustard pot on a tray, though some sets never had a tray, and others were figurals that were made in three parts. For more information, we recommend *Salt & Pepper Shakers IV* by Helene Guarnaccia. See also Black Americana.

Beehives on a tray, ceramic, 3 honey-colored hives w/single bees atop, floral & leaf design embossed on side, 4-pc set..**$35.00**

Cats on a tray, lustre, 3 animated cats w/backs arched, light honey w/orange ears & blue eyes, round tray, 4-pc set..**$75.00**

Chef holding basket & stack of fruit, ceramic, chef is mustard, fruit & basket shakers, Japan, 1950s, 3-pc set...**$40.00**

Chickens, ceramic, honey-colored w/black & red accents, 1 w/head down is mustard, green 'grassy' tray, 4-pc set..**$30.00**

Children & kitten praying at side of bed, ceramic, top of bed lifts off, children are shakers, Japan, 1960s, 3-pc set...**$40.00**

Clowns, porcelain, 2 standing are shakers, 1 seated is mustard, red w/white & yellow accents, Japan, 1930s, 3-pc set...**$40.00**

Corn on a tray, ceramic, 3 'chubby' ears standing upright on green tray, 4-pc set **$40.00**

Dogs on a tray, ceramic, upright on round black tray, yellow dog's head lifts off, blue & pink dog shakers, 4-pc set...**$40.00**

Dogs on a tray, lustre, honey-colored w/rounded ears & lg eyes glancing sideways, white tray, 4-pc set..........**$40.00**

Duck family, lustre, light honey w/blue wing feathers, light green bills, loop handle on duck tray, 4-pc set, $60.00

Dutch mills on a tray, ceramic, white w/black roofs, black & multicolored accents, elongated tray, 4-pc set......**$35.00**

Dutch woman & children, porcelain, woman is mustard, elongated tray, white w/red & green accents, 4-pc set **$75.00**

Fruit on a tray, ceramic, bananas & grape cluster shakers w/peach mustard, oval tray, 4-pc set.....................**$30.00**

Galleons, lustre, 3 galleons w/floral decoration on round tray, Japan, 1930s, 4-pc set.....................................**$50.00**

Indian couple & pueblo, ceramic, he in green she in yellow, pueblo is mustard attached to base, Japan, 1960s, 3-pc set...**$50.00**

Jet plane, lustre, gold-topped mustard & shakers rest in fuselage of white plane, gold wing tips, nose & tail, 4-pc set **$60.00**

Kangaroos, ceramic, in red boxing gloves, mamma's pouch is mustard, boxing-glove spoon handle, on tray, 4-pc set...**$60.00**

Kittens w/ball of yarn, black & white kitten attached to red ball of yarn, kitten shakers & spoon, 3-pc set **$60.00**

Koalas, ceramic, 1 hangs from tree branch & 1 sits atop tree stump which is mustard, 3-pc set **$50.00**

Leprechauns w/pot of gold, ceramic, multicolored leprechaun shakers w/yellow pot on shamrock base, 4-pc set...**$50.00**

Lobsters, ceramic, sitting upright, red shakers w/yellow screw-type bases, yellow tray, 4-pc set **$50.00**

Lock-Ness monster, ceramic, black w/painted-on eyes & nostrils, head & tail shakers, center hump is mustard, 3-pc set **$30.00**

Men seated in chairs in a gondola, lustre, 3-pc set ...**$100.00**

Monks on a tray, ceramic, animated, black robes w/gray accents, black tray w/gray interior, Japan, 1960s, 4-pc set...**$30.00**

Pig, ceramic, stacked, head w/1 ear up & 1 down in honey-colored airbrushing, yellow outfit w/black dots, 3-pc set...**$50.00**

Rabbit, lustre, shaker ears, head lifts off of body, German, 1930s, 3-pc set..**$65.00**

Rabbits, ceramic, upright, head lifts off larger rabbit, black heads w/white bodies, blue eyes, Grafton, 3-pc set **$60.00**

Sailors on a tray, porcelain, 2 w/flags are shakers, 1 looking into mustard pot (attached), Japan, 1930s, 4-pc set **$60.00**

Train engine w/smokestack shakers, ceramic, train in brown tones, white shakers w/floral design gold trim, 3-pc set...**$35.00**

Consolidated Glass

The Consolidated Lamp and Glass Company operated in Coraopolis, Pennsylvania, from 1894 until 1964. At first much of what they made was oil lamps and shades, although they also made Cosmos, a limited line of milk glass tableware decorated with pastel flowers.

By the mid-twenties they were making glassware with 'sculptured' designs, very similar to a line made by a nearby competitor, the Phoenix Glass Company located in Monaca, Pennsylvania. Unless you're a student of these two types of glassware, it's very difficult to distinguish one from the other. The best clue (which is not foolproof) is the fact that most of the time Consolidated applied color to the relief (raised) design and left the background plain, while the reverse was true of Phoenix.

One of their lines was called Ruba Rombic. It has a very distinctive 'cubist' appearance. Shapes are free-form with jutting dimensional planes. It was made in strong colors to compliment its Deco forms, and collectors value anything from this line very highly.

For more information we recommend *Phoenix and Consolidated Art Glass, 1926-1980,* by Jack D. Wilson.

Bowl, Mermaid, plain crystal, 9" $85.00
Candlestick, Catalonian, #1124......................................$35.00
Candlestick, Cockatoo, yellow wash on crystal........$125.00
Cracker jar, Con-Cora, violets on milk glass, 6½" $80.00
Flower bowl, Catalonian, #1130.....................................$85.00
Goblet, Dancing Nymph, 5¼" $85.00

Plate, Bird of Paradise, green wash on crystal, 12", $75.00

Plate, Five Fruits, brown wash, 12" $95.00
Plate, Ruba Rombic, jade, 8" $85.00
Plate, Ruba Rombic, jade green, 8"................................$85.00
Powder jar, Hummingbird, purple wash, 5" dia $75.00
Powder jar, Lovebirds, yellow wash on crystal............$75.00
Sugar bowl, Ruba Rombic, Jungle Green, 3" $150.00
Tumbler, Five Fruits, green wash, footed, 5" $30.00
Tumbler, Ruba Rombic, Sunshine, 9-oz $75.00
Vase, Screech Owl, white wash, 6" $85.00

Cookbooks and Recipe Leaflets

If you've ever read a 19th-century cookbook, no doubt you've been amused by the quaint way the measurements were given. Butter the size of an egg, a handfull of flour, a pinch of this or that — sounds like a much more time-efficient method, doesn't it? They'd sometimes give household tips or some folk remedies, and it's these antiquated methods and ideas that endear those old cookbooks to collectors, although examples from this circa are not easily found.

Cookbooks from the early 20th century are scarce too, but even those that were printed thirty and forty years ago are well worth collecting. Food and appliance companies often published their own, and these appeal to advertising buffs and cookbook collectors alike. Some were die-cut to represent the product, perhaps a pickle or a slice of bread. The leaflets we list below were nearly all advertising giveaways and premiums. Condition is important in any area of paper collectibles, so judge yours accordingly.

For further study, we recommend *A Guide to Collecting Cookbooks* by Colonel Bob Allen, and *Price Guide to Cookbooks and Recipe Leaflets* by Linda Dickenson.

See also Jell-O Collectibles.

ABC of Canapes, R McCrae, 1953 ....$3.50
American Heart Association Cookbook, T Hampson, 1973,
    hardcover, 411 pages..$12.00
Arm & Hammer Baking Soda, Good Things To Eat,
    1930..$5.50
Aunt Jenny's Favorite Recipes, Spry, ca 1940, paperback, 48
    pages...$18.00
Baker's Favorite Chocolate Recipes, 1950, 112 pages....$5.00
Better Homes & Gardens Cookbook, 1939, hardcover ..$15.00
Better Meals for Less, 1930..$12.50
Betty Crocker All Purpose Baking, 1942, paperback, 100
    pages..$4.50
Betty Crocker's Hostess Cookbook, 1967, hardcover, spiral-
    bound, 168 pages...$12.50
Betty Crocker's Parties for Children, 1964, hardcover, spiral-
    bound, 166 pages...$15.00
Bisquick All Star Cookbook, 1935 ....$10.00
Bond Bread, Name Your Favorite Recipe Book, 1935 .$12.50
Borden's Magic Recipes, Borden's milk, 1964...............$1.50
Cake & Frosting, Betty Crocker, 1966, hardcover, 144
    pages...$3.50
Calendar Recipes of Dinners, Crisco, 1923, hardcover, 231
    pages...$8.00
Calumet Book of Oven Triumphs, 1934, 32 pages........$4.50
Casseroles & Compliments w/Minute Rice, General Foods
    Corp, 1966 ....$4.50
Celebrity Recipes, 1961...$4.50
Cheese & Cheese Cookery, T Layton, 1972, 242 pages.$9.50

Chiquita Banana's Recipe Book, 1950, $8.00

Chocolate Cookery, General Foods, 1929, 36 pages $6.50
Come Into the Kitchen Cookbook, Mary & Vincent Price,
    1969, hardcover...$28.00
Cooking w/a French Touch, G Maurois, 1951, 239
    pages...$8.50
Cosmopolitan Cookery, L Deeley, 1945, 167 pages.......$6.00
Cut Up Cakes, Baker's Coconut, 1956 ....$2.50
D-Zerta, 1930, 32 pages...$9.50
Delmonte Fruit Book, 1924, paperback, 32 pages........$3.50
Down on the Farm Cookbook, H Worth, 1943, 322
    pages..$10.00
Downright Delicious Sun-Maid Raisin Recipes, 1949 ..$10.00

Duncan Hines Food Odyssey, 1955, hardcover, 274 pages..**$5.00**

Eggs & Cheese, Spaghetti & Rice, Good Housekeeping, 1958, paperback, 68 pages **$2.50**

Encyclopedia of European Cooking, M Soper, 1962, hardcover, 631 pages **$8.50**

Esquire Party Cookbook, 1965, 314 pages **$8.00**

Family Circle Fish & Poultry, 1955, hardcover, 144 pages..**$4.00**

Famous Recipes for Baker's Chocolate & Breakfast Cocoa, Walter Baker & Co Inc, 1928................**$14.00**

Fannie Farmer Cookbook, 1965, 554 pages.............**$12.00**

Fleischmann's Recipes, 1924, 48 pages.....................**$2.50**

Frigidaire Recipes, 1939, 36 pages **$2.50**

Galloping Gourmet, G Kerr, 1975, hardcover, 284 pages.**$8.50**

Good Housekeeping Book of Meals, 1927, hardcover, 256 pages..**$18.00**

Good Luck Recipes, John F Jelke Co, 1916...........**$15.00**

Good Things To Eat, M Anderson, 1940, 15 pages.......**$3.50**

Green Mountain Cookbook, 1941, 90 pages.............**$12.50**

Harvard Dames Cookbook, 1951, paperback, 199 pages.**$5.00**

Heinz Book of Salads, 1934, paperback.......................**$6.50**

Hood's Cookbook #2, Hood's Sarsaparilla, 16 pages **$5.50**

How To Make Tempting Nutritious Desserts, Mary Mason, 1941 ....**$10.00**

Hunter's Stew & Hangtown Fry, L Perl, 1977, 156 pages **$5.00**

In a Copper Kettle, Armstrong, signed, 1958, hardcover, 116 pages **$5.50**

Incredible Edibles, Lake Forest Park, Washington, 1979, paperback, 124 pages **$4.50**

Joy of Cooking, Irma S Rombauer, 1946, hardcover ...**$15.00**

JR Watkins Co, 1936, hardcover................................**$5.00**

Kate Smith's Favorite Recipes, 1939......................**$12.50**

Kellogg's Cookbook, 1978..**$5.00**

Kerr Home Canning, Kerr, 1943, 56 pages.............**$15.00**

Knox Gelatin Recipes, 1952, 38 pages......................**$8.50**

Ladies' Home Journal Cookbook, 1960, hardcover **$15.00**

Larabee's Best Flour, 1931......................................**$12.00**

Leftovers, 500 Delicious Dishes, Culinary Arts, 1954, paperback **$4.50**

Libby's Fancy Red Alaska Salmon, Libby, McNeill & Libby, can shape, 1935................................**$12.50**

Luchow's German Cookbook, J Mitchell, 1952, hardcover, 224 pages..**$12.50**

Manual of Miracle Cookery, Edison Electric, 1935, paperback, 64 pages **$3.50**

McCall's Cooking Primer, 1953, paperback, 48 pages ...**$3.00**

McCall's Time-Saving Cookery, 1922......................**$14.00**

Meat Curing Made Easy & a New Way To Make Sausage, Morton Salt Co, 1933................................**$12.50**

Miss Minerva's Cookbook, Sampson, 1931 ....**$15.00**

My Better Homes & Gardens Cookbook, 1940, hardcover **$15.00**

New American Cookbook, Wallace, 1946...............**$10.00**

New Metro Cookbook, 1973, paperback, 60 pages.......**$2.50**

Occident Flour Tested Recipes, 1936.....................**$12.00**

Old Mr Boston, 1940, hardcover, 160 pages **$15.00**

Onions Without Tears, J Bothwell, 1950 ....**$5.00**

Pepperidge Farm Cookbook, M Rudkin, 1963, hardcover, 440 pages..**$15.00**

Pillsbury Bake-off, 18th edition, 1967, 96 pages...........**$6.00**

Pillsbury Cookbook, 1941..**$6.50**

Presto Cooker Recipe Book, National Pressure Cooker Co, 1940 ....**$10.00**

Prudence Penny's Cookbook, 1939, hardcover............**$8.50**

Quick & Easy Dinners, Sunset, 1970, paperback, 96 pages..**$4.50**

Recipes & Menus for All Occasions, Frito Co, 1947, 31 pages **$3.50**

Rice, 200 Ways To Serve It, Culinary Arts, 1935 ....**$4.50**

Royal Baker & Pastry Cook, Royal Baking Powder Co, 1906, $15.00

Royal Cookbook, 1935, 64 pages.................................**$5.00**

Rumford Complete Cookbook, L Wallace, 1946, hardcover, 213 pages..**$8.00**

Sally Stokely's Prize Recipes, Stokely Foods, 1935 ....**$4.50**

Simplified Hospitality, Servel, 1932, 47 pages...............**$4.00**

Someone's in the Kitchen w/Dinah, Dinah Shore, 1971, hardcover, 179 pages **$8.50**

Staley's Approved Recipes, William Landers & Sons General Merchandise, Utica Ill, 30 pages, $5.00

Sunset Chefs of the West, 1st edition, 1951, 219 pages.**$10.00**

Take It Easy Before Dinner, R Holberg, 1945, 98 pages..**$4.50**

Tested Recipes w/Blue Ribbon Malt Extract, 1927 .....**$12.50**
Three Meals a Day, Metro Life, 16 pages **$2.50**
Twelve Days of Christmas Cookbook, S Huntley, 1965, 143 pages..**$5.00**
Unusual Old World Recipes, ca 1960, 46 pages **$3.00**
Vermont Maple Recipes, 1952, 87 pages **$5.00**
Watkins Almanac & Home Book, 1868-1936 ....**$12.00**
Westinghouse Sugar & Spice Cookbook, 1951 ....**$3.50**
What's Cookin', J Bailey, 1949 ....**$10.00**
Wilderness Cooking, Berglund, 1973, 192 pages.........**$12.00**
Wolf in Chef's Clothing, Robert H Loeb Jr, 1950, hardcover **$15.00**
World Famous Chefs, F Naylor, 1940 ....**$50.00**
Yacht Club Manual of Salads, 1914............................**$16.00**
100 Glorified Recipes, Carnation Milk, 1930, paperback ..**$3.50**
101 Ways to Prepare Macaroni, La Rosa, 1949............**$10.00**
146 Adventures in Beef Cookery, Swift, 1958, paperback, 98 pages..**$2.50**
2,000 Useful Facts About Food, 1954, paperback.........**$4.50**

Bird in flight, tin, back & strap handle, 3¾x2½".........**$18.00**
Boar, tin, w/handle, 2⅞x5⅞"......................................**$35.00**
Duck, tin, back & strap handle, 4x3"..........................**$18.00**
Dutchman, tin, back & strap handle, 5¼x2¾".............**$40.00**
Eagle, crimped wings, tin, no handle, 4⅛x4½"............**$25.00**
Fish, tin, 5½"...**$35.00**
Hen, tin, back & strap handle, 3⅝x3⅞".......................**$22.00**
Horse, tin, back & strap handle, 3½x2¾"....................**$25.00**
Lady w/bustle, tin, 5"..**$110.00**
Lizard, tin, w/handle, 3⅛x6½"...................................**$45.00**
Maple leaf, red plastic, 1970s-80s...............................**$1.25**
Penquin, standing, tin, back & strap handle, 3⅝x2½".**$24.00**
Rocking horse, tin, back & strap handle, 4¾x4⅜".......**$45.00**
Santa, tin, open back, Germany, 8½x4⅛"....................**$55.00**
Scalloped rectangle, tin, back & strap handle, 3⅞x3"..**$12.00**
Squirrel, tin, lg crimped-edge tail, 5½" **$100.00**
Swan, tin, back & strap handle, 2⅞x2¾".....................**$35.00**
Whale, tin, 3¾"...**$20.00**
Wolf's head, tin, early 1900s, 4½"..............................**$32.00**

Cookie Cutters

Although the early tin cookie cutters from the 1700s are nearly all in museums by now, collectors still occasionally find a nice examples of the thinner handmade cutters from the turn of the century. The smaller, less imaginative examples are worth a minimum of $15.00, and the price increases with size, intricacy and imagination. What you're more apt to find today, of course, are plastic and aluminum cookie cutters. Though certainly not in the same class as the handmade tin ones, they are becoming collectible. Since the first were issued in the early seventies, Hallmark has sold more than 300 different styles, many available for only a short time. Most are worth from $1.00 to $5.00.

Molds, instead of cutting the cookie out, impressed a design into the dough. To learn more about both (and many other old kitchenware gadgets as well), we recommend *300 Years of Kitchen Collectibles* by Linda Campbell Franklin and *Kitchen Antiques, 1790 to 1940*, by Kathryn McNerney.

Girl or bird, metal, flat back, 4", each, $15.00

Cookie Jars

This is an area where we've seen nearly unprecedented growth of both interest and pricing. Rare cookie jars sell for literally thousands of dollars. Even a common jar from a good manufacturer will fall into the $40.00 to $100.00 price range. At the top of the list are the Black-theme jars, then come the cartoon characters such as Popeye, Howdy Doody, or the Flintstones. Any kind of a figural jar from an American pottery is extremely collectible right now.

The American Bisque company was one of the largest producers of these jars from 1930 until the 1970s. Many of their jars have no marks at all; those that do are simply marked 'USA,' sometimes with a mold number. But their airbrushed colors are easy to spot, and collectors look for the molded-in wedge-shaped pads on their bases — these say 'American Bisque' to cookie jar buffs about as clearly as if they were marked.

The Brush Pottery (Ohio, 1946-71) made cookie jars that were decorated with the airbrush in many of the same colors used by American Bisque. These jars are strongly holding their values, and the rare ones continue to climb in price. McCoy, Abingdon, Shawnee, and Red Wing all manufactured lots of cookie jars (their jars are listed in their own categories), and there are lots of wonderful jars by many other companies. Joyce and Fred Roerig's book *The Collector's Encyclopedia of Cookie Jars* covers them all beautifully, and Ermagene Westfall's *An Illustrated Value Guide to Cookie Jars II* is a recent release you won't want to miss.

Warning! The marketplace abounds with reproductions these days. Roger Jensen of Rockwood, Tennessee, is making a line of cookie jars as well as planters, salt and pepper shakers, and many other items which he marks McCoy. Because the 'real' McCoys never registered their trademark, he was able to receive federal approval to begin using this mark in 1992. Though he added '#93' to some of his pieces, the majority of his wares are undated. He is using old molds, and novice collectors are being fooled into buying the new for 'old' prices. Here are some of his reproductions that you should be aware of: McCoy Mammy, Clown, Dalmations, Indian Head; Hull Little Red Riding Hood; Pearl China Mammy; and the Mosaic Tile Mammy. There are sure to be others.

See also Abingdon; McCoy; Regal China; Shawnee; Red Wing.

ABC Bear, bear sitting on blocks marked ABC Cookies, marked Sierra Vista Ceramics, Calif USA on bottom.**$55.00**

Alf, marked Handpainted, Made in USA **$60.00**

Baby Huey, marked USA, American Bisque, minimum value...**$1,500.00**

Ballerina Bear, white w/yellow outfit, hair bow & shoes, marked Metlox Calif USA **$110.00**

Barney & Bam-Bam, marked JD 1992 ....**$95.00**

Barrel of Apples, unmarked, Metlox..........................**$35.00**

Baseball, Official Cookies lettered in blue, bat finial, marked Great American Game c 1991 Pelzam Designs..., Vandor..**$55.00**

Basket of Lemons, marked J-20 USA, Doranne of California...**$40.00**

Beau Bear, white w/pink bow, marked Metlox, Calif USA **$45.00**

Beauty & the Beast, marked Wihoa's Cookie Classic by Rick Wisecarver, R Sims, No 14, 1992.........................**$160.00**

Big Boy, w/cheeseburger, limited edition of 250, Wolfe original, 1992, minimum value **$250.00**

Blue Bird on Stump, marked Made in USA, Metlox **$45.00**

Boy on Pumpkin, unmarked, Metlox, minimum value .**$400.00**

Buddha, marked USA DeForest of California #527......**$70.00**

Cat in Wooden Bucket, Treasure Craft (c) Made in USA, $50.00

Caterpillar, in yellow top hat & red tie, marked 853, California Originals **$40.00**

Christmas Tree w/Mice, marked OCI **$70.00**

Cook Stove, red, unmarked, Twin Winton..................**$40.00**

Cookie Bakery, marked 863 on lid, 863 USA on base, California Originals **$40.00**

Covered Wagon, marked Marcia of California.............**$30.00**

Cow & Calf, in pasture, marked Wihoa's Cookie Classic by Rick Wisecarver #31, 1991, RS **$135.00**

Cross-Eyed Bird, pink & blue, marked C J 6 USA **$165.00**

Cuckoo Clock, stamped William H Hirsch Mfg Co Los Angeles, California...**$55.00**

Cupcake, cherry finial, marked J 54, Doranne of California...**$35.00**

Cylinder w/Duck Finial, marked K/26 USA **$55.00**

Dutch Boy, marked Metlox Calif USA c 87 by Vincent..**$165.00**

ET, unmarked..**$30.00**

Famous Amos, brown sack w/Famous Amos in script & chocolate chip cookie, marked Treasure Craft, Made in USA **$45.00**

Fire Hydrant, bright yellow, marked CJ 50 USA, Doranne of California...**$40.00**

Fire Truck, marked 841, California Originals **$70.00**

Fred & Pebbles, in blue chair, marked Vandor 1989, Made in Japan on paper label..................................**$300.00**

Gingham Dog, blue, marked Made in Poppytrail Calif USA, Metlox..**$130.00**

Girl Cook, stamped #2360, Lefton Reg US Pat Off Exclusive Japan on paper label **$45.00**

Gum Ball Machine, 1¢ Each, green lid & base, marked 890 USA, California Originals.......................................**$40.00**

Hen, blue & white, marked Treasure Craft c Made in USA...**$45.00**

Hen on Nest, marked Twin Winton c Calif USA.........**$50.00**

Hobby Horse, stamped Twin Winton Collector's Series .**$160.00**

Holstein Cow in Pasture, Made in Taiwan on paper label **$30.00**

Howdy Doody, unmarked, Purinton Pottery, from $300.00 to $350.00

Humpty Dumpty, marked 882 on lid & base, California Originals **$55.00**

Jafar (Aladdin), marked c Disney, Treasure Craft........**$55.00**

Jukebox, marked Treasure Craft c Made in USA **$110.00**
Kitten & Beehive, marked USA, American Bisque.......**$40.00**
Koala, marked Made in Poppytrail Calif USA, Metlox.**$120.00**
Koala, marked Maurice Ceramics MP 20 USA.............**$55.00**
Lamb, For Good Little Lambs Only lettered on apron, stamped Twin Winton c San Juan...Collector's Series...........**$110.00**
Lion w/Lollipop, marked 866 on lid, 866 USA on base, California Originals **$40.00**
Little Debbie Snack Cakes, clear glass canister w/red logo on front..**$25.00**
Little Red Riding Hood, marked 320 USA, California Originals **$250.00**
Log Cabin, House of Webster Ceramics, Eastland, Texas stamped on bottom..**$15.00**
M&M's, M&M guys carrying plate of cookies, ball form, marked M&M Mars Inc 1982, Haeger **$60.00**
Magilla Gorilla, marked Twin Winton c San Capistrano, Calif, minimum value **$300.00**
Mouse on Stump, marked 891-892 FS USA on lid & base, California Originals **$35.00**
Mrs Potts (from Beauty & the Beast), marked c Disney, Treasure Craft, Made in USA **$55.00**
Noah's Ark, marked Pat Pend Starnes Calif c on base, Sierra Vista Ceramics..**$140.00**
Noah's Ark, marked 881 USA, California Originals......**$65.00**
Oaken Bucket w/Dipper, marked USA, American Bisque **$70.00**
Panda w/Lollipop, marked Made in Poppytrail Calif USA, Metlox...**$185.00**
Polka Dot Witch, impressed MCMLXXVII, Fitz & Floyd.**$275.00**
Poncho Bear w/Sombrero, white w/yellow poncho, marked Metlox Calif USA **$75.00**

Poodle, marked USA, American Bisque, $70.00

Porky Pig, sitting in chair, marked 1975 Warner Bros.**$85.00**
Pretzel Barrel, unmarked, Metlox **$65.00**
Reclining Frog, marked 704 on lid, 704 USA on base, California Originals **$45.00**
Robot, blue w/red, yellow & black features, marked Japan...**$40.00**
Sailor boy finial, I Love To Eat Except at Mealtimes, Japan, 7"...**$40.00**
Santa Snowman, Made in Taiwan on paper label **$30.00**

School Bus, After School Cookies lettered in black, American Bisque..**$60.00**
Scottie, black w/glossy finish, marked Metlox Calif USA **$110.00**
Skull w/Spider, Ceramichrome, marked Hand-Painted, Made in USA...**$60.00**
Smiling Bear w/Badge, brown w/black features, unmarked, Twin Winton **$45.00**
Snail, w/elf finial, marked Designed by Twin Winton Calif **$135.00**
Snoopy Chef, marked G1958-1966 United Features Syn Inc, Made in Japan...**$235.00**
Strawberry Box, Made in USA Poppytrail Calif on paper label **$55.00**

Sylvester & Tweety Bird, marked Warner Bros Inc, Vandor, 1989, minimum value, $250.00

Tiki, marked Treasure Craft c Made in USA.................**$45.00**
Tommy Turtle, stamped Twin Winton c San Juan Capistrano Calif USA...**$70.00**
Tony the Tiger, plastic, marked Kellogg Co 1968........**$70.00**
Toothache Dog, marked USA, American Bisque, minimum value **$350.00**

Tugboat, Sierra Vista California, $135.00

Uncle Sam Bear, marked Metlox Calif USA, minimum value..**$400.00**

Winnie the Pooh, glossy finish, marked c Disney, Mexico on base $55.00

Wolfe, marked Paw Print, Wolfe Original, Limited Edition $110.00

Yogi Bear, marked Hanna-Barbera Prod Inc 1979, minimum value $400.00

Coors Rosebud Dinnerware

Golden, Colorado, was the site for both the Coors Brewing Company and the Coors Porcelain Company, each founded by the same man, Adolph Coors. The pottery's beginning was in 1910, and in the early years they manufactured various ceramic products such as industrial needs, dinnerware, vases, and figurines, but their most famous line and the one we want to tell you about was 'Rosebud.'

The Rosebud 'Cook 'n Serve' line was introduced in 1934. It's very easy to spot, and after you've once seen a piece, you'll be able to recognize it instantly. It was made in solid colors — rose, blue, green, yellow, ivory, and orange. The rose bud and leaves are embossed and hand-painted in contrasting colors. There are nearly fifty different pieces to collect, and bargains can still be found; but prices are accelerating, due to increased collector interest generated by a new book on the subject called *Collector's Encyclopedia of Colorado Pottery, Identification and Values,* written by Carol and Jim Carlton.

Apple baker, w/lid $45.00
Ashtray, 3½", rare...$175.00
Baking pan, rectangular, 2x12x8" $40.00
Bean pot, w/lid, sm $55.00
Bowl, mixing; handled, 3½-pt $50.00
Bowl, oatmeal; 6"..$25.00
Bowl, pudding; 2-pt...$35.00
Cake knife, 10" $60.00
Cake plate $35.00
Casserole, straight-sided, 2-pt, 5" $45.00

Casserole, w/underplate, 2-pt, $45.00

Casserole, w/underplate, 3½-pt....................................$65.00
Cookie jar, rope handles $110.00

Creamer, 3"...$30.00
Cup & saucer...$35.00
Custard, 4" $15.00
Egg cup...$50.00
Pie plate...$35.00
Platter, 12x9"..$35.00
Refrigerator set, 2 stacking dishes, square w/slightly domed lid $110.00
Salt & pepper shakers, 2½", pr......................................$35.00
Teapot, 2-cup, rare $165.00
Water server, corked stopper, 6-cup $120.00

Cottage Ware

Made by several companies, cottage ware is a line of ceramic table and kitchen accessories, each piece styled as a cozy cottage with a thatched roof. At least three English potteries made the ware, and you'll find pieces marked 'Japan' as well as 'Occupied Japan.' From Japan you'll also find pieces styled as windmills and water wheels, though the quality is inferior. The better pieces are marked 'Price Brothers' and 'Occupied Japan.' They're compatible in coloring as well as in styling, and values run about the same. Items marked simply 'Japan' are worth slightly less.

Bank, coin slot in roof, English.....................................$50.00
Butter dish, square, English...$45.00
Butter pat, embossed cottage, rectangular, Occupied Japan $17.50
Chocolate pot, English..$135.00
Condiment set, salt & pepper shakers w/mustard pot on tray, English, 4-pc set...$45.00
Cookie jar, pink, brown & green, Japan, 8½x5½" $65.00

Cookie jar, round, English, 8", $85.00

Cookie jar, square, English or Occupied Japan **$65.00**
Creamer, windmill, Occupied Japan, 2⅝" **$15.00**
Creamer & sugar bowl, English **$45.00**
Cup & saucer, English **$45.00**
Egg cups, 4 on square tray w/4 compartments, English **$60.00**
Marmalade, lid notched for spoon, English **$35.00**
Platter, oval, English, 12x7½" **$45.00**
Salt & pepper shakers, windmill, Occupied Japan, pr .**$20.00**
Teapot, English or Occupied Japan, 6½"....................**$50.00**
Teapot, Japan, 6½"..**$40.00**
Toast rack, English..**$45.00**

Country Store Collectibles

With the intensity collectors are showing toward anything advertising related, items once used in the 'mom-and-pop' groceries from years gone by are nowadays being bought up and added to collections to imbue a bit of yesteryear ambiance.

See also Advertising; Tobacianna.

Biscuit box, Kennedy's Newtons Biscuit, wood w/paper labels, 8x22x14", G **$65.00**
Cash register, #442 National, ornate brass on oak base, crank handle & tape dispenser on each side, marble shelf, 24", VG **$325.00**
Change tray, glass w/decaled images of Wrigley's gums in change depression, screws at corners, 16¾x18", EX .**$300.00**
Coffee grinder, Enterprise, painted cast iron on wood base, black w/gold trim & floral decor, 12½", VG **$100.00**

Coffee grinder, Fairbanks, Morse & Co, painted cast iron w/painted acanthus leaf design, minor paint loss, 27", VG, $350.00

Display, Baby Ruth/Curtiss Candies, rubber figure of boy wearing lettered sweater pointing to candy bar at feet, 15", VG **$275.00**
Display, Chase & Sanborn's Tea & Coffee, metal, adjustable shelf on vertical stand w/green & gold letters, 33x16x10", VG...**$100.00**
Display, Chief Two Moon Bitter Oil, cardboard trifold, depicts Chief's laboratory & bus w/various medicinals, 39x52", EX...**$150.00**

Display, Esterbrook Pen Nibs, round rotary type w/original product, top lists sizes & assortments, 14x10½" dia, EX...**$200.00**
Display, waist mannequin on pedestal, The 'Marvel' Health Belt, w/cloth belt, 27", G **$35.00**

Display cabinet, Coleman's Mustard, red & black on yellow tin, shaped like lg mustard can, 3 shelves, 16x10x7¼", G, $75.00

Display cabinet, Giblin's Liniment, wood w/stenciled lettering above glass doors, sm bottom drawer, 24x25½x8", G+ **$400.00**
Display cabinet, Munyon's Homoeopathic Home Remedies, tin-sided w/back drawer, portrait on slant top, 14x12", G **$200.00**
Display case, Bonnie-B Hair Nets, 6-sided w/wood base, mirrored front w/Priscilla Dean on panels, 1921, 14x14x11", G **$170.00**
Display case, Cattaraugus Cutlery, oak trapezoid shape w/glass sides, beveled base, 20¼x22x22", VG....**$250.00**
Display case, counter-top, wood w/curved glass front, original condition, 10x18½x12", G **$525.00**
Display case, Paris Garters, stenciled wood w/slanted glass front, 3 shelves, back folds down, 16", G **$30.00**
Display case, Ward's, oak w/glass front stenciled Ward's, single middle shelf, 31x30x24", EX......................**$160.00**
Display case for cheese, oak w/glass sides, round turntable, original condition, 20¼x22x22", VG **$350.00**
Display poster, Damschinsky's Hair Dye, shows strands of real hair, natural & dyed, framed, 19x14" without frame, EX...**$60.00**
Display rack, Card Seed Co, wood w/paper label, 5 stair-step rows w/seed packets, 15x24½", EX.............**$275.00**
Display rack, O-Cedar, wood-grain metal, stair-step type w/O-Cedar lettered on marquee & lettering on sides, 41x14", EX...**$120.00**
Display rack for candy jars, white-painted wire w/13 glass jars, chipping to paint, 58x22x17"........................**$250.00**
Dye cabinet, Diamond Dyes, tin upright w/lettering on knobbed doors promoting product, 16x18¾x6¼", G.................**$50.00**
Dye cabinet, Diamond Dyes, wood w/tin front, shows the evolution of women, rusted tin, wood refinished, 30x22x10", G **$200.00**
Dye cabinet, Perfection Dyes, wood w/tin insert, For Silk, Woolen, Cotton & Feathers, 24¼x17¼x6", EX/NM insert **$900.00**

Exit lamp, embossed ruby glass globe on wall mount, 5½x6" (excluding fixture), EX **$200.00**

Peanut warmer, Defiance, metal w/curved glass window, trapezoid shape on beveled base, 21½x18½x18", VG **$200.00**

Regulator clock, Calumet Baking Powder, Best By Test, wood w/reverse-painted glass panel, 35x17x5", G **$450.00**

Spice cabinet, tin w/mirrored front above 8 sm bins marked w/names of spices, 16x32x13", G.....................**$200.00**

Spool cabinet, JP Coates, counter-top desk type, oak w/4 lettered drawers & lift-up felt desk top, 14x29x21", G, $250.00

Spool cabinet, Royal Society, oak w/glass front, 12 vertical divided pull-out drawers, 35½x19½x19", G **$300.00**

Spool cabinet, Willimatic, oak counter-top desk type w/6 drawers, inlaid leather top, 16x36x24", G **$250.00**

Store bin, Choice Family Tea, tin w/stenciled flowers & bee, 14x11x11", G **$125.00**

Store bin, Dibbit's Toffees, tin, 2 parrots perched on limb on decorative ground, hinged lid, 12x11x7", dia, VG.**$300.00**

Store bin, Forbes Brothers, decorated metal w/curved top, image of horse on front, overall wear, G..............**$55.00**

Store bin, Golden Grains Steel Cut Coffee, painted metal w/hinged slant lid, 9¼x8x6½", G.........................**$185.00**

Store bin, Japan Tea, metal, stenciled & lithographed front, slanted hinged lid, 16x15x13¼", VG+, $155.00

Store bin, Rice's Pan-Dandy Bread, wood w/tin signs on front & slanted lid, footed, metal latch, G...........**$250.00**

Store computing scale, National, weighs goods in brass pan up to 3 lbs, restored, 16x16x6", EX **$350.00**

Store jar, Kis-Me Gum, 4-sided glass w/2 curved sides, paper labels on front & neck, embossed ground lid, 11", EX **$350.00**

Store jar, Ramon's Quality Medicines, round glass w/blue stenciled lettering, blue on yellow tin lid, 7¾", EX **$50.00**

Store jar, slim 4-sided pedestaled jar w/ground fitted teardrop lid, holds candy, 25½x5½", VG.............**$225.00**

Cracker Jack Collectibles

Cracker Jack has been around for over one hundred years. For ninety of those years, there's been a prize inside each box. If you could see the toys from over the years, you'd see the decades of the 20th century unfold. Tanks in wartime, sport's cards and whistles in peacetime, and space toys in the sixties. In addition to the prizes, collectors also look for dealer incentives, point-of-sale items, boxes, cartons, and advertising.

'Cracker Jack' in the following descriptions indicates that the item in question actually carries the Cracker Jack mark.

Sign, die-cut cardboard stand-up featuring Jack & Bingo & 5¢ Cracker Jack box, early, $285.00

Ad, 1919 Saturday Evening Post, color, Cracker Jack, 11x14"..**$18.00**

Button, cast metal w/stud back, features boy & dog, Me & Cracker Jack **$26.00**

Canister, Cracker Jack Commemorative, white w/red scroll, 198s, each **$6.50**

Canister, tin, Cracker Jack Coconut Corn Crisp, 1-lb...**$55.00**

Dealer incentive, jigsaw puzzle, Cracker Jack, 1 of 4, in envelope, 7x10".................................**$35.00**
Dealer incentive, postcard featuring bear, 1 of 16, Cracker Jack, 1907, each **$25.00**
Dealer incentive, tape measure, celluloid, Angelus, oval, 1½"...**$85.00**
Lunch box, embossed tin, Cracker Jack, 1970s, 4x7x9".**$30.00**
Medal, Cracker Jack saleman's award, brass, 1939, scarce..**$125.00**
Popcorn box, store display, Cracker Jack, no contents, 1923...**$65.00**
Premium, baseball bat, wood, Hillerich & Bradsby, Cracker Jack, full size **$125.00**
Premium, oval mirror, Angelus (redhead or blond) on box.**$90.00**
Prize, animals, plastic stand-up, series of 26, Nosco, 1953, each...**$4.00**
Prize, badge, boy & dog, die-cut tin, without tab at top.**$85.00**
Prize, badge, silver-tone die-cast metal, Cracker Jack Jr Detective, 1931, 1¼" **$35.00**
Prize, bank, 3-D book form, red, green or black tin, Cracker Jack Bank, early, 2"..............................**$95.00**
Prize, baseball score counter, Cracker Jack, 3⅜" long..**$145.00**
Prize, book, Birds We Know, Cracker Jack, miniature, 1928 ....**$75.00**
Prize, bookmark, tin, 4 different dogs, Cracker Jack, 2¾", each..**$30.00**
Prize, brooch or pin, tin, various designs on card, Cracker Jack, early, each....................................**$125.00**
Prize, decal, cartoon or nursery-rhyme figure, Cracker Jack, 1947-49.......................................**$7.00**
Prize, dog figure, plastic w/hollow base, series of 10, Cracker Jack, 1954, each............................**$5.00**
Prize, doll dishes, tin-plated, Cracker Jack, 1931, 1¾", 1⅞" & 2⅛" dia **$35.00**
Prize, dollhouse items: lantern, mug, candlestick, etc; no mark, each **$6.50**
Prize, horse & wagon, die-cut tin litho, Cracker Jack & Angelus, 2⅛"...**$65.00**
Prize, Indian headdress, paper, Cracker Jack, early 1920s, 2½"..**$110.00**
Prize, iron-on transfer, sports figure or patriotic, Cracker Jack, 1939, each **$20.00**
Prize, radio lithographed on tin box shape, 1⅛" **$80.00**
Prize, road sign, plastic, series of 10, 1954-60, each......**$3.00**

Prize, rocking horse, orange plastic, 1¾", $3.00

Prize, rocking horse w/boy, inked cast metal, early, 1½" **$29.00**

Prize, sand picture, series of 14, 1967, each **$10.00**
Prize, sled, tin-plated, Cracker Jack, 1931, 2" long **$40.00**
Prize, train engine, lithographed tin, red, 1941............**$18.00**
Prize, whistle, plastic tube w/animals on top, Cracker Jack, 1 of 6, 1950-53, 1⅜" **$7.00**
Prize, whistle, pressed paper, series of 10, Cracker Jack, 1948-49, 1¼x2", each..**$40.00**
Vendor's cap, Cracker Jack, 1930s **$30.00**

Crooksville China

American dinnerware is becoming a very popular field of collectibles, and because many of the more well-established lines such as Fiesta, LuRay, and those designed by Russell Wright have become so expensive, people are now looking for less costly patterns. If you've been at all aware of the market over the past twenty years or so, you know the same thing occurred in the Depression glass field. Lines that we were completely disinterested in during the late sixties have come into their own today.

Crooksville china comes from a small town in Ohio by the same name. They made many lines of dinnerware and kitchen items, much of which carried their trademark, until they closed late in the fifties. One of their more extensive lines is called 'Silhouette,' made in the mid-thirties. It is very similar to a line by Hall China, but you can easily tell the difference. Crooksville's decal is centered by the silhouette of a begging dog. Another nice line is 'House,' so named because of the English cottage featured in the petit-point-style decal. There are many different floral lines, and don't be surprised if you find the same decal on more than one of their standard shapes.

If you'd like to learn more about the various dinnerware companies we've included in this book, we recommed you read *The Collector's Encyclopedia of American Dinnerware* by Jo Cunningham.

California James Poppy, plate, 10", $10.00; casserole, Pantry-Bak-In, 8", $22.00

Apple Blossom, casserole, Pantry-Bak-In, 8" **$28.00**
Apple Blossom, pie baker, Pantry-Bak-In, 10"............**$26.00**
Avenue, plate, La Grande shape, 10¾"........................**$10.00**
Black Tulip, vegetable bowl, divided, hand painted...**$45.00**
Blossom Time, plate, coupe shape, 6" **$40.00**

Blossoms, individual casserole, Fruits shape.................**$8.00**

Blossoms, plate, Fruits shape, 6¾"............................**$8.00**

Blue Blossoms, bean pot.......................................**$50.00**

Border Bouquet, plate, La Grande shape, 10"...............**$8.00**

Calico Flowers, creamer..**$12.00**

Flower Fair, plate, coupe shape, 9"...........................**$10.00**

Homestead in Winter, chop plate, Iva-Lure shape, 10" ..**$16.00**

Hunting, plate, Iva-Lure shape, 12" **$20.00**

Ivy Vine, plate, coupe shape, 10¼" **$8.00**

Little Bouquet, plate, La Grande shape, 9¾" **$8.00**

Petit Point House, casserole (open), 7" **$18.00**

Petit Point House, plate, Fruits shape, 9¾" **$15.00**

Petit Point House, plate, 7¼" **$10.00**

Petit Point House, teapot......................................**$50.00**

Pheasant, plate, 9¾"...**$12.00**

Pink Border, plate, La Grande shape, 10" **$10.00**

Posies, utility bowl..**$8.00**

Rose Garland, gravy boat & liner, 1920s **$15.00**

Roses, serving bowl, Birds shape, 8¾"........................**$12.00**

Scotch Plaid, plate, coupe shape, 10¼" **$8.00**

Silhouette, platter, 11½".......................................**$22.00**

Silhouette, serving tray, 11¾" **$26.00**

Silhouette, tumbler, glass......................................**$26.00**

Silhouette, utility bowl...**$22.00**

Southern Belle, cup & saucer, Iva-Lure shape.............**$10.00**

Trellis, cup saucer...**$16.00**

Trellis, plate, Iva-Glo shape, 8"..............................**$12.00**

Trellis, syrup pitcher, w/lid....................................**$42.00**

Trotter, cup & saucer...**$10.00**

Veggies, pie baker, Pantry-Bak-In, 10".......................**$22.00**

Currier and Ives by Royal

This dinnerware has for the past several years been the focus of a great amount of collector interest. It was made by the Royal China company of Sebring, Ohio, and was given away as premiums for shopping at A&P stores. It is decorated with blue and white renditions of early American scenes by Currier and Ives and so fits not only into the 'country' look now so popular in home decorating but its color schemes as well. Besides the dinnerware, Fire-King baking pans and accessories, glass tumblers, and vinyl placemats were also offered by A&P. Most pieces are relatively easy to find, but the casserole and the teapot are considered 'prizes' by collectors.

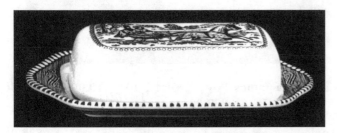

Butter dish, ¼-lb, $25.00

Bowl, cereal; 6⅜" **$7.00**

Bowl, fruit; 5½" **$3.00**

Bowl, lug soup; deep, tab handle, 2¾x4¾" **$20.00**

Bowl, vegetable; 10"...**$20.00**

Bowl, 9"...**$18.00**

Calendar plate, 1970s-85, each...............................**$12.00**

Candle lamp & globe, rare, tall, 3¾" base...................**$30.00**

Casserole w/lid, angle handles **$60.00**

Casserole, w/lid, tab handles, old............................**$100.00**

Creamer **$5.00**

Cup & saucer..**$4.00**

Gravy boat...**$13.00**

Gravy ladle..**$10.00**

Plate, 10½"...**$5.00**

Plate, 7⅜"...**$7.00**

Platter, round, marked, rare, 13" dia.........................**$40.00**

Platter, round, marked, 11" dia **$20.00**

Platter, tab handles, 10½".......................................**$18.00**

Salt & pepper shakers, pr.......................................**$15.00**

Sugar bowl, w/lid **$12.00**

Teapot...**$75.00**

Tumbler, juice...**$10.00**

Tumbler, 13-oz, 5½"...**$12.00**

Czechoslovakian Glass and Ceramics

Established as a country in 1918, Czechoslovakia is rich in the natural resources needed for production of glassware as well as pottery. Over the years it has produced vast amounts of both. Anywhere you go, from flea markets to fine antique shops, you'll find several examples of their lovely pressed and cut glass scent bottles, Deco vases, lamps, kitchenware, tableware and figurines.

More than thirty five marks have been recorded; some are ink stamped, some etched, and some molded in. Paper labels have also been used. *Czechoslovakian Glass and Collectibles* by Diane and Dale Barta and *Made in Czechoslovakia* by Ruth Forsythe are two books we highly recommend for further study.

Ceramics

Bank, black Scotty dog, high gloss finish, 4⅝" **$55.00**

Basket, white glaze w/raised rope design, floral design in center, pedestal feet, 4¼" **$35.00**

Bowl, blue, green, red & tan mottle w/variegated design, 3" **$55.00**

Chocolate pot, orange lustreware, ear-type handle, 9½".**$55.00**

Creamer, orange flowers & green vines on white, orange scalloped design around rim, orange handle, Erphila Art, 4¼" **$70.00**

Dresser box, orange basket-weave design & blue-green ribbon w/flowers in relief, 2½"...................................**$45.00**

Figurine, rearing horse, black w/turquoise mane, tail & hooves, 8"..**$60.00**

Flower frog, orange lustreware w/black trim, 2" **$25.00**

Pitcher, bright yellow w/high gloss finish, ball form, 5¼".**$50.00**

Pitcher, hand-painted raised fruit design on maroon background, ear-type handle, 6½"...............................**$75.00**

Pitcher, purple & orange flowers w/green leaves on white, orange rim & handle, 5½" $60.00

Pitcher, yellow mottle w/multicolored floral design in center, black rim & handle, 6½" $50.00

Plate, orange flower surrounded by green vine in center, orange scalloped design around rim, Erphila Art, 6½" $80.00

Plate, salad; leaf shape w/light green & brownish-yellow leaves, majolica, 7"................................$50.00

Salt box, blue on white w/wooden lid, 6¾x6", $65.00

Sugar bowl (open), white pearl lustre w/shell design, 4 raised feet, 2¼".....................................$55.00

Vase, iridescent blue w/black rim, tall cylinder form w/slightly flared rim & base, 9¼"...................$65.00

Vase, multicolored flower & fruit design on white background, rectangular, 6⅝" $40.00

Vase, multicolored flowers on white background, black rim, bulbous, 6¼" $30.00

Vase, paper overlay w/clear glaze, black trim on scalloped rim, black ear-type handles, 5½"...........$50.00

Vase, red w/black & white scroll design around multicolored flowers, 5"................................$50.00

Vase, sawtooth design in orange to light & dark purple, black rim, 7¼" $130.00

Glassware

Atomizer, blue-painted bottle w/black enameled design, 6¼" $65.00

Atomizer, clear & frosted pink w/enameled decoration, 6¼" $65.00

Bowl, cased, black w/orange interior, 6¼" $95.00

Bowl, cased, white ruffled edge w/applied maroon rim, 6" $135.00

Candle holder/paperweight, cased, varicolored mottle, 1920s, 1¾"..$45.00

Cologne, transparent green, horizontally ridged, 4½" .$65.00

Decanter, clear ball form w/black decoration, applied clear handle, 6½".....................................$95.00

Decanter, clear w/painted floral design, 10½" $60.00

Perfume, black opaque base w/jeweled decoration, black octagon-shaped stopper, 3"....................$85.00

Perfume, graduated bell shape, iridescent amber w/dark blue stripes, faceted drop stopper, 3½"..............$175.00

Perfume, intaglio cut design w/clear cut base, amethyst drop stopper, 6¾" $175.00

Perfume, smoky cut base w/transparent black stopper, 4½" $110.00

Pitcher, cased, yellow w/applied cobalt tricornered rim, 5"...$80.00

Puff box, orange w/gold trim, floral design on lid, 3¾" ..$55.00

Shot glass, clear w/enameled design, 2¼" $25.00

Tumbler, clear w/cobalt threading design & green base, 5".$65.00

Vase, bud; cased, orange w/6 clear feet, gourd form, 8".$50.00

Vase, cased, cobalt w/mottled colors, vertically ridged layers, 4¾" $75.00

Vase, cased, cream color w/applied aqua trim on ruffled rim, vertically ridged hourglass shape, 7¾"...........$95.00

Vase, cased, mottled colors, tall cylinder form w/slightly flared base, 10½"...................................$75.00

Vase, cased, pale blue w/ruffled edge, applied crystal handles, 8" $95.00

Vase, cased, red mottle w/jet rim & applied serpentine, ruffled, 8" $100.00

Vase, cased, red w/applied jet rim & black base, 5" ...$75.00

Vase, cased, varicolored, horizontally ridged layers, 8⅜"..$80.00

Vase, cased, varicolored w/applied 3-footed clear glass pedestal base, 7¼" $80.00

Vase, cased, yellow & brown variegated design w/applied 3-footed jet pedestal base, 7¾" $95.00

Vase, cased, yellow w/brown mottled base, bulbous, 5¾" $65.00

Vase, cased, yellow w/clown design, applied jet rim, 6¼" $65.00

Vase, crystal w/alternating frosted panels, 10" $235.00

Vase, frosted crystal w/coralene design, bulbous, 4½"..$55.00

Vase, multicolored design, 8", $50.00

Dairy Bottles

Between the turn of the century and the 1950s, milk was bought and sold in glass bottles. Until the twenties, the name and location of the dairy was embossed in the glass. After that it became commonplace to pyro-glaze (paint and fire) the lettering onto the surface. Farmers sometimes added a cow or some other graphic that represented the product or related to the name of the dairy.

Because so many of these glass bottles were destroyed when paper and plastic cartons became popular, they've become a scarce commodity, and today's collectors have begun to take notice of them. It's fun to see just how many you can find from your home state — or try getting one from every state in the union!

What makes for a good milk bottle? Collectors normally find the pyro-glaze decorations more desirable, since they're more visual. Bottles from dairies in their home state hold more interest for them, so naturally New Jersey bottles sell better there than they would in California, for instance. Green glass examples are unusual and often go for a premium; so do those with the embossed baby faces. (Watch for reproductions here!) And those with a 'Buy War Bonds' slogan or a patriot message are always popular.

Some collectors enjoy adding 'go-alongs' to enhance their collections, so the paper pull tops, advertising items that feature dairy bottles, and those old cream-top spoons will interest them as well. The spoons usually sell for about $6.00 each. For more information, we recommend *Udderly Delightful* by John Tutton.

Ferndale Dairy, First in Quality, Grand Ledge Mich, amber w/white pyro, 1-qt, $18.00

Alta Crest Farms, Brookfield Mass, cow's head on sides, maroon pyro, square, 1-qt.....................................**$10.00**
AR Parker, Satucket Dairy, East Bridgewater Mass, embossed, round, ½-pt..**$6.50**
Borden's Quality Service (front), Property of Borden's Farm Products Co Inc (back), embossed, round, 1-qt **$7.50**
Braleys (on shoulder), embossed script, square, ½-pt ..**$5.00**
Brookdale Dairy, Seymour Conn, Farmer Producer WF Molsick... & farm-to-residence scene on back, orange pyro, round, 1-qt...**$16.00**
Ca Hayward & Sons, Milford NH, embossed, vertical ribs, round, ½-pt...**$6.00**

Coors Bros Dairy, Cincinnati O, round nurser w/5 cupid-type babies in various scenes, red pyro................**$12.50**
Doberts, Glen Falls NY, orange pyro, round, ¾-oz creamer **$18.00**
Frates Dairy Inc, New Bedford, red pyro, square, 1-qt .**$6.00**
Gascoyne Dairy, embossed, Pat 7-8-30 on base, round, 1-qt...**$80.00**
Gibbs Farm Dairy (on base), embossed, diamond design around neck, round, 1-pt...**$8.50**
Hayward Farms, embossed script, round, 1-pt **$6.00**
Helfand Dairy Products, red pyro, round, ¾-oz creamer.**$16.00**
Horne's Dairy, Milk at It's Best, Fresh From the Farm under barn scene on back, yellow pyro, round 1-qt.......**$16.00**
Indiana Dairy Co, Indiana PA, For Your Next Salad Try Our Delicious Cottage Cheese... on back, black pryo, round, 1-qt...**$30.00**
JB Prescott, P Bedford Mass, embossed, vertical ribs, round, 1-qt...**$6.00**
Morningside Farm, Stockton Cal, sunrise scene w/cow in barnyard on back, orange pyro, round, 1-qt........**$12.00**
Noble's, Thats Good Milk (in shield), embossed, round, 1-qt...**$6.50**
Oakhurst Dairy Co, Protect the Kiddies below scene w/milkman & policeman helping little girl on back, orange pyro, 1-qt **$12.00**
Onatru Farm, Ridgefield Conn, full-bodied goat on back, green pyro, round, 1-qt...**$90.00**
Paiva's Farm Dairy, Dartmouth Mass, clear w/red pyro, round, 1-pt..**$20.00**
Pet Dairy Products Co, laboratory scene in center, red pyro, Pet Dairy Products Co embossed on shoulder, round, 1-qt **$12.00**
Property of Acawam Goat Dairy, Wash, Scald & Return, Pure Goat's Milk on back, embossed, round, ½-pt **$65.00**
Queensboro (embossed) Farm Products, Long Island City NY, 1-pt **$8.00**

Roger E. Brooks & Son, clear w/brown pyro, 1-qt, $18.00

San A Pure Dairy Co, Findlay Ohio, embossed, Pat 7-8-30 on base, round, 1-qt **$90.00**
Sanitary Salad Cream, red & blue pyro, 1-pt.................**$8.00**

Sealtest Dairy Products, Sealtest Pasteurized Products on back, red pyro, round, ½-oz $16.00

Sonny Slope Dairy Cottage Cheese, Spring City PA, lg mouth, orange pyro, round, 12-oz........................$7.50

Stevenson Dairy, Dane Wis, milkman w/tray on back, orange pyro, round, 1-pt $8.50

Sunshine Milk, Bridgeport Conn, sunrise & farm scene in center, orange pyro, round, 1-qt..........................$12.00

Tideys Home Dairy, Eau Claire Mich, Safe Milk Bottled on Our Farm w/cow & barn on back, red pyro, round, 1-qt $18.00

United Farms, Albany NY, embossed lettering & allover diamond design, round, ½-pt...............................$6.50

White Bros, That Creamy Milk (on shoulder), embossed, square, 1-qt..$6.00

Whites Farm, embossed, square, ½-pt.........................$5.00

Wilson Dairy Co, Fine Dairy Products Since 1877 on back, orange pyro, square, ¾-oz.................................$18.00

Witherells Dairy, Rochester NH (front), This Product Bottled in Amber Glass for...(back), yellow pyro, square, 1-qt $10.00

Dakin

Dakin has been in the toy-making business since the 1950s and has made several lines of stuffed and vinyl dolls and animals, but the Dakins that collectors are most interested in today are the licensed characters and advertising figures made from 1968 through the seventies. Originally there were seven Warner Brothers characters, each with a hard plastic body and a soft vinyl head, all under 10" tall. The line was very succesfull and eventually expanded to include more than fifty cartoon characters and several more that were advertising related. In addition to the figures, there are banks that were made in two sizes. Some Dakins are quite scarce and may sell for over $100.00 (a few even higher), though most will be in the $30.00 to $60.00 range.

Condition is very important, and if you find one still in the original box, add about 50% to its value. More are listed in *Schroeder's Collectible Toys, Antique to Modern*, published by Collector Books.

Baby Puss, Hanna-Barbera, 1971, EX+......................$100.00

Bambi, Disney, 1960s, MIP...$35.00

Barney Rubble, Hanna-Barbera, 1970, MIP.................$50.00

Bozo the Clown, MIP...$60.00

Bugs Bunny in Uncle Sam outfit, Warner Bros, 1975, MIP..$60.00

Bullwinkle, Jay Ward, 1976, EX+ $45.00

Daffy Duck, Warner Bros, 1968, EX+ $25.00

Deputy Dawg, Terrytoons, 1977, MIP $60.00

Dewey Duck, red shirt, Disney, MIP $30.00

Dino Dinosaur, hard plastic body w/soft vinyl head, name tag on collar, Hanna-Barbera, 1970, 8", EX..........$40.00

Dog in Suit, Goofy Gram, Have a Dog-Gone Good Time, 1971, 8", EX $40.00

Dudley Do-Right, in cartoon theater box, Jay Ward, M.$75.00

Foghorn Leghorn, Warner Bros, 1970, EX+ $75.00

Glamour Kitty, w/red cape & gold crown, 1978, 5", EX $150.00

Goofy, cloth clothes, Disney, MIP $30.00

Huckleberry Hound, Hanna-Barbera, 1970, MIP $100.00

Huey Duck, green shirt, Disney, MIP $30.00

Jack-in-the-box, bank, 1971, 6", EX.............................$40.00

Laurel or Hardy, w/original tag, 1968, MIP $35.00

Mickey Mouse, Disney, MIP...$30.00

Mighty Mouse, Terrytoons, MIP $175.00

Olive Oyl, molded clothes, in cartoon theater box, 1976, MIB $60.00

Pebbles, Hanna-Barbera, 1971, EX $75.00

Pepe LePew, Warner Bros, 1971, EX+.........................$75.00

Popeye, King Features, 1974, MIP $60.00

Purple Poodle, Goofy Gram, It Was Sweet of You, 1971, 8", EX...$30.00

Roadrunner, Warner Bros, 1968, MIP $30.00

Rocky Squirrel, Jay Ward, 1976, 5", EX+ $30.00

Scooby Doo, Hanna-Barbera, 1971, EX+.....................$75.00

Seal w/ball, bank, 1971, 8", EX $35.00

Second Banana, Warner Bros, 1970, EX+....................$35.00

Snagglepuss, Hanna-Barbera, 1971, EX+....................$100.00

Speedy Gonzales, vinyl w/cloth & felt clothing, 1968, EX, $40.00

Swee' Pea, beanbag, King Features, 1974, EX+ $25.00

Underdog, Leonardo TV, 1976, EX+.............................$85.00

Wile E Coyote, in cartoon theater box, Warner Bros, 1975, MIB $40.00

Woodsy Owl, cloth clothes, 1960s, EX........................$25.00

Yogi Bear, Hanna-Barbera, 1970, MIP.........................$100.00

De Vilbiss

The lovely perfume bottles, lamps, and vanity accessories you'll find marked De Vilbiss were not actually made by that company (De Vilbiss made only the metal hardware), but rather by a variety of glasshouses. Fenton pressed some, so did Cambridge and Imperial. Others were imported from Italy, Czechoslovakia, and West Germany.

They were sold by De Vilbiss both here and abroad. You'll find several variations of the company's paper labels, and rarely one that will be marked 'DeV' in gold enamel.

Values hinge on two factors: the type of glass that was used and the design. The most valuable are those made in Aurene glass by Steuben. (Aurene is primarily found in gold or blue and is characterized by its strong iridescence.) Perfumes with figural stems or those with strong Art Deco influence are usually near the top of the price scale. Gold-colored glass with a crackled appearance was often used, and the smaller, less-strikingly designed examples made of this type of glass are more common.

A good source for further study is *Bedroom and Bathroom Glassware of the Depression Years* by Margaret and Kenn Whitmyer.

Atomizer, black enamel body w/gold decoration, gold encrusted stem & foot over frosted crystal base, 7".**$135.00**
Atomizer, black w/crystal stem & foot, bulb missing, 4¼" **$60.00**
Atomizer, cranberry stain w/gold decoration & foot, 7".**$125.00**
Atomizer, dark green enamel w/black floral decoration, octagon, brass fitting, 5½" **$85.00**
Atomizer, French opalescent, Coin Dot, ball form **$35.00**
Atomizer, lavender enamel, tall stem, 6¼" **$70.00**
Atomizer, orange enamel body w/black & gold decoration, crystal stem & foot, 7¾"......................................**$125.00**
Atomizer, orange enamel w/black & gold decoration, gold encrusted stem & foot, 7½" **$135.00**
Atomizer, orange stain over crystal, tall stem, 6".......**$160.00**
Ginger jar, Chinese red w/gold floral decoration **$95.00**
Perfume bottle, black w/chrome neck **$45.00**

Perfume bottle, green w/gold filigree, 3¼x3½" dia, $40.00

Perfume dropper, crystal w/blue floral decoration......**$30.00**
Perfume dropper, orange enamel on elongated teardrop shape w/round flat base...**$55.00**
Pin tray, orange enamel w/black & gold decoration on oval shape, 3¼x5⅝" **$25.00**
Puff box, gold encrusted bowl-shaped body on round footed base, green enamel dome lid w/gold design.........**$65.00**

Puff box, orange enamel bowl-shaped body on round footed base, orange dome lid w/black & gold decoration, 4¾" dia **$55.00**

Decanters

The first company to make figural ceramic decanters was the James Beam Distilling Company, who now own their own china factory here in the United States. They first issued their bottles in the mid-fifties, and over the course of the next twenty-five years, more than twenty other companies followed their example. Among the more prominent of these were Brooks, Hoffman, Lionstone, McCormick, Old Commonwealth, Ski Country, and Wild Turkey. In 1975, Beam introduced the 'Wheel Series,' cars, trains, and fire engines with wheels that actually revolved. The popularity of this series resulted in a heightened interest in decanter collecting.

There are various sizes. The smallest (called miniatures) hold two ounces, and there are some that hold a gallon! A full decanter is worth no more than an empty one, and the absence of the tax stamp doesn't lower its value either. Just be sure that all the labels are intact and that there are no cracks or chips. You might want to empty your decanters as a safety precaution (many collectors do) rather than risk the possibility of the inner glaze breaking down and allowing the contents to leak into the porous ceramic body.

All of the decanters we've listed are fifths unless we've specified 'miniature' within the description.

Aesthetic Specialties (ASI), Golf, Bing Crosby 39th.....**$25.00**
Aesthetic Specialties (ASI), World's Greatest Hunter...**$30.00**
Anniversary (Marita), Christmas Greeting....................**$12.00**
Anniversary (Marita), John Lennon.............................**$25.00**
Ballantine, Zebra..**$18.00**
Beam, Casino Series, Barney's Slot Machine...............**$20.00**
Beam, Casino Series, Circus Circus Clown..................**$40.00**
Beam, Casino Series, Golden Nugget, 1969.................**$50.00**
Beam, Casino Series, Reno (Prima Donna)...................**$5.00**
Beam, Centennial Series, Alaska Purchase...................**$5.00**
Beam, Centennial Series, Chicago Fire........................**$15.00**
Beam, Centennial Series, Colorado............................**$10.00**
Beam, Centennial Series, Reno....................................**$8.00**
Beam, Centennial Series, San Diego............................**$7.00**
Beam, Centennial Series, Santa Fe.............................**$95.00**
Beam, Club Series, Five Seasons Club.......................**$10.00**
Beam, Club Series, Gem City....................................**$25.00**
Beam, Club Series, Monterey Bay Club.......................**$10.00**
Beam, Club Series, Twin Bridges...............................**$30.00**
Beam, Club Series, Wolverine...................................**$10.00**
Beam, Convention Series, Detroit, 1973 ....**$10.00**
Beam, Convention Series, Houston, 1979 ....**$25.00**
Beam, Convention Series, Minuteman, pewter...........**$50.00**
Beam, Convention Series, Sacramento, 1975 ....**$10.00**
Beam, Convention Series, Showgirl (blond) **$40.00**
Beam, Convention Series, St Louis.............................**$55.00**
Beam, Customer Series, Bohemian Girl......................**$10.00**
Beam, Customer Series, Delco Battery **$25.00**

Beam, Customer Series, Harley-Davidson 85th Anniversary $150.00
Beam, Customer Series, Poulan Chainsaw $25.00
Beam, Executive Series, Bowl, 1986.....................$25.00
Beam, Executive Series, Golden Jubilee, 1977............$10.00
Beam, Executive Series, Holiday Nutcracker, 1990......$40.00
Beam, Executive Series, Mother-of-Pearl, 1979...........$10.00
Beam, Executive Series, Reflections, 1975...................$10.00
Beam, Executive Series, Regency, 1972......................$10.00
Beam, Executive Series, Royal Di Monte, 1957...........$35.00
Beam, Executive Series, Royal Gold Diamond, 1964...$25.00
Beam, Executive Series, Tavern Scene, 1959 ....$50.00
Beam, Executive Series, Twin Doves, 1972.................$24.00
Beam, Foreign Series, Australia, Galah Bird................$25.00
Beam, Foreign Series, Australia, Hobo $12.00
Beam, Foreign Series, Germany, Hansel & Gretel.......$10.00
Beam, Opera Series, Aida, w/base $95.00
Beam, Opera Series, Falstaff, w/base $150.00
Beam, Organization Series, Ahepa............................$5.00
Beam, Organization Series, Ducks Unlimited #10, 1984.$70.00
Beam, Organization Series, Pearl Harbor, 1972 ....$20.00
Beam, Organization Series, Shrine, Rajah Temple.......$20.00
Beam, Organization Series, Telephone #5, pay phone..$50.00
Beam, Organization Series, VFW $10.00
Beam, People Series, Cowboy $25.00
Beam, People Series, Emmet Kelley $35.00
Beam, People Series, Hank Williams Jr $20.00
Beam, People Series, Viking $15.00
Beam, Political Series, Donkey, New York, 1976 ....$10.00
Beam, Political Series, Elephant, San Diego, 1972.......$20.00
Beam, Transportation Series, Caboose, red.................$70.00
Beam, Transportation Series, Space Shuttle $35.00
Beam, Transportation Series, Train, Observation Car..$30.00
Beam, Transportation Series, Train, Passenger Car $40.00
Beam, Wheel Series, Dump Truck.............................$65.00

Beam, Wheel Series, Grant's Locomotive, $90.00

Beam, Wheel Series, Police Tow Truck $60.00
Beam, Wheel Series, 1935 Ford Pickup, Clermont $60.00
Beam, Wheel Series, 1956 Ford Thunderbird, green...$75.00
Beam, Wheel Series, 1957 Chevy Bellair, black hardtop.$95.00
Beam, Wheel Series, 1968 Chevy Corvette, blue or maroon $70.00
Brooks, Animal Series, Northern Raccoon $45.00

Brooks, Animal Series, Panda $18.00
Brooks, Automotive & Transporation Series, 1962 Corvette, Mako Shark...$30.00
Brooks, Automotive & Transportation Series, Snowmobile $12.00
Brooks, Bird Series, Snow Egret $25.00
Brooks, Clown Series, Cuddles, #5 ....$30.00
Brooks, Indian Series, Mudhead, #7 ....$45.00
Brooks, Indian Series, Watermelon, #9 ....$30.00
Brooks, Institutional Series, Golden Pharoah..............$25.00
Brooks, People Series, Betsy Ross $10.00
Brooks, People Series, Casey at the Bat.....................$40.00
Brooks, People Series, Jester.....................................$8.00
Brooks, Sports Series, Georgia Bulldog......................$25.00
Brooks, Sports Series, Tennis Player..........................$12.00
Cyrus Noble, Dolphin..$50.00
Cyrus Noble, Gambler, miniature $12.00
Cyrus Noble, Violinist..$45.00
Cyrus Noble, Walrus Family, miniature $15.00
Cyrus Noble, White-Tail Deer $80.00
Double Springs, Mercedes Benz $25.00
Double Springs, Rolls Royce $25.00
Famous Firsts, #8 National Racer, miniature $25.00
Famous Firsts, Duesenberg $90.00
Famous Firsts, Roulette Wheel...................................$30.00
Grenadier, Appaloosa Horse.....................................$30.00
Grenadier, Billy Mitchell...$40.00
Grenadier, Santa Claus $30.00
Hoffman, Mr Lucky Series, Carpenter........................$35.00
Hoffman, Mr Lucky Series, Carpenter, miniature.........$15.00
Hoffman, Mr Lucky Series, Schoolteacher...................$30.00
Hoffman, Sports Series, Dallas Cheerleader................$30.00
Hoffman, Wildlife Series (Ohrman), Lion & Crane $30.00
Jack Daniels, Belle of Lincoln $30.00
Jack Daniels, Maxwell House.....................................$35.00
Jack Daniels, Tribute to Tennessee.............................$30.00
Kontinental, Gandy Dancer.......................................$20.00
Kontinental, Innkeeper..$25.00
Kontinental, Lumberjack..$25.00
Kontinental, School Marm $30.00
Kontinental, Stephen Foster $20.00
Lionstone, Automotive & Transportation Series, STP Turbocar, red..$45.00
Lionstone, Bicentennial Series, Valley Forge...............$20.00
Lionstone, Bird Series, Owls $25.00
Lionstone, Bird Series, Robin, miniature $18.00
Lionstone, Old West Series, Buffalo Hunter................$30.00
Lionstone, Old West Series, Country Doctor...............$20.00
Lionstone, Old West Series, Indian Tribal Chief $30.00
Lionstone, Old West Series, Judge Roy Bean..............$35.00
Lionstone, Sports Series, Fisherman............................$40.00
McCormick, Confederate Series, Jeb Stuart $60.00
McCormick, Confederate Series, Robert E Lee, miniature...$20.00
McCormick, Confederate Series, Stonewall Jackson, miniature...$20.00
McCormick, Great American Series, Alexander Graham Bell..$25.00

McCormick, Great American Series, Henry Ford $25.00
Michter, Fleetwood Packard..............................$25.00
Mike Wayne, John Wayne Portrait..........................$40.00
Mike Wayne, Pope John Paul $20.00
Mitcher, Conestoga Wagon $50.00
Mitcher, King Tut, miniature $20.00
Mitcher, Stage Coach $15.00
Mitcher, Texas Football $20.00
Mount Hope, American Legion Seaman.......................$25.00
Mount Hope, Fireman #1, PA Volunteer $85.00
Mount Hope, Phila Flyers.................................$65.00
Mount Hope, Snowman......................................$8.00
Old Bardstown, Bulldog...................................$150.00
Old Bardstown, Delta Queen Riverboat.....................$50.00
Old Bardstown, Foster Brooks.............................$15.00
Old Bardstown, Surface Miner $20.00
Old Bardstown, Wildcat #1 ....$40.00
Old Commonwealth, Chief Illini #2 ....$70.00
Old Commonwealth, Coal Miner #1, w/shovel........$100.00
Old Commonwealth, Firefighter #4, Fallen Comrade, miniature.....................................$28.00
Old Commonwealth, Irish, Happy Green $25.00
Old Fitzgerald, Irish, Luck $28.00
Old Fitzgerald, Irish, Sons of Erin......................$18.00
Old Mr Boston, Dan Patch $20.00
Pacesetter, Coca-Cola Truck..............................$180.00
Pacesetter, Ford Tractor.................................$100.00
Pacesetter, International Tractor, miniature.............$50.00
Pacesetter, John Deere Tractor $150.00
Ski Country, Bird Series, Canvasback, Ducks Unlimited...$55.00
Ski Country, Bird Series, Cardinal.......................$65.00
Ski Country, Bird Series, Eagle on Water, miniature ...$50.00
Ski Country, Bird Series, Mallard Family, miniature $40.00
Ski Country, Bird Series, Screech Owl Family $125.00
Ski Country, Bird Series, Widgeon, Ducks Unlimited, miniature.....................................$30.00
Ski Country, Circus Series, Tiger on Ball...............$50.00
Ski Country, Circus Series, Tom Thumb....................$35.00
Ski Country, Indian Series, Deer Dancer..................$120.00
Ski Country, Wildlife Series, Bobcat & Chipmunk.......$75.00
Ski Country, Wildlife Series, Fox Family $70.00
Ski Country, Wildlife Series, Moose......................$110.00

Ski Country, Wildlife Series, Raccoon on Stump, $65.00

Ski Country, Wildlife Series, Skunk Family $65.00
Wild Turkey, Series III, Turkey & Coyote, #10, miniature .$45.00
Wild Turkey, Series III, Turkey & Fox....................$85.00
Wild Turkey, Series III, Turkey & Owl, #8................$90.00
Wild Turkey, Series III, Turkey & Skunk, #12............$85.00

Degenhart

John and Elizabeth Degenhart owned and operated the Crystal Art Glass Factory in Cambridge, Ohio. From 1947 until John died in 1964 they produced some fine glassware; John himself was well known for his superior paperweights. But the glassware that collectors love today was made after '64, when Elizabeth restructured the company, creating many lovely molds and scores of colors. She hired Zack Boyd, who had previously worked for Cambridge Glass, and between the two of them, they developed almost 150 unique and original color formulas.

Complying with provisions she had made before her death, close personal friends at Island Mould and Machine Company in Wheeling, West Virginia, took Elizabeth's molds and removed the familiar 'D in heart' trademark from them. She had requested that ten of her molds be donated to the Degenhart Museum, where they remain today. Zack Boyd eventually bought the Degenhart factory and acquired the remaining molds. He has added his own logo to them and is continuing to press glass very similar to Mrs. Degenhart's.

For more information, we recommend *Degenhart Glass and Paperweights* by Gene Florence, published by the Degenhart Paperweight and Glass Museum, Inc., Cambridge, Ohio.

Beaded Oval Toothpick, Amethyst...........................$17.50
Beaded Oval Toothpick, Vaseline $20.00
Bicentennial Bell, Blue Fire..............................$15.00
Bicentennial Bell, Cobalt $20.00
Bird Salt & Pepper, Opalescent............................$37.50
Bird Salt w/Cherry, Autumn $20.00
Bird Salt w/Cherry, Crown Tuscan $22.50
Bird Salt w/Cherry, Emerald Green $17.50
Buzz Saw Wine, Cobalt $38.00
Chick, Crystal, 2".......................................$15.00
Chick, Lemon Custard, 2".................................$55.00
Chick, Light Powder Blue, 2".............................$25.00
Colonial Drape Toothpick, Light Custard..................$25.00
Colonial Drape Toothpick, Sapphire $20.00
Daisy Button Toothpick, Baby Blue Slag...................$27.50
Daisy Button Toothpick, Vaseline $15.00
Forget-Me-Not Toothpick, April Green......................$25.00
Forget-Me-Not Toothpick, Brownie..........................$15.00
Forget-Me-Not Toothpick, Crystal..........................$13.00
Forget-Me-Not Toothpick, Daffodil.........................$22.50
Forget-Me-Not Toothpick, Peach-Opaque.....................$22.50
Forget-Me-Not Toothpick, Toffee $25.00
Gypsy Pot Toothpick, Bloody Mary $45.00
Gypsy Pot Toothpick, Bluebell $20.00
Gypsy Pot Toothpick, Lavender Blue........................$35.00
Hand, Amethyst..$12.00

Hand, Sapphire $10.00
Hand, Vaseline $10.00
Heart & Lyre Cup Plate, Amethyst, unmarked $10.00
Heart & Lyre Cup Plate, Pink, unmarked $12.50

Heart Box, Baby Green, $30.00

Heart Box, Lavender & Green Slag.......................$37.50
Heart Box, Vaseline $25.00
Heart Toothpick, Amethyst $17.50
Heart Toothpick, Buttercup.................................$30.00
Heart Toothpick, Milk Blue.................................$22.50
Heart Toothpick, Opalescent $22.50
Hen Covered Dish, Baby Blue, 3" $37.50
Hen Covered Dish, Caramel Custard, 3" $55.00
Hen Covered Dish, Forest Green, 3" $22.50
Hen Covered Dish, Sapphire, 3" $22.00
Hobo Shoe, Blue & White Slag...........................$27.50
Hobo Shoe, Caramel Custard Slag $22.50
Kat Slipper, Lemon Custard, unmarked..................$32.50
Kat Slipper, Milk Blue.......................................$28.00
Kat Slipper, Mint Green Opalescent $37.50
Owl, Amethyst $32.50
Owl, Apple Green..$42.50
Owl, Buttercup...$47.50
Owl, Crystal..$16.00
Owl, Fog..$55.00
Owl, Light Ivory $42.50
Owl, Red Carnival..$155.00
Owl, Sapphire $22.50
Owl, Teal...$27.50
Owl, Wanda Blue Opal $47.50
Pooche, Crystal $17.50
Pooche, Gray Tomato...$35.00
Pooche, Ivory..$22.50
Pooche, Sapphire..$15.00

Portrait Plate, Cobalt, $50.00

Pottie Salt, Amethyst $10.00
Pottie Salt, Honey $12.00
Pottie Salt, Nile Green $17.50
Priscilla, Bernard Boyd's Ebony.........................$155.00
Priscilla, Periwinkle..$80.00
Robin Covered Dish, Fawn $58.00
Saw Buzz Wine, Crystal.....................................$15.00
Seal of Ohio Cup Plate, Opalescent $15.00
Skate Shoe, Sapphire $32.50
Texas Boot, Amethyst..$17.50
Texas Boot, Baby Green $22.50
Tomahawk, Amber $18.00
Tomahawk, Emerald Green $25.00
Turkey Covered Dish, Crown Tuscan, 5" $80.00
Wildflower Candy Dish, Crown Tuscan, unmarked $37.50
Wildflower Candy Dish, Twilight Blue.....................$32.50

Depression Glass

Since the early sixties, this has been a very active area of collecting. Interest is still very strong, and although values have long been established, except for some of the rarer items, Depression Glass is still relatively inexpensive. Some of the patterns and colors that were entirely avoided by the early wave of collectors are now becoming popular, and it's very easy to reassemble a nice table setting of one of these lines today.

Most of this glass was produced during the Depression years. It was inexpensive, mass-produced, and was available in a wide assortment of colors. The same type of glassware was still being made to some extent during the fifties and sixties, and today the term 'Depression Glass' has been extended to include the later patterns as well.

Some things have been reproduced, and the slight variation in patterns and colors can be very difficult to detect. For instance, the Sharon butter dish has been reissued in original colors of pink and green (as well as others that were not originial); and several pieces of Cherry Blossom, Madrid, Avocado, Mayfair, and Miss America have also been reproduced. Some pieces you'll see in 'antique' malls and flea markets today have been recently made in dark uncharacteristic 'carnival' colors, which of course are easy to spot.

For further study, Gene Florence has written several informative books on the subject, and we recommend them all: *The Pocket Guide to Depression Glass, The Collector's Encyclopedia of Depression Glass,* and *Very Rare Glassware of the Depression Years.*

Adam, green, bowl, 7¾" $22.50
Adam, green, coaster, 3¾"..................................$18.00
Adam, green, cup..$22.00
Adam, green, pitcher, 32-oz, 8"...........................$42.00
Adam, green, plate, dinner; square, 9" $22.50
Adam, green, plate, salad; square, 7¾".................$12.00
Adam, green, sugar bowl....................................$20.00
Adam, green, tumbler, iced tea; 5½ $42.00
Adam, green, vase, 7½" $47.50

Adam, pink, ashtray, 4½"..................................$22.50
Adam, pink, butter dish...................................$75.00
Adam, pink, cake plate, footed, 10"..............$22.50
Adam, pink, candlesticks, 4", pr $80.00
Adam, pink, creamer.......................................$18.00
Adam, pink, lamp..$247.50
Adam, pink, plate, grill; 9"...........................$18.00
Adam, pink, platter, 11¾"...............................$20.00
Adam, pink, relish dish, divided, 8"..............$18.00
Adam, pink, tumbler, 4½" $27.50
Adam, pink or green, bowl, cereal; 5¾"........$37.50
Adam, pink or green, saucer, square, 6" $7.50
American Pioneer, green, bowl, handled, 5" $18.00
American Pioneer, green, candlesticks, 6½", pr.........$85.00
American Pioneer, green, coaster, 3½"...........$30.00
American Pioneer, green, goblet, wine; 3-oz, 4" $48.00
American Pioneer, green, handled, 9"............$25.00
American Pioneer, green, lamp, tall, 8½".........$102.50
American Pioneer, green, mayonnaise, 4¼"........$90.00
American Pioneer, green, pitcher, 7"..............$210.00
American Pioneer, green, plate, handled, 11½"..........$18.50
American Pioneer, green, plate, 8".................$11.00
American Pioneer, green, saucer $7.00
American Pioneer, green, sugar bowl, 3½"..........$22.50
American Pioneer, pink, bowl, console; 10⅜"........$50.00
American Pioneer, pink, candy jar, 1½-lb..........$85.00
American Pioneer, pink, creamer, 3½".............$20.00
American Pioneer, pink, goblet, water; 8-oz, 6"........$37.50
American Pioneer, pink, ice bucket, 6".............$46.50
American Pioneer, pink, sherbet, 3½" $17.50
American Pioneer, pink, tumbler, juice; 5-oz..........$26.50
American Pioneer, pink, tumbler, 12-oz, 5".......$37.50
American Pioneer, pink, whiskey, 2-oz, 2¼".........$42.50
American Sweetheart, monax, bowl, berry; 9"........$52.00
American Sweetheart, monax, bowl, soup; flat, 9½"...$70.00
American Sweetheart, monax, bowl, vegetable; oval, 11" $65.00
American Sweetheart, monax, cup $10.00
American Sweetheart, monax, plate, bread & butter; 6"..$5.00
American Sweetheart, monax, plate, dinner; 9¾x10¼"..$22.50
American Sweetheart, monax, plate, luncheon; 9" $10.00
American Sweetheart, monax, plate, salver; 12"........$17.50
American Sweetheart, monax, plate, 15½"..............$185.00
American Sweetheart, monax, sherbet, footed, 4¼" $17.00
American Sweetheart, pink, bowl, cereal; 6" $15.00
American Sweetheart, pink, bowl, cream soup; 4½"...$70.00
American Sweetheart, pink, creamer, footed..............$11.00
American Sweetheart, pink, pitcher, 60-oz, 7½".......$525.00
American Sweetheart, pink, platter, oval, 13".........$42.50
American Sweetheart, pink, salt & pepper shakers, footed, pr $262.50
American Sweetheart, pink, saucer...............$5.00
American Sweetheart, pink, sugar bowl (open), footed.$10.50
American Sweetheart, pink, tumbler, 10-oz, 4¾"........$90.00
American Sweetheart, pink, tumbler, 5-oz, 3½"..........$70.00
Anniversary, crystal, bowl, fruit; 9"..............$10.00
Anniversary, crystal, cake plate, 12½"............$7.50
Anniversary, crystal, plate, dinner; 9" $6.00

Anniversary, crystal, sugar lid...................$6.00
Anniversary, crystal, vase, 6½"..................$14.00
Anniversary, pink, bowl, soup; 7⅜"..............$16.00
Anniversary, pink, butter dish.....................$55.00
Anniversary, pink, cup..............................$7.50
Anniversary, pink, relish dish, 8"...............$10.00
Anniversary, pink, wine glass, 2½-oz..........$17.00
Aunt Polly, blue, pitcher, 48-oz, 8"..............$162.50
Aunt Polly, blue, plate, luncheon; 8"............$20.00
Aunt Polly, blue, salt & pepper shakers, pr.............$205.00
Aunt Polly, blue, sugar bowl.......................$32.50
Aunt Polly, blue, tumbler, 8-oz, 3⅝".............$27.50
Aunt Polly, blue, vase, footed, 6½"..............$42.50
Aunt Polly, green, bowl, berry; lg, 7⅞" $19.00
Aunt Polly, green, bowl, 2x4¾"...................$10.50
Aunt Polly, green, butter dish $232.00
Aunt Polly, green, candy dish, 2-handled $60.00
Aunt Polly, green, creamer........................$27.50
Aurora, cobalt, bowl, 4½"..........................$30.00
Aurora, cobalt, creamer, 4½".....................$20.00
Aurora, cobalt, plate, 6½"..........................$11.00
Aurora, cobalt, saucer..............................$6.00
Aurora, cobalt, tumbler, 4¾".....................$20.00
Avocado, green, bowl, oval, 2-handled, 8" $27.50
Avocado, green, bowl, salad; 7½"................$50.00
Avocado, green, bowl, 2-handled, 5¼"..........$30.00
Avocado, green, cake plate, 2-handled, 10¼"............$50.00

Avocado, green, sugar bowl (open), footed, $30.00; plate, sherbet; 6¾", $16.00; plate, luncheon; 8¼", $20.00; cup & saucer, $55.00; tumbler, $175.00

Avocado, green, pitcher, 64-oz....................$835.00
Avocado, pink, bowl, preserve; handled, 7".............$20.00
Avocado, pink, bowl, relish; footed, 6"..........$25.00
Avocado, pink, bowl, 9½"...........................$90.00
Avocado, pink, creamer, footed....................$32.50
Avocado, pink, plate, sherbet; 6¾" $15.00
Avocado, pink, sherbet..............................$50.00
Avocado, pink, tumbler..............................$137.50
Beaded Block, green, bowl, handled, 5½"..................$8.00

Beaded Block, green, bowl, jelly; 2-handled, 4½" **$8.00**
Beaded Block, green, bowl, pickle; 2-handled, 6½"....**$14.00**
Beaded Block, green, bowl, 6" **$12.50**
Beaded Block, green, pitcher, pint jug; 5¼" **$100.00**
Beaded Block, green, plain edge, 7½" **$20.00**
Beaded Block, green, plate, 8¾" **$17.50**
Beaded Block, green, vase, bouquet; 6" **$14.50**
Beaded Block, opalescent, bowl, celery; 8¼" **$20.00**
Beaded Block, opalescent, bowl, flared, 7¼"..........**$19.50**
Beaded Block, opalescent, bowl, unflared, 6¾" **$18.50**
Beaded Block, opalescent, lily; 4½"...................**$20.00**
Beaded Block, opalescent, plate, 7¾" **$11.00**
Beaded Block, opalescent, stemmed jelly, 4½"............**$20.00**
Beaded Block, opalescent, sugar bowl **$26.50**
Block Optic, green, bowl, salad; 7¼" **$22.50**
Block Optic, green, butter dish, 3x5"..................**$47.50**
Block Optic, green, goblet, cocktail; 4"...................**$32.50**

Block Optic, green, pitcher, 54-oz, 8½", $38.00

Block Optic, green, plate, dinner; 9" **$20.00**
Block Optic, green, plate, luncheon; 8" **$6.00**
Block Optic, green, salt & pepper shakers, squatty, pr....**$80.00**
Block Optic, green, sugar bowl, creamer; 3 styles, each .**$15.00**
Block Optic, green, tumbler, flat, 10-oz **$20.00**
Block Optic, green, tumbler, flat, 5-oz, 3½" **$20.00**
Block Optic, green, tumbler, flat, 9-oz **$17.50**
Block Optic, green, whiskey, 2-oz, 2¼" **$26.50**
Block Optic, pink, bowl, berry; 4¼" **$7.50**
Block Optic, pink, bowl, cereal; 5¼"..................**$22.50**
Block Optic, pink, candlesticks, 1¾", pr **$72.50**
Block Optic, pink, candy jar, 6¼" **$100.00**
Block Optic, pink, cup, 4 styles, each **$7.50**
Block Optic, pink, ice bucket **$42.50**
Block Optic, pink, ice tub or butter tub (open) **$85.00**
Block Optic, pink, pitcher, 80-oz, 8" **$70.00**
Block Optic, pink, plate, sherbet; 6"...................**$3.50**
Block Optic, pink, sandwich server, center handle.....**$47.50**
Block Optic, pink, saucer, 2 sizes, each **$8.00**
Block Optic, pink, tumbler, footed, 10-oz, 6" **$22.50**
Block Optic, pink, tumbler, footed, 5-oz, 4" **$15.00**
Block Optic, pink, tumbler, footed, 9-oz **$16.00**
Bowknot, green, bowl, cereal; 5½"...................**$18.00**

Bowknot, green, plate, salad; 7" **$11.00**
Bowknot, green, sherbet, low footed **$15.00**
Bowknot, green, tumbler, 10-oz, 5" **$18.00**
Bubble, blue, bowl, berry; lg, 8⅜".....................**$17.50**
Bubble, blue, bowl, fruit; 4½" **$11.00**
Bubble, blue, bowl, soup; flat, 7¾" **$16.00**
Bubble, blue, creamer **$32.50**
Bubble, blue, plate, dinner; 9⅜" **$7.50**
Bubble, blue, saucer **$2.50**
Bubble, crystal, bowl, cereal; 5¼" **$6.00**
Bubble, crystal, plate, bread & butter; 6¾"...............**$3.00**
Bubble, crystal, platter, oval, 12" **$6.00**
Bubble, crystal, sugar bowl **$6.00**
Bubble, crystal or blue, cup **$4.00**
Bubble, ruby, pitcher, ice lip; 64-oz **$55.00**
Bubble, ruby, tumbler, iced tea; 12-oz **$12.00**
Bubble, ruby, tumbler, juice; 6-oz **$8.00**
Bubble, ruby, tumbler, lemonade; 16-oz...............**$16.00**
Bubble, ruby, tumbler, water; 9-oz **$9.00**
Cameo, green, bowl, berry; lg, 8¼" **$32.50**
Cameo, green, bowl, cereal; 5½" **$30.00**
Cameo, green, bowl, console; 3-footed, 11" **$65.00**
Cameo, green, bowl, cream soup; 4¾".................**$90.00**
Cameo, green, bowl, salad; 7¼" **$50.00**
Cameo, green, cake plate, 3-footed, 10"...............**$20.00**
Cameo, green, candlesticks, 4", pr **$95.00**
Cameo, green, candy jar, low, 4" **$70.00**
Cameo, green, cookie jar................................**$47.50**
Cameo, green, decanter, w/stopper, 10".................**$132.50**
Cameo, green, goblet, water; 6".......................**$47.50**
Cameo, green, goblet, wine; 3½" **$580.00**
Cameo, green, goblet, wine; 4" **$57.50**
Cameo, green, salt & pepper shakers, footed, pr **$65.00**
Cameo, green, saucer w/cup ring.....................**$157.50**
Cameo, green, sherbet, 3⅛" **$14.50**
Cameo, green, tumbler, flat, 10-oz, 4¾" **$25.00**
Cameo, green, tumbler, footed, 11-oz, 5¾"...............**$52.50**
Cameo, green, tumbler, juice; footed, 3-oz **$55.00**
Cameo, green, tumbler, water; 9-oz, 4" **$24.50**
Cameo, green, vase, 5¾" **$152.50**
Cameo, green, vase, 8" **$35.00**
Cameo, yellow, bowl, vegetable; oval, 10" **$37.50**
Cameo, yellow, butter dish **$1,365.00**
Cameo, yellow, creamer, 3¼".........................**$18.00**
Cameo, yellow, cup, 2 styles..........................**$8.00**
Cameo, yellow, plate, closed handles, 10½" **$14.00**
Cameo, yellow, plate, dinner; 9½" **$11.00**
Cameo, yellow, plate, grill; 10½" **$7.00**
Cameo, yellow, plate, luncheon; 8" **$10.50**
Cameo, yellow, plate, sherbet; 6" **$3.50**
Cameo, yellow, plate, square, 8½" **$132.50**
Cameo, yellow, platter, closed handles, 12"...............**$37.50**
Cameo, yellow, relish, 3-part, footed, 7½" **$157.50**
Cameo, yellow, sherbet, 4⅞" **$40.00**
Cameo, yellow, sugar bowl, 3¼" **$15.00**
Cherry Blossom, green, bowl, cereal; 5¾" **$32.50**
Cherry Blossom, green, bowl, soup; flat, 7¾" **$50.00**
Cherry Blossom, green, bowl, 2-handled, 9"...............**$30.00**

Cherry Blossom, green, cake plate, 3-footed, 10¼" **$26.50**
Cherry Blossom, green, coaster **$12.50**

Cherry Blossom, green, cup & saucer, $22.00

Cherry Blossom, green, pitcher, scalloped or round bottom, allover pattern, 36-oz, 6¾"...................................**$55.00**
Cherry Blossom, green, plate, dinner; 9"...................**$22.50**
Cherry Blossom, green, plate, sherbet; 6" **$7.00**
Cherry Blossom, green, saucer.....................................**$6.00**
Cherry Blossom, green, tumbler, flat, pattern around top, 4-oz, 3½"...**$26.00**
Cherry Blossom, green, tumbler, flat, pattern around top, 9-oz, 4¼"...**$22.50**
Cherry Blossom, green, tumbler, footed, allover pattern, 9-oz, 4½"...**$32.50**
Cherry Blossom, pink, bowl, berry; 4¾" **$15.00**
Cherry Blossom, pink, bowl, berry; 8½" **$42.50**
Cherry Blossom, pink, bowl, vegetable; oval, 9"........**$32.50**
Cherry Blossom, pink, creamer....................................**$18.00**
Cherry Blossom, pink, mug, 7-oz **$190.00**
Cherry Blossom, pink, plate, grill; 9"........................**$22.50**
Cherry Blossom, pink, plate, salad; 7".......................**$18.00**
Cherry Blossom, pink, platter, oval, 9".....................**$760.00**
Cherry Blossom, pink, platter, 13" & 13" divided, each..**$60.00**
Cherry Blossom, pink, sherbet.....................................**$16.00**
Cherry Blossom, pink, sugar bowl...............................**$16.00**
Cherry Blossom, pink, tumbler, scalloped foot, allover pattern, 9-oz, 4½"...**$28.50**
Cherryberry, pink or green, bowl, berry; 7½".............**$22.00**
Cherryberry, pink or green, bowl, 6¼".......................**$45.00**
Cherryberry, pink or green, creamer, sm **$18.00**
Cherryberry, pink or green, olive dish, 1-handle, 5"..**$16.00**
Cherryberry, pink or green, pickle dish **$16.00**
Cherryberry, pink or green, pitcher, 7¾" **$147.50**
Cherryberry, pink or green, plate, sherbet; 6"............**$9.00**
Cherryberry, pink or green, sugar lid........................**$52.50**
Cherryberry, pink or green, tumbler, 9-oz, 3⅝"..........**$32.50**
Chinex Classic, ivory, bowl, cereal; 5¾"......................**$6.00**
Chinex Classic, ivory, butter dish................................**$56.00**
Chinex Classic, ivory, cup **$5.50**
Chinex Classic, ivory, plate, dinner; 9¾".....................**$5.00**
Chinex Classic, ivory, saucer..**$3.00**
Chinex Classic, ivory decorated, bowl, soup; flat, 7¾".**$18.00**
Chinex Classic, ivory decorated, bowl, vegetable; 9"..**$22.50**
Chinex Classic, ivory decorated, plate, sherbet; 6¼" **$4.50**

Chinex Classic, ivory decorated, sugar bowl, open.....**$10.00**
Christmas Candy, crystal, bowl, soup; 7⅜"...................**$7.50**
Christmas Candy, crystal, cup **$5.50**
Christmas Candy, crystal, plate, sandwich; 11¼" **$16.00**
Christmas Candy, teal, creamer....................................**$20.00**
Christmas Candy, teal, plate, bread & butter; 6" **$11.00**
Christmas Candy, teal, plate, dinner; 9⅝"....................**$30.00**
Christmas Candy, teal, sugar bowl................................**$20.00**
Circle, green or pink, bowl, flared, 5½" **$11.00**
Circle, green or pink, creamer **$9.50**
Circle, green or pink, goblet, wine; 4½".....................**$13.00**
Circle, green or pink, plate, dinner; 9½".....................**$15.00**
Circle, green or pink, plate, sherbet; 6".......................**$3.00**
Circle, green or pink, sherbet, 4¾" **$7.00**
Circle, green or pink, sugar bowl..................................**$9.00**
Circle, green or pink, tumbler, juice; 4-oz....................**$9.00**
Circle, green or pink, tumbler, water; 8-oz.................**$10.00**
Cloverleaf, green, bowl, dessert; 4" **$20.00**
Cloverleaf, green, candy dish.......................................**$47.50**
Cloverleaf, green, plate, luncheon; 8".........................**$8.00**
Cloverleaf, green, sherbet, footed, 3" **$7.50**
Cloverleaf, green, tumbler, flat, 10-oz, 4"...................**$32.50**
Cloverleaf, green, tumbler, footed, 10-oz, 5¾"...........**$22.50**
Cloverleaf, yellow, bowl, cereal; 5"..............................**$30.00**
Cloverleaf, yellow, bowl, salad; 7"...............................**$47.50**
Cloverleaf, yellow, creamer, footed, 3⅝"....................**$16.00**
Cloverleaf, yellow, cup...**$10.00**
Cloverleaf, yellow, plate, grill; 10¼".............................**$21.50**
Cloverleaf, yellow, plate, sherbet; 6" **$7.50**
Cloverleaf, yellow, salt & pepper shakers, pr...........**$100.00**
Cloverleaf, yellow, sugar bowl, footed, 3⅝" **$16.50**
Colonial, green, butter dish..**$55.00**
Colonial, green, cup **$11.00**
Colonial, green, goblet, cocktail; 3-oz, 4"...................**$26.50**
Colonial, green, goblet, water; 8½-oz, 5¾" **$30.00**
Colonial, green, mug, 12-oz, 4½"...............................**$790.00**
Colonial, green, plate, dinner; 10" **$60.00**
Colonial, green, plate, grill; 10"..................................**$26.50**
Colonial, green, sugar lid...**$20.00**
Colonial, green, tumbler, footed, 10-oz, 5¼" **$47.50**
Colonial, green, tumbler, footed, 5-oz, 4" **$37.50**
Colonial, green, tumbler, water; 9-oz, 4"....................**$21.50**
Colonial, green, whiskey, 1½-oz, 2½".........................**$14.00**
Colonial, pink, bowl, berry; 4½".................................**$13.00**
Colonial, pink, bowl, cereal; 5½".................................**$55.00**
Colonial, pink, bowl, cream soup; 4½".......................**$60.00**
Colonial, pink, bowl, soup; low, 7" **$55.00**
Colonial, pink, bowl, vegetable; oval, 10"...................**$27.50**
Colonial, pink, bowl, 3¾"..**$42.50**
Colonial, pink, platter, oval, 12" **$30.00**
Colonial, pink, salt & pepper shakers, pr **$132.50**
Colonial Block, green or pink, bowl, 7".......................**$18.00**
Colonial Block, green or pink, candy dish, 8½" **$35.00**
Colonial Block, green or pink, creamer **$11.00**
Colonial Block, green or pink, pitcher.........................**$37.50**
Colonial Block, green or pink, sugar lid **$11.00**
Colonial Fluted, green, bowl, cereal; 6" **$8.50**
Colonial Fluted, green, bowl, salad; 6½".....................**$20.00**

Colonial Fluted, green, creamer **$7.00**
Colonial Fluted, green, plate, luncheon; 8" **$6.00**
Columbia, crystal, bowl, cereal; 5" **$16.00**
Columbia, crystal, bowl, low soup; 8" **$18.00**
Columbia, crystal, bowl, salad; 8½" **$18.00**
Columbia, crystal, plate, luncheon; 9½" **$9.50**
Columbia, crystal, tumbler, 9-oz **$24.50**
Columbia, pink, cup **$20.00**
Columbia, pink, plate, bread & butter; 6" **$14.00**
Coronation, pink, bowl, nappy; 6½" **$7.00**
Coronation, pink, plate, luncheon; 8½" **$5.00**
Coronation, pink, plate, sherbet; 6" **$2.50**
Coronation, royal ruby, bowl, berry; 4¼" **$7.00**
Coronation, royal ruby, cup **$7.00**
Cremax, decal decoration, bowl, vegetable; 9" **$14.00**
Cremax, decal decoration, cup **$5.50**
Cremax, decal decoration, plate, bread & butter; 6¼"...**$4.50**
Cremax, ivory, creamer **$5.50**
Cremax, ivory, plate, sandwich; 11½" **$5.50**
Cremax, ivory, sugar bowl (open) **$5.50**
Cube, green, bowl, salad; 6½" **$15.00**
Cube, green, creamer, 3" **$9.00**

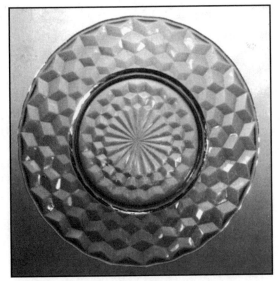

Cube, green, plate, luncheon; 8", $6.50

Cube, green, powder jar, 3-footed **$24.50**
Cube, green, sherbet, footed **$8.00**
Cube, pink, bowl, dessert; 4½" **$6.50**
Cube, pink, butter dish **$60.00**
Cube, pink, cup **$7.50**
Cube, pink, pitcher, 45-oz, 8¾" **$190.00**
Cube, pink, plate, luncheon; 8" **$6.00**
Cube, pink, plate, sherbet; 6" **$4.00**
Cube, pink, salt & pepper shakers, pr **$35.00**
Cube, pink, saucer **$3.50**
Cube, pink, sugar bowl, 2" **$3.00**
Cube, pink, tumbler, 9-oz, 4" **$60.00**
Daisy, amber, bowl, cream soup; 4½" **$13.50**
Daisy, amber, bowl, vegetable; oval, 10" **$17.00**
Daisy, amber, plate, cake or sandwich; 11½" **$13.00**
Daisy, amber, plate, luncheon; 8⅜" **$7.00**

Daisy, amber, plate, sherbet; 6" **$4.00**
Daisy, amber, platter, 10¾" **$15.00**
Daisy, amber, tumbler, footed, 12-oz **$37.50**
Daisy, crystal, bowl, berry; 4½" **$5.50**
Daisy, crystal, bowl, berry; 9⅜" **$15.00**
Daisy, crystal, bowl, cereal; 6" **$11.00**
Daisy, crystal, creamer, footed **$6.00**
Daisy, crystal, plate, grill; 10⅜" **$5.00**
Daisy, crystal, plate, salad; 7⅜" **$4.00**
Daisy, crystal, relish dish, 3-part, 8⅜" **$13.50**
Diamond Quilted, blue, bowl, cream soup; 4¾" **$19.50**
Diamond Quilted, blue, bowl, handled, 5½" **$17.00**
Diamond Quilted, blue, cup **$17.00**
Diamond Quilted, blue, ice bucket **$80.00**
Diamond Quilted, blue, plate, salad; 7" **$9.00**
Diamond Quilted, blue, plate, sherbet; 6" **$6.00**
Diamond Quilted, blue, saucer **$6.00**
Diamond Quilted, blue, sherbet **$15.50**
Diamond Quilted, green, bowl, cereal; 5" **$7.50**
Diamond Quilted, green, candy jar, footed **$60.00**
Diamond Quilted, green, goblet, cordial; 1-oz **$12.50**
Diamond Quilted, green, goblet, wine; 3-oz **$11.00**
Diamond Quilted, green, plate, sandwich; 14" **$13.50**
Diamond Quilted, green, punch bowl & stand **$420.00**
Diamond Quilted, green, sugar bowl **$7.50**
Diamond Quilted, green, tumbler, footed, 12-oz.........**$15.50**
Diamond Quilted, green, tumbler, iced tea; 12-oz **$10.00**
Diamond Quilted, green, tumbler, water; 9-oz **$9.00**
Diana, amber, bowl, cream soup; 5½" **$13.50**
Diana, amber, candy jar **$32.50**
Diana, amber, creamer, oval **$9.00**
Diana, amber, plate, bread & butter; 6" **$3.00**
Diana, amber, salt & pepper shakers, pr **$95.00**
Diana, amber, sherbet **$14.00**
Diana, amber, sugar bowl (open), oval **$8.00**
Diana, pink, ashtray, 3½" **$4.50**
Diana, pink, bowl, cereal; 5" **$9.00**
Diana, pink, plate, sandwich; 11¾" **$22.50**
Diana, pink, saucer **$5.00**
Diana, pink, tumbler, 9-oz, 4⅛" **$42.50**
Dogwood, green, bowl, berry; 8½" **$95.00**
Dogwood, green, bowl, fruit; 10¼" **$185.00**
Dogwood, green, pitcher, decorated, 80-oz, 8" **$475.00**
Dogwood, green, plate, bread & butter; 6" **$8.00**
Dogwood, green, plate, luncheon; 8" **$8.00**
Dogwood, green, sherbet, low footed **$90.00**
Dogwood, green, tumbler, decorated, 12-oz, 5" **$95.00**
Dogwood, pink, bowl, cereal; 5½" **$24.50**
Dogwood, pink, creamer, thick, 3¼" **$20.00**
Dogwood, pink, plate, dinner; 9¼" **$27.50**
Dogwood, pink, plate, salver; 12" **$25.00**
Dogwood, pink, platter, oval, rare, 12" **$370.00**
Dogwood, pink, sugar bowl, thin, 2½" **$16.00**
Dogwood, pink, tumbler, decorated, 10-oz, 4" **$35.00**
Dogwood, pink, tumbler, decorated, 5-oz, 3½" **$265.00**
Doric, green, bowl, cream soup; 2-handled, 5" **$350.00**
Doric, green, bowl, vegetable; oval, 9" **$27.50**
Doric, green, cake plate, 3-footed, 10" **$27.50**

Doric, green, coaster, 3" $17.50
Doric, green, pitcher, footed, 48-oz, 7½" $790.00
Doric, green, platter, oval, 12" $22.50
Doric, green, relish tray, 4x4" $9.00
Doric, green, saucer $4.50
Doric, green, sherbet, footed $14.00
Doric, green, tumbler, footed, 12-oz, 5" $100.00
Doric, pink, bowl, berry; 4½" $7.00
Doric, pink, bowl, cereal; 5½" $42.50
Doric, pink, butter dish $65.00
Doric, pink, creamer, 4" $12.00
Doric, pink, cup $8.00
Doric, pink, plate, grill; 9" $14.00
Doric, pink, plate, salad; 7" $16.50
Doric, pink, plate, sherbet; 6" $4.50
Doric, pink, salt & pepper shakers, pr $32.50
Doric, pink, sugar bowl $12.00
Doric & Pansy, pink, bowl, berry; 4½" $8.00
Doric & Pansy, pink, bowl, handled, 9" $15.50
Doric & Pansy, pink, plate, sherbet; 6" $8.00
Doric & Pansy, ultramarine, cup $17.50
Doric & Pansy, ultramarine, plate, dinner; 9" $27.50
Doric & Pansy, ultramarine, saucer $6.00
Doric & Pansy, ultramarine, sugar bowl, open $135.00
Doric & Pansy, ultramarine, tumbler, 9-oz, 4½" $70.00
English Hobnail, pink or green, ashtray, several shapes, each $22.50
English Hobnail, pink or green, bowl, cream soup $15.50
English Hobnail, pink or green, bowl, several styles, 6" .$14.00
English Hobnail, pink or green, bowls, relish; oval, 8" or 9", ea $20.00
English Hobnail, pink or green, bowls, 2-handled, footed, 8" $55.00
English Hobnail, pink or green, candlesticks, 3½", pr.$37.50
English Hobnail, pink or green, candy dish, 3-footed.$75.00
English Hobnail, pink or green, celery dish, 12" $28.00
English Hobnail, pink or green, cup $18.00
English Hobnail, pink or green, goblet, wine; 2-oz.....$24.00
English Hobnail, pink or green, goblet, 8-oz, 6¼" $25.00
English Hobnail, pink or green, plate, dinner; 10" $25.00
English Hobnail, pink or green, saucer $5.00
English Hobnail, pink or green, tumbler, footed, 12½-oz $25.00
English Hobnail, pink or green, tumbler, iced tea; 12-oz, 5" $26.50
English Hobnail, pink or green, tumbler, 5-oz or 8-oz, 3¾" $16.00
Floragold, iridescent, bowl, cereal; 5½" $32.50
Floragold, iridescent, bowl, salad; 9½" $37.50
Floragold, iridescent, bowl, square, 4½" $6.00
Floragold, iridescent, butter dish $42.50
Floragold, iridescent, coaster/ashtray, 4" $6.00
Floragold, iridescent, cup $6.50
Floragold, iridescent, plate, dinner; 8½" $32.50
Floragold, iridescent, plate, sherbet; 5¾" $11.00
Floragold, iridescent, platter, 11¼" $20.00
Floragold, iridescent, sherbet, low footed $14.00
Floragold, iridescent, tumbler, footed, 11-oz $20.00

Floragold, iridescent, plate or tray, 13½", $20.00

Floragold, iridescent, tumbler, footed, 15-oz $90.00
Floral, green, bowl, salad; 7½" $17.50
Floral, green, candlesticks, 4", pr $80.00
Floral, green, coaster, 3¼" $9.00
Floral, green, compote, 9" $795.00
Floral, green, creamer, flat $15.00
Floral, green, pitcher, lemonade; 48-oz, 10¼" $237.50
Floral, green, plate, dinner; 9" $18.00
Floral, green, plate, grill; 9" $165.00
Floral, green, plate, salad; 8" $11.00
Floral, green, relish dish, 2-part, oval $16.50
Floral, green, vase, tall, 8-sided, 6⅞" $420.00
Floral, pink, bowl, berry; 4" $16.00
Floral, pink, bowl, cream soup; 5½" $710.00
Floral, pink, bowl, vegetable; oval, 9" $17.50
Floral, pink, butter dish $82.50
Floral, pink, cup $12.00
Floral, pink, platter, oval, 10¾" $17.50
Floral, pink, salt & pepper shakers, flat, 6" $47.50
Floral, pink, saucer $10.00
Floral, pink, sherbet $16.00
Floral, pink, sugar bowl $9.00
Floral, pink, tumbler, lemonade; footed, 9-oz, 5¼" $42.50
Floral & Diamond Band, green, bowl, berry; 4½" $9.00
Floral & Diamond Band, green, butter dish $112.00
Floral & Diamond Band, green, pitcher, 42-oz, 8" $95.00
Floral & Diamond Band, green, plate, luncheon; 8" ...$32.50
Floral & Diamond Band, green, sugar bowl, 5¼" $15.00
Floral & Diamond Band, green, tumbler, iced tea; 5" .$37.50
Floral & Diamond Band, pink, compote, tall, 5½" $16.00
Floral & Diamond Band, pink, sherbet $7.00
Floral & Diamond Band, pink, tumbler, water; 4" $20.00
Floral & Diamond Band, pink or green, bowl, nappy; handled, 5¾" $11.00
Florentine No 1, green, bowl, vegetable; w/lid, oval, 9½" $47.50
Florentine No 1, green, coaster/ashtray, 3¾" $17.50
Florentine No 1, green, pitcher, footed, 36-oz, 6½" $40.00
Florentine No 1, green, plate, salad; 8½" $8.00
Florentine No 1, green, saucer $4.00
Florentine No 1, green, sugar bowl $10.00
Florentine No 1, green, tumbler, iced tea; footed $27.50

Florentine No 1, yellow, ashtray, 5½"..............$28.50

Florentine No 1, yellow, bowl, cereal; 6"...........$22.50

Florentine No 1, yellow, butter dish.................$157.50

Florentine No 1, yellow, creamer $12.00

Florentine No 1, yellow, cup..........................$10.50

Florentine No 1, yellow, plate, dinner; 10" $22.50

Florentine No 1, yellow, salt & pepper shakers, footed, pr $55.00

Florentine No 1, yellow, sherbet, 3-oz, footed $12.00

Florentine No 1, yellow, tumbler, juice; footed, 5-oz, 3¾"...$22.00

Florentine No 2, green, candy dish $100.00

Florentine No 2, green, compote, ruffled, 3½".........$22.50

Florentine No 2, green, pitcher, 76-oz, 8" $90.00

Florentine No 2, green, salt & pepper shakers, pr........$42.50

Florentine No 2, green, tumbler, juice; 5-oz, 3½".........$11.00

Florentine No 2, green or yellow, plate, dinner; 10" ...$15.00

Florentine No 2, green or yellow, plate, grill; 10¼".....$11.00

Florentine No 2, yellow, coaster/ashtray, 3¾"...........$22.50

Florentine No 2, yellow, platter, oval, 11".............$20.00

Florentine No 2, yellow, sherbet, footed.................$11.00

Florentine No 2, yellow, tumbler, footed, 5-oz, 3¼" ...$17.50

Flower Garden w/Butterflies, pink or green, ashtray, match-pack holders.......................................$172.50

Flower Garden w/Butterflies, pink or green, bowl, console; footed, 10" $90.00

Flower Garden w/Butterflies, pink or green, bowl, console; rolled edge $80.00

Flower Garden w/Butterflies, pink or green, candlesticks, 8", pr $142.50

Flower Garden w/Butterflies, pink or green, candy dish, 7½"...$132.50

Flower Garden w/Butterflies, pink or green, cheese & cracker set, 4" compote; 10" plate.................$67.50

Flower Garden w/Butterflies, pink or green, cologne bottle, footed, tall, 7½"...................................$170.00

Flower Garden w/Butterflies, pink or green, creamer...$70.00

Flower Garden w/Butterflies, pink or green, cup........$65.00

Flower Garden w/Butterflies, pink or green, plate, dinner; 10"...$42.50

Flower Garden w/Butterflies, pink or green, plate, 2 styles, 8", each...$18.00

Flower Garden w/Butterflies, pink or green, powder jar, footed $105.00

Flower Garden w/Butterflies, pink or green, sandwich server, center handle $65.00

Flower Garden w/Butterflies, pink or green, saucer ...$27.50

Flower Garden w/Butterflies, pink or green, sugar bowl, open...$65.00

Flower Garden w/Butterflies, pink or green, tray, oval, 5½x10" $52.50

Flower Garden w/Butterflies, pink or green, vase, 10" .$132.50

Forest Green, ashtray....................................$4.50

Forest Green, creamer, flat.............................$7.00

Forest Green, pitcher, 3-qt.............................$27.50

Forest Green, plate, luncheon; 8⅜".....................$6.00

Forest Green, saucer....................................$2.50

Forest Green, tumbler, 5-oz.............................$4.50

Forest Green, vase, 6⅜"................................$5.00

Fortune, pink, bowl, dessert; 4½" $5.00

Fortune, pink, candy dish, flat $25.00

Fortune, pink, cup.....................................$5.00

Fortune, pink, plate, sherbet; 6"......................$3.50

Fortune, pink, tumbler, water; 9-oz, 4"................$9.50

Fruits, green, bowl, berry; 8".........................$55.00

Fruits, green, bowl, cereal; 5" $22.50

Fruits, green, pitcher, flat bottom, 7"................$70.00

Fruits, green, saucer..................................$6.00

Fruits, green, tumbler, combination of fruits, 4" $27.50

Fruits, green, tumbler, 12-oz, 5"......................$100.00

Fruits, pink, cup......................................$7.00

Fruits, pink, sherbet..................................$7.00

Georgian, green, bowl, berry; 4½"......................$8.50

Georgian, green, bowl, 6½" $65.00

Georgian, green, butter dish $75.00

Georgian, green, creamer, footed, 3"...................$11.00

Georgian, green, plate, center design only, 9¼".........$22.00

Georgian, green, plate, luncheon; 8" $9.00

Georgian, green, sugar bowl, footed, 3"................$9.50

Georgian, green, tumbler, flat, 9-oz, 4" $50.00

Harp, crystal, coaster $4.50

Harp, crystal, plate, 7" $11.00

Harp, crystal, saucer..................................$6.00

Harp, crystal, tray, rectangular $32.50

Heritage, crystal, bowl, fruit; 10½"...................$15.00

Heritage, crystal, cup.................................$7.50

Heritage, crystal, plate, luncheon; 8".................$9.50

Heritage, crystal, plate, sandwich; 12"................$15.00

Hex Optic, pink or green, bowl, berry; ruffled, 4¼" $6.00

Hex Optic, pink or green, butter dish, 1-lb, rectangular .$70.00

Hex Optic, pink or green, ice bucket, metal handle ...$20.00

Hex Optic, pink or green, pitcher, bottom w/sunflower motif, 32-oz, 5"......................................$22.50

Hex Optic, pink or green, plate, sherbet; 6" $3.00

Hex Optic, pink or green, platter, 11" dia.............$14.50

Hex Optic, pink or green, tumbler, footed, 5¾".........$9.50

Hobnail, crystal, cup..................................$5.00

Hobnail, crystal, goblet, water; 10-oz $7.00

Hobnail, crystal, pitcher, milk; 18-oz.................$20.00

Hobnail, crystal, plate, sherbet; 6"...................$3.00

Hobnail, crystal, tumbler, wine; footed, 3-oz..........$7.50

Holiday, pink, bowl, console; 10¾".....................$92.50

Holiday, pink, bowl, soup; 7¾".........................$42.50

Holiday, pink, candlesticks, 3", pr....................$85.00

Holiday, pink, pitcher, 52-oz, 6¾".....................$32.50

Holiday, pink, plate, chop; 13¾".......................$90.00

Holiday, pink, sandwich tray, 10½".....................$17.50

Holiday, pink, saucer, 2 styles, each..................$5.50

Holiday, pink, tumbler, flat, 10-oz, 4" $20.00

Holiday, pink, tumbler, footed, 6".....................$132.50

Homespun, pink, bowl, cereal; 5".......................$20.00

Homespun, pink, coaster/ashtray $7.00

Homespun, pink, platter, closed handles, 13" $16.50

Homespun, pink, tumbler, footed, 15-oz, 6½"............$25.00

Homespun, pink, tumbler, water; 9-oz, 4"...............$18.50

Indiana Custard, ivory, bowl, soup; flat, 7½"..........$30.00

Indiana Custard, ivory, plate, bread & butter; 5¾".........**$7.50**
Indiana Custard, ivory, plate, luncheon; 8⅞" **$14.50**
Indiana Custard, ivory, saucer......................................**$9.00**
Indiana Custard, ivory, sugar bowl............................**$11.00**
Iris, crystal, bowl, cereal; 5"......................................**$100.00**
Iris, crystal, candy jar...**$102.50**
Iris, crystal, plate, sherbet; 5½"..................................**$15.00**
Iris, crystal, sugar bowl..**$11.00**
Iris, crystal, tumbler, flat, 4".....................................**$105.00**
Iris, iridescent, butter dish, w/lid...............................**$42.50**
Iris, iridescent, goblet, 4-oz, 5¾"..............................**$105.00**
Iris, iridescent, pitcher, footed, 9½"............................**$37.50**
Iris, iridescent, plate, sandwich; 11¾".........................**$27.50**
Jubilee, topaz, bowl, fruit; handled, 9".......................**$105.00**
Jubilee, topaz, creamer...**$22.50**
Jubilee, topaz, cup...**$16.00**
Jubilee, topaz, mayonnaise, w/plate & ladle **$257.50**
Jubilee, topaz, plate, sandwich; 13"............................**$47.50**
Jubilee, topaz, tray, cake; 2-handled, 11" **$42.50**
Lace Edge, pink, bowl, cereal; 6⅜"..............................**$18.50**
Lace Edge, pink, bowl, salad; 7¾"...............................**$20.00**
Lace Edge, pink, bowl, 3-footed, 10½".......................**$185.00**
Lace Edge, pink, candy jar, ribbed **$45.00**
Lace Edge, pink, flower bowl, crystal frog..................**$22.50**
Lace Edge, pink, plate, luncheon; 8¾".........................**$17.50**
Lace Edge, pink, plate, salad; 7¼"...............................**$21.50**
Lace Edge, pink, relish dish, 3-part, 7½".....................**$57.50**
Lace Edge, pink, tumbler, flat, 9-oz, 4½".....................**$18.50**
Laced Edge, blue or green, bowl, divided oval, 11"..**$100.00**
Laced Edge, blue or green, bowl, soup; 7" **$65.00**
Laced Edge, blue or green, creamer............................**$35.00**
Laced Edge, blue or green, plate, bread & butter; 6½"..**$20.00**
Laced Edge, blue or green, sugar bowl......................**$40.00**
Laced Edge, blue or green, vase, 5½".........................**$60.00**
Lake Como, blue scene on white, bowl, soup; flat **$90.00**
Lake Como, blue scene on white, bowl, vegetable; 9¾".**$37.50**
Lake Como, blue scene on white, plate, salad; 7¼" **$18.00**

Laurel, green, cup **$8.00**
Laurel, green, platter, oval, 10¾" **$20.00**
Laurel, green, sugar bowl, short.................................**$8.50**
Laurel, ivory, bowl, 3-footed, 10½".............................**$35.00**
Laurel, ivory, candlesticks, 4", pr..............................**$30.00**
Laurel, ivory, plate, dinner; 9⅛"..................................**$12.50**
Laurel, ivory, salt & pepper shakers **$47.50**
Laurel, ivory, tumbler, flat, 9-oz, 4½"..........................**$32.50**
Lincoln Inn, blue or red, ashtray................................**$18.00**
Lincoln Inn, blue or red, bowl, footed, 10½".............**$42.50**
Lincoln Inn, blue or red, goblet, water........................**$25.00**
Lincoln Inn, blue or red, tumbler, footed, 5-oz **$26.00**
Lincoln Inn, blue or red, vase, footed, 12".................**$137.50**
Lincoln Inn, other than blue or red, bowl, cereal; 6" ..**$10.00**
Lincoln Inn, other than blue or red, bowl, footed, 9¼".**$20.00**
Lincoln Inn, other than blue or red, plate, 9¼"...........**$13.50**
Lincoln Inn, other than blue or red, salt & pepper shakers,
    pr **$137.50**
Lincoln Inn, other than blue or red, tumbler, footed, 9-
    oz **$15.00**
Lorain, green, bowl, berry; 8" **$80.00**
Lorain, green, platter, 11½"..**$25.00**
Lorain, green, relish, 4-part, 8"..................................**$18.50**
Lorain, green, saucer..**$5.00**
Lorain, green, tumbler, footed, 9-oz, 4¾"...................**$20.00**
Lorain, yellow, bowl, salad; 7¼"................................**$60.00**
Lorain, yellow, cup...**$16.00**
Lorain, yellow, sherbet, footed **$30.00**
Lorain, yellow, sugar bowl, footed **$22.50**
Madrid, amber, bowl, vegetable; oval, 10".................**$17.50**

Madrid, amber, butter dish, $65.00

Madrid, amber, cookie jar **$45.00**
Madrid, amber, plate, luncheon; 8⅞"...........................**$9.00**
Madrid, amber, tumbler, footed, 10-oz, 5½"...............**$25.00**
Madrid, green, ashtray, square, 6" **$137.50**
Madrid, green, pitcher, 8-oz, 8½".................................**$210.00**
Madrid, green, platter, oval, 11½"...............................**$16.00**
Madrid, green, saucer **$5.00**
Madrid, green, tumbler, 2 styles, 12-oz, 5½", each **$30.00**
Manhattan, crystal, ashtray, square, 4½".....................**$20.00**
Manhattan, crystal, bowl, closed handles, 8" **$22.50**

Lake Como, blue scene on white, platter, 11", $60.00

Lake Como, blue scene on white, salt & pepper shakers,
    pr...**$40.00**
Laurel, green, bowl, vegetable; oval, 9¾" **$18.50**

146

Manhattan, crystal, pitcher, tilted, 80-oz......................$32.50

Manhattan, crystal, sugar bowl, oval **$11.00**

Manhattan, pink, bowl, fruit; open handle, 9½" **$32.50**

Manhattan, pink, creamer, oval.............................**$11.00**

Manhattan, pink, plate, sherbet; 6" **$47.50**

Manhattan, pink, tumbler, footed, 10-oz.....................**$17.50**

Mayfair (Federal), amber, bowl, vegetable; oval, 10 ".**$27.50**

Mayfair (Federal), amber, creamer, footed..................**$15.00**

Mayfair (Federal), amber, plate, grill; 9½" **$15.00**

Mayfair (Federal), amber, tumbler, 9-oz, 4½"..............**$25.00**

Mayfair (Federal), green, bowl, cereal; 6" **$22.00**

Mayfair (Federal), green, cup.................................**$9.00**

Mayfair (Federal), green, platter, oval, 12" **$30.00**

Mayfair (Federal), green, sugar bowl, footed.............**$16.00**

Mayfair (Open Rose), blue, bowl, low flat, 11¾".........**$65.00**

Mayfair (Open Rose), blue, bowl, vegetable; oval, 9½" .**$65.00**

Mayfair (Open Rose), blue, cake plate, footed............**$60.00**

Mayfair (Open Rose), blue, candy dish, $265.00

Mayfair (Open Rose), blue, cookie jar **$285.00**

Mayfair (Open Rose), blue, cup...............................**$47.50**

Mayfair (Open Rose), blue, pitcher, 80-oz, 8½".........**$190.00**

Mayfair (Open Rose), blue, plate, grill; 9½" **$47.50**

Mayfair (Open Rose), blue, plate, luncheon; 8½".........**$42.50**

Mayfair (Open Rose), blue, salt & pepper shakers, flat, pr **$280.00**

Mayfair (Open Rose), blue, sandwich server, center handle...**$70.00**

Mayfair (Open Rose), blue, tumbler, iced tea; footed, 15-oz, 6½"...**$190.00**

Mayfair (Open Rose), pink, bowl, cream soup, 5" **$40.00**

Mayfair (Open Rose), pink, bowl, fruit; scalloped, 12"..**$50.00**

Mayfair (Open Rose), pink, candy dish.......................**$50.00**

Mayfair (Open Rose), pink, celery dish, divided, 10"..**$185.00**

Mayfair (Open Rose), pink, creamer, footed...............**$25.00**

Mayfair (Open Rose), pink, goblet, cocktail; 3½-oz, 4" ..**$70.00**

Mayfair (Open Rose), pink, plate, sherbet; 6½"...........**$14.00**

Mayfair (Open Rose), pink, platter, oval, open handles, 12" **$26.50**

Mayfair (Open Rose), pink, saucer **$30.00**

Mayfair (Open Rose), pink, sherbet, footed, 4¾" **$80.00**

Mayfair (Open Rose), pink, sugar bowl, footed **$27.50**

Mayfair (Open Rose), pink, tumbler, juice; footed, 3-oz, 3¼"...**$75.00**

Mayfair (Open Rose), pink, tumbler, water; 9-oz, 4¼".**$27.50**

Miss America, crystal, bowl, fruit; straight, 8¾"...........**$32.50**

Miss America, crystal, butter dish **$210.00**

Miss America, crystal, celery dish, oblong, 10½" **$17.50**

Miss America, crystal, goblet, water; 10-oz, 5½" **$22.50**

Miss America, crystal, plate, salad; 8½" **$8.00**

Miss America, crystal, relish, 4-part, 8¾".................**$10.00**

Miss America, crystal, tumbler, iced tea; 14-oz, 5¾"....**$26.50**

Miss America, pink, bowl, vegetable; oval, 10" **$27.50**

Miss America, pink, compote, 5" **$25.00**

Miss America, pink, pitcher, w/ice lip, 65-oz, 8½" **$125.00**

Miss America, pink, plate, grill; 10¼" **$22.50**

Miss America, pink, platter, oval, 12" **$25.00**

Miss America, pink, salt & pepper shakers, pr **$55.00**

Miss America, pink, tumbler, juice; 5-oz, 4" **$42.50**

Moderntone, amethyst, bowl, berry; 5" **$22.50**

Moderntone, amethyst, plate, sandwich; 10½".............**$37.50**

Moderntone, amethyst, plate, sherbet; 5¾" **$6.00**

Moderntone, amethyst, sherbet..............................**$11.00**

Moderntone, amethyst, tumbler, 9-oz......................**$24.00**

Moderntone, cobalt, bowl, cereal; 6½" **$67.50**

Moderntone, cobalt, cup, custard, no handle **$20.00**

Moderntone, cobalt, plate, luncheon; 7¾" **$14.00**

Moderntone, cobalt, platter, oval, 11".......................**$37.50**

Moderntone, cobalt, sugar bowl **$11.00**

Moondrops, red or blue, bowl, casserole; 9¾" **$142.50**

Moondrops, red or blue, bowl, pickle; 7½" **$24.00**

Moondrops, red or blue, candlesticks, w/triple light, 5¼", pr **$97.00**

Moondrops, red or blue, creamer, miniature, 2¾".......**$20.00**

Moondrops, red or blue, decanter, sm, 7¾" **$70.00**

Moondrops, red or blue, goblet, 5-oz, 4¾" **$25.00**

Moondrops, red or blue, plate, bread & butter; 5⅞" ...**$11.00**

Moondrops, red or blue, plate, sandwich; 14"...........**$37.50**

Moondrops, red or blue, platter, oval, 12" **$32.50**

Moondrops, red or blue, sherbet, 2⅝".......................**$17.50**

Moondrops, red or blue, tray, for sugar & creamer, 7½".**$37.50**

Moondrops, red or blue, tumbler, 7-oz, 4⅜"...............**$17.50**

Moonstone, opalescent hobnail, bowl, cloverleaf **$14.00**

Moonstone, opalescent hobnail, bowl, flat, 7¾" **$14.00**

Moonstone, opalescent hobnail, candy jar, 6" **$26.50**

Moonstone, opalescent hobnail, heart bonbon, handle .**$14.00**

Moonstone, opalescent hobnail, plate, luncheon; 8"...**$16.00**

Moonstone, opalescent hobnail, sherbet, footed **$7.00**

Moroccan Amethyst, ashtray, triangular, 6⅝" **$10.00**

Moroccan Amethyst, bowl, fruit; octagonal, 4¾" **$7.00**

Moroccan Amethyst, bowl, w/metal handle, rectangular, 7¾" **$16.00**

Moroccan Amethyst, goblet, juice; 5½-oz, 4⅜" **$9.50**

Moroccan Amethyst, goblet, sherbet; 7½-oz, 4¼" **$8.00**

Moroccan Amethyst, plate, salad; 7¼" **$7.00**

Moroccan Amethyst, tumbler, iced tea; 16-oz, 6½"......**$17.00**

Moroccan Amethyst, tumbler, old-fashioned; 8-oz, 3¼".**$15.00**

Mt Pleasant, black amethyst or cobalt, bowl, fruit; footed, square, 9¼"..**$30.00**

Mt Pleasant, black amethyst or cobalt, bowl, rolled-out edge, 3-footed, 7"......................................**$22.50**

Mt Pleasant, black amethyst or cobalt, bowl, scalloped, footed, 1¾x9"..**$30.00**

Mt Pleasant, black amethyst or cobalt, bowl, 2-handled, square, 6"...**$18.00**

Mt Pleasant, black amethyst or cobalt, candlesticks, single, pr...**$28.00**

Mt Pleasant, black amethyst or cobalt, creamer...........**$20.00**

Mt Pleasant, black amethyst or cobalt, mayonnaise, 3-footed, 5½"...**$27.50**

Mt Pleasant, black amethyst or cobalt, plate, scalloped, 2-handled, 7" **$16.00**

Mt Pleasant, black amethyst or cobalt, plate, w/indent for cup, square, 8¼"......................................**$17.00**

Mt Pleasant, black amethyst or cobalt, salt & pepper shakers, 2 styles, pr **$42.50**

Mt Pleasant, black amethyst or cobalt, sandwich server, center handle **$37.50**

Mt Pleasant, black amethyst or cobalt, sherbet............**$17.00**

Mt Pleasant, black amethyst or cobalt, sugar bowl.....**$20.00**

Mt Pleasant, black amethyst or cobalt, vase, 7¼" **$32.50**

New Century, green, bowl, casserole; 9"....................**$55.00**

New Century, green, butter dish................................**$60.00**

New Century, green, goblet, wine; 2½-oz...................**$25.00**

New Century, green, pitcher, no ice lip, 80-oz, 8"....**$40.00**

New Century, green, pitcher, w/ice lip, 80-oz, 8" **$40.00**

New Century, green, plate, grill; 10".........................**$11.00**

New Century, green, plate, salad; 8½".........................**$9.00**

New Century, green, platter, oval, 11".......................**$16.00**

New Century, green, salt & pepper shakers, pr...........**$37.50**

New Century, green, sherbet, 3" **$9.50**

New Century, green, tumbler, footed, 9-oz, 4⅞" **$20.00**

New Century, green, tumbler, 5-oz, 3½".....................**$11.00**

Newport, amethyst, plate, sherbet; 6", $5.00; sherbert, $13.00; plate, luncheon; 8½", $10.00; bowl, cereal; 5¼", $27.50; tumbler, 4½", $30.00

Newport, amethyst, cup **$10.00**

Newport, amethyst, plate, sandwich; 11½" **$32.50**

Newport, amethyst, salt & pepper shakers, pr............**$40.00**

Newport, amethyst, sugar bowl **$15.00**

Newport, cobalt, bowl, cream soup; 4¾"....................**$18.00**

Newport, cobalt, creamer...**$17.00**

Newport, cobalt, plate, sherbet; 6"...............................**$7.00**

Newport, cobalt, platter, oval, 11¾"...........................**$37.50**

Newport, cobalt, tumbler, 9-oz, 4½"...........................**$32.50**

No 610 Pyramid, pink, bowl, pickle; 9½".....................**$31.50**

No 610 Pyramid, pink, relish tray, handled, 4-part......**$40.00**

No 610 Pyramid, pink, sugar bowl **$24.00**

No 610 Pyramid, pink, tumbler, footed, 11-oz.............**$42.50**

No 610 Pyramid, yellow, bowl, oval, 9½" **$50.00**

No 610 Pyramid, yellow, ice tub, w/lid......................**$630.00**

No 610 Pyramid, yellow, pitcher **$447.50**

No 610 Pyramid, yellow, tumbler, footed, 8-oz **$50.00**

No 612 Horseshoe, green, bowl, vegetable; oval, 10½" .**$20.00**

No 612 Horseshoe, green, plate, grill; 10⅜"................**$55.00**

No 612 Horseshoe, green, platter, oval, 10¾"..............**$22.50**

No 612 Horseshoe, green, sherbet...............................**$15.00**

No 612 Horseshoe, green, tumbler, footed, 12-oz.....**$105.00**

No 612 Horseshoe, green, tumbler, 12-oz, 4¾" **$157.50**

No 612 Horseshoe, green or yellow, bowl, cereal; 6½" .**$22.50**

No 612 Horseshoe, green or yellow, saucer **$6.00**

No 612 Horseshoe, yellow, bowl, berry; lg, 9½" **$32.50**

No 612 Horseshoe, yellow, cup...................................**$11.00**

No 612 Horseshoe, yellow, pitcher, 64-oz, 8½"........**$262.50**

No 612 Horseshoe, yellow, plate, dinner; 10⅜"..........**$20.00**

No 612 Horseshoe, yellow, relish, 3-part, footed **$37.50**

No 612 Horseshoe, yellow, tumbler, footed, 9-oz **$19.00**

No 616 Vernon, green or yellow, cup..........................**$16.00**

No 616 Vernon, green or yellow, plate, luncheon; 8" ...**$9.50**

No 616 Vernon, green or yellow, plate, sandwich; 11".**$26.50**

No 616 Vernon, green or yellow, saucer.......................**$6.00**

No 616 Vernon, green or yellow, sugar bowl, footed.**$24.00**

No 616 Vernon, green or yellow, tumbler, footed, 5".**$32.50**

No 618 Pineapple & Floral, amber, bowl, salad; 7".....**$10.00**

No 618 Pineapple & Floral, amber, bowl, vegetable; oval, 10"...**$20.00**

No 618 Pineapple & Floral, amber, plate, salad; 8⅜" **$9.00**

No 618 Pineapple & Floral, amber, platter, closed handles, 11"...**$19.00**

No 618 Pineapple & Floral, amber, saucer....................**$6.00**

No 618 Pineapple & Floral, crystal, ashtray, 4½".........**$18.00**

No 618 Pineapple & Floral, crystal, bowl, cereal; 6" ...**$25.00**

No 618 Pineapple & Floral, crystal, cup......................**$11.00**

No 618 Pineapple & Floral, crystal, plate, sandwich; 11½"..**$16.00**

No 618 Pineapple & Floral, crystal, plate, sherbet; 6" ...**$6.00**

No 618 Pineapple & Floral, crystal, sherbet, footed **$20.00**

No 622, crystal or teal, bowl, soup; 7½".....................**$12.00**

No 622, crystal or teal, plate, sandwich; 11½" **$14.00**

No 622, crystal or teal, tumbler, water; 9-oz...............**$24.00**

Normandie, amber, bowl, berry; lg, 8½".....................**$16.00**

Normandie, amber, pitcher, 80-oz, 8".........................**$70.00**

Normandie, amber, plate, grill; 11".............................**$15.00**

Normandie, amber, plate, sherbet; 6" **$5.00**

Normandie, amber, salt & pepper shaker, pr.............**$47.50**

Normandie, amber, sugar bowl lid.............................**$85.00**

Normandie, amber, tumbler, iced tea; 12-oz, 5" **$25.00**

Normandie, pink, bowl, vegetable; oval, 10"..............**$32.50**

Normandie, pink, cup...$9.00
Normandie, pink, plate, salad; 8".........................$11.00
Normandie, pink, platter, 11¾"...........................$24.00
Normandie, pink, saucer...$5.00
Normandie, pink, sherbet..$9.00
Old Cafe, pink, pitcher, 80-oz...............................$85.00
Old Cafe, pink, plate, dinner; 10".........................$30.00
Old Cafe, pink, sherbet, low footed.......................$7.00
Old Cafe, pink, tumbler, water; 4".........................$11.00
Old Cafe, ruby, bowl, berry; 3¾"............................$6.00
Old Cafe, ruby, bowl, closed handles, 9"...............$15.00
Old Cafe, ruby, cup..$8.00
Old Cafe, ruby, lamp...$24.50
Old Cafe, ruby, vase, 7¼".......................................$17.50
Old English, green, pink, or amber, bowl, fruit; footed, 9"...$27.50
Old English, green, pink, or amber, candlesticks, 4", pr...$32.50
Old English, green, pink, or amber, candy dish, flat...$47.50
Old English, green, pink, or amber, goblet, 8 oz, 5¾"..$32.50
Old English, green, pink, or amber, pitcher...............$65.00
Old English, green, pink, or amber, sherbet, 2 styles, each...$20.00
Old English, green, pink, or amber, sugar bowl lid....$35.00
Old English, green, pink, or amber, tumbler, footed, 4½"...$22.50
Ovide, black, bowl, berry; 4¾".................................$8.00
Ovide, black, cocktail, fruit; footed.........................$5.00
Ovide, black, cup...$7.00
Ovide, black, sugar bowl (open)..............................$7.00
Ovide, green, candy dish.......................................$22.50
Ovide, green, creamer..$4.00
Ovide, green, plate, luncheon; 8".............................$3.00
Ovide, green, salt & pepper shakers, pr.................$28.50

Oyster & Pearl, pink, candle holder, 3½", $10.00; pink, relish dish, oblong, 10¼", $10.00; pink, bowl, handled, $6.50

Oyster & Pearl, pink, bowl, heart shaped, handled, 5¼"...$8.00
Oyster & Pearl, pink, plate, sandwich; 13½".........$18.00

Oyster & Pearl, ruby, bowl, fruit, 10½"................$47.50
Oyster & Pearl, ruby, bowl, handled, 5¼"............$11.00
Oyster & Pearl, ruby, candle holder, 3½" pr.........$42.50
Parrot, amber, plate, sherbet; 5¾"........................$18.00
Parrot, amber, plate, square, 10¼".......................$47.50
Parrot, amber, platter, oblong, 11¼"....................$60.00
Parrot, amber, saucer...$237.93
Parrot, amber, tumbler, heavy, footed, 5¾"........$122.50
Parrot, green, bowl, berry; 5"................................$22.50
Parrot, green, pitcher, 80-oz, 8½".....................$2,600.00
Parrot, green, plate, dinner; 9"............................$42.50
Parrot, green, sugar bowl......................................$35.00
Parrot, green, tumbler, 10-oz, 4¼".....................$105.00
Patrician, amber, bowl, cereal; 6".........................$24.50
Patrician, amber, cookie jar..................................$85.00
Patrician, amber, pitcher, 75-oz, 8".....................$105.00
Patrician, amber, plate, grill; 10½".......................$15.00
Patrician, amber, saucer..$10.00
Patrician, amber, sugar bowl lid...........................$50.00
Patrician, amber, tumbler, 5-oz, 4".......................$30.00
Patrician, green, bowl, vegetable; oval, 10".........$32.50
Patrician, green, butter dish................................$100.00
Patrician, green, plate, salad; 7½".........................$15.00
Patrician, green, plate, sherbet; 6".........................$8.00
Patrician, green, salt & pepper shakers, pr...........$60.00
Patrician, green, sherbet..$14.00
Patrician, green, tumbler, 14-oz, 5½"...................$40.00
Patrick, pink, candlesticks, pr.............................$152.50
Patrick, pink, goblet, juice; 6-oz, 4¾".................$137.50
Patrick, pink, plate, sherbet; 7"............................$18.00
Patrick, pink, tray, 2-handled, 11".......................$142.50
Patrick, yellow, bowl, fruit; handled, 9"...............$42.50
Patrick, yellow, cheese & cracker set....................$90.00
Patrick, yellow, mayonnaise, 3-pc......................$132.50
Patrick, yellow, sugar bowl...................................$37.50
Petalware, monax, bowl, cereal; 5¾".......................$7.00
Petalware, monax, bowl, cream soup; 4½"............$10.00
Petalware, monax, plate, sherbet; 6".......................$3.00
Petalware, monax, platter, oval, 13".....................$14.00
Petalware, monax, saucer...$2.50
Petalware, pink, creamer, footed............................$8.00
Petalware, pink, cup..$7.00
Petalware, pink, plate, dinner; 9"............................$9.50
Petalware, pink, plate, salver; 11"........................$10.00
Petalware, pink, sugar bowl, footed.......................$8.00
Primo, yellow or green, bowl, 7¾".........................$20.00
Primo, yellow or green, coaster/ashtray.................$8.50
Primo, yellow or green, cup.....................................$9.00
Primo, yellow or green, plate, grill; 10"................$10.00
Primo, yellow or green, saucer................................$4.00
Primo, yellow or green, tumbler, 9-oz, 5¾"...........$17.50
Princess, pink, ashtray, 4½"...................................$85.00
Princess, pink, bowl, cereal or oatmeal; 5"...........$23.50
Princess, pink, bowl, hat shaped, 9½"...................$32.50
Princess, pink, tumbler, iced-tea; 13-oz, 5¼".........$24.00
Princess, pink or green, bowl, salad; octagonal, 9"....$32.50
Princess, pink or green, butter dish.......................$90.00
Princess, pink or green, candy dish.......................$55.00

Princess, pink or green, cookie jar **$55.00**
Princess, pink or green, pitcher, 60-oz, 8" **$50.00**
Princess, pink or green, plate, grill; 9" **$14.00**
Princess, pink or green, plate, sherbet; 5½" **$10.00**
Princess, pink or green, platter, closed handles, 12" ...**$22.50**
Princess, pink or green, salt & pepper shakers, 4½", pr..**$47.50**
Princess, pink or green, sherbet, footed.....................**$20.00**
Princess, pink or green, sugar bowl lid.......................**$20.00**
Princess, pink or green, tumbler, footed, 12½-oz, 6½"..**$80.00**
Queen Mary, crystal, ashtray, oval, 2x3¾"..................**$4.00**
Queen Mary, crystal, candlesticks, double branch, 4½",
  pr **$16.00**
Queen Mary, crystal, celery or pickle dish, 5x10".........**$9.00**
Queen Mary, crystal, plate, sandwich; 12" **$10.00**
Queen Mary, crystal, salt & pepper shakers, pr...........**$20.00**
Queen Mary, crystal, sugar bowl, oval **$6.00**
Queen Mary, crystal, tumbler, footed, 10-oz, 5" **$27.50**
Queen Mary, pink, bowl, 2-handles, 5½"......................**$7.00**
Queen Mary, pink, cigarette jar, oval, 2x3"..................**$8.00**
Queen Mary, pink, cup...**$8.00**
Queen Mary, pink, plate, 6" & 6⅝", each **$5.00**
Queen Mary, pink, relish tray, 4-part, 14" **$17.50**
Queen Mary, pink, saucer **$3.00**
Queen Mary, pink, tumbler, juice; 5-oz, 3½" **$10.00**
Radiance, red or ice blue, bowl, celery; 10" **$22.50**
Radiance, red or ice blue, bowl, pickle; 7" **$20.00**
Radiance, red or ice blue, mayonnaise, 3-pc set **$60.00**
Radiance, red or ice blue, plate, luncheon; 8" **$17.50**
Radiance, red or ice blue, salt & pepper shakers, pr ..**$80.00**
Radiance, red or ice blue, sugar bowl........................**$22.50**
Radiance, red or ice blue, tumbler, 9-oz **$27.50**
Radiance, red or ice blue, vase, crimped, 12".............**$70.00**
Raindrops, green, bowl, cereal; 6" **$8.00**
Raindrops, green, plate, sherbet; 6" **$3.50**
Raindrops, green, salt & pepper shakers, pr.............**$265.00**
Raindrops, green, sugar bowl lid................................**$37.50**
Raindrops, green, tumbler, 4-oz, 3" **$5.00**
Ribbon, black, plate, luncheon; 8".............................**$14.00**
Ribbon, black, salt & pepper shakers, pr **$40.00**
Ribbon, green, bowl, berry; lg, 8" **$25.00**
Ribbon, green, candy dish...**$37.50**
Ribbon, green, sherbet, footed.....................................**$5.50**
Ribbon, green, tumbler, 13-oz, 6½" **$27.50**
Ring, crystal, cocktail shaker......................................**$20.00**
Ring, crystal, creamer, footed......................................**$5.50**
Ring, crystal, plate, sherbet; 6¼" **$2.50**
Ring, crystal, salt & pepper shakers, 3", pr **$18.00**
Ring, crystal, sugar bowl, footed..................................**$5.00**
Ring, crystal, tumbler, cocktail; footed, 3½" **$6.50**
Ring, decorated, bowl, soup; 7" **$14.00**
Ring, decorated, pitcher, 60-oz, 8" **$21.50**
Ring, decorated, sherbet, footed, 4¾" **$9.50**
Ring, decorated, tumbler, iced tea; footed, 6½"..........**$15.00**
Ring, decorated, vase, 8" **$32.50**
Rock Crystal, crystal, candlesticks, tall, 8½", pr...........**$73.00**
Rock Crystal, crystal, creamer, footed, 9-oz **$20.00**
Rock Crystal, crystal, tumbler, juice; 5-oz...................**$16.00**
Rock Crystal, red, candelabra, 3-light, pr...................**$262.50**

Rock Crystal, red, goblet, iced tea; low footed, 11-oz.**$65.00**
Rock Crystal, red, plate, bread & butter; scalloped edge,
  6"..**$17.50**
Rock Crystal, red, sugar bowl, footed, 10-oz **$100.00**
Rock Crystal, red, sundae, low foot, 6-oz **$35.00**
Rose Cameo, green, bowl, berry; 4½" **$9.00**
Rose Cameo, green, sherbet.......................................**$11.00**
Rose Cameo, green, tumbler, footed, 2 styles, 5", each.**$18.00**
Rosemary, amber, bowl, vegetable; oval, 10" **$15.00**
Rosemary, amber, plate, salad; 6¾" **$6.00**
Rosemary, amber, saucer...**$5.00**
Rosemary, amber, sugar bowl, footed **$9.00**
Rosemary, green, bowl, cream soup; 5" **$20.00**
Rosemary, green, creamer, footed **$14.00**
Rosemary, green, platter, oval, 12" **$20.00**
Rosemary, green, tumbler, 9-oz, 4¼"..........................**$30.00**
Roulette, pink, pitcher, 64-oz, 8" **$32.50**
Roulette, pink, tumbler, old-fashioned; 7½-oz, 3¼" **$22.50**
Roulette, pink or green, plate, sandwich; 12"..............**$14.00**
Roulette, pink or green, tumbler, footed, 10-oz, 5½" ..**$25.00**
Roulette, pink or green, whiskey, 1½-oz, 2½" **$15.00**
Round Robin, green or iridescent, bowl, berry; 4" **$5.50**
Round Robin, green or iridescent, plate, sandwich; 12".**$8.00**
Round Robin, green or iridescent, plate, sherbet; 6" **$3.00**
Round Robin, green or iridescent, saucer **$2.50**
Roxana, yellow, bowl, 4½x2⅜"...................................**$10.00**
Roxana, yellow, plate, 6"...**$7.00**
Roxana, yellow, sherbet, footed...................................**$9.00**
Royal Lace, blue, bowl, 3-leg, ruffled edge, 10" **$485.00**
Royal Lace, blue, candlesticks, ruffled edge, pr........**$210.00**

Royal Lace, blue, creamer & sugar bowl, footed, $225.00

Royal Lace, blue, nut dish....................................**$1,000.00**
Royal Lace, blue, plate, sherbet; 6".............................**$12.00**
Royal Lace, blue, platter, oval, 13"..............................**$55.00**
Royal Lace, blue, salt & pepper shakers, pr...............**$242.50**
Royal Lace, blue, sherbet, footed................................**$44.00**
Royal Lace, blue, tumbler, 10-oz, 4⅞" **$110.00**
Royal Lace, pink, bowl, berry; 10"...............................**$27.50**
Royal Lace, pink, bowl, cream soup; 4¾" **$20.00**
Royal Lace, pink, bowl, vegetable; oval, 11"...............**$30.00**
Royal Lace, pink, butter dish **$142.50**
Royal Lace, pink, cookie jar..**$47.50**

Royal Lace, pink, cup $14.00
Royal Lace, pink, pitcher, 86-oz, 8" $80.00
Royal Lace, pink, plate, dinner; 10" $20.00
Royal Lace, pink, tumbler, 5-oz, 3½" $24.00
Royal Ruby, ashtray, square, 4½" $4.00
Royal Ruby, bowl, vegetable; oval, 8" $37.50
Royal Ruby, creamer, footed $9.50
Royal Ruby, pitcher, tilted, 3-qt $37.50
Royal Ruby, plate, dinner; 9" or 9¼", each......$11.00
Royal Ruby, plate, 13¾" $25.00
Royal Ruby, punch bowl & stand $73.00
Royal Ruby, sugar bowl, footed $9.00
Royal Ruby, tumbler, cocktail; 3½" $10.50
Royal Ruby, vase, ball shaped, 4" $5.50
S Patter, amber, bowl, berry; lg, 8½" $16.00
S Pattern, amber, pitcher, 80-oz $95.00
S Pattern, crystal, plate, grill $7.00
S Pattern, crystal, tumbler, 9-oz, 4" $5.50
Sandwich (Hocking), crystal, bowl, cereal; 6" $28.50
Sandwich (Hocking), crystal, cookie jar $37.50
Sandwich (Hocking), crystal, plate, dessert; 7" $10.00
Sandwich (Hocking), crystal, sherbet, footed $8.00
Sandwich (Hocking), crystal, sugar bowl.....$22.50
Sandwich (Hocking), crystal, tumbler, footed, 9-oz $23.50
Sandwich (Hocking), green, bowl, berry; 4⅞" $4.00
Sandwich (Hocking), green, creamer $24.00
Sandwich (Hocking), green, pitcher, juice; 6" $122.00
Sandwich (Hocking), green, saucer...............$13.50
Sandwich (Hocking), green, tumbler, water; 9-oz........$5.50
Sandwich (Indiana), crystal, butter dish, w/dome lid .$22.50
Sandwich (Indiana), crystal, goblet, 9-oz $15.00
Sandwich (Indiana), crystal, pitcher, 69-oz $22.50
Sandwich (Indiana), crystal, plate, bread & butter; 7"...$4.00
Sandwich (Indiana), crystal, plate, sandwich; 13" $11.00
Sandwich (Indiana), crystal, sugar bowl..........$9.50
Sandwich (Indiana), crystal, tumbler, iced-tea; footed, 12-oz................................$11.00
Sandwich (Indiana), crystal, wine; 4-oz, 3" $7.00
Sandwich (Indiana), pink, bowl, console; 9" $17.50
Sandwich (Indiana), pink, candlesticks, 3½", pr..........$15.00
Sandwich (Indiana), pink, decanter & stopper............$90.00
Sandwich (Indiana), pink, sandwich server, center handle................................$27.50
Sharon, amber, bowl, soup; flat, 7½" $42.50
Sharon, amber, bowl, vegetable; oval, 9½"...............$22.50
Sharon, amber, creamer, footed....................$14.00
Sharon, amber, jam dish, 7½" $35.00
Sharon, amber, plate, bread & butter; 6".......$5.00

Sharon, amber, saucer $7.00
Sharon, amber, sugar bowl.............................$9.00
Sharon, amber, tumbler, thick, 12-oz, 5¼" $55.00
Sharon, pink, bowl, berry; 5" $11.00
Sharon, pink, bowl, cereal; 6" $22.50
Sharon, pink, bowl, fruit; 10½" $34.50
Sharon, pink, candy jar.................................$47.50
Sharon, pink, cheese dish, w/lid $850.00
Sharon, pink, cup..$14.00
Sharon, pink, platter, oval, 12½"..................$27.50
Sharon, pink, salt & pepper shakers, pr.......$47.50
Sharon, pink, tumbler, footed, 15-oz, 6½"....$42.50
Sharon, pink, tumbler, thin, 9-oz, 4⅛"..........$32.50
Sierra, green, bowl, vegetable; oval, 9½" $90.00
Sierra, green, creamer....................................$21.50
Sierra, green, cup...$15.00
Sierra, green, platter, oval, 11" $42.50
Sierra, green, salt & pepper shakers, pr $37.50
Sierra, pink, bowl, cereal; 5½" $11.00
Sierra, pink, butter dish $60.00
Sierra, pink, pitcher, 32-oz, 6½" $70.00
Sierra, pink, serving tray, 2-handled.............$15.00
Sierra, pink, sugar bowl lid $16.50
Spiral, green, bowl, berry; lg, 8" $14.00
Spiral, green, bowl, mixing; 7".......................$9.00
Spiral, green, cup..$6.00
Spiral, green, plate, sherbet; 6" $3.00
Spiral, green, platter......................................$25.00

Spiral, green, preserve, $30.00

Spiral, green, saucer..$2.50
Spiral, green, sherbet $4.50
Spiral, green, tumbler, juice; 5-oz, 3" $5.00
Starlight, crystal, bowl, closed handles, 8½"..............$7.00
Starlight, crystal, bowl, salad; 11½"..............$18.00
Starlight, crystal, cup.....................................$5.00
Starlight, crystal, plate, bread & butter; 6" $3.50
Starlight, crystal, plate, sandwich; 13".........$14.00
Starlight, crystal, relish dish $14.00
Starlight, crystal, saucer $2.50
Starlight, crystal, sherbet...............................$13.50

Sharon, amber, salt & pepper shakers, metal tops, 2¾", pr, $40.00

Starlight, crystal, sugar bowl, oval $6.00
Starlight, pink, bowl, cereal; 5½" $9.00
Strawberry, pink or green, bowl, berry; 4" $9.00
Strawberry, pink or green, bowl, salad; 2x6½" $18.00
Strawberry, pink or green, bowl, 2x6¼" $65.00
Strawberry, pink or green, compote, 5¾" $20.00
Strawberry, pink or green, creamer, sm $18.00
Strawberry, pink or green, pickle dish $14.00
Strawberry, pink or green, pitcher, 7¾" $142.50
Strawberry, pink or green, sherbet $8.00
Strawberry, pink or green, sugar bowl lid $47.50
Strawberry, pink or green, tumbler, 9-oz, 3⅝" $30.00
Sunflower, green, cake plate, 3-footed, 10" $16.00
Sunflower, green, creamer $19.50
Sunflower, green, sugar bowl $19.50
Sunflower, green, tumbler, footed, 8-oz, 4¾" $30.00
Sunflower, pink, ashtray, center design only, 5" $10.00
Sunflower, pink, plate, dinner; 9" $15.00
Sunflower, pink, saucer $7.00
Sunflower, pink, trivet, 3-legged, turned-up edge, 7"..$280.00
Swirl, pink, ashtray, 5⅜" $7.00
Swirl, pink, butter dish $185.00
Swirl, pink, candy dish $90.00
Swirl, pink, creamer, footed $8.00
Swirl, pink, plate, sandwich; 12½" $13.50
Swirl, pink, plate, sherbet; 6½" $5.00
Swirl, pink, tumbler, footed, 9-oz $18.00
Swirl, ultramarine, bowl, cereal; 5¼" $16.00
Swirl, ultramarine, bowl, closed handles, footed, 10" .$32.50
Swirl, ultramarine, plate, salad; 8" $15.00
Swirl, ultramarine, sherbet, low footed $18.50
Swirl, ultramarine, sugar bowl, footed $16.00
Swirl, ultramarine, tumbler, 9-oz, 4" $27.50
Swirl, ultramarine, vase, footed, 8½" $27.50
Tea Room, green, bowl, banana split; 7½" $83.00
Tea Room, green, bowl, salad; 8¾" $82.50
Tea Room, green, goblet, 9-oz $75.00
Tea Room, green, pitcher, 64-oz $142.50
Tea Room, green, relish, divided $25.00
Tea Room, green, saucer $27.50
Tea Room, green, sugar bowl, 4" $18.00
Tea Room, green, tumbler, flat, 8½-oz $85.00
Tea Room, green or pink, creamer, 4" $27.50
Tea Room, pink, bowl, celery; 8½" $27.50
Tea Room, pink, bowl, vegetable; oval, 9½" $60.00

Tea Room, pink, cup $47.50
Tea Room, pink, plate, luncheon; 8¼" $30.00
Tea Room, pink, plate, sherbet; 6½" $27.50
Tea Room, pink, salt & pepper shakers, pr $47.50
Tea Room, pink, sundae, footed, ruffled............$70.00
Tea Room, pink, tumbler, footed, 9-oz $32.50
Tea Room, pink, vase, 9" $47.50
Thistle, green, bowl, cereal; 5½" $22.50
Thistle, green, cake plate, heavy, 13" $132.50
Thistle, green, plate, luncheon; 8" $18.00
Thistle, green, saucer $10.00
Thistle, pink, cup, thin $20.00
Thistle, pink, plate, grill; 10¼" $18.00
Twisted Optic, pink or green, bowl, cereal; 5" $6.00
Twisted Optic, pink or green, bowl, salad or soup; 7"..$10.00
Twisted Optic, pink or green, candlestick, pr, 3" $20.00
Twisted Optic, pink or green, creamer................$8.00
Twisted Optic, pink or green, plate, oval, 7½x9" $6.00
Twisted Optic, pink or green, plate, salad; 7"................$3.50
Twisted Optic, pink or green, sandwich server, center handle $20.00
Twisted Optic, pink or green, saucer $2.50
Twisted Optic, pink or green, sherbet $6.50
Twisted Optic, pink or green, sugar bowl $7.00
Twisted Optic, pink or green, tumbler, 12-oz, 5¼".......$9.00
US Swirl, green, bowl, handled, 5½" $10.00
US Swirl, green, candy dish, 2-handled.............$27.50
US Swirl, green, plate, salad; 7⅞" $6.00
US Swirl, green, tumbler, 12-oz, 4⅝" $11.00
US Swirl, pink, bowl, berry; 4⅜" $7.00
US Swirl, pink, bowl, oval, 8¼" $25.00
US Swirl, pink, creamer $16.00
US Swirl, pink, plate, sherbet; 6⅛" $3.50
US Swirl, pink, salt & pepper shakers, pr $42.50
Victory, blue, bowl, cereal; 6½" $28.00
Victory, blue, candlesticks, 3", pr $90.00
Victory, blue, plate, bread & butter; 6" $17.50
Victory, blue, saucer $10.00
Victory, blue, sugar bowl $42.50
Victory, bowl, console; 12" $32.50
Victory, pink, bonbon, 7" $11.00
Victory, pink, cup $9.00
Victory, pink, goblet, 7-oz, 5" $20.00
Victory, pink, gravy boat & platter $175.00
Victory, pink, platter, 12" $27.50
Vitrock, white, bowl, fruit; 6" $6.00
Vitrock, white, plate, luncheon; 8¾" $5.00
Vitrock, white, platter, 11½" $27.50
Vitrock, white, sugar bowl, oval $5.00
Waterford, crystal, bowl, cereal; 5½" $18.00
Waterford, crystal, cup....................................$7.00
Waterford, crystal, pitcher, juice; tilted, 42-oz............$24.00
Waterford, crystal, salt & pepper shakers, 2 styles, pr...$9.50
Waterford, crystal, sherbet, footed $4.50
Waterford, pink, bowl, berry; 4¾" $14.00
Waterford, pink, creamer, oval $11.00
Waterford, pink, plate, dinner; 9⅝" $18.00
Waterford, pink, plate, sandwich; 13¾"...............$26.50

Tea Room, pink, creamer & sugar bowl on tray, $70.00

Waterford, pink, sugar bowl lid, oval...........................$24.00
Waterford, pink, tumbler, footed, 10-oz, 4⅞"...............$20.00
Windsor, crystal, bowl, cereal; 5⅛"............................$9.00
Windsor, crystal, butter dish..$27.50
Windsor, crystal, candy jar..$17.50
Windsor, crystal, compote..$9.00
Windsor, crystal, pitcher, 52-oz, 6¾"............................$14.00
Windsor, crystal, plate, sandwich; handled, 10¼".........$7.00
Windsor, crystal, plate, sherbet; 6"...............................$3.00
Windsor, crystal, saucer..$3.00
Windsor, crystal, sherbet, footed...................................$4.00
Windsor, crystal, tumbler, 9-oz, 4"................................$6.00
Windsor, pink, ashtray, 5¾"..$37.50
Windsor, pink, bowl, boat shape, 7x11¾"....................$32.50
Windsor, pink, bowl, fruit console; 12½".....................$100.00
Windsor, pink, cake plate, thick, 13½".........................$20.00
Windsor, pink, cup...$10.00
Windsor, pink, pitcher, 16-oz, 4½"..............................$105.00
Windsor, pink, plate, salad; 7"......................................$16.00
Windsor, pink, platter, oval, 11½"................................$20.00
Windsor, pink, relish platter, divided, 11½"................$185.00
Windsor, pink, sugar bowl..$26.00
Windsor, pink, tray, 4⅛x9"..$9.00
Windsor, pink, tumbler, 12-oz, 5"................................$27.50

Disney

The largest and most popular area in character collectibles is without doubt Disneyana. There are clubs, newsletters, and special shows that are centered around this hobby. Every aspect of the retail market has been thoroughly saturated with Disney-related merchandise over the years, and today collectors are able to find many good examples at garage sales and flea markets.

Disney memorabilia from the late twenties until about 1940 was marked either 'Walt E. Disney,' or 'Walt Disney Enterprises.' After that time, the name was changed to 'Walt Disney Productions.' Some of the earlier items have become very expensive, though many are still within the reach of the average collector.

During the thirties, Mickey Mouse, Donald Duck, Snow White and the Seven Dwarfs, and the Three Little Pigs (along with all their friends and cohorts) dominated the Disney scene. The last of the thirties' characters was Pinocchio, and some 'purists' prefer to stop their collections with him.

The forties and fifties brought many new characters with them — Alice in Wonderland, Bambi, Dumbo, Lady and the Tramp, and Peter Pan were some of the major personalities featured in Disney's films of this era.

Even today, thanks to the re-releases of many of the old movies and the popularity of Disney's vacation 'kingdoms,' toy stores and department stores alike are full of quality items with the potential of soon becoming collectibles.

If you'd like to learn more about this fascinating field, we recommend *Stern's Guide to Disney Collectibles, First and Second Series*, by Michael Stern; *The Collector's Encyclopedia of Disneyana* by Michael Stern and David Longest; *Character*

Toys and Collectibles and *Toys, Antique and Collectible*, both by David Longest; and *Schroeder's Collectible Toys, Antique to Modern*. All are published by Collector Books.

See also Character and Promotional Drinking Glasses; Character Watches; Games; Pin-Back Buttons; Puzzles; Ramp Walkers; Salt and Pepper Shakers; Toys; TV and Movies; Valentines; Western Heroes.

Alice in Wonderland, figure, Alice, Ceramic Arts Studio, 5" on 3" dia base, M.....................................$125.00
Alice in Wonderland, sewing cards, 4 cards & 2 laces, complete, original productions, Walt Disney Productions, 1951, EX...$60.00
Alice in Wonderland, tea set, china, Walt Disney Productions, 1960s, MIB......................................$95.00
Alice in Wonderland, tea set, complete, 1960s, EX.....$25.00
Bambi, bank, ceramic figure, 7⅛", EX........................$50.00

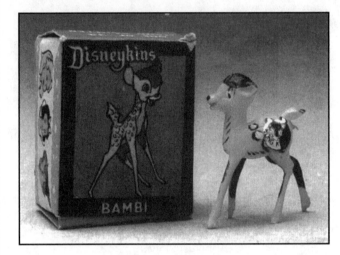

Bambi, Disneykins, Marx, original box, EX, $15.00

Bambi, pencil sharpener, Bakelite, red, worn letters, rare, EX..$85.00
Bambi, soap figure, in original box, EX......................$25.00
Bambi, switch plate, hard plastic, full color, 1949, MIP..$60.00
Bambi & Thumper, planter, EX....................................$25.00
Bashful (Snow White & the Seven Dwarfs), mask, cloth, ca 1938, EX..$35.00
Cinderella, apron pattern, uncut, NM.........................$25.00
Cinderella, glass slipper, M...$50.00
Cinderella, soundtrack, 1965, EX................................$10.00
Clarabelle Cow, book, Walt Disney Enterprises, 1938, EX..$15.00
Disney World, tray, tin, 1970s, 10¾" dia, EX................$12.00
Disneyland, activity set, includes various games, coloring books & crayons, Whitman, 1965, 9x12x1½" box, EX+..$35.00
Disneyland, card set, 66 color-photo scenes to celebrate 10th anniversary, 1965, NM....................................$80.00
Disneyland, charm bracelet, features Mickey, Tinker Bell & Sleeping Beauty's castle, 1950s, MIB....................$35.00
Disneyland, guidebook, 1959, EX................................$25.00
Disneyland Wood Burning Set, complete, American Toys, 1958, 9x16", NMIB...$65.00

Doc (Snow White & the Seven Dwarfs), figure, ceramic, Enesco, 1960s, 4½", NM..**$32.00**

Donald Duck, baby rattle, celluloid, fully embossed, 1940s, EX..**$75.00**

Donald Duck, ball, embossed image of Donald, Sun Rubber, 1940s, minor wear.................................**$40.00**

Donald Duck, ballpoint pen, green plastic w/decals of Donald on gold-tone metal cap, VG+....................**$30.00**

Donald Duck, bank, ceramic, ca 1960s, EX **$30.00**

Donald Duck, bendee, Applause, 5" **$6.00**

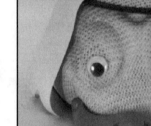

Donald Duck, cap, woven mesh with plastic bill, $40.00

Donald Duck, girl's wallet, Disneyland graphics, 1972 .**$4.00**

Donald Duck, hand puppet, vinyl head w/cloth body, EX..**$25.00**

Donald Duck, handkerchief, shows Donald on skis, EX..**$45.00**

Donald Duck, letter opener, celluloid, 1936, EX.......**$135.00**

Donald Duck, mustard jar, figure w/tin lid, EX...........**$95.00**

Donald Duck, perfume bottle, EX **$40.00**

Donald Duck, PVC, Applause, MOC **$3.00**

Donald Duck, squeeze toy, Dell, EX+...........................**$30.00**

Donald Duck, umbrella, pink w/early Donald figures, Louis Weiss Co, EX..**$200.00**

Donald Duck & Goofy, range set, Good Co, MIB.......**$75.00**

Donald Duck & Nephews, Donald & 2 nephews connected by chain, ceramic, 1960s, 5" & 2½", EX+..............**$30.00**

Dopey (Snow White & the Seven Dwarfs), musical push sweeper, plays Whistle While You Work, Fisher-Price, early, EX **$120.00**

Dopey (Snow White & the Seven Dwarfs), puppet, w/squeaker, Gund, NM..**$25.00**

Dopey (Snow White & the Seven Dwarfs), trinket box, ceramic, Dopey graphics, gold trim, 1960s, 2x2x2½", EX **$60.00**

Dopey & Grumpy (Snow White & the Seven Dwarfs), hairbrush, Walt Disney Enterprises, 1938, VG.............**$60.00**

Dumbo, cookie jar, mouse on lid..............................**$165.00**

Dumbo, pitcher, ceramic, 1950s, EX............................**$45.00**

Fantasia, Jack-in-the-box, NMIB **$165.00**

Fantasia, sound track, 2-album set, 1982, EX.............**$12.00**

Ferdinand the Bull, bank, composition figure in sitting position, 5⅛" **$70.00**

Ferdinand the Bull, sitting figure, hand-painted chalkware, late 1930s-early 40s, 7x8x7", EX.............................**$50.00**

Figaro the Cat, figurine, painted bisque, faded, VG **$50.00**

Geppetto (Pinocchio), soap figure, in original box, VG+ **$65.00**

Goofy, bank, plastic head, 11", VG **$20.00**

Goofy, bendee, Applause, 6", EX.................................**$6.00**

Goofy, marionette, Helm, original box, EX.................**$50.00**

Goofy, nodder, Marx, 1960s, EX **$8.00**

Goofy, pencil sharpener, green w/white plastic, hand crank, Walt Disney Productions, ca 1980, M **$20.00**

Great Mouse Detective, stationery, Disney Studio, 1986, EX...**$6.00**

Happy (Snow White & the Seven Dwarfs), figure, ceramic, Enesco, 1960s, 5", NM..**$35.00**

Jiminy Cricket, balloon, black graphics on color, hourglass shape fits on prepunched cardboard feet, late 1950s-60s, EX+ **$10.00**

Jiminy Cricket, hand puppet, Gund, EX.....................**$25.00**

Jiminy Cricket, mug, pink plastic, eyes appear to move, marked Walt Disney Productions, 1960s, 3¾".......**$14.50**

Jiminy Cricket, record, The Littlest Outlaw, Mickey Mouse Club 61, 78 rpm, M **$40.00**

Jiminy Cricket, wallet, EX..**$25.00**

Jungle Book, pail, colorful graphics, EX **$60.00**

Lady & the Tramp, wallet, vinyl, embossed figures on tan background, EX..**$30.00**

Mad Hatter, figure, soft plastic, Marx, 1950s, EX+ **$15.00**

Mary Poppins, doll, Horsman, 1960s, 12", NMIB.......**$135.00**

Mary Poppins, hand puppet, Gund/Walt Disney, VG .**$25.00**

Mary Poppins, spoon, silver-plated, 1964, M **$20.00**

Mickey & Minnie Mouse, bookends, composition figures, 1970s, 6½", EX, pr..**$95.00**

Mickey & Minnie Mouse, plate & mug, china, Mickey presents gift & bouquet to Minnie, hearts on background, M **$55.00**

Mickey & Minnie Mouse, wall pocket, lustreware, EX+ .**$185.00**

Mickey Mouse, back scratcher, marked Walt Disney World, M **$5.00**

Mickey Mouse, bank, metal suitcase w/Mickey Mouse in circle displaying his name, 3", EX............................**$360.00**

Mickey Mouse, bendee, Durham, 5"............................**$8.00**

Mickey Mouse, book, Mickey Mouse Story Book, 1930s, EX, $150.00

Mickey Mouse, book bank, vinyl & metal, features Mickey on front, 4¼" **$100.00**

Mickey Mouse, candle, illustrated paper wrap, 1930s, 1", M **$95.00**

Mickey Mouse, card game, Old Maid, images of early characters, complete w/instructions, Whitman, 1930s, EX+ **$58.00**

Mickey Mouse, decal, iron-on, 1940s, EX **$6.00**

Mickey Mouse, drinking cup, plastic ice cream cone form, M **$10.00**

Mickey Mouse, gum ball machine, G **$15.00**

Mickey Mouse, iron-on transfer, full-figure Mickey, 1940s, G **$6.00**

Mickey Mouse, Jack-in-the-box, Carnival toys, EX **$55.00**

Mickey Mouse, kaleidoscope, cardboard, 1950s, 6½", EX **$45.00**

Mickey Mouse, pencil box, 1930s, NM, $125.00

Mickey Mouse, soldier set, cardboard target figures w/wooden holders, set of 10, 1930s, EX **$325.00**

Mickey Mouse, spoon, silver-plated metal w/embossed figure of Mickey on handle, 1930s, EX **$25.00**

Mickey Mouse, squeeze toy, Sun Rubber, 1945, NM ...**$65.00**

Mickey Mouse, toy banjo, Carnival Toys, MIP **$28.00**

Mickey Mouse, watering can, tin, features Mickey w/watering can w/name below, G **$225.00**

Mickey Mouse & Donald Duck, pencil case, original contents, G **$25.00**

Mickey Mouse & his friends, grade school reader, 1937, NM **$45.00**

Mickey Mouse & Pluto, place mat, VG **$5.00**

Minnie Mouse, bendee, Applause, 5" **$6.00**

Minnie Mouse, cup, silver-plated, 1930s, EX, $75.00

Minnie Mouse, doll, black plush jointed body w/painted face, hands & shoes, 24", G **$50.00**

Minnie Mouse, pop-up book, Blue Ribbon Books, 1933, EX **$145.00**

Minnie Mouse, puppet, Pelham marionette, MIB, minimum value **$55.00**

Mrs Potts (Beauty & the Beast), cookie jar, Treasure Craft **$60.00**

Pinocchio, bank, plastic, 11", VG **$19.00**

Pinocchio, bendee, Just Toys, 1980s, 4", M **$10.00**

Pinocchio, figure, bisque, Japan, 1940, 4½", EX+ **$25.00**

Pinocchio, puppet, Pelham, NMIB **$75.00**

Pinocchio, thermometer, figural, Bakelite, 1939, NM ..**$65.00**

Pluto, hand puppet, VG **$25.00**

Pluto, jump rope, red, white & blue, 1970s, NM **$12.50**

Pluto, nodder, plastic, Marx, 1960s, EX **$25.00**

Pluto, pencil sharpener, cast metal, paint wear, rare, 1930s, 1½x1⅛" **$140.00**

Pluto, planter, ceramic, Pluto pulling wagon, EX **$50.00**

Pluto, push-button puppet, painted wood, Kohner, 5¼", EX **$80.00**

Rocketter, standee, vinyl w/tags, Applause/Disney, 1991, 9", M **$25.00**

Roger Rabbit, ashtray, w/baby Herman, tin, MIP **$8.00**

Roger Rabbit, bendee, Jessica, LJN, 6", MOC **$30.00**

Roger Rabbit, mug, w/image of Jessica, MIB **$5.00**

Roger Rabbit, stationery, 1987, M **$25.00**

Roger Rabbit, tin, heart shape, 1987, M **$15.00**

Roger Rabbit, yo-yo, Germany, MOC **$8.00**

Scrooge McDuck, bendee, Duck Tales, Just Toys, 4½" .**$5.00**

Shaggy Dog, figures, w/bright gold tags, marked Walt Disney Productions on bottom, Enesco, set of 3, 4", NM in EX box **$65.00**

Sleeping Beauty, book, hard-bound, Disney, 1974, 7x9½", VG+ **$3.00**

Sleeping Beauty, booklet, Walt Disney's Sleeping Beauty Castle, 1957, NM **$60.00**

Sleeping Beauty, Colorforms, 3 actual movie backgrounds on 1 board, few minor pieces missing, 1959, EX ..**$40.00**

Sleeping Beauty, sitting figure, vinyl, 6½", EX **$25.00**

Sneezy (Snow White & the Seven Dwarfs), painted enamel, 1930s, VG **$10.00**

Snow White, planter, ceramic, figure by wishing well, Enesco/Walt Disney Productions, late 1950s-early 60s, 5", NM **$50.00**

Snow White & the Seven Dwarfs, jigsaw puzzle, Jaymar, VG, $12.50

Snow White & the Seven Dwarfs, poster, hallmark, features forest animals & castle, 1970s, 40x28", EX **$12.00**

Snow White & the Seven Dwarfs, song album, Irving Berlin, 46 pages, 1937, G..............................**$50.00**

Snow White & the Seven Dwarfs, toy kitchen appliance set, includes stove, sink & refrigerator, VG.................**$30.00**

Sword in the Stone, stationery, Disney Studio, 1960s, EX .**$8.00**

Three Little Pigs, ashtray, ceramic, 3-D images w/instruments on Art Deco base, 4½x3x3", Japan, 1930s, NM....**$115.00**

Three Little Pigs, mug, ceramic, marked Walt Disney, EX, $75.00

Three Little Pigs, toothbrush holder, painted bisque, center pig at brick piano, pre-war Japan, 4x3½", NM ...**$135.00**

Tinkerbell, cup & saucer, porcelain, Disneyland, 1960s, EX **$30.00**

Tinkerbell, hand puppet, EX.....................................**$20.00**

Tinkerbell, handbag, pink plastic, round w/loop handle & zipper, Disneyland under portrait of Tinkerbell, 5" dia, EX+ **$10.00**

Uncle Scrooge, bank, vinyl, EX..................................**$50.00**

Uncle Scrooge, squeeze toy, Dell...............................**$30.00**

Winnie the Pooh, bulletin board, 27x19", EX **$20.00**

101 Dalmations, bendee, Pongo or Perdita, Just Toys, 1980s, M...**$12.50**

101 Dalmations, party bags, package of 8, MIP............**$8.00**

Dollhouse Furniture

Some of the mass-produced dollhouse furniture you're apt to see on the market today was made by Renwal and Acme during the forties and Ideal in the 1960s. All three of these companies used hard plastic for their furniture lines and imprinted most pieces with their names. Strombecker furniture was made of wood, and although it was not marked, it has a certain recognizable style to it. Remember that if you're lucky enough to find it complete in the original box, you'll want to preserve the carton as well.

Bathinet, pink or blue, Renwal, EX............................**$10.00**

Bathroom sink, pedestal style, pink w/blue fixtures, plastic, 2¼", EX **$6.00**

Bed, oak, simple styling, minor wear, EX...................**$28.00**

Bed, wood, canopy, EX...**$15.00**

Bedside table, pink, Renwal......................................**$5.00**

Blanket chest, lid open, Strombecker, EX...................**$12.50**

Blanket chest, painted wood, Brittany, 3½x13¼x4", EX.**$150.00**

Buffet, brown, Renwal, EX..**$7.00**

Buggy, painted cast iron, Kilgore, 2", $50.00; Ladder, 3", $45.00; Highchair, 3⅛", $45.00; Ironing board, 2", $65.00; Sweeper, 2¼", $50.00

Chair, red w/yellow seat, Renwal **$6.00**

Chaise lounge, Little Hostess....................................**$15.00**

Dining table, w/pictures, Petite Princess, NMIB **$15.00**

Dressing table, w/triple mirror, ivory, Little Hostess, EX.**$10.00**

Dressing table lamps, green w/cream, Strombecker, ¾", EX **$6.00**

Drop-leaf table, gate-leg style, w/2 drawers, Little Hostess, EX..**$18.00**

End table, tier style, Petite Princess **$12.50**

Floor lamp, cream shade, Strombecker **$8.00**

Grand piano, painted cast iron, Arcade, 1920s, VG.....**$65.00**

Grandfather clock, dark wood, Strombecker **$10.00**

Hamper, green, lid opens, Strombecker, EX.................**$6.50**

Highchair, Rosebud, EX...**$10.00**

Icebox, door opens, Strombecker...............................**$18.00**

Ironing board, pink, Renwal **$8.00**

Kitchen chair, green, Strombecker..............................**$5.00**

Kitchen cupboard, Petite Princess, EX.......................**$50.00**

Kitchen stove, gas, Tootsietoy, ca 1930......................**$35.00**

Lawn swing, Kilgore **$25.00**

Planter, brass, w/ferns, Petite Princess, EX **$10.00**

Rocking chair, brown w/tall back, Little Hostess, EX..**$12.50**

Sofa, red, Strombecker, EX..**$11.00**

Tea cart, Petite Princess Fantasy, 1950s, MIB.............**$15.00**

Television, Petite Princess **$65.00**

Towel rack, brass, G..**$75.00**

Vanity & stool, Petite Princess, MIB, $35.00

Vanity bench, blue or pink w/ivory, Little Hostess, EX..**$8.00**
Wash stand, painted tin, EX **$40.00**

Dolls

Doll collecting is one of the most popular hobbies in the United States. Since many of the antique dolls are so expensive, even modern dolls have come into their own, and can be had at prices within the range of most budgets. Today's thrift shop owners know the extent of 'doll mania,' though, so you'll seldom find a bargain there. But if you're willing to spend the time, garage sales can be a good source for your doll buying. Granted most will be in a 'well loved' condition, but as long as they're priced right, many can be redressed, rewigged, and cleaned up. Swap meets and flea markets may sometimes yield a good example or two, depending upon whether the dealer is a professional or someone just trying to peddle his 'junk.'

Modern dolls, those made from 1935 to the present, are made of rubber, composition, magic skin, synthetic rubber, and many types of plastic. Most of these materials do not stand up well to age, so be objective when you buy, especially if you're buying with an eye to the future. Doll repair is an art best left to professionals. But if yours is only dirty, you can probably do it yourself. If you need to clean a composition doll, do it very carefully. Use only baby oil and follow up with a soft dry cloth to remove any residue. Most types of wigs can be shampooed with wig shampoo and lukewarm water. Be careful not to matt the hair as you shampoo, and follow up with hair conditioner or fabric softener. Comb gently and set while wet, using small soft rubber or metal curlers. Never use a curling iron or heated rollers.

In our listings, unless a condition is noted in the descriptions, values are for dolls in excellent condition except for the Cabbage Patch dolls. Those are priced mint in box. (Even if a Cabbage Patch is in super condition but is without its original box, its value would be only about 25% of what we've listed here.)

For further study, we recommend these books, all by Patricia Smith: *Patricia Smith's Doll Values, Antique to Modern; Modern Collector's Dolls* (five in the series), *Vogue Ginny Dolls, Through the Years with Ginny;* and *Madame Alexander Collector's Dolls.* Patikii Gibbs has written the book *Horsman Dolls, 1950 - 1970,* and Estelle Patino is the author of *American Rag Dolls, Straight From the Heart,* both contain a wealth of information on those particular subjects. And if you're into Annalees and Steiffs, you won't want to miss *Teddy Bears, Annalees and Steiff Animals,* by Margaret Fox Mandel. All these references are published by Collector Books.

See also Liddle Kiddles; Barbie and Friends; GI Joe; Shirley Temple; Toys.

American Character, Baby Lou, plastic, molded hair, redressed, 1950, 8" **$20.00**
American Character, Cricket, plastic & vinyl, rooted blond hair w/grow feature, painted blue eyes, all original **$30.00**

American Character, Eloise, cloth w/yarn hair, 1950s, 14".**$285.00**

American Character, Fanny the Fallen Angel, Whimsie, stuffed vinyl, 1960, all original, 20", minimum value, $125.00

American Character, Margaret-Rose, plastic & vinyl, rooted blond hair, sleep eyes, all original, 1966, 17"........**$30.00**
American Character, Puggy, composition, painted eyes, frowning expression, marked Petite, 13"............**$500.00**
American Character, Sally, composition w/molded hair, 1929-35, 12" **$185.00**
American Character, Sally Says, talker, plastic & vinyl, 1965, 19" **$80.00**
American Character, Sweet Sue, vinyl, curly brown hair, original ski outfit, 1955, 17"................................**$325.00**
American Character, Talking Marie, vinyl & plastic w/record player in body, battery-operated, 1963, 18" **$95.00**
American Character, Tiny Tears, hard plastic & vinyl, 1955-62, 8" **$50.00**
American Character, Toddle Loo, vinyl, fully jointed, rooted blond hair, 1961, all original, 18" **$55.00**
American Character, Whimette, plastic & vinyl, rooted red hair, painted green eyes, nude, 1963, 7½" **$30.00**
Annalee, Ballerina Pig, felt, flesh-colored body w/blue tutu & parasol, 1981-82, minimum value **$145.00**
Annalee, bear w/bee on his nose, felt, holding honey pot, 1 of 938, all original, 1986, 18", minimum value....**$200.00**
Annalee, Go Go Girl, felt w/painted features, 10", NM, minimum value **$115.00**
Arranbee, Miss Cody, walker, plastic & vinyl, rooted brown hair, sleep eyes, battery-operated, all original, 10".**$125.00**
Arranbee, Nanette, vinyl, blond wig, original ball gown & fur cape, 1953, 17" **$285.00**
Arranbee, New Happy Tot, vinyl, molded & painted brown hair, blue sleep eyes, redressed, 1955, 16"............**$45.00**
Arranbee, Susan, stuffed vinyl, brown wig, blue sleep eyes, al original, 1952, 15" **$75.00**
Arrow Plastics, Bye-Bye Baby, vinyl & latex, rooted blond hair, sleep eyes, redressed, 1957, 17" **$45.00**
Arrow Plastics, Candy, vinyl, molded hair & clothes, painted eyes, closed mouth, 1958, 8" **$6.00**
Cabbage Patch, Black boy or girl w/pacifier, 1984, MIB, minimum value **$175.00**

Cabbage Patch, Black boy or girl w/shaggy hair, 1983, MIB, minimum value $125.00

Cabbage Patch, boy w/tan shaggy hair & freckles, 1983, MIB..................$150.00

Cabbage Patch, girl w/blond loop ponytail & freckles, 1983, MIB $150.00

Cabbage Patch, girl w/brunette ponytail, single tooth, 1985, MIB, minimum value $200.00

Deluxe Reading, Baby Boo, plastic & vinyl, blond hair, blue sleep eyes, battery-operated cryer, redressed, 1965 .$40.00

Deluxe Reading, Baby Magic, plastic & vinyl, blond hair, sleep eyes, smiles & frowns, redressed, 1966 ....$45.00

Deluxe Reading, Penny Brite, vinyl, rooted blond hair, painted eyes, all original, 1963, 8" $30.00

Deluxe Reading, Susie Homemaker, plastic & vinyl, jointed hips & knees, sleep eyes, 5 teeth, all original, 1966, 21"..................$40.00

Eegee, Baby Susan, nurser, vinyl, molded hair, blue sleep eyes, redressed, 1958, 10½"..................$15.00

Eegee, Baby Tandy Talks, foam & vinyl, pull-string talker, 1960 ....$65.00

Eegee, Ballerina, plastic & vinyl, 1958, 20" $45.00

Eegee, Cuddleskins, nurser, plastic & vinyl, molded hair, inset blue eyes, all original, 1970, 10" $8.00

Eegee, Debutante, plastic & vinyl w/jointed knees, 1958, 28"..................$100.00

Eegee, Georgette, vinyl & cloth, rooted orange hair, green eyes, freckles, all original, 1971, 22"..................$55.00

Eegee, Kid Sister, plastic & vinyl, rooted ash blond hair, painted features & freckles, all original, 9¼".........$15.00

Eegee, Miss Debby, vinyl, rooted long blond hair, blue sleep eyes, original bride outfit, 1958, 14" $30.00

Eegee, Miss Sunbeam, plastic & vinyl, rooted hair, blue sleep eyes, painted teeth, all original, 17"...........$50.00

Eegee, Musical Baby, cloth body, rooted hair, key-wind music box, 1967, 17"..................$25.00

Eegee, Playpen Baby, nurser, plastic & vinyl, rooted blond hair, sleep eyes, all original, 1968, 14" $5.00

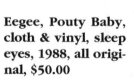

Eegee, Pouty Baby, cloth & vinyl, sleep eyes, 1988, all original, $50.00

Effanbee, Baby Cuddle-Up, oilcloth & vinyl, 2 bottom teeth, all original, 1953, 20" $95.00

Effanbee, Babykin, vinyl w/rooted hair, 10" $30.00

Effanbee, Betty Brite, composition, fur wig, sleep eyes, marked w/name, 1933, 16" $300.00

Effanbee, Dainty Baby, composition & cloth, painted features & hair, 1930s, all original, 10½" $175.00

Effanbee, Dydee Baby, plastic & vinyl, 1950, 15"......$125.00

Effanbee, Gumdrop, plastic & vinyl, all original, ca 1962, 15" $45.00

Effanbee, Honey Bun, vinyl & cloth, rooted blond hair, sleep eyes, redressed, 1967, 17"..................$20.00

Effanbee, Little Lady, cloth w/yarn hair, 1943, 21", minimum value $365.00

Effanbee, Mary Jane, walker, plastic & vinyl, freckled face, 1960, 31"..................$265.00

Effanbee, My Precious Baby, cryer, vinyl & cloth, blond hair, blue sleep eyes, all original, 1960, 20"..........$30.00

Effanbee, Pat-O-Pat, composition & cloth, painted eyes, press stomach & hands pat together, 14"...........$175.00

Effanbee, Patsy, composition, fully jointed, molded hair, painted eyes, 1928, 14"..................$400.00

Effanbee, Patsyette Babies, composition, sleep eyes, all original, 9", each, $265.00

Effanbee, Peaches, vinyl & cloth, rooted blond hair, blue sleep eyes, redressed, 1965, 15"............$50.00

Effanbee, Sugar Plum, vinyl & cloth, rooted brown hair, blue sleep eyes, all original, 1969, 16" $35.00

Effanbee, Susie Sunshine, rooted brown hair, blue sleep eyes, original clothes, 1966, 18"............$75.00

Effanbee, Suzanne, composition, marked w/name, 1940, 14" $275.00

Effanbee, Suzette, composition, marked w/name, 1939, 12"..................$245.00

Effanbee, Twinkie, nurser, vinyl, molded hair, blue sleep eyes, redressed, 1959, 15".....................$25.00

Half doll, Germany, arms & hands extended, china or bisque, 3"..................$145.00

Half doll, Germany, arms extended w/hands attached to figure, papier-mache or composition, 7" $85.00

Half doll, Germany, child figure w/jointed shoulders, papier-mache, 4" $40.00

**Half doll, Germany, 4½",
$125.00**

**Horsman, Nadia Ballerina,
plastic & vinyl, rooted blond
hair, 1987, all original, 11½",
$20.00**

Half doll, Japan mark, 3", minimum value.................**$25.00**
Half doll, Japan mark, 5", minimum value.................**$35.00**
Half doll, Japan mark, 8", minimum value.................**$55.00**
Hasbro, Aimee, plastic & vinyl w/rooted hair, 1972,
    18"...**$55.00**
Hasbro, Leggy Nan, vinyl, brown hair up in lg curls, original
    halter & bell-bottom pants, 1972, 10"....................**$20.00**
Hasbro, Sweet Cookie, vinyl w/rooted hair, all original,
    1972...**$35.00**
Horsman, Answer Doll, vinyl w/rooted hair, head nods,
    10"...**$20.00**
Horsman, Anthony Pipsqueak, plastic & vinyl, rooted brown
    hair, painted features, redressed, 12"..................**$25.00**
Horsman, Baby Tweaks, cloth & vinyl w/inset eyes, 1967,
    20"...**$30.00**
Horsman, Betty Ann, plastic & vinyl, 19"...................**$60.00**
Horsman, Betty Jo, vinyl & plastic, strawberry blond hair,
    1963, 16"...**$30.00**
Horsman, Bootsie, plastic & vinyl, rooted black hair, brown
    sleep eyes, all original, 1969, 12"....................**$10.00**
Horsman, Floppy, foam body & legs, rooted blond hair,
    blue sleep eyes, all original, 1965, 18".............**$30.00**
Horsman, Linda, plastic & vinyl, long rooted hair, sleep
    eyes, all original, 1959, 36"...........................**$100.00**
Horsman, Lullabye Baby, cloth & vinyl, music box in body,
    1964 & 1967, 12"...**$20.00**
Horsman, Mimi Thirsty Baby, fully jointed, dark blond hair,
    glassine eyes, original clothing, 6"..................**$25.00**
Horsman, Molly, plastic & vinyl, rooted brown hair, blue
    sleep eyes, posable head, original clothes, 16".....**$25.00**
Horsman, Penny Pen Pal, plastic & vinyl, blond hair,
    painted eyes, holds pencil, all original, 1970, 18".**$35.00**
Horsman, Pretty Betty, nurser, rooted brown hair, sleep
    eyes, redressed, 1954, 16".............................**$25.00**
Horsman, Renee Ballerina, stuffed vinyl, rooted hair, blue
    sleep eyes, all original, 18"..........................**$45.00**
Horsman, Roberta, composition w/molded hair or wig,
    1937, 14"...**$250.00**
Horsman, Teensie Baby, nurser, plastic & vinyl, painted
    eyes, all original, 1964, 12"..........................**$10.00**
Ideal, April Showers, plastic & vinyl, battery-operated, 1968,
    14"...**$32.00**

Ideal, Baby Belly Button, plastic & vinyl, rooted blond hair,
    painted eyes, redressed, 1970, 9".....................**$25.00**
Ideal, Baby Big Eyes, soft vinyl, rooted curly hair, original
    blanket & nightie, 1954-59, 20".......................**$50.00**
Ideal, Baby Coos, cloth w/plastic head & vinyl limbs,
    molded brown hair, glassine sleep eyes, cries & coos,
    1948, 20"...**$85.00**
Ideal, Baby Crissy, vinyl, rooted auburn hair grows w/arm
    movement, redressed, 1973-76, 24"...................**$40.00**
Ideal, Baby Dreams, cloth & vinyl w/velvet skin, rooted
    blond hair, sleep eyes, 1975-76, 17"................**$30.00**
Ideal, Baby Giggles, vinyl, rooted blond hair, side glanc-
    ing eyes, pull hands together & she giggles, 1967-69,
    18"...**$120.00**
Ideal, Betsy McCall, plastic & vinyl, rooted hair, marked P-
    90, all original, 14"....................................**$295.00**
Ideal, Betsy Wetsy, plastic & vinyl, molded hair, redressed,
    1959...**$55.00**
Ideal, Betty Jane, composition, sleep eyes, open mouth,
    redressed, 1930s-40, 14"...............................**$95.00**
Ideal, Bibsy, vinyl, rooted blond hair, sleep eyes, puckers &
    cries when squeezed, ca 1970, 23"....................**$35.00**
Ideal, Bizzie Lizzie, vinyl, rooted blond hair, sleep eyes, irons,
    vacuums & dusts, battery-operated, 1971-72, 18"....**$40.00**
Ideal, Blessed Event, oilcloth w/vinyl head & limbs, real-
    istic newborn face, changes facial expressions, 1950,
    19"...**$100.00**
Ideal, Bonnie Walker, hard plastic, pin-jointed hips, open
    mouth, flirty eyes, redressed, 23"...................**$50.00**
Ideal, Chew, Chew, Chew Suzy Chew, vinyl, rooted blond
    hair, painted eyes, chews solid food, battery-operated,
    1980, 14"...**$35.00**
Ideal, Cuddly Kissy, vinyl & cloth, puckers up when stom-
    ach is pressed, all original, 1964, 17".............**$60.00**
Ideal, Curly Hair Baby Beautiful, cryer, stuffed cotton
    w/composition limbs, brown mohair wig, all original,
    1947, 24"...**$200.00**
Ideal, Deluxe Kissy, all original, 1962, 22", M.............**$95.00**
Ideal, Happi Returns, w/yellow walker, cloth & vinyl,
    rooted blond hair, laughing mechanism on back,
    1983-84..**$20.00**

Ideal, Honey Moon, cryer, cotton & vinyl, white string hair, painted eyes, all original, 1965, 14" $55.00

Ideal, Lazy Dazy, vinyl & cloth, rooted blond hair, blue sleep eyes, all original, 1971, 12" $20.00

Ideal, Little Miss Revlon, vinyl, fully jointed, rooted blond hair, redressed in bridal gown, 1958-60, 10½" $85.00

Ideal, Magic Lips, vinyl w/vinyl-coated cloth body, blond hair, sleep eyes, 3 teeth, all original, 1955, 24" $95.00

Ideal, Mitzi, plastic & vinyl, rooted reddish-brown hair, blue painted eyes, redressed, 1970 ....$85.00

Ideal, My Bottle Baby, cloth & vinyl, rooted blond hair w/pigtails, pull string for nursing sounds, 1979-80, 14" $25.00

Ideal, Newborn Thumbelina, vinyl & cloth, rooted blond hair, pull string & she squirms, 1968-72, 9" $30.00

Ideal, Patti Playful, soft vinyl puppet doll, rooted platinum hair, 1973, 15" $35.00

Ideal, Penny Playpal, plastic & vinyl, rooted red hair, blue sleep eyes, posable head, 1959, 32", NM $190.00

Ideal, Pretty Curls, w/hair styling kit, vinyl, rooted blond hair, painted eyes, 1980, 12", $35.00

Ideal, Queen of the Ice, fully jointed composition, blond mohair curls, original clothing & skates, 1938-43, 16" $150.00

Ideal, Sara Ann, hard plastic, saran wig, all original, 1952, 14", minimum value...........................$250.00

Ideal, Snuggles, vinyl & cloth, rooted hair, pull string & she snuggles teddy bear or blanket, 1978-81, 12½" $25.00

Ideal, Talking Goody Two Shoes, plastic & vinyl, sleep eyes, battery-operated, all original, 27"...................$200.00

Ideal, Talking Tot, cloth & vinyl, molded hair, key-wind talker, voice box marked Shilling, 1950, 22" $85.00

Ideal, Tickletoes, stuffed cloth w/rubber arms & legs, organdy dress, cries when legs are squeezed, 1931-39, 15" $100.00

Ideal, Tiffany Taylor, top of head swivels to change hair color, all original, 1973, 18"..................$85.00

Ideal, Tiny Kissy, vinyl, press stomach for puckered mouth, all original, 1962, 12" $50.00

Ideal, Tippy Tumbles, vinyl & plastic, rooted hair, stands on head & flips over, battery-operated, 1977, 16½" ...$40.00

Ideal, Toni, plastic, fully jointed, dark brown wig, marked P-90, 1948, redressed, 14" $85.00

Ideal, Tubsy, vinyl & plastic, rooted saran hair, splashes when placed in water, battery-operated, 1967-68, 18" $50.00

Ideal, Twinkle Eyes, soft vinyl, rooted saran ponytail, original pinafore & bonnet, 1957-60, 19" $55.00

Ideal, Upsy-Dazy, vinyl head & foam body, rooted hair, painted features, all original, 1972 ....$20.00

Imperial Crown, Baby Linda, plastic head w/rubber body, original red caracul wig, 1950 ....$70.00

Jolly Toys, Cutie, vinyl, rooted hair in ponytails, sleep eyes, all original, 1965, 14" $25.00

Jolly Toys, Kimberly, plastic & vinyl, rooted blond hair, blue painted eyes, all original, 1972, 14", MIB $8.00

Jolly Toys, Lovely Lisa, vinyl & cloth, rooted white hair, blue sleep eyes, all original, 1962, 15" $5.00

Jolly Toys, Nikki, plastic & vinyl, rooted blond hair, sleep eyes, all original, 1964, 13"................................$15.00

Jolly Toys, Playpen Doll, nurser, plastic & vinyl, rooted hair, original sleeper, 1967, 14" $10.00

Jolly Toys, Trudy, plastic & vinyl, rooted blond hair, blue sleep eyes, all original, 1962, 13" $15.00

Jolly Toys, Twistee, vinyl w/molded foam body, rooted dark hair, black sleep eyes, all original, 1964, 16" $25.00

Kenner, Baby Bundles, 16" $20.00

Kenner, Baby Yawnie, cloth & vinyl, 1974, 15"...........$25.00

Kenner, Black Baby Bundles, all original, 16" $35.00

Kenner, Black Gabbigale, 1972, 18" $45.00

Kenner, Gabbigale, plastic & vinyl, blond hair, painted eyes, battery-operated, all original, 1972, 18".................$45.00

Kenner, Sleep Over Dolly, plastic & vinyl, original gown & cap, w/Skye doll, 1976, 17".....................................$45.00

Knickerbocker, Annie, rigid vinyl, fully jointed, all original, MIB $12.50

Knickerbocker, Beloved Belindy, cloth, all original, 1954, M $300.00

Knickerbocker, Levi's Denim Rag Girl, made of blue denim, 1973, 26", MIB $25.00

Knickerbocker, Sunbonnet Doll Mandy, name on skirt, all original, 1975, 7" $15.00

Lorrie, Bonnie Jean, nurser, plastic & vinyl, rooted blond hair, sleep eyes, all original, 1961, 14"...................$8.00

Lorrie, Cuddly Infant, vinyl & cloth, molded hair, blue sleep eyes, Made by Eugene, redressed, 1963, 14" $10.00

Lorrie, My Baby, plastic & cloth, rooted blond hair, sleep eyes, redressed, 1960, 19"......................................$10.00

Lorrie, Sweet Candy, plastic & vinyl, rooted blond hair, blue sleep eyes, all original, 1964, 19" $8.00

Madame Alexander, Alice in Wonderland, composition, Wendy Ann face, swivel waist, 1930s, 13" $450.00

Madame Alexander, Amish Girl, Americana Series, hard plastic, Wendy Ann face, 1966-69, 8" $400.00

Madame Alexander, Baby Genius, composition & cloth, 1930s-40s, 12", minimum value..........................$150.00

Madame Alexander, Baby Huggams, soft stuffed body, redressed, 1963, 9" $20.00

Madame Alexander, Bad Little Girl, cloth, blue dress, eyes & mouth turned down, 1966, 16" $185.00

Madame Alexander, Carrot Top, cloth, 1967, 21".......**$100.00**

Madame Alexander, Cinderella, Storyland Series, hard plastic, Wendy Ann face, 1990-91, 8"...........................**$60.00**

Madame Alexander, Cissette, hard plastic, dressed as beauty queen w/trophy, 1961, 10"...................................**$200.00**

Madame Alexander, Daisy, Portrette Series, yellow gown w/over-lace, Cissette face, 1987-89, 10"................**$85.00**

Madame Alexander, Dolly Dryper, vinyl, 7-pc layette, 1952, 11"..**$80.00**

Madame Alexander, Elise, hard plastic w/vinyl arms, street clothes, jointed ankles & knees, 1957-64, 16½", minimum value **$220.00**

Madame Alexander, Elise Bridesmaid, 1982-85, all original, 17", minimum value, $400.00

Madame Alexander, Finland, hard plastic, straight legs, Wendy Ann face, marked Alex, 1973-75, 8"..........**$55.00**

Madame Alexander, Goldilocks, plastic & vinyl, blue satin or cotton dress, Mary Ann face, 1980-83, 14"............**$70.00**

Madame Alexander, Heidi, Classic Series, plastic & vinyl, Mary Ann face, 1969-85, 14"...................................**$65.00**

Madame Alexander, Indonesia, hard plastic, straight legs, marked Alex, 1972-75, 8"..**$60.00**

Madame Alexander, Japan, hard plastic, Wendy Ann face, 1968-72, 8"...**$125.00**

Madame Alexander, Kathy Tears, vinyl, closed mouth, 1959-62, 15"...**$70.00**

Madame Alexander, Lissy, hard plastic, dressed as ballerina, jointed knees & elbows, 1956-58, 12"................**$325.00**

Madame Alexander, Maid Marian, Storybook Series, hard plastic, Wendy Ann face, 1989-91, 8"...................**$85.00**

Madame Alexander, Mother Goose, Storybook Series, hard plastic, straight legs, Wendy Ann face, 1986-92, 8"...**$55.00**

Madame Alexander, Natasha, hard plastic, brown & paisley brocade, Jacqueline face, 1989-90, 21"................**$355.00**

Madame Alexander, Old Fashioned Girl, composition, Betty face, 1945-47, 13", minimum value.....................**$475.00**

Madame Alexander, Persia, composition, Tiny Betty face, 1936-38, 7"...**$285.00**

Madame Alexander, Queen Isabella, Americana Series, hard plastic, 1992, 8"..**$80.00**

Madame Alexander, Red Cross Nurse, composition, Tiny Betty face, 1937 & 1941-43, 7"............................**$275.00**

Madame Alexander, Riley's Little Annie, Literature Series, plastic & vinyl, Mary Ann face, 1967, 14"...........**$175.00**

Madame Alexander, Round Up Cowgirl, hard plastic, blue & white outfit, 1992, 8"...**$90.00**

Madame Alexander, Sailorette, Portrette Series, hard plastic, red, white & blue outfit, Cissette face, 1988, 10" ..**$85.00**

Madame Alexander, Scarlett O'Hara, hard plastic, white gown, Wendy Ann face, 1973-91, 8".....................**$65.00**

Madame Alexander, Sulky Sue, hard plastic, Wendy Ann face, marked Alexander, 1988-90, 8"...................**$90.00**

Madame Alexander, Tiny Betty, composition, 1935-42, 7"...**$245.00**

Madame Alexander, Tunisia, hard plastic, Wendy Ann face, marked Alexander, 1989, 8".................................**$80.00**

Madame Alexander, Wendy Ann, composition, painted eyes, 1936-40, 9"...**$325.00**

Marx, Miss Toddler, walker, plastic, molded hair, paper eyes, rollers on bottom of feet, battery-operated, 1965, NM.**$45.00**

Mattel, Baby Beans, vinyl w/beanbag body, blond bangs, blue painted eyes, sewn-on clothes, 1971, 11" **$18.00**

Mattel, Baby First Step, plastic & vinyl, blond hair, sleep eyes, battery-operated, redressed, 1964, 18".........**$35.00**

Mattel, Baby Go Bye Bye, plastic & vinyl, rooted white hair, blue painted eyes, redressed, 1968, 10"................**$25.00**

Mattel, Baby Love Light, battery-operated, 1970, 16" ..**$20.00**

Mattel, Baby Pat-A-Burp, original pink outfit, working.**$30.00**

Mattel, Baby's Hungry, plastic & vinyl, blond hair, blue eyes, battery-operated, all original, 1966, 17"................**$30.00**

Mattel, Baby Secret, vinyl w/foam body, red hair, blue painted eyes, pull-string talker, all original, 1965, 18"...........**$45.00**

Mattel, Baby Walk'n Play, 1968, 11" **$20.00**

Mattel, Baby Walk'n See, all original, 18"....................**$35.00**

Mattel, Bucky Love Notes, press body parts for tunes, all original, 1974, 12" **$30.00**

Mattel, Charmin' Chatty, auburn hair, red, white & blue nautical-style dress w/red knee socks, 1963, 25", MIB ...**$150.00**

Mattel, Chatty Baby, plastic & vinyl, short rooted blond or brown hair, red pinafore over lacy romper, 1962, MIB........**$120.00**

Mattel, Chatty Cathy, blond curly hair w/red headband, blue sleep eyes, redressed, 1960 ....**$35.00**

Mattel, Chatty Cathy, 1960, MIB, $250.00

Mattel, Cheerful Tearful, 1965, 13".............$25.00

Mattel, Hi Dotty, honey-blond hair, brown eyes, original clothes.............$20.00

Mattel, Randy Reader, plastic & vinyl, white hair, blue eyes, battery-operated, redressed, 1967, 19".............$40.00

Mattel, Saucy, twist left arm & her facial expressions change, redressed, 1972, working.............$45.00

Mattel, Shoppin' Sheryl, plastic & vinyl, rooted hair, painted eyes, magnet in right palm, all original, 14½".............$35.00

Mattel, Sister Belle, plastic & cloth, yellow yarn hair, pull-string talker, 1961, all original, 17".............$25.00

Mattel, Sister Small Talk, plastic & vinyl, rooted blond hair, painted eyes & teeth, all original, 1967, 10".............$25.00

Mattel, Talking Baby First Step, plastic & vinyl, painted eyes, battery-operated, all original, 1964, 18".............$45.00

Mattel, Talking Baby Tenderlove, original clothes, working.............$20.00

Mattel, Timey Tell, thick blond curls, blue eyes, original clothes & watch.............$25.00

Mattel, Tiny Chatty Brother, plastic & vinyl, blond hair, blue romper w/matching cap & booties, 1963, MIB...$150.00

Remco, Baby Grow-a-Tooth, all original, 1969, 14".....$30.00

Remco, Baby Laugh Alot, plastic & vinyl, all original, 1970, 16".............$25.00

Remco, Baby This 'n That, vinyl, rooted blond hair, press toes for action, 1976, $35.00

Remco, Hildy Bridesmaid, fully jointed, rooted blond hair, 1966, all original, 4¾".............$12.50

Remco, Jan, fully jointed, black rooted hair, 1965, all original, 5½".............$12.50

Remco, Snugglebun, plastic & vinyl, rooted blond hair, sleep eyes, all original, 1965, 16".............$20.00

Remco, Sweet April, plastic & vinyl, blond hair, complete w/stroller & accessories, 1973, 5".............$14.00

Remco, Sweet April, vinyl, rooted blond hair, stationary eyes, button makes arms move, redressed, 1971, 5½".....$6.00

Remco, Tumbling Tomboy, plastic & vinyl, all original, 1969, 16".............$25.00

Royal, Lisa Toddler, plastic & vinyl, rooted white hair, blue sleep eyes, posable head, all original, 1962, 23" ..$25.00

Royal, Polly, plastic & vinyl, rooted blond hair, blue sleep eyes, all original, 21½".............$40.00

Royal, Raggy Muffin Baby, vinyl, rooted brown hair, blue painted eyes, all original, 1960, 9½".............$8.00

Sayco, Carrie Cries, plastic & vinyl, rooted hair, blue sleep eyes, battery-operated, all original, 1963, 19".........$8.00

Sayco, Play Girl, hard plastic w/latex limbs & cloth body, blue sleep eyes, all original, 1950, 26".............$85.00

Sun Rubber, Sunbabe, nurser, rubber, molded hair, painted eyes, original diaper, 1950, 11".............$45.00

Terri Lee, Baby Linda, vinyl, molded & painted hair, black painted eyes, redressed, 1951, 9".............$185.00

Uneeda, Baby Dana, nurser, plastic & vinyl, all original, 1975, 20".............$25.00

Uneeda, Bride Sue, vinyl, rooted blond hair, blue sleep eyes, all original, 10½".............$35.00

Uneeda, Connie, nurser, plastic & vinyl, rooted red hair, blue sleep eyes, all original, 1968-69, 15".............$15.00

Uneeda, Dollikins, jointed body, original clothes, 1957, 6½".$10.00

Uneeda, Little Sophisticates, vinyl, fully jointed w/various hair colors, eyes closed w/real lashes, 1967, 7½".....$4.50

Uneeda, Littlest So-Soft, vinyl & cloth, rooted brown hair, blue painted eyes, all original, 1970, 6".............$5.00

Uneeda, Magic Meg, plastic & vinyl, rooted blond hair w/grow feature, blue sleep eyes, all original, 1971, 16".........$35.00

Uneeda, Patti-Cake, plastic & vinyl, rooted white hair, blue sleep eyes, key-wind music box, all original, 20"...$8.00

Uneeda, Serenade, talker, vinyl, battery-operated, all original, 1962, 21".............$50.00

Uneeda, Weepsy, nurser, plastic & vinyl, molded hair, painted features, cries when tummy is pressed, all original, 4".$3.00

Vogue, Angel Baby, blond hair, redressed, 1965, 13" .$25.00

Vogue, Angel Baby, vinyl, rooted hair, rooted reddish-blond hair, blue sleep eyes, all original, 1965, 14".........$25.00

Vogue, Baby Burps, nurser, vinyl, fully jointed, rooted hair, painted eyes, all original, 1975, 14".............$30.00

Vogue, Baby Dear, vinyl & cloth, light brown hair, brown sleep eyes, all original, 18".............$35.00

Vogue, Baby Wide Eyes, vinyl, brown sleep eyes, all original, 1976, 16".............$45.00

Vogue, Ginny Ice Skater, plastic, brown sleep eyes, w/skates, all original, 8".............$300.00

Vogue, Littlest Angel, all original, $30.00

Vogue, Precious Baby, vinyl w/rooted hair, sleep eyes, all original, 1975, 12" $45.00
Vogue, Welcome Home Baby, vinyl & cloth, painted hair & eyes, redressed.......................................$125.00

Celebrity Dolls

Lindsay Wagner (Bionic Woman), blue jumpsuit, Kenner, 1976, 12¼", MIB, $50.00

Angela Lansbury (Miss Price from Bedknobs & Broomsticks), fully jointed vinyl, Horsman, 1971, 6¼", NM..........$35.00
Angie Dickinson (Police Woman), fully jointed vinyl, Horsman, 1976, 9", NM....................................$40.00
Babe Ruth, cloth, Hallmark Famous Americans Series I, 1979, original storybook box, M $12.00
Betty Grable, composition, 1940s, 21", NM................$150.00
Brooke Shields, regular version, 1980s, 11½", MIB $30.00
Captain & Tennile, 1970s, 12½", MIB, each $40.00
Cher, blue swimsuit, rooted hair, Mego, 1981, 12", NMIB...$45.00
Cheryl Ladd (Kris from Charlie's Angels), fully jointed vinyl, Mattel, 1978, 11½", MIB........................$50.00
Cheryl Tiegs, Real Model Collection, Matchbox #56412, 1989, MIB $35.00
Christie Brinkley, Real Model Collection, Matchbox #54611, MIB $35.00
Diana Ross, 1970s, 12½", MIB...............................$80.00
Dolly Parton, plastic & vinyl, Eegee, 1987, 18", MIB...$65.00
Dorothy Hamill, vinyl, Ideal, 1977, 12", MIB $75.00
Elizabeth Montgomery (Bewitched), plastic & vinyl, Ideal, 1965, 12", MIB..$200.00
Elizabeth Taylor (Father of the Bride), jointed plastic, Peggy Nisbet, 1970s, 7½", NM..........................$35.00
Ellen Corby (Grandma Walton), fully jointed vinyl, Mego, 1975, 8", NM..$25.00
Erin Moran (Joanie from Happy Days), fully jointed vinyl, Mego, 1976, 8", NM......................................$30.00
Farrah Fawcett, fully jointed vinyl, Mego, 1977, 12¼", NM...$40.00

Joan Collins (Alexis from Dynasty), fully jointed vinyl, World Doll, 1988, MIB.....................................$150.00
Kate Jackson (Sabrina from Charlie's Angels), fully jointed vinyl, Hasbro, 1977, 8½", NM....................$30.00
Kristy McNichol, Mego, 1978, MIB..........................$40.00
Linda Evans (Crystal from Dynasty), fully jointed vinyl, World Doll, 1988, MIB.....................................$150.00
Loretta Swit (Hot Lips Houlihan from M*A*S*H), fully jointed vinyl, FW Woolworth Co, 1976, 8½", NM.............$50.00
Mae West, fully jointed vinyl, Effanbee, 1982, 18", NM.$100.00
Marilyn Monroe, vinyl, silver mesh gown & full-length white mink coat, World Doll, 1983, 16½", NM................$75.00
Marilyn Monroe, 1980s, 11½", MIB, from $50............$100.00
Marla Gibbs (Florence from the Jeffersons), fully jointed vinyl, Shindana, 1978, 15", NM $25.00
Melissa Gilbert (Laura Ingles), vinyl & cloth, Knickerbocker, 1978, 12", NM...$40.00
Michael Jackson, 1980s, 11½", MIB..........................$40.00
Pam Dawber (Mork & Mindy), fully jointed vinyl, Mattel, 1979, 8½", MIB..$60.00
Sally Field (Flying Nun), fully jointed vinyl, Hasbro, 1967, 5", NM..$30.00
Susan B Anthony, cloth, Hallmark Famous Americans Series I, 1979, original storybook box, M.........................$12.00
Susan Dey (Laurie Partridge), vinyl & plastic, brown rooted hair, denim bell-bottoms, Remco, 1973, 19", MIB.$100.00
Tatum O'Neal (from International Velvet), fully jointed vinyl, Kenner, 1979, 11½", NM..........................$40.00

Doorstops

There are three important factors to consider when buying doorstops — rarity, desirability, and condition. Desirability is often a more important issue than rarity, especially if the doorstop is well designed and detailed. Subject matter often overlaps into other areas, and if they appeal to collectors of Black Americana and advertising, for instance, this tends to drive prices upward. Most doorstops are made of painted cast iron, and value is directly related to the condition of the paint. If there is little paint left or if the figure has been repainted or is rusty, unless the price has been significantly reduced, pass it by.

Be aware that Hubley, one of the largest doorstop manufactuers, sold many of their molds to the John Wright Company who makes them today. Watch for seams that do not fit properly, grainy texture, and too-bright paint.

The doorstops we've listed here are all of the painted cast iron variety unless another type of material is mentioned in the description. For further information, we recommend *Doorstops, Identification and Values*, by Jeanne Bertoia.

Amish Man, full figure, solid casting, 8½x3¾", VG....$200.00
Basket of Kittens, marked M Rosenstein, Copyright 1932, Lancaster PA, USA, paint wear, 10x7" $350.00
Begging Boston Terrier, full figure, black & white, 8¾x5", EX $275.00

Blowfish, full figure, salmon & white w/glass eye, Hubley, 8x7¼", VG $300.00

Boston Bulldog, brown glossy finish, glass eyes, Greenblatt Studios, 13x5½", NM $200.00

Boston Terrier w/Paw Up, full figure, black & white, 9½x7", VG...$275.00

Camel, full figure, minor paint wear, 7x9" $270.00

Cat, black w/white paws and red bow tie seated on base, marked Eastern Specialty Mfg Co #62, 7x4½", EX $225.00

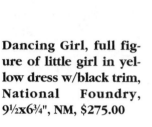

Dancing Girl, full figure of little girl in yellow dress w/black trim, National Foundry, 9½x6¾", NM, $275.00

Donald Duck, full figure of Donald holding stop sign, marked copyright Walt Disney Productions 1971, 8⅜x5¼", NM $200.00

El Capitan, marching soldier w/rifle on base marked El Capitan, 7¾x5¼", EX...$175.00

English Bulldog, seated on base, Bradley & Hubbard, 9½x5½", EX $350.00

Frog on Mushroom, full figure, solid casting, heavy paint wear, 4½x3⅝" $165.00

Fruits & Birds, 2 cardinals & fruit in blue basket, 6½x5½", NM $175.00

Gnome w/Barrel, full figure, minor paint wear, 14½x6¼", EX...$450.00

Horse Jumping Fence, marked Eastern Specialty Co #79, heavy wear to jockey, 7⅞x11¾", EX...................$325.00

Little Bo Beep, full figure on round base, black & white ruffled dress & bonnet, 6¾x5", EX $200.00

Little Boy w/Bear, full figure standing on base, solid casting, Albany Foundry, 5¼x3½", EX $160.00

Marigolds, in blue & white striped flowerpot on blue rectangular base, Hubley, marked 315 Made in USA, 7½x8", VG...$135.00

Monkey on Barrel, green w/yellow features, marked Taylor Cook No 3 1930, paint wear, 8⅜x4⅞" $325.00

Nasturtiums, in black & white striped flowerpot, Hubley, 7¼x6½", NM $125.00

Overhead Swinging Golfer, standing on mound of grass, Hubley, 10x7", NM $285.00

Pekingese, full figure, Hubley, 14½x9", EX...............$425.00

Persian Cat, full figure, Hubley, paint wear, 8½x6½", VG $150.00

Rabbit Eating Carrot, full figure, side view of rabbit in red sweater standing on green base, 8⅛x4⅞", NM ...$345.00

Reclining Kitten, full figure, black w/red & black bow tie, National Foundry, 8⅛x4", NM $200.00

Squirrel, seated on stump eating a nut, black w/glass eye, marked EMIG 1382, 8x5½", NM.........................$175.00

Swan, full figure, solid casting, National Foundry, 5¾x4½", EX $185.00

Tropical Woman, full figure of woman carrying bowl of fruit overhead, 12x6¼", EX..$200.00

Welsch Corgi, seated on base, Bradley & Hubbard, 8¼x5⅞", NM $185.00

Woman Holding Flower Baskets, full figure, marked cJo, minor paint wear, 8x4¾", $200.00

Woman w/Muff, full figure w/head turned right, solid casting, 9¼x5", EX...$200.00

Duncan and Miller Glassware

Although the roots of the company can be traced back to as early as 1865 when George Duncan went into business in Pittsburgh, Pennsylvania, the majority of the glassware that collectors are interested in was produced during the twentieth century. The firm became known as Duncan and Miller in 1900. They were bought out by the United States Glass Company, who continued to produce many of the same designs through a separate operation which they called the Duncan and Miller Division.

In addition to crystal, they made some of their wares in a wide assortment of colors including ruby, milk glass, some opalescent glass, and a black opaque glass they called Ebony. Some of their pieces were decorated by cutting or etching. They also made a line of animals and bird figures. For information on these, see Glass Animals.

Canterbury, ashtray, crystal, 3½x2¾" $6.50

Canterbury, creamer & sugar bowl, lg.........................$24.00

Canterbury, goblet, water; amber $14.00

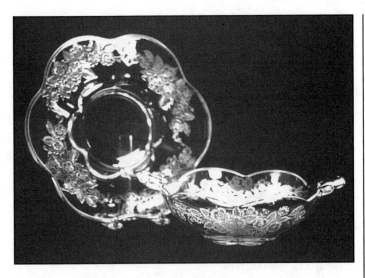

**Canterbury, plate, crystal w/silver overlay, 8",
$16.00; nappy, crystal w/silver overlay, $16.00**

Canterbury, plate, amber, 8" $12.00
Canterbury, sherbet, crystal...$8.50
Caribbean, crystal or amber $5.00
Caribbean, goblet, water; blue....................................$40.00
Caribbean, punch bowl, crystal $85.00
Caribbean, relish, blue, 2-part, 6" $30.00
First Love, candle holders, crystal, 2-light, #30, pr $40.00
First Love, creamer & sugar bowl, crystal, lg...............$45.00
First Love, goblet, crystal...$24.00
First Love, plate, torte; crystal, #111, 13" $65.00
First Love, tumbler, crystal, footed, 5-oz $24.00
Indian Tree, compote, crystal $45.00
Indian Tree, tumbler, crystal, footed $24.00
Murano, candlesticks, crystal, footed, pr.....................$45.00
Murano, nappy, crystal, ruffled rim, 6".......................$20.00
Nautilus, marmalade, green, silver-plated lid...............$65.00
Nautilus, relish, light blue, 3-part, oval, 9¾"...............$65.00

Pall Mall, swan basket, blue opalescent, 9½", $150.00

Plaza, sugar bowl, crystal $15.00
Plaza, tumbler, amber, flat, 12-oz $15.00
Sandwich, ashtray, crystal, 2¼x3½".............................$12.50
Sandwich, bowl, fruit; crystal, flared rim, 12" $50.00
Sandwich, cheese & cracker set, crystal $75.00
Sandwich, cup & saucer, crystal $20.00
Sandwich, nut dish, crystal, 3½" $10.00
Sandwich, pitcher, water; crystal, ice lip................$165.00
Sandwich, plate, crystal, flat edge, 13" $45.00
Sandwich, plate, crystal, 8"...$12.00
Sandwich, relish, crystal, 3-part, ring handle $35.00
Sandwich, tray, crystal, divided, oval, 7"....................$15.00
Spiral Flutes, bowl, amber, flat rim, 7" $8.00
Spiral Flutes, cigarette holder/ashtray, green, footed ..$30.00
Spiral Flutes, compote, green.......................................$25.00
Spiral Flutes, cream soup, crystal.................................$15.00
Spiral Flutes, cup, green, footed $10.00
Spiral Flutes, pickle dish, green, 8½"...........................$15.00
Spiral Flutes, plate, amber, 6"..$4.00
Spiral Flutes, plate, green, 8½"......................................$5.00
Spiral Flutes, sugar bowl, amber....................................$7.00
Spiral Flutes, sweetmeat, green, w/lid......................$125.00
Sylvan, relish, crystal or cobalt, 3-part........................$40.00
Teardrop, bowl, crystal, footed, 11½".........................$35.00
Teardrop, bowl, crystal, oval, 6" $7.00
Teardrop, bowl, salad; crystal, 12".............................$35.00
Teardrop, claret, crystal, 5½"..$16.00
Teardrop, cup & saucer, demitasse; crystal.................$16.00
Teardrop, ice bucket, crystal, w/monogram, footed ...$30.00
Teardrop, nut dish, crystal, 2-part, handled, 6"...........$10.00
Teardrop, relish, crystal, 12"..$20.00
Teardrop, tumbler, crystal, flat, 14-oz........................$18.00
Teardrop, tumbler, crystal, footed, 12-oz $11.00
Terrace, bowl, crystal, 5"..$12.50
Terrace, cordial, crystal..$45.00

Easter Collectibles

The egg (a symbol of new life) and the bunny rabbit have long been part of Easter festivities; and since early in the twentieth century, Easter has been a full-blown commercial event. Postcards, candy containers, toys, and decorations have been made in infinite varieties. In the early 1900s, many holiday items were made of papier-mache and composition and imported to this country from Germany. Rabbits were made of mohair, felt, and velveteen, often filled with straw, cotton, and cellulose.

For more information, we recommend *A Guide to Easter Collectibles* by Juanita Burnett.

Book, Uncle Wiggily Starts Off, by Howard R Garis, paper-
        back, 1940s, EX...$15.00
Candy container, papier-mache, rabbit chef w/lg spoon
        seated atop egg, 1940s, EX....................................$125.00
Candy container, white plastic w/pink neck ribbon, sepa-
        rates below neckline, 1950s, NM $15.00

Decoration, foldout, cardboard & paper, 9", NM, $16.00

Rabbit pulling cart, handcrafted wood, pastel colors, 1940s, VG, $90.00

Dinner bell, ceramic, figural rabbit handle, tulips & Happy Easter 1979 on base, 1970s, NM...........................**$15.00**

Egg, musical, metal, various colors & designs, Mattel, 1950s, each **$35.00**

Egg, plastic w/hand-painted flowers, various colors & designs, 1950s, EX, each...**$10.00**

Pull toy, handcrafted, blue & white checked fabric bunny w/yarn tail, wooden base, 1980s, EX **$20.00**

Rabbit, composition, brown rabbit smoking pipe in red jacket & yellow pants standing on green mottled base, 1940s, NM..**$85.00**

Rabbit, flocked plastic, white w/glass eyes, 1960s-70s, EX..**$12.50**

Rabbit, handcrafted from printed fabric kit, green overalls & hat w/speckled shirt, 1970s, still available, EX+ **$15.00**

Rabbit, handcrafted w/brown upholstery fabric, tan bow tie w/paisley design, button eyes, 1930s, EX+ **$45.00**

Rabbit, mohair & cotton suede, fancy pink & blue sheer dress w/vest & bonnet, 1930s, EX **$150.00**

Rabbit, papier-mache, cloth dress w/paisley print, German, 1940s, EX..**$185.00**

Rabbit, straw-stuffed plush, red felt pants, brown jacket & bow tie, 1930s, EX **$135.00**

Rabbit, stuffed cloth, burnt orange & yellow felt clown suit, celluloid feet, 1920s, EX **$125.00**

Rabbit, tan plush w/pink neck ribbon, button eyes, Gund Mfg Co, 1940s-50s, VG **$40.00**

Rabbit, white corduroy w/pink paws & ears, pink neck ribbon, 1983, 6¼", EX...**$6.50**

Rabbit, white stuffed plush w/red & white checked neck tie, felt facial features, jointed arms & legs, 1980s, EX+ .**$25.00**

Rabbit pulling chicks, papier-mache w/moss cart full of cotton chicks, German, 1930s, EX **$285.00**

Roly Poly, rabbit w/basket of eggs seated atop egg decorated w/flowers, celluloid, Japan, 1920s, EX........**$50.00**

Wind-up, litho tin chick in yellow plastic egg, 1950s, EX **$45.00**

Wind-up, Strutting Bunny by Cragstan, red & white striped pants & yellow jacket, twirls cane, 1930s, G.........**$75.00**

Egg Beaters

There are many types of egg beaters — hand-helds, those with rotary cranks, those that operate on 'squeeze power,' Archimedes up-and-down models — and collectors want them all. Egg beaters are the favorite gadgets in many kitchenware collections, edging out nutmeg graters, spatulas, and can openers. At the turn of the century, every housewife in America owned an egg beater. Pre-packaged, pre-processed foods were a food fifty years into the future. And every inventor felt he/she could make a better beater. As a result, more than 1,000 patents were issued, the first in 1856. Today, most egg beaters are valued at $20.00 or less, but a few approach the $1,000.00 mark. Garage sales and flea markets are wonderful places to find them.

For more information, we recommend *Beat This: The Egg Beater Chronicles* by Don Thornton.

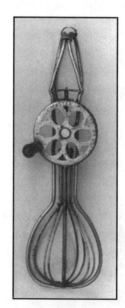

Master, Pat Aug 24, 1909, 10½", $250.00

A&J, rotary, all metal, Pat Oct 9, 1923 Made in USA, 10"..**$12.00**

A&J, rotary w/wooden handle, Pat Oct 9, 1923, Made in USA, 10¾" **$10.00**

Automatic Wire Goods Mfg Co, rotary w/vertical wooden handle, 11"...$15.00

Betty Taplin Egg Beater, baby beater rotary w/vertical wooden handle, 5½"...$15.00

Boun-c-Beater, Archimedes up-&-down beater, Pat Pend, 12½"...$25.00

Dover Egg Beater, cast-iron rotary crank, Pat May 31, 1870, 10"...$75.00

EKCO, Archimedes up-&-down beater w/wooden handle, 10½"..$5.00

High Speed Super Center Drive A&J Pat applied for, rotary w/wooden handle, 11½"..........................$10.00

Landers, Frary & Clark, New Britain, Conn., cast-iron rotary crank, 10¼"...$65.00

No 00 Ladd Beater, rotary crank w/wooden handle, Pat July 7, 1908, Oct 18, 1921, 11"....................$15.00

No 3 Ladd Ball Bearing Beater, rotary crank w/wooden handle, Oct 18, 1921, other Pats Pend, 11" $15.00

Roberts Lightning Mixer, Archimedes up-&-down beater w/snug top in heavy glass jar, Pat Sept 10, 1912, Dorsey, USA, 8".................................$40.00

Super Whirl, Turner & Seymour Mfg Co, Torrington, Conn., USA, rotary crank, plastic handle, 11½"..............$15.00

Taplin Mfg Co New Britain, Conn, rotary w/vertical wooden handle, Pat Dec 9, 1924, Made in USA, 11"..........$10.00

Whippit Cream & Egg Whip Pat No 1705639, Mfg by Duro Metal Products, rotary crank turbine, 13¾" $20.00

Egg Cups

Egg cups were once commonplace kitchen articles that were often put to daily use. Recent trends include changes in dietary patterns that have caused egg cups to follow butter pats and salt dishes into relative obscurity. These small egg holders were commonly made in a variety of shapes from many metals, wood, plastic, and ceramics. They were used as early as ancient Rome and were very common on Victorian tables. Many were styled like whimsical animals or made in other shapes that would specifically appeal to children. Some were commemorative or sold as souvenirs. Still others were part of extensive china or silver services.

They're easy to find today, and though most are inexpensive, some are very pricey! Single egg cups with pedestal bases are the most common, but shapes vary and included doubles, egg hoops, buckets, and sets of many types. Pocillivists, as egg cup collectors are known, are increasing in numbers every day. For more information, contact Joan George, editor of *Egg Cup Collector's Corner*, a quarterly newsletter (see the Newsletters section of the Directory). She will provide titles of reference books, some of which include price lists.

Bone china, single, w/floral design, marked Royal Albert, England..$15.00

Ceramic, bear, lying on his back..................................$5.00

Ceramic, Bunnykins, bucket-shaped single, Royal Doulton $7.50

Ceramic, double, white w/vertical line decoration, marked Adams $9.00

Ceramic, duck, single, multicolor pearlized lustre ware, marked Made in Japan.....................................$8.00

Ceramic, Harlequin, single, yellow $20.00

Ceramic, lion, single, marked Royal Fenton, Staffordshire, England, 2¾" $10.00

Ceramic, orange & white lustre, Japan, 2½", $14.00

Ceramic, single, white w/blue scene, marked Spode England Italian...$12.00

Ceramic, turkey, single, marked France $15.00

Ceramic, white, single, marked Bali Hotel, 3"..............$5.00

China, Azalea pattern, Noritake, 3".............................$65.00

China, Carlton Ware Feet, sm feet sticking out of a white cup $12.50

China, double cup, blue band w/gold trim, Noritake .$16.00

China, floral pattern, gold-lined rim on cup & base......$6.00

China, pastel pink w/green pedestal $8.00

China, Phoenix pattern, double, blue & white, Japan, 3½" $15.00

Fanny Farmer rooster, yellow w/red markings, Fanny Farmer molded into base, 2⅜".............................$15.00

Glass, chick, single, blue opaque, 2¾".........................$20.00

Glass, double, w/concentric ring design, 4¼".............$12.00

Glass, Jadite, double, marked Fire King Oven Ware, Made in USA..$10.00

Ironstone, blue & black geometric design $10.00

Ironstone, double, maroon & floral band, unmarked Homer Laughlin, 1935, 4¾"....................................$8.00

Milk glass, crowing rooster, red waddle........................$6.00

Milk glass, duck, marked Made in France, Modele Depose, Opalex $12.50

Milk glass, swan base, novelty......................................$6.00

Plastic, Bakelite hoop shape, single, gray $8.00

Pottery, tulip shape w/green base................................$10.00

Pottery, w/attached saucer, dark green, marked WK, West German..$10.00

Pressed glass, goose, scalloped top $8.00

Pressed glass, ostrich, smooth top $7.00

Silver, sm (quaill's egg) single w/attached underplate, marked Sterling $5.00

Souvenir, single, pink lustre w/Houses of Parliament transfer, Made in Germany, old, 2½" $5.00

Souvenir, single, white w/transfer design of dice & slots, Las Vegas...$5.00

Wood, single, light wood w/burned-on stripes $2.50

Egg Timers

You've heard of '3-minute eggs' — these were used to time them perfectly. Most of them are figurals, made during the 1930s and '40s, primarily in Germany and Japan. Though many no longer have the time (sand tube), they are easily recognizable by the hole that goes through a portion of the back or the stub of an arm, where the thin glass tube was once connected. Figurals generally range in size from 3" to 5". Most are made of china or bisque.

Amish woman w/churn, painted cast metal, John Wright Inc, 1960s, 2x3" **$20.00**
Bellboy, holding phone w/timer at side, Japan, 3" **$15.00**
Black Boy, ceramic body w/plastic head, 3½" **$50.00**

Black chef, sitting w/timer in right hand, Germany, 3", $45.00

Chef, dressed in white w/timer in right hand, Germany, 3" **$25.00**
Chicks, double, yellow, Goebel, #81501, 1972-79, 2¼" .**$45.00**
Chimney Sweep, Goebel, dated 1972, 3¾" **$45.00**
Dog, sitting upright w/red timer in left paw, Germany, 3½" **$25.00**
Friar Tuck, double, Goebel, #E96, 1960-63, 3½" **$50.00**
Housemaid, w/timer in right hand & cat at side, Germany, 4½" **$20.00**
Mammy, timer in right arm, Occupied Japan, 4" **$45.00**
Oliver Twist, timer at side, embossed lettering on base, Germany, 3¼" **$25.00**
Owl, timer at side, reddish brown w/yellow chest, 1 eye closed, Goebel, #81503, 4½" **$45.00**
Parlor maid talking on telephone, timer at side, Japan, 3" **$12.00**
Rabbits, double, 1 green & 1 blue, Goebel, #E229, 1972-79, 3¾" **$55.00**

Swami, w/green turban & red jacket, timer in right hand, Germany, 3" **$20.00**
Tooled leather pouch holds timer & salt & peppers, marked Souvenir of Canada - 1867 - 1967, Made in Canada, 4", set **$15.00**

Elvis Presley Memorabilia

Since he burst upon the fifties scene wailing 'Heartbreak Hotel,' Elvis has been the undisputed 'King of Rock 'n Roll.' The fans that stood outside his dressing room for hours on end, screamed themselves hoarse as he sang, or simply danced till they dropped to his music are grown-up collectors today. Many of their children remember his comeback performances, and I'd venture to say that even their grandchildren know Elvis on a first-name basis.

There has never been a promotion to equal the manufacture and sale of Elvis merchandise. By the latter part of 1956, there were already hundreds of items that appeared in every department store, drugstore, specialty shop, and music store in the country. There were bubble gum cards, pin-back buttons, handkerchiefs, dolls, guitars, billfolds, photograph albums, and hundreds of other items. You could even buy sideburns from a coin-operated machine. Look for the mark 'Elvis Presley Enterprises' (along with a 1956 or 1957 copright date); you'll know you've found a gold mine.

Due to the very nature of his career, paper items are usually a large part of any 'Elvis' collection. He appeared on the cover of countless magazines. These along with ticket stubs, movie posters, lobby cards, and photographs of all types are sought after today, especially those from before the mid-sixties.

Though you sometime see Elvis 45s with $10.00 to $15.00 price tags, unless the record is in very good to excellent condition this is just not realistic. In fact, the picture sleeve itself (if it's in good condition) will be worth more than the record. The exceptions are, of course, the early Sun label records that collectors often pay $400.00 to $500.00 for, some of the colored vinyls, promotional records, and EPs and LPs with covers and jackets in excellent condition.

For more information refer to *Elvis Collectibles* and *Best of Elvis Collectibles* by Rosalind Cranor, P.O. Box 859, Blacksburg, VA 24063. ($19.95+$1.75 postage each volume.)

Album, sound track from Kissin' Cousins, 1964, EX **$26.00**
Album cover stand-up, Elvis For Everyone!, EX **$40.00**
Balloon, advertises Kid Galahad movie, w/cardboard feet, unused, M **$50.00**
Bracelet, lady's dog tag on card, Elvis Presley Enterprises, M **$28.00**
Bracelet, w/guitar, Elvis picture, broken heart & hound dog charms on card, 1950s, EX **$100.00**
Christmas card, red, green & white, opens to winter scenes of Graceland, marked The Presleys, EX **$65.00**
Coloring sheet, used in contest to promote the film Girls! Girls! Girls!, 1962, EX **$25.00**

Decanter, McCormick, Designer #1 ....**$130.00**
Decanter, McCormick, Designer #2 ....**$180.00**
Decanter, McCormick, Designer #3 ....**$240.00**
Decanter, McCormick, Gold Encore #1 ....**$300.00**
Decanter, McCormick, Gold Encore #2 ....**$250.00**
Decanter, McCormick, Gold Encore #3 ....**$200.00**
Gum card, #45, Preparing To Go on Stage, Bubbles Inc,
   1956, EX..**$10.00**
Gum cards, complete set of 66, Donruss, 1978, NM ...**$25.00**
Key chain, dog tag, available w/2 different chains, M ..**$75.00**
Key chain, record-shaped w/silver portait image of Elvis,
   Holsum Bread ad on back, 1960s, 3" dia, EX **$20.00**
Lobby card, features Elvis from It Happened at the World's
   Fair, MGM, 1963, 11x14", NM..............................**$30.00**

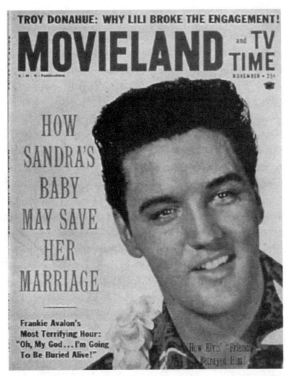

Magazine, Movieland & TV Time, Nov 1961, EX, $20.00

Movie still, black & white image of Elvis in dancing pose
   from Jailhouse Rock, NM.......................................**$20.00**
Movie still, color image from film Happy Girl, EX **$12.00**
Music box, plastic guitar, plays Love Me Tender, late 1970s,
   10" MIB **$35.00**
Necklace, medallion w/Elvis pictured on 1 side & embossed
   autograph on reverse, 1976 Midwest Tour, NM....**$40.00**
Ornament, Hallmark, 1992, MIB **$20.00**
Paper hat, used to promote GI Blues film & record, EX .**$36.00**
Pen, ballpoint, marked From Elvis & The Colonel, NM..**$25.00**
Photo set, #10, black & white photos of Elvis in various west-
   ern poses, sold in dime stores in 1956, set of 4, NM.**$40.00**
Pin, flasher type, Vari-Vue, 3", NM **$23.00**
Pin-back button, Wo'nt (sic) You Be My Teddy Bear, ribbon
   attached, A Epstein Novelty Co, round **$65.00**
Pocket calendar, 1966, EX.......................................**$20.00**
Pocket watch, features Elvis w/guitar, 1970s reissue,
   EX..**$75.00**

Pennant, blue & red on white w/black & white photo, I Love Elvis w/musical notes & hearts, 29", M, $40.00

Postcard, black & white photo of Elvis on motorcycle, Ger-
   many, NM...**$12.00**
Postcard, black & white photo of Elvis serenading Ann-Mar-
   garet in movie scene, Belgium, 1960s, NM **$10.00**
Postcard, color shoulder-length pose of young smiling Elvis,
   England, NM...**$12.00**
Press book, King Creole, Today's Most Exciting Singing Star
   In A Stirring Dramatic Performance!, EX **$125.00**
Puzzle, side view of Elvis w/microphone, 200-pc, 1977,
   11x17", EX **$10.00**
Record sleeve, 45 rpm, Love Me Tender, EX, from $30
   to **$40.00**
Ring, 18k gold-plated adjustable ring w/clear crystal
   cabochon covering color photo, Elvis Presley Enter-
   prises, M **$165.00**
Souvenir folio, Concert Edition, Volume Six, full-length Elvis
   on 1 foot holding microphone, 24 pgs., 8x11", EX..**$25.00**
Special photo folio, Concert Edition, Volume Five, Elvis
   w/microphone in star frame w/red background, 16
   pages, EX...**$30.00**
Standee, features Elvis & Nancy Sinatra in dancing poses for
   movie Speedway, NM..**$95.00**
Vending card, early black & white head shot of Elvis
   w/facsimile autograph, brief biography on back,
   3¼x5¼", NM **$25.00**

Eyewinker

Designed along the lines of an early pressed glass pattern by Dalzell, Gilmore and Leighton, Eyewinker was one
of several attractive glassware assortments featured in the
catalogs of L. G. Wright during the sixties and seventies.
The line was extensive and made in several colors: amber,
blue, green, crystal, and red. It was probably pressed by
Fostoria, Fenton, and Westmoreland, since we know these
are the companies who made Moon and Star for Wright,
who was not a glass manufacturer but a distributing company. Red and green are the most desirable colors and are
priced higher than the others we mentioned. The values
given here are for red and green, deduct about 20% for
examples in clear, amber, or light blue.

Bowl, 4 toes, 2½x5" **$14.00**
Butter dish, 5x7½"...**$38.00**
Compote, fancy pedestal foot, 6¾x7½" **$32.00**

Compote, footed, w/lid, 6¾x4" $28.00
Compote, pedestal foot, w/lid, 8x5" $35.00
Compote, pedestal foot, 5x6" $20.00
Creamer & sugar bowl, 3¾" & 4¼" $40.00
Honey dish, ribbed lid w/patterned edge, 6x5½" $35.00

**Marmalade, w/lid, 5¼x4",
$28.00**

Pickle tray, scalloped edge, 9½" dia $32.00
Salt & pepper shakers, 4", pr $22.00
Sherbet, 4½x3½" $9.00
Tumbler, 8-oz $10.00
Vase, 3-footed, scalloped, 6" $32.00
Water pitcher, 1-qt $38.00

Fast-Food Collectibles

Since the late 1970s, fast-food chains have been catering to their very young customers through their kiddie meals. The toys tucked in each box or bag have made a much longer lasting impression on the kids than any meal could. Today it's not just kids but adults (sometimes entire families) who're clamoring for them. They're after not only the kiddie meal toys but also boxes, promotional signs used by the restaurant, the promotional items themselves (such as Christmas orna-ments you can buy for 99¢, a collector plate, a glass tumbler, or a stuffed animal), or the 'under 3' (safe for children under 3) toys their toddler customers are given on request.

There have been three kinds of promotions: 1) national — every restaurant in the country offering the same item, 2) regional, and 3) test market. While, for instance, a test mar-ket box might be worth $20.00, a regional box might be $10.00, and a national, $1.00. Supply dictates price.

To be most valuable, a toy must be in the original pack-age, just as it was issued by the restaurant. Beware of deal-ers trying to 'repackage' toys in plain plastic bags. Most original bags were printed or contained an insert card. Vacuform containers were quickly discarded, dictating a premium price of $10.00 minimum. Toys without the origi-nal packaging are worth only about one-half to two-thirds as much as those mint in package.

Toys representing popular Disney characters draw cross-collectors, so do Star Trek, My Little Pony, and Barbie toys. It's not always the early items that are the most collectible, because some of them may have been issued in such vast amounts that there is an oversupply of them today. At the same time, a toy only a year or so old that might have been

quickly withdrawn due to a problem with its design will already be one the collector will pay a good price to get.

As I'm sure you've noticed, many flea market dealers are setting out huge plastic bins of these toys, and no one can deny they draw a crowd. It's going to be interesting to see what develops here! If you'd like to learn more about fast-food collectibles, we recommend *Tomart's Price Guide to Kid's Meal Collectibles* by Ken Clee and *The Illustrated Collector's Guide to McDonald's® Happy Meal® Boxes, Premiums, and Promotions©* by Joyce and Terry Lonsonsky whose address is listed in the Directory. The book with 1994 updated values is available from the authors for $9.50 (includes postage).

See also California Raisins.

McDonald's

Books, Look Look Books Happy Meal, Animals of the Sea,
Animals That Fly, Cats in the Wild or Biggest Animals,
1980, each **$30.00**
Box, Circus Wagon Happy Meal, 6 in all, 1979, each .**$50.00**
Box, Cosmic Crayola Happy Meal, 4 in all, 1987, each.**$5.00**
Box, Dukes of Hazzard Happy Meal, 6 in all featuring the
different characters, 1982, each **$25.00**
Box, Mickey's Birthdayland, 5 in all, 1988, each **$4.00**
Box, School Days Happy Meal, 123's, ABC's, History or Sci-
ence, 1984, each...**$6.00**
Box, 101 Dalmations Happy Meal, Barn, Dog's Leashes,
Piano or Staircase, 1991, each **$2.00**
Car, Connectibles Happy Meal, Birdie on trike, Grimace in
wagon, Hamburgler in plane, Ronald in soapbox car,
1991, each..**$8.00**
Cars, Hot Wheels Happy Meal, 18 in all, 1988, each.....**$8.00**
Color Card, Captain, Fry Goblins, Hamburgler, or Ronald,
1977, each..**$10.00**
Comic book, Ronald Lends a Helping Hand, 1978......**$18.00**
Create-A-Face, Grimace, Hamburgler, Mayor or Ronald,
paper, 1978, each...**$8.00**
Cups, Jurassic Park, 6 different, plastic, 1992, each.......**$2.00**
Drinking glass, Mystery Happy Meal, Ronald, Fry Kid or
Birdie, clear, 1983, each **$12.00**

Figure, Mac Tonight, series of 6, 1988, each, $5.00

Figures, Berenstain Bears Happy Meal, Sister w/wagon, Papa w/wheelbarrow, Brother w/scooter or Mama w/cart, 1987, each..**$4.00**

Figures, Carnival Happy Meal, 6 different figures on carnival rides, 1990, MIP, each...**$6.00**

Figures, Flintstone Kids Happy Meal, U-3 Dino, Barney, Fred Betty or Willma as kids, 1987, each.............**$12.00**

Figures, Potato Head Kids Happy Meal, 8 in all, 1992, each...**$3.00**

Figures, Space Aliens, 8 in all, 1979, each......................**$2.00**

Figures, Yo-Yogi! Happy Meal, Yogi, Cindy Bear, Huckleberry or Boo-Boo w/4 different vehicles, 1992, each..........**$5.00**

Frisbee, Ronald & logo on white plastic, 8" dia, M........**$4.00**

Magnifying glass, Duck Tale I Happy Meal, green w/decal, 1987...**$5.00**

Pail, Halloween '85 Happy Meal, 5 in all, 1985, each .**$12.00**

Place mat, Starship Enterprise, 1979, EX+ **$15.00**

Poster, ET w/children, M..**$10.00**

Puppet, hamburger policeman, soft vinyl head w/cloth body, Milton Bradley, 1973, 12x10", EX **$24.00**

Puzzle, frame-tray, Grimace w/Professor, Mayor w/Hamburgler, Captain Crook w/Big Mac or Ronald w/Fry Goblins, 1978, each...**$8.00**

Ring, glow type featuring Ronald or Grimace, w/yellow paper front, 1980, each..**$5.00**

Road map, Washington DC Capital Beltway map shows locations of area restaurants, red & black on white, 1964, 17x22", NM **$20.00**

Stickers, for bicycle fender featuring safety tips, 4 in all, 1977, each..**$8.00**

Stickers, Good Sports Happy Meal, 6 in all, 1984, each ..**$5.50**

Sunglasses, character frames w/colored lenses, MIP, each...**$4.00**

Transfers (iron-on), Fry Goblins, Grimace, Mayor, or Ronald, paper, 1978, each...**$8.00**

Transfers (rub-off), Fortune Burgler, 12 different fortunes, paper, 1977, each...**$8.00**

Wallet, McWrist, 4 in all, 1977, each..............................**$2.00**

Other Fast-Food Chains

Arby's, Barbar's Vehicles, set of 3, MIP **$12.00**

Arby's, figures, Looney Tunes Christmas, series of 3, MIP..**$18.00**

Arby's, puzzles, Barbar's, set of 4, MIP..........................**$20.00**

Arby's, storybooks, Barbar's Calendar set of 3, MIP **$12.00**

Big Boy, action figures, set of 4, MIP **$18.00**

Big Boy, sports figures, set of 3, MIP **$14.00**

Burger King, cups, Teenage Mutant Ninja Turtles, 3 in all, M, each **$2.00**

Burger King, doll, from the Simpsons, stuffed cloth w/vinyl head & cardboard accessories, 5 in all, 1991, each...**$4.00**

Burger King, figure, Peter Pan, European issue, 1993, MIP, each **$10.00**

Burger King, figures, Aladdin, 5 in all, MIP, each..........**$3.00**

Burger King, figures, Top Kids, 4 in all, MIP, each **$2.50**

Burger King, Mini Sports Games, 4 in all, MIP, each.....**$3.00**

Burger King, vehicle, Roger Rabbit in purple vehicle, series of 4, each, $3.00

Burger King, vehicles, Archies, 4 in all, MIP, each, $2.50

Carl Jr's, figures, Addams Family, 4 in all, MIP, each **$6.25**

Carl Jr's, figures, Soccar Stars, 4 in all, MIP, each **$5.00**

Carl Jr's, Mix 'n Match Dinos, 4 in all, MIP, each...........**$6.50**

Dairy Queen, puzzles, Suparsaurus, 4 in all, MIP, each ..**$2.50**

Dairy Queen, refrigerator magnets, 3 in all, each..........**$3.50**

Dairy Queen, wagon, red plastic w/Radio Flyer & Dairy Queen on sides, 4", MIP **$5.00**

Denny's, books, Berenstain Bears, 8 in all, M, each......**$2.00**

Denny's, figures, Flintstones Rock 'n Rollers, 6 in all, MIP, each...**$4.00**

Denny's, puzzle ornaments, Jetsons, 12 in all, MIP, each.**$2.25**

Hardee's, Treasure Trolls, 6 in all, MIP, each.................**$2.75**

Hardee's, Waldo's Straw Buddies, 4 in all, MIP, each ...**$6.00**

Jack-in-the Box, magnets, 3 in all, MIP, each.................**$3.50**

Jack-in-the Box, puzzle books, 3 in all, MIP, each........**$4.25**

Jerry's Restaurants, flicker ring, 1960s, EX....................**$20.00**

Kentucky Fried Chicken, bank, figure of the Colonel w/black decal tie, plastic, late 1960s-early 1970s, 9½x4½", NM **$35.00**

Lift-Up Mystery Game, Big Mac Tic-Tac-Toe, Mayor Word Guess, Professor Dot, or Ronald Maze, 1978, each .**$5.00**

Long John Silvers', I Love Dinosaurs, 4 in all, MIP, each..**$3.50**

Pizza Hut, bendees, Space Aliens, each **$6.00**

Pizza Hut, puppets, Beauty & the Beast, 4 in all, MIP, each..**$4.50**

Pizza Hut, puzzles, Beauty & the Beast, 3 in all, MIP, each..**$4.00**

Roy Rogers, cups, Treasure Trolls, 4 in all, MIP, each ..**$6.00**

Roy Rogers, magnets, Be a Sport, 4 in all, MIP, each....**$5.50**

Wal-Mart, figures, GI Joe & Kid's Meal, Warthog & Wetsuit, MIP, pr...................**$8.00**

Wendy's, cups, Jetsons, plastic, 4 in all, M, each..........**$2.00**

Wendy's, figures, Jetsons the Movie, on scooters, 1990, MIP, each..................**$6.00**

Wendy's, figures, Mighty Mouse, 6 in all, MIP, each.....**$4.00**

Wendy's, Play-Doh Fingles, 4 in all, MIP, each.............**$6.00**

Wendy's, stickers, Where's the Beef? promotion, complete set of 6, MIP **$18.00**

Wendy's, Wild Games, 6 in all, MIP, each **$2.50**

White Castle, bubble makers, Castle Friends, 4 in all, MIP, each..................**$4.25**

White Castle, figures, Glow-in-the-Dark Monsters, 3 in all, MIP, each.................**$3.25**

Fenton Glass

Located in Williamstown, West Virgina, the Fenton company is still producing glassware just as they have since the early part of the century. Nearly all fine department stores and gift shops carry an extensive line of their beautiful products, many of which rival examples of finest antique glassware. The fact that even their new glassware has collectible value attests to its fine quality.

Over the years they have made many lovely colors in scores of lines, several of which are very extensive. Paper labels were used exclusively until 1970. Since then some pieces have been made with a stamped-in logo.

Numbers in the descriptions correspond with catalog numbers used by the company. Collectors use them as a means of identifying subtle variations, such as a goblet with a particular style of stem. If you'd like to learn more about the subject, we recommend *Fenton Glass, The Second Twenty-Five Years*, by William Heacock.

Aqua Crest, bonbon, ruffled, 6" **$12.50**

Aqua Crest, bowl, double-crimped, #7321, 11½"........**$75.00**

Aqua Crest, vase, #36, 4" **$25.00**

Basketweave, basket, ruby, cupped bowl, 6" dia........**$24.00**

Basketweave, bowl, Mandarin red, shallow, 8" **$88.00**

Beaded Melon, creamer, gold overlay, #11..................**$38.00**

Beaded Melon, vase, light green overlay, double-crimped, 3¾".....................**$42.00**

Blue Overlay, basket, #1924........................**$42.00**

Blue Overlay, rose bowl, #711, 4" **$30.00**

Coin Dot, basket, cranberry opalescent, #1925, 10½"..**$130.00**

Coin Dot, bowl, cranberry opalescent, #203, 6" **$65.00**

Coin Dot, bowl, topaz opalescent, #203, 6" **$58.00**

Coin Dot, creamer, blue opalescent, #1461 ....**$30.00**

Coin Dot, vase, cranberry opalescent, #194, 8½".........**$90.00**

Daisy & Button, bell, Lime Sherbet............................**$18.00**

Daisy & Button, bonbon, French opalescent, 5"..........**$15.00**

Daisy & Button, candlesticks, milk glass, 2-light, pr....**$40.00**

Daisy & Button, slipper, pink opalescent, #1995.........**$10.00**

Daisy & Button, vase, milk glass, fan form, footed, 10"..**$35.00**

Dancing Ladies, bowl, cobalt, #900, 12"....................**$150.00**

Dancing Ladies, vase, Mongolian Green, ruffled rim, #901, 8½", $295.00

Diamond Lace, bowl, blue opalescent, #4824, 9½" **$48.00**

Diamond Lace, epergne, topaz opalescent, 4-pc, 10"..**$78.00**

Diamond Optic, base, ruby, fan form, #1502, 8½" **$40.00**

Diamond Optic, creamer & sugar bowl, rose, 3½"......**$40.00**

Dolphin, bowl, moonstone, oval, #1608, 10"..............**$95.00**

Dolphin, compote, ruby, crimped handles, 4"............**$70.00**

Dot Optic, ivy ball, emerald green, #1021 ....**$45.00**

Dot Optic, pitcher, blue opalescent, 4" **$37.50**

Emerald Crest, jug, #711, 6" **$42.00**

Emerald Crest, vase, 4½".....................**$35.00**

Georgian, claret, ruby, #1611, 4½-oz....................**$20.00**

Georgian, cup, amber, #1611....................**$12.50**

Gold Crest, bowl, crimped, 8"...................**$30.00**

Gold Crest, plate, 6¾"....................**$14.00**

Hobnail, ashtray, topaz opalescent, fan form, 5½" **$38.00**

Hobnail, basket, blue opalescent, 4" **$35.00**

Hobnail, bonbon, yellow opalescent, 5½" **$30.00**

Hobnail, bowl, topaz opalescent, double-crimped, #3927, 7" **$50.00**

Hobnail, cigarette lighter, milk glass **$20.00**

Hobnail, creamer & sugar bowl, topaz opalescent, #3900.**$36.00**

Hobnail, cruet, blue opalescent, 4"............................**$32.00**

Hobnail, cruet, milk glass, #3767, 7-oz......................**$28.00**

Hobnail, epergne, pink opalescent, #3701, 4-pc **$60.00**

Hobnail, jug, lime opalescent, 6"...............................**$70.00**

Hobnail, plate, French opalescent, 8" square..............$40.00
Hobnail, tumbler, green opalescent, 6" $26.00
Hobnail, tumbler, milk glass, 8-oz $8.00
Hobnail, vase, blue opalescent, fan form, footed, 6" ..$35.00
Hobnail, vase, emerald green, double-crimped, #3850, 5½"..$30.00
Hobnail, vase, milk glass, pitcher form, #3760 ....$44.00
Hobnail, vase, yellow opalescent, footed, 12" $60.00
Ivory Crest, candle holder, cornucopia form, 6¼".......$35.00
Ivory Crest, vase, crimped, #711, 6" $30.00
Ivory Crest, vase, square top, #201, 5" $45.00
Jade Green, candy dish, footed.....................................$38.00
Jade Green, sugar bowl...$18.00
Jade Green, vase, straight sides, 8"...............................$35.00

Jade Green & Black, batter & syrup pitchers, w/lids, $265.00

Jamestown Blue, powder jar, $90.00

Lilac, biscuit jar, #1681, rare......................................$300.00

Lilac, shell bowl, #9020, 10"...$95.00
Lincoln Inn, compote, light blue...................................$42.50
Lincoln Inn, tumbler, ruby, footed, 5" $30.00
Lincoln Inn, wine, cobalt..$25.00
Orange Tree, candlesticks, custard satin, pr $37.50
Orange Tree, jelly compote, crystal...............................$20.00
Peach Crest, basket, milk glass handle, 6½"................$58.00
Peach Crest, bowl, double-crimped, #7224, 10" $68.00
Peach Crest, vase, crimped, #187, 6" $30.00
Persian Medallion, basket, custard satin, #8238, 8½"...$40.00
Persian Medallion, compote, Lime Sherbet, #8234 ......$20.00
Plymouth, ice bucket, crystal $45.00
Plymouth, sherbet, cobalt, 3½" $18.00
Polka Dot, butter dish, cranberry opalescent, milk glass base...$120.00
Polka Dot, salt & pepper shakers, cranberry opalescent, 3¾", pr $55.00
Rib Optic, vase, lime green opalescent, #184, 11".......$60.00
Rose Crest, vase, #192, 6½" $20.00
Rose Crest, vase, double-crimped, #1924, 4" $25.00
Scroll & Eye, compote, rose pastel, #9021 ....$30.00
Scroll & Eye, plate, rose pastel, #9015.........................$20.00
September Morn, flower frog, crystal $95.00
September Morn, flower frog, light green w/black base .$140.00
Silver Crest, bonbon, crimped, 5½" $10.00
Silver Crest, cake plate, low pedestal base, 13" $35.00
Silver Crest, chip & dip set..$65.00
Silver Crest, compote, ruffled & crimped, 8½"............$17.50
Silver Crest, tidbit tray, 3-tier.......................................$45.00
Silver Crest, tray, chrome center handle, 5½" $18.00
Silver Crest, vase, double-crimped, #1924, 4½" $32.00
Spiral Optic, cruet, cranberry opalescent, clear reeded handle $95.00
Spiral Optic, vase, cranberry opalescent, #3253, 6½" ..$68.00
Swan, bonbon, pink $27.50
Vasa Murrhina, basket, green & blue, 7"......................$75.00
Vasa Murrhina, vase, green & blue, double-crimped, #6454, 4" $48.00
Vasa Murrhina, vase, Rose Mist, fan form, #6457, 7" ...$65.00
Water Lily, basket, Lime Sherbet, #8434, 7" $35.00
Water Lily, candy dish, rosaline, footed, #8480 ....$85.00
Water Lily, jardiniere, custard satin, #8498..................$30.00
Water Lily, pitcher, custard satin, #8464, 30-oz............$35.00
Water Lily, rose bowl, custard satin, #8429..................$20.00

Fiesta

You still can find Fiesta, but it's hard to get a bargain. Since it was discontinued in 1973, it has literally exploded onto the collectibles scene, and even at today's prices, new collectors continue to join the ranks of the veterans.

Fiesta is a line of solid-color dinnerware made by the Homer Laughlin China Company of Newell, West Virginia. It was introduced in 1936 and was immediately accepted by the American public. The line was varied. There were more than fifty items offered, and the color assortment included red (orange-red), cobalt, light green, and yellow. Within a short time, ivory and turquoise were added. (All these are referred to as 'original colors.')

As tastes changed during the production years, old colors were retired and new ones added. The colors collectors refer to as 'fifties' colors are dark green, rose, chartreuse, and gray, and today these are very desirable. Medium green was introduced in 1959 at a time when some of the old standard shapes were being discontinued. Today, medium green pieces are the most expensive. Most pieces are marked. Plates were ink stamped, and molded pieces usually had an indented mark.

In 1986, Homer Laughlin reintroduced Fiesta, but in colors different than the old line: white, black, cobalt, rose (bright pink), and apricot. Many of the pieces had been restyled, and the only problem collectors have had with the new colors is with the cobalt. But if you'll compare it with the old, you'll see that it is darker. Turquoise, periwinkle blue, yellow, and Seamist green have since been added, and though the turquoise is close, it is a little greener than the original. The newest color is lilac

New items that have not been restyled are being made from the original molds. This means that you may find pieces with the old mark in the new colors. When an item has been restyled, new molds had to be created, and these will have the new mark. So will any piece marked with the ink stamp. The new mark is a script 'FIESTA' (all letters upper case), while the old is 'Fiesta.' Compare a few, the difference is obvious. Just don't be fooled into thinking you've found a rare cobalt juice pitcher or individual sugar and creamer set, they just weren't made in the old line.

For further information, we recommend *The Collector's Encyclopedia of Fiesta* by Sharon and Bob Huxford.

Ashtray, '50s colors	$70.00
Ashtray, original colors	$38.00
Ashtray, red or cobalt	$45.00
Bowl, covered onion soup; cobalt or ivory	$450.00
Bowl, covered onion soup; red	$500.00
Bowl, covered onion soup; turquoise	$2,000.00
Bowl, covered onion soup; yellow or light green	$350.00
Bowl, cream soup; '50s colors	$60.00
Bowl, cream soup; med green, minimum value	$2,800.00
Bowl, cream soup; original colors	$35.00
Bowl, cream soup; red or cobalt	$48.00
Bowl, dessert; '50s colors, 6"	$42.00
Bowl, dessert; med green, 6"	$265.00
Bowl, dessert; red or cobalt, 6"	$42.00
Bowl, fruit; '50s colors, 4¾"	$28.00
Bowl, fruit; '50s colors, 5½"	$30.00
Bowl, fruit; med green, 4¾"	$285.00
Bowl, fruit; med green, 5½"	$62.00
Bowl, fruit; original colors, 11¾"	$140.00
Bowl, fruit; original colors, 4¾"	$22.00
Bowl, fruit; original colors, 5½"	$25.00
Bowl, fruit; red or cobalt, 11¾"	$180.00
Bowl, fruit; red or cobalt, 4¾"	$25.00
Bowl, fruit; red or cobalt, 5½"	$28.00
Bowl, individual salad; med green, 7½"	$78.00

Bowl, individual salad; red, turquoise or yellow, 7½".	$60.00
Bowl, nappy; '50s colors, 8½"	$42.00
Bowl, nappy; med green, 8½"	$90.00
Bowl, nappy; original colors, 8½"	$30.00
Bowl, nappy; original colors, 9½"	$40.00
Bowl, nappy; red or cobalt, 8½"	$40.00
Bowl, nappy; red or cobalt, 9½"	$50.00
Bowl, salad; original colors, footed	$190.00
Bowl, salad; red or cobalt, footed	$230.00
Bowl, Tom & Jerry; ivory w/gold letters	$225.00
Candle holders, bulbous, original colors, pr	$70.00
Candle holders, bulbous, red or cobalt, pr	$90.00
Candle holders, tripod, original colors, pr	$325.00
Candle holders, tripod, red, cobalt or ivory, pr	$375.00

Carafe, original colors, $145.00

Carafe, red or cobalt	$185.00
Casserole, '50s colors	$235.00
Casserole, French; standard colors other than yellow.	$450.00
Casserole, French; yellow	$210.00
Casserole, med green	$400.00
Casserole, original colors	$110.00
Casserole, red or cobalt	$160.00
Coffeepot, '50s colors	$220.00
Coffeepot, demitasse; original colors	$185.00
Coffeepot, demitasse; red, cobalt or ivory	$235.00
Coffeepot, original colors	$135.00
Coffeepot, red or cobalt	$175.00
Compote, original colors, 12"	$115.00
Compote, red or cobalt, 12"	$140.00
Compote, sweets; original colors	$50.00
Compote, sweets; red or cobalt	$65.00

Creamer, '50s colors	$30.00
Creamer, individual; red	$145.00
Creamer, individual; turquoise	$235.00
Creamer, individual; yellow	$50.00
Creamer, med green	$50.00
Creamer, original colors	$18.00
Creamer, original colors, stick handle	$40.00
Creamer, original colors, stick handles	$32.00
Creamer, red or cobalt	$24.00
Cup, demitasse; '50s colors	$225.00
Cup, demitasse; original colors	$50.00
Cup, demitasse; red or cobalt	$55.00
Egg cup, '50s colors	$125.00

Egg cup, original colors other than ivory, $42.00

Egg cup, red, cobalt or ivory	$55.00
Lid, for mixing bowl #1-3, any color	$550.00
Lid, for mixing bowl #4, any color	$600.00
Marmalade, original colors	$150.00
Marmalade, red or cobalt	$190.00
Mixing bowl, #1, original colors other than ivory	$90.00
Mixing bowl, #1, red, cobalt or ivory	$120.00
Mixing bowl, #2, original colors	$70.00
Mixing bowl, #2, red or cobalt	$80.00
Mixing bowl, #3, original colors	$80.00
Mixing bowl, #3, red or cobalt	$85.00
Mixing bowl, #4, original colors	$90.00
Mixing bowl, #4, red or cobalt	$95.00
Mixing bowl, #5, original colors	$100.00
Mixing bowl, #5, red or cobalt	$110.00
Mixing bowl, #6, original colors other than ivory	$125.00
Mixing bowl, #6, red, cobalt or ivory	$140.00
Mixing bowl, #7, original colors other than ivory	$160.00
Mixing bowl, #7, red, cobalt or ivory	$185.00
Mug, Tom & Jerry; '50s colors	$85.00
Mug, Tom & Jerry; ivory w/gold letters	$60.00
Mug, Tom & Jerry; red or cobalt	$65.00
Mustard, original colors	$125.00
Mustard, red or cobalt	$170.00
Pitcher, disk juice; gray	$1,200.00

Pitcher, disk juice; red	$250.00
Pitcher, disk water; '50s colors	$200.00
Pitcher, disk water; med green	$600.00
Pitcher, disk water; original colors	$80.00
Pitcher, disk water; red or cobalt	$115.00
Pitcher, ice; original colors	$80.00
Pitcher, ice; red or cobalt	$110.00
Pitcher, jug, 2-pt, '50s colors	$95.00
Pitcher, jug, 2-pt, original colors other than ivory	$50.00
Pitcher, jug, 2-pt, red, cobalt or ivory	$70.00
Plate, '50s color, 10"	$40.00
Plate, '50s colors, deep	$42.00
Plate, '50s colors, 6"	$8.00
Plate, '50s colors, 7"	$11.00
Plate, '50s colors, 9"	$18.00
Plate, cake; light green or yellow	$550.00
Plate, cake; red or cobalt	$600.00
Plate, calender; 1954 or 1955, 10"	$32.00
Plate, calender; 1955, 9"	$38.00
Plate, chop; '50s colors, 13"	$60.00
Plate, chop; '50s colors, 15"	$80.00
Plate, chop; med green, 13"	$110.00
Plate, chop; original colors, 13"	$28.00
Plate, chop; original colors, 15"	$35.00
Plate, chop; red or cobalt, 13"	$38.00
Plate, chop; red or cobalt, 15"	$50.00
Plate, compartment; '50s colors, 10½"	$45.00
Plate, compartment; original colors, 10½"	$28.00
Plate, compartment; original colors, 12"	$50.00
Plate, compartment; red or cobalt, 12"	$45.00
Plate, deep; med green	$90.00
Plate, deep; original colors	$32.00
Plate, deep; red or cobalt	$42.00
Plate, deep; red or cobalt, 10"	$32.00
Plate, med green, 10"	$80.00
Plate, med green, 6"	$15.00
Plate, med green, 7"	$25.00
Plate, med green, 9"	$35.00
Plate, original colors, 10"	$26.00
Plate, original colors, 6"	$4.00
Plate, original colors, 7"	$7.50
Plate, original colors, 9"	$9.00
Plate, red or cobalt, 6"	$6.00
Plate, red or cobalt, 7"	$8.50
Plate, red or cobalt, 9"	$16.00
Platter, '50s colors	$45.00
Platter, med green	$90.00
Platter, original colors	$25.00
Platter, red or cobalt	$35.00
Salt & pepper shakers, '50s colors, pr	$35.00
Salt & pepper shakers, med green, pr	$70.00
Salt & pepper shakers, original colors, pr	$17.00
Salt & pepper shakers, red or cobalt, pr	$23.00
Sauce boat, '50s colors	$60.00
Sauce boat, med green	$95.00
Sauce boat, original colors	$32.00
Sauce boat, red or cobalt	$50.00
Saucer, '50s colors	$5.00

Saucer, demitasse; '50s colors $65.00
Saucer, demitasse; original colors.....................$12.00
Saucer, demitasse; red or cobalt $15.00
Saucer, med green $8.00
Saucer, original colors..$3.00
Saucer, red or cobalt...$4.00
Sugar bowl, '50s colors, 3¼x3½"......................$50.00
Sugar bowl, individual; turquoise $275.00
Sugar bowl, individual; yellow..........................$75.00
Sugar bowl, med green, 3¼x3½".......................$100.00
Sugar bowl, original colors, 3¼x3½" $35.00
Sugar bowl, red or cobalt, 3¼x3½"....................$45.00
Syrup, original colors...$50.00
Syrup, red or cobalt...$235.00
Teacup, '50s colors $35.00
Teacup, med green..$50.00
Teacup, original colors...$22.00
Teacup, red or cobalt $28.00
Teapot, '50s colors, med $210.00
Teapot, med green, med......................................$425.00
Teapot, original colors, lg...................................$120.00

Teapot, original colors, med, $120.00

Teapot, red or cobalt, lg......................................$150.00
Teapot, red or cobalt, med $140.00
Tray, figure-8; cobalt..$60.00
Tray, figure-8; turquoise $190.00
Tray, figure-8; yellow $195.00
Tray, relish; mixed colors, no red......................$175.00
Tray, utility; original colors $30.00
Tray, utility; red or cobalt....................................$35.00
Tumbler, juice; red or cobalt...............................$35.00
Tumbler, juice; Harlequin yellow, dark green or chartreuse,
    each $275.00
Tumbler, juice; original colors $30.00
Tumbler, water; original colors..........................$45.00
Tumbler, water; red or cobalt $55.00
Vase, bud; original colors....................................$50.00
Vase, bud; red or cobalt.......................................$65.00
Vase, original colors, 10" $450.00
Vase, original colors, 12" $540.00
Vase, original colors, 8".......................................$365.00

Vase, red or cobalt, 10" $500.00
Vase, red or cobalt, 12" $635.00
Vase, red or cobalt, 8"...$425.00

Kitchen Kraft

Bowl, mixing; light green or yellow, 10".....................$80.00
Bowl, mixing; light green or yellow, 6".......................$55.00
Bowl, mixing; light green or yellow, 8".......................$70.00
Bowl, mixing; red or cobalt, 10" $90.00
Bowl, mixing; red or cobalt, 6"..................................$60.00
Bowl, mixing; red or cobalt, 8"..................................$80.00
Cake plate, light green or yellow................................$42.00
Cake plate, red or cobalt..$48.00
Cake server, light green or yellow..............................$80.00
Cake server, red or cobalt $90.00
Casserole, individual; light green or yellow, 7½".......$70.00
Casserole, individual; light green or yellow, 8½".......$85.00
Casserole, individual; red or cobalt, 7½"...................$80.00
Casserole, individual; red or cobalt, 8½"..................$130.00

Covered jar, light green or yellow, lg, $210.00

Covered jar, light green or yellow, med...................$190.00
Covered jar, light green or yellow, sm.....................$200.00
Covered jar, red or cobalt, lg $230.00
Covered jar, red or cobalt, med................................$210.00
Covered jar, red or cobalt, sm $225.00
Covered jug, light green or yellow............................$170.00
Covered jug, red or cobalt $180.00
Fork, light green or yellow..$70.00
Fork, red or cobalt $78.00
Metal frame for platter..$22.00
Pie plate, light green or yellow, 10" $38.00
Pie plate, light green or yellow, 9" $35.00
Pie plate, red or cobalt, 10".......................................$42.00
Pie plate, red or cobalt, 9"...$40.00
Salt & pepper shakers, light green or yellow, pr.........$75.00
Salt & pepper shakers, red or cobalt, pr $85.00
Spoon, light green or yellow......................................$75.00
Spoon, red or cobalt..$85.00

Stacking refrigerator lid, ivory.....................$150.00
Stacking refrigerator lid, light green or yellow $45.00
Stacking refrigerator lid, red or cobalt....................$52.00
Stacking refrigerator unit, ivory $150.00
Stacking refrigerator unit, light green or yellow $32.00
Stacking refrigerator unit, red or cobalt......................$36.00

Finch, Kay

Wonderful ceramic figurines signed by artist-decorator Kay Finch are among the many that were produced in California during the middle of the century. She modeled her line of animals with much expression and favored soft color combinations. Some of her models were quite large; but generally they range in size from 12" down to a tiny 2". She made several animal 'family groups' and, though limited, some human subjects as well. After her recent death, values for her work seem to be climbing.

She used a variety of marks and labels, and though most pieces are marked, some of the smaller animals are not; but you should be able to recognize her work with ease, once you've seen a few marked pieces.

For more information, we recommend *The Collector's Encyclopedia of California Pottery* by Jack Chipman.

Ashtray, shaped like dog's head, turquoise.................$25.00
Ashtray, Song of the sea, white shell shape, 5x7" $18.00
Bank, English cottage form, dated 1944, 5½" $100.00
Camel, multicolors, 5"...................................$110.00
Chanticleer, pale multicolors, 10¾" $200.00
Circus monkeys, posed in green & white uniforms, ca 1948, 4", pr...$95.00
Girl, yellow banana curls w/bows, blue pinafore over white dress & pantaloons, black shoes, 5¼" $65.00
Pig, Winkie, 3¾x4"...$55.00
Plate, Santa, 1950, hard to find, 6½"..........................$95.00

Rabbit, white w/black eyes, pink ears & nose, 1946, 2½", $40.00

Santa tumbler or vase, red & white w/black & gold accents, 4¼" $45.00
Vase, footed cylinder narrowing at top, lavender, 9" ..$45.00

Fire-King Dinnerware

This is an area of collecting interest that you can enjoy without having to mortgage the home place. In fact, you'll be able to pick it up for a song, if you keep your eyes peeled at garage sales and swap meets.

Fire-King was a trade name of the Anchor Hocking Glass Company, located in Lancaster, Ohio. As its name indicates, this type of glassware is strong enough to stand up to high oven temperatures without breakage. From the early forties until the mid-seventies, they produced kitchenware, dinnerware, and restaurant ware in a variety of colors. (We'll deal with two of the most popular of these colors, peach lustre and Jadite, later on in the book.) Blues are always popular with collectors, and Anchor Hocking made two, turquoise blue and azurite (light sky blue). They also made pink, forest green, ruby, gold-trimmed lines, and some with fired-on colors. During the late sixties they made Soreno in avocado green to tie in with home decorating trends.

Bubble (made from the thirties through the sixties) was produced in just about every color Anchor Hocking ever made. You may also hear this pattern refered to as Provincial or Bullseye.

Alice was an early forties line. It was made in Jadite and a white that was sometimes trimmed with blue or red. Cups and saucers were given away in boxes of Mother's Oats, but plates had to be purchased (so they're scarce today).

In the early fifties, they produced a 'laurel leaf' design in peach and 'Laurel Gray' lustres (the gray is scarce), followed later in the decade and into the sixties with several lines made of white glass decorated with decals — Honeysuckle, Fleurette, Primrose, and Game Bird, to name only a few. The same white glass was used for lots of kitchen items such as bowl sets, range shakers, grease jars, etc., decorated in bold designs and colors. (See Kitchen Glassware and Reamers.)

So pick a pattern and get going. These are the antiques of the future! If you'd like to study more about Anchor Hocking's dinnerware, we recommend *Collectible Glassware of the 40s, 50s, and 60s*, by Gene Florence.

Alice, cup, white w/red trim, early 1940s...................$12.50
Alice, plate, dinner; white w/red trim, early 40s, 9½" .$20.00
Alice, saucer, white w/red trim, early 1940s $50.00
Azurite Swirl, bowl, fruit or dessert; 1950, 4⅞".............$4.00
Azurite Swirl, bowl, soup plate; 1950, 7⅝"....................$7.00
Azurite Swirl, creamer, flat bottom, 1950 ....$7.00
Azurite Swirl, tumbler, iced tea; 1950, 12-oz...............$6.50
Blue Mosaic, bowl, soup plate; late 1960s, 6⅝" $5.50
Blue Mosaic, cup & saucer, late 1960s $5.50
Blue Mosaic, plate, salad; late 1960s, 7⅜" $4.00
Blue Mosaic, snack tray, rectangular, late 1960s, 6x11".$3.50
Charm, bowl, soup; Azurite, 1950-54, 6" $12.00
Charm, cup, Azurite, 1950-54 ....$3.50
Charm, plate, dinner; Azurite, 1950-54, 9¼"................$12.00
Charm, saucer, Azurite, 1950-54, 5⅜" $1.50
Charm, sugar bowl (open), Azurite, 1950-54 ....$6.50
Fleurette, bowl, dessert; 1958-60, 4⅝" $2.00

Fleurette, cup, 1958-60, 8-oz **$3.50**
Fleurette, plate, dinner; 1958-60, 9⅛" **$3.50**
Fleurette, sugar bowl w/lid, 1958-60 ....**$6.00**
Fleurette, tray, snack; 1958-60, 6x11"............................**$2.50**
Game Bird, ashtray, decal on white, 1959-62, 5¼" **$5.50**
Game Bird, bowl, dessert; decal on white, 1959-62, 4⅝" **$4.00**
Game Bird, creamer, decal on white, 1959-62..............**$7.00**

Game Bird, mug, decal on white, 1959-62, 8-oz, $8.00

Game Bird, plate, dinner; decal on white, 1959-62, 9⅛" .**$6.50**
Game Bird, tumbler, iced tea; decal on white, 1959-62, 11-oz **$7.50**
Golden Anniversary, bowl, vegetable; 22k gold on Ivory White 'Swirl,' 1955-ca 1963, 8¼" **$5.00**
Golden Anniversary, plate, salad; 22k gold trim on Ivory White 'Swirl,' 1955-ca 1963, 7⅜" **$2.50**
Golden Anniversary, plate, salad; 22k gold trim on Ivory White 'Swirl,' 1955-ca 1963, 7⅜" **$2.50**
Golden Anniversary, sugar bowl (open), 22k gold trim on Ivory White 'Swirl,' ear-shaped handles, footed, 1955-ca 1963...**$3.50**
Golden Shell, bowl, cereal; 22k gold trim on white scalloped 'Swirl,' 1963-late 1970s, 6⅜"..........................**$2.50**
Golden Shell, bowl, soup; 22k gold trim on white scalloped 'Swirl,' 1963-late 1970s, 6⅜"....................................**$4.00**
Golden Shell, creamer, footed, 22k gold trim on white scalloped 'Swirl,' 1963-late 1970s **$3.50**
Golden Shell, sugar bowl, footed, 22k gold trim on white scalloped 'Swirl,' 1963-late 1970s **$2.75**
Golden Shell, sugar bowl w/lid, footed, 22k gold trim on white scalloped 'Swirl,' 1963-late 1970s..................**$7.00**
Gray Laurel, bowl, dessert; embossed laurel band around rim, 1952-63, 4⅞" **$4.00**
Gray Laurel, bowl, vegetable; embossed laurel band around rim, 1952-56, 8¼" **$8.50**
Gray Laurel, creamer, embossed laurel band, footed, 1952-63 ....**$4.50**
Gray Laurel, cup & saucer, embossed laurel band, 1952-63 ....**$6.00**
Gray Laurel, sugar bowl (open), embossed laurel band, footed, ear-shaped handles, 1952-63 ....**$4.50**
Honeysuckle, bowl, soup plate; decal on white, 1958-60, 6⅝" **$4.00**
Honeysuckle, platter, decal on white, oval, 1958-60, 9x12" **$10.00**
Honeysuckle, tumbler, iced tea; allover decal on clear glass, 1958-60, 12-oz **$6.00**
Honeysuckle, tumbler, juice; allover decal on clear glass, 1958-60, 5-oz **$3.50**
Ivory Swirl, creamer, flat bottom...................................**$3.50**
Ivory Swirl, sugar bowl, flat bottom **$2.50**
Pink Swirl, bowl, vegetable; 1956, 7¼"........................**$10.00**
Pink Swirl, cup, 1956, 8-oz..**$5.00**
Pink Swirl, saucer, 1956, 5¾" **$1.50**
Primrose, bowl, dessert; decal on white, 1960-62, 4⅝" .**$2.00**
Primrose, bowl, vegetable; decal on white, 1960-62, 8¼" **$7.00**
Primrose, plate, dinner; decal on white, 1960-62, 9⅛" ..**$5.00**
Primrose, tumbler, juice; decal on clear glass, 1960-62, 5-oz...**$4.00**
Primrose, tumbler, water; decal on clear glass, 1960-62, 9-oz...**$5.00**
Sunrise, bowl, vegetable; red trim on Ivory White 'Swirl,' early 1950s, 8¼" **$12.00**
Sunrise, plate, dinner; red trim on Ivory White 'Swirl,' early 1950s, 9⅛"..**$6.50**
Sunrise, platter, red trim on Ivory White 'Swirl,' oval, early 1950s, 9½"..**$13.00**
Turquoise Blue, bowl, berry; 1957-58, 4½" **$6.00**
Turquoise Blue, bowl, vegetable; 1957-58, 8"...............**$14.00**
Turquoise Blue, creamer, 1957-58 ....**$6.00**
Turquoise Blue, deviled-egg plate, gold trim, 1957-58, 9¾" **$15.00**
Turquoise Blue, mug, 1957-58, 8-oz.............................**$10.00**
Turquoise Blue, plate, dinner; 1957-58, 10" **$26.00**
Turquoise Blue, sugar bowl (open), 1957-58................**$6.00**
Wheat, bowl, soup plate; decal on white, 1962-late 1960s, 6⅝" **$4.50**
Wheat, creamer, decal on white, 1962-late 1960s..........**$4.00**

Wheat, decal on white, 1962-late 1960s, 9x12", $10.00

Wheat, plate, dinner; decal on white, 1962-late 1960s, 10" **$4.00**
Wheat, sugar bowl w/lid, decal on white, 1962-late 1960s...**$6.50**
White Swirl, bowl, fruit or dessert; 1953, 4⅞" **$2.50**
White Swirl, cup & saucer, 8-oz....................................**$3.50**
White Swirl, plate, dinner; 9⅛"......................................**$3.00**

Fire-King Ovenware

Anchor Hocking made ovenware in many the same colors and designs as their dinnerware. Their most extensive line (and one that is very popular today) was made in Sapphire Blue, clear glass with a blue tint, in a pattern called Philbe. Most pieces are still very reasonable, but some are already worth in excess of $50.00, so now is the time to start your collection. Gene Florence's book, *Collectible Glassware of the 40s, 50s, and 60s,* is a good source for more information.

Ivory, baking dish, round, 1942-50s, 1½-qt....................**$8.50**
Ivory, baking dish, 1942-50s, 2x10½"............................**$12.50**
Ivory, casserole, knob lid, round, 1942-50s, 1-pt..........**$8.50**
Ivory, custard, 1942-50s, 6-oz.......................................**$3.25**
Ivory, loaf pan, deep, 1942-50, 5⅛x9⅛".......................**$12.50**
Primrose, baking dish, decal on white, rectangular, 1960-62, 8x12½" **$12.50**
Primrose, cake pan, decal on white, square, 1960-62, 8" .**$8.50**
Primrose, casserole, decal on white, knob lid, 1960-62, 2-qt **$12.50**

Primrose, casserole, decal on white, 1960-62, 1½-qt, $14.00

Sapphire Blue, baking dish, individual; 1942-50, 6-oz ..**$5.00**
Sapphire Blue, baking dish, 1942-50, 1½-qt.................**$12.00**
Sapphire Blue, baking dish, 1942-50, 2-qt, 8⅛x12½"...**$35.00**
Sapphire Blue, bowl, measuring; 1942-50, 16-oz.........**$23.00**
Sapphire Blue, bowl, utility; 1½-qt, 1942-50, 8⅜" **$16.00**
Sapphire Blue, casserole, knob lid, 1942-50, 1½-qt.....**$13.00**
Sapphire Blue, custard, 1942-50, 5-oz...........................**$3.25**
Sapphire Blue, pie plate, 1942-50, 1½x9".....................**$8.50**
Sapphire Blue, roaster, 1942-50, 8¾" **$45.00**
Wheat, baking dish, 1962-late 1960s, 2x8x12½" **$11.00**
Wheat, cake pan, decal on white, 8" dia.......................**$8.00**
Wheat, casserole, knob lid, 1962-late 1960s, 1-qt **$7.50**
Wheat, creamer, 1962-late 1960s..................................**$4.00**
Wheat, custard, 1962-late 1960s, 6-oz...........................**$2.50**
Wheat, loaf pan, deep, 1962-late 1960s, 5x9"................**$8.00**

Fisher-Price

Probably no other toy manufacturer is as well known among kids of today than Fisher-Price. Since the 1930s they have produced wonderful toys made of wood covered with vividly lithographed paper. Plastic parts weren't used until 1949, and this can sometimes help you date your finds. These toys were made for play, so very few older examples have survived in condition good enough to attract collectors. Watch for missing parts and avoid those that are dirty. Edge wear and some paint dulling is normal and to be expected.

For more information we recommend *Modern Toys, American Toys, 1930–1980,* by Linda Baker, and *Fisher-Price, A Historical, Rarity Value Guide,* by John J. Murray and Bruce R. Fox (Books Americana).

Allie Gator, #653, VG...**$45.00**
Bouncing Buggy, MIB...**$40.00**
Busy Bee, #325, pull toy, lithographed paper over wood, VG+...**$18.00**
Change-a-Tune Piano, plays 3 songs, 1969, NM..........**$25.00**
Chatter Telephone, MIB **$85.00**

Ducky Cart, #11, EX, $80.00

Fun Jet, 1970, VG..**$20.00**
Humpty Dumpty, MIB..**$40.00**
Jiffy Dump Truck, MIB...**$25.00**
Little Snoopy, MIB...**$50.00**
Mickey Mouse Choo Choo, #485, ca 1949, NM **$135.00**
Mother Goose, #164, VG..**$25.00**
Musical Ferris Wheel, MIB..**$68.00**
Nosy Pup, #445, VG...**$20.00**
Picnic Basket, #677, complete, 1975-79, EX.................**$14.00**
Play Family, Farm, MIB **$125.00**
Play Family Camper, MIB **$40.00**
Play Family School Bus, MIB **$50.00**
Pocket Camera, MIB...**$25.00**
Pony Chime, #132, VG..**$30.00**
Pop-Up-Pal Chime Phone, MIB.................................**$75.00**
Pull-A-Tune Xylophone, #870, wood w/plastic wheels, 1978, VG+...**$10.00**
Running Bunny w/Cart, 1960, EX...............................**$85.00**
Seal, pull toy, EX...**$30.00**
Tailspin Tabby, #455, VG..**$85.00**
Tiny Teddy, 1958, EX **$65.00**
Tumble Tower, MIB...**$40.00**
TV Music Box, 1973, EX..**$45.00**
Uncle Timmy Turtle, #150, NM..................................**$50.00**

Three Men in a Tub, M, $25.00

Fishing Collectibles

This is a hobby that has really caught on over the past several years. There is a national collectors club, newsletters, and several informative books for the serious buyer of old fishing lures.

There have been literally thousands of lures made since the turn of the century. Some have bordered on the ridiculous, and some have turned out to be just as good as the manufacturers claimed. In lieu of buying outright from a dealer, try some of the older stores in your area — you just might turn up a good old lure. Go through any old tackle boxes that might be around; and when the water level is low, check out the river banks.

If you have to limit your collection, you might want to concentrate just on wooden lures, or you might decide to try to locate one of every lure made by a particular company. Whatever you decide, try to find examples with good original paint and hardware.

For further information, we recommend *Old Fishing Lures and Tackle* by Carl F. Luckey.

Abbie & Imbrie Tango, molted red & green on yellow, EX .**$55.00**
Arbogast Jitterbug, wood, white w/red arrow head, EX .**$35.00**
Arbogast Twin Liz, white w/pink heads, MIB.............**$35.00**
Bomber, #409, wood w/pearl finish, MIB...................**$15.00**
Boone Needle Fish, green w/scale finish, EX.............**$20.00**
Creek Chub Baby Plunker, black, glass eyes, EX........**$30.00**
Creek Chub Crawdad, #300, natural crab finish, bead eyes, red legs, MIB.................................**$45.00**
Creek Chub Crawdad, #400, natural crab finish, MIB .**$40.00**
Creek Chub Deepster, #9636, black sucker finish, MIB .**$30.00**
Creek Chub Husky Musky, white w/red head, glass eyes, original box, EX **$75.00**

Creek Chub Injured Baby Minnow, silver flash finish, glass eyes, EX.................................**$15.00**
Creek Chub Injured Minnow, #1502, white w/red head, glass eyes, EX.................................**$22.00**
Creek Chub Injured Minnow, #1518, silver flash finish, glass eyes, EX.................................**$22.00**
Creek Chub Jointed Darter, #4914, yellow w/black & red spots, EX.................................**$15.00**
Creek Chub Pikie, #730, orange w/black spots, red head, glass eyes, MIB.................................**$50.00**
Creek Chub Plunker, silver flash finish, glass eyes, EX.**$20.00**
Creek Chub Pop 'n Dunk, #6325, white w/scale finish, glass eyes, MIB.................................**$145.00**
Creek Chub Surfster, #7200, pikie, glass eyes, MIB.....**$45.00**
Creek Chub Wiggle Fish, perch, glass eyes, EX..........**$65.00**
Devonshire, wood ball-bat shape, brown & yellow, diving lip, EX.................................**$20.00**
Eger Bull Nose Frog, frog-skin finish, EX...................**$85.00**
Heddon's Baby Crab Wiggler, slate back w/silver belly, glass eyes, rare, VG.................................**$55.00**
Heddon's Baby Crab Wiggler, white w/red tail, red glass eyes, VG **$30.00**
Heddon's Crab Wiggler, #1800, green crackle-back, glass eyes, EX.................................**$95.00**

Heddon's Crazy Crawler, gray w/green & black, yellow underside, EX, $25.00

Heddon's Dowagiac Spook, #9100, rainbow finish, glass eyes, VG **$30.00**
Heddon's Midget Digit Spook, #9020-RW, red & white, MIB **$12.00**
Heddon's Punkinseed, #730, sunfish, VG **$40.00**
Heddon's Punkinseed Sinker, #730, crappie, 2-pc, MIB.**$85.00**
Heddon's Scissor Tail, red & white, EX.......................**$18.00**
Heddon's Tiny Spook, #310, plastic bluegill, EX.........**$25.00**
Heddon's Vamp, white w/red nose & tail, glass eyes, EX.**$35.00**

Helin Tackle Co, Flat Fish, orange & gray, original box, EX, $25.00

Jenson Kicker, plastic w/automatic kicking legs, pointed nose, EX..**$20.00**

Martin's Salmon Lure, yellow w/red gill, MIB..............**$20.00**

Paul Bunyon Electro Lure, yellow w/red & green trim, MIB..**$45.00**

Paul Bunyon Ruby Transparent Dodger, ruby & yellow, MIB..**$25.00**

Pflueger Baby Pal-O-Mine, brown w/scale finish, glass eyes, EX..**$25.00**

Pflueger Fantail Squid, red & white, EX **$25.00**

Pflueger Five-Hook Neverfail, green w/scale finish, glass eyes, EX..**$110.00**

Pflueger Globe, white w/red head, EX **$35.00**

Pflueger Three Hook Neverfail, green crackle-back, glass eyes, EX..**$90.00**

Pflueger Wizzard, luminous-red lightning-flash finish, painted eyes, MIB **$50.00**

Shakespeare's Kingfish Wobbler, #6535 WR, white & red, MIB **$75.00**

Shakespeare's Mouse, #6578 T, wood w/tiger stripes, MIB..**$22.00**

Shakespeare's Mouse, #6578 WR, wood, white & red, MIB..**$20.00**

South Bend Baby Surf-Oreno, white w/red head, glass eyes, EX..**$40.00**

South Bend Bass-Oreno, luminous finish, no eyes, VG .**$30.00**

South Bend Crippled Minnow, red & white, glass eyes, EX..**$40.00**

South Bend Fish-O-Bite, plastic, white w/red arrow head, EX..**$10.00**

South Bend Fish-Oreno, aluminum, glass eyes, EX.....**$75.00**

South Bend Musky Surf-Oreno, red & white, glass eyes, rare, EX..**$145.00**

True Temper Crippled Shad, #203, pearl finish, MIB ..**$25.00**

True Temper Speed Shad, #105, black & white, MIB ..**$20.00**

Wilson Super Wobbler, white w/2 red flutes, EX........**$35.00**

Flashlights

Eveready produced some of the earliest flashlights, but since they were invented in 1898, there's been lots of competition. More than 150 additional companies both here and abroad have developed over 1,000 models. Some are figural. For instance, in 1912 Eveready made a vest pocket model styled like a cigarette case, and there's one that looks like a Winchester 20-gauge shotgun shell. Others, like the Bright Star watch flashlight, were novelties, plain and simple. There are at least 45 different categories recognized by today's collectors.

BMG, black USN, w/bull's-eye lens, M.........................**$22.00**

Bright Star, watch light, NM **$75.00**

Burgess Sub, litho, M...**$18.00**

Chase, brass, for vest pocket, EX.................................**$15.00**

Chestlite, green box lantern w/straps, EX...................**$12.00**

Embury, lantern, Pat Jan 10, 1924, EX.........................**$18.00**

Eveready, box lantern, #4706, w/slide switch, lg, EX..**$36.00**

Eveready, canister lantern, #4708, EX..........................**$25.00**

Eveready, Daylo pistol, VG **$24.00**

Eveready, Daylo vest pocket light, w/paper label, original box, NM..**$25.00**

Eveready, electric candle, #1653, 1931, EX **$34.00**

Eveready, for cigarette case, lg, EX..............................**$16.00**

Eveready, for vest pocket, sterling, 1904, NM............**$150.00**

Eveready, glove catch switch, w/3 Pat dates, EX **$55.00**

Eveready, pistol light, gun metal, 1914, EX..................**$36.00**

Franco, for vest pocket, green glass w/button switch, EX **$20.00**

Franco, pistol light, Pat Jan 7 1908, ca 1913, EX.........**$25.00**

Fumalux Flashlight 400, combination flashlight & cigarette lighter, NM..**$15.00**

GOP on the March, lapel light, political w/elephant head, NM..**$12.00**

Homart, w/compass on end cap, VG **$11.00**

Jack Armstrong, blk case, EX **$20.00**

Lightmaster, Art Deco, VG..**$12.00**

Motor Car, electric candle, Made in Hong Kong, NM .**$10.00**

Niagara, green Cub lantern **$14.00**

Peerless, for vest pocket, w/push rod switch, VG.......**$10.00**

Purse Light, rectangular, Pat 1934, 1¼x½x2¾", NM.....**$12.00**

Rayovac, bullet form, VG **$5.00**

Rudolph the Red-Nosed Reindeer, lapel light, NM......**$12.00**

Winchester, copper, marked made in USA, 6¾", EX, $30.00

Winchester, 20-gauge shotgun shell light, NM............**$52.00**

Florence Ceramics

During the forties, Florence Ward began modeling tiny ceramic children as a hobby at her home in Pasadena, California. She was so happy with the results that she expanded, hired decorators, and moved into a larger building where for two decades she produced the lovely line of figurines, wall plaques, busts, etc., that have become so popular today. The 'Florence Collection' featured authentically detailed models of such couples as Louis XV and Madame Pompadour, Queen Elizabeth and King Arthur, Pinkie and Blue Boy, and Rhett and Scarlett. Nearly all of the Florence figures have names which are written on their bases.

Many figures are decorated with 22k gold and lace. Real lace was cut to fit, dipped in a liquid material called slip, and fired. During the firing it burned away, leaving only hardened ceramic lace trim. The amount of lacework that was used is one of the factors that needs to be considered when evaluating a 'Florence.' Size is another. Though most of the figures you'll find today are singles, a few were made as groups, and once in awhile you'll find a lady seated on a divan. The more complex, the more expensive.

If you'd like to learn more about the subject, we recommend *The Collector's Encyclopedia of California Pottery* by Jack Chipman.

Amelia, brown, 9¼" $160.00
Ava, 10" $145.00
Belle, pink...$65.00
Charmaine, white, 9" $135.00
Clarissa, gold trim, 8"...$100.00

Delia, 8", $85.00

Emily, planter...$45.00
Garr, salmon, pink, black & white w/gold, 8½" $110.00
Joy, 6" $85.00
Kay, planter, 6" $50.00
Lantern boy & Blossom girl, flower holders, 9" & 8¼",
    pr $110.00
Lilian, pink, 8" $90.00
Madonna, white w/gold $75.00
Matilda, rose, 8¼"..$90.00
Memories, Grandma sitting in chair, white w/gold...$225.00
Mike, 6½" $125.00
Mimi, planter..$45.00
Nancy, bud vase..$30.00
Pamela, pink $45.00
Planter, white w/feather effect, marked Floraline, square,
    6" $28.00
Polly, planter..$40.00
Prima Donna, maroon $120.00
Roberta, 8¾"...$155.00
Scarlett, 9"...$165.00
Sue, white w/gold..$65.00

Marilyn, purple, 9", $160.00

Sue Ellen..$115.00
Tray, w/rose, handled, 7" $45.00
Vivian, 9½" $150.00

Wall pocket, 7¼", $65.00

Fostoria

This was one of the major glassware producers of the twentieth century. They were located first in Fostoria, Ohio, but by the 1890s had moved to Moundsville, West Virginia. By the late thirties, they were recognized as the largest producers of handmade glass in the world. Their glassware is plentiful today and, considering its quality, not terribly expensive.

Though the company went out of business in the mid-eighties, the Lancaster Colony Company continues to use some of the old molds — herein is the problem. The ever-popular American and Coin Glass patterns are currently in production and even experts have trouble distinguishing the old from the new. Before you invest in either line, talk to dealers. Ask them to show you some of their old pieces. Most will be happy to help out a novice collector. Read *Elegant Glassware of the Depression Era* by Gene Florence. If there is a Fostoria outlet within driving distance, it will be worth your time just to see what is being offered there.

You'll be seeing lots of inferior 'American' at flea markets and (sadly) antique malls. It's often priced as though it is American, but in fact it is not. It's been produced since the 1950s by Indiana Glass who calls it 'Whitehall.' Watch for pitchers with only two mold lines, they're everywhere. (Fostoria's had three.) Remember that Fostoria was hand-made, so their pieces were fire polished. This means that if the piece you're examining has sharp, noticeable mold lines, be leery. There are other differences to watch for as well. Fostoria's footed pieces were designed with a 'toe,' while Whitehall feet have a squared peg-like appearance. The rays are sharper and narrower on the genuine Fostoria pieces, and the glass itself has more sparkle and life. And if it weren't complicated enough, the Home Interior Company has recently offered 'American'-like vases, covered bowls, and a footed candy dish that were produced in a foreign country, but at least they've marked theirs.

Coin Glass was originally produced in crystal, red, blue, emerald green, olive green, and amber. It's being reproduced today in crystal, green, blue, and red. The green and blue are 'off' enough to be pretty obvious, but the red is close. Beware. Here are some (probably not all) of the items currently in production: bowl, 8" diameter; bowl, 9" oval; candlesticks, 4½"; candy jar with lid, 6¼"; creamer and sugar bowl; footed comport; wedding bowl, 8¼". Know your dealer!

Numbers included in our descriptions were company-assigned stock numbers that collectors use as a means to distinguish variations in stems and shapes.

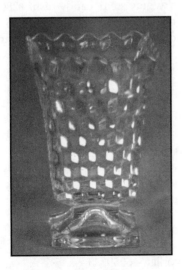

American, clear, vase, #2056, pressed pattern, 6½", $40.00

Alexis, clear, celery tray, #1630, pressed pattern **$16.00**
Alexis, clear, egg cup, #1630, pressed pattern **$9.00**
Alexis, clear, ice jug, #1630, pressed pattern, 3-pt.......**$60.00**
Alexis, clear, nappy, #1630, pressed pattern, 4½".........**$8.00**
Alexis, clear, toothpick holder, #1630, pressed pattern..**$18.00**
Allegro, clear w/gold band, claret, #672, 7½-oz, 5⅞"..**$15.00**
Allegro, clear w/gold band, sherbet, #672, 9-oz.........**$12.00**
Ambassador, clear w/gold band, cordial, #637, 1-oz, 3⅛" **$16.00**
Ambassador, clear w/gold band, sherbet, #637, 7½-oz, 4¾" **$12.00**
American, amber, blue or canary; beer mug, #2056, pressed pattern, 4½".......................................**$40.00**
American, amber, blue or canary; cheese dish, #2056, pressed pattern, footed................................**$90.00**
American, amber, blue or canary; cup, #2056, pressed pattern, footed...**$22.00**
American, amber, blue or canary; jug, #2056, pressed pattern, ice lip, 3-pt, 6½"...............................**$195.00**
American, amber, blue or canary; nappy, #2056, pressed pattern, w/lid, 5"..................................**$95.00**
American, amber, blue or canary; plate, syrup; #2056, pressed pattern, 6"..................................**$27.00**
American, amber, blue or canary; relish, #2056, pressed pattern, 3-part................................**$150.00**
American, amber, blue or canary; rose bowl, #2056, pressed pattern, 3½"....................................**$70.00**
American, amber, blue or canary; tumbler, #2056, pressed pattern, footed, 9-oz, 4⅜"......................**$45.00**
American, clear, ashtray, #2056, pressed pattern, oval, 5½" **$27.50**
American, clear, ashtray, #2056, pressed pattern, oval, 5½" **$27.50**
American, clear, bottle, cordial; #2056, pressed pattern, w/stopper **$100.00**
American, clear, bowl, #2056, pressed pattern, rolled edge, 11½" **$55.00**
American, clear, bowl, #2056, pressed pattern, w/handle, 8½" **$82.00**
American, clear, bowl, fruit; #2056, pressed pattern, footed, 16" **$200.00**
American, clear, cake plate, #2056, pressed pattern, 2 handles..**$35.00**
American, clear, cake salver, #2056, pressed pattern, square **$90.00**
American, clear, cocktail, #2056, pressed pattern, footed, 3-oz **$15.00**
American, clear, comport, #2056, pressed pattern, 8½".**$45.00**
American, clear, jug, #2056, pressed pattern, 3-pt, 8" .**$75.00**
American, clear, nappy, #2056, pressed pattern, tab handles, 9" **$43.00**
American, clear, nappy, fruit; #2056, pressed pattern, 3¾" **$18.50**
American, clear, plate, bread & butter; #2056, pressed pattern, 6" **$8.00**
American, clear, plate, dinner; #2056, pressed pattern, 9½" **$20.00**
American, clear, plate, salad; #2056, pressed pattern, 7".**$12.00**

American, clear, plate, torte; #2056, pressed pattern, 20"..**$115.00**

American, clear, platter, #2056, pressed pattern, oval, 10½"..**$45.00**

American, clear, relish, #2056, pressed pattern, 2-part..**$35.00**

American, clear, sherbet, #2056, pressed pattern, 4½-oz...**$10.00**

American, clear, tidbit, #2056, pressed pattern, metal handle **$45.00**

American, clear, tray, #2056, pressed pattern, oval, 10½"....................**$65.00**

American, clear, tumbler, #2056, pressed pattern, footed, 5-oz **$18.00**

American, red, ashtray, #2056, pressed pattern, square, 5" **$100.00**

American, red, cake stand, #2056, pressed pattern, footed, 12" **$120.00**

American, red, cocktail, oyster; #2056, pressed pattern, 4½"...................**$30.00**

American, red, goblet, #2056, pressed pattern, hexagonal foot, 10-oz **$30.00**

American, red, nappy, #2056, pressed pattern, shallow, 7" **$65.00**

American, red, pitcher, #2056, pressed pattern, 1-pt...**$60.00**

American, red, platter, #2056, pressed pattern, oval, 10½"....................**$110.00**

American, red, vase, #2056, pressed pattern, straight..**$70.00**

American Lady, clear w/blue bowl, cocktail, #5056, 3½-oz, 4" **$10.00**

American Lady, clear w/blue bowl, goblet, #5056, 10-oz, 6⅛" **$12.00**

American Lady, clear w/blue bowl, plate, #5056, 7" **$8.00**

American Lady, clear w/burgundy bowl, sherbet, #5056, 5½-oz, 4⅛" **$20.00**

American Lady, clear w/burgundy bowl, cordial, #5056, 1-oz, 3⅛" **$36.00**

Andover, clear w/encrusted gold band, cordial, #665, 1-oz, 3⅛" **$16.00**

Andover, clear w/encrusted gold band, goblet, #665, 10-oz, 6⅝" **$15.00**

Andover, clear w/encrusted gold band, plate, #665, 8"..**$8.00**

Anniversary, clear w/gold rim, cocktail, #634, 3½-oz, 3⅞" **$10.00**

Anniversary, clear w/gold rim, plate, #634, 8" **$8.00**

Anniversary, clear w/gold rim, sherbet, #634, 6-oz, 4½"..**$12.00**

Announcement, clear w/platinum band, brandy, #666, 3½-oz, 3⅞" **$15.00**

Announcement, clear w/platinum band, plate, #666, 7"..**$8.00**

Announcement, clear w/platinum band, relish, #666, 2-part...................**$13.00**

Astrid, clear, cocktail, #6030, 3½-oz, 5¼" **$10.00**

Astrid, clear, goblet, #6030, 10-oz, 7⅞".............**$12.00**

Astrid, clear, plate, #6030, 7" **$8.00**

Baroque, azure blue or ruby, bowl, #2496, flared, 12".**$66.00**

Baroque, azure blue or ruby, comport, #2496, 5½"....**$40.00**

Baroque, azure blue or ruby, nappy, #2496, square ...**$26.00**

Baroque, azure blue or ruby, sherbet, #2496, 5-oz **$10.00**

Baroque, azure blue or ruby, tray, #2496, 8" **$38.00**

Baroque, clear, bowl, salad; #2496, 10½".............**$25.00**

Baroque, clear, cheese dish, #2496, footed................**$26.00**

Baroque, clear, plate, #2496, 8" **$13.00**

Baroque, clear, saucer, #2496...................**$5.00**

Baroque, clear, sugar bowl, #2496, footed..................**$11.50**

Baroque, clear, tumbler, #2496, footed, 9-oz.............**$15.00**

Baroque, topaz or gold tint, candelabrum, #2496, 2-light, 8¼" **$100.00**

Baroque, topaz or gold tint, nappy, #2496, square **$13.00**

Baroque, topaz or gold tint, platter, #2496, oval, 12"..**$66.00**

Baroque, topaz or gold tint, relish, #2496, 4-part........**$40.00**

Bedford, clear, bonbon, #1000, pressed pattern, 6".....**$10.00**

Bedford, clear, bowl, #1000, pressed pattern, oval, 7"..**$14.00**

Bedford, clear, candy jar, #1000, pressed pattern........**$40.00**

Bedford, clear, custard, #1000, pressed pattern **$8.50**

Bedford, clear, nappy, #1000, pressed pattern, 4½" dia ..**$5.00**

Bedford, clear, tumbler, #1000, pressed pattern **$16.50**

Beloved, clear w/platinum band, bowl, #647, footed, 10" **$25.00**

Beloved, clear w/platinum band, plate, #647, 8" **$8.00**

Beloved, clear w/platinum band, relish, #647, 5-part..**$20.00**

Berkshire, clear, claret, #6105, 7-oz, 6½"...................**$14.00**

Berkshire, clear, goblet, #6105, 11-oz, 7⅛" **$13.00**

Berkshire, clear, plate, #6105, 8".....................**$8.00**

Brazilian, clear, bowl, berry; #600, pressed pattern (2 styles), 8" **$20.00**

Brazilian, clear, nappy, #600, pressed pattern, 4½" **$8.00**

Brazilian, clear, pickle jar, #600, pressed pattern.........**$25.00**

Brazilian, clear, tumbler, #600, pressed pattern **$15.00**

Brilliant, clear, bowl, #1001, pressed pattern, high foot, 6" **$25.00**

Brilliant, clear, bowl, #1871, pressed pattern, 8⅜".......**$15.00**

Brilliant, clear, jug, #1871, pressed pattern, 1-qt..........**$65.00**

Brilliant, clear, measuring cup, #1001, pressed pattern, Boston **$15.00**

Brilliant, clear, nappy, #1001, pressed pattern, 4".........**$6.00**

Brilliant, clear, tidbit set, #1871, pressed pattern, 3-pc..**$20.00**

Brilliant, clear, vase, #1001, pressed pattern, 9"..........**$17.00**

Candlelight, clear w/platinum band, bowl, #652, footed, 10" **$16.00**

Candlelight, clear w/platinum band, plate, #652, 8"......**$8.00**

Candlelight, clear w/platinum band, relish, #652, 2-part.**$15.00**

Caribbean, clear w/gray stem, bowl, #2808, 9"..........**$16.00**

Caribbean, clear w/gray stem, candy dish, #2808, 10".**$20.00**

Caribbean, clear w/gray stem, vase, #2808, 13"..........**$20.00**

Cellini, clear, claret, #6024, 12 Rib Regular Optic, 4-oz, 5¾" **$15.00**

Cellini, clear, goblet #6024, 12 Rib Regular Optic, 10-oz, 7⅛" **$10.00**

Cellini, clear, plate, #6024, plain, 7".....................**$8.00**

Century, clear, bowl, cereal; #2630, 6" **$20.00**

Century, clear, bowl, salad; #2630, 8½".................**$45.00**

Century, clear, comport, #2630, 4⅜"...................**$21.00**

Century, clear, ice bucket, #2630, metal handle, 4⅞"..**$60.00**

Century, clear, plate, #2630, 7"......................**$14.00**

Century, clear, tray, snack; #2630, 10½"................**$25.00**

Century, clear, tray, utility; #2630, handled, 9⅛" **$36.00**

Century, clear, tumbler, #2630, footed, 12-oz, 5⅞"......**$22.00**

Century, clear, vase, #2630, oval, 8½".................**$100.00**

Chalice, clear, goblet, #6059, 11-oz, 5⅜" **$13.00**

Chalice, clear, plate, #6059, 7" **$8.00**

Chateau, clear, sherbet, #6087, 6½-oz, 5⅞" **$5.00**

Coin Glass, amber or olive, ashtray, #1372, 7½" dia....**$28.00**

Coin Glass, amber or olive, bowl, #1372, 8", $50.00

Coin Glass, amber or olive, bowl, nappy; #1372, 4½" .**$35.00**

Coin Glass, amber or olive, cigarette urn, #1372, footed, 3⅜" **$18.50**

Coin Glass, amber or olive, decanter, #1372, w/stopper.**$110.00**

Coin Glass, amber or olive, plate, #1372, 8" **$22.00**

Coin Glass, amber or olive, sugar bowl, #1372, 5⅜" ...**$30.00**

Coin Glass, clear, ashtray, #1372, 10" **$25.00**

Coin Glass, clear, pitcher, #1372, 1-qt **$65.00**

Coin Glass, clear, plate, #1372, 8" **$18.00**

Coin Glass, clear, tumbler, juice; #1372, 9-oz, 3⅝" **$30.00**

Coin Glass, green, ruby or blue; ashtray, #1372, 7½"..**$75.00**

Coin Glass, green, ruby or blue; bowl, #1372, 8" **$135.00**

Coin Glass, green, ruby or blue; cake salver, #1372, 10" **$240.00**

Coin Glass, green, ruby or blue; candy dish, #1372, 6⅜"..**$105.00**

Coin Glass, green, ruby or blue; compote, #1372, footed, 8½"..**$135.00**

Coin Glass, green, ruby or blue; goblet, #1372, 10½-oz ...**$80.00**

Coin Glass, green, ruby or blue; pitcher, #1372, 1-qt.**$195.00**

Coin Glass, green, ruby or blue; sherbet, #1372, 9-oz, 5⅝"..**$50.00**

Colfax, clear, cordial, #6023, 1-oz, 3⅜".......................**$16.00**

Colfax, clear, goblet, #6023, 9-oz, 6⅜" **$12.50**

Colfax, clear, plate, #6023, 8" **$8.00**

Colonial Prism, clear, bowl, #2183, pressed pattern, footed..**$25.00**

Colonial Prism, clear, comport, #2183, pressed pattern, 5½"...**$14.00**

Colonial Prism, clear, dish, #2183, pressed pattern, oval, 7½"...**$10.00**

Colonial Prism, clear, ice tub, #2183, pressed pattern, 4" .**$20.00**

Colonial Prism, clear, nappy, #2183, pressed pattern, shallow, 8"...**$10.00**

Colonial Prism, clear, nappy, #2183, pressed pattern, 3¼"...**$6.00**

Colonial Prism, clear, pitcher, #2183, pressed pattern, ice lip, 3-qt..**$40.00**

Colonial Prism, clear, punch bowl, #2183, pressed pattern **$60.00**

Colony, clear, ashtray, #2412, 3½" **$12.00**

Colony, clear, bowl, cream soup; #2412, 5" **$43.00**

Colony, clear, bowl, fruit; #2412, footed, 10½"...........**$55.00**

Colony, clear, cake salver, #2412, 12" **$45.00**

Colony, clear, candy dish, #2412, 9⅝" **$48.00**

Colony, clear, goblet, #2412, 9-oz, 5⅛" **$18.00**

Colony, clear, nappy, #2412, 4½" dia **$10.00**

Colony, clear, plate, #2412, 8" **$8.00**

Colony, clear, relish, #2412, 2-part, rectangular, 7¼" ..**$16.00**

Contour, clear w/pink, bowl, #2638, square, 8½".......**$16.50**

Contour, clear w/pink, bowl, salad; #2666, 9"............**$18.00**

Contour, clear w/pink, cordial, #6060, 1-oz, 2⅞".......**$22.00**

Contour, clear w/pink, goblet, #6060, 10½-oz, 5⅞".....**$20.00**

Contour, clear w/pink, pitcher, #2666, 1-pt, 5¼".........**$26.00**

Contour, clear w/pink, plate, torte; #2666, 14"...........**$28.00**

Contour, clear w/pink, relish, #2666, 3-part, 10¾" **$16.00**

Coronet, clear, bowl, fruit; #2560, 13" **$19.00**

Coronet, clear, bowl, salad; #2560, 2-part **$23.00**

Coronet, clear, candlesticks, #2560, 4", pr..................**$20.00**

Coronet, clear, plate, torte; #2560, 14".........................**$25.00**

Coronet, clear, relish, #2560, 3-part, 10".....................**$17.00**

Courtship, clear, cocktail, #6051½, 3¼-oz, 3⅞"...........**$12.00**

Courtship, clear, plate, #6051½, 8".................................**$8.00**

Courtship, clear, sherbet, #6051½, 6½-oz, 4⅜"..............**$6.00**

Crystal Twist, clear, cordial, #6101, 1½-oz, 3⅛"...........**$12.00**

Crystal Twist, clear, plate, #6101, 7" **$8.00**

Crystal Twist, clear, tumbler, juice; #6101, footed, 6-oz, 5"...**$6.00**

Diana, clear, bowl, berry; #601, scalloped edge, 7" **$10.00**

Diana, clear, butter dish, #601, scalloped edge **$20.00**

Diana, clear, comport, #601, scalloped edge, 4".........**$10.00**

Diana, clear, salver, #601, scalloped edge, 10" **$35.00**

Drape, clear, bowl, #1300, footed, 8" **$20.00**

Drape, clear, bowl, fruit; #1300, 13" **$35.00**

Drape, clear, comport, #1300, 8" **$20.00**

Drape, clear, plate, #1300, 6" **$6.00**

Drape, clear, sherbet, #1300, footed **$8.00**

Edgewood Ware, clear, bowl, berry; #675, 8".............**$16.50**

Edgewood Ware, clear, butter dish, #675.....................**$44.00**

Edgewood Ware, clear, spooner, #675...........................**$20.00**

Elegance, clear, claret, #6064½, Narrow Rib Optic, 5¾-oz, 5¾"..**$10.00**

Elegance, clear, cocktail, seafood; #6064½, Narrow Rib Optic, 7¾-oz, 3⅝"..**$8.00**

Elegance, clear, goblet, #6064½, Narrow Rib Optic, 9¾-oz, 7"..**$11.00**

Essex, clear, bonbon, #1372..**$4.00**

Essex, clear, comport, #1372, 9".....................................**$15.00**

Essex, clear, nappy, #1372, 7" **$8.00**

Essex, clear, punch bowl, #1372, footed, 10"...............**$35.00**

Essex, clear, tumbler, #1372...**$12.00**

Fairfax, azure or orchid, baker, #2375, oval, 10½" **$75.00**

Fairfax, azure or orchid, cup, #2375, footed **$24.00**

Fairfax, azure or orchid, plate, canape; #2375 ....**$15.00**

Fairfax, clear, baker, #2375, oval, 9"..............................**$22.00**

Fairfax, clear, centerpiece, #2375, oval........................**$22.00**

Fairfax, clear, plate, dinner; #2375, 9" **$10.00**

Fairfax, clear, sauce boat, #2375 ....**$25.00**

Fairfax, rose or green, bowl, #2375, 8" dia **$42.00**

Fairfax, rose or green, bowl, cream soup; #2375, footed .**$30.00**

Fairfax, rose or green, comport, #2375, 7" **$65.00**

Fairfax, rose or green, plate, salad; #2375, 7" **$18.00**

Fairfax, topaz or gold tint, bonbon, #2375...................**$25.00**

Fairfax, topaz or gold tint, plate, grill; #2375, 10".......**$35.00**

Fairfax, topaz or gold tint, platter, #2375, oval, 12".....**$75.00**

Flemish, clear, celery dip, #1913, pressed pattern, lg..**$10.00**

Flemish, clear, jug, #1913, pressed pattern, ½-gal **$30.00**

Flemish, clear, nappy, #1913, pressed pattern, 4"..........**$6.00**

Flemish, clear, pickle jar, #1913, pressed pattern **$28.00**

Flemish, clear, sugar sifter, #1913, pressed pattern **$25.00**

Flemish, clear, toothpick holder, #1913, pressed pattern .**$15.00**

Flemish, clear, vase, #1913, pressed pattern, 8"...........**$12.00**

Frisco, clear, bowl, fruit; #1229, pressed pattern, 9"....**$35.00**

Frisco, clear, butter dish, #1229, pressed pattern.........**$50.00**

Frisco, clear, comport, #1229, pressed pattern, 8" **$12.00**

Frisco, clear, tumbler, #1229, pressed pattern.............**$16.00**

Glacier, clear, ashtray, #2510, acid etched, square **$6.00**

Glacier, clear, bowl, salad; #2510, acid etched, 13".....**$25.00**

Glacier, clear, candlesticks, #2510, acid etched, 3", pr ..**$25.00**

Glacier, clear, cocktail, #2510, acid etched, footed, 4-oz..**$8.00**

Glacier, clear, nappy, #2510, acid etched, flared.........**$15.00**

Glacier, clear, relish, #2510, acid etched, 4-part **$15.00**

Glacier, clear, tumbler, #2510, acid etched, footed, 13-oz **$10.00**

Glacier, clear, vase, #2510, acid etched, 6" **$25.00**

Glamour, clear w/onyx base, claret, #6103, 7½-oz, 5¾"..**$10.00**

Glamour, clear w/onyx base, plate, #6103, 8" **$8.00**

Golden Grail, clear w/encrusted gold band, sherbet, #644, 7¾-oz, 4¾" **$8.00**

Golden Grail, clear w/encrusted gold band, tumbler, juice; #644, footed, 4¾" **$11.00**

Golden Grail, crystal w/encrusted gold band, cordial, #644, 1¼-oz **$14.00**

Greenbrier, clear, cocktail, oyster; #6026, 16 Rib Regular Optic, 4-oz, 3⅝" **$9.00**

Greenbrier, clear, goblet, #6026, 16 Rib Regular Optic, 9-oz, 7⅝" **$12.50**

Greenbrier, clear, plate, #6026, 16 Rib Regular Optic, 8"...**$8.00**

Hartford, clear, bowl, berry; #501, pressed pattern, 5½"..**$12.50**

Hartford, clear, comport, #501, pressed pattern, 4½" ..**$15.00**

Hartford, clear, spooner, #501, pressed pattern...........**$29.00**

Hartford, clear, tumbler, #501, pressed pattern...........**$18.00**

Hermitage, amber, gold tint or green, bowl, #2449, shallow, 10" **$32.00**

Hermitage, amber, gold tint or green, goblet, #2449, 9-oz **$18.50**

Hermitage, amber, gold tint or green, sugar bowl (open), #2449, footed..**$12.50**

Hermitage, amber, gold tint or green, tumbler, #2449, 2-oz **$12.50**

Hermitage, clear, ashtray, #2449 ....**$10.00**

Hermitage, clear, comport, #2449, 6".......................**$18.00**

Hermitage, clear, relish, #2449, 2-part......................**$12.00**

Hermitage, topaz, claret, #2449, 4-oz.......................**$18.00**

Hermitage, topaz, cup, #2449, footed........................**$15.00**

Hermitage, topaz, relish, #2449, 3-part......................**$22.00**

Hermitage, topaz, tumbler, #2449, 5-oz......................**$15.00**

Holiday, clear, coaster, #2643, 4" **$4.00**

Holiday, clear, cocktail mixer, #2643, 30-oz **$25.00**

Illusion, clear, claret, #6111, 7½-oz, 6" **$8.00**

Illusion, clear, plate, #6111, 8" **$8.00**

Invitation, clear w/platinum band, bowl, #660, footed, 10" **$10.00**

Invitation, clear w/platinum band, relish, #660, 5-part..**$12.00**

Jamestown, clear, bowl, salad; #2719, 10"...................**$10.00**

Jamestown, clear, salver, #2719, 10" dia.....................**$35.00**

Jamestown, clear, tumbler, #2719, 12-oz, 5⅛".............**$15.00**

Jamestown, goblet, all colors other than ruby, #2719, 5¾", $12.00

Jamestown, ruby, bowl, dessert; #2719, 4½"................**$38.00**

Jamestown, ruby, relish, #2719, 2-part, 9⅛"................**$40.00**

Jamestown, ruby, sherbet, #2719, 6½-oz, 4¼".............**$16.00**

Jefferson, clear, cordial, #6104, 1½-oz, 5⅝"................**$15.00**

Jefferson, clear, plate, #6104, 8" **$8.00**

Kent, clear, bowl, #2424, 8" **$15.00**

Kent, clear, bowl, fruit; #2424, 11½"..........................**$25.00**

Kent, clear, candy dish, #2424 ....**$20.00**

Legacy, clear w/platinum band, goblet, #635, 11-oz ...**$12.00**

Legacy, clear w/platinum band, saucer, #635 ....**$3.00**

Legacy, clear w/platinum band, sherbet, #635, 7½-oz...**$8.00**

Lincoln, clear, bowl, #1861, pressed pattern, footed, 8".**$32.50**

Lincoln, clear, comport, #1861, pressed pattern, 4½" **$7.50**

Lincoln, clear, pitcher, #1861, pressed pattern, ½-gal..**$44.00**

Louise, clear, bowl, #1121, pressed pattern, footed, 7" .**$14.00**

Louise, clear, comport, #1121, pressed pattern, 4½" ...**$12.50**

Louise, clear, custard, #1121, pressed pattern...............**$6.00**

Louise, clear, nappy, #1121, pressed pattern, 6" **$6.00**

Louise, clear, tumbler, #1121, pressed pattern.............**$15.00**

Lucere, clear, bowl, #1515, pressed pattern, flared, footed, 8"...**$20.00**

Lucere, clear, cordial, #1515, pressed pattern **$10.00**

Lucere, clear, cracker jar, #1515, pressed pattern **$45.00**

Lucere, clear, vase, #1515, pressed pattern, 10"..........**$30.00**

Mademoiselle, clear, cocktail, #6033, 4-oz, 4¼" **$8.00**

Mademoiselle, clear, plate, #6003, 8"..........................**$8.00**

Mayfair, clear, bonbon, #2419, 2 handles...................**$12.50**

Mayfair, clear, plate, dinner; #2419, 10" **$22.00**

Mayfair, topaz, ebony or rose, comport, #2419, 6"......**$22.00**

Mayfair, topaz, ebony or rose, relish, #2419, 5-part **$24.00**

Mayfair, topaz, ebony or rose, saucer, #2419................**$4.50**

Moon Mist, clear w/silver mist stem, goblet, #684, 14-oz.**$12.00**

Moon Mist, clear w/silver mist stem, sherbet, #684, 10-oz.**$7.00**

Moon Ring, clear, cocktail, oyster; #6052, 4½-oz., 3⅞"..**$7.00**

Moon Ring, clear, goblet, #6052, 9¾-oz, 5⅞" **$10.00**

Moon Ring, clear, plate, #6052, 8" **$8.00**

Neo Classic, clear w/colored bowl, claret, #6011, 4½-oz..**$18.00**

Neo Classic, clear w/colored bowl, sherbet, #6011, 5½-oz **$10.00**

Neo Classic, clear w/colored bowl, tumbler, #6011, footed, 10-oz **$12.50**

Niagara, clear, bowl, berry; #793, 7" **$20.00**

Niagara, clear, cordial, #6026½, Niagara Optic, 1-oz, 3⅞" .**$14.00**

Niagara, clear, cruet, vinegar or oil; #793, plain stopper, ea..**$32.00**

Niagara, clear, nappy, #793, 4" **$12.00**

Niagara, clear, nappy, #793, 4½".................................**$14.00**

Niagara, clear, plate, #6026½, Niagara Optic, 7" **$5.00**

Old English, clear, bowl, #1460, footed, 10" **$22.00**

Old English, clear, comport, #1460, 4½"........................**$6.00**

Old English, clear, tumbler, #1460.............................**$16.00**

Patrician, clear, cordial, #6064, 1-oz, 3⅝" **$15.00**

Patrician, clear, goblet, #6064, 9¾-oz, 7" **$11.00**

Patrician, clear, plate, #6064, 8" **$6.00**

Pioneer, amber, comport, #2350, 8" **$12.00**

Pioneer, amber, plate, salad; #2350, 7" **$10.00**

Pioneer, amber, platter, #2350, oval, 15" **$25.00**

Pioneer, green, baker, #2350, oval, 10½" **$18.00**

Pioneer, green, bowl, fruit; #2350, 5" **$9.00**

Pioneer, green, plate, dinner; #2350, 10" **$18.00**

Prelude, clear, plate, #6071, 7" **$5.00**

Prelude, clear, sherbet, #6071, 7-oz, 4¾"........................**$6.00**

Priscilla, clear, bowl, berry; #676, pressed pattern, 8½"..**$27.50**

Priscilla, clear, nappy, #676, pressed pattern, 4½".......**$22.00**

Priscilla, clear, spooner, #676, pressed pattern.............**$21.00**

Puritan, clear, cruet, oil; #1432, pressed pattern, drop or cut stopper, 6-oz **$20.00**

Puritan, clear, sugar sifter, #1432, pressed pattern **$15.00**

Raleigh, clear, bonbon, #2574.....................................**$13.00**

Raleigh, clear, bowl, fruit; #2574, 13" **$19.00**

Raleigh, clear, candlesticks, #2574, 4", pr...................**$15.00**

Rambler, clear, nappy, #1827, pressed pattern, 8".......**$18.00**

Rambler, clear, vase, #1827, pressed pattern, 9"..........**$22.00**

Regal, clear, cruet, oil; #2000, pressed pattern, drop stopper, 8-oz **$25.00**

Regal, clear, goblet, #2000, pressed pattern, 11-oz......**$10.00**

Regal, clear, jug, #2000, pressed pattern, ice lip, ½-gal.**$35.00**

Regal, clear, sherbet, #2000, pressed pattern, footed, 5-oz..**$5.00**

Regal, clear, tray, condiment; #2000, pressed pattern, 5x7" **$15.00**

Regal, clear, tumbler, #2000, pressed pattern, footed..**$10.00**

Fountain Pens

Fountain pens have been made commercially since the 1880s. Today's collector usually prefer those from before 1950, but some of the later ones are collectible as well. Pens by major manufacturers are most desirable, especially Con-klin, Mont Blanc, Parker, Sheaffer, Swan, Wahl-Eversharp, and Waterman. Extra large and extra fancy pens, such as those with silver or gold overlays, filigrees, or mother-of-pearl, are at the top of most collectors' lists and can easily run into several hundreds of dollars, some even thousands. Unless the pen is especially nice and the price is right, avoid buying examples with cracks, missing parts, or other damage, all of which drastically affect value.

For more information, we recommend *The 1992 Official P.F.C. Pen Guide* by Cliff and Judy Lawrence.

Acme, No 6, hard red rubber, gold-filled trim, lever filler, 1925 ....**$200.00**

Aiken Lambert, No 3, hard black-chased rubber, nickel-plated trim, match filler, 1918 ....**$125.00**

Carter INX, No 2223, black w/gold-filled trim, lever filler, 1928 ....**$100.00**

Carter INX, No 5125, blue marble pattern, gold-filled trim, lever filler, 1929 ....**$225.00**

Carter INX Pearltex, red & black marble pattern, gold-filled trim, lever filler, 1930....................................**$250.00**

Chilton, cherry red, gold-filled trim, touchdown filler, 1937 ....**$350.00**

Conklin, No 2, hard black-chased rubber, gold-filled trim, lever filler, 1924 ....**$125.00**

Conklin Endura, black & gold marble pattern, gold-filled trim, lever filler, 1928..**$300.00**

Cronker Ink-Tite, hard black-chased rubber, 1918......**$90.00**

Eagle EP 315, marine green marble pattern, gold-filled trim, lever filler, 1932 ....**$100.00**

Eversharp, black w/gold-filled trim, lever filler, 1943 .**$60.00**

Eversharp Gold Seal Doric, black w/gold-filled trim, lever filler, 1931 ....**$285.00**

Eversharp Skyline, black w/gold-filled trim, lever filler, 1942..**$70.00**

Eversharp Standard Doric, emerald green, gold-filled trim, plunger filler, 1939..**$350.00**

Gold Medal, pearl & black marble pattern, gold-filled trim, lever filler, 1931 ....**$375.00**

John Holland, No 12, gold-filled mounted w/gold-filled trim, lever filler, 1940 ....**$250.00**

John Holland, No 71, hard black-chased rubber, gold-filled trim, hatchet filler, 1915....................................**$250.00**

LeBoeuf, gray & white marble pattern, gold-filled trim, lever filler, 1929 ....**$550.00**

Mont Blanc, No 126S, black w/gold-filled trim, button filler, 1932 ....**$285.00**

Mont Blanc, No 252, black w/gold-filled trim, piston filler, 1955 ....**$195.00**

Mont Blanc, No 324, black-lined pearl, gold-filled trim, button filler, 1934 ....**$350.00**

Moore, No 961C, hard black-lined rubber, gold-filled trim, lever filler, 1925 ....**$350.00**

Moore Pilgrim, No 2070R, gold-filled, lever filler, 1925.**$135.00**

Moore Servo, pearl & black, gold-filled trim, lever filler, 1933 ....**$100.00**

Moore 491C, maroon w/gold-filled trim, lever filler, 1925 ....**$260.00**

Parker, No 20, Lucky Curve in transparent Bakelite, gold-filled trim, 1916 ....**$300.00**

Parker, No 23½, Jack Knife Safety in black hard-chased rubber, nickel-plated trim, button filler, 1920...........**$130.00**

Parker, No 28, Lucky Curve in black hard-lined rubber, gold-filled trim, button filler, 1921 ....**$115.00**

Parker Blue Diamond Major Vacumatic, gold w/pearl stripes, gold-filled trim, vacuum filler, 1941........**$300.00**

Parker Duofold, brown & tan marble pattern, gold-filled trim, button filler, 1930s, $300.00

Parker Duofold Jr, black w/gold-filled trim, button filler, 1930 ....**$140.00**

Parker Duofold Jr, jade green, gold-filled trim, button filler, 1934 ....**$140.00**

Parker Duofold Sr, mandarin yellow, gold-filled trim, button filler, 1930...**$850.00**

Parker Junior Vacumatic, crystal w/gold-filled trim, vacuum filler, 1934..**$300.00**

Parker Lady Duofold, mandarin yellow, gold-filled trim, button filler, 1927 ....**$195.00**

Parker Slender Deluxe Challenger, green w/gold-filled trim, button filler, 1939......................................**$75.00**

Parker Slender Vacumatic, laminated burgundy pearl, gold-filled trim, vacuum filler, 1934 ....**$250.00**

Parker Standard Parkette, burgundy w/gold-filled trim, lever filler, 1936...**$70.00**

Parker 51, black w/Lustraloy cap, chrome-plated, 1951.**$60.00**

Pick Exceptional, No 2005, red w/gold-filled trim, lever filler, 1928...**$175.00**

Sanford Special, hard black-chased rubber, gold-filled trim, lever filler, 1919......................................**$55.00**

Sheaffer, black w/gold-filled trim, lever filler, 1933.....**$85.00**

Sheaffer, No 3-25 C, black w/gold-filled trim, lever filler, 1928 ....**$120.00**

Sheaffer, No 336RM, solid gold, lever filler, 1918......**$400.00**

Sheaffer, No 350, silver pearl stripes, nickel-plated trim, lever filler, 1935.......................................**$60.00**

Sheaffer, No 5-30, jade green, gold-filled trim, lever filler, 1931 ....**$125.00**

Sheaffer, No 875, hard black rubber, gold-filled trim, lever filler, 1921..**$400.00**

Sheaffer Admiral 52S, brown w/gold-filled trim, touchdown filler, 1950...**$45.00**

Sheaffer Lifetime, hard black-chased rubber, solid gold trim, lever filler, 1923 ....**$425.00**

Sheaffer Lifetime, No 1000, golden brown stripes, gold-filled trim, lever filler, 1938.............................**$125.00**

Sheaffer Lifetime Balance, jade green, gold-filled trim, lever filler, 1929.......................................**$350.00**

Sheaffer Lifetime Lady, No C73V, marine green, gold-filled trim, lever filler, 1936........................**$100.00**

Sheaffer PFM III Snorkel, green w/gold-filled trim, touchdown filler, 1959 ....**$200.00**

Sheaffer Signature Snorkel 121 SK-6, black w/14k band, gold-filled trim, touchdown filler, 1952..............**$175.00**

Sheaffer White Dot Triumph, No 1250, black w/gold-trim, plunger filler, 1948..**$125.00**

Sheaffer 20C, hard black-chased rubber, nickel-plated trim, lever filler, 1924 ....**$190.00**

Sheaffer 29MC, hard black rubber, solid gold trim, lever filler, 1924..**$225.00**

Swan, No 2, gold-filled, lever filler, 1922...................**$185.00**

Swan 44 ETN, black w/jade trim, gold-filled trim, lever filler, 1930...**$155.00**

Wahl, No 2, hard black-chased rubber, gold-filled trim, lever filler, 1925...**$65.00**

Wahl Tempoint, No 12, hard black-chased rubber, eye-drop filler, 1919..**$90.00**

Wahl Tempoint, No 75A, hard black-chased rubber, gold-filled trim, lever filler, 1919 ....**$250.00**

Waterman, black w/gold-filled trim, lever filler, 1940s, $95.00

Waterman, No 01855, hard red ripple rubber, gold-filled trim, lever filler, 1930....................................**$375.00**

Waterman, No 312, hard black-chased rubber, nickel-plated trim, twist filler, 1912.....................................**$140.00**

Waterman, No 41, hard black-chased rubber, gold-filled trim, twist filler, 1915....................................**$185.00**

Waterman, No 512, hard black-chased rubber, solid gold trim, eye-drop filler, 1915...................................**$250.00**

Waterman, No 52, hard black-chased rubber, nickel-plated trim, lever filler, 1922..**$95.00**

Waterman, No 55, hard black-chased rubber, nickel-plated trim, lever filler, 1924...**$225.00**

Waterman, No 61, hard black-chased rubber, twist filler, 1915 ....**$285.00**

Waterman, No 94, blue marble pattern, chrome-plated trim, lever filler, 1933 ....**$300.00**

Waterman Crusader, black w/metal cap, chrome-plated steel, lever filler, 1949..**$65.00**

Waterman Ideal, No 52½V, hard black-chased rubber, nickel-plated trim, lever filler, 1925 ....**$75.00**

Waterman 100 Years, jet w/gold-filled trim, lever filler, 1943..**$300.00**

Frames

There always seems to be a market for antique picture frames. Some that seem to sell especially well are the tiny ones that decorators like to group together (these may be made of silver, chrome, glass-bead mosaics, etc.), the large oak frames that are often decorated with gilded gesso reliefs, and the crossed-corner Victorians with the applied leaves.

Black paint w/floral design, embossed brass disks, 3¾" wide, 17x13"......................................**$325.00**

Brass, ornate border, metal back, 6x5"........................**$60.00**

Brass & copper, rope design around edge, round, easel back, 6¼"..**$60.00**

Cast iron, patriotic decoration w/eagle, swords, flags, drum & bugle, WWI era, 9½x6½".....................................**$85.00**

Celluloid, embossed ribbons & garlands, easel back, 4⅛x3¼"..**$25.00**

Chip-carved, worn red paint w/black strip, 4" molding, 18x21"..**$75.00**

Inlaid, light & dark wood, 2" wide, 15x11"...............**$100.00**

Oak, gesso, embossed flower decoration, 18x24".....**$125.00**

Pine w/gilt decor, molded, 1½" wide, 21x24"...........**$150.00**

Pine w/walnut inlaid heart, geometric & diamond design, 2½" wide, 10x8"...**$150.00**

Poplar, mortised, corner blocks, red finish, 1¾" wide, 17x14"...**$100.00**

Pyrographic oak leaves & acorns, 8" dia, $50.00

Sterling, etched flowers in corners, standing, 2x3"......**$75.00**

Walnut Victorian crisscross, carved leaves at corners, 22x18"...**$160.00**

Franciscan Dinnerware

Franciscan is a trade name of Gladding McBean, used on their dinnerware lines from the mid-thirties until it closed its Los Angeles-based plant in 1984. They were the first to market 'starter sets' (four place settings), a practice that today is commonplace.

Two of their earliest lines were El Patio (simply styled, made in bright solid colors) and Coronado (with swirled borders and pastel glazes). In the late thirties, they made the first of many hand-painted dinnerware lines. Some of the best known are Apple, Desert Rose, and Ivy. From 1941 to 1977, 'Masterpiece' (true porcelain) china was produced in more than 170 patterns.

Many marks were used, most included the Franciscan name. An 'F' in a square with 'Made in U.S.A.' below it dates from 1938, and a double-line script F was used in more recent years.

For further information, we recommend *The Collector's Encyclopedia of California Pottery* by Jack Chipman.

Apple, batter bowl, $125.00

Apple, bowl, cereal; footed, from $28 to **$32.00**
Apple, casserole, individual **$45.00**
Apple, chop plate, 14"...**$75.00**
Apple, creamer, regular...**$32.00**
Apple, plate, 8½", from $18 to **$22.00**
Cafe Royal, bowl, fruit; sm..**$9.00**
Cafe Royal, chop plate, 14"...**$56.00**
Cafe Royal, cup & saucer, demitasse; from $32 to **$48.00**
Cafe Royal, platter, 14½"..**$45.00**
Coronado, bowl, cereal..**$12.00**
Coronado, bowl, vegetable; oval.................................**$20.00**
Coronado, butter dish..**$45.00**
Coronado, casserole, w/lid..**$35.00**
Coronado, cup & saucer...**$12.00**
Coronado, nut cup, footed...**$16.00**
Coronado, plate, chop; 12"..**$25.00**
Coronado, plate, 8½"...**$12.00**
Coronado, sherbet **$10.00**
Daisy, bowl, cereal..**$8.00**
Daisy, bowl, vegetable; sm **$10.00**
Daisy, creamer, regular..**$13.00**
Daisy, platter, 12½"...**$32.00**
Desert Rose, bowl, divided oval, 10½x7"....................**$32.50**
Desert Rose, bowl, fruit; sm..**$12.00**
Desert Rose, bowl, rim soup; from $28 to **$38.00**
Desert Rose, compote, lg **$85.00**
Desert Rose, goblet, ceramic, minimum value............**$75.00**

Desert Rose, mixing bowls, (sm, $100.00; med, $125.00; lg, $150.00), 3-pc set, $375.00

Desert Rose, sugar bowl (open), individual; sm..........$75.00
El Patio, bowl, salad; 3-qt..........................$25.00
El Patio, cup.....................................$10.00
El Patio, cup, jumbo..............................$18.00
El Patio, plate, 10½"............................$15.00
El Patio, platter, 13".............................$18.00
El Patio, saucer....................................$4.00
El Patio, saucer, jumbo.............................$8.00
Forget-Me-Not, bowl, bouillon; lug handle, w/lid, sm, from $75 to...$95.00
Forget-Me-Not, plate, 9½", from $12 to............$18.00
Forget-Me-Not, platter, 12½"......................$45.00
Forget-Me-Not, salt & pepper shakers, sm, pr.....$24.00
Forget-Me-Not, tumbler, water; from $25 to........$32.00
Fresh Fruit, bowl, cereal.........................$16.50
Fresh Fruit, creamer & sugar bowl.................$50.00
Fresh Fruit, mug, 7-oz............................$25.00
Fresh Fruit, plate, dinner........................$18.00
Fresh Fruit, platter, 14".........................$45.00
Fresh Fruit, platter, 19½", from $250 to.........$295.00
Fresh Fruit, syrup pitcher, from $65 to...........$80.00
Ivy, cup & saucer, demitasse; from $45 to.........$65.00
Ivy, pickle dish, 10¼"............................$35.00
Ivy, plate, 6½", from $9 to.......................$12.00
Ivy, relish, 3-part, 11"..........................$65.00
Ivy, sugar bowl, w/lid, lg, from $32 to...........$45.00
Ivy, tumbler, juice; from $25 to..................$35.00
Meadow Rose, bowl, cereal.........................$16.50
Meadow Rose, bowl, fruit; sm......................$12.00
Meadow Rose, bowl, vegetable; sm..................$32.00
Meadow Rose, pitcher, milk........................$75.00
Meadow Rose, plate, 10½"..........................$22.00
Meadow Rose, plate, 9½", from $12 to..............$18.00
Meadow Rose, relish, 3-part, 11"..................$65.00
October, baking dish, 1½-qt......................$125.00
October, baking dish, 1-qt........................$95.00
October, bowl, cereal.............................$16.50
October, bowl, rim soup...........................$28.00
October, egg cup..................................$25.00
October, mug, 7-oz................................$22.00
October, pitcher, water...........................$95.00
October, plate, 9½"...............................$18.00
October, platter, 14".............................$65.00
Poppy, bowl, cereal...............................$24.00
Poppy, creamer, regular...........................$48.00
Poppy, cup & saucer, jumbo........................$75.00
Poppy, plate, 10½", from $22 to...................$30.00
Poppy, platter, 12½"..............................$68.00
Poppy, salt & pepper shakers, sm, pr..............$36.00
Starburst, butter dish............................$32.00
Starburst, coffeepot.............................$110.00
Starburst, cup & saucer............................$6.50
Starburst, mug, tall..............................$40.00
Starburst, plate, bread & butter...................$4.00
Starburst, plate, dinner...........................$9.00
Starburst, platter, 15"...........................$32.00
Starburst, relish tray, 3-part....................$27.00
Strawberry, bowl, fruit; sm.......................$12.00

Strawberry, coffeepot, from $95 to...............$125.00
Strawberry, creamer, regular......................$32.00
Strawberry, napkin ring, from $25 to..............$35.00
Strawberry, plate, grill; divided, 10¾", from $95 to...$125.00
Strawberry, salt & pepper shakers, tall, pr, from $45 to.$60.00
Strawberry, tray, 3-tier..........................$75.00

Starburst, bowl, divided vegetable, $18.00; Starburst, salt & pepper shakers, $16.00

Frankoma Pottery

This pottery has operated in Oklahoma since 1933, turning out dinnerware, figurines, novelties, vases, bicentennial plates and plaques, and political mugs in various lovely colors.

Their earliest mark was 'Frankoma' in small block letters; but when fire destroyed the pottery in 1938, all of the early seals were destroyed, so new ones had to be made. The new mark was similar, but slightly larger, and the 'O' (rather than being perfectly round) was elongated. Some of their early wares (1936-38) were marked with a 'pacing leopard'; these are treasured by collectors today. By the mid-1950s the mark was no longer impressed by hand but instead became part of the mold. Paper labels have been used since the late forties, and since 1942 nearly every item has had an impressed mold number.

In 1954, Frankoma began digging their clay from another area of the neighboring countryside. The early clay had been a light golden brown color; it was mined near the town of Ada, and collectors refer to this type of clay as 'Ada' to distinguish it from the red-firing Sapula clay that has been used since 1954.

Their glazes have varied over the years due in part to the change in the color of the clay, so with a knowledge of the marks and color variances, you can usually date a piece with a fair amount of accuracy. If you'd like to learn more, we recommend *Frankoma Pottery, Value Guide & More,* by Susan Cox.

Ashtray, Fish, #T-8, 1962-76, 7"....................................$20.00
Bean pot w/lid, Barrel, #97V..$35.00
Bookends, Charger Horse, #420, Ada clay, black onyx, pr $195.00
Bookends, seated figure (without base), signed Taylor #425, pr $750.00
Bottle vase, #V1, FE..$105.00
Bowl, Four-Leaf Clover, #223, 6" $10.00
Candle holders, double, #304, Ada clay, Desert Gold, pr..$35.00
Carafe, w/lid, any color..$25.00
Christmas card, Prayer for Peace, 1970 ....$25.00
Christmas card, Yellow Ribbon, 1980..........................$50.00
Christmas card, 1955-56, each.......................................$75.00

Ewer, #V-15, Prairie Green, 1983, 12", $75.00

Flower holder, Elephant, turquoise, #180, 3½"..........$150.00
Jewelry, Cacti pin, any glaze...$45.00
Lazy Susan, Wagon Wheel, #94FC, Woodland Moss...$65.00
Mask, Oriental woman, #133, 4¾" $100.00
Mug, Donkey, Centennial Red, 1976 ....$35.00
Mug, Elephant, Prairie Green..$45.00
Mug, Plainsman, #5CL, green, 12-oz.............................$6.00
Pitcher, Ada clay, Aztec, 2-qt $35.00
Pitcher, Wagon Wheel, #94-D, Ada clay, 2-qt.............$35.00
Plate, Bob White Quail, first Wildlife series, 1972.....$100.00
Plate, Buffalo, last Wildlife series, 1979.....................$70.00
Plate, Christmas, King of Kings, 1970 ....$90.00

Plate, Christmas, Wise Men Rejoice, 1982 ....$40.00
Salt & pepper shakers, pumas, Red Bud, 3", pr..........$50.00
Salt & pepper shakers, snails, #558-H, Ada clay, Desert Gold, pr..$12.50
Sculpture, Bucking Bronco, #121, no stepped base, early glaze, 5"..$175.00
Sculpture, Cocker Spaniel, 8½", any glaze $75.00
Sculpture, Greyhound, 6 petals on black base, 1983 reproduction, 14" $85.00
Sculpture, Pekingese, pot & leopard mark, 7¾"........$195.00

Sculpture, Puma, black, Ada clay, $85.00

Sculpture, Swan, Rosetone, miniature $50.00
Tray, oval, #36, 1955-64, 12" $45.00
Trivet, Spanish Iron, #3TR, square, 6" $12.00
Vase, Cactus, Red Bud, #4..$40.00
Vase, ringed cylinder, #72, 10½"..................................$12.50
Wall plaque, Peter Pan, marked SAI on reverse, 6".....$95.00
Wall pocket, acorn, green & brown, #190 ....$25.00
Wall pocket, boot, green, #133.....................................$25.00
Wall pocket, Phoebe, Ada clay, Prairie Green, #730, 7".$125.00

Fruit Jars

Did you know that we have Napoleon to thank for the invention of the fruit jar? History has it that it was because of a reward he offered to anyone who could come up with a palatable way of preserving food for him and his army during wartime. The money was claimed by a fellow by the name of Appert in 1812, whose winning ideas have been altered or copied more than 4,000 times since.

One of the more successful adaptations ever conceived was patented by John Mason on November 30, 1858. His jar wasn't perfect, but many years and several improvements later (after he'd sold the rights to a company who subsequently let them expire), the Ball Brothers picked it up and began to market them nationwide. They were made by the thousands and are very common today. Just remember that most of them date to the twentieth century (not to 1858, which is simply the patent date), and unless they're made in an uncommon color, they're worth very little. Most fruit jars are clear or aqua blue; other colors, for instance emerald green, amber, cobalt, milk glass, or black, are unusual. Values are based on condition, age, rarity, color, and special features.

Globe (on side), Pat May 25, 1886 (on lid), amber, 1-qt, $60.00

Anchor Mason's Patent (roped letters on anchor), clear, rare, 1-qt..$25.00

ARS (in fancy script), aqua, rare, 1-qt.....................$85.00

Atlas E-Z Seal, blue, 1-qt......................................$15.00

Atlas E-Z Seal, squatty shape, blue, rare, 1-pt............$18.00

Atlas Good Luck (T Boss Dimples), clear, ½-pt..........$18.00

Atlas HA E-Z Seal, clear, 1-pt $6.00

Atlas Jr Mason, clear, ½-pt....................................$18.00

Atlas Mason's Patent Nov 30th 1858, aqua..................$12.00

Bagley & Co Ltd Knottingley & London (on lid), light green, fluted, ½-pt...$15.00

Baker Bros & Co Baltimore, MD, aqua, wax sealer, 1-qt .$40.00

Ball (underlined) Ideal, (Fisher the Fisher Years 1941-1946 on side), clear, 1-qt......................................$50.00

Ball (underlined) Ideal, blue, ½-gal............................$12.00

Ball (underlined) Improved Ghost Mason, 1-pt...........$20.00

Ball (underlined) Special, blue, 1-qt...........................$8.00

Ball (underlined) The First Copper-Related Zinc Penny Blanks Nov 1981 Greenville...Tenn, clear, 1-pt.....$38.00

Ball Improved Mason's Patent 1858 (on 4 lines), aqua, 1-pt...$20.00

Ball Mason Patent, clear, 1-qt..................................$6.00

Ball Mason's Pat N Patent Nov 30th 1858, aqua, rare, 1-qt $38.00

Ball Perfect Mason (block letters), 1-qt $20.00

Ball Sure Seal Pat July 14 1908, blue, 1-qt..................$8.00

Bamberger's Mason Jar, blue, 1-pt............................$18.00

Boyd Perfect Mason, aqua, 1-qt $6.00

Brockway Sure Grip Mason, clear, 1-qt......................$4.00

Clark's Peerless (in circle), ½-gal $20.00

Cohansey (arched), aqua, ½-pt................................$100.00

Dallas (in small incised letters), brown, 1-qt...............$45.00

Decker's Iowana Mason City, Iowa, Pat'd July 14 1908, clear, 1-qt..$25.00

Dillon G Co Fairmont Ind (on base), green, wax sealer, 1-qt...$35.00

Drey Improved Everseal, clear, ½-gal.........................$12.00

Eagle (circled by patent dates), aqua, whittled lid, rare, 1qt...$128.00

Economy (Portland Ore on base), 1-qt.........................$4.00

Economy Sealer Pat'd Sept 15th 1885, aqua, wax sealer, 1-qt...$20.00

Empire, clear, ½-pt..$25.00

Everlasting (jar in flag), aqua, rare, ½-gal...................$22.00

Foster Sealfast, clear, 1-pt.....................................$3.00

Genuine Mason (in flag), light green, 1-pt..................$10.00

Geo D Brown & Co, clear, rare, 1-pt.........................$48.00

GJCo (in double lines), aqua, dome lid, rare, ½-gal....$48.00

Green Mountain (in frame), 1-qt..............................$15.00

H&R (on base), green, wax sealer, ½-gal....................$20.00

Haines 1 Improved March 1 1870, aqua, rare, 1-qt ...$100.00

Hawley Glass Co (Hawley PA on base), 1-qt..............$10.00

Imperial Pat April 20 1858, aqua, no closure, rare, ½-gal...$30.00

King (on banner below crown), clear, twin side clamps, 1-qt...$12.00

Knox (K in keystone) Mason, clear, zinc lid, 1-qt $5.00

L&W (front), aqua, rare, 1-qt.....................................$48.00

Leotric (in circle), aqua, 1-qt..................................$8.50

Lustre RE Tongue & Bros Inc Phila (in circle), aqua, 1-pt $14.00

Macomb Pottery Co Pat Jan 24 1899 Macomb, Ill (on base), white...$35.00

Mason (underlined w/loop), clear, 1-qt.......................$6.00

Mason CFJ Improved, aqua, midget $20.00

Mason's Cross Improved, aqua, 1-pt.........................$12.00

Mason's GCCo Patent Nov 30th 1858, aqua, 1-pt $14.00

Mason's Improved, #520/525, light emerald green, aqua insert, midget...$48.00

Mason's Improved (hourglass on reverse), aqua, midget ..$90.00

Mason's Improved (over cross), aqua, midget............$25.00

Mason's N Patent Nov 30th 1858, aqua, 1-qt $15.00

Mason's Patent 1858, #910/1010, sun-colored amethyst, screw lid, 1-qt..$16.00

Mason's Patent 1858 (ball in script on reverse), aqua, ½-gal..$15.00

Mason's SGCo Patent Nov 30th 1858, aqua, ½-gal $12.00

Mason's 1 Large Patent Nov 30th 1858, aqua, midget .$35.00

Mason's 15 (underlined) Patent Nov 30th 1858, aqua, ½-gal..$20.00

Midland Mason, clear, 1-qt......................................$6.00

National (in script), clear, ½-gal..............................$18.00

Ohio (small HI) Quality Mason, clear, 1-pt..................$8.50

Pacific Mason, clear, 1-qt.......................................$20.00

Patent Applied For (SK & Co around N in star on base), aqua, wax sealer, ½-gal $75.00

Peoria Pottery (on base), brown, 1-qt.......................$35.00

Presto Supreme, clear, ½-gal....................................$5.00

Quick Seal (in circle), blue, 1-qt...............................$3.00

Safe Seal Made in Canada, clear, ½-gal $6.00

Safety Valve (on base), clear, ½-pt............................$28.00

Sanford (on base) One Quart, clear, no band...............$6.00

Sealfast, clear, ½-pt...$8.00

Silicone Glass Co Pitts PA, aqua, 1-qt.......................$15.00

Smalley Nu-Seal Trademark, clear, ½-pt.....................$35.00

Smalley's Nu Seal (in diamonds), clear, 1-qt................$8.00

Standard (W McC & Co on reverse), aqua, wax sealer, 1-qt...$18.00

Swayzee's (fleur-de-lis) Improved Mason, aqua, ½-gal .**$12.00**
The Gem (hourglass on reverse), aqua, 1-qt **$15.00**
The Mason (The in tail of M), aqua, 1-qt **$10.00**
The Queen (circled by patent dates), aqua, rare, 1-qt...**$42.50**
The Whitney Mason Pat'd 1858, aqua, 1-qt.................**$20.00**
Trademark Banner Warranted, aqua, 1-qt....................**$12.00**
Victory (in shield on lid), 1-qt...**$5.00**
Victory 1925 (on lid) Reg'd, clear, ½-pt.......................**$15.00**
Wallaceburg Gem, clear, 1-pt..**$8.00**
Wears (in oval), aqua, 1-qt..**$12.00**
Weideman Boy Brand Cleveland, clear, 1-qt **$8.00**
Western Stoneware Co Monmouth Ill (on lid), white,
    1-pt..**$25.00**
Whiteall Tatum & Co, clear, rare, ½-gal **$50.00**
Wm Frank & Sons Pitts (on base), aqua, wax sealer,
    1-qt..**$28.00**

Fry Oven Glassware

First developed in 1920, Ovenglass was a breakthrough in cooking methods, allowing the housewife to cook and serve in the same dish. The glassware was advertised as 'iridescent pearl' in color; today we would call it opalescent. Some pieces were decorated with engraved designs, and these are more valuable. It carried one of several marks; most contained the 'Fry' name, and some included a patent number as well as a mold number. (Though these might be mistaken for the date of manufacture, they're not!)

A matching line of kitchenware was also made — platters, sundae dishes, reamers, etc. — but these were usually marked 'Not Heat Resistant Glass' in block letters.

The company was sold in 1934, but the glassware they made is being discovered by collectors who will cherish it and preserve it for years to come.

To learn more about this subject, we recommend *The Collector's Encyclopedia of Fry Glassware* by the H.C. Fry Glass Society and *Kitchen Glassware of the Depression Years* by Gene Florence.

Casserole, transparent green, #1938, 7", $80.00

Baker, apple or custard; Pearl, bowl shape w/thick banded
    rim, sm round base, 4¾"...**$15.00**
Baker, Pearl, straight-sided round shape w/thick rim, flat
    bottom, 6"...**$20.00**
Bean pot, Pearl, tall straight side w/rounded bottom, knob
    lid, 1-pt...**$45.00**
Bread baker, Pearl, rectangular w/thick rim & flat bottom,
    5"..**$55.00**
Cake plate, transparent cobalt blue, round w/recessed rim,
    3-footed **$85.00**
Casserole, Pearl w/green trim, oval, knob finial, flat bottom,
    7"..**$45.00**
Cream soup, Pearl, footed w/loop handles 5¼" **$45.00**
Cup & saucer, Pearl, #1969 ....**$40.00**
Grill plate, Rose, 3-part, 10½" **$40.00**

Measuring cup, #1933, 1-cup, $45.00

Pie plate, Pearl, in footed metal holder, engraved, 9½"..**$30.00**
Pitcher, milk; crystal w/transparent cobalt blue lid, 4-sided
    w/angled handle **$50.00**
Platter, Pearl, round w/flat rim, engraved design in center,
    17"..**$50.00**
Ramekin, Pearl, straight-sided w/thick rim, flat bottom,
    2½" **$30.00**
Reamer, transparent canary yellow, tall fluted sides w/loop
    handle, flat bottom **$250.00**
Reamer, transparent emerald green, fluted straight sides
    w/side spout & tab handle, flat bottom.................**$30.00**
Roaster, Pearl, oval w/domed lid, tab handles,
    7½x10x14"...**$150.00**
Rolling pin, crystal w/transparent cobalt blue handles..**$200.00**
Snack set, royal blue, plate w/cup rest, w/cup, 6x7" ..**$50.00**
Trivet, Pearl, 3-footed round shape, 8"........................**$15.00**
Vegetable dish, Pearl, round w/thick rim, divided, 9¾".**$30.00**

Fulper

Founded around the turn of the century, the Fulper Pottery entered into the art pottery market about 1909 and produced a considerable quantity of fine art ware vases, bowls, lamps, etc., many of which were styled in the Arts and Crafts tradition and glazed in outstanding color combinations and textures. Today these pieces are evaluated on the basis of form, size, and glaze. Most pieces are marked in ink under the glaze or with a paper label.

Bookends, open books, pr..**$300.00**
Bowl, blue-green w/semigloss drips on light matt pepper gray, 7½"..**$115.00**
Bowl, cat's-eye glaze, ribbed exterior, shaped edge, #472, 4x15"..**$260.00**
Bowl, centerpiece; glossy drip over matt oatmeal, marked, 5x11"..**$170.00**
Bowl, copper overlay, handled, 3"........................**$395.00**
Candlesticks, mustard to dark green crystalline, 16", pr.**$425.00**
Chamberstick, green gloss glaze w/blue highlights, 7" ..**$200.00**
Flower frog, green crystalline on brown crystalline base, 4"..**$150.00**
Flower frog, mushroom shape, green & gun-metal gray, 3" **$45.00**

Jug, blue crystalline on olive, 8", $375.00

Jug, musical; gun-metal crystalline on green flambe, 9½"..**$135.00**
Vase, #T25, cucumber crystalline, step-down shape w/Arts & Crafts handles, 7x9" **$325.00**
Vase, #661, butterscotch flambe, footed classical form, 12" **$475.00**
Vase, blue crystalline, vertical black mark, miniature, 4".**$150.00**
Vase, blue-green matt glaze, ink stamp, 7½" **$150.00**
Vase, bud; #018, blue & brown flambe on blue speckle, 5½", pr..**$275.00**
Vase, bud; brown w/blue flambe drip glaze over yellow, 7"..**$170.00**
Vase, copper dust, rim-to-width akimbo Deco handles, 5½"...**$325.00**
Vase, green crystalline, 3 lug handles, 7"...................**$295.00**
Vase, green crystalline drip glaze, hexagonal, 11" **$275.00**
Vase, mirror black, handled, horizontal mark, 7½" **$85.00**
Vase, olive, blue & gray flambe on speckled mustard, 5" .**$175.00**

Vase, purple, matt glaze, ink stamp, 6½" **$130.00**
Vase, purple matt glaze, early, 3½"............................**$75.00**
Vase, Rose matt glaze, vertical ink mark, 8" **$170.00**
Vase, roses in high relief on blue, marked, 6x6½"....**$180.00**
Vase, watermelon pink & green matt glaze, handled, ink stamp, 7½"..**$145.00**
Vase, wheat over mirror black, ink stamp, 7½".........**$150.00**
Vase, wisteria, mirror black, embossed mark, 6½"....**$120.00**
Wall pocket, double, mirror black, 3 handles, 6½x8"..**$235.00**

Vase, irridescent green streaks, 10½", $275.00

Furniture

A piece of furniture can often be difficult to date, since many 17th- and 18th-century styles have been reproduced. Even a piece made early in the 20th century now has enough age on it that it may be impossible for a novice to distinguish it from the antique. Even cabinetmakers have trouble identifying specific types of wood, since so much variation can occur within the same species; so although it is usually helpful to try to determine what kind of wood a piece has been made of, results are sometimes inconclusive. Construction methods are usually the best clues. Watch for evidence of 20th-century tools — automatic routers, lathes, carvers, and spray guns.

To learn about furniture and accessories from the twenties, thirties, and forties, we recommend *Furniture of the Depression Era* by Robert and Harriett Swedberg.

Armchair, carved hardwood frame w/red velvet upholstery, late 1920s, 39x31", $225.00

Armchair, barrel style, black leather upholstery tufted on sides & back, solid oak frame..............................**$225.00**

Armchair, child's, ladderback, old black repaint, worn cane seat, 25¼"..**$85.00**

Armchair, French style, carved frame w/green floral silk brocade upholstery, minor stains, 43"......................**$300.00**

Armchair, ladderback w/5 graduated slats, turned finials, rush seat, 44"...**$450.00**

Armchair, maple, ladderback w/4 arched slats, shaped arms, refinished, 46"...**$750.00**

Armchair, oak frame w/green crushed velvet upholstery, ornate crest w/center face, lion's head at end of armrests, 44"..**$575.00**

Armchair, Queen Anne, hardwood w/cherry finish, vase-shaped splat, new rush seat, scrolled arms, turned legs, 42½"..**$385.00**

Armchair, Windsor, spindle back, shaped arms w/turned arm posts, saddle seat, splayed legs w/bulbous turnings, 34½"..**$495.00**

Bed, day; curly maple w/walnut headboard, old mellow finish, upholstered cushion, 24x77"........................**$500.00**

Bed, day; English, walnut, carved & turned legs & posts, 67" long **$1,100.00**

Bed, day; old hickory, original caned fold-down back & seat, 74" long..**$475.00**

Bed, oak, wide paneled head & footboard, applied machine carvings, heavy crest, 76" headboard, 33" footboard..**$500.00**

Bed, poplar w/red & black grain paint, round rope side rails, 48", mattress size approx 69½x50½"...........**$600.00**

Bed, rope; maple w/curly head & footboards, turned posts, refinished, 46x53" **$550.00**

Bench, French style, carved frame w/tapestry-weave upholstered seat, 45"..**$400.00**

Bench, oak, splat back, shaped arms, 37x50x20"......**$400.00**

Bench, piano; oak, flat top, built-in adjustment for various heights, Standard Piano Bench Co, Chicago, 20½x25"..**$145.00**

Bench, settle; old blue repaint, half spindle back & shaped crest, scrolled arms, plank seat, turned legs, 72" long..**$900.00**

Bench, Windsor, poplar w/old dark paint & yellow striping, oblong top, splayed turned legs w/sm knob feet, 13¾" **$165.00**

Bookcase, oak, grotesques on stiles, 2-door, 59x30x17" .**$850.00**

Bookcase, oak, 2 doors w/brass pull & escutcheon, 5 shelves, top shelf reeded, apron forms into feet, 57½x36½" **$750.00**

Bookcase, oak, 4 stacked sections w/hinged glass doors, refinished..**$650.00**

Cabinet, china; French style, gilt w/hand-painted scenes, curved glass, 63x30" **$600.00**

Cabinet, china; oak, convex glass panels, claw feet, 63x45" **$1,100.00**

Cabinet, china; walnut veneer panels & drawer front, hardwood frame & base, 3 curly maple overlay designs, 1920s, 65" **$325.00**

Cabinet, curio; oak, Victorian, molding on crest & above base, 2 drawers, 71"..**$750.00**

Cabinet, china; crotch mahogany veneer on drawer & lower doors, convex glass on upper doors, 1930s, 67x36", $325.00

Cabinet, curio; 2 shelves & drawers, hand-painted flowers on cornice & drawers, 1930s, 66x19" **$475.00**

Cabinet, oak, moderate bow-front w/2 doors, 3 shelves, side posts form feet, 54x36".......................................**$485.00**

Cabinet, oak, Seller's, porcelain work surface & pull-down tambour door, 1920s, 70x41", $950.00

Candlestand, Chippendale, hardwood w/red repaint, round 1-board top, turned column, tripod base w/snake feet, 27½"..$700.00

Candlestand, Chippendale, maple, cutout ovolo corners, curled base, tripod base w/snake feet, turned column, 15¼"..$750.00

Candlestand, Country, cherry, 2-board top, turned column, tripod base, 28x18"..$200.00

Candlestand, Country Chippendale, birch, 1-board top, tripod base w/snake feet, 16x15"..$335.00

Candlestand, Country Hepplewhite, birch, 2-board top, tripod base, 30x22x15"..$385.00

Candlestand, wrought iron, tripod base w/twisted stem, adjustable arm w/2 brass sockets, early 1900s, 63".$300.00

Chair, Bentwood, curved & splayed back, Fischel Czeck Mrfer stamped under round seat, 34"..$65.00

Chair, child's; oak, 4-baluster back w/wide slat top, front stretcher, 29½"..$75.00

Chair, English Chippendale, mahogany, scroll back, slip seat, 37"..$275.00

Chair, ladder; oak, bird's-eye maple & walnut, iron & brass fixtures, opens into 4 steps, 37"..$60.00

Chair, side; Country, hardwood w/old dark brown finish, vase-shaped splat, worn rush seat, 36"..$125.00

Chair, side; European style, carved frame w/worn leather seat, 52"..$145.00

Chair, side; Hepplewhite style, mahogany, carved slats, upholstered seat, refinished, 36"..$95.00

Chair, side; maple w/worn rush seat, vase-shaped splat w/carved ears, turned legs w/tassel feet, refinished, 40½"..$275.00

Chair, side; Mission style, oak w/traces of green paint, banister back, original green fabric seat, 36"..$55.00

Chair, side; oak, hourglass shape splat w/pressed design in headpiece, quarter-sawn veneer seat, 3 front stretchers, 38"..$150.00

Chair, side; oak, loop back w/turned ball & button spindles, new cane seat, 2 front stretchers, 33"..$40.00

Chair, side; oak, slat back, restored caning, tapered legs, front & side stretchers, 32"..$200.00

Chair, side; oak, spindle back, upholstered seat, wide front stretcher w/3 turned stretchers on each side, 46"..$75.00

Chair, side; oak w/dark stain, vase-shaped splat w/applied shell medallion, pressed paper seat, 3 front stretchers, 33"..$95.00

Chair, side; Victorian style, oak w/new upholstery, applied pineapple carving on wide crest, 38½"..$225.00

Chair, side; Windsor, bamboo, old black repaint, age crack in seat, 33"..$95.00

Chair, side; Windsor, bow-back w/7 spindles, shaped seat, bamboo turnings, 'H' stretcher, dark finish, 34"...$150.00

Chair, side; Windsor, spindle back & shaped crest, saddle seat, splayed base w/bulbous turning, refinished, 37"..$385.00

Chair, vanity; diamond-matched satinwood veneer back, selected hardwood frame, floral upholstery, 1938, 32x25"..$95.00

Chair set, oak, pressed-carved back w/central splat & saddle seat, 4 for..$600.00

Chest, American Empire, mahogany, figured mahogany veneer, step-back top, 3 drawers, 40"..$425.00

Chest, American Empire, walnut & curly maple, 9 drawers, scroll feet & pilasters, 68"..$600.00

Chest, blanket; curly maple, square corner posts, paneled ends, replaced lid, 34"..$650.00

Chest, blanket; pine & poplar w/green repaint over blue, dovetailed case, applied lid moldings, bracket feet, 25"..$325.00

Chest, blanket; pine & poplar w/red & black grain paint, dovetailed case & lid, bracket feet, 22x35"..$550.00

Chest, blanket; poplar & walnut w/original red & black grain paint, w/till, 28x49x25"..$350.00

Chest, blanket; poplar w/worn red flame graining, dovetailed case, bracket feet & till, w/lid, 23½x36½".$385.00

Chest, cedar covered w/mohair upholstery, late 1930s, 19x36"..$225.00

Chest, Chippendale, cherry, 4 dovetailed & beaded drawers, repaired ogee feet, 35x40x21"..$2,650.00

Chest, Country, pine w/red stain, 5 graduated drawers, replaced bracket feet, refinished, 56"..$1,250.00

Chest, Country Empire, cherry, 4 dovetailed drawers, turned half columns, replaced pulls, 52"..$385.00

Chest, Country Hepplewhite, cherry, 4 dovetailed drawers, cut-out feet w/scrolled veneer apron, refinished, 39⅜"..$1,485.00

Chest, Country Sheraton, walnut, paneled sides, turned feet w/castors, 31x44x22"..$685.00

Chest, Hepplewhite, cherry, 5 overlapping dovetailed draws, replaced brass handles, French feet, refinished, 42¼"..$950.00

Chest, Hepplewhite-style, mahogany, inlay outlines on drawers & back rail, brass pulls, 1920s, 38x42", $425.00

Chest, miniature; walnut & cherry, 4 drawers w/porcelain knobs, short chamfered feet, 15"..$440.00

Chest, New England, pine w/red flame grain paint, 4 dove-tailed drawers w/replaced wood knobs, scrolled apron, 39¼" **$850.00**

Chest, oak w/incised lines, 3 drawers, straight apron, 32x40x28" **$235.00**

Chest, window seat; cedar w/plain walnut veneer top & sides, figured walnut veneer front & decorations, 1930s, 21x48", $225.00

Chiffonier, golden oak, adjustable beveled mirror held by serpentine posts, 2 sm drawers above 4 lg, brass pulls, 72" **$375.00**

Chiffonier, oak, plain & quarter-sawn, adjustable beveled mirror held by serpentine posts, 4 dovetailed drawers, 72" **$750.00**

Church pew, golden & dark stained oak finish, incised cross on each outside panel, 57" long **$195.00**

Commode, bird's-eye maple veneer & selected hardwoods, 3 drawers & 1 door w/brass pulls, 1920s **$275.00**

Commode, oak, sm splashboard w/narrow apron, bow-front drawer w/brass pulls, front ledge curved, 29" **$135.00**

Commode, oak, towel bar between 2 reeded posts w/ball finials, 3 drawers w/ornate brass pulls, bracket feet, 53x30" **$265.00**

Cupboard, corner; Country, poplar, 2 6-pane doors over 2 paneled doors, 2-pc, 79x55" **$775.00**

Cupboard, corner; mahogany w/12 panes of glass, 1930s, 71x32" **$525.00**

Cupboard, corner; walnut, 6-pane door over 3 drawers & 2 paneled doors, 87x56" **$1,250.00**

Cupboard, Country, pine, open top w/paneled door in base, butterfly shelves & molded cornice, mellow refinish, 81½" **$2,200.00**

Cupboard, Country, pine, 4 paneled doors, 2 drawers, simple tiered cornice, refinished **$750.00**

Cupboard, Country, poplar, 4 paneled doors, 3 drawers & pie shelf, cut-out feet, shaped apron, refinished, 90½" ...**$650.00**

Cupboard, linen press; English, oak w/inlay, 2 doors over 4 drawers, 2-pc, 72x42" **$650.00**

Cupboard, pewter; walnut, paneled door, open shelves, no cornice, 71x47" **$800.00**

Cupboard, Southern walnut w/poplar ends, step-back type w/pie shelf, 4 paneled doors, scalloped apron, refinished, 79" **$1,400.00**

Desk, Country, pine, open top w/2 drawers over slant lid, 1-board door, 57x24" **$700.00**

Desk, Country Chippendale, curly maple, slant front, 4 drawers, fitted interior, 42x36" **$4,800.00**

Desk, English Regency style, walnut w/vinyl top, 5 drawers, 30x51x28" **$275.00**

Desk, table type; bleached mahogany top, sides & drawer front, birch hardwood base, early 1940s, 30x36" .**$175.00**

Dresser, American Empire, mahogany w/flame graining, ogee mirror, 4 drawers, 75" **$8,500.00**

Footstool, curly maple w/red stain, lyre form **$300.00**

Footstool, pine, old reddish-brown paint, cut-out feet, 8¾x24½x8" **$135.00**

Footstool, walnut w/scrubbed finish, scalloped apron, cut-out feet, 9x16" **$300.00**

Hall tree, hardwood w/brass hooks, old finish, 72" ..**$150.00**

Love seat rocker, ladderback, new black & beige taped seat, refinished, 44" long..**$200.00**

Magazine stand, hard-wood w/hand-painted parrot motif, 2 pockets, 1920s, 22x15", $65.00

Parlor couch, dark stained oak frame & feet, reupholstered in brocade, 81" long **$425.00**

Pie safe, Country, poplar, 12 tin panels, 1 dovetailed drawer, 54x39x16½"...**$500.00**

Pie safe, Country, walnut, 12 punched tin panels, double door, 50x40x18" **$1,000.00**

Pie safe, yellow pine, 12 tin panels w/Masonic designs, tapered legs, worn finish, 51x41½" **$900.00**

Rocker, golden oak, shallow-pressed crest, flattened arrow-shaped spindles, reupholstered seat, 36" **$175.00**

Rocker, golden oak, spindle back w/pressed design on crest & tops of stiles, saddle seat, 2 front stretchers, 45" **$185.00**

Rocker, oak, fan-back w/spool-turned spindles, curved headpiece w/applied edge carvings, saddle-curved seat, 34" **$225.00**

Rocker, oak, straight crest over spindle back, curved arms & legs...**$250.00**

Rocker, oak, wide pressed headpiece w/ornate design, 7 spindles, bowed saddle seat, 35" **$185.00**

Rocker, oak & elm, pressed back w/6 spindles, saddle seat, posts under armrests, legs & stiles, 39" **$175.00**

Rocker, oak w/brocade upholstery, applied pineapple crest, swan-carved arm fronts, fluted seat apron, 41"...**$325.00**

Stand, bed; cherry, 1 nailed drawer, replaced 2-board top, refinished, 28x20x21"...**$300.00**

Stand, bed; cherry & poplar, 1 dovetailed drawer, replaced top, 38x19x16" $175.00

Stand, Country, cherry, poplar & curly maple, turned legs, 1-board top, dovetailed drawer w/glass pull, refinished, 29"...$300.00

Stand, Country, curly maple w/dark finish, square 1-board top, mortised apron, turned legs, 28½" $700.00

Stand, Country, pine & poplar w/salmon repaint & green striping, 2-board top, 2 dovetailed drawers, turned legs, 28½"...$200.00

Stand, Country, walnut, round 1-board tilt top, turned column, 4-part feet, 26¼x18" dia $200.00

Stand, Country Empire, walnut, applied ornaments on 1-board top & leg posts, 2 dovetailed drawers, refinished, 30"...$150.00

Stand, night; cherry, 2 paneled doors & 1 drawer w/brass pulls, ornate carved feet, 1930s, 28x22" $345.00

Stand, oak, round top over shaped base shelf, 4 turned splay legs...$250.00

Stand, poplar w/worn flame graining, 1-board top, 1 drawer w/brass pull, 28x20x20" $275.00

Stand, walnut w/figured veneer, checkerboard drop-leaf top, 29x17x18" $135.00

Stool, oak, round 2-board seat, heavy twisted wire base, 24x12" dia $95.00

Table, card; English Sheraton, mahogany w/ebony line inlay on apron, bamboo turned legs, 27x36" $150.00

Table, coffee; mahogany frame w/leather tooled cloverleaf-shaped top, 1930s, 19x28"...................................$165.00

Table, coffee; mahogany veneered w/acid-etched blue mirror top, late 1930s, 16x30"....................................$225.00

Table, dining; oak, lg pedestal w/claw & ball feet, some carving, round..$1,200.00

Table, dining; oak, lg pedestal w/4 cut-out scroll legs, round...$650.00

Table, dining; oak, pedestal w/4 paw ft, little carving, round $650.00

Table, dressing; Empire style, mahogany veneer, w/mirror, 28½x37¾x23" $165.00

Table, drop leaf; cherry, S-shaped end aprons w/bird's-eye veneer, 1 w/concealed drawer, turned legs, refinished $350.00

Table, drop leaf; Country Sheraton, cherry, 1 dovetailed drawer, refinished, 20x36x17"...............................$550.00

Table, drop leaf; Country Sheraton, cherry & birch, 2 drawers w/brass ring pulls, rope-carved legs, refinished, 28½"...$650.00

Table, drop leaf; Empire, cherry w/old finish, shaped leaves, 6 turned & reeded legs, minor age cracks, 29" ...$200.00

Table, drop leaf; mahogany, 1-board top, 5 drawers w/brass pulls, rope-carved legs & stretcher, 1920s, 30x25" .$325.00

Table, extension; plain-sliced round oak veneer top, quarter-sawed oak veneer apron & base, 1920s, 28x42" dia $375.00

Table, kitchen drop leaf; maple w/porcelain top, 1 drawer, Sellers, 1930s, 31x20x36".....................................$175.00

Table, library; English Regency, mahogany, spiral rope legs, 28x54"...$395.00

Table, library; Italian style, mahogany veneer, cabriole legs, 60½"...$250.00

Table, library; oak, colonial style, 2-board oval top, pillar base w/scrolled feet, 28x48" $395.00

Table, library; oak, lyre pillars & scroll feet, 1920s, 30x40"...$245.00

Table, occasional; hand-painted Oriental pagodas & peacock on octagonal top, wheel-type base, 1920s, 30x30", $265.00

Table, occasional; mahogany veneer top w/solid mahogany scalloped edge, hardwood tripod base, 1930s, 27x24" dia $165.00

Table, occasional; round tooled leather top w/hardwood tripod base, 1930s, 20x14" dia................................$175.00

Table, occasional; tilt top, white w/hand-painted flowers & gold-trimmed outline, 1920s, 27x23" dia.............$320.00

Table, tavern; Country Hepplewhite, hardwood, hickory & pine, 1-board top, 27x40x24" $500.00

Table, tavern; Queen Anne, maple & pine, stretcher base w/mortised & pinned apron, turned legs w/button feet, 24"..$2,500.00

Table, tea; Chippendale, mahogany, 1-board tilt top, snake feet, 35" dia $700.00

Table, tea; Country Hepplewhite, maple & cherry, tilt top, spade feet, refinished, 28x25" $500.00

Table, tea; English Chippendale, mahogany, round tilt top, turned column, tripod base w/snake feet, 28x27¼" dia $200.00

Table, tea; walnut, round 2-board top, turned column, tripod base w/spider legs, refinished, 28¾x26" dia $165.00

Table, work; Country Chippendale, walnut, 3-board top, beaded corners, refinished, 41x30"...........................$800.00

Table, work; Country Hepplewhite, pine, 3-board top, beveled edge drawer w/porcelain pull, tapered legs, refinished, 31" $450.00

Table, work; pine & birch w/old refinish, mortised & pinned apron, dovetailed drawer & board top, turned legs, 29¾"...$1,320.00

Table, work; poplar, 2-board top, 2 dovetailed drawers, turned legs, refinished, 29x55x32".......................$600.00

Table, writing; Empire, rosewood veneer w/inlay, brass feet, 29x28x16"...$650.00

Vanity, striped walnut veneer on top, sides & drawer fronts, zebra wood veneer between 4 drawers, round mirror, 1930s...$395.00

Wardrobe, yellow pine w/mellow refinish & traces of white paint, raised panel doors, molded cornice, bracket feet, 77"...$400.00

Wash stand, oak, sm mirror in lyre frame w/simple press carving, drawer over 2 doors, sm.......................$350.00

Wash stand, poplar & hardwoods, orig brown graining on yellow, 38x30x15"...$140.00

Games

Games from the 1870s to the 1970s and beyond are fun to collect. Many of the earlier games are beautifully lithographed. Some of their boxes were designed by well-known artists and illustrators. Many times these old games are appreciated more for their artwork than for their entertainment value. Some represent a historical event or a specific era in the social development of our country. Characters from the early days of radio, television, and movies have been featured in hundreds of games designed for children and adults alike.

If you're going to collect games, be sure that they're reasonably clean, free of water damage, and complete. Most have playing instructions printed inside the lid or on a separate piece of paper that include an inventory list. Check the contents, and remember that the condition of the box is very important too.

If you'd like to learn more about games, we recommend *Toys, Antique and Collectible,* by David Longest, *Toys of the Sixties* by Bill Bruegman, and *Schroeder's Collectible Toys, Antique to Modern.*

When sizes are listed with board game descriptions, they indicate the dimensions of the boxes.

See also TV Characters.

Across the Continent, metal trains, Parker Bros, 1952, VG+ .$35.00

Addams Family Cartoon, Milton Bradley, 1973, EX.....$28.00

Adventures of Rin-Tin-Tin, Transogram, 1955, G $35.00

Anagrams, MCL, 1900, EX $26.00

Animal Race, 6 lg animals, Milton Bradley, 1920s, EX..$85.00

Apple's Way, Milton Bradley, 1974, VG $25.00

As the World Turns, Transogram, 1957, EX $35.00

Assembly Line, Selchow & Righter, 1960s, EX+...........$35.00

Baretta, The Street Detective, Milton Bradley, 1976, M in EX box..$26.00

Barney Miller, complete, Parker Bros, 1976, EX.........$15.00

Batman, card game, Ideal, NM....................................$45.00

Batman, Milton Bradley, 1966, EX $35.00

Behind the 8-Ball, Selchow & Righter, 1960s, EX.......$18.00

Ben Casey MD, Transogram, 1961, EX.........................$22.00

Beverly Hillbillies, card game, Set Back, Milton Bradley, 1963, NMIB...$25.00

Black Beauty, Transogram, 1953, VG+ $22.00

Bonanza, rummy card game, Parker Bros, VG+ $35.00

Branded, Milton Bradley, 1950s, G $25.00

Camelot, Parker Bros, 1930, VG+ $26.00

Captain America, Milton Bradley, 1977, VG+.............$18.00

Captain Kangaroo, card game, Noah's Ark (Old Maid), complete, mid-1960s, EX..$15.00

Careers, Parker Bros, 1950s, F......................................$20.00

Charlie's Angels, Cheryl Ladd photo on box, Milton Bradley, 1978, NM $18.00

Crazy Clock, Ideal, 1960s, EX.......................................$65.00

Dark Shadows, Whitman, NM in EX box $25.00

Disney's Fantasyland, complete, 1958, EX $40.00

Disney World Fire Engine, card game, Russell, ca 1963, MIB...$45.00

Disneyland Monorail, Parker Bros, 1960s, NM.............$38.00

Disneyland Riverboat, complete, Parker Bros, 1965, EX .$20.00

Dragnet, target game, Badge 714 Triple Fire, complete, Knickerbocker, #643, 1955, NMIB $225.00

Easy Money, Milton Bradley, 1936, EX+......................$35.00

Eddie Cantor, Tell It to the Judge, Milton Bradley, 1930s, EX...$45.00

Fairies Cauldron (tiddley winks), Parker Bros, 1920s, VG+ .$28.00

Finance, Parker Bros, 1936, EX+ $35.00

Freddy Krueger, sealed, NOES, MIB............................$8.00

Game of India, Milton Bradley, 1910, 15x15", EX........$35.00

A-Team, Parker Bros, 1984, M in EX box, $10.00

GI Joe Combat Infantry Game, complete w/15 combat cards, GI Joe action figure & accessories, NM, $80.00

Gidget Fortune Telling, card came, Milton Bradley, 1960s, EX..$22.00

Gilligan's Island, New Adventures, 1974, NM............$31.00

Gomer Pyle, Transogram, 1961, EX.........................$35.00

Group Therapy, GT Associates, 1969, EX+ $28.00

Hee Haw Target Game, Milton Bradley, 1973, EX.......$28.00

Hickety Pickety, Parker Bros, 1930s, EX $28.00

Hitch Hiker, Whitman, 1937, EX.............................$135.00

Hollywood Squares, complete, Ideal, 1974, EX+ $8.00

Honeymooners, sealed, VIP Corp/TRS Inc, 1968, MIB.$15.00

Ilya Kuriakan, card game, Milton Bradley, 1960, ...$22.00

James Bond, Action Episode, EX+ $5.00

James Bond, Thunderball, Milton Bradley, 1970s, EX.$38.00

James Bond Secret Agent, Milton Bradley, 1960, EX...$22.00

Jetsons, Milton Bradley, 1985, EX $10.00

Jungle Book, Parker Bros, 1960, EX $20.00

Kukla & Ollie, Parker Bros, 1962, EX $32.00

Let's Make a Deal, Ideal, 1970s, EX........................$15.00

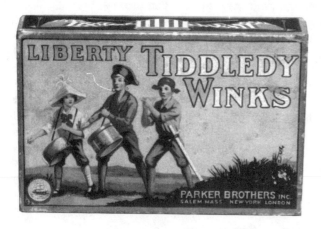

Liberty Tiddledy Winks, Parker Bros, EX, $35.00

Life of the Party, Rosebud, 1930s, EX..........................$35.00

Little Red Bushy Tail, Parker Bros, 1930, EX+ $38.00

M*A*S*H, Milton Bradley, 1981, EX.............................$15.00

M*A*S*H Trivia, #4154, Golden, 1984, NMIB $15.00

Man from UNCLE, card game, Milton Bradley, 1960, EX...$18.00

Merry Steeple Chase, Ottman, 1910, 8x8", EX..............$35.00

Mighty Mouse, Parker Bros, 1964, 10x20" box, EX......$50.00

Monopoly, Parker Bros, 1935 edition, EX $35.00

Munsters, card game, Milton Bradley, 1960s, EX+.......$45.00

Murder She Wrote, Warren, 1985, EX.......................$10.00

National Velvet, Transogram, 1961, EX $30.00

No Time For Sergeants, Ideal, 1964, VG+ $22.00

Nutty Mads' Bagatelle, Marx, 1960s, EX $32.00

O'Grady's Goat, Milton Bradley, 1959, EX $28.00

Official Basketball, Toy Creations, 1940, EX...............$48.00

Pathfinders, David Jansen, Milton Bradley, 1977, EX ..$24.00

Pebbles & Bamm-Bamm Turn Over Race, Transogram, 1962, MIB $115.00

Peter Pan, Transogram, 1950s, VG+ $24.00

Petticoat Junction, complete, Toycraft, 1963, EX.........$75.00

Pirate & the Traveler, Milton Bradley, 1950s, EX.........$15.00

Planet of the Apes, sealed, Milton Bradley, 1974, MIB..$55.00

Popeye, card game, complete set of 72, Parker Bros, EX...$5.00

Popeye Magnetic Fishing Game, Transogram, 1958, VG+.$33.00

Popeye Pinball, litho tin w/several characters, 1950s, MIP..$38.00

PT Boat 109, Ideal, 1960s, VG+ $22.00

Public Assistance, Hammerhead, 1980, M $45.00

Rambo, P-38 Dart Gun & Target, Arco, 1985, MOC $9.00

Red Ryder, Whitman, new platform, 1939, EX............$65.00

Risk, Parker Bros, wooden pieces, 1959, EX...............$30.00

Scooby Do, Where Are You?, Milton Bradley, 1973, EX...$22.00

Scooby Do & Scrappy Do, Haunted Castle, Milton Bradley, 1983, EX..$9.00

Shindig, Remco, 1965, EX......................................$35.00

Simpsons, Mystery of Life, Cardinal, NM....................$15.00

Snoopy Come Home, Milton Bradley, 1966, EX.........$20.00

Snuffy Smith Board Game, Milton Bradley, NM...........$45.00

Sorry, Parker Bros, 1950s, EX.................................$15.00

Spinette, Milton Bradley, 1930, EX...........................$22.00

Spingo & Whirlette, Transogram, $32.00

Spoof Card Game, Milton Bradley, 1930s, EX..............$25.00

Stop & Shop, All Fair, 1920s, EX..............................$55.00

Superman, card game, Ideal, NM..............................$45.00

Thinking Man's Golf, 3M, 1960s, EX..........................$22.00

Tiddle Tennis Jr, Schoenhut, 1930, EX......................$35.00

Tiny Tim, signed by Tiny, Parker Bros, 1960s, EX $55.00

Tom & Jerry, Milton Bradley, 1977, EX $15.00

Touring, Parker Bros, 1930, EX................................$22.00

Twenty-One, Lowell, 1950s, EX................................$28.00

Twiggy, Milton Bradley, EX.....................................$45.00

Uncle Wiggily, Parker Bros, 1967, MIB......................$35.00

Welcome Back Kotter, Milton Bradley, 1970s, EX.......$18.00

What's My Line, Lowell, 1950s, EX $35.00

Whoppee, card game, Milton Bradley, 1930s, EX........$24.00

Woody Woodpecker Travel Game, 1950s, NM...........$45.00

Yogi Bear, Milton Bradley, 1971, VG+ $18.00

Zip-Top, Deluxe, 1930s, EX $32.00

Gas Station Collectibles

Items used and/or sold by gas stations are included in this specialized area of advertising memorabilia. Collector interest is strong here, due to the crossover attraction of these items to both advertising fans and automobilia buffs as well. Over the past few years, there have been several large auctions in the east that featured gasoline-related material, much of which brought very respectable selling prices.

If you're interested in learning more about these types of collectibles, we recommend *Huxford's Collectible Advertising* by Sharon and Bob Huxford.

See also Ashtrays.

Air Meter, Arno, model 30 C #10050, red & silver cast iron, footed, 14x6", NM **$190.00**

Air pump, red, black & white painted metal, Air lettered vertically on base, crank handle on meter head, 51x9", NM ...**$475.00**

Atlas, Chevron Travel Club, USA-Canada, unused.......**$10.00**

Ballpoint pen, Amoco, retractable, red, white & black, EX...**$20.00**

Bank, Amoco 586, oil can shape w/3 gold bands at top, Amoco oval above 586, Special Piston & Valve Stem Oil, 3", NM **$10.00**

Bank, Atlas Battery, metal, EX **$22.00**

Bank, Esso, tanker truck, Save At Your Esso Dealer, red plastic, 1950s or 1960s, VG......................................**$40.00**

Banner, Amoco Winter Lubricants, oval snow-covered sign looms over silhouetted car, Your Car Needs..., cloth, 35x38", NM **$85.00**

Banner, Kendall Motor Oil, repeated white logos on red bands above & below red Kendall Motor Oil on white, 37x57", EX+ **$10.00**

Banner, Texaco, w/star logo, red & white on black, 29x42½", EX, $45.00

Blotter, Texaco Motor Oil, pictures early auto, driver & garage man, unused, 6x3½", EX **$10.00**

Booklet, Chevron, car care guide & lube chart, 1970, EX **$15.00**

Bookmark w/ruler, Richfield, features logo of all stations accepting company credit cards, EX......................**$6.00**

Calendar, Esso, 1953, May through December w/various scenes, 29½x16", EX **$30.00**

Calendar, Magnolia Maximum Mileage Gasoline, 1932, shows lg October page w/sm September & November below, 24x15", EX+..**$65.00**

Calendar, STP, 1965, early Indy cars surround winner's circle scene w/full pad below flanked by STP cans, VG+ **$40.00**

Calendar, Texaco, 1941, pictures woman above Texaco signs & symbols, January/February sheets, 19x9½", EX..**$20.00**

Calendar, Union Oil, 1941, Santa Claus cover, unused, EX..**$40.00**

Cap, Gulf, tan attendant's type w/black bill, round Gulf patch, EX **$110.00**

Cap, Texaco, winter style w/fur-type ear flaps & bill, logo patch on bill, EX+ **$80.00**

Car-care guide & lube chart, Chevron, 1970, EX **$15.00**

Chalkboard, Atlantic Motor Oil on panel above board, red, white & blue pressed board, 15x17", EX..............**$55.00**

Clock, neon, Quaker State Motor Oil, green & black numbers (1-12) & lettering on white, green metal frame, 21" dia, EX **$500.00**

Clock, Prestone, silver numbers (1-12) & lettering on blue metal, 10" dia, EX...**$40.00**

Clock, RPM Motor Oils, 3-9-12 & line marks around red & blue logo on white square cardboard face, metal frame, 16x16", G..**$100.00**

Clock, Texaco Motor Oil, star logo in center on white ground, glass lens w/metal rim, 14½" dia, EX **$425.00**

Coloring Book, Esso Happy Motoring, features 22 historic cities, unused, 1963, 8½x10¾", EX+.......................**$20.00**

Cup, Shell, folding plastic, NM...............................**$10.00**

Decal, Amalie Motor Oil, Push lettered above product can, 6x3½", NM **$18.00**

Dip-stick clip, Sinclair Oil, oil can shape, EX..............**$10.00**

Display, Anco Blades & Arms, features windshield wiper, 19x15", EX **$10.00**

Display, Firestone Battery Cables, hangs on wall, 8 hooks to hold cables, red & white, tin, 8x20", EX+..............**$40.00**

Display, Permalube Oil, demonstrates need for oil change, 7x6", VG **$150.00**

Display cabinet, Auto-Lite Spark Plugs, painted metal w/glass front, advertising marquee above, 29x13", VG+ **$45.00**

Display case, AC Spark Plugs, cylinder shape w/lg spark-plug graphic giving off rays over AC, 17", EX **$125.00**

Display for gas pump, Esso, embossed image of tiger's head & paws, plastic, 1960, 18x16x4", EX **$28.00**

Display rack, Goodyear Tires, tin, 1950s-60s, 25", NM ..**$80.00**

Display rack, Mobiloil SAE 50 Filpruf, holds 8 embossed glass bottles w/spouts, coiled handle, wire feet, 19x22x19", NM, $900.00

Display rack, Prestone Anti-Freeze, Nothing Else Like It, metal w/embossed cream lettering, 4-legged, 20x21x16", VG..$60.00

Display rack, Sunoco A To Z Lubrication, light-up, red, white & blue porcelain, 1920-30, 36x29", EX......$400.00

Display rack, Thermoid Fan Belts, wood panel w/advertising above 10 hooks, some soiling & scratches, EX.......$20.00

Gasoline pump nozzle, brass, w/box, 15" long, NM...$30.00

Globe, Atlantic Gasoline, Atlantic lettered on wide center band in red, white & blue, glass case, 16½", VG+.$150.00

Globe, Atlantic Imperial, emblem logo on round lens w/gill body, 13½" dia, EX body w/NM lens $395.00

Globe, Cities Service Oils, metal body w/clover-leaf logo on white lens, 1928, 15" dia, EX.............................$250.00

Globe, Essoline, 2-sided, Essloine lettered over circluar band, glass w/inserted metal band, 21x18x6", VG.........$115.00

Globe, Gulf, hull body, 13½" dia, EX+ $425.00

Globe, Kendall De Luxe, Kendall lettered above De Luxe in script, red-painted Capcolite body, 13½" dia, EX+ ..$205.00

Grease can, Amoco Motor Grease, logo above cream & black lettering, green background, pry lid, EX.....$15.00

Grease can, Phillips 66, ca 1940s logo, #1 size, EX.....$18.00

Map holder, Atlantic Flying A Maps, metal, red w/Flying A emblem above Maps lettered in black, 36x9", NM ..$95.00

Map holder, Calso Gasoline Road Maps, red-painted metal, 3-tier, 20x12½", EX, $95.00

Map holder, Cities Service Road Aids, dark green w/white lettering & logo on metal, 3-tier, 20x12½", VG $80.00

Mechanical pencil, Amoco American Gas, oil sample in end, Permalube Service, red, white & black, EX...........$25.00

Mug, Esso, the Esso tiger's face in orange, white & brown on milk glass, Anchor Hocking, 1970s, 3½", VG+ ..$8.00

Oil can, Air Chief Motor Oil, product name & plane on white, Guaranteed 100%... on red, screw lid & handle, 2-gal, VG..$80.00

Oil can, Harley-Davidson Motorcycles Genuine Oil, For Two Cycle Motors, emblem-type logo, 1-pt, EX $160.00

Oil can, Indian Motorcycle Oil, 3-banded w/Premium lettered in center on 'explosive'-type graphic, 1-qt, EX..$170.00

Oil can, Marathon Motor Oil, frontal view of 3 runners nearing finish line w/lettering above & below, handled, 2-gal, VG...$210.00

Oil can, Mobil Handy Oil, red Mobil horse logo, plastic spout, 4-oz, EX...$10.00

Oil can, Oilzum Medium Gas Engine Cylinder Oil, shows Oilzum man logo, 5-gal, VG+ $210.00

Oil can, Quaker Maid, waxed cardboard, 1-qt, some scratches $35.00

Oil can, Red Indian Aviation Motor Oil, Indian head in profile above lettering, 1-qt, 6½x4" dia, EX.............$400.00

Oil can, Star Zero-Flo Motor Oil, shows open touring car w/lettering above & below, overall rust w/minor dents, 2-gal $125.00

Oil Can, Texaco Home Lubricant, star logo w/illustration of house above lettering, tall squirt spout, 3-oz, 6", EX...$65.00

Oil can, Texaco Outboard Motor Oil, boat motor w/product name in green & red on white, screw lid, 1935-45, 1-qt, EX...$15.00

Oil can, Traffic Motor Oil, traffic light above product name, blue & white, pour spout & handle, 1939-52, 2-gal, EX $45.00

Oil can, Veedol Motor Oil, 5-qt, 9½x6½" dia, EX........$30.00

Oil can, Veedol 10-30 Motor Oil, flying A logo upper right of lettering, some denting w/scratches & rust, 5-qt....$40.00

Paperweight, Hood Tires, 2-sided die-cut tin litho figure of the Hood Tire man w/flag on square lead base, 4⅜", EX+ $475.00

Patch, features the Michelin man in blue & white w/gold trim, 3x3", EX...$3.00

Pencil clip, Standard Oil $8.00

Pocket lighter, Marathon logo, Zippo.........................$25.00

Pump, Valvoline Motor Oil, green w/black hose, round painted-tin sign above, 1925-40, 34", EX............$160.00

Pump plate, Amlico Regular Gasoline, Regular lettered on green band, Amlico... above & below, porcelain, 10" dia, EX $95.00

Pump sign, Atlantic White Flash, white & black on red, Atlantic above round White Flash logo, metal, 17x13", M $125.00

Pump sign, Dixie Gasoline, crossed Confederate flags above Dixie, blue & red on yellow, red border, porcelain, round, EX $170.00

Pump sign, Texaco, fireman's helmet & star logo w/product name above, red, gold & black porcelain, ca 1940, 12x8", NM..$150.00

Radio, Sinclair Dino Supreme Gasoline, red transistor type resembling modern pump, 4x2½", EX..................$40.00

Radio, white plastic rectangular shape w/2 front knobs, features AC Fire Ring Spark Plugs logo, Admiral, 6x10", EX...$120.00

Scrapper, Sweney Motor Oil, product name on wooden handle, 3½x2¼", EX..$20.00

Sign, Cities Service Motor Oil, flange, 2-sided, oil can right of Cities Service Oil Sold Here..., tin, 12x22", VG $165.00

Sign, Delco Batteries, Delco lettered vertically above encircled battery, orange background, tin, framed, 70x19", EX...$35.00

Sign, Dixie Motor Oil, counter-top, illuminated reverse-painted glass lens in metal case picturing oil can, 14", EX **$250.00**

Sign, Flying 'A' Service, embossed tin, red & white w/black accents, ca 1962-70, 40x56", NM, $400.00

Sign, Goodyear Tires, 2-sided, elongated diamond w/flag above winged foot flanked by Good & Year, porcelain, 31x53", EX **$40.00**

Sign, Sunoco, flange, 2-sided, Sunoco Charge Accounts Honored, black & white porcelain, 1950s-60s, 18x14", VG...**$80.00**

Sign, Union Gasoline, 2-sided, shield logo above Speed & Power, red & blue on white, 26x32", VG............**$175.00**

Thermometer, Bowes Seal Fast Radiator Chemicals, The Famous 500 Line, black & red on white-painted metal, 38½", EX **$100.00**

Thermometer, Champion Spark Plugs, spark plug shape, wood, 21x15", VG..**$425.00**

Thermometer, Havoline, free-standing painted cast-metal building representing 1933-34 World's Fair, 4½", EX.......**$150.00**

Thermometer, Standard Oil, enamel, EX......................**$25.00**

Thermometer, Texaco, painted metal, blue & red on white, bulb at left of Texaco lettered vertically, logo above, 24", EX..**$120.00**

Tie pin, brass-colored Goodyear figural blimp, EX.....**$15.00**

Geisha Girl China

During the decade before the turn of the century, Western interest in Oriental and Japanese artwork, home furnishings, and accessories had increased to the point that imports were unable to keep pace with demand. In the country of Japan, years of internal strife and the power struggle that resulted had diverted the interests of the feudal lords away from the fine porcelains that had been made there for centuries, and many of the great kilns had closed down. As a result, many tiny household kilns sprang up around the country, worked by both skilled artisans and common laborers, all trying to survive in a depressed economy.

The porcelain they designed to fill the needs of this market was decorated with scenes portraying the day-to-day life of the Japanese people. There were hundreds of different patterns, some simple and others very detailed, but common to each were the geishas. So popular was the ware with the American market that its import continued uninterrupted until WWII. Even after the war, some of the kilns were rebuilt, and a few pieces were manufactured during the Occupied Japan period.

Each piece of this porcelain has a border of a particular color. Some colors are connected with certain time periods, and collectors often use this as a method of dating their pieces. For instance, reds, maroon, cobalt blue, and light and nile green borders were early. Pine green, blue-green, and turquoise were used after about 1917 or so, and in the late 1920s and '30s, a light cobalt was popular. Some pieces from the Occupied era have a black border. Border colors are given directly after pattern names in our descriptions.

Even if you're not sure of the name of your pattern, you can use the following listings as a general guide. If you'd like to learn more about this porcelain and its many variations, we recommend *The Collector's Encyclopedia of Geisha Girl Porcelain* by Elyce Litts.

Basket vase, Bamboo Trellis, green & brown w/gold highlights, 8½" **$75.00**

Biscuit jar, Basket of Mums B, red w/gold highlights, melon ribs, 3-footed, $65.00

Bowl, berry; Chinese Coin, Washday reserve **$15.00**

Bowl, Garden Bench K, green w/gold highlights, 9-lobed, 2¼x8¾" **$75.00**

Bowl, master nut; Basket A, dark apple green, 9-lobed, 3-footed, 6" **$35.00**

Bowl, master nut; Ribbon Parasol, red-orange w/gold highlights **$20.00**

Bowl, Pointing D, red-orange w/gold buds, 5¼".........**$12.00**

Bowl, rice; Samurai Dance, red-orange w/gold highlights **$18.00**

Celery dish, Boat Festival, blue w/gold lacing, 13" **$32.00**

Chocolate pot, Battledore, ewer form, yellow-green, 9".**$85.00**

Chocolate pot, Battledore, yellow-green, ribbed conical body, 9½" **$65.00**

Cookie jar, Meeting B, cobalt & red w/gold highlights ..**$75.00**

Cup & saucer, chocolate; Garden Bench C, cobalt border **$15.00**

Cup & saucer, demitasse; Bamboo Trellis, red-orange w/gold buds **$12.00**

Cup & saucer, demitasse; Plum Blossom Branch, red-orange w/gold highlights **$20.00**

Dish, Slowpoke, pattern in reserve, red w/gold highlights, footed, 8" **$55.00**

Egg cup, Cherry Blossom Ikebana, red **$10.00**

Hair receiver, Bamboo Trellis, red-orange **$25.00**

Mint dish, Seamstress, floral shape, w/handles, 5½x4"..**$14.00**

Mustard jar, Gardening, blue-green w/red handles & finial..**$28.00**

Nappy, Mother & Daughter, dark turquoise w/gold highlights, lobed..**$35.00**

Plate, Battledore, red-orange, swirled w/scalloped rim, 6¼"...**$20.00**

Plate, Bird Cage, red-orange w/gold highlights, 6" **$12.00**

Plate, Visitor to the Court, blue w/gold highlights, Japan, 7¼" **$22.00**

Pot, demitasse; Fan D, pattern in reserve....................**$85.00**

Spooner, Vantine's Blue, scalloped edge, Vantine **$40.00**

Sugar bowl, Boy w/Scythe, cobalt w/gold highlights..**$18.00**

Sugar bowl, Mother & Daughter, red w/gold **$15.00**

Vase, Bamboo Trellis, red-orange, 4½", pr..................**$25.00**

GI Joe

The first GI Joe was introduced by Hasbro in 1964. He was 12" tall, and you could buy him with blond, auburn, black or brown hair in four basic variations: Action Sailor, Action Marine, Action Soldier, and Action Pilot. There was also a Black doll as well as representatives of many other nations. By 1967, Joe could talk, all the better to converse with the female nurse who was first issued that year. The Adventure Team series (1970 - 1976) included Black Adventurer, Air Adventurer, Talking Astronaut, Sea Adventurer, Talking Team Commander, Land Aventurer, and several variations. At this point, their hands were made of rubber, making it easier for them to hold onto the many guns, tools, and other various accessories that Hasbro had devised. Playsets, vehicles and articles of clothing completed the package, and there were kid-size items designed specifically for the kids themselves. The 12" dolls were discontinued by 1976.

Brought out by popular demand, Hasbro's 3¾" GI Joes hit the market in 1982. Needless to say, they were very well accepted. In fact, these smaller GI Joes are thought to be the most successful line of action figures ever made. Loose (removed from the original packaging) figures are very common, and even if you can locate the accessories that they

came out with, most are worth only about $3.00 to $10.00. It's the mint-in-package items that most interest collectors, and they pay a huge premium for the package. There's an extensive line of accessories that go along with the smaller line as well. Many more are listed in *Schroeder's Collectible Toys, Antique to Modern*, published by Collector Books.

12" Figures and Accessories

Figure, Shore Patrol, dark molded hair, complete w/accessories, #7612, 1967, EX, $250.00

Adventure Team Capture Copter, helicopter w/claws, pontoons, winch & net, EX in VG+ box....................**$100.00**

Adventure Team Sea Wolf Submarine, complete, EX in torn box..**$120.00**

Armband, Medic's, EX **$15.00**

Bayonet, Japanese soldier's, EX..................................**$75.00**

Bazooka, Green Beret's, w/2 shells, EX......................**$28.00**

Beret, French Soldier's, EX..**$50.00**

Boots, Crash Crew's, silver, EX **$6.00**

Combat set, complete w/first-aid pouch, trenching tool, mess kit, canteen & cover, pistol, belt & manual, MIP **$220.00**

Coveralls, Action Pilot's, orange, G..............................**$4.00**

Depth gauge, fits on wrist, EX....................................**$18.00**

Dog tag w/chain, Adventure Team's, plastic, EX........**$15.00**

Field phone, Air Police's, gray, EX **$45.00**

Figure, Action Marine, in dress uniform, molded auburn hair, replaced hat, broken trigger guard on rifle.........**$100.00**

Figure, Action Pilot, in orange jumpsuit & blue fatigue hat, molded hair, lightly worn paint on hair **$80.00**

Figure, Action Sailor, in work shirt & blue jeans, molded hair, EX **$75.00**

Figure, Adventure Team Set, Sky Dive to Danger outfit w/accessories, brown hair & beard, hard hands, papers & comic, EX **$130.00**

Figure, Astronaut, in space suit & helmet, gloves, boots, pack & tether cord, EX....................................**$145.00**

Figure, Combat Marine, in camouflage outfit, helmet, boots, cartridge belt, pack, grenades & flare gun, 1976, EX+ **$185.00**

Figure, Deep Freeze, in fur parka, gold pants & snow boots, w/sm pull sled, goggles & flare gun, molded hair, 1976, EX+ **$190.00**

Figure, Deep Sea Diver, auburn molded hair, missing gloves, o/w complete, NM **$150.00**

Figure, French Resistance Fighter, w/most accessories, missing rifle & medal, EX **$140.00**

Figure, Green Beret, complete accept for scarf, blond molded hair, EX+ **$190.00**

Figure, Land Adventurer, brown hair & beard, hard hands, no clothes or accessories..**$45.00**

Figure, Man of Action, in shirts, pants, hat & boots w/insignia & dog tag, hard hands, EX in VG+ box **$180.00**

Figure, Scuba Diver, 3-piece blk wet suit w/flippers, molded hair, EX..**$175.00**

Figure, Talking Adventure Team Commander, in outfit w/dog tags, gun & holster, flocked hair & beard, EX in VG box **$170.00**

Figure, Talking Man of Action, in original outfit, brown hair, no beard, working, VG+......................................**$70.00**

Flame thrower, Marine's, green, EX..........................**$25.00**

Flight suit, no helmet sticker, MIP **$120.00**

Hat, Air Cadet's, EX **$25.00**

Helmet, Air Police's, w/strap, EX...............................**$45.00**

Helmet, Navy Attack, blue, w/strap, EX......................**$35.00**

Jacket, Army Field, green, EX.....................................**$20.00**

Jet helicopter, Action Soldier's, green, Irwin, complete, EX **$120.00**

Jumpsuit, LSO, EX...**$25.00**

Mess kit (Action Series), w/sticker, MOC....................**$55.00**

Mine detector set, complete w/4 metal land mines, EX.....**$60.00**

Motorcycle w/sidecar, brown, Irwin, no decals, VG.**$125.00**

Outfit, High Voltage Escape, black jumpsuit w/silver set, face mask, wrist meter, wire cutters & warning sign, MIB.**$60.00**

Pants, Action Soldier MP #7525, Ike style, brown, EX..**$75.00**

Pants, Air Force Dress, snap needs repair, VG **$10.00**

Searchlight for jeep, EX **$15.00**

Shorts, Desert Patrol's, jeep driver, EX **$30.00**

Sleeping bag, no sticker, MOC....................................**$30.00**

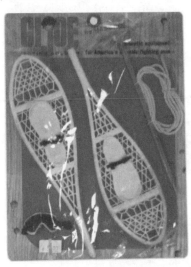

Snow gear, Action Soldier's, complete w/snow shoes, goggles, pick & rope, Hasbro, 1964, NMOC, $55.00

Stretcher, Medic's, NM **$30.00**

3¾" Figures and Accessories

Air Defense Pack, 1985, MOC....................................**$15.00**

Air Skiff, w/Zanzibar figure & ID card, EX.................**$18.00**

Attack Cannon, 1982, M on EX+ card.........................**$26.00**

Battle Force 2000 Vector (jet), M in sealed EX box.....**$24.00**

Bivoac Battle Station, 1983, EX **$6.00**

Cobra Battle Copter, w/Heli-Viper figure, pink, 1992, MOC **$7.00**

Cobra Jet Pack, 1987, MOC..**$11.00**

Cobra Rifle Range, 1984-85, MOC..............................**$10.00**

Conquest, Python Patrol, M in worn box.....................**$6.00**

Dreadnok Swampfire, 1986, MIB **$15.00**

Figure, Ace Driver, 1983, EX......................................**$15.00**

Figure, Ace Pilot, 1983, MOC.....................................**$25.00**

Figure, Alley Viper, 1989, MOC..................................**$18.00**

Figure, Backblast, 1989, MOC.....................................**$15.00**

Figure, Baroness, 1983, MOC......................................**$25.00**

Figure, Bazooka, 1983-85, MOC..................................**$25.00**

Figure, Blizzard, w/accessories, missing ID, 1988 ....**$5.00**

Figure, Buzzer, 1984, MOC...**$20.00**

Figure, Captain Grid Iron, 1990, MOC........................**$10.00**

Figure, Clutch, 1983, M in EX+ package **$35.00**

Figure, Cobra Pogo, 1987, EX......................................**$15.00**

Figure, Crimson Guard, w/accessories, 1985, $7.00

Figure, Cross Country, w/accessories, 1986, EX **$10.00**

Figure, Deep Six, 1988, MOC......................................**$10.00**

Figure, Dusty, 1985, MOC **$30.00**

Figure, Free Fall, 1990, MOC......................................**$12.00**

Figure, Gung Ho, 1986, MOC **$15.00**

Figure, Iceburg, 1986, MOC..**$25.00**

Figure, Jinx, 1987, MOC **$15.00**

Figure, Laser Voper, 1990, MOC.................................**$12.00**

Figure, Leatherneck, 1986, MOC.................................**$25.00**

Figure, Monkey Wrench, 1986, MOC **$20.00**

Figure, Monkey Wrench, no accessories, 1986, $6.00

Figure, Muskrat, 1988, MOC.......................................$18.00
Figure, Outback, 1987, MOC......................................$18.00
Figure, Q-Force Aqua Trooper, Action Force, MOC......$8.00
Figure, Scoop, 1989, MOC..$12.00
Figure, Sub-Zero, 1990, MOC....................................$12.00
Figure, Thunder, w/accessories, 1984, MOC.............$20.00
Figure, Tunnel Rat, w/accessories & ID, 1987, EX......$10.00
Figure, Whirlwind, Action Force, MOC.......................$30.00
Figure, Z Force Sapper, Action Force, MOC.................$8.00
Figure, Zarana, w/earrings, 1986, MOC.....................$25.00
Hydro Sled, MIB...$10.00
LCV Recon Sled, 1986, MOC.....................................$14.00
Machine Gun, Pac Rat, 1983, MIB.............................$10.00
Missle Defense Unit, 1984, MOC...............................$18.00
Mobile Command Center, MIB...................................$40.00
Pocket Patrol Pack, 1983, M on EX card.....................$10.00
Pulverizer, MIB..$10.00
Q-Force Battle Gear, Action Force, MOC.......................$3.00
Raider, NMIB..$25.00
Sea Lion, w/pilot, Action Force, MOC........................$35.00
Sky Hawk, 1989, MIB..$15.00
SWAT Assault Mission Gear, complete, 1993, M...........$8.00
Tiger Paw, Tiger Force, 1988, MOC............................$18.00

Glass Animals and Figurines

Nearly every glasshouse in America has produced beautiful models of animals and birds — many are still being made today. Heisey was one of the largest manufacturers, and some of their more expensive figures are valued at $2,000.00 and higher. As these companies closed, the molds were often bought by others who used them to press their own lines. Although some are marked so that you can identify the maker, many are not, and even advanced collectors are sometimes unable to make a positive identification.

Unless you're sure of what you're buying, we recommend you read *Glass Animals of the Depression Era* by Lee Garmon and Dick Spencer.

American Glass Co, Boxer Dog, lying down, crystal, 3⅞"..$60.00

American Glass Co, Jumping Horse, bookend, crystal, hollow base, 8"...$50.00
Cambridge, Draped Lady, flower frog, amber satin, 8½".$185.00
Cambridge, Frog, crystal satin...................................$25.00
Cambridge, Heron, flower frog, crystal, 12"..............$100.00
Cambridge, Lion, bookend, crystal, hollow base, 6x5"..$120.00
Cambridge, Pouter Pigeon, bookend, tail fanned out, crystal, hollow base, 5½"..$60.00
Cambridge, Rose Lady, flower frog, amber, 8½".......$185.00
Cambridge, Swan, ebony, 8½".................................$140.00
Cambridge, Swan, light emerald, 3"...........................$40.00
Co-Operative Flint Glass Co, Bear, 2-piece dish, amber, 1928...$325.00
Co-Operative Flint Glass Co, Elephant, 2-piece dish, ruby, 1930, rare, 4½x7"...$175.00
Duncan & Miller, Fat Goose, crystal, 6½"................$275.00
Duncan & Miller, Heron, crystal satin, 9"................$110.00
Duncan & Miller, Swan, open back, crystal w/engraved design, 7"...$70.00
Duncan & Miller, Sylvan Swan, open back, yellow opalescent, 7½"...$100.00
Duncan & Miller, Tropical Fish, ashtray, yellow opalescent, 3½" long..$50.00
Fenton, Butterfly, candle holder, souvenir issue, ruby carnival, 1989, 7½" long...$85.00
Fenton, Donkey, daisies on custard, #5125, 1978, 4½"..$40.00
Fenton, Elephant, flower bowl, teal blue, #1618, 1929, 6½x9"..$375.00
Fenton, September Morn Nymph, flower frog, milk glass, 6¼"...$120.00
Fostoria, Bird, candle holder, crystal, signed Fostoria, 1½".$12.50
Fostoria, Duckling, head back, amber, #2632/405, 1965-73, 2½"..$12.50
Fostoria, Hen, 2-piece dish, aqua, 1960s.................$120.00
Fostoria, Lyre, bookend, crystal, Regency pattern, #2601, 1942-44, 7"...$65.00
Fostoria, Mama Rabbit, light blue, 1973, 2⅛".............$30.00
Fostoria, Seal, topaz, #2531, 1935-36, 3⅞"..............$120.00
Fostoria, Standing Deer, blue, #2589, w/label, 1980, 4⅜".$40.00
Heisey, Chick, head up, crystal, 1948-49, 1x1⅜"........$70.00
Heisey, Colt, standing, crystal, 1940-52, 5x3"............$85.00
Heisey, Fish, match holder, crystal, 1944-46, 3x2¾"..$135.00
Heisey, Horse Head, bookend, crystal, 1937-55, 6⅞x6¼".$110.00
Heisey, Horse Head, stopper, crystal, 4"....................$65.00
Heisey, Piglet, crystal, ⅞x1½"...............................$100.00
Heisey, Ringneck Pheasant, crystal, 1942-53, 5x12"..$120.00

Heisey, Rooster, vase, crystal, 6½", $90.00

Heisey, Toy Horse Head, bookend, cobalt, 1985, 3½"..**$35.00**

Imperial, Baby Rabbit, head down, milk glass, 1977, 2⅜" **$25.00**

Imperial, Owl, 2-piece jar, Horizon Blue carnival w/glass eyes, 6½"..**$40.00**

Imperial, Scolding Bird, crystal & satin combination, signed Virginia B Evans, 1949, 5" **$165.00**

Imperial, Sittin' Duck, caramel slag, 1969-78, 4½".......**$40.00**

Imperial, Standing Piglet, Ultra Blue, made for Mirror Images, 1983, ⅞" **$40.00**

Imperial, Swan, caramel slag, 1969, 8" long................**$75.00**

Imperial, Tiger, paperweight, jade green, 1980, 8" long..**$80.00**

Imperial, Venus Rising, Ruby Sunset, ribbed base, made for Mirror Images, marked IG-81, 6½"........................**$25.00**

Indiana Glass Co, Walking Panther, blue, rare, 3x7".**$225.00**

KR Haley, Bird on Stump, crystal, 1945-60s, 6" **$15.00**

KR Haley, Horse & Rider (Lady Godiva), bookend, crystal, 6"..**$40.00**

KR Haley, Jumping Horse, crystal, hollow base, 1947, 7½x9½"..**$50.00**

LE Smith, Duck, ashtray, black glass, 6½" long...........**$10.00**

LE Smith, Fighting Cock, amberina, 1960s, 9".............**$40.00**

LE Smith, Fighting Cock, butterscotch w/brown to red swirls, 1960s, 9"..**$85.00**

LE Smith, Goose Girl, amber, 1950s, 8"......................**$55.00**

LE Smith, Queen Fish, aquarium, crystal, 15" long, $225.00

LE Smith, Sparrow, head up, crystal, 1950s, 3½".........**$15.00**

New Martinsville, Baby Bear, head turned, crystal, 3" ..**$50.00**

New Martinsville, Clipper Ship, bookends, crystal, 1938, 5¾", pr...**$85.00**

New Martinsville, Gazelle, leaping, crystal w/frosted base, 8¼"..**$55.00**

New Martinsville, Pelican, crystal, 8"..........................**$85.00**

New Martinsville, Seal, w/lg ball, crystal, 1938-51, 7" .**$65.00**

New Martinsville, Swan, ashtray/bowl, crystal w/cobalt head & neck, Janice S-Line, 1940-70, 6½" long..............**$30.00**

New Martinsville, Swan, console bowl, emerald w/crystal neck, 11" long...**$25.00**

Paden City, Rooster, head down, crystal, Barth Art, 8¾".**$85.00**

Paden City, Rooster (Chanticleer), pale blue, ca 1940, 9½"...**$175.00**

Viking, Angelfish, amber, #1301, 1957, 6½"................**$65.00**

Viking, Dog, orange, #1323, 1960s, 8"........................**$45.00**

Viking, Rooster, avocado, Epic Line, 1960s, 9½" **$45.00**

Viking, Seal, persimmon, 9¾" long..............................**$15.00**

Westmoreland, Bird in Flight, amber marigold, 4¼" long...**$25.00**

Westmoreland, Bulldog, Black Mist w/gold-painted collar & rhinestone eyes, ca 1910, 2½" **$35.00**

Westmoreland, Butterfly, Green Mist, 2½" wide.........**$22.00**

Westmoreland, Penguin on Ice Floe, Brandywine Blue Mist **$35.00**

Westmoreland, Robin, crystal, 1" ground bottom, 3¼" long...**$20.00**

Westmoreland, 1,000 Eye Turtle, 2-piece cigarette box, crystal w/flashed ruby, lavender & yellow, 7¾" long ..**$50.00**

Glass Knives

Popular during the Depression years, glass knives were made in many of the same colors as the glass dinnerware of the era — pink, green, light blue, crystal, and once in awhile even amber, forest green or white. Some were decorated by hand with flowers or fruit. Collectors will accept reground, resharpened blades as long as the original shape has been maintained. By their very nature, they were naturally prone to chipping, and mint condition examples are scarce.

Prices are volatile and inconsistent across the country. These knives were distributed more heavily throughout the West Coast (many were sold at the San Francisco World's Fair), so prices are generally lower there.

Aer-flo, crystal, decorative diamond design embossed on handle, 7½"..**$25.00**

Aer-flo, green, decorative diamond design embossed on handle, 7½"..**$30.00**

Block pattern on handle, green, 8¼"............................**$30.00**

Butter, amber handle w/crystal blade **$20.00**

Butter, crystal handle w/blue blade.............................**$25.00**

Candlewick, crystal, ornate handle, 8½" **$325.00**

Dagger, crystal, hand-painted flowers, 9¼"................**$75.00**

Dur-X, crystal, embossed flower & leaf design, 9¼", $22.00

Plain handle, green, 9¼"...**$30.00**

Rose Spray, crystal, 8½", MIB.....................................**$16.00**

Rose Spray, pink, 8½"..**$65.00**

Steel-ite, pink, sm checks & L imprinted on handle....**$65.00**

Stonex, green, ribs on handle, 8¼", minimum value...**$55.00**

Stonex, white, ribs on handle, 8¼".............................**$135.00**

Thumbguard, Westmoreland, crystal, hand-painted flowers & leaves on handle, 9¼"..**$25.00**

Thumbguard, Westmoreland, crystal, ribs on handle, 9¼" **$150.00**
Vitex, blue, embossed stars & diamond pattern on handle, 9¼" **$20.00**
Vitex, crystal, embossed stars & diamond pattern on handle, 8½" **$10.00**

Glass Shoes

Little shoes of glass were made as early as 1800. In 1886 a patent was issued to John E. Miller for his method of pressing a glass slipper. George Duncan pressed a shoe in the Daisy and Button pattern, and soon every glasshouse in the country was following in their 'footsteps.' Even today, contemporary glass artists like Boyd and Mosser are making shoes very much like the older ones. You'll find shoes of every color and design imaginable. Some have been used to convey an advertising message. There are ladies' slippers and men's house shoes, high-top shoes and roller skates, babies' booties, 'wooden' shoes, shoes with lids, and shoes that are bottles.

To learn more about them all, we recommend *Shoes of Glass* by Libby Yalom.

See also Boyd Crystal Art Glass; Degenhart.

Martini boot, transparent blue, Pilgrim Glass Co, 7½x5½" long, $26.00

Baby bootee, allover 'knitted' pattern w/scalloped top, blue, King Glass Co, 2⅝x3⅝" **$49.00**
Baby bootee, front w/horizontal ribbing, rest in diamond pattern, 2 flowers at opening, crystal, King Glass Co, 2⅝" **$30.00**
Boot, ribbed pattern w/tassel & hobnail top, opaque light-blue, slightly hollowed sole & heel **$80.00**
Boot jar on round base, embossed snowflake design on lid, amber, 1880s, 2¾x3" **$70.00**
Boot w/cuff & spur, purple & white slag, Challinor, Taylor & Co (?), ca 1890, 3¼x4" **$53.00**

Bow slipper, Daisy & Button pattern, amberina, Kanawha Glass Co **$10.00**
Cat slipper, Daisy pattern (no buttons), crystal, amber or blue, w/advertising, Columbia Glass Co, ca 1887, 3x5⅞" **$42.00**
High shoe w/buttons on right, horizontally ribbed, amber, ca 1880, 4¼x4¼" **$42.00**
Kitten slipper, Daisy & Button pattern, pink opalescent, #1995, Fenton **$12.50**
Kitten slipper, hobnail pattern, blue opalescent, Fenton **$25.00**
Large shoe, w/6 lace holes, amber w/clear solid heel, advertising on sole, George Duncan & Sons **$45.00**
Man's slipper pipe holder, plain dark amethyst, 1950s, 1½x5⅛" **$20.00**
Roller skate, Daisy & Button pattern, blue, Central Glass Co, 3¼x5⅜" **$65.00**
Sandal, Daisy & Button pattern w/plain sole, vaseline, Bryce Bros (?), 1880s, 1⅜x4½" **$38.00**
Shoe, Dutch type, crystal, Baccarat Co **$130.00**
Shoe on toboggan, pointed toe in Cane pattern, crystal, snowshoes embossed on front of toboggan, Bryce Bros, 2¼x5" **$110.00**

Goebel

The Hummelwork Porcelain Manufactory (the same company that produces Hummel figures) has been located in Rodental, in the area formerly referred to as West Germany since 1871. In addition to the Hummels, they're also famous for their Disney characters, Art Deco pieces, bird and animal figures, and two types of novelty kitchenware lines designed as Friar Tuck (brown-robed) monks and Cardinal (red-robed) monks.

The Goebel marks are indicative of particular time periods; see the section on Hummels for information concerning marks.

Ashtray, Friar Tuck, ZF43/II, stylized bee mark **$40.00**
Ashtray, poodle, RT167, full bee mark **$50.00**
Bank, Friar Tuck, SD29, stylized bee mark **$50.00**
Bookends, Dutch boy & girl kissing, XS116-A&B, crown mark, pr **$85.00**
Bottle, clown w/mandolin, white w/red details, crown mark **$75.00**
Cigarette holder, Friar Tuck, RX110, stylized bee mark.**$75.00**
Cookie jar, Friar Tuck, SD29, full bee mark, 9" **$350.00**
Creamer, orange elephant, S487, double crown mark, 6¼" **$75.00**
Decanter, Friar Tuck, KL95, 3-line mark **$50.00**
Egg cup, Friar Tuck, E95A, stylized bee mark **$20.00**
Egg timer, single; Cardinal Tuck, E104, 3-line mark..**$150.00**
Figurine, dwarf on pig, FX17, full bee mark **$75.00**
Figurine, elf on back w/knees up, fly on his nose, full bee mark, 4" **$85.00**
Figurine, Madonna bust, HM52, full bee mark **$65.00**
Figurine, nurse, FF320, 1971, 8" **$55.00**

Figurine, peacock, yellow, green & tan feathers on black, 1984, 16" long..$90.00

Figurine, Putting on the Dog, girl w/2 dachshunds, full bee mark, $75.00

Flask, Friar Tuck, KL97, stylized bee mark $60.00
Jug, Cardinal Tuck, S141-2/0, stylized bee mark, 2½" .$75.00
Jug, Cardinal Tuck, S141/1, stylized bee mark, 4".....$125.00
Jug, Friar Tuck, S141/0, full bee mark, 4" $30.00
Match holder & striker, Friar Tuck, RX104/B, stylized bee mark..$40.00
Mustard pot, Friar Tuck, S183, stylized bee mark, 3¾"..$20.00
Napkin ring, Friar Tuck, X98, stylized bee mark $50.00
Pitcher, bear head form, brown, full bee mark $40.00
Tray, Friar Tuck, T69, stylized bee mark......................$50.00
Wall pocket, umbrella, VP82, crown & bee mark, 7¼" .$75.00

Graniteware

Though it really wasn't as durable as it's name suggests, there's still lots of graniteware around today, though much of it is now in collections. You may even be able to find a bargain or two. The popularity of the 'country' look in home decorating and the exposure it's had in some of the leading decorating magazines has caused graniteware prices, especially on rare items, to soar in recent years.

It's made from a variety of metals coated with enameling of various colors, some solid, others swirled. It's the color, the form, and of course the condition that dictate value. Swirls of cobalt and white, purple and white, green and white, and brown and white are unusual, but even solid gray items such as a hanging salt box or a chamberstick can be expensive because pieces like those are rare. Decorated examples are uncommon — so are children's pieces and salesman's samples.

For further information, we recommend *The Collector's Encyclopedia of Graniteware, Colors, Shapes, and Values,* by Helen Greguire.

Bowl, lg black & white swirl, white interior, black trim, rare, 2½x6¾" dia, M..$135.00
Bowl, lg blue & white mottle, white interior, labeled US Standard Quality Enameled Ware..., 2½x6" dia, M......$100.00
Bowl, solid white w/cobalt trim, eyelet for hanging, labeled Tru-Blu Quality Enamelware..., 2½x7" dia, M.......$45.00
Bucket, lg green vein-type mottle on white, light green trim, wooden bail, marked Elite Austria Reg'd, 10x8½" dia, VG...$210.00

Bucket, 2-tone gray mottling, straight-sided w/bail handle, 4½x5", EX, $110.00

Candlestick, solid yellow, black trim & ring handle, 1¾x5¾" dia, G $65.00
Chamber pot, lg blue & white mottle, white interior w/sm blue flecks, riveted strap handle, 4¾x9⅜" dia, VG..........$125.00
Coaster/ashtray, solid green, orange or blue, labeled This Is a Suporcel Superior Porcelain..., rare, ¾x3" dia, M....$75.00
Coffee biggin, solid white w/cobalt trim, squatty shape, 8x4¾" dia, NM...$145.00
Coffee boiler, brown & white mottle (relish pattern), cobalt trim, riveted handle, wire bail, rare, 11x9" dia, NM $225.00
Coffeepot, lg blue & white swirl, white interior, black trim & handle, rare, 11x6½" dia, NM.............................$395.00
Coffeepot, lg cobalt & white swirl, white interior, black trim & wooden handle, ribbed design on lid, 10x6¾" dia, M...$365.00
Coffeepot, light blue & white med mottle, cobalt trim, metal thumb rest, riveted handle, rare, 5½x3½" dia, NM...$365.00
Cream can, deep sea green shading to moss green, white interior, riveted wire ears, rare, 7⅝x4" dia, NM ..$265.00

Cream can, grayish-blue & white med swirl, black trim & ears, wooden bail, w/lid, 7½x4" dia, VG **$265.00**

Cream can, med gray mottle, wire bail & lock cover, rare, 5¾x3¼" dia, NM....................**$225.00**

Cream can, solid blue w/white interior, darker blue trim & ears, wire bail, rare, 6x3" dia, M **$195.00**

Creamer, blue & white mottle (relish pattern), dark blue trim, riveted handle, rare, 4½x3⅝", NM.............**$225.00**

Creamer, lg blue & white mottle, bluish-gray interior, riveted handle, squatty shape, rare, 6x3¾", VG **$395.00**

Cup, blue & white med swirl, white interior, black trim & handle, rare, 2¾x3⅞", VG.....................**$90.00**

Cup, lg aqua & white swirl, white interior, cobalt trim, riveted strap handle, flared, rare, 2⅜x3¾" dia, G+..**$95.00**

Cup, lg white & light blue swirl, black trim & handle, 2x4⅜" dia, NM...............................**$65.00**

Cup, lg yellow & white mottle, black trim, ca 1960, 2x3⅛" dia, M...............................**$45.00**

Cup, lg yellow & white mottle, black trim, ca 1960, 2x3⅛" dia, M...............................**$45.00**

Cup, old red & white swirl, white interior, red trim & handle, rare, 2x2⅞" dia, NM....................**$525.00**

Cuspidor, blue & white med swirl, white interior, black trim, seamed body, 4¼x7¾" dia, VG **$265.00**

Cuspidor, sm blue & white mottle, white interior, 2-pc, 4½x9¾" dia, NM..............................**$265.00**

Custard cup, solid green w/cream interior, rare, 2¼x3⅝" dia, M.....................................**$55.00**

Custard cup, solid white w/green trim, marked Savory Ware, rare, 2⅜x4" dia, M.........................**$55.00**

Dipper, lg gray mottle, riveted handle, 2⅝x6⅛" dia, NM.....................................**$65.00**

Dish pan, lg blue & white mottle, white interior, dark blue trim & handles, oval, 16⅞x12¾", NM **$270.00**

Funnel, lg brown & white swirl, white interior, black trim & riveted handle, squatty shape, rare, 5½x6" dia, G+......**$260.00**

Funnel, lg lavender blue & white swirl, white interior, black trim & handle, squatty shape, rare, 5½x5⅞" dia, NM **$135.00**

Funnel, solid red w/white interior, applied handle & spout, 6¼"x5" dia, NM.......................**$40.00**

Griddle, lg gray mottle, embossed National, eyelet on handle for hanging, marked Royal Granite, Nesco, 11" dia, NM **$125.00**

Measure, blue shading to lighter blue, white interior, black trim & handle, riveted handle, rare, 4⅜x3¾" dia, G+.....**$185.00**

Measure, lg aqua & white swirl, white interior, cobalt trim, riveted spout & strap handle, rare, 5x3⅝" dia, NM....**$295.00**

Measure, sm blue & white mottle, white interior, light blue trim, riveted strap handle, rare, 2⅞x2¼" dia, VG..**$185.00**

Measure, solid cobalt w/white interior, riveted lip & strap handle, rare, 4¾x3½" dia, G+.................**$95.00**

Measuring cup, blue & white med mottle, white interior, graduated ¼-cup measurements, riveted handle, rare, VG......................................**$145.00**

Milk pan, old red & white swirl, white interior, blue trim, rare, 2x8⅜" dia, G+..............................**$400.00**

Milk pitcher, lg gray mottle, weld handle, squatty shape, 6⅞x4½" dia, NM.........................**$185.00**

Mold, lg cobalt & white swirl, white interior, fluted edge, rare, 2¼x4¾" dia, NM **$435.00**

Mug, deep sea green shading to moss green, white interior, riveted handle, rare, 2½x3⅜" dia, M.....................**$65.00**

Mug, lg blue & white mottle, white interior, black trim & handle, 2⅞x3⅜" dia, NM......................**$65.00**

Mug, lg brown & white swirl, white interior, cobalt trim, riveted handle, rare, 3⅛x4" dia, G+ **$135.00**

Mug, lg red & white swirl, white interior, black trim, ca 1950, 3½x3¾" dia.................................**$45.00**

Mug, sm blue & white mottle, white interior, cobalt trim, rare, 2⅞x2¾" dia, NM.............................**$95.00**

Pan, lg pink & white mottle, white interior, cobalt trim, marked HW 20, rare, 2¾x8¼" dia, VG **$235.00**

Pie plate, blue & white med mottle, white interior, 9⅝" dia, VG...**$55.00**

Pie plate, green & white mottle (relish pattern), white interior, cobalt trim, rare, 9½" dia, G+ **$25.00**

Pie plate, lg blue & white swirl, white interior, black trim, 10¾" dia, VG.................................**$95.00**

Pie plate, lg green & white swirl, white interior, dark blue trim, rare, 8¾" dia, NM **$110.00**

Pie plate, solid cream w/green trim, 10" dia, G+.........**$25.00**

Pitcher, lg dark gray mottle, ice lip, rare, 7½x5" dia, NM...**$225.00**

Pitcher, white w/blue flecks, black trim, Bakelite-type handle, marked GHC (General Housewares Co), 6½x5" dia, VG..**$70.00**

Plate, lg yellow & white mottle, black trim, ca 1950, 10¼" dia, M...**$40.00**

Platter, lg blue & white swirl, white interior, blue trim, Blue Diamond Ware, rare, oval, 10⅞x14", NM...........**$365.00**

Platter, lg multicolored swirl, rare, oval, 8⅝x13¾", G+.**$975.00**

Pudding pan, lg gray mottle, labeled La Fayette Quality Ware, Made in USA, Moore Enameling..., 2x5¼" dia, M **$50.00**

Pudding pan, solid red w/black trim, white interior, 2¾x9¾" dia, NM...**$30.00**

Sauce pan, lg blue & white mottle, white interior, black trim & rolled flat handle, convex, 5¼x10" dia, VG.....**$165.00**

Sauce pan, med gray mottle, riveted handle, rare, 7¾x6" dia, G+ **$135.00**

Sauce pan, solid yellow, white interior, black trim & handle, ca 1960, G+...**$20.00**

Saucer, light blue & white med mottle, white interior, rare, 1x4¾" dia, VG................................**$55.00**

Slop bucket, lg red & white mottle, white interior, red trim, riveted wire ears, wooden bail, rare, 12x9⅝" dia, NM..**$495.00**

Soup ladle, blue & white med swirl, white interior, black trim & handle, 13⅜x3⅝" dia, M............................**$75.00**

Spoon, lg green & white mottle, white bowl, rare, 9½", G+...**$115.00**

Strainer, lg gray mottle, 3 spatula feet, 8-sided, 3¾x8" dia, NM **$165.00**

Sugar bowl, lg red & white mottle, black trim, squatty shape, rare, ca 1980, 4½x4" dia, M **$65.00**

Sugar bowl, solid red w/black trim, ca 1970, 5x3⅜" dia, G+ **$30.00**

**Tea steeper, blue & white swirl w/black side handle, 6",
G, $365.00**

Tea strainer, lg blue & white splash-type mottle inside &
  out, screen bottom, rare, ¾x4" dia, NM $220.00
Tea strainer, solid white, fancy perforated bottom, triangular
  shape, rare, 4", NM $95.00
Teapot, brown shading to lighter brown, white interior, riv-
  eted handle, rare, 9x5¼" dia, NM $225.00
Teapot, cobalt w/white veins (chicken wire pattern), white
  interior, marked Patent, 5¾x4⅝" dia, VG............$135.00
Teapot, lg pink & white swirl, white interior, pink trim, rare,
  8½x4½" dia, VG $430.00
Teapot, lg yellow & white swirl, white interior, black trim,
  ca 1960, 8x5" dia, G+...$120.00
Teapot, med blue & white swirl, white interior, black trim & riv-
  eted handle, squatty shape, rare, 5¼x5" dia, NM......$265.00
Teapot, sm brown & white mottle, black trim, black
  wooden bail, 6¼x4⅛" dia, NM................................$75.00
Teapot, white w/band of violets, leaves & reddish-brown
  bands, metal trim, squatty shape, 7½x6" dia, NM.$295.00
Tureen, lg gray mottle, dome-shaped lid, oval, 10½x16¼",
  G+ $195.00
Wash basin, lg blue & white spatter, white interior, black
  trim, eyelet for hanging, 2⅝x10¼" dia, VG $125.00
Wash basin, lg blue & white swirl, white interior, cobalt trim,
  Blue Diamond Ware, rare, 3¼x11¾" dia, NM $165.00
Wash basin, white w/gold bands, black trim, labeled Lisk
  Warranted No 2..., brass eyelet for hanging, 12" dia,
  VG..$60.00

Griswold Cast-Iron Cooking Ware

Late in the 1800s, the Griswold company introduced a
line of cast iron cooking ware that was eventually distributed on a large scale nationwide. Today's collectors appreciate the variety of skillets, cornstick pans, Dutch ovens, and
griddles available to them, and many still enjoy using them
to cook with.

Several marks have been used, most contain the Griswold name, though some were marked simply 'Erie.'

If you intend to use your cast iron, you can clean it
safely by using any commercial oven cleaner. (Be sure to
re-season it before you cook in it.) A badly pitted, rusty
piece may leave you with no other recourse than to remove
what rust you can with a wire brush, paint the surface
black, and find an alternate use for it around the house. For
instance, you might use a kettle to hold a large floor plant
or some magazines. A small griddle or skillet would be
attractive as part of a wall display in a country kitchen.

For more information, we recommend *Griswold Cast
Collectibles* by Bill and Denise Harned.

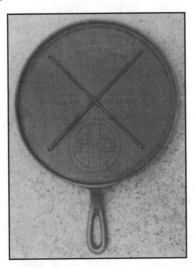

Griddle, #8/738, round, ca 1920, $65.00

Barbecue grill, #10 (base #180, grill #821, coal tray #820), footed
  kettle type, w/bail handle, 1922-57, 12¼" dia $110.00
Bread-stick pan, #23/955, ca 1930 ....$80.00
Broiler, #875, gridiron type, handled, 1891-1954, 10½"
  dia $125.00
Brownie pan, #19/966, 6 ball-shaped connected cups w/tab
  handles, 1900-30s, 1x4⅝x7¾"..............................$125.00
Cake mold, #866, lamb figure, MIB..........................$140.00
Candy mold, #100/#960 (lg), Hearts & Star, square hanger,
  1920-30s, ¼x7¾" dia $115.00
Cornbread pan, #21/961, ca 1930 ....$90.00
Corncake pan, #283, box reads Crisy Corn Cake Pan, 7
  corn-shaped molds, tab handles, 1x7⅝x14"........$120.00
Danish cake pan or egg poacher, #32/962, 7 molds,
  rimmed, 1935-57, 1¾x9¼" $55.00
Double boiler, #A702, wooden lid finial & handles w/hang
  rings, 1910-30s, 2-qt..$40.00
Dutch oven, #8, w/glass lid, bail holes in tab handles, 1930-
  40s, MIB..$130.00
Dutch oven, #8/2568, hinged lid, ribbed tab handles, 1940-
  50s, 4½-qt, 10⅛" dia..$55.00
Dutch oven, chuck wagon; #10/310, w/flanged lid, bail han-
  dle, 3-legged, 1951, 4⅞x10¾" dia $140.00

Fruit or lard press, #2, 1910-1938, 2-qt **$75.00**

Gem pan, French roll; #17/6140, 6 molds, tab handles, 1900-30s, 1x6x7½" **$75.00**

Gem pan, muffin or cupcake; #12/951, 11 cups, 1930, ¾x7⅜x10⅞" **$210.00**

Griddle, #110/203, round w/shallow rim & 2 pour spouts, handled, 1915-39, ¾x12¼" **$95.00**

Griddle, #18/1108, rectangular w/tab handles, 1939-57, 10x16¾" **$42.00**

Griddle, #6/606, round, 1928, 7¼" dia **$50.00**

Kettle, #7/789, bail handle, ring hanger, footed, 1900-30, 6-qt, 9½" dia **$65.00**

Kettle, #8/811X, flat bottom, bail handle, ring hanger, 1915, 1909-1940, 7-qt **$70.00**

Kettle, #9, bulged sides & flared rim, bail w/wooden handle, ring hanger, footed, 1880-1932, 9-qt, 10¾" dia ...**$130.00**

Kettle, table service; #00/100, footed w/tab handle & iron bail, 1930-40s, 2x4" **$38.00**

Munk pan, #33 G, round w/7 cups, handled, 1920s, 1¼x9½" dia **$135.00**

Pancake or plett pan; #34/2930A, round & flat w/short rim & pour spout, 7 shallow cups, handled, 1925-57, ⅝x9½" **$100.00**

Patty bowl, #871, rimmed bottom, 2 spouts, bail handle..**$100.00**

Patty irons, various designs, 1900-1957, shallow, w/handle, 3" dia, set of 2 ....**$35.00**

Popover pan, #10/949, 11 cups, 2 oval cutouts at each end, 1⅝x7⅝x11⅛" **$75.00**

Roaster, #3/643 (#644 lid), oval w/end handles, 1924-57, 4-qt, 3⅛x8x12¾" **$95.00**

Roaster trivet, #3, oval, 1920-40 ....**$30.00**

Safety cooker, #8/858, bail handle, flat bottom, 1919-40.**$75.00**

Sauce pot, #A703, wooden lid finial & handle w/hang ring, 1910-30s, 3-qt **$40.00**

Scotch bowl, #3/781, round w/square pour spout & bail handle, 1915, 4¼x10¼" dia...............................**$60.00**

Skillet, #7/721, marked Victor, 1910-30, 1⅝x9½" dia...**$65.00**

Skillet, #80/1103, marked Double Skillet Top, Erie PA USA w/Griswold trademark, $100.00

Skillet, all-in-one dinner; #8/1008, 3 compartments, 1930-39, 2¼x10½" **$75.00**

Skillet, breakfast; #666, square w/3 compartments, handled, 1934-51, 1x9" **$45.00**

Skillet, egg; #53, square w/handle at corner, 1⅛x4¾".**$30.00**

Skillet, fish; #15/1013, oval, w/lid, 1938-57, ¼x9¾x15"..**$140.00**

Skillet, hotel; #20, oval w/open handles at ends, w/lid, 1938-57 ....**$180.00**

Skillet, snack; #42, 1⅛x7½" **$75.00**

Steak platter, #951, oval w/raised flat rim, iron or chrome, 1933-57, 12x8⅜" **$55.00**

Trivet, #1740, lg star, 6" dia **$20.00**

Trivet, 5-legged round shape w/cut-out design, 7" dia .**$90.00**

Turk-head pan, #20/953, 11 2" dia cake molds on grid frame, 1910-30, 1x7½x10⅜" **$125.00**

Waffle iron, #11/363, square w/bail handle, low base, coiled handle, 1922-40s **$95.00**

Waffle iron, #708/708AF, Heart & Star pattern, bail handle on base, coiled handle on pan, 1920-51, 8" dia..**$132.00**

Waffle iron, #8, American, 1893-1901, 8½" pans **$140.00**

Wax ladle, side spout, marked Erie, 1880-1930s, 8" long..**$35.00**

Yankee bowl, #4/786, bail handle, ring hanger, 1897-1935 ....**$75.00**

Haeger Pottery

Many generations of the Haeger family have been associated with the ceramic industry. Starting out as a brickyard in 1871, the Haeger Company (Dundee, Illinois) progressed to include artware in their production line as early as 1914. That was only the beginning. In the thirties they began to make a line of commercial artware so successful that as a result a plant was built in Macomb, Illinois, devoted exclusively to its production.

Royal Haeger was their premium line. Its chief designer was Royal Arden Hickman, a talented artist and sculptor who worked in mediums other than pottery. For Haeger he designed a line of wonderfully stylized animals and birds, high-style vases, and human figures and masks with extremely fine details.

Paper labels were used extensively before the mid-thirties. Royal Haeger ware has an in-mold script mark, and their Flower Ware line (1954-1963) is marked 'RG' (Royal Garden).

For those wanting to learn more about this pottery, we recommend *Collecting Royal Haeger* by Lee Garmon and Doris Frizell.

Ashtray, boomerang shape, #1006, 12" long **$5.00**

Ashtray, hexagon shape, #138, 8½" long....................**$5.00**

Candle holder, cornucopia, #R-312, 5½", each **$6.00**

Candle holder, water lily shape, #3288, 4", each **$6.00**

Candy box, calla lily on lid, #R-431, 7½" dia **$10.00**

Cigarette box, w/lid, #R-560, 7" long........................**$10.00**

Console bowl, acanthus, white w/gold trim, #R-819, 14" long...**$10.00**

Console bowl, beaded, #R-476, 15" long.....................**$8.00**

Console bowl, lg swan shape, #R-955, 11".................**$20.00**
Console bowl, petal shape on base, #R-816, 10½" **$10.00**
Dish, sm leaf shape, #R-126A, 11" **$6.00**
Figurine, bucking bronco w/cowboy, #R-424, 13" **$45.00**
Figurine, crowing rooster, amber, 10" **$20.00**
Figurine, Egyptian cat (head down), #R-493, 6½"........**$15.00**
Figurine, elephant w/trunk up, #R-785, 5" **$12.00**
Figurine, garden girl sitting, #R-1179, 14" long............**$25.00**
Figurine, gypsy girl standing w/2 baskets, #R-1224, 16½"...**$65.00**
Figurine, pheasants, #R-130, 12" long, pr....................**$24.00**
Figurine, sleeping cocker pup, #R-776, 6" long...........**$15.00**
Figurine, tiger, black, #R-314X, 11"..............................**$45.00**
Flower frog, frog w/turned head, #R-838, 4½" **$20.00**
Flower holder, stylized colt, #R-235, 12" **$35.00**
Pitcher, trout form, #R-595, 8"......................................**$25.00**
Planter, black panther, #R-683, 18" long **$20.00**
Planter, double racing horses, #R-883, 11" long **$40.00**
Planter, fawn, #617, 6½" **$8.00**

Planter, mermaid, #505, 21" long, $45.00

Planter/bookend, moon fish, #1240, 10", each **$25.00**
Platter, fish shape, stoneware, #854-H, 18" long.........**$10.00**
Table lamp, bison on rectangular base, bird finial, #5171, 23½" **$50.00**
TV lamp, leaping gazelle, 13½".....................................**$25.00**
Vase, basket shape, #R-386, 12"..................................**$20.00**
Vase, gazelle head, #R-857, 12" **$20.00**
Vase, swan shape, #R-713, 8".......................................**$15.00**
Vase, trout form, #R-284, 7" **$18.00**
Vase/planter, double conch shell, #R-322, 7½"...........**$20.00**
Wall pocket, fluted fan shape in green art glaze.........**$25.00**
Wall pocket, Oriental lady seated, deep yellow trimmed in gold, 12" **$40.00**

Hall China Company

Hall China is still in production in East Liverpool, Ohio, where they have been located since around the turn of the century. They have produced literally hundreds of lines of kitchen and dinnerware items for both home and commercial use. Several of these in particular have become very collectible. They're especially famous for their teapots, some of which were shaped like automobiles, basketballs, donuts, and footballs. Each teapot was made in an assortment of colors, often trimmed in gold. Many were decaled to match their dinnerware lines. Some are quite rare, and collecting them all would be a real challenge.

During the 1950s, Eva Zeisel designed dinnerware shapes with a streamlined, ultra modern look. Her lines, Classic and Century, were used with various decals as the basis for several of Hall's dinnerware patterns. She also designed kitchenware lines with the same modern styling. They were called Casual Living and Tri-Tone. All her designs are popular with today's collectors.

Although some of the old kitchenware shapes and teapots are being produced today, you'll be able to tell them from the old pieces by the backstamp. To identify these new issues, Hall marks them with the shaped rectangular 'Hall' trademark they've used since the early 1970s.

For more information, we recommend *The Collector's Encyclopedia of Hall China* by Margaret and Kenn Whitmyer.

Acacia, bowl, Radiance, 9" **$20.00**
Acacia, stack set, Radiance...**$90.00**
Arizona, bowl, fruit; Tomorrow's Classic, 5¼" **$4.00**
Arizona, celery dish, Tomorrow's Classic, oval...........**$12.00**
Arizona, cup, Tomorrow's Classic..................................**$6.00**
Arizona, egg cup, Tomorrow's Classic **$22.00**
Arizona, plate, Tomorrow's Classic, 11" **$8.00**
Beauty, bean pot, New England, #4..........................**$100.00**
Blue Blossom, ball jug, #3..**$50.00**
Blue Blossom, bowl, Thick Rim, 6" **$30.00**
Blue Blossom, leftover, loop handle **$90.00**
Blue Blossom, shirred egg dish **$60.00**
Blue Bouquet, bowl, flat soup; D-style, 8½"................**$18.00**
Blue Bouquet, bowl, fruit; D-style, 5½".........................**$6.00**
Blue Bouquet, bowl, Radiance, 6" **$12.00**
Blue Bouquet, casserole, Radiance..............................**$32.00**
Blue Bouquet, creamer, Boston....................................**$11.00**
Blue Bouquet, drip jar, Thick Rim **$28.00**
Blue Bouquet, gravy boat, D-style................................**$28.00**

Blue Bouquet, jug, Radiance, $70.00

Blue Bouquet, plate, D-style, 8¼" $9.00
Blue Bouquet, platter, D-style, oval, 13¼" $26.00
Blue Bouquet, salt & pepper shakers, handled, pr......$30.00
Blue Bouquet, sugar bowl, Boston...............................$20.00
Blue Bouquet, teapot, Boston.....................................$125.00
Blue Floral, bowl, 7¾"...$12.00
Blue Floral, bowl, 9"...$16.00
Blue Garden, batter jug, Sundial................................$195.00
Blue Garden, canister, Radiance.................................$130.00
Blue Garden, casserole, #1, Sundial $40.00
Blue Garden, salt & pepper shakers, handled, pr $18.00
Blue Willow, bowl, finger; 4"..$25.00
Blue Willow, casserole, 7½" $60.00
Bouquet, baker (open), Tomorrow's Classic, 11-oz $15.00
Bouquet, bowl, onion soup; w/lid, Tomorrow's Classic .$32.00
Bouquet, bowl, soup; coupe shape, Tomorrow's Classic,
    9" $10.50
Bouquet, candlestick, Tomorrow's Classic, 8".............$35.00
Bouquet, cup & saucer, after dinner; Tomorrow's Clas-
    sic $12.00
Bouquet, egg cup, Tomorrow's Classic $26.00
Bouquet, plate, Tomorrow's Classic, 8".........................$6.50
Buckingham, butter dish, Tomorrow's Classic.............$65.00
Buckingham, casserole, Tomorrow's Classic, 2-qt.......$35.00
Buckingham, salt & pepper shakers, Tomorrow's Classic,
    pr $20.00
Cactus, bowl, Five Band, 6"..$16.00
Cactus, bowl, Radiance, 6"...$18.50
Cactus, creamer, Viking..$20.00
Cactus, salt & pepper shakers, handled, pr.................$35.00
Cameo Rose, bowl, cereal; tab handles, 6¼"................$8.00
Cameo Rose, bowl, vegetable; round, 9" $20.00
Cameo Rose, butter dish, ¼-lb $45.00
Cameo Rose, cup $8.00
Cameo Rose, plate, 8"..$8.00
Cameo Rose, platter, oval, 15½" $22.50
Cameo Rose, teapot, 8-cup $55.00
Caprice, bowl, cereal; Tomorrow's Classic....................$5.50
Caprice, bowl, fruit; footed, Tomorrow's Classic, lg....$25.00
Caprice, casserole, Tomorrow's Classic, 1¼-qt............$20.00
Caprice, cup, Tomorrow's Classic $5.00
Caprice, plate, Tomorrow's Classic, 11".......................$11.00
Carrot/Golden Carrot, bowl, batter; Five Band............$55.00
Carrot/Golden Carrot, bowl, Radiance, 10".................$38.00
Clover/Golden Clover, casserole, Radiance $40.00
Clover/Golden Clover, jug, #5, Radiance.....................$35.00
Crocus, ball jug, #3 ....$85.00
Crocus, bowl, flat soup; D-style, 8½"...........................$20.00
Crocus, bowl, Radiance, 7½"...$16.50
Crocus, coffeepot, w/glass dripper, Five Band $55.00
Crocus, creamer, Meltdown...$38.00
Crocus, custard...$12.50
Crocus, gravy boat, D-style $28.00
Crocus, mug, flagon style $45.00
Crocus, plate, D-style, 9" $14.00
Crocus, platter, D-style, oval, 13¼" $28.00
Crocus, saucer, St Denis $9.00
Crocus, stack set, Radiance $140.00

Crocus, tray, metal, oval..$24.00
Eggshell, bowl, Blue Dot, Thin Rim, 7¼".....................$18.00
Eggshell, bowl, salad; Red or Green Dot, 8¾"............$20.00
Eggshell, mustard, Red or Green Dot...........................$32.00
Fantasy, ball jug, #2...$115.00

Fantasy, batter jug, 5½x10½", $250.00

Fantasy, bean pot, #4, New England..........................$115.00
Fantasy, bowl, cereal; Tomorrow's Classic, 6" $6.00
Fantasy, butter dish, Tomorrow's Classic $50.00
Fantasy, casserole, Tomorrow's Classic, 2-qt $25.00
Fantasy, custard, Thick Rim..$16.50
Fantasy, platter, Tomorrow's Classic, 11"....................$11.00
Fantasy, vinegar cruet, Tomorrow's Classic $24.00
Fern, bowl, soup; Century, 8" $6.50
Fern, bowl, vegetable; Century, 10½"..........................$15.00
Fern, casserole, Century $22.00
Fern, cup, Century $4.50
Fern, jug, Century $12.00
Fern, plate, Century, 6" $2.50
Five Band, bowl, Cadet Blue, 7¼" $10.00
Five Band, bowl, red/cobalt, 6" $11.00
Five Band, casserole, red/cobalt, 8"............................$32.00
Five Band, cookie jar, red/cobalt..................................$75.00
Five Band, jug, red/cobalt, 5".......................................$32.00
Flamingo, bowl, batter; Five Band................................$90.00
Flamingo, salt & pepper shakers, Five Band, pr..........$40.00
Floral Lattice, ball jug, #3 ....$100.00
Floral Lattice, canister, Radiance $100.00
Floral Lattice, casserole, #101, round...........................$35.00
Frost Flowers, bowl, coupe soup; Tomorrow's Classic,
    9" $10.00
Frost Flowers, celery dish, oval, Tomorrow's Classic ..$14.00
Frost Flowers, gravy boat, Tomorrow's Classic...........$20.00
Frost Flowers, plate, Tomorrow's Classic, 11".............$11.00
Gold Label, bowl, Thick Rim, 7½".................................$12.00
Gold Label, casserole, #101, round..............................$27.00
Golden Glo, baking shell, 4"...$5.00
Golden Glo, casserole, duck knob $30.00
Golden Glo, creamer, Boston $11.00
Harlequin, butter dish, Tomorrow's Classic $60.00
Harlequin, celery dish, Tomorrow's Classic $13.00
Harlequin, plate, Tomorrow's Classic, 6"......................$3.00

Heather Rose, bowl, E-style, oval, 9¼".................**$15.00**
Heather Rose, bowl, vegetable; w/lid, E-style **$28.00**
Heather Rose, cookie jar, Flare.........................**$35.00**
Heather Rose, cup, E-style..............................**$6.00**
Heather Rose, plate, 10"................................**$7.00**
Heather Rose, saucer **$2.00**
Holiday, bowl, coupe soup; 9"..........................**$8.00**
Holiday, cup, Tomorrow's Classic.......................**$6.50**
Holiday, plate, 8".....................................**$5.00**
Meadow Flower, ball jug, #3............................**$80.00**
Meadow Flower, bowl, Thick Rim, 7½"....................**$20.00**
Meadow Flower, cookie jar, Five Band...................**$150.00**
Meadow Flower, drip jar, Thick Rim **$28.00**
Medallion, bowl, #3, ivory, 6".........................**$3.50**
Medallion, bowl, #5, Lettuce, 8½"......................**$11.00**
Medallion, creamer, Chinese Red **$12.00**
Medallion, jug, ice lip, Lettuce, 4-pt **$20.00**
Medallion, salt & pepper shakers, ivory, pr **$24.00**
Morning Glory, bowl, straight-sided, 7½"...............**$20.00**
Morning Glory, bowl, Thick Rim, 8½"....................**$16.50**
Mulberry, ashtray, Tomorrow's Classic **$5.50**
Mulberry, cup, Tomorrow's Classic......................**$6.00**
Mulberry, plate, Tomorrow's Classic, 11" **$7.00**
Mulberry, teapot, Tomorrow's Classic, 6-cup............**$70.00**
Mullberry, bowl, lg salad; Tomorrow's Classic, 14½" ..**$17.00**
Mums, bowl, D-style, oval, 10¼"........................**$25.00**
Mums, bowl, D-style, round, 9¼"........................**$25.00**
Mums, bowl, fruit; D-style, 5½"........................**$5.00**
Mums, bowl, salad; D-style, 9".........................**$20.00**
Mums, casserole, Medallion **$38.00**
Mums, coffeepot, Terrace...............................**$65.00**
Mums, creamer, Medallion **$15.00**
Mums, drip jar (open), #1188...........................**$32.00**
Mums, pie baker **$26.00**
Mums, plate, D-style, 6"...............................**$3.00**
Mums, stack set, Radiance..............................**$80.00**
No 488, ball jug, #3...................................**$90.00**
No 488, bowl, flat soup; D-style, 8½".................**$20.00**
No 488, casserole, Medallion **$35.00**
No 488, leftover, square **$70.00**
No 488, plate, D-style, 8¼"............................**$9.00**
No 488, platter, D-style, oval, 11½" **$20.00**
No 488, shirred egg dish **$32.00**
Orange Poppy, baker, French fluted **$17.00**
Orange Poppy, bowl, cereal; C-style, 6"................**$14.00**
Orange Poppy, bowl, flat soup; C-style, 8½" **$18.50**
Orange Poppy, coffee dispenser, metal **$28.00**
Orange Poppy, plate, C-style, 9".......................**$12.50**
Orange Poppy, pretzel jar **$90.00**
Orange Poppy, salt & pepper shakers, handled, pr **$30.00**
Orange Poppy, waste basket, metal **$38.00**
Pastel Morning Glory, bean pot, New England #4 ....**$100.00**
Pastel Morning Glory, bowl, cereal; D-style, 6" **$9.50**
Pastel Morning Glory, cake plate.......................**$20.00**
Pastel Morning Glory, cup, St Denis....................**$32.00**
Pastel Morning Glory, jug, Donut style **$120.00**
Pastel Morning Glory, plate, D-style, 10"..............**$23.00**
Pastel Morning Glory, platter, D-style, 11¼" **$19.00**

Pastel Morning Glory, teapot, New York, ...**$135.00**
Peach Blossom, bowl, baker (open); Tomorrow's Classic,
    11-oz...**$10.00**
Peach Blossom, bowl, fruit; Tomorrow's Classic, 5¼"...**$5.00**
Peach Blossom, bowl, onion soup; Tomorrow's Classic .**$22.00**
Peach Blossom, egg cup, Tomorrow's Classic **$22.00**
Peach Blossom, sugar bowl, Tomorrow's Classic **$12.00**
Pine Cone, bowl, fruit; E-style, 5¼" **$5.50**
Pine Cone, bowl, vegetable (open); Tomorrow's Classic,
    8¾" **$15.00**
Pine Cone, casserole, Tomorrow's Classic, 2-qt..........**$30.00**
Pine Cone, cup, E-style...............................**$8.00**
Pine Cone, plate, Tomorrow's Classic, 11".............**$10.00**
Pine Cone, plate, Tomorrow's Classic, 6"..............**$3.50**
Primrose, bowl, cereal; E-style, 6¼"..................**$5.00**
Primrose, bowl, E-style, oval, 9¼" **$14.00**
Primrose, creamer, E-style............................**$6.50**
Primrose, cup, E-style **$6.50**
Primrose, plate, E-style, 10".........................**$7.00**
Primrose, saucer, E-style.............................**$1.50**
Primrose, sugar bowl, E-style.........................**$13.00**
Red Poppy, bowl, D-style, oval, 10¼"..................**$23.00**
Red Poppy, bowl, flat soup; D-style, 8½"..............**$17.00**
Red Poppy, bread box, metal, 3 styles.................**$35.00**
Red Poppy, clock, teapot shape, plastic...............**$60.00**
Red Poppy, creamer, Daniel **$14.00**

**Red Poppy, drip jar, Radiance, $20.00; salt & pepper
shakers, Teardrop, pr, $28.00**

Red Poppy, jug, Radiance, #5 ....**$25.00**
Red Poppy, match safe.................................**$32.00**
Red Poppy, plate, D-style, 10" **$32.00**
Red Poppy, plate, D-style, 7¼"........................**$5.50**
Red Poppy, sugar bowl, Daniel **$20.00**
Rose Parade, bowl, salad; 9"..........................**$30.00**
Rose Parade, drip jar, tab handles **$25.00**
Rose White, bean pot, tab handles.....................**$50.00**
Rose White, bowl, straight-sided, 7½".................**$12.50**
Rose White, creamer, Pert **$12.50**
Rose White, custard, straight-sided **$14.00**
Royal Rose, bowl, straight-sided, 6".................**$15.00**
Royal Rose, drip jar, Thick Rim.......................**$22.00**
Royal Rose, salt & pepper shakers, handled, pr **$15.00**

Sears' Arlington, bowl, cereal; E-style, 6¼" **$5.00**
Sears' Arlington, bowl, E-style, oval, 9¼" **$13.00**
Sears' Arlington, bowl, flat soup; E-style, 8" **$8.00**
Sears' Arlington, plate, E-style, 6¼" **$2.50**
Sears' Arlington, plate, E-style, 9¼" **$5.00**
Sears' Arlington, platter, E-style, oval, 11¼" **$13.00**
Sears' Monticello, bowl, vegetable; w/lid, E-style **$30.00**
Sears' Monticello, gravy boat, w/underplate, E-style ...**$16.50**
Sears' Monticello, plate, E-style, 8" **$4.00**
Sears' Monticello, platter, E-style, oval, 11¼" **$12.00**
Sears' Monticello, sugar bowl, E-style **$13.00**
Sears' Mount Vernon, bowl, flat soup; E-style, 8" **$11.00**
Sears' Mount Vernon, cup, E-style **$6.50**
Sears' Mount Vernon, plate, E-style, 10" **$8.50**
Sears' Mount Vernon, plater, E-style, oval, 13¼" **$15.00**
Sears' Richmond, bowl, fruit; E-style, 5¼" **$5.00**
Sears' Richmond/Brown-Eyed Susan, bowl, E-style, oval,
   9¼" **$14.00**
Sears' Richmond/Brown-Eyed Susan, cup, E-style **$6.00**
Sears' Richmond/Brown-Eyed Susan, pickle dish, E-style,
   9" **$5.00**
Sears' Richmond/Brown-Eyed Susan, plate, E-style, 9¼".**$6.00**
Serenade, baker, French fluted **$12.50**
Serenade, bowl, D-style, round, 9¼" **$20.00**
Serenade, bowl, oval, D-style...................................**$14.00**
Serenade, bowl, salad; D-style, 9" **$15.00**
Serenade, creamer, Moderne....................................**$10.00**
Serenade, plate, D-style, 8¼" **$5.00**
Serenade, pretzel jar **$85.00**
Serenade, saucer, D-style...**$2.00**
Shaggy Tulip, bean pot, #4, New England...................**$90.00**
Shaggy Tulip, casserole, Radiance **$30.00**
Shaggy Tulip, jug, #3, w/lid, Radiance **$55.00**
Shaggy Tulip, stack set, Radiance..............................**$100.00**
Silhouette, bean pot, #4, New England **$115.00**
Silhouette, bowl, D-style, flared, 3⅝"........................**$12.00**
Silhouette, bowl, flat soup; D-style, 8½"...................**$18.50**

Silhouette, bowl, mixing; Medallion, 7½", $16.00; bowl, mixing; Medallion, 8½", $22.00

Silhouette, bowl, 9", Radiance.....................................**$21.00**
Silhouette, bread box, metal **$70.00**
Silhouette, cake safe, metal..**$32.00**
Silhouette, coffeepot, Medallion **$100.00**
Silhouette, leftover, rectangular **$40.00**
Silhouette, plate, D-style, 6" **$5.50**
Silhouette, platter, D-style, oval, 11¼" **$20.00**
Silhouette, salt & pepper shakers, handled, pr............**$90.00**

Silhouette, saucer, St Denis **$9.00**
Silhouette, teapot, Streamline...................................**$225.00**
Spring, ashtray, Tomorrow's Classic **$5.00**
Spring, bowl, lg salad; Tomorrow's Classic, 14½".......**$18.00**
Spring, candlestick, Tomorrow's Classic, 8" **$25.00**
Spring, celery dish, Tomorrow's Classic, oval.............**$11.00**
Spring, coffeepot, Tomorrow's Classic, 6-cup.............**$50.00**
Spring, platter, Tomorrow's Classic, 17" **$25.00**
Springtime, bowl, fruit; D-style, 5½"..........................**$5.00**
Springtime, bowl, Thick Rim, 7½" **$13.00**
Springtime, cake plate **$15.00**
Springtime, coffeepot, Washington.............................**$35.00**
Springtime, jug, Radiance, #6.....................................**$23.00**
Springtime, plate, D-style, 6" **$3.50**
Springtime, plate, D-style, 9" **$8.00**
Springtime, platter, D-style, oval, 11¼".......................**$13.50**
Springtime, salt & pepper shakers, handled, pr...........**$14.00**
Stonewall, casserole, Radiance..................................**$30.00**
Stonewall, coffeepot, drip; china................................**$150.00**
Stonewall, salt & pepper shakers, handled, pr **$36.00**
Sunglow, bowl, soup; Century, 8" **$9.00**
Sunglow, bowl, vegetable; Century, 10½"...................**$13.00**
Sunglow, butter dish, Century....................................**$28.00**
Sunglow, creamer, Century **$7.00**
Sunglow, plate, Century, 10¼" **$7.00**
Sunglow, platter, Century, 15"....................................**$16.00**
Tri-Tone, bowl, individual salad; Zeisel **$14.00**
Tri-Tone, leftover, Zeisel **$30.00**
Tulip, bowl, cereal; D-style, 6" **$12.00**
Tulip, bowl, Radiance, 9" **$20.00**
Tulip, bowl, Thick Rim, 7½"...**$15.00**
Tulip, casserole, Thick Rim **$35.00**
Tulip, cup, St Denis **$32.00**
Tulip, gravy boat, D-style **$25.00**
Tulip, plate, D-style, 9" **$10.00**
Tulip, platter, D-style, 11¼" **$14.00**
Wild Poppy, bowl, Radiance, 6" **$20.00**
Wild Poppy, casserole, #103, oval..............................**$100.00**
Wild Poppy, cookie jar, Five Band...............................**$200.00**
Wild Poppy, creamer, New York...................................**$28.00**
Wild Poppy, custard, Radiance....................................**$15.00**
Wild Poppy, leftover, square..**$80.00**
Wildfire, baker, French fluted **$17.00**
Wildfire, bowl, straight-sided, 6".................................**$11.00**
Wildfire, bowl, Thick Rim, 8½" **$22.00**
Wildfire, casserole, Thick Rim.....................................**$28.00**
Wildfire, coffee dispenser, metal **$20.00**
Wildfire, custard...**$22.00**
Wildfire, gravy boat, D-style..**$22.00**
Wildfire, platter, D-style, oval, 13¼" **$22.00**
Wildfire, sugar bowl, Pert..**$28.00**
Yellow Rose, baker, French fluted................................**$15.00**
Yellow Rose, bowl, flat soup; D-style, 8½" **$13.00**
Yellow Rose, bowl, fruit; D-style, 5½" **$5.00**
Yellow Rose, coffeepot, Norse....................................**$60.00**
Yellow Rose, cup, D-style **$8.00**
Yellow Rose, plate, D-style, 6" **$3.00**
Yellow Rose, platter, D-style, oval, 13¼".....................**$20.00**

Teapots

Airflow, 6-cup, 'Special' gold-decorated colors............**$50.00**

Aladdin, 6-cup, light blue w/gold trim, round opening, $50.00

Albany, 6-cup, 'Special' gold-decorated cobalt............**$55.00**
Automobile, 6-cup, red...**$650.00**
Baltimore, 6-cup, Gold Label maroon **$45.00**
Bellvue, 2-4 cup, solid colors......................................**$14.00**
Boston, 6-cup, gold-decorated Dresden blue **$65.00**
Cleveland, 6-cup, gold-decorated emerald green **$60.00**
Donut, 6-cup, gold-decorated turquoise...................**$225.00**
French, 4-6 cup, gold-decorated colors.......................**$50.00**
Hollywood, 6-cup, Hi-black w/Gold Label decoration..**$40.00**
Hook Cover, 6-cup, cadet blue **$25.00**
Illinois, 6-cup, gold-decorated maroon **$140.00**
Los Angeles, 8-cup, milk-glass glaze w/floral decal
    band **$100.00**
Manhattan, 2-cup, cobalt, side handle..........................**$65.00**
Melody, 6-cup, gold-decorated cobalt........................**$175.00**
Moderne, 6-cup, ivory **$20.00**
Nautilus, 6-cup, gold-decorated turquoise **$120.00**
New York, 6-cup, matt pink w/Gold Label decoration ...**$35.00**
Philadelphia, 7-10 cup, gold-decorated canary............**$35.00**
Rhythm, 6-cup, gold-decorated canary.........................**$70.00**
Star, 6-cup, gold-decorated cobalt **$75.00**
Streamline, 6-cup, 'Special' gold-decorated canary......**$60.00**
Sundial, 6-cup, cobalt...**$120.00**
Surfside, 6-cup, 'Special' gold-decorated emerald green .**$135.00**
Windshield, 6-cup, white w/bird decal, gold trim.....**$160.00**

Hallmark Ornaments

Some of the Hallmark Christmas ornaments that have been made since they were first introduced in 1973 are worth many times their original price. This is especially true of the first one issued in a particular series. For instance, Cardinals, first in the Holiday Wildlife series issued in 1982 has a value today of $400.00 (MIB).

If you'd like to learn more about them, we recommend *The*

Secondary Price Guide to Hallmark Ornaments by Rosie Wells. Our values are for ornaments that are mint and in their original boxes.

Adorable Ornaments, Betsy Clark, #QX 157-1, by Donna Lee, 1975, 3½"..**$250.00**
Adorable Ornaments, Mrs Santa, #QX 156-1, by Donna Lee, 1975, 3½"..**$270.00**
Angel, #QX 110-1, white glass ball, 1974 ....**$70.00**
Angel Tree Topper, #QSD 230-2, country-style wood-look angel in cream, pink, turquoise & gold, 1977.....**$350.00**
Angel Tree Topper, #QTT 710-1, fabric & porcelain, gold accents on wings & gown, 1984 ....**$35.00**
Baby-Sitter, #QX 253-1, green glass ball w/mice having fun w/baby-sitter, Thank Heaven for Baby-Sitters Like You, 1984 ....**$14.00**
Beary Smooth Ride, #QX 480-5, handcrafted, teddy bear riding colorful tricycle, by Linda Sickman, 1985........**$20.00**
Beauty of America, Seashore, #QX 160-2, white glass ball, Christmas Is the Warmth of Goodwill..., 1977 ......**$30.00**
Bell Wreath, #QX 420-9, brass holly wreath w/7 sm bells, by Linda Sickman, 1983 ....**$30.00**
Betsy Clark, #QX 305-6, blue cameo, Tis the Season for Trimming Trees & Making Merry Memories, 1982.**$28.00**
Betsy Clark, #QX 423-5, handcrafted, Betsy & fawn looking at tree, by John Francis (Collin), 1981 ....**$70.00**
Betsy Clark, #XHD 100-2, white glass ball w/5 girls caroling around Christmas tree, 1973................................**$80.00**
Big on Gardening, #QX 584-2, handcrafted, elephant in red apron w/flowerpot & tools, by LaDene Votruba, 1993, 2½"...**$14.00**
Brass Santa, #QX 423-9, front & back view of Santa's head, by Ed Seale, 1983...**$16.00**
Cactus Cowboy, #QX 411-2, handcrafted, smiling green cactus wrapped in red lights, by Peter Dutkin, 1989, 3½"...**$40.00**
Caroling Bear, #QX 140-1, handcrafted, brown bear in red & green striped scarf singing duet w/bird, Carols 1980..**$145.00**
Chatty Penguin, #QX 417-6, plush, squeaker, colorful penguin in red Santa cap, by Ken Crow, 1986, 3⅝" ...**$22.00**
Chickadees, #QX 204-1, white glass ball, Christmas 1976..**$35.00**
Chiming In, #QX 436-6, handcrafted, squirrel atop brass chimes, by Sharon Pike, 1990, 5"..........................**$24.00**
Christmas Chickadees, #QX 204-7, gold glass ball w/2 chickadees enjoying holly berries, Beauty Is a Gift..., 1979..**$30.00**
Christmas is Love, #XHD 106-2, white glass ball w/2 angels playing mandolins in shades of green & lavender, 1973 ....**$65.00**
Christmas Magic, #QX 810-2, white satin ball w/gnome-like Santa ice skating, ...Christmas Magic's in the Air, 1981..**$22.00**
Christmas Mouse, #QX 134-2, white satin ball w/mice decorating their tree, Tinsel & Lights Make..., 1977......**$65.00**
Christmas Treats, #QX 507-5, beveled glass, colorful candy canes & candies on white, 1985, 3¼" **$18.00**

Colors of Christmas, Angel, #QX 354-3, acrylic stained-glass look, red dress & halo w/gold hair & wings, 1978...**$50.00**

Cozy Goose, #QX 496-6, handcrafted, by Sharon Pike, 1990, 3⅛"......**$14.00**

Cuddly Lamb, #QX 519-9, handcrafted, detailed texturing & white flocking, by Anita Marra Rogers, 1991 ....**$14.00**

Currier & Ives, #QX 112-1, white glass ball w/winter farmstead & horse-drawn sleigh, 1974, pr **$55.00**

Currier & Ives, #QX 164-1, white satin ball w/farmhouse & buildings, 1975 ....**$45.00**

Currier & Ives, #QX 250-1, white blown glass ball, American Winter Scenes, Evening, Christmas 1984..............**$18.00**

Daughter, #QX 212-1, white glass ball w/1 kitten napping & 1 playing w/ornament, A Daughter Is the Sweetest Gift, 1980 ....**$30.00**

Deer Disguise, #QX 426-5, handcrafted, 2 kids peeking out from reindeer costume, by Bob Siedler, 1989.......**$22.00**

Elvis Presley, 1992, 4½", from $20.00 to $25.00

Embroidered Stocking, #QX 479-6, fabric, quilted red stocking trimmed w/lace, by Linda Sickman, 1983 ....**$16.00**

Feliz Navidad, #QX 416-1, handcrafted, gray burro in sombrero carrying package & bottle brush tree, by Duane Unruh, 1988...**$25.00**

Filled w/Fudge, #QX 419-1, handcrafted, mouse in ice-cream cone filled w/chocolate, by Ed Seale, 1988 ....**$20.00**

First Christmas Together, #QX 205-4, white glass ball w/man & wife taking sleigh ride, ...Written in Our Hearts, 1980 ....**$22.00**

First Christmas Together, #QX 302-6, acrylic Christmas tree, 1982, 4¼" **$16.00**

Flights of Fantasy, #QX 256-4, blue glass ball w/birds taking elves on flight, 1984.................................**$16.00**

Forest Frolics, #QLX 725-4, handcrafted w/lights & motion, forest friends on seesaw, by Sharon Pike, 1992, 4⅛" **$50.00**

Friendship, #QX 203-9, white glass ball w/ice skating scene & sleigh ride scene, There Is No Time Quite Like..., 1979 ....**$30.00**

Frosted Images, Dove, #QX 308-1, acrylic, dove in flight, 1980 ....**$32.00**

Frosty Friends, #QX 482-2, handcrafted, little E/skimo & friend paddling red kayak, by Ed Seale, 6th in series, 1985 ....**$55.00**

Garfield, #QX 230-3, blue chrome glass ball w/Garfield carving design in ice, ...Happy New Year Too!, 1990 .**$12.00**

General Store, #QLX 705-3, handcrafted light-up, by Donna Lee, Christmas Trees 50¢, 1986 ....**$60.00**

Gentle Fawn, #QX 548-5, handcrafted, flocked fawn wearing holly ribbon, 1989 ....**$18.00**

Gingham Dog, #QX 402-2, sewn fabric, blue & white w/red bow, 1981, 3" **$20.00**

Gone Wishin', #QX 517-1, handcrafted, Santa napping in silver boat w/package hooked on line, by Donna Lee, 1992 ....**$20.00**

Good Cheer Blimp, #QXL 704-6, handcrafted w/blinking lights, by Linda Sickman, 1987.......................**$55.00**

Grandaughter, #QX 216-3, white satin ball w/little girl decorating tree, Never Far From Thought..., 1978........**$35.00**

Grandmother, #QX 260-2, gold glass ball, Grandmother Is Another Word for Love, 1977.................................**$45.00**

Heavenly Dreamer, #QX 417-3, handcrafted, angel in brass halo sleeping in acrylic cloud, by Donna Lee, 1986.**$30.00**

Here Comes Santa Series, Santa's Express, #QX 143-4, handcrafted, Santa in locomotive, 2nd in series, 1980.**$175.00**

High Top-Purr, #QX 533-2, handcrafted, brown kitten tucked in red sneaker, by Ed Seale, 1993 ....**$16.00**

Holiday Chimes, Snowflake, #QX 165-4, chrome-plated, by Linda Sickman, 1981 ....**$28.00**

Holiday Highlights, Christmas Magic, acrylic, rabbit looking at ornament, ...Season of Magical Moments, 1982.**$30.00**

Holiday Highlights, Love, #QX 304-7, acrylic heart shape, Time of Memories & Dreams... in silver foil, 1979.**$95.00**

Ice Fairy, #QX 431-5, acrylic & handcrafted, white ice fairy holding snowflake, by Donna Lee, 1981, 4⅛".......**$70.00**

Jack Frost, #QX 407-9, handcrafted, Jack Frost painting scrolls on windowpanes, 1983, 3¾".......................**$58.00**

Jesus Loves Me, #QX 315-6, acrylic, happy bunny in etched frosted design, by Joyce Pattee, 1990, 2¾" dia......**$15.00**

Joan Walsh Anglund, #QX 205-9, white satin ball w/children hanging stockings, The Smallest Pleasure..., 1979 .**$40.00**

Jolly Hiker, #QX 483-2, handcrafted, Santa w/backpack, bedroll & candy cane walking stick, by Bob Siedler, 1986 ....**$25.00**

Kitty Mischief, #QX 474-5, handcrafted, yellow & white kitten w/real ball of yarn, by Peter Dutkin, 1985, 2".**$24.00**

Little Whittler, #QX 469-9, handcrafted, Santa carving reindeer toy, by Peter Dutkin, 1987 ....**$25.00**

Merry-Mint Unicorn, #QX 423-4, porcelain, unicorn balancing on peppermint candy, by Anita Marra Rogers, 1988...**$20.00**

Mouse Wagon, #QX 476-2, handcrafted, white mouse in little red wagon bearing gift of cheese, 1985, 2"......**$55.00**

Norman Rockwell, #QX 166-1, white satin ball w/Santa writing in book & looking through telescope, 1975 ...**$65.00**

Norman Rockwell, #QX 202-3, red soft-sheen satin ball, ...Smiles are Bright, Child's Delight, It's Christmas, 1982..........**$25.00**

North Pole Nutcrackers, Franz the Artist, #QX 526-1, Franz w/paint palette, by Linda Sickman, 1992, 4⅝" **$16.00**

Nostalgia Ornaments, Peace on Earth, #QX 223-1, by Linda Sickman, Christmas 1976, 3¼" dia **$135.00**

Notes of Cheer, #QX 535-7, handcrafted, flocked brown bear w/keyboard, by Bob Siedler, 1991, 1¾".......**$15.00**

Open Me First, #QX 422-6, handcrafted, child opening box w/kitten inside, 1986 ....**$25.00**

Peace on Earth, #QX 341-4, red oval cameo w/old-world ivory angel playing harp, 1984.....................**$20.00**

Peanuts, #QX 205-6, white satin ball, features Linus w/wreath & the rest of the gang singing, Joy to the World, 1978.....................**$65.00**

Peppermint Mouse, #QX 401-5, sewn fabric, white w/red & white striped outfit, 1981, 3" **$25.00**

Puppy Love, #QX 448-4, handcrafted, terrier w/brass tag in wicker basket, 2nd in series, by Anita Marra Rogers, 1992, $35.00

Rainbow Brite & Friends, #QX 268-2, clear glass ball w/Rainbow Bright & Sprites against stars & snowflakes, 1985 ....**$20.00**

Reindeer Champs, Dancer, #QX 480-9, handcrafted, Dancer in skates, by Bob Siedler, 2nd in series, 1987.......**$50.00**

Santa Bell, #QX 148-7, hand-decorated porcelain, bell inside black boots, 1982.....................**$60.00**

Sparkling Snowflake, #QX 547-2, brass, lacy design w/etched layers, by Joyce A Lyle, 1989................**$18.00**

Special Delivery, #QX 415-6, handcrafted, penguin w/gift of sardines, by Bob Siedler, 1986.....................**$20.00**

Special Friends, #QX 372-5, acrylic, doll & bear, Special Friends Bring... in etched letters, by Don Palmiter, 1985.....................**$12.00**

Stitches of Joy, #QX 733-6, handcrafted, mama rabbit in blue gown doing needlepoint, by Julia Lee, 1990, 2½" ..**$25.00**

Sweet Star, #QX 418-4, handcrafted clip-on, squirrel nibbling on cherry in star-shaped cookie, by Ed Seale, 1988 ....**$22.00**

Teacher, #QX 301-6, clear acrylic apple w/green leaves & red print, To a Special Teacher 1982, 3½"............**$15.00**

Ten Years Together, #QX 258-4, bone china bell, frosty blue winter scene inside oval, 1984, 3".........................**$20.00**

Trumpet Panda, #QX 471-2, handcrafted, flocked panda playing red trumpet, by Ed Seale, 1985, 2" **$20.00**

Twirl-Abouts, Angel, #QX 171-1, angel rotates on brass pin in center of Christmas tree, by Linda Sickman, 1976 ....**$155.00**

Uncle Sam, #QX 449-1, pressed tin, Uncle Sam holding teddy bear, by Linda Sickman, 1984, 5" **$45.00**

Well-Stocked Stocking, #QX 154-7, handcrafted, red & white stocking filled w/toys, 1981, 4½" **$70.00**

Word of Love, #QX 447-7, porcelain, Love sculpted in contemporary design w/red heart dangling in the O, 1987 ....**$16.00**

Yarn & Fabric, Angel, #QX 162-1, blue w/white wings & pinafore holding green wreath, 1980, 5" **$10.00**

Yarn Ornament, Caroler (little girl), #QX 126-1, green w/white muff & green hat, 1975, 4½"....................**$25.00**

Yarn Ornament, Elf, #XHD 79-2, 1973, 4½" **$25.00**

Yarn Ornament, Mrs Santa, #XHD 75-2, 1973, 4½" **$28.00**

Yarn Ornament, Snowman, #XHD 104-1, plaid scarf & black top hat, 1974, 4¾" **$25.00**

Yarn Ornament, Soldier, #XHD 81-2, blue w/red hat, boots & bands, 1973, 4½" **$25.00**

Yesteryears, Drummer Boy, #QX 184-1, wood-look designs in old world character, 1976 ....**$140.00**

Halloween

Next to Christmas, you probably have more happy childhood recollections of Halloween than any other holiday of the year. If somehow you've managed to hang onto some old party decorations or one of the jack-o'-lanterns that we used to collect candy in, you already have a good start on a collection that you'll really enjoy.

Decoration, black cat, crepe paper fold-out type, 1940s, 15", $35.00

Candy container, chick bellhop, Germany, 7½", NM .**$180.00**

Candy container, jack-o'-lantern, plastic, open top, 4½", EX **$25.00**

Candy container, witch & jack-o'-lantern, plastic, M ...**$20.00**

Clicker, moon & devil shape, 2", EX **$15.00**

Clicker, owl, black cat & moon shape, T Cohn, 3", EX.**$22.00**

Clicker, owl shape, US Metal Toy, VG **$16.50**

Decoration, black cat, die-cut foil, 8x14", EX..............**$20.00**

Decoration, howling black cat & quarter moon, die-cut, 9", NM **$50.00**

Decoration, owl, die-cut, HE Luhrs, 9", NM **$20.00**

Decoration, skeleton, die-cut, Beistle, 12", EX............**$18.00**

Decoration, witch, die-cut cardboard, Merri-Lei, 8x8", NM **$30.00**

Decoration, witch in haunted house, die-cut, HE Luhrs, 8", M **$25.00**

Figure, witch, molded plastic, 5" **$15.00**

Hat, paper, black cats, Germany, 13x6", M **$25.00**

Hat, paper, witch, black cat & jack-o'-lantern, 14", EX..**$16.00**

Horn, jack-o'-lantern, cats & witches, US Metal Toy, 11", NM **$22.00**

Lantern, devil's head, pressed cardboard, American, EX...**$120.00**

Lantern, pumpkin face, pressed cardboard, 5½"..........**$65.00**

Lantern, skull shape, 4-sided, NM............................**$95.00**

Noisemaker, clown face on metal, wood handle, Kirchof, 4" dia, EX **$20.00**

Noisemaker, goblins & witch, tin, ratchet type, EX.....**$20.00**

Noisemaker, Spanish dancer, tin, ratchet type, EX......**$10.00**

Pin, jack-o'-lantern w/blinking eye, MOC **$32.00**

Tambourine, black cats & moon over fence, tin, 6", EX **$65.00**

Tambourine, witch face, tin, T Cohn, 7", VG..............**$40.00**

Treat bucket, Hulk figure, green plastic, 1970s, EX.....**$22.50**

Treat bucket, Popeye characters on yellow plastic, 1970s, EX **$25.00**

Halloween Costumes

If you can find one of these still in the original box and the price is right, buy it! During the fifties and sixties, Collegeville and Ben Cooper made these costumes to represent popular TV and movie characters of the day, and these are the more collectible.

Donald Duck, Collegeville, complete w/original box, NM, $30.00

Bart Simpson, Ben Cooper, complete, M **$10.00**

Batman, Japan, 1989, MIB.......................................**$20.00**

Beetlejuice, mask only, rubber, 1988, M **$40.00**

Boss Hog, Ben Cooper, 1982, MIB............................**$35.00**

Captain America, Ben Cooper, 1977, NMIB **$20.00**

Chewbacca, Ben Cooper, MIB..................................**$40.00**

Cone Head, mask only, M...**$28.00**

Daniel Boone, Collegeville, 1960s, M........................**$16.50**

Doc, Einson-Freeman, mask only, paper, 1937, EX.....**$20.00**

Donny Osmond, Ben Cooper, 1977, MIB **$25.00**

Ewok, Ben Cooper, complete, EX **$16.00**

Farrah Fawcett, Collegeville, complete, 1977, EX........**$50.00**

Frankenstein, Ben Cooper, 1973, MIB........................**$50.00**

Fred Flintstone, complete, 1973, EX **$25.00**

Girl From UNCLE, complete, Halco/MGM, 1960s, NMIB, $160.00

Grumpy, Einson-Freeman, mask only, paper, 1937, EX **$20.00**

Hawkeye, M*A*S*H, complete, 1981, EX....................**$20.00**

Hee Haw Country Bumpkin, Ben Cooper, 1976, NM..**$30.00**

Huckleberry Hound, complete, 1960, EX....................**$65.00**

I Dream of Jeannie, 1974, original box, EX.................**$16.00**

King Kong, Ben Cooper, 1976, M **$20.00**

Lily Munster, Ben Cooper, complete, 1964, EX **$75.00**

Lt Worf, Ben Cooper, complete, 1987, EX **$20.00**

Morticia, Ben Cooper, 1965, MIB..............................**$225.00**

Pinocchio, Gillette Blue Blade, mask only, paper, 1939, EX...**$15.00**

Police Woman, MIB...**$15.00**

Road Runner, Collegeville, complete, 1973, M **$30.00**

Six Million-Dollar Man, complete, 1974, EX................**$30.00**

Spiderman, Ben Cooper, 1972, MIB **$50.00**

Spock, complete, 1975, EX.......................................**$65.00**

Strawberry Shortcake, complete, 1980, EX...................**$5.00**

SWAT, 1975, NMIB **$15.00**

Tom Terrific, Halco, complete, 1957, NM **$80.00**

Ultra Man, 1971, NM..**$70.00**

Witchiepoo, Collegeville, complete, 1971, EX **$65.00**

Wonder Woman, Ben Cooper, MIB............................**$25.00**

Woody Woodpecker, complete, 1970, EX....................**$8.50**

Yoda, Don Post, mask only, MIP...............................**$40.00**

Harker Pottery

Harker was one of the oldest potteries in the country. Their history can be traced back to the 1840s. In the thirties, a new plant was built in Chester, West Virginia, and the company began manufacturing kitchen and dinnerware lines, eventually employing as many as three hundred workers.

Several of these lines are popular with collectors today. One of the most easily recognized is Cameoware. It is usually found in pink or blue decorated with white silhouettes of flowers, though other designs were made as well. Colonial Lady, Red Apple, Amy, Mallow, and Pansy are some of their other lines that are fairly easy to find and reassemble into sets.

If you'd like to learn more about Harker, we recommend *The Collector's Encyclopedia of American Dinnerware* by Jo Cunningham and *The Collector's Guide to Harker Pottery* by Neva Colbert.

Old Vintage, plate, dinner; 10", $8.00

Amy, bean pot, individual	$8.00
Amy, creamer & sugar bowl (open)	$16.00
Amy, stack set, w/lid	$35.00
Amy, teapot	$35.00
Blue Blossoms, salt & pepper shakers, pr	$16.00
Boyce, pitcher, gold-trimmed handle	$35.00
Calico Tulip, creamer & sugar bowl	$20.00
Cameo, cup & saucer, Shell Shape	$10.00
Cameo, pie baker, Carv-Kraft	$20.00
Cameo, plate, Shell shape, 9"	$10.00
Cameo, platter, oval	$18.00
Cameo, teapot	$27.00
Cherry Blossom, platter	$8.00
Colonial Lady, batter pitcher	$32.00
Colonial Lady, casserole	$27.00
Colonial Lady, 'Drips' jar	$18.00
Colonial Lady, syrup pitcher	$22.00
Cottage, casserole	$15.00
Cottage, plate, 8¼"	$6.00

Cottage, salad fork	$20.00
Deco-Dahlia, jug, utility; 6"	$18.00
Deco-Dahlia, pie baker	$20.00
Deco-Dahlia, server	$16.00
Enchantment, creamer	$8.00
Enchantment, sugar bowl	$10.00
English Countryside, custard	$5.00
English Countryside, jar, tall	$27.00
Forest Flowers, bowl, serving	$4.00
Ivy Vine, platter, oval, Gadroon shape	$18.00
Jessica, bowl, utility	$30.00
Lisa, bowl, utility, Arches shape	$25.00
Mallow, bowl, 7½"	$8.00
Mallow, 'Lard' jar, w/lid	$20.00
Mallow, serving spoon	$25.00
Old Vintage, bowl, vegetable; 8"	$12.00
Old Vintage, cup & saucer, Gadroon shape	$10.00
Old Vintage, soup, flat; 8"	$8.00
Pansy, salt & pepper shakers, pr	$28.00
Pastel Tulip, plate, Gadroon shape	$6.00
Red Apple I, pitcher, utility; Modern Age shape	$35.00
Red Apple I, teapot, lid missing	$10.00
Red Apple II, bowl, swirl w/red trim, 9"	$30.00
Red Apple II, bowl, utility, 10"	$30.00
Rose I, pie baker	$20.00
Rose I, plate, 6"	$4.00
Rose II, cake server	$20.00
Rose II, custard	$4.00
Rose Spray, bowl, cream soup; tab handles	$10.00
Rose Spray, cup & saucer	$10.00
Rose Spray, plate, round, 6"	$4.00
Royal Rose, cake plate & server, Gadroon shape	$15.00

Ruffled Tulip, tray, self-handled, 11¾", $25.00; pitcher, w/lid, Arches shape, $28.00

Slender Leaf, plate, 8"	$6.00
Springtime, plate, 10"	$6.00
Springtime, saucer, Gadroon shape	$3.00
Swirl Leaf, coffee server	$35.00

Harlequin Dinnerware

This is another line of solid-color dinnerware made by the Fiesta people, Homer Laughlin. Harlequin was less-expensive, designed to cater to the dimestore trade. In fact, it was sold exclusively through the F.W. Woolworth Company. It was introduced to the public in the late 1930s, and records indicate that production continued until near the middle of the 1960s.

Like Fiesta, Harlequin is very Deco in appearance. But in contrast to Fiesta's ring handles, Harlequin's are angular, as are many of its shapes. The band of rings, though similar to Fiesta's, is set farther away from its rims. Harlequin isn't nearly as heavy as Fiesta, and it was never marked.

Some of its colors are more desirable to collectors than others, so they're worth more. Two values are given for each item we've listed. The higher values apply to these colors: maroon, gray, medium green, spruce green, chartreuse, dark green, rose, mauve blue, red, and light green. Lower values are for items in turquoise and yellow.

Harlequin animals were made during the forties. There were six: a cat, a fish, a penguin, a duck, a lamb, and a donkey. They were made in maroon, spruce green, mauve blue, and yellow. These were reproduced by other companies. If you find one trimmed in gold, you've probably got a 'maverick.' If you find one in a color not listed, you're very lucky — these are worth twice as much as one in a standard color.

In 1979, complying with a request from the Woolworth company, HLC reissued a line of new Harlequin. It was made in original yellow and turquoise, medium green (slightly different than the original shade), and coral (an altogether new color). Some pieces were restyled, and the line was very limited. If you find a piece with a trademark, you'll know it's new.

If you'd like to know more about Harlequin, it's included in *The Collector's Encyclopedia of Fiesta* by Sharon and Bob Huxford.

Ashtrays, basket weave, high (left), $45.00; regular, high (right), $45.00; saucer, maroon (back), $75.00

Ashtray, basket-weave, low	$30.00
Ashtray, regular, low	$32.00

Bowl, cream soup, high	$22.00
Bowl, cream soup, low	$18.00
Bowl, fruit, high, 5½"	$9.00
Bowl, fruit, low, 5½"	$6.00
Bowl, individual salad, high	$32.00
Bowl, individual salad, low	$18.00
Bowl, mixing; Kitchen Kraft, mauve blue, 8"	$110.00
Bowl, mixing; Kitchen Kraft, red or green, 6"	$80.00
Bowl, mixing; Kitchen Kraft, yellow, 10"	$110.00
Bowl, nappy, high, 9"	$28.00
Bowl, nappy, low, 9"	$18.00
Bowl, oval baker, high	$26.00
Bowl, oval baker, low	$18.00
Bowl, 36s, high	$28.00
Bowl, 36s, low	$18.00
Bowl, 36s, oatmeal, high	$18.00
Bowl, 36s, oatmeal, low	$12.00
Bowl, 36s, spruce green, maroon, or med green	$55.00
Butter dish, high, ½-lb	$100.00
Butter dish, low, ½-lb	$80.00
Candle holders, high, pr	$200.00
Candle holders, low, pr	$170.00
Casserole, high	$125.00
Casserole, low	$75.00
Casserole, med green	$350.00
Creamer, individual, high	$20.00
Creamer, individual, low	$13.00
Creamer, novelty, high	$25.00
Creamer, novelty, low	$16.00
Creamer, regular, high	$14.00
Creamer, regular, low	$8.00
Creamer, w/high lip, any color	$80.00
Cup, demitasse; high	$85.00
Cup, demitasse; low	$30.00
Cup, demitasse; med green	$150.00
Cup, lg, any color	$125.00
Egg cup, double, high	$22.00
Egg cup, double, low	$15.00
Egg cup, single, high	$24.00
Egg cup, single, low	$17.00
Marmalade, any color	$130.00
Nut dish, basket-weave, high	$12.00
Nut dish, basket-weave, low	$8.00
Perfume bottle, any color	$80.00
Pitcher, jug, high, 22-oz	$50.00
Pitcher, jug, low, 22-oz	$30.00
Pitcher, med green, 22-oz	$135.00
Pitcher, service water; high	$75.00
Pitcher, service water; low	$40.00
Plate, deep, high	$20.00
Plate, deep, low	$15.00
Plate, deep, med green	$50.00
Plate, high, 10"	$24.00
Plate, high, 6"	$4.50
Plate, high, 7"	$6.50
Plate, high, 9"	$12.00
Plate, low, 10"	$14.00
Plate, low, 6"	$3.50

Plate, low, 7"	$4.50
Plate, 9", low	$7.00
Platter, high, 11"	$18.00
Platter, high, 13"	$25.00
Platter, low, 11"	$12.00
Platter, low, 13"	$16.50
Relish tray, mixed colors	$225.00
Salt & pepper shakers, high, pr	$18.00
Salt & pepper shakers, low, pr	$13.00
Sauce boat, high	$25.00
Sauce boat, low	$20.00
Saucer, demitasse; high	$15.00
Saucer, demitasse; low	$9.00
Saucer, high	$3.50
Saucer, low	$2.00
Sugar bowl, high	$25.00
Sugar bowl, low	$15.00
Syrup, other standard colors	$210.00
Syrup, red, yellow, mauve blue	$200.00
Teacup, high	$10.00
Teacup, low	$7.50
Teapot, high	$110.00
Teapot, low	$60.00
Tumbler, high	$45.00
Tumbler, low	$35.00
Tumbler, w/car decal	$55.00

Hartland Plastics, Inc.

The Hartland company was located in Hartland, Wisconsin, where during the fifties and sixties they made several lines of plastic figures: Western and Historic Horsemen, Miniature Western Series, and the Hartland Sport Series of Famous Baseball Stars. Football and bowling figures and religious statues were made as well. The plastic, virgin acetate, was very durable and the figures were hand painted with careful attention to detail. They're often marked.

For more information, there is a chapter on Hartland in *Collecting Toys* by Richard O'Brien (Books Americana). See also *Schroeder's Collectible Toys, Antique to Modern* (Collector Books).

Annie Oakley & Palomino, w/saddle, hat & gun, EX	$175.00
Bat Masterson, w/cane, hat & pistol, EX	$200.00
Bill Longley the Texan, no horse or accessories, 6½", VG	$38.00
Brave Eagle, w/horse, no accessories, 9½", VG	$75.00
Brave Eagle, w/horse & accessories, 9½", EX	$225.00
Bret Maverick, w/hat & guns, EX	$170.00
Buffalo Bill, w/horse, US Mail saddle, hat & guns, EX, from $215 to	$245.00
Bullet, #700, 6", MIB	$75.00
Champ Cowgirl, red shirt & white pantskirt, NM	$60.00
Chief Thunder Cloud, w/horse & accessories, NM, from $115 to	$150.00
Chris Colt, missing accessories, EX	$80.00
Cochise, on black & white horse w/saddle, NM	$100.00

Dale Evans & Buttermilk, complete, EX	$150.00
Dan Troop, no accessories, EX	$135.00
Don Drysdale, G	$110.00
General Custer, w/horse, flag, saddle & sword, EX, from $185 to	$225.00
Horse, grazing mare, chestnut	$35.00
Horse, w/molded-on saddle & bridle, 6¼", EX	$15.00
Jim Bowie, w/horse & accessories, EX	$150.00
Johnny Yuma, w/horse & accessories, EX	$315.00
Lawman Gunfighter, w/hat & guns, complete, EX	$160.00
Little Leager Bat Boy, 4", M	$265.00

Lone Ranger on Silver, 9½", EX, $175.00

Matt Dillon's Horse, for sm figure, EX	$22.50
Paladin, w/horse & accesssories, no hat, 5½", NM	$40.00
Polo Pony, gray, EX	$35.00
Roger Maris, NM	$200.00
Roger Maris, 25th-Anniversary edition, MIB	$60.00
Tufking (horse) & Jockey, w/saddle, EX, from $60 to	$85.00
Ward Bond (Wagon Train), complete, NM	$195.00

Head Vases

These are fun to collect, and prices are still reasonable. You've seen them at flea markets — heads of ladies, children, clowns, even some men and a religious figure now and then. A few look very much like famous people — there's a Jackie Onassis vase by Inarco that leaves no doubt as to who it's supposed to represent!

They were mainly imported from Japan, although a few were made by American companies and sold to florist shops to be filled with flower arrangements. So if there's an old flower shop in your neighborhood, you might start your search with their storerooms.

If you'd like to learn more about them, we recommend

Head Vases, Identification and Values, by Kathleen Cole.

Baby, Inarco, #E3156, blond-haired girl w/pink bow, head slightly turned, pink ruffled collar, 5½"................$27.50

Baby, Inarco (paper label) #E4392, red-haired boy holding telephone wearing Hello Gran'pa bib, 6"..............$37.50

Child, #609, blond-haired girl in black graduation cap, 5¼"...$32.50

Child, Enesco (paper label), 1 of 4 Delsey Tissue girls, blond hair w/pastel flower, hands holding flowers, 5"....$42.50

Child, Inarco, #E1247, blond-haired girl wearing Santa hat, head tilted, 4"......................................$32.50

Child, Inarco, #E1579, praying, blond hair & red robe, 1964, 6"...$32.50

Child, Inarco, #E2965, blond hair w/2 braids & bangs, head slightly tilted, yellow scarf, 7"..................$42.50

Child, Relpo, #2010, blond-haired boy in blue cap, blue shirt w/white collar, 7".............................$65.00

Child, unmarked, blond hair w/ponytail, brown bodice w/applied flower on white collar, 5½"...............$37.50

Clown, Inarco, #E2320, blond hair, red & white polka-dot bow tie & black hat, 5"............................$27.50

Clown, National Potteries (paper label), red cone style hat w/white ball, white ruffled collar w/red trim, 7"..$37.50

Lady, Ardco (paper label), blond hair, head tilted, blue bodice w/applied flowers, pearl necklace & earrings, 6".....$32.50

Lady, Enesco, blond hair, brown fur collar, 6", $40.00

Lady, Inarco, #E-191, blond hair, pink bodice w/white scalloped collar & feather hat, pearl necklace & earrings, 5½"...$42.50

Lady, Inarco, #E1753, brown upswept hair, black lacy bodice, pearl necklace & earrings, hand to chin, 6½"...$48.50

Lady, Inarco, #E190/S, blond, black bodice & hat w/white bow, pearl necklace & earrings, hand under chin, 1961, 4¾"...$32.50

Lady, Japan, light brown hair, green scalloped bodice & hat, hand to cheek, 7"..................................$48.50

Lady, Lefton, blond bouffant hair, green bodice, pearl necklace & earrings, green-gloved hand up, 6"..........$42.50

Lady, Napco, #C2633C, blond hair, black hat w/white dotted bow, black bodice, pearl earrings, missing pearl necklace, 6", $40.00

Lady, Napco, #C3141B, red hair w/lg flower above right ear, pearl necklace & earrings, 1958, 6½".................$52.50

Lady, Napco, #C4891A, red hair, black scalloped bodice & hat, pearl earrings & bracelet, hand to cheek, 1961, 8½"...$125.00

Lady, Napcoware, #6429, red bouffant hair, blue bodice w/white daisies, pearl earrings, blue-gloved hand up, 7½"...$52.50

Lady, Napcoware #C348, blond hair, black hat, bodice & glove, pearl earrings, eyes closed, 7".............$42.50

Lady, Parma, #A219, blond bouffant hair, green bodice, pearl earrings & necklace, 8½"......................$155.00

Lady, Relpo, #K1335, white banana curls, white ruffled bodice w/bow & gold highlights, 8".................$125.00

Lady, Relpo, #2055, blond banana curls, green bodice w/white scalloped collar, pearl necklace & earrings, hand up, 6"...$47.50

Lady, Relpo #A-1229, blond in tall hat of pink flowers, white bodice, gloved hands at tilted face, eyes open, 6½"...$37.50

Lady, Rubens, #482, blond side-swept hair, green bodice w/ruffled collar, pearl necklace & earrings, hand to cheek, 5"...$27.50

Lady, Rubens, #501, blond w/wraparound braid, white bodice w/gold-trimmed flowers, pearl necklace & earrings, 6½"..$48.50

Lady, Thames (paper label), blond hair, pink bodice w/white ruffled collar, wide-brimmed hat, 5½"....$32.50

Lady, Tilso, red hair, head tilted, red scalloped bodice & hat, pearl earrings, hand to chin, 6"..................$27.50

Lady, unmarked, #3854, light brown upswept hair, head turned, blue ruffled bodice, pearl necklace & earrings, 6½" **$47.50**

Lady, unmarked, black hair, yellow bodice w/gold-trimmed bow, large beret-type hat, 7½" **$47.50**

Lady, unmarked, red upswept hair w/applied multicolored flowers, pink ruffled bodice, diamond earrings, 7½" **$42.50**

Lady, unmarked, short black hair, head tilted, green bodice w/applied gold sequins, 7¼" **$47.50**

Lady, Vcagco (paper label), blond hair, slightly tilted head, pink bodice & head scarf, 6" **$42.50**

Teen girl, Brinn's (paper label), #2 TP-2444, blond, white bodice w/brown stars, Love choker & pearl earrings, 7½" **$56.50**

Teen girl, Inarco, #E5626, blond banana curls w/yellow bow, green bodice, heart necklace & pearl earrings, hand up, 7" **$67.50**

Teen girl, Japan, blond side ponytail, green bodice w/white trim, pearl earrings, 7" **$47.50**

Teen girl, Nancy Pew (paper label), blond girl holding red telephone to ear, white ruffled collar w/red trim, 6" **$37.50**

Teen girl, Napcoware, #C7294, light brown hair, blue bodice, pearl necklace, 7½" **$85.00**

Teen girl, Napcoware, #C8493, long red hair w/yellow headband, yellow bodice w/white collar, pearl earrings, 5½" **$32.50**

Teen girl, Rubens, #4121, blond w/wraparound braid & 2 pink bows, pink bodice w/white collar, pearl necklace, 6" **$32.50**

Teen girl, unmarked, #50/425, red hair w/black ribbon, head tilted, orange bodice w/collar, 8" **$85.00**

Teen girl, unmarked, brown flipped-up hair w/pink bow, head tilted, pink bodice, pearl necklace & earrings, 7½" ..**$75.00**

Heisey Glass

From just before the turn of the century until 1957, the Heisey Glass Company of Newark, Ohio, was one of the largest, most successful manufacturers of quality tableware in the world. Though the market is well established, many pieces are still reasonably priced; and if you're drawn to the lovely patterns and colors that Heisey made, you're investment should be sound.

After 1901, much of their glassware was marked with their familiar trademark, the 'Diamond H' (an H in a diamond), or a paper label. Blown pieces are often marked on the stem instead of the bowl or foot.

Numbers in the listings are catalog reference numbers assigned by the company to indicate variations in shape or stem style. Collectors use them, especially when they buy and sell by mail, for the same purpose. Many catalog pages (showing these numbers) are contained in *The Collector's Encyclopedia of Heisey Glass* by Neila Bredehoft. This book and *Elegant Glassware of the Depression Era* by Gene Florence are both excellent references for further study.

See also Glass Animals.

Charter Oak, clear, bowl, finger; #3362.....................**$10.00**
Charter Oak, clear, plate, dinner; #1246, 6" **$27.50**
Charter Oak, pink, comport, footed, #3362, 7" **$55.00**

Charter Oak, pink, goblet, high footed, #3362, 8-oz, $30.00

Chintz, clear, bowl, finger; #4107 ....**$8.00**
Chintz, clear, creamer, 3 dolphin-shaped feet **$20.00**
Chintz, clear, ice bucket, footed **$75.00**
Chintz, clear, mayonnaise, dolphin-shaped feet, 5½"..**$65.00**
Chintz, clear, plate, bread & butter; square, 6" **$6.00**
Chintz, clear, plate, luncheon; square, 8"....................**$18.00**
Chintz, clear, platter, oval, 14" **$65.00**
Chintz, clear, tray, celery; 13".....................................**$18.00**
Chintz, yellow, bowl, mint; footed, 6" **$30.00**
Chintz, yellow, stem, sherbet; 5-oz..............................**$17.50**
Chintz, yellow, tumbler, iced tea; #3389, 12-oz **$30.00**
Crystolite, clear, ashtray, square, 3½" **$4.00**
Crystolite, clear, bonbon, 2-handled, 7½" **$15.00**
Crystolite, clear, bowl, dessert; 5½" **$12.00**
Crystolite, clear, bowl, flower; deep, oval, 13" **$30.00**
Crystolite, clear, bowl, individual nut; handled, 3" **$15.00**
Crystolite, clear, bowl, preserve; 5" **$12.00**
Crystolite, clear, bowl, salad; 10" **$47.50**
Crystolite, clear, candlestick, 2-light **$25.00**
Crystolite, clear, cigarette box, w/lid, 4"......................**$17.00**
Crystolite, clear, cigarette holder, round **$17.50**
Crystolite, clear, cup, punch or custard..........................**$7.00**
Crystolite, clear, mayonnaise underplate, oval, 8" **$20.00**
Crystolite, clear, mustard jar, w/lid..............................**$37.00**
Crystolite, clear, plate, salad; 9" **$9.00**
Crystolite, clear, plate, sandwich; 14" **$35.00**
Crystolite, clear, plate, torte; 11" **$24.00**
Crystolite, clear, relish tray, leaf shape, 4-part, 9"........**$25.00**
Crystolite, clear, salt & pepper shakers, pr...................**$30.00**
Crystolite, clear, saucer **$5.00**
Crystolite, clear, sugar bowl (open), individual...........**$15.00**

Crystolite, clear, tray, celery; rectangular, 12" $35.00
Crystolite, clear, tumbler, pressed, 10-oz......................$70.00
Crystolite, clear, urn, flower; 7"..................................$75.00
Crystolite, clear, vase, 12"..$225.00
Crystolite, ladle, plastic..$7.50
Empress, alexandrite, plate, bouillon liner..................$20.00
Empress, alexandrite, plate, 8".................................$65.00
Empress, alexandrite, saucer, square.........................$25.00
Empress, bowl, nappy; 4½"......................................$12.50
Empress, cobalt, plate, square, 7".............................$55.00
Empress, green, bowl, flower; rolled edge, 9"............$42.00
Empress, green, bowl, mint; dolphin-footed, 6".........$30.00
Empress, green, bowl, vegetable; oval, 10".................$55.00
Empress, green, cup, bouillon; 2-handled....................$33.00
Empress, green, plate, muffin; upturned sides, 12" $70.00
Empress, green, plate, 2-handled, square, 13"............$55.00
Empress, pink, bowl, cream soup $26.00
Empress, pink, bowl, dessert; 2-handled, oval, 10" $45.00
Empress, pink, candlestick, low, 4-footed, 2-handled.$35.00
Empress, pink, comport, oval, 7"...............................$70.00
Empress, pink, cup..$27.00
Empress, pink, plate, 6"..$11.00
Empress, pink, stem, sherbet; 4-oz............................$22.00
Empress, yellow, ashtray...$90.00
Empress, yellow, bowl, cream soup; w/square liner...$30.00
Empress, yellow, bowl, flower; dolphin-footed, 11" ...$75.00
Empress, yellow, bowl, nappy; 8"..............................$35.00
Empress, yellow, bowl, relish; 3-part, center handled, 7".$50.00
Empress, yellow, creamer, dolphin-footed..................$30.00
Empress, yellow, grapefruit, w/square liner $30.00
Empress, yellow, marmalade, w/lid, dolphin-footed...$80.00
Empress, yellow, plate..$10.00
Empress, yellow, plate, 9" $35.00
Empress, yellow, relish tray, 4-part, 16" $75.00
Empress, yellow, saucer, after dinner........................$10.00
Empress, yellow, sugar bowl (open), dolphin-footed, 3-handle..$30.00
Empress, yellow, tray, celery; 10" $22.00
Greek Key, clear, bowl, individual almond; footed.....$25.00
Greek Key, clear, bowl, nappy; 8"..............................$37.50
Greek Key, clear, butter dish, individual.....................$30.00
Greek Key, clear, creamer, hotel, oval $30.00
Greek Key, clear, egg cup, 5-oz.................................$60.00
Greek Key, clear, pitcher, 1-pt...................................$75.00
Greek Key, clear, plate, 5"...$11.00
Greek Key, clear, plate, 6½"......................................$15.00
Greek Key, clear, stem, 7-oz......................................$75.00
Greek Key, clear, sugar bowl (open) $25.00
Greek Key, clear, tumbler, flared rim, 7-oz.................$22.00
Greek Key, clear, tumbler, straight sides, 13-oz $42.00
Ipswich, clear, bowl, finger; w/underplate $20.00
Ipswich, clear, stem, goblet; 10-oz $750.00
Ipswich, clear, stem, oyster cocktail; 4-oz.................$20.00
Ipswich, clear, tumbler, footed, 12-oz $30.00
Ipswich, clear, tumbler, footed, 5-oz.........................$30.00
Ipswich, cobalt, bowl, flower; footed, 11" $250.00
Ipswich, green, creamer $42.50
Ipswich, pink, plate, square, 7"..................................$25.00

Ipswich, yellow, sugar bowl $37.50
Ipswich, yellow, tumbler, footed, 8-oz........................$40.00
Lariat, clear, bowl, individual nut; 4"..........................$20.00
Lariat, clear, candlestick, 1-light.................................$15.00
Lariat, clear, creamer...$15.00
Lariat, clear, ice tub...$75.00
Lariat, clear, plate, buffet; 21".....................................$90.00
Lariat, clear, plate, salad; 7".......................................$7.00
Lariat, clear, stem, oyster cocktail; blown, 4½-oz $15.00
Lariat, clear, stem, pressed, 9-oz................................$20.00
Lariat, clear, stem, wine; blown, 2½-oz.......................$25.00
Lariat, clear, sugar bowl (open)...................................$15.00
Lariat, clear, tumbler, iced tea; footed, 12-oz.............$18.00
Lariat, clear wine, stem, wine; pressed, 3½-oz............$20.00
Lodestar, Dawn, ashtray...$70.00
Lodestar, Dawn, bowl, #1565, 6¾" $45.00
Lodestar, Dawn, bowl, flower, deep; 12".....................$75.00
Lodestar, Dawn, bowl, sauce dish; #1626, 4½"...........$35.00
Lodestar, Dawn, creamer...$50.00
Lodestar, Dawn, plate, 8½"..$65.00
Lodestar, Dawn, relish, 3-part, 7½"..............................$55.00
Lodestar, Dawn, tumbler, juice; 6-oz............................$35.00
Minuet, clear, bell, dinner; #3408................................$60.00
Minuet, clear, bowl, mint; footed, 6"............................$15.00
Minuet, clear, bowl, pickle/olive; 13"............................$30.00
Minuet, clear, candlestick, #112, 1-light.......................$25.00
Minuet, clear, plate, luncheon; 8"................................$15.00
Minuet, clear, plate, salad; 7"......................................$10.00
Minuet, clear, stem, water; #1511, 9-oz........................$30.00
New Era, clear, candelabrum, w/2 #4044 bobeche & prisms, 2-light..$55.00
New Era, clear, flower; 11"...$25.00
New Era, clear, pilsner, 8-oz..$25.00
New Era, clear, plate, bread & butter; 5½x4½"............$12.00
New Era, clear, saucer $5.00
New Era, clear, stem, claret; 4-oz $15.00
New Era, clear, stem, high cocktail; 3½-oz $10.00
New Era, clear, tray, celery; 13"...................................$30.00
New Era, clear, tumbler, soda; footed, 12-oz...............$12.50
Octagon, clear, bonbon, turned sides, #1229, 6" $5.00
Octagon, clear, cup, after dinner $5.00
Octagon, clear, plate, 10½"..$17.00
Octagon, clear, tray, #500, 4-part, 12"..........................$7.00
Octagon, green, bowl, mint; #1229, 6" $17.00
Octagon, green, plate, 14"..$35.00
Octagon, green, saucer, #1231 ....$7.00
Octagon, orchid, cheese dish, 2-handled, #1229, 6"....$15.00
Octagon, orchid, plate, cream soup liner.....................$12.00
Octagon, orchid, saucer, after dinner $12.00
Octagon, pink, bowl, jelly; #1229, 5½".........................$12.00
Octagon, pink, bowl, soup; flat, 9"...............................$15.00
Octagon, pink, creamer, hotel $15.00
Octagon, pink, dish, frozen dessert; #500 ....$15.00
Octagon, pink, plate, sandwich; #1229, 10" $20.00
Octagon, pink, tray, celery; 9" $10.00
Octagon, yellow, plate, bread; 7"..................................$9.00
Octagon, yellow, plate, muffin; turned sides, #1229, 12" $30.00

Octagon, yellow, sugar bowl (open), hotel $15.00
Old Colony, clear, bowl, finger; #4075.....................$5.50
Old Colony, clear, bowl, flower; footed, 2-handled, 8½" $32.00
Old Colony, clear, cigarette holder, #3390..................$16.00
Old Colony, clear, plate, bouillon..............................$5.00
Old Colony, clear, plate, round, 9" $15.00
Old Colony, clear, plate, sandwich; 2-handled, square, 13" $35.00
Old Colony, clear, stem, cocktail; #3380, 3-oz.............$13.00
Old Colony, clear, stem, short soda; #3380, 10-oz.........$7.00
Old Colony, clear, tumbler, juice; footed, #3390, 5-oz..$7.00
Old Colony, cobalt, cigarette holder, #3390.............$100.00
Old Colony, green, bowl, flared, footed, 13" $45.00
Old Colony, green, bowl, salad; 2-handled, round, 10" $47.50
Old Colony, green, bowl, triplex, 7"...........................$28.00
Old Colony, green, grapefruit; 6".................................$35.00
Old Colony, green, plate, square, 6" $18.00
Old Colony, green, stem, claret; #3390, 4-oz $32.50
Old Colony, green, stem, parfait; #3380, 5-oz..............$17.00
Old Colony, green, tray, hors d'oeuvre; 2-handled, 13".$55.00
Old Colony, pink, bowl, cream soup; 2-handled $20.00
Old Colony, pink, bowl, nappy; 4½"............................$10.00
Old Colony, pink, plate, round, 4½"..............................$6.00
Old Colony, pink, plate, square, 10½"..........................$50.00
Old Colony, pink, platter, oval, 14" $35.00
Old Colony, pink, stem, oyster/cocktail; #3380, 4-oz..$13.00
Old Colony, pink, stem, tall soda; #3380, 10-oz $21.00
Old Colony, yellow, bowl, dessert; 2-handled, oval, 10".$50.00
Old Colony, yellow, bowl, jelly; footed, 2-handled, 6" .$25.00
Old Colony, yellow, cup $32.00
Old Colony, yellow, plate, muffin; 2-handled, round, 12" $70.00
Old Colony, yellow, plate, 6" $15.00
Old Colony, yellow, saucer, square or round.............$10.00
Old Colony, yellow, stem, claret; #3380, 4-oz $40.00
Old Colony, yellow, stem, oyster cocktail; #3390, 3-oz..$20.00
Old Colony, yellow, tray, sandwich; center handle, 12".$75.00
Old Sandwich, clear, comport, 6" $37.50
Old Sandwich, clear, stem, footed, 10-oz......................$9.00
Old Sandwich, cobalt, ashtray, individual...................$35.00
Old Sandwich, crystal, ashtray, individual....................$7.00
Old Sandwich, green, flower block, #22 ....$35.00
Old Sandwich, green, stem, claret; 4-oz......................$27.50
Old Sandwich, green, tumbler, iced tea; 12-oz............$40.00
Old Sandwich, green, tumbler, toddy; 6½-oz $22.00
Old Sandwich, pink, bowl, finger $50.00
Old Sandwich, pink, creamer, oval $20.00
Old Sandwich, pink, parfait, 4½-oz $15.00
Old Sandwich, yellow, bowl, flower; footed, 12" $50.00
Old Sandwich, yellow, cup $65.00
Old Sandwich, yellow, plate, ground bottom, square, 6"..$10.00
Old Sandwich, yellow, stem, wine; 2½-oz $45.00
Orchid, clear, ashtray, 3" $27.50
Orchid, clear, bowl, crimped, 10"................................$65.00
Orchid, clear, bowl, dressing; 2-part, w/ladle, oval, 8"..$52.50

Orchid, clear, bowl, finger; #3309 or #5025................$65.00
Orchid, clear, bowl, flower; crimped, Waverly shape, 12" $55.00
Orchid, clear, bowl, gardenia; Queen Ann shape, 9"..$60.00
Orchid, clear, bowl, honey/cheese; footed, Queen Ann shape, 6½" $32.50
Orchid, clear, bowl, mint; footed, Queen Ann shape, 5½" $30.00

Orchid, clear, butter dish, ¼-lb, $315.00

Orchid, clear, candlestick, 1-light, Mercury shape.......$32.50
Orchid, clear, candlestick, 2-light, Waverly shape.......$50.00
Orchid, clear, comport, footed, Waverly shape, 6"......$45.00
Orchid, clear, relish, 3-part, round, 7" $45.00
Orchid, clear, salt & pepper, shakers, pr....................$60.00
Orchid, clear, vase, 12"...$600.00

Orchid, clear, mayonnaise w/underplate, 2-pc set, $55.00

Plantation, clear, ashtray, 3½" $30.00
Plantation, clear, bowl, jelly; flared, 6½" $18.00
Plantation, clear, bowl, nappy; 5½".............................$15.00
Plantation, clear, celery, 2-part, 13" $35.00
Plantation, clear, creamer, footed $25.00
Plantation, clear, cup, punch $25.00
Plantation, clear, mayonnaise, w/liner, 5¼" $45.00
Plantation, clear, plate, demi-torte; 10½"....................$40.00
Plantation, clear, plate, salad; 7" $15.00
Plantation, clear, relish, 3-part, 11" $60.00
Plantation, clear, saucer...$5.00
Plantation, clear, stem, oyster cocktail; blown, 4½".....$25.00
Plantation, clear, tray, condiment; 8½" $22.50
Pleat & Panel, clear, bowl, chow-chow; 4" $5.00
Pleat & Panel, clear, bowl, grapefruit/cereal; 6½".........$5.00

Pleat & Panel, clear, marmalade, 4¾".................**$10.00**

Pleat & Panel, clear, stem, footed, 7½-oz....................**$10.00**

Pleat & Panel, green, bowl, bouillon; 2-handled, 5"....**$15.00**

Pleat & Panel, green, creamer, hotel **$30.00**

Pleat & Panel, green, saucer....................................**$5.00**

Pleat & Panel, green, tumbler, iced tea, ground bottom, 12-oz **$20.00**

Pleat & Panel, pink, bowl, vegetable; oval, 9"............**$30.00**

Pleat & Panel, pink, plate, 6"....................................**$8.00**

Pleat & Panel, pink, stem, sherbet; footed, 5-oz...........**$8.00**

Pleat & Panel, pink, tray, compartmented spice; 10"...**$25.00**

Provincial, clear, bowl, bonbon; 2-handled, upturned sides, 7" **$12.00**

Provincial, clear, bowl, nappy; 5½"..........................**$12.00**

Provincial, clear, coaster, 4"....................................**$8.00**

Provincial, clear, plate, cheese; footed, 5"...................**$10.00**

Provincial, clear, stem, sherbet/champagne; 5-oz........**$10.00**

Provincial, clear, tumbler, iced tea; 12-oz, footed **$17.00**

Provincial, green, bowl, individual nut/jelly **$35.00**

Provincial, green, plate, luncheon; 8"..........................**$50.00**

Provincial, green, tumbler, juice; footed, 5-oz **$50.00**

Queen Ann, clear, bowl, bonbon, 6"..........................**$10.00**

Queen Ann, clear, bowl, grapefruit; square top, ground bottom, 6" **$9.00**

Queen Ann, clear, bowl, individual nut; dolphin-footed **$15.00**

Queen Ann, clear, bowl, pickle/olive; 2-part, 13" **$15.00**

Queen Ann, clear, bowl, preserve; 2-handled, 5"........**$12.00**

Queen Ann, clear, creamer, dolphin-footed **$15.00**

Queen Ann, clear, grapefruit, w/square liner **$15.00**

Queen Ann, clear, plate, bouillon liner **$4.00**

Queen Ann, clear, plate, 4½" **$5.00**

Queen Ann, clear, plate, 7" **$8.00**

Queen Ann, clear, salt & pepper shakers, pr.............**$50.00**

Queen Ann, clear, saucer, square **$3.00**

Queen Ann, clear, sugar bowl (open), individual **$15.00**

Ridgeleigh, clear, ashtray, round................................**$5.00**

Ridgeleigh, clear, basket, bonbon..............................**$11.00**

Ridgeleigh, clear, bowl, jelly; divided, 2-handled, 6" ..**$12.75**

Ridgeleigh, clear, bowl, nappy; bell or cup shape, 4½".**$7.00**

Ridgeleigh, clear, box, flower; 8"...............................**$25.00**

Ridgeleigh, clear, cigarette holder, round....................**$7.50**

Ridgeleigh, clear, coaster or cocktail rest **$5.00**

Ridgeleigh, clear, cup, punch....................................**$10.00**

Ridgeleigh, clear, individual nut................................**$9.00**

Ridgeleigh, clear, plate, cheese; 2-handled, 6"...........**$11.00**

Ridgeleigh, clear, plate, 6"..**$7.00**

Ridgeleigh, clear, salt dip, individual.........................**$13.00**

Ridgeleigh, clear, stem, oyster cocktail; pressed..........**$15.00**

Ridgeleigh, clear, stem, sherbet; blown, 5-oz **$15.00**

Ridgeleigh, clear, stem, wine; pressed........................**$32.00**

Ridgeleigh, clear, tray for individual sugar & creamer .**$12.50**

Ridgeleigh, clear, tumbler, juice; blown, 5-oz.............**$24.00**

Ridgeleigh, clear, vase, 3½".....................................**$22.00**

Rose, clear, bowl, dressing; 2-part, Waverly shape, oval, 6½"...**$65.00**

Rose, clear, bowl, flower; Waverly shape, 11".............**$67.50**

Rose, clear, bowl, lily; Queen Ann shape, 7"...............**$50.00**

Rose, clear, bowl, mint; footed, 5½"...........................**$35.00**

Rose, clear, bowl, salad; Waverly shape, 9" **$95.00**

Rose, clear, candlestick, 3-light, Cascade shape, #142..**$77.50**

Rose, clear, creamer, footed, Waverly shape **$27.50**

Rose, clear, mayonnaise, 2-handled, Waverly shape, 5½" **$55.00**

Rose, clear, plate, demi-torte; Waverly shape, 11".......**$65.00**

Rose, clear, plate, salad; Waverly shape, 7" **$20.00**

Rose, clear, plate, sandwich; Waverly shape, 14".......**$90.00**

Rose, clear, plate, service; Waverly shape, 10½" **$75.00**

Rose, clear, saucer, Waverly shape............................**$15.00**

Rose, clear, sugar bowl, footed, Waverly shape **$25.00**

Rose, clear, tray, celery; Waverly shape, 12"...............**$65.00**

Rose, clear, vase, violet; footed, Waverly shape, 3½"..**$95.00**

Saturn, clear, ashtray..**$9.00**

Saturn, clear, bowl, celery; 10"..................................**$15.00**

Saturn, clear, bowl, nappy; 4½"................................**$5.00**

Saturn, clear, comport, 7"..**$30.00**

Saturn, clear, mayonnaise..**$8.00**

Saturn, clear, saucer...**$5.00**

Saturn, clear, stem, parfait; 5-oz................................**$10.00**

Saturn, clear, tumbler, soda; 12-oz **$10.00**

Saturn, limelight green, bowl, baked apple **$65.00**

Saturn, limelight green, mayonnaise............................**$80.00**

Saturn, limelight green, plate, 6"................................**$35.00**

Saturn, limelight green, stem, fruit cocktail; 4-oz........**$75.00**

Stanhope, clear, bowl, finger; blown or plain, #4080....**$5.00**

Stanhope, clear, bowl, mint; 2-handled, w/ or w/o knobs, 6"..**$15.00**

Stanhope, clear, bowl, nappy; handled, w/ or w/o knob, 4½"..**$15.00**

Stanhope, clear, cigarette box, w/lid, w/ or w/o knob ..**$45.00**

Stanhope, clear, plate, relish; 3-part, 2-handled, w/ or w/o knob..**$30.00**

Stanhope, clear, stem, cocktail; pressed, 3½"..............**$10.00**

Stanhope, clear, stem, goblet; pressed, 9-oz...............**$20.00**

Stanhope, clear, stem, wine; pressed, 2½" **$20.00**

Stanhope, clear, tray, celery; 2-handled, w/ or w/o knob..**$12.50**

Twist, amber or yellow, grapefruit, footed...................**$30.00**

Twist, clear, bowl, individual nut.................................**$5.00**

Twist, clear, cheese dish, 2-handled, 6" **$20.00**

Twist, clear, saucer...**$3.00**

Twist, green, bowl, mint; 2-handled, 6" **$18.00**

Twist, green, sugar bowl, footed **$37.50**

Twist, green, tumbler, flat, ground bottom, 8-oz.........**$21.00**

Twist, pink, baker, oval, 9" **$20.00**

Twist, pink, plate, cream soup liner **$7.00**

Twist, pink, tray, pickle; ground bottom, 7" **$15.00**

Victorian, clear, bottle, oil; 3-oz................................**$35.00**

Victorian, clear, bowl, triplex, w/flared or cupped rim.**$80.00**

Victorian, clear, cigarette holder & ashtray, individual.**$20.00**

Victorian, clear, comport, cheese................................**$17.50**

Victorian, clear, plate, liner for finger, 6" **$10.00**

Victorian, clear, stem, oyster cocktail; 5-oz.................**$15.00**

Victorian, clear, tumbler, bar; 2-oz............................**$35.00**

Waverly, candlestick, 2-light **$40.00**

Waverly, clear, bowl, gardenia; 10" **$20.00**

Waverly, clear, bowl, salad; 7"...................................**$17.00**

Waverly, clear, box, chocolate; w/lid, 5".....................$60.00
Waverly, clear, creamer, footed $20.00
Waverly, clear, plate, cheese; footed, 5½"..................$20.00

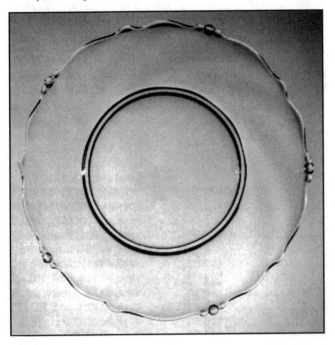

Waverly, clear, plate, dinner; 10½", $45.00

Waverly, clear, plate, salad; 7" $6.00
Waverly, clear, salt & pepper shakers, pr $50.00
Waverly, clear, stem, cocktail; 3½-oz $25.00
Yeoman, amber, cigarette box.................................$100.00
Yeoman, amber, plate, cheese; 2-handled $25.00
Yeoman, amber, saucer..$10.00
Yeoman, amber, sugar bowl, w/lid $40.00
Yeoman, clear, ashtray, handled, 4" $10.00
Yeoman, clear, creamer..$10.00
Yeoman, clear, orchid, bowl, fruit; oval, 9" $55.00
Yeoman, clear, plate, 7"...$5.00
Yeoman, clear, stem, soda; 5-oz $9.00
Yeoman, clear, tray, celery; 9" $16.00
Yeoman, green, bowl, lemon; round or oval, 5".........$18.00
Yeoman, green, egg cup $39.00
Yeoman, green, tumbler, whiskey; 2½-oz....................$12.00
Yeoman, orchid, platter, oval, 12" $33.00
Yeoman, orchid, stem, parfait; 5-oz...............................$30.00
Yeoman, pink, bowl, finger $11.00
Yeoman, pink, cruet, oil; 4-oz $50.00
Yeoman, pink, plate, divided center handled, oval, 10½".$26.00
Yeoman, pink, saucer...$5.00
Yeoman, pink, stem, 8-oz $12.00
Yeoman, yellow, bowl, nappy; 4½"................................$10.00
Yeoman, yellow, cup, after dinner $30.00
Yeoman, yellow, tray, relish; 3-part, 13" $32.00

Holly Hobbie and Friends

Back in the late 1960s, Holly Hobbie was a housewife and mother who also happened to be an artist who used her children as models for her drawings. A friend who had long admired her work suggested that she send some of her drawings to the American Greetings Company. What came of that contact is very obvious! Since then, more than 400 items have been licensed. Today there's a Holly Hobbie newsletter and club, whose members are devoted to collecting anything related to or designed by Holly Hobbie.

Knickerbocker produced dolls in cloth, vinyl, and bisque until they went out of business in 1982. There were four different sizes for Holly, Heather, Carrie, Amy, and Robby: 9", 16", 27", and 33". You'll often find these at garage sales, but not always in good condition. Should you find one still new in the box, expect to pay $10.00 for the 9" doll and up to $30.00 for the 33" cloth dolls. Played-with, soiled dolls are worth much less, perhaps only one-tenth as much.

About 95% of all items are signed either HH, H Hobbie, or Holly Hobbie. This trademark will help you identify the genuine Holly Hobbie merchandise. Other companies have put out look-alike items, so beware!

See the Directory for information concerning the Holly Hobbie club and newsletter.

Book, Art of Holly Hobbie, Random House, 1986, minimum value $25.00
Butter dish, Sharing Something Good To Eat Is Twice the Pleasure Twice the Treat, beige & brown, footed, round, 1980 ....$7.50
Canister, glass, Happiness Starts in Sunny Hearts, Holly w/umbrella, sm $5.00
Cup, It's a Grand Old Day for Being Happy, footed, 1974..$7.50
Doll, cloth, made from Simplicity pattern #6248, 17" ..$10.00

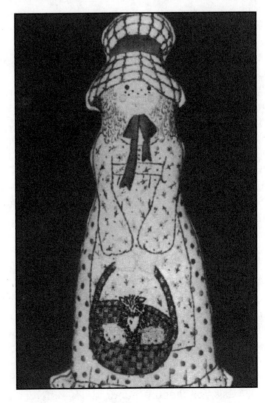

Doll, embroidered, made from Simplicity pattern #6248, 17", $15.00

Doll, vinyl, red hair, original green outfit & straw hat, Knickerbocker, marked KTC 1975/Made in Taiwan, 11" **$12.00**

Drinking glass, There's a Special Glow at Christmas, Holly beside Christmas tree, Coca-Cola logo **$2.50**

Figurine, girl holding packages, Deluxe HHF, 1973....**$95.00**

Figurine, Happy Hearts, Series III, girl w/cat & ball of yarn, porcelain, miniature...**$12.50**

Figurine, One & Only, Series VII, ballerina kneeling, porcelain, miniature **$12.50**

Plate, A Kindness Is Remembered Long After It Is Done, 4" dia **$5.00**

Plate, A Mother's Love Just Grows & Grows, Mother's Day 1975, 10" dia..**$10.00**

Plate, A Smile Reflects a Happy Heart, light green edge, 10" **$10.00**

Plate, Christmas Is All That's Bright & Beautiful, 1975, 10" dia **$10.00**

Plate, Classic Edition, Everyone Needs a Lazy Day Once in a While, 10" dia..**$22.50**

Plate, Classic Edition, Love Is the Good Cooks Secret Ingredient, 10" dia **$22.50**

Plate, Four Seasons Series, Summer Is a Song Anyone Can Sing, 6¼" dia..**$25.00**

Plate, Freedom Series, It's a Star Spangled Day When You Share It w/a Friend, 10" dia....................................**$15.00**

Plate, Friendship Makes the Rough Road Smooth, light green edge, 10" dia **$10.00**

Plate, Good Friends Are Sunshine on a Rainy Day, dark green edge, 10" dia **$15.00**

Plate, Happiness Is Found in Little Things, dark green edge, 10" dia..**$15.00**

Plate, Happy Is the Home That Welcomes a Friend, 6" dia **$6.00**

Plate, Start Each Day in a Happy Way, light blue trim, 10" dia **$18.00**

Tile, Happiness Is Having Someone To Care For, wood frame, 1973, 8x8"...**$8.00**

Tile, Start Each Day in a Happy Way, oval, 5x6"...........**$8.00**

Tray, Start Each Day in a Happy Way, Holly & Heather, metal, round **$4.00**

Vase, Happy Is the Home That Welcomes a Friend, ruffled top, 6" **$6.00**

Vase, Start Each Day in a Happy Way, straight, 1973, 8½" **$7.50**

Homer Laughlin China Co.

Since well before the turn of the century, the Homer Laughlin China Company of Newell, West Virginia, has been turning out dinnerware and kitchenware lines in hundreds of styles and patterns. Most of their pieces are marked either 'HLC' or 'Homer Laughlin.' As styles changed over the years, they designed several basic dinnerware shapes that they used as a basis for literally hundreds of different patterns simply by applying various decals and glaze treatments. If you find pieces stamped with a name like Virginia Rose,

Rhythm, or Nautalis, don't assume it to be the pattern name; it's the shape name. Virginia Rose, for instance, was decorated with many different decals. If you have some you're trying to sell through a mail or a phone contact, it would be a good idea to send the prospective buyer a zerox copy of the pattern.

For more information, we recommend *Homer Laughlin China, An Identification Guide,* by Darlene Nossman and *The Collector's Encyclopedia of Homer Laughlin Pottery* by Joanne Jasper.

See also Fiesta; Harlequin.

Britanny, bowl, nappy; 10"...**$16.00**
Britanny, chop plate **$10.00**
Britanny, plate, 9"...**$9.00**
Britanny, tea saucer **$3.00**
Britanny, teacup **$5.00**
Brittany, bowl, deep, 5"...**$10.00**
Brittany, dish, 13"...**$18.00**
Cavalier, bowl, fruit..**$4.00**
Cavalier, dish, 15"...**$20.00**
Cavalier, plate, square, 8" **$9.00**
Cavalier, plate 6" **$6.00**
Cavalier, sugar bowl **$15.00**
Cavalier, teapot..**$35.00**
Century, after dinner cup **$15.00**
Century, after dinner saucer...**$10.00**
Century, bowl, baker; 8"..**$18.00**
Century, bowl, fruit...**$4.00**
Century, bowl, nappy; 9"...**$20.00**
Century, cake plate, 11½"...**$20.00**
Century, dish (oval well), 11".......................................**$18.00**
Century, egg cup, double...**$20.00**

Century, plates, grapes, 10", $15.00; Mexicana, 10", $25.00

Century, teapot...**$75.00**
Coronet, bowl, baker..**$25.00**
Coronet, pickle dish...**$14.00**
Coronet, plate, 8" **$9.00**
Coronet, platter, 11" **$16.00**
Coronet, tea saucer **$4.00**
Coronet, teacup..**$6.00**
Debutante, bowl, fruit..**$5.00**
Debutante, bowl, nappy; 10" **$16.00**
Debutante, pie server **$30.00**

Debutante, plate, 6" $4.00
Debutante, platter, 11" $16.00
Debutante (Skytone), coupe soup $7.50
Debutante (Skytone), plate, 9" $9.00
Debutante (Skytone), salt & pepper shakers, pr..........$18.00
Debutante (Suntone), creamer $17.50
Debutante (Suntone), dish, 13" $25.00
Debutante (Suntone), egg cup, double $15.00
Duraprint, coupe soup...................................$7.00
Duraprint, plate, 6" $6.00
Duraprint, plate, 9" $9.00
Duraprint, tidbit tray, tiered $40.00
Duraprint (Charm House), salt & pepper shakers $15.00
Duraprint (Charm House), sugar bowl........$18.00
Duraprint (Charm House), teapot................$40.00
Eggshell Georgian, after dinner cup $12.00
Eggshell Georgian, after dinner saucer........$10.00
Eggshell Georgian, bowl, baker; 9" $15.00
Eggshell Georgian, bowl, nappy; 10" $18.00
Eggshell Georgian, chop plate, 14" $25.00
Eggshell Georgian, creamer $12.00
Eggshell Georgian, dish, 15" $25.00
Eggshell Georgian, pickle dish......................$8.00
Eggshell Georgian, plate, 10" $11.00
Eggshell Georgian, salt & pepper shakers, pr..........$20.00
Eggshell Nautilus, bowl, baker; 10" $16.00
Eggshell Nautilus, bowl, oatmeal; 6" $10.00
Eggshell Nautilus, chop plate, 14" $20.00
Eggshell Nautilus, dish, 15" $20.00
Eggshell Nautilus, plate, 10" $10.00
Eggshell Nautilus, sauce boat........................$18.00
Eggshell Nautilus, tea saucer $3.00
Eggshell Nautilus, teacup...............................$4.00

Eggshell Nautilus, teapot, Priscilla pattern, $45.00

Empress, bowl, baker; 8".................................$12.00
Empress, bowl, cream soup $16.00
Empress, bowl, fruit, 6" $8.00
Empress, bowl, nappy (sm round bowl).....................$10.00
Empress, bowl, nappy; 8"................................$12.00
Empress, bowl, oatmeal; 6" $8.00
Empress, butter dish $55.00
Empress, celery tray, 11" $25.00
Empress, coffee cup...$10.00

Empress, coffee saucer $8.00
Empress, dish, 12"...$14.00
Empress, dish, 17"...$25.00
Empress, dish, 7"...$9.00
Empress, plate, 6"..$5.00
Empress, plate, 9"..$9.00
Empress, sauce boat, double handles.........................$50.00
Empress, tea saucer...$4.00
Empress, teacup...$7.00
Jade, bowl, baker..$20.00
Jade, bowl, oatmeal; 36's $10.00
Jade, bowl, 36's, deep $15.00
Jade, dish, 15" $30.00
Jade, plate, 10" $15.00
Jade, plate, 7" $9.00
Jade, plate, 9" $11.00
Jade, sauce boat...$20.00
Jade, tea saucer..$5.00
Jade, teacup..$8.00
Jade, teapot..$60.00
Kwaker, bowl, baker; 11"................................$20.00
Kwaker, bowl, fruit; 5"....................................$5.00
Kwaker, bowl, nappy; 10"...............................$16.00
Kwaker, bowl, oyster; 1¼-pt $20.00
Kwaker, cake plate, 10"...................................$18.00
Kwaker, coffee cup...$10.00
Kwaker, dish, 12"...$16.00
Kwaker, egg cup...$18.00
Kwaker, plate, 10"..$10.00
Kwaker, sauce boat..$18.00
Liberty, bowl, oatmeal; 6"...............................$8.00
Liberty, creamer $10.00
Liberty, pickle dish..$12.00
Liberty, plate, 7"..$5.00
Liberty, platter, 11½"......................................$15.00
Liberty, sugar bowl $15.00
Liberty, teapot $50.00
Marigold, bowl, 5"...$8.00
Marigold, casserole $40.00
Marigold, cream soup $18.00
Marigold, cream soup saucer $12.00
Marigold, dish, 13"...$20.00
Marigold, plate, 10"...$12.00
Marigold, plate, 8"...$8.00
Marigold, sauce boat..$20.00
Marigold, teacup $4.50
Nautilus, bowl, fruit $6.00
Nautilus, bowl, oatmeal; 6"..............................$8.00
Nautilus, bowl, 30's, 6" $10.00
Nautilus, casserole $45.00
Nautilus, creamer $16.00
Nautilus, plate, 10"..$9.00
Nautilus, plate, rare, 8"...................................$12.00
Nautilus, sauce boat...$20.00
Nautilus, sauce boat underplate......................$8.00
Nautilus, sugar bowl..$18.00
Newell, bowl, fruit; 5".....................................$6.00
Newell, bowl, nappy; 8"...................................$12.00

Newell, bowl, oyster; 1¼-pt $20.00
Newell, butter dish................................$60.00
Newell, dish, 9" $12.00
Newell, jug, 36's, 1½-pt $30.00
Newell, plate, coupe; 7" $7.00
Newell, plate, 6" $10.00
Newell, plate, 9" $11.00
Newell, platter, 8" $8.00
Orleans, bowl, baker; 9" $20.00
Orleans, bowl, fruit $7.00
Orleans, creamer $16.00
Orleans, pickle dish $12.00
Orleans, plate, 6" $5.00
Orleans, platter, 11" $16.00
Orleans, sugar bowl (open) $18.00
Piccadilly, casserole $35.00
Piccadilly, cream soup $10.00
Piccadilly, cream soup saucer $8.00
Piccadilly, plate, 10" $10.00
Piccadilly, plate, 7" $7.00
Piccadilly, teapot $40.00
Ravenna, bowl, deep, 5"............................$10.00
Ravenna, bowl, oatmeal; 6" $10.00
Ravenna, plate, 10" $14.00
Ravenna, plate, 7" $8.00
Ravenna, platter, 11" $18.00
Ravenna, sugar bowl (open) $16.00
Ravenna, tea saucer $4.00
Ravenna, teacup $6.00
Republic, bone dish $20.00
Republic, bowl, baker; 10" $16.00
Republic, bowl, oatmeal; 6½"........................$9.00
Republic, casserole $35.00
Republic, dish, w/lid, 8" $20.00
Republic, dish, 12" $15.00
Republic, dish, 15" $22.00
Republic, jug, 42's, 1-pt $24.00
Republic, plate, 9" $8.00
Republic, platter, 7" $10.00
Republic, sugar bowl, 4"...........................$15.00
Republic, tureen, oyster; 8" $40.00
Rhythm, bowl, fruit $4.00
Rhythm, bowl, soup/cereal; 5½" $7.00
Rhythm, casserole $40.00
Rhythm, jug, 2-qt..................................$20.00
Rhythm, sauce boat $12.00
Rhythm, spoon rest................................$100.00
Rhythm, tidbit tray $30.00
Skytone, plate, dessert; Stardust pattern $5.00
Skytone, plate, dinner; Stardust pattern...........$10.00
Skytone, plate, saucer; Stardust pattern $4.00
Swing, butter dish $50.00
Swing, dish, 15" $24.00
Swing, plate, 6" $5.00
Swing, plate, 9" $10.00
Swing, sauce boat $18.00
Swing, saucer $3.00
Swing, teacup $5.00

Theme, chop plate, 14" $30.00
Theme, dish, 14" $20.00
Theme, plate, square, 8" $9.00
Theme, plate, 10" $10.00
Theme, sugar bowl $16.00
Theme, teapot $50.00
Trellis, after dinner cup $17.00
Trellis, bowl, baker; 8" $18.00
Trellis, bowl, oatmeal; 30's, 6" $15.00
Trellis, dish, 13" $30.00
Trellis, sauce boat $23.00
Virginia Rose, after dinner cup $12.00
Virginia Rose, bowl, nappy; 8" $15.00
Virginia Rose, bowl, oatmeal; 6" $6.00
Virginia Rose, cake plate $18.00
Virginia Rose, cream soup..........................$14.00
Virginia Rose, creamer $10.00
Virginia Rose, dish, 13" $16.00

Virginia Rose, mixing bowls, 3-pc set, $75.00

Virginia Rose, plate, 8" $10.00
Virginia Rose, sugar bowl..........................$15.00
Virginia Rose, tray, w/handles $25.00
Wells, bowl, fruit $5.00
Wells, casserole $45.00
Wells, cream soup $16.00
Wells, cream soup saucer $8.00
Wells, creamer $14.00
Wells, jug, w/lid, 42's $30.00
Wells, plate, 7" $7.00
Wells, plate, 9" $12.00
Wells, sauce boat $20.00
Wells, teacup $5.00
Wells, teacup saucer $4.00
Yellowstone, bowl, deep, 6" $15.00
Yellowstone, bowl, nappy; 8" $14.00
Yellowstone, bowl, oatmeal; 36's $8.00
Yellowstone, butter dish...........................$50.00
Yellowstone, cake plate $24.00
Yellowstone, creamer $14.00
Yellowstone, grapefruit $15.00
Yellowstone, plate, deep, 9" $10.00

Yellowstone, plate, 5" **$6.00**
Yellowstone, plate, 7" **$8.00**
Yellowstone, relish dish **$20.00**
Yellowstone, teapot **$40.00**

Yellowstone (Raymond), platter, 8", $14.00

Hull

Hull has a look of its own. Many lines were made in soft, pastel matt glazes and modeled with flowers and ribbons, resulting in a very feminine appeal.

The company operated in Crooksville (near Zanesville), Ohio, from just after the turn of the century until they closed in 1985. From the thirties until the plant was destroyed by fire in 1950, they preferred the soft matt glazes so popular with today's collectors, though a few high gloss lines were made as well. When the plant was rebuilt, modern equipment was installed which they soon found did not lend itself to the duplication of the matt glazes, so they began to concentrate on the production of glossy wares, novelties, and figurines.

During the forties and fifties, they produced a line of kitchenware items modeled after Little Red Riding Hood. Some of this line was sent to Regal China, who decorated Hull's whiteware. All of these pieces are very expensive today. (See also Little Red Riding Hood.)

Hull's Mirror Brown dinnerware line made from about 1960 until they closed in 1985 was very successful for them and was made in large quantities. Its glossy brown glaze was enhanced with a band of ivory foam, and today's collectors are finding that its rich colors and basic, strong shapes just as attractive now as it was back then. In addition to table service, there are novelty trays shaped like gingerbread men and fish, canisters and cookie jars, covered casseroles with ducks and hens as lids, vases, ashtrays, and mixing bowls. It's easy to find, and though you may have to pay 'near book' prices at co-ops and antique malls, because it's just now 'catching on,' the bargains are out there. It may be marked Hull, Crooksville, O; HPCo; or Crestone.

If you would like to learn more about this subject, we recommend *The Collector's Encyclopedia of Hull Pottery* by Brenda Roberts and *Collector's Guide to Hull Pottery, The Dinnerware Lines*, by Barbara Loveless Gick-Burke.

Ashtray, Tropicana, colorful Caribbean figure on cream, green trim, glossy finish, 1959, #T52, 10" wide ..**$245.00**
Basket, Camellia, embossed flowers on basket-weave background, green shading to cream, matt finish, 1943-44, #107, 8" **$235.00**
Basket, Ebb Tide, shell form, black & maroon w/chartreuse handle & interior, glossy finish, #E-11, 16½" **$185.00**
Basket, Iris, embossed flowers on yellow shading to pink, matt finish, 1940-42, #408, 7" **$225.00**
Basket, Rosella, embossed flowers on ivory, glossy finish, fluted rim & handle, 1946, #R-12, 7" **$200.00**
Basket, Tulip, embossed flowers on pink shading to blue, matt finish, 1938-41, #102-33, 6" **$195.00**
Bell, Sun-Glow, embossed pink flowers on yellow, glossy finish, rope handle, unmarked, 6¼" **$90.00**
Bonbon, Wild Flower, embossed flowers on pink & cream, matt finish, handled, 1942-43, #65, 7" **$250.00**
Bowl, Regal, green shading to white, glossy finish, scalloped rim, 1960, unmarked, 6½" **$15.00**
Candle holder, Butterfly, embossed butterfly & floral motif on cream, glossy & matt finish, footed, 1956, #B22, 2½" **$40.00**
Candle holder, Calla Lily, dusky green shading to cinnamon, matt finish, ring handle, 1938-40, unmarked, 2¼" **$70.00**
Candle holder, Iris, embossed flowers on pink shading to blue, matt finish, 1940-42, #411, 5" **$60.00**
Candle holder, Orchid, embossed flowers on pink shading to blue, matt finish, 1939-41, 4" **$75.00**
Candle holder, Woodland, embossed flowers on yellow shading to rose, ring handle, 1949-50, #W30, 3½"..........**$55.00**
Console bowl, Bow-Knot, embossed flowers on pink, cream & blue, matt finish, fluted rim, 1949-50, #16, 13½" **$250.00**
Console bowl, Calla Lily, dusky green, yellow & cinnamon-colored shading, matt finish, ruffled, 1938-40, #590/32, 13" **$125.00**
Console bowl, Wild Flower, embossed flowers on pink, cream & blue, matt finish, 1942-43, #70, 12", minimum value **$225.00**
Cornucopia, Magnolia, embossed flowers w/gold trim on ivory, glossy finish, 1947-48, #H-10, 8½" **$75.00**
Cornucopia, Rosella, embossed flowers on coral, glossy finish, 1946, #R-13, 8½" **$90.00**
Cornucopia, Royal Woodland, turquoise w/white spatter, black trim, glossy finish, 1955-57, #W10, 11" **$60.00**
Cornucopia, Sun-Glow, embossed flowers on yellow, glossy finish, 1948-49, #96, 8½" **$45.00**
Dish, Mayfair, leaf shape, yellow w/glossy finish, 1958, #86, 10" **$30.00**
Ewer, Butterfly, embossed butterfly & floral motif on cream, glossy & matt finish, angle handle, 1956, #B15, 13½" **$145.00**

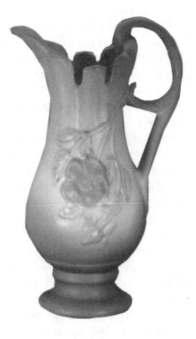

Ewer, Dogwood, embossed flowers on pink shading to blue, matt finish, 1942-43, #505-6½ (actual height is 8½"), $250.00

Ewer, Tokay, embossed leaf & grape design on cream, glossy finish, ear-type handle, 1958, #13, 12" **$195.00**

Ewer, Tropicana, colorful Caribbean figure on cream, glossy finish, angle handle, 1959, #T56, 12½", minimum value..**$275.00**

Ewer, Tulip, embossed flowers on pink shading to blue, 1938-41, #109, 8"..**$185.00**

Figurine, cactus cat, yellow w/glossy finish, #964, 2¾".**$28.00**

Figurine, colt, black w/blue tail & mane, glossy finish, 1954, unmarked, 5½"..**$55.00**

Figurine, dachshund, black w/glossy finish, 1952, 14" long **$165.00**

Figurine, dancing girl, pink & cream w/glossy finish, 1938, #955, 7"..**$45.00**

Figurine, rabbit, green w/glossy finish, #968, 6"..........**$30.00**

Figurine, Swing Band Tuba Player, yellow pants & hat w/green coat, cream tuba & skin tones, glossy finish, 6½", $80.00

Flower bowl, Medley, green shading to orange, 1962, #44, round, 4½" **$15.00**

Flower frog, hippopotamus, yellow shading to pink, glossy finish, 1951, #83, 3½"..**$25.00**

Flowerpot & saucer, Tulip, embossed flowers on blue, matt finish, 1938-41, #116-33, 6"............................**$95.00**

Flowerpot & saucer, Tulip, embossed flowers on yellow to blue, matt finish, 1938-41, #116-33, 4¼" **$85.00**

Flowerpot & saucer, Woodland, embossed flowers on yellow, rose-colored saucer, matt, fluted rim, 1949-50, #W11, 6" **$145.00**

Jardiniere, Camellia, embossed flowers on cream shading to blue, matt finish, fluted rim, 1943-44, #114, 8¼"...**$250.00**

Jardiniere, Iris, embossed flowers on cream, matt finish, 1940-42, #413, 5½" **$155.00**

Jardiniere, Iris, embossed flowers on pink shading to blue, matt finish, 1940-42, 9" **$325.00**

Jardiniere, Poppy, embossed flowers on cream shading to pink, matt finish, 1943-44, #608, 4¾"....................**$90.00**

Jardiniere, Sun-Glow, embossed flowers on yellow, glossy finish, 1948-49, #98, 7½"..**$45.00**

Jardiniere, Water Lily, embossed flowers on pink shading to green, matt finish, 1948-49, #L-24, 8½", $300.00

Jardiniere, Woodland, embossed flowers on cream shading to green, matt, fluted rim, ring handles, 1949-50, #W7, 5½" **$125.00**

Jardiniere, Woodland, embossed flowers w/gold highlights on cream, glossy finish, gold ring handles, #W7, 5½"....**$75.00**

Planter, bandana duck, dark green & wine w/polka-dot bandana, glossy finish, 1951-54, #76, 3½" **$90.00**

Planter, clover shape, dark green & wine, glossy finish, 1951-54, 4½" **$30.00**

Planter, Coronet, swan, chartreuse, yellow & green w/glossy finish, 1959, #213, 6½x10" **$40.00**

Planter, kitten, cream w/pink highlights, glossy finish, #965, 7½" **$45.00**

Planter, Medley, teddy bear, orange w/glossy finish, 1962, #811, 7"...**$40.00**

Planter, pink w/veiled decor, glossy finish, #F3, 8½"..**$30.00**

Rose bowl, Iris, embossed flowers on yellow shading to pink, matt finish, 1940-42, #412, 4".........................**$65.00**

Teapot, Water Lily, embossed flowers w/gold highlights on cream, glossy finish, gold handle & finial, #L-18, 6"...**$125.00**

Vase, Bow-Knot, yellow flowers embossed on aqua shading to cream & green, matt finish, 6½", $175.00

Vase, bud; Orchid, embossed flowers on pink shading to blue, matt finish, 1939-41, #306, 6¾".................**$120.00**

Vase, bud; Tulip, embossed flowers on blue, matt finish, integral handles, 1938-41, #104-33, 6" **$80.00**

Vase, Calla Lily, embossed flowers on green, yellow & pink shading, bulbous, matt finish, 1938-40, #540/33, 6"..**$85.00**

Vase, Calla Lily, embossed flowers on pink shading to blue, matt finish, angle handles, #560, 13" **$235.00**

Vase, Camellia, embossed flowers on cream, matt finish, bulbous, ring handles, 1943-44, #135, 6¼"............**$85.00**

Vase, Dogwood, embossed flowers on cream, matt finish, 1942-43, #517, 4¾" **$60.00**

Vase, Fantasy, pink w/light blue trim, glossy finish, bulbous, 1957-58, #39, 12"...**$30.00**

Vase, Iris, embossed flowers on yellow, matt finish, 1940-42, #402, 4¼" **$55.00**

Vase, Lily, embossed flowers on pink shading to blue, matt finish, fluted rim, 1940-42, #404, 8½" **$135.00**

Vase, Magnolia, embossed flowers on ivory, glossy finish, gold trim & handles, 1947-48, #H-6, 6½"...............**$45.00**

Vase, Magnolia, embossed flowers on pink, cream & blue shading, matt finish, fluted rim, 1946-47, #22, 12½" **$200.00**

Vase, Poppy, embossed flowers on cream shading to pink, matt finish, angle handles, 1943-44, #607, 6½" ...**$125.00**

Vase, Poppy, embossed flowers on pink shading to blue, intregral handles, matt finish, 1943-44, #606, 8½"..........**$175.00**

Vase, Rosella, embossed flowers on coral, glossy finish, bulbous, 1946, #R-2, 5" **$40.00**

Vase, Rosella, embossed flowers on coral, glossy finish, heart shape, 1946, #R-8, 6½" **$95.00**

Vase, Sun Valley, tulip form on round base, ivory w/glossy finish, 1956-57, #162, 11½" **$35.00**

Vase, Sun-Glow, embossed flowers on pink, glossy, slightly bulbous w/flared rim, ear-type handles, 1948-49, #93, 6½"...**$45.00**

Vase, Thistle, embossed flowers on blue, matt finish, angled handles, 1938-41, #51, 6½" **$55.00**

Vase, Tokay, embossed leaf & grape design on cream, glossy finish, hourglass form w/diagonal handles, 1958, #12, 12"...**$70.00**

Vase, Tulip, embossed flowers on yellow shading to blue, matt finish, 3-ring handles, 1938-41, 6" **$85.00**

Wall pocket, Bow-Knot, whisk broom shape, embossed flowers on cream shading to blue, matt finish, 1949-50, #B-27, 8"...**$145.00**

Wall pocket, flying goose, dark green & wine, glossy finish, #67, 6" **$45.00**

Wall pocket, heart shape, embossed flowers on coral, glossy finish, 1946, #R-10, 6½" **$95.00**

Wall pocket, Royal Woodland, conch shell, turquoise w/white spatter, black trim, glossy finish, 1955-57, #W13, 7½"..**$45.00**

Wall pocket, Woodland, conch shell, embossed flowers on cream, matt finish, #W13, 7½"..............................**$145.00**

Window box, Dogwood, embossed flowers on pink shading to blue, matt finish, 1942-43, #508, 10½" long, minimum value **$140.00**

Window box, Sun Valley, light pink w/glossy finish, scalloped edge, 1956-57, #153, 12½" long..................**$35.00**

Dinnerware

Avocado, bean pot, individual; #624, 12-oz **$8.50**

Avocado, bowl, fruit; #603, 5¼" **$5.00**

Avocado, bowl, fruit; #633, 6" **$6.00**

Avocado, casserole (open), individual; #613, French handle, 12-oz **$5.00**

Avocado, dish, divided vegetable; #642, 10¾x7¼" **$12.00**

Avocado, pie plate, #666, 9¼" dia **$22.00**

Avocado, plate, luncheon; #699, 9⅜"..........................**$8.50**

Avocado, plate, salad; #601, 6½" **$5.00**

Avocado, salt & pepper shakers, #615 & 616, w/cork, 3¾", pr...**$12.00**

Avocado, saucer, #698, 5⅞"..**$4.00**

Avocado, sugar bowl, #619, 12-oz **$8.50**

Brown Ring, bean pot, #5410.......................................**$30.00**

Brown Ring, bowl, mixing; #5440, 10" **$20.00**

Brown Ring, casserole, #5428, round **$30.00**

Brown Ring, cheese server, #5462................................**$18.00**

Brown Ring, plate, dinner; #5400 ....**$10.00**

Brown Ring, platter, #5441, oval..................................**$16.00**

Brown Ring, sugar bowl, #5419....................................**$12.00**

Centennial, bowl, cereal; #571, brown w/ivory trim, American Bald Eagle imprinted in center, 5¾" **$50.00**

Centennial, casserole, #586, brown w/ivory trim, American Bald Eagle imprinted in center, 4½x11" **$100.00**

Centennial, mug, #572, brown w/ivory trim, American Bald Eagle imprinted in center, 4"..................................**$50.00**

Centennial, sugar bowl, #582, brown w/ivory trim, American Bald Eagle imprinted in center, 3¾" **$50.00**

Country Belle, baker, #6567, ivory w/blue stenciled flower & bell design **$30.00**

Country Belle, bean pot, #6410, ivory w/blue stenciled flower & bell design **$30.00**

Country Belle, bowl, soup or salad; #6403, ivory w/blue stenciled flower & bell design, 12-oz......................**$8.50**

Country Belle, custard cup, #6476, ivory w/blue stenciled flower & bell design.....................................**$8.00**

Country Belle, pitcher, #6470, ivory w/blue stenciled flower & bell design, 36-oz...................................**$40.00**

Country Belle, plate, dinner; #6400, ivory w/blue stenciled flower & bell design **$12.00**

Country Belle, platter, #6441, ivory w/blue stenciled flower & bell design, oval **$25.00**

Country Belle, sugar bowl, #6419, ivory w/blue stenciled flower & bell design **$16.00**

Country Squire, bowl, mixing; #107, green agate w/white trim, 8¼" **$15.00**

Country Squire, chip 'n dip leaf, #121, green agate w/white trim, 15x10½".....................................**$30.00**

Country Squire, dish, divided vegetable; #142, green agate w/white trim, 10¾x7¼"...............................**$22.00**

Country Squire, ice jug, #114, green agate w/white trim, 2-qt..**$28.00**

Country Squire, plate, salad; #101, green agate w/white trim, 6½" **$5.00**

Country Squire, sugar bowl, #119, green agate w/white trim, 12-oz **$12.00**

Crestone, butter dish, #361, turquoise, ¼-lb...............**$20.00**

Crestone, carafe, #305, turquoise, 2-cup **$35.00**

Crestone, casserole, #307, turquoise, 32-oz................**$25.00**

Crestone, custard cup, #314, turquoise, 6-oz **$10.00**

Crestone, gravy boat, #310, turquoise, 10-oz **$20.00**

Crestone, pitcher, #325, turquoise, 38-oz **$45.00**

Crestone, plate, bread & butter; #304, turquoise, 6½" ...**$5.00**

Crestone, plate, dinner; #300, turquoise, 10¼"...........**$12.00**

Crestone, plate, luncheon; #331, turquoise, 9⅜"............**$8.50**

Heartland, baker, #467, ivory w/yellow trim, brown stenciled heart design in center, rectangular **$30.00**

Heartland, bean pot, #410, ivory w/yellow trim, brown stenciled heart design in center..................**$35.00**

Heartland, bowl, #438, ivory w/yellow trim, brown stenciled heart design in center, 8"....................**$20.00**

Heartland, casserole, #428, ivory w/yellow trim, brown stenciled heart design in center..................**$35.00**

Heartland, cheese server, #463, ivory w/yellow trim, brown stenciled design in center......................**$18.00**

Heartland, coffee cup, #471, ivory w/yellow trim, brown stenciled heart design in center, stemmed...........**$10.00**

Heartland, plate, salad; #401, ivory w/yellow trim, brown stenciled heart design in center **$8.00**

Heartland, sugar bowl, #419, ivory w/yellow trim, brown stenciled heart design in center **$15.00**

Mirror Almond, bowl, mixing; #836, caramel trim, 6" .**$12.00**

Mirror Almond, plate, luncheon; #804, caramel trim, 8½"..**$8.00**

Mirror Almond, bowl, vegetable; #867, caramel trim, tab handles, $16.00; Plate, steak; #841, oval, 9x11¾", $18.00; Salt & pepper shakers, #887/#888, caramel tan, pr, $26.00

Mirror Almond, plate, salad; #801, caramel trim, 6½"....**$6.00**

Mirror Almond, ramekin, #806, caramel trim, 2-½-oz....**$8.00**

Mirror Almond, vinegar cruet, #808, caramel trim, 5¾".**$25.00**

Mirror Brown, baker, #568, square, 3-pt **$10.00**

Mirror Brown, bean pot, individual; #524, 12-oz...........**$5.00**

Mirror Brown, bowl, fruit; #503, 5¼" **$3.00**

Mirror Brown, bowl, mixing; #536, 6" **$6.00**

Mirror Brown, bowl, mixing; #538, 8" **$12.00**

Mirror Brown, bowl, salad; #508, w/rooster imprint, oval..**$12.00**

Mirror Brown, bowl, soup or salad; #569, 6½" **$6.00**

Mirror Brown, butter dish, #561, ¼-lb **$6.00**

Mirror Brown, carafe, #505, 2-cup...........................**$22.00**

Mirror Brown, casserole, #507, 32-oz.......................**$15.00**

Mirror Brown, casserole, #544, 2-pt..........................**$18.00**

Mirror Brown, casserole, individual; #527, French handle, 1980s **$6.50**

Mirror Brown, cheese server, #582 ....**$18.00**

Mirror Brown, custard cup, #576, 6-oz **$8.00**

Mirror Brown, ice jug, #514, 2-qt.............................**$20.00**

Mirror Brown, mustard jar, #551, 12-oz.......................**$7.00**

Mirror Brown, pie plate, #566, 9½" dia **$22.00**

Mirror Brown, plate, dinner; #500, 10¼" **$5.00**

Mirror Brown, plate, luncheon; #531, 8½".....................**$8.50**

Mirror Brown, plate, luncheon; #599, 9⅜"....................**$8.50**

Mirror Brown, plate, salad; #501, 6½" **$3.00**

Mirror Brown, platter, #557, w/rooster imprint, oval ..**$40.00**

Mirror Brown, salad server, #583, rectangular, 11x6½" ..**$15.00**

Mirror Brown, salt & pepper shakers, #587/#588, mushroom shapes, 3¾", pr...**$10.00**

Mirror Brown, saucer, #598, 5⅞".............................**$3.00**

Mirror Brown, vinegar server, #585 ....**$18.00**

Mirror Brown, water jug, #509, 5-pt **$25.00**

Provincial, bean pot, #710, brown w/white trim, 2-qt.**$40.00**

Provincial, bowl, fruit; #703, brown w/white trim, 5¼"..**$10.00**

Provincial, bowl, mixing; #707, brown w/white trim, 8¼".**$22.00**

Provincial, ice jug, #714, brown w/white trim, 2-qt **$32.00**

Provincial, plate, dinner; #700, brown w/white trim, 10¼" **$14.00**

Provincial, sugar bowl, #719, brown w/white trim, 12-oz **$16.00**

Ridge, cup, #204, tawny w/ivory trim, 8-oz **$5.00**

Ridge, mug, #102, gray w/ivory trim, 10-oz **$5.00**

Ridge, mug, #302, walnut w/ivory trim, 10-oz **$5.00**

Ridge, plate, dinner; #100, gray w/ivory trim, 10¼" **$8.00**

Ridge, plate, dinner; #300, walnut w/ivory trim, 10¼" ..**$8.00**

Ridge, plate, salad; #201, tawny w/ivory trim, 7¼" **$5.00**

Ridge, saucer, #305, walnut w/ivory trim, 6" **$5.00**

Ridge, sugar bowl, #109, gray w/ivory trim, 8-oz **$10.00**

Ridge, vegetable server, #208, tawny w/ivory trim, 32-oz, 7½x2½" **$10.00**

Tangerine, bean pot, individual; #924, ivory trim, 12-oz .**$10.00**

Tangerine, casserole (open), individual; #913, French handle, 12-oz **$6.00**

Tangerine, dish, divided vegetable; #942, ivory trim, 10¾x7¼" **$20.00**

Tangerine, pie plate, #966, ivory trim, 9¼" dia **$20.00**

Tangerine, plate, dinner; #900, ivory trim, 10¼" **$8.00**

Tangerine, sugar bowl, #919, ivory trim, 12-oz **$10.00**

Hummels

Hummels have been made in Rodental, (West) Germany since 1935. All have been inspired by the drawings of a Franciscan nun, Sister M. Innocentia. They're commonplace today, both on the retail level and the secondary market. You'll find them in any fine gift shop. In addition to the figurines, a line of collector plates and bells have been made as well.

The figurines have been in demand by collectors for many years, and some are very valuable. It's sometimes difficult to determine what prices you should be paying. Even if the figure is currently in production, the law of supply and demand may cause retail prices to fluctuate as much as 50% in different parts of the country. Several marks have been used over the years, and generally speaking, the older the mark, the more valuable the piece. But if a particular piece happens to be hard to find, scarcity may override the age factor.

Here are some of the marks you'll find: 1) Crown WG — a two-lobed crown over the letters 'W and G,' one superimposed over the other, 1934-1950; 2) full bee — a realistically styled bee within a large 'V,' with variations, 1940-56; 3) stylized bee — bee (represented by a solid circle having triangular wings) within a large 'V,' with variations, mid-1950s until around 1965; 4) 3-line mark — same stylized bee plus three lines of words to the right: c by/W. Goebel/W. Germany; 5) Goebel bee or last bee — stylized bee in 'V' above and toward the right end of 'Goebel/W. Germany,' 1970-80; 6) missing bee — simple 'Goebel/W. Germany' (no bee), mid-eighties to present.

For further information we recommend *Hummel Figurines and Plates, A Collector's Identification and Value Guide*, by Carl Luckey.

#III/57, Chick Girl, candy box, 3-line mark, 5¼" **$135.00**

#III/63, Singing Lesson, candy box, 3-line mark, 5¼" ..**$145.00**

#III/69, Happy Pastime, candy box, last bee, 6" **$145.00**

#10/I, Flower Madonna, white, stylized bee, 9½" **$120.00**

#110/0, Let's Sing, 3-line mark, 3¼" **$95.00**

#111/1, Wayside Harmony, last bee, 5", $230.00

#114, Let's Sing, ashtray, last bee, 3½x6¾" **$100.00**

#12/2/0, Chimney Sweep, 3-line mark, 4" **$65.00**

#125, Vacation Time, plaque, stylized bee, 4¾x4" **$165.00**

#129, Band Leader, last bee, 5¼" **$160.00**

#13/2/0, Meditation, last bee, 4¼" **$90.00**

#134, Quartet, plaque, full bee, 6x6" **$325.00**

#139, Flitting Butterfly, plaque, crown mark, 2½x2½" .**$265.00**

#142/I, Apple Tree Boy, 3-line mark, 6" **$185.00**

#145, Little Guardian, stylized bee, 3¾" **$115.00**

#153/0, Auf Wiedersehen, 3-line mark, 5¼" **$165.00**

#163, Whitsuntide, last bee, 7¼" **$225.00**

#165, Swaying Lullaby, plaque, stylized bee, 5¼x4½" .**$135.00**

#167, Angel w/Bird, font, crown mark, 4¼x3¼" **$135.00**

#172/0, Festival Harmony, last bee, 8" **$175.00**

#180, Tuneful Goodnight, plaque, 3-line mark, 4¾x4" .**$150.00**

#185, Accordion Boy, full bee, 5¼" **$225.00**

#188, Celestial Musician, full bee, 7" **$300.00**

#195/2/0, Barnyard Hero, 3-line mark, 4" **$125.00**

#197/2/0, Be Patient, full bee, 4¼" **$200.00**

#2/0, Little Fiddler, full bee, 6" **$225.00**

#20, Prayer Before Battle, 3-line mark, 4¼" **$135.00**

#200/I, Little Goat Herder, 3-line mark, 5¼" **$175.00**

#206, Angel Cloud, font, stylized bee, 4¾x2¼" **$250.00**

#21/0, Heavenly Angel, full bee, 4¼" **$140.00**

#217, Boy w/Toothache, last bee, 5½" **$160.00**

#224/III, Wayside Harmony, table lamp, 3-line mark, 9½" **$275.00**

#240, Little Drummer, full bee, 4¼" **$165.00**

#246, Holy Family, font, stylized bee, 4x3" **$60.00**

#248, Guardian Angel, font, stylized bee, 5½x2¼" **$60.00**

#25, Angelic Sleep, candle holder, 3-line mark, 3½x5"..**$140.00**
#262, Heavenly Lullaby, last bee, 3½x5" **$130.00**
#265, Hear Ye, Hear Ye, plate, 1972, 7½" dia.............**$50.00**
#28/II, Wayside Devotion, 3-line mark, 7½" **$300.00**

#305, The Builder, last bee, 1970s, 5½", $200.00

#308, Little Tailor, last bee, 5½" **$140.00**
#315, Mountaineer, 3-line mark, 5¼"........................**$150.00**
#319, Doll Bath, 3-line mark, 5¼"..............................**$170.00**
#321, Wash Day, last bee, 5¾"....................................**$175.00**
#322, Little Pharmacist, 3-line mark, 6" **$185.00**
#33, Joyful, ashtray, stylized bee, 3½x6" **$95.00**
#340, Letter to Santa Claus, last bee, 7"...................**$225.00**
#344, Feathered Friends, last bee, 4¾" **$180.00**
#35/0, Good Shepherd, font, full bee, 2¼x4¾"............**$60.00**

#399, Valentine Joy, 1979, 5⅝", $275.00

#4, Little Fiddler, 3-line mark, 4¾".............................**$120.00**
#43, March Winds, last bee, 5"......................................**$95.00**
#45/0, Madonna w/Halo, full bee, 10½"......................**$95.00**
#5, Strolling Along, last bee, 4¾" **$110.00**
#51/3/0, Village Boy, full bee, 4" **$125.00**

#54, Silent Night, candle holder, 3-line mark, 4¾x5½".**$200.00**
#56/B, Out of Danger, last bee, 6¼"..........................**$225.00**
#6/0, Sensitive Hunter, full bee, 4¾" **$165.00**
#60/A&B, Farm Boy & Goose Girl, bookends, stylized bee, 6", pr...**$275.00**
#66, Farm Boy, 3-line mark, 5¼" **$185.00**
#67, Doll Mother, stylized bee, 4¾"............................**$175.00**
#73, Little Helper, stylized Bee, 4¼" **$110.00**
#75, White Angel, font, crown mark, 1¾x3½" **$145.00**
#78/I, Infant of Krumbad, full bee, 2½".......................**$55.00**
#8, Bookworm, stylized bee, 4" **$160.00**
#81/2/0, School Girl, full bee, 4¼" **$185.00**
#84/0, Worship, 3-line mark, 5" **$135.00**
#85/0, Serenade, last bee, 4¾" **$100.00**
#91/A&B, Angel at Prayer, font, crown mark, 4¾x2", pr..**$225.00**
#93, Little Fiddler, plaque, stylized bee, 5⅛x4¾".......**$125.00**
#97, Trumpet Boy, full bee, 4¾" **$150.00**

Ice-Cream Molds

Normally made of pewter (though you might find an aluminum example now and then), these were used on special occasions and holidays to mold ice cream (usually single servings) into a shape that was related somehow to the celebration — bells and snowmen at Christmas time, eggs and flowers at Easter, and cupids and rings for Valentine's Day or weddings, for instance. They were designed with two or three hinged sections, so that the ice cream could be removed with ease.

Stork w/baby, #1151, hinged, 5¼", $115.00

Apple, E-239...**$25.00**
Auto, E-1080, 3" **$65.00**
Boat, S&Co, 5" long **$25.00**
Calla lily, #210, 3-part **$35.00**
Chick in egg, #600, vertical, 4".......................................**$35.00**
Christmas bells, 5 in mold, hinged, 2-piece, ca 1900s.**$45.00**
Cow, #659...**$20.00**
Cucumber, E-226...**$25.00**
Duck, 4"..**$65.00**
Football, #381, 3-piece..**$30.00**
Football, E-1159 ....**$25.00**

Grape cluster, E-278...$20.00
Heart w/cupid, E&Co, 3¾" $45.00
Hen, 3¾"...$85.00
Medallion, E-270, passion flower relief $32.00
O'possum, 5" long $115.00
Petunia, 3" $25.00
Potato, K-154...$35.00
Pumpkin, E-309..$25.00
Rotary Club emblem, E-1110...................................$28.00
Santa, E-962...$85.00
Santa Claus, E-991...$50.00
Soldier, 5⅝"...$45.00
Spade playing card, 4" $60.00
Waffle, E-842 ....$55.00
Wedding ring, E-1142 ....$30.00

Imperial Glass

Organized in 1901 in Bellaire, Ohio, the Imperial Glass Company made carnival glass, stretch glass, a line called NuCut (made in imitation of cut glass), and a limited amount of art glass within the first decade of the century. In the mid-thirties, they designed one of their most famous patterns (and one of their most popular with today's collectors), Candlewick. Within a few years, milk glass had become their leading product.

During the fifties, they reintroduced their NuCut line in crystal as well as colors, marketing it as 'Collector's Crystal.' In the late fifties they bought molds from both Heisey and Cambridge. The glassware they reissued from these old molds was marked 'IG,' one letter superimposed over the other. When Imperial was bought by Lenox in 1973, an 'L' was added to the mark. The company changed hands twice more before closing altogether in 1984.

In addition to tableware, they made a line of animal figures, some of which were made from Heisey's molds. *Glass Animals of the Depression Years* by Lee Garmon and Dick Spencer is an wonderful source of information and can help you determine the value and the manufacturer of your figures.

Numbers in the listings were assigned by the company and appeared on their catalog pages. They were used to indicate differences in shapes and stems, for instance. Collectors still use them.

For more information on Imperial in general, we recommend *Imperial Glass* by Margaret and Douglas Archer and *Elegant Glassware of the Depression Era* by Gene Florence.

See also Carnival Glass; Candlewick; Glass Animals.

Bowl, Crochet Crystal, 7", $30.00

Basket, purple slag w/milk glass handle, #156, 5½"....$35.00
Bowl, Collector's Crystal, cranberry, #737A, 8½" $45.00
Bowl, Grape, purple slag, crimped, #62C, 9"...............$48.00
Bowl, Pillar Flute, blue, 10"......................................$55.00
Bowl, Rose, jade slag, crimped, 3-toed, #74C, 8" $48.00
Box, lion, caramel slag, w/lid, #159 ....$160.00
Box, rooster, purple slag, w/lid, #158 ....$140.00
Cake plate, Old Williamsburg, footed, #341/67D, 11".$35.00
Candle holder, Dolphin, caramel slag, #779, 5"..........$40.00
Candle holder, Hoffman House, amber, #46, 4¾" $20.00
Candle holder, Pillar Flute, blue, 2-light.....................$20.00
Celery dish, Pillar Flute, ruby, oval...........................$40.00
Compote, Lace Edge, purple slag, crimped, 4-toed, #274C, 7"...$45.00
Creamer, Fancy Colonial, pink...................................$15.00
Creamer & sugar bowl, Grape, Rubigold Carnival, footed, #831 ....$28.00
Cup & saucer, Pillar Flute, blue $35.00
Decanter, Collector's Crystal, #612............................$35.00
Goblet, purple slag, #593 ....$32.00
Goblet, Scroll, amber, #322, 11-oz.............................$25.00
Jar, American, amber, #282, lg $25.00

Mayonnaise, Cape Cod, clear, 3-piece set, $40.00

Mug, Storybook, caramel slag, satin $35.00
Plate, Fancy Colonial, Reef Aqua, 7½".........................$14.50

Pitcher, Old Williamsburg, 6", $80.00; Stem, goblet; Old Williamsburg, 6½", $12.00; Stem, wine, Old Williamsburg, 5½", $10.00

Plate, Pillar Flute, blue, 8½" $15.00
Plate, Rose, milk glass, #1950/10D, 10½" $25.00

Relish, Pillar Flute, blue, oval..................$16.50
Salt & pepper shakers, Salz & Pfeffer, Rubigold Carnival .$50.00
Sherbet, Grape, milk glass, glossy, #1950/473 ....$10.00
Tumbler, Big Shot, ruby, 14-oz...................$18.00
Vase, Free-Hand, gold w/stretched & ruffled top, 9" ..$160.00
Vase, Loganberry, milk glass, 10" $30.00

Imperial Porcelain

Figurines representing Paul Webb's Blue Ridge Mountain Boys were made by the Imperial Porcelain Corporation of Zanesville, Ohio, from the late 1940s until they closed in 1960. You'll see some knocking on outhouse doors by ashtrays, drinking from a jug of 'moonshine' as they sit by washtub planters, or embossed in scenes of mountain-life activity on mugs and pitchers. Imperial also made the Al Capp Dogpatch series and a line of twenty-three miniature animals, 2" tall and under, that they called American Folklore miniatures.

Ashtray, Barrel of Wishes, w/hound, #106..................$75.00
Ashtray, hillbilly & skunk, #103 ....$75.00
Decanter, Ma leaning over stump, w/baby & skunk, #104 ....$95.00
Decanter, outhouse, man & bird, #100..................$75.00
Figurine, man leaning on tree trunk, #101, 5" $90.00
Figurine, man on hands & knees, 3" $95.00
Figurine, man sitting w/chicken on his knee, 3" $95.00
Hot pad, Dutch boy w/tulips, IP mark, round............$30.00
Jug, Willie & snake, #101 ....$75.00
Mug, ma handle, #94, 4¼"..................$95.00
Mug, man handle, signed Paul Webb, #29, 4¾" $45.00
Mug, man w/yellow beard & red pants on handle, #94, 4¼" $95.00

Mug, Mt Rug Cutting, #94, 6", $95.00

Planter, dog sitting by tub, IP mark, #106..................$75.00
Planter, man w/chicken on knee, washtub, #105......$110.00
Planter, man w/jug & snake, #110, 4½"..................$65.00
Planter, outhouse, man & bird, #100..................$75.00

Salt & pepper shakers, Ma & Old Doc, pr, $95.00

Salt & pepper shakers, standing pigs, IP mark, 8", pr.$95.00

Indiana Glass Carnival Ware

In the mid-1980s, the Indiana Glass Company produced a line of iridescent 'new carnival' glass, much of which was embossed with grape clusters and detailed leaves reminescent of the old Northwood carnival. It was made in blue, marigold, and green and was evidently a good seller for them, judging from the amount around today. They also produced a line of 'press cut' iridescent glass, some of which can be found in red as well as the other colors mentioned. Collectors always seem to gravitate toward lustre-coated glassware, whether it's old or recently made, and there seems to be a significant amount of interest in this line.

It's a little difficult to evaluate, since you see it in malls and at flea markets with such a wide range of 'asking' prices. On one hand, you'll have sellers who themselves are not exactly sure what it is they have, but since it's 'carnival' assume it should be fairly pricey. On the other hand, you have those who've just 'cleaned house' and want to get rid of it. They may have bought it new themselves and know it's not very old and wasn't expensive to start with. This is what you'll be up against if you decide you want to collect it.

Over the last ten years, the collectibles market has changed. Nowadays, some shows' criteria regarding the merchandise they allow to be displayed is 'if it's no longer available on the retail market, it's OK.' I suspect that this attitude will become more and more widespread. At any rate, this is one of the newest interests at the flea market/antique mall level, and if you can buy it right (and like its looks), now is the time!

Bowl, fruit; wide oval shape w/embossed grapes & vines, lg..**$22.50**

Butter dish, stick-type; embossed grapes & vines **$18.00**

Candy dish, paneled cylinder w/embossed grapes & vines, w/lid, 7½x5", $12.00

Compote, embossed grapes & vines, 10x8½" **$22.00**

Compote, jelly; thumbprint rim......................................**$9.00**

Covered dish, hen on nest **$18.00**

Creamer & sugar bowl on tray, embossed grapes & vines..**$15.00**

Egg plate, embossed grapes & vines **$10.00**

Egg plate, Press Cut design..**$12.00**

Goblet, water; embossed grapes....................................**$8.00**

Pitcher, embossed grapes & vines, pedestal foot, 10".**$25.00**

Tumbler, embossed grapes & vines, scarce, 5½".........**$10.00**

Vase, red, Press Cut design, footed, 9".........................**$20.00**

Jadite Glassware

For the past few years, Jadite has been one of the fastest-moving types of collectible glassware on the market. It was produced by several companies from the 1940s through 1965. Many of Anchor Hocking's Fire-King lines were available in the soft opaque green Jadite, and Jeannette Glass as well as McKee produced their own versions.

It was always very inexpensive glass, and it was made in abundance. Dinnerware for the home as well as restaurants and a vast array of kitchenware items literally flooded the country for many years. Though a few rare pieces have become fairly expensive, most are still reasonably priced, and there are still bargains to be had.

For more information we recommend *Kitchen Glassware of the Depression Years* and *Collectible Glassware of the 40s, 50s, and 60s,* both by Gene Florence.

Ashtray, 6-sided, Jeannette **$8.00**

Bowl, #G309, deep w/thick rim, Restaurant Ware (Fire-King), Anchor Hocking, 10-oz, 1950-56..................**$8.00**

Bowl, batter; banded rim w/pour spout, curved handle w/straight top, flat bottom, Anchor Hocking........**$18.00**

Bowl, dessert; Charm line (Fire-King), Anchor Hocking, square, 4¾" **$7.00**

Bowl, mixing set; Swirl line (Fire-King), Anchor Hocking, set of 4: 6" to 9"..**$40.00**

Bowl, mixing; Swedish Modern line (Fire-King), Anchor Hocking, 3-qt, 11" **$20.00**

Bowl, oatmeal; Jane-Ray line (Fire-King), Anchor Hocking, 5⅞", 1945-63 ....**$7.00**

Bowl dessert; scalloped rim, Shell line (Fire-King), Anchor Hocking, 4¾", 1964-72 ....**$3.00**

Bud vase, horizontal ridges, flat bottom, flared rim, Jeannette **$15.00**

Butter dish, dark Jadite, rectangular w/Butter embossed on lid, Jeannette, 1-lb...**$45.00**

Butter dish, green rectangular tray w/clear lid, Anchor Hocking, ¼-lb..**$20.00**

Butter dish, rectangular Jadite bottom w/white metal top depicting advertising, Ask For...Always Good!, 1-lb.**$25.00**

Butter dish, rectangular w/ribbed decoration on lid, McKee, 2-lb..**$45.00**

Canister, light or dark, Coffee on smooth band above horizontal ridges, flat bottom, metal lid, Jeannette, 40-oz....**$70.00**

Canister, square sides tapering to flat bottom, flat lid w/recessed handle, black lettering, Jeannette, 29-oz.**$35.00**

Creamer, Charm line (Fire-King), Anchor Hocking, 1950-54..**$10.00**

Creamer, Jane-Ray line (Fire-King), Anchor Hocking, 1945-63 ....**$5.00**

Cup, #G299, extra heavy, Restaurant Ware (Fire-King), Anchor Hocking, 7-oz, 1950-56..............................**$6.00**

Cup, demitasse; Jane-Ray line (Fire-King), Anchor Hocking, 1945-63 ....**$13.50**

Grease jar, rectangular w/Drippings in black lettering, flat lid & bottom, thick rim, McKee, 4x5" **$75.00**

Measure, 2-cup, light Jadite, Sunflower in bottom, banded rim, curved handle w/straight top, flat bottom, Jeannette **$18.00**

Measure, 2-cup, pour spout, curved handle w/straight rim, flat bottom, McKee..**$15.00**

Measure, 4-cup, cylindrical w/flat bottom, pour spout, no handle **$350.00**

Measuring set, ¼-cup to 1-cup, cup shapes w/tab handles, no spouts, flat bottoms, Jeannette, 4-piece **$65.00**

Mug, #G212, Restaurant Ware (Fire-King) Anchor Hocking, 7-oz, 1950-56 ....**$8.00**

Mug, embossed decoration on side tapering to thick-rimmed bottom, Anchor Hocking.......................................**$20.00**

Pitcher, alternating diagonal embossed bead & ridge design, flat bottom, ear-shaped handle, Anchor Hocking, 16-oz **$15.00**

Plate, #G292, 3-compartment, Restaurant Ware (Fire-King), 9⅝", 1950-56..**$6.00**

Plate, dinner; Alice line (Fire-King), Anchor Hocking, 9½", early 1940s..**$15.00**

Plate, dinner; Charm line (Fire-King), Anchor Hocking, 9¼", 1950-54 ....**$20.00**

Plate, dinner; scalloped rim, Shell line (Fire-King), Anchor Hocking, 10", 1964-72...**$6.00**

Plate, salad; Jane-Ray line (Fire-King), Anchor Hocking, 7¾", 1945-63 ....**$6.00**

Platter, Charm line (Fire-King), Anchor Hocking, 8x11", 1950-54 ....**$20.00**

Reamer, dark, footed boat shape w/swirled cone, loop handle, Jeannette...**$25.00**

Reamer, embossed Sunkist on straight sides w/flat bottom, squared handle, ridged cone, McKee **$22.00**

Reamer, footed boat shape w/pointed swirled cone, loop handle, McKee, 5¼" **$55.00**

Refrigerator dish, floral decoration around rectangular dish, flat lid w/recessed handle, flat bottom, Jeannette, 5x5" **$20.00**

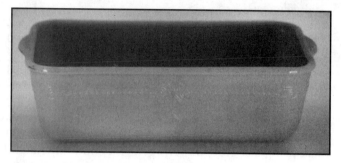

Refrigerator dish, Philbe design, no lid, 9½" long, $25.00

Toiletry shakers, smooth top half w/black lettering, horizontal ribbing at bottom, black lid, Jeannette, each **$90.00**

Japan Ceramics

This category is narrowed down to the inexpensive novelty items produced in Japan from 1921 to 1941 and again from 1947 until the present. Though Japanese ceramics marked Nippon, Noritake, and Occupied Japan have long been collected, some of the newest fun-type collectibles on today's market are the figural ashtrays, pincushions, wall pockets, toothbrush holders, etc., that are marked 'Made in Japan' or simply 'Japan.' In her new book called *Collector's Guide to Made in Japan Ceramics*, Carole Bess White explains the pitfalls you will encounter when you try to determine production dates. Collectors refer to anything produced before WWII as 'old,' and anything made after 1952 as 'new.' Backstamps are inconsistent as to wording and color, and styles are eclectic. Generally, items with applied devices are old, and they are heavier and thicker. Often they were more colorful than the newer items, since fewer colors mean less expense to the manufacturer. Lustre glazes are usually indicative of older pieces, especially the deep solid colors. When lustre was used after the war, it was often mottled with contrasting hues.

Imaginative styling and strong colors are what give these Japanese ceramics their charm, and they also are factors to consider when you make your purchases. You'll find all you need to know to be a wise shopper in *Made in Japan Ceramics, Identification & Values*, by Carole Bess White.

Bell, chef holding bottle, white w/green trim & brown bottle, glossy finish, 3" **$18.00**

Bell, Dutch girl, multicolored w/tan lustre skirt, 3¼" ..**$15.00**

Bird feeder, owl shape, tan & blue lustre, red eyes, 3".**$20.00**

Bonbon, frog on lily pad, tan & blue lustre, 4¾" **$30.00**

Bookends, dog seated on a book, green glossy finish, 3¾", pr...**$25.00**

Bookends, elephant on ball, green crackle glaze, 9", pr.**$85.00**

Bookends, lady skier, multicolored w/matt finish, 6", pr **$30.00**

Bowl, serving; tan & blue lustre finish, 2¾x8¼" dia **$25.00**

Cache pot, black & white cat w/ball of yarn, glossy finish, 4¼" **$12.50**

Cache pot, calico pig, white w/multicolored design, glossy finish, 3¼" **$15.00**

Cache pot, double; boys in fez between pots, yellow lustre w/multicolored figure, 4"................................**$25.00**

Cache pot, man w/camel, tan lustre w/multicolored figures, 2½" **$12.50**

Cache pot, mandolin player, yellow lustre w/multicolored figure, 4" **$12.50**

Cache pot, rabbit pulling cart, multicolored w/glossy finish, 3½" **$15.00**

Cache pot, Scottie dog, white & shades of blue w/glossy finish, 4" **$20.00**

Cache pot, tiger on barrel, tan & yellow matt finish, 5"...**$12.50**

Cache pot, 2 men in sombreros, tan lustre w/multicolored figures, 4½"..**$12.50**

Candlesticks, green & white crackle glaze, 4¾", pr.....**$35.00**

Candlesticks, skeleton head on book, bisque, 2½", pr.**$30.00**

Canister, multicolored flowers on cream crackle glaze, hexagonal, 4¾"...**$25.00**

Creamer & sugar bowl, seated dogs, blue lustre, gold tails form handles, 4½", pr, $50.00

Donkey, orange glossy finish, Japan, 6½" **$50.00**

Figurine, bunny atop egg, multicolored w/matt finish, 4¼" **$12.50**

Figurine, calico dog, white w/multicolored spots, glossy finish, 4½" **$15.00**

Figurine, colonial couple at dresser w/mirror, multicolored w/gold highlights, glossy finish, 7½" **$30.00**

Figurine, dog on shoe, black & brown glossy finish, 2½"..**$8.50**

Figurine, dogs w/watering can on round base, multicolored w/matt finish, 2¼" **$10.00**

Figurine, elephant, yellow lustre w/red trunk, 2½"…..**$10.00**

Figurine, kitten w/ball of yarn, white w/green & red features & blue yarn, glossy finish, 2¼" …………….**$10.00**

Figurine, lady holding skiis, multicolored w/matt finish, rare, 7¾" ………………………………………………**$50.00**

Figurine, lady w/parasol, orange & cream ruffled dress, glossy finish, 3¾" ………………………………**$15.00**

Figurine, scottie dog w/violin, orange glossy finish, 4¼" ……………………………………………**$15.00**

Figurine, seated bunny rabbit, white lustre finish, 2" ….**$8.50**

Figurine, sleeping cat, tan lustre w/orange bow, 5" long, $25.00

Fishbowl castle, green, orange & blue glossy finish, 2½"…………………………………………………**$12.50**

Flask, girl standing in life preserver, bisque, inscribed Life Preserver, 4¾", minumum value …………………**$50.00**

Flower basket, cream & blue w/embossed flowers, glossy finish, 4", minimum value………………………**$20.00**

Flower bowl, circle of swans form rim, hand-painted scene in center, tan & blue lustre, 8" dia, minimum value …**$85.00**

Flower bowl, swans & lily pads in relief on rim, tan, teal & white lustre, 8" dia …………………………**$60.00**

Flower frog, bird on stump, orange lustre w/multicolored bird, 4½"………………………………………**$15.00**

Hair receiver, Geisha girl & multicolored flowers on white, glossy finish, 2½" ………………………………**$60.00**

Hair receiver, violets on white, glossy finish, 2¾" …….**$50.00**

Humidor, green & yellow crackle glaze w/multicolored floral design, 6"…………………………………**$40.00**

Mayonnaise set, Art Deco, green & cream w/yellow & orange flowers, lustre finish, 3¼"………………**$40.00**

Mayonnaise set, green & opal lustre w/multicolored floral design, scalloped rim, 3-piece set, 3½"…………**$40.00**

Mayonnaise set, lotus shape, yellow & orange matt finish w/white lustre interior, 3-piece set, 6¾" dia………**$30.00**

Napkin ring, baby chick, yellow lustre, 2½" …………**$18.00**

Nut cup, colonial girl w/basket, green, orange & white glossy finish, 3¾" ……………………………**$15.00**

Nut cup, dog in clown suit beside basket, multicolored w/matt finish, 4"………………………………**$18.00**

Pincushion, banjo player seated in chair, multicolored w/matt finish, rare, 3½"………………………**$50.00**

Pincushion, cocker spaniel w/basket on his back, green & yellow lustre, rare, 4"…………………………**$30.00**

Pincushion, dachshund, black w/white eyes, glossy finish, 2½" ………………………………………………**$18.00**

Pincushion, dog facing left, Art Deco style w/tan lustre, green base, 2½"………………………………**$15.00**

Pincushion, dog w/bucket, brown & white glossy finish w/red neck ribbon, yellow matt bucket, 3¼"……**$12.50**

Pincushion, dog w/radio, yellow & tan lustre, rare, 3"..**$30.00**

Pincushion, man w/accordion, multicolored glossy finish w/tan lustre accordion & base, 3¾"……………**$20.00**

Pincushion, man w/top hat, black, orange & blue matt finish, 4"………………………………………**$30.00**

Pincushion, monkey w/orange, multicolored matt finish, 2¼" ………………………………………………**$15.00**

Pincushion, pelican, blue & yellow matt finish, 2½" …**$15.00**

Pincushion, sailor boy, seated w/1 knee up & hand to cheek, bisque, rare, 3¼" ………………………**$25.00**

Pitcher, Art Deco, orange w/yellow flowers, matt finish, 6"………………………………………………**$40.00**

Pitcher, begging dog, brown, black & white w/glossy finish, inscribed Souvenir of Splitrock Lighthouse, 6½"..**$40.00**

Pitcher, horse head, brown & black glossy finish, 4½" ..**$20.00**

Place card holder, dog seated on base looking up, tan lustre w/orange spots, rare, 2¾"………………………**$28.00**

Planter, green w/Art Deco style shamrocks & tulips, glossy finish, 4", minimum value………………………**$30.00**

Planter, green w/embossed flowers, glossy finish, 6" wide………………………………………………**$20.00**

Planter, multicolored birds & flowers on cream crackle glaze, 5"…………………………………………**$20.00**

Planter, pink & blue w/vertical ribs, fluted rim, glossy finish, 3"………………………………………………**$10.00**

Planter, yellow crackle glaze w/embossed elephants, 3¾" ………………………………………………**$15.00**

Plaque, Hawaiian girl, multicolored w/orange lustre skirt, 6"………………………………………………**$35.00**

Powder jar, girl holding skirt up forms lid, yellow & blue lustre, 5½"………………………………………**$60.00**

Powder jar, green & orange airbrushed glaze, black & white dog finial, 2½", minimum value…………………**$40.00**

Powder jar, orange & pink lustre, multicolored clown finial, ball form, 7¼", minimum value…………………**$125.00**

Salt box, embossed flowers on basket-weave design, matt finish, 5¼" ……………………………………**$35.00**

Soap dish, elephant w/dish on his back, green matt finish, 3"………………………………………………**$18.00**

Sugar shaker, Art Deco, orange & blue lustre w/multicolored flowers, gold top, 6¼"………………………**$30.00**

Teapot, Art Deco, orange, yellow & green lustre, black diamond shape lid finial, 7", minimum value…………**$75.00**

Teapot, blue & white lustre w/multicolored floral motif, 6½"………………………………………………**$40.00**

Teapot, elephant figure, blue lustre w/multicolored motif, 6¾"………………………………………………**$45.00**

Teapot, Pekingese dog, paw forms spout, tail forms handle, green matt finish, rare, 6¾" ……………………**$145.00**

Toast rack, yellow, orange & green matt finish, 8" long………………………………………………**$25.00**

Tulip shape, orange lustre, Japan, 1¾"………………**$20.00**

Vase, alternating tan & blue lustre panels, 5" $22.00

Vase, bird on tree trunk, brown w/multicolored bird, glossy finish, 6½"..$25.00

Vase, brown w/enameled flowers, glossy finish, bulbous w/flared rim & base, ring handles at rim, 7½" $20.00

Vase, bud; yellow lustre w/multicolored 'siesta' figure, 3¾"..$12.00

Vase, colonial lady holding basket, green & white glossy finish, 7½"...$30.00

Vase, cream crackle glaze w/multicolored poppies, ball form, 5½"...$45.00

Vase, figural lady in green dress holding white basket, glossy finish, red mark, 7½", $30.00

Vase, monkey trio, blue, orange & cream lustre, 2¾" .$12.50

Vase, multicolored poppies & tan lustre accents on black matt glaze, rare, 6" $50.00

Vase, multicolored w/dragon motif, bulbous, 13".....$225.00

Vase, orange w/black & white Art Deco motif around top, glossy finish, bulbous, 6"..$50.00

Vase, pixie beside lily, multicolored w/glossy finish, 3¾"..$18.00

Vase, Satsuma type, frog trio, green & orange glossy finish, 7½", minumum value...$40.00

Vase, Satsuma type w/Oriental figure, bulbous, 3½"...$15.00

Vase, seated clown, green & white lustre w/multicolored polka dots, 3¼"..$20.00

Vase, tulips, multicolored w/glossy finish, scrolled tan lustre base, 6" $30.00

Whisk broom, dog's-head handle in yellow lustre w/red bristles, 2"...$20.00

Jell-O Collectibles

'America's Most Famous Dessert' (Jell-O's first advertising slogan) was first concocted nearly a century ago. The name 'Jell-O' was originally used by the Genesee Pure Food Company in 1900. It was well advertised and quickly accepted by the American public. Sales that amounted to a quarter of a million dollars in 1902 grew to reach the million-dollar mark in only four years. During that span of time, the company printed recipe folders and booklets and ran advertising in national magazines. Jell-O became a household word.

The first of many recipe books was published in 1904, and the company added two more flavors to the original four. At that time, they also developed a new product, Ice Cream Powder. The first souvenir spoon (there were two styles), souvenir dish (there were also two of these), and Jell-O molds appeared in 1906. Today any Jell-O related item is becoming very collectible. Especially good are the recipe books and magazine ads illustrated by such famous artists as Rose O'Neill, John Newton Howitt, and Norman Rockwell. Many other well-know artists and illustrators lent their talents to designing the covers as well.

In 1923 the Jello-O Company Inc. was organized, which in two years was sold to the Postum Cereal Company Inc. By 1929 that company owned fourteen different food companies. To better reflect the diversified nature of its business, the name was changed to General Foods Corporation.

The recipe booklets kept coming — sometimes at the rate of several a year. In 1932 the company's radio broadcast, 'General Foods Cooking School of the Air,' offered them to listeners everywhere. They sponsored the 'Wizard of Oz' show in 1933, adapting four titles from Frank Baum's series and incorporating into them advertising illustrations and a section of recipes. The 'Jack Benny Show' replaced 'The Wizard of Oz' from 1934 until 1942. During the 1937 season General Foods published a radio show premium titled 'Jack & Mary's Jell-O Recipe Book' featuring caricatures of Jack and Mary on the soft cover.

For more information we recommend 'A Guide to Collecting Cookbooks' by Col. Bob Allen, who provided us with this narrative material.

Recipe Booklets

1905, Jell-O The Dainty Dessert, pictures encircled bust portrait of the Jell-O girl..$100.00

1906, Jell-O Ice Cream Powder, pictures the Jell-O girl w/tray of goodies...$55.00

1909, Desserts of the World $60.00

1912, America's Most Famous Dessert, lady on phone saying 'Yes, Jell-O, please..; O'Neill illustration..................$55.00

1912, What Six Famous Cooks Say of Jell-O, America's Most Famous Dessert $55.00

1915, Jell-O & the Kewpies, pictures the Jell-O girl & kewpies making dessert, O'Neill illustration...............$55.00

1918, New Talks About Jell-O, shows the Jell-O girl seated at desk $25.00

1922, It's So Simple, a Norman Rockwell cover illustration of Grandma making Jell-O w/2 children watching ...**$20.00**

1924, Polly Put the Kettle On, We'll All Make Jell-O, pictures colonial family at hearth, by Maxfield Parrish.......**$55.00**

1924, The Jell-O Girl Gives a Party, illustrated by Rose O'Neill, $55.00

1926, The Charm of Jell-O, shows lady in green dress w/tray & Jell-O mold..**$25.00**

1927, Through the Menu With Jell-O, illustrated by Linn Ball, $15.00

1928, Secrets of the Automatic Refrigerator, illustrated by Giro..**$15.00**

1929, The Complete Jell-O Recipe Book.....................**$15.00**

1930, Quick & Easy Jell-O Wonder Dishes **$15.00**

1933, What You Can Do With Jell-O, second printing ..**$10.00**

1934, The Scarecrow & the Tin Wood-man **$75.00**

1935, Recipes for Lucious Ice Cream, Quick, Economical **$15.00**

1937, Jack & Mary's Jell-O Recipe Book, 1st edition ...**$50.00**

1937, Jack & Mary's Jell-O Recipe Book, 3rd edition ..**$15.00**

Miscellaneous

Dish, 2 variations **$150.00**

Mailing envelope, 1908..**$25.00**

Mold, individual **$3.00**

Molds, fancy shapes, early 1900s, each **$35.00**

Molds, fancy shapes, family size, each, from $10 to .**$20.00**

Product boxes, ca 1920s, each, $3.00

Spoon, 2 variations, each **$25.00**

Jewelry

Though the collectible jewelry frenzy of a few years ago seems to have subsided a bit, better costume jewelry remains a strong area of interest on today's market. Signed pieces are especially good. Check for makers' marks on metal mounts. Some of the better designers are Hobé, Haskell, Monet, Trifari, Weiss, and Eisenberg.

Early plastic pieces (Lucite, Bakelite, and celluloid, for example) are very collectible. Some Lucite is used in combination with wood, and the figural designs are especially desirable. The better rhinestone jewelry, especially when it's signed, is a good investment as well.

There are several excellent reference books available, if you'd like more information. Lillian Baker has written several: *Art Nouveau and Art Deco Jewelry, An Identification and Value Guide; Twentieth Century Fashionable Plastic Jewelry;* and *50 Years of Collectible Fashion Jewelry.* Other books: *Collecting Rhinestone Colored Jewelry* by Maryanne Dolan and *The Art and Mystique of Shell Cameos* by Ed Aswad and Michael Weinstein.

Barrette, Florentine gold-tone alternating leaf design on rectangular bar w/a single pearl accent, Sarah Coventry, 1950, $25.00

Bracelet, antique gold-tone 'Harvest Wheat' design, Sarah Coventry, 1950 ....**$35.00**

Bracelet, black faceted rhinestones w/clear rhinestone 'crescent-moon' settings every fourth one, Sarah Coventry, 1960 ....**$40.00**

Bracelet, butterscotch Bakelite bangle carved w/various 'hash-mark' designs, 1970....................................**$50.00**

Bracelet, hinged, sterling silver w/bird & bamboo designs, ⅝" wide **$115.00**

Bracelet, lapis blue Thermoset plastic cuff, 1935.........**$45.00**

Bracelet, magenta Lucite free-form bangle, 1960.........**$95.00**

Bracelet, marbled dark amber Bakelite bangle w/5 round copper inserts imprinted w/ 4 'swastika' designs on each, 1950 ....**$85.00**

Bracelet, red & black Thermoset free-form bangle, marked KJL **$45.00**

Bracelet, sterling heart w/filigree border on chain, Jewel Art, 1940 ....**$65.00**

Bracelet, 4 sterling silver flower blossoms w/mother-of-pearl stone centers over 4 lg chain links, Kreisler **$80.00**

Bracelet, 5 yellow glass scarabs on chain **$35.00**

Bracelet, 6 marbled lavender Lucite triangles w/rounded corners set in white-metal leaf design, 1960 ....**$55.00**

Bracelet, 6 red Lucite squares linked w/gold-tone chain, 1950 ....**$45.00**

Bracelet, 9 etched & engraved leaves linked in a single row, Beau, ca 1940 ....**$55.00**

Bracelet & earring set, clip-on, rhodium rectangles designed of ribbed half-circles & bars, Sarah Coventry, 1960 ....**$125.00**

Brooch, aqua-blue plastic flower w/yellow center set in silver-tone rhodium w/stem & 2 leaves, 1960 ....**$35.00**

Brooch, hand-painted accents in center of wreath of carved butterscotch Bakelite leaves, 1930 ....**$45.00**

Brooch, multicolored abstract mask shape, signed Missoni, 1980 ....**$75.00**

Brooch, multicolored faceted stones forming star encircled by more stones, Kramer, 1950 ....**$40.00**

Brooch, ribbon design w/prong-set & faceted clear rhinestones, Mimi, 1960, $45.00

Brooch, multicolored plastic, glass & Lucite clustered 'gems,' marked W Germany, 1960-70.................................**$65.00**

Brooch, sterling repousse w/open leaf & berry design, Danecraft, 1950 ....**$65.00**

Brooch & earring set, turquoise enamel & plastic turquoise stones set in a rhodium flower design, Emmons, 1960 ....**$35.00**

Buckle, 2 elephants of marbled amber plastic facing each other w/trunks together, 2-piece, 1935 ....**$55.00**

Buckle, 2 red Catalin plastic apples w/hand-painted green stems, 1936-41...**$125.00**

Buckle, dark amber Bakelite circle w/allover carved circle design, 1-piece w/hasp, 1930, $65.00

Cameo, black & white, 1⅞"....................................**$30.00**

Charm, ivory plastic cat figure w/sm balls on body surface, ruffled collar, 1½"...**$15.00**

Dress clip, Catalin plastic in carved ivory & green 'zigzag'-designed triangle, 1936-1941 ....**$75.00**

Dress clip, deeply carved green Bakelite leaf design, 1935...**$45.00**

Dress clip, diamond shape w/lg faceted clear rhinestones set in sterling w/gold wash, Eisenberg, 1930-40.**$125.00**

Dress clip, green carved Bakelite w/leaf design, 1930s, 1⅜" **$20.00**

Dress clip, red Bakelite cat sitting in profile w/carved features, painted-on yellow collar & yellow & black eye, 1⅝" **$50.00**

Earrings, clip-on, baguette-cut clear rhinestones set in a rhodium apple design with 2 sm leaves on stem, Trifari, 1950, $35.00

Earrings, clip-on, black Thermoset star shapes w/white borders, marked KJL..**$35.00**

Earrings, clip-on, elongated cluster of frosted & clear light purple wired-on beads, Alice Caviness, 1970-75 ..**$55.00**

Earrings, clip-on, faceted & bezel-set gemstones set in antiqued gold-tone filigree leaf shape, Hobe, 1948, 1¾x1" **$95.00**

Earrings, clip-on, hand-painted gold-electroplated shell design w/gold accents, Mosell, 1960 ....**$35.00**

Earrings, clip-on, red button shape w/clear rhinestones, 1935 ....**$45.00**

Earrings, clip-on, red tassels attached by gold-tone chain links to domed caps, 1940....................................**$35.00**

Earrings, clip-on, red teardrops hanging from red & clear rhinestone clusters set in gold-tone metal, M Hall, 1955-60 ....**$100.00**

Earrings, clip-on, 2 overlapping 'boomerang' shapes w/blue enamel on copper, Renoir, 1950-55......................**$35.00**

Earrings, coiled fuchsia Bakelite w/rhinestone centers, 1930s, 1" dia **$15.00**

Earrings, dark amber oval hoop shapes, marked Trifari, 1970 ....**$45.00**

Earrings, fuchsia Bakelite knot motif, 1930s, ¾" dia **$15.00**

Earrings, pierced, green marbled Bakelite hoops, 1930s, 1" dia **$15.00**

Earrings, screw-on, bezel-set blue zircons, amethyst, peridot & topaz in gold-tone mounting, 1945, 1x1½" **$85.00**

Earrings, screw-on, red faceted Bakelite buttons, ⅝" dia..**$25.00**

Earrings, sm shell shapes in electroplated gold, Christian Dior, 1965 ....**$35.00**

Earrings, wired turquoise & blue glass stones set in round gilded filigree mounting, Miriam Haskell, 1940 ....**$65.00**

Earrings, 2 green & orange molded Thermoset leaves w/metal center vein & branch accented w/tiny rhinestones, 1935 ....**$35.00**

Earrings & bracelet set, yellow Thermoset oval shapes set in decorative metal, bracelet has 6 ovals, 1950 ....**$55.00**

Hair ornaments, 3 vertical rows of 6 yellow flowers w/clear rhinestone centers on clear sticks, 1935, 8", pr.....**$45.00**

Hat ornament, 2 brown Deco triangles w/clear rhinestones & 'hash-mark' cutouts on connecting rod, 1930 ...**$30.00**

Necklace, alternating orange Bakelite & wood triangle shapes separated by gold-tone beads, 1930.........**$65.00**

Necklace, amber glass cylindrical beads w/clear spacers, 54" long...**$35.00**

Necklace, beaded w/3 clear Lucite squares separated by single beads, Encore, 1970....................................**$45.00**

Necklace, black chunky faceted Bakelite beads, short, 1930s **$20.00**

Necklace, clusters of tiny purple flowers w/white centers separated by purple beads & clusters of green leaves...**$35.00**

Necklace, cross w/colored plastic stones & simulated pearl center in enameled rhodium mounting, Emmons, 1970, 24" **$35.00**

Necklace, double strand of simulated baroque pearls w/gray spacer beads, long **$50.00**

Necklace, marbled green Bakelite beads w/gold spacers, 1930s, 12"...**$35.00**

Necklace, red faceted oval Bakelite beads, 50" long.**$125.00**

Necklace, round & square beige tortoise-shell celluloid beads w/long curved pieces in front, short, 1930s **$25.00**

Necklace, turquoise Thermoset beads combined w/wood & painted cork beads connected by sm gold-tone beads, ca 1950..**$45.00**

Necklace, 22 14k-gold beads on trace-link chain, 1950, 20" long..**$125.00**

Necklace, 4 strands of Australian 'aurora borealis' beads in varying faceted shapes w/gold ball spacers, 1960.**$135.00**

Necklace, 4 strands of gold-tone chain, Trifari, 1965 ..**$55.00**

Necklace & earring set, gold-electroplated signets & hearts, necklace can be worn as belt, Napier, 1950 ....**$195.00**

Pendant, cross in antiqued filigreed rhodium w/applied beading, 1977, Emmons **$20.00**

Pendant, figural pewter bunny w/animated features, blue eyes & gold-tone eyeglasses, JJ, 1950...................**$45.00**

Pin, anchor & rope design in blue enamel w/gold-electroplated rope & trim, Trifari, 1955 ....**$35.00**

Pin, basket design set w/baquette & pear-shaped topaz-colored 'flowers' in clear rhinestone basket, Trifari, 1955-65..**$45.00**

Pin, black Bakelite 6-sided beveled shape w/red round center, 1930..**$20.00**

Pin, black vintage auto w/white running board & fenders accented w/clear rhinestones, marked Lea Stein Paris, 1950 ....**$85.00**

Pin, blackamoor bust of painted enamel on gold-tone metal w/colorful rhinestone accents, Boucher, 1960......**$85.00**

Pin, butterfly shape w/multicolored blue stones set in gold-tone metal w/gold-tone antennae, Kramer, 1960 .**$65.00**

Pin, carved black Catalin sailfish w/painted eyes, 1936-41 1 ....**$65.00**

Pin, celluloid cockatoo in shades of ivory, rose & blue w/red faceted stones, 1935....................................**$55.00**

Pin, clear rhinestones set in rhodium 'Tinlizzy' design, Emmons, 1970..**$35.00**

Pin, electroplated gold-tone figural peacock w/clear rhinestone accents, Coro, 1950.....................................**$75.00**

Pin, enamel on sterling silver circle, white fleur-de-lis design on royal blue background, 1½" dia **$50.00**

Pin, faceted 6-sided shape in black Bakelite w/red center, 1930 ....**$55.00**

Pin, faux cabachons & rhinestones set in gold-tone crown shape, Emmons, 1960...**$35.00**

Pin, figural bird in flight in combination of polished wood & carved translucent plastic, unmarked, 1935 ....**$65.00**

Pin, figural Christmas tree highlighted w/multicolored faceted stones appearing to be candles & ornaments, Weiss, 1960...**$35.00**

Necklace, rhinestones set in gold-tone filigree flowers on chain set w/sets of 4 & single rhinestones, unmarked, $110.00

Pin, figural fish w/blue and green painted enamel on gold-tone metal, Boucher, 1955, $60.00

Pin, 'fireworks' design w/alternating pearl & pink stone 'streamers,' pink stone & pearl cluster in center, BSK, 1955 .... **$45.00**

Pin, fob type w/dark red Lucite heart shape attached by chain to red & clear bar, 1935 .... **$55.00**

Pin, gold-electroplated pansy shape w/clear rhinestone border & cultured pearl in center, Pat Pend 3453, Boucher, 1960 .... **$45.00**

Pin, gold-tone 'coat-of-arms' design, M Haskell **$75.00**

Pin, gold-tone double bow shape w/deep red & clear rhinestones on bowknot, Mazer **$185.00**

Pin, gold-tone dragonfly w/yellow enameling, Trifari, 1960 .... **$45.00**

Pin, gold-tone figural bulldog, Trifari, ca 1965 .... **$20.00**

Pin, green carved Bakelite Scottie dog, 1935, $95.00

Pin, heavy-cast & hand-stippled acorn & oak leaf design in burnished gold-tone metal, Jeanne, 1950-60 .... **$45.00**

Pin, lg red enameled flower w/5 curled petals, rhinestone accents on stamen & leaves, Trifari, 1960 .... **$65.00**

Pin, mouse on ice skates, gold-tone w/enameled orange windswept scarf & yellow sweater, JJ, 1970 .... **$15.00**

Pin, orange, brown, green & ivory Catalin plastic rectangles & triangles on yellow rod, 1936-41 .... **$75.00**

Pin, peacock on birdbath, antiqued sterling w/florentine finish, blue & green stones on tail, red stone crown, Theda **$110.00**

Pin, 'Rainbow Star' design w/'aurora borealis' stones set in gold-tone metal w/cultured pearl center, Emmons, 1950 .... **$30.00**

Pin, red carved & scrolled Bakelite, 2x¾" **$25.00**

Pin, red variegated Bakelite dachshund, 3½" long **$25.00**

Pin, rhodium curled-leaf shape w/pave-set baguette-cut clear rhinestones, Boucher, 1960 .... **$45.00**

Pin, silver flamenco dancer in full layered skirt & puffed sleeves holding maracas, marked Silver Mexico, 1950 .... **$25.00**

Pin, simulated baroque pearl set in gold-electroplated branch w/many 'pointy' ends, Castlecliff, 1960 .... **$55.00**

Pin, sterling silver repousse leaf shape, Danecraft, 1940. **$55.00**

Pin, stretch-carved purple Lucite figural bird w/rhinestone eye, 1935 .... **$55.00**

Pin, stylized flower w/pronged amber glass stone & clear rhinestones set in patented gold-tone, Sarah Coventry, 1950 .... **$85.00**

Pin, stylized gold-tone scarecrow w/simulated pearl head, tassle-like chain legs, Emmons, 1960 .... **$30.00**

Pin, stylized lamb, black enamel in oxidized brass outline w/allover brass 'curlicues,' Emmons, 1960 .... **$15.00**

Pin, 3 blue faceted stones set on stems of gold wash over sterling 'tied' together w/gold bow, Coro, 1960 ... **$45.00**

Pin, 3 simulated moonstones & 2 blue faux gemstones on gold-electroplated leaf & scroll mounting, Van Dell, 1960 .... **$95.00**

Pin, 3-D red-brown accordion w/paper keys **$60.00**

Pin & earring set, clip-on, gold-electroplated coiled bamboo design w/white enameled petals, Boucher, 1950 . **$65.00**

Ring, 'aurora borealis' pave-set stones in gold-tone diamond shape, Emmons, 1950 .... **$30.00**

Ring, carved red-orange Bakelite leaf design, 1930s ... **$28.00**

Ring, orange marbled Bakelite **$20.00**

Ring, 1-color Catalin w/stylized floral carving **$35.00**

Ring, 10k-gold double hearts (side by side), 3mm band, 1940 .... **$35.00**

Ring, 14k-gold Tiffany-style mounting w/25ct round ruby **$95.00**

Ring, 14k yellow gold filigree w/oval jade stone in multiclaw setting w/each claw a fleur-de-lis, early 20th Century **$225.00**

Ring, 2-color Catalin w/inlaid Deco stripe design **$45.00**

Scarf pin, clear rhinestones set in rhodium open-diamond shape, Standard, 1950 .... **$25.00**

Scarf pin, double bow design in gold-tone rope, Cadoro, 1955 .... **$15.00**

Scarf pin, gold-electroplated lion's head w/ring through nose, Accessocraft, 1955-65, $75.00

Scarf pin, rhodium tassel design on each end, reproduction of mid-Victorian era pin, Emmons, 1950 .... **$35.00**

Josef Originals

Figurines of lovely ladies and a variety of whimsical animals marked Josef were designed by Muriel Josef George of Arcadia, California, from 1946 until she retired in the late 1970s. Until the '60s, they were produced in California. But production costs were increasing, and in order to stay competitive, she found it necessary to contract the work out to a Japanese manufacturer. After Muriel retired, her partner, George Good, continued to produce her designs as well as new ones of his own creation. Eventually the company was sold to Applause, and they use the Josef molds yet today.

Those made before Muriel retired are the most collectible. You'll be able to recognize them by these characteristics: the girls all have black eyes and the animals were all done in a glossy finish. (Later girls have red-brown eyes and some of the newer animals may have a flocked coat.) Watch for a soon-to-be-released book on this subject by Jim and Kaye Whitaker. It will be published by Collector Books.

Birthday Girl #15, yellow gown, black eyes, Japan.....**$33.00**
Birthday Girl #2, pink dress w/bear, black eyes, Japan .**$27.00**
Birthstone Doll, January, pink gown, red stone, Japan.**$20.00**
Cho Cho, Chinese lady, white & pink kimono, holding fan, Japan, 10½" **$100.00**
Christmas Belle, girl holding package, California, 3"...**$30.00**
Christmas Music Box, Santa Claus w/bag, Japan.........**$75.00**
Doll of the Month, w/birthstone, California, 3¼", from $30.00 to..**$35.00**
Elephant, w/flower, Japan, 5" **$33.00**
Frogs, gr, various poses & sizes...................................**$14.00**

Gabriella, blue gown & brown coat, California, 5¾", $60.00; Jacques, pink suit & gray vest, California, 5¾", $60.00

Happy Birthday Music Box, girl in pink dress.............**$80.00**
Hippo, bug on head, 2½"...**$20.00**
Joseph II, pink suit w/hat, lace front, gold cane **$55.00**
Kangaroo, w/baby in pouch, Japan, 6" **$40.00**
Ladybug, Japan, 2½"...**$14.00**
Little International, England, green & brown dress, holding gold hoop, Japan, 4"...**$27.00**
Little International, France, pink, white & blue clothing, Japan, 4" **$33.00**
Little International, Hawaii, white dress, holding pineapple in basket, Japan, 4" **$30.00**
Love Story, Romance Series, lady in pink dress, holding letter, Japan, 8"..**$115.00**
Mice, semi-gloss, various poses & sizes, Japan, each..**$17.00**

Rabbits, various poses, 3 to 5", each **$16.00**
Southern Belle, pink dress w/hat, Japan, 3½"..............**$29.00**

Jukeboxes

Because so many suppliers are now going to CD players, right now the market is full of jukeboxes from the past twenty-five years that you can usually buy very inexpensively. One as recent as these in good working order should cost you no more than $500.00. Look for one that has a little personality (some from the early seventies are fairly 'funky'), and if you're buying it for your own use and particularly enjoy hearing the 'oldies,' you'll find it to be one of the best investments you've ever made. Look in the Yellow Pages under 'Amusements' or 'Arcade Machines' to locate a supplier in your area.

The older models are another story. They've been appreciated by collectors for a long time, as their prices indicate. The forties was an era of stiff competition among jukebox manufacturers, and as a result many beautiful models were produced. Wurlitzer's 1015 with the bubble tubes (see our listings) is one of the most famous and desirable models ever made. It's being made again today as the 'One More Time.'

Buying a completely restored vintage jukebox will be an expensive move. You're not only paying for parts that are sometimes hard to find but hours upon hours of hard work and professional services involved in refinishing the chrome and paint.

There are several books on the market that offer more information; two that we'd recommend are: *A Blast from the Past! Jukeboxes*, by Scott Wood and *An American Premium Guide to Jukeboxes and Slot Machines* by Jerry Ayliffe.

Seeburg Symphonola, model 146M, wood case w/hard plastic dome, side light tunnels, plays 78 rpm records, 56", G+, $650.00

AMI #200, 1957, NM **$900.00**
AMI Streamliner, 1938, EX original **$2,800.00**
Packard Manhattan, 1945, EX original **$2,200.00**
Rockola #1422, 1946, EX original **$1,650.00**
Rockola #1434, EX original **$1,200.00**
Rockola #1468, EX original **$1,600.00**
Rockola #456, 1974, NM......................................**$550.00**
Rockola Empress, 1959, EX original......................**$1,500.00**
Rockola Monarch, 1938, EX original.......................**$850.00**
Seeburg #100C, 1950, EX original.........................**$850.00**
Seeburg Gem, 1938, EX original...........................**$1,650.00**
Seeburg Select-O-Matic 200 Console, complete w/100
    records **$880.00**
Wurlitzer #1015, 1946, EX original **$7,500.00**
Wurlitzer #1050, 1972, NM......................................**$4,500.00**
Wurlitzer #1650, restored **$750.00**
Wurlitzer #3100, EX original **$450.00**
Wurlitzer #42, 1942, VG **$4,000.00**
Wurlitzer #51, counter-top model, 1937, NM.........**$1,800.00**
Wurlitzer #700, 1940, EX original **$2,800.00**
Wurlitzer #750-E, 1940, EX original **$5,750.00**
Wurlitzer Ambassador, 1949, EX original...............**$2,500.00**
Wurlitzer P-12 #9714, walnut case, 1936, EX original...**$900.00**

Keen Kutter

The E.C. Simmons Company used 'Keen Kutter' as a trade name on an extensive line of tools, knives, and other hardware items made by them from about 1870 until the mid-'30s. The older items are especially collectible, so is advertising material such as catalogs, calendars, and wooden packing boxes.

For more information, we recommend *Keen Kutter*, an illustrated guide by Elaine and Jerry Heuring.

See also Knives.

Calendar, pictures little girl w/doll on her shoulder, 1944, full pad, $165.00

Can opener...**$25.00**
Draw knife, K4, 4" blade **$55.00**
Drill, hand; hollow brass handle, holds fluted drill points or
    twist drills, revolving cap w/compartments **$60.00**
Emblem, cast iron **$40.00**
File, half-round; wood handle **$12.00**
Garden hoe **$35.00**
Garden tool rack, metal, marked Keen Kutter Lightweight
    Garden Tools **$200.00**
Grinder, meat; K112, lg size w/separate base plate, sliding
    base & thumb screw **$35.00**
Gun holster, leather, emblem in lower left corner **$125.00**
Hammer, brick; head length: 8½" **$45.00**
Hammer, EC Simmons, round neck, curved claw, 20-oz .**$35.00**
Hammer, tack...**$25.00**
Ice shaver, K33...**$95.00**
Letter opener, knife blade w/leather cover..............**$75.00**
Level, KK0, brass top plate, 24" **$30.00**
Level, KK3, cast-brass tips & top plate, adjustable, 12".**$60.00**
Level, K618, cast iron, adjustable, 18", minimum value.**$125.00**
Mallet, rubber; minimum value...........................**$55.00**
Nail apron, Shapleigh's Keen Kutter.....................**$90.00**
Padlock, EC Simmons, emblem shaped w/plain shackle ..**$120.00**
Plane, block; KK9½, adjustable, 6" **$40.00**
Plane, block; K140, adjustable w/removable side fence, minimum
    value **$175.00**
Plane, block; K220, iron, adjustable, old style cap, 7½"..**$35.00**
Plane, KK4½, iron, smooth bottom, 10", minimum value..**$50.00**
Plane, K31, wood bottom, 24" **$60.00**
Pliers, combination; K51-8.................................**$20.00**
Pliers, combination; K51-8.................................**$20.00**
Pocketknife, #A102, melon tester, ivory-like handle, 1-blade,
    Diamond Edge, 5¾" **$40.00**
Pocketknife, #1719½, easy opener, metal handle, 1-blade,
    EC Simmons, 3⅜" **$55.00**
Pocketknife, #1898¾, Texas toothpick, brown bone handle,
    1-blade, EC Simmons, 5" **$175.00**
Postcard, advertising Keen Kutter lawn mower, shows
    mother & daughter looking at mower.................**$100.00**
Ratchet, utility...**$55.00**
Reamer, K126, for reaming pipe & counter sinking **$30.00**
Rule, K312, steel, 12" **$40.00**
Rule, 8-fold; K504, enameled yellow, Pat June 5, 1900.**$130.00**

Saw, hand; K88S, for tool box, 20", $50.00

Saw, stair builder's; KK6, crucible steel blade, applewood
    handle **$150.00**
Saw set, K10 ....**$20.00**
Scissors, 6½" **$12.00**
Screwdriver, brass ferrule, 6"...........................**$30.00**
Screwdriver, K50, 8" blade **$20.00**

Shears, barber's; 8½"..................................$12.00

Shears, sheep; engraving of man shearing sheep, marked Made in England $50.00

Sign, porcelain flange, emblem shape, EC Simmons, Keen Kutter Cutlery & Tools, double-sided, M............$500.00

Spoke shave, K95, concave cutter $60.00

Square, K18, 12"..$40.00

Square, sliding T-bevel; logo on blade, wood handle, 6" blade $40.00

Square, tri & mitre; cast-iron handle, 6" blade.............$30.00

Square, tri & mitre; logo on blade, wooden handle, 7½"...$25.00

Staple puller, head length: 2⅝"......................$35.00

Straight razor, K15, black handle w/logo...................$35.00

Wrench, pipe; interchangeable jaw $35.00

Wrench, steel, w/logo, 10"..............................$35.00

Kentucky Derby Glasses

Since the 1940s, every running of the Kentucky Derby has been commemorated with a drinking glass. Race fans have begun to collect them, and now some of the earlier glasses are worth several hundred dollars.

1940s, aluminum...$400.00

1940s, plastic Beetleware, from $2,500 to..............$3,500.00

1945, short...$800.00

1945, tall..$300.00

1948 ....$125.00

1949 ....$125.00

1950 ....$300.00

1951 ....$375.00

1952, Gold Cup..$125.00

1953 ....$85.00

1954 ....$100.00

1955 ....$85.00

1956, from $150 to.......................................$250.00

1957 ....$75.00

1958, Gold Bar...$150.00

1958, Iron Liege $150.00

1959 ....$70.00

1960, $65.00

1961 ....$85.00

1962 ....$60.00

1963-65, each $40.00

1966-67, each $35.00

1968 ....$38.00

1969 ....$32.00

1970 ....$45.00

1971-72, each $28.00

1973 ....$30.00

1974, mistake..$16.00

1974, regular, $14.00

1975..$8.00

1976 ....$12.00

1976, plastic..$10.00

1977..$7.50

1978-79, each $10.00

1980 ....$15.00

1981..$8.00

1982..$7.00

1983..$7.00

1984-85, each..$6.00

1986..$7.00

1986 ('85 copy) $15.00

1987-89, each..$5.00

1990, each..$4.00

1991-94 ....$3.50

Kentucky Derby Festival Glasses

1960s...$150.00

1984 ....$15.00

1987 ....$10.00

1988-1989..$8.00

1990-1991..$6.00

1992...$5.00

1993, very few made $75.00

1994..$5.00

Kentucky Derby Shot Glasses

1945	**$1,000.00**
1987, black, 3-oz	**$350.00**
1987, clear, 1½-oz	**$200.00**
1987, frosted, 1½-oz	**$225.00**
1987, red, 3-oz	**$500.00**
1988, 1½-oz	**$40.00**
1988, 3-oz	**$50.00**
1989, 1½-oz	**$35.00**
1989, 3-oz	**$40.00**
1990, 1½-oz	**$30.00**
1991, 1½-oz & 3-oz, each	**$25.00**
1992, 1½ & 3-oz, each	**$10.00**
1993, 1½ & 3-oz, each	**$8.00**
1994, 1½ & 3-oz, each	**$6.00**

King's Crown Thumbprint Line

Back in the late 1800s, this pattern was called Thumbprint. It was made then by the U.S. Glass Company and by Tiffin, one of the companies who were a part of that conglomerate, through the 1940s. U.S. Glass closed in the late fifties, but Tiffin reopened in 1963 and reissued it. Indiana Glass bought the molds, made some minor changes, and during the 1970s, they made this line as well. Confusing, to say the least! Gene Florence's *Collectible Glassware of the 40s, 50s, and 60s,* explains that originally the thumbprints were oval, but at some point Indiana changed theirs to circles. And Tiffin's tumblers were flared at the top, while Indiana's were straight. Our values are for the later issues of both companies.

Compote, 7¼x9" dia, $25.00

Bowl, bonbon; crimped, 2-handled, 10½"	**$35.00**
Bowl, crimped, footed	**$25.00**
Bowl, finger; 4"	**$15.00**
Bowl, wedding or candy; footed, 6" dia	**$25.00**
Bowl, wedding or candy; w/lid, footed, 10½"	**$65.00**
Lazy Susan, w/ball-bearing spinner, 8½x24" dia	**$100.00**
Plate, salad; 7⅜"	**$12.00**
Plate, torte; 14½"	**$40.00**
Relish, 5-part, 14"	**$55.00**
Stem, cocktail; 2¼-oz	**$12.50**
Stem, oyster cocktail; 4-oz	**$12.50**
Stem, sundae or sherbet; 5½-oz	**$10.00**
Tumbler, iced-tea, footed, 12-oz	**$17.50**
Tumbler, juice; footed, 4-oz	**$10.00**

Kitchen Appliances

If you've never paid much attention to old kitchen appliances, now is the time to do just that. Check in Grandma's basement — or your mother's kitchen cabinets, for that matter. As styles in home decorating changed, so did the styles of appliances. Toasters, coffee makers, waffle irons, and popcorn poppers are just a few examples of collectible small appliances. Some have wonderful Art Deco lines, while others border on the primitive.

Most of those you'll find will still work, and with a thorough cleaning you'll be able to restore them to their original 'like-new' appearance. Missing parts may be impossible to replace, but if it's just the cord that's gone, you can usually find what you need at any hardware store.

Even larger appliances are collectible and are often used to add the finishing touch to a period kitchen.

Blender, Knapp Monarch Liquidizer, Art Deco style, 1940s, EX	**$50.00**
Broiler, Farberware, chrome, 3-prong plug, 1920s	**$22.00**
Coffeepot, Manning-Brown, electric, chrome & Bakelite	**$125.00**
Deep fryer, Fryrite, EX	**$12.50**
Egg cooker, Hankscraft #599, china base, 1930s	**$42.50**
Hot plate, Universal Thermax, wooden handle, 1920s	**$24.00**
Mixer, Gilbert Polar Cub, gray-painted metal, 10", EX	**$60.00**
Mixer, Hamilton Beach, 10-speed deluxe, milk glass bowl	**$25.00**
Mixer, Hamilton Beach G, Bakelite handle, 1930s, EX	**$40.00**
Popcorn popper, Berstead #302, chrome w/glass lid, EX	**$50.00**
Popcorn popper, Monarch Teenie Weenie, EX	**$55.00**
Refrigerator, General Electric, motor on top, 1930s, 64"	**$365.00**
Teakettle, Mirro, internal heating element, 1930s, 4-qt.	**$22.00**
Toaster, General Mills #GM 5 A, Bakelite handles, 1940s	**$45.00**
Toaster, Hotpoint #125T22, EX	**$45.00**
Toaster, Kenmore, 2-slice, chrome, 1940s	**$25.00**
Toaster, Marian Giant #66 Flip Flop, chrome, EX	**$55.00**
Toaster, Montgomery Ward & Co #94-KW 2298-B, 1930s	**$20.00**

Toaster, Proctor #1405 ....**$85.00**
Toaster, Star Rite Extra Fast **$50.00**
Toaster, Toast-O-Later, EX **$160.00**
Toaster, Westinghouse #TT-23 ....**$50.00**
Waffle iron, Dominion, 2 wells, chrome w/wooden handles, 1940s **$35.00**
Waffle iron, Knapp-Monarch, nickel w/wooden handle, 1930s, sm **$25.00**
Waffle iron, Landers, Frary & Clark **$45.00**
Waffle iron, Manning-Bowman Twin-O-Matic, Bakelite stand **$75.00**

Waffle iron, Westinghouse, ceramic base, Fuji pattern, $50.00

Whipper, Knapp Monarch, chrome motor housing, 1930s, 7" **$22.00**

Kitchen Gadgets

Whether you're buying them to use or to decorate with, you'll find good examples just about anywhere you go at prices that won't wreck your buying budget. From the 19th century, cast-iron apple peelers, cherry pitters, and food choppers were patented by the hundreds, and because they're practically indestructible, they're still around today. Unless parts are missing, they're still usable and most are very efficient at the task they were designed to perform.

A collection of egg beaters can be very interesting, and you'll find specialized gadgets for chores no one today would even dream of doing. Some will probably leave you in doubt as to their intended use.

If this area of collecting interests you, you'll enjoy *300 Years of Kitchen Collectibles* by Linda Campbell and *Kitchen Antiques, 1790-1940*, by Kathryn McNerney.

Apple peeler, cast iron, RP Scott & Co, Pat 1879, $85.00

Apple corer, tin, tubular handle, 6" **$15.00**
Apple peeler, cast iron, clamp-on style, 2-gear, unmarked, dated 1872 ....**$85.00**
Apple peeler, cast iron, Hudson **$65.00**
Apple peeler, cast iron, Lockley & Howland, Pat June 17 & December 5, 1856 ....**$80.00**
Apple peeler, cast iron, White Mountain, Goodell Co...**$55.00**
Bread knife, steel blade, open cast-iron handle **$20.00**
Butter scales, red & white, Dazey, 1920s, EX **$65.00**
Can opener, advertising, Pet Milk, tin **$15.00**
Can opener, cast iron & steel, Peerless Pat Feb 11 90, 6¼" long **$10.00**
Can opener, cast-iron cow figural, tail curls on handle, Victorian **$40.00**
Can opener, electric, Dazey **$30.00**
Can opener, iron w/loop handle, Never-Slip, Pat Nov 12, '02 ....**$20.00**
Can opener, steel w/wooden handle, Vaughan's Easy Cutter, 1900s **$10.00**
Cheese slicer, green-painted metal, Handi-Kraft, 5½x5½" .**$30.00**
Cherry seeder, cast iron, Enterprise, 1903 ....**$65.00**
Cherry seeder, cast iron, marked Pat Date Apr 9, 1867 .**$90.00**
Cherry seeder, cast iron, 3-legged, hand crank, Pat Nov 17, 1863 ....**$75.00**
Cherry seeder, Rollman Mfg Co No 8, 1900s, 12" **$40.00**
Chopper, wrought-iron blade, wooden handle **$50.00**
Chopper, wrought iron mounted to thick board, swivels, maple handle...**$85.00**
Chopper, 6 blades in bell shape, iron handle.............**$30.00**

Churn, #102, unmarked, 1-qt, $285.00

Churn, cast iron & glass, clamp-on style, Universal #15, 1-qt **$350.00**
Churn, Dazey #40, Pat date, 1-gal...............**$75.00**
Churn, Lightning Butter Machine, Pat Feb 6, 1917, 2-qt **$110.00**
Churn, wood w/old red paint, wrought-iron handle, 13x12x12½" **$175.00**
Cornstick pan, Krusty Korn Kobs, Wagner...1920, miniature **$80.00**

Crimper, bone wheel, wood handle, 5½" **$30.00**

Crimper, open lead wheel, iron shaft, wood handle, 7¾" **$25.00**

Cutter, biscuit; advertising, Forbes Quality Baking Powder, tin **$10.00**

Cutter, biscuit; green plastic, Bonnie Ware, 1930s, 2¼"..**$8.00**

Cutter, biscuit; Kreamer, strap handle **$8.00**

Cutter, biscuit; tin, arched rolled-edge strap handle, 1890s **$15.00**

Cutter, kraut; oval iron blade, wooden handle...........**$60.00**

Cutter, kraut; 2 blades in scalloped pine board, 5¾x15" **$180.00**

Egg beater, Cassidy Fairbanks, turbine type **$20.00**

Egg beater, Dunlap Sanitary..**$20.00**

Egg beater, Improved Keystone..................................**$165.00**

Egg beater, metal, push-down type, 11" **$35.00**

Egg beater, ratchet type, Art-Beck **$40.00**

Egg beater, Taplin, 1908...**$35.00**

Egg beater, tin wheel w/6 wire loops, wooden handle, 1900s...**$70.00**

Egg beater, turbine type, ca 1930, 9½", $25.00

Egg beater, turbine type, Washburn Co **$25.00**

Egg beater, United Royalties, Pat 1929, green wooden handle..**$30.00**

Egg beater, vertical, blue & white knob, Pat 10-9-03 ..**$20.00**

Egg poacher, tin, Kreamer embossed on handle, $60.00

Egg separator, advertising, Town Talk Flour, tin.........**$15.00**

Egg separator, round tin bowl w/slots, Gem, 1889, 3¼" dia **$40.00**

Flour scoop, advertising, Jenny Wren Ready Mixed Flour, tin..**$10.00**

Funnel, tin, copper tipped, rolled edge, 1800s, 20".....**$35.00**

Grater, hand-punched tin in wood frame, 1840s, 14x4¾" **$85.00**

Grater, ironstone, light gray, curved top, 5½" **$55.00**

Grater, nutmeg; round crank style w/lg black knob .**$110.00**

Grater, nutmeg; tin, The Boye, mechanical, 5¾" long.**$85.00**

Grater, nutmeg; tin & wood, Edgar, Pat through Nov 10, 1896 ....**$85.00**

Grater, pierced tin, pine back w/cut-out handle, 13½" long..**$135.00**

Grater, tin w/cast-iron frame, rotary type w/hand crank, Climax, 10" **$35.00**

Grater, tin w/heavy wire frame, 3 surfaces, hinged door, 1910 ....**$35.00**

Grater, 2 metal-toothed blades w/wooden frame, Norlund Corn, 12" **$20.00**

Grinder, brass & cast iron, late 1800s, 7½"...................**$65.00**

Grinder, brass & cast iron, Standard Werk, late 1800s, 7½" long..**$40.00**

Grinder, cast iron, table-top type, American #20.........**$12.50**

Grinder, cast iron, table-top type, Pomeroy's #10 ....**$15.00**

Grinder, cast iron, table-top type, Puritan #10.............**$12.50**

Grinder, Universal LFC Pat 1897 ....**$35.00**

Herb masher/butter tamper, maple, 5⅞" dia mushroom-shaped base..**$45.00**

Ice crusher, chrome & black, standing type, Dazey....**$25.00**

Ice pick, steel w/metal ferrule, square wooden handle, 1900s **$7.50**

Jar opener/lifter, iron, Iron Hottongs, lg **$12.00**

Juicer, metal, wall mount, Dazey..................................**$30.00**

Meat pounder, cast iron half-circle w/frets, wooden handle, 1800s **$100.00**

Mixer, heavy wire, ratchet type, Horlick's...................**$38.00**

Orange squeezer, wood, 2-part, hinged, 1890s, 11" long **$75.00**

Pepper mill, brass, Germany, illegible mark, 1880s-1900s, 7½" **$40.00**

Pot scrubber, linked chain, 6x6", $30.00

Potato masher, iron bottom w/holes, wood handle, 16".**$25.00**
Potato masher, tiger-striped maple handle, 1850s, 12½" .**$85.00**
Potato masher, twisted iron w/black wooden handle, ca 1890, 9½" **$30.00**
Potato masher, zigzag mashers work w/fulcrum action, 11½"...**$55.00**
Potato peeler, tin back, unmarked Hamlinite, Pat July 20, 1920 ....**$48.00**
Raisin seeder, Enterprise, Aug 20, 1895, tall w/curved shank **$58.00**
Raisin seeder, Everett, wood w/7 curved wires, 1889-93...**$75.00**
Raisin seeder, Gem, dated December 1924, 1895.......**$80.00**
Rolling pin, clear glass, Roll Rite cap...........................**$30.00**
Rolling pin, curly maple, 15¼" **$50.00**
Rolling pin, metal center w/oval cutouts, wooden handles **$32.00**
Rolling pin, wood, round bulbous handles, EX patina, 1-piece, 18½" **$32.00**
Sifter, rotary type w/metal handle & green wood knob, 1-cup **$10.00**
Sifter, tin, Bromwell, ca 1925, 5-cup............................**$25.00**
Sifter, wood w/iron crank, drawer in base, 1840s, 15¼" .**$210.00**
Slicer, vegetable; WH Baldwin, Pat Oct 3, 1871, sm ...**$35.00**
Strawberry huller, nickel-plated brass, Boston Huller, 1894.**$8.50**
Timer, cast-iron pilgrim figure, Tillie the Time, original box **$25.00**

Kitchen Glassware

Though there's still lots of this type of glassware around, some harder-to-find items and pieces in the more desirable colors and types of glass often bring unbelievably high prices. We've listed a cross section of values here, but you'll really need to study a good book before you decide to do much investing. One of the best is *Kitchen Glassware of the Depression Years* by authority Gene Florence.

See also Fry Oven Glassware; Jadite Glassware; Fire King Ovenware; Glass Knives; Reamers; Peach Lustre Glassware.

Apothecary jar, transparent green, shouldered cylinder w/lid, flat bottom **$30.00**

Batter jug, cobalt w/silver lid & handle, McKee, $80.00

Batter jug, crystal w/green lid, square shape w/vertical ribbing at corners, angled handle, flat bottom **$35.00**
Batter jug, transparent green, bulbous body w/vertical fluting, recessed handle, flat lid, flat bottom, Jenkins #570 ....**$130.00**
Bowl, batter; fired-on white bottom & handle w/red band around rim & spout **$12.50**
Bowl, batter; transparent green, sides curve down to sm round base, 2 spouts, tab handle, Tufglas............**$35.00**
Bowl, batter; transparent green, vertical panels, pour spout, handled, Anchor Hocking **$20.00**
Bowl, beater; Chalaine blue, rolled rim w/pour spout, tapered sides, sm round base, 4" **$60.00**
Bowl, crushed fruit; crystal, tab handle, Bohner's Pat Feb 22, 1898 ....**$25.00**
Bowl, mixing; Chalaine blue, rolled rim w/vertical ribbing, 9" **$85.00**
Bowl, mixing; custard, plain rim, 9" **$18.00**
Bowl, mixing; Delphite blue, flat wim, square base, Pyrex, 12" **$20.00**

Bowl, mixing; multicolored tulips on white, Anchor Hocking, 9½", $16.00

Bowl, mixing; transparent cobalt blue, thick rolled rim, sm round base, 6" **$18.00**
Bowl, mixing; transparent green, overlapping rim, vertical fluting, sm square base, Anchor Hocking, 9".......**$15.00**
Bowl, mixing; transparent green, thick rim, slightly tapering w/horizontal bands, 9½"..................................**$25.00**
Bowl, mixing; transparent pink, Hex Optic design, flat rim, 9" **$22.00**
Bowl, mixing; transparent pink, overlapping rim, vertical ribbing, sm square base, Federal Glass, 6½" **$8.00**
Bowl, mixing; transparent red, plain, w/thick rim, sm round base, 7¾" **$60.00**
Bowl, mixing; transparent ultramarine, fluted sides, flat scalloped rim, 'Jennyware' by Jeannette, 8" **$35.00**
Bowl, mixing; white, horizontal ridges, 3 red lines around rim, Anchor Hocking, 10" **$10.00**
Bowls, mixing; fired-on colors, Pyrex, set of 4 ....**$20.00**
Butter dish, amber, rectangular w/vertical ribbing, tab handles, Federal Glass, 1-lb..........................**$35.00**
Butter dish, transparent green, straight sides w/flat bottom, tab handles, flat lid, Jeannette, 2-lb **$125.00**
Butter dish, transparent pink, ribbed lid on tray, ¼-lb ..**$30.00**
Butter dish, transparent red tray w/crystal lid, ¼-lb .**$105.00**

Cake plate, transparent pink, round w/snowflake design, footed...**$20.00**

Canister, caramel, bowl shape w/tapered sides, flat lid, 40-oz **$65.00**

Canister, cereal; clambroth green, 4-sided w/vertically ribbed oval panels, diagonal silver paper label, knob lid, 47-oz...**$45.00**

Canister, cereal; Delphite blue, 4-sided w/black lettering, recessed handle on flat lid, 29-oz, 5" **$150.00**

Canister, Chalaine blue, round w/slightly tapering sides, flat bottom & lid, 10-oz..**$40.00**

Canister, crystal, raised dot design on oval panels, round metal lid, lg **$15.00**

Canister, crystal, 4-sided w/green silhouetted 'Taverne' scene, round corners w/horizontal ribbing, green metal lid, lg...**$25.00**

Canister, flour; crystal, ball shape w/flat bottom, embossed lettering, metal lid, 128-oz.....................................**$40.00**

Canister, flour; white, ball shape w/flat front & back, blue circle design & lettering, lid w/ball finial, Vitrock **$25.00**

Canister, sugar; caramel, square w/oval panels, black lettering & lid, 48-oz **$85.00**

Canister, sugar; dark amber ball shape w/metal lid..**$110.00**

Canister, sugar; transparent forest green, 4-sided w/diagonal ribbing, silver label, metal lid, Owens-Illinois...........**$22.50**

Canister, tea; dark amber, 4-sided w/vertically ribbed arched panels, embossed lettering, metal lid **$70.00**

Canister, tea; fired-on green, shouldered, flat bottom, black letters & design on flat front, metal lid, Hazel Atlas **$18.00**

Casserole, dark amber, round w/flat rim, flat bottom, angled cut-out finial on dome lid, Cambridge **$30.00**

Casserole, Emerald-Glo, round green bowl w/gold-tone metal lid, green finial...**$25.00**

Coaster, transparent cobalt blue, round **$5.00**

Cookie jar, peacock blue, barrel shape w/flat lid, tab handles, LE Smith, $80.00

Cookie jar, transparent green, etched floral design on barrel shape, tab handles, flat lid, LE Smith....................**$100.00**

Creamer & sugar bowl stacking set, transparent pink, square w/angled handles, w/lid...**$50.00**

Cruet, frosted clambroth white, red & black rooster decal marked vinegar or oil, clear crystal stopper, each..**$15.00**

Cruet, transparent amber, straight-sided body w/panels, flat bottom, pointed stopper..**$26.00**

Cruet, transparent forest green, bulbous w/panels, clear stopper..**$35.00**

Cup, transparent green, slick handle **$8.00**

Custard, fruit design on white, 6-oz, $4.00; Refrigerator dish, 4½x4½", $8.00; Refrigerator dish, 4¼x8¼", $12.00

Decanter, transparent green, bulbous shape w/horizontal ribbing, flat bottom, w/stopper, Anchor Hocking....**$350.00**

Decanter, transparent peacock blue, long neck w/bulbous body, flat bottom, rounded 'arrowhead'-shaped finial, Imperial **$30.00**

Decanter w/4 shot glasses, crystal, bulbous w/rooster-head stopper, red waddle at pour spout, red-trimmed glasses ..**$35.00**

Egg cup, crystal cup w/opaque black base **$10.00**

Egg cup, light amber, Paden City...................................**$8.00**

Egg cup, transparent yellow, Hazel Atlas **$5.00**

Funnel, transparent yellow, CW Hart **$35.00**

Gelatin mold, transparent green, round & fluted w/tapered side..**$15.00**

Grease jar, opaque white w/red sailboat decoration, marked Drippings, crystal lid, McKee, 16-oz **$35.00**

Grease jar, opaque yellow, plain bowl shape, flat lid w/recessed handle, Anchor Hocking **$40.00**

Grease jar, white, bowl shape w/vertical fluting, slightly domed lid w/recessed knob, w/label....................**$20.00**

Horseradish jar, crystal, fancy 'tulip' shape w/round base, knob lid, embossed lettering................................**$10.00**

Ice bucket, transparent green, plain top half w/embossed design around bottom half, metal handle **$35.00**

Ice bucket (open), opaque black, round w/straight sides tapering to flat bottom, scrolled handles...............**$50.00**

Ice tub (open), transparent peacock blue, swirled design on sides slightly tapering to flat bottom, tab handles .**$30.00**

Instant coffee container, crystal, bulbous shape w/sterling lid & base, etched lettering **$25.00**

Ketchup, crystal w/green plastic cone top, from 'Serve U Set' Medco #86 ....**$15.00**

Ladle, opaque black, round cup w/metal rim, flat bottom, arched handle...**$20.00**

Ladle, punch; transparent green, round bowl w/spout, curved handle **$40.00**

Marmalade, crystal w/green plastic lid, from 'Serve U Set' Medco #86 ....**$6.00**

Marmalade, Emerald-Glo, straight-sided w/flat bottom, metal dome lid w/green glass finial...............................**$18.00**

Match holder, Delphite blue, round cup w/rolled rim & base, Matches lettered in black...............................**$75.00**

Mayonnaise, Emerald-Glo, green bowl w/gold-tone metal liner, metal spoon...**$18.00**

Measure, 1-cup, Delphite blue, side tab handle w/hole.**$45.00**

Measure, 1-cup, fired-on red, straight-sided w/3 spouts, ear-shaped handle, Hazel Atlas...................................**$35.00**

Measure, 1-cup, transparent green, sides taper, 3-spout, closed handle, Federal..**$32.50**

Measure, 1-qt, crystal pitcher w/slightly flared thick bottom, thick ear-shaped handle **$30.00**

Measure, 2-cup, clambroth green, curved sides, w/handle, Anchor Hocking...**$100.00**

Measure, 2-cup, fired-on green, cup shape, ear-shaped handle, pour spout.......................................**$10.00**

Measure, 2-cup, red or black Diamond Check design on white bowl shape w/spout & handle, McKee.......**$30.00**

Measure, 2-cup, transparent pink, ribbed cup shape, thick ear-shaped handle, Anchor Hocking.....................**$35.00**

Measure, 2-cup, transparent pink, straight-sided w/thick bottom, ear-shaped handle, US Glass.......................**$150.00**

Measure, 2-cup, white Vitrock, w/pouring spout, ear-shaped handle, flat lid **$40.00**

Measure, 4-cup, custard, pitcher shape.......................**$30.00**

Measure, 4-cup, transparent green, 'Kold or Hot,' straight sided pitcher, 'finger-grip' handle **$55.00**

Mug, clambroth green, straight-sided, lg ribbed handle.**$30.00**

Mug, opaque black, straight-sided w/rolled rim & loop handle, footed **$22.00**

Mug, root beer; transparent pink, straight-sided w/angled handle, vertical panels w/rounded ends **$25.00**

Mug, transparent peacock blue, paneled, tall & flared w/thick ear-shaped handle...................................**$25.00**

Napkin holder, frosted crystal....................................**$40.00**

Napkin holder, white, SLEN-DR-FOLD........................**$55.00**

Pie plate, Delphite blue, flat rim, Pyrex, 10"..............**$18.00**

Pitcher, milk; transparent cobalt blue, paneled, straight-sided, ear-shaped handle..**$85.00**

Pitcher, transparent green, straight-sided w/vertical panels on thick round base, ear-shaped handle, Jenkins.......**$40.00**

Pitcher, transparent ultramarine, deeply fluted w/smooth band around rim, 'Jennyware' by Jeannette, 36-oz **$100.00**

Platter, meat; dark amber, footed oval shape w/stylized tree design, Fry...**$50.00**

Pretzel jar, transparent pink, round w/vertical panels, flat bottom, w/lid, Anchor Hocking.............................**$65.00**

Refrigerator dish, Chalaine blue, rectangular w/straight sides, flat lid, 4x5"..**$40.00**

Refrigerator dish, clambroth green, oval w/vertical ribbing, flat bottom & lid, 8" **$30.00**

Refrigerator dish, fired-on black, oval w/vertical fluting, flat lid w/recessed handle, 7" **$15.00**

Refrigerator dish, opaque yellow, square w/tab handles, no lid, 7¼"...**$30.00**

Refrigerator dish, round w/'quilted' design, sides taper slightly, flat lid, 8-oz **$25.00**

Refrigerator dish, Delphite blue, Jeannette, 4¼x4¼", $42.00; Salt & pepper shakers, metal tops, 6¼", pr, $35.00

Refrigerator dish, transparent cobalt blue, square, recessed knob on flat lid, 4½x5"..**$40.00**

Refrigerator dish, transparent green, Hex Optic design on straight sides, tab handles, w/lid, Jeannette, 4½x5".**$18.00**

Refrigerator dish, transparent pink, round & fluted, tapering sides, flat lid w/recessed handle, Jeannette, 16-oz .**$28.00**

Refrigerator stack set, opaque white w/red Dutch children, round, flat lids, set of 3..**$35.00**

Relish dish, Delphite blue, divided oval w/tab ends, Pyrex **$20.00**

Rolling pin, amethyst, blown **$130.00**

Rolling pin, cobalt blue, blown **$160.00**

Rolling pin, custard, metal screw-on end...................**$300.00**

Rolling pin, milk glass, w/portrait, Use Columbus Flour, 18" **$85.00**

Rolling pin, transparent forest green **$125.00**

Salt & pepper shakers, custard, 4-sided w/arched panels, black lettering, metal lid, pr **$20.00**

Salt & pepper shakers, forest green, bulbous w/flat bottom, metal dome lid, pr **$17.50**

Salt & pepper shakers, transparent red, 4-sided w/flat bottoms, red metal lids, Anchor Hocking, 1960s, pr..**$35.00**

Salt & pepper shakers, white Vitrock, ball shape w/flat front & back, red tulip design w/lettering, red metal lids, pr **$20.00**

Salt bowl, crystal, round w/fluted sides, metal lid, lg .**$20.00**

Salt bowl, fired-on yellow, round w/paneled sides, red lid w/yellow ball knob, Gemco...................................**$8.00**

Salt bowl, transparent green, round w/straight sides, embossed lettering on lid w/recessed handle, 6" $165.00

Salt shaker, clambroth white, octagonal, w/metal lid, each **$15.00**

Sanitary jar, transparent green, cylindrical, flat lid w/knob finial...**$135.00**

Server, clambroth white, round w/straight sides, flat rim, 9⅞" dia...**$12.00**

Server, clambroth white, square w/straight sides & flat rim, 10½" **$12.00**

Shaker, cinnamon; crystal, 4-sided w/embossed lattice design around blue Dutch boy, red lettering & lid, 16-oz...**$10.00**

Shaker, cinnamon; custard, 4-sided w/arched panels, black lettering, metal cap **$25.00**

Shaker, flour; Chalaine blue, 2 sides w/arched panels, black lettering, metal lid **$70.00**

Shaker, spice; crystal, 4-sided w/vertical ribbing, metal lid, smooth label panel, Sneath **$10.00**

Shaker, sugar; dark amber, plain w/rolled base & rim, pour spout in metal lid **$90.00**

Shaker, sugar; fired-on yellow w/red metal lid, Gemco..**$15.00**

Shaker, sugar; transparent green, Hex Optic design w/metal cap, Jeannette Glass...**$165.00**

Soap dish, transparent yellow, deep sides w/flat rim, ridged bottom **$18.00**

Soap dish, transparent peacock blue, rectangular, Home Soap Co **$22.50**

Soup cup, fired-on colors, square w/rounded corners, handled, each **$2.50**

Spoon & fork, crystal w/transparent green handles, set.**$40.00**

Straw holder, transparent peacock blue, cylinder w/flat bottom, ball finial on dome lid, ca 1950s **$200.00**

Sundae dish, transparent green, scalloped rim, footed..**$15.00**

Syrup, crystal w/blue plastic lid & handle, paper label: No-Drip Server, sm...**$6.00**

Syrup, crystal w/green plastic lid & handle, from 'Serve U Set' Medco #86 ....**$15.00**

Syrup, transparent green, swirl design on slightly flared body, curved handle, metal lid, Anchor Hocking.**$40.00**

Teakettle, crystal, horizontally ribbed ball shape w/flat bottom, metal spout, glass handle, Glasbake **$25.00**

Trivet, transparent red, round w/embossed 'spoke' design, raised rim, footed...**$40.00**

Tumbler, crystal, Crisscross design, 9-oz **$30.00**

Tumbler, crystal, fluted, tapering, 'Jennyware' by Jeannette, 8-oz **$20.00**

Tumbler w/straw, opaque black, slightly tapering sides w/flat bottom, McKee **$20.00**

Water bottle, forest green, smooth neck w/horizontally ribbed bulbous body, flat lid.................................**$25.00**

Water bottle, transparent cobalt blue, shouldered, sm round metal lid, 64-oz, 10" **$55.00**

Water dispenser, clambroth green, chrome spigot, crystal top...**$55.00**

Knives

Knives have been widely collected since the 1960s. The most desirable are those from before WWII, but even some made since then have value. Don't try to clean or sharpen an old knife, collectors want them as found. Of course, mint unused knives are preferred, and any apparent use or damage greatly reduces their value. Our prices are for those in near mint to mint condition.

For more information we recommend *Sargent's American Premium Guide to Knives and Razors, Identification and Values*, by Jim Sargent and *The Standard Knife Collector's Guide* by Ron Stewart and Roy Ritchie.

See also Keen Kutter.

Browning, #805, Featherweight Composite series, 1-blade, 4" **$32.00**

Browning, camping, multi-item unit, German made, 3½"...**$45.00**

Case, #GS222, doctor's knife, goldstone handle, 2-blade, Case Brad Pa **$450.00**

Case, #02244, slick black handle, 2-blade, Tested XX, 1920-40, 3¼"...**$120.00**

Case, #06267, rough black handle, 2-blade, Tested XX, 1940-50, 3¼"...**$150.00**

Case, #22055, slick black handle, 2-blade, XX, 1940-64, 3½"...**$50.00**

Case, #32098F, Sea Beast, yellow composition handle, 2-blade, Tested XX, 1920-40, 5½" **$225.00**

Case, #4220, peanut handle, 2-blade, Tested XX, WR Case & Sons, 2⅞"...**$300.00**

Case, #5254, trapper, stag handle, 2-blade, XX, 1940-64, 4⅛"...**$200.00**

Case, #5393, stockman, stag handle, 3-blade, Tested XX, 1920-40, 4"...**$310.00**

Case, #62044F, green bone handle, 2-blade, Tested XX, 1920-40, 3¼"...**$150.00**

Case, #6249, Copperhead, red bone handle, 2-blade, XX, 1940-64, 4"...**$125.00**

Case, #6250, Bradford Bonanza, bone stag handle, 2-blade, XX, 1940-64, 4⅜"...**$200.00**

Case, #6269, Congress, green handle, 2-blade, XX, 1940-55, 3"...**$125.00**

Case, #63052, Congress whittler, green bone handle, 3-blade, Tested XX, 1920-40, 3½" **$900.00**

Case, #6332, bone handle, 3-blade, USA, 1965-69, 3⅝"..**$40.00**

Case, #6345, green bone handle, 3-blade, Tested XX, 1920-40, 3⅝"...**$250.00**

Case, #6394½, green bone handle, 3-blade, Tested XX, 1920-40, 4¼"...**$1,000.00**

Case, #640045R, Scout, black plastic handle, 4-blade, XX, 1940-50, 3⅝"...**$30.00**

Case, #64045R, Scout, green bone handle (no shield), 4-blade, Tested XX, 1940-50, 3¾" **$175.00**

Case, #64052, Congress, red bone handle, 4-blade, XX, 1940-50, 3½"...**$150.00**

Case, #6445R, utility, rough black handle, 4-blade, Tested XX, 1920-40, 3¾"...**$200.00**

Case, #6592, transitional, green bone handle, 5-blade, Tested XX, 3⅞"...**$18.00**

Case, #82099R, Senator/lobster, genuine pearl handle, 2-blade, Tested XX, 1920-40, 2⅞" **$150.00**

Case, #8222, pearl handle, 2-blade, Case Bros Little Valley NY, 3¼" **$275.00**

Case, #83089SCI, lobster scissors, genuine pearl handle, 3-blade, XX, 1940-64, 3" **$135.00**

Case, #8361FSC, pearl handle, 3-blade, Tested XX, 1920-40, 2⅞" **$350.00**

Case, #92058, Birdseye, French pearl handle, 2-blade, Tested XX, 1920-40, 3¼" **$125.00**

Case, #93042, whittler, imitation pearl handle, 3-blade, Tested XX, 1920-40, 3¼" **$400.00**

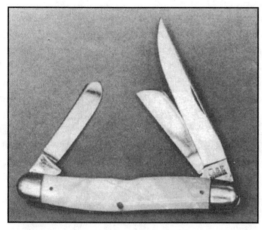

Case, #93047, cracked ice handle, 3-blade, Tested XX, 1920-40, 3⅞", $250.00

Case, #9490R, imitation pearl handle, 4-blade, Tested XX, 1920-40, 3⅜" **$225.00**

Pal Cutlery, lobster, metal handle, 2-blade, USA tang stamp, 2¼" **$50.00**

Pal Cutlery, pen, candy-stripe handle, 1-blade, tang stamp, 3" **$20.00**

Pal Cutlery, stockman, bone handle, 2-blade, 1-punch, tang stamp, 4" **$80.00**

Pal Cutlery, swell-end jackknife, red pyremite handle, tang stamp, 2-blade, 3⅜" **$50.00**

Pal Cutlery, toothpick, candy-stripe handle, 2-blade, tang stamp, 5" **$125.00**

Queen, #10, jackknife, Rogers bone handle, 2-blade, Queen & Crown, 3⅝" **$65.00**

Queen, #14, peanut, winterbottom bone handle, 2-blade, 2¾" **$25.00**

Queen, #15, Congress, winterbottom bone handle, 2-blade, 3½" **$25.00**

Queen, #18, jackknife, winterbottom bone handle, 2-blade, Big Q, 4" **$50.00**

Queen, #19, trapper, winterbottom bone handle, 2-blade, Queen Steel, 4⅛" **$85.00**

Queen, #20, Texas toothpick, Rogers bone handle, 2-blade, 1,200 made, 5" **$45.00**

Queen, #22, Barlow, brown bone handle, 2-blade, 3½" **$45.00**

Queen, #35, serpentine, rough black handle, 3-blade, 2⅝" **$30.00**

Queen, #36, lockback, Rogers bone handle, 1-blade, Queen, 4½" **$75.00**

Queen, #39, folding hunter, winterbottom bone handle, 2-blade, Queen Steel, 5¼" **$65.00**

Queen, #4, sleeveboard, smoked pearl handle, 2-blade, 3⅜" **$125.00**

Queen, #46, fisherman's, winterbottom bone handle, 1-blade, 1 scaler, Queen Steel, 5" **$35.00**

Queen, #48, whittler, winterbottom bone handle, 3-blade, Queen Steel, 3½" **$45.00**

Queen, #52, moose, winterbottom bone handle, 2-blade, Queen Steel, 4½" **$40.00**

Queen, #55, pen, green Rogers bone handle, 1-blade, Queen Steel, 200 made, 3¼" **$30.00**

Queen, #8415, canoe, stag handle, 2-blade, 3⅝" **$35.00**

Remington, #RB45, Barlow (spay), brown bone handle, 2-blade, 3⅜" **$175.00**

Remington, #RS3333, Scout, brown bone handle, acorn-shaped shield, 4-blade, 3¾" **$250.00**

Remington, #R1103, brown bone handle, 2-blade, 3⅜"..**$135.00**

Remington, #R1123, brown bone handle, bullet shield, 2-blade, 4½" **$1,200.00**

Remington, #R1182, black handle, 2-blade, 4½"........**$125.00**

Remington, #R165, jackknife, yellow scale handle, 2-blade, 3½" **$125.00**

Remington, #R213, jackknife, easy-open handle, 2-blade, 3⅝" **$200.00**

Remington, #R273, Texas jackknife, brown handle w/acorn shield, 2-blade, 4" **$200.00**

Remington, #R3, bone handle, 1-blade, 3⅜" **$80.00**

Remington, #R3115, serpentine, imitation ivory handle, 2-blade, 4" **$135.00**

Remington, #R3273, cattle, brown bone handle, 3-blade, long pull, 3¾" **$275.00**

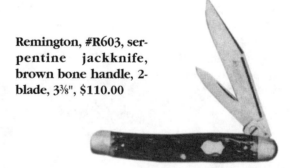

Remington, #R603, serpentine jackknife, brown bone handle, 2-blade, 3⅜", $110.00

Remington, #R64, lobster, metal handle, 3-blade, 3⅛" .**$75.00**

Remington, #R718, hawkbill, cocobolo handle, 2-blade, 3⅝" **$125.00**

Winchester, #1051, Texas jackknife, celluloid handle, 1-blade, 4¼" **$300.00**

Winchester, #1201, jackknife, nickel silver handle, 1-blade, 3⅜" **$190.00**

Winchester, #1608, cocobolo handle, 1-blade, 3⅜" **$70.00**

Winchester, #1611, mariner's, cocobolo handle, 1-blade, 3¼" **$80.00**

Winchester, #1905, jackknife, stag handle, 1-blade, 4½" **$150.00**

Winchester, #1924, powder horn, stag handle, 1-blade, 3½" **$320.00**

Winchester, #1936, toothpick, brown bone handle, 1-blade, 5" $350.00

Winchester, #2087, serpentine jack, shell celluloid handle, 1-blade, 3" $130.00

Winchester, #2099, jackknife, pink celluloid handle, 2-blade, 3⅜" $150.00

Winchester, #2201, Senator, nickel silver handle, 2-blade, 3¼" $75.00

Winchester, #2314, Wharncliffe, pearl handle, 2-blade, 2⅞" $150.00

Winchester, #2330, pen, pearl handle, 2-blade, 3¼" ..$125.00

Winchester, #2356, lobster, pearl handle, 2-blade, 3" $110.00

Winchester, #3008, cattle, white celluloid handle, 3-blade, 3⅝" $300.00

Winchester, #3025, premium stockman, blue abalone celluloid handle, 3-blade, 3½" $175.00

Winchester, whittler, green celluloid handle, 3-blade, 3¾" $275.00

Edwin M. Knowles

This was one of the major chinaware manufacturers that operated in the Newell, West Virginia, area during the first half of the century. You'll find their marks on a variety of wares.

One of their most popular and collectible lines is 'Fruits,' marketed under the trade name of Sequoia Ovenware through Montgomery Ward in the 1930s. Its shapes are quaintly styled and decorated with decals of a red apple, a yellow pear, and some purple grapes. They made at least three of their own versions of the Mexican-style decaled ware that is so popular today and in the late thirties produced some dinnerware that is distinctly Art Deco.

For more information, we recommend *The Collector's Encyclopedia of American Dinnerware* by Jo Cunningham.

Fruits, shaker, $30.00; pitcher, $12.00

Daisies, platter, oval..$8.00
Deanna, bowl, lug soup; yellow $6.00

Deanna, coffee server, green $37.00
Deanna, plate, 10", blue $8.00
Deanna, sugar bowl, pastel blue $10.00
Fruits, salt & pepper shakers, pr.........................$24.00
Fruits, server...$20.00
Golden Wheat, saucer, Yorktown Shape.............$3.00
Leaf Spray, plate, fluted rim, 8".........................$3.00
Penthouse, casserole...$30.00
Penthouse, gravy boat...$10.00
Picket Fence, tea cup..$8.00
Pink Pastel, sugar bowl $4.00
Poppy, plate, 7"..$4.00
Sleeping Mexican, cup, after dinner $15.00
Tia Juana, bowl, utility...$30.00
Tia Juana, salt & pepper shakers, pr $20.00
Tia Juana, soup, flat, 8".......................................$15.00
Tia Juana, tray, round w/tab handles $20.00
Tulip, cookie jar...$35.00
Tulip, pie baker...$15.00
Tulip Time, bowl, vegetable $12.00
Yorktown, salt & pepper shakers, cobalt, pr $16.00
Yorktown, teapot, Mango red $45.00

Labels

Each one a work of art in miniature, labels of all types appeal to collectors through their colorful lithography and imaginative choice of graphics representative of the product or the producer. Before cardboard boxes became so commonplace, wooden crates were used to transport everything from asparagus to yams. Cigar boxes were labeled both on the outside and in the lid. Tin cans had wonderful labels with Black children, lucious fruits and vegetables, animals, and birds. Some of the better examples are listed here. Many can be bought at much lower prices.

Can, Altus Pineapple, sunrise over mountains & valley .$15.00
Can, Burnham Applesauce, red apples & lettering on ivory background w/gold trim............................$3.50
Can, Chevron Sauerkraut, 2 lg cabbages.......................$6.00
Can, Del Monte Asparagus, asparagus bunch, blue tie & red logo $3.00
Can, Del Monte Peaches, sliced peaches in blue & white china bowl.....................................$2.00
Can, Delicious Pie Fruits, fox jumping over stream.......$4.00
Can, Duff's Molasses, gingerbread man & sugar cane...$5.00
Can, Elk Brand Prunes, elk head & prunes on red background $6.00
Can, Fern Park Hominy, factory scene & bowl of hominy on red background........................$2.00
Can, Hartland String Beans, rose bouquet & bunch of string beans..$14.00
Can, Holly Asparagus Tips, embossed holly leaves & berries, gold trim $2.50
Can, Log Cabin Tomatoes, men outside cabin in forest .$12.00
Can, Meadow Brook Peaches, sliced peaches in cut glass bowl on red background.....................$3.00

Can, Mother Goose Tomatoes, Mother Goose flying on a goose **$10.00**

Can, Orrco Pimentos, Egyptian bird & red peppers on green background..**$3.00**

Can, Paradise Tomatoes, embossed bird of paradise **$8.00**

Can, Quail Pineapples, quail on fence & bowl of berries..**$8.00**

Can, Red Moon Sweet Peas, red crescent man logo w/pea pods in background..**$3.00**

Can, Today's Fruit Cocktail, Deco style w/3 bowls of fruit cocktail on white background..............................**$3.00**

Can, White Frost Pineapple, campsite w/tent in forest, fancy border **$8.00**

Cigar box, inner lid; Boma, Black man wearing fur coat, 6x9" **$14.00**

Cigar box, inner lid; Canadian Club, 1950s, 7x8", $3.00

Cigar box, inner lid; Edmund Halley, astronomer & telescope, 6x9" **$10.00**

Cigar box, inner lid; Jewel, bust portrait of woman in lg purple hat, 6x9" **$12.50**

Cigar box, inner lid; Juan Y Julia, lovers embracing, 6x9" **$6.00**

Cigar box, inner lid; La Flor de Victor, bald eagle feeding chick in nest, 6x9"..**$14.00**

Cigar box, inner lid; New Day, sunrise over tobacco field, 6x9" **$4.00**

Cigar box, inner lid; Season's Greetings, snow-covered pine branches, 6x9" **$3.00**

Cigar box, inner lid; smiling man holding cigar **$12.00**

Cigar box, inner lid; view of Swiss mountain village, 6x9" **$6.00**

Cigar box, outer; Argus, Viking surrounded by gold arrows, 4½x4½" **$2.00**

Cigar box, outer; Duckey Darling, young woman wearing white veil, 4½x4½" **$8.00**

Cigar box, outer; Gral, angel directing prince & horse, 4½x4½" **$12.00**

Cigar box, outer; La Confession, Latin couple enjoying cigars, 4½x4½"..**$8.00**

Cigar box, outer; Milwaukee Leader, black & white floral bouquet on red background, 4½x4½" **$10.00**

Cigar box, outer; Royal Gem, woman dressed in regal costume, 4½x4½"..**$6.00**

Cigar box, outer; Toledana, woman surrounded by gold leaves, 4½x4½" **$8.00**

Cigar box, outer; Zirella, woman wearing white veil, 4½x4½" **$12.00**

Crate, All American, Washington apples, shield w/stars & stripes on black panel, yellow & white lettering on blue, 9x11".**$5.00**

Crate, Best Strike Apples, Pajaro Valley, 9x11", $35.00

Crate, Big Chief, Canadian apples, colorful image of Indian in full headdress, 9x11" **$10.00**

Crate, Big Jim, California pears, caricature of Big Jim & yellow logo on blue background, 8x11" **$3.00**

Crate, Butler's Supreme, Washington apples, white & green 3-D lettering on blue background, 9x11" **$2.50**

Crate, Camel, California pears, Arab & camel facing orange sun, 7½x11" **$3.00**

Crate, Chickie Asparagus, baby chick & lg asparagus bunch on blue background..**$4.00**

Crate, Clipper Brand Cranberries, ships at sea..............**$5.00**

Crate, Co-ed, California oranges, girl in graduation cap & gown on purple background, 10x11" **$4.00**

Crate, Dulcis, Spanish citrus, blue, orange & gold Art Deco design..**$6.00**

Crate, Ensign Brand, California apples, flag on bright yellow background, 9x10½" **$4.00**

Crate, Envoy, California lemons, gold-winged blue circle on orange & blue background, 9x12" **$3.50**

Crate, Eureka, Florida citrus, Indian playing flute, 9x9" ..**$5.00**

Crate, Forever First, California pears, 3 pears, holly & light blue script logo on black background, 8x11" **$4.00**

Crate, Four Star, Washington apples, lg '4' & 4 stars on blue background, orange lettering, 9x11"....................**$2.00**

Crate, Grizzly Island Asparagus, sunset scene w/grizzly bear on orange background, red AK logo....................**$12.00**

Crate, Jack Rabbit Yams, lg rabbit in triangle, 9x9" **$3.00**

Crate, K-O, Washington apples, boxing fist & arm punching out of black background, blue border, 9x11" **$10.00**

Crate, Kaweah Maid, California lemons, Indian squaw, 9x12" **$5.00**

Crate, King Pelican Lettuce, green pelican wearing crown on black background **$3.00**

Crate, Lochinvar, California oranges, gallant knight riding off w/maiden, 10x11" **$7.50**

Crate, Morjon, California apples, blue triangle & red apple on yellow background, 9x11" **$2.00**

Crate, Prodigio, Spanish citrus, little boy peeking around door **$25.00**

Crate, Quality First, peaches, 2 peaches on green background, 7x8" **$12.00**

Crate, Red Bird, California oranges, red phoenix-type bird in wreath, 10x11" **$3.00**

Crate, Redman, Washington apples, Indian & cave drawings on red background, 9x11" **$4.00**

Crate, River Maid, California pears, Dutch girl beside windmill w/boat sailing past, 8x11" **$3.00**

Crate, Safe Hit Vegetables, baseball player hitting ball toward fan-filled stands **$3.00**

Crate, Sea Grape, Florida citrus, seaside rainbow & fruit crate, 9x9" **$4.00**

Crate, Sun Garden, California oranges, sunrise scene, 10x11¾" **$12.00**

Crate, Sutter Maid Asparagus, blue goose logo & lg gold letters on black background....................................**$2.50**

Crate, Sweet Lue, yams, little girl in field holding yam .**$2.50**

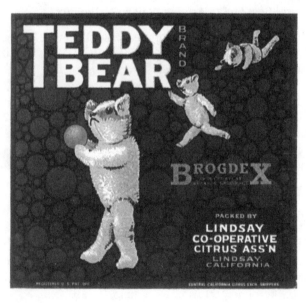

Crate, Teddy Bear Citrus, Brogdex, 9x11", $20.00

Crate, Unicorn, California oranges, unicorn running through field, 10x11¾" **$14.00**

Crate, Ventura Maid, California lemons, Art Deco woman holding lemons, 10x11¾" **$15.00**

Crate, Waldorf, Washington apples, bellhop in green suit carring oversized apple on tray, 9x11" **$3.00**

Crate, Weeks, Oregon pears, pear on branch & red script logo on blue background, 8x11"..............................**$5.00**

Crate, Yuba Orchard, California pears, white lettering & 2 pears on blue flag background, 8x11"....................**$2.00**

Lug box, Battle Axe Grapes, knight in armor w/weapon..**$2.00**

Lug box, Florita Grapes, dancing Senorita w/tamborine..**$2.00**

Lug box, Golden Gate Grapes, sm sketch of the Golden Gate Bridge & red script lettering on blue background ...**$2.00**

Lug box, Palo Alto (various fruits), tall redwood tree & white lettering on red background **$4.00**

Lug box, White House Melon, vignette of the White House & white lettering on red background **$3.00**

Lefton China

Made-in-Japan ceramics marked Lefton (a Chicago-based importer/distributor) are among the newest collectibles around today, especially the three lines we've featured below: Cat, Blue Bird, and Young Lady. All were done in the same combination of colors. Blue is predominate: the cat's face is blue; of course, the bird is blue, and blue was used for the young blond lady's bow tie and the flower atop her red and white hat. I remember all of these lines from the '50s and '60s. They may have a stamped mark or a paper label.

See also Cookie Jars.

Tea set, Young Lady, $65.00; Cookie jar, $45.00

Cookie jar, Cat..**$45.00**

Creamer, Cat, #1508...**$15.00**

Cup, Blue Bird, #284..**$5.00**

Dish, white shell shape on low pedestal foot, applied pink flowers, gold trim, #841.......................................**$15.00**

Egg cup, Blue Bird, #282..**$5.00**

Jam jar, Young lady, #323 ....**$10.00**

Planter, Blue Bird, unmarked...**$8.00**

Planter, Pig, white hobnail w/applied roses & leaves, rosebud eyes, 6" long **$25.00**

Planter, Rooster, 8x7½", $25.00

Powder box, ornate banjo shape, pink body w/flower design, gold trim & gold-tone metal handle, 7½".**$50.00**
Salt & pepper shakers, Cat, #1521, pr.............................**$15.00**
Salt & pepper shakers, Young Lady, pr........................**$15.00**
Sugar bowl (open), Cat **$15.00**
Teapot, Cat **$35.00**
Vase, hand cupped together w/red-painted fingernails, applied flowers at wrists, 5½" **$15.00**

Letter Openers

Interesting as a grouping or singularly as a decorative accent, old letter openers are easy to find and affordable. They've been made in just about any material you can think of — some very fancy, others almost primitive. If you like advertising, you'll want to add those with product or company names to your collection.

Brass, engraved ship on handle, 9" **$25.00**
Brass, National Foundry, St Louis **$18.00**
Brass, Victorian-style lion handle................................**$45.00**
Bronze, Mechanics Savings Bank, Manchester NH......**$20.00**
Celluloid, bust of Napoleon, tan, worn brown hat, 7¾"..**$30.00**
Celluloid, embossed violets & leaves, 10" **$16.00**
Chrome, fluted **$12.50**
Copper, embossed bronco w/rider, 1940s **$10.00**
Ivory, w/stanhope...**$60.00**
Pewter, nude w/sword, 9"..**$45.00**
Sterling, Nouveau flowers **$60.00**
Whalebone, sword form, 4¼", EX..................................**$25.00**

Brass, gargoyle handle, marked, 9", $25.00

Plastic, Fuller Brush, figural handle, $8.00

License Plates

Some of the early porcelain license plates are valued at more than $500.00. First-year plates (the date varies from state to state, of course) are especially desirable. Steel plates with the aluminum 'state seal' attached range in value from $150.00 (for those from 1915-20) down to $20.00 (for those from the early forties to 1950). Even some modern plates are desirable to collectors who like those with special graphics and messages.

1911, Iowa...**$150.00**
1912, Minnesota **$125.00**
1916, Maine **$35.00**
1916, South Dakota..**$45.00**
1920, Arkansas **$140.00**
1920, North Dakota..**$20.00**
1921, New Hampshire **$13.50**
1921, Oklahoma..**$140.00**
1923, Vermont **$13.50**
1925, Wyoming **$25.00**
1926, Washington State...**$28.00**
1928, Kentucky...**$50.00**
1928, Ohio..**$14.50**
1928, Oregon..**$25.00**
1929, Nebraska...**$15.50**
1930, New Jersey **$20.00**
1930, New York **$14.50**
1932, Maryland **$23.00**
1934, Michigan, pr **$25.00**
1935, Conneticut **$13.50**
1935, Massachusetts, lock tab, tab cut......................**$40.00**
1936, Tennessee, state shaped **$70.00**
1939, Utah **$30.00**
1942, Kansas, sunflower **$30.00**
1943, California, 'V' tab...**$20.00**
1944, Illinois, soybean **$12.50**
1944, Pennsylvania..**$9.50**
1944, Virginia, soybean **$25.00**
1946, Mississippi **$35.00**
1946, Wisconsin **$12.50**
1947, Idaho, skier **$125.00**

1948, Illinois, composition, $8.00

1948, Indiana...**$7.50**
1950, Hawaii..**$75.00**
1954, Alabama...**$15.50**

1955, Florida	**$20.00**
1955, Louisiana	**$30.00**
1956, Delaware, stainless	**$20.00**
1959, Rhode Island	**$17.00**
1961, Nevada	**$17.50**
1961, Washington DC, inaugural	**$60.00**
1962, Texas	**$6.00**
1963, New Mexico	**$9.50**
1963, South Carolina	**$6.50**
1964, Arizona	**$8.50**
1966, Alaska, Totem Pole	**$25.00**
1976, North Carolina, First in Freedom	**$10.50**
1990, Georgia, Peach	**$6.50**

Liddle Kiddles

These tiny little dolls ranging from ¾" to 4" tall were made by Mattel from 1966 until 1979. They all had posable bodies and rooted hair that could be restyled, and they came with accessories of many types. Some represented storybook characters, some were flowers in perfume bottles, some were made to be worn as jewelry, and there were even spacemen 'Kiddles.' Our prices are for dolls still mint and in their original packaging. If only the package is missing, deduct 25%. If the doll is dressed but has none of the original accessories, deduct 75%.

For more information, we recommend *Modern Collector's Dolls,* by Pat Smith.

Alice in Wonderliddle, 1967, minumum value	**$150.00**
Anabelle Autodiddle, #3770	**$45.00**
Beat-A-Diddle, Sears Exclusive, 1967, 3½"	**$150.00**
Bugs Bunny Skediddler, #3822, rare	**$85.00**
Calamity Jiddle, #3506, w/horse	**$70.00**
Carrying case, round or rectangular, sm	**$40.00**
Cinderiddles Palace, 1966, minimum value	**$45.00**
Cookin' Hiddle, #3846	**$45.00**
Greta Grape, #3728, Canadian version	**$40.00**
Greta Griddle, #3508	**$75.00**
Heather Hiddlehorse Skediddle, red hair, w/horse, 1967, minimum value	**$75.00**
Honeysuckle Kologne, #3704	**$30.00**
Kampy Kiddle, #3753, w/fishing gear, 1968	**$60.00**
Lady Crimson, #A3840, w/tag	**$100.00**
Laffy Lemon Kola Kiddle, blond hair, 1967, minimum value	**$40.00**
Larky Locket, blond hair, 1966, minimum value	**$25.00**
Liddle Diddle, #3503, checked pajamas	**$60.00**
Liddle Middle Muffet, #3545	**$150.00**
Lilac Locket, #3540	**$25.00**
Lola Liddle, #3504	**$75.00**
Lorelei Locket, #3717, 1976	**$25.00**
Loretta Locket, #3722, 1976	**$25.00**
Lorna Locket, #3535, fits in gold locket w/red stones & dark blue top, 1967	**$25.00**
Orange Ice Kone, #3654	**$40.00**
Orange Meringue, #3585, name sticker missing	**$25.00**

Peter Paniddle, 1966, minimum value	**$150.00**
Rosemary Roadster, #3642	**$100.00**
Sheila Skediddle, #3765, from $40 to	**$50.00**
Sizzly Friddle, #3513, polka-dot outfit	**$45.00**
Slipsy Sliddle, #3754	**$75.00**
Surfy Skiddle, #3517, pink vinyl bikini, sunglasses & surfboard, 1967	**$65.00**
Sweet Pea Kologne, #3705	**$25.00**
Tiny Tiger Animiddle, 1968, minimum value	**$45.00**

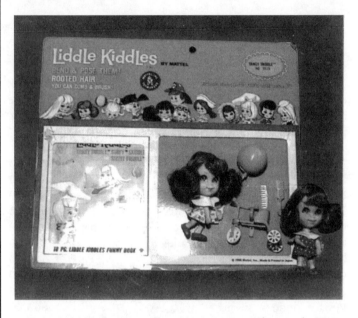

Trikey Triddle, #3515, floral dress, from $75 to $100.00

Tutti-Frutti Kone, #3655	**$40.00**
Violet Kiddle Kologne, lavender hair, minimum value	**$25.00**

Little Golden Books

Everyone has had a few of these books in their lifetime; some we've read to our own children so many times that we still know them word for word. Today they're appearing in antique malls and shops everywhere, and when they're found in good condition, dust jacket intact, first editions from the 1940s may go as high as $30.00.

The first were printed in 1942. These are recognizable by their blue paper spines (later ones had gold foil). Until the early 1970s, they were numbered consecutively; after that they were unnumbered.

First editions of the titles having a 25¢ or 29¢ cover price can be identified by either a notation on the first or second pages, or a letter on the bottom right corner of the last page (A for 1, B for 2, etc.). If these are absent, you probably have a first edition.

Condition is extremely important. To qualify as mint, these books must look just as good as they looked the day they were purchased. Naturally, having been used by children, many show signs of wear. If your book is just lightly soiled, the cover has no tears or scrapes, the inside pages have only small creases or folded corners, and the spine is still strong (though its cover may be missing), it will be worth about half as much as one in mint condition. Additional damge would of course lessen the value even more.

A series number containing an 'A' refers to an activity book, while a 'D' number identifies a Disney story. Our values are for first editions, unless specifically stated otherwise in the description.

For more information, we recommend _Collecting Little Golden Books_ by Steve Santi.

A Day at the Beach, #110, 1951, 28 pages, M.............**$15.00**
Ali Baba, #323, 1958, 24 pages, M **$10.00**
Babes in Toyland, #D97, VG...**$10.00**
Baby Dear, #466, 1962, 24 pages, M............................**$15.00**
Baby's House, #80P (puzzle on back cover), 1950, 28 pages, M...**$35.00**
Bozo the Clown, #446, 1961, 24 pages, M **$10.00**
Broken Arrow, #299, 1957, 24 pages, M.......................**$8.00**
Bugs Bunny, #312, 1949, 24 pages, M...........................**$6.00**
Bugs Bunny Gets a Job, #136, 1952, 28 pages, M..........**$8.00**

Bunny Book, #D111, 1951, 24 pages, M, $15.00

Car & Truck Stamps, #A20, 1957, 20 pages, M **$10.00**
Chip, Chip, #28, 1947, 42 pages, M **$15.00**
Chipmunks' Merry Christmas, #375, 1959, VG **$5.00**
Christmas Carol, #595, 1946, 24 pages, M **$4.00**
Cinderella's Friends, #D115, 7th edition, G...................**$2.50**
Come Play House, #44, 1948, 42 pages, M **$20.00**
Doctor Squash, #157, 1952, 28 pages, M......................**$12.00**
Donald Duck's Safety Book, #D41, 1954, 28 pages, M..**$20.00**
Fish, #5023, 1959, 56 pages, M **$12.00**
Five Little Firemen, #64, 1948, NM **$15.00**
George Finds a Grandpa, #196, 1954, 28 pages, M.....**$18.00**
Gunsmoke, #320, 1958, 24 pages, M............................**$15.00**
Happy Birthday, #123, full of party favors, only American 35¢ Little Golden Book, 1952, 42 pages, M...........**$25.00**
Hiawatha, #D31, 1952, 28 pages, M **$15.00**
Howdy Doody & the Princess, #135, 1952, 1st printing, VG **$11.50**
Huckleberry Hound Builds a House, #376, 4th edition, VG..**$5.00**

Jiminy Cricket Fire Fighter, #D50, 1956, 24 pages, M..**$18.00**
Just Watch Me, #104, 1975, 24 pages, M **$4.00**
Lassie & the Big Cleanup Day, #572, 1972, 2nd printing, VG **$2.50**
Leave It to Beaver, #347, 1959, 24 pages, M...............**$25.00**
Little Mommy, #569, 1967, 24 pages, M **$20.00**
Mickey Mouse & the Missing Mouseketeers, #D57, 1956, M..**$12.00**
My Baby Sister, #340, 1951, 24 pages, M....................**$18.00**
My Kitten, #163, 1954, 28 pages, M **$12.00**
My Little Golden Book of Manners, #460, 1968, 5th edition, G **$1.00**
Nurse Nancy, #154, (Band-Aids pasted to title page), 1952, 28 pages, M **$25.00**
Paper Dolls, #A3, 1955, 20 pages, M **$25.00**
Peter & the Wolf, #D10, 1948, 4th edition, VG...........**$12.00**
Peter & the Wolf, #D5, 1947, 42 pages, M **$12.00**
Quick Draw McGraw, #398, 1960, 24 pages, M..........**$12.00**
Return to Oz, Dorothy Saves..., #105-56, 1985, 1st printing, VG **$4.50**
Road Runner, A Very Scary Lesson, #122, 1976, 2nd printing, G **$1.00**
Roy Rogers, #177, 1953, 28 pages, M **$18.00**
Rudolph the Red Nose Reindeer, #331, 1958, G............**$3.00**
Ruff & Ready, #378, 1959, 24 pages, M **$7.00**
Rusty Goes to School, #479, 1962, NM........................**$10.00**
Sly Little Bear, #411, 1960, 24 pages, M.......................**$8.00**
Smokey Bear & the Campers, #423, 2nd edition, G **$3.00**
Smokey the Bear, #224, 1955, 28 pages, M..................**$15.00**
Snow White & Rose Red, #228, 1955, 28 pages, M **$10.00**
Snow White & the Seven Dwarfs, #D66, 29th printing, VG..**$1.00**
Steve Canyon, #356, 1959, 24 pages, M.......................**$15.00**
Surprise for Sally, #84, 1950, 42 pages, M...................**$15.00**
Tarzan, #549, 1964, 24 pages, M..................................**$16.00**
The Lion's Paw, #367, 1959, 24 pages, M....................**$12.00**
The Lone Ranger, #263, 1956, 24 pages, M..................**$18.00**
The Love Bug, #D130, 1974, 24 pages, M....................**$10.00**
The Road to Oz, #144, 1951, 28 pages, M....................**$20.00**
The Taxi That Hurried, #25, 1948, 5th edition, VG.......**$6.00**
Thumper, #D119, 1942, 24 pages, M **$10.00**
Tom & Jerry, #117, 1951, 28 pages, M........................**$10.00**

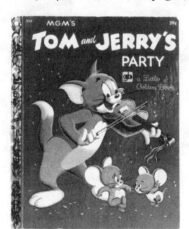

Tom & Jerry's Party, #235, NM, $8.00

Tootle, #21, 1945, 42 pages, M **$18.00**

Top Cat, #453, 1962, 24 pages, M.................................**$15.00**
Whales, #171, 1978, 24 pages, M.................................**$5.00**
What If, #130, 1951, 28 pages, M................................**$10.00**
Woody Woodpecker, #330, 1952, 24 pages, M.............**$5.00**
3 Little Kittens, #1, 1942, 42 pages, M **$25.00**

Little Red Riding Hood

This line of novelty cookie jars, canisters, mugs, teapots, and other kitchenware items was made by both Regal China and Hull. Any piece today is expensive. There are several variations of the cookie jars. The Regal jar with the open basket marked 'Little Red Riding Hood Pat. Design 135889' is worth about $250.00. The same with the closed basket goes for about $25.00 more. An unmarked Regal variation with a closed basket, full skirt, and no apron books at $600.00. The Hull jars are valued higher, about $350.00 unless they're heavily decorated with decals and gold trim, which can add as much as $250.00 to the basic value.

A companion piece, the wolf on the basketweave jar is valued at $950.00; it was also made by Regal.

The complete line is covered in *The Collector's Encyclopedia of Cookie Jars* by Joyce and Fred Roerig.

Butter dish...**$395.00**
Canister, salt...**$1,100.00**
Canister, sugar, flour, or coffee, each.......................**$650.00**
Canisters, spice; each...**$650.00**
Cracker jar, skirt held wide, 8½"..............................**$550.00**
Creamer, tab handle **$225.00**
Creamer & sugar bowl, head pour, w/lid...................**$700.00**
Creamer & sugar bowl (open), side spout, pr..........**$300.00**
Match safe, wall hanging.......................................**$800.00**
Milk pitcher, ruffled skirt, w/apron, rare, 8½"......**$3,000.00**
Milk pitcher, standing, 8" **$265.00**
Planter, standing, wall hanging................................**$475.00**
Salt & pepper shakers, standing, rare, 4½", pr..........**$850.00**
Salt & pepper shakers, standing, 3¼", pr **$75.00**

Salt & pepper shakers, standing, 5¼", pr, $150.00

Sugar bowl, crawling..**$225.00**
Teapot **$365.00**

Lu Ray Pastels

This was one of Taylor, Smith, and Taylor's most popular lines of dinnerware. It was made from the late 1930s until sometime in the early '50s in five pastel colors: Windsor Blue, Persian Cream, Sharon Pink, Surf Green, and Chatham Gray.

If you'd like more information, we recommend *The Collector's Encyclopedia of American Dinnerware* by Jo Cunningham.

Bowl, fruit; 5½" **$4.50**
Bowl, mixing; lg...**$75.00**
Bowl, salad; lg...**$40.00**
Bowl, soup; 8"...**$12.50**
Bowl, tab handle, 6"..**$13.50**
Bowl, vegetable; 9"...**$10.00**
Casserole **$60.00**
Coffeepot, demitasse; ovoid....................................**$95.00**
Creamer, demitasse; ovoid **$22.00**
Cup & saucer, demitasse **$18.00**
Cup & saucer, demitasse; straight sides.....................**$25.00**
Egg cup..**$12.00**
Nut dish..**$35.00**
Pitcher, bulbous w/flat bottom **$40.00**
Pitcher, juice; ovoid..**$110.00**
Plate, chop; 14"..**$27.50**
Plate, serving; tab handle **$25.00**
Plate, 10"...**$12.50**
Plate, 6"..**$2.00**
Plate, 9"..**$7.50**
Platter, oval, 11½"...**$10.00**
Platter, oval, 13"...**$10.00**
Relish, 4-part...**$60.00**
Salt & pepper shakers, pr..**$10.00**
Sauce pitcher..**$22.50**
Sugar bowl, demitasse; ovoid **$24.00**

Teapot, flat-top spout, $45.00

Tidbit, 2-tier...**$30.00**

Tumbler, water..$45.00
Vase, bud; 2 styles, each $175.00

Lunch Boxes

Character lunch boxes made of metal have been very collectible for several years, but now even those made of plastic and vinyl are coming into their own.

The first lunch box of this type ever produced featured Hopalong Cassidy. Made by the Aladdin company, it was constructed of steel and decorated with decals. But the first fully lithographed steel lunch box and matching thermos bottle was made a few years later (in 1953) by American Thermos. Roy Rogers was its featured character.

Hundreds have been made, and just as is true in other areas of character-related collectibles, the more desirable lunch boxes are those with easily recognizable, well-known subjects — western heroes; TV, Disney, and cartoon characters; and famous entertainers.

Values given in our listings are for boxes in excellent condition. For metal boxes this means that you will notice only very minor defects and less than normal wear. Plastic boxes may have a few scratches and some minor wear on the sides, but the graphics are completely undamaged. Vinyls must retain their original shape; brass parts may be tarnished, and the hinge may show signs of beginning splits. If the box you're trying to evaluate is in any worse condition than we've described, to be realistic, you must cut these prices rather drastically. Values are given for boxes without matching thermoses. If you'd like to learn more, we recommend *A Pictorial Price Guide to Metal Lunch Boxes and Thermoses* by Larry Aikins.

Metal

America On Parade, Aladdin, 1976............................$40.00
Archies, Aladdin, 1969..$55.00
Batman, Aladdin, 1966 ....$110.00

Battlestar Galactica, Aladdin, 1978, $38.00

Berenstain Bears, American Thermos, 1983.................$25.00
Beverly Hillbillies, Aladdin, 1963...............................$110.00
Boston Bruins, Okay, 1973...$475.00
Bozo, Aladdin, 1963 ....$280.00
Buck Rogers, Aladdin, 1979 ....$30.00
Cartoon Zoo, Universal, 1963 ....$320.00
Children, Okay, 1974..$210.00
Cowboy in Africa, King Seeley Thermos, 1968, EX...$190.00
Daniel Boone, Aladdin, 1965 ....$120.00
Dick Tracy, Aladdin, 1967 ....$130.00
Doctor Doolittle, Aladdin, 1968 ....$80.00
Dukes of Hazzard, Aladdin, 1983 ....$45.00
Evil Knievel, Aladdin, 1974 ....$40.00
Fess Parker, King Seely Thermos, 1965.....................$140.00
Flipper, King Seely Thermos, 1966............................$140.00

Flying Nun, 1968, $75.00

Gene Autry, Universal, 1954 ....$200.00
Grizzly Adams, Aladdin, 1977 ....$60.00
Gunsmoke (double LL's), Aladdin, 1959 ....$400.00
Hector Heathcote, Aladdin, 1964...............................$200.00
Hopalong Cassidy, Aladdin, 1952 ....$160.00
HR Puff 'n Stuff, Aladdin, 1970 ....$90.00
Jungle Book, Aladdin, 1968..$65.00
King Kong, American Thermos, 1977..........................$45.00
Kung Fu, King Seely Thermos, 1974 ....$50.00
Lawman, King Seely Thermos, 1961..........................$100.00
Looney Tunes TV, American Thermos, 1959.............$220.00
Man From UNCLE, King Seely Thermos, 1966..........$140.00

Masters of the Universe, 1983, $10.00

Mod Floral, Okay Industries, 1975..............................$230.00
Munsters, King Seely Thermos, 1965.......................$160.00
Nancy Drew Mysteries, King Seely Thermos, 1977 .....$35.00
Orbit, King Seely Thermos, 1963..............................$210.00
Peanuts, King Seely Thermos, 1966...........................$35.00
Pete's Dragon, Aladdin, 1978 ....$35.00
Pinocchio, Aladdin, 1971 ....$80.00
Plaid Scotch, Ohio Art, 1962 ....$60.00
Play Ball, King Seely Thermos, 1969 ....$80.00
Racing Wheels, King Seely Thermos, 1977 ....$50.00
Rat Patrol, Aladdin, 1967 ....$80.00
Red Barn (open doors), American Thermos, 1958 ......$65.00
Rough Rider, Aladdin, 1973.......................................$55.00
Saddlebag, King Seely Thermos, 1977.......................$130.00
Secret Agent, King Seely Thermos, 1968...................$95.00
Sesame Street, Aladdin, 1983.....................................$7.00

Sleeping Beauty, 2 handles, rare, $250.00

Snoopy, King Seely Thermos, 1968 ....$40.00
Speed Buggy, King Seely Thermos, 1974....................$35.00
Stars & Stripes, Aladdin, 1970 ....$70.00
Strawberry Land, Aladdin, 1985 ....$35.00
Super Heroes, Aladdin, 1976......................................$45.00
Tarzan, Aladdin, 1966 ....$90.00
Thundercats, Aladdin, 1985 ....$10.00
UFO, King Seely Thermos, 1973................................$75.00
Welcome Back Kotter, Aladdin, 1977.........................$40.00
Woody Woodpecker, Aladdin, 1972............................$90.00

Plastic
ABC, Taiwan, unknown year $12.00
Astrokids, Brazil, 1988 ....$30.00
Barnaby Bear w/blackboard, United Kingdon, 1987...$20.00
Beach Bronto, Aladdin, 1984 ....$50.00
Bear Box, Cipsa Mexico, 1988 ....$10.00
Big Jim, Thermos, 1976 ....$60.00
Bozostuffs, Deko, 1988..$40.00
Camera, Taiwan, 1986 ....$15.00
Care Bears, Aladdin, 1986 ....$10.00
Chiclets, Thermos, 1987...$40.00
Cinderella, Aladdin, 1992 ....$10.00
Curiosity Shop, Thermos, 1972 ....$45.00
Dinosaur, Taiwan, 1988..$20.00
Dr Pepper, Taiwan, 1982..$35.00

Dune, Aladdin, 1984 ....$40.00
Food Fighters, Aladdin, 1988 ....$20.00
Ghostbusters, Deka, 1986..$20.00
Gumby, Thermos, 1986 ....$25.00
Hot Wheels, Thermos, 1984 ....$15.00
Inspector Gadget, Thermos, 1983..............................$15.00
Keebler, Taiwan, 1978 ....$35.00
LA Gear Club, Taiwan, 1987 ....$25.00
Levi's, Taiwan, 1985..$30.00
Lunch Break, Taiwan, 1986 ....$30.00
Mad Balls, Aladdin, 1986 ....$15.00
Masters of the Universe, Thermos Canada, 1985,....... $25.00
Mermaid, Thermos, 1989 ....$15.00
Mickey & Donald, Aladdin Canada, 1984...................$25.00
Miss Piggy's Safari Van, Superseal, 1989 ....$20.00
Movie Monsters, Aladdin Canada, 1979......................$80.00
Nosey Bears, Aladdin, 1988..$12.00
Roller Games, Thermos, 1989 ....$25.00
School Bus, Taiwan, 1986 ....$20.00
Shirt Tales, Thermos, 1981 ....$10.00
Smurfs, Thermos, 1981 ....$10.00
Snorks, Thermos, 1984 ....$12.00
Sport Goofy, Aladdin, 1986..$40.00
Sunkist, Taiwan, 1987 ....$30.00
Taxi, Thermos, 1985 ....$20.00
Train, Taiwan, 1988 ....$15.00
Turtles, Thermos, 1990 ....$10.00
Where's Waldo, Thermos, 1990 ....$10.00
Wild Fire, Aladdin, 1986...$15.00

Vinyl
All American, Bayville, 1976 ....$120.00
Annie, Aladdin, 1981 ....$55.00
Barbie & Francie, King Seely Thermos, 1965..............$95.00
Barnum's Animals, Adco Liberty, 1978 ....$60.00
Boston Red Sox, Ardee, 1960s $140.00
Coca-Cola, Aladdin, 1980 ....$140.00
Dawn, Aladdin, 1971 ....$140.00
Denim, King Seely Thermos, 1970s............................$50.00
Deputy Dawg, Thermos, 1964 ....$550.00
Fawn, unknown, 1960s $140.00

Ford 1910, unknown maker, $45.00

Goat Butt, Ardee, 1965 ....$160.00
Haunted House, Dart, 1979.............................$85.00
I Love a Parade, Bayville, 1970.....................$130.00
Jr Deb, Aladdin, 1960 ....$175.00
Kodak II, Aladdin, 1970s $95.00
Lion in Van, King Seely Thermos, 1978 .....$145.00
Mary Ann, Aladdin, 1960 ....$75.00
Mr Peanut Snap Pack, Dart, 1979...................$90.00
Penelope & Penny, Gary, 1970s $120.00
Pony Tail, King Seely Thermos, 1960.........$185.00
Princess, Aladdin, 1963................................$140.00
Sabrina, Aladdin, 1972 ....$230.00
Shari Lewis, Aladdin, 1963 ....$470.00
Snow White, unknown, 1967.........................$285.00
Squares (blue), unknown company & year $60.00
Tammy, Alladin, 1964....................................$240.00
Tina Teen, unknown, 1960s...........................$210.00
White Psychedelic, Thermos, 1962 ....$475.00

Thermoses

Astronauts, Thermos, 1986.............................$10.00
Battle Kit, Aladdin, 1965................................$55.00
Beach Party (pink), Deka, 1988........................$5.00
Black Hole, Aladdin, 1979...............................$30.00
Brady Bunch, King Seely Thermos, 1970 ......$90.00
Buck Rogers, Aladdin, 1979 ....$20.00
Care Bears, Aladdin, 1984................................$5.00
Charlie's Angels, Aladdin, 1978......................$15.00
Colonial Bread Van, unknown, 1984..............$40.00
Corsage, King Seely Thermos, 1970................$30.00
Cracker Jack, Aladdin, 1969 ....$25.00
Dark Crystal, King Seely Thermos, 1982 ......$10.00
Denim, King Seely Thermos, 1970s................$20.00
Dick Tracy, Aladdin, 1989 ....$5.00
Disco, Aladdin, 1979.......................................$25.00
Doctor Doolittle, Aladdin, 1968 ....$45.00
Dynomutt, King Seely Thermos, 1977 ....$30.00
Ed Grimley, Aladdin, 1988................................$8.00
Fall Guy, Aladdin, 1981...................................$12.00
Flag-O-Rama, Universal, 1954 ....$60.00
Flipper, King Seely Thermos, 1966................$60.00
Flying Nun, Aladdin, 1968................................$75.00
Fox & the Hound, Aladdin, 1981 ....$10.00
Fraggle Rock, Thermos, 1987............................$8.00
Geoffrey, Aladdin, 1981..................................$10.00
How the West Was Won, King Seely Thermos, 1979..$30.00
Hugga Bunch, Aladdin Hallmark, 1984 ....$5.00
Jr Miss, Aladdin, 1966....................................$15.00
Menudo, Thermos, 1984..................................$10.00
Monster in My Pocket, Aladdin, 1990............$10.00
Muppets (dome), Thermos, 1981......................$5.00
New Zoo Revue, Aladdin, 1970s.....................$55.00
Princess, Aladdin, 1963..................................$55.00
Rambo, King Seely Thermos, 1985 ....$5.00
Roller Games, Thermos, 1989 ....$10.00
Sabrina, Aladdin, 1972...................................$85.00
Satellite, King Seely Thermos, 1960 ....$70.00

Six Million Dollar Man, Aladdin, 1978...........$25.00
Sky Commanders, Thermos, 1987......................$5.00
Snorks, Thermos, 1984.....................................$5.00
Speed Buggy, King Seely Thermos, 1974........$20.00
Star Wars, King Seely Thermos, 1978.............$12.00
Tiger w/Umbrella, Neevel, unknown year.......$15.00
Toppie, American Thermos, 1957....................$750.00
Wag's 'n Whiskers, King Seely Thermos, 1978 ...$12.00
Wonderful World on Ice, Aladdin, 1982...........$7.00
WWF, Thermos, 1986 ....$10.00
Ziggy's, Aladdin, 1979....................................$40.00
18-Wheeler, Aladdin, 1978 ....$25.00

Maddux of California

Founded in Los Angeles in 1938, Maddux not only produced ceramics but imported and distributed them as well. They supplied chainstores nationwide with well-designed figural planters, TV lamps, novelty and giftware items, and during the mid-1960s their merchandise was listed in every major stamp catalog. Because of an increasing amount of foreign imports and an economic slowdown in our own country, the company was forced to sell out in 1976. Under the new management, manufacturing was abandoned, and the company was converted solely to distribution. Collectors have only recently discovered this line, and prices right now are affordable though increasing.

Planter, rearing horse, 10x7½", $25.00

Bowl, #3017, seashell $15.00
Figurine, #912/#913, Chinese pheasants, air-brushed colors, 11", pr $30.00
Figurine, #923, swans, black matt glaze, 10½", pr.......$25.00
Figurine, #924, standing stag, natural colors, 12½".......$15.00
Figurine, #932, rooster, 10½"...........................$30.00

Figurine, #971, flamingo, winging, 12" $45.00
Figurine, #972/#973, bulls, 1 w/head up & 1 w/head down, red, 11" long, pr.........................$40.00
Figurine, #982, prancing horse.................$20.00
Planter, #515, pink flamingo, 10½" $45.00
TV lamp, #810, prancing stallion, 12" $30.00
TV lamp, #826, pr of cockatiels $50.00
TV lamp, #839, flying mallard, natural colors $30.00
TV lamp, #841, 3-D planter w/head of Christ.............$20.00
TV lamp, #844, prairie schooner (covered wagon), 11" ..$40.00
Vase, #221, swan, white, 12"........................$20.00

Magazines

There are lots of magazines around today, but unless they're in fine condition (clean, no missing or clipped pages, and very little other damage); have interesting features (cover illustrations, good advertising, or special-interest stories); or deal with sports greats, famous entertainers, or world-reknowned personalities, they're worth very little, no matter how old they are. Address labels on the front are acceptable, but if you find one with no label, it will be worth about 25% more than our listed values. See also Movie Stars, Magazines; TV Guides.

Air Trails, 1941, November, G+.........................$3.50
Amateur Photography, 1917, August 10, G $5.00
Amazing Stories, 1929, June, Coblentz, Verne, Hays, G.$20.00
Amazing Stories, 1977, October, Bischoff, Busby, EX ...$3.00
American Home, 1949, January, Dollar Stretching issue, EX...................$6.00
American Home, 1962, October, Dennis Day, G-.........$2.50
American Photography, 1930, August, VG $7.00
Arizona Highways, 1958, April, Sulphur Springs Valley, VG $4.00
Auto Age, 1953, October, Hudson Super Jet Road Test, VG...................$10.00
Avon Fantasy Reader, 1947, February, Pratt, Howard, VG...................$11.00
Banana Republic, 1986, Summer, Voices From Africa, EX $2.50
Better Homes & Gardens, 1974, October, Mexico travel, Greek foods, G+...................$3.00
Big Song Magazine, 1943, March, Betty Grable & Caesar Romero cover, EX...................$4.00
Brief, 1953, June, Winston Churchill article, VG...........$4.50
Catholic Digest, 1950, September, Tommy Henrich on cover, EX...................$5.00
Collectibles Illustrated, 1983, September/October, Beatles cover, stamps, Lucille Ball, plates, NM.................$10.00
Collector's Weekly, 1973, August 14, cast-iron toys, dolls, chess items, VG...................$2.00
College Laughs, 1958, June, girl athlete cover, EX.........$6.00
Collier's, 1905, September, bear & buzzard, Lyendecker illustration, EX...................$20.00
Collier's, 1957, January 4, Grace Kelly's pregnancy, VG .$5.00
Complete TV, 1957, May, Elvis Presley's New Love, VG .$8.00

Confidential, 1955, May, Rory Calhoun; A Convict?, VG..$6.00
Confidential, 1958, December, The Murder Truman Won't Talk About, EX...................$7.00
Coronet, 1946, June, Blondie short story, EX.............$4.50
Cosmopolitan, 1893, Columbian Expo cover, EX.......$35.00
Cosmopolitan, 1952, October, Queen Elizabeth cover, EX $20.00
Country Gentleman, 1928, December, Santa cover, VG..$8.00
Country Life, 1931, September, EX $5.00
Eerie, 1981, September, Frazetta cover, EX...................$6.00
Ellery Queen, 1956, June, Eberhart, Harte, Hare, Simeon, VG...................$4.00
Ellery Queen, 1973, June, Christie, Hoch, Mathieson, G+...................$3.00
Ellery Queen, 1976, June, Christie, Hoch, Pronzini, Fish, VG...................$2.50
Ellery Queen, 1980, February 11, Doyle cover, G+.......$2.50
Ellery Queen, 1984, January, Bensen (Adler/Holmes pastiche), Bradbury, VG...................$4.50
Esquire, 1956, July, Father's Day, EX...................$10.00
Esquire, 1973, March, Fat City Follies, EX $6.00
Eve, 1950, November, Can't Tell a Woman by Her Legs, VG...................$8.00
Family Circle, 1940, March 8, Eleanor Powell & Fred Astaire cover, G-...................$2.00
Family Circle, 1975, March, Maple Sugaring, VG..........$3.00
Famous Fantastic Mysteries, 1939, December, Farley — The Radio Man (1,2), G+ $12.00
Famous Fantasy Memories, 1940, December, McMorrow — The Sun Makers, G $10.00
Famous Fantasy Memories, 1942, December, Farley — The Golden City, G- $6.00
Fear, 1960, May, Collins, Jales, Mathieson, Ellson, VG ..$9.00
For Men Only, 1972, March, Asphalt Angels, VG $5.00
Forum, 1926, July, KKK article, EX $3.00
Foto, 1950, September, China Dolls, VG $8.00
Glance, 1950, April, Are You Blackmail Bait?, VG.........$8.00
Gold Bulletin, 1982, July, Liquid Golds, Enamelling on Gold, VG+...................$2.50
Good Housekeeping, 1918, July, Jessie Wilcox Smith cover, VG...................$20.00
Good Housekeeping, 1938, January, Deanna Durbin articles, EX...................$14.00
Good Housekeeping, 1945, August, baby cover, EX.....$6.00
Good Housekeeping, 1959, July, Ingrid Bergman cover, VG...................$6.00
Gourmet, 1969, August, French Wines, VG+ $3.50
Harper's Bazaar, 1936, June, Erte cover, EX $50.00
Highway Traveler, 1944, October/November, North Carolina, VG...................$6.00
Hitchcock Mystery, 1981, October 14, Martin, Pronzini, Brittain, VG...................$3.00
Homicide Detective, 1956, February, EX...................$6.00
House & Garden, 1964, April, The Drinks of Ireland, Frozen Food Cookbook, G $3.00
House & Garden, 1969, April, Dutch treats, VG $4.00
House & Garden, 1975, November, 775 Gift Suggestions, VG+...................$5.00

House Beautiful, 1946, December, Golden Jubilee, EX **$6.00**

Illustrated Mechanics, 1935, November, Wood Finishing, Waste Baskets, VG **$2.00**

Inside Detective, 1943, January, Decoy in Cell 13, worn .**$3.00**

Inside Detective, 1953, April, Don't Tease Me Baby..., VG...**$6.00**

Intellectual Digest, George Bernard Shaw, VG+ **$3.25**

Jack & Jill, 1960, January, Howdy Doody, Clarabell & Buffalo Bill cover, EX **$20.00**

Kirk Collector, 1972, Fall, silver collecting, EX **$3.00**

Ladies' Home Journal, 1902, August, EX **$12.50**

Ladies' Home Journal, 1912, December, Parrish cover, EX **$80.00**

Ladies' Home Journal, 1957, August, Motherhood Possible for Many Women, EX **$5.00**

Ladies' Home Journal, 1966, April, Sophia Loren, VG.**$40.00**

Ladies' Home Journal, 1968, February, That 'Bonnie & Clyde' Girl Faye Dunaway, EX.................................**$6.00**

Ladies' Home Journal, 1969, November, LBJ's Own Story — The Day Kennedy Was Shot, EX.............................**$5.00**

Liberty, 1973, Fall, Marilyn Monroe cover, EX.............**$12.50**

Life, 1937, February 22, Trotsky exile in Mexico article, EX...**$4.00**

Life, 1937, September 27, Nelson Eddy cover, EX.......**$15.00**

Life, 1938, December 5, showgirls of yesteryear cover, EX...**$5.00**

Life, 1938, Shirley Temple cover & story, EX..............**$35.00**

Life, 1939, March 6, Tallulah Bankhead cover, EX, $8.00

Life, 1939, December 11, Betty Grable cover, VG+.....**$10.00**

Life, 1942, November, war cover, EX **$4.00**

Life, 1944, April 17, Esther Williams cover, VG.............**$7.50**

Life, 1944, August 14, War in Europe, G **$5.00**

Life, 1946, July 29, Vivien Leigh cover, EX..................**$35.00**

Life, 1947, February 17, Army in Arctic article, EX **$4.00**

Life, 1948, November 22, Truman cover, G **$7.50**

Life, 1950, July 18, flying saucers, VG **$6.00**

Life, 1956, June 25, Mickey Mantle cover, EX.............**$17.50**

Life, 1959, November, Jackie Gleason cover, EX...........**$7.00**

Life, 1964, August 7, Marilyn Monroe cover, EX, $50.00

Life, 1964, March 6, Cassius Clay cover, NM...............**$17.50**

Life, 1969, April 18, Mae West cover, G+ **$8.00**

Life, 1970, October 23, Muhammad Ali cover, EX.......**$10.00**

Life, 1971, March 5, Frazier & Ali cover, VG...............**$10.00**

Life, 1972, November 3, Joe Namath cover, VG **$9.50**

Life, 1981, May, Reagan's attempted assassination, EX.**$10.00**

Literary Digest, 1922, July 29, Rockwell cover, NM.....**$17.50**

London Magazine, 1954, July, Kitchen — A Cottage in Cornwall, VG+...**$7.50**

Look, 1937, December 21, Shirley Temple, VG...........**$20.00**

Look, 1937, July 20, movie censorship, Tarzan, EX.....**$15.00**

Look, 1937, May, Jean Harlow, Prohibition, VG+........**$12.50**

Look, 1937, October 26, Hollywood Tragedies, Rudy Vallee, VG+...**$9.00**

Look, 1937, September 28, the movie 'Hurricane,' EX ..**$9.00**

Look, 1938, June 7, Dionne Quints, VG+.....................**$12.50**

Look, 1938, March 15, the movie 'Flash Gordon,' EX .**$20.00**

Look, 1939, December 5, Hitler, VG..............................**$9.00**

Look, 1939, July 18, Vivien Leigh/Clark Gable in 'Gone With the Wind,' EX **$17.00**

Look, 1940, February 27, Rita Hayworth, Superman, VG+ **$90.00**

Look, 1940, July 30, Hitler, Paulette Goddard, VG+ **$10.00**

Look, 1940, September 24, Charlie Chaplin, VG+..........**$9.25**

Look, 1942, June 30, Submarines, VG **$9.00**

Look, 1943, March 23, Lt Clarke Gable, VG **$9.50**

Look, 1943, November 30, Pearl Harbor plus 2 years, VG...**$9.00**

Look, 1944, March 21, US WACS, Invasion, Eisenhower, Count Basie, VG...**$8.00**

Look, 1945, December 25, Burns & Allen, Japan, VG ...**$8.00**

Look, 1946, May 28, Nagasaki, VG **$8.00**

Look, 1946, October 29, 10th Anniversary Edition, Basil Rathbone, VG...**$20.00**

Look, 1947, August 5, Roosevelt vs Stalin/Russia, Frank Sinatra, VG+ **$9.00**

Look, 1947, February 4, Stalin, Stork Club, VG.............**$8.00**

Look, 1949, July 19, Mary Martin's South Pacific Fashion Fad, EX **$7.00**

Look, 1950, August 1, How Truman Got To Be President, EX **$7.00**

Look, 1954, September 7, Gable cover and article, G . **$15.00**

Look, 1961, January 31, Clark Gable/Marilyn Monroe, VG. **$17.50**

Look, 1964, July 28, NY Nightlife, VG **$5.00**

Look, 1965, August 10, Kennedy by Sorensen, Part 1, EX **$9.50**

Look, 1967, February 21, Death of a President, Part 3, VG+ **$7.00**

Manhunt, 1953, Spillane, Kane, Deming, Hunter, G+ . **$10.00**

Manhunt, 1954, September, Heatter, Weldman, Hunter, Taylor, G+ **$6.00**

Master Detective, 1942, January, Case of the Spectral Figure, VG **$6.00**

McCall's, 1949, July, Eleanor Roosevelt Tells Her Story, EX **$5.00**

McCall's, 1959, June, The Groucho Marx Story, VG **$4.00**

McCall's, 1968, June, Jacqueline Kennedy, EX **$5.00**

McCall's, 1969, Fabulous Ford Women, VG **$4.00**

McCall's, 1969, June, Edward, Duke of Windsor, VG **$3.00**

McCall's, 1970, March, The Occult Explosion, Behind the Sharon Tate Murders, G- **$4.00**

Mobsters, 1953, February, EX **$20.00**

Mother Earth News, 1982, July/August, Safe & Sane Garden Pest Control, VG+ **$3.50**

Motor Trend, 1953, August, Woodill Wildfire, EX **$10.00**

Motor Trend, 1959, August, Driving Tomorrow's Cars, VG **$8.00**

Motor Trend, 1960, February, 1960s Hottest — Chevy or Ford?, VG **$6.00**

Mystery Digest, 1957, May, Vol 1, #1, EX **$5.00**

Mystic Magazine, 1953, November, Palmer, Phillips, Benson, G **$7.00**

National Geographic, 1922, May, England by Canoe, EX+ **$9.50**

National Geographic, 1937, November, America's First Settlers, Mecca, EX **$6.00**

National Geographic, 1940, August, Britain at War, VG+ .. **$7.00**

National Geographic, 1940, December, India, Coca-Cola advertising on back cover, VG+ **$7.00**

National Geographic, 1940, January, Denmark, South Hampton GB, The Everglades, EX **$6.00**

National Geographic, 1945, April, England's Treasures, Paris, The Crimea, VG+ **$7.00**

National Geographic, 1953, June, Lewis & Clark, London Bridge, VG **$2.00**

National Geographic, 1959, June, Germany, Hawaii, VG **$2.00**

National Geographic, 1959, May, Normandy, Amazon, VG **$3.00**

National Geographic, 1962, June, Glenn's Earth Orbits, G **$5.00**

National Geographic, 1965, September, US Air Force, Walk in Space, VG+ **$7.00**

National Geographic, 1974, January, Golden Treasure, Laos, VG **$4.00**

National Geographic, 1975, September, Mark Twain, Greenland, VG **$2.00**

National Geographic, 1981, May, The Arctic, Australia, EX **$4.50**

National Lampoon, 1972, March, Travel Through Time, EX **$3.50**

National Lampoon, 1976, September, humor, cartons, etc, VG **$4.00**

New West, 1976, April 26, Gov Jerry Brown, Los Angeles, EX **$6.00**

New West, 1976, October 25, Stallone, VG **$3.50**

New West, 1976, September 27, Palisades High School Class of '65, VG+ **$4.00**

Newsweek, 1976, July 4, Our America, special issue, VG **$4.00**

Newsweek, 1981, April 13, President Reagan's Close Call, VG **$5.00**

Panorama, 1980, February, Television Today & Tomorrow, VCRs, VG+ **$5.00**

Parents, 1942, September, VG **$3.00**

Penthouse, 1971, October, Charles Schulz interview, VG . **$5.00**

Penthouse, 1973, December, Groucho Marx interview, 1974 calendar, EX **$6.50**

Penthouse, 1976, July, Stephen King's 'The Ledge,' Gore Vidal **$9.00**

Penthouse, 1983, April, Jimmy Carter interview, VG **$7.00**

People, 1986, May 6, Bette Davis cover, EX **$3.00**

Personal Romances, 1945, March, Someday I'll Marry You, VG **$5.00**

Philip Morris, 1987, Summer, Dolly Parton cover, VG+... **$3.00**

Philip Morris, 1989, March/April, Mickey Mantle cover, EX **$5.00**

Photo Exhibit, 1957, July, Vol 1, #1, EX **$5.00**

Planet Stories, 1939, Winter, Reynolds, Pratt, Davies, Wiggins, VG **$25.00**

Playboy, 1960, January, Stella Stevens centerfold, G... **$25.00**

Playboy, 1964, January, Marilyn Monroe Remembered, VG **$30.00**

Playboy, 1970, December, Wodehouse, Buckley, Dan Blocker, VG **$10.00**

Playboy, 1973, December, Bob Hope interview, Tennessee Williams, Varga girl, VG **$12.00**

Playboy, 1974, December, Robert Redford interview, Larry King, Varga girl, G+ **$6.00**

Playboy, 1981, September, Bo Derek cover, VG+ **$10.00**

Playboy, 1983, May, Nastassi Kinski cover, Ansel Adams interview, VG+ **$6.00**

Playgirl, 1973, July, George Maharis centerfold, Karen Black, Frank Sinatra, EX **$80.00**

Playgirl, 1974, December, Burt Reynold's cover & interview, Woody Parker centerfold, EX **$45.00**

Playgirl, 1974, May, Sean Connery, Marlon Brando, Japan, EX **$20.00**

Playgirl, 1976, August, Robert Redford cover, EX **$30.00**

Popular Mechanics, 1934, October, Midget Auto Racing Cars, VG **$8.00**

Popular Mechanics, 1942, November, Miracle on Wheels, VG **$8.00**

Popular Mechanics, 1945, Shop Notes, VG **$5.00**

Popular Mechanics, 1952, January, 50th Anniversary issue, VG **$5.00**

Popular Mechanics, 1955, August, '55 Desoto, Uranium Hunt, Space, G+ **$3.00**

Post, 1966, April 23, Sonny & Cher, VG **$3.00**

Prevue, 1983, September, Mark Hammill, EX **$4.00**

Radio News, 1929, August, airship cover by H Brown, G **$8.00**

Real Stories, 1945, October, Journey to Paradise, VG **$6.00**

Rebel, 1984, January, John F Kennedy assassination story, EX **$12.50**

Red Cross Magazine, 1918, June, Rockwell cover, EX.**$37.50**

Redbook, 1977, March, The Occult, Margaret Meade, VG+ **$5.00**

Roaring Twenties, 1955, pictorial cover, EX **$7.00**

Rolling Stone, 1975, November 23, Pattie Hearst story, EX **$17.50**

Rolling Stone, 1985, May 9, Madonna, VG **$3.00**

Rolling Stone, 1987, February 12, Pee Wee Herman, VG ..**$3.00**

Saga, 1976, October, Space 1999 article, VG **$10.00**

Saturday Evening Post, 1921, May 28, girl & kite, EX..**$12.50**

Saturday Evening Post, 1930, May 24, Gary Cooper cover, EX **$45.00**

Saturday Evening Post, 1940, October 5, Will Rogers cover, VG **$7.50**

Saturday Evening Post, 1942, August 29, P-38 Aircraft cover, VG **$7.00**

Saturday Evening Post, 1945, October 27, article & photo about Japanese surrender, VG **$5.00**

Saturday Evening Post, 1960, June 5, Richard Nixon cover, VG **$5.00**

Saturday Evening Post, 1964, December, Johnny Unitas cover, EX **$5.00**

Saturday Evening Post, 1967, March, VG **$3.00**

Saturday Evening Post, 1980, December, Muppet cover, EX **$6.00**

Saturday Evening Post, 1980, July/August, Marijuana, Gene Kelly, Phil Donahoe, VG+ **$5.00**

Saucy Stories, 1945, April, cartoons & jokes, EX **$5.00**

Science & Mechanics, 1939, April, VG **$3.00**

Scientific American, 1984, November, Rain Forests, Cathedral Structures, VG **$4.00**

Scriber's, 1899, January, T Roosevelt/Rough Rider cover, EX **$8.00**

See, 1955, September, Are You a Security Risk?, VG **$8.00**

Seventeen, 1948, August, Back to School, VG **$4.00**

Short Wave & Television, 1937, January, Hugo Gernsback Editor, G+ **$15.00**

Sight & Sound, 1954, April, Greta Garbo cover, EX **$6.50**

Skeptic, 1975, March/April, America's Survival, VG **$5.00**

Skeptic, 1975, September/October, Who Killed JFK?, VG **$20.00**

Smithsonian, 1991, August, Paris Art Exhibition, w/11 color plates, VG+ **$6.00**

Soldier of Fortune, 1982, May, articles on weapons & war, VG **$3.00**

Soldier of Fortune, 1982, May, VG **$8.00**

Southern Living, 1967, June, Six Flags Over Georgia, VG **$5.00**

Sport, 1962, January, Jimmy Brown cover, EX **$5.00**

Sports Illustrated, 1956, September 24, football special, NM **$10.00**

Sports Illustrated, 1960, April 10, baseball issue, EX ...**$18.00**

Sports Illustrated, 1970, September 14, Top 20 College Ball, EX **$10.00**

Successful Farming, 1929, July, cover by Victor Anderson, VG **$4.00**

Sunset, 1935, September, Dionne Quints article, EX ...**$10.00**

Suspense (American release), 1951, Spring, Carr, Bradbury, Tenn, G+ **$6.00**

This Month, 1962, February, Vol 1, #1, EX **$4.00**

Time, 1962, August 24, Russian Cosmonauts, VG **$1.00**

Time, 1964, January 3, Martin Luther King cover, $30.00

Today's Housewife, 1925, October, EX **$6.00**

Top Notch, 1925, October 15, VG **$7.00**

Trains, 1961, September, train articles & ads, EX **$8.00**

Travel & Holiday, 1983, November, Reno, Ankara, VG+ .**$4.00**

Travel & Holiday, 1984, February, New England, EX **$4.50**

True, 1967, February, The Secret Nazi Surrender, VG ...**$4.00**

True Confessions, 1938, June, His Bride's Secret, VG ...**$8.00**

True Story, 1955, November, Teenage Bottle Party, VG..**$4.00**

True Story, 1957, April, What Every Wife Wants, VG **$4.00**

TRW Space Log, 1968, Winter, Soviet Space Program, EX **$5.00**

Twilight Zone, 1985, April, Sterling's Night Gallery Guide, EX **$8.00**

Twilight Zone, 1986, December, Stephen King interview, Koonnz, Burleson, EX **$10.00**

Twilight Zone, 1986, Poltergeist II preview, EX **$8.00**

Uncensored, 1956, June, Sex in Our Hospitals?, VG **$8.00**

US, 1977, May 3, Paul Newman cover, EX **$4.00**

Venture, 1964, October, Hong Kong, NM **$12.00**

Venture, 1968, June, Dublin Horse Show, 3-D Europe map, EX+ **$10.00**

Weird Tales, 1946, September, Lovecraft, Quinn, Block, Hamilton, G+..**$10.00**

Weird Tales, 1947, May, Cummings, Tenn, Quinn, Jacobi, G+ **$10.00**

Whisper, 1950, March, Sammy Davis Jr & Kim Novak cover, VG **$8.50**

Wilson Quarterly, 1984, Spring, Blacks in America, VG ..**$5.00**

Wisconsin Magazine, 1923, March, EX **$5.00**

Woman's Day, 1940, September, Jimmy Stewart article, J Edgar Hoover on military training, VG **$6.00**

Woman's Day, 1941, May, Army Draftees, G+ **$5.00**

Woman's Day, 1943, July, eagle & flag cover, EX **$4.00**

Woman's Day, 1957, July, Grace Kelly, Mystic Seaport, French Cuisine, G+ **$5.00**

Woman's Home Companion, 1949, September, Is Chastity Outlawed?, VG **$4.00**

Woman's Home Journal, 1955, February, Joan Crawford, VG **$4.00**

Woman's World, 1940, March, EX **$4.00**

Woman's World, 1991, December 17, Marilyn Monroe cover, VG+ **$7.00**

Wonder Stories, 1933, October, Hinton, Harris, Kelly, Thebault, G+ **$12.50**

World Progress, 1986, Winter, International Terrorism, EX **$4.50**

World War II, 1993, May, Warsaw Ghetto, EX.............**$3.75**

Writer's Digest, 1981, December, Block, Bradbury, Van Vogt, Asimov, VG+ **$6.00**

Yank, 1944, December 22, Sad Sack & Santa cover, VG.**$8.00**

Majolica

Vast amounts of majolica were made by potters both here and in England from the Victorian era until the early 1900s (and much later in France and Germany), so it has roots in a much earlier time period than we generally deal with in this publication, but there are many examples of it still around today, and because it is such an interesting field, we want to at least touch on it.

Broadly defined, majolica is a lead-glazed pottery with relief designs taken from nature. Colors are nearly always vivid. Figural pieces are common. Much of it is unmarked, but items that are will be stamped with names like Winton, George Jones, Sarreguemines, Griffin Smith and Hill (Etruscan), Wedgwood, and Fielding. Of course, if a mark is present, the design very detailed, and the color good, majolica can be expensive. But many of the smaller pieces are very beautiful and can sometimes still be picked up at reasonable prices, especially the lighter-weight French and German items.

For more information, we recommend *The Collector's Encyclopedia of Majolica* by Mariann Katz-Marks.

Basket, floral pattern on turquoise w/brown trim & handle, lavender interior, 6" long....................**$300.00**

Basket, light green basketweave pattern w/lavender ribbon-tied handle & interior, 10" long **$300.00**

Bowl, brown shell shape w/turquoise interior, shell-shaped feet, signed Holdcroft, 9" dia **$200.00**

Bowl, Pond Lily, green, footed, J Holdcroft impressed on bottom, 11" dia..**$200.00**

Bowl, Shell & Seaweed, lavender interior, scalloped edge, Etruscan, 8½" dia **$300.00**

Bowl, vegetable; Wardle Bird & Fan, lavender interior, footed, English registry mark, 10" long **$285.00**

Bread tray, twin shell on waves, 14" long................**$350.00**

Butter pat, begonia leaf on basketweave, 3" dia **$22.00**

Butter pat, wicker pattern, green w/beige border, Etruscan, 3" dia...**$45.00**

Cake stand, leaf on turquoise, yellow trim, low pedestal base, 9" dia..**$165.00**

Cheese dish, allover mottle w/wheat handle, 5¾x9¾" long..**$185.00**

Compote, grape leaf on brown background, 4½x8½" dia...**$165.00**

Compote, Pineapple, turquoise interior, 4¾x9" dia...**$165.00**

Cup & saucer, Bamboo & Floral, turquoise background, pink interior **$165.00**

Cuspidor, floral, yellow background, lavender interior, 7" .**$225.00**

Dish, fan shape, dragonfly & prunus branch on turquoise background, 6" **$95.00**

Dish, Morning Glory & Picket Fence, green interior, 9" dia...**$110.00**

Jardiniere, Pond Lily, white & green on brown, lavender interior, footed, 8" **$245.00**

Mug, Lily, lavender interior, green ear-type handle, footed, 4"..**$165.00**

Mug, Picket Fence & Floral, green interior, ring handle, 3¾"...**$140.00**

Mug, sunflower on cobalt, lavender interior, 3½" **$140.00**

Pitcher, Banana Leaf, brown w/embossed turquoise floral pattern at top, lavender interior, 6¼"....................**$95.00**

Pitcher, bent tree trunk, turquoise w/lavender interior, V-shaped handle, 7" **$145.00**

Pitcher, Bird & Basketweave, turquoise & brown, scalloped edge, bulbous bottom, ear-type handle, 8½" **$150.00**

Pitcher, cream; Butterfly & Bamboo, lavender interior, 3" **$165.00**

Pitcher, cream; Corn, pink interior, green ear-type handle, 4" **$175.00**

Pitcher, cream; Floral & Corn, pink interior, brown V-shaped handle, 4½"...**$70.00**

Pitcher, Dogwood, brown background, turquoise interior, green handle, Holdcroft, 9"..................................**$250.00**

Pitcher, Dogwood, mottled background, brown rectangular handle, 5½" **$225.00**

Pitcher, fern on bark, pewter top, 7"........................**$175.00**

Pitcher, floral on cobalt, lavender interior, brown handle, 8" **$145.00**

Pitcher, sheaves of wheat, yellow & brown on green, pink interior, 6"..**$95.00**

Pitcher, syrup; Bow & Floral, pewter top, ear-type handle, 8¼"...**$195.00**

Pitcher, syrup; mottled w/pewter top, marked Morley & Co, Wellsville OH, 8¼"...**$175.00**

Pitcher, Zinnias, dragon handle, 10½", $450.00

Plate, Bamboo & Basketweave, mottled center, unmarked, 7¾" dia...**$55.00**

Plate, bird in flight, turquoise background, attributed to J Holdcroft, 8½" dia...**$160.00**

Plate, bow on basketweave, turquoise background, 6" dia...**$110.00**

Plate, Chrysanthemum, impressed Wedgwood, 9" dia..**$200.00**

Plate, Classical Series, Etruscan, GSH monogram mark, 9", $150.00

Plate, Dogwood, turquoise background, 8" dia.........**$110.00**

Plate, Geranium, pink, white & green on brown, scalloped edge, 9"..**$175.00**

Plate, lobster & vegetables, turquoise w/white border, impressed Wedgwood, 8¾" dia **$200.00**

Plate, Morning Glory, turquoise background, lobed edge, 9"...**$135.00**

Plate, mottled center w/reticulated border, Wedgwood, 8¾" dia...**$125.00**

Plate, mottled w/basketweave border, impressed Wedgwood, 9" dia..**$125.00**

Plate, oyster; basketweave & seaweed, cobalt & yellow, impressed Minton, 9" long **$300.00**

Plate, strawberry blossoms, lavender background, 8"..**$135.00**

Plate, Water Lily, George Jones, 8" **$135.00**

Platter, Banana Leaf & Bows, white background, 14½" long...**$225.00**

Platter, begonia & floral, cobalt background, open handles, 11½" long **$175.00**

Platter, Blackberry, white background, Clifton Decor mark, 13" dia..**$185.00**

Platter, flying crane & water lily, cobalt background, 10½" dia..**$150.00**

Platter, raspberry pattern w/mottled center, open handles, 11¾" long **$175.00**

Sugar bowl, leaf & bow, open handles, 4" **$145.00**

Sugar bowl, Shell & Seaweed, fish finial & handles, 5" .**$250.00**

Sugar bowl, Wild Rose, green rose finial, Etruscan, marked M13, 3¾" dia...**$175.00**

Waste bowl, flying ducks on ivory background, lavender interior, 5½" dia..**$125.00**

Marbles

Antique marbles can be very expensive (some are worth more than $1,500.00) and variations are endless. In his books *Antique and Collectible Marbles, Machine-Made and Contemporary Marbles*, and *Everett Grist's Big Book of Marbles*, author Everett Grist thoroughly describes and pictures each type. These books are a must if you plan on doing much in the way of buying or selling marbles.

Mr. Grist divides antique marbles into several classes: 1) Transparent Swirls, of which he lists six types (Solid Core, Latticinio Core, Divided Core, Ribbon Core, Lobed Core, and Coreless) 2) Lutz or Lutz-type, having bands containing copper flecks which alternate with colored or clear bands 3) Peppermint Swirl, made with red, white, and blue opaque glass 4) Indian Swirl, made of black glass with multicolored surface swirls 5) Banded Swirl, opaque or transparent, having wide swirling bands 6) Onionskin, given an overall mottled appearance by its spotted swirling lines or lobes 7) End of Day, single pontil, allover spots, 2-colored or multicolored 8) Clambroth, evenly spaced swirled lines on opaque glass 9) Mica, transparent color with mica flakes added 10) Sulphide, usually made of clear glass (though colored examples may be found), containing figures

In addition to the glass marbles, there were those made of clay, pottery, china, steel, and various types of semi-precious stones.

Then come the machine-made marbles! Most of these defy description. Many are worth no more than 50¢, but some of the harder-to-find colors and those with well-defined color placement may run from $10.00 up to $20.00. The better Guineas (Christensen agates with small multicolored specks instead of swirls) go for as much as $200.00, and the comic character marbles made by Peltier range from

$60.00 to $80.00, except for Betty Boop and Kayo which are worth $100.00 to $150.00 each.

As for condition, it is all-important. An absolutely mint marble is very rare and may be worth as much as three to five times more than one in near-mint condition. Marbles in only 'good' condition, having large chips and cracks, may be worth half (or less) of near-mint values. The same is true of one that has been polished, regardless of the improvement the polishing makes. Unless specifically noted, our values are for marbles in at least excellent condition.

Artist-made, crown filigree & peppermints, contemporary, by Bill Burchfield, 1", M **$35.00**

Artist-made, swirl or end-of-day, contemporary, by Mark Matthews, 1½", M..............................**$60.00**

Banded Opaque, semiopaque w/translucent pink bands, ¾", NM **$40.00**

Banded Swirl, cobalt w/wide bands of yellow, red & white, ¾", NM...**$30.00**

Clambroth, black opaque base w/white & gray stripes, ⅞", NM **$80.00**

Clambroth, opaque black base w/white stripes, ¾", M..**$60.00**

Comic Strip, Betty Boop or Kayo, Peltier, M.............**$200.00**

Divided Core Swirl, blue-tinted glass w/3 red, white & blue inner bands, 3 sets of white outer bands, 1¼", NM..**$80.00**

Divided Core Swirl, blue-tinted glass w/4 wide 3-color inner bands, 4 sets of multicolored outer bands, 1⅞", NM..**$150.00**

End-of-Day, 4-panel onionskin w/mica, yellow w/2 red & green panels, 1½", NM...........................**$75.00**

End-of-Day, onionskin Lutz, pink & white core, ½", NM **$90.00**

End-of-Day, onionskin w/mica, opaque core w/transparent blue & red splotches, 1½", EX **$110.00**

Indian, slag-type, opaque black base w/dark red bands, ¾", NM..**$40.00**

Latticinio Swirl, alternating yellow & white core w/6 outer bands, 2", NM.....................................**$125.00**

Latticinio Swirl, white core w/alternating green & white outer bands under translucent pink, 2", NM.......**$150.00**

Latticinio Swirl, white core w/4 multicolored outer bands, 1½", NM..**$100.00**

Latticinio Swirl, yellow core w/6 red & white outer bands, 1⅝", NM..**$100.00**

Lutz, clear w/blue swirl, ⅞", EX..............................**$110.00**

Machine-made, carnelian oxblood, Akro Agate, ½" to ¾", M **$100.00**

Machine-made, lemonade & oxblood, Akro Agate, ½" to ¾", M **$75.00**

Machine-made, light aqua slag w/rotating white spirals, MF Christensen & Son, ⅝", M...........................**$50.00**

Machine-made, oxblood swirl, Akro Agate, ½" to ¾", M..**$20.00**

Machine-made, purple slag, melted pontil, ⅞", NM **$40.00**

Machine-made, red & white, American Christensen Agate, ⅝", M **$65.00**

Machine-made, transparent brown w/opaque swirls, MF Christensen & Son, ¾", M.............................**$35.00**

Machine-made, triple-twist corkscrew, Akro Agate, ½" to ¾", M **$10.00**

Onionskin, white w/blue, red & green specks, 1⅜", M..**$150.00**

Onionskin w/mica, ¾", $85.00

Solid core swirl, red, green & yellow core w/white outer bands, 1¾", $150.00

Solid Core Swirl, red, white, green & blue core w/4 sets of greenish-yellow outer bands, 1⅜", M **$100.00**

Solid Core Swirl, 3-section multicolored core w/3 sets of yellow outer bands, blue-tinted glass, 1½", NM **$150.00**

Sulfide, duck seated on mound of grass, 1¼", NM......**$50.00**

Sulfide, male lion standing on mound of grass, 1⅛", NM **$100.00**

Sulfide, rabbit sprinting over grass, 1⅞", NM............**$150.00**

Sulfide, squirrel eating a nut, 1⅜", M.......................**$80.00**

Match Covers

Only two or three match covers out of a hundred have any value to a collector. Of that small percentage, most will be worth considerably less than $10.00. What makes a match cover collectible? First of all, it must be in mint condition. Collectors prefer to remove the staples and the matchsticks and to store them in special albums for protection. Secondly, those with the striker on the front are preferred. These predate the mid-1970s, when new laws were passed that resulted in the striker being moved to the back cover.

General categories include restaurants, hotels and motels, political, girlies, and sports stars and events.

The American Match Cover Association publishes a book with information on both pricing and identification. See the Directory under Newsletters for the address of the Front Striker Bulletin.

Aladdin Candy Shop, 211 Mass Ave, Boston MA, front strike..**$5.50**

Anheuser-Busch, horse-drawn wagon on front, front strike, NM..**$7.00**

Artcraft Engineering Mfg Co, black & white photo of 2 jets, front strike **$5.00**

Baby Ruth 5¢, Curtiss Candies, Rich in Pure Dextrose..., front left strike..**$6.00**

Blue Parrot Patio, Oak Park Ill, colorful parrot, front strike $7.50

Colgate, Let Me Live in the House..., front strike, original cellophane package $6.00

Cotton Club, Broadway at 48th St, drawing of nude natives dancing, front strike $6.00

Famous Kernwood Cafe & Coffee Shop, Malden MA, front strike $3.00

Marlboro Cigarettes, 20 for 20 Cents, front strike $7.50

McCutcheon's Cocktail Lounge, Niagara Falls, girl in swimsuit across sticks, front strike...............$8.50

Merry Christmas & Happy New Year Baltimore & Ohio RR, pictures carolers, front strike...............$10.00

Miller High Life Beer, front features product name, bottles on ice shown on reverse, front strike, NM...............$5.00

Nature's Remedy Vegetable Laxative, front strike...............$3.00

Overnight Motor Transportation Co, truck & polar bear logo on side, front strike...............$4.50

Pabst Blue Ribbon Beer, pictures a bottle, each stick shaped like a bottle, front strike $18.50

Quaker State Oil Refining Co, Indianapolis IN, front strike...............$2.00

Rival Dog Food, dog at ship's wheel, front strike...............$4.50

Virginia Tuberculosis Association, front strike $4.50

1973 Sugar Bowl, Notre Dame 24 — Alabama 23, Irish helmets, front strike $6.00

Match Safes

'Smalls' are always fun to collect. They appeal to people whose space for displaying collectibles is limited, whether due to cramped living quarters or simply because they already have so many collections. But match safes are 'big' on interest because they've been used to advertise products, commemorate special events, and even to promote political candidates. They can be distinguished from other small cases by the rough-textured panel used as a striking surface for the matches.

Advertising, Sterling Refining Co, aluminum, barrel shape, Boiler Compound, Special Paints..., 2½", $30.00

Advance Thresher, celluloid wrapped, multicolored graphics, 2¾x1½", EX...............$140.00

Advertising, Edgeworth Tobacco, tin litho, striker on bottom, 2½x3⅛", EX...............$5.00

Advertising, Huntley & Palmer, brass, biscuit shape, 2⅛" dia, VG...............$165.00

Advertising, International Tailoring, plated brass, Indian on lid, striker on both ends, 2⅞x1⅜", EX...............$37.00

Advertising, National Lead, celluloid wrapped, multicolored graphics, 2⅝x1½", VG...............$45.00

Advertising, Red Top Rye, thermoplastic, slip top, 2⅞x1⅛", EX...............$65.00

Advertising, Schlitz Beer, leather wrapped, w/cigar cutter, 2¾x1½", EX...............$85.00

Advertising, Union Cigar Makers, celluloid wrapped, blue graphics, 2½x1½"...............$70.00

Agate, book shape w/brass trim, 1¾x1¼"...............$110.00

Columbian Expo, plated brass, medallion on figural ear of corn, 2½x1", EX...............$275.00

Filigree, silver w/floral motif, 2½x1½", EX...............$135.00

Gladstone bust, plated brass, figural, 2½x1¼", EX $195.00

Ivory, book shape w/applied sterling initial, 1⅞x1⅛", EX...............$135.00

Lady in boat motif, stamped Sterling, 2¼x1¾", EX...............$130.00

Love's Flight, celluloid wrapped, multicolored graphics, Whitehead & Hoag, 2¾x1½", EX...............$135.00

Oriental dragon, brass, quasi-figural, dome lid, 2½x1¼", EX...............$245.00

Pen box, brass, embossed D Leonardt, 2⅛x2⅝x¾", EX .$50.00

Shoe figural w/glass stones in sole, wire laces, silver-plated, 1⅜x2⅝", EX...............$265.00

Shoe figural w/striker on heel, aluminum, flat-type, 2⅞x1¼", EX...............$75.00

Superdux, hard rubber, cylindrical, 3¼x1¼", EX...............$25.00

US Arms w/bullet & target, silver-plated, 2⅝x1½", EX.$125.00

1893 Chicago World's Fair, Bryant & May Wax Vesta, tin litho design, 1¾x6¼", VG...............$65.00

McCoy Pottery

This is probably the best-known of all American potteries, due to the wide variety of goods they produced from 1910 until the pottery finally closed only a few years ago.

They were located in Roseville, Ohio, the pottery center of the United States during the first half of the century. They're most famous for their cookie jars, of which were made several hundred styles and variations. Some of the rarer, more desirable jars are 'Mammy with Cauliflowers,' 'Leprechaun,' and 'Hillbilly Bear,' any one of which is worth at least $1,000.00. Many are in the $200.00 to $400.00 range, and even the most common jars generally bring $30.00 to $40.00. Condition is important, not only in regard to hairlines and chips but paint as well. Many of the early jars were painted over the glaze with 'cold' (unfired) paint which over the years tends to wear off. Be sure to evaluate the amount of remaining 'cold' paint when you buy or sell.

In addition to the cookie jars, McCoy is well-known for their figural planters, novelty kitchenware, and dinnerware. A line introduced in the late 1970s is beginning to attract collectors — a glossy brown stoneware-type dinnerware with frothy white decoration around the rims. Similar lines of brown stoneware was made by many other companies,

Hull and Pfaltzgraff among them. See Hull and/or Pfaltzgraff for values that will also apply to McCoy's line.

They used a variety of marks over the years, but with little consistency, since it was a common practice to discontinue an item for awhile and then bring it out again decorated in a manner that would be in sync with current tastes. All of McCoy's marks were 'in the mold.' None were ink stamped, so very often the in-mold mark remained as it was when the mold was originally created. Most marks contain the McCoy name, though some of the early pieces were simply signed 'NM' for Nelson McCoy (Sanitary and Stoneware Company, the company's original title). Early stoneware pieces were sometimes impressed with a shield containing a number. If you have a piece with the Lancaster Colony Company mark (three curved lines — the left one beginning as a vertical and terminating as a horizontal, the other two formed as 'C's contained in the curve of the first), you'll know that your piece was made after the mid-70s when McCoy was owned by that group. Today even these later pieces are becoming collectible.

If you'd like to learn more about this company, we recommend *The Collector's Encyclopedia of McCoy Pottery* by Sharon and Bob Huxford.

Beware of *new* cookie jars marked McCoy. It seems that McCoy never registered their trademark, and it is now legally used by a small company in Rockwood, Tennessee. Not only do they use the original mark, but they are reproducing some of the original jars as well. If you're not an experienced collector, you may have trouble distinguishing the new from the old. Some (but not all) are dated #93, the '#' one last attempt to fool the novice, but there are differences to watch for. The new ones are slightly smaller in size, and the finish is often flawed. The company is also using the McCoy mark on jars never produced by the original company, such as Little Red Riding Hood and the Luzianne mammy.

Basket, embossed flowers, Rustic glaze, scalloped edge, marked...$35.00
Bean pot, bright flowers on black, ring-type handles, unmarked $30.00
Bean pot, yellow w/hammered effect, ring handles & lid finial, footed, marked $25.00
Bookends, lilies, marked, pr $55.00
Bowl, shouldered type, ivory w/pink & blue bands, marked USA, lg...$45.00
Bowl, shouldered type, ivory w/pink & blue bands, unmarked, sm $30.00
Cache pot, 2 pink & white flower forms on green base, marked...$40.00
Casserole, ivory w/green lid, tab handles, marked $30.00
Cookie jar, Bananas, yellow bunch of bananas w/brown stem finial, marked..$125.00
Cookie jar, Basket of Eggs, off-white w/white eggs forming lid, marked 0274 McCoy USA, 1977-79.................$45.00
Cookie jar, Basket of Strawberries, white w/red strawberries forming lid, marked McCoy USA, 1978 ....$75.00
Cookie jar, Bobby Baker, white w/blue eyes, holding red spoon, marked #183, McCoy USA, 1974-79..........$75.00

Cookie jar, Burlap Bag w/red bird finial, marked 158 USA, 1972 ....$75.00
Cookie jar, Cat on Basketweave, pink w/black & white cat lid, Cookies lettered in black, marked McCoy USA, 1956-57 ....$85.00
Cookie jar, Chilly Willy, penguin in blue & white hat, scarf & mittens, marked 155 USA, 1986-89 ....$40.00
Cookie jar, Christmas Tree, star finial, marked, minimum value $550.00
Cookie jar, Circus Horse, black w/red & white details, marked..$235.00

Cookie jar, Coalby Cat, black, $375.00

Cookie jar, Coffee Grinder, 1961-68 ....$40.00

Cookie jar, Colonial Fireplace, embossed hearth on front of rectangular shape, clock finial, marked USA, $95.00

Cookie jar, Cookie Jug, brown top w/woven rope-type tan base, marked...$30.00
Cookie jar, Cookie Log, squirrel on stump, unmarked, 1967..$60.00
Cookie jar, Country Stove (or Potbellied Stove), black w/red & gold details, marked $40.00
Cookie jar, Davy Crockett, marked USA, 1957, minimum value $500.00
Cookie jar, Drum, red w/black band at top & bottom, sm drum finial, marked $75.00
Cookie jar, Fortune Cookie, Chinese lantern form, red, white & black, marked...$75.00

Cookie jar, Frontier Family, brown-washed scene, 1960. **$50.00**

Cookie jar, Gingerbread Boy, embossed figure in reserve w/multicolored cookie shapes, marked **$70.00**

Cookie jar, Granite Coffeepot, blue & white w/wire bail, unmarked, 1974-75 .... **$100.00**

Cookie jar, Granny, lady w/glasses & hands folded, hair bun forms lid, marked USA.. **$85.00**

Cookie jar, Hillbilly Bear, sitting on stump, multicolored paint, marked, minimum value **$900.00**

Cookie jar, Hot Air Balloon, brown & yellow, marked 353 USA, 1985-86 .... **$35.00**

Cookie jar, Kissing Penguins, white w/black & red features, marked McCoy, 1946 .... **$85.00**

Cookie jar, Kookie Kettle, black w/gold trim, bail handle, marked.. **$30.00**

Cookie jar, Milk Can w/Gingham Flowers, marked 333 USA **$50.00**

Cookie jar, multicolored fruit on blue, unmarked, 1942.. **$40.00**

Cookie jar, Oaken Bucket, marked USA **$35.00**

Cookie jar, Owl, brown w/black & white features, marked 204 McCoy USA, 1978-79.................................... **$40.00**

Cookie jar, Puppy w/Sign, black, brown & cream, marked McCoy USA, 1961-62... **$95.00**

Cookie jar, Raggedy Ann, marked 151 USA, 1972-75 .. **$65.00**

Cookie jar, Rooster, yellow & brown, marked McCoy USA, 1956-58 .... **$125.00**

Cookie jar, Snoopy on Doghouse, marked USA & stamped United Features Syndicate..., 1970 .... **$275.00**

Cookie jar, Teakettle, hammered bronze, 1961-67 ...... **$25.00**

Cookie jar, Tepee, Indian in doorway, straight top, marked.. **$325.00**

Cookie jar, Thinking Puppy, brown, marked 272, McCoy USA, 1977-79 .... **$40.00**

Cookie jar, Timmy Tortoise, yellow butterfly finial, 1977-80.. **$32.00**

Cookie jar, Tulip, white flowerpot form w/red tulip finial, marked McCoy USA, 1958-59.............................. **$190.00**

Cookie jar, Turkey, tail spread, head & neck form lid, natural colors, marked.. **$185.00**

Cookie jar, Uncle Sam's Hat, red, white & blue upturned hat w/stars & stripes, marked USA **$235.00**

Cookie jar, Windmill, blue w/pink rosebud finial, marked **$150.00**

Cookie jar, Wishing Well, Wish I Had a Cookie lettered on front, marked.. **$45.00**

Cookie jar, Woodsy Owl, figure w/green hat & pants playing guitar, marked USA **$250.00**

Cookie jar, Wren House, brown & green on tan, half of roof removes, bird finial, marked **$150.00**

Creamer, brown, V-shaped handle, marked **$10.00**

Creamer, dog figural, green, marked, 1950s **$70.00**

Creamer, embossed water lilies on brown, ear-type handle, unmarked **$30.00**

Creamer, Sunburst Gold, marked........................... **$25.00**

Crock, white, CV Cry Co on rim **$16.00**

Custard cup, green w/embossed vertical ribs, unmarked.. **$8.00**

French casserole, brown, yellow & ivory mottle, marked.. **$15.00**

French casserole, pink w/black lid, stick handle, marked, 1-pt.. **$15.00**

Jardiniere, embossed acorns on green, unmarked **$40.00**

Jardiniere, embossed birds in flight on ivory, unmarked, sm **$20.00**

Jardiniere, embossed ferns on brown, unmarked........ **$40.00**

Mug, barrel shape w/embossed bands, green, ear-type handle, marked **$15.00**

Mug, embossed grapes medallion on green, ear-type handle, unmarked **$25.00**

Novelty, baseball glove, tan, unmarked **$35.00**

Novelty, deer on base, white, unmarked **$15.00**

Novelty, swan, Sunburst Gold, open back **$20.00**

Pitcher, Antique Rose pattern on white, marked........ **$25.00**

Pitcher, embossed angelfish on green, lg ear-type handle, unmarked **$45.00**

Pitcher, embossed cloverleaves on yellow, marked, 1948, $30.00

Pitcher, embossed water lilies on green, fish handle, unmarked **$55.00**

Pitcher, green, bulbous top, ear-type handle, unmarked.. **$30.00**

Pitcher, yellow, ball form, unmarked, 1950s **$30.00**

Planter, Antique Rose pattern on sprinkling can figural, white w/gold trim, marked **$20.00**

Planter, baby cradle, pink, unmarked **$20.00**

Planter, bunny holding carrot, yellow w/pink facial features, marked, rare **$50.00**

Planter, butterfly, green **$25.00**

Planter, conch shell, ivory w/pink highlights, unmarked... **$16.00**

Planter, doe & fawn on base, white, marked............... **$22.00**

Planter, duck, yellow w/orange beak, unmarked.......... **$8.00**

Planter, Dutch shoe, yellow w/pink flower in relief, marked, 1947 .... **$20.00**

Planter, elephant, trunk up, pink, unmarked.............. **$22.00**

Planter, fish, green, pink & ivory, marked **$225.00**

Planter, hand holding bowl, white, marked............... **$30.00**

Planter, parrot beside planter, green, unmarked **$22.00**

Planter, pelican, light green, marked.......................... **$25.00**

Planter, prowling lion, green, unmarked **$40.00**

Planter, squirrel w/nut, brown, marked **$18.00**

Planter, turtle w/open back, green, marked **$40.00**

Salt & pepper shakers, cucumber & mango, unmarked, 1954, pr.. **$40.00**

Salt box, embossed flowers on basketweave pattern, green & cream, unmarked **$110.00**

Tankard, barrel shape w/embossed bands, green, ear-type handle, marked **$60.00**

Teapot, black & white cat w/paw up for spout, tail forms handle, 1971 ....**$70.00**

Teapot, embossed cherries & leaves on light green, ball form, ear-type handle, unmarked **$55.00**

Vase, basket form, brown, cream & shades of green, marked, 1954, $35.00

Vase, cornucopia; yellow w/embossed flowers at base, marked...**$18.00**

Vase, double tulip, marked **$38.00**

Vase, embossed flowers on blue, slightly flared rim, unmarked **$25.00**

Vase, embossed flowers on pink heart shape, footed.**$30.00**

Vase, embossed sailboats on blue, flared rim, square base, marked..**$30.00**

Vase, embossed tulip on green, integral handles, marked **$24.00**

Vase, embossed water lilies on green, lizard handles, bulbous, unmarked **$45.00**

Vase, green w/vertical ribs, cylinder form, marked, 10"..**$25.00**

Vase, Hobnail pattern on green, slightly flared rim, footed, marked..**$25.00**

Vase, pillow form, pink, marked **$15.00**

Vase, pink w/applied green leaf, marked, 1955 ....**$35.00**

Vase, ram's head figural, light green, marked..............**$80.00**

Vase, sunflower in basket, unmarked **$38.00**

Vase, Uncle Sam, yellow, marked, 1943......................**$45.00**

Wall pocket, bunch of grapes resting on green leaves .**$45.00**

Wall pocket, fan shape, Sunburst Gold, marked **$40.00**

Wall pocket, leaf, pink & ivory, marked **$25.00**

Wall pocket, leaves & berries **$60.00**

Wall pocket, mailbox, green, marked **$50.00**

Wall pocket, owls on trivet, brown & yellow, marked .**$35.00**

Wall pocket, umbrella, yellow w/green handle, marked .**$30.00**

Metlox Pottery

Founded in the late 1920s in Manhattan Beach, California, this company initially produced tile and commercial advertising signs. By the early thirties, their business in these areas had dwindled, and they began to concentrate their efforts on the manufacture of dinnerware, figurines, and kitchenware.

Carl Romanelli was the designer responsible for modeling many of the figural pieces they made during the late thirties and early forties. These items are usually imprinted with his signature and are very collectible today.

Poppytrail was the trade name for their kitchen and dinnerware lines. Among their more popular patterns were California Ivy, Red Rooster, Homestead Provincial, and the later embossed patterns, Sculptured Grape, Sculptured Zinnia, and Sculptured Daisy.

Some of their lines can be confusing. There are two 'rooster' lines, Red Rooster (red, orange, and brown) and California Provincial (this one is in dark green and burgundy), and two 'homestead' lines, Colonial Homestead (red, orange, and brown like the Red Rooster line) and Homestead Provincial. Just remember the Provincial patterns are done in dark green and burgundy. If you'd like to learn more about this pottery, we recommend *The Collector's Encyclopedia of California Pottery* by Jack Chipman and *Collector's Encyclopedia of Metlox Pottery* by Carl Gibbs.

Bowl, berry; Red Rooster Provincial, sm **$8.00**

Bowl, cereal; California Ivy, 7"......................................**$15.00**

Bowl, cereal; California Strawberry, 5¾" **$10.00**

Bowl, cereal; Homestead Provincial **$10.00**

Bowl, Provincial Fruit, tab handles, 5" **$10.00**

Bowl, salad; Homestead Provincial, 11" **$25.00**

Bowl, Sculptured Daisy, deep, 7" **$10.00**

Bowl, Tropicana, low **$35.00**

Bowl, vegetable; California Strawberry, w/lid............**$45.00**

Bowl, vegetable; Sculptured Grape, 9¼" **$30.00**

Bowl, Yorkshire, ca 1939, 6"......................................**$15.00**

Bread plate, Red Rooster Provincial............................**$6.00**

Bread tray, Homestead Provincial..............................**$30.00**

Bread tray, Red Rooster Provincial **$28.00**

Butter dish, Provincial Fruit..**$25.00**

Butter dish, Red Rooster Provincial **$35.00**

Canisters, California Provincial, set of 4 ....**$195.00**

Carafe, California Aztec, w/lid, 18" **$95.00**

Chop plate, Sculptured Grape, round, lg **$40.00**

Coaster, California Mobile **$10.00**

Coffeepot, California Strawberry................................**$50.00**

Coffeepot, Homestead Provincial................................**$40.00**

Coffeepot, Red Rooster Provincial **$45.00**

Cookie jar, Barrel of Apples, $65.00

Cookie jar, Bear w/Sombrero......................................**$65.00**
Cookie jar, Blue Bird on Stump, Made in USA **$50.00**
Cookie jar, Circus Bear...**$165.00**
Cookie jar, Cow, w/butterfly & flowers **$325.00**
Cookie jar, Fido..**$65.00**
Cookie jar, Lamb's Head, crier in lid **$135.00**
Cookie jar, Mona Dinosaur **$130.00**
Cookie jar, Orange, Made in USA................................**$45.00**
Cookie jar, Slenderella...**$75.00**
Cookie jar, Wheat Shock **$45.00**
Creamer, California Ivy..**$12.00**
Creamer, Red Rooster Provincial.................................**$10.00**
Cup, Provincial Fruit...**$10.00**
Cup, Red Rooster Provincial..**$10.00**
Cup & saucer, California Mobile **$25.00**
Cup & saucer, Golden Blossom **$12.00**
Cup & saucer, Sculptured Grape **$20.00**
Figurine, Poppets by Poppytrail Tina partially glazed
    stoneware, Helen Slater, ca 1970 ....**$25.00**
Figurine, rooster, satin white, Carl Romanelli, 8¾"......**$75.00**
Gravy boat, California Aztec **$22.00**
Gravy boat, Sculptured Grape, w/undertray................**$35.00**
Match holder, California Provincial..............................**$65.00**
Miniature, elephant, Carl Romanelli **$95.00**
Miniature, hippo, Carl Romanelli **$75.00**

Miniature, monkey, turquoise & rust glaze, ca 1939, 4½", $60.00

Miniature, seal, Carl Romanelli **$65.00**
Pitcher, California Provincial, 1-qt **$25.00**
Pitcher, California Strawberry, 6" **$22.00**
Pitcher, milk; Sculptured Daisy, 6"..............................**$35.00**
Pitcher, Sculptured Grape, lg **$45.00**
Plate, bread; Red Rooster Provincial.............................**$6.00**
Plate, California Ivy, 10¼" **$15.00**
Plate, California Mobile, 10" **$20.00**
Plate, California Provincial, 9".....................................**$12.00**
Plate, California Strawberry, 6".....................................**$5.00**
Plate, Provincial Blue, 10"...**$12.00**
Plate, Provincial Blue, 7½"..**$8.00**
Plate, Provincial Fruit, 10½"..**$15.00**
Plate, Sculptured Daisy, 10½".......................................**$10.00**
Plate, Yorkshire, ca 1939, 6½".....................................**$15.00**

Platter, California Aztec, oval, 9½" **$18.00**
Platter, Provincial Blue, 11"...**$22.00**
Platter, Provincial Fruit, 14"...**$22.00**
Platter, Red Rooster Provincial, 11"..............................**$30.00**
Platter, Sculptured Daisy, 14".......................................**$30.00**
Relish dish, Homestead Provincial, divided **$25.00**
Salt & pepper shakers, California Strawberry, pr........**$12.00**
Salt & pepper shakers, Sculptured Grape, pr..............**$15.00**
Soup, California Provincial, flat....................................**$18.00**
Soup, Sculptured Daisy, flat...**$18.00**
Stein, Red Rooster Provincial **$45.00**
Sugar bowl, California Ivy...**$15.00**
Teapot, California Strawberry.......................................**$45.00**
Vase, angelfish form, Carl Romanelli, ca 1940, 8½".....**$65.00**
Vase, bud; Mosaic **$20.00**
Vase, Tropicana, teardrop shape **$50.00**
Water can, California Provincial....................................**$28.00**

Plate, dinner; Red Rooster Provincial, 10", $25.00

Military Awards

These items are being sought out by a growing number of passionate collectors, and many are beginning to appreciate at an unbelievable pace. There are hundreds of types to look for. Check boxes of memorabilia at estate sales and auctions and attend specialized militaria shows. There is no shortage of these as yet, and you should be able to put together a very interesting collection for a modest investment.

Aerial Achievement Medal, full size, NM.....................**$45.00**
Air Force Armed Forces Reserve Ribbon, EX................**$2.00**
Air Force Combat Readiness Medal, miniature, EX **$10.00**
Air Force Flight Nurse Badge, full size, EX **$6.00**
Air Force Flight Surgeon Badge, miniature **$5.00**
Air Force Good Conduct Medal, miniature, EX.............**$8.00**

Air Force Meritorious Achievement Medal, w/ribbon, full size, EX...$25.00

Air Force Military Merit Medal, w/ribbon, full size, EX .$15.00

Air Force Officer Air Crew Senior Badge, full size, EX..$6.50

Air Force Outstanding Civilian Service Medal, full size, NM...$50.00

Armed Forces Expeditionary Medal, miniature, EX.......$6.50

Army Cuban Pacification Medal, 1906-1909, w/ribbon, miniature, EX...$15.00

Army Distinguished Service Cross, miniature, EX........$16.00

Army Distinguished Service Medal, w/ribbon, full size, EX...$90.00

Army Reserve Achievement Medal, w/ribbon, full size, EX...$20.00

Canadian WWII Service Medal, 1939-45, w/ribbon, full size, EX...$45.00

Coast Guard Arctic Service Medal, miniature.................$6.00

Coast Guard Armed Forces Reserve Medal, full size, NM...$35.00

Coast Guard Combat Action Ribbon, EX........................$2.00

Coast Guard Reserve Good Conduct Medal, w/ribbon, full size, EX...$30.00

Department of State Meritorious Honor Medal, full size, EX...$140.00

Marine Corps Armed Forces Reserve Medal, full size, NM...$25.00

Marine Corps China Relief Expedition Medal, w/ribbon, 1900, miniature, EX...$15.00

Marine Corps Good Conduct Medal, w/ribbon, miniature, EX...$10.00

Marine Corps Philippine Campaign 1899-1903 Medal, w/ribbon, miniature, EX...$15.00

National Guard Armed Forces Reserve Ribbon, EX.......$2.00

Navy Armed Forces Reserve Medal, miniature, EX........$6.00

Navy Expeditions Medal, w/ribbon, full size, EX $15.00

Navy Expert Rifleman Medal, miniature.......................$6.00

Navy-Marine Corps Medal, full size, NM.....................$25.00

Office of the Secretary of Defense Meritorious Civilian Service Medal, full size, NM...$50.00

South Vietnam Civic Action Medal, w/ribbon, full size, EX...$25.00

Spanish War Veterans Encampment Medal, 22nd annual, 1925, EX...$45.00

Vietnam Service Medal, miniature, EX..........................$6.50

Vietnam Service Medal, w/ribbon, miniature, EX........$10.00

Virginia National Guard Commendation Medal, full size, EX...$20.00

Woman's Army Service Corps Medal, full size, NM.....$20.00

WWI New Haven Connecticut Medal for Service, Whitehead & Hoag Mfg Co, in original box, EX.....................$35.00

WWII Marine Corps Occupation Medal, miniature, EX..$15.00

WWII Victory Medal, miniature, EX..............................$6.00

Model Kits

By and far the majority of model kits were vehicular, and though worth collecting, especially when you can find them still mint in the box, the really big news are the figure kits. Most were made by Aurora during the 1960s. Especially hot are the movie monsters, though TV and comic strip character kits are popular with collectors, too. As a rule of thumb, assembled kits are priced about half of a conservatively priced mint-in-box kit. For more information, we recommend *Aurora History and Price Guide* by Bill Bruegman.

Ace, Hughes OH-6 Cayuse, #200, sealed, MIB $5.00

Adams, Chuck Wagon, #K235, 1958, NMIB $20.00

Adams, Ranch Wagon, #K232, unassembled $15.00

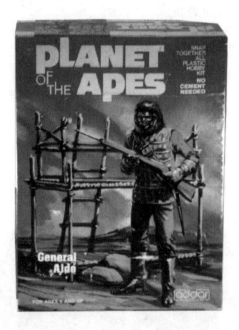

Addar, Planet of the Apes, 1973, MIB, $45.00

AHM, Northrop 5B, #FJ-4, sealed, MIB........................$15.00

Airfix, Boeing 727, #3173-6, MIB $10.00

Airfix, Lunar Module, #393, unassembled $20.00

Airline, Miles Master, #4904, 1964, sealed, MIB..........$10.00

Airline, Westland Wallace, 1964, MIB..........................$12.00

AMT, Munster Koach, 1964, assembled & painted, 7" long $90.00

AMT, 1963 Chevy Impala, #6723, partially assembled..$50.00

AMT/Ertl, Starship Enterprise (Next Generation), MIB..$15.00

Aurora, Allosaurus, assembled, EX $35.00

Aurora, American Astronaut, MIB $90.00

Aurora, Batman, #467, assembled................................$50.00

Aurora, Boeing F4B-4FF, #122-69, unassembled $40.00

Aurora, Cro-Magnon Woman, MIB $35.00

Aurora, Dr Deadly, #631, assembled, no base.............$35.00

Aurora, Dracula, 1962, assembled $45.00

Aurora, Giant Bird, MIB...$40.00

Aurora, Hulk, Comic Scenes series, MIB $45.00

Aurora, Lone Ranger, #188, Comic Scenes series, 1974, sealed, MIB...$35.00

Aurora, Mr Hyde (under street light), Monsters of the Movies, 1975, sealed, MIB $90.00

Aurora, Spiderman, assembled....................................$80.00

Aurora, US Marine, factory assembled........................$75.00

Aurora, Wonder Woman, #479, assembled...............$250.00
Aurora, 1963 T-Bird, sealed, MIB................................$25.00
Bandai, Shado Interceptor, MIB.................................$15.00
Dark Horse, King Kong, MIB.......................................$75.00
Ertl/Esci, F/A-18 Hornet, #4072, MIB.........................$10.00
Fundimensions, Colossal Mantis, MIB $65.00
Geometric, Captain Picard (Star Trek The Next Generation),
   MIB $45.00
Graphitti, Lobo Statue, MIB.....................................$125.00
Halcyon, Narcissus, MIB...$35.00
Hawk, Huey's Hot Rod, #538, unassembled $40.00
Horizan, Iron Man, MIB..$25.00
Horizon, Bride of Frankenstein, unassembled.............$25.00
Imai, Batmobile, #B1397, unassembled......................$50.00
Kaiyodo, Alien Warrior, MIB.....................................$195.00
Kaiyodo, Freddy Krueger, MIB $45.00
Lindberg, Destroyer Escort, #753, unassembled $20.00
Lindberg, Star Probe Space Shuttle, 1976, MIB...........$18.00
Max Factory, Vamore, MIB..$45.00
Monogram, Buck Rogers, #6031, unassembled, NMIB..$45.00
Monogram, Dragon Wagon, #6746, unassembled $50.00
MPC, Darth Vader Action Model (bust type w/sounds &
   lights), 1978, sealed, NMIB....................................$55.00
MPC, Fonzie & His Bike, #1-0634, unassembled $50.00
MPC, Incredible Hulk, 1978, sealed, MIB....................$45.00
MPC, Monkeemobile (PA), MIB..................................$120.00
MPC, Star Wars ROTJ, 3-pc set, MIB...........................$15.00
Multiple, World's Greatest Stage Illusions Disappearing
   Lady, fully operates when assembled, 1966, M in EX+
   box..$125.00
Nitto, Pop-up Jeep, motorized, 1970s, MIB.................$25.00
Pyro, Rolls Royce, #C349, sealed, MIB $10.00

Pyro, VW Sun Roof Sedan, Deluxe Classics, MIB, $25.00

Remco, Flintstones Motorized Paddy Wagon, M in EX
   box $250.00
Renwal, Human Skeleton, #803, unassembled $50.00
Revell, Beatnik Bandit, MIB $20.00
Revell, Tingo the Noodle-Topped Stroodle (Dr Seuss),
   NMIB $50.00
Revell, 1957 Chevy, #H1284, unassembled $25.00
Testors, Huey's Hut Rod, MIB......................................$20.00
Tsukuda, Endoskeleton, chrome, MIB.........................$30.00

Monster Collectibles

TV shows like Land of the Giants, Lost in Space, The Munsters, Addams Family, Twilight Zone, and Outer Limits have spawned some great monster toys that collectors are zeroing in on today. Universal Studios are responsible for some as well, and it's not just the monster figures that are collectible but board games, puzzles, Halloween costumes, coloring books, and gum cards too.

Frankenstein, bendee, Ahi, 1974, 4" MOC...................$25.00
Frankenstein, glow putty, Laramie, 1979, MOC $8.00
Frankenstein, monster ball, Illco, 1980s, MOC.............$5.00
Frankenstein, night light, ceramic head flashes, Hamilton, 6",
   EX...$30.00
Frankenstein, Wolfman, Creature, Mummy & Dracula,
   Horrorscope Magic Drawing Slate, Lowe, 1963, 14x8",
   NM $60.00
Freddy Krueger, doll, posable, 12", 1988, MIB $25.00
Freddy Krueger, glove, w/bendable & movable fingers,
   MOC...$25.00
Godzilla, figure, posable plastic, 1985, 14", NM............$8.00
Godzilla, Pocket Hero Set, Yutaka, MIP.....................$15.00
Mummy, bendee, Novelty Mfg, 1979, 5¼", NMOC......$24.00
Mummy, figure, Kenner, MIP $8.00
Mummy, iron-on transfer, Universal Monsters, 1964,
   MOC...$25.00
Mummy, paint-by-number set, complete w/oil paints &
   brushes, Crafthouse, 1975, sealed, MIB................$28.00
Vampire, kit, Toy 'n' Things, MIP $5.00

Moon and Star

Moon and Star (originally called Palace) was first produced in the 1880s by John Adams & Company of Pittsburgh. But because the glassware was so heavy to transport, it was made for only a few years. In the 1960s, Joseph Weishar of Wheeling, West Virginia, owner of Island Mould & Machine Company, reproduced some of the original molds and incorporated the pattern into approximately forty new and different items. Two of the largest distributors of this line were L.E. Smith of Mt. Pleasant, Pennsylvania, who pressed their own glass, and L.G. Wright, of New Martinsville, West Virginia, who had theirs pressed by Fostoria, Fenton, and Westmoreland. Both companies carried a large and varied assortment of shapes and colors. Several other companies were involved in its manufacture as well, especially of the smaller items. All in all, there may be as many as one hundred different pieces, plenty to keep you involved and excited as you do your searching.

The glassware is already very collectible, even though it is still being made on a limited basis. Colors you'll see most often are amberina (yellow shading to orange-red), green, amber, crystal, light blue, and ruby. Pieces in ruby and light blue are most collectible and harder to find than the other colors, which seem to be abundant. Purple, pink, cobalt, amethyst, tan slag, and light green and blue opalescent were made, too, but on a lesser scale.

Current L.E. Smith catalogs contain a dozen or so pieces that are still available in crystal, pink, cobalt (lighter than the old shade), and these colors with an iridized finish. A new color was introduced in 1992, teal green, and the water set in sapphire blue opalescent was pressed in 1993 by Weishar Enterprises. Cranberry Ice (light transparent pink) was introduced in 1994.

Our values are given for ruby and light blue. For amberina, green, and amber, deduct 30%. These colors are less in demand and unless your prices are reasonable, you may find them harder to sell.

Ashtray, patterned moons at rim, star in base, 6-sided, 5½"..**$12.00**

Butter dish, allover pattern, scalloped foot, patterned lid & finial, 6x5½" dia **$45.00**

Cake salver, allover pattern w/scalloped rim, raised foot w/scalloped edge, 5x12" **$50.00**

Candle holders, allover pattern, flared foot w/scalloped edge, 6", pr..**$30.00**

Compote, allover pattern, raised foot, patterned lid & finial, 7½x6" **$40.00**

Compote, allover pattern, raised foot on stem, patterned lid & finial, 10x8"...**$50.00**

Compote, allover pattern, raised foot on stem, patterned lid & finial, 12x8"...**$70.00**

Compote, allover pattern, scalloped foot on stem, patterned lid & finial, 8x4" dia **$35.00**

Compote, allover pattern, scalloped rim, footed, 5½x8" .**$35.00**

Compote, allover pattern, scalloped rim, footed, 5x6½" .**$18.00**

Compote, allover pattern, scalloped rim, footed, 7x10" ..**$45.00**

Console bowl, allover pattern, scalloped rim, flared foot w/flat edge, 8" dia..**$25.00**

Creamer, allover pattern, raised foot w/scalloped edge, 5¾x3" **$30.00**

Creamer & sugar bowl (open), disk foot, sm **$25.00**

Cruet, vinegar; 6¾", $35.00

Decanter, bulbous w/allover pattern, plain neck, foot ring, original patterned stopper, 32-oz, 12" **$50.00**

Goblet, water; plain rim & foot, 5¾" **$12.00**

Goblet, wine; plain rim & foot, 4½" **$10.00**

Jelly dish, allover pattern, patterned lid & finial, stem foot.**$35.00**

Jelly dish, allover pattern, patterned lid & finial, stemmed foot, 10½" **$45.00**

Jelly dish, patterned body w/plain flat rim & disk foot, patterned lid & finial, 6¾x3½" dia............................**$30.00**

Nappy, allover pattern, crimped rim, 2¾x6" dia **$18.00**

Oil lamp, 12", $85.00

Pitcher, water; patterned body, straight sides, plain disk foot, 1-qt, 7½"..**$65.00**

Relish bowl, 6 lg scallops form allover pattern, 1½x8" dia .**$16.00**

Relish dish, allover pattern, 1 plain handle, 2x8" dia ..**$18.00**

Relish tray, patterned moons form scalloped rim, star in base, rectangular, 8" long.....................................**$18.00**

Salt & pepper shakers, allover pattern, metal tops, 4x2" dia, pr...**$25.00**

Salt cellar, allover pattern, scalloped rim, sm flat foot...**$8.00**

Sherbet, patterned body & foot w/plain rim & stem, 4¼x3¾"..**$12.00**

Soap dish, allover pattern, oval, 2x6" **$12.00**

Spooner, allover pattern, straight sides, scalloped rim, raised foot, 5¼x4" dia **$30.00**

Sugar bowl, allover pattern, patterned lid & finial, sm flat foot, 5¼x4" dia **$30.00**

Sugar bowl, allover pattern, straight sides, patterned lid & finial, scalloped foot, 8x4½" **$35.00**

Sugar shaker, allover pattern, metal top, 4½x3½" dia .**$25.00**

Syrup, allover pattern, metal top, 4½x3½" **$25.00**

Toothpick holder, allover pattern, scalloped rim, sm flat foot..**$10.00**

Tumbler, iced tea; no pattern at flat rim or on disk foot, 11-oz, 5½"..**$14.00**

Tumbler, juice; no pattern at rim or on disk foot, 5-oz, 3½"...**$10.00**

Tumbler, no pattern at rim or on disk foot, 7-oz, 4¼" ..**$12.00**

Mortens Studio

During the 1940s, a Swedish sculpturer by the name of Oscar Mortens left his native country and moved to the United States, settling in Arizona. Along with his partner, Gunnar Thelin, they founded the Mortens Studios, a firm that specialized in the manufacture of animal figurines. Though he preferred dogs of all breeds, horses, cats, and wild animals were made, too, but on a much smaller scale.

The material he used was a plaster-like composition molded over a wire framework for support and reinforcement. Crazing is common, and our values reflect pieces with a moderate amount, but be sure to check for more serious damage before you buy. Most pieces are marked with either an ink stamp or a paper label.

Airdale, standing, tan w/black details, 5x5" $65.00
Beagle, standing, ivory, tan & black, paper label, 6x6" $70.00
Bedlington Terrier, standing, ivory & black, 6½x4¾", M $80.00
Chihuahua, sitting, 3½x3" $75.00
Chow pup, recumbent, tan & brown, 3x3" $50.00
Cocker Spaniel puppy, ivory w/black spots, 3¾x3" $40.00

Collie, standing, tan & ivory, 6x7", $85.00

Dalmation, #812, sm $45.00
Dalmation, standing, 7½x5½" $80.00
Doberman, standing, 6x7" $70.00
French Poodle, standing, ivory w/black features, 5x5", M $75.00
Great Dane, recumbent, black on tan, 7½x6½" $75.00
Mexican Chihuahua, sitting, tan w/black details, 3x3½"..$55.00
Pekingese, standing, 3½x4½" $80.00
Pointer, sitting, ivory w/black spots, 4x4¾" $65.00
Samoyed, sitting, ivory w/black eyes & nose, 4x4½", M $70.00
Scottish Terrier, sitting, black & charcoal, 4½x6" $75.00
St Bernard, standing, 6½x8½" $100.00

Morton Pottery

Morton, Illinois, was the location for six potteries that operated there at various times over the course of nearly a hundred years. The first was established by six brothers by the name of Rapp, who immigrated to America from Germany. Second- and third-generation Rapps followed in the tradition that had been established by their elders in the late 1870s.

The original company was titled Morton Pottery Works and was later renamed Morton Earthenware Co. It was in business from 1877 until 1917. The second to be established was Cliftwood Art Potteries, Inc. (1920-1940). The Morton Pottery Company opened in 1922 and became the longest running of the six, having operated for more than fifty-four years by the time Midwest Potteries incorporated in 1940. They were in business for only four years. The last to open was the American Art Pottery who operated from 1947 until 1961. Various types of pottery was made by each — Rockingham and yellowware in the early years, novelties and giftware from the 1920s on.

To learn more about these companies, we recommend *Morton's Potteries: 99 Years,* by Doris and Burdell Hall.

American Art Potteries

Figurine, squirrel, brown & gray spray........................$16.00
Flower bowl, rectangular w/frog or turtle frog, green & yellow spray effect.......................................$22.00
Planter, baby shoes on heart base, blue & pink..........$22.00
Planter, bunny on stump, natural colors.....................$14.00
Planter, pheasant, natural colors................................$25.00
Planter/vase, conch shell, blue & white spray effect, 6"...$14.00
Planter/vase, teddy bear on 3 blocks (ABC), white w/hand-painted decor.......................................$15.00
TV lamp, black panther on log...................................$22.00
TV lamp, conch shell, yellow & brown.......................$20.00
Wall pocket, apple on leaf, red & green.....................$15.00
Wall pocket, plum, lg...$12.00

Cliftwood Art Potteries, Inc.

Bookends, tree trunk w/applied birds, brown drip glaze, pr...$90.00
Bowl, console; white matt glaze w/pink interior, applied dolphin base, 8x5x14" $95.00
Compote, pink, applied dolphin base, 6x8"................$85.00
Figurine, bear, natural colors, miniature, rare, 3½x5½" ..$70.00
Figurine, billikin, cobalt, 8" $75.00
Figurine, cat, reclining, cobalt, 4½".........................$25.00
Figurine, elephant, natural colors, miniature, rare, 3½x5½" $75.00
Figurine, lion, natural colors, miniature, rare, 3½x5½".$80.00
Figurine, lioness, natural colors, miniature, rare, 3½x5½" $80.00
Vase, turquoise matt glaze, applied dolphin base, 10" ...$65.00
Wall pocket, tree-trunk form, brown drip...................$65.00
Wine jug, bulbous, blue mulberry drip glaze, swirl decor..$48.00

Midwest Potteries Inc.

Ashtray, hand shape w/applied saucer, 14k gold........**$22.00**
Bust, Art Deco lady, white & platinum, 8½" **$75.00**
Figurine, female dancer, white w/gold, 8½" **$25.00**
Figurine, gazelle, brown & tan spray effect, 12¾".......**$35.00**
Figurine, road runner, mauve & blue spray effect, 12" ..**$30.00**
Lamp, urn w/tassel handles, blue w/gold, 12" **$25.00**
Planter, broken egg, tripod base, gold, 6"...................**$15.00**
Planter, elephant, yellow w/blue drip glaze, 4x6".......**$10.00**
Planter, lioness, green, 3½x5½" **$10.00**
Planter, mountain goat, green...**$8.00**
Vase, bud; hand form, tan matt glaze, 4½" **$14.00**
Wall pocket, corner type, underglazed mums on white,
5½"..**$14.00**

Morton Pottery Company

Amish Pantry Ware, baking nappy set, canary yellow,
6-pc **$70.00**
Amish Pantry Ware, refrigerator bowls, canary yellow, stack-
ing, set of 3 ....**$100.00**
Au gratin dish, red & blue spatter on white.................**$50.00**
Bank, hen, white w/brushed black trim.......................**$30.00**
Christmas, mug, natural colors.....................................**$15.00**
Christmas, nut cup, natural colors **$10.00**
Christmas, Santa plate, natural colors, 8" **$30.00**
Coffeepot, Coffee Time w/clock face, yellow..............**$22.00**
Creamer & sugar bowl, hen & rooster, white w/brushed
black trim **$25.00**
Pitcher, milk; red & blue spatter on white w/advertising.**$48.00**
Sauce warmer, yellow sauce boat w/yellow candle holder,
4-oz..**$15.00**
Syrup, floral w/gold decor **$38.00**
Teapot, Teatime w/clock face, burgundy **$22.00**

Morton Pottery Works-Morton Earthenware Co.

Bank, shoe, yellow w/red roof, 7x6", $30.00

**Cookie jar, turkey w/chick finial, brown w/red wattle,
$125.00**

Milk jug, brown Rockingham, 6-pt **$100.00**
Nappy, yellow ware, plain, 10"....................................**$45.00**
Nappy, yellow ware, plain, 4"......................................**$32.00**
Nappy, yellow ware, plain, 6"......................................**$36.00**
Pie baker, brown Rockingham, 10" **$100.00**
Pie baker, brown Rockingham, 8" **$80.00**
Pie baker, yellow ware, 7" **$70.00**
Pitcher, cobalt, miniature, 3¼" **$55.00**
Stein, brown Rockingham w/German motto, 6".........**$65.00**
Stein, embossed German dancers, yellow & white spray,
10"..**$30.00**
Wall pocket, scoop, white w/hand-painted flowers....**$12.00**

Motion Lamps

Though some were made as early as 1920 and as late as the '70s, motion lamps were most popular during the '50s. Most are cylindrical with scenes such as waterfalls and forest fires and attain a sense of motion through the action of an inner cylinder that rotates with the heat of the bulb. Linda and Bill Montgomery have written a book called *Motion Lamps, 1920s to the Present*, containing full-page color photographs and lots of good information if you'd like to learn more about these lamps.

Airplanes, plastic, Econolite, 1958, 11", from $85 to .**$100.00**
Antique Cars, plastic, Econolite, 1957, 11", from $85 to .**$100.00**
Christmas Tree, paper, Econolite, 1951, 15", from $60 to.**$75.00**
Forest Fire, plastic, Econolite, 1955, 11", from $60 to..**$80.00**
Forest Fire, plastic, LA Goodman, 1956, 11" from $65 to..**$75.00**
Fountain of Youth, Boy, Econolite, 1950, 11", from $75
to..**$90.00**
Marine Scene, glass, ship & lighthouse, Scene in Action,
1930s, from $100 to **$150.00**
Marine Scene, glass & pot metal, Scene in Action, Chicago,
Il, 1931, 10"..**$75.00**

Merry-Go-Round, Econolite, Roto-Vue Jr, 1950, 10", from $90 to...**$125.00**

Merry-Go-Round, red plastic, Econolite, Disney, 1955, from $150 to...**$200.00**

Mill Scene, plastic Econolite, 1956, 11", from $75 to ...**$90.00**

Niagara Falls, glass & metal, Scene In Action, 1930s, from $100 to...**$150.00**

Niagara Falls, plastic, Econolite, 1955, 11", from $75 to .**$80.00**

Niagara Falls, plastic, LA Goodman, 1957, 11", from $55 to...**$70.00**

Ocean Creatures, plastic, LA Goodman, 1955, 11", from $80 to **$100.00**

On the Bayou, Econolite, picture frame, 1953, 10", $90.00

Oriental Fantasy, plastic, LA Goodman, 1957, 11", from $75 to...**$90.00**

Pot-Bellied Stove, plastic figural, Econolite, 1962, 14" **$85.00**

Santa & Reindeer, plastic, LA Goodman, 1957, 11", from $75 to...**$100.00**

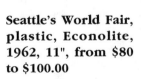

Seattle's World Fair, plastic, Econolite, 1962, 11", from $80 to $100.00

Ships, bronze & plastic, Rev-O-Lite, 1930s, 10", from $80 to...**$110.00**

Snow Scene w/Church, plastic, Econolite, 1957, 11", from $75 to...**$90.00**

Tropical Fish, plastic Econolite, 1954, 11", from $55 to.**$70.00**

Water skiers, plastic, Econolite, 1958, 11", from $100 to **$125.00**

Movie Stars

Americans have been fans of the silver screen stars since the early days of movies. Cashing in on their popularity, manufacturers took full advantage of the moment by filling stores with merchandise of all types — coloring books, paper dolls, games, and toys for the children; calendars, books, magazines, and pin-up posters for more mature fans. The movies themselves generated lobby cards (11" x 14" scenes on cardboard, usually issued in sets of eight), press books (given to theatre owners, containing photos of posters and other types of promotional items available to them), and posters (the most common of which are the 1-sheet, measuring 41" x 27"), all of which are very collectible today. Be sure an item is authentic before you invest much money in it; there are many reproductions.

See also Autographs; Magazines; Paper Dolls; Posters; Puzzles; Sheet Music; Shirley Temple; Trade Cards; Western Heroes.

Marilyn Monroe, figurine, 1990, 3½", M, $40.00

Abbott & Costello, figure, Sports Impressions, Who's on First, porcelain, limited edition, 1988, MIB **$90.00**

Allan Ladd, tablet, Allen on cover w/facsimile signature, 1950s, 8x10", unused, EX **$10.00**

Basil Rathbone, movie stills, Pursuit to Algiers (Holmes & Watson, Spider Woman (Holmes), 1945/1950, EX, pr **$15.00**

Betty Grable, program from Hello Dolly Road Show, EX...**$18.00**

Bing Crosby, board game, Call Me Lucky, Parker Bros, 1954, VG...**$25.00**

Bruce Lee, black-light poster, collage of Enter the Dragon Graphics, 1974, 21x32", EX+ **$25.00**

Bruce Lee, gum card set, 12 cards, complete, NGP, EX..**$25.00**

Burt Lancaster, press kit, Atlantic City, 1981, EX **$25.00**

Burt Reynolds, press kit, The Best Little Whore House in Texas, 1982, EX...**$35.00**

Charlie Chaplin, coloring book, mostly colored, Saalfield, 1941, G+ **$40.00**

Charlie Chaplin, postcard, English, early 1900s, EX **$30.00**

Charlton Heston, lobby card, Airport 1975, 11x14", EX...**$18.00**

Clark Gable & Ava Gardner, press book, Mogambo, 1953, EX..**$40.00**

Dean Martin & Jerry Lewis, decal, color photo, 1950s, 3x5", sealed, MIP **$28.00**

Dean Martin & Jerry Lewis, movie program, 16-page magazine w/photos, behind the scenes info & bio's, 1950s, EX...**$20.00**

Deanna Durbin, songbook, Favorite Songs & Arias, black & white photo cover & inside photos, bio & notes, 1939, EX...**$25.00**

Douglas Fairbanks, lobby card, The Nut, close-up, 11x14", EX+ **$125.00**

Elizabeth Taylor, book, National Velvet, color photo dust jacket w/Miss Taylor, hard-bound, 304 pages, 1945, EX...**$25.00**

Elizabeth Taylor, coloring book, Whitman, 1950, some pages colored, EX+ **$25.00**

Elizabeth Taylor, movie program from Cleopatra, VG ..**$18.00**

Fred Astaire & Ginger Rogers, Gershwin song book & picture from movie Shall We Dance?, 1937, EX.........**$20.00**

Gabby Hayes, tablet, unused **$18.00**

Gloria Jean, display card for hair bows w/2 unused bows, Exclusive Creations, 1930s-40s, EX+ **$24.00**

Grace Kelly, View-Master set, Miss Kelly's wedding to Prince Rainier, #417A, 1956, EX..**$35.00**

Groucho Marx, coaster, Grouch Marx & an All-Star Variety Show for Pabst Blue Ribbon Beer (Marx not pictured), 1940s, EX+ **$30.00**

Jackie Coogan, movie flyer promoting Tom Sawyer, EX...**$12.00**

James Cagney, window card, The West Point Story, 1950, EX...**$45.00**

James Dean, album, A Tribute to James Dean, music from East of Eden, Rebel Without a Cause & Giant, 1950s, EX **$35.00**

Joan Crawford, handkerchief, promoting film Ice Follies of 1939 w/MGM logo & facsimile autograph, foil label, EX...**$85.00**

John Wayne, playing cards, NRFB...............................**$20.00**

Judy Garland, sheet music from Me & My Gal, EX........**$8.00**

Lana Turner, paperback book, illustrated, black & white photos, NM...**$12.00**

Laurel & Hardy, dolls, painted vinyl w/movable arms & legs, cloth clothes, Dakin, 8" Stan/7" Ollie, EX+, pr......**$40.00**

Loretta Young, scrapbook, full of memorabilia, 61 pages, EX...**$35.00**

Lucille Ball, decal, glossy color picture for wood, fabric or glass, 1950s, 4x5", MIP...**$45.00**

Lucille Ball, dress pattern, Lucy pictured on front of envelope, ca 1940, EX...**$15.00**

Mae West, stage program, Diamond Lil, 18 pages, 1950, 8½x11", EX...**$30.00**

Marilyn Monroe, ad, for diet pills **$475.00**

Marilyn Monroe, book, A Composite View, Wangenknecht, hardcover, dust jacket....................................**$100.00**

Marilyn Monroe, book, Marilyn Monroe Story by Joe Franklin & Laurie Palmer, soft-bound, 1953.......**$375.00**

Marilyn Monroe, book, Strange Death of Marilyn Monroe, Kapell, soft cover, 1964 ....**$125.00**

Marilyn Monroe, cardboard standee of Marilyn wearing wind-blown dress from The Seven Year Itch, 36" plus, EX.**$25.00**

Marilyn Monroe, earrings, MOC...................................**$10.00**

Marilyn Monroe, McCormick Whiskey decanter, M...**$475.00**

Marilyn Monroe, paperback book, Seven Year Itch, features Marilyn on cover, ca 1955, EX **$12.00**

Marilyn Monroe, photograph, scene of Marilyn riding horse toward camera, 1961, EX.......................................**$25.00**

Marilyn Monroe, plate, Royal Orleans, MIB **$60.00**

Marilyn Monroe, playing cards, dated 1956, MIP (sealed) **$17.50**

Marilyn Monroe, pocket mirror, Marilyn in bathing suit, 2x3", M...**$5.00**

Marilyn Monroe, T-shirt, from Gentleman Prefer Blondes, Manhattan background, 1987 ....**$15.00**

Marilyn Monroe, tapestry, Seven Year Itch pose on felt, 38x53", M...**$125.00**

Paul Newman, blow-up pillow, 1970s, M **$12.00**

Rita Hayworth & Burt Lancaster, press book, Separate Tables, EX..**$32.00**

Ryan O'Neal, pin-back button, Bary Landon, 1977, EX.**$5.00**

Sean Connery, lobby card set, Diamonds Are Forever, 1971, 11x14", EX..**$70.00**

Sonja Henie, sheet music from One in a Million, EX ..**$20.00**

Three Stooges, fan club kit, 1959, EX.........................**$35.00**

Three Stooges, hand puppet, Larry, painted vinyl head w/printed cloth body, 1950s-60s, 10x8½", NM ...**$100.00**

Vivian Leigh, lobby card, Gone w/the Wind, 1939, 11x14", EX, $400.00

Vivian Leigh & Laurence Oliver, playbill, Caesar & Cleopatra/Anthony & Cleopatra, 40 pages, 1952, EX-......**$20.00**

WC Fields, bank, plastic figure, MGM, 7½".................**$15.00**

WC Fields, bookends, plastic bust figures, 8", pr **$30.00**

Magazines

Before the late 1930s, the covers of many movie magazines were often illustrated with portraits of the stars by such well-known artists as James Montgomery Flagg, Rolf Armstrong, Earl Chandler Christie, and many others. But when *Photoplay* broke tradition by featuring a photograph of Ginger Rogers in 1937, a new era began. There were scores of different magazines, each contained stories about a top Hollywood personality. Some of these features were explicit and often exaggerated. The ads they contained portrayed the stars plugging their favorite products — cigarettes, a particular brand of liquor, etc. Some factors to consider when evaluating a vintage movie magazine are: who is on the cover, who the articles are about and their content, the photos the magazine contains, and of course, condition.

Modern Screen, 1949, April, Jane Wyman & cocker spaniel on cover, VG+..**$18.00**

Modern Screen, 1954, September, Marilyn Monroe cover, Marilyn Talks About Joe & Babies, VG+ **$30.00**

Modern Screen, 1961, June, Elizabeth Taylor, EX.......**$10.00**

Modern Screen, 1964, February, Sandra Dee, Carol Baker, Natalie Wood, NM..**$12.00**

Modern Screen, 1964, July, Jackie Kennedy cover, Beatles Movie Review, VG **$10.00**

Modern Screen, 1976, April, Burt Reynolds & Lauren Hutton cover, EX **$8.00**

Motion Picture, 1931, April, Clara Bow, VG+.............**$50.00**

Motion Picture, 1940, May, Joan Blondell in swimsuit, VG **$16.00**

Motion Picture, 1946, January, Rita Hayworth & daughter, VG..**$20.00**

Motion Picture, 1949, August, Ann Blyth, EX.............**$14.00**

Motion Picture, 1949, March, Elizabeth Taylor, EX, $15.00

Motion Picture, 1955, May, Debbie Reynolds & Eddie Fisher, EX..**$14.00**

Motion Picture, 1958, November, Tony Curtis & Janet Leigh, G+ **$6.00**

Motion Picture, 1965, March, Debbie Reynolds & children, VG+..**$8.00**

Movie Classic, 1935, August, Dolores Del Rio, VG+....**$26.00**

Movie Fan, 1949, October 9, Gregory Peck, VG+.......**$20.00**

Movie Life, 1943, May, Veronica Lake, VG+ **$20.00**

Movie Life, 1944, December, Judy Garland, VG+........**$18.00**

Movie Life, 1949, July, Doris Day, VG+.......................**$15.00**

Movie Life, 1960, May, Cary Grant, Connie Stevens, G+ .**$8.00**

Movie Life, 1980, May, Steve McQueen, VG+ **$6.00**

Movie Life Yearbook, 1969, #45, VG **$12.00**

Movie Mirror, 1968, March, EX....................................**$8.00**

Movie Play, 1954, January, Jane Powell cover, pinup calendar, EX..**$20.00**

Movie Screen Yearbook, 1955, #2, Kim Novak, VG **$18.00**

Movie Spotlight, 1951, November, Gordon McRae cover, EX..**$20.00**

Movie Star Parade, 1944, November, Deanna Durbin cover, EX+..**$20.00**

Movie Star Parade, 1945, October, NM.......................**$25.00**

Movie Story, 1938, May, Jeanette McDonald & Nelson Eddy, VG + ...**$25.00**

Movie Story, 1941, May, Bette Davis & George Brent, VG **$22.00**

Movie Story, 1943, July, Sonja Henie, VG **$18.00**

Movie Story, 1945, October, Betty Grable, VG **$24.00**

Movie Story, 1946, December, Gregory Peck, VG.......**$25.00**

Movie Story, 1946, October, NM..................................**$22.00**

Movie Story, 1949, August, Montgomery Clift & Olivia de Havilland, G+ **$10.00**

Movie Story Yearbook, 1948, #7, Loretta Young cover, VG **$18.00**

Movie World, 1968, May, Frank Sinatra & Mia Farrow, VG+..**$8.00**

Movieland, 1943, May, Betty Grable, G+.....................**$20.00**

Movieland, 1944, August, Sonny Tufts, Van Johnson, Marilyn Maxwell, EX **$22.00**

Movieland, 1945, March, Gregory Peck cover, 12-year-old Liz Taylor, VG+ **$20.00**

Movieland, 1945, May, Ingrid Bergman, VG **$16.00**

Movieland, 1956, October, Elizabeth Taylor, Jimmy Dean, EX..**$14.00**

Movies, 1942, May, Joan Fontaine, VG+......................**$18.00**

Movies, 1945, July, Gloria de Haven, VG+...................**$14.00**

Movies, 1946, August, Betty Hutton, EX......................**$14.00**

New Stars Over Hollywood, 1946, August, Peggy Cummins, G+ **$7.00**

New Stars Over Hollywood, 1946, October, Donna Reed, G+ **$7.00**

Photo Screen, 1971, August, Dean Martin & family, EX ..**$6.00**

Photoplay, 1933, October, Ruby Keeler, VG...............**$25.00**

Photoplay, 1935, June, Irene Dunn, VG **$26.00**

Photoplay, 1939, August, Alice Faye, VG+..................**$25.00**

Photoplay, 1946, August, June Allyson, VG **$20.00**

Photoplay, 1948, September, Alan Ladd, VG+............**$14.00**

Photoplay, 1953, February, Marilyn Monroe cover, Is Hollywood Carrying Sex Too Far?, NM $40.00
Photoplay, 1955, November, Kim Novak, VG.............$10.00
Photoplay, 1956, April, Grace Kelly, VG+ $12.00
Photoplay, 1957, February, Rock Hudson, VG+ $10.00
Photoplay, 1960, November, EX.............................$14.00
Photoplay, 1961, August, Tuesday Weld, VG................$8.00
Photoplay, 1963, February, Marilyn Monroe cover, We Grant Marilyn's Last Wish, EX.......................................$25.00
Photoplay, 1967, August, Barbara Stanwyck, VG+ $8.00
Picture Play, 1936, May, Ginger Rogers, VG+.............$26.00
Picture Play, 1937, April, Myrna Loy, VG+ $14.00
Real Screen Fun, 1938, January, Helen Dell, G+...........$8.00
Real Screen Fun, 1942, July, showgirl cover, VG...........$8.00
Romantic Movie Stories, Carole Lombard by Mozert, VG+ $45.00
Romantic Movie Stories, Joan Blondell, EX.................$42.00
Screen Album, 1939, Olivia de Havilland, EX.............$26.00
Screen Album, 1950, Summer, #51, Jane Powell, VG+..$16.00
Screen Annual, 1951, Elizabeth Taylor, VG.................$16.00
Screen Book, 1935, March, Claudette Colbert, VG $25.00
Screen Book, 1939, September, Paulette Goddard, EX..$28.00
Screen Guide, 1936, October, Ginger Rogers, VG+.....$36.00
Screen Guide, 1942, March, Ann Sheridan, VG+ $14.00
Screen Guide, 1943, January, Dorothy Lamour, EX.....$25.00
Screen Guide, 1946, June, Lizabeth Scott, EX $22.00
Screen Life, 1941, November, Gene Tierny, EX...........$26.00
Screen Life, 1965, January, Paul Newman, 4 Fights the Beatles Won't Talk About, VG+......................................$8.00
Screen Parade, 1969, June, Jackie, Elvis, Sidney Poitier, Natalie Wood, Sophia Loren, NM $12.00
Screen Play, 1933, July, May West, VG+ $16.00
Screen Romances, 1932, January, Norma Shearer, G+ ..$32.00
Screen Romances, 1941, April, Mickey Rooney, VG....$18.00
Screen Stars, 1946, October, Ida Lupino, VG+.............$15.00
Screen Stories, 1949, June, June Allyson & James Stewart, VG $14.00
Screen Stories, 1951, January, Van Johnson & Katheryn Grayson, VG+...$14.00
Screen Stories, 1954, April, Ann Blyth, VG+ $14.00
Screen Stories, 1957, October, Natalie Wood, VG+.....$10.00
Screen Stories, 1959, July, Rock Hudson, VG.............$8.00
Screen Stories, 1960, June, Sandra Dee, EX $8.00
Screen Stories, 1961, December, Nancy Kwan, EX........$8.00
Screen Stories, 1961, January, Great Stars, Where Are They?, VG $8.00
Screen Stories, 1963, September, Janet Leigh cover, NM..$12.00
Screen Stories, 1964, December, Audrey Hepburn, VG+....$6.00
Screen Stories, 1966, March, James Stewart in The Flight of the Phoenix, EX $10.00
Screen Stories, 1967, November, Julie Christie, EX........$7.00
Screen Stories, 1971, May, Patty Duke, VG+ $7.00
Screenland, 1944, December, Veronica Lake, VG+ $18.00
Screenland, 1946, May, Betty Hutton, G+....................$8.00
Screenland, 1949, May, Tyrone Power & wife, EX $18.00
Screenland, 1951, July, Jeanne Crain, VG+ $14.00
Silver Screen, 1931, February, Nancy Carroll, VG+......$28.00
Silver Screen, 1937, November, Madeline Carroll, VG+..$16.00

Silver Screen, 1939, October, Garbo cover, When Greta Isn't Garbo, G..$12.00
Silver Screen, 1944, September, Susan Hayward, VG..$12.00
Silver Screen, 1945, June, Ingrid Bergman, EX $24.00
Silver Screen, 1948, Ava Gardner cover, VG...............$16.00
Silver Screen, 1948, June, Joan Fontaine, EX $16.00
Silver Screen, 1952, February, Marilyn Monroe cover, EX+ $40.00
Silver Screen, 1967, March, Mia Farrow, Nancy Sinatra, VG+ $6.00
Star Album, 1948, Esther Williams, portraits & bio's of the stars, VG $20.00

New Martinsville Glass

Located in a West Virginia town by the same name, the New Martinsville Glass Company was founded in 1901 and until it was purchased by Viking in 1944 produced quality tableware in various patterns and colors that collectors admire today. They also made a line of glass animals which Viking continued to produce until they closed in 1986. In 1987 the factory was bought by Mr. Kenneth Dalzell who reopened the company under the title Dalzell-Viking. He used the old molds to reissue his own line of animals, which he marked 'Dalzell' with an acid stamp. These are usually priced in the $50.00 to $60.00 range. Examples marked 'V' were made by Viking for another company, Mirror Images. They're valued at $15.00 to $35.00.

See also Glass Animals.

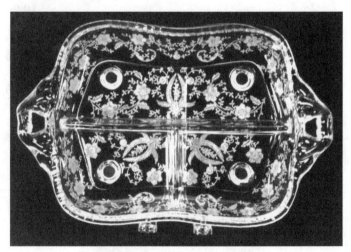

Prelude, relish, 3-part, $55.00

Florentine, bowl, nut; etched, center handle, #4429, 11"..$18.00
Florentine, candlesticks, double, #4429, pr..................$26.00
Georgian, creamer, green, 4" $15.00
Georgian, cup & saucer, green $12.50
Georgian, sugar bowl, green, 3" $40.00
Hostmaster, tumbler, ruby, 4¼"...................................$11.00
Hostmaster, wine, ruby, 4x2½" $11.00
Janice, banana boat, red, low footed, 12" $125.00
Janice, basket, crystal w/red handle, 4-footed, 6½".....$50.00
Janice, bonbon, med blue, handled, 7" $45.00

Janice, cup, light blue...$15.00
Janice, tumbler, ruby, footed...............................$30.00
Moondrops, tumbler, red or cobalt, 4⅜" $35.00
Mt Vernon, decanter, w/8 footed 1-oz cordials, 11-oz.$195.00
Nautilus, bookends, pr $60.00
Oscar, tumbler, amber w/platinum trim $5.50
Palmette Band, salt & pepper shakers, blue opaque, 2½",
　pr $60.00
Prelude, candlestick, single, 5".............................$24.00
Prelude, cordial..$20.00
Princess, compote, stemmed.................................$20.00
Princess, server, center handle.............................$22.00
Radiance, cordial, amber, 1-oz.............................$26.00
Radiance, creamer, ice blue $30.00
Radiance, pitcher, amber, 64-oz $125.00
Radiance, plate, luncheon; amber, 8" $10.00
Radiance, plate, luncheon; ice blue, 8" $16.00
Radiance, relish, amber, 2-part, 7" $13.00
Radiance, salt & pepper shakers, red, pr $80.00
Radiance, tumbler, amber, 9-oz $17.50
Twenty Rib, salt & pepper shakers, ruby, footed pillar
　shape, 3⅜", pr $110.00

Newspapers

Papers that cover specific events, whether historical, regarding well-known political or entertainment figures, natural disasters of unusually large proportions, or catastropic events of any nature, are just the type that people tend to keep, and they're also the most collectible. Those that carry first-report accounts are more valuable than those with subsequent reporting. Other factors that bear on value are where the article appears (front page is best), how visual it is (are there photographs or a large headline), and whether it is from a small town or city paper.

An authentic copy of The New York Herald's April 15, 1865, 10 AM edition, reporting the assassination of Lincoln is rare and expensive, valued at about $2,000.00. There are thousands of reprints around today, in at least nineteen different versions, so beware! To help you detect one of these reproductions before you mortgage the farm to buy it, send for *A Primer on Collecting Old & Historic Newspapers*. $2.00 and an SASE to NCSA, Box 19134-S, Lansing, MI 48901, will get you this 32-page pamphlet that is a goldmine of information on where to buy and sell newspapers, how to grade their condition, and their approximate values. For instance, did you know that historical content has much more bearing on the value of a newspaper than age? It's true! In fact, age has little relevance. On the other hand, condition is extremely important. Even if yours is historically significant, if it's fragile and stained, don't expect to get more than a few dollars for it. A knowledgeable collector may not be interested in buying it at all.

In our descriptions, headlines are in quotes, storylines are not.

1929, October 29, Stock Market Crashes, Cleveland News,
　complete, VG $100.00

1935, August 17, Will Rogers Killed in Plane Crash, Detroit
　Free Press, complete, VG $35.00
1936, August 4, Jesse Owens Sets Olympic Mark, Lancaster
　(Ohio) Eagle Gazette, incomplete.........................$20.00
1939, February 15, World's Fair, 'Golden Gate International Exposition' section of San Francisco Examiner,
　EX...$20.00
1940, April 9, Nazis Invade Scandinavia, The Patriot (Harrisburg PA), complete, VG $25.00
1940, May 10, Churchill Becomes Prime Minister, Honolulu
　Star Bulletin, complete, VG...................................$70.00
1941, December 8, 'Japanese Start War on US by Suprise
　Attack on Hawaii,' New York Times, complete, G.$35.00
1941, December 8, 'US at War,' SF Chronicle, 3 photo pages
　including ½-page map, 1st section only...............$35.00
1941, December 8, 'US Declares War,' Long Beach Press-
　Telegram, outer leaf only, VG...............................$35.00
1941, June 3, New York Times, Death of Lou Gehrig, complete, VG $175.00
1942, January 18, Carole Lombard Killed in Plane Crash,
　Chicago Herald American, complete, VG.............$80.00
1943, February 25, 'Rommel Armor in Full Retreat,' San Jose
　Mercury Herald, incomplete, G............................$14.00
1944, June 6, D-Day, Cincinnati Post, complete, EX ...$30.00
1945, April 12, 'FDR Dead,' San Fransisco News, w/photo,
　outer leaf only, EX...$20.00
1945, April 14, Truman Takes Helm, Philadelphia Inquirer,
　complete, G+..$15.00
1945, August 14, 'Jap Radio Announces Complete Surrender,' 1st section only, EX...$30.00
1945, August 14, 'Japs Surrender,' Akron Beacon Journal, 8-
　page souvenir edition, VG.....................................$11.00
1945, August 15, 'Peace! Victory!,' Los Angeles Times, outer
　leaf only, minor flaws, EX $33.00
1945, August 9, 'New Atom Attack' headlines relating the
　bombing of Hiroshima, New York Journal American,
　complete, EX..$30.00
1945, August 9, Hiroshima Bombing, Russia starts war on
　Japan, Honolulu Advertiser, complete, minor flaws ..$20.00
1945, May 8, V-E Day, San Francisco Examiner, complete,
　EX..$35.00

1948, August 17, 'Babe Ruth, Baseball's Greatest Player, Dies,' Boston Post, EX, $75.00

1948, November 18, 'Congressman Nixon Visited Rosemead,' Alhambra (CA) Park Review, 4 pages, EX.$12.50
1948, November 3, 'Truman Elected President as Democrats
　Win Senate & House,' outer leaf only $18.00

1951, March 19, 'Reds Back Over 38th,' Honolulu Advertiser, 16 pages, incomplete................................$11.00

1952, November 5, 'Ike Wins — Tops FDR,' 1st section, EX................................$18.00

1955, April 6, 'Churchill Resigns as Prime Minister,' LA Times, outer leaf only................................$12.00

1956, July 26, Andrea Doria Sinking at Sea, Detroit Times, complete, VG................................$40.00

1957, May 3, 'Senator McCarthy Dies in Hospital,' Montreal Gazette, 1st section only, NM................................$16.00

1962, August 6, 'Marilyn Monroe Is Dead, An Overdose of Pills,' San Francisco Chronicle, nearly complete, EX................................$40.00

1962, February 20, 'Glenn Orbits Earth 3 Times; Home Safe,' Berkeley Gazette, complete, EX................................$18.00

1963, November 23, 'Kennedy Dead, Assassin Flees After Shooting,' LA Times, NM................................$30.00

1963, November 23, 'Kennedy Slain on Dallas Street; Johnson Becomes President,' Dallas Morning News, complete, VG................................$30.00

1964, October 20, Ex-President Hoover Dies, Daily Tribune, Covina CA, 1st section only, EX................................$10.00

1968, November 6, 'Nixon Wins,' LA Herald Examiner, minor flaws, 1st section only, EX................................$13.00

1969, July 21, 'Man Walks on Moon,' LA Times, 4 sections, EX................................$24.00

1969, July 21, 'Our Space Heroes First Men To Walk on...Moon,' Post-Standard, Syracuse NY, 1st section only, EX................................$18.00

1969, March 28, 'Eisenhower Dies,' San Francisco Examiner, photo & story inside, NM................................$13.00

1972, December 27, 'Nation Mourns Truman,' news of survivors of plane crash in Andes (movie), 1st section only, EX................................$10.00

1976, April 6, 'Howard Hughes Dies,' Los Angeles Examiner, 2 sections, EX................................$16.00

1976, July 4, 'Happy Birthday America Let Freedom Ring,' Los Angeles Examiner, special sections only, NM................$11.00

1977, August 17, Death of Elvis Presley, Commercial Appeal, complete, EX................................$50.00

1989, October 18, 'Killer Quake,' Sacramento Bee, complete, EX................................$10.00

Niloak Pottery

This company operated in the Little Rock area of Arkansas from the turn of the century until 1947 (when it was converted to a tile company which is still in existence). It was founded by Charles Hyten, whose partner was a former Rookwood potter, Arthur Dovey. It was originally known as the Hyten Pottery, renamed Eagle Pottery soon after that, and finally was incorporated in 1911 as the Niloak Pottery Company. Niloak (the backwards spelling of kaolin, a type of clay) is best known today for their Mission Ware line, characterized by swirled colors of natural and artificially dyed clay. Though other companies made swirled pottery, none were as successful as Hyten, who received a patent for his process in 1928. Except for a few rare examples, Mission Ware was glazed only on the inside.

Facing financial difficulties at the onset of the Depression, the company changed ownership and began to manufacture a more extensive line of molded wares, including figural planters, vases, jardineres, clocks, and some tile.

Several marks were used, all of which include the company name, and paper labels were used as well.

Vase, cobalt, vertical ribs, fluted rim, 12", $65.00

Ashtray, pink w/blue overspray, 1½x3½" dia..............$25.00

Ashtray, solid blue, recessed diamond below pegasus in low relief, Arkansas lettered in upper left, 4¼x3½".....$75.00

Basket, cobalt, basketweave pattern in low relief, handled, 4"................................$25.00

Basket, tan w/blue overspray, handled, 6½"..............$80.00

Bowl, Mission Ware, swirled colors, 2"........................$85.00

Bowl, peacock blue, scalloped edge, 2¾x5½" dia.......$40.00

Chamber stick, Mission Ware, swirled colors, 4".......$150.00

Creamer, pink w/blue overspray, petal design in low relief, ear-type handle, 5"................................$40.00

Creamer, pink w/blue overspray, 4¼"........................$30.00

Ewer, solid blue w/tulip in low relief, 10¾"...............$55.00

Flower frog, ivory, pelican atop base, 6¾"..................$35.00

Flower frog, Mission Ware, swirled colors, 1¼x4" dia.$90.00

Flower frog, yellow turtle w/high gloss finish, 1½x4¾".$30.00

Jug, yellow w/high gloss finish, 4½"..........................$30.00

Mug, Mission Ware, swirled colors, ear-type handle, 5½"..$300.00

Novelty, canoe, pink w/blue overspray, 5½" long......$45.00

Novelty, wishing well, cobalt, 8½"..............................$45.00

Pin dish, flower shape, pink w/blue overspray, 4" dia .$20.00

Pitcher, yellow w/blue overspray, Lewis glaze, repeating rings in center, 10"................................$60.00

Planter, camel, cobalt, 3¾"..$35.00

Planter, deer facing left, cobalt, 5"............................$30.00

Planter, dove, ivory, 9"................................$110.00

Planter, duck, pink w/blue overspray, 4"....................$25.00

Planter, Mission Ware, swirled colors, footed, 2½x7½" dia................................$220.00

Planter, rocking horse, cobalt, 6¼" **$90.00**
Planter, squirrel, yellow w/blue overspray, 6".............**$25.00**
Plate, salad; pink w/blue overspray, petal design in low relief, 8" **$40.00**
Shot glass, Mission Ware, swirled colors, 2¼"...........**$85.00**
Sugar bowl (open), pink w/blue overspray, petal design in low relief, 4" **$30.00**
Tumbler, Mission Ware, swirled colors, slightly flared rim, single groove at base, 4¼"......................**$95.00**
Vase, bud; Mission Ware, swirled colors, single groove in center, flared base, 8¼" **$135.00**

Vase, Mission Ware, spherical, 6½", $200.00; Vase, 6¾", $180.00

Vase, Mission Ware, swirled colors, bulbous, 10¾" ..**$260.00**
Vase, Mission Ware, swirled colors, bulbous w/slightly flared rim, 9" **$210.00**
Vase, Mission Ware, swirled colors, cone shape on flat round base, 9½" **$265.00**
Vase, Mission Ware, swirled colors, cylinder form, 9¾" .**$225.00**
Vase, Mission Ware, swirled colors, waisted cylinder form, 10¼" **$200.00**
Vase, peacock blue, flared & ruffled rim, 4¼" **$30.00**
Vase, peacock blue, Lewis glaze, bulbous, 6¾"...........**$50.00**
Vase, pink w/blue overspray, bulbous w/flared rim, 10" **$95.00**
Vase, pink w/blue overspray, fan form on round base, 7"...**$40.00**
Vase, sea green, Stoin glaze, bulbous w/applied handles, 9¼" **$120.00**
Vase, yellow, bulbous w/ear-type handles, 6".............**$55.00**
Wall pocket, Mission Ware, swirled colors, cone shape, 6" **$235.00**

Nippon

In 1890, the McKinley Tariff Act was passed by congress, requiring that all items of foreign manufacture be marked in 'legible English' with the name of the country of origin. In compliance, items imported from Japan were marked 'Nippon,' the Japanese word for their homeland. For many years, this was acceptable. In 1921, however, the United States government reversed its position and instructed their custom agents to deny entry to imported items bearing only the Nippon mark. The transition was slow, but ultimately the Japanese were forced to add or substitute the English word 'Japan' in their trademarks.

This was an era of prosperity in our country, a time when even laboring families had money to spend on little niceties. The import business was booming. Japanese-made porcelains were much more inexpensive than similar items from Germany and Austria, and as a result, it was imported in vast quantities. It was sold at fairs, through gift stores, five and ten cent stores, Sears and Roebuck, and Montgomery Ward.

Today Nippon is an active area of buying and selling among collectors. Quality varies from piece to piece. The more desirable pieces are those with fine art work and lavish gold overlay. The term moriage used in the descriptions that follow refers to a decorating method where soft clay is piped on with a squeeze bag, similar to decorating a cake with icing. Items with animals in relief, children's dinnerware, unusual forms (such as hanging hatpin holders, for instance), and those with out-of-the-ordinary decorative themes are good to invest in.

If you'd like to learn more about this subject, we recommend *The Collector's Encyclopedia of Nippon Porcelain* (there are three volumes) by Joan F. Van Patten.

Chocolate pot, 6-sided urn shape w/heavy gold moriage design, solid gold handle, blue mark, 9¾", $225.00

Ashtray, figural boy seated on edge of square dish, blue mark, 6" **$200.00**
Ashtray, round w/2 protruding rests, lion's head in profile in center, green mark, 4½" dia **$100.00**
Ashtray, stylized rabbit & floral design, banded top & bottom, green mark, 3¼" dia,....................**$90.00**
Ashtray, triangular shape w/horse's head in profile, green mark, 4½" **$100.00**
Bonbon dish, round, house on stilts over water scene on lid, blue mark, 5" dia **$150.00**
Bonbon dish, round w/sailboats on water near shoreline on lid, green mark, 5½" dia **$175.00**

Butter dish, round lid w/straight sides on round plate, floral design, green mark, 7¾" dia..................................$160.00

Cake set, lg gold-handled plate w/6 smaller plates, Arabs on camels w/palm trees, gold rims, green mark......$225.00

Candy dish, hunt scene on inside of fluted rim w/moriage trim, footed, blue mark, 12" $200.00

Celery dish, Indian in canoe in center of bowl, Indian-style design around edge, green mark, 12" long.........$210.00

Child's cup & saucer, embossed doll face, blue mark.$75.00

Child's dish, heart shape w/doll face, gold rim, blue mark, 5¼" $125.00

Child's tea set, teapot, creamer & sugar bowl w/4 cups, saucers & plates, Dutch design, gold trim, blue mark $300.00

Chocolate set, pot w/4 cups & saucers, white w/deep pink rose design, heavy gold trim, green mark, 9" $350.00

Compote, round w/moriage floral decor on shaded background, Oriental-style handles, blue mark, 4" dia ..$90.00

Compote, woodland scene in center of bowl w/scalloped rim, pedestal foot, green mark, 3½x6½"..............$225.00

Cookie/cracker jar, footed bulbous body w/knob finial on lid, rose decor, gold trim, green mark, 7" $250.00

Cracker jar, Indian in canoe w/Indian-style design around top, green mark, 8½"...$325.00

Creamer & sugar bowl, moriage floral decor on footed bowl shapes, 4½" (including finial)..............................$225.00

Cruet, Dutch sailboats near shore, loop handle, green mark, 7¼" $325.00

Cup & saucer, demitasse; mug type w/ear-shaped handle, cobalt w/gold decor, green mark, 2" $60.00

Dish, basket shape w/boating & landscape scene, moriage design on handle, brown trim around rim, green mark, 7" long $110.00

Dish, figural bird on decorated rim, blue mark, 6".$135.00

Egg cup, white w/blue Oriental landscape, 2½".........$50.00

Egg server, 6 egg rests on plate w/scalloped edge, center handle, floral design w/gold trim, blue mark, 6¼" dia $155.00

Ferner, round dish w/molded Pharaoh handles & Egyptian design on straight sides, rolled rim, green mark, 8½" dia $350.00

Hatpin holder, deep rose design on white, gold trim, 4¾" $65.00

Hostess set in box, black lacquer w/cranes in flight on box lid, dogwoods on 4 plates & bowl, gold trim, blue mark..$135.00

Humidor, lion's head w/acorn & leaf design, green mark, 5½" $500.00

Inkwell w/pen rest, rectangular w/floral design, green mark, 3½" $215.00

Lemonade set, pitcher & 6 cups, rose design on off-white background, gold trim, green mark.....................$280.00

Match holder & ashtray combination, round w/hieroglyphic design, green mark, 3½"..$225.00

Mug, geese flying off from marsh, moriage trim, green mark, 5½" $250.00

Nut bowl, 6-sided w/scalloped rim, owl decor in center, molded square handles, green mark, 7¾"..........$175.00

Peanut set, long self-handled bowl w/6 sm bowls, black lacquer w/Oriental bird & floral motif, gold trim, green mark..$135.00

Plaque, head of moose w/trees & acorn motif, green mark, 5½" $275.00

Plaque, hunt scene, green mark, 10"...................$325.00

Plate, cobalt rim w/white center, gold & floral design, blue mark, 7½" dia $90.00

Plate, cobalt w/gold decor around rim & in center, green mark, 8½" dia $150.00

Relish dish, divided w/figural bird center handle, rose & leaf decor, green mark, 7¾" long.............................$225.00

Ring holder, white hand reaching up on round plate, rose & moriage design, blue mark, 3½" $80.00

Salt & pepper shakers, woodland scene on cylinder shapes w/flared bottoms, slightly domed tops, green mark, 2½", pr..$85.00

Shaving mug, landscape scene, flared rim, circular handle, green mark, 4"..$155.00

Sugar shaker, 6-sided, rose design on white w/gold moriage trim on black, blue mark, 5" $150.00

Syrup pitcher w/underplate, pink roses w/heavy gold moriage design & trim, solid gold handle, green mark, 6"..$160.00

Talcum powder flask, floral design w/gold top, blue mark, 5" $170.00

Tea set, teapot, creamer & sugar bowl w/8 cups & saucers, floral design w/gold trim, green mark, 5½" $230.00

Tea strainer, rose design on white w/gold trim around scalloped rim, handle & bottom, blue mark, 6" long .$160.00

Tea tile, octagon shape w/Dutch girl under umbrella by brick wall, green mark, 5½" dia $90.00

Teapot, individual; flower basket w/ribbon on side, floral design around lid, gold finial & trim, blue mark, 4¾"............$95.00

Toast rack, rectangular w/dainty floral design on white, lime green edge w/gold trim, blue mark, 8¼" long....$140.00

Vase, basket w/yellow floral design, moriage trim, green mark, 6x7¼" $225.00

Vase, footed bulbous shape w/moriage dragon design, fluted rim, angled handles, blue mark, 6"..........$150.00

Vase, urn shape w/jonquils, braided rope & moriage trim, green mark, 9½"..$325.00

Vase, urn shape w/moriage geisha girls, gold trim, Oriental man on reverse, 9½", $200.00

Wall pocket, horn shape w/shaded pink floral design w/moriage outline, scalloped rim, blue mark, 7" .$200.00

Noritake

Before the government restricted the use of the Nippon mark in 1921, all porcelain exported from Japan (even that made by the Noritake Company) carried the Nippon mark. The company that became Noritake had its beginning in 1904, and over the years experienced several changes in name and organization. Until 1941 (at the onset of WWII) they continued to import large amounts of their products to America. (During the occupation, when chinaware production was resumed, all imports were to have been marked 'Occupied Japan,' though because of the natural resentment on the part of the Japanese, much of it was not.)

Many variations will be found in their marks, but nearly all contain the Noritake name. If you'd like to learn more about this subject, we recommend *The Collector's Encyclopedia of Noritake* (there are two books in the series) by Joan Van Patten.

Bowl, desert scene w/camel & rider, gold trim & handles, green M-in-wreath mark, 8" dia **$70.00**

Bowl, mallard in flight on rim of orange lustre bowl, red M-in-wreath mark, 9" wide......................................**$325.00**

Bowl, sailing ship in center, lavender border & open handles, red M-in-wreath mark, 7¾" dia **$50.00**

Bowl, shell form w/grape & leaf design in center, gold trim, footed, red M-in-wreath mark, 10" wide **$65.00**

Bowl, shell form w/scenic interior, 2 handles, green M-in-wreath mark, 11" long..**$85.00**

Butter dish, pink azaleas on white, gold trim & lid finial, red M-in-wreath mark, 6" dia......................................**$70.00**

Cake plate, daisies on white background, brown & tan border, gold handles, red M-in-wreath mark, 10" dia ..**$60.00**

Candy dish, basket shape w/floral design on white, lavender scalloped rim w/gold trim, red M-in-wreath mark, 5" dia **$70.00**

Candy dish, clover shape w/butterflies in center, gold ring handles, red M-in-wreath mark, 7" wide **$70.00**

Candy dish, heart shape w/scenic interior, sm ring handle, green M-in-wreath, 4½" long.................................**$25.00**

Candy dish, indented sides w/twisted handle, footed, 6½" long, $80.00

Dresser doll, orange lustre dress & green hat holding multicolored bouquet, red M-in-wreath mark, 6"........**$285.00**

Flower frog, yellow & blue fish atop orange lustre base, red M-in-wreath mark, 4½".......................................**$235.00**

Honey jar, multicolored flowers on white lustre beehive w/raised gold bees & finial, red M-in-wreath mark, 4½" **$70.00**

Inkwell, colonial girl in tiered dress, green M-in-wreath mark, 4½" **$285.00**

Lemon dish, green leaves & raised lemon inside rim, red M-in-wreath mark, 5¾" wide **$40.00**

Lobster dish, w/10¾" underplate, red M-in-wreath mark, $130.00

Matchbox holder, gold bear seated atop peach lustre base, 3¼"...**$165.00**

Pin dish, tan lustre dog seated in lavender dish, M-in-wreath mark, 2¾" dia **$50.00**

Plate, floral & scroll design on white, yellow trim, red M-in-wreath mark, 8½" dia...**$30.00**

Salt & pepper shakers, hen on nest, yellow w/black trim on scalloped edge, green M-in-wreath mark, 2½" ...**$100.00**

Tray, tan center w/raised flowers around blue rim, red M-in-wreath mark, oval, 8¼" long **$50.00**

Vase, multicolored lustre pheasant w/tail fanned out on orange lustre base, red M-in-wreath mark, 5¼"..**$100.00**

Wall pocket, cone shape w/leaves & various fruit molded in relief, red M-in-wreath mark, 8"..........................**$185.00**

Wall pocket, 3 baby birds w/open mouths in orange lustre nest, green M-in-wreath mark, 6½" wide **$265.00**

Novelty Clocks

The largest producers of these small clocks were Lux, Keebler, Westclox, and Columbia Time. Some had moving parts, others a small pendulette. They were made of wood, china, Syroco (a pressed wood product), and eventually plastic. Until the late 1940s when electric-powered novelties were made by the Mastercrofter Company, they were all wind-up. The last Lux clocks were made in the mid-1950s.

Beer barrel drinkers, non-animated, Lux Pendulette, minimum value **$275.00**

Birdcage w/rhinestones on stand, Germany................**$40.00**

Bobbing bird, animated, Lux Pendulette, from $20 to .**$25.00**
Clock on top of elephant, Regent...........................**$250.00**
Cocker Spaniel, animated, Lux Pendulette, from $300 to..**$350.00**
Cuckoo pendulette, Lux **$35.00**
Cupid in wreath on top, porcelain dial, New Haven .**$100.00**
Dog by doghouse, pewter, bee movement, Ansonia ..**$60.00**
Dog looks out of his house, sunflower on top, Waterbury..**$70.00**
Hunting scene, non-animated, Lux Pendulette, from $65 to..**$85.00**
Man rides St Bernard w/Victory on collar, Regent **$105.00**
Organ grinder, animated, Lux.....................................**$125.00**
Owl w/blinking eyes, Germany, 1930s, 8"................**$195.00**

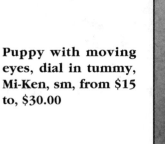

Puppy with moving eyes, dial in tummy, Mi-Ken, sm, from $15 to, $30.00

Puppy w/moving eyes, dial in tummy, Tezuka, 6" ...**$175.00**
Scholar on bench, animated, French **$85.00**
Tape measure, Lux, EX...**$30.00**
Totem-pole pendulum, eyes move, Japan **$85.00**
US Capitol, non-animated, Lux Pendulette, from $325 to...**$350.00**

Occupied Japan Collectibles

Some items produced in Japan during the period from the end of WWII until the occupation ended in 1952 were marked Occupied Japan. No doubt much of the ware from this era was marked simply Japan, since obviously the 'Occupied' term caused considerable resentment among the Japanese people, and they were understandably reluctant to use the mark. So even though you may find identical items marked simply Japan or Made in Japan, only those with the more limited Occupied Japan mark are evaluated here.

Assume that the items described below are ceramic unless another material is mentioned. For more information, we recommend *The Collector's Encyclopedia of Occupied Japan* (there are five in the series) by Gene Florence.

Bowl, bunch of fruit on white, gold trim, reticulated border, 7" dia..**$14.00**
Bowl, green leaf shape w/2 white daisies, gold trim, marked Pico **$8.50**
Casserole, dogwood on light beige, gold handles, 7¾x12"...**$38.00**
Cigarette box, Oriental men carry box w/dragon head on lid, 6⅜"...**$24.00**
Cigarette box, wood w/3 sections marked Lucky Strike, Camel & Chesterfield, 5x3½"...................**$35.00**
Cup, tulip shape, blue & white w/green leaf-shape handle, marked Merit China **$10.00**
Cup & saucer, allover blue & white floral design........**$12.50**
Cup & saucer, black w/gold trim, marked Noritake....**$12.50**
Cup & saucer, Blue Willow.......................................**$18.00**
Cup & saucer, crab apple design on white, Ucagco China..**$10.00**
Cup & saucer, demitasse; Oriental house scene on white..**$5.00**
Cup & saucer, demitasse; Oriental scene w/lady **$10.00**
Cup & saucer, demitasse; white lacy flower design on black, HB in diamond mark.......................**$12.50**
Cup & saucer, dragon design on purple, gold trim, marked Lucky China..**$16.50**
Cup & saucer, Florida souvenir, ocean scene on white, gold trim, C-over-M mark...................**$10.00**
Cup & saucer, pink & white floral design on tan, gold trim, marked Trimont China.................**$12.50**
Cup & saucer, pink roses on white, gold trim, marked Merit **$8.00**
Cup & saucer, violets on white, gold trim & ornate handle, marked Spring Violets...................**$16.00**
Dish, fish shape, circle K mark **$12.50**
Doll, celluloid, molded blond hair, ivory lace dress also marked, 7"..**$55.00**
Doll, celluloid, molded brown hair, nude, 4¾" **$14.00**
Egg cup, Blue Willow, 3¾"...**$22.00**
Figurine, angel w/horn, bisque, 5" **$25.00**
Figurine, ballerina in orange net dress, 4½"................**$24.00**
Figurine, Black shoeshine boy, 5½".............................**$45.00**

Figurine, boy with accordion, 6", $12.50

Figurine, boy w/begging dog, Hummel type, 5" **$38.00**

Figurine, boy w/boxing gloves, 4½"...........................**$14.00**

Figurine, boy w/broken sprinkler, seated on round base, Hummel type, 4½" **$32.00**

Figurine, boy w/parrot, 5".......................................**$12.50**

Figurine, boy w/tuba, 3½"..**$6.00**

Figurine, cat w/fiddle, tan w/blue jacket & orange fiddle, 2¼"..**$7.50**

Figurine, colonial couple, 5½", $35.00

Figurine, colonial girl w/song book, marked Ucagco China w/emblem, 5¾"...**$30.00**

Figurine, cupid w/donkey, bisque, 4" **$25.00**

Figurine, dog w/hat & pipe, 3½" **$12.50**

Figurine, dog w/horn, 3½"...**$8.50**

Figurine, elf on caterpillar **$14.00**

Figurine, frog w/violin, bisque, 4¼" **$18.00**

Figurine, girl holding doll, 4¼" **$14.00**

Figurine, girl w/accordion, rabbit at her feet, 4½".......**$10.00**

Figurine, Indian in canoe w/plastic flowers.................**$20.00**

Figurine, lady bug w/bat, 2¼"....................................**$8.00**

Figurine, lady w/balloons, 5½"................................**$45.00**

Figurine, Spanish guitar player, 4¼" **$10.00**

Figurines, Oriental couple in prayer, marked Mariyama, 7⅝", pr...**$40.00**

Figurines, Oriental couple in red robes, 6⅛", pr..........**$45.00**

Gravy boat, dogwood on light beige, gold trim & handle..**$16.00**

Jewelry box, metal dragon design, crown mark, 4x7".**$25.00**

Jewelry box, metal piano shape w/pink velvet interior, world-with-wings mark, 2½x3" **$16.50**

Lamp base, colonial lady lifting skirt, porcelain w/metal socket..**$35.00**

Lamp base, colonial man holding bouquet, porcelain w/metal socket, 10" **$30.00**

Match holder, black coal hod shape w/floral decor....**$12.50**

Mug, lady w/fork, 2¾"..**$16.50**

Planter, child playing violin on fence..........................**$10.00**

Planter, duck pulling cart, 3x5"...................................**$7.50**

Planter, duck wearing black top hat, 6½x6" **$14.00**

Planter, flamingo w/basket.......................................**$12.50**

Planter, Oriental girl pushing cart, 4" **$12.50**

Planter, ox pulling cart, 2½x7"..................................**$10.00**

Planter, rabbit pulling cart, light blue, 2½x6"..............**$14.00**

Planter, swan on blue base, 3"....................................**$6.00**

Plaque, colonial couple, light green border w/gold scroll design, bisque, marked Paulex, 6½x6" **$45.00**

Plaque, upsidedown monkey, light green outfit, bisque, 5"..**$35.00**

Plate, allover floral design on white, gold trim, marked Ardalt, Lenwile China No 3160, 4½" **$6.50**

Plate, birds of paradise scene w/peach lustre border .**$14.50**

Plate, Blue Willow, marked w/crown emblem, 9".......**$14.00**

Plate, cabin scene w/chickens **$20.00**

Plate, dragon design on rust, CK emblem....................**$6.00**

Plate, Geisha girl, gold trim, marked No 6078 Ardalt Hand Painted..**$25.00**

Plate, lg gold-trimmed flower on pink, marked Trimont China Hand Painted..**$20.00**

Plate, Oriental scene, gold trim, K-in-circle mark, 7½"..**$12.00**

Plate, pink flowers on white, blue border **$10.00**

Plate, yellow flower on white, gold trim, Ucagco China, Floral B mark..**$14.00**

Plate, yellow hibiscus on white, reticulated border, 8¼" ..**$20.00**

Platter, crab apple design on white, Ucagco China, oval, 15" **$25.00**

Platter, dogwood on light beige, gold trim, 13½".......**$16.00**

Powder jar, blue w/rose finial, porcelain, 3½"............**$14.00**

Powder jar, heart shape w/windmill scene, porcelain, 2¾" **$12.00**

Purse, basket bottom w/multicolored beaded top, drawstring closure, 7½x7"..**$65.00**

Ring box, Wedgwood type **$20.00**

Salt & pepper shakers, baseball players, pr **$25.00**

Salt & pepper shakers, bride & groom, pr **$25.00**

Salt & pepper shakers, chicks in basket, pr **$22.00**

Salt & pepper shakers, corncobs, pr...........................**$12.50**

Salt & pepper shakers, Humpty Dumpty, marked Ardalt, Lenwile China, pr..**$55.00**

Salt & pepper shakers, Indians in canoe, pr **$25.00**

Salt & pepper shakers, Niagara Falls souvenir, metal, 3", pr **$16.00**

Salt & pepper shakers, squirrels, pr...........................**$14.00**

Saucer, iris on black, gold trim **$3.00**

Scarf, multicolored tulips on brown & beige, turquoise border, silk, 18½x48"...**$45.00**

Shelf sitter, ballerina in net dress, 5" **$25.00**

Shelf sitter, boy w/accordion, 4"................................**$14.00**

Shelf sitter, fishing couple on bench, bisque, 4".........**$18.00**

Sugar bowl, birds & flowers on peach lustre glaze, KA in diamond mark...**$16.00**

Sugar bowl, crab apple design on white, Ucagco China.**$12.50**

Sugar bowl, tomato w/green stem lid finial.................**$14.50**

Tablecloth, red plaid w/yellow & blue stripes, sewn-in tag, 48x48" **$45.00**

Teapot, tomato w/green spout & handle, marked Maruhon Ware, 4½" **$42.00**

Toby mug, bearded man, 2¾".......................**$20.00**

Toby pitcher, bartender holding 2 mugs, 4⅞" **$35.00**

Toothpick holder, dog in barrel......................**$6.00**

Toothpick holder, dog w/pitcher......................**$8.00**

Toy, dog, celluloid squeaker, tan w/red neck ribbon.**$10.00**

Toy, Fancy Dan the Juggling Man, clown balancing top hat on his nose, wind-up, original box.......................**$85.00**

Toy, kangaroo, wind-up, original box........................**$65.00**

Toy, tool set, rubber, 6-piece set on original card.......**$45.00**

Toy, turtle, metal wind-up, black w/red & gold shell.**$22.00**

Vase, cornucopia; white w/pink roses in relief, footed, Lamore China **$35.00**

Vase, fancy gold design on white w/flowers in relief, bulbous w/ruffled rim, 10⅛".......................**$55.00**

Vase, green w/white polka dots, bulbous....................**$10.00**

Vase, multicolored flowers on white w/pink rose in relief at top, gold trim, Meiko China, 3½"..........................**$14.00**

Vase, Oriental man on brown background, bulbous, 4¾"..**$20.00**

Vase, Wedgwood type, 2⅝" **$10.00**

Old MacDonald's Farm

This is a wonderful line of novelty kitchenware items fashioned as the family and the animals that live on Old MacDonald's Farm. It's been popular with collectors for quite some time, and prices are astronomical, though they seem to have stabilized, at least for now. But I've found shakers at a garage sales and spice jars that were way underpriced at a small flea market, and at these prices, just one good find can make your day.

These things were made by the Regal China Company, who also made some of the Little Red Riding Hood items that are so collectible, as well as figural cookie jars, 'hugger' salt and pepper shakers, and decanters. The Roerig's devote a chapter to Regal in their book *The Collector's Encyclopedia of Cookie Jars* and, in fact, show the entire Old MacDonald's Farm line.

Canister, flour, cereal, coffee or cookie; med, each, $225.00

Butter dish, cow's head **$225.00**
Canister, cookies, lg...**$325.00**
Canister, pretzels, peanuts, popcorn, chips, tidbits; lg, each **$325.00**
Canister, salt, sugar or tea; med, each.......................**$225.00**
Canister, soap, lg **$325.00**
Cookie jar, barn **$250.00**
Creamer, rooster **$110.00**
Grease jar, pig...**$175.00**
Pitcher, milk...**$400.00**
Salt & pepper shakers, boy & girl, pr.........................**$75.00**
Salt & pepper shakers, churn, pr **$65.00**
Salt & pepper shakers, feed sacks w/sheep, pr.........**$165.00**
Spice jar, sm, each **$100.00**
Sugar bowl, hen..**$125.00**
Teapot, duck's head **$250.00**

Opalescent Glass

Opalescent glass is press molded in many patterns and colors, but the characteristic common to all of it is its white (or opalescent) rims, developed through the application of a strong acid to those areas. It was made early in the century by many American glasshouses, and it isn't at all uncommon to find a piece from time to time at estate sales, flea markets, or even garage sales, for that matter. Colors are more valuable than clear, and examples of major patterns are usually worth more than those with few or no matching pieces.

If you'd like to learn more about the subject, we recommend *The Standard Opalescent Glass Price Guide* by Bill Edwards.

Alaska, creamer, blue **$75.00**
Alaska, cruet, vaseline or canary **$260.00**
Alaska, pitcher, white..**$320.00**
Alaska, sugar bowl, blue **$160.00**
Arabian Nights, syrup, white......................................**$185.00**
Argonaut Shell, salt & pepper shakers, vaseline, pr..**$110.00**

Argonaut Shell, sauce bowl, blue, $45.00

Astro, bowl, canary, 8" **$40.00**
Autumn Leaves, bowl, white.......................................**$30.00**
Barbells, bowl, green...**$42.00**
Beaded Cable, bowl, footed, green **$32.00**
Beaded Drapes, banana bowl, footed, green..............**$37.00**

Beaded Ovals in Sand, nappy, blue $38.00

Beaded Ovals in Sand, sugar bowl, blue $225.00

Beaded Ovals in Sand, toothpick holder, green $180.00

Beaded Shell, creamer, white.....................................$60.00

Beaded Shell, salt & pepper shakers, green $135.00

Beaded Shell, sugar bowl, white $160.00

Beaded Stars, bowl, green...$45.00

Beaded Stars, bowl, white...$30.00

Beatty Honeycomb, creamer, white $40.00

Beatty Honeycomb, mustard pot, blue.......................$90.00

Beatty Honeycomb, pitcher, blue $175.00

Beatty Honeycomb, pitcher, white $130.00

Beatty Honeycomb, sauce bowl, blue.........................$28.00

Beatty Honeycomb, sugar bowl, white $70.00

Beatty Rib, butter dish, blue.....................................$180.00

Beatty Rib, mug, white $30.00

Beatty Rib, salt & pepper shakers, blue, pr.................$65.00

Beatty Rib, spooner, blue..$50.00

Beatty Rib, toothpick holder, white............................$28.00

Beatty Rib, tumbler, blue...$45.00

Beatty Swirl, celery vase, blue $75.00

Beatty Swirl, master bowl, white $38.00

Beatty Swirl, pitcher, blue...$175.00

Berry Patch, nappy, w/dome base, green....................$40.00

Blossom & Palms, bowl, blue $42.00

Blown Drape, pitcher, green..$150.00

Blown Drape, tumbler, green $40.00

Blown Twist, syrup, white $155.00

Blown Twist, tumbler, blue..$50.00

Brideshead (English), butter dish, blue $75.00

Brideshead (English), creamer, blue............................$57.00

Brideshead (English), sugar bowl, blue.......................$60.00

Bubble Lattice, bride's basket, cranberry $120.00

Bubble Lattice, finger bowl, green..............................$30.00

Bubble Lattice, sugar bowl, white $65.00

Bull's Eye, bowl, blue..$40.00

Button Panels, bowl, white $30.00

Buttons & Braids, bowl, blue $45.00

Buttons & Braids, pitcher, white $125.00

Christmas Pearls, salt & pepper shakers, blue $95.00

Christmas Snowflake, tumbler, cranberry..................$100.00

Chrysanthemum Base Swirl, master bowl, cranberry .$100.00

Chrysanthemum Base Swirl, mustard pot, white $100.00

Chrysanthemum Base Swirl, toothpick holder, blue ...$85.00

Circle Scroll, jelly compote, white $100.00

Circle Scroll, pitcher, green or white.........................$400.00

Circle Scroll, tumbler, green..$85.00

Coin Spot, celery vase, cranberry $160.00

Coin Spot, compote, blue...$50.00

Coin Spot, syrup, white..$135.00

Colonial Stairsteps, creamer, blue..............................$90.00

Colonial Stairsteps, sugar bowl, blue..........................$90.00

Consolidated Crisscross, mustard pot, white.............$145.00

Consolidated Crisscross, sauce bowl, cranberry $55.00

Consolidated Crisscross, tumbler, cranberry $110.00

Coral, bowl, blue $40.00

Daffodills, pitcher, white $170.00

Daisy & Fern, butter dish, green.................................$210.00

Daisy & Fern, cruet, blue $180.00

Daisy & Fern, sugar bowl, white $65.00

Daisy Dear, bowl, white...$30.00

Daisy in Crisscross, tumbler, blue...............................$55.00

Daisy May (Leaf Rays), bonbon, blue or green $30.00

Daisy May (Leaf Rays), bonbon, white.......................$16.00

Desert Garden, bowl, white $20.00

Diamond & Oval Thumbprint, vase, green.................$35.00

Diamond Spearhead, mug, green $50.00

Diamond Spearhead, sauce bowl, blue or green.........$30.00

Diamond Spearhead, tumbler, cobalt $60.00

Dolly Madison, butter dish, green $320.00

Dolly Madison, master bowl, blue $50.00

Dolly Madison, pitcher, white....................................$295.00

Dolphin Petticoat, candlesticks, vaseline, pr.............$12.00

Double Greek Key, mustard pot, white $135.00

Double Greek Key, pickle tray, blue..........................$110.00

Double Greek Key, spooner, white.............................$65.00

Dragon lady, rose bowl, white....................................$26.00

Dragon Lady, vase, blue..$40.00

Drapery (Northwood), cruet, white............................$140.00

Drapery (Northwood), pitcher, white.........................$150.00

Drapery (Northwood), tumbler, white $18.00

Duchess (English), cruet, white $140.00

Duchess (English), pitcher, vaseline..........................$150.00

Duchess (English), tumbler, vaseline.........................$25.00

Everglades, creamer, white $70.00

Everglades, salt & pepper shakers, blue, pr.............$230.00

Everglades, tumbler, blue, vaseline or canary...........$70.00

Fan, creamer, green...$60.00

Fan, sauce bowl, blue..$28.00

Fan, sugar bowl, green..$160.00

Fern, celery vase, blue..$100.00

Fern, finger bowl, cranberry $90.00

Fern, sauce bowl, white..$25.00

Flora, butter dish, blue $250.00

Flora, creamer, blue..$90.00

Flora, cruet, white..$400.00

Flora, jelly compote, canary.......................................$115.00

Flora, spooner, white..$80.00

Fluted Scrolls, epergne, white, sm.............................$80.00

Fluted Scrolls, puff box, blue.....................................$55.00

Fluted Scrolls, sauce bowl, canary............................$20.00

Frosted Leaf & Basket, butter dish, canary...............$240.00

Frosted Leaf & Basket, spooner, blue........................$130.00

Fruit Patch, compote, vaseline or canary $65.00

Gonterman (Adonis) Swirl, creamer, blue..................$80.00

Gonterman (Adonis) Swirl, sugar bowl, blue $200.00

Gonterman (Adonis) Swirl, toothpick holder, amber.$150.00

Grape & Cable, centerpiece bowl, white $110.00

Grape & Cherry, bowl, blue..$50.00

Hearts & Flowers, bowl, white...................................$35.00

Hearts & Flowers, compote, blue $75.00

Hobnail (Hobbs), cruet, white $170.00

Hobnail (Hobbs), finger bowl, cranberry...................$90.00

Hobnail (Hobbs), spooner, blue or white...................$90.00

Hobnail (Northwood), mug, white $70.00

Hobnail (4-Footed), creamer, vaseline or canary.........$70.00

Hobnail (4-Footed), sugar bowl, canary or vaseline .**$120.00**
Hobnail & Panelled Thumbprint, sauce bowl, blue **$35.00**
Hobnail & Panelled Thumbprint, tumbler, vaseline **$65.00**
Hobnail in Square (Vesta), creamer, white **$70.00**
Hobnail in Square (Vesta), sauce bowl, white.............**$20.00**
Hobnail in Square (Vesta), tumbler, white.................**$30.00**
Holly, bowl, white, 10"...**$65.00**
Honeycomb, pitcher, blue..**$200.00**
Honeycomb, tumbler, blue **$50.00**
Honeycomb & Clover, creamer, blue.........................**$100.00**
Honeycomb & Clover, master bowl, white..................**$40.00**
Honeycomb & Clover, tumbler, green **$75.00**
Idyll, master bowl, green...**$50.00**
Idyll, sugar bowl, white...**$80.00**
Idyll, tray, white **$75.00**
Inside Ribbing, celery vase, white **$25.00**
Inside Ribbing, salt & pepper shakers, blue, pr..........**$90.00**
Inside Ribbing, toothpick holder, canary **$18.00**
Intaglio, butter dish, blue...**$450.00**
Intaglio, butter dish, white.......................................**$200.00**
Intaglio, spooner, white..**$35.00**

Interior Panel, fan vase, amber opalescent, $40.00

Inverted Fan & Feather, creamer, white.....................**$100.00**
Inverted Fan & Feather, sauce bowl, blue **$45.00**
Inverted Fan & Feather, sugar bowl, white...............**$190.00**
Iris w/Meander, pickle dish, green.............................**$70.00**
Iris w/Meander, pitcher, white...................................**$260.00**
Iris w/Meander, tumbler, white **$55.00**
Jackson, butter dish, blue...**$200.00**
Jackson, candy dish, blue..**$45.00**
Jackson, master bowl, white **$60.00**

Jewel & Fan, bowl, green..**$35.00**
Jewel & Flower, white..**$195.00**
Jewelled Heart, compote, blue **$125.00**
Jewelled Heart, pitcher, white....................................**$95.00**
Jewelled Heart, sauce bowl, green **$25.00**
Jolly Bear, bowl, green..**$100.00**
Lady Caroline (English), basket **$58.00**
Leaf Mold, master bowl, cranberry...........................**$120.00**
Leaf Mold, spooner, cranberry..................................**$110.00**
Leaf Mold, sugar shaker, cranberry **$320.00**
Lords & Ladies, creamer, blue....................................**$55.00**
Lords & Ladies, sugar bowl (open), blue **$60.00**
Lorna, vase, blue..**$30.00**
Lustre Flute, butter dish, white **$125.00**
Lustre Flute, sauce bowl, blue **$25.00**
Lustre Fruit, sugar bowl, white **$90.00**
Many Loops, green **$30.00**
Mary Ann, vase, white..**$35.00**
Northern Star, banana bowl, blue or green.................**$70.00**
Old Man Winter, basket, blue, sm **$55.00**
Over-All Hob, celery vase, white.................................**$45.00**
Over-All Hob, mug, vaseline.......................................**$70.00**
Over-All Hob, spooner, canary **$55.00**
Palm Beach, butter dish, vaseline or canary **$260.00**
Palm Beach, creamer, blue..**$75.00**
Palm Beach, master bowl, blue **$70.00**
Palm Beach, sugar bowl, blue **$120.00**
Panelled Holly, pitcher, white....................................**$300.00**
Panelled Holly, salt & pepper shakers, blue, pr........**$105.00**
Panelled Holly, tumbler, white **$45.00**
Panelled Sprig, cruet, white **$115.00**
Pearl Flowers, nut bowl, footed, green **$35.00**
Pine Cones & Leaves, bowl, white **$50.00**
Poinsettia, fruit bowl, blue **$70.00**
Poinsettia, pitcher, 2 shapes, green **$195.00**
Poinsettia, tumbler, green..**$40.00**
Polka Dot, pitcher, white, rare..................................**$100.00**
Polka Dot, tumbler, blue...**$65.00**
Polka Dot, tumbler, white...**$20.00**
Prince William (English), plate, blue, oval **$40.00**
Prince William (English), sugar bowl (open), vaseline or
    canary **$50.00**
Princess Diana (English), creamer, blue.....................**$50.00**
Princess Diana (English), crimped plate, blue **$40.00**
Princess Diana (English), salad bowl, vaseline or canary.**$70.00**
Queen's Crown (English), compote, low, blue...........**$45.00**

Question Mark, compote, with Georgia Bell exterior, blue, $50.00

Regal (Northwood), master bowl, white **$30.00**

Regal (Northwood), pitcher, white $210.00
Regal (Northwood), salt & pepper shakers, blue, pr...$90.00
Reverse Drapery, plate, green......................................$36.00
Reverse Drapery, vase, white..$16.00
Reverse Swirl, celery vase, vaseline............................$145.00
Reverse Swirl, master bowl, cranberry $75.00
Reverse Swirl, mustard pot, cranberry........................$95.00
Ribbed Spiral, creamer, blue $60.00
Ribbed Spiral, cup & saucer, white..............................$55.00
Ribbed Spiral, novelty bowl, blue.................................$40.00
Richelieu (English), basket, w/handle, canary............$65.00
Richelieu (English), cracker jar, blue..........................$180.00
Richelieu (English), jelly compote, blue......................$65.00
Scroll w/Acanthus, creamer, green $45.00
Scroll w/Acanthus, sauce bowl, blue or green $20.00
Seaspray, nappy, green $32.00
Seaweed, master bowl, white $35.00
Seaweed, salt & pepper shakers, blue, pr..................$110.00
Seaweed, sugar shaker, white......................................$160.00
Somerset (English), juice pitcher, blue, 5½"................$50.00
Somerset (English), tumbler, 3"...................................$25.00
Spanish Lace, cruet, blue...$230.00
Spanish Lace, jam jar, white $170.00
Spanish Lace, pitcher, 3 shapes, vaseline or canary, from
    $195 to...$300.00
Spanish Lace, sauce bowl, blue $22.00
Spanish Lace, tumbler, vaseline or canary $60.00
Squirrel & Acorn, vase, green $60.00
Stripe, condiment set, blue..$350.00
Stripe, pitcher, white $140.00
Stripe, tumbler, white $28.00
Stripe (Wide), cruet, blue...$160.00
Stripe (Wide), syrup, white $160.00
Sunburst on Shield, creamer, white $35.00
Sunburst on Shield, tumbler, blue $100.00
Swag w/Brackets, master bowl, blue............................$70.00
Swag w/Brackets, salt & pepper shakers, white, pr..$125.00
Swag w/Brackets, tumbler, vaseline or canary $55.00
Swastika, tumbler, white $50.00
Swirl, cheese dish, white..$210.00
Swirl, master bowl, cranberry $65.00
Swirl, pitcher, blue..$125.00
Swirl, tumbler, blue $25.00
Swirling Maze, salad bowl, white $40.00
Thousand Eye, pitcher, white $80.00
Thousand Eye, salt & pepper shakers, pr $65.00
Thousand Eye, sugar bowl, white $80.00
Three Fruits, bowl, blue $70.00

Tokyo, salt & pepper shakers, green, pr.....................$70.00
Tokyo, sauce bowl, blue $20.00
Tokyo, tumbler, white $40.00
Water Lily & Cattails, master bowl, blue $55.00
Water Lily & Cattails, plate, white................................$46.00
Wild Bouquet, creamer, white $40.00
Wild Bouquet, salt & pepper shakers, green, pr $80.00
Wild Bouquet, tumbler, blue $100.00
Wild Rose, banana bowl, white $25.00
Wild Rose, mug, blue $28.00
William & Mary (English), creamer, blue $50.00
William & Mary (English), sugar bowl (open), blue....$50.00
Windows (Plain), pitcher, various shapes, white.........$96.00
Windows (Swirled), creamer, blue $80.00
Windows (Swirled), cruet set, white............................$100.00
Windows (Swirled), master bowl, cranberry..............$100.00
Winterlily, vase, footed, white $30.00
Wreath & Shell, master bowl, white $55.00
Wreath & Shell, salt dip, vaseline or canary................$80.00
Wreath & Shell, spooner, vaseline or canary $65.00

Pacific Clay Products

This company was formed by the consolidation of several small California potteries. In the early twenties, they produced stoneware staples from local clay taken from their own mines. Their business, along with many others, suffered at the onset of the Depression, and taking note of Bauer's success, they initiated the production of earthenware dishes which they marketed under the trade name Hostess Ware. During the next decade they developed several dinnerware lines in both vivid colors and pastel glazes as well as artware such as vases, figurines, flowerpots, and large architectural sand jars and birdbaths. 1942 saw the end of all pottery manufacture, due to the company's commitment to full-time defense work. Today they are located in Corona, California, where they specialize in the production of roof tile.

If you're interested in learning more about this company, we recommend *The Collector's Encyclopedia of California Pottery* by Jack Chipman.

Figurine, stylized bird in satin white, circular in-mold mark, $50.00

Tokyo, plate, footed, blue, $55.00

Baby plate, 3 sections w/bunny design border, 1934, 9" .**$65.00**

Baking dish, w/wood clamp-on handle, 8¾"...............**$65.00**

Coffeepot, after dinner; Ring style, Sierra white **$70.00**

Creamer & sugar bowl (open), Ring style, closed handles, sm **$25.00**

Cup, Ring style, lg...**$24.00**

Custard cup, early Ring style, in-mold mark...............**$24.00**

Egg cup, early Ring style **$40.00**

Jar, Ring style, straight-sided, w/lid, in-mold mark, 5" ..**$60.00**

Jug, ball shape, plain **$55.00**

Pie plate, delphinium blue, w/clamp-on handle, 11" dia .**$65.00**

Pitcher, Ring style, 2-qt...**$60.00**

Plate, dinner; plaid...**$30.00**

Teapot, early Ring style, apricot **$50.00**

Tray, Ring style, tab handles, 15" dia........................**$50.00**

Tumbler, ball shape, 5" **$18.00**

Tumbler, Ring style, straight body w/flared rim, 4".....**$18.00**

Black Forest, bowl, pink, handled, 9" **$60.00**

Black Forest, cup & saucer, black...............................**$80.00**

Black Forest, mayonnaise, green, w/ladle...................**$95.00**

Black Forest, vase, green, 6½" **$75.00**

Crow's Foot, bowl, amber, square, 4¼"........................**$8.00**

Crow's Foot, bowl, console; amber, 3-footed, 11½" **$30.00**

Crow's Foot, bowl, cream soup; amber.......................**$10.00**

Crow's Foot, bowl, ruby, 9½".....................................**$75.00**

Crow's Foot, candy dish, ruby, w/lid **$50.00**

Crow's Foot, creamer, ruby.......................................**$25.00**

Crow's Foot, cup & saucer, amber................................**$5.00**

Crow's Foot, plate, amber, 6" **$2.00**

Crow's Foot, plate, luncheon; ruby **$16.50**

Crow's Foot, plate, ruby, square, 6"............................**$4.00**

Crow's Foot, platter, amber, oval...............................**$10.00**

Vase, hand-decorated bird motif, stamped mark, ca 1939, 8¼", $50.00

Vase, low urn shape w/handles, early 1930s, 5" **$60.00**

Paden City Glass

Operating in this West Virginia city from 1916 until 1951, this company is best known to collectors for their many handmade lines of colored dinnerware such as we have listed here. They almost never marked their glass, making it very difficult to identify.

A line of glass animals and birds was also made here; see also Glass Animals and Figurines.

Ardith, tray, green, center handle **$60.00**

Crow's Foot, platter, ruby, 9½", $50.00

Crow's Foot, tumbler, water; cobalt............................**$55.00**

Cupid, cake salver, pink, footed...............................**$140.00**

Cupid, candle holders, green, pr **$135.00**

Cupid, compote, pink or green, 6¼" **$65.00**

Cupid, sugar bowl, pink or green, footed, 4¼" **$75.00**

Gadroon, candle holders, clear, double, 5½", pr, $125.00

Gothic Garden, cake plate, yellow, handled, 10" **$40.00**

Gothic Garden, plate, handled, 10" **$45.00**

Lela Bird, compote, pink, Archaic shape, 6"................**$95.00**

Lela Bird, ice bucket, green $115.00
Mrs B, candlesticks, light blue, low, flat, pr.............$25.00
Mrs B, cup & saucer, ruby........................$10.00
Mrs B, plate, ruby, 8¼" $8.00
Nora Bird, plate, pink or green, 8" $20.00
Orchid, bowl, ruby, footed, 10" $90.00
Orchid, vase, ruby, 8½" $110.00
Peacock & Wild Rose, bowl, pink, rolled edge $80.00
Peacock & Wild Rose, cake plate, pink, footed, 10" ...$45.00
Peacock & Wild Rose, compote, pink, 6¼"................$65.00
Peacock & Wild Rose, ice bucket, pink $130.00
Peacock & Wild Rose, tray, pink, center handle.........$90.00
Peacock & Wild Rose, vase, pink, 8½"...................$140.00
Peacock Reverse, bowl, fruit; cobalt w/ebony foot, 4½x9½"..........................$95.00
Peacock Reverse, creamer & sugar bowl, pink.........$135.00
Peacock Reverse, saucer, cobalt $15.00
Penny Line, cup & saucer, ruby.................$10.00
Penny Line, goblet, ruby, 4¾" $10.00
Penny Line, salt & pepper shakers, amber, pr...........$10.00
Penny Line, water goblet, ruby.................$20.00

Paden City Pottery

Founded in 1907, this company produced many dinnerware and kitchenware lines until they closed in the 1950s. Many were decaled, in fact this company is credited with originating the underglaze decal process.

One of their most collectible lines is called Caliente. It was Paden City's version of the solid-color dinnerware lines that became so popular in the thirties and forties. Caliente's shapes were simple and round, but its shell-like finials, handles, and feet did little to enhance its Art Deco possibilities, which the public seemed to prefer at that time. As a result, it never sold in volume comparable to Fiesta or Bauer's Ring, but you should be able to rebuild a set eventually, and your efforts would be well worthwhile. If you'd like to see photographs of this line and many others produced by Paden City, see *The Collector's Encyclopedia of American Dinnerware* by Jo Cunningham.

Acacia Flowers, creamer, Shell-Crest shape, footed $12.00
Acacia Flowers, sugar bowl, Shell-Crest shape, footed .$12.00
American Beauty, cup & saucer, Minion shape...........$15.00
American Beauty, plate, serving; Minion shape...........$12.00
Caliente, cream soup $15.00
Caliente, creamer $15.00
Caliente, plate, dinner.........................$10.00
Caliente, salt & pepper shakers, pr............$16.00
Caliente, teapot $48.00
Duchess, plate, dinner; round..................$8.00
Duchess, plate, salad; Regina shape $5.00
Far East, creamer, Shell-Crest shape, footed $12.00
Far East, plate, Shell-Crest shape, 9".........$8.00
Far East, sugar bowl, Shell-Crest shape, footed $14.00
Jonquil, creamer, floral pattern on ivory $6.50
Jonquil, plate, salad; Regina shape $6.00

Jonquil, sugar bowl, floral pattern on ivory, handled....$6.50
Modern Orchid, bowl, sauce; round...............$4.50
Modern Orchid, plate, round, sm $4.50
Morning Glory, creamer, Shenandoah Ware.............$8.00
Morning Glory, teapot, Shenandoah Ware.............$35.00
Nasturtium, creamer, Shell-Crest shape $10.00
Nasturtium, plate, dinner; Shell-Crest shape $6.50
Nasturtium, sugar bowl, Shell-Crest shape............$14.00
Paden Rose, plate, bread & butter; 6" dia $4.00
Paden Rose, platter..............................$14.00
Patio, bowl, sauce; Shell-Crest shape $6.00
Patio, plate, dinner; Shell-Crest shape $8.00
Posies, cup & saucer............................$8.00
Rust Tulip, plate, dinner; Shell-Crest shape.................$8.00

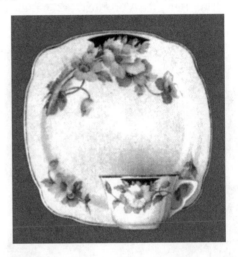

Springblossom, cup, $6.00; plate, dinner, $10.00

Yellow Rose, cup & saucer, Minion shape.................$12.00
Yellow Rose, plate, salad; Minion shape.......$8.00
Yellow Rose, sugar bowl.........................$10.00

Paper Dolls

One of the earliest producers of paper dolls was Raphael Tuck of England, who distributed many of their dolls in the United States in the late 1800s. Advertising companies used them to promote their products, and some were often included in the pages of leading ladies' magazines.

But over the years, the most common paper dolls have been those printed on the covers of a book containing their clothes on the inside pages. These were initiated during the 1920s and because they were inexpensive, retained their popularity even during the Depression years. They peaked in the 1940s, but with the advent of television in the fifties, children began to loose interest. Be sure to check old boxes and trunks in your attic, you just may find some waiting for you.

But what's really exciting right now are those from more recent years — celebrity dolls from television shows like 'The Brady Bunch' or 'The Waltons,' the skinny English model Twiggy, and movie stars like Rock Hudson and Debbie Reynolds. Just remember that cut sets (even if all original components are still there) are worth only about half the price of dolls in mint, uncut, originial condition.

If you'd like to learn more about them, we recommend *Collector's Guide to Paper Dolls* (there are two in the series) and *Collector's Guide to Magazine Paper Dolls,* all by Mary Young. Other references: *Collecting Toys #6* by Richard O'Brien, *Schroeder's Collectible Toys, Antique to Modern,* and *Toys, Antique and Collectible,* by David Longest.

Aladdin, #1606, Western, 1992, M **$3.00**
Alice in Wonderland, Dress the Mad Hatter in Bell-Bottoms!,
    1976, M **$35.00**
Annette Funicello, Whitman, 1958, EX **$30.00**
Annie the Movie, #4330, Milton Bradley, 1983, MIB ...**$12.50**
Archie's Girls, Betty & Veronica, #2764, Lowe, 1964,
    NM **$22.00**

Ava Gardner, Authorized Edition, 1949, M, $100.00

Baby Betsy, #1964, Whitman, 1967, NM **$15.00**
Baby Bumpkins, #1957, Whitman, 1969, NM **$10.00**
Baby Kim, #1969, Whitman, 1962, NM **$20.00**
Baby Sparkle Plenty, Whitman, 1971, M **$25.00**
Baby Tender Love, #1949, Whitman, 1947, NM **$12.00**
Bedknobs & Broomsticks, 1971, M **$20.00**
Betsy McCall, #4744, Whitman, 1971, M **$20.00**
Betty Boop Goes to Hollywood, marked KFS/BS Ltd, cut-&-
    punch dolls w/5 outfits, 1984, M **$5.00**
Beverly Hillbillies (Ellie May), Watkins-Stratmore, 1960s,
    NM **$32.00**
Bonnie Braids, #2724, Saalfield, 1951, EX **$25.00**
Brady Bunch (Greg & Marsha), Whitman, VG **$35.00**
Children From Other Lands, #2089, Whitman, M **$12.50**
Chitty Chitty Bang Bang, 1968, NM **$30.00**
Crissy Fashion & Hairstyle Boutique, #1996, Whitman, 1970,
    NM **$20.00**
Debbie Reynolds, 1960, EX **$25.00**
Dinah Shore & George Montgomery, M **$35.00**
Dolls of All Nations, Merrimack, 1980, EX **$6.00**

Eight Little Playmates, Lowe, 1944, NM **$12.50**

Elizabeth Taylor, Authorized Edition, 1949, M, $100.00

Family Affair (Buffy), 1968, M **$40.00**
First Family (Reagans), M **$12.50**
Flintstones (Fred & Wilma), Wonder Books, 1974, M ..**$35.00**
Freckles & Sniffles, #1959, Whitman, 1972, NM **$12.00**
Gilda Radner, 1979, NM **$10.00**
Ginghams at Home & at School, #1837, Whitman, NM ..**$15.00**
Ginghams Visit Grandma, #1987, Whitman, EX **$10.00**
Grace Kelly, Whitman, 1955, NM **$25.00**
Heart Family, Mattel, 1985, EX **$6.00**
Hollywood Fashion Dolls, #2242, Saalfield, 1942, VG.**$35.00**
John Wayne, 1981, M..**$10.00**
Junior Miss, #250, Saalfield, 1942, NM **$20.00**
Katie's Country Store, #7319F, Western, 1978, EX **$3.50**
Littlest First Born, #1964, Whitman, 1971, M **$5.00**
Magic Mary, #4010-1, Milton Bradley, 1960, NM **$12.00**
Marge's Little Lulu, #1970, Whitman, 1971, NM **$20.00**
Marilyn Monroe, dated 1979, M **$10.00**
Mary Poppins, 1973, M **$30.00**
Mickey & Minnie Steppin' Out, #1986, Whitman, 1977,
    NM **$10.00**
Miss America, #1978, Whitman, 1973, NM **$12.00**
Mother Goose, #4422, Artcraft, EX............................**$12.00**
My Buddy, A Real Pal, Western, 1986, M **$3.50**
Pat Boone, #1968, Whitman, 1959, EX **$15.00**
Patty's Party, #175, Stevens Publishing, 1960s, NM........**$2.50**
Peachy & Her Puppets, #1966, Whitman, 1974, NM......**$8.00**
Pipi Longstocking, NM...**$7.50**
Princess Diana, Western, 1985, EX **$5.00**
Punky Brester, #1532, Golden Press, 1986, M...............**$3.50**
Riders of the West, #2716, Saalfield, 1950, NM..........**$35.00**
Sabrina & the Archies, #1978, Whitman, 1971, NM **$20.00**
Sally & Jane, Lowe, 1964, NM **$12.50**
Sesame Street, #1994, Whitman, 1976, NM..................**$10.00**
Skating Stars, #2105, Whitman, 1954, VG **$15.00**
Snow White, Whitman, 1974, NM **$25.00**

Sunshine Family, #1995, Whitman, 1978, NM $7.50

Tiny Chatty Twins, #1985, Whitman, 1963, EX............$16.00

Tiny Thumbelina, Whitman, 1963, M $31.00

Toodles the Toddler, #1341, Saalfield, 1966, M $12.50

Tricia Nixon, #4248, Artcraft, 1970, NM.....................$16.00

Valerie with Growin' Pretty Hair, Whitman, 1974, M $5.00

Waltons, Whitman, 1975, M $40.00

Welcome Back Kotter, Toy Factory, 1976, MIB $25.00

White House Party Dresses, #1550, Merrill, 1961, EX..$25.00

Woody Woodpecker & Andy Panda, #1391, Saalfield, 1968, NM $22.00

Yogi Bear & Girlfriend Cindy, Wonder Books, 1974, M.$25.00

Raggedy Ann & Andy, Whitman, 1978, 13x10", M, $9.00

Paperback Books

Here is a field that you can really have some fun with. These are easy to find, but you may have to spend some time going through many to find some really good ones. Most collectors prefer those that were printed from around 1940 until the late 1950s. Obviously you could buy thousands, so you may prefer to limit your collection to a particular author, genre, publisher, or illustrator. Be particular about the condition of the books you buy. For more information, refer to *Huxford's Collectible Paperback Books* by Bob and Sharon Huxford.

All My Pretty Ones, Roger Hall, Midwood 105, 1961, EX.$6.50

All Our Yesterdays, Jean Lissette Arceste, Bantam 11350X, paperback original, 1978, EX $10.00

Anything for Kicks, Thomas Vail, Merit Books 602, paperback original, photo cover, 1962, VG $4.00

Assignment Ankara, Edward S Aarons, Gold Medal D 1630, 1966, 4th printing, VG...$3.50

Benefit Performance, Richard Sale, Dell 252, 1948, 1st printing, G $3.50

Big Heat, William P McGivern, Pocket 981, 1954, EX ...$8.00

Bitter Ending, Alexander Irving, Dell 289, cover art by F Kenwood Giles, 1949, VG $6.00

Bloody Gold, Peter Dawson, Bantam 2585, 1963, 1st edition, EX..$10.00

Book of Dreams, Jack Vance, DAW 416, 1981, 1st edition, EX..$2.50

Brass Cupcake, John D MacDonald, Gold Medal 124, paperback original, 1950, VG $50.00

Bridget Loves Bernie, Paul W Fairman, Lancer 74-795, 1972, 1st printing, VG $2.50

Casbah Killers, Nick Carter, Award A 560X, 1969, 1st printing, EX $3.00

Case of the Drowsy Mosquito, Erle Stanley Gardner, Pocket 75523, 1969, 10th printing, EX $4.50

City of Illusions, Ursula K Le Guin, Ace G 626, 1967, 1st edition, G...$2.50

Cold Poison, Stuart Palmer, Pyramid F 1040, 1964, VG.$4.00

Court of Shadows, Giles Jackson, Handi-Book 25, paperback original, 1944, 1st edition, rare, EX.............$40.00

Cross-Eyed Bear Murders, Dorothy B Hughes, Dell 48, 1944, VG..$10.00

Dame's the Game, Al Fray, Popular G 431, VG.............$6.50

Danger Within, Michael Gilbert, Dell 870, VG...............$5.00

Day New York Went Dry, Charles Einstein, Gold Medal K 1446, 1964, 1st printing, G.................................$5.50

Dead Man's Tale, Ellery Queen, Pocket 6117, 1961, EX..$4.00

Death of a Postman, John Creasey, Berkley F 1167, 1965, 1st printing, VG..$3.25

Devil's Mistress, Kenneth Thomas, Gold Medal S 802, 1958, 2nd edition, VG...$10.00

Dirty Harry, Phillip Rock, Bantam S 7329, 1971, 1st printing, EX..$2.00

Doll Maker, Sarban, Ballantine 431K, paperback original, 1960, VG..$7.50

Don't Dig Deeper, William Francis, Lion 123, paperback original, 1953, EX...$20.00

Erotic Traveler, Richard Burton, Berkley S 1509, 1968, 1st printing, EX..$5.00

Firebug, Robert Bloch, Regency RB 101, cover art by artist, signed, 1961 ....$38.50

Flight of the Horse, Larry Niven, Ballantine 23487, paperback original, 1973, EX...$15.00

Footsteps in the Night, Dolores Hitchens, Perma M 4261, 1962, EX..$4.00

Free Country, Warren Dearden, Grove Press B 318Z, 1971, 1st printing, EX..$6.50

From the Sea & the Jungle, Robert Carse, Popular G 102, 1952, EX..$5.00

Garden of Fear, Robert E Howard, Crawford, EX..........$8.00

Gate of Time, Philip Jose Farmer, Belmont B50-717, 1966, EX..$15.00

Girl in Every Bush, AJ Davis, Vega Book 51, paperback original, 1961, VG...$15.00

Golden Girl, Ian Flander, Novel Book 7N765, 1965, 1st edition, scarce, EX...$30.00

Gun Hand, Frank O'Rourke, Ballantine 35, 1953, VG ...$6.50

Han Solo's Revenge, Brian Daley, Ballantine 29840, 1980, EX..**$3.50**

Harvard Has a Homicide, Timothy Fuller, Dell 54, cover illustration by G Gregg, 1944, scarce, VG+, $45.00

Hippie Harlot, Toni O'Brien, Cougar 829, paperback original, 1967, VG.....................................**$20.00**

Honor Thy Godmother, RT Larkin, Lancer 78-703, paperback original, 1972, VG **$6.00**

Housekeeper's Daughter, DH Clark, Avon 336, 1951, VG **$5.00**

How Sleeps the Beast, Don Tracy, Lion 45, 1950, VG ..**$15.00**

I Lost My Girlish Laughter, Jane Allen, Avon 345, paperback original, 1951, 1st edition, EX **$42.50**

In the Face of My Enemy, Joseph H Delaney, Baen 55993, 1985, VG **$3.50**

Jade-Eyed Jungle, Carter Brown, Signet G 2355, 1963, VG..**$4.00**

Jailbait Jungle, Wenzell Brown, Belmont 90-265, 1962, 1st edition, scarce, EX **$20.00**

Johnny Bogan, Leonora Baccante, Popular 423, 1952...**$6.00**

Joy House, Day Keene, Lion 210, paperback original, 1954, VG..**$25.00**

Jungle Kids, Evan Hunter, Dell 4331, 1967, VG..........**$10.00**

Letter From the Earth, Mark Twain, Crest R 647, 1963, 2nd printing, G **$4.00**

Love Kitten, Lester Lake, All Star 520, paperpack original, 1962, VG...**$7.50**

Love Pirate, Jason Stuart, Bee Line 529, 1968, 1st edition, EX **$12.50**

Lovers, Philip Jose Farmer, Ballantine 507, paperback original, 1961, VG...**$8.00**

Lure for Love, James Clayford, Quarter Book 28, paperback original, 1949, EX......................................**$82.00**

Man Without a Planet, Lin Carter, Ace G 606, 1966, 1st edition, VG **$8.00**

Memory of Love, Bessie Breuer, Avon 196, cover art by Ann Cantor, paperback original, 1949, 1st edition, EX...**$60.00**

Merry Month of May, James Jones, Dell 05588, 1972, 1st printing, VG **$4.00**

Miracle on 34th Street, Valentine Davies, Pocket 903, 1952, VG..**$10.00**

Moby Dick, Herman Melville, Pocket PL 28, 1955, VG .**$2.50**

Murder for Two, GH Coxe, Dell 276, VG.....................**$4.50**

Murder on the Links, Agatha Christie, Dell D 288, 1959, EX..**$3.50**

Mystery House, Kathleen Norris, Pocket 453, 1947, EX...**$5.50**

Mystery of Dr Fu Manchu, Sax Rohmer, World Dist 905, 1960, 2nd printing, VG **$5.50**

Night of Fire & Snow, Alfred Coppel, Crest 212, EX **$6.00**

Night of Light, Philip Jose Farmer, Berkley S 2249, 1972, 2nd edition, EX......................................**$2.00**

Old Trade of Killing, J Harris, Banner 60101, VG **$5.00**

One Monday We Killed Them All, John D MacDonald, Gold Medal S 1177, 1961, VG................................**$14.00**

Passport to Terror, Max Daniels, Avon T 423, 1960, 1st edition, EX..**$8.00**

Plain Murder, CS Forester, Dell 30, paperback original, 1954, 1st printing, VG **$5.00**

Plastic Nightmare, Richard Neely, Ace 67095, 1969, VG..**$4.50**

Policewoman, Dorothy Uhnak, MacFadden 60-203, 1965, VG..**$5.50**

Quickness of the Hand, Jim Mayo, Pan G 203, 1959, VG..**$7.00**

Red Moon, Ron Goulart, Warner 75-610, 1974, 1st edition, EX..**$8.00**

Rings of Tantalus, Richard Avery, Gold Medal P 3307, 1975, 1st printing, VG **$2.00**

Rockabilly, Harlan Ellison, Gold Medal S 1161, 1961, 1st edition..**$60.00**

Rooming House, Berton Roueche, Lion 141, paperback original, 1953, scarce, EX **$36.00**

Search the Sky, Frederik Pohl, Ballantine 61, 1954, 1st edition, VG..**$12.00**

Secret Adversary, Agatha Christie, Bestseller B 48, 1944, 1st printing, EX..**$10.00**

Shadow of the Ship, Robert Franson, Ballantine 30688, 1983, VG..**$3.50**

Silver Mistress, Peter O'Donnell, Pan 24360, 1980, 3rd edition, VG..**$4.00**

So Strange Our Love, Joseph Heron, Newsstand U 159, 1961, 1st edition, EX..**$14.00**

Spellstone of Shaltus, Linda E Bushyager, Dell 18274, 1980, 1st edition, EX..**$9.50**

Stardust Voyages, Stephen Tall, Berkley, 1975, 1st edition, EX..**$5.00**

Starseekers, David Garnett, Berkley S 1956, cover art by P Lehr, paperback original, 1971, EX......................**$5.00**

Steel Mirror, Donald Hamilton, Dell 473, 1948, 1st printing, EX..**$6.00**

Stories From the Twilight Zone, Walter Gibson, Bantam A 2046, 1960, G..**$6.50**

Sweetheart of the Razors, Peter Cheyney, Ace H 226, 1958, VG..**$8.50**

Talisman, King & Straub, Berkley 08181, 1985, 1st printing, VG..**$3.00**

Tarzan & Forbidden City, Edgar Rice Burroughs, Ballantine U2020, 1964, 1st printing, EX......................**$10.00**

Tarzan & the Jewels of Opar, Edgar Rice Burroughs, Ace F 204, VG..**$4.00**

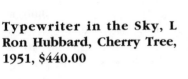

The Hills of Creation, Neil Elliott Blum, Regency, 1962, VG+, $42.00

This Woman, Albert Idell, Red Seal 9, 1952, 1st edition, EX **$15.00**

To Love, To Hate, Fay Adams, Gold Medal 333, paperback original, 1953, VG **$70.00**

Too French & Too Deadly, Henry Kane, Avon 672, 1955, 1st edition, EX.......................................**$12.50**

Trouble Rider, Thomas Thompson, Ballantine 74, 1954, EX **$12.00**

Troubled Midnight, Rodney Garland, Lion LL 128, 1956, EX **$10.00**

Typewriter in the Sky, L Ron Hubbard, Cherry Tree, 1951, $440.00

Walk to the End of the World, Suzy Charnas, Ballantine 25661, 1977, 3rd printing, G **$2.50**

When the Star Kings Die, John Jakes, Ace G 656, 1967, 1st printing, G **$2.50**

Whisper Her Name, Howard Hunt, Gold Medal 268, paperpack original, 1952, 1st printing, VG **$7.50**

Whistle for the Crows, Dorothy Eden, Ace K 184, 1963, 1st US edition, VG.......................................**$6.00**

White Death, Robert Sheckley, Bantam 2685, 1963, 1st edition, EX...**$15.00**

Wind & the Lion, John Milius, Award 1468, paperback original, 1975, EX..**$5.00**

Young Frankenstein, Gilbert Pearlman, Ballantine 24268, 1974, VG **$4.00**

Young Loves, Julian Halevy, Dell 9856, 1964, 1st printing, EX **$2.00**

Young Man of Paris, Henri Caley, Berkley G 28, cover art by Victor Kalin, paperback original, 1956, 1st edition, VG **$28.00**

Zarsthor's Bane, Andre Norton, Ace, 1978, 1st edition, EX **$6.00**

Paperweights

The most collectible weights on the market today are the antique weights, those made from 1845 to 1870 and those made by contemporary artists like Rick Ayotte and Paul Ysart. There are many types — millefiori, sulfides, and those that contain fruit and animals. These are usually very expensive. Among the lower-priced weights are those that were sold through gift stores, made in American glasshouses and studios, China, Murano, Italy, and Scotland.

Ayotte, Rick; berry bouquet on clear ground, 3½"....**$850.00**

Ayotte, Rick; Christmas poinsettias on clear ground, 1991, 3¼"...**$600.00**

Ayotte, Rick; poppy bouquet on clear ground, 1992, 3¾"...**$850.00**

Baccarat, clematis flowers on faceted cobalt ground, 1969, 3⅛"...**$685.00**

Baccarat, Dupont type, interlaced trefoil garland, 1930s..**$400.00**

Baccarat, millefiori circles surround center canes w/arrowheads, 3"...**$1,050.00**

Baccarat, Napoleon III etched into amber-flashed base, faceted, 3¼"...**$450.00**

Baccarat, purple & yellow pansy w/central millefiori cane, green leaves & stem, clear background, star-cut base, 2¾", $300.00

Baccarat, Queen Elizabeth & Prince Philip sulfide on amethyst ground, 1953 ....**$125.00**

Baccarat, scramble w/variations of multicolored latticinio twists, 2½" **$450.00**

Baccarat, spaced concentric millefiori over translucent green ground, starburst center, 2"....................................**$550.00**

Baccarat, wild strawberry on clear, slightly off center, 2¾"...**$1,000.00**

Banford, Bobby; dahlia & buds on dark purple ground, 3¼" **$625.00**

Banford, Bobby; pink flower w/6 buds, leaves & knotweeds, 1992, 3⅛"...**$600.00**

Banford, Bobby; 3 yellow & orange flowers on black ground, 3-4" **$600.00**

Banford, Bobby; 6 pink & white Hawthorn blossoms & buds, 1992, 3⅛"...**$550.00**

Banford, Ray; amethyst iris in yellow & white overlay basket, 3-4" **$1,400.00**

Banford, Ray; 5 pink & white roses on cobalt ground, 4"..**$850.00**

Banford, Ray; 5 ruby red roses on latticinio ground & torsade, 1992, 3⅛"...................................**$800.00**

Clichy, spaced millefiori, pink & green Clichy rose w/in 17 complex canes, 2¼".........................**$575.00**

Clichy, 3-color swirl...........................**$1,200.00**

Donofrio, Jim; black raspberries w/leaves on branch, 1992, 3½"..**$750.00**

Eblehare, Drew; millefiori canes in pink & lime stave basket, moss ground........................**$185.00**

Grubb, Randy; blue, purple & red dahlia bouquet on clear ground, 3⅜"....................................**$375.00**

Grubb, Randy; compound grapes on clear ground, 3¼"..**$375.00**

Grubb, Randy; purple dahlia on clear ground, 1987, 3"..**$250.00**

Grubb, Randy; purple grape cluster on clear ground, 1991, 3"..**$265.00**

Kaziun, Charles; blue, gold & white pansy, gold foil bee on purple, 2⅛".................................**$950.00**

Kaziun, Charles; blue & white flower & buds on red & white jasper ground, K cane, 2¼"..........**$320.00**

Kaziun, Charles; miniature pedestal w/K cane & gold K on pink torsade, 1½", $500.00

Kaziun, Charles; yellow & orange snake on dark green opaque w/goldstone, 2¼"......................**$900.00**

Lundberg, Steven; Japanese blue iris w/sword-like leaves..**$320.00**

Lundberg, Steven; red hibiscus on clear ground, 1991, 3¼"..**$250.00**

Lundberg, Steven; salmon hibiscus w/stamen & leaves on clear...**$250.00**

Manson, William; lizard & flowers, 1991, 3½"..........**$600.00**

Manson, William; 3 Christmas candles, leaves & millefiori garland on amethyst, 3½"...............**$375.00**

Manson, William; 5-petal pink & white flower over white latticinio, 1992, 3"............................**$300.00**

New England Glass, posy garland on latticinio, 2¼".**$850.00**

New England Glass, spaced concentric on latticinio basket, 2½"..**$350.00**

New England Glass, 5 pears & 4 cherries on latticinio ground, 3"..**$850.00**

Parabelle, millefiori heart & matching garland on muslin ground, limited edition.......................**$185.00**

Parabelle, multicolored millefiori in concentric pattern, 1989, 3"..**$265.00**

Perthshire, crown, twisted ribbons & filigree alternate, 1990, miniature......................................**$245.00**

Perthshire, multicolored butterfly silhouette cane centers pattern milleflori, 3⅛"...................**$95.00**

Perthshire, nosegay on pink & chartreuse latticinio, 1977, 2¼"..**$225.00**

Perthshire, patterned millefiori w/horse silhouette, 1982, 2½"..**$175.00**

Rosenfeld, Ken; coleus bouquet of yellow & blue on clear ground, 3⅝"..................................**$500.00**

Rosenfeld, Ken; daffodils on blue ground, 3¼".........**$500.00**

Rosenfeld, Ken; floral bouquet on clear ground, 1987, 3"...**$325.00**

Rosenfeld, Ken; pumpkin patch, 3".......................**$350.00**

Rosenfeld, Ken; tomatoes on vine w/leaves, 1992, 3½"..**$400.00**

Rosenfeld, Ken; 5 multicolored flowers on earth ground w/roots & green foliage......................**$550.00**

Rosenfeld, Ken; 8 flowers in 4 colors & 9 purple flowers on earth ground, 1991, 3½".............**$600.00**

Salazar, Daniel; butterfly over clematis....................**$250.00**

Salazar, Daniel; white crane & blue sky, 2½"............**$275.00**

Smith, Gordon; 2 black raspberries & green berry w/pink blossom, 3¼"..............................**$800.00**

Smith, Gordon; 3 dogwood flowers w/twisted leaves, 1992..**$750.00**

Smith, Gordon; 5 strawberries w/buds on blue ground, 1992..**$800.00**

St Louis, clematis on white swirl latticinio ground, white starburst center, 2"...................**$1,100.00**

St Louis, flower on orange ground, 1973, 3"............**$350.00**

St Louis, pear w/2 green leaves on white ground, faceted top, 1993..............................**$250.00**

St Louis, upright bouquet on green leaves, honeycomb faceted, 2"..............................**$650.00**

St Louis, 2 cherries & leaves on stem on light blue ground, faceted top, 1993..................**$250.00**

Tarsitano, Debbie; 12 pink buds & white flower sprigs tied w/bow, blue ground, 2¾".............**$550.00**

Trabucco, Jon & David; flowers & buds on blue, 1988, 3"..**$300.00**

Trabucco, Jon & David; pink rose & 4 buds w/6 light blue blooms, 3"................................**$300.00**

Trabucco, Jon & David; 2 upright black & white orchids, 3⅛"..**$400.00**

Trabucco, Jon & David; 8 blueberries w/pink flowers & buds, 1992, 3½"..............................**$400.00**

Trabucco, Victor; morning-glory bouquet on clear ground, 1992, 3¼"................................**$600.00**

Trabucco, Victor; yellow rose & buds on cobalt, 3⅜"..**$600.00**

Whittemore, Francis D; calla lilies on blue ground, 1970s, 2½"..**$350.00**

Ysart, Paul; dragonfly in gold & red millefiori & white latticinio on cobalt, 3¼"..**$650.00**
Ysart, Paul; white flower garland on dark green, 2⅞"..**$825.00**

Peach Lustre Glassware

Fire-King made several lines of peach lustre glassware that have been causing lots of excitement among today's collectors. Peach lustre was their white glassware with a fired-on iridescent gold finish (called 'copper-tint' when applied to their ovenware line).

Their first pattern, introduced in 1952 was ('laurel leaf') Peach Lustre. It consisted of a cup and saucer, creamer, sugar bowl, vegetable bowl, dessert bowl, soup bowl, dinner and salad plates, and an 11" serving plate. It was made until about 1965.

Lustre Shell was introduced in the late 1960s. By this time, Peach Lustre was used to describe the finish of the glassware rather than a particular pattern. Lustre Shell, as the name suggests, was a swirled design. In addition to the pieces mentioned above, a 13" platter and a demitasse cup and saucer were added to the assortment. A set of nested mixing bowls were also avilable.

You'll find baking dishes, bowls and mugs in other styles, vases, and miscellaneous items in this glassware too; all are collectible and at this point, at least, none are very expensive. If you'd like to learn more about Peach Lustre, we recommend *Collectible Glassware from the 40s, 50s, and 60s* by Gene Florence.

Baking dish, Copper-Tint (white interior), 1958-71, 8x12½"..**$10.00**
Bowl, dessert; Lustre Shell (scalloped edge), 1965-76, 4¾"...**$4.00**
Bowl, dessert; Royal Lustre (ribbed), 4¾"..................**$4.00**
Bowl, divided vegetable; Copper-Tint (white interior), tab handles, 1958-71, 11¾".......................................**$8.00**
Bowl, mixing; Beaded Rim, 1950-64, 8⅜"..................**$10.00**
Bowl, mixing; Colonial Rim, 1960-71, 6"......................**$80.00**
Bowl, mixing; Swirl, 8", 1949-72................................**$12.00**
Bowl, soup plate; Lustre Shell (scalloped rim), 1965-76, 7⅝"..**$5.00**

Bowl, vegetable; Three Bands, 1950s, 8¼"...................**$6.00**
Cake Pan, Copper-Tint (white interior), round, 1958-71, 8"..**$8.00**
Casserole, Copper-Tint, oval w/au gratin lid, 1958-71, 1½-qt...**$6.00**
Casserole, Copper-Tint (white interior), knob lid, 1958-71, 1-qt...**$8.00**
Cup, Peach Lustre (laurel band), 1952-63, 8-oz.............**$3.50**
Cup, Royal Lustre (ribbed), 1976 ....**$4.00**
Cup & saucer, demitasse; Lustre Shell (scalloped rim), 1965-76 ....**$12.50**
Custard, Copper-Tint, (white interior), 1958-71, 6-oz....**$4.00**
Loaf pan, Copper-Tint (white interior), 1958-71, 5x9"...**$6.00**
Pie plate, Copper-Tint (white interior), 1958-71, 9".......**$5.00**
Plate, dinner; Royal Lustre (ribbed), 1976, 10"...............**$8.00**
Plate, salad; Three Bands, 1950s, 7¾"...........................**$4.00**
Plate, serving; Peach Lustre (laurel band), 1952-63, 11"..**$9.00**
Platter, Royal Lustre, oval, 1976, 9½x13" **$8.00**
Platter, Three Bands, oval, 1950s, 9x12".......................**$8.00**
Sugar bowl, Three Bands, 1950s...................................**$4.00**
Sugar bowl (open), Peach Lustre (laurel band), footed, 1952-63..**$3.50**

Peanuts Collectibles

Charles M. Schultz first introduced the world to the *Peanuts* cartoon strip in 1950. Today it appears in more than 2,000 newspapers across the United States. Its popularity naturally resulted in the manufacture of hundreds of items, each a potential collectible. Books, toys, movies, and theme parks have been devoted to entertaining children and adults alike through the characters of this cartoon — Linus, Snoopy, Lucy, and Charlie Brown.

If you're going to collect *Peanuts* items, be sure to look for the United Features Syndicate logo and copyright date. Only these are authentic. The copyright date (in most cases) relates not to when an item was made but to when the character and the pose in which he is depicted first appeared in the strip.

If you'd like to learn more about this subject, we recommend *The Official Price Guide to Peanuts Collectibles* by Freddi Margolin and Andrea Podey.

Cookie cutters, Charlie Brown, Snoopy, Linus & Lucy, plastic, 1971, MIB, set of 4, $100.00

Bowl, vegetable; Lustre Shell, 8½", $7.00

Bobblehead, papier-mache, Determined, 1979, Snoopy as Santa, Snoopy as Flying Ace, Lucy or Charlie Brown, each, $25 to...$35.00

Bobblehead, papier-mache, Determined, 1979, Snoopy sitting, from $15 to...$25.00

Book, Cartoonist Cookbook, Hobler Dornan & Co Inc Publishers, introduction by Jame A Beard, 1966, from $60 to...$65.00

Cookie jar, Snoopy as chef, Determined, 1978, from $135 to...$150.00

Cookie jar, Snoopy lying on his back on top of his house, One of the Great Joys of Life..., Con Agra, 1976, from $250 to...$300.00

Figure scene, papier-mache, Lucy at psychiatrist booth, Psychiatric Help 5 Cents, Dr Is In/Out, from $50 to ..$60.00

Game, board; Snoopy a Dog-On Funny Game, Selchow & Righter #66, 1959, from $60 to..............................$65.00

Ice bucket, baseball scene w/ Charlie Brown, Snoopy, Peppermint Patty, etc, Schmid, 1972, from $225 to ..$275.00

Magnet, rubber, Simon Simple, 1971–72, each, from $5 to...$6.00

Musical, Christmas tree w/Lucy, Charlie, Snoopy, Sally, Linus around it, plays Joy to the World, Schmid, 1984, from $200 to...$275.00

Musical, ice bucket, plays Love Story, Schmid, 1972, from $250 to..$300.00

Musical, nativity scene, 6 figures w/musical créche, plays Der Tannenbaum, Willitts #440380, from $175 to......$200.00

Musical, Snoopy as sailor, plays Anchors Aweigh, Schmid, 1986, from $125 to..$135.00

Musical, Snoopy in blue Thunderbird as Joe Cool, Woodstock sitting on back tire, plays Don't Be Cruel, Willitts, 1989 ....$165.00

Musical, Snoopy in nightshirt w/teddy bear, plays My Favorite Things, 1986, from $125 to....................$135.00

Musical, Snoopy in red Corvette, Woodstock as hood ornament, plays Puppy Love, Willitts, 1988, from $150 to...$175.00

Nodder, papier-mache, Lego, 1960, name on base: Lucy, Linus or Charlie Brown, each, from $50 to...........$75.00

Nodder, papier-mache, Lego, 1960, name on base: Pigpen, from $65 to...$85.00

Nodder, papier-mache, Lego, 1960, name on base: Schroeder, from $60 to......................................$75.00

Nodder, papier-mache, Lego, 1960, name on base: Snoopy, from $45 to...$75.00

Ornament, ceramic, Snoopy as a clown, Determined, 1975, from $30 to...$40.00

Ornament, ceramic, Snoopy dressed as an angel, Determined, dated 1978, from $35 to....................................$45.00

Ornament, ceramic, Snoopy from Transylvania, wearing top hat & cape, Determined, 1977, from $30 to..........$40.00

Ornament, ceramic, Snoopy standing, holding North Pole sign, dated 1978, from $35 to.................................$45.00

Ornament, ceramic, Snoopy w/bag of French fries, Determined, 1982, from $30 to $40.00

Ornament, ceramic, Snoopy w/bag of toys, in Santa cap, by chimney, Determined, dated Merry Christmas 1979, from $35 to...$45.00

Tea set, tray, 2 cups & saucers, cake plate, Chein, 1970, from $135 to..$150.00

Toy, Deluxe Peanuts Playset, plastic, Lucy doll at psychiatrist booth, Snoopy doll, Charlie doll, Determined, 1977, from $50 to..$65.00

Toy, Fun Figures, rubber, Snoopy as artist, Determined, early 1980s, each...$5.50

Toy, Official Peanuts baseball, facsimile signatures only, Wilson Sporting Goods, 1967 (only), in graphic box, $175 to...$235.00

Toy, Official Peanuts baseball, images of Snoopy & others, Wilson Sporting Goods, 1967 (only), in graphic box, $200 to...$275.00

Toy, Snoopy & His Motorcycle Snap-Tite Kit, battery operated, Monogram, 1971, from $85 to....................$125.00

Toy, Snoopy Electric Comb & Brush, battery-operated Snoopy in boat, comb & brush are oars, Kenner, 1978, from $45 to..$50.00

Toy, Snoopy Family Car (Mystery Car) Snoopy driving, Lucy, Peppermint Patty, Charlie & Woodstock, blinking lights, MIB $85.00

Toy, Snoopy Skiddler & His Sopwith Camel, in vinyl carrying case, Mattel, #4954, from $150 to.................$195.00

Nodder, Snoopy as the Red Baron, 1966, 3¾", EX, $35.00

Pennsbury Pottery

From the 1950s throughout the '60s, this pottery was sold in gift stores and souvenir shops up and down the Pennsylvania Turnpike. It was produced in Morrisville, Pennsylvania, by Henry and Lee Below. Much of the ware was hand painted in multicolor on caramel backgrounds, though some pieces were made in blue and white. Most of the time, themes centered around Amish people, barber shop singers, roosters, hex signs, and folky mottos.

Much of the ware is marked, and if you're in the Pennsylvania/New Jersey area, you'll find lots of it. It's fairly prevalent in the Mid-West as well and can still sometimes be found at bargain prices. If you'd like to learn more about this pottery, we recommend *Pennsbury Pottery Video Book* by Shirley Graff and BA Wellman.

Ashtray, 'It Wonders Me,' 5"...$22.00
Ashtray, pink tulip, octagonal, 3¼x5"...........................$15.00
Ashtray, 2 Amish people $20.00
Bowl, cereal; Pennsylvania Hex, 5½" $15.00
Bowl, Dutch figures & sayings, 11¼" $40.00
Bowl, Folk Art, round, 11" $30.00
Bowl, Folk Art, 5½"..$22.00
Bread plate, Wheat $50.00
Butter dish, Red Rooster...$35.00
Candle holder, Red Rooster $40.00
Candlesticks, hummingbird on flower, 5", pr $145.00
Canister, Pennsylvania Hex, wooden lid, 6½" $60.00
Cheese & cracker set, Red or Black Rooster, 3½x11"..$50.00
Cigarette box, Red Rooster, 2½x4¼"............................$30.00
Coaster, Olson..$16.00
Coffeepot, Folk Art, 6-cup, 8½" $50.00
Creamer & sugar bowl, Folk Art, 4".............................$30.00
Cup & saucer, Pennsylvania Hex..................................$20.00
Figurine, Sparrow, 3x3½"...$45.00
Gravy boat, Black Rooster...$30.00

Mug, beer; Amish couple, 5", $30.00

Mug, beer; fisherman..$25.00
Mug, beer; Sweet Adeline $30.00
Pitcher, Amish man, 2" $20.00
Pitcher, Amish woman, 4" $25.00
Pitcher, Red Rooster, 7¼"...$50.00
Plaque, 2 birds over heart, 7x5".....................................$25.00
Plate, Courting Buggy, 8" $25.00
Plate, Folk Art or Pennsylvania Hex, 10".......................$30.00
Plate, Red Rooster, 10"...$40.00
Platter, Folk Art, oval, 10½"...$25.00
Salt & pepper shakers, Amish heads, pr.........................$55.00
Sugar bowl, Amish man & woman, 4".............................$25.00
Tile, Eagle, 6x6" $30.00

Wall pocket, 'God Bless Our Mortgaged Home,' 6½" .**$40.00**
Wall pocket, blue flowers & leaves, green border, 6½x6½"...**$40.00**

Pitcher, Red Rooster, 5", $30.00

Pepsi-Cola

People have been enjoying Pepsi-Cola since before the turn of the century. Various logos have been registered over the years; the familiar oval was first used in the early 1940s. At about the same time, the two 'dots' between the words Pepsi and Cola became one, though more recent items may carry the double-dot logo (indicated by '=' in our descriptions), especially when they're designed to be reminiscent of the old ones. The bottle cap logo came along in 1943 and with variations was used through the early sixties.

Though there are expensive rarities, most items are still reasonable, since collectors are just now beginning to discover how fascinating this line of advertising memorabilia can be. There are three books in the series called *Pepsi-Cola Collectibles* written by Bill Vehling and Michael Hunt, which we highly recommend. Another good reference is *Introduction to Pepsi Collecting* by Bob Stoddard.

Apron, 1950s, canvas, vendor's waist apron w/Pepsi-Cola across front, red & blue on white, 22", NM...........**$42.00**
Ashtray, glass, bottle cap logo above Lafayette Beverages, NH..., oval, NM **$110.00**
Bank, 1945, embossed plastic, upright 5¢ vending machine, Drink Ice Cold Pepsi=Cola, Marx, 7x3", MIB **$185.00**
Baseball cards, 1989, set of 12 Mark McGuire cards distributed 1 card per 12-can carton, M.........................**$35.00**
Bottle, paper label, Pepsi=Cola, EX **$20.00**
Bottle, 1974, clear w/red & white label, 16-oz, EX........**$8.50**
Bottle carrier, 1940s, bottle cap image, Family Case, 59¢, 10x16", EX **$65.00**
Bottle opener, 1930s, tin bottle shape, 4", EX.............**$35.00**
Cake carrier, metal, red, white & blue w/Pepsi logo, 9x11" dia, EX **$50.00**

Calendar, 1947, Pepsi-Cola Presents Paintings Of The Year, complete, metal strip at top, EX.............................$50.00

Calendar, 1950, 6 pages featuring 2 months & girls in various poses, artist signed, metal strip at top, 22x13", EX ..$135.00

Clock, 1954, double glass, Say Pepsi Please, 15" dia, EX..$175.00

Clock, 1960s, metal frame w/plastic lens, Pepsi logo at 12 w/numbers 3, 6 & 9, 18x14", EX.............................$65.00

Coaster, 1940s, cork, Pepsi=Cola logo in red, white & blue, 4" dia, NM...$22.00

Decal, 1960, bottle cap on yellow background, Have A Pepsi below, 12x12", EX..$25.00

Fan, 1940, cardboard w/wood handle, America Keeps Cool..., features Pepsi & Pete, NM, $110.00

Hat, soda jerk; 1970s, paper, Have A Pepsi Day!, red, white & blue, adjustable, EX...$4.00

Kaleidoscope, 1970s, can shape, EX.............................$25.00

Menu board, 1950s, tin, Special Today at top, bottle cap & Hits The Spot below, 30x19½", EX, A $200.00

Menu board, 1951, Pepsi-Cola Hits The Spot, 20x30", EX $85.00

Miniature 6-pack, 1950s, vertical white & blue striped carton & 6 bottles, bottle cap logo & printed Pepsi-Cola, NM...$60.00

Miniskirt, 1960s, Feeling Free, EX...............................$25.00

Paperweight, etched glass, bottle cap shape w/vertical Pepsi-Cola oval logo, NM...$55.00

Pin, 1942, metal, Pepsi=Cola embossed on bar attached to ball, Scholastic Softball Champions, 1x1¼", NM ...$45.00

Playing cards, 1951, complete w/box.............................$50.00

Poster, 1989, Indiana Jones & the Last Crusade, 35x23", EX $8.50

Radio, 1950s, upright vending machine, Pepsi-Cola across top, leather case, 7", NM $140.00

Radio, 1970s, bottle shape w/oval Pepsi-Cola label, 8½", NM...$35.00

Sign, 1940, easel back, gloss-coated cardboard, We Use...Pepsi=Cola...Exclusively In Making Rum Drinks, 12x6", M...$200.00

Sign, 1940s, cardboard, girl holding glass, Pepsi=Cola bottle cap on left shoulder, 24x36", NM $175.00

Sign, 1940s, embossed tin, Drink Pepsi=Cola, 12 Ounces 5¢, Peps You Up..., red, yellow & blue, 18x28", VG.$170.00

Sign, 1940s, tin, self framed, Enjoy Pepsi=Cola, Bigger Better, 48x24", VG $275.00

Sign, 1940s, tin flange, 2-sided, Ice Cold & Sold Here lettered above & below red Pepsi=Cola on white wavy band, NM, $425.00

Sign, 1950, celluloid, bottle cap w/Drink Pepsi=Cola Now!, 9" dia, G $250.00

Sign, 1950s, cardboard, Be Sociable, Have A Pepsi & bottle cap upper right of 2 couples, horse & dog, 26x38", EX $145.00

Sign, 1950s, embossed tin, Drink...Delicious Delightful, green background w/red border, 3½x9⅞", M.....$180.00

Sign, 1950s, light-up & revolving, plastic w/metal frame, Take Home Pepsi, The Light Refreshment, 16x12", NM ...$200.00

Sign, 1950s, tin (Mexican), girl by table w/bottles in bowl, Pepsi-Cola button in right corner, 20x30", EX $250.00

Sign, 1950s, tin flange (Mexican), Tome Pepsi-Cola, EX .$575.00

Sign, 1951, die-cut cardboard stand-up, woman holding glass w/Pepsi-Cola disk logo near bottom, 20x48", EX..$100.00

Sign, 1960, mirror glass sign, shows lady w/bottle in hand looking in mirror, 6x14", G $30.00

Sign, 1967, easel back, celluloid, Say Pepsi Please, 10x12", M...$45.00

Thermometer, 1956, tin, Have A Pepsi on white V-shaped field tapering to slanted bottle cap, 27", NM.......$200.00

Thermometer, 1973, tin, stylized Pepsi cap logo top & bottom, squared corners, 28", NM.............................$35.00

Toy hot dog wagon, 1940s, plastic w/detachable man & umbrella, bottle logo on sides, Ideal, NMIB, ...$500.00

Toy truck, 1958, tin, Ny-Lint w/various logos in cargo bed, enclosed top & back, open sides, 16", EX $175.00

Toy van, 1950s, tin, bottle & round Pepsi-Cola logo on top, script logo on sides, friction, 4", NM $225.00

Tray, 1939, tilted bottle over US map, Bigger & Better, Coast To Coast & Pepsi=Cola on rim, 11x14", NM $550.00

Tray, 1955, deep-dish, Coney Island scene, plain rim, 12" dia, NM **$45.00**

Tray, 1955, deep-dish, Coney Island scene, plain rim, 12" dia, NM **$45.00**

Tray, 1970s, deep-dish, 3 bottles on ice, lettering inside rim, 13" dia, EX................................**$20.00**

Vendor cap, 1960, paper, Be Sociable, Have A Pepsi, EX..**$5.00**

Perfume Bottles

Here's an area of bottle collecting that is right now coming into its own. Commercial bottles, as you can see from our listings, are very popular. Their values are based on several factors, for instance: is it sealed or full, does it have its original label, and is the original package or box present.

Figural bottles are interesting, especially the ceramic ones with tiny regal crowns as their stoppers.

Commercial Perfumes

Ambush, Dana, clear w/paper label, embossed mark on base, glass stopper, 2" **$25.00**

Amou-Daria, Revillon, 3-tiered crystal shaped like a log cabin, Made in France etched in bottom, 4x4" ..**$60.00**

Anais Anais, Cacharel, milk glass w/floral label, screw-on cap, 4" **$15.00**

Apple Blossom, Helena Rubenstein, clear cylindrical form w/3 sections, paper label, 2⅞" **$45.00**

April Showers, Cheramy, clear w/green Bakelite screw-on cap & tassel, 1930s, 2¼" **$45.00**

Arpege, Lanvin, clear w/gold neck, black glass intaglio stopper, marked Lanvin France on bottom, 6¾"..........**$65.00**

Asuma, Coty, frosted ball-form w/molded flowers, ribbed ball stopper, original box, 2¼"............................**$175.00**

Ave Maria, Prince Matchabelli, clear crown shape w/metal screw-on cap, miniature **$25.00**

Ave Maria, Prince Matchabelli, clear crown shape w/gold enamel, ball stopper, label on bottom, 3¼", $175.00

Balalaika, Lucien LeLong, clear gourd shape w/hot pink label, pink screw-on cap, 8"..................................**$35.00**

Balalaika, Lucien LeLong, clear w/gold enameled swirl design, gold label, conforming stopper, 4" **$75.00**

Blue Grass, Elizabeth Arden, clear w/blue & silver label, glass stopper molded w/mare & colt, original box, 2½"..**$175.00**

Blue Smoke, Goubaud, light blue modernistic faceted shape w/gold label, 5⅛"..**$45.00**

Christian Dior, crystal urn shape w/handles, enameled label, Made in France etched in bottom, 6⅞".................**$80.00**

Cordon D'Argent, Elizabeth Hartley, clear hourglass shape w/royal blue & gold label, black plastic cap, 1⅞" ..**$16.00**

Crepe de Chine, Millot, heavy crystal w/foil label, Lucite cap, 2¾"..**$35.00**

Danger, Ciro, stacked rectangles w/black Bakelite cap, 3"..**$60.00**

Dark Brilliance, Lentheric, clear w/gold enameled lettering, gold ball cap, black & gold box, 1½" **$100.00**

Dreamy, Luzier, clear round bottle w/plastic flame-type cap, gold label on bottom, 2½"...............................**$15.00**

Duchess of York, Prince Matchabelli, clear crown shape w/metal cap, label on bottom, 1¼".......................**$25.00**

Emeraude, Coty, clear w/green & gold label, screw-on cap, 4¾" **$25.00**

Essence Imperial Russe, Lengyel, clear crown shape w/green collar, glass & cork stopper, 3¾" **$12.00**

Essence Rare, Houbigant, clear glass resembling column of ice, silver label on stopper, 6½"..........................**$145.00**

Estee Lauder's Private Collection, frosted gourd shape, label on bottom, w/contents, 1⅞"................................**$25.00**

Fantasque, Riviera, clear w/hot pink & gold label, black plastic screw-on cap, miniature **$12.00**

Femme du Jour, frosted glass w/dancing nymph molded on front, metal cap, purse size, w/original box **$50.00**

Flowers of Devonshire, Mary Dunhill, spherical w/8 ridged sections, label around neck.....................................**$80.00**

Francois, clear w/ivory & black label, tassel around neck, ivory-colored Bakelite cap, 2⅜" **$22.00**

Gamin, Gragonard, gold-covered urn shape, 2⅜" **$90.00**

Gardenia, Lander, clear w/colorful label, green ribbed cap, 5¼" **$15.00**

Gardenia, Lander, clear w/gold label, green plastic jewel-like cap, 4⅝"..**$25.00**

Golden Shadows, Evyan, clear bell shape w/molded vertical lines, gold label, handle-shaped stopper, 3¼" **$60.00**

Guerlinade, Guerlain, heavy crystal, Baccarat, no label, conforming stopper, 7½" **$195.00**

Heaven Scent, Helena Rubenstein, frosted angel, gold cap, label on bottom, 2½" **$55.00**

Heure Intime, Vigny, clear w/embossed squares, triangular silver label, faceted stopper, 4" **$55.00**

Ideal, Houbigant, clear w/gold enameled label, bronze metal cap, 2¾"..**$14.00**

Imprevu, Coty, clear w/gold enameled lettering, glass stopper, 2⅝" **$25.00**

Impromptu, Lucien LeLong, clear & frosted futuristic shape, label at neck & base, 4½"....................................**$150.00**

Jabot, Lucien LeLong, clear glass bell shape w/drapery design, gilded wood cap, original box, 1½" **$185.00**

Joy, Jean Patou, black glass w/gold label, long dauber w/red button stopper, 2¼" **$25.00**

L'Aimant, Coty, clear w/fishscale motif & gold label, frosted stopper, contained in plastic world globe on metal base **$100.00**

L'Air du Temps, Nina Ricci, clear w/Lalique dove stopper, 3½"..**$85.00**

L'Or, Coty, clear teardrop shape, conforming stopper, Baccarat emblem on base, 6"..........................**$75.00**

L'Origan, Coty, clear w/embossed label, gold metal cap, 1¾"..**$35.00**

La Vierge Folle, Gabilla, clear w/crosshatch design, no label, original box, 5½"..................................**$85.00**

Le Gui, Duvelle, opaque green w/metallic label, cylindrical, 6½"..**$100.00**

Le Vertige, Coty, clear w/gold label around neck, fluted stopper, original box, 3"................................**$135.00**

Lily of the Valley, Dralle, Hamburg, cylindrical w/8 frosted panels & 8 clear, gold label on front, ground stopper, 4"..**$70.00**

Lily of the Valley, Ronni, clear w/gold label, maroon plastic screw-on cap, 2⅛"....................................**$15.00**

Madam Rochas, clear w/enameled label, faceted sides, white plastic cap, 2⅜"....................................**$20.00**

Maxim's of Paris, black glass w/gold enameled design, gold neck cord, red plastic stopper, 12"..........**$175.00**

Miracle, Lentheric, clear & frosted glass w/Art Deco design , label on front & back, original box, 2½".............**$145.00**

Miracle, Lentheric, clear w/etched floral design, label on neck cord, w/contents, sealed, 7"....................**$80.00**

Miss de Rauch, De Rauch of Paris, clear w/20-ribbed dome stopper, footed, 3¼"..................................**$15.00**

Miss Dior, Christian Dior, clear w/enameled label, plastic screw-on cap, 1⅝"....................................**$25.00**

Monico, clear w/white enameled lettering, frosted glass stopper w/cork tip, 2¾"................................**$50.00**

Most Precious, Evyan, textured heart shape w/metal label, screw-on cap, 2¼"....................................**$35.00**

New Horizons, Ciro, clear w/blue enameled lettering, eagle stopper, 2¾"..**$45.00**

Nocturnes, Caron, clear w/round plastic stopper, rectangular, 2⅜"..**$15.00**

Nuit de Noel, Caron, black glass rectangular shape w/label around shoulder, conforming stopper, 4⅜"..........**$30.00**

Oeillet Fane, Grenoville, clear w/gold label, frosted rooster stopper, 3"..**$175.00**

Oh La La, clear waisted form w/black enameled lettering, frosted fan-shaped stopper, 4½"..................**$65.00**

Ombre Rose, Brosseau, frosted glass octagon w/molded snowflakes & abstract designs, ball stopper, w/contents, 12"..**$250.00**

Opalia, L Clavel, clear w/black & gold label, black plastic screw-on cap, 1¼"....................................**$12.00**

Orchidee Bleue, Cordey, clear w/ivory-colored Bakelite cap, no labels, 1"..**$35.00**

Pois de Senteur de Chez Moi, clear w/paper label, green enameling on stopper, 6"................................**$65.00**

Quelque Fleurs, Houbigant, clear w/metallic-type flowered label, mushroom stopper, 4¾x4½"..................**$60.00**

Rosee d'Arabie, Alain Steven, clear w/green paper label, glass stopper, w/contents, 2"........................**$20.00**

Royal Secret, Germaine Monteil, clear w/gold enameled label, white plastic screw-on cap, 1¾"..........**$22.00**

Ruffles, Oscar de la Renta, clear boat shape w/enameled lettering, tall rectangular stopper, 10¼"..........**$165.00**

Safari, Ralph Lauren, clear w/cut glass appearance, plastic cap w/faux silver & tortoise shell design, 10".....**$165.00**

Secret of Suzanne, clear w/enameled label, ribbed neck & shoulder, ground glass stopper, 2¾"..........**$65.00**

Shalimar, Guerlain, draped urn-shaped bottle w/frosted sides, rose-bud stopper, 4¾"........................**$25.00**

Spellbound, Lynette, crackle glass w/dark gold cone-shaped cap, label around neck & on front, round, ca 1944, 4½"..**$30.00**

Styx, Coty, clear w/gold label, frosted glass stopper molded w/thorns, original gold foil box..........................**$150.00**

Succes Foo (Smash Hit), Schiaparelli, white glass w/allover green enameling, gold trim, fig leaf shape, marked, 3", $750.00

Surrender, Ciro, clear faceted diamond-shape w/labels on side, conforming stopper, 3½"......................**$65.00**

Sweet Pea, Renaud, clear w/blue stripes, brass cap, w/original red leather case, 2¼"............................**$45.00**

Sweet Pea, Renaud, green glass flask shape w/gold labels, pointed stopper, 3½"................................**$175.00**

Tailspin, Lucien LeLong, clear w/red & gold neck label, embossed logo on metal screw-on cap, 5"..........**$18.00**

Toujours Fidele, D'Orsay, clear pillow form w/enameled lettering, molded dog on stopper, signed Cristal Nancy, 3½"..**$200.00**

Town, Helena Rubenstein, round tiered bottle w/black enameled label, flame stopper, 1936, 7¾"............**$70.00**

White Shoulders, Evyan, clear w/gold label, gold rose-shaped cap, w/contents, 1¾"........................**$22.00**

Wind Song, Prince Matchabelli, clear crown shape w/enameled label, gold plastic cap, w/contents, 2½"........**$20.00**

With Pleasure, Caron, clear keg shape w/gold enameled lettering & bands, Baccarat emblem on base, 1947, 3½"..**$175.00**

Woodhue, Faberge, clear w/brown & cream label, white 8-sided cap, w/contents, 2⅜"........................**$35.00**

Zigane, Corday, clear violin shape w/hot pink label, pink screw-on cap, 4"..**$35.00**

Miscellaneous

Blown glass, cobalt, 12-sided, flared mouth, smooth base, 6½"..**$75.00**

Blown glass, gold, green & orange swirls on white, gold mercury glass base & stopper, 3¼"..................**$65.00**

Blown glass, yellow heart shape, gold mercury glass stopper w/long dauber, 2⅜" $80.00

Cut glass, green to clear w/prism & mirror cuttings, faceted stopper, 6x3" $135.00

Cut glass, ruby panels w/gold highlights, ornate stopper, 7x3¾" $150.00

Cut-out brass over glass, round screw-on cap, purse-size $20.00

Enameled sterling, light green w/pink roses, ca 1915, 2" $110.00

Figural, duck, clear w/multiple facets around ovoid shape to form body, duck's head forms stopper, 6½".......$100.00

Figural, elephant, white ceramic w/red eyes & mouth, metal crown stopper, impressed Germany & #13293, 3"..$85.00

Figural, fan, porcelain w/multicolored flowers & gold highlights, metal crown stopper, Sitzendorf mark, 2½" .$65.00

Figural, inkwell, amber & clear glass overlay w/clear top & neck, amber & clear stopper, 2½" $100.00

Figural, lady holding urn, ceramic w/multicolored paint, crown stopper, signed Limoges, 6".....................$125.00

Figural, Pierette w/ruffled collar & bouquet, ceramic w/multicolored paint, Germany, 3½" $125.00

Italian glass, red cased in light yellow, ball shape w/long & slender stopper, 10¼" $100.00

Milk glass, vertical ribs w/swirling stars, 8".................$24.00

Opalescent white glass, octagonal panels w/enameled flowers & gold leaves, 3"...$145.00

Pink glass w/conforming stopper, Art Deco style, 5½" .$25.00

Pez Candy Dispensers

Though Pez candy has been around since the late 1920s, the dispensers that we all remember as children weren't introduced until the 1950s. Each had the head of a certain character — a Mexican, a doctor, Santa Claus, an animal, or perhaps a comic book hero. It's hard to determine the age of some of these, but if yours have tabs or 'feet' on the bottom so they can stand up, they were made in the last ten years. Though early on, collectors focused on this feature to evaluate their finds, now it's simply the character's head that's important to them. Some have variations in color and design, both of which can greatly affect value. For instance, Batman may have a blue hood and a black mask, or both his mask and his hood may match; sometimes they're both black and sometimes they're blue. (The first one is the most valuable, but not much more than the all-black variation.)

Condition is important; watch out for broken or missing parts. If a Pez is not in mint condition, most are worthless. Original packaging can add to the value, especially if it is one that came out on a blister card. If the card has special graphics or information, this is especially true. Early figures were sometimes sold in boxes, but these are hard to find. Nowadays you'll see them offered 'mint in package,' sometimes at premium prices. But most intense Pez collectors say that those cellophane bags add very little if any to the value.

For more information, refer to *A Pictorial Guide to Plastic Candy Dispensers Featuring Pez* by David Welch, *Schroeder's Collectible Toys, Antique to Modern,* and *Collecting Toys #6* by Richard O'Brien.

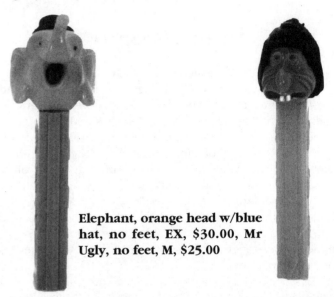

Elephant, orange head w/blue hat, no feet, EX, $30.00, Mr Ugly, no feet, M, $25.00

Bandit, NMIP $15.00
Batman, no feet, MIP $15.00
Bugs Bunny, no feet, NMIP..$15.00
Captain America, MIP $35.00
Charlie Brown, w/feet, M $7.00
Clown, w/chin, no feet, M $40.00
Daffy Duck, no feet, MIP..$15.00
Donald Duck, no feet, loose, M....................................$7.00
Donkey, gray, NMIP $20.00
Dr Skull, M...$10.00
Droopy Dog, w/feet, painted ears, MOC $6.50
Engineer, no feet, EX..$40.00
Girl, blond hair, M $15.00
Hulk, dark green, no feet, MIP $20.00
Indian, w/feet, whistle head, MOC..............................$6.50
Kola, no feet, M $30.00
Maharajah, no feet, EX $35.00
Mickey Mouse, no feet, NMIP $15.00
Miss Piggy, American, MIP $3.00
Panda, no feet, M..$25.00
Parrot, w/feet, whistle head, MOC...............................$6.50
Pilot, no feet, EX...$55.00
Pluto, no feet, MIP $12.00
Policeman, no feet, M...$40.00
Pumpkin, no feet, loose, M...$12.00
Roadrunner, w/feet, MOC $7.00
Rooster, M..$22.00
Rudolph, no feet, M...$25.00
Scrooge McDuck, no feet, M.......................................$25.00
Semi Tractor, NMIP $2.00
Skull, no feet, NM $12.00
Smurfette, loose, M...$10.00
Snoopy, w/feet, NMIP $15.00
Snowman, no feet, NMIP..$15.00
Spiderman, no feet, EX...$12.00
Tom (Tom & Jerry), w/feet, NMIP...............................$15.00

Tweety Bird, w/feet, MOC **$7.00**
Wile E Coyote, w/feet, NMIP **$30.00**
Woodstock, w/feet, NMOC **$15.00**

Pfaltzgraff Pottery

Pfaltzgraff has operated in Pennsylvania since the early 1800s making redware at first, then stoneware crocks and jugs, yellowware and spongeware in the twenties, artware and kitchenware in the thirties, and stoneware kitchen items through the hard years of the forties. In 1950 they developed their first line of dinnerware, called Gourmet Royal (known in later years as simply Gourmet). It was a high-gloss line of solid color accented at the rims with a band of frothy white, similar to lines made later by McCoy, Hull, Harker and many other companies. Although it also came in pink, it was the dark brown that became so popular. Today these brown stoneware lines are one of the newest interests of young collectors.

The success of Gourmet was just the inspiration that was needed to initiate the production of the many dinnerware lines that have become the backbone of the Pfaltzgraff company.

A giftware line called Muggsy was designed in the late 1940s. It consisted of items such as comic character mugs, ashtrays, bottle stoppers, children's dishes, a pretzel jar, a cookie jar, etc. All of the characters were given names. It was very successful and continued in production until 1960. The older versions have protruding features, while the later ones were simply painted on.

For further information, we recommend *Pfaltzgraff, America's Potter,* by David A. Walsh and Polly Stetler, published in conjunction with the Historical Society of York County, York, Pennsylvania.

Gourmet Royal, bowl, cereal; 5½" **$5.00**
Gourmet Royal, bowl, soup; 2¼x7¼" **$5.00**
Gourmet Royal, butter dish, 1¼-lb...............**$14.00**
Gourmet Royal, casserole, round.................**$18.00**
Gourmet Royal, cheese shaker, bulbous, 6¾"............**$15.00**
Gourmet Royal, cruet, coffeepot shape, fill by spout, 5" .**$15.00**
Gourmet Royal, flour scoop, tapers down to open end, 7½"
   long...**$12.00**
Gourmet Royal, meat platter, 13¾x9⅝" **$25.00**
Gourmet Royal, plate, dinner; 10" **$10.00**
Gourmet Royal, salt & pepper shakers, pr **$8.50**
Gourmet Royal, sugar bowl..........................**$8.00**
Muggsy, ashtray **$125.00**
Muggsy, cigarette server..............................**$125.00**
Muggsy, clothes sprinkler bottle, Myrtle, black, from $200
   to...**$250.00**
Muggsy, clothes sprinkler bottle, Myrtle, white, from $125
   to...**$175.00**
Muggsy, cookie jar, character face, minimum value .**$250.00**
Muggsy, jigger, w/handle, sm, from $40 to.................**$50.00**
Muggsy, mug, action figure (golfer, fisherman, etc), any,
   from $65 to...**$80.00**

Muggsy, mug, Black action figure **$125.00**

Muggsy, mug, character face, any, from $35 to $40.00

Muggsy, tumbler **$60.00**
Muggsy, utility jar, hat lid, from $175 to **$200.00**
Village, butter dish, ¼-lb...................................**$14.00**
Village, canister set, set of 4................................**$85.00**
Village, creamer...**$6.00**
Village, custard cup..**$4.50**
Village, mustard jar **$10.00**
Village, plate, dinner; 10½"................................**$6.00**
Village, platter, oval, 14"..................................**$10.00**
Village, sugar bowl **$6.00**

Phoenix Bird Pottery

This is a type of blue and white porcelain dinnerware that has been imported from Japan since the early 1900s. It is decorated with the bird of paradise and stylized sprigs of Chinese grass. You'll find several marks on the older pieces. The newer ones, if marked at all, carry a paper label; backgrounds are whiter and the blue more harsh.

For more information, we recommend *Phoenix Bird China* by Joan Collett Oates.

Bowl, fruit; scalloped, 9" **$65.00**

Candlestick, scalloped ring handle, 2x5", $95.00

Casserole, round **$135.00**
Creamer, bell form, #6......................................**$20.00**
Creamer & sugar bowl, w/lid, #20............................**$45.00**
Cup & saucer, chocolate; scalloped..........................**$25.00**

Egg cup, double, 3¼" **$18.00**
Gravy boat, Nippon, #2 ....**$75.00**
Gravy ladle, 6" **$45.00**
Hot-water pot & cover, #1 ....**$65.00**
Ice-cream dish, oval w/inverted scallops **$35.00**
Mustard pot **$45.00**
Pitcher, lemonade; bulbous **$145.00**
Pitcher, water; bell shape **$135.00**
Plate, dinner; 9¾" **$50.00**
Plate, hand-painted, scalloped rim, 7¼" **$35.00**
Platter, 12" **$50.00**
Salt & pepper shakers, 6-sided, pr **$25.00**
Sugar bowl, Nippon, #11 ....**$30.00**
Teapot, #10 ....**$55.00**
Tureen, oval, w/lid **$135.00**
Water tankard, bell shape **$135.00**

Powder box, Hummingbirds, blue **$100.00**
Sugar bowl, Lacy Dewdrop, blue wash, w/lid **$65.00**
Vase, Astor, mother-of-pearl design on tan over milk glass, 7" **$85.00**
Vase, Batchelor Button, satin milk glass w/green in background areas, 7" **$170.00**
Vase, Bicentennial, crystal w/red, white & blue design **$50.00**
Vase, Fern, crystal w/blue in background areas, 7" **$80.00**
Vase, Jewel, milk glass w/green background areas, 5" .**$100.00**
Vase, Madonna, milk glass w/tan in background areas, mother-of-pearl design, 10" **$200.00**
Vase, Primrose, milk glass w/green in background areas, 8¾" **$350.00**
Vase, Wild Rose, milk glass with wine in background areas, mother-of-pearl design, 10!/2" **$245.00**
Vase, Zodiac, milk glass w/med blue in background areas, frosted design, 10" **$500.00**

Phoenix Glass

Though this company has operated in Monaca, Pennsylvania, from 1880 until the present (it's now a division of the Newell Group), collectors are primarily interested in the sculptured glassware lines they made during the thirties and forties. These quality artware items were usually made in milk glass or crystal with various color treatments or with a satin finish. Most of the time, the backgrounds were colored and the relief designs left plain. The glassware was never signed, instead the company used paper labels in the shape of a phoenix bird.

For more information, refer to *Phoenix and Consolidated Art Glass* by Jack D. Wilson.

**Vase, umbrella; Thistle, white, 1930s, 18",
$450.00**

Bowl, Diving Girl, frosted design on lavender, oblong.**$250.00**
Bowl, Lacy Dew Drop, pink on milk glass, square, 8x8".**$45.00**
Candlesticks, Sawtooth, dark blue on milk glass, pr.**$140.00**
Comport, Moon & Star, pearl lustre on milk glass, 8" .**$45.00**

Pie Birds

Popular since Victorian times, a pie bird is a hollow figure used in the middle of the pie to allow steam to vent through the top crust. They're glazed inside and out and were made as various types of birds, as elephants, and sometimes as chefs and bakers. At least one hundred 'new' pie birds are on the market today, and the number is growing. Many of these are more expensive than the old ones, and if you can't live without them in your collection and must buy them, far be it from me to discourage free enterprise. As far as we know, most of the new designs are original — just don't be fooled into buying them for old ones. There are new black birds everywhere, though. They'll have yellow beaks and protruding white-dotted eyes. If they're on a white base and have an orange beak, they're old.

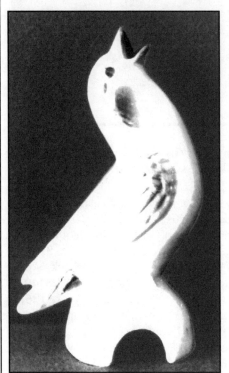

**Singing canary,
pink or green
multicolor,
4½", $45.00**

Benny the Baker, Cardinal China, ceramic..................**$65.00**
Black bird, yellow beak, white dot eyes, Japan, new ...**$5.00**
Black bird on white base, ceramic **$30.00**
Canary, yellow w/pink lips **$18.00**
Duck, long-necked, yellow, blue or pink w/black accents, US..**$22.50**
Elephant, ceramic..**$40.00**
Granny Pie Baker, Lorrie Design, Japan.....................**$23.00**
Rooster, Cleminson, multicolored..............................**$18.00**
Songbird, blue or pink, ceramic **$22.50**
White bird, blue dot eyes, Japan, new **$5.00**

Pierce, Howard

Mr. Pierce was a potter who had his own studio in Claremont, California, where from the 1940s until he died a few years ago he designed distinctively styled sculptures of animals, birds, and human figures that were sold in gift shops and department stores nationwide. Many of his animal 'families' were sold in pairs or three-piece sets.

You may also find examples of vases and lamps with openings containing small animals or plant forms. Most of his work, except for some of the smaller animals, was marked.

If you'd like to learn more about Howard Pierce and his work, *The Collector's Encyclopedia of California Pottery* by Jack Chipman contains a chapter devoted to him.

Quail family, brown w/brown speckles on white breasts, stamped, 3-piece set, $100.00

Ashtray, bowl shape w/3-pointed rim, lava glaze **$55.00**
Bear, gray mottled glaze, 1950s, 6".............................**$40.00**
Bust, lady's head, hair longer on left side, square base, brown, 7"...**$125.00**
Bust, stylized lady's head, hands cupped by cheek, square base, brown agate, in-mold mark, ca 1956, 10½".**$140.00**
Cat family, stylized, 3-piece **$125.00**
Fawn, sitting, head turned to side w/ears up, gray, various glazes, in-mold 'Pierce,' 7½"..................................**$38.00**
Fish, usually w/vertical stripes, stamp mark 'Howard Pierce,' 5" & 3¼", 2-piece set..**$85.00**

Giraffes, standing w/heads up on rectangular bases, brown agate, 1950s, 10½", pr...**$62.00**
Girl & boy on irregular-edged base, 4½".....................**$35.00**
Girl w/book seated on stump, 2 holes for flowers or use as a pencil holder, 6½"..**$60.00**
Girl w/dog on irregular-edged base, 4½".....................**$40.00**
Girl w/pot, right hand holding up bottom of skirt, gray glaze, 9" **$75.00**
Gondola bowl, brown on white, 5x9½"..........................**$38.00**
Heron on base, experimental blue glaze, 9½"...........**$160.00**
Monkey, brown mottled glaze, 6"................................**$35.00**
Owl magnet, brown glaze, ca 1989, 2½".....................**$12.00**
Pelican, beak not touching body, 8½"..........................**$75.00**
Penguin, black & white, ca 1953, 7"............................**$45.00**
Pigeon, white w/brown head & bottom, 1950s, 7½"...**$25.00**
Vase, burgundy w/high glaze green interior, irregular lip, incised 'Howard Pierce P-5 Calif,' 3½"..................**$35.00**
Vase, cylinder shape w/mottled green shading from bottom to top, 7¼"..**$30.00**

Pin-Back Buttons

Literally hundreds of thousands of pin-back buttons are available; pick a category and have fun! Most fall into one of three fields — advertising, political, and personality related, but within these three broad areas are many more specialized groups. Just make sure you buy only those that are undamaged, are still bright and unfaded, and have well-centered designs and properly aligned printing. The older buttons (those from before the 1920s) may be made of celluloid and the cardboard backing printed with the name of a company or a product.

See also Political.

Rocky Lane, 1¼", $12.00; Monte Hale, 1¼", $12.00; Bill Elliott, 1¼", $12.00

A&P, Growing w/America above & For 75 Years below encircled logo flanked by 2 men holding dates (1859-1934), 3" dia, EX.....................$16.00

American Hereford Breeders Association arched above head image of Hereford bull, black & white, 1910s, 1¾" dia, EX...............................$18.00

Annie A New Musical, Annie's full image leaning on the letter N in Annie, black & white, 3½" dia, M.............$3.00

Bette Midler, I Saw Bette At The Palace arched above illustrated waist-length image of her singing, 1970s-80s, 2" dia......................$16.00

Budweiser, This Is Budweiser Month lettered below eagle logo, red & white, early 1900s, 1¾" dia, EX..........$16.00

Buick, I'm A Buick Man, white lettering on red, round, EX........................$21.00

Buster Brown Walking Club, logo w/lettering above & below Tread Straight arrow, red, white & blue, 1920s, oval, EX......................$25.00

Cadillac, Now! A Cadillac For Only $1,345 lettered on red & white background, 1" dia........................$15.00

Carnation Cream, image of product can, multicolored, early 1900s, 1¼" dia, EX.......................$28.00

Casper the Friendly Ghost, 1950s, M...........................$20.00

Challenger, hexagonal image of space shuttle bordered by shuttle name & astronauts' names, 2¼" dia, M........$5.00

Cocker Power, image of Joe Cocker showing bicep muscle w/lettering above & below, early 1970s, 2¼" dia, EX..........................$12.00

Davy Crockett, photo head image encircled by Fess Parker As Davy Crockett, brown & white, 1950s, 1¼" dia, EX......................$25.00

DeSoto, white pennant w/Welcome lettered in red above DeSoto Plymouth Homecoming in white on red background, 2" dia, EX.......................$15.00

Dick Clark, head image above white band w/his signature, green & white, 1960s, 3" dia, EX..........................$18.00

Disney's Caribbean Beach Resort, head image of Goofy encircled by lettering, M....................$5.00

Disneyland & Thumper's Easter Egg Hunt 1984 lettered at left of Thumper the rabbit, multicolored, 3" dia, EX.....$10.00

Donald Duck, image of Donald w/lighted birthday candle on his head w/1934-1984 birthday message, 2½" dia, EX..........................$12.00

Elsie's Bagel & Cream Cheese Club, Junior Member arched above Elsie's head & bagel, mulitcolored, 1930s, 1¼" dia, EX........................$28.00

Evel Knievel, rocket-type craft encircled by Snake River Canyon September 8, 1974, multicolored, 2½" dia, EX.........................$16.00

Fabian, name in script, no image, early 1960s, 1" dia, EX.........................$15.00

Fonzy, The Fonz lettered at left of image, 1¼" dia, M...$3.00

Ford, Be Wise... lettered above image of touring car, Drive a Ford below, red, white & blue, 1910s, 1¼" dia.....$75.00

Ford, Have A Ford Summer, 1972, EX.......................$3.00

Ford Mustang's 20th Anniversary, 1984, 3" dia, EX........$5.00

Ford V8 arched above America's Choice '34 superimposed over Ford grille close-up, round, EX....................$80.00

General Dwight D Eisenhower, bust image w/name encircled by stars & stripes, red, white, blue & black, 1940s, 1¼", EX................................$6.00

Greatful Dead, figure on armadillo w/Greatful Dead, Houston, Texas, July 1981 lettered above, red, white & blue, 2¼".........................$2.00

Halloween, lg orange jack-o'-lantern image, 1920s, 1¼" dia.........................$12.00

Hopalong Cassidy In The Daily News, illustrated head image encircled by lettering, 1950s, 2" dia, EX.....$25.00

Howdy Doody, It's Howdy Doody Time lettered above Howdy's smiling face, orange & black, 2" dia, M...$3.00

HP Hood & Sons Milk, head image of cow in landscape encircled by lettering, multicolored, 1920s, 1¼" dia, EX......................$16.00

Indian Apple-Us Gloves, apple logo in center, banded edge, 1930s, ⅞" dia, EX............................$10.00

Jiminy Cricket, pictures Jiminy in center encircled by I've Got Environmentality, Earth Day 1992, 2½" dia......$9.00

Johnny Thunder, Famous Western Stuntmen arched above image w/signature, yellow & black, 1¾", M............$2.00

Karma Biscuits, bust image of girl holding product, multicolored, round, EX........................$20.00

King Arthur Flour, features multicolored image of King Arthur on horse, ca 1896, ⅞", EX....................$45.00

Latest Greatest Plymouth lettered on flag in center, Four Years Better... above, round, EX.........................$25.00

Leave It To Beaver, image of June & Ward Cleaver, 1½" dia, M.........................$2.00

M*A*S*H, features the cast w/M*A*S*H lettered above, black & white, 1¾", M........................$2.00

Mascot Cereal, The Lightning Warrior lettered around image of Rin-Tin-Tin, ¾" dia, NM.......................$16.00

Metropolitan Life Insurance Co, company name in blue center e/building, lettering on rim, ⅞" dia, EX.............$6.00

MIA Missing or Prisoner, black question mark in center of white silhouette of man's head in profile, 1¾" dia, EX.........................$12.00

Mickey Mouse, I Grew Up On lettered above image of Mickey posed as band leader, name lettered below, 1½" dia, EX........................$15.00

Mickey Mouse Seed Shop, Mickey posed as gardener saying Let's Grow America, ...Wonderful World of Gardening, 3" dia, EX.........................$50.00

Nash, I Am Voting For arched above Nash in script, For '49 below, red on white, edge chips, 1½".....................$10.00

Nash, There's None As New As Nash in red lettering on white, round, EX................................$20.00

Penney's Back To School Days, lettering around boy & girl walking to school, red & black on white, 1930s, 1¼" dia, EX.........................$15.00

Peter & Gordon Fan Club, black & white image of the duo encircled by lettering, 1½" dia, EX.........................$16.00

Philip Morris, bellhop yelling Vote For Philip Morris, ca 1930s, round, EX................................$35.00

Pontiac, logo in center w/Pontiac lettered above, A General Motors Masterpiece below, red & blue on white, 2" dia, EX.........................$25.00

Pontiac, 2 birds on a branch w/1 watching the other sing It's Spring, Get a Pontiac, multicolored, 1930s, ⅞" dia, EX..................$15.00

Red Comb Poultry Foods, rooster's head encircled by lettering, black & white w/red, early 1900s, 1¼" dia, EX..................$18.00

Red Goose Shoes, Red Goose Club Member lettered above & below centered logo, red on white, 1940s, 1¼" dia, EX..................$15.00

Remington-UMC, white on red, round, VG..................$15.00

Rolling Stones, black & white close-up photo image of group w/name lettered below, 1960s, 3½" dia, EX..................$50.00

Roy Rogers & Trigger, close-up image w/lettering below, black & yellow, 1¾" dia, M..................$6.00

Shaun Cassidy, close-up frontal view w/As Joe Hardy under signature, 3" dia, M..................$6.00

Snow White Jingle Club, image of Snow White & the 7 Dwarfs encircled by lettering, red, white & blue, 1938, 3" dia, EX..................$150.00

Sunset Carson, black & white slightly turned pose w/name on white curved band below, 1950s, 1¾" dia, EX..................$25.00

Swift's Golden Neck Layer lettered above proud hen flanked by 2 baskets of eggs, 1930s, 1½" dia, EX..................$12.00

Winchester, bull's-eye target w/W on inner circle, Always shoot... on outer circle, 1" dia, NM..................$32.00

Kellogg's Pep Pins

Chances are if you're over forty, you remember them, one in each box of PEP (Kellogg's wheat-flake cereal that was among the first to be vitamin fortified). There were eighty-six in all, each carrying the full-color image of a character from one of the popular cartoon strips of the day — Maggie and Jiggs, the Winkles, Dagwood and Blondie, Superman, Dick Tracy and many others. Very few of these cartoons are still in print.

The pins were issued in five sets, the first in 1945, three in 1946, and the last in 1947. They were made in Connecticut by the Crown Bottle Cap Company, and they're marked PEP on the back. You could wear them on your cap, shirt, coat, or the official PEP pin beenie, a orange and white cloth cap made for just that purpose. The Superman pin — he was the only D.C. Comics Inc. character in the group — was included in each set.

Not all are listed below. These are the most valuable. If you find an unlisted pin, it will be worth from $10.00 to $15.00. Values are given for pins in near mint condition.

Andy Gump..................$15.00
BO Plenty..................$30.00
Dagwood..................$35.00
Dick Tracy..................$30.00
Felix the Cat..................$75.00
Flash Gordon..................$30.00
Jiggs..................$25.00
Little King..................$15.00
Little Moose..................$15.00

Maggie..................$25.00
Mama De Stross..................$30.00
Mama Katzenjammer..................$25.00
Olive Oyl..................$30.00
Orphan Annie..................$25.00
Phantom..................$75.00
Popeye..................$30.00
Superman..................$35.00
Winkles Twins..................$75.00
Winnie Winkle..................$15.00

Pinup Art

Some of the more well-known artists in this field are Vargas, Petty, DeVross, Elvgren, Moran, Ballantyne, Armstrong, and Phillips, and some enthusiasts pick a favorite and concentrate their collections on just his work. From the mid-thirties until well into the fifties, pinup art was extremely popular. Female movie stars from this era were ultra-glamorous, voluptous, and very sensual creatures, and this type of media influence naturally impacted the social and esthetic attitudes of the period. As the adage goes, 'Sex sells.' And well it did. You'll find calendars, playing cards, magazines, advertising, and merchandise of all types that depict these unrealistically perfect ladies. Though not all will be signed, most of these artists have a distinctive, easily identifiable style that you'll soon be able to recognize.

Calendar, Marilyn Monroe posed in black lace, 1954, 15x9", EX, $80.00

Ad for Jantzen Bathing Suits, Skip the Flattery Darling, man & woman, June 1938, NM..................$15.00

Blotter, salesman's sample, Drawing Attention, girl w/easel & brush, Gillette Elvgren, 1950s, 4x9", NM..................$10.00

Blotter, salesman's sample, redhead on divan wearing yellow dress & white fur jacket, Billy DeVorss, 8¾x3¾", NM..................$10.00

Blotter, w/1953 calender, No Kisses & a Girl & Her Honey Are Soon Parted, brunette in sunsuit, Earl Moran, 4x3", NM..................$10.00

Book, Pinup, A Modest History, Mark Garbor, 1972, hard-bound, minor wear to dust jacket, EX...................**$35.00**

Book, Playboy's Vargas Girls, Playboy Press, copyright 1972, paperback, NM...**$45.00**

Book, Playboy's Vargas Girls, Playboy Press, copyright 1972, hard-bound, w/dust jacket, NM **$65.00**

Book, Sirens, Chris Achilleos, Dragon's World Ltd, 1st edition, 1986, paperback, NM **$15.00**

Calendar, Playboy's Playmate, features Jayne Mansfield, 1960, NM **$120.00**

Calendar, Vargas Art, in original glassine envelope, EX.**$75.00**

Calendar print, Mother May I Go Out & Swim, brunette girl wearing a white towel, signed Earl Moran, 1945, 14x5", EX...**$25.00**

Calendar print, Sheer Delight, woman in sheer negligee at fireplace, Elvgren, 1940s, 14x11", NM..................**$25.00**

Calendar sheet, blond in sheer red slip, 1947, 12x9", M **$12.50**

Calendar top, Hook, Line & Sinker, redhead in halter top, shorts & straw hat w/fishing pole, Walt Otto, 13½x11", EX...**$20.00**

Cartoon, I Suppose This Bum Check Is Your Idea of a Joke!, Esquire, April 1937, Petty, EX...............................**$14.00**

Cartoon, Mind If I Phone My Husband?, blond w/telephone, Esquire, December 1935, Petty, EX.......................**$14.00**

Gatefold, blond in sheer white teddy holding telephone, Esquire, December 1941, NM.............................**$30.00**

Gatefold, Curves Are Trumps, Esquire, July 1941, Alberto Vargas, EX **$25.00**

Gatefold, Esquire's Lady Fair, Denise Darcel in low-cut evening dress & white gloves, Mike Ludlow, 1955, 18x13", NM...**$16.50**

Gatefold, kneeling blond in short navy jacket holding sailor doll, Esquire, July 1941, NM..................................**$30.00**

Gatefold, redhead in tennis outfit on yellow background, True, February 1945, NM **$25.00**

Greeting card, fully dressed girl undresses as card unfolds, Earl Macpherson, open: 17x24", EX.......................**$12.00**

Greeting card, WWII, features Chicago Sun Purple Heart Girl on cover, EX **$8.00**

Key chain telescope viewer, view of girl when held to light, extends to 1¼", EX...**$12.50**

Magazine print, blond in sheer white gown & silver heels, Esquire, September 1940, Vargas, 14x9½", NM.....**$12.50**

Magazine print, blond watching lightning through curtain, Esquire, April 1936, 14x10", M **$16.00**

Mutoscope card, blond in military uniform being chased by unseen pursuer, Zoe Mozert, 1940s, NM **$8.00**

Mutoscope card, Heads Up, redhead w/alluring eyes on black background, Rolf Armstrong, 5¼x3¼", EX **$8.50**

Mutoscope card, On the Beam, brunette in low-cut costume w/straw hat tied around her neck, Rolf Armstrong, EX...**$10.00**

Poster, The Petty Girl, blond in maroon teddy, 22x14", VG **$50.00**

Print, Favorite Model, nude blond woman in classic pose, rust & pink background w/yellow highlights, 1945, 10x8", EX **$20.00**

Print, Figures Don't Lie, redhead on scales wearing black teddy & heels, Louis F Dow Co, 9½x7½", NM......**$15.00**

Print, Golden Dreams, nude Marilyn Monroe on red background, ca 1935, 10x8", EX **$45.00**

Print, portrait of pretty redhead looking over her shoulder, signed DeVross, framed..**$35.00**

Print, Twinkle Toes, brunette in 2-piece swimsuit sitting on diving board, blue background, 6x4½", EX..........**$15.00**

Program from Ice-Capades, saluting redhead in Marine's uniform w/baton on front cover, George Petty, 1944, 11x8½", VG...**$30.00**

Record album jacket, He Really Digs Jazz & Music for the Boyfriend, Decca #DL8314, Petty girl in bikini, rare, VG **$25.00**

Shot glass, Playboy Playmate w/key painted on glass, 1960s, M **$40.00**

Planters Peanuts

The personification of the Planters Company, Mr. Peanut has been around since 1916, adding a bit of class and dash to all their advertising efforts. Until the company was sold in 1961, he was a common sight on their product containers and at special promotional events. He was modeled as salt and pepper shakers, mugs, whistles, and paperweights. His image decorated neckties, playing cards, beach towels, and T-shirts. Today he has his own fan club, a collectors' organization for those who especially enjoy this area of advertising memorabilia.

Just about everyone remembers the Planter's Peanut jars, though they're becoming very scarce today. There are more than fifteen different styles and shapes, and some have been reproduced. The earliest, introduced in 1926, was the 'pennant' jar. It was octagonal, and the back panel was embossed with this message: 'Sold Only in Printed Planters Red Pennant Bags.' A second octagonal style carried a paper label instead. Pennant jars marked 'Made in Italy' are reproductions, beware!

Ashtray, Mr Peanut in bisque standing beside peanut shell, Mr Peanut stamped on base, 4½x3", EX..............**$120.00**

Bank, Mr Peanut figure, plastic, 8½", from $18 to **$22.00**

Bank, painted cast-iron Mr Peanut figure w/legs straight, round base, 11½", G **$30.00**

Belt buckle, brass, features Mr Peanut, 1970, M **$25.00**

Belt buckle, tan plastic, pictures Mr Peanut & guns, child size, 2x4", EX..**$45.00**

Bookmark, die-cut cardboard figure of Mr Peanut, speckled orange, black & white, 1920s-30s, 8x3", EX..........**$15.00**

Canister, embossed plastic figural peanut w/Planters in script along side, stands upright, reissue, 11x5x5", NM..**$8.00**

Charm bracelet w/1 charm, M.....................................**$40.00**

Coasters, commemorating Planters 75th Anniversary, Mr Peanut logo, cork base, set of 3, M **$10.00**

Coloring book, Around the World w/Mr Peanut, features Mr Peanut standing before world map, Book No 3, 7x10", EX...**$15.00**

Cookbook, Cooking the Modern Way, 40 pages, includes original mailer depicting Mr Peanut, 1948, 8½x5½", NM..**$25.00**

Costume, tan plastic body w/embossed gold lettering on black hat, 47x18" dia, $500.00

Display, clear amber plastic head of Mr Peanut w/blue hat, 1960s, 12x10" dia, EX................................**$40.00**

Doll, Mr Peanut, cloth, 19", EX **$18.00**

Jar, Clipper, original lid..**$150.00**

Jar, Fish Bowl, rectangular label................................**$150.00**

Jar, Football, peanut finial...**$300.00**

Jar, glass w/embossed peanuts on 4 corners, peanut finial on lid, 13x8", EX...**$150.00**

Jar, octagon, pennant 5¢, 8 sides embossed.............**$800.00**

Jar, octagonal, pennant 5¢, 7 sides embossed..........**$250.00**

Jar, pennant 5¢, paper label.......................................**$175.00**

Jar, Please Keep, Mr Peanut, 1930s............................**$65.00**

Jar, running peanut, worn siver paint, w/lid, 12x8" dia, VG..**$250.00**

Jar, square, peanut finial, Planters embossed each side.**$150.00**

Jar, Streamline, tin lid **$65.00**

Jar, 6-sided, printed square label **$60.00**

Key-chain charm, Mr Peanut, 2¼"..................................**$5.00**

Lapel pin, die-cut tin lithograph of Mr Peanut, 1½", NM..**$18.00**

Lighter, Bic, features Mr Peanut, unused, M **$12.00**

Marbles in plastic bag, 1940s-50s, EX.........................**$25.00**

Mug, white ceramic w/Planters lettered under Mr Peanut figure, gold trim, pointed handle, 6½x3½" dia at rim, NM..**$25.00**

Nut chopper, fits 8-oz Planters can.............................**$20.00**

Nut dish, Mr Peanut standing in center, gold-tone metal, M...**$50.00**

Paint book, features Washington through Eisenhower w/Kennedy insert, 32 pages, 1960, 10½x7½", NM..**$24.00**

Peanut bag, paper, Mr Peanut promoting Salted Peanuts at right of tall flag lettered Pennant, 6x3", NM............**$8.00**

Peanut bag, paper, The Peanut Store, lettering over diamond graphics w/Mr Peanut lower left, 80-oz, NM **$15.00**

Peanut butter maker, 1967, M.....................................**$40.00**

Plate, features Mr Peanut, pewter type, 1 of 3000, 1970s, 6" dia, EX **$35.00**

Playing cards, Planters Tavern Nuts, complete, NM **$15.00**

Pocketknife, flat gold peanut w/raised lettering, Taylor Cutlery Co, Nov 2, 1976, 2⅞" closed, NM..................**$27.00**

Punchboard, product name & 5¢ above cans flanking listed numbers on white background, punchboard below, unused, NM...**$60.00**

Ramp walker, Mr Peanut figure, plastic, 1984, 3", M...**$30.00**

Ruler, wood, Eat a 5¢ Bag, 12", EX............................**$20.00**

Sack, black & red image of Mr Peanut on brown burlap, 1950s-60s, 2-lb, 14x8", NM **$30.00**

Salt & pepper shakers, Mr Peanut figural, tan & black plastic, 4", pr...**$18.00**

Salt & pepper shakers, red plastic Mr Peanut figures, 3", pr, $10.00

Serving spoon, Mr Peanut figure molded on front & back of handle, metal, 1950s, 5", NM...............................**$25.00**

Snack dish & 4 cups, gold designs on bottom & sides of 6" metal plate w/Mr Peanut in center, 3" cups, EX+.**$45.00**

Straw, white plastic w/3-D Mr Peanut mouthpiece, 8", NM..**$10.00**

Swizzle stick, blue plastic w/Mr Peanut **$4.00**

Whistle, tan plastic w/Mr Peanut, 2½"..........................**$8.00**

Wristwatch, recent-issue presentation watch given to salesman, Mr Peanut on dial, crinkled leather buckle strap, NM..**$25.00**

Plastics

Early plastics such as Bakelite, Catalin, gutta percha, and celluloid are not new to collectors, and most of us realize the value of the wonderful radios and jewelry items, but did you know that even plastics from after WWII are becoming collectible as well? The market is not yet well established, and here's an area where you will be able to make some good buys well before the public in general while prices are still low.

Because plastic was such an inexpensive material, manufacturers produced literally thousands of household items with the intent of very short-term appeal. Their theory was simple: replace existing models with new ones that varied just enough to stimulate sales. Buyers would be willing to throw out the old and replace with the new, since most items were very cheap. As a result, new colors, new styles, and new looks epitomized the public's fascinations and fads. Pop beads, flying saucer lamps, and kitchenware items in streamlined shapes all had their time in the spotlight.

Items that you may want to buy are interesting pieces of jewelry, well-designed kitchenware and appliances, and things that relate to celebrities, Disney characters, advertising, or special holidays. Whatever aspect of plastic collecting you personally enjoy should afford you good shopping and lots of satisfaction.

See also Jewelry; Catalin Napkin Rings.

Ashtray, Catalin, marbled light green, square, 4½" **$30.00**
Bottle opener, Catalin, chrome plate w/red, green or amber handle **$10.00**
Bridge pencil holder, celluloid, pearlescent ivory on black animal **$60.00**
Butter mold, Catalin, green, amber or brown w/floral carvings, 2½" **$32.00**
Cake breaker, Catalin, red, green or amber handle, CJ Schneider **$4.00**
Checkers, Catalin, red & black, full set in box............**$32.00**
Chopsticks, Catalin, ivory, pr **$3.00**
Cigarette box, Catalin, cylindrical w/chrome inserts, 4½" **$40.00**
Cigarette holder, Catalin, multicolored or w/rhinestones, long..**$25.00**
Clock, Bakelite, dark brown Deco mantel type w/wind-up alarm **$60.00**
Clock, Cataline, scalloped case, electric alarm, Sessions, 4¼" dia **$52.00**
Corkscrew, Catalin, chrome w/red, green or amber handle **$12.50**
Crib toy, Catalin, 11 multicolored spools on string, 1940s..**$50.00**
Crib toy, Catalin body, clown, loalin head, Tykie Toy ..**$60.00**
Dice, Catalin, ivory or red, ¾" , pr..................................**$2.00**
Dice cup, Catalin, leather or cork lined **$30.00**
Drawer pull, Catalin, 2-color octagon w/inlaid dot **$3.00**
Dresser mirror, celluloid, oval beveled glass w/ivoroid handle, 13"..**$30.00**
Dresser set, celluloid, marbled amberoid & green, 7-piece .**$70.00**
Egg beater, Catalin, red, green or amber handle **$16.00**
Flatware, Catalin, 1-color handle, 3-piece matched place setting..**$7.50**
Flatware, celluloid, green pearl on black handle, 3-piece set..**$9.00**
Gavel, Catalin, ivory, lathe turned **$18.00**
Inkwell, Catalin, amber, single well, Carvacraft Great Britian **$70.00**
Lamp base, Catalin, brass w/amber Deco design, 10".**$30.00**
Letter opener, Catalin, Deco design w/black & amber stripes **$20.00**
Letter opener, Catalin, marbled light green dagger shape **$20.00**
Manicure set, celluloid, 4 mini-tools in tube holder w/painted floral design..**$35.00**

Memo pad, Catalin, amber, Carvacraft Great Britain ...**$45.00**
Nail brush, Catalin, dark amber turtle shape, 3½" **$16.00**
Nail brush, Catalin, marbled light green, 2½x1½"..........**$8.00**

Napkin holder, red chef figure holding black kettle & skillet, Papol Plastic Inc, $25.00

Pencil sharpener, Catalin, orange, no decal, ¾x1".......**$30.00**
Pencil sharpener, Catalin, red scotty w/carved details on black base..**$30.00**
Penholder, Bakelite, black, streamlined **$22.50**
Penholder, Catalin, amber & black striped Deco design .**$35.00**
Picture frame, Catalin, amber & red Deco style, 6x7" .**$45.00**
Picture frame, Lucite, clear square Deco style, 6"........**$14.00**
Poker-chip rack, Catalin, cylindrical w/50 chips, 2½" .**$85.00**
Powder box, Catalin, amber & black fluted round shape, 2½"..**$45.00**
Purse, Lucite, clear box style..**$45.00**
Salad servers, Catalin, chrome w/ivory, black or brown handles, pr..**$30.00**
Salt & pepper shakers, Catalin, amber & ivory mushroom shape, 1⅞", pr..**$25.00**
Salt & pepper shakers, Lucite, translucent red, 4", pr..**$12.00**
Shaving brush, Catalin, amber, red or green...............**$18.00**
Spatula, Catalin, stainless steel w/amber, green or red handle **$5.00**
Strainer, Catalin, red, green or amber handle, 2¾"........**$4.00**
Swizzle stick, Catalin, amber or red baseball-bat shape ..**$4.00**
Syrup pitcher, Catalin, glass w/green, red or amber handle..**$18.00**
Thermometer, Catalin, amber & dark green rectangle, Taylor, 4" **$45.00**
Writing set, Catalin, marbled black, green or amber Deco design, 5-piece in original box **$150.00**

Playing Cards

Here is another collectible that is inexpensive, easy to display (especially single cards), and very diversified. Among the endless variations are backs that are printed with reproductions of famous paintings and pinup art, carry advertising of all types, and picture tourist attractions and world's fair scenes. Early decks are scarce, but those from the forties on are usually more attractive anyway, so pick an area that interests you most and have fun! Though they're usually not dated, you may find some clues that will help you to determine an approximate date. Telephone numbers, zip codes, advertising slogans, and patriotic messages are always helpful.

Everett Grist has written an informative book, *Advertising Playing Cards*, which we highly recommend to anyone interested in playing cards with any type of advertising.

Advertising

Blue Bonnet Margarine, Blue Bonnet girl & lettering at top & bottom on blue background, MIB **$12.50**

Budweiser Beer, resembles beer can, MIB....................**$8.50**

Camel Cigarettes, resembles cigarette package, MIB...**$12.50**

Campbell's Chunky Soup, resembles can of soup, white lettering on red, ...Ready To Serve, MIB....................**$5.00**

Du Pont, gold logo on navy background w/2-line gold border, MIB....................**$4.00**

Early Times Whiskey, bottle of whiskey on bright yellow background, Just Mention My Name in black, MIB..**$8.50**

Eckerd Drug Stores, product name in white oval on black background, white border, MIB....................**$4.00**

Evinrude, shield logo on blue background w/white border, MIB **$16.50**

Gerber, round image of the Gerber baby on red background, MIB **$8.50**

Goodrich Silvertowns, lettering & logo at both ends on red background, white line border, MIB....................**$6.50**

Holiday Inn, hotel sign on white background w/black border, MIB....................**$6.50**

Jos Nesser Motors Inc, shows elderly man talking to boy in baseball uniform, Dealers In High Grade Cars..., MIB....................**$16.50**

Keebler Zesta Saltine Crackers, resembles box of crackers, MIB **$12.50**

Life Savers, 3 rows of assorted life savers, MIB **$6.50**

Merchant's National Bank & Trust Co, single rose on white w/gold & red line border, MIB **$6.50**

Owl Drug Store, lettering above & below owl logo, complete, ca 1900-08, EX+, $210.00

Sheboygan Sausage Co, white lettering on red w/white, black & red border, ...Quality Sausage, Sheboygan Wis, MIB....................**$6.50**

Vantage Cigarettes, resembles cigarette package, MIB..**$6.50**

Games, Tarot, Magic and Miscellaneous

Canasta, white on green w/sm fleur-de-lis in each corner, complete, EX....................**$3.50**

Glob-Astral, color drawings & fortunes on each card, 1937, NMIB....................**$15.00**

Make a Million, double-deck, pirate theme on back, ca 1934, MIB **$16.50**

Mythological Zoo, D Martin, creatures on back, 1971, MIP....................**$50.00**

New Art Tarot, colorful design on each card, Knapp, 1929, MIB....................**$175.00**

Old Maid, Milton Bradley #4172, old, complete w/instructions & original box, VG....................**$12.50**

Rummy, Parker Bros, 1942, 44 cards & 16-page rule booklet, NMIB....................**$10.00**

Space Race, Edu-Cards, 1969, MIB....................**$3.50**

Stardust, Stanley minatures, black & white dog on barrel on back, original box, EX....................**$10.00**

Modern Decks

Aircraft Spotter I, red rider backs, 1942, MIB..............**$35.00**

Aquarius, astrological sign on backs, MIB....................**$4.00**

Baraja Taurina, Casero, 52 portraits of bullfighters, 1965, MIB **$16.50**

Clydesdales, color photos on each card, 1984, MIB....**$10.00**

Country Music, color photos of stars on each card, 1978, NMIB....................**$6.50**

Grand Prix, Lirola designs, Grimaud, 1973, MIB.........**$14.00**

Journey to the West, China, various character on each card, NMIB....................**$10.00**

Kennedy Cards, Kennedy family members on courts, 1963, MIB **$18.50**

Party Pack, naughty cartoons on backs, 1953, oversized, NMIB....................**$20.00**

Salvidor Dali, France, colorful designs w/gold edges, 1969, MIB....................**$85.00**

Survival, information for survival or first aid on each card, non-standard, 1974, MIB....................**$4.50**

Tally-Ho #43, pinochle deck, Dougherty, 1960s tax stamp, MIB....................**$8.00**

Tee-Up, Creative Cards, cartoons on back, 1963, MIB ..**$14.00**

Texas White House, tourist information on each card, square corners, 1966, MIB....................**$16.50**

Pinups

Elvgren, double-deck, beach scenes on back, original box, EX....................**$30.00**

Elvgren, double-deck, girl holding record & girl reading letter, NMIB....................**$35.00**

Elvgren, hula girls on back, ad at bottom, MIB..........**$25.00**

Elvgren, lady reading in bed, blue background w/gold edge, MIB **$25.00**

Elvgren, lady w/records sitting on cushion, yellow background w/gold edge, NMIB **$25.00**

Elvgren, lady w/roses, sealed box, M....................**$35.00**

Elvgren, Number To Remember, pinup girls on backs, NMIB..**$25.00**
Esquire, canasta, double-deck, pinup girls on back, original box, VG **$22.00**
Esquire, lady in leopard bikini, NMIB........................**$30.00**
Esquire, nude redhead by flowers, ca 1945, original box, EX..**$20.00**
Marilyn Monroe, nude photos of Marilyn, original box, EX..**$18.50**
Pherson, double-deck, girls w/playing cards, MIB......**$25.00**

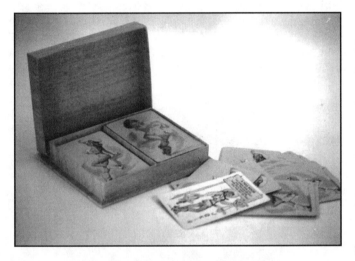

Wipsey Fish Co, double-deck, western pinup girls on back, complete, 1947, MIB, $35.00

Souvenir

Hawaii, color photos repeat each suit, 1980, MIB.......**$10.00**
Hawaiian Heritage, photos of Hawaiian history, 1982, MIB..**$16.50**
Las Vegas Club, blue logo on white background, original box, EX **$3.50**
Lover's Leap, Rock City, standard faces, 1930s, original box, EX..**$6.50**
New York World's Fair, color drawings on each card, gold edges, 1964-65, M **$12.50**
North Dakota, double-deck, scenic, 1950s, NMIB.......**$15.00**
Reno, night scenes on back, 1950s, NM......................**$22.00**
Rocky Mountains, scenic w/gold edges, 1940, NMIB..**$22.00**
San Francisco, Golden Gate Bridge scenes, 1950s, MIB.**$12.50**
Texas Centennial, 100th Anniversary, standard faces, gold border, 1936, M..**$15.00**
Washington, Arco Playing Card Co, cherry trees in blossom w/Washington Monument in background, MIB......**$8.50**
XIII Commonwealth Games, standard faces, 1986, MIB..**$14.00**

Transportation

Amtrak, red, white & blue logo at top & bottom on white background, red border, MIB................................**$8.50**
Delta Airlines, Miami in red above lady in straw hat, bright yellow background, MIB **$12.50**

Delta Airlines, New Orleans in yellow above man playing trumpet, blue background, MIB..........................**$12.50**
Eastern Airlines, Eastern & logo in white on blue w/white line border, MIB..**$12.50**

Moore-McCormack Lines, MIB, $12.50

New York Central Railroad, palisades scene, original box, VG..**$20.00**
North American Van Lines, NA logo in red & blue on white w/red border, MIB..**$7.50**
Norwegian Carribean Lines, double-deck, cruise ship sketch on silver & gold background, MIB..........................**$8.50**
Pan Am, photo image of an elephant beside stream at sunset, MIB..**$8.50**
RC Cola, blue & red logo on white, MIB......................**$6.50**
Rock Island, black & white logo on red w/gold border, MIB..**$18.50**
Soo-Line, logo on red background, MIB......................**$8.50**
Trans Caribbean, purple-tone photo of a DC-8, 1960s, NMIB..**$25.00**
TWA, logo & white feather design on gold, MIB..........**$6.50**
United Airlines, Fly the Friendly Skies of United in white on red, MIB..**$6.50**

Political Memorabilia

From 1840 until 1896 when celluloid (cellos) buttons appeared, American voters showed support for presidential candidates and their platforms by wearing sulfide brooches, ferrotype pins, mechanical badges, silk ribbons and other lapel devices. Today some of these are valued at thousands of dollars. Celluloid pin-backs were made until the 1920s; many are attractively and colorfully designed, and their values hinge on scarcity, historical significance, and of course condition. Most (but not all) buttons since then have been produced by lithography directly on metal disks (lithos). Jugates are those that feature both the presidential and the vice-presidential candidates and are generally preferred by collectors, but there are several specialty areas that are also desirable such as state and local, third party, and 'cause' types.

Many buttons have been reproduced, but because of a bill passed by Nixon called 'The Hobby Protection Act,' the reproductions are all marked. A set distributed by the American Oil company in 1972 can be confusing, however. Look on the edge of the button for this mark: 'A-O-1972.' Don't buy buttons that have been tampered with, because unscrupulous dealers sometimes try to scratch off or paint over the 'Reproduction' mark. When these marks are on the paper backing, they may paint that too, so beware.

Besides buttons, look for pamphlets, leaflets, flyers, tickets, electoral ballots, and hand cards used to promote candidates to the presidency. Even memorabilia from the past few decades is something you'll want to hang on to, especially items dealing with Kennedy, Nixon (Watergate) — and, who knows, maybe even Perot.

See also Watch Fobs.

Ashtray, I Like Ike, ceramic, red, white & blue, square.**$12.00**
Balloon, Truman For President, black on white **$25.00**
Coaster, I Like Ike in bold red letters in center, cork....**$5.00**

Coaster, Wendell L Willkie bust in blue tones encircled by red rim, 3" dia, $20.00

Coloring book, JFK, caricature cartoons inside, unused.**$35.00**
Fan, I'm a Fan of Bush & Quayle in 1992 w/photo on red, white & blue cardboard shield shape **$8.00**
Inauguration ticket, Eisenhower-Nixon, pictures the White House in center of oval photos............................**$20.00**
Inauguration ticket, Reagan-Bush, America A Great New Beginning, 1981 in center of oval photos, w/original stub **$8.50**
License plate, Coolidge For President in red on white, red line border...**$120.00**
License plate, Hoover For President in blue on white, blue line border..**$40.00**
License plate, LBJ For the USA, red, white & blue **$25.00**
License plate, Nixon-Agnew in blue on white, blue line border..**$20.00**
Matchbook, black & white photo left of Draft George Wallace For President in red & blue **$6.00**
Matchbook, Elect Dewey & Warren on red above black & white photo, Join a Great Team on blue below ...**$12.00**

Matchbook, Veterans For Nixon in red & blue on white ..**$8.00**
Pamphlet, Kennedy For President below lg photo, For California..., For America... above, white lettering on red & blue...**$16.00**
Pamphlet, Nixon's Program For Success, photo on yellow, blue lettering **$10.00**
Penknife, Reagan-Bush, 1980, elephant symbol, blue plastic handle **$15.00**
Pin-back button, America's First Lady, Jacqueline Kennedy surrounds black & white photo, blue & red border **$75.00**
Pin-back button, Bush 1988 on red & white border surrounds black & white photo **$3.00**
Pin-back button, Clinton-Gore For New Leadership in white on blue surrounds black & white photos................**$4.00**
Pin-back button, Democrats For Dwight D Eisenhower on blue & red bands surrounds black & white photo .**$45.00**

Pin-back button, flasher type featuring Agnew & Nixon, 2½" dia, $15.00

Pin-back button, Ford-Dole for Pres-V Pres, 1976 surrounds black & white photos, red background...................**$3.00**
Pin-back button, Give Ike a Republican Congress above & below photo on red, white & blue shield.............**$20.00**
Pin-back button, Goldwater in '64 surrounds black & white photo, gold background...**$4.00**
Pin-back button, Harding & Coolidge in white letters on blue center band, red background...........................**$8.50**
Pin-back button, I'm For Nixon surrounds black & white oval photo, blue background **$5.00**
Pin-back button, Jimmy Carter 76 arched above black & white photo, white background..............................**$4.00**
Pin-back button, John F Kennedy For President surrounds black & white photo **$8.00**
Pin-back button, Johnson & Humphrey on blue below black & white photos...**$5.00**
Pin-back button, Junior Ike & Dick Club in red & white flanked by black & white photos, red border.......**$35.00**
Pin-back button, McGovern For President 1972, blue & white **$4.00**
Pin-back button, McKinley in bold letters on center band, America First... arched above & below, red, white & blue...**$25.00**

Pin-back button, Ohio Loves the Reagans arched above black & white photo **$5.00**

Pin-back button, Perot For President in '92 surrounds photo & flag **$5.00**

Pin-back button, Reagan-Bush surrounds black & white photos, gold background **$4.00**

Pin-back button, Stevenson For President surrounds blue & white checked flag, red background **$35.00**

Pin-back button, Taft in bold blue letters on white center band, red background **$10.00**

Pin-back button, Theodore Roosevelt for President surrounds black & white photo **$40.00**

Pin-back button, USA Likes LBJ surrounds black & white photo in red outline of the United States **$5.00**

Pin-back button, Willkie For President in red letters surrounds black & white photo, white background ..**$40.00**

Pin-back button, Win w/Barry Goldwater surrounds black & white photo, patriotic border **$12.00**

Pin-back button, 100% Hoover American on red, white & blue background **$25.00**

Pocket mirror, RFK Destined To Become President surrounds photo, red, white & blue **$35.00**

Ribbon, Independence Missouri Truman Reception Committee in blue on white paper....................................**$40.00**

Ribbon, Women Volunteers For Nixon, St Joseph County in red on light blue satin **$30.00**

Sticker, Brooks, Willkie & Green lettered on red, white & blue bands, round...**$8.00**

Sticker, Vote For Nixon, The Future You Save May Be Your Own in red on white, rectangular..........................**$5.00**

Toy, Watergate Bug, mechanical plastic, w/original box **$40.00**

Postcards

Postcards are generally inexpensive, historically interesting, graphically pleasing, easy to store, and very easy to find. They were first printed in Austria in 1986, where they were very well accepted. In this country, souvenir cards were printed for the Columbian Exposition in 1892, and postcards became the rage.

Until WWI, they remained very collectible, with many being preserved in special postcard albums. Even today postcards rank near the top of paper collectibles, second only to stamps.

Today's collectors often specialize in certain types of postcards. Themes that are particularly worth investing in are advertising, industry, transportation, and entertainment. Other popular cards deal with certain holidays, Black Americana, and patriotism. Some collectors prefer the work of a particular illustrator such as Ellen Clapsaddle, Frances Brundage, Rose O'Neill, Raphael Tuck, Charles Dana Gibson, and Philip Boileau. Don't forget how important condition is with any type of paper collectible. Even though many of these cards are sixty to ninety years old, they must be in excellent shape to have value, whether used or unused.

Many old postcards are worth very little. Some of the more collectible examples are listed here. There are several books available for further study, we recommend *The Collector's Guide to Postcards* by Jane Wood and *Postcards, Mail Memories,* by John M. Kaduck.

Advertising, Bromo-Seltzer, black & white photo of horse-drawn wagon w/bottle & lettering on wagon, EX..**$30.00**

Advertising, Cherry Smash, Black servant serving Cherry Smash on the lawn of Mt Vernon, EX **$40.00**

Advertising, Colt Firearms Co, printed photo of the Colt Museum, 1953, VG..**$16.00**

Advertising, Continental Tires, comical image of dogs around sausage vendor, German, EX **$35.00**

Advertising, Fisk, pictures little boy & dog skidding along side speeding tire, 'To Skid or Not To Skid,' EX, $30.00

Advertising, Hochschild, Kohn & Co, pictures a horse-drawn buggy, Baltimore's Best Store, EX..........................**$35.00**

Advertising, Kellogg's Rice Krispies, mechanical, swing-out panels w/scenes of Snap!, Crackle! & Pop!, VG....**$10.00**

Advertising, Krokodil Restaurant, pictures waitress kissing a crocodile, German, NM **$35.00**

Advertising, McKee High Grade Refrigerators, mother & daughter beside refrigerator, Don't You Want Something Good?, EX..**$30.00**

Advertising, Nestle's Baby Meal, chromolitho, naked baby getting out of horse-drawn buggy, German, EX...**$35.00**

Advertising, Pabst Brewing Co, aerial view of the factory, 1935, EX..**$3.00**

Advertising, Silver Slipper Saloon, dance hall design, We Mail It, You Address It, red & black, 1950s, NM.....**$6.50**

Advertising, Winchester Shells, salesman's advance notice from Clark-Rutka-Weaver Co, black & white, EX .**$40.00**

Animal, A Great View, 4 kittens in a basket, EX............**$3.00**

Animal, bear leaning on a tree, I'm So Lonesome Without You Honey, I Can't Bear It Any Longer, EX............**$2.50**

Animal, bear washing clothes, Monday, This Little Bear Washes Clothes, Bernhardt Wall, EX **$5.00**

Animal, calico cat w/bow & flowers around her neck, Good Luck & Many Happy Returns, EX...........................**$4.00**

Animal, side view of a crowing rooster, EX..................**$4.00**

Animal, 3 kittens playing w/bouquet of flowers, EX.....**$3.00**

Earl Christy, elegant girl in wide-brimmed hat holding bouquet of roses, VG $6.50

Earl Christy, girl at ship's wheel, VG $6.50

Fantasy, frog playing guitar for mermaid, EX $20.00

Fantasy, 2 winged children in nest surrounded by flowers, EX..$6.00

Harrison Fisher, The Wedding, wedding scene, VG ...$10.00

Harrison Fisher, Vanity, lady looking in hand mirror, EX $12.50

Harrison Fisher, woman in profile admiring ring in box, EX $12.50

Hold-to-Light, Absecom Light House & US Life Saving Station, Atlantic City, NJ, multicolored, EX $35.00

Hold-to-Light, Alone, woman walking across board above water, EX $15.00

Hold-to-Light, Luna Park, Coney Island NY, multicolored, EX $35.00

Hold-to-Light, Town Hall & Castle St, Liverpool, VG ..$25.00

Holiday, A Happy Easter Tide, bunny pulling little girl in cart, VG...$2.50

Holiday, A Jolly Halloween, little girl dressed as witch holding black cat & jack-o'-lantern, Ellen Clapsaddle, EX $10.00

Holiday, A Merry Christmas, woman overloaded w/gifts, Ellen Clapsaddle, EX...$8.00

Holiday, A Merry Christmas, 3 children building a snowman, EX..$4.50

Holiday, Best Easter Wishes, little girl in bonnet holding basket of flowers, Ellen Clapsaddle, EX $8.00

Holiday, Christmas Greetings, little girl having breakfast in bed, Frances Brundage, EX $10.00

Holiday, Christmas Greetings, Santa giving little girl a doll, VG $7.50

Holiday, Halloween, witch & black cat riding broom...$8.00

Holiday, Halloween Greetings, little boy standing in front of window w/black cat leering at him, Ellen Clapsaddle, EX...$8.00

Holiday, New Year Greetings, gnomes setting clock at midnight, EX...$5.00

Holiday, St Patrick's Day, Kissing the Blarney Stone, postmarked 1914, EX, $5.00

Holiday, Thanksgiving Day Greetings, woman carrying tray w/baked turkey, Frances Brundage, EX..................$8.00

Holiday, Valentine Greetings, Dutch boy holding a heart, VG $1.50

Holiday, Valentines Day, 2 children seated in chair, It's Made For Us I Do Declare..., embossed, Mary Evans Price, EX...$4.00

Holiday, Wishing You A Happy Thanksgiving, Dutch children pointing at large turkey, Ellen Clapsaddle, VG $6.50

Katherine Gassaway, curly-haired baby w/pacifier, 1 Year, EX $6.00

Katherine Gassaway, little girl mailing a letter, I Send My Love By Mail, EX...$6.00

Patriotic, eagle atop flag, Your Flag & My Flag, The Flag That Flies Above..., EX...$5.00

Patriotic, Lincoln Centennial Souvenir 1809-1909, Lincoln's Emancipation Proclamation, EX, $25.00

Patriotic, 4th of July, little boy in uniform holding flag, VG $6.50

Photo, Chalmers Motor Co, Detroit MI, EX $14.00

Photo, Cincinnati Northern Railroad Bridge, Franklin OH, VG $6.00

Photo, Ferry Between Davenport IA & Rock Island IL, VG $3.00

Photo, Lake Shore & B&O Depot, Gary IN, EX.............$5.00

Photo, Lillian Russell in Victorian-style portrait, EX.......$5.00

Posters

Posters are popular among many collectors, not only as an alternative to more expensive art forms but also because they seem to be appreciating very quickly.

Though you may not find a Cheret or a Lautrec, there are many kinds of contemporary posters that are well worth your attention. Hundreds of movie posters can be bought for less than $100.00, many for less than $25.00. Of course, those featuring the Hollywood legends like Marilyn Monroe or James Dean are bringing in thousands of dollars at auction. Posters from early monster movies are hot as well, and some are estimated to be worth tens of thousands of dollars! The most available size is about 41" x 27"; collectors refer to them as 1-sheets.

Though not as easy to find, posters from the WWII era are well worth looking for. They will vary in price from about $20.00 up to several hundred or more. Look for fine graphics, artists' signatures, interesting subject matter, and, of course, good condition.

Advertising, Ingersol Watch Co, features boy w/His First Watch, 19x11", VG $90.00

Advertising, Lighthouse Footwear, pictures reptile shoe, Warhol, 1979, 45x30", M.......................................$115.00

Advertising, Williamtic Thread, pictures girl w/dog, 20x24", EX $275.00

Circus, Adam Forepaugh & Sells Bros, shows circus scene w/cars, 13x17½", EX $75.00

Circus, Cole Bros, Quarter Million Pounds of Elephants, 1-sheet, EX..$175.00

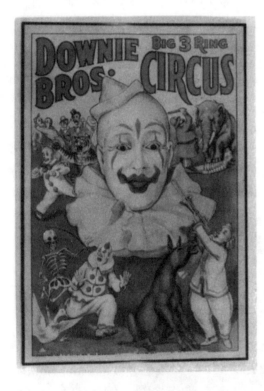

Circus, Downie Bros Big 3 Ring Circus, clown head encircled by circus acts, Epic Litho Co, metal frame, 41x28", EX, $400.00

Circus, Olympia Circus & Xmas Fair, features clown w/ball reading Here We Are Again, fold marks, 32x23", VG $60.00

Circus, Skippy & Bum, pictures elephant & clown, Erie Litho, 1-sheet, EX...$130.00

Circus, Tom Mix, Menagarie of Wild Beasts, 1934, 1-sheet, EX $280.00

Magic, Alexander The Man Who Knows, man's head wrapped in turban, lettering above & below, ragged edge, soiling, 42x28" $85.00

Magic, Irving the Magician, Oriental Oddities, 42x14", EX $65.00

Magic, Sorcar, World's Greatest Magician, 1952, 29x18½", EX..$225.00

Magic, Willard the Wizard, Night of Enchantment, Hunter's, 24x8", EX..$175.00

Movie, Aliens, Sigorney Weaver, Ripley/Newt, 1986, 1-sheet, EX..$50.00

Movie, Beauty & the Beast, animated, 1991, 1-sheet, EX $20.00

Movie, Being There, Peter Sellers, 1980, 1-sheet, EX ..$25.00

Movie, Big Jake, John Wayne, 1971, ½-sheet, VG $20.00

Movie, Charro!, Elvis Presley, 1969, 1-sheet, NM.........$35.00

Movie, Clambake, Elvis Presley, 1967, 1-sheet, EX......$40.00

Movie, Funniest Man in the World, Charles Chaplin, 1968, 1-sheet, EX...$25.00

Movie, Hard To Kill, Steven Seagal, 1990, 1-sheet, EX..$20.00

Movie, Inside Daisey Clover, Natalie Wood, Christopher Plummer, Robert Redford, 1966, 1-sheet, M.........$20.00

Movie, Irma La Douce, Jack Lemmon & Shirley MacLaine, 1962, 1-sheet, EX..$35.00

Movie, It's a Mad Mad Mad World, Spencer Tracy, 1963, 1-sheet, EX..$20.00

Movie, Last Time I Saw Paris, Elizabeth Taylor, Van Johnson, 1954, 1-sheet, VG+...$60.00

Movie, Marked Trails, Hoot Gibson & Bob Steel, 1944, ½-sheet, EX..$250.00

Movie, Moonraker, Roger Moore as James Bond, 1979, 1-sheet, EX..$15.00

Movie, Nevada Smith, Steve McQueen & all-star cast, 1966, 1-sheet, EX..$20.00

Movie, North by Northwest, Cary Grant, directed by Alfred Hitchcock, 1959, 1-sheet, EX...............................$125.00

Movie, Pack Up Your Troubles, Laurel & Hardy, 1932, 1-sheet, EX..$350.00

Movie, Raiders of the Lost Ark, Harrison Ford, 1981, 1-sheet, EX..$20.00

Movie, Red River, John Wayne, 1948, ½-sheet, EX ...$275.00

Movie, Tall in the Saddle, John Wayne, 1944, ½-sheet, EX $285.00

Movie, The Alamo, John Wayne, 1967, 1-sheet, EX $25.00

Movie, The Cyclops, James Craig & Gloria Talbot, 1957, 1-sheet, EX..$65.00

Movie, The Third Voice, Edmond O'Brien, Julie London, 1-sheet, VG...$15.00

Mystic, Carter the Great, The Modern Priestess of Delphi, 3 sections glue together, 78x42", $500.00

Theater, And a Nightingale Sang, Demoney & Stahl, 1989, 46x30", M..$55.00

Theater, John Sheridan, Strobridge, 30x20", EX..........$90.00

Theater, The Girl on the Barge, Carl Laemmle & Rupert Hughes, illustrated image of girl on water, minor soiling, 22x14"..$25.00

Theater, The Pirates of Penzance, shows various scenes of play, borders trimmed, 23¾x17¾", VG, $50.00

Travel, Batumi, features Russian scene, 40x24½", VG.**$100.00**

Travel, Eastern Airlines, features Mickey Mouse, framed, 1983, NM **$55.00**

Travel, Normandy, French National Railroad, pictures countryside, Dufy, 1952, 39x24", NM...........................**$140.00**

WWI, Be Patriotic, Sign Your Country's Pledge To Save Food, patriotic lady w/outstretched arms, 28x20", EX **$90.00**

WWI, Hun or Home?, Buy More Liberty Bonds, Edward Duetsch Litho Co, 1918, 30x20", EX **$40.00**

WWI, Ring It Again, Buy US Gov't Bonds, Third Liberty Loan, Sackett & Wilhelms Corp, 30x30", EX.........**$50.00**

WWI, The Hun - His Mark & red hand print above Blot It Out w/Liberty Bonds, signed J Allen St John, 29¼x19", EX, $30.00

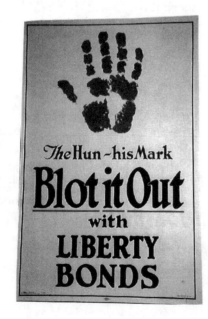

WWII, A Careless Word...A Needless Sinking, by Anton Otto Fisher, 1942, 27x22", VG+ **$95.00**

WWII, Assurance for Your Men of the Navy, 32x24", VG **$85.00**

WWII, Buy a Share in America, by H Billings, 40x28", VG **$90.00**

WWII, Give War Bonds, shows Christmas tree covered w/bonds, Snider, 1943, ½-sheet, M......................**$30.00**

WWII, Let Em Have It, features sailors loading charges, 14x19", EX **$20.00**

WWII, The Marines Have Landed, pictures marine hitting beachhead, by JM Flagg, 40x30", VG **$225.00**

Precious Moments

These modern collectibles are designed by Samuel J. Butcher and produced in the orient by the Enesco company. You'll see them in gift stores and card shops all across the nation. They were introduced less than fifteen years ago, and already some are selling on the secondary market for as much as five or six times their original retail price. Each piece is marked, and like the Hummel figures to which they're sometimes compared, the older retired items are the most valuable. Their figurines, bells, ornaments, and plates all portray children actively engaged in a particular pursuit, and many have an inspirational message.

If you'd like to learn more, we recommend *Precious Moments Secondary Market Price Guide* by Rosie Wells.

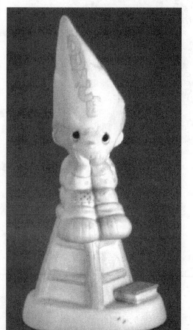

Figurine, Nobody's Perfect, 1982, 7¼", $70.00

Bell, May Your Christmas Be Merry, girl w/bird, #524182, Vessel mark, 1991 ....**$35.00**

Container, Jesus Loves Me, boy holding teddy bear, #E-9280, Hourglass mark, 1982 ....**$55.00**

Doll, Candy, girl clown, #100455, Olive Branch mark, 1986 ....**$250.00**

Figurine, Blessings From My House to Yours, girl in snow looking at birdhouse, #E-0503, Fish mark, 1983...**$80.00**

Figurine, Dropping In for Christmas, boy ice skating, #E-2350, Cross mark, 1984..................**$65.00**

Figurine, Friendship Grows When You Plant a Seed, girl w/watering can, #524271, Vessel mark, 1991 ....**$45.00**

Figurine, God Sent His Son, girl looking into manger, #E-0507, Cedar Tree mark, 1987 ....**$80.00**

Figurine, He Careth for You, boy helping lamb, #E-1377B, no mark, 1976 ....**$130.00**

Figurine, How Can I Ever Forget You, elephant w/string around neck, #526924, Vessel mark, 1991 ....**$20.00**

Figurine, Let Heaven & Nature Sing, angel w/song book & bird, #E-0532, Cross mark, 1984..................**$45.00**

Figurine, Make a Joyful Noise, girl w/goose, #E-1374G, Hourglass mark, 1982 ....**$50.00**

Figurine, Peace on Earth, boy on globe, #E-2804, Triangle mark, 1981..................**$150.00**

Figurine, Scent From Above, girl w/skunk, #100528, Cedar Tree mark, 1987 ....**$70.00**

Figurine, Sharing a Gift of Love, girl w/bluebird, #527114, Vessel mark, 1990 ....**$45.00**

Figurine, Summer's Joy, girl holding rose, #12076, Cross mark, 1984..................**$100.00**

Figurine, Time Heals, nurse w/alarm clock, #523739, G Clef mark, 1992 ....**$38.00**

Figurine, Tubby's First Christmas, pig w/chicken on his back, #525278, G Clef mark, 1992 ....**$15.00**

Figurine, Unto Us a Child Is Born, boy & girl w/book, #E-2013, Fish mark, 1983..................**$100.00**

Frame, God's Precious Gift, baby girl, #12041, Flower mark, 1988 ....**$38.00**

Frame, Jesus Loves Me, girl holding bunny, #E-7171, Hourglass mark, 1982..................**$55.00**

Frame, The Lord Bless You & Keep You, #E-7166, fish mark, $25.00

Frame, Loving You, girl holding heart, #12025, Dove mark, 1985 ....**$45.00**

Frame, Wedding Arch, Bridal series, #102369, Bow & Arrow mark, 1989..................**$30.00**

Ornament, Our First Christmas Together, bride & groom in car, #525324, Flame mark, 1990..................**$28.00**

Ornament, Serve w/a Smile, tennis boy, #102431, Flower mark, 1988..................**$25.00**

Ornament, Shepherd of Love, angel w/lamb, #102288, Cedar Tree mark, 1987 ....**$25.00**

Plate, Blessings From Me to Thee, girl looking in birdhouse, #523860, Vessel mark, 1991..................**$60.00**

Plate, I'm Sending You a White Christmas, girl at mailbox, #101834, Olive Branch mark, 1986 ....**$55.00**

Plate, Loving Thy Neighbor, mother wrapping bread, #E-2848, Cross mark, 1984..................**$40.00**

Plate, Our First Christmas Together, girl knitting tie for boy, #E-2378, Dove mark, 1985..................**$35.00**

Plate, Summer's Joy, girl holding rose, #12114, Cross mark, 1984..................**$75.00**

Thimble, God Is Love, Dear Valentine, girl holding heart, #100625, Flower mark, 1988..................**$12.00**

Thimble, The Lord Bless You & Keep You, bride, #100633, Dove mark, 1985..................**$25.00**

Premiums

From the early thirties until the advent of TV, kids hurried home to tune in their favorite radio show. They were glued to the set for the thirty-minute program, and these bigger-and-better-than-life heroes were a very real part of their lives. They agonized over cliff-hanger episodes and were always vastly relieved when Tom Mix (or whoever) was rescued from the 'bad guys' the very next day. These radio superstars were made even more real to children through the premiums they could obtain for nothing more than a box top or an inner label and a few pennies for postage. Secret manuals, signet rings, decoders, compasses, flashlights, pocketknives, and badges were just a few of the items available. Who could have known that by the nineties, some of these would be worth hundreds of dollars!

See also Character Collectibles; Cracker Jack Collectibles; Pin-Back Buttons.

Batman, temporary tattoo transfer, Coca Cola/Hong Kong, 1992, M **$10.00**

Battlestar Galactica, collector cards, Wonder Bread, 1978, EX..................**$6.50**

Beatles, 8mm movie, A Hard Days Night, mail-in offer, plain box w/printing on side, 100 ft, EX+ **$35.00**

Buck Rogers, badge, gold-tone, Solar Scouts, Cream of Wheat, 1935-36, VG **$90.00**

Buck Rogers, book, Buck Rogers in the 25th Century, Kellogg's, 1933, EX..................**$100.00**

Buffalo Bill, ring, brass, pictures Buffalo Bill, radio premium, 1950s, EX..................**$50.00**

Captain Marvel, key chain, 1944-47, EX..................**$55.00**

Captain Marvel, membership code card, 1941, EX......**$45.00**

Captain Midnight, cup, red plastic w/decal of Captain Midnight, premium from Ovaltine & radio show, 4" (w/lid: $45), $25.00

Captain Midnight, Official Secret Code Book & Membership Manual, Ovaltine, 1940-41, EX.............................**$110.00**

Captain Midnight, photo of the Captain w/hand showing the 'Secret Ring,' Skelly, 1939, EX.................................**$15.00**

Captain Video, Space Men, plastic, 12 different, came in Post Raisin Brand, EX, each **$10.00**

Davy Crockett, ring, brass, pictures Davy Crockett, radio premium, 1950s, EX..**$25.00**

Davy Crockett, ring, plastic, NM **$10.00**

Dick Daring, jigsaw puzzle, underground view of mountain, Quaker Oats, 1933-34, EX **$65.00**

Dick Tracy, badge, Secret Service Patrol Sergeant, NM..**$40.00**

Dick Tracy, membership badge, Secret Service Patrol Second Year Member, NM...**$18.00**

Dragnet, whistle, plastic, black, radio premium, 1960s, EX+...**$7.00**

Frank Buck, Adventure Club pin-back button, from Bring 'Em Back Alive radio show, EX **$20.00**

Gene Autry, photograph, black & white, Homogenized Bond Bread, in plastic holder, 1949, NM **$15.00**

Green Hornet, ring, rubber, Fritos giveaway, VG+......**$40.00**

Hopalong Cassidy, bank, plastic bust, EX....................**$20.00**

Hopalong Cassidy, premium folder, EX.......................**$20.00**

Hopalong Cassidy, wallet, 1950s, VG **$45.00**

Howdy Doody, badge, Howdy Doody for President, diagonal, EX **$30.00**

Howdy Doody, cup, features Howdy Doody promoting Ovaltine, EX **$45.00**

Howdy Doody, mask, Wheaties, EX..............................**$10.00**

Howdy Doody, ring, Poll-Parrot premium, NM **$30.00**

Little Orphan Annie, mug, green w/cartoon graphic, dome lid, EX **$50.00**

Little Orphan Annie, decoder pins from the Secret Society, 1936, 1937 & 1938, premiums from radio show, each, $25.00

Little Orphan Annie, Secret Society manual, w/original mailing envelope, 1935, EX...**$60.00**

Lone Ranger, blotter, 1938-40, EX.................................**$10.00**

Lone Ranger, flashlight ring, EX...................................**$35.00**

Lone Ranger, mask, Merita Bread, 1934-38, EX **$40.00**

Lone Ranger, masks, 8 of the Lone Ranger & Tonto, 6 of the 'bad guys,' Wheaties, 1951-56, EX, each **$25.00**

Lone Ranger, postcard, features Lone Ranger on Silver going at a fast gallop, Merita Bread, early 1950s, EX......**$20.00**

Lone Wolf Tribe, bracelet, 1932, EX **$60.00**

Lone Wolf Tribe, watch fob, Wrigley's Gum, 1932, EX.**$28.00**

Lum & Abner, Family Almanac, 1938, radio premium, EX..**$8.00**

Red Goose, ring, round flat top w/cover that swings to the side to expose the Red Goose, EX **$55.00**

Rin-Tin-Tin, beanie, EX+ **$50.00**

Rin-Tin-Tin, cavalry hat, NM+ **$70.00**

Rin-Tin-Tin, pennant, EX+..**$65.00**

Rocky Jones Space Ranger, membership pin-back button, ca 1953, EX...**$35.00**

Rocky Lane, sundial watch, Carnation Malted Powder, EX..**$32.00**

Rootie Kazootie, membership card, early TV puppet show, EX..**$22.00**

Roy Rogers, branding iron ring, Quaker Oats radio premium, 1950s, NM...**$120.00**

Roy Rogers, microscope ring, Quaker Oats radio premium, 1949, NM **$120.00**

Roy Rogers, Nellybell badge, tin, Post Raisin Brand radio premium, 1950s, MIP **$20.00**

Roy Rogers, poster, Post Cereals, 1950s, NM **$95.00**

Sgt Preston & Yukon King, pedometer, plastic w/paper label featuring duo, EX...**$35.00**

Sgt Preston & Yukon King, photo, w/facsimile salutation & signature, 8½x11", EX **$20.00**

Sgt Preston & Yukon King, whistle, w/cord, engraved signature, EX..**$40.00**

Singing Lady, punch-out circus, designed by Vernon Grant, Kellogg's, 1936, EX **$110.00**

Skippy, cereal bowl, white ceramic featuring Skippy in cartoon graphics, Wheaties radio premium, EX........**$30.00**

Sky King, code writer, Spy Dectecto, radio premium, 1940s, EX..**$55.00**

Sky King, Electronic Television ring w/12 pictures, EX..**$100.00**

Sky King, Magni-Glo writing ring, gold-tone w/fold-out pen & magnifier, secret compartment, 1949, VG **$75.00**

Sky King, 2-Way Tele-Blinker, EX **$75.00**

Space Patrol, balloon, features rocket-ship graphics, w/envelope, Ralston, EX **$110.00**

Space Patrol, Buzz Cory Color Book, Ralston premium, EX.....................**$35.00**

Space Patrol, handbook (original), Ralston, EX..........**$85.00**

Space Patrol, handbook (reprint), Ralston, EX............**$15.00**

Space Patrol, phones, w/original string & mailer, Ralston, M in EX package **$205.00**

Straight Arrow, ring, name flanks embossed face, Nabisco, 1950, EX.....................**$40.00**

Superman, belt & buckle, plastic, 1940s-early 50s, EX .**$280.00**

Superman, pin-back button, Action Comics, late 1930s-early 40s, EX.....................**$65.00**

Tom Mix, badge, Dobie County Siren Sheriff, no pin, VG **$25.00**

Tom Mix, glow-in-the-dark compass & magnifier, Ralston, NM **$70.00**

Tom Mix, marbles, original bag, M.....................**$75.00**

Tom Mix, photo in silver frame, EX **$75.00**

Tom Mix, ring, Look-Around, cereal premium, EX+ .**$125.00**

Tom Mix, wooden gun, EX.....................**$125.00**

Wild Bill Hickock, Treasure Guide & Map, Kellogg's, EX.....................**$55.00**

Win Lose or Draw, game, cereal premium, 1988, sealed, MIP **$3.00**

Purinton Pottery

The Purinton Pottery Company moved from Ohio to Shippenville, Pennsylvania, in 1941 and began producing several lines of dinnerware and kitchen items hand painted with fruits, ivy vines, and trees in bold brush strokes of color on a background reminiscent of old yellowware pieces. The company closed in 1959 due to economic reasons.

Purinton has a style that's popular today with collectors who like the country look. It isn't always marked, but you'll soon recognize it's distinct appearance. Some of the rarer designs are Palm Tree and Pheasant Lady, and examples of these lines are considerably higher than the more common ones. You'll see more Apple and Apple and Pear pieces than any, and in more diversified shapes.

Apple, bowl, spaghetti; 14½" **$50.00**

Apple, plate, chop; 12" **$40.00**

Apple, platter, 12" **$30.00**

Apple, tumbler, short.....................**$14.00**

Apple, tumbler, 12-oz **$12.00**

Chartreuse, jam & jelly.....................**$20.00**

Chartreuse, salt & pepper shakers, jug form, pr **$15.00**

Fruit, bowl, vegetable; 8".....................**$12.00**

Fruit, cookie jar **$50.00**

Intaglio, cookie jar **$65.00**

Intaglio, mug, jug form, 8-oz.....................**$40.00**

Intaglio, mug, juice; 5-oz.....................**$14.50**

Intaglio, server, rectangular, 11" **$35.00**

Ivy, butter dish, ¼-lb.....................**$50.00**

Kent, jug, souvenir.....................**$50.00**

Maywood, bowl, fruit; 12".....................**$50.00**

Maywood, range set, 3-piece **$60.00**

Palm Tree, canister.....................**$100.00**

Pennsylvania Dutch, pickle dish, 6" **$25.00**

Pennsylvania Dutch, plate, lap; 8½", $35.00; cup, $20.00

Plaid, beer mug, 16-oz.....................**$50.00**

Plaid, coffeepot, 8-cup.....................**$50.00**

Plaid, creamer **$10.00**

Plaid, cruet, square **$20.00**

Plaid, platter, 11".....................**$20.00**

Plaid, teapot, 6-cup.....................**$30.00**

Ribbon Flower, bowl, fruit; 12".....................**$50.00**

Tulip, coffee server **$75.00**

Purses and Vanity Bags

Purses from the late 1800s through the '20s and '30s have long been collectible, but they're not as scarce as you might think. You'll still be able to find some nice examples at many flea markets and antique malls. Some of the very early purses were covered allover with fine glass or cut steel beads. Flowers, birds, scenics or geometric designs were popular. By the turn of the century, the design was stylized and Victorian, like you see in stained glass windows and lamp shades from that period. Instead of beads, mesh became the material of preference. Some mesh purses were simply left plain to reflect the beauty of the metal itself, but many featured enameling. Sometimes the framework was sterling silver, and small semiprecious stones were added. Whiting and Davis was one of the larger manufacturers; Mandalian was another. Most purses with the mark of either of these companies are worth $150.00 at a very minimum. During the '50s, purses made of Lucite or some other plastic became popular. Nowadays these are often priced from $40.00 on up, depending upon style, color, condition, and whether or not the label of the manufacturer is present. As a general rule, expect to pay $70.00 and up for beaded or metal mesh bags and $40.00 to $100.00 for tooled leather or alligator hide.

For more information, we suggest *Antique Purses, A History, Identification, and Value Guide, Second Edition,* by Richard Holiner.

Cloisonne & gold-tone, red, green & blue stones on white enameled lid, gold silk tassel & carrying cord, oval, 5x2½" **$450.00**

Lucite, Elgin, marbleized white, envelope closure, swinging handle w/cut-out design each end, w/carryall, 4x4½" long...**$300.00**

Lucite, marbleized brown with piano hinge, teardrop clasp, inside mirror, $45.00

Lucite, Wilardy Original, clear w/gold tulle & sparkles, envelope closure & swinging handles, carryall on lid, 4x7" long **$295.00**

Lucite, Wilardy Original, tortoise color w/envelope closure & swinging handles, complete w/carryall case, 4x7" long...**$225.00**

Mesh, gilt, filigree flowers set w/multicolored stones on lid, lined interior, 3¼" dia **$80.00**

Mesh, gilt w/red, green & yellow stones set in filigree lid, silk-lined interior, finger-ring chain, 1930s-40s, 3" dia ..**$125.00**

Mesh, gold-tone, yellow cloisonne lid decorated w/hand-painted roses, chain handle, 1930s, 9½x4½".......**$285.00**

Mesh, gun metal w/finger-ring chain, oval, 3x1¾" **$135.00**

Mesh, silver-tone w/attached compact on chain handle, 5x8" long..**$175.00**

Mesh, silver-tone w/blue cabochon thumbpiece, compact centered on front lid, Whiting & Davis, 1920s, 7½x2¾" **$200.00**

Mesh, tap-sift ivory-tone beadlite w/ivory & green enameled round lid, lined interior, 1930s, 3½" **$100.00**

Pewter-colored filigree metal w/marcasites & blue stones, gray moire lining, blue stones set in tassel & chain, 4¾" **$400.00**

Silk, multicolored w/pearls & red stones on gold-tone lid, metal jeweled tassel & chain, 8-sided, 3½x2¾" dia **$400.00**

Velvet, black, embossed flower set w/red stones on lid, lined interior, 1940s-50s, 5" dia...........................**$110.00**

Velvet, black w/rhinestone-studded lid, lined interior, 1940s-50s, 5" dia **$135.00**

Puzzles

The first children's puzzle was actually developed as a learning aid by an English map maker, trying to encourage the study of geography. Most 19th-century puzzles were made of wood, rather boring, and very expensive. But by the Victorian era, nursery rhymes and other light-hearted themes became popular. The industrial revolution and the inception of color lithography combined to produce a stunning variety of themes ranging from technical advancements, historical scenarios, and fairy tales. Power saws made production more cost effective, and wood was replaced with less expensive cardboard.

As early as the twenties and thirties, American manufacturers began to favor character-related puzzles, the market already influenced by radio and the movies. Some of these were advertising premiums. Die-cutters had replaced jigsaws, cardboard became thinner, and now everyone could afford puzzles. During the Depression they were a cheap form of entertainment, and no family get-together was complete without a puzzle spread out on the card table for all to enjoy.

Television and movies caused a lull in puzzle making during the fifties, but advancements in printing and improvements in quality brought them back strongly in the sixties. Unusual shapes, the use of fine art prints, and more challenging designs caused sales to increase.

If you're going to collect puzzles, you'll need to remember that unless all the pieces are there, they're not of much value, especially those from the 20th century. The condition of the box is important as well. Right now there's lots of interest in puzzles from the fifties through the seventies that feature popular TV shows and characters from that era.

To learn more about the subject, we recommend *Character Toys and Collectibles* and *Toys, Antique and Collectible*, both by David Longest, *Toys of the Sixties, A Pictorial Guide* by Bill Bruegman, and *Schroeder's Toys, Antique to Modern* (Collector Books).

Wonder Woman's Capture, frame-tray, wooden, 16 pieces, TM & DC Comics, 1979, 11½x9⅜", $10.00

Addams Family, jigsaw, Addams Family Mystery, Milton Bradley, complete, 1965, EX $35.00

Alien, jigsaw, 250 pieces, 1979, 14½x36", NMIB..........$20.00

Archies, jigsaw, Whitman, 1972, EX.....................$8.00

Banana Splits, jigsaw, Whitman, 1968, G $35.00

Batman, frame-tray, Batcave scene, Headbusters in Spanish, Whitman, 1966, 11x14", NM $35.00

Batman, jigsaw, APC, 82 pieces, 1976, 11x11", VG $45.00

Battlestar Galactica, jigsaw, Viper Launch, 140 pieces, Parker Bros, 1978, 14x18", EX...........................$20.00

Beatles, jigsaw, Beatles in Pepperland, 650+ pieces, complete, EX............................$150.00

Beatles, jigsaw, United Kingdom, shows the group in chairs on stage, 340 pieces, original box, 11x17", EX ..$225.00

Beetle Bailey, sliding tile, Roalex, 1960s, NMOC.........$25.00

Beverly Hillbillies, frame-tray, Ellie May, Jaymar, 1963, M....................................$25.00

Black Hole, frame-tray, Whitman, 1979, NM.................$6.00

Blondie, jigsaw, Dagwood's in Trouble, 100 pieces, Jaymar, 1960, 8x10" box, NM.............................$22.00

Bugs Bunny, frame-tray, Elmer & other characters in garden, Jaymar, 11x14", EX.............................$30.00

Captain Kangaroo, frame-tray, Captain & Mr Green Jeans as king & court jester, sealed, Fairchild, 1971, M......$20.00

Cinderella, frame-tray, w/coach & castle in background, EX+ $4.00

Close Encounters of the Third Kind, We Are Not Alone, jigsaw, #100, 108 pieces, 11x16", EX $9.00

Daffy Duck & Elmer Fudd, frame-tray, complete, 1977, EX................................$10.00

Daffy Duck & Elmer Fudd, jigsaw, 100 pieces, Milton Bradley, 1973, 14x18", VG+.........................$8.00

Dark Crystal, jigsaw, 250 pieces, M in worn box...........$4.00

Davy Crockett, jigsaw, Indian Fighter, over 60 pieces, Jaymar, 1956, 8x10" box, VG+ $12.00

Dick Tracy, jigsaw, Mr Tracy reviews police lineup, 100 pieces, Jaymar, 1961, 8x10" box, EX+ $22.00

Donny & Marie Osmond, frame-tray, Whitman, 1977, EX $5.00

Dr Doolittle, frame-tray, posed w/eye chart, Whitman, EX+ $9.00

Dracula, frame-tray, 11 pieces, Universal Studios, M.....$5.00

Dukes of Hazzard, jigsaw, 200 pieces, complete, 1982, EX $10.00

Eight Is Enough, jigsaw, sealed, APC, 1978, MIB $20.00

Flintstones, frame-tray, Pebbles & Bamm-Bamm riding Dino, Whitman, 1964, 11x14", EX+ $25.00

Flipper, frame-tray, Whitman, 1965, EX+ $12.00

Frankenstein, frame-tray, Universal Studios, 11 pieces, M..$5.00

Fury, frame-tray, Whitman, 1960s, NM $18.00

Gene Autry, frame-tray, original sleeve, 12x15", EX+..$55.00

Hong Kong Phooey, jigsaw, 70 pieces (1 missing), HG Toys, 1974, 10x14", G+ $5.00

Hopalong Cassidy, frame-tray, photo w/horse, 1950, EX...................................$35.00

Laverne & Shirley, jigsaw, HG Toys, 1976, NMIB........$15.00

Lone Ranger & Tonto, frame-tray, both on horseback, Whitman, 1954, 15x11", NM....................$35.00

Marvel Super Heroes, jigsaw, 100 pieces, Milton Bradley, 1966, 8x12" box, NMIB....................$80.00

Mary Poppins, frame-tray, Flying Kites, 1965, EX........$10.00

Milton the Monster, frame-tray, 1966...........................$15.00

Mod Squad, jigsaw, 500 pieces, Milton Bradley, 1969, 5x10" box, NM....................................$40.00

Monkees, jigsaw, Monkees Waterskiing, 340 pieces, Fairchild, 1967, G+.............................$25.00

Munsters, sliding tile, shows family, 2½" square..........$35.00

Nancy Drew Mysteries, jigsaw, 121 pieces, APC, 1978, 11x11", EX $8.00

Peanuts, jigsaw, 100 pieces, Milton Bradley, 1976, 16x11", EX....................................$12.00

Phantom, sliding tile, sealed, Ja-Ru, 1985, MIP $14.00

Playland Child's Picture Puzzle, jigsaw, features a Popeye scene w/all of the characters, lg pieces, Jaymar, EX, $125.00

Popeye, frame-tray, Popeye & pirates w/Olive Oyl & Sweet Pea, Jaymar, 1950s, 11x14", EX+ $25.00

Prince Valiant, frame-tray, Built Rite, 1954, 10x13", NM .$115.00

Puss 'n Boots, jigsaw, HG Toys, NM in canister $14.00

Rin-Tin-Tin, jigsaw, Whitman Jr, 1956, EX $25.00

Robin Hood, frame-tray, Richard Green & Alan Wheatly in sword fight, Built-Rite, 1956, 11x14", VG+ $25.00

Rocketeer, jigsaw, Movie Poster, Golden & Golden, 300 pieces, 1991, MIB....................................$14.00

Rootie Kazootie, frame-tray, complete, 1955, EX.........$30.00

Roy Rogers, frame-tray, complete, 1953, VG $20.00

Sgt Preston & Yukon King, frame-tray, Milton Bradley, #4508, rare, 1954, VG+ $60.00

Shogun, jigsaw, The Great Mazinga, 150 pieces, NM..$15.00

Shotgun Slade, jigsaw, shows star on rock w/rifle, complete, 1960, NMIB................................$38.00

Snow White & the Seven Dwarfs, frame-tray, group outside cottage, Jaymar, 1940s, 11x14", EX+ $24.00

Space Kidettes, jigsaw, complete, Whitman, 1968, EX ..$18.00

Space Patrol, frame-tray, features crew & spaceship, Milton Bradley, 1950, 11x14", EX....................$70.00

Spiderman, sliding tile, Belgium, 1978, 6½x8", EX $5.00

Stingray, frame-tray, 1966, NM......................**$30.00**
Super Six, jigsaw, complete, Whitman, 1969, EX in G box..**$15.00**
Sword in the Stone, jigsaw, 1963, EX.....................**$18.00**
Tammy, jigsaw, 100 pieces, 1964, 14x18", EX............**$15.00**
Top Cat, frame-tray, Whitman, 1961, EX................**$25.00**
Wild Bill Hickock, frame-tray, EX.....................**$22.00**
Winky Dink, jigsaw, pictures pirate gang, over 60 pieces, Jamar, 1950s, NM in EX box................................**$40.00**
Wyatt Earp, frame-tray, waist-length portrait, Whitman, 1958, 15x11", NM...**$30.00**
Zorro, frame-tray, pictures Zorro in Mexican villa, Whitman, 1957, 11x14", EX..............................**$32.00**

Quilts

Early quilts were considered basic homemaking necessities. They were used not only on the bed for warmth but also to hang over the windows and walls for extra insulation from gusty winter winds and on the floor as mattresses for overnight guests. Even into the thirties and forties they were made primarily to be used. But most of the contemporary quilts, of course (though they may be displayed with care as a bed covering), are designed and made as showpieces, some of them requiring several months of steady work to complete. Quilts from any circa are collectible and should be judged on condition, craftsmanship, intricacy of design, and color composition.

Though modern quilt artists sometimes devise some very unique methods of dying, printing, and construction, basically there are four types of quilts: 1) crazy — made up of scraps and pieces of various types of materials and sometimes ribbons sewn together in no specific design; 2) pieced — having intricate patterns put together with pieces that have been cut into specific shapes; 3) appliqued — made by applying a cut-out design (sometimes of one piece, sometimes pieced) to background material that is basically the size of the finished quilt; 4) trapunto — having a one-piece top lined with a second layer of loosely woven fabric through which padding is inserted to enhance the stitched pattern.

Nowadays you can't go to any flea market or department store, for that matter, without seeing new quilts that have been imported from China. At retail these are priced as low as $50.00 up to $200.00 in the more exclusive outlets. Upon examination you'll see poor workmanship and large, careless quilting stitches that are in sharp contrast to the fine sewing done by an accomplished quilter.

If you like quilts, you'll want to get these books: *Collecting Quilts* by Cathy Gaines Florence and *Gallery of American Quilts, 1849-1988* and *Arkansas Quilts*, both published by The American Quilter's Society.

Appliqued, Butterfly, off-white block pattern w/orange & brown stripes, polyester & cotton, 1989, 95x100" .**$500.00**
Appliqued, Ducks Shadow, orange, yellow, green & teal on white, cotton w/top layer of voile, 1987, 40x40"..**$120.00**
Appliqued, Ducky Doodle, yellow duck on orange w/purple borders, cotton, 1983, 45x60"........................**$345.00**
Appliqued, Falling Leaves, multicolor on white, polyester & cotton, polyester fiberfill batting, 1989, 84x85"..**$175.00**
Appliqued, Garden of Tulips, multicolored flowerpots in block pattern, cotton blend, sheet lining, 1989, 86x108", NM...**$450.00**
Appliqued, Hearts, tan print & dusty blue on unbleached muslin, Polyfil batting, 1989, 26½x26"...................**$70.00**
Appliqued, Pennsylvania Dutch, multicolored, muslin & polyester-cotton blend, Polyfil batting, 1989, 84x105"..**$700.00**
Appliqued, Poppies, green, red & off-white w/poppies in block pattern, Mountain Mist batting, 1989, 48x48"..........**$110.00**
Appliqued, red poppies w/yellow centers & green leaves, 12 repeats, embroidered detailing, diamond quilting, 1930, VG...**$285.00**
Appliqued & embroidered, Floral Medallion, multicolor on white, cotton batting, scalloped edges, 1930s, 74x86"..**$1,350.00**
Appliqued & machine-pieced, Uncle Sam, copyright Country Threads Pattern, red, navy, green & black, 1989, 31x31"..**$145.00**
Hand-embroidered & quilted, Butterflies, multicolored w/off-white background & blue sashing, cotton, 1989, 74x87½"...**$345.00**
Hand-pieced, Churn Dash, navy mini-print churns w/mini print, 2" red sashing, blue corner blocks, 1880, 70x82", G-..**$200.00**
Hand-pieced, Cobblestones, variegated prints w/off-white lining, cotton blends, machine-quilted, 1989, 72x84".**$175.00**
Hand-pieced, Corn & Beans, mixed calico prints around old red blocks, 1880, 70x84", G **$200.00**
Hand-pieced, Drunkard's Path, pink & white, heavy quilting, sawtooth border, 1930, 70x78", G **$150.00**
Hand-pieced, Flower Garden, multicolored prints, fence around each garden, shaped sides, 1930, 76x86", EX...**$325.00**
Hand-pieced, Grandmother's Flower Garden, multicolored cotton, scalloped edge, 1980, 96x72" **$245.00**
Hand-pieced, Indian Summer, cream muslin & burnt orange, cotton, muslin backing, bias bound, 1920s, 72x78".**$345.00**
Hand-pieced, Little Red School House, red, black & white block pattern, white trim, polyester batting, 1989, 72x87"..**$400.00**
Hand-pieced, Lone Star, light & dark prints on blue field, 6" border, 1930s, never used, 75x82".....................**$275.00**
Hand-pieced, Mosaic, yellow print triangles w/green & rust on white, pointed border, 1930, 70x80", EX.......**$185.00**
Hand-pieced, Nine Patch w/a Flair, various prints w/bright yellow, cotton, polyester batting, 1986, 60x80" ..**$200.00**
Hand-pieced, Ocean Waves, multicolored, white backing, binding & background, Mountain Mist batting, 1988, 78x88" **$375.00**
Hand-pieced, Ocean Waves, red & white mini print, medallion quilting in center, 1900, 67x82", EX............**$375.00**
Hand-pieced, Old Maid's Puzzle, earth tones, red stripes, 6" blocks, straight quilting, 1880, 80x80", EX.........**$250.00**

Hand-pieced, Pineapple, navy, wine & calicos w/black border, cotton, 1940s, 81x81" $450.00

Hand-pieced, School House, blue on white w/blue border, cotton blend, 1989, 80x98"..................................$345.00

Hand-pieced, Spring Blossom, blue print w/rose & white solids, broadcloth, polyester batting, 1989, 98x87", $240.00

Hand-pieced, Star Bouquet, multicolored prints & solids w/muslin backing, scalloped edge, 1989, 87x75".**$225.00**

Hand-pieced, Stepping Stones, wine calico set w/white in 8" blocks, navy & red mini-print blocks between, unused, 1900 ....$200.00

Hand-pieced, Trip Around the World, variegated prints & solids, polyester batting, 1989, 69x86"................**$200.00**

Hand-pieced, Tumbler, variegated prints & yellow, cotton, muslin backing & double-bias binding, 1990, 85x95" **$230.00**

Hand-pieced, Turkey Tracks, rose, tan & caramel prints on rose polka dot field, diamond quilting, 1920s, 65x82", VG..**$150.00**

Hand-pieced, 6-Point Star, tumbling blocks effect, 7" stars, strong colors, 1900, 74x82", EX............................**$175.00**

Hand-quilted, Hearts & Dolls, pink, white & blue, polyester & cotton, Dacron batting, eyelet ruffle, 1989, 62x46" **$145.00**

Hand-quilted, My Jungle Buddies, multicolored jungle animals on blue, cotton blend, polyester batting, 1991, 45x39"..**$100.00**

Hand-quilted, Nosegay of Flowers, pastels w/blue-green borders, muslin background & back, cotton batting, 1930s, 78x89" **$375.00**

Hand-quilted, slate blue, cotton & polyester, Dacron batting, scalloped edge, reversible, 1990, 80x96"............**$345.00**

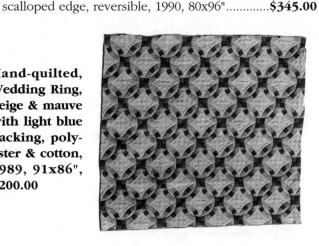

Hand-quilted, Wedding Ring, beige & mauve with light blue backing, polyester & cotton, 1989, 91x86", $200.00

Machine-pieced, Alternating Block, blue, red & green w/matching plaid, wool blends w/flannel backing, 1989, 96x77"...**$290.00**

Machine-pieced, Amish Shadows, black & purple, cotton, Mountain Mist batting, 1990, 66x86"....................**$270.00**

Machine-pieced, Amish style, black & 3 shades of blue, blue backing, cotton batting, 1989, 44x44"..................**$150.00**

Machine-pieced, Broken Star, shades of lavender on white, polyester & cotton, polyester batting, 1988, 91x91" **$575.00**

Machine-pieced, Circles & Stars, multicolored w/off-white lining, polyester fluff batting, 1989, 76x88".........**$225.00**

Machine-pieced, Color Crayons, multicolored prints & white, cotton, Mountain Mist batting, 1990, 37x55" **$65.00**

Machine-pieced, Country Scraps, multicolored & white triangles w/blue border, cotton & polyester, 1990, 30x30"..**$115.00**

Machine-pieced, Crazy Patch, multicolored prints, solids, checks, etc, gray lining, polyester batting, 1988, 74x84"..**$200.00**

Machine-pieced, Double Irish Chain, blue muslin w/rust, blue & brown cotton print, polyester batting, 1984, 50x50" **$175.00**

Machine-pieced, Double Irish Chain, pink & lavender on white, white eyelet trim, polyester batting, 1988, 44x48"..**$175.00**

Machine-pieced, Fans, shades of blue on white, cotton, polyester batting, 1990, 80x94" **$275.00**

Machine-pieced, Giant Dahlia, solids & prints in pinks & greens, pink binding, Mountain Mist batting, 1988, 60" dia **$300.00**

Machine-pieced, Lone Star, shades of blue on white, cotton & polyester, polyester batting, 1990, 94x100" **$400.00**

Machine-pieced, Lone Star, solids & prints in shades of mauve on ecru, polyester & cotton, 1989, 87x104"...........**$500.00**

Machine-pieced, Ohio Star, navy & red design on off-white block pattern, cotton & polyester, 1987, 105x90", $500.00

Machine-pieced, Ohio Star, navy & white, cotton, feather wreath quilting, Mountain Mist batting, 1990, 85x96" **$345.00**

Machine-pieced, Ohio Star Images, lilac, peach & ecru tapestry, cotton w/polyester batting, octagonal, 1989, 25x25" **$85.00**

Machine-pieced, Patriotic Squares, checked design w/blue border, cotton blends, polyester batting, 1991, 35x40" .**$100.00**

Machine-pieced, Rail Fence, yellow, red & blue, cotton & polyester, reversible, 1989, 110x92" **$225.00**

Machine-pieced, Reverse Roman Square, wine, white & blue, cotton & polyester, Polyfil batting, 1989, 74x88" **$175.00**

Machine-pieced, Rocky Mountain Rainbow, pastels, cotton, crosshatch quilting, Mountain Mist batting, 1989, 98x102" **$300.00**

Machine-pieced, Sheep, blue plaids in diamond block pattern w/red hearts, rail fence border, cotton, 1989, 77x94" **$400.00**

Machine-pieced, Snails Trails, light & dark prints, cotton blend, double-bias binding, Dacron batting, 1990, 91x102" **$345.00**

Machine-pieced, Texas Star, rose, white & mint green w/white trim, cotton, 1985, 108x110" **$455.00**

Machine-pieced, Variable Star, shades of pink on print background, cotton, polyester batting, 88x104" **$460.00**

Machine-pieced, Windmill, cream & 3 shades of peach, cotton & polyester, polyester batting, 1990, 85x98" ..**$385.00**

Machine-pieced, 6-Point Stars, multicolor on white w/green, white & yellow border, cotton, 1988, 88x94" **$345.00**

Quimper

This is a type of enamel-glazed earthenware made in Quimper, France, since the 1600s. They still operate there today, so some of their production falls into the time period we've geared this price guide to — 1930s on. Since its inception, the company has undergone several management and name changes, and since 1983 it has been owned by Americans.

Most of the ware you'll see is decorated by hand with colorful depictions of peasant men and women on a yellowware background. Besides dinnerware, they also made vases, figurines, tiles, and bookends.

If you'd like to learn more about the subject, we recommend *Quimper Pottery: A French Folk Art Faience* by Sandra V. Bondhus.

Bell, bagpipe form w/peasant man, unglazed clapper, HQF, 3½" **$110.00**

Bowl, lady w/bud sprigs, HBQ, square, 2½x5¼" **$25.00**

Bowl, vegetable; man & lady, w/lid, horseshoe handles, HQ, 6" **$120.00**

Cache pot, rooster & floral decoration, HBQF, flaking, 3" **$90.00**

Coffeepot, man & lady, hexagonal, HQF, 8", EX......**$140.00**

Compote, man w/walking stick, scalloped, HR Quimper, 4x8½" **$185.00**

Cup & saucer, demitasse; peasant man, HQF, chipped .**$40.00**

Egg cups, man & lady, Ordinaire, HQF, 4¼", pr **$55.00**

Holy water font, Decor Riche pattern, peasant lady, fleur-de-lis, HR Quimper, 9", $325.00

Jam pot, peasant man & fir tree, straw handle, HB, restored, 2½" **$65.00**

Mug, lady w/flowers, HQF, glaze chips, 6" **$45.00**

Pin tray, lady & fir tree, red 'S' design, HBQ, 4⅞x3" ...**$40.00**

Pitcher, peasant man w/ship & floral decoration, HBQ, 6½" **$90.00**

Plate, lady by fence, Malicorne colors, PBX, 4¾" **$85.00**

Plate, 3 yellow roses w/floral garlands, sponged rim, HQ, 8" **$65.00**

Platter, lady w/garland border, HQF, age line, 13¾x9" .**$130.00**

Porringer, lady knitting, Malicorne colors, handle, PBX, pierced, 7½" **$45.00**

Powder jar, lady's portrait, Ivoire Corbeille, HQ, 4" dia .**$55.00**

Sugar bowl, peasant lady & fir tree, handles, HBQ, 4¼x5¼" **$50.00**

Tea bag holder/spoon rest, bagpipe shape, peasant man, HQ, 3" **$55.00**

Teapot, man & lady, blue-striped handle, HQ, 8" **$200.00**

Tureen, peasant lady, Ordinaire, HQF, new, 9½x10¼" .**$100.00**

Vase, bud; lady & floral decoration, cornucopia form, HQ, 3½" **$55.00**

Vase, geometric design w/flowers, Henriot Quimper, recent, 10x5" **$30.00**

Vase, quintal; man w/flute, 5 openings, HQ, 3½", EX...**$55.00**

Wall pocket, man w/horn, bagpipe shape, HR Quimper, 8½", EX..**$120.00**

Radios

Vintage radios are those made from 1920 through the fifties. The most desirable and those whose values have been increasing the most consistently are the streamlined Deco styles, novelties, and of course the harder-to-find sets. But experts tell us that as the older sets become more scarce and expensive, even some transistors are beginning to attract radio collectors.

There are several basic types: 1) breadboard — having exposed tubes and other components that are simply attached to a rectangular board; 2) cathedral — vertical shape with a rounded or peaked top; 3) console — floor model consisting of a cabinet on legs or a tall rectangular case; 4) portable — smaller set made to be used at any location; 5) table — general term referring to sets of all shapes and sizes designed to be used atop a table; 6) novelty — having an unusual case such as a bottle or a camera, or one depicting a popular character — Mickey Mouse, for instance.

The primary factor to consider when evaluating a radio is condition. Whether or not it plays, be sure that all parts are present. Cabinet condition is important as well, and even though it is unrealistic not to expect a few nicks and scratches, be sure there are no cracks, chips, or other highly visible damage. These are the criteria our evaluations are based on.

If you'd like to learn more, we recommend *The Collector's Guide to Antique Radios, Vols 1 and 2*, and *Collector's Guide to Transistor Radios*, all by Sue and Marty Bunis. Also refer to *Collecting Transistor Novelty Radios, A Value Guide*, by Robert F. Breed.

Admiral, #Y-2027, beige 'Super 7' table transistor w/front off-center dial & right/left lattice grills, battery/BC, 1960 ....**$25.00**

Admiral, #4P28, turquoise portable AM transistor w/perforated grille, right dial & thumbwheel knob, battery, 1957 ....**$40.00**

Admiral, #5S22AN, plastic table model w/right front curved dial & off-center circular louvers, 2 knobs, AC, 1953 ....**$35.00**

Admiral, #581, portable transistor w/perforated grille, right front dial knob & right side knob, battery, AM, 1959...**$25.00**

Admiral, #63-A11, walnut console w/slanted front dial, tuning eye & lower vertical grille bars, 5 bands, AC, 1940...**$125.00**

Admiral, #7L12, red portable transistor w/right side dial knob & stylized 'V' front grille, battery, AM, 1958..........**$45.00**

Admiral, #7M16, white & yellow portable transistor w/right front dial over perforated grille, handled, battery, AM, 1958 ....**$30.00**

Air Castle, #REV248, plastic table model w/curved upper slide-rule dial, front horizontal louvers & 3 knobs, AC/DC, 1951...**$50.00**

Air Castle, #607-314, plastic table model, lg front dial flanked by horizontal decorative lines, 2 knobs, AC/DC, 1951 ....**$35.00**

Air Castle, #782.FM-99-AC, plastic table model w/lower front slide-rule dial, lg upper grille & 2 knobs, AC, 1955..**$35.00**

Air Castle, #9008W, plastic table model w/left vertical wrap-over grille bars, right dial & 2 knobs, AC/DC, 1950 ..**$45.00**

Air King, #5H110, plastic table model w/right front round dial, left lattice grille & 2 knobs, AC, 1946...........**$45.00**

Airline, #GEN-1120C, portable transistor w/right front round dial knob & logoed lower grille, handled, battery, AM, 1959 ....**$30.00**

Airline, #04WG-754C, wood table model w/front center cylinder dial, 6 push buttons & upper grille w/cutouts, battery...**$50.00**

Airline, #15BR-1535B, plastic table model w/lower front slide-rule dial, upper quarter-moon louvers & 4 knobs, $50.00

Airline, #62-288, plastic 'Miracle' table model w/right dial above 6 push buttons, tuning eye, right side knob...**$125.00**

Airline, #93BR-460A, wood table model, lower front slide-rule dial, upper horizontal grille bars, 2 knobs, battery, 1940 ....**$45.00**

American Bosch, #650, wood console, upper front dial, lower grille w/center vertical bars, 4 knobs, w/shortwave, AC, 1936 ....**$95.00**

Amrad, #81, wood 'Serenata' console highboy w/inner front dial, double doors, stretcher base, AC, 1929.......**$125.00**

Apex, #12B, wood console w/curved front dial, grille w/Gothic cutouts, 6 legs & stretcher base, AC, 1932 ....**$150.00**

Arvin, #140-P, 2-tone portable w/slide-rule dial, 2 knobs on top, lattice grille & handle, battery, AC/DC , 1947...**$35.00**

Arvin, #358T, plastic table model w/left arched dial over horizontal wrap-around louvers, 2 knobs, 1948 ...**$45.00**

Arvin, #7595, 2-tone plastic portable tranistor w/right front round dial, swing handle, battery, AM, 1960 ....**$30.00**

Arvin, #950T2, plastic trapezoid-shaped table model w/upper right round dial & knob over checkered grille, AC/DC, 1958...**$30.00**

Atwater Kent, #80, wood cathedral w/arched dial, upper cloth grille w/cutouts, twisted side columns, 3 knobs, AC, 1931, $450.00

Automatic, #CL-100, plastic table model w/right square dial, left alarm clock & center vertical wrap-over bars, AC, 1959 ....$35.00

Automatic, #TT528, plastic portable w/right front dial, left lattice grille & top right thumbwheel dial, handled, 1957...$45.00

Belmonr, #4B17, wood table model w/lower front slide-rule dial, upper vertical grille openings & 2 knobs, battery, 1946 ....$30.00

Bendix, #111, walnut plastic table model w/slide-rule dial, vertical grille bars & 2 knobs, rear hand-hold, AC/DC, 1949 ....$40.00

Bendix, #55L2, ivory plastic table model w/slide-rule dial, vertical grille bars & 2 knobs, rear hand-hold, AC/DC..$40.00

Bendix, #753M, wood table model w/lower sm slide-rule dial, lg front glass clock face, 5 knobs, AC, 1953 .$65.00

Benrus, metal table model w/right-side dial knob & lg front clock face, left volume knob, AC, 1955.................$50.00

Bulova, #100, plastic table model w/left dial & clock, right metal grille, side knobs, step-down top, AC, 1957 .$40.00

Channel Master, #6506, plastic portable transistor w/right front dial, left metal perforated grille, battery, 1960...........$40.00

Channel Master, #6536, walnut table model, right clock & slide-rule dial, left lattice grille, 4 knobs, AM/FM, 1960 ....$25.00

Colonial, #T345, wood cathedral w/lower front arched dial & upper cloth grille w/cutouts, 3 knobs $175.00

Columbia, #400R, red plastic portable transistor w/right window dial, circular grille w/vertical bars, battery, AM, 1960 ....$25.00

Concord, #1-513, plastic portable w/right rectangular dial, patterned grille & 3 knobs, handled, battery/AC/DC, 1949 ....$35.00

Concord, #1-611, leatherette portable w/slide-rule dial, horizontal grille bars & 2 knobs, battery/AC/DC, 1948..$30.00

Continental, #SW-7, portable transistor w/slide-rule dial, perforated grille, swing handle, w/shortwave, battery, 1960 ....$35.00

Coronado, #RA37-43-9240A, wood table model w/phonograph, lift top, right side dial, lg front grille, AC, 1955...$25.00

Coronado, #RA37-43-9240A, wood table model w/phonograph, lift top, right side dial & lg front grille, AC, 1955 ....$25.00

Coronado, #RA48-9898A, portable transistor, leather case, right dial, lattice grille w/cutouts, handle, battery, AM, 1959 ....$30.00

Crosley, #11-109U, plastic table model w/center front dial, inner checkered grille & crest, 2 knobs, AC/DC, 1952...$60.00

Crosley, #56TX, cream plastic table model w/right front square dial above 3 knobs, wrap-around grille bars, 1946 ....$50.00

Crosley, #62-148, wood tombstone table model with lower front round airplane dial, upper grille with cutouts, inlay, AC, $130.00

Crosley, #8H1, wood console w/upper front round dial, lower cloth grille w/cutouts, w/shortwave, AC, 1934 ....$125.00

Crown, #TR-875, portable transistor w/slide-rule dial, perforated grille, telescoping antenna, w/shortwave, battery, 1960 ....$25.00

Delco, #R-1410, luggage-type portable w/front slide-rule dial, 2 knobs & handle, battery/AC/DC, 1948.......$35.00

Delco, #1107, wood tombstone w/'airplane' dial & cloth grille w/3 vertical bars, 4 knobs, w/shortwave, AC, 1935...$125.00

Detrola, #383, cloth-covered portable w/right front square dial, left grille & 2 knobs, handled, battery/AC/DC, 1941...$30.00

Detrola, #576-1-6A, wood table model w/upper slanted slide-rule dial, cloth grille w/vertical bars & 3 knobs, AC/DC, 1946...$60.00

Dewald, #A-509, plastic table model, slide-rule dial, horizontal louvers, 1 front/1 side dial, w/shortwave, AC/DC, 1948 ....$40.00

Dewald, #K-544, portable transistor w/leather case, right front horseshoe dial, left grille, handled, battery, AM, 1957 ....$40.00

Echophone, #80, walnut cathedral, arched dial w/escutcheon, decorative pressed-wood grille, 3 knobs, AC, 1931 ....**$275.00**

Emerson, #BM-215, 2-tone wood table model w/right front dial & left horizontal louvers, 2 knobs, AC/DC, 1938......**$45.00**

Emerson, #CL-256, wood 'Strad' table model w/off-center dial, left horizontal louvers, cut-out top, AC/DC, 1930..**$425.00**

Emerson, #F-133, 2-tone wood table model w/right front gold dial, horizontal 3-bar grille, w/shortwave, AC/DC, 1936 ....**$85.00**

Emerson, #547A, brown plastic table model w/front slide-rule dial below louvered grille, 2 knobs, AC/DC, 1947, $40.00

Emerson, #555, 'All-American' plastic portable transistor, left lattice grille, thumbwheel knobs, battery, AM, 1959 ....**$35.00**

Emerson, #747, plastic portable w/right front dial, horizontal grille bars, thumbwheel knob, handled, battery, 1954 ....**$35.00**

Emerson, 2-tone Catalin table model w/round dial, center panel w/checkered grille, 2 knobs, AC/DC, 1946 ..**$175.00**

Emmerson, #A-130, wood table model w/Ingraham case, right dial, left cloth grille w/horizontal bars, 2 knobs, AC, 1936 ....**$45.00**

Fada, #C-34, leatherette portable w/flip-open front, inner dial, vertical grille bars, handled, battery/AC/DC, 1941....**$55.00**

Fada, #43, wood cathedral table model w/ornate pressed-wood front, arched window dial, scalloped top..**$265.00**

Fada, #845, plastic Deco table model w/right round dial, horizontal grille bars & 2 knobs, handled, AC/DC, 1950..**$185.00**

Fairbanks-Morse, wood console, upper round dial w/automatic tuning, lower cloth grille w/vertical bars, AC, 1937..**$165.00**

Farnsworth, #BT-68, leatherette portable w/fold-down front, inner dial, grille & 2 knobs, handled, battery/AC/DC, 1946 ....**$45.00**

Farnsworth, #GT-065, plastic table model, slanted dial, cloth grille, vertical fluting & 2 knobs, handled, AC/DC, 1948..**$45.00**

Federal, #1028T, wood table model w/rounded corners, right square dial & left square grille w/inverted corners, 3 knobs..**$45.00**

Firestone, #4-A-3, plastic 'Diplomat' table model w/right dial & left vertical grille bars w/lower loops, AC/DC, 1948..**$65.00**

Firestone, #4-A-86, wood console w/pull-out phonograph drawer, inner right slide-rule dial, 4 knobs, FM, AC, 1951 ....**$80.00**

Firestone, #4-C-29, plastic portable w/tubes & transistors, right dial & left checkered grille, handled, battery, 1956 ..**$50.00**

Garod, #5A4, plastic 'Thriftee' table model w/upper slanted slide-rule dial, lower horizontal grille bars, 1948..**$40.00**

General Electric, #A-64, wood tombstone w/arched top, center horizontal pointer dial, upper grille cutouts, 4 knobs, 1935..**$140.00**

General Electric, #C-415C, plastic table model w/clock above slide-rule dial, right & left vertical grills, AC, 1958 ....**$30.00**

General Electric, #M-51-A, 2-tone wood tombstone w/square 'airplane' dial, cloth grille w/vertical bars, 4 knobs, 1935..**$125.00**

General Electric, #P715-D, metal & leatherette portable transistor w/dial above perforated grille, pull-up handle, 1958 ....**$30.00**

General Electric, #P750A, portable transistor w/leather case, right-side dial knob, front lattice grille, AM, 1958.**$40.00**

General Electric, #P800A, plastic portable transistor, right dial w/magnifier, left lattice grille, center knob, AM, 1959..**$35.00**

General Electric, #201, cream plastic table model w/lower front dial & upper metal crisscross grille, 2 knobs, 1946..**$45.00**

General Electric, #411, plastic table model w/lg front dial & left vertical grille bars, 2 knobs, 1950................**$35.00**

General Electric, #440, plastic table model, arched dial above bar w/2 thumbwheel knobs at ends over bar grille, 1954..**$45.00**

General Motors, #250A, 'Little General' wood cathedral w/cloth cut-out grille above window dial, 3 knobs, AC, 1931 ....**$250.00**

Gilfillan, #66B, 'Overland' leatherette portable w/double front doors, copper grille, knobs, handle, battery/AC/DC, 1946..**$50.00**

Gloritone, #26-P, wood cathedral, cloth grille w/cutouts above center window dial w/escutcheon, 3 knobs, 1929..**$200.00**

Grantline, #502, 'Series A' plastic Deco table model w/right dial, left arched grille above horizontal bars, side knob..**$120.00**

Grunow, #588, wood table model w/flat top & rounded corners, left wrap-around grille w/horizontal bars, 3 knobs, 1937 ....**$85.00**

Halson, #T10, wood table model w/right front dial, left cloth grille w/Deco cutouts, 2 knobs, AC, 1937............**$45.00**

Hoffman, #C503, wood console w/phonograph, inner slide-rule dial, 5 knobs, 6 push buttons, lift top, 2 shortwaves, 1948..**$95.00**

Jackson-Bell, #4, wood cathedral, cloth grille w/cutouts above front window dial w/escutcheon, 3 knobs............**$200.00**

Jewel, #5057U, plastic 'Wakemaster' table model w/center clock, right slide-rule dial, checkered grille, 5 knobs, 1950 ....**$45.00**

Jewel, #940, plastic table model w/lattice grille between right front dial & left clock, 6 knobs, AC **$30.00**

Kadette, #44, red plastic 'Jewel' table model w/right front dial, center grille w/cutouts, 2 knobs, AC/DC, 1935.....**$300.00**

Knight, #5H-565, plastic table model w/lower round dial over graduated vertical bars, 2 knobs, AC/DC, 1951..**$25.00**

Knight, #6K-718, 2-tone leatherette portable w/center front round dial, 2 knobs, handled, battery/AC/DC, 1953...**$35.00**

Knight, #68B-151K, rectangular wood table model w/right oval dial & left cloth grille w/cutouts, 4 knobs, battery, $60.00

Kolster, #K-140, wood lowboy console w/upper dial, lower grille w/cutouts, doors, 6 legs, 10 tubes, AC, 1932...**$185.00**

Lafayette, #FS-122, portable transistor w/upper front thumbwheel dial, lower perforated grille, battery, AM, 1959 ....**$25.00**

Lee, #400, table model w/red flocked case, right half-moon dial printed on flocking, 2 plastic knobs, 1948...**$150.00**

Majestic, #353, wood 'Abbeywood' console w/phonograph, ornate Charles II design w/lift top, front dial & knobs, 1932 ....**$235.00**

Majestic, #6G780, plastic transistor w/left front dial above V-shaped metal perforated dial, battery, AM............**$35.00**

Majestic, #92, walnut highboy console, fold-open doors, oval grille w/cutouts above window dial, 3 knobs, AC, 1929 ....**$140.00**

Mantola, #R-78162, wood console w/pull-out phonograph drawer, inner right slide-rule dial, 4 knobs, FM, AC, 1948 ....**$75.00**

Mitchell, #1268R, plastic upright table model w/square clock above horizontal bars & left dial knob, AC, 1951.**$40.00**

Motorla, #68X11Q, 2-tone plastic model w/slanted slide-rule dial above geometric grille, 2 knobs, AC/DC, 1949 ....**$65.00**

Motorola, #X11E, portable transistor w/rear swing-out stand, dial above perforated grille w/'M' logo, battery, AM, 1960 ....**$30.00**

Motorola, #5M1, metal 'Playmate Jr' portable w/flip-up front, inner dial, 2 knobs, handle, battery/AC/DC, 1950..**$45.00**

Motorola, #53C1B, plastic table model w/left alarm clock, right front dial, 3 knobs, footed, 1954 ....**$30.00**

Motorola, #57A, red plastic table model w/center 'M' logo over horizontal grille bars, right & left tuning & volume knobs **$25.00**

Olympic, #501, 2-tone wood table model w/phonograph, lift-up top, right front square dial above 3 knobs, left grille, AC..**$35.00**

Olympic, #808, portable transistor w/right front dial, lg lattice grille, 2 knobs, handled, AM, battery, 1960....**$25.00**

Packard-Bell, #65A, wood table model, right front square dial, left cloth grille w/horizontal bars, 3 knobs, handle, 1940 ....**$50.00**

Packard-Bell, #771, wood table model, upper slanted slide-rule dial, crisscross grille, 4 knobs, w/shortwave, AC, 1948 ....**$40.00**

Philco, #E-810-124, plastic table model w/rounded corners, round dial over checked panel, perforated grille, footed, 1957 ....**$20.00**

Philco, #37-38, wood 'shouldered' tombstone w/cut-out grille above round center dial, 4 knobs, battery, 1937 ...**$80.00**

Philco, #37-630, wood console w/recessed front, upper round dial, lower cloth grille w/3 vertical bars, 4 knobs, 1937 ....**$135.00**

Philco, #38-9, wood table model w/rounded left side, round dial, cloth grille w/Deco cutouts, 4 knobs, AC, 1938 ....**$80.00**

Philco, #48-206, leatherette table model w/plastic louvered escutcheon, rounded corners, 2 knobs, AC/DC, 1948, $45.00

Philco, wood cathedral w/center window dial, upper grille w/scrolled cutouts, 7 tubes, 3 knobs, AC............**$300.00**

Pilot, #X3, wood table model w/squared top corners & rounded bottom corners on base, slanted slide-rule dial, AC/DC..**$40.00**

Radiola, #517, 2-tone wood table model w/rounded top corners, slanted slide-rule dial above horizontal bars, 1942...**$50.00**

Raytheon, #T2500, portable leatherette transistor, w/2 top knobs & handle, front grille w/crest, battery, AM, 1956 ....**$110.00**

RCA, #BX-57, plastic portable, 'alligator' panels, slide-rule dial above louvered bars, top handle, battery/AC/DC, 1950 ....**$40.00**

RCA, #120, wood cathedral, upper cut-out grille above 2 window dials, 2 knobs, AC, 1933 ....**$225.00**

RCA, #2-C-521, plastic table model w/right round dial, left alarm clock, center horizontal bars, 5 knobs, AC, 1953...**$20.00**

RCA, #8X521, maroon plastic table model w/lg round top dial, front horizontal louvered grille, right side knob, 1948 ....**$55.00**

RCA, #9-Y-7, wood table model w/phonograph, lift top, front slide-rule dial above horizontal grille bars, AC, 1949 ....**$30.00**

Regency, #TR-1, plastic portable transistor, round dial, dotted grille, thumbwheel knob, battery, AM, 1955, minimum value **$250.00**

Roland, #54B, plastic table model w/front center round dial over lg horizontal louvers, 1 lower knob.............**$20.00**

Sentinel, #314W, plastic trapezoid-shaped table model w/rounded corners, slide-rule dial above wrap-around louvers, 1948 ....**$45.00**

Silvertone, #1582, wood cathedral cut-out grille above arched dial, 5 knobs, 7 tubes..............................**$260.00**

Silvertone, #2002, ivory metal table model w/right round dial over crisscross grille, lower left knob, AC, 1950...**$50.00**

Silvertone, #3001, brown plastic table model w/upper thumbwheel dial, V-shaped cloth grille above checked panels, 1954...**$35.00**

Silvertone, #9250, red plastic portable transister w/back stand, upper triangle dial, lower perforated grille, AM, 1959 ....**$25.00**

Sonora, #RDU-209, wood table model w/upper slide-rule dial, waterfall front w/horizontal louvers, 3 knobs, AC/DC, 1946...**$45.00**

Sonora, #610, plastic portable transistor w/right dial & left lattice grille, thumbwheel knob, battery, AM, 1958 .....**$30.00**

Sparton, #10, wood 'shouldered' tombstone w/cut-out grille above arched dial, 3 knobs, 7 tubes, AC, 1931...**$125.00**

Steelman, $450, plastic table model w/right round dial, left round alarm clock, center vertical grille bars, AC, 1952 ....**$25.00**

Sterling, #LS-4, plastic portable, w/right thumbwheel dial, diagonal perforated chrome grille, top handle, battery...**$40.00**

Stewart-Warner, #R-1301-A, wood tombstone w/rounded step-down top, cut-out grille above round dial, 4 knobs..**$160.00**

Stewart-Warner, #9002-B, plastic table model w/upper slanted slide-rule dial, lower horizontal louvers, 3 knobs, 1948 ....**$40.00**

Stromberg-Carlson, #1101, plastic table model w/raised top, slide-rule dial above wrap-around louvers, 2 knobs..**$50.00**

Stromberg-Carlson, #115, wood console, upper octagonal dial, lower cut-out cloth grille, w/shortwave, battery, 1936 ....**$110.00**

Sylvania, #1102, red plastic table model w/right-side dial knob, front lattice grille, left side switch, AC/DC, 1957..**$25.00**

Sylvania, #5P11R, plastic portable transistor w/left window dial, front horizontal grille bars, battery, AM, 1960..**$35.00**

Tele-Tone, #109, plastic table model w/circle cut-out grille above slide-rule grille, 2 knobs, AC/DC, 1946......**$45.00**

Telechron, #8H59, plastic 'Musalarm' trapezoid-shaped table model, clock left of circle cut-out grille, knobs below, 1950 ....**$45.00**

Toshiba, #6TR-92, portable transistor, round case w/floral design, dial above grille, handled, battery, AM, 1959...**$125.00**

Trav-Ler, #5054, sm square table model w/rounded corners, right front dial w/left horizontal louvers, 2 knobs, 1948..**$80.00**

Truetone, #D2810, plastic table model w/upper slanted slide-rule dial, lower cloth grille, 2 knobs, AC/DC, 1948 ....**$40.00**

Westinghouse, #H-138, wood console w/horizontal louvers above slide-rule dial, 4 knobs & 6 push buttons, AC, 1946 ....**$100.00**

Westinghouse, #H-653P6, plastic portable transistor w/round dial over 2-toned checked & perforated grille, AM, 1958 ....**$25.00**

Westinghouse, #H-656P5, portable transistor w/checked grille above round dial resting in bow-tie design, AM, 1959 ....**$30.00**

Westinghouse, #WR-678, portable 'Carryette' w/brown & white cloth cover, front dial, handled, battery/AC/DC, 1940 ....**$30.00**

Zenith, #Y-723, plastic table model, bowed sides, front off-center round dial over checked grille, side knob, AM/FM, 1956 ....**$35.00**

Zenith, #288, 2-tone wood Deco tombstone w/cut-out grille above window dial, 6 knobs, w/shortwave, AC, 1934..**$175.00**

Zenith, #5-C-01, plastic 'Consoltone' table model w/right front dial, left cloth grille, 5 tubes, 1946................**$45.00**

Zenith, #6-D-516, plastic table model, right dial over horizontal wrap-around louvers, 2 knobs, top handle, footed, 1940..**$45.00**

Novelty

Annie, molded bust images of Annie & Sandy atop her name on red & white striped base, Prime Designs, Hong Kong, 5x5"..**$35.00**

Big Bird in nest, Sesame Street logo on brown nest, strap handle, Muppets Inc, Hong Kong, 7¾x4¾" dia **$25.00**

Blabber Puppy, plastic 'wrinkled' body in begging pose w/light brown flocking, PowerTonic/Nasta, Hong Kong, 8x4" **$25.00**

CP Huntington Locomotive, black w/red & gold trim, Hong Kong, 5x11"...**$35.00**

Cylon Warrior (Battlestar Galactia), 3-D silver-tone head, face plate flashes w/sound, Vanity Fair, Hong Kong, 1979 ....**$25.00**

Eveready Classic, vertical unit w/black-cat logo, 9 KUSA lettered above The World's Choice for Dependability, China..**$25.00**

Football w/kicking tee, 'Official' Wilson football on orange tee, Hong Kong, 6¼x3½" dia **$22.50**

Garfield w/Odie charm, Garfield's yellow face w/'toothy' smile, black strap handle, Durhan Industries, Hong Kong, 4x3"..**$45.00**

Globe, 5¼" dia globe on 4½" dia cream-colored base, early 2-transistor, Omsco Lite, Japan.............................**$45.00**

Goofy (look-alike) on wagon, 'Goofy' seated on front of flat car w/trunk in back, Hong Kong, 7x7" **$20.00**

Gumby & Pokey, cream-colored vertical AM/FM transistor w/image of Gumby & Pokey on front perforated grille, Lewco, China..**$20.00**

Hawaiian Punch, Punchy figure, plastic, 1970s, 6", M.**$40.00**

He-Man/Skeletor, 2-sided w/heads of He-Man & Skeletor on lettered base, strap handle, PowerTonic/Nasta, Hong Kong **$20.00**

Hello Kitty, red vertical shape w/rounded corners featuring white molded kitty w/red bow, Samrio Co, Taiwan, 6x4"..**$18.00**

Hershey's Syrup, newer brown plastic bottle shape w/bowed sides & flat back & front w/label, Hong Kong, 8¼x4¼" **$40.00**

Holly Hobbie, figure w/arms resting on 1930s cathedral radio, American Greetings, Hong Kong, 7½x6" **$35.00**

Jaguar grille, chrome-look w/hood ornament atop grille & logo over front vertical bars **$40.00**

Jukebox, Rockola model #1426 in shades of green, yellow & brown, AM/FM w/cassette player, Hong Kong, 11½x7½" **$60.00**

Kent Cigarettes, top flips up on pack to expose controls, Hong Kong, 3¼x2¼" **$40.00**

Kermit the Frog, 2-D bust image of Kermit dressed in tux w/head resting in hand, Nasta, Hong Kong, 1984, 4¼x5" **$45.00**

Kraft Macaroni & Cheese, box image on 1 side, dinosaurs & dinosaur-shaped macaroni on other, plastic, 4x3", M **$20.00**

Little Lulu, 2-D head image w/strap handle, J Swedlin Inc, Hong Kong, 7x5¼"...**$50.00**

Masters of the Universe, features weapons atop lettered base, Nasta, Hong Kong, 5x4½"............................**$25.00**

Mickey Mouse, big-eared head version resting on 2 molded bars, WDP & Philgee International, Hong Kong, 4x5"...**$50.00**

Money Talks (Blabber series), shaped as dollar bill w/Money Talks lettered below image of Washington, Nasta, Hong Kong..**$45.00**

Princess of the Power Castle, image of princess in molded castle, strap handle, Mattel/Nasta, Hong Kong, 1985, 8x4" **$35.00**

Rabbit, 2-D image of running rabbit in black & white, strap handle, Hong Kong, 7⅜x6½" **$25.00**

Safeguard Soap, box shape marked Beige Safeguard Deodorant Soap, Hong Kong, 2½x3¼".................**$25.00**

Shell Logo, yellow 3-D shell shape w/red Shell lettered across front, trademark of Shell Oil Co, Hong Kong, 4¾x5"..**$100.00**

Soccer ball, black & white ball on round black base, AM/FM, Hyman Products, Hong Kong, 1987, 4½" dia **$25.00**

Spiderman, round red plastic w/black face image, strap handle, PowerTronics/Nasta, Hong Kong, 5" dia **$16.00**

Stutz Bearcat (ca 1914), metal body w/plastic undercarriage, Japan, 4½x10½" **$50.00**

Superman, features Superman coming out of green phone booth, Vanity Fair/DC Comics, Hong Kong, 1978, 7x3"..**$55.00**

Tony the Tiger, 1980, 7", MIB, $30.00

Transformers, vertical radio featuring Transformer w/movable legs & arms, Hasbro/Nasta, Hong Kong, 1984, 5x2¾" **$18.00**

Tune-a-Bear, brown & white bear w/red fabric bow tie, Hong Kong, 7x4"..**$20.00**

VW Police Car, green w/white fenders, Police lettered in white on side, white siren, red light on top, Hong Kong, 4x6" **$35.00**

Railroad Collectibles

Prices continue to rise as this hobby gains in popularity. It is estimated that almost two hundred different railway companies once operated in this country, so to try to collect just one item representative of each would be a real challenge. Supply and demand is the rule governing all pricing, so naturally an item with a marking from a long-defunct, less-prominent railroad generally carries the higher price tag.

Railroadiana is basically divided into two main categories, paper and hardware, with both having many subdivisions. Some collectors tend to specialize in only one area — locks, lanterns, ticket punches, dinnerware, or timetables, for example. Many times estate sales and garage sales are good sources for finding these items, since retired railroad employees often kept such memorabilia as keepsakes. Because many of these items are very unique, you need to get to know as much as possible about railroad artifacts in order to be able to recognize and evaluate a good piece. For more information, we recommend *Railroad Collectibles, 3rd Edition,* by Stanley L. Baker.

See also Playing Cards.

Ashtray, Pullman, brown Bakelite w/white lettering, deep-dish, 4¼" dia...**$15.00**

Badge, cap; Amtrak Assistant Conductor in black letters, red & blue logo on gold finish, 1¾x3".........................**$30.00**

Badge, cap; Rock Island Brakeman, black enamel logo & title raised on silver background, arched top, rare, 1¼x3¾"..**$65.00**

Badge, cap; Union Pacific Brakeman, silver finish, rectangular w/raised border, 1⅛x4"....................................**$35.00**

Badge, Duluth Missabe & Iron Range, Special Officer 254, chrome-plated steel, 6-point star...........................**$90.00**

Badge, Duluth Missabe & Northern, nickel-plated, 1935 Employee, oval, 1⅛x2"..**$25.00**

Badge, Northern Pacific, Deputy Sheriff, nickel-plated, marked St Paul Stamp Works, 6-point star, 2½"....**$95.00**

Badge, Union Pacific Waiter, plastic shield shape, marked Whitehead Hoag, 1½x1½"....................................**$10.00**

Baggage check, Baltimore & Ohio, brass, capitol dome logo, 1½x2½"..**$40.00**

Baggage check, Northern Pacific, brass, Yellowstone Park Line logo, 2¼x2½"...**$45.00**

Book, Commodore Vanderbilt, An Epic of the Steam Age, Wheaton J Lane, Alfred Knoff publisher, 1942, hard-bound...**$15.00**

Book, Moody's Steam Railroad, 1950, hard-bound, 1,448 pages...**$20.00**

Book, Story of American Railroads, Stewart H Holbrook, Crown Publishers, 5th printing, 1959, hard-bound..**$10.00**

Book, Twentieth Century Manual of Railway Commercial & Wireless Telegraphy, Fred L Meyer, 9th edition, hard-bound..**$27.50**

Builder's plate, cast bronze, Baldwin Locomotive Works, Philadelphia PA, Serial No, August 1913, scarce, 3½x9".........**$200.00**

Calendar, Chicago & Northwestern, 1937, lg logo across top, full pad, 23x15"...**$20.00**

Calendar sheet, Great Northern, 1928, full-color portrait of Little Plume by W Langdon Kinn, 22x10".............**$40.00**

Calendar sheet, Northern Pacific, 1970, repro painting of diesel freight train coming through tunnel, 25¾x20½"...**$6.00**

Can, oil; Great Northern Railway incised on handle, stop-flow lever, Eagle, 30½"...**$48.00**

Can, oil; Northern Pacific Railway, spout top w/screw-on filler cap top center, bail handle, Eagle, 11x8¾" dia...**$36.00**

Can, oil; Pennsylvania Railroad, embossed Keystone logo on front, J-Urbana...**$35.00**

Can, water; Burlington Route, embossed logo on front, lift-off lid, cap on spout, wire handle, 9½x7½" dia....**$35.00**

Coin, embossed locomotive, Oriental lettering, 1972, 2¼" dia, MIB, $25.00

Cup, Pennsylvania Railroad, tin, Keystone logo embossed on front, rounded bottom, 2¼x4¼" dia.................**$25.00**

Door handle, box car; Chicago & Northwestern, cast iron, 3 bolts each end marked C&NW M8805, early 1900s, 10" long...**$20.00**

Funnel, Great Northern Railroad embossed on interior of mouth, tin, 5¼" dia, 6½" long.............................**$18.00**

Headrest, Illinois Central in script at buttonholes, brown on tan, 15x15½"...**$10.00**

Bell/ashtray, Southern Pacific, brass, 8", $160.00

Blanket, Great Northern Railway, brown & tan checked design w/early logo top center, scarce, 53x81"..**$250.00**

Lamp, compartment; Pullman, electric, brass wall plate w/extended light socket, white plastic shade, 7½".**$55.00**

Lamp, switch stand; Northern Pacific, cannonball-type w/4 plastic lenses, Adlake embossed on top, cast iron base, 5" dia..**$35.00**

Lamp, wall mount or table; Union Pacific, V-shaped tin base, backplate curves forward, embossed UPRR, 2½"......**$65.00**

Lantern, Burlington Route on lid, Adlake Kero Pat 3-59 on bottom, wire ring base w/oil pot insert, 3¼" red globe..**$50.00**

Lantern, Erie Railroad on lid, CT HAM Mfg Co, 39 Railroad... on twist-off base, steel wire ring base, 5" clear globe...**$150.00**

Lantern, New York, Haven & Hartford, stamped Dietz Vesta NY, tubular frame w/wire ring base, 4¼" clear globe...**$65.00**

Lantern, Pullman, nickel-plated brass, Adams & Westlake Co... on bottom, dome top w/bail, 5" clear globe..........**$450.00**

Lapel pin, Brotherhood of Locomotive Engineers, 10k gold, raised steam locomotives in center, Bastian Bros Co, oval..**$37.50**

Lapel pin, Burlington Route—Fifty Years Service, 14k gold, raised letters around red & black logo, ½" dia......**$30.00**

Lapel pin, Southern Pacific Lines, lettering around & across track & sunset in center, ⅝" dia............................**$22.00**

Lock, signal; Baltimore & Ohio, white metal, RACO raised at side, takes hexagon wrench-type key...................**$15.00**

Lock, signal; New York, Chicago & St Louis, Yale cast in circle, Yale & Towne Mfg Co on shackle, square.....**$15.00**

Lock, Southern Pacific, brass, Sunset logo cast on front, round bottom, takes flat key.................................**$85.00**

Lock, switch; Denver & Santa Fe, brass heart shape, Eagle Lock Co Terryville, Conn, USA stamped on front shackle..**$200.00**

Lock, switch; Erie Railroad, steel, Slaymaker S-diamond on key drop, brass rivets, 1966 on rear shackle.........**$12.00**

Luggage sticker, Burlington Route, yellow & violet cut-out profile of Buffalo Bill, Yellowstone Park via Cody Road, 3x4"..**$15.00**

Luggage sticker, Santa Fe, blue & silver field w/red Indian & silver logo in center, Super Chief, 3x3¾"..................**$4.50**

Magazine, Brotherhood of Locomotive Engineers Journal, Vol XXX, No 4, April, 1896......................................**$8.00**

Magazine, New York Central & Hudson River, Four-Track News, Vol IV, No 4, April, 1903.............................**$4.00**

Magazine, Railroad Stories, May, 1932..........................**$3.50**

Magazine, Railroad Trainmen's Journal, Vol XXI, No 3, March, 1904..**$4.50**

Manual, Official Guide to Railways, August 1945, softbound..**$30.00**

Map, Burlington North, roll-down, US map w/road system in red, logo in lower right, Rand McNally, 1971, 62x39"..**$12.00**

Map, Chicago & Northwestern, tourist's map of US, dated 2-53, 32x19"...**$6.00**

Map, Union Pacific, roll-down, US map w/road system in red, logo in upper right, Rand McNally, recent, 62x40"..**$17.50**

Measure, Missouri Pacific embossed on front, tin, wide spout w/grip handle, 8-oz...................................**$25.00**

Menu, Chicago, Burlington & Quincy, litho of children frolicking w/gold napkin ring on back, 1876, rare, 7x5½", $75.00

Money sack, Chicago North Shore & Milwaukee, Return To...Ill $500 in black on white, cotton, 8½x14"....**$15.00**

Napkin, Rock Island Lines, logo & Californian arched at top, magenta on tan pinstripe around border, 11¾x14¾"..**$15.00**

Neckerchief, Railroad Brotherhood, cotton, various Brotherhood logos & motifs in white on dark blue field, 20x24"...**$10.00**

Pass, Baltimore & Ohio, ornate w/train vignette in brown, 1873...**$30.00**

Pass, Buffalo, Rochester & Pittsburgh, shaded orange, 1894...**$18.00**

Pass, Chicago, St Paul, Minneapolis & Omaha, light blue w/logo, 1902...**$10.00**

Pass, employee's; Chicago & Northwestern, 30 Day Pass, pink stock paper, 1884, 3x4¼"...............................**$12.00**

Pass, employee's; Missouri, Kansas & Texas Railway, One Trip Only, tan stock paper, 1906, 3x5"...................**$8.00**

Pass, Milwaukee Lake Shore & Western, logo in circle, 1892...**$22.00**

Pass, St Paul & Pacific, plain w/gold digits, 1876........**$30.00**

Pass, Texas & Pacific, Complimentary, light blue w/ornate graphics, 1876...**$22.00**

Pencil, Pullman Co, gold lettering on blue, blue lead, unsharpened, hexagon, 7" long.............................**$2.00**

Pencil clip, Brotherhood Railroad Trainmen, red & white emblem w/green 'T,' celluloid button below metal holder..**$5.00**

Pin-back button, Amtrak, blue & red logo, Tracks are Back! in black on white, 2¼" dia...................................**$5.00**

Pin-back button, Northern Pacific, Yellowstone Park logo in red & black on off-white, 1¾" dia..........................**$12.00**

Pin-back button, Order of Railway Conductors, tin litho, blue & white lettering w/caboose in center, 1⅛" dia.....**$10.00**

Pin-back button, Railroad Centennial, 1848-1948, Chicago Ill, illustration of trains & people around edge, 1⅝" dia ..**$12.00**

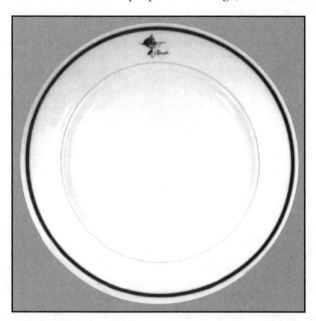

Plate, dinner; Chicago, Burlington & Quincy, Chessie, ivory w/blue trim, 9¾", $150.00

Postcard, A Delicious Northern Pacific Breakfast, pictures a table setting, menu & logo at bottom....................**$20.00**

Postcard, Chicago Rock Island & Pacific, illustration of passenger station, Royal Series....................................**$10.00**

Rule book, Minneapolis & St Louis Railway Co, gold on red, hard-bound, May 1, 1953 ....**$10.00**

Shop cloth, Milwaukee Road, logo & Work Safely, Wipe Out Accidents in blue on orange, 14x17".......................**$8.00**

Step stool, New York Central, metal, NYC System embossed on both sides, Morton Mfg Co **$160.00**

Switch key, Ann Arbor Railroad, brass, marked 479 Adlake...**$20.00**

Switch key, Chicago Great Western, brass, marked Adlake, unused..**$18.50**

Switch key, Terminal Railroad Association, brass, marked 9918 Adlake...**$30.00**

Tag, Erie Railroad, brass, marked 416 JC, octagon......**$12.00**

Tag, Great Northern, brass, marked GNRY 208, dotted border design, 1¼" dia **$8.00**

Token, Baltimore & Ohio, aluminum, 2 locomotives & Century of Progress, Chicago, 1933, penny inserted in center...**$15.00**

Torch, Burlington Route, teapot style, embossed logo on sides, tubular handle, 4½", $60.00

Token, New Haven, aluminum, streamlined locomotive in center, Compliments... & horn of plenty motif on reverse, scarce...**$18.00**

Towel, Great Northern Railway woven in white on red stripe, 15x27"...**$18.00**

Uniform button, Main Line Special, side view of steam engine in center, ⅞" dia..**$10.00**

Uniform button, New York & Boston Line Express, silver dome-type, Scovill Mfg Co Waterbury stamped on back......**$22.00**

Uniform button, Union Pacific, silver dome-type, FG Clover Co New York stamped on back..............................**$4.00**

Utility box, Northern Pacific Railway embossed on front, tin, hinged lid, 3x4½x8½" **$12.00**

Dining Car Collectibles

Ashtray, Chesapeake & Ohio, Buffalo china, front reads George Washington's Railroad..., rectangular, 3½x7½"..........**$85.00**

Bowl, cereal; Chicago & Northwestern, Buffalo China, cluster of oranges in center, Golden State at top, 6½" **$95.00**

Bowl, cereal; Union Pacific, Syracuse china, tan w/Challenger lettered in yellow & brown script, 6¼" **$25.00**

Bowl, Chicago & Northwestern, International silver hollowware, marked 05085, footed, 4¼" dia..............**$35.00**

Butter pat, New York, New Haven & Hartford, china, blue-gray w/pinstripes & kneeling nude figure cameos, 3½"..**$95.00**

Cap, waiter's; flat white paper w/blue Frisco logo & stripe, 3½x11" **$12.00**

Carafe, Soo Line, clear w/etched banner logo, cut glass neck w/bulbous bottom, 9"..**$150.00**

Champagne, New York Central, clear glass w/white frosted logo, knob style stem, 4½x3½" dia **$20.00**

Coffeepot, Baltimore & Ohio, International silver hollowware, regular spout, marked 05097, 10-oz....**$100.00**

Cordial, New York Central, clear w/gold logo, plain stem, 4" **$40.00**

Creamer, Boston & Albany, Syracuse china, white w/tan & green draped border design, 4½" **$150.00**

Creamer, Great Northern, International silver hollowware, hinged lid, marked 05082, 1946, 4-oz...................**$55.00**

Creamer, Union Pacific, International silver hollowware, marked 05045B, 1955, 8-oz, 4"..............................**$50.00**

Cup, bouillon; Southern Pacific, china, white w/individual wildflowers & black pinstripe border, 5¾"............**$30.00**

Cup & saucer, demitasse; Canadian National, Royal Doulton, yellow maple leaf w/brown pinstripe border.....**$125.00**

Cup & saucer, demitasse; Chicago, Burlington & Quincy, Syracuse china, Violets & Daisies motif..............**$125.00**

Cup & saucer, demitasse; Union Pacific, Scammell china, white w/blue scrollwork on scalloped edge.......**$150.00**

Cup & saucer, Illinois Central, Syracuse china, coral w/floral motif & white border..**$50.00**

Dish, Maine Central, Syracuse china, white w/black & orange pinstripe border, black logo top center, oval, 5¾x8¼" **$85.00**

Egg cup, Great Northern, Syracuse china, floral design w/pinstripe border, footed, 2¼"..........................**$100.00**

Goblet, Union Pacific, clear w/frosted shield logo, ball stem, footed, 5½" $15.00

Gravy boat, Denver & Rio Grande Western, Syracuse china, ivory w/blue pinstripe border, 6" $150.00

Gravy boat, Pennsylvania Railroad, Scammell china, ivory w/pink flowers & mint green border, railroad backstamp, 6" long $75.00

Knife, butter; Northern Pacific, International silver, long hollow handle w/stainless blade, 3¼".............$20.00

Knife, fruit; Southern Pacific, International silver, curved stainless blade, 5".............$25.00

Menu, breakfast; Illinois Central, Panama Limited, early steam engine to modern diesel on cover, 1963, 9x6".............$5.00

Menu, dinner; Spokane, Portland & Seattle, photo of Bonneville Dam Spillway on cover, 1957, 11x7".............$10.00

Menu, luncheon; Burlington Route, streamliner Zephyr on cover, 1943, 9x6".............$5.50

Menu, luncheon; Great Northern Railway, Oriental Limited, Indian chief riding black horse on cover, 1949, 10x6½".............$25.00

Menu holder, Great Northern, International silver hollowware, pierced sides w/2 pencil holders, marked 00295, 1946.............$95.00

Menu holder, Illinois Central, Wallace silver hollowware, pierced sides w/2 pencil holders, marked 01753.............$65.00

Menu holder, Rock Island Lines, International silver hollowware, winged Golden Rocket logo, marked 05094.............$175.00

Napkin, Milwaukee Road, lg red logo, rectangular, 7½x4¼".............$1.50

Napkin, Seaboard, heart logo w/Silver Meteor in brown, wide gray lace-effect border w/brown stripe.............$2.00

Plate, dinner; Atlantic Coast Line, china, ivory w/gray outer band, railroad backstamp, 1945, 9".............$60.00

Plate, dinner; Baltimore & Ohio, Shenango china, diesel-electric #51 1937 locomotive on border, 2nd issue, 9".............$75.00

Plate, dinner; New York Central, Syracuse china, white w/brown vertical lines, 9".............$75.00

Plate, dinner; Pennsylvania Railroad, Scammel china, white w/red pinstripe border & Keystone logo, 9".............$85.00

Plate, salad; Canadian National, china, white w/turquoise border, CNR intertwined in center, 5½".............$40.00

Plate, salad; Illinois Central, Syracuse china, coral w/floral motif & white border, 5½".............$25.00

Plate, salad; Union Pacific, Syracuse china, tan w/Challenger lettered in yellow & brown script, 6¼".............$50.00

Platter, Great Northern, china, mountain & lake scene w/flowers in the foreground, railroad backstamp, oval, 7x9".............$55.00

Platter, New York New Haven & Hartford, china, blue-gray w/pinstripes & kneeling nude figure cameos, 5½x8¼".............$60.00

Platter, Southern Pacific, Syracuse china, white w/floral border, Sunset logo top center, 8½x12¼".............$100.00

Platter, Western Pacific, Shenango china, tan w/red feathers & black lettering, 6x9".............$50.00

Sauce boat, Union Pacific, International silver hollowware, stylized Winged Streamliner logo, marked 0235, 1947, 6" long.............$60.00

Sauce dish, Gulf Mobile & Ohio, Syracuse china, white w/shaded pink border & logo, 4½".............$45.00

Sherbet, Northern Pacific, International silver hollowware, marked SF0161, footed, 1930, 3½x3½" dia.............$50.00

Shot glass, Union Pacific, clear w/frosted shield logo, 2½".............$10.00

Spoon, bouillon; Great Northern, International silver, intertwined logo.............$16.00

Spoon, iced tea; Chicago, Milwaukee, St Paul & Pacific, International silver.............$18.00

Stir stick, New Haven Railroad, blue glass w/ball ends.............$30.00

Stir stick, Union Pacific, red w/gold shield logo, oval top.............$2.00

Sugar bowl, Boston & Maine, International silver hollowware, arrow logo, marked 03800, 6-oz.............$95.00

Sugar packet, Northern Pacific, flat paper packet w/red & black Monad logo, 2x2½".............$3.00

Sugar tongs, Northern Pacific, International silver.......$75.00

Tray, bread; Santa Fe Route, Reed & Barton silver hollowware, #1610, oval, 6¼x13¼".............$130.00

Tray, celery; Union Pacific, Scammell china, white w/blue scrollwork on scalloped edge, 5½x12".............$65.00

Tumbler, Canadian Pacific, clear glass w/white enameled beaver & shield logo, 4".............$12.00

Tumbler, Chicago, Milwaukee, St Paul & Pacific, clear glass w/etched box logo, 4¾x2½" dia.............$25.00

Razors

One of the factors that should be considered when determining the worth of an old straight razor is the handle material. Ivory is perferred over celluloid, and the more decorative, the better. Plain celluloid-handled razors, unless their blades are well marked, are really worth very little. But when embellished with an animal, a nude, an automobile, etc., they often go for prices in the $30.00 to $50.00 and up range. Other materials that were used to make handles were bone, buffalo horn, mother-of-pearl, wood, aluminum, and sterling silver.

After 1880, hollow-ground blades (concave in cross-section) took the place of the older, wedge-shaped blades. This will sometimes help you determine the age of your razor.

If you'd like to learn more about them, we recommend *Sargent's American Premium Guide to Knives and Razors, Identification and Values,* by Jim Sargent.

Black Demon, sterling devil on celluloid handle, EX..$20.00

Case Brothers, candy-stripe handle, square point, Tested XX, EX.............$225.00

Case Brothers, tortoise bamboo handle, square point, EX.............$160.00

Cattaraugus Cutlery Co, blue handle, white liners, square point, EX.............$30.00

Curvfit the Woman's Razor, gold plated, Pat 1945, NMIB .**$15.00**

East St Louis BS Co Germany, brown & cream handle, fancy bolsters, EX..**$20.00**

Eversharp Schick Injector, gold plated, white & tan handle, 4½", EX **$12.50**

Fein Stahl Solingen, white composition handle w/fancy inlay, etched gold-wash blade, EX.........................**$25.00**

Gem, gold plated w/white handle, 1940s, w/original plastic case, 5⅛", EX..**$10.00**

Genco Heavy Geneva NY USA, black hard rubber handle, metal ends, EX **$5.00**

Geneva Cutlery Co Geneva NY, red & pink Bakelite handle, EX...**$12.00**

Gillette Blue Band, blue w/black letters, 1930s, VG ...**$10.00**

Joseph Allen & Sons Sheffield, scrolls & geometric design on handle, etched blade, EX..................................**$35.00**

Kane Cutlery, red transparent handle, hollow point, EX...**$40.00**

Lion Razor Works Germany, black handle, etched eagle on blade, EX **$22.00**

Oxford, faux ivory handle w/windmill scene, etched blade, EX...**$65.00**

Red Point, Utica Knife & Razor Co, rubber inlaid handle, VG..**$12.00**

Robeson Shuredge, black celluloid handle, hollow-ground blade, EX **$35.00**

Schatt & Morgan Co Titusbille PA, slick black handle, EX...**$35.00**

SR Droescher, scroll handle, Our Star etched in blade, EX...**$55.00**

Valet Auto Strop Model C, 4⅛", NM **$15.00**

Wade & Butcher's Hollow Ground, Sheffield, $25.00

Weck Bantam E Weck & Co, red-marbled ivory celluloid handle, EX...**$10.00**

Weck Bantam E Wick & Co NY, red over ivory handle, EX...**$12.00**

Worthington, Cleveland, faux ivory handle w/German silver inlay, EX **$45.00**

Wostenholm Geo & Son Wtd IXL Sheffield, celluloid handle w/scroll design, EX **$8.50**

Reamers

Reamers have been around since the mid-1700s. They've been made in silver, fine china, wood, pottery, and glass, in plain basic styles, patented models with hand-cranks, and as unusual figurals. Before soda pop became such a convenience, fruit juices were routinely served at social gatherings. Sunkist reamers were introduced around 1915 and until the sixties were cranked out in hundreds of styles and color variations. Many other companies followed suit, and novelty reamers were imported from Japan and Germany as well. Then came the age of convenience foods and the demise of the reamer.

Today some of the rarer reamers are worth hundreds of dollars. We've listed some of those you're more apt to find here; but if you want more information, we recommend that you read *Kitchen Glassware of the Depression Years* by Gene Florence.

Anchor Hocking, clambroth green, side spout & tab handle, pointed cone, flat bottom...................................**$125.00**

Anchor Hocking, fired-on black, vertically ribbed w/side spout, tab handle, flat bottom..............................**$15.00**

Anchor Hocking, transparent deep green, pitcher set, lg bulbous shape w/horizontal ribbing around middle .**$70.00**

Anchor Hocking, transparent green, vertical ribbing w/smooth rim, loop handle, footed......................**$20.00**

Federal Glass, transparent amber, fluted sides w/smooth rim, loop handle, footed.......................................**$20.00**

Federal Glass, transparent green, smooth-sided, tab handle, flat bottom, sm **$15.00**

Federal Glass, transparent pink, verticallly ribbed panels alternate w/smooth panels, loop handle, footed..**$30.00**

Fleur-de-lis, red/orange swirl slag, straight side w/embossed design, swirled cone, angled & curved handle, flat bottom...**$425.00**

Foreign, transparent forest green, square w/vertical ribbing at diagonal corners, corner tab handle, marked Argentina **$135.00**

Foreign, transparent pink, boat shape w/embossed floral design, pointed cone, closed handle...................**$100.00**

Hazel Atlas, cobalt blue, concave w/Crisscross design, loop handle, swirled cone, flat bottom.........................**$275.00**

Hazel Atlas, crystal, Crisscross design on slightly tapered base, side spout & tab handle, flat bottom, sm.....**$12.00**

Hazel Atlas, fired-on red measuring cup set, opaque white reamer, footed...**$45.00**

Hazel Atlas, opaque white, fluted side w/side spout & tab handle, swirled cone, flat bottom **$40.00**

Hazel Atlas, opaque white decorated cup sets, footed, each..**$38.00**

Hazel Atlas, opaque white w/red trim, fluted side w/side spout, tab handle, pointed cone, flat bottom........**$25.00**

Hazel Atlas, transparent green, 4-cup pitcher set w/8 panels arched at top, thick rim, flat bottom, marked A&J, 2-piece...**$35.00**

Hazel Atlas, transparent pink, concave w/Crisscross design, loop handle, swirl cone, flat bottom, lg **$250.00**

Hazel Atlas, transparent pink, 2-cup measuring set, bowl shape w/ear-shaped handle & opposite spout, footed, 2-piece...**$125.00**

Indiana Glass, crystal, concave w/vertical fluting, smooth rim, side spout, loop handle, flat bottom, embossed ASCO... ....**$20.00**

Indiana Glass, transparent green, smooth band around rim w/vertical fluting below, recessed cone, side spout, tab handle $20.00

Jeannette, crystal, horizontal ribbing w/beads around base of cone, side spout & tab handle, flat bottom $10.00

Jeannette, transparent ultramarine blue, footed boat shape, loop handle, ridged cone, $110.00

Lindsey, transparent pink, Lindsey embossed on thick straight side, ribbed cone, angled handle, flat bottom $425.00

McKee, custard w/red trim, footed boat shape w/swirled pointed cone, loop handle, embossed McK.........$20.00

McKee, opalescent white, embossed Sunkist, marked Made in USA on base, $85.00

McKee, opaque Delphite blue, footed boat shape, swirled cone w/rounded top, loop handle, embossed McK $275.00

Tufglas, light or dark crystal, straight smooth side w/slick handle & side spout, flat bottom $85.00

US Glass, decorated crystal, 2-cup measuring set, footed bowl shape w/thick ear-shaped handle, 2-piece, each set $25.00

US Glass, frosted green, 2-cup set w/plain sides, thick band around rim, ear-shaped handle, footed, transparent cone $25.00

US Glass, transparent pink, paneled tub shape w/metal swing handle, 2-piece..$200.00

US Glass, transparent pink, pitcher set, horizontal ribbing above & below bulbous body, ear-shaped handle, w/lid, 3-piece $275.00

US Glass, transparent turquoise blue, tub shape w/horizontal bands, slick handle, rounded bottom, 2-piece.....$100.00

Valencia, opaque white, embossed lettering, ribbed cone w/flat top, squared handle $100.00

Valencia, transparent green, plain side, ribbed cone w/flat top, squared handle..$85.00

Westmoreland, crystal decorated w/oranges or lemons, fluted w/smooth rim, upturned handle, flat bottom, each $65.00

Records

Records are still plentiful at flea markets and some antique malls, though not to the degree they were a year or so ago. Garage sales are sometimes a great place to buy old records, since most of what you'll find there have been stored more carefully by their original owners.

There are two schools of thought concerning what is a collectible record. While some collectors prefer the rarities — those made in limited quantities, by an unknown who later became famous, or those aimed at a specific segment of music lovers — others like the vintage Top-10 recordings. Now that they're so often being replaced with CDs, we realize that even though we take them for granted, the possibilty of their becoming a thing of the past may be reality tomorrow.

Whatever the slant your collection takes, learn to visually inspect records before you buy them. Condition is one of the most important factors to consider when assessing value. To be judged as mint, a record may have been played but must have no visual or audible deterioration — no loss of gloss to the finish, no stickers or writing on the label, no holes, no skips when it is played. If any of these are apparent, at best it is considered to be excellent and its value is at least 50% lower. Many of the records you'll find that seem to you to be in wonderful shape would be judged only very good, excellent at the most, by a knowledgeable dealer. Sleeves with no tape, stickers, tears, or obvious damage at best would be excellent; mint condition sleeves are impossible to find unless you've found old store stock.

It's not too uncommon to find old radio station discards. These records will say either 'Not for Sale' or 'Audition Copy' and may be worth more than their commercial couterparts.

Rather than to try to list enough 45s to give you a general feel for the market, let me say this. You'll find them at garage sales and flea markets everywhere at prices from 10 for $1.00 up to $3.00 or $4.00 each. But if you'd rather buy from a used record dealer who has them cleaned, graded, and sorted by artist, expect to pay considerably more because of the time and effort expended by the dealer. I've dragged home thousands bought a box full at a time and for awhile had a great time doing my own sorting. But I'm 'over it,' and now I'd much rather pay more for the ones that have proven to be a little hard to find.

If you'd like more information, we recommend *American Premium Record Guide* by L.R. Docks.

33⅓ rpm

Acuff, Roy; Favorite Hymns, MGM 3707, VG..............$10.00
Acuff, Roy; Treasure of Country Hits, Hichory 147, NM..$40.00
Animals, Animal Tracks, MCA 4305, VG+ $25.00
Anka, Paul; Diana, ABC Paramount 420, VG $15.00
Association, Windy, Warner Brothers 45103, M............$4.00
Atkins, Chet; Picks on the Beatles, RCA 3531, NM $20.00
Bare, Bobby; The Best of..., RCA 3479, NM................$50.00
Belafonte, Harry; Calypso, RCA 1248, VG..................$30.00
Berry, Chuck; Rockin' at the Hop, Chess 1448, VG.....$30.00
Bill Haley & the Comets, Greatest Hits, MCA 161, NM..$12.00
Bostic, Earl; Dancetime, King 525, NM......................$75.00
Brown, Savoy; A Step Forward, Parrot 71029, NM $15.00
Chad & Jeremy, 5+10=15, Fidu 101, NM $40.00
Chad Mitchell Trio, The Best of..., Kapp 1334, VG+ ...$30.00
Checker, Chubby; Twist With..., Parkway 7001, VG ...$20.00
Cher, All I Really Want To Do, Imperial 9292, VG......$20.00
Collins, Tyler; Whatcha Gonna Do?, RCA 9062, NM....$10.00
Cramer, Floyd; The Best of..., RCA 2888, VG..............$25.00
Cristie, Lou; Lightnin' Strikes, MCA 4360, NM.............$25.00
Denny, Martin; The Best of..., Liberty 5502, VG+ $25.00
Diana Ross & the Supremes, Cream of the Crop, Motown
    695, NM $25.00
Domino, Fats; Million Sellers by Fats, Imperial 12195,
    NM $30.00
Donavon, Catch the Wind, Hickory 123, VG $10.00
Dudley, Dave; Talk of the Town, Mercury 20970, M ..$40.00
Eddy, Duane; $1,000,000.00 Worth of Twang, Jamie 3014,
    VG $25.00
Eric Burdon & the Animals, Every One of Us, MCA 4553,
    NM $25.00
Four Freshmen, A Today Kind of Thing, Liberty 6542,
    VG+ $25.00
Four Seasons, Gold Vault of Hits, Philips 600-196, VG .$20.00
Foxx, Redd; Laff of the Party, Dootone 214, G+..........$15.00
Francis, Connie; Sings Award Winning Motion Picture Hits,
    MCA 4048, NM $40.00
Gore, Lesley; Sings of Mixed-Up Hearts, Mercury 20849,
    NM $50.00
Guess Who, Canned Heat, RCA 4157, NM $15.00
Hamilton, Roy; You'll Never Walk Alone, Epic 3294, G- .$5.00
Herman's Hermits, The Best of..., MCA 4315, NM.......$25.00
Jan & Dean, Golden Hits, Liberty 3248, G+ $20.00
Jefferson Airplane, Takes Off, RCA 3584, VG+ $25.00
Jones, Jack; Call Me Irresponsible, Kapp 3328, VG+...$30.00
Lance, Major; Major's Greatest Hits, Okeh 14110, NM..$100.00
Limelighters, The Slightly Famous, RCA 2393, NM $50.00
Mayall, John; Live in Europe, London 589, NM $15.00
Nelson, Ricky; Ricky, Imperial 9048, VG....................$50.00
New Vaudeville Band, Winchester Cathedral, Fontana
    67560, NM..$40.00
Paul & Paula, Sing for Young Lovers, Philips 200-078,
    NM..$45.00
Pitney, Gene; Only Love Can Break a Heart, Musicor 2003,
    G $5.00
Platters, Life Is Just a Bowl of Cherries, Mercury 20589,
    NM..$75.00

Presley, Elvis; Elvis, RCA 1382, G+ $50.00
Randolph, Boots; More Yakety Sax, Monument 8037,
    NM $50.00
Reeves, Jim; Talkin' to Your Heart, RCA 2339, NM $50.00
Richie, Lionel; Lionel Richie, Motown 6007, NM $8.00
Rivers, Johnny; JR Rocks the Folks, Imperial 9293, VG.$20.00
Smothers Brothers, The Two Sides of..., Mercury 20675,
    EX..$5.00
Snow, Hank; Sings Your Favorite Country Hits, RCA 3317,
    EX..$40.00
Supremes, I Hear a Symphony, Motown 643, EX........$20.00
Tillotson, Johnny; The Tillotson Touch, MCA 4224, NM .$40.00
Van Dyke, Leroy; Walk On By, Mercury 20682, VG+ .$50.00
Vee, Bobby; BV, Liberty 3181, NM $30.00
Williams, Roger; Greatest Hits, Kapp 3260, NM..........$40.00
Young, Neil; Harvest, Reprise 2032, NM $15.00
Zentner, Si; Up a Lazy River, Liberty 3216, EX $30.00

78 rpm

Alabama Jug Band, Crazy Blues, Decca 7042, VG.......$10.00
Allen Brothers, Browns Ferry Blues, Bluebird 5403, EX..$8.00
Ambassadors, It Had To Be You, Vocalion 14792, G+..$8.00
American Quartet, Mocking Bird Rag, Victor 17204,
    G+ $8.00
Ames Brothers; You You You, RCA 5325, G+ $5.00
Aristocrats, Vagabonds, Argo 5275, G+ $10.00
Arkansas Charlie, He Was a Traveling Man, Vocalion 5298,
    EX..$15.00
Arthur Pryor's Band; Darama, Victor 4133, G+ $20.00
Autry, Gene; South of the Border, Columbia 20242,
    VG..$30.00
Autry, Gene; Take Me Back to My Roots & Saddle, Vocalion
    4172, G+ $25.00
Autry, Gene; The Horse With the Easter Bonnet, Columbia
    194, G+ $20.00
Avalon, Frankie; De De Dinah, Chancellor 1011, VG .$15.00
Bang Boys, When Lulu's Gone, Vocalion 03372, EX...$40.00
Bennett, Buster & His Band; Got Too Much Insurance,
    Columbia 3727, VG..$25.00
Berry, Richard; Good Love, RPM 477, NM $25.00
Blake, Charlie; Jackson Country, Supertone 9559, EX..$15.00
Brooks, Billy; Freight Train Blues, Columbia 15614-D,
    EX..$30.00
Brown, Charles; Risin' Sun, Aladdin 3176, NM $10.00
Buckner, Joe; Eventime, Vee-Jay 125, VG+................$20.00
Butcher, Dwight; Alarm Clock Blues, Victor 23802, EX .$40.00
Carolina Playboys, There's a New Moon Over My Shoulder,
    Sonora 7005, G+...$10.00
Carson Robinson Trio, Moonlight on the Colorado, Banner
    07711, VG $5.00
Charms, Heaven Only Knows, Deluxe 6000, G+.........$25.00
Como, Perry; Juke Box Baby, RCA 6427, G+ $5.00
Copas, Cowboy (Pappy); Filipino Baby, King 505, VG.$15.00
Corn Cobb Crushers, Dill Pickle Bag, Champion 16373,
    VG...$30.00
Cornell, Don; The Bible Tells Me So, Coral 61467, G ...$5.00
Counts, Darling Dear, Dot 1188, NM $30.00

Cramer Brothers, Simpson County, Broadway 8180, VG $20.00

Crosby, Bing; White Christmas, Decca 18429, G+ $10.00

Dalhart, Vernon; The Crepe on the Old Cabin Door, Victor 20387, G+ $8.00

Davis Trio, Sleepy Hollow, Paramount 3238, VG $15.00

Dee, Mercy; One Room Country Shack, Specialty 458, G .$10.00

Delegates, The Convention, Vee-Jay 212, NM $30.00

Dells, Time Makes You Change, Vee-Jay 258, VG $25.00

Dillard, Varetta; Promise Mr Thomas, Savoy 1160, VG..$20.00

Dixie String Band, Soldier's Joy, Silvertone 3516, VG ...$7.00

Dixon, Floyd; Wine Wine Wine, Aladdin 3135, VG $20.00

Doggett, Bill; High Heels, King 4732, NM...................$20.00

Draper, Rusty; Free Home Demonstration, Mercury 70167, G- $3.00

Eckstine, Billy; If That's the Way You Feel, Deluxe 2001, VG $5.00

Elbert, Donnie; What Can I Do?, Deluxe 6125, NM.....$25.00

Flamingo's, Would I Be Crying, Checker 853, VG.......$20.00

Fontane Sisters, Hearts of Stone, Dot 15265, G+ $5.00

Four Fellows, Angels Say, Glory 236, NM $25.00

Four Knights, Just in Case You Change Your Mind, Decca 48026, G+ $10.00

Four Tunes, I Understand Just How You Feel, Jubilee 5132, EX..$25.00

Four Vagabonds, Pleasure Is All Mine, Apollo 1039, EX $25.00

Foxx, Redd; Song Plugging, Dootone 385, NM $20.00

Foxx, Redd; The Jackasses, Authentic 390, NM $20.00

Gaylords, The Little Shoemaker, Mercury 70403, G+ $6.00

Georgia Crackers, A Broken Doll, RCA 591, VG+ $20.00

Gershwin, Elinore at Piano, Rhapsody in Blue, Vogue R725, photo record, EX, $65.00

Golden, Bobby; Turkey in the Straw, Columbia 1291, G+..$8.00

Grady Family, Carolina's Best, Columbia 15633-D, VG..$10.00

Green, Lil; What's the Matter With Love?, Bluebird 8754, G+ $7.00

H-Bomb Ferguson, Preachin' the Blues, Savoy 848, VG+..$25.00

Harris, Phil & His Orchestra; One-zy Two-zy, Ara 136, G $5.00

Hayes, Linda; Yes! I Know, Hollywood 244, NM.........$25.00

Hill, David; Jellybean, Aladdin 3354, VG+ $15.00

Ink Spots, The Gypsy, Decca 18817, G+......................$10.00

Irvan, Chris & the Sparks, Make a Little Love, RPM 417, VG $25.00

Jackson, Al; It Ain't Gonna Be Like That, Roost 608, NM...$40.00

Johnson, Lonnie; Watch Snoopy, Bluebird 0732, NM .$30.00

Jones, Grandpa; It's Raining Here This Morning, King 502, VG+..$25.00

Kidwell, Don; Don't Put Your Heart Up for Sale, MGM 11774, VG+...$25.00

King, Earl; My Love Is Strong, Ace 3278, VG $5.00

King Pleasure, Red Top, Prestige 821, G+.....................$10.00

Lanin's Orchestra, In a Boat for Two, Edison, G+ $15.00

Lazy Larry, The Gay Caballero, Cameo 9019, G+ $5.00

Lovett Sisters, Until I Lost You, VG+ $10.00

Mac, The Bum Song, Victor 40054, G+.........................$8.00

Magic Stars, Stand by Me, Phoenix 009, VG $15.00

Mayfield, Percy; Please Send Me Someone To Love, Specialty 375, G- $3.00

Midnighters, Partners for Life, Federal 12251, VG $25.00

Milburn, Amos; All Is Well, Aladdin 3293, VG............$20.00

Mills Brothers, There's No One but You, Decca 18834, G+...$10.00

Moody, James; Over the Rainbow, Prestige 896, NM..$10.00

Moore, Kenzie; Let It Lay, Specialty 456, NM............$25.00

Moore, Marta; Yo Yo Yo, Deluxe 6038, NM $30.00

Moran & Mack, Two Black Crows, Columbia 935, G+..$10.00

Murray, Billy; That's Why I Never Married, Victor 16851, G+ $10.00

Nuggers, Anxious Heart, Capitol 3052, NM.................$25.00

Page, Patti; I Went to Your Wedding, Mercury 5899, G-..$3.00

Paul, Les & Mary Ford; Vaya con Dios, Capitol 2486, VG+..$20.00

Pee Wee Hunt, 12th Street Rag, Capitol 15105, VG.....$10.00

Presley, Elvis; Good Rockin' Tonight, RCA 6381, VG..$60.00

Presley, Elvis; Love Me Tender, RCA 6643, VG $50.00

Price, Jimmie; Waiting for the Train, Cameo 9219, G+..$15.00

Prince, Sam & His Texas Blusicians; Lead Me Daddy Straight to the Bar, Decca 8649, VG...............................$30.00

Red Callender Sextet, Dolphin Street Boogie, Federal 9095, NM $25.00

Reed, Lula; Watch Dog, King 4688, G+ $10.00

Rhambo, Bo; Dianne, Cash 1047, G $5.00

Richards, Jack; Dungaree Doll, Broadway 318, G $3.00

Ritter, Tex; Jealous Heart, Capitol 179, G-...................$5.00

Rogers, Roy; I'll Be Honest With You, Decca 6016, G+ .$10.00

Royal Marimba Band; Blue Danube Waltz, Columbia 1845, G+...$10.00

Scott, Jimmy; Something From a Fool, Brunswick 84000, G+...$10.00

Shirley & Lee, I Feel Good, Aladdin 3338, EX **$20.00**

Six Teens, A Casual Look, Flip 315, NM...................**$25.00**

Spaniels, Do-Wah, Vee-Jay 131, NM..........................**$40.00**

Spiders, Witchcraft, Imperial 911, VG.....................**$20.00**

Stewart, Cal; Uncle Josh & the Sailor, Columbia 2854,
G+...**$10.00**

Sugar Boy, I Bowed on My Knees, Checker 795, NM.**$25.00**

Sykes, Roosevelt; Hush on Hush, Imperial 914, VG....**$20.00**

Tatum, Art; The Shout, Decca 468, G+.........................**$5.00**

Terry, Sonny; Early Morning Blues, Capitol 15237,
VG...**$20.00**

Thomas, John & His Orchestra, Rib Tips, Checker
809, VG **$15.00**

Thompson, Hank; Yesterday's Mail, Capitol 15132, VG.**$20.00**

Thorpe, Jimmy & His Orchestra; A Sinner I Will Be, Deluxe
2016, G+ **$15.00**

Three Flames, Cling to Me Baby, Columbia 37935,
VG+ **$25.00**

Travis, Merle; Information Please, Capitol 40072, G+....**$5.00**

Tuttle, Wesley; Tho' I Tried, Capitol 267, G+.................**$5.00**

Tyler, Big 'T'; Sadie Green, Aladdin 3384, EX..............**$25.00**

Vaughn, Sarah; Banana Boat Song, Mercury 71020, G..**$20.00**

Ward, Billy & the Dominoes; These Foolish Things Remind
Me of You, Federal 12129, G+ **$8.00**

White, Josh; Evil Hearted Man, Keynote 542, G+ **$20.00**

Willis, Bob & His Texas Playboys; End of the Line, MGM
10898, VG...**$20.00**

Extended Play

Ames Brothers, I Don't Know Why/For Sentimental Rea-
sons, stereo, RCA 4213, VG+...................................**$6.00**

Armstrong, Louis; Pennies From Heaven/Long Long Jour-
ney, RCA 1443, VG..**$8.00**

Basie, Count; Everday/It's Sand Man, ABCP 223, G+ **$4.00**

Belafonte, Harry; Scarlet Ribbons/Sylvie, RCA 9131,
VG **$3.25**

Boone, Pat; Autumn Leaves/Cold Cold Heart, Dot
1069, G+...**$250.00**

Brown, Les; Till Then/Summertime in Venice, Decca 34753,
VG **$4.00**

Campbell, Glen; Homeward Bound/Mary in the Morning,
Capitol, 54, G+ **$2.00**

Cash, Johnny; I Walk the Line/Orange Blossom Special,
Columbia 9478, G+ **$12.00**

Cole, Nat 'King'; Unforgettable/For Sentimental Reasons,
Capitol 1-357, G+ **$6.00**

Como, Perry; I'll Be Home for Christmas/God Rest Ye Gen-
tlemen, RCA 1050, G+...**$2.50**

Crosby, Bing; White Christmas/I'll Be Home for Christmas,
Decca 34184, G+ **$8.00**

Cugat, Xavier; Medias de Seda/Gypsy Aira, RCA 0014,
G+..**$3.25**

Eddy, Duane; Detour/Lonesome Road, Jamie 301, VG.**$26.00**

Elgart, Les; Sophisticated Swing/Gang That Sang Heart of
My Heart, Columbia 1820, G+................................**$6.50**

Everly Brothers, Let It Be Me/Til I Kissed You, Cadence 121,
G+ **$10.00**

Faith, Percy; McArthur Park/Scarborough, Columbia 9706,
VG+...**$9.00**

Fisher, Eddie; April Showers/Call It Madness, RCA 547-0326,
G+ **$6.50**

Ford, Tennessee Ernie; Let the Lower Lights Be Burning/My
Task, Capitol 3-756, VG+.......................................**$4.50**

Franchi, Sergio; Summertime in Venice/Autumn in Rome,
RCA 2657, VG **$5.00**

Garner, Erroll; Other Voices/This Is Always, Columbia
10141, VG...**$12.00**

Gleason, Jackie; Somebody Loves Me/Nearness of You,
Capitol 4-509, VG...**$4.00**

Goodman, Al; South Pacific Medley/Kiss Me Kate Medley,
Camden 339, NM...**$4.00**

Goodman, Benny; Call Me Impossible/Them There Eyes,
Cap 2157, VG **$5.00**

Grant, Gogi; Why Was I Born/On the Sunny Side of the
Street, RCA 4112, VG **$20.00**

Griffith, Andy; Make Yourself Comfortable/Swan Lake, com-
edy, Capitol 1-630, VG...**$20.00**

Harp, Martha Lou; Harbor Lights/When You're a Long Way
from Home, Columbia 1578, G+ **$5.50**

Henderson, Skitch; In a Sentimental Mood/Mood Indigo,
RCA 1401, NM **$3.50**

Herman, Woody; Blue Flame/Blue Moon, Columbia 1612,
G+ **$2.50**

Hirt, Al; Alley Cat/You Took Advantage of Me, RCA 3337,
G+ **$1.50**

Ink Spots, If I Didn't Care/For Sentimental Reasons, Wal-
dorf, VG..**$16.00**

Ives, Burl; Yesterday/Scarlet Ribbons, Decca 34554, VG+.**$15.00**

James, Joni; You Belong to Me/You're Foolin' Someone,
MGM 1616, G+ **$6.00**

Jones, Quincy; After Hours/In Crowd, Mercury 658,
G+ **$6.50**

Jones, Spike; That Old Black Magic/Love in Bloom, RCA
288, VG...**$24.00**

Kingston Trio, When I Was Young/Who's Gonna Hold Her
Hand, Capitol 2-1407, VG+ **$14.00**

Laine, Frankie; September in the Rain/Sleepy Old River,
Mercury 3001, G+..**$6.00**

Lanza, Mario; Hit Songs From Student Prince/Serenade
Beloved, RCA 1837, G+ **$10.00**

Lombardo, Guy; Concerto/April Showers, Decca 2002,
VG+...**$8.00**

London, Julie; Don't Take Your Love From Me/It's the Talk
of the Town, Liberty 3-3-12, VG **$10.00**

Mancini, Henry; Mr Lucky/Lightly Latin, RCA 4363, G+ .**$5.50**

Mantovani, Indian Summer/Sweethearts, London 6074,
VG+...**$6.00**

Martin, Dean; That's Amore/Come Back to Sorrento, Capitol
1-481, VG...**$12.00**

Mathis, Johnny; Will I Find My Love Today/Let Me Love
You, Columbia 10281, VG....................................**$12.00**

Matino, Al; Fascination/Crying in the Chapel, Capitol 2362,
VG **$4.00**

Miller, Glenn; Devil May Care/Don't Sit Under the Apple
Tree, RCA 0123, VG **$4.00**

Miller, Glenn; Johnson Rag/My Isle of Golden Dreams, RCA 3002, G+ **$6.00**

Mills Brothers, Basin St Blues/Carnival in Venice, Decca 2118, G+ **$10.00**

Nelson, Ricky; Be-Bop Baby/Honeycomb, Imperial 153, G+...**$20.00**

Paul, Les & Mary Ford; Mister Sandman/I Need You Now, Capitol 1-9121, G+ **$6.00**

Presley, Elvis; Jailhouse Rock/I Want To Be Free, RCA EPA 4144, G+ **$14.00**

Presley, Elvis; Loving You/Teddy Bear, RCA EPA 1-1515, VG **$60.00**

Presley, Elvis; So Glad You're Mine/Ready Teddy, RCA EPA 993, VG **$28.00**

Rich, Charlie; Big Boss Man/Life Has Its Ups & Downs, Epic 1065, VG+...**$11.00**

Sands, Tommy; Too Young/Ring My Phone, Capitol 848, G+...**$6.00**

Shore, Dinah; Hostess With the Mostess/Like Me, RCA 19-0002, VG **$6.50**

Sinatra, Frank; My Funny Valentine/They Can't Take That Away From Me, Capitol 1-488, G **$3.00**

Sinatra, Frank; Three Coins in the Fountain/Young at Heart, Capitol 1583, VG **$12.00**

Three Suns, Sweet & Low/Out of Nowhere, RCA 3075, VG.**$6.50**

Welk, Lawrence; Girl Friend/Marie, Coral 81101, VG+ .**$8.00**

Welk, Lawrence; Moonlight Bay/Yoo Hoo, Coral, 82014, VG **$12.00**

Picture Sleeves

Ames Brothers, Hello Again, RCA 7680, VG **$10.00**

Arnold, Eddy; Last Word in Lonesome Is Me, RCA 8818, VG **$8.00**

Avalon, Frankie & Annette; Merry Christmas, Pac Star 569, NM **$8.00**

Avalon, Frankie; Just Ask Your Heart, Chancellor 1040, G+ **$10.00**

Belafonte, Harry; Banana Boat/Day-O, RCA 6771, G+ ..**$5.00**

Benton, Brook; Another Cup of Coffee, Mercury 72266, VG+...**$10.00**

Boone, Pat; Walking the Floor Over You, Dot 16073, G+ **$5.00**

Browne, Jackson; For a Rocker, Asylum 69764, M........**$2.00**

Cash, Johnny; Guess Things Happen That Way, Sun 295, VG **$12.00**

Checker, Chubby; Let's Limbo Some More, Parkway 862, VG **$10.00**

Cole, Nat 'King'; Ramblin' Rose, Capitol, 4804, VG **$5.00**

Creedence Clearwater Revival, Run Through the Jungle, Fantasy 641, G+...**$3.50**

Darin, Bobby; While I'm Gone, Atco 6133, G+.............**$7.00**

Def Leppard, Rocket, Mercury 872 614, NM **$2.00**

Donovan, Mellow Yellow, Epic 10098, VG **$8.00**

Eddy, Duane; Lonely Boy, Lonely Guitar, RCA 8180, VG **$11.00**

Everly Brothers, Lucille, Warner Brothers 5163, EX.....**$25.00**

Fleetwood Mac; Gypsy, Warner Brothers 29918, VG **$5.00**

Four Seasons, Patch of Blue, Philips 40662, G+ **$10.00**

Gore, Lesley; She's a Fool, Mercury 72180, VG **$12.00**

Go-Go's, We Got the Beat, IRS 9903, NM **$5.00**

Humperdinck, Engelbert; Sweetheart, London 40054, VG+...**$4.00**

James, Sonny; My Love, Capitol 2782, VG **$5.00**

Joel, Billy; Uptown Girl, Columbia 04149, VG+.............**$2.00**

John, Elton; Mama Can't Buy You Love, MCA 41042, VG **$4.00**

Jones, Tom, Love Me Tonight, London 40038, VG........**$4.00**

Lee, Brenda; My Dreams, Decca 31628, VG **$11.00**

Bee Gees, Woman in You/Stayin' Alive, 1983, EX, $3.00

McCartney, Paul; Take It Away/I'll Give You a Ring, Columbia 18-03018, 1982, EX, $5.00

Presley, Elvis; Are You Sincere?, RCA PB-10998, VG+...**$9.00**

Presley, Elvis; Good Luck Charm, RCA 47-7992, VG...**$15.00**

Presley, Elvis; Suspicious Minds, RCA 47-9764, VG **$9.00**

Revere, Paul & the Raiders; Good Thing, Columbia 43907, M...**$12.00**

Rogers, Jimmie, Secretly, Roulette 4070, VG **$8.00**
Seeger, Bob; Tryin' To Live My Life Without You, Capitol 5042, NM...**$2.00**
Sherman, Bobby; Together Again, Metromedia 240, VG.**$40.00**
Springfield, Dusty; Stay Awhile, Philips 40180, VG **$5.00**
Stewart, Rod; I Don't Want To Talk About It, Warner Brothers 3373, VG .,...**$3.00**
Twitty, Conway; Rose, Elektra 69854, NM.....................**$2.00**

Vinton, Bobby; Just As Much As Ever/Another Memory, Epic 5-10266, VG, $4.50

Vinton, Bobby; Please Love Me Forever, Epic 10228, VG ..**$4.00**

Red Wing Potteries, Inc.

For almost a century, Red Wing, Minnesota, was the center of a great pottery industry. In the early 1900s, several local companies merged to form the Red Wing Stoneware Company. Until they introduced their dinnerware lines in 1935, most of their production centered around stoneware jugs, crocks, flowerpots, and other utilitarian items. To reflect the changes made in '35, the name was changed to Red Wing Potteries, Inc. In addition to scores of lovely dinnerware lines, they also made vases, planters, flowerpots, etc., some with exceptional shapes and decoration.

Some of their more recognizable lines of dinnerware and those you'll most often find are Bob White (decorated in blue and brown brush strokes with quail), Tampico (featuring a collage of fruit including watermelon), Random Harvest (simple pink and brown leaves and flowers), and Village Green (or Brown, solid-color pieces introduced in the fifties). Often you'll find complete or nearly complete sets, and when you do, the lot price is usually a real bargain.

If you'd like to learn more about the subject, we recommend *Red Wing Stoneware, An Identification and Value Guide,* and *Red Wing Collectibles,* both by Dan and Gail DePasquale and Larry Peterson.

Art Ware

Ash receiver, figural elephant **$60.00**
Ash receiver, pelican w/mouth open, brown **$60.00**
Ashtray, red-wing form w/embossed feathers **$38.00**
Ashtray, 75th Anniversary, 1953..................................**$135.00**
Bank, the Hamm's bear holding up Hamm's Beer sign, From the Land of the Sky Blue Water, 1960s **$225.00**
Clock, Mammy figure, hangs on wall........................**$125.00**
Figurine, lady w/tambourine, cinnamon, 10"............**$175.00**
Figurine, reclining draped lute player w/doe, maroon, #2507...**$195.00**
Jug, Egyptian, brown, miniature **$40.00**
Sewer pipe, advertising **$50.00**
Trivet, 1858-1958, yellow..**$70.00**
Vase, cherubs & garlands, Brushware, marked **$100.00**
Vase, Deco style, green, #1359 ....**$50.00**

Vase, stylized humans w/relief outlines, gold & caramel, #M3013, 15", $350.00

Cookie Jars

Bob White, unmarked **$80.00**
Carousel, unmarked..**$350.00**
Crock, white **$25.00**
Dutch Girl, yellow w/brown trim **$60.00**
Friar Tuck, green, marked..**$150.00**
Friar Tuck, yellow, unmarked **$60.00**
Jack Frost, unmarked, minimum value.........................**$600.00**
King of Tarts, white, unmarked **$350.00**

Peasant design, painted embossed figures on brown .**$60.00**
Pierre (chef), pink, marked..................................**$250.00**
Pineapple **$100.00**

Dinnerware

Bob White, beverage server & stand, 14"..................**$95.00**
Bob White, butter dish, ¼-lb.............................**$75.00**
Bob White, cruets, vinegar & oil; pr....................**$150.00**
Bob White, Lazy Susan...................................**$125.00**

Bob White, plate, dinner; $12.00

Brittany, bowl, buffet...................................**$42.00**
Capistrano, bowl, vegetable; divided **$20.00**
Country Garden, bread tray **$48.00**
Country Garden, plate, 8"................................**$10.00**
Driftwood, creamer.......................................**$12.00**
Driftwood, plate, dinner.................................**$10.00**
Frontenac, trivet..**$50.00**
Lanterns, cup & saucer **$10.00**
Lotus, plate, 7½"..**$7.00**
Lotus, teacup..**$8.00**
Lute Song, nappy **$15.00**
Magnolia, rim soup **$10.00**
Morning-Glory, creamer & sugar bowl......................**$12.00**
Morning-Glory, platter, 13"..............................**$16.00**
Orleans, water pitcher **$70.00**
Pepe, beverage server, w/lid.............................**$45.00**
Pepe, plate, 10"...**$12.00**
Random Harvest, plate, 10" **$13.00**
Round-Up, bowl, salad; 6" **$40.00**
Round-Up, bowl, salad; 9½"...............................**$80.00**
Round-Up, casserole, sm.................................**$130.00**
Round-Up, plate, dinner..................................**$30.00**
Round-Up, plate, salad **$18.00**
Smart Set, bowl, salad **$100.00**
Smart Set, cocktail tray **$45.00**
Smart Set, marmite, w/lid, handled.......................**$28.00**
Tampico, casserole **$60.00**
Tampico, coffee mug **$45.00**
Village Green, bean pot, 2-qt............................**$25.00**

Village Green, bowl, cereal..............................**$15.00**
Village Green, bowl, rimmed soup.........................**$16.00**
Village Green, bowl, sauce...............................**$8.50**
Village Green, butter dish **$25.00**
Village Green, gravy boat w/tray.........................**$25.00**
Village Green, plate, salad; 8"..........................**$8.50**
Village Green, salt & pepper shakers, pr **$20.00**

Stoneware

Bean pot, Boston style, Albany slip, marked MN, ½-gal .**$125.00**
Bowl, mixing; blue bands on white, lg **$70.00**
Bowl, red & blue sponging on saffron **$75.00**
Bowl, white w/blue bands on rim..........................**$70.00**
Butter crock, low style, white, marked RW, 10-lb **$75.00**
Butter jar, low style, Albany slip, marked RW, 1-lb.....**$80.00**
Chamber pot, blue bands on white, unsigned.............**$125.00**
Churn, birch leaves & #8, 8-gal........................**$350.00**
Churn, red wing & #2 on white, marked RWUS, 2-gal..**$225.00**
Cooler, Ice Water, red wing & #3 in cobalt, marked RW, 3-gal **$425.00**

Jug, advertising Dells Extra Tea & Coffee, unsigned, ½-pt, $150.00

Jug, common w/ball top, Albany slip, marked MN, 1-gal .**$50.00**
Jug, common w/funnel top, Albany slip, marked MN, 1-gal .**$85.00**
Jug, common w/standard top, Albany slip, marked MN, ½-gal **$60.00**
Jug, fancy w/white & brown ball top, marked MN, 1-pt..**$50.00**
Jug, molded seam w/wide mouth, white, marked RW, 1-qt.**$45.00**
Jug, shoulder type w/cone top, white, marked RW, 1-gal..**$60.00**
Jug, shoulder type w/dome top, brown & salt glaze, 1-gal.**$75.00**
Jug, shoulder type w/funnel top, brown & salt glaze, 1-gal.**$80.00**
Jug, syrup; cone top, white, marked MN, ½-gal **$70.00**
Milk pan, Albany slip..................................**$85.00**
Pitcher, barrel form, Albany slip, marked RW **$125.00**
Pitcher, milk; Russian style, Albany slip, 1-gal............**$90.00**
Spittoon, salt glaze, unsigned **$200.00**

Regal China

Perhaps best known for their Beam whiskey decanters, the Regal China company (of Antioch, Illinois) also produced some exceptionally well-modeled ceramic novelties, among them their 'hugger' salt and pepper shakers, designed by artist Ruth Van Tellingen Bendel. Facing pairs made to 'lock' together arm-in-arm, some huggies are signed Bendel while others bear the Van Tellingen mark. Another popular design is her Peek-a-Boo Bunny line, depicting the coy little bunny in the red and white 'jammies' who's just about to pop his buttons.

See also Old MacDonald's Farm.

Bendel Shakers

Bears, white w/brown & pink trim, pr	**$125.00**
Bunnies, white w/black & pink trim, pr	**$135.00**
Kissing pigs, gray w/pink trim, lg, pr	**$275.00**
Love Bugs, burgundy, lg, pr	**$140.00**
Love Bugs, burgundy, sm, pr	**$70.00**
Love Bugs, green, sm, pr	**$55.00**

Cookie Jars

Cat	**$450.00**
Clown, multicolor	**$575.00**
Diaper Pin Pig	**$450.00**
Dutch Girl, blue accents	**$500.00**
French Chef	**$300.00**
Goldilocks, blue accents	**$275.00**
Humpty Dumpty, red bottom	**$275.00**

Peek-a-Boo, cookie jar, $1,300.00; matching salt and pepper shakers, sm. pr, $225.00

Regal Majorette	**$275.00**

Van Tellingen Shakers

Bears, yellow w/rose accents, pr	**$18.00**
Black dogs, pr	**$85.00**
Bunnies, white w/pink accents, pr	**$18.00**
Dutch boy & girl, pr	**$35.00**
Mary & gray lamb, pr	**$50.00**

Peek-a-Boo, all white, lg, pr	**$325.00**
Peek-a-Boo, all white, sm, pr	**$165.00**
Peek-a-Boo, peach trim, rare, lg, pr	**$475.00**
Peek-a-Boo, peach trim, sm, pr	**$250.00**
Peek-a-Boo, red dots, lg, pr	**$425.00**
Peek-a-Boo, white w/burgundy trim, sm, pr	**$275.00**
Peek-a-Boo, white w/gold trim, lg, pr	**$425.00**
Sailor & mermaid, multicolored, pr	**$150.00**
White dogs, pr	**$50.00**
Yellow ducks w/black spots, pr	**$35.00**

Miscellaneous

Banks, kissing pigs, Bendel, pr	**$325.00**
Salt & pepper shakers, Alice in Wonderland, matches cookie jar, rare, pr	**$625.00**
Salt & pepper shakers, Clown, matches cookie jar, rare, pr	**$275.00**
Salt & pepper shakers, Dutch girls, matches cookie jar, rare, pr	**$275.00**
Salt & pepper shakers, Goldilocks, matches cookie jar	**$150.00**

Riviera Dinnerware

A sister to the Fiesta line, Riviera was made by The Homer Laughlin China Company from 1938 until just before 1950. It was a thinner line, unmarked, and inexpensive. Their major marketing outlet was the Murphy Company chain of dime stores. Its pieces are squared with shaped rounded corners. Colors are mauve blue, red, yellow, light green, and ivory.

If you'd like to learn more about Riviera, we recommend *The Collector's Encyclopedia of Fiesta* by Sharon and Bob Huxford.

Bowl, baker; 9"	**$18.00**
Bowl, cream soup; w/liner in ivory	**$80.00**
Bowl, fruit; 5½"	**$9.00**
Bowl, nappy; 9¼"	**$20.00**
Bowl, oatmeal; 6"	**$28.00**
Bowl, utility; ivory	**$45.00**
Butter dish, cobalt or turquoise, from $185 to	**$200.00**
Butter dish, colors other than cobalt & turquoise, ¼-lb	**$100.00**
Butter dish, ½-lb	**$90.00**

Casserole, $85.00

Creamer $8.00
Cup & saucer, demi; ivory...........................$50.00
Jug, covered..$100.00
Jug, open, ivory, 4½".....................................$85.00
Pitcher, juice; mauve blue..........................$175.00
Plate, deep..$18.00
Plate, 10"..$35.00
Plate, 6"...$7.00
Plate, 7"...$8.00
Plate, 9"...$13.00
Platter, closed handles, 11¼"......................$18.00
Platter, in cobalt, 12"...................................$50.00
Platter, 11½"..$15.00
Salt & pepper shakers, pr............................$18.00
Sauce boat..$18.00
Saucer..$3.00
Teacup...$8.50
Teapot...$100.00
Tidbit, 2-tier, in ivory..................................$70.00
Tumbler, handled...$55.00
Tumbler, handled, in ivory.........................$115.00
Tumbler, juice..$42.00

Rock 'n Roll Memorabilia

Ticket stubs and souvenirs issued at rock concerts, posters of the artists that have reached celebrity status, and merchandise such as dolls, games, clothing, etc., sold through retail stores during the heights of their careers are just the thing that interests rock 'n roll fans. Some original, one-of-a-kind examples — for instance, their instruments, concert costumes, and personal memorabilia — often sell at the large auction galleries in the East where they've realized very high-dollar hammer prices.

See also Beatles Collectibles; Elvis Presley Memorabilia; Magazines; Pin-Back Buttons; Records.

Bee Gees, tour book, 1979, 24 pages, NM.................$15.00
Bruce Spingsteen, book, Born To Run, w/photos, 176 pages, 1979, EX..$5.00
Bruce Springsteen, color photo, 8x10" $6.00
Cyndi Lauper, gum card set, 33 cards, complete, Topps, 1985, EX..$8.00
Dave Clark Five, souvenir booklet, 1960s, 28 pages, 9x12½"...$25.00
David Bowie, concert poster, German Sounds & Visions Tour, 1990 ....$26.00
David Lee Roth, scarf, from 1988 Skyscraper Tour, EX.$5.00
Dick Clark, book, Twenty Years of Rock 'n Roll, Buddha Records Inc, 24 pages, 1953-1973, EX.................$50.00
Donny Osmond, keepsake photo & activity book, unused, Artcraft, 1973, NM...$12.00
Donny Osmond, nodder, NMIB.................................$25.00
Ed 'Cookie' Burns, comb, 1959, MOC......................$55.00
Elton John, tour book, 1975, 28 pages, EX+ $16.00
Fabian, pillow, cloth w/printed graphics, 1950s-60s, 11x11", EX...$65.00
Frankie Avalon, pillow, stuffed, 1950s-60s, 10x10", EX.$130.00
Freddie & the Dreamers, gum card set, 66 cards, complete, Donruss, 1965, NM...$95.00
Hermann's Hermitts, charm bracelet, 5 photos on chain, 1950s, EX...$40.00
Jackson Five, pennant, We Love the Jacksons w/black & white group photo, felt, 1970s, 11x29", EX...........$55.00
Jackson Five, pillow, VG.................................$32.50
KISS, backpack, KISS photo on red canvas, 1977, 13x16", NM $36.00
KISS, eraser, MIP...$12.00
Kiss, gum cards, set of 44, complete, 1978, EX $20.00
KISS, program, 1977-78 World Tour, VG $35.00
Led Zeplin, concert poster, bright colors, 1979, 18x22", EX...$100.00
Michael Jackson, belt, 1980s, M.................................$12.00

Dick Clark, writing tablet, 1950s, EX, $12.00

Michael Jackson, doll, Thriller outfit, 1982, 11½", MIB, $40.00

Michael Jackson, playing cards, MOC **$15.00**

Michael Jackson, stickers, Super Sticker series, set of 13, Topps, 1984, 5x7", NM **$30.00**

Monkees, book, Private Picture Book, fan club offer, Laufer, 32 pages, 8½x11", NM **$75.00**

Monkees, bubble gum pack, 5 cards from More of the Monkees series, Donruss, 1968, unopened, NM **$15.00**

Monkees, charm bracelet, gold-tone metal chain w/4 1" dia portraits, Raybert Products, 1967, MOC.................**$40.00**

Monkees, finger puppets, Mickey, Peter & David, Remco, 1970, 5", set of 3, minimum value, $60.00

Monkees, tambourine, 1960s, M **$55.00**

New Kids on the Block, gum card set, 1st series, 88 cards w/22 stickers, complete, Topps, 1990, M **$12.00**

New Kids on the Block, posable figures, Danny or Jordan, 6", MIB, each **$5.00**

Partridge Family, photo album/activity book, 1973, M..**$25.00**

Paul McCartney & Wings, card set, Back to the Egg, set of 5 black & white photos, EX+ **$14.00**

Ricky Nelson, photo, facsimile signature, sent by studio to fan, 1958, 5x7", NM...**$28.00**

Rolling Stones, fan club kit..**$10.00**

Rolling Stones, poster, 38x27", EX **$12.00**

Rolling Stones, sheet music songbook, Big Hits, 6 pages w/color photos, VG+ **$25.00**

Shaun Cassidy, scrapbook, w/photos, 187 pages, 1978, EX **$3.00**

Rookwood

Although this company was established in 1879, it continued to produce commercial artware until it closed in 1967. Located in Cincinnati, Ohio, Rookwood is recognized today as the largest producer of high-quality art pottery ever to operate in the United States.

Most of the pieces listed here are from the later years of production, but we've included some early pieces as well. With few exceptions, all early Ohio art pottery companies produced an artist-decorated brown-glaze line — Rookwood's was called Standard. Among their other early lines were Sea Green, Iris, Jewel Porcelain, Wax Matt, and Vellum.

Virtually all of Rookwood's pieces are marked. The most familiar mark is the 'reverse R'-P monogram. It was first used in 1886, and until 1900 a flame point was added above it to represent each passing year. After the turn of the century, a Roman numeral below the monogram indicated the current year. In addition to the dating mark, a die-stamped number was used to identify the shape.

The Cincinnati Art Galleries held two large and important cataloged auctions in 1991. The full-color catalogs contain a comprehensive history of the company, list known artists and designers with their monograms (as well as company codes and trademarks), and describe each lot thoroughly. Collectors now regard them as an excellent source for information and study.

Ashtray, #1139, rook on side, Bengal Brown, 1949, 4"..**$125.00**

Bookends, #2655, owls, brown bloss, 1948, 6", pr....**$240.00**

Bookends, #2998, puppies, brown gloss, 1953, 5x5", pr **$250.00**

Bookends, Oriental woman in lotus pose, McDonald, 1918, pr **$200.00**

Bookends, rook on open book, taupe & dark blue, 1943, 6½", pr **$200.00**

Bowl, #1288, incurvate w/reticulated ferns, green shading to pink, matte glaze, 2¾x6½" **$275.00**

Bowl, #2568, 4 floral panels embossed on yellow, matte glaze, 1922, 8" **$70.00**

Bowl, #366Z, carnations carved in blue & red, matte glaze, S Toohey, 1904, 3x5" **$550.00**

Bowl, #643D, canoe shape, pink & gray, wax matte glaze, 1922, 8" long **$70.00**

Bowl, #923, swirl carving, blue on yellow, matte glaze, W Hentschel, 1913, 7" **$200.00**

Bowl, seminude at each end, white w/blue interior, marked LA, 1927, 7" **$550.00**

Candle holder, #653, wild roses, standard glaze, C Bonsall, handled, 1903, 2¾" **$300.00**

Candlestick, #1192, embossed flowers on blue, matte glaze, petal cup, 1922, 7" **$150.00**

Creamer, #47, floral spray on peach & white, S Toohey, 1887, 2" **$150.00**

Figurine, #2628, seated nude, white matte glaze, L Abel, 1925, 4x5" **$350.00**

Figurine, #6981, bird, white & gray gloss, 10" **$240.00**

Figurine, boxer dog, brown & blue gloss, L Abel, 1934, 4½" **$400.00**

Flowerpot, pink & yellow tulips on blue gloss, porcelain, Shirayamadani, 1946...**$750.00**

Jar, Oriental-style hexagon, blue gloss, dome lid, 1928, 8" **$120.00**

Mug, #354C, carved circles on light green, matte glaze, 1902...**$150.00**

Pitcher, #251, floral design on peach, A Sprague, 1889, 8½" $425.00

Pitcher, floral design, griffin handle, wax matte, signed Louise Abel, 1927, lg, $850.00

Stein, #1014D, carved abstract floral design, wax matte, signed AP, 1907, 7" $300.00

Teapot, band of ships, salmon on white, porcelain, S Sax, 1912, 4x8" $375.00

Tile, oak tree & lake carving, 3-color matte glaze, unmarked, 18x12" $400.00

Vase, #1123, flat black crystalline w/maroon interior, 1922, 6" $375.00

Vase, #1552D, geometric design at top on light green w/rust, vellum glaze, 1911, 9" $350.00

Vase, #2093, yellow, matte glaze, curved banding forms panels & foot, 1921, 3" $80.00

Vase, #2129, 4-petal flowers alternating w/leaves, vellum glaze, 9" $180.00

Vase, #2191, flowers carved on pastels, vellum glaze, Shirayamadani, 1931, 5" $550.00

Vase, #2404, embossed peacock feathers on light blue, matte glaze, 1927, 6" $260.00

Vase, #2472, embossed cattail band, pink gloss, 1955, 5".. $85.00

Vase, #2482, embossed leaf on dark blue, matte glaze, 1920, 12" $210.00

Vase, #2762, beaded motif at top & base, wax matte glaze, 4-sided, 4" $55.00

Vase, #2811, tiny flowers embossed on blue, matte glaze 5-sided, 1925, 4" $75.00

Vase, #6183F, bluebirds & flowers on white gloss, porcelain, 1944, 5" $350.00

Vase, #6199F, red & gray flowers on white, porcelain, E Barrett, 1946, 4x5" $350.00

Vase, #6306, pink & blue drip glaze on tan, pink interior, 1932, 7" $300.00

Vase, #6434, embossed daisies on green gloss, 1953, 5". $85.00

Vase, #6444, berries & leaves embossed on blue, matte glaze 1914, 6" $85.00

Vase, #6614, black w/white glossy drip glaze, bisque, 1960, 4" $70.00

Vase, #778, dark burgundy gloss, 1947, 10" $200.00

Vase, #8303, brown & blue feathered gloss, 1932, 4"..**$130.00**

Vase, #934, geometric flowers carved on brown, matte glaze, gourd form, 13x9" **$600.00**

Vase, berries on ivory band on purple background, matte glaze, C Steinle, 1916, 5" **$375.00**

Vase, carved grapevine band on dark blue-green, vellum glaze, S Sax, 1915, 9¾" **$850.00**

Vase, cherry blossoms on blue shading to pink, vellum glaze, C Steinle, 1919, 4½" **$300.00**

Vase, cherry blossoms on pink w/white band at top, vellum glaze, Hurley, 1920, 10" **$700.00**

Vase, cream & blue flowers & leaves on brown, iris glaze, J Jensen, 1944, 8" **$850.00**

Vase, daffodils on pink shading to green, iris glaze, EN Lincoln, 1910, 6½x3½" **$1,100.00**

Vase, embossed flowers, rose w/green matte overglaze, angle handles, 1915, 4" **$150.00**

Vase, floral design, purple & green on brown, wax matte, MH McDonald, 1925, 8½x3½" **$350.00**

Vase, grapes & vines on blue shading to pink, iris glaze, L Asbury, 1907, 7¾x3¾" **$800.00**

Vase, Greek Key band on light green wash over rose, vellum glaze, 1907, 4" **$300.00**

Vase, light & dark blue drip glaze, square form w/handles, footed, 1945, 10" **$125.00**

Vase, nasturtiums at shoulder, iris glaze, 1903, 6x3".**$850.00**

Vase, pansies, porcelain, ET Hurley, spherical, 1946, 4x5" **$450.00**

Vase, pink roses on blue shading to green to pink, vellum glaze, MH McDonald, 1913, 6x3½" **$600.00**

Vase, roses on gray, iris glaze, S Coyne, 1904, 5½"... **$500.00**

Vase, tulips, blue-lined red & yellow on rose, wax matte, signed, 1925, 8" **$500.00**

Vase, Venini handkerchief shape, brown & blue drip glaze, 1960, 9x8" **$240.00**

Vase, white cloud design on black, bisque, L Holtkamp, 1952, 6" **$225.00**

Roselane Pottery

Beginning as a husband and wife operation in the late 1930s, the Roselane Pottery Company of Pasadena, California, expanded their inventory from the figurines they originally sold to local florists to include a complete line of decorative items that eventually were shipped to Alaska, South American, and all parts of the United States.

One of their lines was the Roselane Sparklers. Popular in the fifties, these small animal and bird figures were airbrush decorated and had rhinestone eyes. They're fun to look for and not at all expensive.

If you'd like to learn more, there's a chapter on Roselane in *The Collector's Encyclopedia of California Pottery* by Jack Chipman.

Bowl, Chinese Modern, square w/cut-out pedestal foot, late 1940s, 2½x6¼" **$18.00**

Figurine, baby owl, Sparkler series, very dark brown glaze, plastic eyes, 1960s-70s, 3½" **$8.00**

Figurine, boy w/dog, 5½"......................................**$12.00**

Figurine, fawn, Sparkler series, plastic eyes, ca 1965, $8.00

Figurine, girl w/bouquet, in-mold mark, sm..............**$12.00**

Figurine, male Bali dancer, in-mold mark, 11" **$40.00**

Figurine, stylized deer w/head down, 6" **$18.00**

Figurines, stylized pheasants in Howard Pierce-like brown on white matt glaze, ceramic seed pearl eyes, 7¾" pr **$50.00**

Sculpture, modern elephant figure on wood block, brown lustre glaze, early 1950s, 8"...............**$100.00**

Vase, Chinese Modern, plain, 8" **$24.00**

Rosemeade

The Wahpeton Pottery Company of Wahpeton, North Dakota, chose the trade name Rosemeade for a line of bird and animal figurines, novelty salt and pepper shakers, bells, and many other items which were sold from the 1940s to the '60s through gift stores and souvenir shops in that part of the country. They were marked with either a paper label or an ink stamp; the name Prairie Rose was also used.

Ashtray, Minnesota state, Lake of the Woods **$65.00**

Ashtray, North Dakota state, Kiwanis..........................**$55.00**

Basket, pink, twist handle, sm....................................**$30.00**

Bell, flamingo..**$195.00**

Bell, tulip form, $175.00

Bookends, wolfhounds, wine-colored, pr..................**$280.00**

Figurine, duck, miniature **$85.00**

Figurines, fighting cocks, miniature, pr.....................**$150.00**

Figurines, penguins, miniature, set of 3 ....**$45.00**

Figurines, seals, miniature, set of 3............................**$45.00**

Flower frog, fish...**$55.00**

Flower frog, heron..**$30.00**

Flower frog, pheasant..**$95.00**

Incense burner, elephant **$200.00**

Planter, squirrel on log...**$30.00**

Planter, swan...**$30.00**

Plaque, fish..**$130.00**

Salt & pepper shakers, begging dogs, light reddish brown, pr..**$30.00**

Salt & pepper shakers, bluebirds, pr **$175.00**

Salt & pepper shakers, bull's heads, pr **$85.00**

Salt & pepper shakers, bulldog's heads, golden brown w/black collars, pr **$50.00**

Salt & pepper shakers, cacti, tall ridged shape w/single pink budding flower, pr **$50.00**

Salt & pepper shakers, donkey's heads, pr **$45.00**

Salt & pepper shakers, elephants, reddish brown, pr .**$75.00**

Salt & pepper shakers, muskies, pr **$200.00**

Salt & pepper shakers, parrots, pr **$80.00**

Salt & pepper shakers, pink flamingos, pr.................**$150.00**

Salt & pepper shakers, robins, pr **$180.00**

Salt & pepper shakers, Siamese cats, pr.......................**$60.00**

Salt & pepper shakers, strutting roosters, pr.............**$150.00**

Spoon rest, rooster..**$75.00**

Vase, boot shape, blue matte, 6½"..............................**$50.00**

Roseville Pottery

This company took its name from the city in Ohio where they operated for a few years before moving to Zanesville in the late 1890s. They're recognized as one of the giants in the industry, having produced many lines of the finest in art pottery from the beginning to the end of their production. Even when machinery took over many of the procedures once carefully done by hand, the pottery they produced continued to reflect the artistic merit and high standards of quality the company had always insisted upon.

Several marks were used over the years as well as some paper labels. The very early art lines often carried an applied ceramic seal with the name of the line (Royal, Egypto, Mongol, Mara, or Woodland) under a circle containing the words Rozane Ware. From 1910 until 1928 an Rv mark was used, the 'v' being contained in the upper loop of the 'R.' Paper labels were common from 1914 until 1937. From 1932 until they closed in 1952, the mark was Roseville in script, or R USA. Pieces marked RRP Co Roseville, Ohio, were not made by the Roseville Pottery but by Robinson Ransbotton of Roseville, Ohio. Don't be confused. There are many jardiniers and pedestals in a brown and green blended glaze that are being sold at flea markets and antique malls as Roseville, that were actually made by Robinson Ransbottom as late as the 1970s and '80s. That isn't to say they don't have some worth of their own, but don't buy them for old Roseville.

Most of the listings here are for items produced from the 1930s on — things you'll be more likely to encounter today. If you'd like to learn more about the subject, we recommend *The Collector's Encyclopedia of Roseville Pottery, Vols 1 and 2,* and *The Catalog of Early Roseville,* all by Sharon and Bob Huxford.

Apple Blossom, ewer, #318, white blossoms & branches on blue bulbous shape, flared base, twig handle, 15". **$275.00**

Apple Blossom, hanging basket, white blossoms & branches on green bowl, twig handles, relief mark **$125.00**

Apple Blossom, vase, #387, white blossoms & branches on pink cylinder, twig handles, 9" **$100.00**

Aztec, pitcher, decorated gray squatty bulbous body on round base, artist-signed L, 5½" **$300.00**

Baneda, console bowl, blue band w/colorful pod, flower & leaf design on 6-sided bowl w/base, curved handles, 13" **$225.00**

Baneda, vase, blue band w/colorful pod, flower & leaf design on mottled pink bulbous shape, sm curved handles, 5½" **$200.00**

Bittersweet, basket, #810, bittersweet decor on textured shaded pink boat shape, twig handle, 10" **$125.00**

Bittersweet, planter, #868, bittersweet decor on textured mint green elongated box w/twig handles, 8" long **$50.00**

Blackberry, vase, colorful blackberry decor on squatty bulbous shape w/flat bottom, plain rim, angled handles, 4" **$225.00**

Blackberry, wall pocket, colorful blackberry decor on textured green fan shape, paper label **$450.00**

Bleeding Heart, ewer, #972, floral decor on tan bulbous form w/cut-out design at neck, curved handle, round base, 10" **$125.00**

Bleeding Heart, wall pocket, #1287, floral decor on shaded blue V-shape w/angled appendage, relief mark, 8" **$250.00**

Bushberry, bowl, #411, berry & leaf decor on green horizontally textured ball shape w/twig handles, 4"... **$60.00**

Bushberry, cornucopia, #154, berry & leaf decor on horizontally textured tan & green, relief mark, 8" **$50.00**

Bushberry, vase, cone shape on round base, V-shaped handles, 8", $125.00

Carnelian I, candlesticks, cup on round flared base, scroll handles, aqua blue drip glaze on turquoise, Rv stamp, 3", pr **$45.00**

Carnelian I, console bowl, med blue drip glaze on light blue round shape w/3-ring base, 2-handled, Rv stamp, 14" dia **$85.00**

Carnelian I, fan vase, tan drip glaze over lighter tan, vertical ridges w/scalloped rim, handled, dome base, Rv mark, 8" **$45.00**

Carnelian II, pillow vase, heavily textured blue drip glaze on lighter blue glaze, flat bottom, curved handles, 5" **$60.00**

Carnelian II, vase, squatty bulbous body w/textured green & rose drip glaze on trumpet neck, handled, flat bottom, 10" **$125.00**

Cherry Blossom, candlesticks, cherry blossoms on deep tan cup on base w/vertical bar design, curved handles, 4", pr **$250.00**

Cherry Blossom, jug vase, cherry-blossom design on deep tan w/vertical cream-colored bar design, sm curved handles, 7" **$150.00**

Clemana, vase, 4-sided w/angled handles, geometric floral design on blue shading, 7" **$125.00**

Clematis, double bud vase, #194, white clematis flower connecting 2 Ciel Blue cylinders on round bases, relief mark, 5" **$50.00**

Clematis, tea set, #5, floral decor on tan & green teapot, sugar bowl & creamer, relief mark **$225.00**

Columbine, bowl, #401, floral decor on blue bowl angled around middle, flat bottom, sharply angled handles, 6" **$40.00**

Columbine, vase, #20, floral decor on tan cylinder shading to green angled bottom w/round base, angled handles, 8" **$70.00**

Corinthian, ashtray, twisted grape decor on band above vertical cream & green fluting, 3 rests on flat cream rim, Rv, 2" **$70.00**

Corinthian, vase, twisted grape & fruit decor on band above cream & green fluting on bulbous body, Rv mark, 10½" **$110.00**

Cosmos, basket, white flower design on blue fan shape on flared pedestal, handle slightly pointed in middle, 12" **$300.00**

Cosmos, bowl, #376, white flower design on green ball shape, sm round handles by irregular rim, 6" **$75.00**

Cremona, bowl, mottled pink octagon shape w/rim curving inward, sm blossom & leaf design, paper label, 9" across **$60.00**

Dahlrose, bowl, oval w/green angled handles, band of ivory flowers & green leaves on mottled tan, paper label, 10" **$120.00**

Dahlrose, vase, 4-sided flared rim & short base, band of flowers & green leaves at top, paper label, 6" **$125.00**

Dawn, vase, #826, stylized floral decor on wide pink cylinder w/square base & handles, plain rim, impressed mark, 6" **$90.00**

Dawn, vase, #827, stylized floral decor on yellow inverted teardrop shape w/square base & handles, plain rim, 6" **$90.00**

Dogwood I, vase, blossoms on brown branches on textured green bulbous body tapering to flat bottom, straight rim, 6" **$110.00**

Dogwood I, wall pocket, V-shaped w/dogwood blossoms on brown branches on textured green background, Rv stamp **$150.00**

Dogwood II, boat planter, white dogwood blossoms on black branches on smooth green background, 6" .**$95.00**

Dogwood II, bud vase, smooth green horn shape w/white dogwood blossoms on black branches around base, 8"..**$70.00**

Donatello, basket, banded cherub design on vertically fluted bulbous body w/tall pointed handle, 15"............**$300.00**

Donatello, compote, banded cherub design on vertically fluted pedestal base, Rv stamp, 4" **$95.00**

Donatello, double-bud vase on panel w/cherub design connecting short & tall vertically fluted cylinders, 5" .**$65.00**

Dutch, mug, decaled w/3 children & dog, ear-type handle, 5", $85.00

Dutch, tankard, Dutch couple on tall ivory cylinder slightly flaring to flat bottom, curved handle, pour spout, 11½" **$165.00**

Earlam, candlesticks, 4-sided w/tan cup on mottled turquoise flared base, scrolled handle, 6", pr........**$65.00**

Earlam, urn vase, bulbous form w/handles in mottled green & turquoise w/tan interior, 6" **$85.00**

Falline, urn vase, green 'pea-pod' design on tan shading to brown, sm round handles at top, 8"....................**$250.00**

Ferella, bowl, turquoise & curdled rose on round shape cut-out & shell designs around rim & short pedestal base, 12"..**$350.00**

Ferella, vase, curdled tan on tall angled body w/curved handles, cut-out & shell design around rim & base, 9" .**$350.00**

Florentine, basket, urn shape w/textured panels alternating w/leaf & berries on tan, flared base, handled, Rv stamp, 8"..**$165.00**

Florentine, wall pocket, textured panel flanked by leaf & berry design on beige V-shape, Rv stamp, 9½" ..**$150.00**

Foxglove, conch shell, #426, sprig of flowers on pink shell, relief mark, 6"...**$60.00**

Foxglove, cornucopia, #164, sprig of flowers on green, relief mark, 8" **$55.00**

Freesia, candle holder, #1161, tan straight-sided cup on straight-sided base w/white floral decor, angled handles, 4½" **$70.00**

Freesia, cookie jar, #4, white & pink floral design on green urn shape, knob lid & angled handles, relief mark, 10" **$250.00**

Freesia, vase, #120, white floral decor on shaded blue slightly bulbous cylinder, angled handles, no lip, 7" **$75.00**

Fuchsia, bowl, #346, floral decor on shaded tan, curved handles, no lip, impressed mark, 4" **$65.00**

Fuchsia, pitcher, #1322, floral decor on ball shape w/curved handle, ice lip, impressed mark, 8" **$275.00**

Futura, vase, ball shape w/flared rim on 4-sided base w/4 columns, blue w/colored circles decor, paper label, 8" **$450.00**

Futura, vase, tapered w/6 deeply fluted points w/alternate glossy pink & gray glaze, stepped base, paper label, 8" **$300.00**

Gardenia, basket, #608, white floral decor on Seafoam fan shape w/scalloped rim, curved handle, round base, 8" **$100.00**

Imperial I, basket, leaf & loop design on round textured green body w/smooth loop handle, 6"..................**$95.00**

Imperial II, wall pocket, tan w/'splotchy' green center pocket flanked by 2 sm pockets, paper label.....**$275.00**

Iris, bowl, #359, bulbous shape w/angled handles, iris decor on tan shading to brown at sm round base, 5" ..**$150.00**

Iris, ewer, #926, bulbous shape w/stacked handle, iris decor on pink shading to green around base, 10"........**$200.00**

Ivory II, candelabrum, Velmoss II shape #1116, satin ivory finish, 5 cups, 5½"....................................**$150.00**

Ivory II, vase, satin ivory on 'Savona' shape w/vertical ribbing, short pedestal base, angled handles, 6".......**$60.00**

Ixia, basket, #346, floral design on turquoise, angled handle, flared base, impressed mark, 10"........................**$150.00**

Ixia, bowl, #326, floral design on pink & turquoise bulbous shape, closed pointed handles, no lip on rim, 4".**$45.00**

Jonquil, basket, floral design on mottled tan angled body w/tall pointed green handle, 9" **$200.00**

Jonquil, bowl, white & green jonquil design on textured tan ground, curved handles, flat bottom, green interior, 5½" **$100.00**

Juvenile, creamer, Sunbonnet Girl on ivory, orange band, gold Rv stamp, 3½"...**$85.00**

Juvenile, egg cup, yellow chick on ivory w/light green band around rim, pedestal base, 3" **$225.00**

Juvenile, mug, standing rabbit on ivory background w/light green band around rim, Rv stamp, 3"....................**$75.00**

Juvenile, plate, yellow duck decor on ivory w/turquoise bands, rolled rim, 8" **$125.00**

La Rose, bowl, textured cream backgound w/swags of green leaves caught up w/pink roses, beaded rim, Rv stamp, 9" dia..**$70.00**

La Rose, double bud vase, textured cream background w/swags of green leaves & pink roses, Rv stamp ..**$75.00**

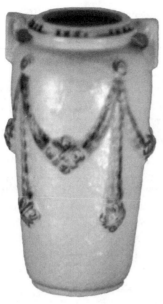

La Rose, vase, textured cream background with swags of green leaves & pink roses, 2 handles at rim, 6", $75.00

Monticello, vase, stylized trumpet flowers around top, ring handles, 6", $150.00

Laurel, vase, laurel & vertically ribbed panels on turquoise cylinder widening to flat bottom, angled handles, 8"..**$130.00**

Laurel, vase, laurel design & vertically ribbed panels on turquoise V-shape, closed handles near base, 6½".**$120.00**

Luffa, bowl, white floral & leaf design on horizontal wavy-ridged green bowl, round base, sm angled handles, 4" **$80.00**

Luffa, vase, white floral & leaf design on tan & green horizontal wavy-ridged body, flat bottom, angled handles, 7"..**$125.00**

Lustre, vase, glossy pink lustre finish on tall cylinder shape tapering inward to flat bottom, paper label, 10"...**$75.00**

Magnolia, bowl, #665, blossoms on black branches on textured green bowl, flat bottom, angled handles, lip rim, 3"..**$40.00**

Magnolia, mug, #3, blossoms on black branches on textured blue cup, round base, angled handle, relief mark, 3" **$60.00**

Magnolia, planter, #389, blossoms on black branches on textured blue elongated box curving to base, angled handles, 8"..**$100.00**

Mayfair, bowl, #1110, high-gloss beige glaze over embossed petal & pistil design on straight-sided bowl, 4" **$25.00**

Mayfair, tankard, #1107, impressed leaf design on tall brown cylinder on round base, fancy handle, 12"...........**$75.00**

Ming Tree, console bowl, #528, white blossoms & branch on blue irregular-shaped bowl w/twig handles, 10" long **$65.00**

Ming Tree, vase, #581, white blossoms & branch on cylindrical green body, twig handles, 6" **$45.00**

Mock Orange, bowl, #900, white blossoms on shaded yellow, closed handles, 4"..**$35.00**

Mock Orange, planter, white blossoms on tall 4-sided blue planter, slightly flared rim, footed, relief mark **$55.00**

Monticello, vase, angled shape w/curved handles, band w/stylized trumpet flowers around top, 4"...........**$75.00**

Monticello, vase, plain rim, flat bottom w/curved handles, band w/stylized trumpet flowers around top, 9"..**$225.00**

Morning Glory, bowl, allover morning-glory design on bulbous shape w/plain rim, angled handles, paper label, 4" **$200.00**

Morning Glory, vase, allover morning-glory design on cylinder fanned at top, flared base, stacked angled handles, 7" **$225.00**

Moss, candlesticks, #1107, tall blue cup on flared base w/moss motif, angled handles, impressed mark, 4½", pr **$90.00**

Moss, console bowl, elongated w/angled handles, moss motif on pink shading to blue, 13"....................**$175.00**

Mostique, bowl, geometric flowers & berries on textured beige background, glossy interior, flat bottom, Rv stamp, 2½" **$45.00**

Orian, bowl vase, blue ball shape on slightly flared base, curved handles, plain rim, paper label, 6" **$100.00**

Orian, vase, tan cylinder flaring to bulbous body, 2 rings on flared base w/hint of blue, handled, 12"............**$150.00**

Panel, candle holders, floral design on green cup w/flat round base, Rv stamp, 6", pr................................**$65.00**

Panel, pillow vase, w/angled handles, tan floral panel on brown, Rv stamp, 6" **$95.00**

Peony, vase, #168, floral decor on tan & green textured urn w/straight neck, round base, angled handles, relief mark, 6" **$45.00**

Peony, wall pocket, #1293, white floral motif on blue textured V-shape w/fancy rim, curved handles, relief mark, 8" **$150.00**

Persian, creamer & sugar bowl, 4-sided & footed w/pale floral decor on cream background, angled handles .**$140.00**

Pine Cone, boat basket, #410, pine cone motif on blue shaded to white on irregular shape, tan interior, twig handle, 10" **$350.00**

Pine Cone, pitcher, pine cone design on blue ball shape w/straight-sided base, irregular lip, twig handle, 8" **$400.00**

Pine Cone, planter, #468, pine cone decor on elongated 4-sided shape, dark brown 2-step base, decorative corners, 3½"..**$110.00**

Pine Cone, triple candle holder, #1106, 3 cups (from sm to lg) on pine cone base, 5½", each **$200.00**

Poppy, basket, #347, poppy design on pink shading to blue, loop handle, 10"..**$150.00**

Poppy, wall pocket/candle holder, #1291, pocket flanked by sm candle holders connected by leaves, 9" **$225.00**

Primrose, jug vase, #767, white floral & green leaf design on turquoise, angled stacked handles, flat bottom, 8" .**$125.00**

Primrose, vase, #765, floral & leaf design on turquoise V-shape w/irregular rim & 4-sided base, angled handles, 8"..**$150.00**

Rosecraft, vase, glossy yellow glaze on cylinder w/short round base, sm square handles at rim, Rv stamp, 8"........**$100.00**

Rosecraft Hexagon, vase, dark green w/Arts & Crafts medallion, handles, 6", $150.00

Rosecraft Vintage, urn vase, banded beige & orange grape design on dark brown, Rv stamp, 8" **$225.00**

Rozane, jug, #888, squatty bulbous shape w/top handle, floral decor on shades of brown, marked Rozane RPCo, 4½"..**$225.00**

Rozane, mug, #886, floral decor on shades of brown to dark gold, marked Rozane RPCo, 4½" **$200.00**

Rozane, paperweight, rectangular shape w/rounded edges & corners, floral decor on shades of brown, Rozane Ware seal...**$250.00**

Rozane, vase, bulbous shape w/pointed handles, floral decor on shaded dark brown, marked w/Rozane Ware seal, 4" **$150.00**

Rozane (1917), compote, rose decor on pitted green background of rimless bowl on thick pedestal base, stamped, 5"..**$70.00**

Russco, bowl vase, blue w/decorative vertical panels front & back, octagonal rim, round base, stacked handles, 6½" **$60.00**

Russco, bud vase, trumpet shape w/decorative vertical panels front & back on handled base in shades of light tan, 8"..**$75.00**

Silhouette, cigarette box, square shape w/floral design on recessed background on rose, relief mark **$50.00**

Silhouette, fan vase, #783, profile of seated nude on recessed background on shaded blue, relief mark, 7"...**$225.00**

Snowberry, candle holders, #1CS-1, berry sprigs on blue sqatty bulbous shape, angled handles, pr.............**$45.00**

Snowberry, console bowl, #1BL1, sprigs of white berries on green & gold boat shape w/pointed rim, angled handles, 10"...**$75.00**

Sumflower, vase, yellow & green sunflower design on cylinder curving inward at rim, sharply angled handles, 6"..**$175.00**

Sunflower, jardiniere, round tapering to flat bottom, yellow & green sunflower design w/tan rim, paper label, 9"...**$375.00**

Teasel, basket, #349, stylized teasel design on white cylinder w/flared petal rim, pedestal base, handled, 10"....**$45.00**

Thornapple, candle holders, #1117, cup w/thornapple design resting on leaf-shaped base, twig handle, 2½", pr **$75.00**

Thornapple, planter, #262, round w/straight sides, angled handles, thornapple & leaf design on brown shaded to tan, 5"...**$60.00**

Topeo, vase, tapered pink & green beaded design on mottled blue ball shape, upright rim, flat bottom, 6" **$135.00**

Topeo, vase, vertical tapered bead design on dark red shape that flares then tapers to flat bottom, upright rim, 9½"..**$200.00**

Tourmaline, bowl vase, #283, ball shape w/sm straight base, horizontally ribbed panels around top, paper label, 5" **$60.00**

Tuscany, candlesticks, cup on handled base, mottled pale turquoise w/berry & leaf design on handles, no mark, 4", pr **$50.00**

Tuscany, console bowl, elongated w/2 rounded & 2 flat sides , mottled pink & white, no mark, 11" long..**$75.00**

Velmoss II, double cornucopia vase, leaf design on 2 blue upright cornucopias on round vase, paper label, 8½"...**$85.00**

Velmoss II, vase, leaf decor on blue cylinder w/angled handles, no lip, 6" **$75.00**

Velmoss Scroll, bowl, incised rose decor on ivory squatty bowl w/short straight-sided rim & base, 2½x9" dia...**$75.00**

Velmoss Scroll, vase, incised rose decor on ivory cylinder w/slightly bowed sides, short round base, 6" **$90.00**

Water Lily, basket, #382, cream water lily on tan bowl shading to round brown base, irregular rim, angled handles, 12"..**$175.00**

Water Lily, cornucopia, #178, pink water lily on horizontally textured background, 8" **$60.00**

White Rose, bowl, #387, floral design on shaded pink & green ball shape w/loop handles, no lip on rim, 4"..**$50.00**

White Rose, ewer, #993, floral decor on blue bulbous body, long neck w/cut-out design, straight base, curved handle, 15"...**$225.00**

Wincraft, circle vase, #1053, tree trunk & branches in cut-out center of mottled green circle on brown base, 8" ..**$60.00**

Wincraft, vase, #282, white tulip decor on mottled blue shaded to darker blue square base, relief mark, 8" .**$55.00**

Windsor, planter w/frog, low elongated diamond shape w/sharply angled handles, mottled red-brown, paper label, 16"...**$175.00**

Windsor, vase, double bulbous body w/lg curved handles, blue w/fern design, paper label, 7"....................**$300.00**

Wisteria, console bowl, pink & green wisteria motif on textured blue & tan elongated shape, angled handles, 12"....**$250.00**

Wisteria, vase, pink & green wisteria on textured blue & tan ball shape, angled handles, flat bottom, 7½" **$300.00**

Zephyr Lily, console boat, #475, cream floral decor on swirl-textured green & tan elongated dish, 10" long **$90.00**

Zephyr Lily, vase, #137, white floral decor on blue swirl-textured bulbous body w/trumpet neck, curved handles, 10"..**$110.00**

Royal Copenhagen Figurines

The Royal Copenhagen Manufactory was established in Denmark in the late 1800s and since that time has produced quality china dinnerware, vases, collector plates, and the figurines such as we've listed here. They're very appealing, high in quality, and extremely collectible.

Nude at pool, #1532, $150.00

Bird preening, #1041 ....**$35.00**

Boy at lunch, #865...**$175.00**

Boy on barrel, #3647 ....**$110.00**

Boy w/gourd, #4539..**$225.00**

Boy w/horn, #3689 ....**$105.00**

Dachshund puppy, recumbent, #856 ....**$275.00**

Dog, seated, #259, 8"...**$250.00**

Farm girl, #815 ....**$200.00**

Girl w/basket & jug, #815 ....**$200.00**

Girl w/doll, #1938, 5¼"..**$285.00**

Goat Lady, #694 ....**$350.00**

Goose Girl, #527 ....**$250.00**

Icelandic Falcon, #263 ....**$300.00**

Koala Bear, #5402..**$275.00**

Lady w/wool sweater, #1251 ....**$120.00**

Lambs, #2769..**$110.00**

Little girl modeling new dress, 8" **$140.00**

Man seated wearing tam-o'-shanter, 8" **$295.00**

Man w/2 calves, #1858 ....**$375.00**

Milkmaid, #2017...**$195.00**

October, #4532..**$275.00**

Old lady w/prayer book, 9" **$125.00**

Pan playing pipes, #1736 ....**$235.00**

Pan w/frog, #1713...**$215.00**

Pardon Me, #2372...**$295.00**

Penguin, #3003, 3" **$65.00**

Rabbit, #4676..**$245.00**

Robin, fat, #1166, 2¾"..**$75.00**

Seal, #1441 ....**$140.00**

Two children, #1761 ....**$625.00**

Two Ducks, signed P Cerald, 7x7" **$170.00**

Two Girls in garden, #1316..**$325.00**

Royal Copley

This is a line of planters, wall pockets, vases, and other novelty items, most of which are modeled as appealing animals, birds, or human figures. They were made by the Spaulding China Company of Sebring, Ohio, from 1942 until 1957. The decoration is underglazed and airbrushed, and some pieces are trimmed in gold (which can add 25% to 50% to their values). Not every piece is marked, but they have a style that is distinctive. Some items are ink stamped; others have (or have had) labels.

Examples are readily found, and prices are still low. Unmarked items may often be found at a bargain. Some people choose a particular animal to collect. For instance, if you're a cat lover, they were made in an extensive assortment of styles and sizes. Teddy bears are also popular; you'll find them licking a lollipop, playing a mandolin, or modeled as a bank, for instance. Wildlife lovers can collect deer, pheasants, fish, and gazelles, and there's a wide array of songbirds to be had as well.

If you'd like more information, we recommend *Royal Copley* written by Leslie Wolfe, edited by Joe Devine.

Ashtray, affectionate birds on heart shape, yellow & blue, raised letters on bottom, 5½" **$16.00**

Ashtray, bird on lily pad, pink & blue, green stamp, 5" dia..**$10.00**

Ashtray, bow & ribbon, blue w/black lettering, Watch Those Ashes Friend, signed w/raised letters, 5" dia **$20.00**

Bank, farmer pig, pink bibs & blue neckerchief, paper label, 5½"..**$35.00**

Bank, pig in cream shirt w/blue bow tie, For My Cruise in black on shirt, green stamp, 7½".............................**$32.00**

Bank, rooster, multicolored, Chicken Feed lettered at base, paper label, 7½" **$40.00**

Bowl, perched bird on scalloped rim, yellow shading to pink, green stamp, 4" **$10.00**

Cigarette holder, mallard duck, paper label, 3" **$10.00**

Figurine, baby lark, paper label, 3⅝" **$18.00**

Figurine, cat, black w/white paws & face, pink neck ribbon, paper label, 8" **$28.00**

Figurine, cockatoo on stump, blue, paper label, 7¼" ..**$26.00**

Figurine, cocker spaniel, light brown w/white paws, paper label, 7¾" **$18.00**

Figurine, dancing lady, light gray & yellow dress, 8" ..**$40.00**

Figurine, deer on sled, paper label, rare, 6½" **$25.00**

Figurine, hen, black & white on green base, paper label, 7¼" **$35.00**

Figurine, hen, paper label, 6" **$18.00**

Figurine, kingfisher on stump, yellow & brown, paper label, 5" **$22.00**

Figurine, mallard duck, paper label, 7" **$18.00**

Figurine, nuthatch on stump, paper label, 4½" **$14.00**

Figurine, Oriental girl holding vase, paper label, 7½" ..**$15.00**

Figurine, parrot on stump, blue w/pink head, paper label, 8" **$26.00**

Figurine, sparrow on stump, paper label, 5" **$14.00**

Figurine, swallow on heavy double stump, paper label, 7½", $25.00

Figurine, teddy bear w/sucker, brown w/white face & paws, paper label, 5½" **$38.00**

Figurine, thrush on stump, pink & teal, paper label, 6½" ..**$16.00**

Figurine, wren on stump, paper label, 6¼" **$16.00**

Lamp, pig in blue trousers w/blue & white striped shirt, paper label, 6½" **$45.00**

Lamp, praying child in pink gown, paper label, 7¾" ..**$32.00**

Lamp base, birds on tree trunk, 11" **$30.00**

Pitcher, embossed daffodils on yellow shading to teal, ear-type handle, green stamp, 8" **$26.00**

Pitcher, embossed pome fruit on shades of blue, green stamp, 8" **$30.00**

Pitcher, floral decal on white, gold stamp, 6¼" **$10.00**

Planter, bird-track design on gray w/pink trim, paper label, 4½" **$12.00**

Planter, birdhouse w/bird, paper label, rare, 5¼" **$45.00**

Planter, cat playing cello, paper label, 7½" **$40.00**

Planter, cocker spaniel beside basket, paper label, 5½" ..**$15.00**

Planter, deer & fawn, paper label, 8¼" **$24.00**

Planter, deer on stump, paper label, 8" **$20.00**

Planter, dog in picnic basket, earth tones, paper label, 7¾" **$16.00**

Planter, dog on stump w/string bass, paper label, rare, 7" ..**$50.00**

Planter, duck, Stuffed Animal series, white w/green polka dots, paper label, 6" **$25.00**

Planter, duck & wheelbarrow, paper label, rare, 8" **$14.00**

Planter, Dutch girl holding bucket, paper label, 6" **$15.00**

Planter, elephant w/ball, paper label, 6" **$20.00**

Planter, elf & shoe, paper label, 6" **$20.00**

Planter, embossed ivy on cream, footed, paper label, 4¼" **$8.00**

Planter, embossed philodendron on cream, footed, paper label, 4¼" **$8.00**

Planter, hummingbird on flower, paper label, 5¼" **$18.00**

Planter, Indian boy & drum, multicolored w/gold highlights, 6½" **$15.00**

Planter, kitten beside book, paper label, 6½" **$20.00**

Planter, kitten in cradle, paper label, rare, 7½" **$40.00**

Planter, Laura's Twig, white on black, paper label, 5" ..**$16.00**

Planter, mailbox & duck, paper label & US Mail lettered on mailbox, rare, 6¾" **$40.00**

Planter, mallard duck, multicolored w/gold highlights, 7¾" **$28.00**

Planter, nuthatch on stump, paper label, 5½" **$14.00**

Planter, Oriental boy w/lg basket on his back, paper label, rare, 8" **$28.00**

Planter, Oriental girl beside basket, signed w/raised letters, 7¾" **$14.00**

Planter, palomino horse head, cream w/shades of brown, paper label or green stamp, 6¼" **$18.00**

Planter, playful kitten & boot, paper label, 7½" **$30.00**

Planter, praying angel, paper label, 6¼" **$18.00**

Planter, puppy in basket, paper label, 7" **$18.00**

Planter, reclining cat, white w/pink features & gray ribbon, paper label, 5¾x7½" **$40.00**

Planter, resting poodle, pink w/white collar, paper label, 6½" **$30.00**

Planter, rib & cornice pattern, gray & yellow, paper label, 3½" **$10.00**

Planter, ribbed, green, raised letters on bottom, 4⅛" ..**$10.00**

Planter, ribbed, yellow, raised letters on bottom, 3½" ..**$8.00**

Planter, teddy bear, brown & cream w/pink neck ribbon, paper label, 8" **$34.00**

Planter, teddy bear on tree stump, paper label, 5½" ..**$20.00**

Planter/plaque, Home Is Where the Heart Is surrounded by dogwood flowers in relief on chartreuse, 4½" **$15.00**

Planter/plaque, multicolored hen on white, signed w/raised letters, 6¾" dia..**$20.00**

Planter/wall pocket, Chinese boy in wide-brimmed hat, 7½" **$20.00**

Planter, teddy bear w/sucker, black & white w/pink neck ribbon & sucker, paper label, 8", $45.00

Planter/wall pocket, hat shape, pink w/embossed yellow flowers, signed w/raised letters, 7" **$20.00**

Razor blade receptacle, red & white barber pole w/gold top, paper label, 6¼" **$25.00**

Vase, embossed bamboo & green leaves on cream, cylinder form, paper label, 8" **$12.00**

Vase, embossed black floral leaf & stem design on pink, cylinder form, paper label, 8" **$12.00**

Vase, embossed dragon on chartreuse, Oriental style, footed, paper label, 5½" **$10.00**

Vase, embossed fish on chartreuse, Oriental style, footed, paper label, 5½" **$10.00**

Vase, embossed ivy w/gold trim on chartreuse, footed, 8" **$12.00**

Vase, embossed ribbon & bow on yellow shading to green, footed, paper label, 6½" **$12.00**

Vase, fish form, red, white & blue, paper label, rare, 6" .**$35.00**

Vase, Happy Anniversary decal w/gold trim on dark green, cylinder form, 8" **$28.00**

Vase, praying angel in relief on star shape, yellow & white, paper label, 6¾" **$22.00**

Vase, rooster, multicolored, paper label, 7" **$18.00**

Vase, running gazelles in relief on rectangular shape, chartreuse & green, paper label, 6" **$12.00**

Vase, stylized flowers on black, cylinder form, paper label, 8¼" **$10.00**

Vase, stylized leaves on yellow, bulbous, paper label, 5½" **$8.00**

Window box, embossed ivy w/gold trim on chartreuse, footed, 4x7" **$10.00**

Royal Doulton

Probably the best-known producers of figurines, character jugs, and series ware ever to exist, the Royal Doulton Company was established in 1815 and continues today to make quality items that are sold through fine gift stores and distributors worldwide.

Kingsware (1899-1946) was a brown-glazed line decorated with drinking scenes. A popular line of collector plates, twenty-four in all, was called the Gibson Girl series. Made from 1901 until sometime in the forties, it was decorated in blue and white with scenes that portrayed a day in the life of 'The Widow and Her Friends.' From 1908 until the early 1940s, they produced Dickensware, decorated with illustrations from Charles Dickens. Robin Hood and Shakespeare were both introduced around 1914, and their Bunnykin series has been made since 1933.

The first character figures were made in 1913 and have remained very popular with collectors ever since. They are not only marked, but each character (and variation) is assigned an identifying number which is printed on the base following the prefix letters 'HN.' Factors that bear on the value of a figurine are age, detail, color, and availability. The presence of an artist's signature or a 'Potted' (pre-1939) mark adds to it as well.

Many collectors favor the bird and animal figures. They were made in a full-size line (having 'HN' prefixes) as well as miniatures (which have a 'K' prefix). Popular domestic breeds are usually valued higher than the more generic animals.

Toby and character jugs were introduced in the 1930s. Both styles are marked with numbers in a 'D' series; the character jugs are made in three sizes (large, small, and miniature). Occasionally you may find a jug with an 'A' mark which, though apparently used for only factory identification purposes, usually boosts its value to some extent. Dates found on the bottom of some jugs are merely copyright dates, not necessarily production dates.

Animal, boxer, #2643, 6½" **$150.00**
Animal, bulldog pup, K-2 .... **$100.00**
Animal, cat, character **$225.00**
Animal, cocker spaniel, #1109, black & white, med .**$135.00**
Animal, corgi, #1559, sm **$110.00**
Animal, dachshund, #1140, med **$275.00**
Animal, Doberman pinscher, #1117, sm **$175.00**
Animal, dog chewing slipper, #2654, 3¼" **$75.00**
Animal, elephant, #2644, 5½" **$100.00**
Animal, English setter, #1050, med **$145.00**
Animal, foxhound, K-7, 2½" **$75.00**
Animal, French poodle, #2631, med **$185.00**
Animal, Irish setter, #1056, sm **$145.00**
Animal, pig lying down w/head up, #2648, 1¾" **$175.00**
Animal, Scottish terrier w/bone in mouth **$75.00**
Bunnykins, cup & saucer, Feeding the Baby **$85.00**
Bunnykins, cup & saucer, Santa Claus **$95.00**
Bunnykins, figurine, Bedtime, #103, yellow **$85.00**
Bunnykins, figurine, Jogging, #22 .... **$45.00**
Bunnykins, figurine, mother bunny sweeps **$45.00**
Bunnykins, figurine, Soccer Player, #116 .... **$75.00**
Bunnykins, Harry & Herold **$40.00**
Bunnykins, mug, Gardening **$85.00**
Bunnykins, plate, baby's, Toast for Tea Today **$120.00**
Bunnykins, plate, oatmeal; Going Shopping **$70.00**

Bunnykins, plate, Watering the Flowers, 7½" **$85.00**
Bunnykins, tumbler, mother swings baby, 1950s **$100.00**
Character jug, Anne of Cleves, D6728, lg..................**$145.00**
Character jug, Anthony & Cleopatra, D6728, lg.........**$145.00**

Character jug, Aramis, D6441, 7½", $125.00

Character jug, Auld Mac, D6253, miniature.................**$55.00**
Character jug, Catherine Howard, D6645, lg **$145.00**
Character jug, Chelsea Pensioner, D6817, lg **$125.00**
Character jug, City Gent, D6185, lg...........................**$110.00**
Character jug, Collector, D6796, lg...........................**$180.00**
Character jug, Davy Crockett & Santa Anna, D6729, lg.**$145.00**
Character jug, Falstaff, D6795, lg **$130.00**
Character jug, Farmer John, D5788, lg **$160.00**
Character jug, Gardener, D6634, sm...........................**$80.00**
Character jug, Gone Away, D6531, lg **$120.00**
Character jug, Granny, D6520, miniature **$55.00**
Character jug, Izaac Walton, D6404, lg **$110.00**
Character jug, Jane Seymour, D6646, lg....................**$135.00**
Character jug, Jarge, D6295, sm...............................**$180.00**
Character jug, Johnny Appleseed, D6372, lg **$365.00**

Character jug, Mad Hatter, D6790, limited edition, sm..**$125.00**
Character jug, Mae West, D6688, lg..........................**$130.00**
Character Jug, Mr Micawbar, D6138, miniature **$55.00**
Character jug, Napoleon & Josephine, D6750, limited edition, lg **$135.00**
Character jug, Neptune, D6548, lg............................**$100.00**
Character jug, Paddy, D5768, sm **$55.00**
Character jug, Pearly King, D6760, lg.......................**$100.00**
Character jug, Porthos, D6516, miniature....................**$45.00**
Character jug, Rip Van Winkle, D6517, sm **$45.00**
Character jug, Robinson Crusoe, D6539, sm **$45.00**
Character jug, Sairey Gamp, D5528, sm......................**$55.00**
Character jug, Tam O'Shanter D6632, lg **$130.00**
Character jug, Town Crier, D6544, miniature.............**$135.00**
Character jug, Walrus & Carpenter, D6600, lg **$145.00**
Chatacter jug, Veteran Motorist, D6633, lg...............**$115.00**
Figurine, Affection, HN2236.....................................**$125.00**
Figurine, Alexandra, HN2398....................................**$140.00**
Figurine, All Aboard, HN2940 ....**$125.00**
Figurine, Ascot, HN2356..**$185.00**
Figurine, Bachelor, HN2319......................................**$225.00**
Figurine, Bess, HN2002 ....**$225.00**
Figurine, Blithe Morning, HN2065 ....**$200.00**
Figurine, Boatman, HN2417......................................**$150.00**
Figurine, Bon Appetit, HN2444.................................**$165.00**
Figurine, Breezy Day, HN3162..................................**$120.00**
Figurine, Bridesmaid, HN2874 ....**$110.00**
Figurine, Captain, HN2260, 9½" **$250.00**
Figurine, Centurion, HN2726 ....**$185.00**
Figurine, Charlotte, HN2421.....................................**$150.00**
Figurine, Christine, HN2792 ....**$275.00**
Figurine, Christmas Morn, HN1992...........................**$235.00**
Figurine, Country Lass, HN1991................................**$125.00**
Figurine, Embroidering, HN2855 ....**$175.00**
Figurine, Fair Maiden, HN2211 ....**$175.00**
Figurine, Fiona, HN2694...**$125.00**

Character jug, Long John Silver, D6386, sm, $55.00

Figurine, Fortune Teller, HN2159, $450.00

Figurine, Gay Morning, HN2135 .... $275.00

Figurine, Genie, HN2989 .... $150.00

Figurine, Good Catch, HN2258 .... $140.00

Figurine, Grace, HN2318 .... $135.00

Figurine, Grand Manner, HN2723 .... $185.00

Figurine, Her Ladyship, HN1977 .... $300.00

Figurine, Huckleberry Finn, HN2927 .... $100.00

Figurine, January, HN2697 .... $110.00

Figurine, Jersey Milkmaid, HN2057 .... $200.00

Figurine, Judge, HN2443 .... $165.00

Figurine, Lambing Time, HN1890 .... $195.00

Figurine, Lifeboat Man, HN2764 .... $180.00

Figurine, Loretta, HN2337 .... $130.00

Figurine, Lunchtime, HN2485 .... $155.00

Figurine, May, HN2711 .... $130.00

Figurine, Melanie, HN2271 .... $150.00

Figurine, Merry Christmas, HN3096 .... $115.00

Figurine, Milkmaid, HN2057 .... $150.00

Figurine, New Companions, HN2770 .... $175.00

Figurine, Officer of the Line, HN2733 .... $225.00

Figurine, Old King Cole, HN2217 .... $495.00

Figurine, Old Meg, HN2494 .... $215.00

Figurine, Omar Khayyam, HN2247 .... $150.00

Figurine, Patricia, HN2715 .... $155.00

Figurine, Pearly Boy, HN2035 .... $165.00

Figurine, Pope John Paul, HN2888 .... $125.00

Figurine, Pretty Polly, HN2768 .... $115.00

Figurine, Rag Doll Seller, HN2944 .... $150.00

Figurine, Silks & Ribbons, HN2017 .... $165.00

Figurine, Sleeping Beauty, HN3079 .... $155.00

Figurine, Stitch in Time, HN2352 .... $200.00

Figurine, Sweet Violets, HN3175 .... $90.00

Figurine, Tinker Bell, HN1677 .... $100.00

Figurine, Toymaker, HN2250 .... $350.00

Figurine, Traveler's Tale, HN3185 .... $95.00

Figurine, Twilight, HN2265, $225.00

Figurine, Veronica, HN1517 .... $355.00

Figurine, Victoria, HN2417 .... $175.00

Figurine, Wigmaker of Williamsburg, HN2239 .... $185.00

Flambe, cat, #9, 4¾" $130.00

Flambe, Confucious, #3314 .... $195.00

Flambe, duck, #395, 2½" $125.00

Flambe, King Penguin, #84, 6" $130.00

Flambe, owl, #2249 .... $200.00

Flambe, rabbit w/ears up, #113 .... $70.00

Flambe, tiger, #809, 6" $450.00

Flambe, vase, #1613, woodcut, 6½" $110.00

Flambe, vase, #1618, veined, 13¼" $265.00

Flambe, Wizard, #3121 .... $120.00

Flambe, wolf sitting w/tail around legs, 5" $100.00

Series Ware, ashtray, Dutch People, marked, 3⅝" dia. $38.00

Series Ware, bowl, Bobby Burns, 7½" dia. $150.00

Series Ware, box, Robin Hood, rectangular, 2x3x4½". $150.00

Series Ware, coffeepot, Morrish Gate, marked, 6¾" .. $150.00

Series Ware, cup & saucer, Don Quixote $50.00

Series Ware, cup & saucer, Mad Hatter $125.00

Series Ware, match holder, monks in profile, 2½" $95.00

Series Ware, mug, Moreton Hall, court scene, D1898. $135.00

Series Ware, pitcher, Coaching Days, 6" $195.00

Series Ware, pitcher, Night Watchman, 8" $105.00

Series Ware, plate, Fat Boy, Dickensware, 2nd mark,
    10½" $125.00

Series Ware, plate, Gibson Girl, Miss Babbles Brings the
    Paper $130.00

Series Ware, plate, Windsor Castle, 10½" $55.00

Series Ware, toothpick holder, sunset scene, handled .. $90.00

Series Ware, tray, Under the Greenwood Tree, 11x5". $110.00

Series Ware, vase, Gleaners & Gypsies, 2" $80.00

Series Ware, vase, Sydney Carton, Dickensware, handled,
    7" $185.00

Stoneware, ashtray, Courage's Ale $60.00

Stoneware, creamer & sugar bowl, Slater's Patent $125.00

Stoneware, humidor, hunting figures in relief, marked,
    5x4⅛" $155.00

Stoneware, lawn fountain, pelican figure, 15" $325.00

Stoneware, pitcher, blue & brown on brown, incised Islamic
    leaves, 5" $180.00

Stoneware, pitcher, tan tapestry w/red, gold & white trim,
    3⅜" $45.00

Stoneware, ring dish, brown & tan owl figure, 4x3¼". $170.00

Stoneware, teapot, floral tapestry, marked, 5x4½" $150.00

Stoneware, vase, blue mottling on blue-green, embossed
    flowers, Lambeth, 6½" $85.00

Stoneware, vase, white & brown on tan, applied cherry
    blossoms, 6" $300.00

Toby jug, Cap'n Cuttle, D6266, 4½" $185.00

Toby jug, Charrington, One Toby Leads to Another. $350.00

Toby jug, Cliff Cornell, tan, 9" $435.00

Toby jug, Falstaff, 8½" $145.00

Toby jug, Huntsman, D6320, 7½" $150.00

Toby jug, Old Charlie, seated, sm $175.00

Toby jug, Sir Francis Drake, D6660, 9" $145.00

Toby jug, Sir Winston Churchill, D6175, 4" $75.00

Toby jug, Squire, D6319 .... $270.00

Ruby Glass

Red glassware has always appealed to the buying public, and today there are lots of collectors who look for it. It's been made for more than one hundred years by literally every glasshouse in the country, but most of what's out there today was made during the Depression era though the decade of the seventies. Anchor Hocking made lots of it; they called their line 'Royal Ruby.'

If you like this type of glassware, we recommend you read _Ruby Glass of the 20th Century_ by Naomi Over.

See also Depression Glass; Eyewinker; Moon and Star.

Basket, scalloped rim, yellow handle, 4½" **$65.00**
Bowl, Oyster & Pearl, Anchor Hocking, 6½" **$20.00**
Cake plate, Sandwich, Indiana, 13" **$90.00**
Candlestick, Viking, swan neck, 6¼" **$28.00**
Candy dish, Sweetheart, LG Wright, 3¾"....................**$22.00**
Door stop, Alley Cat, 11¼" **$40.00**
Fairy lamp, Sweetheart, LG Wright, 4½"....................**$30.00**
Figurine, bird, Swedish glass, 4" **$18.00**
Figurine, elephant, Swedish glass, 5" **$18.00**

Mint dish, $20.00

Nappy, Royal Ruby, Anchor Hocking, 6½" **$10.00**
Paperweight, apple, Viking, 3¾".........................**$20.00**
Pickle dish, Royal Ruby, Anchor Hocking, 1940s, 7"...**$18.00**
Pie plate, Pyrex, 9½".....................................**$50.00**
Pitcher, High Point, Anchor Hocking, 80-oz **$45.00**
Plate, Oyster & Pearl, Anchor Hocking, 13½" **$44.00**
Salt & pepper shakers, Mirror & Rose, LG Wright, 3¼",
  pr...**$22.00**
Saucer, American, Macbeth-Evans **$27.00**
Sherbet, Anchor Hocking **$8.00**
Snack set, Fan, Anchor Hocking............................**$12.00**
Tray, Anchor Hocking, 14" **$27.00**
Tumbler, Georgian, Anchor Hocking, 9-oz **$8.00**
Vase, Elite, Westmoreland, 8½"............................**$28.00**
Vase, fan form, 8½"......................................**$45.00**
Wine goblet, Czechoslovakia, 5-oz.........................**$20.00**

Ruby-Stained Souvenirs

These were popular at fairs around the turn of the century up until the 1920s, and even today they're not at all hard to find. You'll find them with names, dates, and sometimes an inscription, all etched onto the ruby-flashed pattern glass at the direction of the souvenir buyer.

Bell, St Louis, 7" **$80.00**
Butter dish, Button Arches **$80.00**
Creamer, Arched Oval, miniature **$30.00**
Creamer, Heart Band, miniature **$30.00**
Cruet, Sunken Honeycomb, Mother, 1893 World's Fair...**$95.00**

Goblet, Toledo O 1907, 4", $35.00

Mug, Button Arches, 1904 St Louis Exposition **$45.00**
Mug, Diamond Point Band................................**$35.00**
Mug, Heart, Eureka Springs Crescent Hotel **$35.00**
Mug, Heart Band, Oxford MI **$42.00**
Pin dish, heart shape **$35.00**
Spooner, Button Arches, Sister, 1897...................**$40.00**
Toothpick holder, Scalloped Swirl.....................**$40.00**
Toothpick holder, Shamrock............................**$45.00**
Toothpick holder, Trophy **$25.00**
Toothpick holder, Witch's Kettle **$18.00**
Tumbler, Atlantic City, 1898..........................**$50.00**
Tumbler, Pavonia......................................**$55.00**
Wine, Honeycomb.......................................**$35.00**

Russel Wright Designs

One of the country's foremost industrial designers, Russel Wright, was also responsible for several dinnerware lines, glassware, and aluminum that have become very collectible. American Modern, produced by the Steubenville Pottery Company (1939-1959) is his best known and most popular today. It had simple, sweeping lines that appealed to tastes of that period, and it was made in a variety of solid colors. The most desirable are: Canteloupe, Glacier, Bean Brown, and white.

Double our values for these colors. Chartreuse is represented by the low end of our range, Cedar, Black Chutney and Seafoam by the high end, and Coral and Gray near the middle.

Iroquois China made his Casual line, and because it was so serviceable, it's relatively easy to find today. It will be marked with both Wright's signature and 'China by Iroquois.'

To price Brick Red and Aqua Casual, double our values; for Avocado use the low end of the range. Canteloupe, Oyster, and Charcoal are valued at 50% more than prices listed.

Wright's aluminum ware is highly valued by today's collectors, even though it wasn't so well accepted in its day, due to the fact that it was so easily damaged.

If you'd like to learn more about the subject, we recommend *The Collector's Encyclopedia of Russel Wright Designs* by Ann Kerr.

American Modern

Bowl, divided vegetable; from $75 to **$80.00**
Bowl, salad; from $70 to **$75.00**

Butter dish, from $155 to $165.00

Carafe (stoppered jug), from $150 to **$165.00**
Celery dish, from $23 to **$25.00**
Coffeepot, AD; from $55 to **$65.00**
Creamer **$10.00**
Cup, from $10 to..**$12.00**
Divided relish, from $150 to **$175.00**
Gravy boat, 10½", from $18 to......................................**$20.00**
Lug soup, from, $12 to **$15.00**
Pitcher, w/lid, from $150 to **$165.00**
Plate, dinner; 10", from $8 to..**$10.00**
Plate, salad; 8", from $10 to...**$12.00**
Platter, 13¼", from $20 to...**$25.00**
Salad fork & spoon, from $85 to....................................**$95.00**
Sauce boat, 8¾", from $25 to **$30.00**
Snack server, from $150 to...**$160.00**
Sugar bowl, w/lid, from $12 to **$14.00**
Teapot, 6x10", from $65 to...**$75.00**
Tumbler, child's, from $55 to **$60.00**
Bowl, cereal; 5", from $7 to..**$8.00**

Casual

Bowl, divided vegetable; 10", from $35 to **$40.00**
Bowl, flat soup; 21-oz, rare, from $32 to......................**$35.00**
Bowl, fruit; 5½", from $6 to...**$8.00**
Bowl, salad; 10", from $28 to **$30.00**
Bowl, soup; 11½-oz, from $15 to...................................**$18.00**
Bowl, vegetable; 36-oz, from $18 to..............................**$20.00**

Butter dish, ½-lb, from $60 to **$65.00**
Casserole, deep tureen; 4-qt, from $60 to **$65.00**

Coffeepot, AD; 4½", from $50 to $75.00

Creamer, stacking; from $10 to **$12.00**
Cup & saucer, AD; from $75 to.....................................**$80.00**
Gravy bowl, 12-oz, from $10 to.....................................**$12.00**
Mug, 13-oz, from $45 to **$55.00**
Plate, bread & butter; 6½", from $4 to.........................**$5.00**
Plate, dinner; 10", from $8 to **$10.00**
Plate, luncheon; 9½", from $7 to..................................**$8.00**
Plate, salad; 7½", from $8 to...**$10.00**
Platter, 12¾", from $20 to...**$25.00**
Salt & pepper shakers, stacking; pr, from $10 to........**$12.00**
Teacup & saucer, from $12 to.......................................**$15.00**

Glassware

American Modern, cordial, 2-oz, from $35 to **$38.00**
American Modern, dessert dish, 2", from $35 to..........**$40.00**
American Modern, goblet, 10-oz, from $35 to **$40.00**
American Modern, tumbler, iced tea; 13-oz, from $25 to .**$30.00**
Iroquois, tumbler, water; 11-oz, from $30 to **$35.00**
Iroquois Pinch, tumbler, juice; 6-oz, from $30 to **$35.00**
Old Morgantown, coctail, 3-oz, from $25 to **$30.00**
Old Morgantown, sherbet, 5-oz from $25 to **$30.00**
Old Morgantown, wine, 4-oz, from $25 to...................**$30.00**

Highlight

Bowl, vegetable; oval, from $55 to **$60.00**
Butter dish, from $100 to **$125.00**
Creamer, from $25 to..**$30.00**
Mug, from $30 to **$30.00**
Plate, bread & butter; from $8 to **$10.00**
Salt & pepper shakers, pr, from $45 to **$50.00**
Sugar bowl, from $25 to..**$30.00**

Knowles

Bowl, fruit; 5½" **$8.00**
Bowl, serving; oval, 12¼" **$28.00**

Bowl, soup/cereal; 6¼"................................$10.00
Compote, deep, 7x12½" $70.00
Pitcher, cream $14.00

Pitcher, 9¼", $70.00

Plate, bread & butter; 6¼" $6.00
Plate, dinner; 10¾"...................................$15.00
Plate, salad; 8¼" $10.00
Platter, oval, 13" $18.00
Salt & pepper shakers, pr...........................$24.00

Plastic

Black Velvet, bowl, divided vegetable $22.00
Black Velvet, onion soup, w/lid $30.00
Copper Penny, platter.................................$18.00
Copper Penny, sugar bowl...........................$13.00
Flair, bowl, vegetable, shallow oval $12.00
Flair, tumbler..$15.00
Home Decorator, lug soup...........................$12.00
Home Decorator, sugar bowl........................$13.00
Meladur, cup, 7-oz....................................$8.00
Meladur, saucer, rare $3.00
Residential, cup...$6.00
Residential, lug soup $12.00

Spun Aluminum

Bain Marie server.....................................$400.00
Bowl $75.00
Flower ring...$125.00
Hot relish server $175.00
Ice bucket..$75.00
Tidbit tray $85.00
Vase, 12"...$110.00

Waste basket $110.00

Sterling

Bowl, salad; 7½", scarce $12.00
Celery dish, 11¼" $18.00
Creamer, individual; 3-oz $12.00
Cup, demitasse; rare, 3½" $45.00
Pitcher, cream; 9-oz $12.00
Plate, bread & butter; 6¼" $5.00
Platter, oval, 7½" $14.00
Saucer, 6¼" $4.00

White Clover (for Harker)

Bowl, cereal/soup; clover decoration.............$14.00
Casserole, clover decoration, 2-qt................$50.00
Dish, vegetable (open); 7½"..........................$20.00
Plate, bread & butter; color only, 6" $6.00
Plate, salad; color only, 7⅝"........................$9.00
Platter, clover decoration, 13¼" $30.00

Salem China

This company operated in Salem, Ohio, from 1920 until the fifties, producing various lines of dinnerware, most of it marked with some form of the company name and various logos. The pattern name was often included in the mark. Styles naturally changed from decade to decade and ranged from very formal lines heavily encrusted with gold to very simple geometric shapes glazed in solid colors.

For more information, we recommend *The Collector's Encyclopedia of American Dinnerware* by Jo Cunningham.

Basket of Tulips, creamer.............................$10.00
Basket of Tulips, saucer.................................$3.00
Colonial, ashtray w/Farberware 'basket' frame............$15.00
Formal, plate, salad......................................$3.00
Mandarin Red, creamer, Streamline shape $10.00
Mandarin Red, sugar bowl, Streamline shape.............$10.00

Maple Leaf, plate, 9", $4.00

Rust Tulip, plate, square, 6" **$3.00**
Rust Tulip, plate, 7" **$3.00**
Sailing, plate, dinner **$6.00**
Sailing, sugar bowl, Streamline shape **$10.00**
Standard, plate, dessert **$4.00**
Standard, plate, dinner **$6.00**
Summer Day, cup & saucer **$6.00**
Tulip, cup & saucer **$6.00**
Yellowridge, plate, octagon, 9" **$6.00**

Salt Shakers

Probably the most common type of souvenir shop merchandise from the twenties through the sixties, salt and pepper shaker sets can be spotted at any antique mall or flea market today by the dozens. Most were made in Japan and imported by various companies, though American manufacturers made their fair share as well.

'Miniature shakers' are hard to find and their prices have risen faster than any others. They were made by Arcadia Ceramics (probably an American company). They're under 1½" tall, some so small they had no space to accommodate a cork. Instead they came with instructions to 'use Scotch tape to cover the hole.'

Advertising sets and premiums are always good, since they appeal to a cross section of collectors. If you have a chance to buy them on the primary market, do so. The F&F Mold & Die Works of Dayton, Ohio, made plastic shakers (as well as other kitchenware items) with painted details for such companies as Quaker Oats, Kools Cigarettes, and Ken-L Ration Pet Food. You'll find Aunt Jemima and Uncle Mose, Willie and Millie Penguin, and Fido and Fifi with the F&F mark. The Black couples (there are two sizes) will range in value from $50.00 to $65.00. The others are about $12.00 per pair. F&F also made Luzianne Mammy shakers (so marked) for the tea company — they're worth about $175.00 (the green-skirted version), and a set representing the Campbell Kids that usually go for about $50.00.

There are several good books on the market. We recommend *Salt and Pepper Shakers, Identification and Values, Vols I, II, III and IV*, by Helene Guarnaccia; and *The Collector's Encyclopedia of Salt and Pepper Shakers, Figural and Novelty, First and Second Series*, by Melva Davern.

See also Black Americana; Condiment Sets; Regal China; Rosemeade.

Advertising

Amoco gas pumps, plastic, red, 1950s, pr **$30.00**
Big Boy figure & double-decker hamburger on blue plate, ceramic, 1990s, USA, 5" Big Boy, 2¼" hamburger, pr.**$20.00**
Blue Sunoco gas pumps, plastic, blue & white w/blue & yellow decals, 1950-60 era, pr **$30.00**
Borden's Elsie & Elmer, decaled ceramic heads on white teakettle shapes w/handles, 1940s, pr **$25.00**
Borden's Elsie & her twins, ceramic, seated Elsie smiling down at twins resting in her crossed legs, pr **$50.00**

Budweiser's Bud Man figures, plastic, red w/blue capes, yellow belts & red shoes, lettered chests, 1991, 3½", pr **$18.00**
Campbell Kids, ceramic, red & white, lg range size w/Campbell girl in chef's hat & apron decaled on front, pr.**$15.00**
Evinrude motors, plastic, motors rest on transparent amber stands, given as employee Christmas gifts, pr **$125.00**
Firestone tire shapes, ceramic, lettered Firestone & US Rubber, pr **$40.00**
Hamm's Beer bear figures, ceramic, black & white bears holding Hamm's labels, 1 pours from top, other from nose, 5", pr **$125.00**
Inlet Valley Farms Inc milk bottles, glass, company name lettered on side, pr.................................**$10.00**
Marathon Mile-Maker gas pumps, plastic, white w/red, white & blue decals, pr **$35.00**
New Era Potato Chips cans, metal, yellow w/woman's form in black silhouette next to red & black lettering, pr.**$8.00**
Pabst Blue Ribbon Beer steins, dark blue glass w/paper labels, silver-tone metal caps, pr....................**$10.00**
Philgas tanks, green w/Philgas lettered diagonally on front, pr...**$20.00**

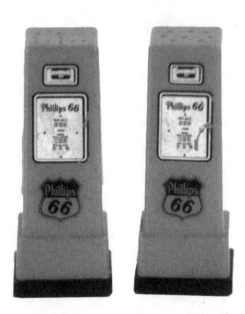

Phillips 66 gas pumps, plastic, orange w/black logo & base, 2¼", pr, $22.00

Planters' Mr Peanut figures, ceramic, yellow peanut bodies w/legs crossed in seated Indian style, Taiwan, 1992, 5", pr...**$10.00**
Seagram's 7, plastic, red crowned 7's on white oval bases w/Seagram's lettered in red, pr **$8.00**
Sprite soda cans, Sprite lettered diagonally on green label, pr...**$6.00**

Animals, Birds and Fish

Alligators, ceramic, animated, 1 upright, 1 crawling, golden brown, wearing yellow hats & black bow ties, glossy, pr...**$6.00**

Antelope, bone china, realistic, 1 standing w/head down, 1 resting, dark gray & white, pr **$22.00**

Basset hounds, ceramic, both sitting, 1 howling, white w/brown, pr **$22.00**

Bear cubs on rocking horse, ceramic, 2-piece yellow horse w/dots, girl on front half, boy on back half, 2-piece set **$10.00**

Bears, ceramic, hugging rocking bears, 1 white & 1 reddish brown w/black accents, 1-piece **$12.00**

Bears, ceramic, mother bear looking up at baby bear sitting in crook of her lifted arm, gray w/white & gold accents, pr **$10.00**

Bears, ceramic, sitting upright, 'stuffed' teddy bears w/seam stitching, 1 brown & white, 1 black & white, pr ...**$10.00**

Bird on a nest, ceramic, mamma bird lifts off to reveal 2 egg shakers in nest, 4-piece set **$8.00**

Bird on stump, ceramic, yellow & white bird on tree stump w/blue flowers, gold accents, Poinsettia Studio, 3-piece set **$18.00**

Birds in eggshell holder, ceramic, blue birds w/yellow breasts & black beaks in blue shells, center handle, lustre, pr **$12.00**

Blue Jays, ceramic, 1 w/wings spread looking sideways, other huddled w/wings slightly open, blue w/yellow bellies, pr **$9.00**

Boxer dogs, ceramic, realistic, 1 standing, 1 sitting, golden airbrushing w/brown-black faces, removable collars, pr.**$20.00**

Bunny huggers, ceramic, white w/gold accents, orange ears hanging down, bug eyes, pr **$8.00**

Cat carrier, red clay, posed w/rump up holding 2 buckets, black w/metallic-gold accents, 3-piece set **$10.00**

Cat on block of ice, ceramic, shivering kitty w/arms & legs crossed atop block of ice, pr.................................**$12.00**

Cats, ceramic, 1 sitting upright & the other resting, black lustre w/red ears & mouth, gold eyes, pr **$10.00**

Chickens, ceramic, black & white stripes w/red combs & waddles, green bases, pr **$10.00**

Collie dogs, ceramic, realistic looking in standing position, brown on white, pr..**$18.00**

Cows, ceramic, animated, standing w/legs spread & backs arched, pink & white w/dark gray accents, pr........**$8.00**

Dachshunds, ceramic, resembling pull toys w/heads & tails up, brown, black & yellow w/red 'wheels,' pr **$15.00**

Dalmation pups, ceramic, realistic, 1 sitting, 1 standing, white w/black spots & ears, pr **$22.00**

Dog couple, ceramic, he in gold jacket, black pants & brown shoes, she in gold & pink layered dress, pair, $15.00

Dogs, clear glass, sitting upright, glass heads unscrew, pr..**$15.00**

Donkey carrier, metal, copper-tone donkey w/barrel shakers attached to back, pr **$10.00**

Ducks, ceramic, carved wood look w/black breasts, red heads & brushed bodies, pr **$8.00**

Ducks, ceramic, yellow ducks w/flat sides resembling rocking toys, blue wings, orange bills & tails, green rockers, pr..**$15.00**

Elephant, ceramic, sitting upright w/trunk up, marked GOP, light blue glaze, head separates from body, 2-piece set...**$30.00**

Elephant carrier, ceramic, standing upright w/bundles of wood as shakers hanging from shoulders, brown tones, 3-piece set...**$10.00**

Elephants, bone china, both in stride, 1 w/trunk up, 1 curled under, gray & white airbrushing, black toes, glossy, pr...**$22.00**

Elephants, ceramic, animated, sitting upright w/trunks up, white w/gray, pink & gold airbrushing, red collars, pr...**$10.00**

Fish, ceramic, resting on 3 fins, orange w/green brushstroke design & white dots, white 'seams' w/black 'stitching,' pr..**$12.00**

Fish couple, ceramic, standing upright on tails, he in blue hat & yellow tie, she in yellow hat, glossy, pr......**$12.00**

Fish nodders, ceramic, 2 fish on base lettered 'Even a fish would't get caught if he kept his mouth shut,' 3-piece set...**$35.00**

Fish on tray, ceramic, white & yellow bodies w/black stripes, gold accents, yellow tray, Poinsettia Studio, 3-piece set...**$18.00**

Fish w/polka dots, ceramic, animated pose w/human features, tails up, white w/red dots & metallic gold trim, pr..**$12.00**

Foxes, ceramic, realistic, sitting upright, 1 w/front paws up, rich brown & white, glossy, pr...............................**$8.00**

Frog & toadstool, ceramic, toadstool w/smiling face on stem nestled into stomach of lime green frog, glossy, 2-piece set...**$6.00**

Frogs, ceramic, stylized shape in white w/green & pink floral & leaf design, w/tray of same design, 3-piece set ...**$8.00**

Giraffe heads, ceramic, realistic, 1 looking up & the other looking down, gold w/golden brown spots, pr....**$10.00**

Goats, bone china, realistic, standing billy goat, resting nanny goat, white w/black hooves & features, gold horns, pr **$20.00**

Gorillas in a cage, ceramic, amimated courting couple in honey-colored airbrushing, he w/flowers, wire cage, 3-piece set...**$10.00**

Horse heads, silver-tone metal, pr **$15.00**

Horse musicians, ceramic, playing sax & accordion, she dressed in gold & pink & he in blue & black, glossy, pr..**$18.00**

Horses, ceramic, stylized standing form, cream w/brown mane & eyes, pr **$6.00**

Kitten in a basket, ceramic, white kitten sticking its paw through blue basket, 2-piece set **$15.00**

Kittens, pot metal, sitting upright, 1 painted white w/red bow, 1 painted black w/red bow, pink ears, pr...**$12.00**

Monkey & baby nodders, ceramic, mamma seated w/arms wrapped around baby, heads nod in different directions, 3-piece set **$50.00**

Monkey & telephone, ceramic, brown monkey using early black upright desk phone, 2-piece set.................**$15.00**

Monkey couple, ceramic, dressed for the tropics, she in pink w/dots & he in blue on palm tree stand, glossy, 3-piece set...**$15.00**

Monkeys, ceramic, 'See No Evil' & 'Speak No Evil' sitting on base w/'Hear No Evil' handle, 3-piece set............**$15.00**

Monkeys, ceramic, standing looking sideways, dressed in suits w/vests reading 'I am Salt' & 'I am Pepper,' German, pr **$20.00**

Mouse couple, ceramic, dressed to go, she in pink dress & white hat, he in yellow & blue w/black hat, glossy, pr...**$10.00**

Mouse couple & cheese, plastic, both upright on cheese base, he dressed in orange, she dressed in pink, 3-piece set...**$15.00**

Mouse on bowling ball, ceramic, animated gray mouse w/pink & black accents atop black bowling ball, glossy, 2-piece set...**$18.00**

Mouse playing drums, animated pink felt-like body appearing to beat on 2 yellow 'drum' shakers on yellow base, 3-piece set...**$5.00**

Owls, ceramic, stylized oval shapes w/embossed feathers, shades of brown & gold w/black brows, eyes & feet, pr...**$8.00**

Peacocks, ceramic, stylized forms resting on feet & tails, looking up, light green w/gold accents, pr...........**$15.00**

Pelicans, heavy metal, white w/lg orange open beaks, looking up, green bases lettered Miami, pr.................**$30.00**

Penguins, ceramic, chubby fellows wearing red neck scarves sitting, looking up, glossy, pr....................**$10.00**

Penguins, handblown glass, painted black & white striped bodies, orange beaks & feet, 1 lg, 1 sm, pr **$20.00**

Penguins, silver-tone metal, both upright w/smooth sleek features, pr **$18.00**

Pig bride & groom nodders, ceramic, he in black top hat, coat & bow tie, she in pink bow w/yellow bouquet, 3-piece set...**$125.00**

Ponies, bone china, both in stride, gray w/white airbrushed spots & manes, matte, pr.......................**$22.00**

Poodles in a basket, 1 gray & 1 white w/pink accents in basket w/floral design & gold trim, 3-piece set ...**$18.00**

Rabbits, bone china, realistic, 1 sitting upright w/front paws up, 1 hopping, looking back, white w/pink ears, pr **$20.00**

Rabbits, wood, egg-shaped heads on tapered cylindrical bodies, white heads w/black features, red & blue bodies, pr...**$8.00**

Rabbits on motorcycles, ceramic, white w/pink shirts, blue head bands & pants sitting on green motorcycles, pr..**$20.00**

Rainbow trout, ceramic, realistic, appearing to jump from water, shades of brown w/spots, blue water base, pr...**$12.00**

Roosters, ceramic, carved wood-look w/flat sides, shades of green w/red comb & yellow beak, matte, pr........**$15.00**

Roosters, ceramic, stylized crowing roosters w/exaggerated necks, shades of yellow w/red, few brown spots, red bases, pr **$10.00**

Scotty dogs, ceramic, sitting upright begging, 1 white & 1 black w/gold trim, pr, $8.00

Sheep, ceramic, realistic, standing ram & resting ewe, white w/black hooves & features, ram has golden horns, pr.**$22.00**

Skunk, ceramic, elongated w/head resting on front paws, black w/scalloped white stripe, 1-piece **$8.00**

Snails, bone china, white shells w/blue accents, blue & white bodies, white tray w/blue floral design, pr...**$8.00**

Squirrels, silver-tone metal, both upright holding acorns, smooth sleek features, pr **$12.00**

Swans on log, metal, natural looking, sitting on curved log w/bills resting on breasts, pr.................................**$10.00**

Tigers, ceramic, animated, sitting upright, yellow w/black stripes, exaggerated cheeks & chins, pr **$10.00**

Toucans, ceramic, heads & open beaks looking upward, lustre, pr **$15.00**

Turkeys, ceramic, black male & female w/white, red & yellow accents, glossy, pr..**$10.00**

Turtles, silver-tone metal, standing stiff legged, rounded embossed shells, pr **$10.00**

Wild boars, wood, stylized carving, from Africa, pr **$8.00**

Character

Felix the Cat, ceramic, posed w/arms behind back, black w/white 'beady' eyes, 1930s, sm, pr....................**$100.00**

Ferdinand the Bull, ceramic, black & white Ferdinand sitting among flowers on green base, matte, pr...............**$35.00**

Fred & Wilma Flintstone, ceramic, both standing in front of stone slabs, 1991, pr **$30.00**

Garfield heads, ceramic, Garfield w/'toothy' grin & eyes half closed, pr..**$18.00**

Goofy & Donald Duck, ceramic, Goofy w/legs wrapped around yellow apple & Donald w/carton of milk, newer, glossy, pr..**$15.00**

Hare & the tortoise, ceramic, hare asleep on back w/arms crossed, upright tortoise 'sneaking' past, Vallona Star, pr **$30.00**

Huey & Dewey, some crazing, pr..............................**$35.00**

Humpty Dumpty, ceramic, Humpty Dumpty sitting on brick wall, looking up, 2-piece set **$12.00**

Humpty Dumpty characters, ceramic, 1 is artist w/eyes closed, 1 is mailman, Norcrest H 714, pr **$30.00**

Kermit & Miss Piggy magic trick, ceramic, Kermit contemplating sawing Miss Piggy in half, she in white trunk, pr **$18.00**

Knothead & Splinter from Woody Woodpecker cartoons, ceramic, both carrying white 6-sided shakers, lettered bases, pr **$30.00**

Little Miss Muffet & the Spider, bone china, black burgundy & gold accents, black spider on white w/green, pr **$28.00**

Little Miss Muffet w/bowl of curds & whey, ceramic, she appearing to fall off her 'tuffet,' Vallona Star, pr ..**$30.00**

Little Red Riding Hood & the Wolf, ceramic, both on bases marked 'Never Never Land,' pr **$45.00**

Maggie & Jiggs outhouses, ceramic, white w/blue roofs, names lettered in gold w/gold trim, pr **$35.00**

Mammy & Pappy Yokum, ceramic, pipe-smoking Mammy in plaid skirt, Pappy in red & white striped shirt, patched jeans, pr..**$100.00**

Mickey Mouse in car, ceramic, Mickey in yellow car waving, 1989, pr..**$15.00**

Moon Mullins, ceramic, wearing off-white suit incised w/checks & black top hat, 1 w/black tie & 1 w/red, pr...**$25.00**

Paul Bunyan & Babe the bull, ceramic, Babe is blue w/name on rump, Paul stiffly posed in red & blue on lettered base, pr **$25.00**

Pebbles & Bam-Bam, ceramic, Pebbles crawling & Bam-Bam holding club, pr **$22.00**

Pinocchio, Japan, 1960s, EX+, pr **$30.00**

Raggedy Ann & Andy, ceramic, standing, he in white shirt w/green dots, blue pants, she in white dress w/pink dots, pr **$22.00**

Sad Sack, chalkware, 1 posed in green military hiking garb & 1 in brown Army uniform w/hand up, marked bases, 1940s, pr **$35.00**

Sewing machines, pot metal, 1 black & 1 white w/painted floral designs, pr **$12.00**

Smokey Bear seated, ceramic, wearing blue suits & yellow hats, pr, $25.00; Smokey Bear heads, ceramic, wearing yellow hats lettered Smokey, honey brown airbrushing w/white cheeks & nose, lg, pr, $25.00

Winnie the Pooh & Eeyore, Winnie riding Eeyore, pr .**$65.00**

Woody Woodpecker & his girlfriend, cold paint, Woody in saluting pose, girlfriend in shy pose w/head turned, 1990, pr...**$45.00**

Fruit, Vegetables and Other Food

Artichoke & head of cauliflower, porcelain, both upright, realistic colors & details, pr **$8.00**

Banana & pineapple boxers, ceramic, fruit heads w/human bodies wearing boxing gloves & shorts, pr...........**$15.00**

Cabbage girls, ceramic, realistic heads w/yellow hair wrapped on 'cabbage' hats, cabbage bodies, glossy, pr **$10.00**

Carrots, ceramic, bunch of 3 carrots standing on end, green tops, pr **$12.00**

Cookies, ceramic, chocolate sandwich type w/white centers, Cookies embossed across front, lg, pr...................**$20.00**

Corn, ceramic, 2 half-shucked ears lying side-by-side, 1-piece **$10.00**

Corn people, ceramic, corn bodies w/human heads, pr.**$8.00**

Corn people, ceramic, realistic upright ears in black shoes & painted-on smiling facial features, looking up, pr.**$10.00**

Cucumbers, ceramic, 1 cucumber resting on side of the other, green w/yellow ends, 1-piece **$10.00**

Egg heads, plastic, 1 crying & 1 smiling, upper half yellow, lower half light blue, white shoes, pr...................**$10.00**

Eggplant & cabbage referees, ceramic, human bodies w/vegetable heads wearing black & white striped shirts & whistles, pr **$20.00**

Grape clusters, mold-blown glass, 1 clear w/brown stem, 1 blue, w/inverted interior funnels, pr **$22.00**

Ice-Cream Cones, ceramic, light yellow cones w/yellow over white tops, pr..**$8.00**

Onion heads, ceramic, smiling facial features w/closed eyes curved up, rosy cheeks, pr.....................................**$10.00**

Oranges, ceramic, realistic looking w/3 green leaves on top, glossy, pr **$12.00**

Pea pods on leaf tray, ceramic, natural looking in shades of green, 3-piece set...**$15.00**

Peach & tomato baseball players, ceramic, human bodies in baseball uniforms w/vegetable & fruit heads, pr..**$20.00**

Peanut couple, ceramic, both w/wide-eyed expressions, she in green hat w/pink bow trim, he in black hat & glasses, pr, $12.00

Pineapple heads, ceramic, wide-eyed smiling features w/green tops, pr **$10.00**

Potatoes, ceramic, potato bodies w/facial features & a spoon & fork for arms, marked Latke Pepper & Latke Salt, pr..**$18.00**

Potatoes, ceramic, resting on sides w/flat bottoms, brown semigloss finish, pr **$5.00**

Pretzels, ceramic, 'salted' twisted type, J Rayton, California, glossy, pr..**$12.00**

Radishes, ceramic, resting on sides, glossy red w/short green tops, pr..**$8.00**

Squash person, ceramic, smiling squash head separates from human body w/gold-trimmed collar & green pants, 2-piece set..**$20.00**

Strawberries, ceramic, berries w/screw-on leaf bases, glossy, pr..**$10.00**

Strawberries on the vine, ceramic, realistic upright clusters of berries surrounded by brownish-green leaves, pr..**$10.00**

Tomato couple, ceramic, she looking up, white bows on shoes, lg 'leafy' hairdo, he w/open-mouthed smile, brown shoes, pr..**$10.00**

Holidays and Special Occasions

Anniversary, bone china, birds & floral bows on white hearts w/gold trim & feet, marked Happy Anniversary in script, pr..**$10.00**

Birthday cake & present, ceramic, white round cake embossed w/Happy Birthday, white present w/embossed black ribbon, pr..**$14.00**

Children dressed for St Patrick's Day, ceramic, dressed in shades of green w/embossed cloverleafs on base & skirt, pr..**$12.00**

Christmas carolers, ceramic, 2 boys in black top hats & scarves, white robes & red shoes, 1 w/book, 1 w/accordion, pr, $12.00

Christmas elephants, ceramic, both wearing Santa's hats, 1 w/eyes closed, 1 looking sideways, gold trim, pr .**$12.00**

Christmas elves, ceramic, boy & girl in red & white striped hats & outfits, he w/gift, she w/ornament, pr.......**$12.00**

Christmas ornaments, ceramic, 1 red ball & 1 green ball w/metal tops for hooks, pr..**$8.00**

Christmas soldiers, ceramic, w/white beards wearing red & white uniforms holding rifles, pr **$20.00**

Easter egg & bunny, ceramic, egg resting on end decorated w/flowers & green & yellow band, white bunny, pr..**$10.00**

Easter eggs, ceramic, resting on sides, decorated in Easter colors, pr..**$10.00**

Easter eggs, plastic, solid purple & yellow tops w/glitter water in bottoms, Applause, 1991, pr..**$8.00**

Jack-o'-lanterns, ceramic, wearing black witches' hats w/green & yellow bands, smiling facial expressions, 1980, pr..**$12.00**

Pilgrim girl & turkey, ceramic, girl in orange dress & white apron & hat, multicolored turkey, pr..**$12.00**

Pilgrim squirrels, ceramic, he holding acorn, she holding flowers, Hallmark, pr..**$10.00**

Pilgrims, ceramic, both in black & white w/blond hair, he holding corn, Hallmark, pr..**$10.00**

Santa & Mrs Claus in spaceships, ceramic, both hanging out of portholes, white w/red stripes, pr..**$22.00**

Santas, ceramic, animated expressions, 1 standing, 1 sitting w/legs spread, both holding candy canes, Fritz & Floyd, pr..**$25.00**

Santas, ceramic, stylized w/distinct V-shaped beards marked Merry Christmas & Happy New Year, Holt-Howard, 1950s, pr..**$20.00**

Valentine hearts, ceramic, 2 red heart shakers resting on floral base w/gold-trimmed arrow, 3-piece set **$12.00**

Valentine's Day hearts, ceramic, red hearts w/embossed arrows tilted on red bases, pr **$10.00**

Wedding couple, he in black & white w/top hat on arm, she in dress & veil made of netting, wire alter base, 3-piece set..**$25.00**

Witch & jack-o'-lantern, ceramic, gray witch w/black hat & purple cape holding yellow broom, smiling pumpkin, pr..**$12.00**

Household Items

Alarm clocks, wood, round w/tree-bark edging, peg feet, dome ringers, marked Time for Pepper, Time for Salt, pr..**$8.00**

Basket of laundry & iron, ceramic, light gold basket w/blue & rust-colored clothes, blue iron w/white handle, pr ..**$22.00**

Blenders, plastic, chrome-colored bases w/clear containers, black lids, pr..**$22.00**

Candles, wood, red 'flames' on short tapered candles w/bark, marked 'S' & 'P,' pr..**$10.00**

Canning jars, plastic w/rubber sealing rings & 'metal' locks, pr..**$10.00**

Clock & dust pan couple, ceramic, human bodies, clock seated in blue overalls, dust pan in pink dress, PY Japan, pr..**$18.00**

Coffeepot on stove, ceramic, white pot w/blue spattering on white stove w/black trim, pr.....................................**$12.00**

Heating radiators, pot metal, 1 white & 1 black w/painted tulips, pr......................................**$12.00**

Irons, plastic, resting upright, chrome-colored w/black handles, pr.....................................**$10.00**

Milk cans, pot metal, 1 white & 1 black w/floral design, marked milk, pr....................................**$12.00**

Milk cans, wood, 1 white & 1 black, Milk lettered in green above 3 flowers & grass, pr.............................**$10.00**

Oil lamp, ceramic, white w/pink floral design, gold trim, shade lifts off handled base, 2-piece set................**$12.00**

Outdoor water pump & wash tub, plastic, black w/gold trim, 2-piece set.....................................**$22.00**

Pot & kettle on stove, red clay, multicolored stove w/fancy 6-footed base, 3-piece set.....................................**$18.00**

Rocking chairs, pot metal, 1 black & 1 white w/painted floral design, pr....................................**$12.00**

Rolltop desk & stuffed chair, ceramic, golden brown desk, white chair featuring yellow flowers w/blue centers, pr....................................**$12.00**

Sofa & chair, natural wood square shapes, pr **$8.00**

Spool of thread & sewing basket, ceramic, wood-look spool w/red thread, yellow basket, pr............................**$22.00**

Teapot heads, ceramic, wearing pink hats w/black bills & top knots, golden hair, embossed & incised facial features, pr **$12.00**

Telephone, ceramic, 1950s desk type w/green receiver on yellow base, black-numbered dial, 2-piece set, $14.00

Toaster, plastic, black & white slices of bread in black & white toaster, 3-piece set.....................................**$12.00**

Vegetable graters, ceramic, shades of gray w/'S' & 'P' marked in red, pr.....................................**$15.00**

Miniatures

Aladdin on flying carpet & lamp, ceramic, purple lamp & white Aladdin & carpet w/multicolored accents, pr.**$26.00**

Ball & jack-in-the-box, ceramic, white ball w/blue & pink swirled effect, gold-trimmed jack-in-the-box, pr...**$26.00**

Barbecue pit & picnic table, ceramic, stone pit in shades of gray, green table w/white tablecloth, pr **$25.00**

Bathtub & kettle, ceramic, white tub w/'water,' gold soap holder, pink cloth, spattered kettle, pr...................**$26.00**

Body buried in sand w/beach umbrella, white body w/gold pail & hand shovel, blue & white umbrella, pr **$28.00**

Change purse & pocket watch, ceramic, wine-colored purse w/gold trim, white & gold face w/gold case, pr...**$26.00**

Chocolate candies in paper wrap, ceramic, rectangular metallic gold piece & 1 reddish-brown bonbon, fluted paper, pr....................................**$25.00**

Coffeepot & cup of coffee, ceramic, round 'glass' container w/metallic gold handle, white cup & saucer, pr...**$25.00**

Cowboy boots, ceramic, reddish brown w/gold trim, pr **$18.00**

Creel & catch of the day, ceramic, honey gold basket w/metallic gold latch, pile of white fish w/gray shading, pr....................................**$26.00**

Diary & love letters, ceramic, pink diary w/gold trim, white letters tied w/light pink bow, pr...........................**$25.00**

Dog & bowl of food, ceramic, white long-haired dog w/rear up & head resting on front paws looking at food, pr **$26.00**

Garden gate & hat, ceramic, vine-covered archway over open gate, white hat w/blue accents, gold trim, pr **$25.00**

Graduation cap & diploma, ceramic, black cap w/gold trim, white rolled-up diploma w/gold ends & tie, pr....**$25.00**

Ice skates & sled, ceramic, white skates w/shades of brown, gold blades, brown sled w/gold runners, 2-piece set.**$25.00**

Ice-cream maker & dish of ice cream, ceramic, brown bucket-type maker, gold trim, white plate w/gold fork, pr....................................**$25.00**

Mouse & trap, ceramic, gray mouse w/pink ears & gold trim, white trap w/yellow cheese & gold trim, pr **$28.00**

Oyster & lobster, ceramic, black shell w/white trim open to show pearl, red lobster w/black eyes, pr...............**$26.00**

Pipe & slippers, ceramic, cream & black pipe w/gold trim, wine-colored slippers, pr..**$25.00**

Roller skates, ceramic, white w/shades of brown, gold wheels, pr....................................**$22.00**

Sausage & eggs, ceramic, 2 sausage links sitting on plate of eggs (sunny side up), pr..**$28.00**

Shaving brush & mug, ceramic, upright brush w/shaving cream on end, spattered mug overflowing w/suds, pr.........**$25.00**

Stack of pancakes & syrup dispenser, ceramic, on white plate w/gold knife & fork, pr................................**$25.00**

Stop sign & car, ceramic, red sign on white post, bluish purple car, pr **$25.00**

Telescope & planet Saturn, ceramic, gold planet w/white ring, black & gold telescope, pr............................**$25.00**

Violin & accordion, ceramic, wine-colored violin, honey-colored accordion w/black & white keyboard, pr.....**$26.00**

People

Alcatraz heads, ceramic, scruffy heads on black & white striped bases lettered Alcatraz w/prisoner numbers, glossy, pr **$12.00**

Baseball players, ceramic, worried batter eyeing catcher, both w/lg red lips, white uniforms w/red & blue trim, pr..**$18.00**

Bellhops, porcelain, standing w/heads tilted holding a card, green shirts, white pants, red hats, pr **$35.00**

Boxing babies, ceramic, w/lg bellies wearing only diapers w/gold boxing gloves & green slippers, pr...........**$10.00**

Boy & girl, plastic, red boy & blue girl on white & black bases that fit together like puzzle pieces, pr.........**$15.00**

Chef couple, ceramic, short & chubby bodies, she w/dead goose, he w/dead chicken, white uniforms, Germany, pr...**$20.00**

Clowns, ceramic, Emmet Kelly look-alikes holding canes & wearing brown derby hats, red jackets & plaid pants, pr **$24.00**

Clowns, ceramic, 1 clown dancing on back of the other, 1 in stripes & 1 in dots, pr...............................**$14.00**

Clowns, ceramic, 1 in yellow & red standing w/legs spread, 1 in green & yellow doing handstand, pr **$16.00**

Cowboy nodder, porcelain, kneeled w/guns drawn, head in green hat & right hand w/gun nod, 3-piece set .**$150.00**

Cowboy on bull, ceramic, young ferocious rider w/guns drawn on brown bull w/white horns & hooves, he in red & blue, pr...**$18.00**

Dapper couple, ceramic, standing, early 1900s style of dress in white w/metallic gold accents, pr **$18.00**

Dutch girls, porcelain w/lustre finish, orange dresses, white aprons, yellow scarves & shoes, gold hats, Japan, pr **$40.00**

Fishing couple, porcelain, he in black hat & boots w/pipe, she w/hands on hips, orange dress, white apron, German, pr **$40.00**

Girl skiers, ceramic, on white bases holding skis upright next to bodies, 1 hand in pocket, red sweaters, blue pants, pr **$20.00**

Happy & Mad nodders, ceramic, connected bodies, 1 green & brown, 1 pink & blue, 3-piece set...................**$125.00**

Heart girls, ceramic, posed on knees wearing black & white hearts, blond hair, pr...**$12.00**

Indian couple in canoe, ceramic, busts of chief & squaw sitting on wood-looking base, 3-piece set.................**$14.00**

Indian on horse, ceramic, realistic multicolored Indian on black & white horse, pr..**$20.00**

Kissing Dutch couple, ceramic, she in blue & white, he in red & white, pr, $12.00

Mexican couple, ceramic, standing, she in white dress & yellow sombreo, hands on hips, he w/yellow serape, pr **$8.00**

Mexican girls, ceramic, stylized design w/red sombreros, white jackets w/white, red & yellow decorated skirts, Elbee, pr **$12.00**

Nuns, ceramic, stylized oval-shaped bodies in black & white w/blue airbrushing, pr...**$15.00**

Oriental carrier, ceramic, farmer carrying 2 baskets w/pigs heads, he dressed in red hat, yellow jacket, blue pants, pr **$24.00**

Oriental girl w/urn of fruit, ceramic, she holding fruit in 1 hand, black hair, green, red & blue clothing, pr ..**$20.00**

Pixie chefs, ceramic, 1 holding pan & yellow chick, the other w/fish & pie server, red shoes, gold trim, Napco, pr..**$12.00**

Roly Poly couple, plastic, looking sideways, he in black painted-on hat, both in red & blue, she w/white apron, pr..**$15.00**

Western couple, ceramic, stylized bodies, she in yellow hat & vest, w/black whip, he in black hat & vest, w/guns, pr..**$12.00**

Winking cowboy head, ceramic, w/cigarette, white hat, black hair, red tie, hat separates from head, 2-piece set **$18.00**

Souvenir

Beale St, ceramic, black-glazed musicians on white lamp-post base marked Beale St in black, 3-piece set...**$12.00**

Bonneville Dam Oregon, ceramic, tall rectangular shapes w/'split' scene of dam on both, 'S' & 'P' imprinted on top, pr, $12.00

Brown Derby, heavy pottery, hats representing the Brown Derby restaurant in Hollywood California, reddish brown, pr...**$10.00**

Canada, chalkware, animated features, 1 w/eyes & mouth closed, 1 w/'toothy' grin & eyes open, on marked bases, pr **$15.00**

Idaho Spuds, ceramic, potato heads w/facial features & wearing crowns marked Idaho, 'Spud' w/Salt & Pepper on bases, pr..**$10.00**

Las Vegas clowns, ceramic, standing w/hands behind backs, white w/red mouths, black card symbols & lettering, pr **$12.00**

Loretta Lynn's Dude Ranch, ceramic, white cowboy hats w/black lettering & branding symbols, pr **$15.00**

Minnesota, ceramic, shaped as the state w/name embossed & on front, light green, pr......................................**$10.00**

Movieland Wax Museum, gold-tone metal, 2 Rolls Royce cars on tray embossed w/car & name, pr **$25.00**

New York City, ceramic, satchels w/Statue of Liberty & the Empire State Building on sides, yellow handles, pr..**$12.00**

New York World's Fair, silver & gold-toned metal, 2 globes on tray embossed w/city & globe, cut-out lettering, 3-piece set..**$12.00**

Old City Gateway, St Augustine Florida, bisque, gate tower shakers on stone wall base, 3-piece set....................**$20.00**

Ozarks, ceramic, brown jugs w/painted faces of a pipe-smoking 'ma' & 'pa' in profile, marked 'S' & 'P,' pr...........**$8.00**

Peggy's Cove Nova Scotia, ceramic, lighthouse split down the middle, embossed & incised lettering, pr **$12.00**

Pennsylvania Turnpike, ceramic, winking orange-shaped head, removable brown hat w/gold paper label, pr..**$12.00**

Punxsutawney PA, ceramic, groundhogs sitting upright w/lettered bellies, reddish brown w/dark brown accents, pr **$15.00**

Remember Pearl Harbor, chalkware, the USS Arizona sinking into blue water on marked rectangular bases, pr **$20.00**

Reno Nevada, ceramic, slot machines in white w/gray & red accents, marked Salt & Pepper & Reno Nevada, pr .**$12.00**

Seattle World's Fair 1962, ceramic, white egg shapes w/'book' shapes protruding from top, blue design & lettering, pr **$25.00**

Space Needle Seattle Washington, porcelain, shaped as Space Needle in red & yellow w/lettered bases, pr............**$12.00**

Washington DC, ceramic, shaped as Washington Monument on round green bases, lustre, pr.............................**$18.00**

Miscellaneous

Alien in spaceship, ceramic, green creature seated in round yellow spaceship, Vallona Star, pr.........................**$45.00**

Barn & silo, ceramic, red w/black roofs & window trim, 1970s, pr...**$10.00**

Baseball bat & glove, ceramic, green hat attached to bat, baseball in golden brown glove, glossy, pr **$18.00**

Baseballs on stands, ceramic, white balls w/black & red 'stitching,' on black square stands, pr....................**$12.00**

Beer steins, ceramic, colorful scene in center w/lustred rim & base, angled handles, no lids, pr **$10.00**

Cigarette pack & matchbook, white open pack w/Oldfield Cigarettes embossed on front, red book w/black striker, pr..**$12.00**

Bowling pin people, ceramic, upper half red, lower half white, white & black painted-on features & lettering, Japan, pr, $12.00

Circus wagon w/horse, ceramic, white w/yellow, green & brown accents, gold trim, Poinsettia Studios, 2-piece set **$18.00**

Confederate caps, ceramic, dark blue w/Confederate flags decaled on top, crossed rifles in gold on front, pr.**$10.00**

Egg-cup couple, ceramic, shakers are hats sitting on egg cup heads, painted features w/embossed eyelashes, 4-piece set...**$18.00**

Golf balls on tees, ceramic, white balls on yellow tees w/green grassy bases, pr.......................................**$15.00**

Gum-ball machines, clear plastic globes w/red tops & red & black bases, pr...**$15.00**

Gun & holster, yellow ceramic, pr................................**$15.00**

Hats, ceramic, yellow bowler & black top hat, glossy, pr **$12.00**

Ink bottle & ink blob, ceramic, solid black, glossy, Treasure Craft, 2-piece set **$25.00**

Lighthouses, ceramic, red & white striped bodies on round brick bases w/black accents, tops are blue & yellow, pr **$8.00**

Logging truck, ceramic, 3 chained logs on gray wheels hooked to lime green cab, pr **$12.00**

Magnet & bar, ceramic, red horseshoe-shaped magnet w/gray bar, pr **$15.00**

Playing cards, ceramic, w/embossed human features & arms, king-of-spades & queen-of-hearts, 1988, pr...........**$15.00**

Pool balls, plastic, 1 solid blue w/white dot marked 2, 1 white w/red stripe & white dot marked 11, pr.....**$22.00**

Shoe houses, ceramic, white w/toes pointed up showing blue soles & heels, green roofs w/red chimneys, red laces, pr **$8.00**

Sphinx, ceramic, deep gold w/green headdress & paws, glossy, 1-piece..**$20.00**

Train engine & coal car, ceramic, engine is green w/red coal car, pr **$14.00**

Schoop, Hedi

One of the most successful California ceramic studios was founded in Hollywood by Hedi Schoop, who had been educated in the arts in Berlin and Germany. She had studied not only painting but sculpture, architecture, and fashion design as well. Fleeing Nazi Germany with her husband, the famous composer Frederick Holander, Hedi settled in California in 1933 and only a few years later became involved in producing a line of novelty giftware items so popular that it was soon widely copied by other California companies. She designed many animated human figures, some in matched pairs, some that doubled as flower containers. All were hand painted and many were decorated with applied ribbons, sgraffito work, and gold trim. To a lesser extent, she modeled animal figures as well. Until fire leveled the plant in 1958, the business was very productive. Nearly everything she made was marked.

If you'd like to learn more about her work, we recommend *The Collector's Encyclopedia of California Pottery* by Jack Chipman.

Bowl, lady's figure at side, skirt is bowl , #418, 13" **$70.00**
Bowl, shell form, pink w/gold trim, 12".......................**$32.00**

Candle holder, Mermaid, ca 1950, 13½", $150.00

Cookie jar, Queen, rare...**$175.00**
Figurine, lady holding shell-shaped bowl above her, 13"...**$45.00**
Figurine, Southern Belle, 12½"....................................**$50.00**
Figurines, Dutch boy & girl, 10½", pr.........................**$75.00**
Figurines, Oriental w/instrument, boy & girl, 10½", pr .**$95.00**
Figurines, Siamese dancers, tinted bisque w/high glaze & gold overglaze, stamped, ca 1947, 14", pr **$100.00**

Flower holder, peasant woman figural, 12" **$40.00**
Planter, geisha girl w/umbrella, blue, #223.................**$50.00**
Planter, hobby horse, 5"...**$45.00**
Planter, seated cat wearing bow w/applied bell..........**$50.00**
Tray, King of Diamonds, multicolored incised suit card design, in-mold mark..**$40.00**
Vase, crowing cock, tinted clay body w/transparent high glaze & gold overglaze, ca 1949, 12"....................**$55.00**
Vase, fan form w/gold trim, 10"...................................**$30.00**

Scottie Dog Collectibles

Collectors of Scottie dog memorabilia have banded together to form a club called Wee Scots, which holds regional and national shows each year. There's also a quarterly newsletter called the *Scottie Sampler* that includes historical data, current market prices, photographs, ads, and feature articles. They're interested in anything with Scottie dogs — advertising items, magazine covers, postcards, glassware, ceramic figures, and household items.

Book, Jock the Scot, Alice Grant Rosman, 1930 ....**$30.00**
Book, The Story of Buttons, Marguerite Kirmse illustrator **$65.00**
Bookends, Art Deco Scottie heads, white alabaster, 6½", pr...**$75.00**
Bookends, head figures, composition wood, pr..........**$35.00**
Bottle holder, advertising Black & White Scotch Whiskey, papier-mache w/race car image............................**$55.00**
Chalkboard, child's, circus figures & Scottie dog at top .**$45.00**
Clock, pendulum, 2 white dogs & black movable Scottie head..**$225.00**
Display, advertising Red Heart Dog Food, cardboard w/Robert Dickey illustration **$40.00**
Dog's feeding dish, ceramic w/Scotties in relief, UHL .**$125.00**
Dusting powder, yellow cardboard box w/multicolored Scotties, sm size **$30.00**
Figurine, opalescent glass by Sabino........................**$100.00**
Lamp, mother Scottie w/3 puppies in basket, painted pot metal..**$50.00**
Mailbox, Scottie head, cast-iron wall-type, 12x6" **$75.00**

Paperweight, cast iron, full figure on base marked Hamilton Foundry, 2½x3½", $35.00

Paperweight, Scotties w/movable dice, cast iron, Hubley **$150.00**

Planter, green spinning wheel w/black Scottie, McCoy..**$25.00**

Pull toy, Scottie on red wheels, composition wood, Hubley **$35.00**

Radio, Remler w/plastic Scottie decoration...............**$300.00**

Tumbler, black Scotties in 4 different poses, red wicket trim, Federal Glass Co **$5.00**

Sebastians

These tiny figures were first made in 1938 by Preston W. Baston and sold through gift stores, primarily in the New England area. When he retired in 1976, the Lance Corporation chose one hundred designs which they continued to produce under Baston's supervision. Since then, the discontinued figures have become very collectible.

Baston died in 1984, but his son, P.W. Baston, Jr., continues the tradition.

The figures are marked with an imprinted signature and a paper label. Early labels (before 1977) were green and silver foil shaped like an artist's palette; these are referred to as 'Marblehead' labels (Marblehead, Massachusetts, being the location of the factory), and figures that carry one of these are becoming hard to find and are highly valued by collectors.

Abe Lincoln, head up **$100.00**

America Remembers Family Sing, $100.00

Ben Franklin...**$60.00**
Clown, #130A **$75.00**
Colonial Glass Blower **$25.00**
Cow Hand **$45.00**
Deborah Franklin...**$65.00**
Dilemma, #82 ....**$150.00**
Family Feast...**$75.00**
Gabriel...**$75.00**
Gardener Woman **$200.00**
George & the Hatchet..**$300.00**

James Madison, pewter..**$45.00**
Jesse Buffun **$125.00**
John Smith & Pocahontas..**$115.00**
Martha Washington...**$45.00**
Merchants Warren Sea Captain, #329 ....**$150.00**
Mr Sheraton..**$200.00**
Mrs Cratchit **$50.00**
Old Salt **$45.00**
Phoebe **$125.00**
Priscilla Alden..**$50.00**
Romeo & Juliet, pr **$100.00**
Royal Bengal Lancer **$200.00**
Self-Portrait **$35.00**
Slalom **$100.00**

Sewing Collectibles

Once regarded simply as a necessary day-to-day chore, sewing evolved into an art form that the ladies of the 1800s took much pride in. Sewing circles and quilting bees became popular social functions, and it was a common practice to take sewing projects along when paying a visit. As this evolution took place, sewing tools became more decorative and were often counted among a lady's most prized possessions.

Of course, 19th-century notions have long been collectible, but there are lots of interesting items from this century as well. When machine-made clothing became more readily available after the 1920s, ladies began to loose interest in home sewing, and the market for sewing tools began to drop off. As a result, manufacturers tried to boost lagging sales with novelty tape measures, figural pincushions, and a variety of other tools that you may find hard to resist.

Retail companies often distributed sewing notions with imprinted advertising messages; these appeal to collectors of advertising memorabila as well. You'll see ads for household appliances, remedies for ladies' ills, grocery stores, and even John Deere tractors.

See also thimbles.

Book, Mary Thomas Embroidery, text on applique, monograms, smocking, etc, black & white pictures, 304 pages **$8.00**

Book, Story of a Silkmill, Belding Bros publishers, 1914, 30 pages, EX...**$10.00**

Button hook, sterling silver handle w/repousse design, 6" **$25.00**

Buttonhole cutter, brass w/sliding retractable knife, scalloped brass design on both sides, Pat Sept 3, 1872 ....**$55.00**

Crochet hook, bone handle w/steel working end.......**$35.00**

Darner, amber glass blown into foot shape.................**$65.00**

Darner, black-painted wood w/sterling silver handle, sm **$50.00**

Darner, child's, blue-painted wood **$25.00**

Darner, dark green glass blown into ball shape, 5¼"..**$75.00**

Darner, sterling silver w/geometric design around daisy & leaves, sm **$75.00**

Darner, wood w/cherry stain, mushroom-shaped working
end..**$40.00**

Emery, black fabric cat's head w/red ribbon around neck,
white painted eyes, 1⅜x1¼"...................................**$25.00**

Emery, cream-colored silk face w/pink silk turban, painted
facial features, 1½" dia...**$65.00**

Emery, green taffeta heart shape, 2"..........................**$35.00**

Emery, ivory w/mother-of-pearl head.........................**$25.00**

Finger guard, gold-plated w/raised flower design, marked c
Carol Bradley, 1975..**$25.00**

Glove hook, ivory teardrop handle w/2½" metal hook..**$25.00**

Measure, basket of fruit, celluloid, 1½" wide, $75.00

Measure, brass teapot form w/scalloped effect on handle,
self-winding..**$165.00**

Measure, duck, china, yellow w/blue wings................**$40.00**

Measure, fish shape, gray plastic, 4½"........................**$45.00**

Measure, house shape, celluloid, tan w/red roof & detailed
green shrubbery, 2"..**$60.00**

Measure, Indian boy's head, celluloid, 1¾x1¼" dia.....**$25.00**

Measure, sterling silver, engraved Emily Dec 25, 1915..**$65.00**

Mending kit, red leather shoe w/blue laces, opens to hold 5
spools of thread & aluminum thimble...................**$45.00**

Mending kit, suede roll-over top w/bullet-type holder,
unmarked...**$25.00**

Needle case, Art Deco Bakelite, white w/black design &
ends, 3"..**$25.00**

Needle case, brass cylinder form w/brown marbled pattern,
top turns to release needle, 2½"............................**$45.00**

Needle case, fish shape, ivory....................................**$75.00**

Needle case, ivory w/carved dragon-butterfly, 3¾".....**$70.00**

Needle case, pink fabric heart shape, 4x4½"..............**$35.00**

Needle case, smooth ivory cylinder, 3⅜"....................**$40.00**

Needle case, spool shape w/bronze head, Wheeler & Wilson...**$25.00**

Needle case, sterling silver w/repousse design on both
sides, 2¼x2¼"..**$165.00**

Needle dispenser, wood barrel shape, German patent, 5
needle sizes..**$40.00**

Pattern, Butterick dress, 1930s.................................**$8.50**

Pin holder, red satin mitten shape, 3½x1¾"...............**$35.00**

Pincushion, bootie shape, gilt metal, 2¾x1¾"............**$50.00**

Pincushion, canoe shape, cream-colored celluloid w/silk
print fabric, blue bow at each end.......................**$85.00**

Pattern, Pictorial Review, #4408, lady's coat, 1925, $8.00

Pincushion, clamp-on, ivory w/padded top, unmarked.**$60.00**

Pincushion, egg shape, composition, 3 ball feet, 3x4½"..**$60.00**

Pincushion, heart shape, black & blue woven straw-type
fabric, beveled-edge mirror on reverse.................**$80.00**

Pincushion, woman's high-heeled shoe, leather w/beaded
trim...**$40.00**

Reel holder, peach w/painted line drawing of bird on
branch, celluloid w/tassel on end, tubular............**$25.00**

Scissors, brass, stork handles, unmarked, 7"...............**$15.00**

Scissors, green enamel over sterling w/painted flowers,
4½"...**$45.00**

Scissors, mother-of-pearl dolphin-shaped handles, chrome
blades, 10¾"..**$135.00**

Sewing kit, green Bakelite w/carved spool of thread,
w/thread reel..**$25.00**

Sewing kit, painted wood scene w/elf & mushroom, flower pincushion, mushroom darner, thimble in bucket, 3", $35.00

Sewing kit, red heart shape, w/sm scissors, zipper closure..**$8.00**

Spool case, sterling silver, beaded borders, notch inside for thread, 1¼x1" dia **$135.00**

Tatting shuttle, ivory...**$40.00**

Tatting shuttle, sterling, raised oval cartouche on both sides...**$85.00**

Thimble case, acorn shape, walnut w/grooves around pull-off cap, unmarked..**$70.00**

Thimble case, cloisonne, china **$25.00**

Thimble case, egg shape, brass w/chain for chatelaine, 2½x2" **$100.00**

Thimble case, egg shape, sterling silver, Russian......**$135.00**

Thimble case, Plexiglas, 6 shelves w/11 thimble posts on each, sliding door, 12x8½" **$40.00**

Thimble case, sterling silver, allover pierced design w/plain top for engraving, Webster Co............................**$140.00**

Thimble case, sterling treasure chest figural, 8 applied carnelian stones around sides, 2 handles each side, unlined...**$125.00**

Thread barrel, ivory **$40.00**

Thread case, sterling silver w/fancy flower & scroll design, England..**$135.00**

Thread winder, blue glass, tubular, 1½x2½" **$75.00**

Thread winder, ivory, flat rectangular shape, 2"..........**$45.00**

Thread winder, ivory, unmarked **$20.00**

Tweezers, French ivory handle, 6"................................**$6.50**

Winding clamp, ivory w/netting knob & spool peg....**$75.00**

Shawnee Pottery

In 1937, a company was formed in Zanesville, Ohio, on the suspected site of a Shawnee Indian village. They took the tribe's name to represent their company, recognizing the Indians to be the first to use the rich clay from the banks of the Muskingum River to make pottery there. Their venture was very successful, and until they closed in 1961, they produced many lines of kitchenware, planters, vases, lamps, and cookie jars that are very collectible today.

They specialized in figural items. There were 'Winnie' and 'Smiley' pig cookie jars and salt and pepper shakers; 'Bo Peep,' 'Puss 'n Boots,' 'Boy Blue,' and 'Charlie Chicken' pitchers; Dutch children; lobsters; and two lines of dinnerware modeled as ears of corn.

Values sometimes hinge on the extent of an item's decoration. For instance, a 'Smiley' pig cookie jar with no decoration is valued at a minimum of $50.00, while one with a painted neckerchief and a few scattered flowers or cloverleaves may be worth $200.00. Add brown trousers and gold trim and the value zooms to $375.00 And while a 'Bo Peep' pitcher is basically worth $95.00, the addition of some decals and gold about doubles it. Most items will increase by 50% to 200% when heavily decorated and gold trimmed.

Not all of their ware was marked Shawnee; many pieces were simply marked USA with a three- or four-digit mold number. If you'd like to learn more about this subject, we recommend *The Collector's Guide to Shawnee Pottery* by

Duane and Janice Vanderbilt; *Shawnee Pottery, Identification & Value Guide,* by Jim and Bev Mangus; and *Collecting Shawnee Pottery* by Mark E. Supnick.

Bank, bulldog, white w/rose & blue features, green eyes...**$150.00**

Bank, Howdy Doody on pig, white w/rose & blue shading, marked USA Bob Smith......................................**$350.00**

Bowl, fruit; Corn Queen, marked Shawnee 92, 6".......**$40.00**

Bowl, mixing; Corn King, marked Shawnee 5, 5" **$25.00**

Bowl, mixing; Lobster Ware, 5" dia **$30.00**

Bowl, mixing; Lobster Ware, 9" dia **$45.00**

Bowl, mixing; Valencia, 10" **$25.00**

Bowl, soup or cereal; Corn King, marked Shawnee 94.**$50.00**

Butter dish, Lobster Ware...**$75.00**

Casserole, Corn Queen, marked Shawnee 74, lg.........**$50.00**

Casserole, Valencia, 8½"..**$55.00**

Coffeepot, Pennsylvania Dutch, marked USA 52.......**$135.00**

Coffeepot, Sunflower, marked USA, minimum value, $125.00

Cookie jar, blue jug form, marked USA, minimum value.**$75.00**

Cookie jar, Corn King, marked Shawnee 66, minimum value **$185.00**

Cookie jar, Drum Major, marked USA 10, minimum value **$400.00**

Cookie jar, Dutch Boy (Jack), white w/blue stripes & tie, marked USA, minimum value **$140.00**

Cookie jar, Dutch Boy (Jack), white w/decals & gold highlights, hand-painted flowers on back, marked USA, minimum value **$250.00**

Cookie jar, Dutch Girl (Jill), floral decals & gold trim, marked USA, minimum value **$275.00**

Cookie jar, Dutch Girl (Jill), hand-painted tulips, floral decals & gold trim, marked USA, minimum value..........**$285.00**

Cookie jar, Fruit Basket, airbrushed fruit on yellow basket, gold trim, marked Shawnee 84, minimum value.**$200.00**

Cookie jar, Hexagon, blue basketweave design, marked USA, minimum value **$50.00**

Cookie jar, Jo Jo the Clown, gold trim, marked Shawnee 12, perfect, no damage on ball, minimum value **$600.00**

Cookie jar, Jo Jo the Clown, marked Shawnee 12, minimum value **$375.00**

Cookie jar, light yellow bean pot shape w/snowflake design, marked USA, minimum value **$50.00**

Cookie jar, light yellow Fernware, octagon, marked USA, minimum value **$75.00**

Cookie jar, Little Chef, 4-sided, green w/embossed 'Cookies' & chef, marked USA, minimum value **$120.00**

Cookie jar, Muggsy, white w/blue scarf tied around jaw, gold trim, marked Pat Muggsy USA, minimum value, $650.00

Cookie jar, owl, gold trim, marked USA, minimum value .**$250.00**

Cookie jar, Puss 'n Boots, gold, w/decals, marked Pat Puss 'n Boots, minimum value **$375.00**

Cookie jar, Puss 'n Boots, rose-colored bow, blue trim, marked Pat Puss 'n Boots, minimum value **$165.00**

Cookie jar, Sailor Boy, white w/blond hair & gold trim, marked USA, minimum value **$600.00**

Cookie jar, Sailor Boy, white w/floral decals & gold trim, blond hair, marked USA, minimum value **$650.00**

Cookie jar, Smiley the Pig, allover chrysanthemum design, gold trim, marked USA, minimum value **$375.00**

Cookie jar, Smiley the Pig, allover shamrock design, marked USA, minimum value **$200.00**

Cookie jar, Smiley the Pig, gold trim, no decals, marked USA, minimum value **$325.00**

Cookie jar, Smiley the Pig, white w/blue bib, marked USA, minimum value **$200.00**

Cookie jar, Winnie the Pig, red collar, gold highlights, marked USA, minimum value, $400.00

Cookie jar, Winnie the Pig (Clover Bud Winnie), green collar, marked Pat Winnie USA, minimum value **$350.00**

Cookie jar, 4-sided, hand-painted flowers on yellow, gold trim, marked USA, minimum value **$125.00**

Creamer, elephant, white w/floral decals & gold trim, marked Pat USA **$165.00**

Creamer, elephant, white w/gold trim, marked Pat USA **$115.00**

Creamer, Pennsylvania Dutch, ball form, marked USA 12 .... **$50.00**

Creamer, Puss 'n Boots, green & yellow shading w/rose-colored bow, marked Shawnee 85 .... **$55.00**

Creamer, Puss 'n Boots, white w/gold trim, marked Pat Puss 'n Boots **$125.00**

Creamer, Smiley the Pig, white w/peach flower, marked Pat Smiley **$50.00**

Creamer, Smiley the Pig, yellow w/blue bib, gold trim, marked Shawnee 86 .... **$135.00**

Creamer, White Corn Ware, marked USA, 12-oz **$35.00**

Figurine, fawn, unmarked, 4½" **$12.00**

Figurine, rabbit, white w/floral decals & gold trim ...**$125.00**

Figurine, southern girl, light blue, marked USA, 4½" ..**$10.00**

Figurine, tumbling bear, white w/floral decals & gold trim **$115.00**

Flower frog, swan on high base, lavender, unmarked, 4¼" **$25.00**

Flower frog, turtle, light green, unmarked, 4x5" **$20.00**

Flowerpot & saucer, embossed tulips on pink, marked USA, 4½" **$8.00**

French casserole, Lobster Ware, 10-oz **$15.00**

French casserole, Lobster Ware, 2-qt **$35.00**

Goblets, gold, marked Hand Decorated 24 Karat Gold, pr **$175.00**

Ice server, pink elephant, w/original rubber seal, marked Shawnee 60, minimum value **$125.00**

Jardiniere, embossed tulips on light blue, marked USA, 5" **$10.00**

Match holder, Fernware, yellow, marked USA **$75.00**

Mug, Corn King, marked Shawnee 69, 8-oz................**$50.00**

Nappie, Valencia, 8½" **$16.00**

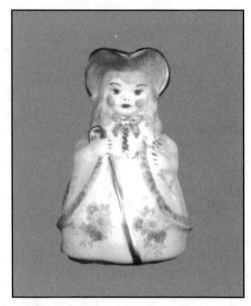

Pitcher, Bo Peep, white w/blue bonnet & floral decals, gold trim, marked Pat Bo Peep, $200.00

Pitcher, Bo Peep, yellow, rose & blue shading, gold trim, marked Shawnee 47 ....**$175.00**

Pitcher, Boy Blue, blue, yellow & rose shading, gold trim, marked Shawnee 46 ....**$175.00**

Pitcher, Chanticleer Rooster, floral decals & gold trim, marked Chanticleer................................**$235.00**

Pitcher, Chanticleer Rooster, solid gold, marked Chanticleer **$285.00**

Pitcher, Fruit, ball form, marked Shawnee 80..............**$60.00**

Pitcher, Smiley the Pig, clover bud design, marked Pat Smiley USA..**$145.00**

Pitcher, Smiley the Pig, white w/peach & blue flowers, gold trim, marked Pat Smiley **$220.00**

Planter, bird on shell, marked USA **$18.00**

Planter, canopy bed, marked Shawnee 734................**$85.00**

Planter, Chihuahua & doghouse, marked Shawnee USA **$22.00**

Planter, circus wagon, marked USA **$35.00**

Planter, covered wagon, marked USA 514, sm............**$10.00**

Planter, cradle, embossed flower, marked USA..........**$30.00**

Planter, elf & shoe, marked Shawnee 765....................**$14.00**

Planter, lamb, gold trim, marked USA 724....................**$25.00**

Planter, mouse & cheese, gold trim, marked USA 705..**$25.00**

Planter, panda & cradle, marked Shawnee USA 2031..**$45.00**

Planter, rabbit w/turnip, marked USA 703....................**$20.00**

Planter, southern girl w/basket, blue, marked USA.....**$10.00**

Planter, squirrel & stump, gold trim, marked Shawnee 664 ....**$25.00**

Planter, watering can, embossed flower on cream, marked USA **$15.00**

Plate, Corn Queen, Shawnee #68, 10" **$35.00**

Plate, Valencia, 10¾"..**$15.00**

Platter, Corn Queen, marked Shawnee 96, 12"............**$50.00**

Salt & pepper shakers, Bo Beep & Sailor Boy, sm, pr ..**$18.00**

Salt & pepper shakers, Bo Peep & Sailor Boy, gold trim, sm, pr..**$50.00**

Salt & pepper shakers, Cottage, marked USA 9, sm, rare, pr **$225.00**

Salt & pepper shakers, Dutch boy & girl, floral decals & gold trim, lg, pr..............................**$145.00**

Salt & pepper shakers, Farmer Pigs, white w/hand-painted features & gold trim, sm, pr **$60.00**

Salt & pepper shakers, flowerpots, sunflowers in rose-colored pots, gold trim, sm, pr **$40.00**

Salt & pepper shakers, milk cans, floral decals & gold trim, sm, pr..**$50.00**

Salt & pepper shakers, milk cans, sm, pr....................**$18.00**

Salt & pepper shakers, Muggsy, white w/blue scarf tied around chin, lg, pr..**$125.00**

Salt & pepper shakers, Muggsy, white w/blue scarf tied around chin, gold highlights, sm, rare, pr..........**$125.00**

Salt & pepper shakers, Owls, plain **$18.00**

Salt & pepper shakers, Pennsylvania Dutch, jug form, range size, pr **$75.00**

Salt & pepper shakers, Smiley the Pig, blue bib, floral decals & gold trim, lg, rare, pr **$250.00**

Salt & pepper shakers, Smiley the Pig, peach bib, sm, pr **$55.00**

Salt & pepper shakers, Smiley the Pig, white w/red bib, lg, pr **$100.00**

Salt & pepper shakers, Swiss boy & girl, w/gold trim, lg, pr..**$70.00**

Salt & pepper shakers, wheelbarrows, gold trim, sm, pr.**$55.00**

Salt & pepper shakers, White Corn Ware, gold trim, 3¼", pr **$60.00**

Salt & pepper shakers, White Corn Ware, 3¼", pr.......**$25.00**

Salt & pepper shakers, Winnie & Smiley, blue bibs, sm, pr **$55.00**

Salt & pepper shakers, Winnie & Smiley, red bibs w/gold trim, sm, pr..**$95.00**

Salt box, Fernware, yellow, marked USA....................**$75.00**

Sugar bowl, bucket shape, white w/blue trim, marked USA, $40.00

Sugar bowl, Corn King, marked Shawnee 78 ....**$30.00**
Sugar bowl, Valencia **$12.00**
Sugar bowl (open), cream w/snowflake design, ring handles, marked USA..**$15.00**
Sugar bowl (open), light yellow w/flower & fern design, marked 78...**$15.00**
Sugar bowl (open), Pennsylvania Dutch, jug form, marked USA **$70.00**
Sugar bowl (w/lid), Clover Bud, marked USA.............**$85.00**
Sugar bowl (w/lid), Sunflower, marked USA................**$35.00**
Sugar shaker, White Corn Ware, marked USA............**$45.00**
Teapot, Clover Bud, gold trim, marked USA **$160.00**
Teapot, Clover Bud, marked USA................................**$100.00**
Teapot, Cottage, marked USA 7..................................**$325.00**
Teapot, elephant, light green, marked USA **$225.00**
Teapot, Granny Ann, lavender w/gold trim, marked Pat Granny Ann USA..**$200.00**
Teapot, Granny Ann, peach apron, marked USA **$95.00**
Teapot, light green w/snowflake design, marked USA .**$25.00**

Teapot, Pennsylvania Dutch, marked USA 18, 18-oz, $75.00

Teapot, solid gold w/embossed rose, marked USA ..**$100.00**
Teapot, Sunflower, gold trim, marked USA **$140.00**
Teapot, Tom Tom, rose & blue shading, gold trim, marked Tom the Piper's Son Pat USA..............................**$185.00**
Teapot, white w/blue flower & gold highlights, marked USA **$55.00**
Teapot, white w/blue leaves & floral decals, gold trim, marked USA **$65.00**
Teapot, white w/embossed pink rose, marked USA ...**$45.00**
Teapot, white w/heart-shaped flower, marked USA ...**$45.00**
Tumbler, Valencia, 10-oz..**$25.00**
Utility jar, white basketweave pattern w/blue rope trim, marked USA **$80.00**
Vase, blue w/swirled design, bulbous w/fluted rim, marked USA, 5"..**$14.00**
Vase, burlap pattern, marked USA 879, 9" **$16.00**
Vase, cornucopia style on square base, plain white, marked USA, 3½"...**$8.00**
Vase, deep rose w/embossed design, bulbous w/slightly flared rim, ear-type handles, marked USA, 5".......**$10.00**
Vase, embossed flowers & leaves w/gold trim on off-white, slightly flared rim, marked USA 1225, 5"...............**$20.00**
Vase, embossed wheat on white, scalloped rim, marked USA 1266, 6"..**$18.00**

Vase, fan shape w/embossed blue flower, marked USA 1264, 4" **$14.00**
Vase, Valencia, 10"...**$18.00**
Vase, white w/embossed wheat, marked USA 1208....**$16.00**
Wall pocket, grandfather clock, brown & yellow w/gold highlights, marked USA 1261 ....**$50.00**
Wall pocket, Scotty dog, unmarked..........................**$35.00**

Sheet Music

Flea markets are a good source for buying old sheet music, and prices are usually very reasonable. Most examples can be bought for less than $5.00 More often than not, it is collected for reasons other than content. Some of the cover art was done by well-known illustrators like Rockwell, Christy, Barbelle, and Starmer, and some collectors like to zero in on their particular favorite, often framing some of the more attractive examples. Black Americana collectors can find many good examples with Black entertainers featured on the covers and the music reflecting an ethnic theme.

You may want to concentrate on music by a particularly renowned composer, for instance George M. Cohan or Irving Berlin. Or you may find you enjoy covers featuring famous entertainers and movie stars from the forties through the sixties. At any rate, be critical of condition when you buy or sell sheet music. As is true with any item of paper, tears, dog ears, or soil will greatly reduce its value.

If you'd like a more thorough listing of sheet music and prices, we recommend *The Sheet Music Reference and Price Guide* by Anna Marie Guiheen and Marie-Reine A. Pafik and *The Collector's Guide to Sheet Music* by Debbie Dillon.

Abraham, Irving Berlin, 1942 ....**$10.00**
Absence Makes the Heart Grow Fonder, Gillespie & Dillea, 1939..**$3.00**
Advice, Royden Barrie & Molly Carew, 1935 ....**$2.00**
Afraid of the Moon, RL Thompson & L Roberts, 1944...**$5.00**
After All Is Said & Done, Dave Ringle, 1931 ....**$5.00**
An Ordinary Couple, Rodgers & Hammerstein II, Movie: The Sound of Music, J Andrews & C Plummer photo cover, 1959..**$5.00**
Anchors Away (Song of the Navy), Charles Zimmerman, 1942..**$5.00**
And So To Sleep Again, Joe Marsala & Sunny Skylar, Patti Page photo cover, 1951 ....**$5.00**
And This Is My Beloved, Robert Wright & Chet Forrest, Musical: Kismet, 1953...**$5.00**
Anything You Can Do, Irving Berlin, Movie: Annie Get Your Gun, 1946 ....**$5.00**
Backwards, Turn Backward, Dave Coleman, 1954........**$5.00**
Ballerina, Bob Russell Carl Sigman, Harry Cool photo cover, 1947..**$5.00**
Ballin' the Jack, Jim Burris Chris Smith, Movie: That's My Boy, Dean Martin & Jerry Lewis photo cover, 1951 ....**$5.00**
Bargain Day, William Roy, Rosemary Clooney signed photo, Im-Ho cover artist-signed, 1949 ....**$5.00**
Barnara Polka, Sev Kocicky & F Kovarik, 1940 ....**$5.00**

Bartender Bill, McKenna, Pfeiffer cover artist, 1930 ....**$10.00**

Be Anything, Irving Gordon, Eddy Howard photo cover, 1952..**$5.00**

Be Honest With Me, Gene Autry & Fred Rose, 1941.....**$5.00**

Bean Song, Ray Stanley, Eillen Barton photo cover, 1956...**$5.00**

Boin-n-n-ng, Sam Stept, Kay Kyser photo cover, 1947..**$5.00**

Bonaparte's Retreat, Pee Wee King, Kaye Starr photo cover, 1949...**$3.00**

Boogie Blues, Gene Krupa & Ray Biondi, Gene Krupa photo cover, 1946 ....**$3.00**

Born Free, Don Clarke & John Barry, Roger Williams photo cover, 1966 ....**$5.00**

Boy Named Sue, Shel Silverstein, Johnny Cash photo cover, 1969...**$5.00**

Bring Back the Thrill, Ruth Poll & Peter Rugolo, Eddie Fisher photo cover, 1950 ....**$3.00**

C'est Si Bon, Jerry Seelen & Henri Betti, 1950 ....**$2.00**

Call of the Canyon, Billy Hill, 1940..............................**$3.00**

Can't Take My Eyes Off of You, Bob Crewe & Bob Gaudio, 1967..**$3.00**

Canadian Sunset, Norman Gimbel & Eddie Heywood, 1956...**$2.00**

Carlotta, Cole Porter, Movie: Can Can, 1943 ....**$5.00**

Comforter, Thomas Moore & Charles Fonteyn Manney, 1938...**$5.00**

Coney Island Baby, Peter Alonzo, 1962 ....**$5.00**

Dear Old Donegal, Steve Graham, Irish, 1942 ....**$2.00**

Deck of Cards, T Texas Tyler, Wink Martin photo, JoJo cover artist, 1952 ....**$10.00**

Deep in the Heart of Texas, Don Swander & June Hershey, The Three Suns photo cover, 1941 ....**$3.00**

Dig Down Deep, Walter Hirsch, Sano Marco & Gerald Marks, War Bond Song, 1942................................**$20.00**

Divorce Me COD, Merle Travis & Cliffe Stone, Lawrence Welk photo cover, 1946..**$3.00**

Do I Love You, Cole Porter, Movie: DuBarry Was a Lady, 1943 ....**$5.00**

Down t' Uncle Bill's, Hoagy Carmichael & Johnny Mercer, 1934...**$5.00**

Dream, Dream, Dream, John Redman & Lou Ricca, 1946.**$3.00**

Enchanted Sea, Frank Metis & Randy Starr, 1959...........**$5.00**

Estelle, Frankie Carle, 1930 ....**$5.00**

Evelina, Harold Arlen & EY Harburg, 1944 ....**$5.00**

Fire & Rain, James Taylor, James Taylor photo cover, 1969...**$5.00**

Fishing for the Moon, Eddie Seiler, Sol Marcus & Guy Wood, 1950 ....**$5.00**

Fool That I Am, Floyd Hunt, 1946 ....**$3.00**

For Sentimental Reasons, Dick Watson & William Best, Eddy Howard photo cover, 1946................................**$3.00**

Girl Who Came From Paris, Charlie Tobias & Carlos Maduro, 1941..**$3.00**

Girl With the Dreamy Eyes, Michael Carr & Eddie Pola, 1935...**$5.00**

Give Me a Hundred Reasons, Ann Jones, 1949.............**$5.00**

Go Away Little Girl, Carole King, Donny Osmond photo cover, 1962 ....**$5.00**

Guy Named Joe, Jim Carhart, & Bus Davis, Gertrude Lawrence photo cover, 1945 ....**$5.00**

Gypsy in Me, Cole Porter, Movie: Anything Goes, 1934 .**$5.00**

Half As Much, Curley Williams, Rosemary Clooney photo cover, 1951 ....**$3.00**

Handful of Stars, Jack Lawrence & Dan Shapiro, 1940..**$5.00**

Happy Holiday, Irving Berlin, 1942 ....**$5.00**

Have Mercy, Buck Ram & Chick Webb, 1939...............**$5.00**

**Hello Dolly, David Merrick Presents Carol Channing...,
Edwin H Morris & Co, pink & blue cover, 1964, NM, $15.00**

Hey, Good-Lookin', Cole Porter, Movie: Something for the Boys, 1942 ....**$5.00**

High on a Windy Hill, Joan Whitney & Alex Kramer, 1940 ....**$5.00**

Hillbilly Fever, George Vaughn, Kenny Roberts photo cover, 1950...**$5.00**

Holiday Inn, Irving Berlin, 1942....................................**$5.00**

Home Is Where the Heart Is, Dave Kapp & Charles Tobias, cover artist Im-Ho, Sammy Kaye photo cover, 1947 .**$3.00**

Homework, Irving Berlin, Musical: Miss Liberty, 1949 ..**$5.00**

I Could Write a Book, Lorenz Hart & Richard Rogers, Musical: Pal Joey, 1940 ....**$5.00**

I Couldn't Stay Away From You, Ben Raleigh & Bernie Wayne, Frankie Carle photo cover, 1948 ....**$3.00**

I Cross My Fingers, Kent & Farrar, Percy Faith photo cover, 1949...**$5.00**

I Don't Know How To Love Him, Tim Rice & Andrew Lloyd Webber, Musical: Jesus Christ Superstar, 1970........**$5.00**

I Don't See Me in Your Eyes Anymore, Bennie Benjamin & George Weiss, Perry Como photo cover, 1949 ....**$3.00**

I Don't Wanna Do It Alone, Bill Hampton & George Duning, 1949..**$3.00**

I Dream of Jeanie With the Light Brown Hair, Stephen Foster, 1938...**$15.00**

I Feel the Earth Move, Carole King, Carole King photo cover, 1971...**$3.00**

I Found the Answer, Johnny Lange, 1957 ....**$3.00**

I Get So Lonely, Pat Ballard, 1954 ....$2.00

I Got Rhythm, Ira & George Gershwin, 1930.................$5.00

I'll Be Around, Alec Wilder, Mills Brothers photo cover, 1942..$3.00

I'm Henry the Eighth I Am, Fred Murry & RP Weston, Herman Hermits photo cover, 1965.....................................$3.00

I'm Late, Bob Hilliard & Sammy Fain, Movie: Alice in Wonderland (Disney), 1951 ....$10.00

I'm My Own Grandpa, Latham Dwight & Moe Jaffe, 1947.$3.00

I Understand, Jim Gannon & Mabel Wayne, Tommy Dorsey photo cover, 1941 ....$3.00

I Walk Alone, Herbert W Wilson, 1943 ....$5.00

I Wanna Be Free, Tommy Boyce & Bobby Hart, Monkees photo cover, 1966 ....$10.00

I Want To Hold Your Hand, Beatles, 1978 ....$25.00

I Went Down to Virginia, Sammy Gallop & David Saxon, 1948..$3.00

I Went Out of My Way, Helen Bliss, 1941.....................$3.00

I Wonder What's Become of Sally, Ager, Yellen & Bornstein Inc, Al Jolson photo cover, 1924, EX, $10.00

If We Could Be A-L-O-N-E, Milton Drake, Al Hoffman & Jerry Livingston, Fred Waring photo cover, 1950....$3.00

In the Blue of Evening, Tom Adair & D Artega, Frank Sinatra photo cover, 1942.......................................$3.00

In the Middle of the Night, Nick Aquaviva & Ted Varneck, 1957..$3.00

In the Moon Mist, Jack Lawrence, Randy Brooks photo cover, cover artist Nick, 1946 ....$3.00

It Might Have Been, Cole Porter, Movie: Something To Shout About, 1943...$5.00

It Pays To Be Ignorant, Tom Howard Jr, 1944...............$3.00

It's a Big Wide Wonderful World, John Rox, 1940 ....$3.00

It's a Lovely Day Tomorrow, Irving Berlin, 1939...........$5.00

It's a Sin, Fred Rose & Zeb Turner, 1948.....................$3.00

It's All in the Game, Daws & Sigman, 1951...................$3.00

It's Been a Long Time, Sammy Cahn & Jule Styne, Bing Crosby photo cover, 1945..$3.00

Jones Boy, Mann Curtis & Vic Mizzy, 1935 ....$3.00

Josephine, Gus Kahn, Wayne King & Burke Rivens, Johnny Long photo cover, 1937...$5.00

Judy, Hoagy Carmichael & Sammy Lerner, 1934 ....$3.00

Just a Blue Serge Suit, Irving Berlin, Cesareo & Irving Berlin cover artist, 1945..$8.00

Just an Old Love of Mine, Peggy Lee & Dave Barbour photo cover, 1947...$5.00

Just Ask Your Heart, Joe Ricci, Frankie Avalon photo cover, 1959..$3.00

Just Between Friends, Robert Mellin & Gerald Rogers, 1955...$3.00

Kentucky Waltz, Brook, Bill Monroe, Bill Monroe photo cover, 1946..$3.00

Kid With the Rip in His Pants, Jack Owens, 1944..........$5.00

Kinda Peculiar Brown, J Burke & J Van Heusen, 1943 .$3.00

Kiss Me Goodnight, Bud Green & Jesse Greer, Guy Lombardo photo cover, 1935 ....$5.00

Kiss Me Kate, Cole Porter, Musical: Kiss Me Kate, 1948.$5.00

Knowing You, Wood, Eckstein & Henneman, 1948......$3.00

Left Right Out of Your Heart, Shuman & Garson, Patti Page photo cover, 1943 ....$3.00

Let Freedom Ring, Shelly & Mossman, Starmer & Patriotic cover artist, 1940 ....$10.00

Let It Snow, Sammy Cahn & Jule Styne, Griff Williams photo cover, 1945 ....$3.00

Let Me Go Lover, Jeny Lou Carson & Al Hill, Joan Weber photo cover, 1954 ....$3.00

Let's Be Friendly, Sammy Fain & Paul Francis Webster, Movie: Hollywood or Bust, 1956.............................$5.00

Let's Get Together, Merchant, 1950 ....$3.00

Let's Go to Church, Steve Allen, Jimmy Wakely & Margaret Whiting photo cover, 1950 ....$5.00

Let's Not Talk About Love, Cole Porter, Movie: Let's Face It, 1943...$5.00

Let's Start the New Year Right, Irving Berlin, 1942........$5.00

Let the Rain Pour Down, Foster Carling, Movie: Song of the South (Disney), 1946 ....$10.00

Let There Be Love, Ian Grant & Lionel Rand, 1940 ....$3.00

Little Boy's Christmas, Claire, Elliot & Hettel, 1959........$3.00

Little Child, Wayne Shanklin, 1953 ....$3.00

Little Dancers, Lawrence Binton & Richard Hageman, 1935 ....$3.00

Little Flower, Sidney Becket, 1952 ....$3.00

Little Old Church in England, Irving Berlin, 1941.......$10.00

Little Old Mill, Pelosi, Ilda & Towers, 1947 ....$3.00

Little Small Town Girl, Jules Loman & Hugo Rubens, 1945...$3.00

Little White Cloud That Cried, Johnnie Ray, Johnnie Ray photo cover, 1951 ....$3.00

Lovelier Than Ever, Frank Loesser, Musical: Where's Charlie?, 1948...$5.00

Lover's Roulette, Charyl Edmonds, Jonah Thompson & Paul Raoul Arenas, Mel Torme photo cover, 1966..........$5.00

Lullaby of Birdland, George Shearing, 1952.................$3.00

Macnamara's Band, John J Stamford & Shamus O'Connor, 1940..$5.00

Manhattan Serenade, Harold Anderson, Louis Alter, 1942.$5.00

Many a New Day, Rogers & Hammerstein II, Musical: Oklahoma, Holley cover artist, 1943................................**$5.00**

Many Tears Ago, Jenny Lou Carson, 1945.....................**$3.00**

Marianne, Terry Gilkyson, Easy Rider photo cover, 1955 ....**$5.00**

Marry the Man Today, Jo Sterling, Abe Burrows & Frank Loesser, Musical: Guys & Dolls, 1950 ....**$5.00**

Mary's Lullaby, Rev FJ West, SJ & Achille P Bragers, 1943 ....**$3.00**

Minute Waltz, Frederick Chopin, Diana Lynn photo cover, 1945..**$3.00**

Mister & Mississippi, Irving Gordon, Patti Page photo cover, 1951..**$3.00**

Music From Across the Way, Carl Sigman & James Last, Andy Williams photo cover, 1970 ....**$3.00**

Muskrat Rumble, Ray Gilbert & Edward Kid Ory, Dennis Day photo cover, 1950 ....**$5.00**

Mutual Admiration Society, Matt Dubey & Harold Karr, Musical: Happy Hunting, Ethel Merman photo cover, 1956..**$5.00**

My Buddy's Girl, Herb Newman & Murry Schwimmer, 1956 ....**$3.00**

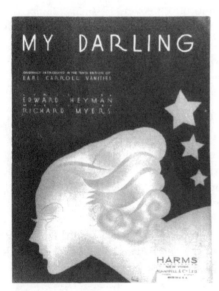

My Darling, Edward Heyman & Richard Myers, Art Deco cover, 1932, EX+, $15.00

My Little Angel, Dazz Jordan & Gordon Charles, Four Lads photo cover, 1956 ....**$3.00**

My Mind's, Ullman & Simon, 1940..............................**$3.00**

My Mother's Waltz, Dave Franklin, Bing Crosby photo cover, 1945 ....**$5.00**

My One & Only One, Robert Mellin & Guy Wood, 1953.**$3.00**

Near to You, Richard Adler & Jerry Ross, Movie: Damn Yankees, 1955 ....**$3.00**

Neath the Stars & Stripes, RS Morrison, 1943 ....**$5.00**

Need You, Johnny Blackburn & Mitchell & Lew Porter, Gordon McRae photo cover, 1949............................**$3.00**

Never a Day Goes By, Walter Donaldson, Peter DeRose & Mitchell Parrish, Guy Lombardo photo cover, 1943 .**$3.00**

Never Gonna Let You Go, Cynthia Weil & Barry Mann, 1981 ....**$3.00**

New Moon & an Old Serenade, Abner Silver, Martin Block & Sam Coslow, Tommy Dorsey photo cover, 1939.....**$3.00**

Nighty-Night, Leslie Beacon, Alvino Rey & King Sisters photo cover, 1941 ....**$3.00**

Ninna-Nanna, Wm A Reilly, 1944................................**$5.00**

No Letter Today, Frankie Brown, Gene Autry photo cover, 1943..**$3.00**

No Star Is Lost, Fred Fisher, Sammy Kaye photo cover, 1939..**$5.00**

No Two People, Frank Loesser, Movie: Hans Christian Anderson, Danny Kaye photo cover, 1951 ....**$10.00**

Oklahoma, Rodgers & Hammerstein II, Musical: Oklahoma, Holley cover artist, 1943 ....**$5.00**

Old Glory, Johnny Mercer & Harold Arlen, Movie: Star Spangled Rhythm, Crosby, Hope, Lamour & many more stars, 1942..**$10.00**

Old Man, Irving Berlin, Movie: White Christmas, Crosby, Kaye, Clooney & Ellen photo cover, 1942 ....**$10.00**

Once in Love With Amy, Frank Loesser, Musical: Where's Charlie?, Ray Bolger caricature, 1948....................**$10.00**

One Dozon Roses, Dick Jurgens, Country Washburn Roger Lewis & Walter Donovan, 1942................................**$3.00**

One Finger Melody, Al Hoffman, Kermit Goell & Fred Spielman, Frank Sinatra photo cover, Barbelle cover artist, 1950..**$3.00**

One Last Kiss, Lee Adams & Charles Strause, Movie: Bye Bye Birdie, 1960 ....**$3.00**

One Little Candle, J Maloy Rosch & George Mysels, Perry Como signed photo cover, 1951 ....**$10.00**

Only for Americans, Irving Berlin, Musical: Miss Liberty, 1949..**$10.00**

Oop Shoop, Shirley Gunter & the Queens, Crew Cut photo cover, 1954..**$3.00**

Orange Colored Sky, Milton Delugg & Willie Stein, 1950..**$3.00**

Paris Wakes Up & Smiles, Irving Berlin, Musical: Miss Liberty, 1949..**$10.00**

Party's Over, Betty Comden, Adolph Green & Jule Styne, Movie: Bells Are Ringing, J Holiday & D Martin photo cover, 1956..**$5.00**

Pearly Shells, Webley Edwards & Leon Pober, 1964 .....**$5.00**

Peony Bush, Meredith Wilson, 1949 ....**$3.00**

Personality, Johnny Burke & Van Heusen, Movie: Road to Utopia, Bing Crosby, Bob Hope & Dorothy Lamour photo cover, 1945 ....**$10.00**

Peter Gunn, Henry Mancini, TV theme music, 1958......**$5.00**

Petite Waltz, EA Ellington, Phyllis Claire & Joe Heyne, Guy Lombardo signed photo cover, 1950 ....**$10.00**

Pianissimo, Bernie Benjamin & George Weiss, Perry Como photo cover, 1947 ....**$5.00**

Pretend, Lew Douglas, Cliff Parman & Frank Lavere, Ralph Marterie photo cover, 1952............................**$2.00**

Promises, Al Hoffman, Milton Drake & Jerry Livigston, Guy Lombardo photo cover, J Geyler cover artist, 1945..**$3.00**

Pussy Cat Song, Dick Manning, 1948............................**$5.00**

Put On a Happy Face, Lee Adams & Charles Strouse, Movie: Bye Bye Birdie, 1960 ....**$5.00**

Put That Ring on My Finger, Sunny Skylar & Randy Ryan, 1945...**$3.00**

Put Your Head on My Shoulder, Paul Anka, 1958.........**$3.00**

Rags to Riches, Richard Alder & Jerry Ross, Tony Bennett photo cover, 1953 ....**$3.00**

Remember When, Buck Ram & Mickey Addy, 1945......**$2.00**

Riders in the Sky, Stan Jones, Burl Ives photo cover, 1949 ....**$3.00**

Riding on a Rainbow, Berkeley Graham & Carley Mills, 1951 ....**$3.00**

Right Kind of Love, Mabel Wayne & Kermit Goell, 1943 .**$3.00**

Road to Morocco, Johnny Burke & Nan Heusen, Movie; Road to Morocco, Hope, Crosby & Lamour photo cover, 1952...**$5.00**

Rock-A-Bye Your Baby...Dixie Melody, Joe Young, Sam Lewis & J Schwartz, Movie: Jolson Story, J Lewis photo cover, 1946 ....**$5.00**

Rockin' Chair, Hoagy Carmichael, 1941.....................**$3.00**

Rogue River Valley, Hoagy Carmichael, 1946 ....**$3.00**

Rollin' Stone, Mack Gordon, Perry Como photo cover, 1951 ....**$3.00**

Room Full of Roses, Tim Spencer, 1949 ....**$3.00**

Salt Water Cowboy, Redd Evans, 1944 ....**$3.00**

San Fernando Valley, Gordon Jenkins, Bing Crosby photo cover, 1943 ....**$3.00**

Santa Claus for President, Peter Tinturin, 1947 ....**$3.00**

Say It With Firecrackers, Irving Berlin, 1942................**$10.00**

Say Yes, Erik Satie, 1953...**$3.00**

Silver in the Moon, HA Pooley, 1945..........................**$3.00**

Singin' in the Saddle, Sherwin, Ann Sheridan photo cover, 1944..**$3.00**

Sioux City Sue, Dick Thomas & Ray Freedman, Bing Crosby photo cover, Cesareo cover artist, 1945.................**$5.00**

Sit Down You're Rocking the Boat, Jo Swerling, Abe Burrows & Frank Loesser, Musical: Guys & Dolls, 1950...**$5.00**

Sixteen Tons, Merle Travis, 1947................................**$3.00**

Skylark, Johnny Mercer & Hoagy Carmichael, 1942......**$3.00**

Slowly With Feeling, Don George & Mark 'Moose' Charlap, 1955...**$5.00**

Someone To Love, Bob Warren, 1945 ....**$3.00**

Somethin' Stupid, C Carson Parks, Frank & Nancy Sinatra photo cover, 1967 ....**$2.00**

Something Old, Something New, Ramez Idriss & George Tibbles, Frank Sinatra photo cover, 1946 ....**$3.00**

Somewhere Along the Way, Sammy Gallop & Kurt Adams, Nat King Cole photo cover, 1952...........................**$5.00**

St Louis Blues, WC Handy, Movie: St Louis Blues, Nat King Cole photo cover, 1942...**$5.00**

Star Eyes, Don Raye & Gene DePaul, Movie: I Dood It, Red Skelton & Eleanor Powell photo cover, 1943..........**$5.00**

Stars & Stripes on Iwo Jima, Bob Wills & Cliff Johnson, Bob Wills photo cover, 1945 ....**$10.00**

Steam Heat, Richard Adler & Jerry Ross, Musical: Pajama Game, 1954...**$3.00**

Stella by Starlight, Victor Young, 1946.......................**$5.00**

Sunrise, Sunset; Sheldon Harnick & Jerry Bock, Movie: Fiddler on the Roof, 1964...**$2.00**

Sunshine Cake, Johnny Burke & Van Heusen, Movie: Riding High, Bing Crosby photo cover, 1950.....................**$5.00**

Sweet Old-Fashion Girl, Bob Merrill, 1956...................**$3.00**

Sweet Violets, JK Emmet, 1940 ....**$3.00**

Tattletale, Jack Lawrence, Bob Schaeffer & Irving Rose, 1941 ....**$5.00**

Teddy Bears' Picnic, Jimmy Kennedy & John W Bratton, Cesareo cover artist, 1947 ....**$5.00**

Tell Me a Story, Larry Stork & Maurice Sigler, Sammy Kaye photo cover, 1948 ....**$2.00**

Tell Me Why, Al Alberts & Marty Gold, Four Aces photo cover, 1951 ....**$5.00**

Tenderly, Jack Lawrence & Walter Gross, 1946.............**$2.00**

Tennessee Saturday Nights, Billy Hughes, Red Foley photo cover, 1947 ....**$3.00**

Tennessee Waltz, Redd Stewart & Pee Wee King, Patti Page photo cover, 1948 ....**$5.00**

Texarkana Baby, Cottonseed Clark & Fred Rose, Eddy Arnold signed photo cover, 1948....................**$5.00**

Thanks for Your Letter My Darling, Jay Burnett & Gladys Lane, Dinah Shore photo cover, 1942 ....**$5.00**

That's Where I Came In, Charles Tobias & Peter DeRose, Perry Como photo cover, 1946 ....**$3.00**

Theme From the Monkees, Tommy Bruce & Bobby Hart, Monkees photo cover, 1966 ....**$5.00**

There I Go, Hy Zaret & Irving Weiser, Im-Ho cover srtist, 1940...**$3.00**

There Is a Tavern in the Town, Harry Henneman, 1942 ....**$5.00**

There Must Be Someone for Me, Cole Porter, Movie: Can Can, 1943 ....**$5.00**

Thing, Charles R Grean, Phil Harris photo cover, 1950.**$5.00**

This Is the Night, Redd Evans & Lewis Bellin, 1946......**$3.00**

This Old House, Stuart Hamblen, 1954 ....**$3.00**

Those Things Money Can't Buy, Ruth Poll & Al Goodhart, Sammy Kaye photo cover, 1947...............................**$3.00**

Three Bells, Bert Reisfeld & Jean Villard Gilles, 1948....**$3.00**

Three Coins in a Fountain, Sammy Cahn & Jule Styne, Movie: Three Coins..., C Webb, D McGuire & others photo cover, 1954 ....**$5.00**

Tom Dooley, Ed Jackson, 1958....................................**$3.00**

Tomorrow, Cole Porter, Movie: Leave It to Me, 1938....**$2.00**

Too Darn Hot, Cole Porter, Musical: Kiss Me Kate, 1948 ....**$5.00**

Too Good To Be True, Eliot Daniel & Buddy Kaye, Movie: Fun & Fancy Free (Disney), 1947 ....**$10.00**

Too Young, Sylvia Dee & Sid Lippman, Nat King Cole photo cover, 1951 ....**$3.00**

Toy Trumpet, Movie: Rebecca of Sunnybrook Farm, Shirley Temple photo cover, 1944 ....**$10.00**

Trolley Song, Hugh Martin & Ralph Blane, Movie: Meet Me in St Louis, Judy Garland photo cover, 1944.........**$15.00**

Under the Bridges of Paris, Dorcas Cochran & Vincent Scotto, 1953 ....**$2.00**

Waitin' for My Dearie, Alan Jay Lerner & Frederick J Loewe, Movie: Brigadoon, 1947...............................**$3.00**

Wanderin' Sammy Kaye, Sammy Kaye photo cover, 1950 ....**$3.00**

Shell Pink Glassware

Here's something new to look for this year — lovely soft pink opaque glassware made by the Jeannette Glass Company for only a short time during the late 1950s. Prices, says expert Gene Florence, have been increasing by leaps and bounds! You'll find a wide variance in style from piece to piece, since the company chose shapes from several of their most popular lines to press in the satiny shell pink. Refer to *Collectible Glassware from the 40s, 50s, and 60s,* by Mr. Florence for photos and more information.

Bowl, Florentine, footed, 10" $25.00
Bowl, Gondola Fruit, 17½" $25.00
Bowl, Holiday, footed, 10½" $40.00
Bowl, Lombardi, plain center, 4-footed, 10⅞".............$25.00
Cake stand, Harp, 10" $30.00
Candle holders, Eagle, 3-footed, pr $65.00
Candy dish, Floragold, 4-footed, 5¼" $20.00
Compote, Windsor, 6" $20.00
Creamer, Baltimore Pear...$14.00
Powder jar, 4¾" $30.00
Punch bowl, 7½-qt..$50.00
Relish, Vineyard, 4-part, octagonal, 12".......................$40.00
Sherbet, Thumbprint, stemmed, 5-oz $10.00
Sugar bowl, Baltimore Pear, footed..............................$10.00
Tray, Harp, 2 handles, 12½x9¾" $50.00
Tray, Venetian, 6-part, 16½" $30.00
Tumbler, juice; Thumbprint, footed, 5-oz $8.00
Vase, heavy bottom, 9"...$65.00
Vase, 7"...$35.00

Shirley Temple

Born April 23, 1928, Shirley Jane Temple danced and smiled her way into the hearts of America in the movie *Stand Up and Cheer.* Many, many successful roles followed and by the time Shirley was eight years old, she was #1 at the box offices around the country. Her picture appeared in publications almost daily, and any news about her was news indeed. Mothers dressed their little daughters in clothing copied after hers and coifed them with Shirley hairdos.

The extent of her success was mirrored in the unbelievable assortment of merchandise that saturated the retail market. Dolls, coloring books, children's clothing and jewelry, fountain pens, paper dolls, stationery, and playing cards are just a few examples of the hundreds of items that were available. Shirley's face was a common sight on the covers of magazines as well as in the advertisements they contained, and she was featured in hundreds of articles.

Though she had been retired from the movies for nearly a decade, she had two successful TV series in the late fifties, *The Shirley Temple Story-Book* and *The Shirley Temple Show.* Her reappearance caused new interest in some of the items that had been so popular during her childhood, and many were reissued.

Always interested in charity and community service,

Shirley became actively involved in a political career in the late sixties, serving at both the state and national level.

If you're interested in learning more about her, we recommend *Shirley Temple Dolls and Collectibles* by Patricia R. Smith and *Toys, Antique and Collectible,* by David Longest.

Book, Favorite Tales of Long Ago, Random House, 3rd
    printing, 1958, VG...$8.00
Book, Little Colonel, Saalfield, EX $40.00

Book, Shirley Temple at Play, #1712, full-color pictures of Shirley, 1935, EX, $40.00

Book, Shirley Temple Christmas Book, Saalfield #1770,
    1937, VG...$20.00
Book, Shirley Temple's Storytime Favorites, Random House,
    1962, EX..$10.00
Book, Shirley Temple Through the Day, Saalfield, photo
    illustrations throughout, 1936, NM.........................$55.00
Book, Stars & Films of 1937, Daily Express, NM.........$30.00
Bookmark, photo & 20th Century Fox logo on heavy card-
    board, from Spain, EX...$12.50
Charm, Shirley holding dress out, enameled, 1930s, mini-
    mum value...$60.00
Christmas card, Hallmark, dated 1935, EX $28.00
Coloring book, Little Princess, 1939, 15x11", EX $110.00
Coloring book, Shirley Temple Crossing the Country,
    M $25.00
Comic page ad, Shirley advertising Quaker Puffed Wheat,
    Boston Sunday Globe, March 6, 1938, EX, minimum
    value..$15.00
Creamer, cobalt glass, M..$35.00
Doll, dressed as Cinderella, vinyl, 1961, 15", M.........$300.00
Doll, dressed as Heidi, vinyl, Ideal, MIB....................$200.00
Doll, dressed as Stowaway, vinyl, Ideal, 1982, 8", MIB.$45.00
Doll, in Stand Up & Cheer dress, vinyl, 1973, 16", MIB..$200.00
Doll clothes hanger, light blue cardboard, marked Hol-
    lywood Cinema Fashions, 1930s, EX, minimum
    value..$10.00
Drawing book, Saalfield #1725, 1935, EX, minimum
    value..$35.00

Embroidery set, Gabriel #311, 1960, NMIB $20.00
Fan, premium for Royal Crown Cola, 1930s, M $25.00
Figurine, Shirley as Captain January, bisque, 6½".......$65.00
Figurine, silver & gold plaster caricature, 1930s, 3¾", EX.$200.00
Handkerchief, features Shirley as The Little Colonel, NM...$35.00
Magazine, Film Collector's World, August 1, 1977, EX..$10.00
Magazine, Parents, October 1938, EX........................$16.50
Magazine, True Story, April 1936, EX $15.00
Magic slate, Shirley Temple Treasure Board, Saalfield #8806, 1959, EX...$25.00
Mug, cobalt glass, M $35.00
Paper dolls, 36" doll & 5 dresses, 1930s, worn $70.00
Party invitations, Wanna Come to a Party?, Freelance, 1973, MIP $8.50
Pin-back button, My Friend Shirley Temple lettered around portrait, red background, 1930s, minimum value .$35.00
Playing cards, image of Shirley playing drums, MIB ...$65.00
Poster, That Hagen Girl, featuring Shirley & Ronald Reagan, 1947, 40x27", VG, minimum value........................$25.00
Pot holder, features Shirley as Wee Willie Winkie, embroidered, 1930s, 5x5", EX, minimum value...............$15.00
Scrapbook, family photo on front, spiral-bound, 1950s, EX, minimum value $15.00
Scrapbook, Saalfield #1714, 1935, NM.....................$25.00
Sheet music, from movie Since You Went Away, EX..$15.00
Sheet music, I'll Be Seeing You, EX $95.00
Sheet music, Polly-Wolly-Doodle, Sam Fox Pub Co, 1935, EX $20.00
Song album, Sing with Shirley Temple, 1935, EX, minimum value $25.00
Stationery, ca 1930, MIB..$65.00
String holder, plaster, 1930s, EX, minimum value $25.00
Writing tablet, Western, 1935, M................................$40.00

Doll, blue & white striped dress & red headband, composition, all original including button, 17", EX, $450.00

Shot Glasses

Shot glasses come in a wide variety of colors and designs. They're readily available, inexpensive, and they don't take lots of room to display. Most sell for $5.00 and under, except cut glass, for which you would probably have to pay $100.00. Carnival glass examples go for about $50.00, pressed glass for about $75.00. Colored glass, those with etching or gold trim, or one that has an unusual shape — squared or barrel form, for instance — fall into the $3.00 to $7.00 range. Several advertising shot glasses, probably the most common type of all, are described in our listings. Soda advertising is unusual and may drive the value up to about $12.00.

For more information, we recommend *Shot Glasses: An American Tradition,* by Mark Pickvet.

Fox Home Liquor Store, black enameled fox & lettering, $3.00

A Real Kicker!, tinted glass w/black enameled design of football player kicking ball, 1959.............................$3.50
An Eye Opener, red & black enameled eye design & lettering, 1940s..$3.50
Antique 6 Year Old Kentucky Bourbon, gold lettering, 1970s...$4.50
Arizona Wildcats, multicolored mascot & lettering, 1980s.$3.00
Atlas Whiskey, A Dillman & Co Milwaukee, etched white lettering...$15.00
Brobst & Markling & Co, Wholesale Wines & Liquors, Bar Supplies..., barrel-shaped $20.00
Carolina Beach NC, blue lighthouse scene & lettering, 1970s...$3.00
Carstairs, red & white seal & lettering, 1950s.................$3.00
Cheap Shot, black lettering, 1980s $3.00
Chicago Cubs, blue & red logo, 1980s $4.00
Chicago Drug & Chemical Assn, Christmas Banquet 1940, Kimble Glass Co, blue enameled lettering $12.50

Clover Brook The Lucky Whiskey, etched white lettering & 4-leaf clover **$15.00**

Compliments of the Santa Clara Wine Co, Indianapolis IN, gold lettering & rim...**$25.00**

GB Baker, High Ball, slanted lettering, 16 panels inside .**$15.00**

Green Mountain, Kansas City MO, gold lettering & rim.**$25.00**

Happy Days Are Here Again, black mule w/lettering arched above, 1930s..**$3.00**

Here's Fun, shows 2 men facing each other w/drink in hand, pre-1960 ....**$35.00**

Iowa Hawkeyes, black & yellow logo, 1980s **$3.00**

Kansas, The Sunflower State, multicolored lettering & sunflower in shield, 1980s..**$3.50**

King Edward VII, Straight Whiskey, JG Philpott Co, Port Huron, Mich USA, barrel-shaped **$18.00**

Marlin Club Whiskey, etched white lettering & sunrise scene **$18.50**

Miller High Life, green, red & yellow logo, 1980s **$4.00**

Moss Wood, Woolner Bros Distillery, Peoria IL on reverse...**$15.00**

O'So Good Kansas City MO, gold lettering & rim **$30.00**

Red Top Rye, gold script lettering & rim.....................**$30.00**

Rohrers Liquor Store, etched lettering **$12.00**

Scotch, gold & white scroll design, 1960s **$4.00**

Texas, The Lone Star State, red outline of Texas & flag on reverse, 1970s...**$3.00**

University U of B Budweiser, red lettering, 1980s.........**$4.00**

You Bet Your Life We're Democrats!, red lettering, 1964..**$3.00**

7-Up, You Like It — It Likes You, green & orange logo, 1980s...**$10.00**

Silhouette Pictures

These novelty pictures are familiar to everyone. Even today a good number of them are still around, and you'll often see them at flea markets and co-ops. They were very popular in their day and never expensive, and because they were made for so many years (the twenties through the fifties), many variations are available. Though the glass in some is flat, others were made with curved glass. Backgrounds may be foil, a scenic print, hand tinted, or plain. Sometimes dried flowers were added as accents. But the characteristic common to them all is the subject matter reverse painted on the glass. People (even complicated groups), scenes, ships, and animals were popular themes. Though quite often the silhouette was done in solid black to create a look similar to the 19th-century cut silhouettes, colors were sometimes used as well.

In the twenties, making tinsel art pictures became a popular pastime. Ladies would paint the outline of their subjects on the back of the glass and use crumpled tinfoil as a background. Sometimes they would tint certain areas of the glass, making the foil appear to be colored. This type is popular with with today's collectors.

If you'd like to learn more about this subject, we recommend *The Encyclopedia of Silhouette Collectibles on Glass* by Shirley Mace.

Convex Glass

Baby playing w/his toes, 'This Little Piggy,' full color, Benton Glass Co, signed Charlotte Becker, 8x6".........**$30.00**

Boy tipping his hat, multicolored flowers at his feet, gold background, Peter Watson's Studio, 5" dia............**$15.00**

Colonial lady playing piano, black on cream, Benton Glass Co, 8x6" **$35.00**

Colonial lady shooting bow & arrow, full-color background, Benton Glass Co, 5x4" **$18.00**

Colonial man playing violin, black on white, Benton Glass Co, 5x4" **$18.00**

Couple at pond watching swans, full color, Benton Glass Co, 5x4" **$12.00**

Couple building a swowman, snow-covered mountains & blue sky beyond, Benton Glass Co, 5x4" **$20.00**

Couple dancing w/landscape beyond, full-color background, Benton Glass Co, 8x6" **$35.00**

Couple looking at Japanese lanterns, full color, Benton Glass Co, 5x4", $12.00

Horse & jockey jumping fence, black & red on wood-look background, Peter Watson's Studio, 5" dia............**$15.00**

Kitten beside pond watching a bird, black on cream, Benton Glass Co, 5x4" **$18.00**

Lady serving a drink to man on horse, black on cream surrounded by birds & flowers, Benton Glass Co, 5x4".**$18.00**

Lady w/rose & parasol on a garden path, black on white, Benton Glass Co, 5x4" **$15.00**

Man smoking pipe while reading the newspaper, black on white, Benton Glass Co, 5x4"...............................**$18.00**

Romantic couple beside stream, full-color background, Benton Glass Co, 5x4"...**$18.00**

Romantic couple in flower garden, full color, Benton Glass Co, 5x4" **$12.00**

Romantic couple on park bench, full color, Benton Glass Co, marked Copr S Colef 12-1-41 & signed Roy, 8x6" **$18.00**

Sailing ship, black on white, Benton Glass Co, 5x4"...**$18.00**

Spanish couple in flower garden, full-color background, Benton Glass Co, 5x4" **$18.00**

Flat Glass

Autumn Bouquet, full-color image, Reliance, signed Smith Frederick, 11x7" **$30.00**

Bouquet of flowers, full-color flowers on earth tones, C&A Richards, 3½x3" **$10.00**

Bouquet of flowers, tinsel art, 8x5" **$10.00**

Boy fishing w/dog sitting beside him, dried flowers pressed in background, Fisher & Flowercraft, 4x4"..........**$15.00**

Colonial lady at fireplace lighting candle, gold foil background, Art Publishing Co, marked Stock #268, 10x8" **$16.50**

Colonial lady caught in rain storm, 'A Fickle Wind,' black on yellow, Reliance, 4x3".........**$16.00**

Cowboys going toward mountain trail, advertising Jones Dairy Co, full-color image, w/thermometer, Newton Mfg Co, 5x4" **$15.00**

Dutch girl holding flowers, tinsel art, 10x8".........**$25.00**

Flowers & butterfly in scalloped oval, white background, Art Publishing Co, signed Best Wishes...April, 1936, 12x8".........**$12.00**

Girl kissing letter, 'The Love Letter,' plaster, Buckbee-Brehm Co, oval, 9x7" **$8.00**

Goldilocks & the Three Bears, full-color image, Reliance, 11x7" **$35.00**

Lady at spinning wheel, 'The Spinning Wheel,' black w/purple highlights on gold, Buckbee-Brehm, 10x7" **$30.00**

Lady watering flowers, 'Happy in Her Garden,' West Coast Picture Co, 8x5½" **$20.00**

Little girl watering flowers, black on white, Reliance, 5x6" **$22.00**

Little Red Riding Hood, black on white, Reliance, 10x8"..**$25.00**

Man tipping hat to lady on swing, black on silver foil background, Deltex, 10x8" **$35.00**

Man tipping hat to lady w/parasol, 'The Meeting,' black on gold, Buckbee-Brehm, unmarked, 7x5"................**$16.50**

Man tipping his hat, 'Beau Brummel,' Reliance, 7x5"..**$12.00**

Old Lady Who Lived in a Shoe, full color, Reliance, 11x7" **$35.00**

Romantic couple in a landscape, 'Lovers,' black on gold foil background, Deltex, 10x8" **$35.00**

Romantic couple on bench, 'The Trysting Place,' black on white, Reliance, 4x4"................**$16.00**

Romantic couple standing on bridge, dried flowers pressed in background, Flowercraft, 10x4"................**$22.00**

Romantic couple w/lady seated on swing, C&A Richards, copyright 1937, signed Eileen Virginia Dowd, 5" dia **$25.00**

Sailing ship, 'Homeward Bound,' black on cream, Reliance, marked T-3, 5x4" **$16.00**

US flag, advertising West Side Motors, Studebaker..., Colors That Never Run, marked made in USA & Forever, 5½x4½" **$10.00**

Silver Flatware

You may have inherited a set of silver flatware with a few pieces missing, or you may become interested in collecting a pattern simply because you find yourself drawn to its elegance and the quality of its workmanship. Whatever the reason, if you decide to collect silver flatware, you'll be interested in learning of the many matching services advertise in the trade papers listed in the back of this book.

Popular patterns are the most expensive, regardless of their age, due simply to collector demand. Monogrammed pieces are hard to sell and are worth only about half price.

English King, twelve 6-piece place settings plus 2 tablespoons, Tiffany, $3,500.00

Aegean Weave, place fork, Wallace **$20.00**

Aegean Weave, teaspoon, Wallace............**$15.00**

Antique Lily, oyster ladle, Whiting, 11½" **$235.00**

Arabesque, demitasse spoon, JR Wendt.........**$20.00**

Arabesque, serving spoon, gold-washed bowl, Whiting, sm.........**$95.00**

Avalon, chocolate spoon, International.........**$25.00**

Avalon, pickle fork, International **$55.00**

Avalon, sugar tongs, International.........**$45.00**

Brocade, butter spreader, International.........**$14.00**

Brocade, cheese server, International.........**$15.00**

Brocade, cocktail fork, International **$12.00**

Brocade, gravy ladle, International.........**$48.00**

Buttercup, ice cream fork, Gorham **$40.00**

Buttercup, pierced nut spoon, Gorham.........**$55.00**

Canterbury, bouillon spoon, Towle.........**$30.00**

Canterbury, iced-tea spoon, Towle.........**$35.00**

Chantilly, butter spreader, Gorham **$14.00**

Chantilly, cocktail fork, Gorham............**$14.00**

Chantilly, demitasse spoon, Gorham.........**$15.00**

Chantilly, luncheon fork, Gorham.........**$20.00**

Chantilly, parfait spoon, Gorham, 8¼" **$35.00**

Chantilly, salad fork, Gorham **$20.00**

Chantilly, seafood fork, Gorham	$22.00
Chantilly, sugar tongs, Gorham	$50.00
Chrysanthemum, butter pat, Tiffany	$135.00
Chrysanthemum, dinner fork, Tiffany	$85.00
Chrysanthemum, olive fork, Towle	$95.00
Clovelly, butter spreader, Reed & Barton	$12.00
Clovelly, knife, Reed & Barton, 9½"	$20.00
Clovelly, sugar spoon, Reed & Barton	$15.00
Colonial, salad fork, Tiffany	$48.00
Colonial, sardine fork, Gorham	$60.00
Courtship, butter spreader, International	$12.00
Courtship, cold-meat fork, International	$48.00
Courtship, jelly server, International	$16.00
Courtship, teaspoon, International	$10.00
Cupid, teaspoon, Reed & Barton	$20.00
Diamond, pickle fork, Reed & Barton	$25.00
Diamond, sugar shell, Reed & Barton	$30.00
Diamond, sugar tongs, Reed & Barton	$35.00
Fairfax, demitasse spoon, Gorham	$15.00
Fairfax, iced-tea spoon, Gorham	$20.00
Fairfax, jelly server, Durgin	$20.00
Fairfax, salad fork, Gorham	$15.00
Fairfax, sugar tongs, Durgin	$55.00
Fairfax, teaspoon, Gorham	$12.00
Fiorito, salad fork, Reed & Barton	$50.00
Fiorito, teaspoon, Reed & Barton	$25.00
Fontainebleau, master salt spoon, Gorham	$40.00
Fontainebleau, sugar shell, Gorham	$65.00
Fontainebleau, sugar spoon, Gorham	$65.00
Fontana, salad fork, Towle	$20.00
Fontana, sugar spoon, Towle	$16.00
Fontana, tablespoon, Towle	$38.00
French Provincial, baby fork, Towle	$16.00
French Provincial, gravy ladle, Towle	$48.00
French Provincial, nut spoon, Towle	$24.00
French Provincial, tablespoon, Towle	$42.00
French Regency, cheese cleaver, Wallace	$22.00
Georgian, butter spreader, Towle	$35.00
Georgian, luncheon knife, Towle	$50.00
Georgian, salad fork, Towle	$50.00
Golden Aegean Weave, cheese cleaver, Wallace	$22.00
Golden Aegean Weave, pizza cutter, Wallace	$28.00
Golden Aegean Weave, salad fork, Wallace	$35.00
Golden Aegean Weave, sugar spoon, Wallace	$30.00
Grand Baroque, fork, Wallace, 7⅜"	$30.00
Grand Colonial, cheese cleaver, Wallace	$22.00
Grand Colonial, cream soup, Wallace	$25.00
Grand Colonial, iced-tea spoon, Wallace	$24.00
Grand Colonial, place fork, Wallace	$30.00
Grand Colonial, place knife, Wallace	$25.00
Grand Colonial, salad fork, Wallace	$28.00
Grand Colonial, teaspoon, Wallace	$22.00
Gypsy, luncheon fork, Shiebler	$25.00
Hanover, sugar tongs, Gorham	$50.00
Imperial Chrysanthemum, dessert spoon, Gorham	$40.00
Imperial Chrysanthemum, dinner fork, Gorham	$50.00
Imperial Chrysanthemum, luncheon fork, Gorham	$35.00
Imperial Chrysanthemum, oyster fork, Gorham	$20.00
Imperial Chrysanthemum, sugar tongs, Durgin	$85.00
Imperial Chrysanthemum, teaspoon, Gorham	$35.00
King Edward, dinner fork, Whiting	$45.00
King Edward, luncheon fork, Whiting	$35.00
King Edward, tablespoon, Whiting	$60.00
King George, butter spreader, Gorham	$45.00
King George, dessert spoon, Gorham	$65.00
King George, dinner knife, Gorham	$35.00
King Richard, cheese server, Towle	$25.00
King Richard, fork, Towle, 7¼"	$30.00
King Richard, spoon, Towle, 6"	$20.00
La Parisienne, egg spoon, Reed & Barton	$24.00
La Parisienne, luncheon knife, Reed & Barton	$35.00
Lancaster, cold-meat fork, Gorham	$65.00
Lancaster, gravy ladle, Gorham	$85.00
Lancaster, luncheon fork, Gorham	$38.00
Lancaster, master butter knife, Gorham	$25.00
Lark, nut spoon, Reed & Barton	$20.00
Lark, pie server, Reed & Barton	$22.00
Lark, sugar spoon, Reed & Barton	$18.00
Legato, butter spreader, flat handle, Towle	$18.00
Legato, cream soup, Towle	$35.00
Legato, pickle fork, Towle	$28.00
Legato, salad fork, Towle	$30.00
Les Six Fleurs, butter pick, Reed & Barton	$85.00
Les Six Fleurs, dinner fork, Reed & Barton	$65.00
Lily, bouillon spoon, Whiting	$40.00
Lily, dinner fork, Whiting	$75.00
Lily, dinner knife, Whiting	$75.00
Lily, luncheon fork, Whiting	$45.00
Lily, sugar spoon, Whiting	$65.00
Lily, teaspoon, Whiting, sm	$20.00
Lily of the Valley, demitasse spoon	$20.00
Lily of the Valley, luncheon knife	$55.00
Louis XV, bonbon, Whiting	$35.00
Louis XV, butter fork, Whiting	$35.00
Louis XV, cold-meat fork, Whiting, 7½"	$50.00
Louis XV, dinner fork, Whiting	$25.00
Louis XV, sardine fork, Whiting	$35.00
Lucerne, sugar tongs, Wallace	$40.00
Lucerne, teaspoon, Reed & Barton	$18.00
Lyric, butter spreader, Gorham	$12.00
Lyric, cream soup, Gorham	$16.00
Lyric, fork, Gorham, 7¼"	$16.00
Lyric, sugar spoon, Gorham	$16.00
Madeira, butter spreader, Towle	$10.00
Madeira, master butter spreader, Towle	$15.00
Madeira, salad fork, Towle	$18.00
Majestic, cocktail fork, Alvin	$30.00
Majestic, dinner knife, Alvin	$28.00
Maryland, breakfast knife, Gorham	$20.00
Maryland, sugar spoon, Gorham	$35.00
Meadow Rose, master butter spreader, Towle	$30.00
Meadow Rose, steak carving set, Towle	$60.00
Minuet, cucumber server, International	$40.00
Minuet, poultry shears, International	$60.00
Mt Vernon, fork, Lunt, 7¼"	$12.00
Mt Vernon, teaspoon, Lunt, 5¾"	$12.00

Mythologique, bouillon, Gorham..............$35.00
Mythologique, dessert spoon, Gorham $50.00
Mythologique, tablespoon, Gorham $95.00
Nuremberg, egg spoon, Alvin....................$25.00
Old Atlanta, cheese server, Wallace $25.00
Old Baronial, bouillon spoon, Gorham........$16.00
Old Baronial, butter spreader, Gorham........$12.50
Old Baronial, fork, Gorham, 6⅞"...............$16.00
Old Baronial, fruit spoon, Gorham..............$18.00
Old Colonial, dessert spoon, Towle............$30.00
Old Colonial, luncheon fork, Towle............$30.00
Old Colonial, salt spoon, Towle.................$10.00
Old Colonial, steak knife, Towle................$30.00
Old English, pastry fork, Towle.................$25.00
Old Lace, master butter, Towle..................$12.00
Old Lace, sugar spoon, Towle....................$14.00
Old Lace, teaspoon, Towle........................$10.00
Old Master, iced-tea spoon, Towle..............$25.00
Old Master, luncheon fork, Towle..............$22.00
Old Master, salt spoon, Towle...................$10.00
Old Master, teaspoon, Towle.....................$16.00
Old Newbury, butter spade, Towle..............$70.00
Old Newbury, cocktail fork, Towle..............$20.00
Old Newbury, sauce ladle, Towle...............$40.00
Old Orange Blossom, demitasse spoon, Alvin...........$30.00
Old Orange Blossom, seafood fork, Alvin $25.00
Pansy, butter spreader, flat handle, International........$20.00
Pansy, dinner fork, International $28.00
Paul Revere, gravy ladle, Towle.................$55.00
Paul Revere, preserve server, Towle $45.00
Persian, fish server, engraved, Tiffany, 11" $38.00
Persian, ice-cream scoop, Tiffany $80.00
Pointed Antique, luncheon fork, Reed & Barton.........$28.00
Pointed Antique, salad fork, Reed & Barton $30.00
Queen Elizabeth I, lasagna server, Towle....................$30.00
Queen Elizabeth I, pie server, Towle $30.00
Radiant, dinner fork, Whiting....................$35.00
Radiant, seafood fork, Whiting..................$22.00
Radiant, teaspoon, Whiting.......................$20.00
Rambler, salt spoon, Towle.......................$10.00
Rambler, teaspoon, Towle.........................$10.00
Repousse, lettuce fork, Kirk......................$65.00
Repousse, pie server, Kirk........................$145.00
Rococo, berry spoon, Dominick & Haff.......................$75.00
Rococo, mustard ladle, Dominick & Haff....................$50.00
Romance of the Sea, cheese cleaver, Wallace............$22.00
Romance of the Sea, salt spoon, Wallace....................$12.00
Romance of the Sea, soup spoon, Wallace, oval.........$40.00
Romance of the Sea, steak knife, Wallace....................$28.00
Rose Point, grapefruit, Wallace.................$18.00
Rose Point, iced-tea spoon, Towle..............$22.00
Rose Solitaire, baby fork, Towle................$18.00
Rose Solitaire, butter spreader, Towle..........$15.00
Rose Solitaire, soup spoon, Towle...............$22.00
Saratoga, coffee spoon, Tiffany..................$35.00
Saratoga, fish knife, flat handle, Tiffany.......$110.00
Sculptured Rose, luncheon fork, Towle..........$20.00
Sculptured Rose, sugar spoon, Towle $15.00

Sculptured Rose, teaspoon, Towle...............$12.00
Sea Rose, dessert spoon, Gorham...............$25.00
Sea Rose, fork, Gorham, 7⅜"...................$20.00
Sea Rose, pie server, Gorham $25.00
Sea Rose, teaspoon, Gorham....................$10.00
Shenandoah, cheese cleaver, Wallace..........$22.00
Shenandoah, teaspoon, Wallace $12.00
Silver Spray, cold-meat fork, Towle.............$34.00
Silver Spray, sugar spoon, Towle................$15.00
Silver Spray, tablespoon, Towle..................$30.00
Sir Christopher, salt spoon, Wallace $10.00
Sir Christopher, steak knife, Wallace...........$28.00
Sir Christopher, teaspoon, Wallace $20.00
Southwind, gravy ladle, Towle...................$36.00
Southwind, jelly spoon, Towle $16.00
Southwind, place fork, Towle.....................$22.00
Southwind, salad fork, Towle.....................$20.00
Southwind, sugar spoon, Towle..................$15.00
Southwind, tablespoon, Towle....................$32.00
Spanish Lace, luncheon knife, Wallace.....................$14.00
Spanish Lace, teaspoon, Wallace...............$14.00
St Cloud, dessert spoon, Gorham $25.00
St Cloud, teaspoon, Gorham.....................$25.00
Strasbourg, ice-cream spoon, Gorham........................$28.00
Strasbourg, luncheon fork, Gorham $18.00
Strasbourg, master salt spoon, Gorham.......$35.00
Versailles, bouillon spoon, Gorham.............$26.00
Versailles, coffee spoon, Gorham $20.00
Versailles, egg spoon, Gorham $20.00
Versailles, ice-cream fork, Gorham..............$40.00
Viking, sugar tongs, Alvin, 3¾"................$35.00
Violet, dessert spoon, Whiting $25.00
Violet, dinner fork, Wallace $32.00
Violet, teaspoon, Towle............................$22.50
Watteau, gravy ladle, Durgin.....................$90.00
Watteau, ice-cream spoon, Durgin..............$35.00
Watteau, sugar shell, Durgin.....................$40.00
Waverly, horseradish spoon, Wallace..........................$45.00
Waverly, sardine tongs, Wallace.................$120.00

Silver-Plated Flatware

When buying silver-plated flatware, avoid pieces that are worn or have been monogrammed. Replating can be very expensive. Matching services often advertise in certain trade papers and can be very helpful in helping you locate the items you're looking for. One of the best sources we are aware of is *The Antique Trader*; they're listed with the trade papers in the back of this book.

If you'd like to learn more about the subject, we recommend *Silver-Plated Flatware, Revised Fourth Edition*, by Tere Hagan.

Alhambra, cocktail fork $8.00
Alhambra, fruit knife................................$8.50
Alhambra, ladle, 10¾".............................$65.00

Ambassador, cream soup spoon.....................................$4.00
Ambassador, ice-cream fork................................$20.00
Arbustus, salad fork..$12.50
Ballad, gravy ladle...$15.00
Berkshire, sugar tongs..$25.00
Camelia, cocktail fork..$3.50

Cardinal, dinner fork, Wallace, $8.00

Cardinal, salad fork, Wallace.................................$8.00
Carnation, cocktail fork.......................................$10.00
Carnation, luncheon fork......................................$10.00
Charter Oak, gravy ladle......................................$25.00
Charter Oak, salad fork, Rogers.............................$35.00
Colony, cold-meat fork...$20.00
Continental, seafood fork.......................................$6.00
Daffodil, ice-cream fork.......................................$20.00
Daffodil, seafood fork...$10.00
Fair Oak, salad fork..$5.00
First Love, cold-meat fork.....................................$25.00

First Love, iced-tea spoon, $15.00

Flair, coffee spoon...$7.50
Flair, dinner knife..$8.50
Floral, dinner fork, Wallace..................................$12.00
Floral, salad fork, Wallace...................................$20.00
Floral, seafood fork, Wallace.................................$14.00
Floral, teaspoon, Wallace......................................$8.00
Flower de Luce, dinner fork, Oneida.........................$18.00
Flower de Luce, dinner knife, Oneida........................$18.00
Grosvenor, bouillon...$5.50
Grosvenor, fruit spoon...$5.50
Grosvenor, pickle fork..$8.00
Hawthorne, pastry fork, Oneida................................$3.50
Heritage, cold-meat fork......................................$20.00
Holly, seafood fork..$25.00
Holly, tomato server...$85.00
Joan, salad fork, Wallace.......................................$6.00
La Vigne, bouillon spoon......................................$10.00
La Vigne, butter spreader, Rogers............................$20.00
La Vigne, citrus spoon, gold-washed, Rogers $25.00
La Vigne, demitasse spoon....................................$12.00
Lovely Lady, berry spoon, Holmes & Edwards, lg.......$10.00
Lovely Lady, salad fork, Holmes & Edwards................$8.50
Morning Star, iced-tea spoon $8.00
Moselle, dinner fork...$10.00
Moselle, luncheon knife.......................................$12.00
Moselle, tablespoon..$35.00

Moselle, teaspoon, $18.00

New Century, berry spoon, gold-washed.....................$34.00
New Century, pie server.......................................$35.00
Old Colony, gravy ladle.......................................$20.00
Old Colony, pickle fork, long handle.......................$14.00
Poppy, cream ladle...$18.00
Poppy, gravy ladle...$20.00
Sheraton, fruit spoon $5.50
Sierra, ice-cream fork...$15.00
South Seas, demitasse spoon...................................$6.00
Springtime, sugar tongs.......................................$20.00

Slot Machines

Coin-operated gambling machines have been around since before the turn of the century. There are many types. One-arm bandits, 3-reelers, uprights, trade stimulators, and bell machines are some of the terms used to describe them. Until the Johnson Act was signed by Harry Truman in 1951, the slot machine industry was thriving. This bill prohibited the shipment of slots into states where they were illegal and banned them from all military installations in the country. One by one nearly every state in the union outlawed gambling devices, and soon the industry was practically non-existent.

Today, it is legal to own an 'antique' slot machine in all but eight states: Alabama, Connecticut, Hawaii, Indiana, South Carolina, Tennessee, and Nebraska and Rhode Island (who's views are uncertain.) Check your state's laws before you buy; the age of allowable machines varies from fifteen to thirty years.

Values of slots range from several hundred to thousands of dollars. If you decide to invest in this hobby, you'll need to study a good book on the subject. One we would recommend is *An American Premium Guide to Jukeboxes and Slot Machines* by Jerry Ayliffe.

Bally Draw Bell, console model, 1946, EX original.**$1,500.00**
Caille Console Bell, 1937, EX original....................**$1,200.00**
Caille Dough Boy Bell, 1935, EX original **$1,500.00**
Dollar Pace, 1940s, EX original..............................**$1,200.00**
Exhibit Supply Races, console model, 1937, VG original..**$500.00**
Groetchen Corona Blue Bell, 1950, EX original........**$650.00**
Jennings Chrome Bell Diamond Front, 1939, VG original..**$1,600.00**
Jennings Electro Bell, w/vendor, 1930, EX original.**$1,800.00**
Jennings Improved Century Bell, 1933, EX original .**$1,800.00**
Jennings Lucky Chief Bell, 1945, EX original.........**$1,700.00**
Jennings Silver Moon Chief, 1941, restored, NM **$1,500.00**
Jennings 5¢ Sun Chief, EX original.......................**$1,500.00**

Jennings 50¢ Standard Chief, VG original, $1,000.00

Keeney Track Time, console model, 1937, NM original **$1,500.00**
Mills Chrome Bell Diamond Front, 1939, VG original.**$1,600.00**
Mills QT Firebird, 1934, EX original **$1,600.00**
Mills Skyscraper, restored, M **$2,350.00**
Mills 25¢ Black Cherry, restored, M **$2,150.00**
Mills 25¢ Golden Nugget, open front, EX original **$950.00**
Mills 5¢ Burning Cherry, 1937, EX original............**$1,800.00**
Mills 5¢ Poinsettia, EX original **$1,750.00**
Pace All Star Comet, EX original **$1,650.00**
Pace Bantam, 1938, EX original.............................**$1,400.00**
Pace 25¢ Comet, EX original **$1,550.00**
Superior Golden Bell, 1934, EX original **$2,200.00**

Snow Domes

Snow dome collectors buy them all, old and new. The older ones (from the thirties and forties) are made in two pieces, the round glass globe that sits on a separate base. They were made here as well as in Italy, and today this type is being imported from Austria and the Orient.

During the fifties, plastic snow domes made in West Germany were popular as souvenirs and Christmas toys. Some were half-domes with blue backs; others were made in bottle shapes or simple geometric forms.

There were two styles produced in the seventies. Both were made of plastic. The first were designed as large domes with a plastic figure of an animal, a mermaid, or some other character draped over the top. In the other style, the snow dome itself was made in an unusual shape.

Snow domes have become popular fun-type collectibles, and Nancy McMichael has written an illustrated book called, of course, *Snow Domes*, which we recommend if you'd like to read more about the subject. Also refer to *The Collector's Guide to Snow Domes* by Helene Guarnaccia.

Advertising

Air Canada, airplane flying over city in dome on yellow footed base, EX..**$16.00**
American Express Vacations, dome w/advertising against blue ground, '800' number on white footed base, EX **$15.00**
Gordon Hart Truck Line, clear globe on black trapezoid base w/gold lettering, shows Hart truck against cityscape, EX **$40.00**
IBM, dome w/white prototype computer against light blue European map, footed base, EX **$25.00**
Maurer-Reifen Technic Service, dome w/penguin holding Uniroyal tire, white w/blue advertising, white footed base, EX **$12.00**
Universal Studios, New York skyline w/King Kong in background in dome on white base, EX........................**$10.00**
WDR, smiling man in front of Villa Hammerschmidt building in dome on white footed base, EX **$15.00**

Character

Barber the Elephant, storybook character by Jean de Brunoff, in dome on white footed base marked Barber, EX...**$15.00**
Bugs Bunny, plastic, Bugs seated holding globe between legs, shows Elmer Fudd & Sylvester, EX **$90.00**
Felix the Cat, dancing Felix w/top hat & cane in tall dome on black base w/star design, Standing Ovations, 1987, EX...**$15.00**
Flintstones, Fred, Pebbles, Bam Bam & Dino in front of gateway lettered Bedrock city in dome on white footed base, EX..**$25.00**

Little Mermaid, tall dome on round black base marked Disney Collections, 1986, Bully, EX, $18.00

Lone Ranger Round-Up, Lone Ranger tries to lasso cow, 4" glass ball on round black base w/early decal, Drier, 1940s, M **$123.00**

Marilyn Monroe, Marilyn in director's chair surrounded by memorabilia, glass dome on black base w/signature, Enesco, EX.......................................**$35.00**

Mickey Mouse, black & white Mickey in stride in dome on round black base, Bully, 1977, EX......................**$18.00**

Paul Bunyan & His Blue Ox Babe, blue ground in dome on white footed base, EX......................................**$15.00**

Pluto, glass globe on round wood base, Kurt Adler, EX.**$15.00**

Snoopy, Snoopy wearing red hat & scarf in dome on round base w/plate marked Hup Hup Hup, Willits, 1966, EX......................................**$20.00**

Wizard of Oz, Dorothy, Toto & friends in clear dome on red base w/gold paper label, EX...............................**$15.00**

Figurals

Alligator, dark brown alligators on seesaw in globe belly, marked New Orleans, EX....................................**$12.00**

Apple, bookworm atop red apple marked #1 Teacher, EX..**$10.00**

Cat Playing Drum, plastic, blue cat in Christmas hat & scarf beating on drum w/Santa in center, EX **$20.00**

Church, red w/white snowy roof, white base & green trim, EX..**$25.00**

Coffeepot, clear plastic w/boy playing in snow, EX ...**$15.00**

Dolphin, plastic, dolphin atop globe containing dolphins on base resembling blue waves, marked Galveston Island, EX..**$15.00**

Heart, New York City skyline against red in heart-shaped dome on black round base marked New York, EX..**$14.00**

Sailor, plastic, sailor w/yellow beard, black hat & orange shirt, pipe, Queen Mary in globe belly, black boots, EX...**$40.00**

Statue of Liberty, name plaque & statue against dark blue ground in tall dome on white base, EX.................**$10.00**

Holidays and Special Occasions

Birth Announcement, stork perched on seesaw w/2 new-borns against blue ground in plastic dome on white footed base, EX.......................................**$8.00**

Birthday, boy & girl w/cake on platform marked Happy Birthday against blue ground in plastic dome on footed base, EX.......................................**$8.00**

Christmas, Rudolph in glass dome on plastic base, paper label, Driss, EX....................................**$40.00**

Christmas, Santa emerging from chimney w/toy bag in pointed dome, white round base, Unieboek BV, 1980, EX..**$12.00**

Christmas, Santa on sled in bell-shaped dome on white base, EX.......................................**$10.00**

Christmas, snowman sitting by Christmas tree in pointed dome on red base marked Merry Christmas, Unieboek, EX..**$12.00**

Easter, yellow chick in egg-shaped globe on basket base, Midwest Imports, 1988, EX.........................**$8.00**

Halloween, vampire w/orange cape in dome on round black base, EX.......................................**$10.00**

Halloween, witch on house & other characters in tall dome on black round base, marked Trick or Treat!, EX.**$10.00**

Halloween, 3 ghosts in round dome atop jack-o'-lantern, EX..**$8.00**

Santa standing w/deer over shoulders, plastic, Santa on Reindeer in globe belly, EX...........................**$18.00**

Sitting Santa, plastic, Santa holding dome w/green & yellow bow, EX......................................**$18.00**

Valentine's Day, red heart in cylinder shape w/flat back, slot for personal photo, gold glitter, pink base, EX.....**$14.00**

Wedding, Good Luck banner wrapped around bottom of bride & groom cutting cake in dome w/white footed base, EX......................................**$10.00**

Souvenir

Arizona, the Grand Canyon State, roadrunner against mountainous desert scene in dome on white footed base, EX......................................**$8.00**

Calgary Zoo, name plaque & 2 resting tigers in grass against black ground in dome on round black base, EX..**$12.00**

Cedar Point, name plaque & amusement park against dark blue ground in globe on red pedestal base, EX ...**$12.00**

Florida, colorful palm trees & sea gulls in dome on white footed base, EX......................................**$8.00**

Grand Canyon National Park, name plaque & pack mule by canyon wall against blue ground in plastic dome, white base, EX......................................**$15.00**

Hoover Dam, name plaque & dam against blue ground in plastic dome on white base, EX......................**$10.00**

Indy 500, colorful Indy car before full grandstand against black ground on black base w/white lettering, EX .**$12.00**

Kansas, buffalo standing on base marked Kansas in front of pine trees in dome on white base, EX **$10.00**

New York Aquarium, penguin & other sea creatures swimming in rectangular dome on blue base w/white lettering, EX....**$8.00**

New York City, red apple shape w/city scene in center, round white base, EX, $15.00

Reno, Nevada, cowboy at the gate to the city in dome on white base, EX **$12.00**

Sea World of Florida, name plaque & row of penguins against snowy hill & dark blue sky, EX **$10.00**

South Dakota, name plaque & buffalo standing before pine trees against blue ground in dome on white base, EX **$10.00**

West Virginia, black bear in front of red map in dome on black Lucite base marked West Virginia, EX **$8.00**

Miscellaneous

Ashtray, snow baby in glass globe on round black Bakelite ashtray, EX **$70.00**

German-made dome, angel on skis in dome on white footed base, EX **$10.00**

German-made dome, deep-sea diver on sea horse against blue ground in plastic dome on white footed base, EX **$6.00**

German-made dome, lg ice-cream cone in front of palm trees in dome on white footed base, EX **$10.00**

Glass dome, golfer in globe on wood base, EX **$25.00**

Ink stamp, Teenage Mutant Ninja Turtles in tall dome w/ink stamp on bottom, M, minimum value......................**$5.00**

Key chain, pink flamingo in dome on white base w/ball-link chain, EX **$10.00**

Pencil twirler, the Simpsons, a Simpson character in tall dome fitted over end of pencil, MOC, minimum value **$5.00**

Religious dome, Crucifixion, 3 mourners at foot of cross, tall plastic dome on white base, EX............................**$10.00**

Ring Toss Bottle, pink flamingo & colorful rings in clear plastic bottle w/blue cap, EX **$7.00**

Sport dome, Chicago Cubs name plaque & ball cap before ballpark crowd in dome on white base, EX............**$8.00**

Soda Bottles

The earliest type of soda bottles were made by soda producers and sold in the immediate vicinity of the bottling company. Many had pontil scars, left by a rod that was used to manipulate the bottle as it was blown. They had a flat bottom rather than a 'kick-up,' so for transport, they were laid on their side and arranged in layers. This served to keep the cork moist, which kept it expanded, tight, and in place. Upright the cork would dry out, shrink, and expel itself with a 'pop,' hence the name 'soda pop.'

Until the thirties, the name of the product or the bottler was embossed in the glass or printed on a paper label (sometimes pasted over reused returnable bottles). Though a few paper labels were used as late as the sixties, nearly all bottles produced from the mid-thirties on had painted-on (pyro-glazed) lettering, and logos and pictures were often added. Imaginations ran rampant. Bottlers waged a fierce competition to make their soda logos eyecatching and sales inspiring. Anything went! Girls, airplanes, patriotic designs, slogans proclaiming amazing health benefits, even cowboys

and Indians became popular advertising ploys. This is the type you'll encounter most often today, and collector interest is on the increase. Look for interesting, multicolored labels, rare examples from small-town bottlers, and those made from glass other than clear or green. If you'd like to learn more about them, we recommend *The Official Guide to Collecting Applied Color Label Soda Bottles* by Thomas E. Marsh.

Paper labels were used to some extent from the thirties into the sixties, sometimes pasted over reused returnable bottles.

Embossed Soda Bottles

AM&B Co, Waco TX, Registered Monterrey... on aqua glass, applied lip, 8½" **$10.00**

Bacon's Soda Works Sonora Cal, light green glass w/blob top, 7" **$10.00**

Billings EL Sacramento Ca Geiser Soda, aqua glass, 7½" **$8.00**

Clarke & Co New York, dark green glass, cylindrical, 8" .**$16.50**

Clarke & White New York, olive green glass w/applied top, 7½" **$32.00**

Congress & Empire Spring Co, green glass w/applied top, 8" **$30.00**

Crystal Soda Water Co, blue glass w/applied top, cylindrical, 7¾" **$10.00**

Dr Pepper Good for Life, 10-2-4 O'clock, clear glass w/crown top, 6½-oz..**$5.00**

Eagle Soda, green glass w/applied top, cylindrical, 7".**$10.00**

Henry Kuck Savannah GA, green glass w/blob top & iron pontil, 7¼" **$20.00**

Jackson Napa Soda, light green glass w/applied lip, cylindrical, 7" **$4.00**

Lewis Soda Bottles Sacramento, clear glass, slender form, 8½" **$8.50**

Priest Natural Soda, light green glass, cylindrical, 7½" .**$12.00**

Samuel Soda Bottling Works St Helena Calif, aqua glass w/applied top, 9" **$5.00**

Sun-Rise Soda Works Sacramento Cal, aqua glass, 7½".**$6.00**

Yuba Bottling Works, aqua glass, cylindrical, 8"............**$5.00**

Painted-Label Soda Bottles

A-Treat, Premium Beverages, embossed ribs at shoulder, clear glass, 7-oz..**$6.50**

All Star Cola, lettering on front & on shoulder, clear glass, 12-oz **$8.50**

Black Kow, cow logo & Just a Swell Treat on green glass, 12-oz **$25.00**

Cascade Ginger Ale, lettering & line design on green glass, 7-oz **$8.00**

Cloverdale, 4-leaf clover above product name on clear glass, 1-qt **$8.00**

Colonial, colonial woman on clear glass, 12-oz..........**$10.00**

Crystal Very Fine Beverages, clear glass, 12-oz **$6.00**

Double-Dry, banner on shield, embossed ribs at shoulder & neck, green glass, 10-oz **$9.50**

Fiz Specialty Beverages, bubble design & lettering on green glass, 1-qt..**$8.00**

Get Up, logo & white rings on green glass, 8-oz...........$6.00

Heart Club, lettering in heart on clear glass, 12-oz........**$8.00**

Hi Ho, boy holding Hi Ho banner on clear glass, 7-oz.**$15.00**

Joe Louis Punch, sunburst design on clear, 7-oz.........**$10.00**

Kleer Kool Beverages, hand holding glass w/pouring bottle on clear, 12-oz...**$12.00**

Kool-Aid, First in Flavor on clear glass, 1-qt................**$20.00**

Lyons Root Beer, lion logo above product name on clear glass, 10-oz...**$8.00**

Mason's Root Beer, Drink above Mason's lettered in lg M, horizontal ribs, amber glass, 1-qt...........................**$16.50**

Mission Charge Up, logo & embossed swirls, green glass, 7-oz **$10.00**

My Pic Beverages, product name & Statue of Liberty on clear glass, 10-oz...**$15.00**

Nealer's Beverages, product name on leaf, embossed ribs around neck & shoulder, clear glass, 7-oz...........**$10.00**

Nemo Beverages, Our Jumbo Value lettered on elephant, clear glass, 7-oz...**$30.00**

O-So Beverages, O-So Good! on 4-leaf clover, clear glass, 7-oz **$6.00**

Paul's Beverages, vertical ribs, clear glass, 7-oz.............**$6.00**

Polka Dot Beverages, product name on polka dots, King Size on neck, clear glass, 10-oz...............................**$8.00**

Quality's Fine Beverages, product name on ornate design, clear glass, 7-oz...**$6.00**

Rose, pictures a rose & Family Beverage on line design, clear glass, 7-oz...**$8.00**

Rose Valley, clear glass, 1-qt, $8.00; Saturn Club Soda, clear glass, 1-qt, $20.00

Royal Crown Cola, diamond logo, vertical ribs, clear glass, 8-oz **$5.00**

Sperky, product name superimposed over clown on green glass, 7-oz...**$15.00**

Universe, product name above planets, clear glass, 7-oz.**$20.00**

Variety Club Beverages, swirled ribs at shoulder, clear glass, 10-oz **$6.00**

Yaky's, round logo on clear glass, 7-oz.........................**$6.00**

Soda-Pop Memorabilia

A specialty area of the advertising field, soft drink memorabilia is a favorite of many collectors. Now that vintage Coca-Cola items have become rather expensive, interest is expanding to include some of the less widely known flavors — Grapette, Hires Root Beer, and Dr Pepper, for instance.

If you want more pricing information, we recommend *Huxford's Collectible Advertising* by Sharon and Bob Huxford. See also Coca-Cola; Pepsi.

Bottle, syrup; Cherry Smash, label under glass, metal cap, 11½", VG **$125.00**

Bottle, syrup; Hires, label under glass, metal cap, 11½", EX **$375.00**

Bottle cap, Moxie, metal w/cork lining, pictures the Moxie man, 1950s, NM...**$8.00**

Bottle opener, Orange-Crush, chrome-plated, pictures Crushy & bottle of Crush Dry, pocket-size, M **$15.00**

Calendar, NuGrape, 1957, complete, EX....................**$25.00**

Calendar, Orange-Crush, 1946, shows girl w/panda bear, Drink Orange-Crush on diamond logo, full pad, 31x16", NM..**$155.00**

Calendar, Royal Crown Cola, 1955, woman holding RC bottle & young couple in circular inset behind her, full pad, VG **$30.00**

Can, Ma's Root Beer, steel, EX.....................................**$4.00**

Clock, Canada Dry, 12-3-6-9 w/dots surrounds logo, metal frame w/plastic face, 16x16", EX..........................**$35.00**

Clock, Dr Pepper, neon, Dr Pepper logo below hands, square, EX **$250.00**

Clock, Grapette Soda, glass w/metal frame, 1-12 surrounds horizontal oval reading Enjoy Grapette Soda, round, EX...**$250.00**

Clock, Hires, glass w/metal frame, 1-12 surrounds Drink Hires Root Beer on dot, round, EX.....................**$240.00**

Clock, Hires Root Beer, #s 1-12 around Drink Hires Root Beer, round w/glass lens & metal frame, EX......**$250.00**

Clock, Kist Beverages, glass w/painted wood case, 1-12 surrounds advertising, electric, ca 1931, 15½x15½", G..**$45.00**

Clock, Orange-Crush, glass w/wood frame, reverse-painted advertising below, 36x19", G, 175.00

Clock, 7-Up on colorful sun & rainbow logo above 12-3-6-9 on yellow, light-up w/metal frame & glass lens, 18x12", EX..**$45.00**

Decal, Sprite, pictures hand holding bottle, 1963, 14", EX **$8.00**

Dispenser, bottle; Hires, tin, dark blue w/white lettering, bottles dispense at bottom, 19", VG **$125.00**

Dispenser, Buckeye Root Beer, porcelain, foaming soda glass transfer on all sides, rare, ovoid, 17x7½" dia, EX **$500.00**

Dispenser, Grape Kola, porcelain figure-8 shape, 5¢ script logo above cluster of grapes, 20x9", EX.............**$800.00**

Dispenser, Hires, porcelain hourglass shape, Drink Hires, It Is Pure, original pump, 14x7½" dia, VG.............**$325.00**

Dispenser, Mission Grapefruit Juice, green conical glass bowl set on round cast base, 12½x6½" dia, VG ...**$90.00**

Doll, A&W Root Beer, plush, 4", M **$10.00**

Door plate, Squirt, Drink Squirt on yellow splash above tilted bottle, embossed tin, 1941, 8½x3½", EX **$80.00**

Door push bar, Hires, bottle cap at left of It's High Time For Hires Root Beer, 30" long, G **$15.00**

Door push plate, Bireley's Beverages, Drink above labeled bottle, NM..**$100.00**

Door push plate, Kik Cola, porcelain, white w/red Kik Cola in shadowed letters, Le Cola Des Families, 3x10", EX...**$38.00**

Drinking glass, Moxie, embossed Moxie flag logo, flared rim, fluted bottom, NM...**$50.00**

Fan, Mission Orange, cardboard on wooden handle, yellow, orange & blue w/oranges, Keep Cool With..., EX..**$35.00**

Fan, Moxie, cardboard, lady in hat tipping full glass, 1920s, 9x8", NM **$60.00**

Fan hanger, Orange Kist, Kist character w/bottle, Take It From Me..., 8¼x6", EX **$14.00**

Fan pull, B-1 Lemon-Lime Soda, cardboard, B-1 on white dot above Lemon-Lime Soda on red, EX.............**$10.00**

Globe, Hires, milk glass w/brown lettering, Drink Hires, 8½", EX **$185.00**

Ice-cream scoop, Hires, plastic, white w/black lettering, EX **$10.00**

Menu board, Canada Dry, crown logo & Champagne Of Ginger Ales above chalkboard, vertical w/rounded corners, EX **$30.00**

Menu board, Drink Double Cola on red oval w/star bursts on blue band above chalkboard, 28x20", NM.......**$75.00**

Menu board, Green Spot Orange Drink, tin, drink being poured in several glasses above black menu area, 27x17", NM **$75.00**

Menu board, Hires, tin, Drink Hires left of tilted bottle above chalkboard, 29x16", NM...........................**$125.00**

Menu board, Kist Beverages, pictures labeled bottle, G...**$65.00**

Menu board, Mason's Root Beer, tin, Mason's lettered on M left of Root Beer, white & black on yellow, 27x19", NM..**$80.00**

Menu board, NuGrape & tilted bottle above chalkboard, tin, vertical w/rounded corners, VG.............................**$30.00**

Mirror, Dixi-Cola, Enjoy Dixi-Cola... on panel below mirror, 14x6", EX **$40.00**

Mirror, Orange-Crush, Crushy figure at top, ...Carbonated Beverage lettered below, 11x9", NM **$100.00**

Mug, Hires, ceramic barrel shape w/flared base, pointing Hires boy & Drink Hires Root Beer above, reproduction, NM...**$45.00**

Mug, Moxie, ceramic hourglass shape w/handle, Moxie embossed on 1 side, NM..**$60.00**

Photo album, Dr Pepper, Tales of Tokyo, gold geisha & logo on red cover, w/schedule of 1977 Bottler's Convention, M..**$10.00**

Sign, Canada Dry, product name lettered over crown emblem, embossed die-cut tin, 15x14", M.............**$45.00**

Sign, Canada Dry Ginger Ale, heavy cardboard wall hanger, image of old bottle & hamburger platter, 1964, 12x13", EX..**$20.00**

Sign, Dad's Old Fashioned Root Beer, painted embossed tin, name on diagonal band w/Drink & In Bottles, 19x27", EX..**$190.00**

Sign, Dad's Root Beer, depicts bottle cap, ca 1940s, 29", NM..**$115.00**

Sign, Moxie, die-cut tin, bust of girl w/bottle offering glass, Moxie panel below, 2 hanger holes in head, 7x6¼", VG **$300.00**

Sign, 7-Up lettered on green triangle, embossed tin, 13", NM..**$140.00**

Straw holder, clear glass, metal lid, common, 10", EX .**$150.00**

Straw holder, Dr Pepper, glass w/chrome top & holder, 11½", EX **$25.00**

Thermometer, B-1 Lemon-Lime Soda, embossed tin, logo & lettering on striped background, 1950s, 16x4½", EX **$45.00**

Thermometer, Bubble Up, pictures bottle, 16x6", G ...**$45.00**

Thermometer, Bubble Up, tin, pictures labeled bottle, 16x6", G **$45.00**

Thermometer, Dr Pepper, bottle cap shape, G...........**$95.00**

Thermometer, Mission Orange, tin, lg bottle on white, 17x5", NM **$75.00**

Thermometer, 7-Up, porcelain, pictures labeled bottle & The Fresh Up Family Drink..., 15", EX, $65.00

Thermometer, Moxie, tin, bottle & round logo above ...Good At Any Temperature, Moxie boy below, 25½x9½", VG..**$300.00**

Thermometer, Nesbitt's California Orange, painted & stenciled tin, lettering above bulb w/bottle below, 27", VG **$80.00**

Thermometer, Orange-Crush, blue & orange, bottle cap above numbered bulb, tin, rounded corners, 1950s, 16x6", EX+ **$60.00**

Thermometer, Royal Crown Cola, ...Best By Taste-Test above bulb & bottle, embossed tin, EX................**$70.00**

Thermometer, Squirt, name on diagonal band above numbered bulb & bottle, embossed tin, round corners, 1960, 14x6", NM...**$45.00**

Tray, Cherry Blossoms, bottle in white oval, In Bottles Only, oblong, EX..**$75.00**

Tray, Hires, pointing Hires boy w/frothy mug flanked by lettering, C Shonk litho, 13½" dia **$450.00**

Tray, Kist Beverages, sailor girl next to lg bottle on sailboat, NM **$250.00**

Tray, Moxie, lady w/glass on dark blue, lettering on light blue rim w/gold trim, 6" dia, EX, $300.00

Tray, Nehi, shows lg bottle & bather caught up in ocean wave, labeled rim top & bottom, vertical rectangle, VG+ **$160.00**

Tray, NuGrape, woman standing in moonlight holding bottle, American Artworks, 13¼x10½", VG................**$55.00**

Tray, Orange-Julep, bathing beauty holding glass & parasol, lettering on rim, 13¼x10½", EX **$135.00**

Souvenir Spoons

Before the turn of the century, collecting silver spoons commemorating towns, states, fairs, holidays, and famous people became popular. Huge quantities were produced, and many are now found on the antiques and collectibles circuit, still interesting to later generations of collectors. There are many types of spoons; some are gold-washed, some enameled. Handles may be figural, representing something especially noteworthy about a particular area or state (for instance, a gold miner from Nevada or a salmon from Washington), or they may have a cut-out design. Indians and nudes are unusual, and along with the more interesting designs — past presidents, war memorials, or fraternal emblems, for instance — usually carry the higher price tags.

Maryland, eagle on handle, plain bowl, 1914, $10.00

Anderson SC, scroll design & monogram on handle, Anderson SC lettered in bowl **$12.50**

Blue Rapids, simple floral design on handle, Blue Rapids lettered in bowl..**$12.50**

Charleston WV, cut-out capitol building on handle, plain bowl..**$14.50**

Chattanooga TN, beaded scroll design on handle, etched scene of Lookout Mountain in bowl......................**$9.50**

Chicago IL, bust of Columbus & World's Fair on handle, embossed fisheries building in bowl.....................**$12.50**

Chicago IL, Chicago in ornate letters & scroll & leaf design on handle, embossed fountain in bowl.................**$12.50**

Chicago IL, raised pansies on handle, Chicago in fancy script in bowl **$16.50**

Cincinnati OH, cut-out flower on handle, raised fountain & 1905 in bowl..**$18.00**

Colorado, cut-out flowers on handle, plain bowl........**$12.50**

Dayton OH, scroll design & 1897 on handle, Dayton OH lettered in bowl $7.50

Denver CO, mule & state flower on handle, state capitol engraved in bowl $9.50

Emmelsburg IA, raised floral design on handle, Emmelsburg IA etched in bowl $16.00

Gunston Hall VA, cutout of Gunston Hall on handle, plain bowl $7.50

Harrisburg PA, heavy floral design on handle, state capitol building & Harrisburg lettered in bowl $14.00

Hawaii, 50 State Hawaii USA lettered on handle, plain bowl, 1959 ....$14.50

Honolulu HI, cut-out hula girl & ukelele on handle, plain bowl $15.00

Hot Springs AK, scroll design on handle, etched army/navy hospital in bowl $16.50

Idaho, raised flowers & Idaho lettered on handle, plain bowl $7.50

Kalamazoo MI, state seal & flower on handle, Kalamazoo lettered in bowl $14.50

Knott's Berry Farm CA, cut-out wagon train on handle, plain bowl, 1950 ....$12.50

Lansing MI, filigree handle, Lansing 1892 lettered in bowl $14.50

Los Angeles CA, Indian head w/corn on handle, etched poinsettia in bowl $28.00

Mansfield IL, heavy floral design on handle, Mansfield lettered in bowl $12.50

Mexico, cut-out gaucho on handle, plain bowl $9.50

Mexico City, floral design on handle, etched bullfight scene in bowl $7.50

Milwaukee WI, state seal & trees on handle, Milwaukee WI lettered in bowl $14.50

Missouri, state seal & horse on handle, plain bowl.....$12.00

Murdo SD, state seal & grapes on handle, Murdo SD lettered in bowl $8.00

New Mexico, state seal & New Mexico lettered on handle, plain bowl $7.00

New Orleans LA, floral design on handle, carnival scene in bowl $8.00

New York NY, cut-out skyline of New York on handle, Statue of Liberty engraved in bowl $40.00

Newton KS, flower & scroll design on handle, Newton KS lettered in bowl $12.50

Niagara Falls, cattail handle, Niagara lettered in bowl ..$9.50

North Dakota, state seal on handle, plain bowl............$7.50

Oakland CA, state seal & US seal on handle, etched oak tree in bowl $12.50

Ocean City MO, sailboat, lighthouse & embossed flowers on handle, embossed sailboat in bowl $12.50

Oregon, log truck & trees on handle, plain bowl........$12.50

Oregon, sea lions & coastal scene on handle, plain bowl..$6.50

Ottawa Canada, enameled maple leaves on handle, Ottawa lettered in bowl $7.50

Palm Springs CA, Palm Springs enameled on handle, plain bowl $6.00

Plymouth MA, cutout of Priscilla Alden on handle, plain bowl $7.50

Quebec Canada, enameled seal & crown on handle, embossed city scene in bowl $12.50

Reno NV, cowboy & horse embossed on handle, plain bowl $7.50

Salem MA, cut-out witch on handle, plain bowl, ca 1930..$18.50

San Antonio TX, scroll design on handle, etched Alamo scene in bowl $12.50

San Diego CA, floral design on handle, San Diego CA lettered in bowl $6.50

San Francisco CA, Chinese lantern on handle, plain bowl $9.50

San Francisco CA, Ghirardelli square on handle, plain bowl, ca 1950..$9.50

San Francisco CA, Golden Gate Bridge & cable car on handle, plain bowl $7.50

Saratoga FL, floral design on handle, engraved Indian & teepee in bowl $22.00

Spokane WA, bust of George Washington on handle, relief of Spokane Falls in bowl $17.50

Spokane WA, scroll design & monogrammed M on handle, Spokane lettered in bowl $12.50

St Paul MN, lg sheaf of wheat on handle, St Paul MN lettered in bowl $15.00

St Petersburg FL, cut-out pelican on handle, plain bowl.$7.50

Syracuse NY, scroll design on twisted handle, Syracuse NY lettered in bowl $9.50

Tacoma WA, George Washington on handle, Mt Tacoma scene etched in bowl $16.50

Tiajuana Mexico, Indian head, teepee & hatchets on handle, Tiajuana Mexico lettered in bowl....................$14.50

Trinidad CO, cut-out flowers on handle, Trinidad CO lettered in bowl $16.50

Vicksburg MS, scroll design on handle, Vicksburg MS lettered in bowl $12.00

Washington DC, embossed flowers on handle, US Capitol embossed in bowl $12.50

Woodland CA, embossed flowers on handle, Woodland CA lettered in bowl $14.50

Yosemite CA, mountain scene & Yosemite lettered on handle, plain bowl $8.00

Space Collectibles

Even before the first man landed on the moon, the idea of space travel had always intrigued us. This is an area of collecting that is right now attracting lots of interest and includes not only serious documentary material, but games, toys, puzzles, and models as well.

See also Toys, Space.

Astronaut Pilot Wings, 1963, MOC..............................$25.00

Book, Mariner 6 & 7 Pictures of Mars, NASA #SP-263, hardbound w/cloth binding, 159 pages, 1971, VG $40.00

Book, punch-out; Space Rockets, 1958, M..................$30.00

Book, Question & Answer Book About Space, Random House, EX $5.00

Booklet, Earth Orbital Science in the 70s, NASA #EP-83, 28 pages, EX......................................**$5.00**

Bubble bath, Space Scouts Stardust, each pack features planet, boxed set of 20, 1950s, 5x10", NM in EX box.............................**$165.00**

Ceiling light shade, gold & white space graphics on white glass, ca early 1950, scarce, 13x13", M **$68.00**

Christmas ornaments, ceramic spaceship, set of 3 different, Japan, 1960s, 3" to 4", M.........................**$25.00**

Clicker, Space Gun, plastic, w/whistle, 5", NM............**$20.00**

Coloring book, Moon Rockets, 1950s, M......................**$25.00**

Coloring book, Sky Rocket, unused, Lowe, 1959, NM .**$15.00**

Coloring book, Zedo in Space, 1950s, EX....................**$20.00**

Drink mixer, plastic rocket-shaped container w/straw, United Plastic Corp, 1952, 9", NM in NM box.......**$85.00**

Goblet, Apollo Moon Landing, red, white & blue graphics on clear glass, M **$22.00**

Juice carafe, graphics of the Apollo missions on clear glass w/white plastic cap, Libbey, 7¾", M.......................**$30.00**

Key chain, yellow plastic spaceman, 1950s, 2", M.......**$15.00**

Membership card, Junior Rocket Rangers, official member of Rod Brown of the Rocket Rangers, 1950s, 2½x4", NM..**$15.00**

Paint-By-Number set, Space Traveler, unused, 1950s, EX **$100.00**

Party Streamers, spaceship graphics, 1950s, NM..........**$20.00**

Pencil case, Rocket Patrol Deluxe, heavy cardboard w/lithographed paper space scene, American Pencil, 1950, 7x10", EX+ **$70.00**

Pencil topper, rubber astronaut's head in space helmet w/visor up, sold through 25¢ gumball machines, 1960s, 1½", M..**$5.00**

Pocketknife, w/whistle, marked Space Rocket, NM **$45.00**

Poster, Historic Moon Landing, from photo taken by Apollo astronauts while on moon, Rand McNally, 24x18", MIP **$5.00**

Trading cards, Space Ventures, Moon-Stars series, embossed set of 36, 1991, EX **$65.00**

Trading cards, Space Ventures, NASA photos, 1st series, set of 110, complete, 1991, EX....................................**$50.00**

Sports Collectibles

When the baseball card craze began sweeping the country a decade ago, memorabilia relating to many types of sports began to interest sports fans. Ticket stubs, uniforms, autographed baseballs, sports magazines, and game-used bats are prized by baseball fans, and some items, depending on their age or the notoriety of the player or team they represent, may be very valuable. Baseball and golfing seem to be the two sports most collectors are involved with, but basketball is gaining ground. There are several books on the market you'll want to read if you're personally interested in either: *Value Guide to Baseball Collectibles* by M. Donald Raycraft and R. Craig Raycraft, *Collector's Guide to Baseball Memorabilia* by Don Raycraft and Stew Salowitz, and *The Encyclopedia of Golf Collectibles* by John M. Olman and Morton W. Olman.

Kenner's Starting Lineup figures were first produced in 1988. They sell at retail for $5.00 to $8.00 or so, on the secondary market they often carry price tags of $25.00 to $50.00, some much higher. Two of the top-prized figures are Nolan Ryan (card #94) which is worth about $275.00 (MIB) and John Stockton (card #72), valued at about $400.00. Besides the baseball figures, football and basketball series have been made as well, and in 1993, hockey was added. Original packaging is very important. If you're going to collect 'em, be critical of its condition.

Another facet of sports collecting centers around the bobbin' head papier-mache dolls that represent sports teams and their mascots. They were made in Japan during the 1960s up to about 1972. They're about 7" high and very colorful. Depending on scarcity and condition, expect to pay as little as $25.00 and as much as $100.00 for each. A few were modeled in the likeness of a particular sports star, and those are a different story! A Roger Marris sold at auction this year for $400.00.

See also Autographs; Baseball Cards; Hartland; Magazines; Pin-Back Buttons; Puzzles; Sports Pins; View Master.

Trading cards, Space Ventures, Space Shots Series I, set of 110, 1990, MIB, $60.00

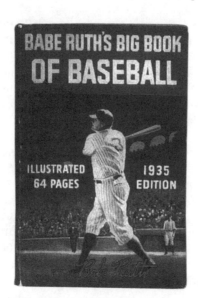

Book, Babe Ruth's Big Book of Baseball, 1935, compliments of Quaker Oats, personally autographed by Babe, $325.00

Book, Baseball Is a Funny Game, Joe Garagiola, w/autograph, 1960, EX..**$25.00**

Book, Collier's Quick & Easy Guide to Golf, Robert Scharff, 1963, EX..**$12.50**

Book, Holy Cow!, Harry Carey, 1989, EX....................**$20.00**

Book, Major League Baseball: Technique & Tactics, Ethan Allen, 1938, EX..**$30.00**

Book, Sports Star: George Brett, SH Burchard, 1982, EX..**$20.00**

Book, Willie Mays, Coast to Coast, 1963, EX **$25.00**

Book, Young Sportsman's Guide to Golf, Donald Smith, 1961, EX..**$14.00**

Calendar, Philadelphia Phillies, 1978 National League East Division Champs, Steve Carlton on cover, EX **$10.00**

Coin set, set of 48 w/full-color photos of Canseco, Jackson, Gooden, Boggs, etc, Topps, 1987, complete, EX..**$15.00**

Fan, commemorating St Louis Cardinals 1982 World Championship, multicolored, ball park shape w/wooden handle, 1982, EX **$6.50**

Film, 16mm, Football Parade, 1948, EX......................**$250.00**

Film, 8mm, This Is Baseball, #3024, EX....................**$10.00**

Gambling card (boxing), used to bet on televised boxing matches, multicolored, 1950s, VG **$100.00**

Game, Bob Feller's Big League Baseball Game, $130.00

Media guide, Boston Red Sox, 1980, EX **$6.00**

Media guide, Los Angeles Dodgers, 1968, EX..............**$20.00**

Media guide, Philadelphia Phillies, 1979, EX **$8.00**

Media guide, St Louis Cardinals, 1956, EX **$30.00**

Photo, Joe Louis in his classic boxing stance, black & white, signed, 1940s, 5x7", NM **$15.00**

Pocketknife, baseball bat shape, plastic w/embossed baseball & Boston, 2 blades, baseball attached to chain, 1960s, VG **$75.00**

Poker chip, embossed clay, shows golfer in knickers swinging club, 1930s, 1½" dia, G..................................**$8.50**

Postcard, Clearwater Stadium, linen, 1950s, VG **$4.50**

Postcard, 1974 National League All Star Team at Pittsburgh, EX..**$4.00**

Poster, Doug Flutie (1984 Heisman trophy winner), full color w/6 action photos, 1984, 23x17½", EX **$10.00**

Poster, Michael Jordan, full color, marked Michael Jordan, Chicago Bulls, Copyright: Marketcom, Official..., 20x16", M **$4.50**

Program, 1960 World Series, Pittsburgh Pirates/New York Yankees, EX..**$100.00**

Program, 1971 World Series, Pittsburgh Pirates/Baltimore Orioles, EX..**$25.00**

Program, 1984 World Series, Detroit Tigers/San Diego Padres, EX..**$6.00**

Schedule, Philadelphia Phillies Spring Training, cardboard, 1965, EX..**$15.00**

Score card, Twins vs Yankees, Mantle, Maris & Berra scored, 1963, EX..**$30.00**

Swizzel stick, golf club, red, blue or green plastic, G ...**$2.50**

Swizzle stick, baseball bat, green plastic, marked Man It's a Hit, Early Times Distillery Co, Louisville KY, G **$5.00**

Tally card (baseball), book form w/pull-tab card, red, green, blue & black, 1940s, G **$100.00**

Ticket, Oakland A's vs Minnesota Twins, Sept 22, 1975, VG..**$3.50**

Ticket, Orange Bowl Big 8 Championship, Missouri vs Oklahoma, Nov 16, 1968, EX..................................**$30.00**

Ticket, Tiger Stadium lower deck box, Sept 2, 1973, G .**$2.50**

Ticket, 1983 World Series at Memorial Stadium, Game 7, EX **$25.00**

Token (golf), brass, marked Ball-O-Matic South Bend Indiana, golfer swinging club on reverse, 1970s?, EX.**$10.00**

Yearbook, Atlanta Braves, 1970, EX **$20.00**

Yearbook, San Francisco Giants, 1965, EX..................**$35.00**

Yearbook, Seattle Mariners, 1985, EX..........................**$12.00**

Bobbin' Head Dolls

Atlanta Falcons, Merger Series, gold round base, team name & NFL decals **$25.00**

Baltimore Colts, gold round base, 00 on sleeves, realistic face, 1966-68 ....**$45.00**

Boston Red Sox, white round base, team name on decal, 1961-62, rare, miniature..................................**$210.00**

Chicago Cubs, mascot, white square base, embossed team name, 1961-62, rare **$325.00**

Chicago White Sox, gold round base, team name on decal, 1962-64, $55.00

Cincinnati Reds, mascot, gold round base, team name on decal, 1967-72, rare..**$80.00**

Cleveland Browns, brown ceramic round or square base, embossed team name on chest, NFL on base, 1961-62, scarce **$95.00**

Cleveland Indians, mascot, white square base, embossed team name, 1961-62, rare **$285.00**

Denver Broncos, gold round base, team name & AFL decals, ear pads on helmet.....................................**$120.00**

Detroit Tigers, mascot, white round base, team name on decal, 1961-62, rare, miniature.............................**$300.00**

Henry Aaron, caricature, plastic, 1975, original box....**$25.00**

Houston Oilers, gold round base, team name & AFL decal, 1966-67, rare...**$75.00**

Little League Baseball Boy, bank, boy sitting on half base-ball, early 1960s, rare...**$125.00**

Los Angeles Dodgers, white square base, embossed team name, 1961-62, rare **$125.00**

Los Angeles Rams, gold round base, 00 on sleeves, realistic face, 1966-68 ....**$45.00**

Milwaukee Braves, mascot, green round base, team name on decal, 1962-64, rare **$160.00**

Milwaukee Braves, mascot, white round base, team name on decal, 1961-62, rare, miniature **$275.00**

Minnesota Vikings, purple ceramic square or round base, embossed team name on chest, 1961-62...............**$35.00**

New York Mets, Black player, green round base, team name on decal, 1962-64...**$350.00**

New York Mets, blue square base, team name on decal, 1960-61, rare..**$200.00**

New York Yankees, gold round base, team name on decal, 1967-72, scarce..**$70.00**

New York Yankees, white square base, embossed team name, 1961-62, rare **$140.00**

Philadelphia Eagles, green ceramic square or round base, 1960 Champions embossed on base, 1961-62, scarce **$80.00**

San Francisco Giants, white round base, team name on decal, 1961-62, rare, miniature.............................**$175.00**

Umpire, various teams, white round base, boyish grin & curved hat, early 1960s, minimum value.............**$100.00**

Washington Redskins, Merger Series, gold round base, team name & NFL decals, rare **$80.00**

Kenner Starting Lineup Figures

Bo Jackson, 1990, 4", MIP **$18.00**
Brett Saberhagen, 1988, 4", MIP....................................**$18.00**
Darryl Strawberry, 1990, 4", MIP...................................**$10.00**
Dave Madagan, 1991, 4", MIP **$14.00**
Don Mattingly, 1988, 4", MIP...**$24.00**
Dwight Gooden, 1991, 4", MIP **$12.00**
George Brett, 1988, 4", MIP..**$24.00**
Kal Daniels, 1989, 4", MIP..**$12.00**
Ken Griffey Sr, 1988, 4", MIP..**$40.00**
Kevin Mitchell, 1990, 4", MIP...**$10.00**
Kirby Puckett, 1989, 4", MIP...**$10.00**
Mark Davis, 1989, 4", MIP **$16.00**

Orel Hershiser, 1989, 4", MIP **$24.00**
Paul Molitor, 1988, 4", MIP...**$15.00**
Ricky Jordan, 1990, 4", MIP..**$16.00**
Roberto Kelly, 1990, 4", MIP...**$20.00**
Ryne Sandberg, 1991, 4", MIP...**$10.00**
Terry Steinbach, 1989, 4", MIP..**$35.00**
Wade Boggs, 1989, 4", MIP..**$10.00**
Will Clark, 1991, 4", MIP...**$10.00**

Sports Pins

Major league sponsers distribute these pins free to each fan who comes through the gate to see the game on the night that specific sponser is featured. Overruns are sold at participating businesses until the supply is exhausted. Our values are for mint condition pins and cards.

A's, California Egg Commission, 1986 & 1987, 1 pin each year, each...**$10.00**

A's, California Raisins, 1990, w/card...........................**$20.00**

A's, Fire Fighter Appreciation Night, 1992...................**$18.00**

A's, Oscar Meyer, 1991 ....**$20.00**

A's, Unocal, 1991, set of 5 w/cards.............................**$10.00**

Angels, California Egg Commission, 1986 through 1989, 1 pin each year, each...**$10.00**

Angels, Prime Ticket, 1993, w/pennant.........................**$6.00**

Angels, Snapple, Dean Chance-Cy Young Award, 1994, w/card...**$7.00**

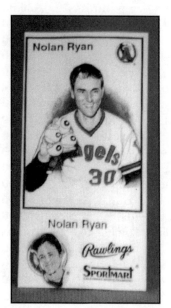

Angels, Sport Mart/Rawl-ings, Nolan Ryan & 4 No Hitters, 1992, set of 4 w/cards (1 shown), $60.00

Braves, Chevron, 1993 & 1994, w/cards, each...............**$8.00**
Braves, Coca-Cola, 1990, w/card **$10.00**
Brewers, Country Time Lemonade, 1993, set of 3.......**$10.00**
Brewers, Unocal, 1988, set of 4 ....**$20.00**
Brewers, US Oil Co Inc, 1991, set of 4 w/cards...........**$24.00**
Cardinals, Coca-Cola, 1991 ....**$15.00**
Cardinals, Coca-Cola, 1993, set of 3 w/cards **$35.00**
Cardinals, Coca-Cola/National, 1992, set of 10 w/cards ..**$55.00**
Cardinals, Levi Strauss, 1988...**$7.00**

Cardinals, Levi Strauss, 1990 ....**$18.00**
Cardinals, Quiktrip, 1994..**$10.00**
Cubs, Builders Square, 1994, set of 2 w/cards **$4.00**
Cubs, Connie's Pizza, 1994, w/card **$4.00**
Cubs, Florsheim, 1994, w/card...................................**$4.00**
Cubs, Kemper, 1994, w/card......................................**$4.00**
Cubs, Marathon, 1994, w/card...................................**$4.00**
Cubs, Unocal, 1988, set of 4.....................................**$18.00**
Cubs, Unocal, 1989, set of 4.....................................**$16.00**
Cubs, Unocal, 1990, set of 4.....................................**$12.00**
Cubs, Unocal, 1993, set of 4.....................................**$12.00**
Dodgers, Unocal, United Way Centennial, 1990, w/card .**$8.00**
Dodgers, Unocal, 1987, set of 6 w/cards....................**$18.00**
Dodgers, Unocal, 1988, set of 6 w/cards....................**$12.00**
Dodgers, Unocal, 1989, set of 6 w/cards....................**$12.00**
Giants, California Egg Commission, 1987.....................**$12.00**
Giants, Chevron, 1989, set of 3 w/cards.....................**$30.00**
Giants, Chevron, 1990, set of 4 w/cards.....................**$20.00**
Giants, Chevron, 1991, set of 3 w/cards.....................**$18.00**
Giants, Coca-Cola, 1993, w/card **$20.00**
Giants, Equitable Old Timers Game, 1989 ....**$8.00**
Giants, Opening Day, 1993, w/card **$10.00**
Giants, Until There's a Cure Foundation, 1994, w/card.**$8.00**
Indians, Sunoco, 1991, set of 5 w/cards......................**$25.00**
Indians, Sunoco, 1992 & 1993, set of 4 w/cards each year, each set..........................**$20.00**
Indians, Unocal, 1988 through 1990, set of 4 each year, each set, from $18 to **$20.00**
Mariners, Chevron, 1992, set of 5 w/cards...................**$25.00**
Mariners, Dairy Queen, 1993, set of 5 w/cards............**$20.00**
Mariners, McDonalds, 1993, set of 3 w/cards **$10.00**
Mariners, Red Apple Farms, 1990, set of 5 w/cards **$40.00**
Mariners, Unocal, 1988, set of 4 w/cards **$12.00**
Marlins, Bumble Bee Seafoods, Inc, 1993, w/card **$75.00**
Marlins, Winn Dixie Super Market, 1993, set of 4 w/cards **$85.00**
Mets, Chemical Bank, 1993, set of 2 w/cards **$10.00**
Mets, Chemical Bank, 1994, set of 5 w/cards **$20.00**
Mets, Sharp Electronics, 1990, set of 4 w/cards...........**$25.00**
Orioles, Coca-Cola, 1993, w/card **$10.00**
Orioles, Country Time Lemonade, 1993, set of 5 ....**$15.00**
Orioles, Gatorade, All-Star Fan Fest, 1993....................**$7.00**
Orioles, Toyota, 1989, set of 3 w/cards.......................**$30.00**
Orioles, Toyota/Memorial Stadium Commission, 1991, set of 2 w/cards..**$25.00**
Padres, California Egg Commission, 1987 ....**$7.00**
Padres, Equitable Old Timers Series, July 20, 1990.......**$6.00**
Padres, Great American Bank, 1986 & 1987, w/card, each...**$10.00**
Padres, San Diego Cable Sports Network, 1989 & 1991, set of 3 each year, each set.........................**$30.00**
Padres, San Diego Cable Sports Network, 1991, set of 3 ....**$30.00**
Padres, Vons/Coca-Cola, 1990 through 1992, 1 pin each year w/card, each..........................**$12.00**
Pirates, Block Buster Video, 1991 & 1992, set of 5 w/cards each year, each set, from $25 to **$35.00**
Pirates, Gatorade, 1994, set of 4 w/cards...................**$20.00**

Pirates, TCBY Yogurt, 1990, set of 5 w/cards............**$40.00**
Rangers, Chevron, 1990, set of 4 w/cards...................**$20.00**
Rangers, Dr Pepper, 1993, set of 4 w/cards................**$24.00**
Rockies, Coca-Cola, 1994, set of 7 w/cards.................**$21.00**
Rockies, Coca-Cola/7 Eleven, 1993, set of 13 w/cards.**$80.00**
Royals, Phillips 66, 1990 through 1993, set of 2 w/cards each year, each set, from $18 to **$20.00**
Royals, Western Auto, 1989, set of 3 w/cards...............**$35.00**
Tigers, Little Caesars, 1992, set of 3 w/cards............**$18.00**
Tigers, Little Caesars, 1993, set of 5 w/cards............**$25.00**
Tigers, Unocal, 1989, set of 4....................................**$16.00**
Tigers, Unocal, 1990, set of 4....................................**$12.00**
Twins, Gatorade, 1992, w/card **$12.00**
Twins, Norwest/Olympic Festival, 1990 ....**$10.00**
Twins, Star Tribune, Homer Hanky, 1987 ....**$7.00**
Twins, Unocal, 1989, set of 4....................................**$16.00**
White Sox, Burger King, 1993, w/card **$8.00**
White Sox, Coca-Cola, Jr Fan Club, 1993 ....**$10.00**
White Sox, Coca-Cola, 1989, set of 6 w/cards **$35.00**
White Sox, Coca-Cola, 1990, set of 5 w/cards **$25.00**
White Sox, Scott Peterson Ballpark Franks, 1991 through 1993, set of 4 w/cards each year, each set, from $12 to **$16.00**
White Sox, Scott Peterson Ballpark Franks, 1992, set of 4 w/cards **$16.00**
White Sox, Unocal, 1994, w/card..............................**$5.00**
Yankees, Chemical Bank, 1994, w/card **$6.00**

Stanford Corn

Teapots, cookie jars, salt and pepper shakers, and other kitchen and dinnerware items modeled as ears of yellow corn with green shucks were made by the Stanford company, who marked most of their ware. The Shawnee company made two very similar corn lines; just check the marks to verify the manufacturer.

Cookie jar, $85.00

Butter dish	$45.00
Creamer & sugar bowl	$45.00
Pitcher, 7½"	$55.00
Relish tray	$35.00
Salt & pepper shakers, pr	$25.00
Spoon rest	$25.00
Teapot	$60.00

Stangl Birds

The Stangl Pottery Company of Flemington and Trenton, New Jersey, made a line of ceramic birds which they introduced in 1940 to fulfill the needs of a market no longer able to access foreign imports, due to the onset of WWII. These bird figures immediately attracted a great deal of attention. At the height of their production, sixty decorators were employed to hand paint the birds at the plant, and the overflow was contracted out and decorated in private homes. After WWII, inexpensive imported figurines once again saturated the market, and for the most part, Stangl curtailed their own production, though the birds were made on a very limited basis until as late as 1977.

Nearly all the birds were marked. A four-digit number was used to identify the species, and some pieces were signed by the decorator. An 'F' indicates a bird that was decorated at the Flemington plant.

Allen Hummingbird, #3634, 3½"	$65.00
Bird of Paradise, #3408, 5½"	$100.00
Blue Jay w/peanut, #3716, 10¼"	$550.00
Blue-Headed Vireo, #3448, 4¼"	$65.00
Broadtail Hummingbird, #3629, 4½"	$135.00
Broadtail Hummingbird w/blue flower, #3626, 6"	$150.00
Cerulean Warbler, #3456, 4¼"	$65.00
Chickadees (group), #3581, 5½x8½"	$225.00

Cockatoo, #3580, 8⅞", $140.00

Cockatoo, #3405, 6"	$65.00
Cockatoos, #3405D, old, 9½"	$175.00
Cockatoos, #3405D, revised, 9½"	$125.00
Flying Duck, #3443, 9"	$275.00
Gazing Duck, #3250, 3¾"	$100.00
Goldfinches (group of 4), #3635, 4x11½"	$200.00
Gray Cardinal, #3596, 4¾"	$90.00
Hen, yellow, #3446, 7"	$160.00
Hummingbirds, #3599D, 8x10½"	$270.00
Key West Quail Dove, #3454, 9"	$315.00
Kingfisher, #3406, 3½"	$75.00
Love Bird, #3400, revised, 4"	$65.00
Oriole, #3402, revised, 3¼"	$60.00
Orioles, #3402D, revised, 5½"	$150.00
Painted Bunting, #3452, 5"	$100.00
Parula Warbler, #3583, 4¼"	$60.00
Preening Duck, #3250, 2¾"	$100.00
Prothonatary Warbler, #3447, 5"	$85.00
Quacking Duck, #3250, 2¾"	$65.00
Red Faced Warbler, #3594, 3"	$70.00
Red Starts, #3490D, 9"	$175.00
Red-Headed Woodpecker, #3752D, glossy pink, 7¾"	$275.00
Rieffers Hummingbird, #3628, 4½"	$135.00
Rivoli Hummingbird w/red flowers, #3627, 6"	$150.00
Rooster, #3445, 9"	$180.00
Rufous Hummingbird, #3585, 3"	$60.00
Standing Duck, #3250, 3¼"	$100.00
Western Tanagers, #3750D, 4¾"	$360.00
Wilson Warbler, #3597, 3½"	$50.00
Wren, #3401, 3½"	$55.00
Yellow Warbler, #3850, 4"	$90.00

Stangl Dinnerware

The Stangl Company of Trenton, New Jersey, grew out of the Fulper company that had been established in Flemington early in the 1800s. Martin Stangl, president of the company, introduced a line of dinnerware in the 1920s. By 1954, 90% of their production centered around their dinnerware lines. Until 1942, the clay they used was white firing, and decoration was minimal, usually simple one-color glazes. In 1942, however, the first of the red-clay lines that have become synonomous with the Stangl name was created. Designs were hand carved into the greenware, then hand painted. More than one hundred different patterns have been cataloged. From 1974 until 1978, a few lines previously discontinued on the red clay were reintroduced with a white clay body. Soon after '78, the factory closed.

If you'd like more information on the subject, read *The Collector's Encyclopedia of American Dinnerware* by Jo Cunningham.

Amberglo, coffee server	$50.00
Blueberry, bowl, coupe soup; 7½"	$22.00
Blueberry, bowl, fruit; 5½"	$16.00
Blueberry, plate, 10"	$15.00

Chicory, bread plate $36.00
Chicory, egg cup......................................$12.00
Chicory, plate, 10".................................$16.00
Colonial, custard cup $8.00
Country Garden, plate, 8".......................$10.00
Daisy, bowl, nut; 4½" $12.00
Daisy, bowl, vegetable; oval, 10"...............$25.00
Daisy, plate, 10" $22.00
Deco Delight, creamer, silver-green $40.00
First Love, bowl, 5½" $8.00
First Love, butter dish $25.00
First Love, plate, 8" $8.00
Fruit, plate, 10" $18.00
Fruit & Flowers, chop plate, 12½" $35.00
Fruit & Flowers, creamer.........................$16.00
Fruit & Flowers, relish dish $36.00
Fruit & Flowers, saucer............................$7.00
Fruits, bowl, soup; 7½"............................$20.00
Garden Flower (Morning Glory), bowl, cereal; 5½" $15.00
Garden Flower (Rose), plate, 10"...............$17.00
Garland, butter dish................................$35.00
Garland, cup...$14.00
Golden Blossom, plate, 8".........................$8.00
Lyric, bowl, vegetable; round, 8" $30.00
Lyric, cup...$12.00
Lyric, sugar bowl.....................................$20.00

Magnolia, dinner plate, $10.00

Mountain Laurel, bowl, cereal; 5½" $14.00
Mountain Laurel, teapot............................$46.00
Orchard Song, mug, tall $25.00
Sculptured Fruit, bowl, 10"........................$35.00
Star Flower, bowl, vegetable; w/lid, 8" $52.00
Star Flower, plate, 8"................................$10.00
Star Flower, sugar bowl.............................$14.00
Thistle, plate, bread & butter.....................$6.00

Star Trek Memorabilia

Trekkies, as fans are often referred to, number nearly 40,000 today, hold national conventions, and compete with each other for choice items of Star Trek memorabilia, some of which may go for hundreds of dollars.

The Star Trek concept was introduced to the public in the mid-1960s through a TV series which continued for many years in syndication. An animated cartoon series (1977), the release of six major motion pictures (1979 through 1989), and the success of 'Star Trek, The Next Generation,' television show (Fox network, 1987) all served as a bridge to join two generations of loyal fans.

Its success has resulted in the sale of vast amounts of merchandise, both licensed and unlicensed, such as clothing, promotional items of many sorts, books and comics, toys and games, records and tapes, school supplies, and party goods. Many of these are still available at flea markets around the country. An item that is 'mint in box' is worth at least twice as much as one in excellent condition but without its original packaging.

For more information, refer to *Modern Toys, American Toys, 1930-1980,* by Linda Baker and *Schroeder's Collectible Toys, Antique to Modern* (Collector Books).

Activity book, Star Trek Action Toy Book, 1976, EX...$15.00
Bank, Captain Kirk or Mr Spock, Play Pal, 1975, each..$42.00
Belt buckle, Paramount, 1979, M $8.00
Birthday party decorations, Happy Birthday w/Enterprise, Mr Spock, Captain Kirk & Dr McCoy, 1978, sealed, MIP..$30.00
Book, Make Your Own Costume, patterns, 1979, EX+ .$12.00

Book, Mission to Horatius, Whitman Authorized Edition, 1968, EX, $15.00

Book, Star Trek The Motion Picture, Gene Roddenberry, signed, EX..$50.00
Calendar, Ballantine, 1976, NMIB $25.00

Comic book, Star Trek V, The Final Frontier, #1 issue, DC Comics, 1989, M..**$5.00**

Communicators, Remco, 1967, MIB, from $125 to $160.00

Costumes, Captain Kirk or Mr Spock, Collegeville, 1967..**$32.00**

Decanter, Mr Spock bust, 1979, MIB..........................**$45.00**

Dictionary, Klingon language, M....................................**$6.00**

Doll, Captain Kirk, stuffed body w/vinyl head, Knicker-bocker, 1979, 12", VG...**$10.00**

Earrings, Enterprise outlined on clear Lucite block, Aviva, pr...**$5.00**

Figural paint set, Star Trek, The Motion Picture, features Mr Spock or Captain Kirk figures, Whitling, 1979, MOC, each...**$20.00**

Figure, Captain Picard (Next Generation), vinyl, w/stand, 11", MIB...**$15.00**

Figure, Dr McCoy, Star Trek V, Galoob, 1989, M in EX box...**$45.00**

Figure, Klingon (Next Generation), PVC, Presents, 1992, 4", MOC...**$4.00**

Figure, Mr Spock, PVC, Presents, 1992, 4", MIP..........**$4.00**

Flashlight, Ray Gun, Larami Corp, 1968, 7½x10¾", MOC.**$16.00**

Frisbee, Remco, 1967...**$32.00**

Game, Star Trek Pinball, plastic, 14", VG+..................**$30.00**

Globe, Enterprise shape, lights up, NM in EX box, M.**$55.00**

Greeting cards, set of 6, 1980, MIP..............................**$10.00**

Gum card set, Star Trek II, 100 cards, complete, Monty Gum, M...**$75.00**

Lobby card set, Star Trek The Next Generation, Zanart, M...**$12.00**

Magazine, Deep Space 9, #1, M....................................**$6.00**

Magic Putty, Larami, 1979...**$6.00**

Magnet, shaped like Enterprise, MIP............................**$2.00**

Mug, features Scotty, Star Trek Collector, Presents, 1992, MIB...**$10.00**

Napkin, cartoon graphics, MIP..**$5.00**

Necklace, Enterprise on chain, 1976, NMOC..............**$18.00**

Ornament, Shuttlecraft Galileo, Hallmark, MIB...........**$30.00**

Patch, Star Fleet, NM on EX card..................................**$10.00**

Pencil topper, Presents, 1992, MIP.................................**$4.00**

Phaser gun (Next Generation), Playmates, MIP...........**$12.00**

Plate, Captain Kirk or Mr Spock, blue-rimmed, 1985-89, 8½" dia...**$62.00**

Postcard, USS Enterprise, Trotter Photo, 1977, 3x5"......**$3.00**

Program, Star Trek III, color photos, 1984, EX.............**$5.00**

Puzzle, Star Trek I, The Enterprise, 250 pcs, 1979, 20x14", EX...**$15.00**

Spock's ears, painted plastic, 1976, MOC....................**$14.00**

Spoon, Captain Kirk, Mr Spock, Dr McCoy or Scotty..**$20.00**

Sticker, Save Star Trek - Write NBC, Star Trek Enterprises, 1968, 4x13"...**$3.00**

Sticker book, Jeopardy at Jutterdon, Whitman, 1979, NM...**$10.00**

Stickpin, I Am a Trekkie, Lincoln Enterprises, 1976......**$6.00**

T-Shirt, Deep Space 9, M...**$15.00**

Tote bag, gray plastic w/abstract drawing of Enterprise on both sides, from April 1976 convention, EX..........**$10.00**

Trading card tin, 25th Anniversary, Impel, empty, M..**$20.00**

TV tray, Star Trek, The Motion Picture, features Mr Spock, 1979, EX...**$25.00**

Vehicle, Klingon Warship, The Motion Picture, Dinky, NM on VG card...**$25.00**

Wall clock, depicts the Enterprise, electric, ASA Inc, 1974, 8" dia...**$35.00**

Water gun, Aviva, 1979...**$25.00**

Star Wars

In the late seventies, the movie 'Star Wars' became a box office hit, most notably for its fantastic special effects and its ever-popular theme of space adventure. Two more movies followed, 'The Empire Strikes Back' in 1980 and 'Return of the Jedi' in 1983. After the first movie, an enormous amount of related merchandise was released. A large percentage of these items was action figures, made by the Kenner company who included the logo of the 20th Century Fox studios (under whom they were licensed) on everything they made until 1980. Just before the second movie, Star Wars creator, George Lucas, regained control of the merchandise rights, and items inspired by the last two films can be identified by his own Lucasfilm logo. Since 1987, Lucasfilm, Ltd., has operated shops in conjunction with the Star Tours at Disneyland theme parks.

What to collect? First and foremost, buy what you yourself enjoy. But remember that condition is all important. Look for items still mint in the box. Using that as a basis, if the box is missing, deduct at least half. If a major accessory or part is gone, the item is basically worthless. Learn to recognize the most desirable, most valuable items. There are lots of Star Wars bargains yet to be had!

Activity book, Empire Strikes Back, 1980, VG+.............**$5.00**

Bank, Emperor's Royal Guard, EX.................................**$15.00**

Bank, Jabba the Hutt figure, painted ceramic, Sigma, MIB...**$50.00**

Bedspread, cotton, blue background w/characters, 1977, twin size, NM...**$31.00**

Belt buckle, features C-3PO & R2-D2, EX **$12.00**

Book & record set, Star Wars, from original movie, 24-page book w/45 rpm record, Read-Along Books, 1977, M **$10.00**

Child's bowl & cup, plastic, Empire Strikes Back, NMIP . **$15.00**

Coloring book, Return of the Jedi, Kenner, M **$8.00**

Comic book, Star Wars, 1st issue, 1977, M **$16.00**

Doll, Paploo, plush, lg, MIB **$45.00**

Doll, R2-D2, plush, EX **$20.00**

Doll, Wicket W Warrick, plush, EX **$18.00**

Eraser, Darth Vader figure, MIP **$4.00**

Felt-tip marker, Darth Vader figure, remove head to write, 1983, M **$4.00**

Figure, Amanaman, Power of the Force, Kenner, MOC . **$95.00**

Figure, Barada, w/coin, Power of the Force, Kenner, MOC **$45.00**

Figure, Biker Scout, w/coin, Power of the Force, MOC .. **$30.00**

Figure, Boba Fett, Star Wars, Kenner, 1977, 13", MIB . **$220.00**

Figure, Bossk, Return of the Jedi, Kenner, MOC **$30.00**

Figure, Darth Vader, Kenner, 12", MIB **$195.00**

Figure, Death Star Droid, Return of the Jedi, MOC **$40.00**

Figure, Emperor, Return of the Jedi, Kenner, 3¾", MOC **$20.00**

Figure, Gamorrean Guard, Return of the Jedi, Kenner, 1983, 3¾", MOC **$20.00**

Figure, Imperial Commandor, Return of the Jedi, Kenner, 3¾", MOC **$18.00**

Figure, Jawa, complete w/accessories, Star Wars, Kenner, 1979, 12", EX **$50.00**

Figure, Leia Organa, in Bespin gown, Return of the Jedi, Kenner, MOC **$50.00**

Figure, Luke Skywalker, as Jedi Knight, Return of the Jedi, Kenner, 3¾", MOC **$35.00**

Figure, Luke Skywalker, in Bespin outfit, Empire Strikes Back, Kenner, M on EX card **$65.00**

Figure, Rancor Monster, Return of the Jedi, Kenner, 10", MIB **$35.00**

Figure, R2-D2, w/pop-up light saber, w/coin, Power of the Force, 3¾", M on EX card **$100.00**

Figure, Teebo, Return of the Jedi, Kenner, 1983, 3¾", MOC **$25.00**

Figurine, Wickett, painted ceramic, MIB **$35.00**

Game, Escape From Death Star, Kenner, 1977, NM **$18.00**

Game, Yoda the Jedi Master, unused, Kenner, MIB **$25.00**

Gum cards, complete set of 66, 1st series, Topps, 1977, EX **$30.00**

Gum cards, 3rd series, complete set of 132, OPC, 1978, NM **$50.00**

Lamp, R2-D2 figure, VG+ **$75.00**

Napkins, Empire Strikes Back, 16 in all, 1980, MIP **$7.00**

Picture frame, Darth Vader, painted ceramic, Sigma, MIB **$35.00**

Placemats, set of 2 featuring R2-D2 & C-3PO, Empire Strikes Back, NMIP **$25.00**

Playset, Creature Cantina, Kenner, EX in VG box **$65.00**

Playset, Degobah Action, Empire Strikes Back, unused, Kenner, 1981, MIB **$75.00**

Playset, Ewok Village, Return of the Jedi, Kenner, 1983, 21" box, NM in EX box **$85.00**

Playset, Imperial Attack Base, complete, no box, EX .. **$25.00**

Poster, lithographed cardboard, A Long Time Ago...Star Wars, 20th Century Fox, 1977, 24x38", NM **$65.00**

Puppet, Yoda, M in EX box **$35.00**

Puzzle, frame-tray; Return of the Jedi, 1983, 11x8", EX+ . **$8.00**

Puzzle book, Return of the Jedi, Happy House, NM ... **$40.00**

Record tote, Star Wars, VG+ **$12.00**

Shoelaces, Star Wars, MIP **$8.00**

Stickers, Empire Strikes Back, 1st series, complete set of 33, Topps, 1980, NM **$50.00**

Stickers, 1st series, complete set of 11, Topps, 1977, EX+ **$20.00**

Figure, Stormtrooper, molded plastic, jointed at hips & shoulders, Kenner, 1979-80, 12", M, $125.00

Teapot, R2-D2, porcelain, white w/blue features, EX+, $100.00

Vehicle, Darth Vader Star Destroyer, Empire Strikes Back, Kenner, MIB **$125.00**

Vehicle, Imperial Cruiser, Star Wars, die-cast metal & plastic, Kenner, 1979, 7", M in EX box............................**$140.00**
Vehicle, Jedi Tri-Pod Cannon, MIB..............................**$12.00**
Vehicle, Rebel Transport, w/applied decals, Empire Strikes Back, Kenner, NMIB..**$70.00**
Vehicle, X-Wing Fighter, die-cast metal & plastic, Star Wars, Kenner, 1978, 5", M on EX card............................**$125.00**

Stauffer Figurines

Figures of children marked 'Designed by Erich Stauffer' are very much like Hummels. From a distance, they're look-alikes, and very good ones at that. But the activities they portray are different than any Hummel, and the quality is not the same. Compared to most of the other unmarked Hummel-like figures you see today, though they're much better than average, and they're becoming quite collectible. Stauffer's figures were imported from Japan by Arnart Imports Inc. of New York in the late 1950s. They range from 4½" to 10" high and may have from one to three children on a single base. (Singles are common, groups are in the minority.) Most interesting, of course, are the figures that incorporate a prop — for instance, a goose or two, an animal, a snow shovel, a doll, or a musical instrument. The groups sometimes have a rather large base, while some of the single figures have flat backs and look almost like bookends.

Variations exist, and you may find that without keeping notes, it's easy to end up with duplicates! They're all numbered, but those numbers can be confusing! Sometimes a figure was reissued in other sizes. Even though everything else was identical, each different size was assigned a new model number. And you may have several different figures all having the same number which, in this case, is a series number, not a model number.

Various marks were used in addition to the one already mentioned. Sometimes the number is prefixed by an 'S' or a 'U.' In addition to the name, some carry a crossed arrow mark and others a crown. A sticker was also used: 'Original Arnart Creation, Japan,' with the image of a bee. (Some of the smaller figures marked with the crown and 'Arnart, 5th Avenue, Handpainted,' are not of the same good quality and are thought to be earlier.)

A good rule of thumb for pricing the average child figure is $3.00 to $4.00 an inch (in height), depending on the activity portrayed, the props involved, and of course, condition.

Boy blowing horn, sitting, #1554 (Arnart), no label, 5½" w/4" dia base **$18.00**
Boy holding hat full of flowers, 'Pretty Please,' #S8564, 9½"..**$28.00**
Boy in bowler hat sitting playing violin, 'Music Time,' #U8543, 6"..**$18.00**
Boy playing violin, 'Music Time,' #U8543, 6½"...........**$18.00**
Boy playing violin, #2613, no label, 5".......................**$15.00**
Boy w/artist's palette, sitting, 'Bohemian,' #2613 (Arnart), 4¾"..**$15.00**

Boy w/axe beside him, #8518, no label, 5½"..............**$15.00**

Boy w/axe holding logs, 'Chores,' #8564, 9½", $28.00, Boy w/2 girls dancing in a circle, 'Dancing Time,' #55/2029, $25.00

Boy w/carrot & rake, 'Farm Chores,' #55/1542, 4⅜"....**$12.00**
Boy w/knapsack, kneeling, #U8517, no label, 5" **$15.00**
Boy w/rake, #U8541, no label, 6¾" **$20.00**
Boy w/shovel, 'Life on the Farm,' #U8541, 6¾"...........**$20.00**
Boy w/umbrella, handle on other hand, 'Woodland Frolics,' #U8518, 5½"..**$18.00**
Boy w/umbrella, kneeling, #S8517, no label, 5" **$15.00**
Girl holding boy doll, 'Play Time,' #U8561, 7½"..........**$28.00**
Girl playing accordion, sitting, #2613, no label, 5"......**$15.00**
Girl w/artist's palette, sitting, 'Little Bohemian,' #U8543, 6"...**$20.00**
Girl w/basket over arm, #U8541, no label, 6¾"..........**$18.00**
Girl w/knapsack on back holding orange, #1538 (Arnart), 4¼"...**$10.00**
Girl w/spade in hand, sitting, 'Young Folks,' #U8515, 6½"...**$18.00**
Girl w/spade in hand, sitting, #2623 (Arnart), no label, 4½"...**$12.00**
Two Girls side by side, 'Dancing Time,' #55/1556, 5½".**$22.00**

Steiff Animals

These stuffed animals originated in Germany around the turn of the century. They were created by Margaret Steiff, whose company continues to operate to the present day. They are identified by the button inside the ear and the identification tag (which often carries the name of the animal) on their chest. Over the years, variations in the tags and buttons help collectors determine approximate dates of manufacture.

Teddy bear collectors regard Steiff bears as some of the most valuable on the market. When assessing the worth of a bear, they use some general guidelines as a starting basis, though other features can come into play as well. For instance, bears made prior to 1912 that have long gold mohair fur start at a minimum of $75.00 per inch. If the bear has dark brown or curly white mohair fur instead, that figure may go as high as $135.00. From the 1920 to 1930 era, the price would be about $50.00 minimum per inch. A bear (or any other animal) on cast iron or wooden wheels starts at $75.00 per inch; but if the tires are hard rubber, the value is much lower, at $27.00 per inch.

It's a fascinating study which is well-covered in _Teddy Bears and Steiff Animals, First and Second Series,_ by Margaret Fox Mandel.

Bear, beige mohair, fully jointed, black bead eyes, ca 1950, 3½", NM..**$275.00**

Bear, beige mohair, glass eyes, brown floss nose, mouth & claws, felt pads, 1940-50, 9", NM......................**$325.00**

Bear, squeaker, beige mohair, fully jointed, glass eyes, chest tag reads Original Teddy, 1950s, 14", EX, minimum value..**$550.00**

Bear, squeaker, honey mohair, fully jointed, dark brown floss nose, mouth & claws, 1950-55, 8", EX........**$275.00**

Bear, squeaker, short gold mohair, fully jointed, glass eyes, floss nose, mouth & claws, 1930-40, 6½", EX.....**$225.00**

Bear, white mohair, fully jointed, black bead eyes, brown floss nose & mouth, 1950s, rare, 3¼", EX...........**$275.00**

Bear, Zotty, platinum frosted mohair, fully jointed, glass eyes, embroidered nose & claws, felt mouth & pads, 11", EX..**$195.00**

Beaver, Nagi, tan mohair, bristly back, plastic eyes, felt paws, ears, feet & tail, original tag, 3½", EX, $65.00

Bison, short brown mohair w/long pile hump, tail & head, brown glass eyes, ruled felt horns, 1960s, 11x15", EX **$375.00**

Cat, Cosy Siam, Siamese, dralon, blue eyes, rivet-type ear button, original blue ribbon & tag, 1970s, 9", M...**$75.00**

Cat, Siamese, silky mohair, jointed neck, blue eyes, tag reads Made in US Zone Germany, rare, ca 1950, 9", M..**$550.00**

Cat, Snurry, mohair w/brown tabby markings, curled position, embroidered slits for sleeping eyes, rare, 1964, 5½", M..**$225.00**

Cat, Susi, gray & white cotton plush, jointed neck, green glass eyes, original red rayon bow, w/chest tag, 1930s, 7", M..**$375.00**

Cat, Tabby, gray & white mohair, tan collar w/bell & tag, 1950s, 3¼", G................................**$85.00**

Cat, Topsy, short pile mohair w/tabby markings, green glass eyes, pink rayon ribbon w/brass bell, ca 1964, 3½x5", M..**$95.00**

Cow, mohair w/Hereford markings, black & white glass eyes, open felt mouth, well-formed felt udders, 6½x9", EX **$100.00**

Deer, Bambi, velvet w/mohair insets on chest, ears & tail, glass eyes, w/button, 8", VG **$95.00**

Dog, Cockie, cocker spaniel, black & white mohair, glass eyes, open felt mouth, ca 1957, 8½", M, minimum value..**$225.00**

Dog, fox terrier, tan velour w/brown spots, brown glass eyes, leather collar w/attached paper tag, 10x13", VG **$200.00**

Dog, Foxy, fox terrier, white, black & brown mohair, glass eyes, sewn-in tag reads US Zone Germany, 1945-52, rare, NM..**$275.00**

Dog, silver & brown long pile mohair, shank-type brown glass eyes trimmed in black, embroidered nose & claws, 8x12", NM..**$300.00**

Dog, Tessie, schnauzer, gray mohair, swivel head, glass eyes, floss nose, mouth & claws, 1950s, 11x14", M, minimum value..**$250.00**

Giraffe, mohair, steel structure, black glass eyes, open felt mouth, ca 1968, 31", M.......................**$375.00**

Goldfish, Flossy, yellow & orange mohair, glass eyes, open felt mouth, original tag, 1965-78, 5", EX, minimum value, $55.00

Guinea pig, dralon & cotton, black & white plastic eyes, black embroidered nose & mouth, 1965, 5", EX...**$35.00**

Lamb, Lamby, white wooly mohair, glass eyes, red ribbon & bell, EX **$75.00**

Lamb, white wooly plush, green glass eyes, red floss nose & mouth, felt-lined ears, 1950s, 8½", M.....................**$75.00**

Lion, Lea, mohair w/airbrushed markings & claws, orange glass eyes, w/chest tag, 1957-69, M.....................**$150.00**

Lobster, red, cream & orange mohair, black bead eyes, 12", EX **$195.00**

Panther, lounging, black dralon, yellow glass eyes, rose floss nose, 1973-80, 20", M.................................**$150.00**

Pig, pink felt, blue glass eyes, floss nose & mouth, 1970s, 2¾x4", M...**$55.00**

Pony, mohair, brown glass eyes, red floss bridle, red leather saddle, synthetic bristle mane & tail, 5", EX..........**$65.00**

Porcupine, dralon & cotton, black bead eyes, painted face, corduroy stomach, w/button, 1965, 4", EX............**$35.00**

Rabbit, lying, brown & white mohair, jointed neck, glass eyes, red bow, chest tag, 1960s, 4½" long, M, minimum value **$65.00**

Rabbit, white & brown mohair, brown glass eyes, original tan neck ribbon, bell missing, 1950, 5½x10", NM.**$75.00**

Rooster, multicolored mohair, black bead eyes, felt tail & feet, 6", EX...**$75.00**

Seal, white mohair w/blue spots, plastic eyes, pink nose, brown mouth, w/button, 8" long, NM...................**$95.00**

Tiger, mohair, green glass eyes, pink embroidered nose, paper chest tag, ca 1972, 13½" long, EX **$125.00**

String Holders

Before Scotch tape made string obsolete, every household and business had a string holder of sorts. Some were made of cast iron, for heavy duty office work or for use in general stores and groceries. Others were frivolous and decorative, perhaps modeled as a human face or a big red apple, and made of various materials such as plaster or ceramic.

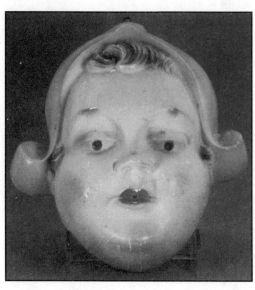

Dutch girl, chalkware, 8", VG, $35.00

Bell shape, counter top, green glass w/tin bottom, 5¾", EX **$145.00**

Bird, ceramic, yellow on green string nest..................**$30.00**

Black Porter, Fredricksburg Art Pottery, 6½", M........**$150.00**

Cat's face, Holt Howard China, 1958...........................**$17.50**

Cat's head w/ball of yarn, white head & front paws trimmed in gold, pink yarn, marked Japan, EX **$30.00**

Dutch boy w/pipe, chalkware, EX paint.....................**$45.00**

Mammy figure, brown-skinned w/polka-dot dress & plaid apron, Japan, 1930s, 6½", EX.............................**$180.00**

Old lady in rocker, chalkware **$32.00**

Tabby, cast iron, multicolored paint, 1880s, 5⅝".......**$385.00**

Top hat w/face, chalkware, EX paint **$45.00**

Swanky Swigs

These glass tumblers ranging in size from 3¼" to 4¾" were originally distributed by the Kraft company who filled them with their cheese spread. They were primarily used from the 1930s until sometime during the war, but they were brought out soon after and used to some extent until the late 1970s. Many were decorated with fired-on designs of flowers, 'Bustling Betty' scenes (assorted chores being done by a Gibson-type Betty), 'Antique' patterns (clocks, coal scuttles, lamps, kettles, coffee grinders, spinning wheels, etc.), animals (in their 'Kiddie Cup' line), or solid colors of red, yellow, green, and blue (Fiesta ware look-alikes).

Even the lids are collectible and are valued at a minimum of $3.00, depending on condition and the advertising message they convey.

For more information, we recommend *Collectible Glassware of the 40s, 50s, and 60s* and *The Collector's Encyclopedia of Depression Glass, Eleventh Edition*, both by Gene Florence.

Squirrel & deer, brown, 3¾", $4.00

Antique pattern, churn & cradle, orange, 3¼".................**$8.50**

Antique pattern, coffee grinder & plate, green, 3¼"......**$8.50**

Bustling Betsy, all colors, 3¼", each $8.50
Carnival, yellow or red, 3½" $5.00
Cornflowers #1, light blue, 3¼" $8.50
Cornflowers #2, light blue, 3¼" $8.50
Cornflowers #2, yellow, 3¼" $8.50
Daisies, red, white & green, 4½" $14.50
Daisies, red & white, 3¾" $24.00
Forget-Me-Nots, blue, red or yellow, 3½" $3.00
Forget-Me-Nots, yellow, w/label, 3½" $10.00
Jonquils, yellow, 4½" $14.50
Tulips #3, light blue or yellow, 3¾" $3.50
Tulips #3, red, 4½" $14.50
Tulips in pots #1, black, 3½" $4.00
Tulips in pots #1, blue, 3½" $4.00
Violets, purple, 3¼" $8.50
Violets, purple, 4½" $14.50

Syracuse Dinnerware

Until 1970, the Onandaga Pottery Company produced many lines of beautiful china dinnerware for home use. Located in Syracuse, New York, they are still in business, but the tablewares they make today are for commercial use only (hotels, restaurants, airlines, etc.). They marked their china with the trade name Syracuse, and in 1966 they adopted that name for their company in order to more easily identify with the fine chinaware lines for which they had become famous.

Each piece is marked with a dating code that will help you determine just when your pattern was produced. In her book *Lehner's Encyclopedia of U.S. Marks on Pottery, Porcelain, and Clay*, Lois Lehner gives the details of this code. Nine columns of information and mark facsimiles are given as well, and if you're interested in learning more about Syracuse china, this is probably the best source available for study.

Apple Blossom, cup & saucer $36.00
Apple Blossom, plate, salad $20.00
Arcadia, cup & saucer $22.00
Arcadia, platter, 12" $45.00
Avalon, cup & saucer, gold trim $32.00
Avalon, plate, 10" $25.00
Baroque Gray, bowl, vegetable; w/lid, sm $40.00
Baroque Gray, plate, dinner $25.00
Bombay, coffeepot $100.00
Bombay, cup & saucer $34.00
Bracelet, plate, 10¼" $35.00
Bracelet, platter, 12" $50.00
Briarcliff, bowl, vegetable; w/lid, 8" $85.00
Briarcliff, plate, 10" $25.00
Carvel, bowl, vegetable $55.00
Carvel, platter, 14" $65.00
Carvel, platter, 16" $85.00
Celest, cup & saucer $36.00
Celeste, plate, salad $18.00
Clover, bowl, vegetable; round, w/lid, 8" $85.00
Clover, plate, salad; 8" $16.00

Coralbel, bowl, soup $25.00
Coralbel, cup & saucer $24.00
Coralbel, plate, bread & butter $15.00
Coralbel, plate, salad $16.00
Countess, platter, lg $55.00
Gardinia, plate, dinner $25.00
Governor Clinton, cup & saucer $38.00
Jefferson, bowl, rimmed soup $25.00
Jefferson, gravy boat $65.00
Jefferson, plate, 10" $28.00
Jefferson, platter, 14" $75.00
Lady Mary, plate, 9¾" $20.00
Lady Mary, platter, 8" $30.00
Lyric, bowl, fruit; sm $20.00
Lyric, cup & saucer $32.00
Madame Butterfly, plate, bread & butter $16.00
Meadow Breeze, cup & saucer $30.00
Meadow Breeze, sugar bowl, w/lid $55.00
Monticello, bowl, vegetable $56.00
Monticello, cake plate $48.00
Monticello, gravy boat $58.00
Orchard, plate, dinner $25.00
Orleans, creamer & sugar bowl $65.00
Orleans, platter, 12" $50.00
Rosalie, plate, 10" $30.00
Rose Marie, bowl, salad $18.00
Rose Marie, platter, 16" $76.00
Selma, cup & saucer $34.00
Selma, plate, salad $18.00
Sherwood, cup & saucer $36.00
Sherwood, platter, med size $48.00
Silhouette, plate, 10½" $30.00
Silhouette, plate, 8" $20.00
Stansbury, bowl, cream soup; w/underplate $30.00
Stansbury, cup & saucer $32.00
Stansbury, plate, salad; 8" $16.00
Suzanne, bowl, dessert; 7" $18.00
Suzanne, bowl, fruit; sm $22.00
Victoria, cup & saucer $36.00
Victoria, platter, 12x9" $70.00
Woodbine, bowl, 6½" $16.00
Woodbine, cup & saucer $20.00
Woodbine, plate, 8" $10.00

Telephones

Where better can the advancement of technology be demonstrated than by comparing the large wood and metal wall phones of the late 1870s to the very small plastic portables of today. We've listed a few of the older styles, but remember, the values we give you are retail. If you're buying to sell, you'll first need to examine them and try to determine how much refurbishing you'll need to do. Many times dealers who specialize in old telephones will pay only 25% to 35% of retail.

Novelty phones have been popular for the past fifteen years or so, and many of them are now being seen on the secondary market. Especially good are character- and advertising-related models.

AT&T, candlestick, 1915, EX.....................................**$125.00**
AT&T, Trimline, rotary dial, 1968, M **$10.00**
Automatic Electric, beige 3-slotted pay phone, 1950s, EX...**$150.00**
Cracraft, oak wall type, complete.............................**$225.00**
Kellogg, candlestick & box, no dial...........................**$145.00**
Kellogg Switchboard, Supply Signal Corps, US Army, in case...**$35.00**
Monarch, upright desk stand w/cast-iron base, 1904, EX.**$300.00**
Stromberg-Carlson, clear plastic desk type, 1930s, EX.**$35.00**
Stromberg-Carlson, intercom, Bakelite, black, EX **$65.00**
Swedish American, wood wall type, EX **$250.00**
Western Electric, #102, cradle type w/dial.................**$145.00**
Western Electric, #202, gold metal cradle type, 1931, EX...**$175.00**
Western Electric, #205, black variation, 1938, EX......**$115.00**

Western Electric, candlestick, 11½", EX, $115.00

Western Electric, non-dial cradle type, oval base........**$45.00**
Western Electric, space-saver wall type, no dial, 1920s..**$35.00**

Novelty

AC Spark Plug, push buttons in base, 10½", EX..........**$80.00**
Charlie the Tuna, MIB **$35.00**
Cigarette pack, opened Salem package, 5½", EX **$65.00**
Crayon, standing crayon form w/'Crayon Communicator' on label, marked Made by Tote, 1983 ....**$42.00**
Crest Toothpaste, Crest man on round base, dark blue w/speckles, 1980s, 11", NMIB **$40.00**
Gas pump, 1930s style, push buttons under base, EX ..**$65.00**
Ghostbusters, NMIB..**$60.00**
Keebler Elf, 1980s, NM **$80.00**
Kermit the Frog, reclining in chair w/foot cradling receiver, 11½", 1983 ....**$280.00**
Mickey Mouse, standing w/hand cradle, marked Disney & American Telecommunications, 14½", NM........**$280.00**
Pizza Inn's Pizza Baker, mustached man in white apron on round base, MIB **$90.00**
Popeye, seated vinyl figure on duffle bag w/keg of spinach on shoulder, 1982, EX **$80.00**

Poppin' Fresh, arms extended to hold receiver, plastic, 1980s, 14", M...**$125.00**
Punchy, comical figure for Hawaiian Punch, plastic, 1980s, 11", NM...**$155.00**
Raid Bug, push buttons in base, 9", NM **$100.00**
Ronald McDonald, plastic figure, 1985, 10", NM.........**$95.00**
Shoe Fashion Fone, lady's hig-heeled shoe, marked Columbia Telecommunications, 5¾", 1987, NM..............**$80.00**
Stars & Stripes, candlestick type, EX..........................**$40.00**
Tang Lips, round base, very scarce, EX+ **$200.00**
7-Up Can, push buttons in bottom of can, made by Enterprex, 6¼", EX..**$40.00**
7-Up Spot, standing on black checkered base, plastic, 1990, 12", M...**$55.00**

Televisions

If you're too young to remember what the very early TV sets looked like, screens were very small. Some measured only 7" — a few even less. In 1938 a miniature unit designed to be held in the hand was on display in London. It had an earphone to amplify the sound, and the screen was a tiny 2" square. By the late forties, luxurious home entertainment consoles were available, complete with glide-out turntables, hidden radios mounted on fold-out doors, and a big 10" 'direct view' screen, all for only $499.95.

Today pre-WWII TVs sometimes sell for as much as $4,000.00. Unusual cabinet models from the forties may go as high as $300.00. Generally, any kind of vintage TV with a screen less than 14" is very collectible. Supply, demand, and of course, condition are the most important price-assessing factors. Our values are given for sets in fine condition and in working order.

If you'd like to see photos of these and many more fascinating early TVs (and learn what they're worth as well), we recommend *Classic TVs, Pre-War Through 1950s,* by Scott Wood, and *Poster's Radio & Television Price Guide, 1920-1990*, by Harry Poster.

Admiral, 1949, #20X136, wood table top w/12" screen centered above 4 knobs, $100.00

Admiral, 1948, #17T12, mahogany Bakelite w/7" screen left of grille & knobs **$150.00**

Admiral, 1948, #19A11, black Bakelite tabletop, w/7" screen at left of waffled grille & knobs **$150.00**

Admiral, 1949, wood console, upright w/10" screen above knobs & cloth-covered speaker w/wooden X design **$75.00**

Arvin, 1950, #4080T, metal table top w/mahogany front, 8" screen flanked by 2 knobs at bottom..................**$150.00**

General Electric, 1949, #10T1, black Bakelite table top w/shouldered top, 10" screen above grille flanked by 4 knobs **$10.00**

General Electric, 1949, #811, wood console w/10" screen above 4 knobs & cloth-covered grille under diamond design **$125.00**

Motorola, 1949, #V773, table-top leatherette, round 7" screen at right of louvered grille w/knobs below **$150.00**

Motorola, 1950, #7VT2, brown Bakelite table top, round 7" screen at right of cloth-covered grille, knobs below **$125.00**

Motorola, 1951, light wood footed console w/17" screen above 2 knobs & cloth-covered grille **$150.00**

Motorola, 1958, #17T32BZ, metal portable, 17" screen w/side knobs..**$75.00**

National, 1949, #TV7M, metal table top w/7" screen flanked by rectangular grilles, knobs below, square corners **$200.00**

Philco, 1948, #48-1001, walnut table top w/10" screen at left of bar grille, knobs below, curved top................**$125.00**

Philco, 1949, #49-702, mahogany table top w/7" screen above 4 knobs on bar grille, curved top.............**$225.00**

Philco, 1950, #50-T-702, Bakelite table top w/7" screen above knobs & dial on horizontal bar grille **$250.00**

Philco, 1950, #50-T1632, wood footed console w/16" screen above 4 knobs & cloth-covered grille w/metal diamond design **$50.00**

Philco, 1960, #H-2010 Safari, 1st transistor w/2" screen, side knobs, leather case w/swing handle **$150.00**

Philco, 1960, #10L60 Predicta Series, wood w/light-colored rectangular base w/horizontal ribbing, 21" screen, top knobs...**$150.00**

Sony, 1961, #8-301W, transistor portable w/top handle, 8" screen, knobs on top...**$125.00**

Stromberg Carlson, 1958, #TC-10H, Manhattan wood portable w/10" round screen at left of knobs & dial, rounded corners...**$125.00**

Zenith, 1948, #28T925E Biltmore, blond wood table top w/10" round screen flanked by knobs & metal decoration below **$175.00**

Zenith, 1950, #24H21, wood footed console w/19" round screen above knobs & cloth-covered grille w/diamond design **$175.00**

Thimbles

Collectors can give you several reasons for their fascination with these small basic tools of needlework. First, many are very beautiful — tiny works of art in their own right. Enameling, engraving, and embossing are seen on thimbles made of metals such as gold, silver, brass, and pewter; and there are china thimbles that have been hand painted. Many were made as souvenirs or as keepsake gifts to mark a special occasion. In the 19th century when social functions for ladies often revolved around their needlework projects, a fine, fancy thimble was a status symbol.

Some collectors are intrigued by the inscriptions they find. Many suggest a glimpse into a thimble's history. For instance, 'Mother, 12-25-01' inside a lovely gold thimble conveys a scene around a turn-of-the-century Christmas tree and a loving child presenting a special gift to a cherished parent.

Others simply like the older thimbles because to them they evoke a bit of nostalgia for a bygone era. But new thimbles are collectible as well. Bone china thimbles from England commemorating Charles' and Diana's marriage, Olympiad XXIII done in blue and white Jasperware by Wedgwood, hand-decorated examples with a 'Christmas 1982' message, and Norman Rockwell thimbles by Gorham are just a few examples of those that are 'new' yet very collectible.

If you'd like to read more about them and see hundreds shown in large, full-color photographs, we recommend *Antique and Collectible Thimbles and Accessories* by Averil Mathis.

RCA, 1954, #CT 100, footed wood console color model, 15" screen above knobs & cloth-covered grille under wood bar design, $600.00

Brass w/abalone inlaid floral design, $12.00

Brass, applied butterfly, unmarked..............................$15.00
Brass, bells & holly on band, unmarked.....................$25.00
Brass, Greek key design on band, unmarked.............$18.00
Brass, stars in hexagons on band, Austria...................$15.00
Brogan, Quaker type, gold w/plain band marked USA .$140.00
Brogan, sterling silver w/fleur-de-lis on band.............$40.00
China, hand-painted hummingbirds & flowers, England.$12.50
China, hand-painted roses, gold trim, unmarked $15.00
Eleanor Brand, sterling silver w/pierced design, scalloped
    edge, marked ECB $30.00
Gabler, sterling silver w/bee, birds & flowers on band, 8-
    point star mark, Germany.......................................$56.00
Glass, hand-painted butterfly, scalloped edge, unmarked.$15.00
Glass, hand-painted flowers, scalloped edge, unmarked .$12.50
Goldsmith-Stern, sterling silver w/basket-weave design on
    band, marked GSC..$30.00
Goldsmith-Stern, sterling silver w/fancy scrolls on gold
    band, marked GSC..$50.00
Goldsmith-Stern, sterling silver w/paneled band, marked
    GSC $30.00
H Muhr's Sons, sterling silver w/rope design below plain
    band, crown mark...$30.00
Ketcham & McDougall, sterling silver w/diamond-
    shaped knurling, paneled band w/scroll design,
    marked KMD $42.00
Ketcham & McDougall, sterling silver w/embossed cherubs
    on band, marked KMD...$135.00
Ketcham & McDougall, sterling silver w/palmated design on
    band, marked KMD $32.00
Metal, diamond-shaped knurling, plain band, Poland...$6.50
Nicholas Gish, pewter merry-go-round figural $20.00
Simons Brothers, sterling silver w/floral design on band,
    marked USA $25.00
Simons Brothers, sterling silver w/flower & scroll design on
    gold band, Simons shield mark.............................$50.00
Simons Brothers, sterling silver w/geometric design below
    plain band, marked USA $30.00
Simons Brothers, sterling silver w/Mother lettered in script
    on band, Simons shield mark..................................$40.00
Sterling silver, beading below plain band, unmarked.$28.00
Sterling silver, embossed image of Mt Vernon,
    unmarked..$40.00

**Sterling silver, filigree
design, unmarked,
Portugal, $38.00**

Sterling silver, enameled scenic design on band, Ger-
    many..$45.00
Sterling silver, various buildings on band, unmarked .$35.00
Stern Brothers, sterling silver w/allover knurling, anchor
    mark...$35.00
Webster Co, sterling silver w/paneled band, marked W
    Co..$35.00
10k Gold, scenic design on band, unmarked $100.00
14k Gold, scenic design on band, unmarked $125.00

Tiffin Glass

This company was originally founded in 1887 in Tiffin,
Ohio, and later became one of several that was known as
the U.S. Glass Company. U.S. Glass closed in the early sixties, and the plant reopened in 1963 under the title of the
Tiffin Art Glass Company.

They have made many lovely lines of tableware and
decorative items, but they are probably most famous for
their black satin glass which was produced in the twenties.

Byzantine, cordial $35.00
Byzantine, plate, 10½" $35.00
Cadena, bowl, grapefruit; footed $20.00
Cadena, bowl, pickle; 10"...$12.50
Cadena, champagne, 6½" $17.00
Cadena, cream soup $20.00

Cadena, creamer, footed, pink or yellow, $25.00

Cadena, finger bowl, footed, yellow $23.00
Camelot, goblet, water...$10.00
Cerice, cocktail...$22.00
Cerice, creamer, footed $25.00
Cerice, sugar bowl $25.00
Cerice, sundae, #071..$18.00
Cerice, tumbler, juice; footed, #071 ....$18.00
Chardonnay, champagne...$17.00
Cherokee Rose, cake plate, center handle, 12½"........$35.00
Cherokee Rose, centerpiece bowl, 13" $65.00
Cherokee Rose, cordial, 1-oz $55.00

Cherokee Rose, mayonnaise, w/ladle & liner $45.00
Cherokee Rose, relish, 3-part, 6½" $25.00
Cherokee Rose, vase, bud; 6" $25.00
Classic, cocktail $35.00

Classic, creamer & sugar bowl, crystal, each, $35.00

Classic, parfait $45.00
Classic, plate, 7½" $18.00
Classic, sherbet, pink $30.00
Classic Shawl Dancer, tumbler, iced tea; cone shape...$20.00
Eternally Yours, goblet, water..$15.00
Eternally Yours, wine $15.00
Flanders, bonbon, 2 handles, pink $40.00
Flanders, candlsticks, pink, pr $120.00
Flanders, celery dish, 11" $25.00
Flanders, cheese & crackers, pink $85.00
Flanders, creamer, pink...$100.00
Flanders, decanter..$150.00
Flanders, finger bowl, w/liner...$17.00
Flanders, nut cup, blown, footed.....................................$30.00
Flanders, oil bottle, w/stopper, yellow $175.00
Flanders, whiskey $32.00
Flying Nun, parfait $38.00
Fontaine, champagne, green..$30.00
Fontaine, parfait, Twilight w/crystal stem $45.00
Fontaine, tumbler, ice tea; Twilight, footed $48.00
Fuchsia, ashtray, w/cigarette rest, 2¼x3¾"....................$20.00
Fuchsia, bell, 6" $65.00
Fuchsia, bowl, salad; deep, #5902, 9¾".........................$50.00
Fuchsia, creamer, individual; #5831, 2⅞" $35.00
Fuchsia, pitcher, w/lid, #194...$325.00
Fuchsia, tumbler, water; #15083, 9-oz, 5¼"...................$25.00
Fuchsia, vase, bud; #14185, 8¼" $35.00
Heirloom, goblet, water...$10.00
Huntington, sherbet, tall..$12.00
Julia, claret, amber, 6⅛"..$35.00
Julia, plate, amber, 10" $20.00
June Night, cocktail, #17392...$27.00
June Night, cordial, #17403 ....$45.00
June Night, goblet, water; #17392...................................$24.00
Kilarney, cornucopia, 11½" $225.00
La Fleure, plate, yellow, 7¼" $15.00
La Fleure, saucer, yellow $5.00
Manchester, goblet, water $22.00
Manchester, wine $25.00
Mansard, champagne..$12.00
Persian Night, cordial, #17403..$45.00

Persian Pheasant, cordial...$45.00
Persian Pheasant, sherry, wide mouth.............................$25.00
Princess, vase, 4" $22.50
Rambler Rose, cocktail, pink, #188.................................$40.00
Riveria, wine..$24.00
Rosalind, candlesticks, yellow or brown, pr $90.00
Rosalind, cup & saucer, blown, yellow $18.00
Roselyn, plate, yellow, 10½" $35.00
Swedish Modern, vase, blown, #17350, 11½" $55.00
Sylvan, comport, cheese; green $15.00
Wistaria, cordial, #17477...$45.00
Wistaria, goblet, water; #17394 ....$25.00

Tobacco Collectibles

Until lately, the tobacco industry spent staggering sums on advertising their products, and scores of retail companies turned out many types of smoking accessories such as pipes, humidors, lighters, and ashtrays. Even though the smoking habit isn't particularly popular nowadays, collecting tobacco-related memorabilia is!

See also Ashtrays; Cigarette Lighters; Labels.

Belt buckle, Red Man Tobacco, EX $15.00
Cigar box, Lucky Lindy & Spirit of St Louis airplane on lid, repaired, EX $200.00
Cigar box, Winnie Winkle portrait on inside lid, EX.$225.00
Cigar cutter, Browns Mule Tobacco, cast-iron lever type w/embossed lettering, w/original wooden box, 7½x20x5½", NM $100.00
Cigar cutter, Crane's Havanna Smokers, paper labels under glass dome w/key-wind cutter, 4½x7x8¼", VG ..$175.00

Cigar cutter & match vendor, cast-iron counter-top cutter w/original plating, 8x6x7", VG, $400.00

Cigar holder, banded agate, w/velvet-lined leather box, M...$45.00
Cigar tin, Intermission Little Cigars, lettering & logo on red, white & blue shaded colors, flat w/square corners, EX+ $25.00
Cigar tin, Prime Puff Little Cigars, cream lettering on blue, flat w/square corners, EX+ $40.00

Cigarette carton, Barking Dog Cigarettes, w/bulldog logo & lettering on neutral background, empty, EX+.......**$30.00**

Cigar tin, Sunset Trail, 5½x6x4", VG, $250.00; Cigar tin, Black Fox, round canister type, 5¼" dia, G, $225.00

Cigarette carton, Philip Morris, bellboy yelling Call for Philip Morris America's Finest Cigarette, EX....................**$45.00**

Cigarette holder, amber Bakelite, unused...................**$30.00**

Cigarette holder, chrome ball-shaped cup on 2-step square base, marked Chase, 2½"......................................**$45.00**

Cigarette holder, meerschaum, dragon design.............**$35.00**

Cigarette papers, Blanca, cardboard pack...................**$12.00**

Cigarette papers, Dukes Mixture, blue background **$8.00**

Cigarette papers, Half & Half, Burley & Bright.............**$6.00**

Cigarette papers, Hi-Plane, shows single-engine plane.**$12.00**

Cigarette papers, White Seal **$10.00**

Cigarette papers, Yum-Yum **$50.00**

Cigarette tin, flat (20), Carmen Cigarettes, pictures half-length portrait of lady w/fancy border, VG+ **$40.00**

Cigarette tin, flat (50), Davros Cigarettes, VG+ **$70.00**

Cigarette tin, flat (50), Kool Mild Menthol Cigarettes lettered on cream, penguin in lower right corner, VG **$100.00**

Cigarette tin, Hignett's Golden Butterfly, 100 Gold Tipped Magnums Cigarettes, embossed, 2x4x7½", VG ...**$100.00**

Dispenser, Zig-Zag Cigarette Papers, image of hands rolling cigarette above Easy To Roll Your Own..., metal, 6", EX...**$65.00**

Display, Kool Cigarettes, cardboard carton w/light green, white & black graphics, EX.....................................**$60.00**

Display, the Bull Durham bull figure on base w/embossed lettering, For Three Generations..., 17¾x22x7½", EX...**$1,600.00**

Display, Three Castles Cigarettes, wood & cardboard, Three Castles lettered on marquee, product box on base, 11x10", EX...**$50.00**

Display rack for pipes, Yellow Bole Pipes, round metal 2-tiered holders w/ad panels, round base, 18", EX+ **$135.00**

Door push, The Old Reliable lettered above 'Peg Top' cigar w/5¢ below, brown on cream, vertical rectangle, 12½x4", EX..**$135.00**

Game, Marlboro, poker dice in leather pouch, MIB....**$35.00**

Humidor, figural hen, multicolored painted pottery, 10"...**$80.00**

Humidor, La Plaina Cigars, brass, EX **$75.00**

Humidor, Mi Lola Cigar, glass w/embossed lettering, round w/flat knob lid, NM **$30.00**

Lunch pail, George Washington Cut Plug, red, white & dark blue w/oval portrait, rectangular w/wood handle, lg, EX+ **$70.00**

Lunch pail, George Washington Cut Plug, red, white & light blue w/portrait, rectangular w/wire handle, sm, VG+ **$50.00**

Lunch pail, Just Suits, red w/BL (Buchanan & Lyall) seal & gold lettering, rectangular w/wire handle, VG+ ...**$45.00**

Lunch pail, Winner Cut Plug Tobacco, early race car scene w/lettering, wire handle, 4x8x5¼", VG, $200.00

Pipe, blown-glass bowl & stem, hand-painted floral design..**$50.00**

Pipe, burled wood bowl & reservoir, stem w/nickle-plated trim, Czechoslovakia, EX....................................**$45.00**

Pipe, clay, General Pershing in cape forms bowl, England, 7", EX...**$15.00**

Pipe, meerschaum, horn stem, Bakelite mouthpiece, 8½", EX...**$75.00**

Pipe, meerschaum, horses in relief against flower, 8", EX...**$115.00**

Pipe stand, bronze, pipe rest leaning on back of nude figure in diving pose on 2-step rectangular base **$150.00**

Pocket tin, flat, Lucky Strike, red seal on green w/gold trim, rectangular w/square corners, 2½x4½", EX+.........**$65.00**

Pocket tin, flat, Lucky Strike, red seal on green w/gold trim, rectangular w/rounded corners, 2½x4½", EX........**$55.00**

Pocket tin, flat, Quill Smoking Tobacco, gold lettering & trim on blue, rectangular w/square corners, 2½x4½", EX+ **$155.00**

Pocket tin, flat, Three States Mixture, Kentucky, Virginia, & Louisiana lettered on wavy bands, slip lid, oval, EX+ **$400.00**

Pocket tin, upright, American Granulated Cut Plug, product name & ornate graphics on green background, VG.**$180.00**

Pocket tin, upright, Bagley's Old Colony Mixture Smoking Tobacco, white w/red oval bust portrait of a woman, G **$80.00**

Pocket tin, upright, Buckingham Tobacco, ornate graphics, slip lid, NM..**$165.00**

Pocket tin, upright, Bull Dog Cut Plug Tobacco, bulldog in oval w/product name above & below, slip lid, G ..**$90.00**

Pocket tins, upright, Guide Pipe & Cigarette Tobacco, features outdoorsman smoking pipe, VG, $140.00; Honey Moon Rum-Flavored Smoking Tobacco, features pipe & cigarette in oval inset, VG, $200.00

Pocket tin, upright, Hi-Plane Smooth Cut Tobacco, features white 2-engine plane on red, EX+ **$50.00**

Pocket tin, upright, Model Extra Quality Smoking Tobacco, red w/mustached man smoking pipe, NM............**$60.00**

Pocket tin, upright, Union Leader Smoking Tobacco, red w/Uncle Sam (without pipe) portrait in white oval, EX+ **$135.00**

Pocket tin, upright (short), Bagdad Smoking Short Cut Pipe Tobacco, bearded man wearing fez in profile on blue, EX+ **$125.00**

Pocket tin, upright (short), Buckhorn & Cigarette Case lettered above & below head of buck on red background, EX+ **$75.00**

Pocket tin, upright (short), Eve Cube Cut, features Eve at the apple tree w/lettering, Globe Tobacco Co, VG+..**$150.00**

Punchboard, features Hiram's General Store w/various brands of cigarettes & 5¢ cigars, 1 hole punched, VG **$70.00**

Punchboard, Lucky Strike, Chesterfield & Camel packs featured, Spend Your Pennies Here & lady's portrait above, unpunched **$45.00**

Ruler, Phillip Morris Cigarettes, thin plastic w/colorful image of bellboy, 1940s, 6" scale, 2x6¼", NM.................**$22.00**

Sign, Chesterfield Regular & King-Size Cigarettes, 2-sided tin flange, Buy Here on red oval above unopened pack, EX+ **$35.00**

Sign, Heart of Havana Harvester 5¢ Cigar, oval tin hanger w/rolled rim featuring lady's head in heart shape, 13x9", EX **$140.00**

Sign, Imperial Club 5cts Cigars, embossed painted tin, full cigar box at right of lettering, banded edge, 10x13½", VG..**$60.00**

Sign, Philip Morris, bellboy w/oversized pack of cigarettes, Buy 'em Here!, Call For King Size..., tin, 14x12", NM........**$75.00**

Sign, Raleigh Cigarettes, Now At Popular Prices above product name & open pack, Save B&W Coupons below, tin, 14x20", NM **$65.00**

Sign, Missing Miss Cigar, tin w/curled corners, features stock image of pretty girl, 14½x14½", VG+, $325.00

Store bin, Sure Shot Chewing Tobacco, metal, features Indian w/pulled bow, yellow, red & blue, 7½x15x10", VG, $550.00

Store bin, Sweet Cuba Fine Cut Tobacco, metal w/slanted lid, encircled girl in profile on curved front, 8x8x10", VG.**$95.00**

Store bin, Sweet Mist Tobacco, oval image of children at fountain, product name above & below, square slip lid, VG..**$165.00**

Store jar, La Palina Cigars, round paneled glass jar w/embossed lettering, product name on black wood base, 8", VG..**$120.00**

Thermometer, Camel Cigarettes, embossed painted tin, open pack w/Camels Sold Here, Have A Real Cigarette, 14x6", VG+..**$40.00**

Thermometer, Fatima Cigarettes, yellow porcelain w/black, red & white, arched top & straight bottom, 27½x7", EX+ **$200.00**

Thermometer, Mail Pouch Tobacco, Treat Yourself To The Best, white on dark blue porcelain, square corners, 72x18", G **$275.00**

Thermometer, Winston Cigarettes, The Taste Is Tops flanked by open packs of cigarettes, Winston arched above, 9" dia, NM **$35.00**

Tip tray, Opia Cigar, veiled lady in crescent moon surrounded by poppies & stars, product name on rim, 4¼" dia, EX..**$100.00**

Tip tray, Pippins 5¢ Cigar, apple graphics w/tab handle, 5⅜", VG+ **$230.00**

Tobacco tag, Best Navy, wavy banner shape.................**$5.00**

Tobacco tag, Big Foot...**$60.00**

Tobacco tag, Bookers KY Burley, shaped like tobacco leaf...**$10.00**

Tobacco tag, Golden Slipper, shape like low-heeled shoe **$10.00**

Tobacco tag, Jack the Ripper **$25.00**

Tobacco tag, Log Barn, square w/diagonal corners **$60.00**

Tobacco tag, Old Medford, shaped like wooden barrel..**$20.00**

Tobacco tin, Dutch Masters, Dutchmen seated around table, product name on band above, canister w/slip lid, 6x5" dia, EX **$30.00**

Tobacco tin, Forest & Stream Pipe Tobacco, black & cream on red, canister w/gold screw lid, 4", EX+............**$50.00**

Tobacco tin, Full Dress Pipe & Cigarette Tobacco, cream on gold, shows man in tuxedo, canister w/slip lid, 6x5", EX+ **$330.00**

Tobacco tin, Mayo's Cut Plug, dark blue paper label w/gold lettering, rectangular w/rounded corners, slip lid, 4x6", EX+ **$75.00**

Tobacco tin, Penn's Tobacco, Penn's Spells Quality & quill pen tip on hinged lid, square w/round corners, 2½x6x6", G **$30.00**

Tobacco tin, Plow Boy, paper label w/farm boy sitting on plow reading & smoking, canister w/slip lid, 6x5" dia, VG **$50.00**

Tobacco tin, Prim Puff Mild Little Cigars, blue w/cream lettering & trim, square, flat, NM...............................**$45.00**

Tobacco tin, Sensation Cut Plug, gold lettering on dark blue w/gold, slip lid, rectangular w/rounded corners, 4x6", VG+ **$35.00**

Tobacco tin, Tuxedo Tobacco, Specially Prepared For Pipe & Cigarette, gold on green, canister w/slip lid, 6x4" dia, EX **$100.00**

Toothbrush Holders

These figural novelties have been made in the likenesses of many storybook personalities, and today all are very collectible, especially those representing popular Disney characters. Most are made of bisque and are decorated over the glaze. Condition of the paint is an important consideration when trying to arrive at an evaluation.

Andy Gump & Min, standing arm in arm, painted bisque, marked FAS, Japan, 4x3¼" **$85.00**

Bellhop, lustre glaze, head cocked to side, toothbrushes stored in pants pockets, Japan, 6¾"......................**$60.00**

Bonzo-type, green w/red features, glossy finish, 5½", minimum value **$100.00**

Boy in big hat riding spotted elephant, Japan, 6"........**$50.00**

Calico dog, hole for toothbrushes in top of head, Japan, 4" **$5.00**

Cowboy, arms folded, cactus by side, toothbrushes stored in holsters, Japan, 5" **$65.00**

Doc, figural, Doc Says Brush Your Teeth, EX.............**$70.00**

Donald Duck, tipping his hat, bisque, multicolored, marked WED, prewar Japan, 5x3", NM...........................**$175.00**

Dutch girl beside barrel, multicolored w/matte finish, Japan, 2½" **$12.50**

Elephant seated on base, blue, yellow & orange lustre, tube tray, Japan, 5½" **$55.00**

Fiddler Pig, Genuine Walt Disney Copyright, made for British market, 4", EX...**$45.00**

Froggy singing & strumming banjo, legs wide apart, Japan, 6" **$50.00**

Giraffe, tan & white glossy finish, tube tray, Japan, 6".**$55.00**

Kissing Dutch couple, blue Delft-like glossy finish, tube tray, Japan, 6" **$55.00**

Kissing Dutch couple, red, white & blue, Japan, 6" **$55.00**

Little Orphan Annie & Sandy, standing, painted bisque, prewar Japan, 4x2", NM...**$95.00**

Lone Ranger, chalkware, 1940s, NM...........................**$85.00**

Man in black top hat, black jacket, red pants, white dog w/brown spots beside him, Japan, 5½".................**$60.00**

Mickey, Minnie & Pluto, sitting on couch, painted bisque, prewar Japan, 4x4½", M **$250.00**

Moon Mullins & Kayo, painted bisque, early, 4", EX ..**$85.00**

Penguin, w/tube tray, Japan, 5½" **$60.00**

Rabbit w/1 lopped ear standing between upright tubes for brushes, Japan, 6½"..**$60.00**

Scottie dogs, seated, black & yellow, inscribed Diamond Cleaners..., 5¼" **$75.00**

Skippy, ceramic, 5½", NM **$110.00**

Snow White, standing, porcelain, Great Britain, 6", NM **$200.00**

Soldier boy, black hat & pants, red jacket, Japan, 6" ..**$50.00**

Teacher w/book & cane, brown, blue & black glossy finish, Japan, 5½"...**$55.00**

Three Little Pigs, center pig at brick piano, painted bisque, prewar Japan, 4x3½", M **$140.00**

Two Scotty dogs, 1 red, 1 black, on base before yellow holder, Japan, 5" **$80.00**

Toothpick Holders

These have long been collected, so you may not find them often, but occasionally the old pressed glass toothpick holders turn up at flea markets and co-ops. There are lots of reproductions around, though, so beware. Unless you're sure of what you're doing, ask the dealer. Most are very honest. Besides pressed, cut and art glass, they've also been made in china, bisque and various metals.

Atlas, etched design...**$30.00**

Beatty Honeycomb, blue opalescent...........................**$60.00**

Bull's-Eye & Fan, green **$42.00**

Daisy & Button, vaseline, flared scalloped top...........**$30.00**

Fine-Cut, blue hat shape **$30.00**

Fleur-de-Lis shape...**$25.00**

Heisey, custard, gold-outlined winged scroll pattern, scalloped rim, $195.00

King's Crown	$20.00
Lacy Medallion, green w/gold (has been reproduced)	$35.00
National's Eureka	$28.00
Paneled Grape	$45.00
Simplicity Scroll, gold tint	$20.00
Trophy, emerald green	$22.00
US Rib, emerald green	$35.00

Toys

Toy collecting has long been an area of very strong activity, but over the past decade it has really expanded. Many of the larger auction galleries have cataloged toy auctions, and it isn't uncommon for scarce 19th-century toys in good condition go for $5,000.00 to $10,000.00 and up. Toy shows are popular, and there are clubs, newsletters, and magazines that cater only to the needs and wants of toy collectors. Though once buyers ignored toys less than thirty years old, in more recent years, even some toys from the eighties are sought after.

Condition has more bearing on the value of a toy than any other factor. A used toy in good condition with no major flaws will still be worth about half (in some cases much less) than one in mint (like new) condition. Those mint and in their original boxes will be worth considerably more than the same toy without its box.

There are many good toy guides on the market today including: *Teddy Bears and Steiff Animals* by Margaret Fox Mandel; *Toys, Antique and Collectible*, and *Character Toys and Collectibles*, both by David Longest; *Modern Toys, American Toys, 1930 to 1980,* by Linda Baker; *Collecting Toys, Collecting Toy Trains* and *Collecting Toy Soldiers*, all by Richard O'Brien; *Toys of the Sixties* by Bill Bruegman; *Collector's Guide to Tootsietoys* by David E. Richter, and *Schroeder's Collectible Toys, Antique to Modern* (Collector Books).

See also Action Figures; Barbie and Her Friends; Breyer Horses; Bubble Bath Containers; Character Collectibles; Disney Collectibles; Fast Food Toys and Figurines; Fisher-Price; GI Joe; Halloween Costumes; Hartland; Liddle Kiddles; Model Kits; Paper Dolls; Star Trek; Star Wars; Steiff Animals; Trolls.

Action Figures and Accessories

Back in 1964, Barbie dolls were sweeping the feminine side of the toy market by storm. Hasbro took a risky step in an attempt to capture the interest of the male segment of the population. Their answer to the Barbie craze was GI Joe. Since no self-respecting boy would admit to playing with dolls, Hasbro called their boy dolls 'action figures,' and to the surprise of many, they were phenomenally successful. Today action figures generate just as much enthusiasm among toy collectors as they ever did among little boys.

Action figures are simply dolls with poseable bodies. The original GI Joes were 12" tall, but several other sizes were made over the years, too. Some are 8" to 9", others 6", and 3¾" figures have been favored in recent years. GI Joe was introduced in the 3¾" size in the '80s and proved to be unprecedented in action figure sales. (See also GI Joe.)

In addition to the figures themselves, each company added a full line of accessories such as clothing, vehicles, play sets, weapons, etc. — all are avidly collected. Be aware of condition! Original packaging is extremely important. In fact, when it comes to the recent issues, loose, played-with examples are seldom worth more than a few dollars.

Action Jackson, figure, white w/black hair & beard, complete, Mego, 1974, 8", MIB, $25.00

A-Team, Command Chopper, M	$20.00
A-Team, figure, Cobra, MOC	$5.00

A-Team, figures, Bad Guys, Galoob, 1984, 3¾", M set of 4 ....**$25.00**

A-Team, figures, Hannibal, Face or Murdock, 6½", M, each...**$14.00**

Action Jackson, outfit, Jungle Safari, original box, 1974, EX **$8.00**

Action Jackson, outfit, Secret Agent, original box, 1974, EX **$8.00**

Action Jackson, outfit, Surf & Scuba, for 8" figure, Mego, 1971, MIB **$13.00**

Action Jackson, Rescue Pack, Mego, MIB **$15.00**

Addams Family, figure, Gomez, Morticia, Pugsley, Lurch, Grandpa or Uncle Fester, Playmates, 1992, MIB, each...**$10.00**

Alien, figure, Atax, Kenner, MIP **$15.00**

Alien, figure, Bull Allen, Kenner, MIP **$8.00**

Alien, figure, Corporal Hicks, Kenner, 1993, MOC.....**$15.00**

Alien, figure, Scorpion, Kenner, MIP **$8.00**

Alien, Space Marine Stinger XT-37, Kenner, M **$14.00**

Antlar, figure, vinyl, Bandai, MIP..............................**$10.00**

Aquaman, figure, Mego, 8", M **$30.00**

Arachnophobia, figure, Big Bob Spider, Remco, 1990, MOC **$15.00**

Baragon, figure, Bandai, vinyl, MIP...........................**$20.00**

Batman, Batcave, Toy Biz, MIB **$35.00**

Batman, Batcycle, Kenner, MIP....................................**$8.00**

Batman, Dark Knight Sonic Neutralizer, Kenner, MIB..**$35.00**

Batman, figure, Keaton face, 1st issue, Toy Biz, 1989, MOC...**$25.00**

Batman, figure, Riddler w/Question Mark Launcher, #64700, Kenner, 1993, M **$8.00**

Batman, figure, w/cape, Applause, 1991, 11½", EX.....**$18.00**

Batman, Stunt Cycle, 1974, MOC **$65.00**

Batman Returns, figure, Catwoman, Kenner, MOC **$10.00**

Battlestar Galactica, Cylon Raider, Mattel, missing pilot, 12 firing missiles..**$20.00**

Battlestar Galactica, figure, Adama, Mattel, 1978, 4", M on NM card..**$27.00**

Battlestar Galactica, figure, Ovion, Mattel, 1978, MOC..**$18.00**

Battlestar Galactica, Medic Kit, Mattel, MOC...............**$10.00**

Beatlejuice, figure, Old Buzzard, Kenner, MIP **$15.00**

Beetlejuice, Gross-Out Meter, Kenner, MIP.................**$10.00**

Beetlejuice, Vanishing Vault, Kenner, MIP **$8.00**

Big Jim, All-Terrain Vehicle, Space series, MIB...........**$40.00**

Big Jim, Camper Gear, #8868, 1970s, MOC...................**$7.50**

Big Jim, figure, basic version, original red shorts, no package, EX...**$16.00**

Big Jim, Gyrocopter, Big Jim/004 Secret Agent series, MIB **$18.00**

Big Jim, outfit, Attack Vehicle Driver, MIB.................**$12.00**

Big Jim, play set, Devil River Trip, 1970s, MIB...........**$35.00**

Bionic Woman, outfit, Floral Delight, 1970s, MOC........**$6.00**

Blackstar, figure, w/laser light action, Galoob, 1983, MOC...**$10.00**

Blackstar, spaceship, Galoob, 1983, MIB **$20.00**

Bravestar, figure, Skull Walker, MIB...........................**$8.00**

Buck Rogers, figure, Ardella, Mego, 1979, 3¾", MOC .**$15.00**

Buck Rogers, figure, Tigerman, Mego, 1979, 3¾", M.....**$5.00**

Buck Rogers, figures, Draco, Mego, 1979, 3¾", MOC, $20.00; Killer Kane, Mego, 1979, 3¾", MOC, $20.00

Buck Rogers, figure, Twili, Mego, 1979, 3¾", MOC.......**$4.00**

Captain Action, outfit, Steve Canyon jumpsuit, Ideal, EX.**$15.00**

Captain Planet, figure, Applause, 12", MIP..................**$15.00**

Captain Planet, figure, Argos Bleak, MOC **$20.00**

Captain Planet, figure, Sly Sludge, MOC **$20.00**

Captain Planet, Toxic Dump, MIB **$15.00**

Captain Power, Communication Station, Mattel, 1987, MIB.**$16.00**

Captain Power, figure, Corporal Pilot Chase, 1987, 3¾", MOC...**$12.00**

Chuck Norris, figure, in any of 7 outfits, MOC, each **$5.00**

Crash Dummies, figure, Skid the Kid, Tyco, MIP..........**$8.00**

Crash Dummies, figures, Vince & Larry, MOC, pr **$28.00**

Fighting Yank, figure, Mego, 1974, 12", MIB **$20.00**

Fighting Yank, outfit, Marine Dress #3367, MIB **$5.00**

Ghostbusters, Ecto 1A Ambulance, 1980s, MIB **$25.00**

Happy Days, figure, Fonzie, Mego, 1978, 8", MOC **$25.00**

Happy Days, Fonzie's Motorcycle, Mego, 1978, 8", MIB .**$50.00**

He-Man, Doomcopter, Mattel, M **$10.00**

He-Man, figure, Artilla, Mattel, 1990, MOC **$12.00**

He-Man, figure, Butthead, Mattel, 1990, M..................**$12.00**

He-Man, figure, w/mini-comic, Mattel, 1989, 5½", MOC.**$10.00**

He-Man, Terroclaw Vehicle, Mattel, 1989, M **$14.00**

Johnny Apollo, figures, Jane or Johnny, Marx, 1968, M, each..**$125.00**

Johnny West, figure, Jane, complete, Marx, M in VG box, $35.00

Major Matt Mason, figure, Mattel, 1969, MOC............**$135.00**

Major Matt Mason, figure, Sergeant Storm, w/helmet, Mattel, EX..**$55.00**

Major Matt Mason, Laser Rifle, G **$10.00**

Major Matt Mason, Space Sled, Mattel, EX **$10.00**

Major Matt Mason, Space Station, complete w/instructions, no box, Mattel, 1966-68, EX **$95.00**

Major Matt Mason, vehicle, Space Crawler, EX............**$30.00**

Man from UNCLE, TV Action Figure Apparel, complete, Gilbert, 1965, MIB, $35.00

Masters of the Universe, Attack Trak, MIB..................**$15.00**

Masters of the Universe, Dragon Walker, MIB.............**$15.00**

Masters of the Universe, figure, Scareglow, MOC........**$20.00**

Masters of the Universe, figure, Thunder Punch, MOC.**$15.00**

Masters of the Universe, Land Shark, MIB **$15.00**

Masters of the Universe, Masters Weapon Pak, MIB **$5.00**

Micronauts, figure, Pharoid Space Warrior, w/time chamber, Mego, 1977, MOC **$10.00**

Micronauts, figure, Time Traveler, 1976, 3¾", MOC....**$12.00**

Micronauts, Hydro Copter, MIB **$20.00**

One Million BC, figure, Mada, Mego, 1976, 8", M **$20.00**

One Million BC, figure, Orm, Mego, 1976, 8", MOC ...**$40.00**

One Million BC, figure, Tyrannosaurus Rex, Mego, MIB...**$100.00**

Planet of the Apes, figure, Soldier Ape, Bend 'n Flex, Mego, 5", M on VG card, $35.00

Planet of the Apes, figures, Dr Zaius, Zira or Cornelius, Mego, 8", MOC, each.......................................**$55.00**

Planet of the Apes, Treehouse, for 8" figures, complete, unused, Mego, 1967, NM....................................**$145.00**

Raiders of the Lost Ark, figure, Toht, Kenner, MIP......**$10.00**

Rambo, Combat Set, Largo, 1985, MOC **$15.00**

Rambo, figure, Coleco, 1986, 6", MOC **$10.00**

Rambo, Savage Strike Cycle, for 6" figure, Coleco, 1986, MIP **$10.00**

Robocop, figure, Nightfighter, Kenner, MIP................**$10.00**

Robocop, figure, Nitro, MOC...**$8.00**

Robocop, Robo 1 Vehicle, Kenner, MIP......................**$25.00**

Robotech, figure, Robotech Master, Matchbox, 1985, 3¾", MOC...**$5.00**

Six Million-Dollar Man, Bionic Transport & Repair Station, Kenner, 1975, sealed, MIB....................................**$50.00**

Six Million-Dollar Man, figure, Steve Austin, Kenner, 1975, 12½", MIB **$40.00**

Space 1999, figures, Dr Russell or Commander Koeig, Mattel, 1975, 9", MOC, each **$55.00**

Space 1999, Moon Base Alpha Control Room & Launch Monitor Center, for 9" figures, complete, Mattel, NMIB....**$40.00**

Spiderman, Energized Copter, 1978, MIB....................**$85.00**

Spiderman, figure, Toy Biz, MOC **$9.00**

Super Heroes, figure, Batman, Mego, 8", MOC...........**$30.00**

Super Heroes, figure, Incredible Hulk, Mego, 8", MOC..**$20.00**

Super Heroes, figure, Jor-el, Mego, 1979, 8", MOC **$15.00**

Super Heroes, figure, Lex Luther, Mego, 1979, 8", MOC.**$15.00**

Super Heroes, figures, Superman, Mego, 3¾", M, $12.00; Robin, Mego, 3½", M, $12.00

Super Heroes, figure, Superman, Mego, 1979, 8", MOC..**$25.00**

Super Heroes, figure, Wonder Woman, Mego, 1979, 8", MOC..**$80.00**

Super Powers, figure, Flash, Kenner, MOC.................**$10.00**

Super Powers, figure, Joker, w/mini comic, Kenner, 1984, M..**$40.00**

Super Powers, figure, Orion, Kenner, MOC................**$22.00**

Super Powers, figure, Para Demon, Kenner, MIP **$8.00**
Super Powers, figure, Tyr, Kenner, MOC **$70.00**
Super Powers, figure, Wonder Woman, Kenner, MOC .**$15.00**
Teenage Mutant Ninja Turtles, figure, Footsoldier, movie version, MOC **$15.00**
Teenage Mutant Ninja Turtles, figure, Krang, Playmates, 1989, MOC..**$12.00**
Teenage Mutant Ninja Turtles, figure, Mona Lisa, Playmates, MOC...**$8.00**
Teenage Mutant Ninja Turtles, figure, Wacky Action Mouser, MOC...**$15.00**
Teenage Mutant Ninja Turtles, Sludgemobile, MIB........**$5.00**
Terminator 2, figure, John Conner, Kenner, MOC......**$12.00**
Terminator 2, Mobile Assault Vehicle, Kenner, MIP **$12.00**
Toxic Crusaders, Apocalype Helicopter, MIB **$12.00**
Toxic Crusaders, figures, any of 7 characters, Playmates, 1991, MIP, each..**$10.00**
Toxic Crusaders, Toxic Surf Surfer Vehicle, MIB **$8.00**
Ultraman, figures, Gerukidon, Majaba or Bogun, MOC, each **$10.00**
Voltron, figure, Hagger the Witch, MOC **$6.00**
Voltron, figure, King Zarkon, MOC **$6.00**
Voltron, Skull Tank, MIB **$10.00**
Waltons, farmhouse playset, vinyl, complete, no box, Mego, 1975-76, M **$50.00**
Waltons, figures, John Boy & Mary Ellen, Mego, 1975-76, 8", MIB, pr..**$35.00**
World's Greatest Super Knights, castle playset, complete, Mego, 1975-76, EX+ **$90.00**
World's Greatest Super Knights, figure, Black Knight, unused, Mego, 1975-76, 8", MIB **$75.00**
World's Greatest Super Knights, figure, King Arthur, Mego, 1975-76, 8", MIB....................................**$75.00**
X-Force, figures, Cable, Gideon, Shatterstar or Warpath, Toy Biz, MOC, each **$15.00**
X-Men, figure, Gambit, Toy Biz, MOC **$15.00**
X-Men, figure, Storm, Toy Biz, MOC **$20.00**
X-Men, figure, Wolverine, 2nd edition, 1990, MOC.....**$12.00**
X-Men, Wolverine Stunt Cycle, 1991, MIB **$20.00**

Airplanes

It was well into the second decade of the 20th century before toy manufacturers tested the waters with areonautical toys. The first airplanes were basically bulky, inert replicas of early models. By the 1950s, though, Japanese manufacturers were designing detailed, battery-operated airplanes that could taxi and turn, make whirring motor noises, and had lights that actually worked.

Acorn, American Airlines DC-3, silver & red w/plastic props, friction, 13x14", NM in VG box **$95.00**
Bachmann, B-58 Hustler, #8365, 1/260 scale, VG........**$12.00**
Bachmann, F-104 Starfighter, #8304:69, 1/210 scale, NMIB.**$10.00**
Bandai, American Airlines DC-7, lithographed tin, friction, 9x11" wingspan, EX+..**$175.00**
Boycraft, Graf Zeppelin, painted steel w/silver finish, metal wheels, 1931, 25" **$275.00**

G-A MYT, Passenger Plane, twin-engine, slight wear & scuffs, 18x20", EX..**$300.00**
Girard, airplane w/pilot, tin w/bull's-eye wing decals, wind-up, 12½" **$325.00**
Ideal, Yankee Scout Airplane, gold, removable 19½" wing, G- **$200.00**
Japan, TWA Jetliner, friction, 1970s, 14"....................**$135.00**
Japan (TT), Pan Am 747 Jet, red, white & blue, w/original box, 15x13", NM **$75.00**
Marx, Aeroplane (Bomber), blue & silver lithographed tin, 2 props, balloon tires, NM in G box......................**$400.00**
Mecanno, Seaplane, w/pilot, double-winged, 20" wingspan, VG+..**$300.00**
Mettoy, Super Skyliner, red & yellow lithographed tin w/blue trim, wind-up motor turns props & wheels, 16¾", VG..**$325.00**
Pyro Plastics, F-7U Cutlass, 1960s **$10.00**
Renwal, Bomber plane, #777, plastic w/wing decals, props spin, 1950s, NM in EX box................................**$125.00**
Renwal, P-38 Lightning Fighter, plastic, manually spinning props, marked Lockheed, 1950s, 5x7", NM in G+ box **$90.00**
Schieble, Biplane, yellow w/tin pilot, rudder swivels, prop turns, wind-up, working, 15", VG......................**$325.00**
Steelcraft, Akron Zeppelin, silver, 25", G **$130.00**
Tootsietoy, Boeing 707 Jet, no landing gear, EX.........**$33.00**
Wyandotte, PAA China Clipper, metal props, wood wheels, 13" **$360.00**
Yone, American Air DC-3, red, white, silver & blue, twin-engine, 9x7", EX+ **$245.00**

Arnold, Flying Wonder, complete w/box, 1950s, 18" wingspan, EX, $250.00

Battery-Operated Toys

It is estimated that approximately 95% of the battery-operated toys that were so popular from the forties through the sixties came from Japan. The remaining 5% were made in the United States by other companies. To market these toys in America, many distributorships were organized. Some of the largest were Cragstan, Linemar, and Rosko. But even American toy makers such as Marx, Ideal, Hubley, and Daisy sold them under their own names, so the trademarks you'll find on Japanese battery-operated toys are not necessarily that of the manufacturer, and it's sometimes just about impossible to determine the specific company that actually made them. After peaking in the sixites, the Japanese toy industry began a decline, bowing out to competition from the cheaper die-cast and plastic toy makers.

Remember that it is rare to find one of these complex toys that have survived in good, collectible condition. Batteries caused corrosion, lubricants dried out, cycles were interrupted and mechanisms ruined, rubber hoses and bellows aged and cracked, so the mortality rate was extremely high. A toy rated good, that is showing signs of wear but well taken care of, is generally worth about half as much as the same toy in mint (like new) condition. Besides condition, battery-operated toys are rated on scarcity, desirability, and the number of 'actions' they preform. A 'major' toy is one that has three or more actions, while one that does only one or two is considered 'minor.' The latter, of course, are worth much less.

Cragstan, Beep-Beep Greyhound Bus, rubber tires, ca 1950, 20", M in worn box, $180.00

Alps, Antique Gooney Car, 4 actions, 1960s, MIB **$150.00**
Alps, Balloon-Blowing Monkey, 5 actions, 1950s, 11".**$100.00**
Alps, Barney the Drumming Bear, 1950s, MIB **$195.00**
Alps, Busy Shoe-Shining Bear, 5 actions, 1950s, NM ..**$225.00**
Alps, Clown the Magician, lithographed tin, vinyl & cloth, original box, 11", EX..**$270.00**
Alps, Cola-Drinking Bear, working, 1950s, VG............**$55.00**
Alps, Fido the Xylophone Player, 6 actions, 1950s, 8¾", EX **$180.00**
Alps, Happy Santa (walking), 5 actions, 1950s, 11", VG+ **$200.00**
Alps, Honda Accord, tin & plastic, 1970s, MIB............**$45.00**
Alps, Monkey Artist, 5 actions, 1950s, VG **$200.00**
Alps, Picnic Bear, 5 actions, 1950s, M in EX box **$180.00**
Alps, Princess the French Poodle, 5 actions, 1950s, EX .**$50.00**
Alps, Reading Bear, 5 actions, 1950s, 9", EX..............**$175.00**
Alps, Rock 'n Roll Monkey, plush face, strums guitar & dances while singing into lighted microphone, 12", NMIB...**$295.00**
Alps, Shoe Shine Joe, 6 actions, 1950s, NM **$200.00**

Alps, Sightseeing Bus, 3 actions, 1960s, M in NM box.**$125.00**
Alps, Warpath Indian, 3 actions, 1950s, EX **$120.00**
Arnold, Police Car, painted tin, manual remote control, steering mechanism, working, original box, 10", EX **$100.00**
Bandai, Cycling Daddy, 1960s, 10", MIB....................**$250.00**
CK, Musical Jolly Chimp, 1960s, MIB **$95.00**
Cragstan, Cap-Firing Tank, lithographed tin & plastic, camo paint, cap action, working, original box, 8¾", VG+..**$30.00**
Cragstan Anti-Aircraft Tank, MIB **$225.00**
Cragstan Freight Train, complete w/track, working, ca 1950s, NMIB...**$200.00**
ET, Professor Owl, 5 actions, 1950s, 8", EX **$250.00**
Haji, My Fair Dancer, 1950s, 10½", MIB....................**$275.00**
Hubley, Mr Magoo Car, painted & lithographed tin, plastic, cloth & painted vinyl, makes sounds, working, 9", VG+...**$200.00**

Japan, Royal Cub, plush-over-tin bear walks, baby lifts bottle to mouth & cries, NMIB, $250.00

K, M-35 Tank, moves w/rotating turret, makes gun noise, 9", NMIB..**$129.00**
KO, Air Mail Helicopter, tin & plastic, pilot moves head & arms, 2 spinning rotors, 10", NM in EX box........**$175.00**
KO, Volkswagon w/Visible Engine, 1960s, MIB........**$175.00**
Linemar, Army Radio Jeep, 4 actions, 1950s, 7", NM.**$160.00**
Linemar, Disney Acrobat (Donald Duck), painted celluloid, swings on lithographed tin & wire frame, original box, 9", EX...**$450.00**

Linemar, Mickey the Acrobat, celluloid Mickey on high-bar, 9", NMIB, $550.00

Linemar, Mickey the Acrobat, lithographed tin w/painted celluloid figure, working, original box, 9", EX....**$400.00**
Linemar, Sleeping Baby Bear, 6 actions, 1950s, NM..**$350.00**
Linemar, Sneezing Bear, plush, lifts tissue to nose, 10", VG+..**$185.00**

Linemar, Spanking Bear, 6 actions, 1950s, EX **$250.00**

LJN, Magnum PI Rough Riders Torture Tail, side-wheel action, working lights, 1982, M in NM box **$40.00**

Marusan, Jolly Pianist, 5 actions, 1950s, 8", NM......**$180.00**

Marusan, Magic Man Clown, 1950s, MIB **$625.00**

Mattel, Bart Simpson w/Skateboard, 6½" figure on 6" skateboard, remote control, EX **$25.00**

MT, Big Ring Circus Truck, 3 actions, EX **$250.00**

MT, Broadway Trolley, tin, working, 1950s, EX **$95.00**

MT, Desert Patrol Jeep, 4 actions, 1960s, 11", NM.....**$150.00**

MT, Goodtime Charlie, 7 actions, 1960s, NM in EX box **$220.00**

MT, Great Western Train, 3 actions, EX **$85.00**

MT, Mickey Mouse Locomotive, 4 actions, 1960s, NM in VG box...**$200.00**

MT, Overland Express, 1950s, MIB............................**$60.00**

MT, Radar Tank, advances w/clicking noise, light blinks, antenna rotates, NMIB, $200.00

MT, Santa Copter, 3 actions, 1960s, M in NM box.....**$150.00**

MT, Tinkling Trolley, 4 actions, 1950s, MIB..............**$195.00**

MT, Walking Donkey, tin & fur, working, 1950s, G....**$25.00**

Remco, Flying Dutchman, 1960s, NMIB.....................**$125.00**

Remco, Shark-U-Control Racing Car, 1961, NMIB **$95.00**

Remco, Showboat, 1960s, EX....................................**$125.00**

Remco, Whirlybird, NMIB **$80.00**

Remco, Wizard of Oz Tin Man, 21", MIB..................**$375.00**

Rock Valley, Circus Lion, 4 actions, missing cane & carpet, 1950s, 11", EX **$285.00**

RTV, Drinking Bear on Barrel, 1960s, VG...................**$50.00**

S&E, VIP Busy Boss Bear, plush & cloth bear sits behind lithographed tin desk, dial phone, original box, VG.**$230.00**

SAN, Smoking Grandpa, in rocking chair, 4 actions, 1950s, M in VG box **$275.00**

SH, Hysterical Harry, 1960s, VG **$125.00**

SH, Old Fashioned Car, 4 actions, 1950s, NM.............**$80.00**

SH, Piston Bulldozer, tin & plastic, w/driver, working, 1970s, EX...**$45.00**

Sonsco, Funland Cup Ride, 3 actions, 7", MIB...........**$375.00**

Taiyo, Highway Patrol Police Car, 1960s, MIB.............**$85.00**

TN, American Air 747, silver, red, white & blue, engines light as plane moves, 14x12", NM.......................**$85.00**

TN, Ball-Blowing Train #7021, 3 actions, 1950s, NM...**$95.00**

TN, Charlie Weaver Bartender, 1960s, 12", MIB **$100.00**

TN, Circus Jet, 1950s, MIB......................................**$185.00**

TN, Express Line Train, 3 actions, 1950s, EX **$95.00**

TN, Frankenstein Monster, 4 actions, 1960s, NM......**$250.00**

TN, Highway Drive, 1950s, MIB **$125.00**

TN, John's Farm Truck, 7 actions, 1950s, MIB..........**$325.00**

TN, Knitting Grandma, 3 actions, 1950s, 8½", M **$250.00**

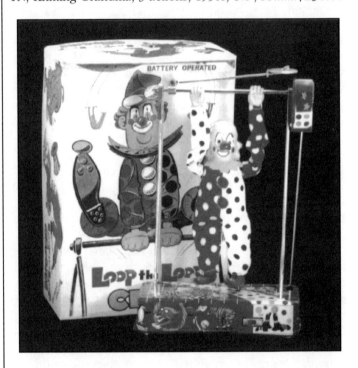

TN, Loop-the-Loop Clown, 10½", MIB, $100.00

TN, Magic Bulldozer, 3 actions, 1950s, MIB...............**$175.00**

TN, Miss Friday the Typist, lithographed tin, rubber & cloth, bell & typing actions, NMIB **$225.00**

TN, Shaking Old-Timer Car, tin, working, 1960s, EX..**$85.00**

TN, Skipping Action, 2 actions, 1960s, NM in EX box..**$100.00**

TN, Surrey Jeep, lithographed tin w/fabric-fringed top, MIB **$185.00**

TN, Turn-O-Matic, 1960s, NMIB...............................**$175.00**

TN, Veteran Car, 3 actions, 1950s, MIB.....................**$185.00**

TN, Windy the Circus Elephant, TN, EX **$125.00**

Tomiyama, Flying Circus, 2 bears swing above net, each has magnets in paws, 3rd bear alternates between them, rare, NMIB, $1,350.00

Tomiyama, Gino Neapolitan Balloon Blower, 5 actions, 1960s, M in EX box..............................$225.00

TPS, Stunt Plane, MIB..............................$275.00

Y, Begging Puppy, working, 1960s, G $25.00

Y, Blushing Willie, working, 1960s, 10", EX.............$40.00

Y, Captain Blushwell, tin, vinyl & cloth, hat bounces, pours drink, blushes & eyes roll, non-working, 11", EX in NM box..............................$65.00

Y, Drinking Dog, 4 actions, 1950s, NM..............$150.00

Y, Grandpa Car, 4 actions, 1950s, MIB.............$150.00

Y, Happy 'n Sad Magic Face Clown, 5 actions, 1960s, NM $220.00

Y, Ol' Sleepy Head Rip, 7 actions, 1950s, EX $220.00

Y, Teddy the Boxing Bear, 5 actions, 1950s, EX $220.00

Yanoman, Pepi Tumbling Monkey, 1960s, MIB $100.00

Yonezawa, Hungry Baby Bear, tin & plush, mother feeds baby who kicks & cries when bottle is gone, 9", EX $200.00

Yonezawa, Marshal Wild Bill, w/tin hat, remote control, 11", NM in EX box $275.00

Boats and Ships

Toy boats were first produced on a large scale during the first World War. They remained popular for about a decade, and when World War II broke out, scaled-down models of battleships were made to appeal to little wood-be sailors. Some of the larger manufacturers were Dent, Bing, Orkin Craft, Liberty Plaything, and Arnold.

Arnold, ocean liner, painted tin, red, black & white, 1 stack, clockwork, working, light crazing, missing mast, 6", VG..............................$70.00

Bing, ocean liner, painted tin, red, white, blue & orange w/lithographed deck, 2 stacks, clockwork, working, 6", G+..............................$400.00

Dent, Adirondack paddle-wheeler, poor repaint, 14½".$325.00

Fleischmann, ocean liner, painted tin, red & black hull, 2 stacks, w/white superstructure, clockwork, working, 11", VG $200.00

Fleishmann, cruise liner, painted tin, clockwork, repainted, lifeboats missing, 21", G $248.00

Hess, warship, lithographed tin, red, white & gray w/gold trim, weighted flywheel, working, original box, 9½", VG+ $325.00

Ideal, pirate ship, missing crow's nest & wheel..........$90.00

Ives, destroyer, painted tin, 2-tone dark green & olive green, clockwork, working, no lifeboats or deck parts, 12", G+, $350.00

Ives, gunboat, gray w/2 stacks & 1 cannon, 2 masts, clockwork, 10", VG+ $350.00

Ives, New York ocean liner, red & black w/tan deck, 13½", G- $275.00

Ives, submarine, painted tin, clockwork, 10", G+.....$175.00

Liberty Playthings, fireboat, 22", EX....................$300.00

Liberty Playthings, freighter, 27", EX....................$300.00

Liberty Playthings, sea scooter, 14", EX....................$200.00

Liberty Playthings, speed boat w/Outboard, 16", EX ..$135.00

Liberty Playthings, sportster, 16", EX....................$125.00

Liberty Playthings, tugboat & scow, 24", EX.............$125.00

Liberty Playthings, twin cockpit speed boat, 14", EX.$175.00

Mengel, Miss America, wood w/metal accessories, decaled lettering, 1930s, 15", G+ $140.00

Orkin Craft, dingy, 22", EX..............................$250.00

Orkin Craft, runabout, 22", EX..............................$300.00

Sutcliffe, speedboat, w/decals & windshield, original key, flag & keyhole cover, 1950s, 12½", NM in EX box $85.00

Wyandotte, SS America, tin ship on wood wheels, 1930s, VG..............................$150.00

Wyandotte, US Navy battleship, tin w/metal wheels, 1930s, EX..............................$90.00

Farm Toys

Since the decade of the twenties, farm machinery manufacturers have contracted with many of the leading toy companies to produce scale models of their machines. Most were made on a 1/16 scale, but other sizes have been made as well.

Tractor, red & cream die-cast metal, 1/16 scale, Cockshutt, Golden Arrow, MIB, $50.00

Cattle truck, cast iron, Kenton, ca 1938, 8", NM $110.00

Corn sheller, die cast, 1/8 scale, Ertle #4968, MIB.......$20.00

Manure spreader, w/teams of horses, McCormick-Deering, Arcade..............................$110.00

Plow or spreader, Case, 3/16 scale, #476/#492, Ertl, MIB..............................$10.00

Thresher, painted cast iron, Fordson, Arcade, 1928, 6", EX..............................$125.00

Tractor, #5020 Custom John Deere, EX....................$80.00

Tractor, #7710 Custom Ford, EX....................................$70.00

Tractor, cast iron, blue w/white rubber tires, missing driver's head, 1 replaced tire, Arcade, 3⅛", EX.................$35.00

Tractor, die cast, w/high lift, John Deere, 1950s, 13".$150.00

Tractor, Farmall M, die cast, 1/12 scale, metal wheels w/rare shovel attachment, Hubley, 1952 model, EX $95.00

Tractor & dump trailer, painted cast iron, Allis Chalmers, Arcade, 8", EX..$75.00

Tractor & dump wagon, cast iron, Allis-Chalmers, red w/green trailer, rubber tires, Arcade, 2x3x8", EX .$75.00

Trailer, 4-wheel, Arcade, 3¼", EX..................................$45.00

Truck, steel w/7 plastic animals, Structo, 20", M.......$100.00

Wagon, Arcade, 3½", EX..$40.00

Wagon, red & green paint, McCormick-Deering, Arcade, 12½", G...$85.00

Wagon, w/2 horses, McCormick-Deering, Arcade, EX.$160.00

Guns

One of the best-selling kinds of toys every made, toy guns were first patented in the late 1850s. Until WWII, most were made of cast iron, though other materials were used on a lesser scale. After the war, cast iron became cost prohibitive, and steel and die-cast zinc were used. By 1950, most were made either of die-cast material or plastic. Hundreds of names can be found embossed on these little guns, a custom which continues to the present time. Because of their tremendous popularity and durability, today's collectors can find a diversity of models and styles, and prices are still fairly affordable.

See also Western Heroes.

Daisy Bull's-Eye Cap Gun, blue w/wood grips, 1960s, VG+..$95.00

Daisy Buzz Barton BB Gun, VG+..............................$115.00

Daiya Astronaut Rocket Gun, lithographed tin, sparks, late 1950s, 9¼", VG...$35.00

Hawkeye Automatic Pistol, die cast, original box, 1950s, VG..$20.00

Hubley Automatic Cap Pistol, #290, die cast, brown checkered grips, 1956, 6½", NM $50.00

Hubley Double-Barreled 'Flintlock' Cap Gun, metal & wood-grain plastic, 1950s, 10", NM......................$35.00

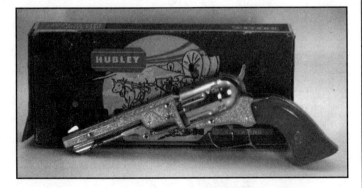

Hubley Pioneer Pistol Repeating Cap Shooter, metal w/Bakelite handle, M in EX box, $135.00

Hubley Tiny Tommy Machine Gun, 10¼" long, MIB, $50.00

Ives Crack C27.1, japanned cast iron, VG $45.00

Ives Liberty L7.1.1, japanned cast iron, VG...............$125.00

Kenston Western Cap Gun, cast iron, 1935, 8", EX+ ...$50.00

Kilgore Falcon Pocket Pistol & Holster, die cast, uses roll caps, 1950s, MIB $45.00

Kilgore Mountie Cap Gun, late 1950s, MIB.................$85.00

Kilgore 6-shooter, cast iron, revolving disk, slider release, light rust, 1934, 6½", VG......................................$165.00

King BB Gun, VG+ $65.00

Knickerbocker Mare's Laig Water Gun, white, gold & black plastic, missing filler cap, 1960, 15", VG...............$25.00

Kusan Western Heritage Texan Cap Gun, die cast, 1970s, MOC...$25.00

Lone Star Gun-Fighting Holster Set, die cast, silver finish, brown plastic grips, red & white holster, 1960s, NMIB..$55.00

Maco USA Machine Gun, #198/250, red & yellow plastic, mounted on tripod, fires plastic bullets, 1950s, 12", MIB $135.00

Marx Air Defense Laser Rifle, sparking action, 1970s, MIB $25.00

Marx Bullet-Firing Snub-Nose Pistol, die cast w/black paint finish, revolving cylinder, fired, 1960, 6", VG $55.00

Marx Burp Gun, #3310, green & black plastic, battery-operated (uses 1 D cell), NMOC $20.00

Marx G-Man Machine Gun, lithographed tin & plastic, sparker needs flint, EX+ $75.00

Marx Secret Agent, die cast, original box, 1969, EX+ ..$45.00

Mattel Agent Zero-M Snap-Shot Camera Pistol, plastic diecast works, unfired, 1964, 7½", NM $35.00

Mattel Cowboy in Africa Cap Gun & Holster, Black Fanner 50, embossed antelope head on stag grips, 1960s, EX $75.00

Midwest Long Tom Dart Gun, #PD-1, black painted pressed steel, missing darts, 1950s, 11", NMIB $35.00

Nichols Colt Special Cap Gun, die cast, chrome w/black plastic grips, 1950s, 7", G $25.00

Nichols Spitfire #100, die cast w/plastic stock, hip mini rifle style, plastic stock, 1950s, MIB.............................$35.00

Nichols Stallion 38 Cap Pistol, die cast, w/strip of 6 2-pc cartridges & box of caps, 1951, 9½", VG...................$75.00

Park Space Squirt Gun, plastic, 5", NM.......................$20.00

Remco Hamilton Invader Cap Pistol, w/grenade launcher, 1959, MIB $65.00

Remco Space Gun Set, 1 red & 1 gray, 1960s, VG $25.00

Stevens Buddy Cap Gun, cast iron, 1930s, 6¼", EX.....$65.00

Stevens Hero H8.3.2, nickle-plated, VG $25.00

Stevens Pioneer Cap Gun, metal, unused, 8", MIB......$45.00

Superior Rocket Gun, silver, NM $70.00
Topper Johnny Eagle Magumba Pistol, plastic, single action w/removable clip action, 11", VG......................$45.00
Wyandotte Dart Gun, pressed steel w/chrome, 1940s, VG...$10.00
Wyandotte Western Gun, lithographed tin sparkler, 12x7", MIB $55.00

Ramp Walkers

Though ramp-walking figures were made as early as the 1870s, ours date from about 1935 on. They were made in Czechoslovakia from the twenties through the forties and in this country during the fifties and sixties by Marx, who made theirs of plastic. John Wilson of Watsontown, Pennsylvania, sold his worldwide. They were known as 'Wilson Walkies' and stood about 4½" high, but the majority has been imported from Hong Kong.

Baby Teeny Toddler, plastic baby girl, Dolls Inc, lg, EX.$50.00
Baby Walk-a-Way, plastic, Marx, lg, EX.......................$40.00
Boy walking behind girl, plastic, lg, EX+ $45.00
Bull, plastic, EX...$15.00
Chicks & Easter egg, plastic, EX $30.00
Chipmunks playing drum & horn, plastic, EX $30.00
Clown, wood & composition, Wilson, EX....................$30.00
Cowboy riding horse, plastic w/metal legs, sm, EX $20.00
Donald Duck w/nephews in wagon, plastic, Disney, EX...$35.00
Dutch boy & girl, plastic, EX.......................................$30.00
Elephant, wood & composition, Wilson, EX................$30.00
Farmer w/wheelbarrow, plastic, EX $20.00
Figaro the Cat w/ball, plastic, EX $25.00
Goofy riding hippo, plastic, Disney, EX......................$40.00
Horse, yellow plastic w/rubber ears & string tail, lg, EX $30.00
Indian Chief, wood & composition, Wilson, EX..........$45.00

Jetsons, Astro & George, Hanna-Barbera, Marx, NM, $100.00

Jiminy Cricket w/cello, plastic, Disney, from $25.00 to.$30.00
Little Red Riding Hood, wood & compostion, Wilson, EX $35.00
Marty's Market Lady w/shopping cart, EX...................$35.00
Milk Cow, plastic, Marx, lg, NM..................................$40.00
Olive Oyl, wood & compositon, Wilson, NM...........$150.00
Oriental couple, 1960s, NM...$25.00

Penguin, wood & composition, Wilson, EX................$25.00
Popeye & Wimpy, plastic w/spring on heads, 1964, 4", M..$65.00
Santa Claus & snowman, faces on both sides, EX.......$40.00
Top Cat & Benny, Marx, 1950s, EX+ $75.00

Lady pushing buggy, plastic, Made in USA, 3", NM, $20.00

Robots

As early as 1948, Japanese toy manufactuers introduced their toy robots. Some of the best examples were made in the fifties, during the 'golden age' of battery-operated toys. They became more and more complex, and today some of these in excellent condition may bring well over $1,000.00. By the sixties, more and more plastic was used in their production, and the toys became inferior.

Electric Robot & Son, red & black plastic with silver accents, with buzzer & Morse code on back of head, Marx, 14½x5", EX, $195.00

Dynamic Fighter Robot, working, Japan, 1960s, MIB..**$85.00**

Empire-Monster Robot, battery-operated, working, Taiwan, MIB **$45.00**

Engine Robot, battery-operated, working, 1960s, MIB.**$85.00**

Fighting Robot, plastic w/tin chest plate, advances, stops & fires gun, makes sounds, SH/Japan, 10" NM in VG+ box **$125.00**

Giant Robot, silver w/red feet & accents, battery-operated, 17", EX+..**$340.00**

Gun Robot, plastic & tin newer version, Taiwan, 1970s, MIB...**$125.00**

High-Wheel Robot, black- & red-painted tin & plastic, sparking action, clockwork, working, Japan, 9", MIB .**$395.00**

Joker Billiken Robot, wind-up, 1980s, MIB................**$145.00**

Laughing Robot, plastic, bump-&-go action, neck stretches as lights flash, laughs, battery-operated, Waco, MIB..**$495.00**

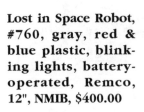

Lost in Space Robot, #760, gray, red & blue plastic, blinking lights, battery-operated, Remco, 12", NMIB, $400.00

Lost in Space Robot, plastic, battery-operated, AHI/Azar Hamway, Hong Kong, 1977, 10", NMIB..............**$160.00**

Mechanical Robot, lithographed tin w/yellow, red & blue plastic arms, sparking action, clockwork, w/box, 6", VG+..**$100.00**

Mighty Robot, lithographed tin & plastic, clockwork, sparking action, Noguchi/Japan, 1960s, 5¼", MIB.......**$145.00**

Planet Robot, red- & black-painted tin & plastic, wind-up, sparking action, working, original box, KO, 1960s, 8¾", VG..**$250.00**

Robert the Robot, talker w/turn crank, silver & red plastic, working, original box, Ideal, 14", VG.................**$110.00**

Robot & Son, silver & red-painted plastic, w/light & Morse-code buzzer, battery-operated, non-working, w/box, Marx, G...**$160.00**

Robot Captain, lithographed tin & plastic, sparking action, wind-up, scarce, Yone/Japan, 6", VG+ in NM box.**$135.00**

Robot 2500, battery-operated, MIB............................**$100.00**

Rudy the Robot, Remco, 1960s, NMIB **$175.00**

Saturn Robot, plastic, battery-operated, working, 1970s, MIB **$35.00**

Sparky Robot, painted tin, silver body w/red feet & ears, sparking action, clockwork, working, w/box, KO, 7¾", G+ **$160.00**

Star Strider Robot, battery-operated, MIB..................**$225.00**

Steele Robot, battery-operated, Marx **$475.00**

Talking Robot, battery-operated, working, HK, 1970s, MIB **$45.00**

Venus Robot, lithographed tin & plastic, clockwork, working, w/box, Japan, 5½", EX..............................**$200.00**

Walking Robot, tin, sparking action, wind-up, SY/Japan, 7", NM in EX box **$245.00**

Zeroid Robot, Zintar or Zerak, Ideal, 1968, EX............**$25.00**

Zoomer the Robot, black & silver painted tin, w/light, battery-operated, working, Japan, 7½", VG+ **$400.00**

Slot Car Racers

Kids in the '70s were really into slot car racing. Any family with boys had a track set up in the family room or the basement, and that's where the neighborhood kids congregated. Slot cars ranged in size from the very small HO scale models up to some that were about 10" long. Transformers supplied the track with electricity that was conducted to the motors of the cars via a wire receptor that made the connection.

Eldon, #78602 1966 Dodge Charger (from set #48), 1/32 scale, red, M, from $25 to $35.00

Aurora, #1357, Buick Riviera, HO scale, white, NM **$40.00**

Aurora, #1375, Ford GT, HO scale, green & white, M .**$35.00**

Aurora, #1376, Porsche 906, HO scale, yellow, MIB ...**$30.00**

Aurora, #1382, Ford J Car, HO scale, blue & black, MIB **$35.00**

Aurora, #1389, Cougar, HO scale, yellow, M..............**$42.00**

Aurora, #1399, Dune Buggy w/top, HO scale, white, MIB...**$45.00**

Aurora, #1403, Cheetah, HO scale, green, M..............**$40.00**

Aurora, #1430, Flamethrower Ford J, HO scale, white & blue, MIB..**$35.00**

Aurora, #1478, Tuff Ones Firebird, HO scale, yellow & black, M..**$45.00**

Aurora, #1481, Tuff Ones Dino Ferrari, red, white & green, M **$35.00**

Aurora, #1541, Jaguar Convertible, HO scale, blue, MIB.**$75.00**

Aurora, #1546, Mercedes, HO scale, hardtop, white & black, NM **$75.00**

Aurora, #1554, Hot Rod Coupe-VIB, HO scale, lemon yellow & red, MIB...**$80.00**

Aurora, #6203, Porsche 934 Turbo #81 AFX, HO scale, white, MIB...**$20.00**

Cox, LaCucaracha, 1/24 scale, kit, unused, M.............**$35.00**

Eldon, #1350 Chaparral, 1/32 scale, white, G **$15.00**

Eldon, #1518-11B Dune Buggy, 1/32 scale, purple, EX...**$40.00**

Lionel, BRM Racing Car Formula I, 1/32 scale, red or green, M **$25.00**

Lionel, Copper Racing Car, 1/32 scale, yellow, M **$25.00**

Lionel, Jaguar D, 1/32 scale, light blue, some decal flaking, M **$35.00**

Strombecker, #9590, Chettah #58, 1/32 scale, orange, MIB **$50.00**

Strombecker, Ford GT, 1/32 scale, yellow, 1970s, MIB.**$25.00**

Strombecker, Ford J Car, 1/32 scale, yellow, MIB **$25.00**

Tyco, #3937, Army Jeep, US-1 Trucking, olive drab, MIB **$25.00**

Tyco, #3941, Exxon Tank Tailer, US-1 Trucking, MIB.**$10.00**

Tyco, #3942, DuPont Tank Trailer, US-1 Trucking, MIB .**$12.00**

Tyco, #7063, Mazda Miata MX-5, HO scale, red & green, twin pack, MIB...**$50.00**

Tyco, #8563, Corvette Silversteak #9 CH, HO scale, chrome & pink, MIB..**$25.00**

Tyco, #8964, Buick Stockcar, #33 Skoal Bandit, HO scale, white w/green numbers, M, $40.00

Tyco, Canon Formula #2, 442 X2, HO scale, white, blue & yellow, MIB **$30.00**

Tyco, Roadline Flatbed Trailer, US-1 Trucking, MIB ...**$10.00**

Tyco, Smith's Box Trailer, US-1 Trucking, MIB............**$10.00**

Space Toys

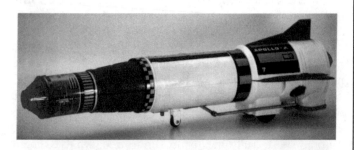

Apollo X Moon Challenger, red, white & blue plastic, battery-operated, Japan, 16" long, M in G box, $150.00

Astro-Sound Satellite Talking Space Toy, EX in VG box..**$60.00**

Cape Canaveral Satellite Tracking Truck, replaced antenna, EX **$200.00**

Flying Saucer, tin & plastic, working, Y/Japan, 1960s, MIB **$95.00**

Gama Space Tank, w/original box, EX **$300.00**

Golden Sonic the Mysterious Spaceship, Tigrett, NMIB .**$125.00**

Holdraketa Spaceship, friction, w/box, 16", EX..........**$40.00**

King Flying Saucer, 3 actions, KO, 1960s, 7½" dia, NMIB..**$150.00**

Lunar Hovercraft, TPS, 8", EX in VG+ box.................**$325.00**

Lunar Traffic Control, MIB **$110.00**

New Space Capsule, astronaut pops up, tin body w/plastic dome, marked United States & NASA, SH, 8", EX in EX box **$245.00**

Out of This World Flying Saucer, aluminum saucer circles around box, Wilson, 1950s, NM in EX box........**$175.00**

Solar X Rocket, lithographed tin, several actions & sounds, battery-operated, TN, 15", EX in NM box...........**$165.00**

Space Cruiser, black-painted tin, working, 1 wheel resoldered, w/box, Japan, 9", VG **$75.00**

Space Frontier Apollo 12, tin & plastic, revolving nose & tail, hatch opens to spaceman w/camera, 18", EX+ in VG+ box..**$150.00**

Space Patrol NASA Capsule, lithographed tin w/plastic figure in bubble-top cockpit, friction, MT/Japan, 7" long, EX, $190.00

Space Patrol XII, tank, VG+ **$185.00**

Space Patrol 2019 Saucer, MIB................................**$200.00**

Space Ship X-5, MT, MIB.......................................**$95.00**

Space Shuttle, working, MT/Japan, 1960s, MIB **$55.00**

Space Station, X-2, MIB...**$175.00**

Space 1999 Eagleship, plastic w/metal axles, AHI, 1976, 7", EX..**$20.00**

Space 1999 Moon Car, yellow, w/2 spacemen, friction, working, AHI, 1976, MOC **$45.00**

Star Hawk Spaceship w/Zeroid, Ideal, MIB **$95.00**

Super Sonic Space Rocket, NMIB **$625.00**

Two Stage Rocket Launching Pad, MIB **$525.00**

USA-NASA Apollo Space Ship, tin, bump-&-go action, battery-operated, MT, 9½", NMIB **$220.00**

X-7 Flying Saucer, lithographed tin, battery-operated, Japan, 7½" dia, EX, $110.00

Teddy Bears

Though the top-of-the-line collectible bears are those made by Steiff, there have been several other companies who's teddies are just about as high on many collectors' want lists. Hermann, Ideal, Schuco are just a few, and even high-quality bears produced during the past ten years have collector potential; so with that in mind, hang on to more modern bears as well.

American, brown & gold cotton plush, long hard-stuffed free-standing legs, early 1940s, 25".........................$45.00
American, long rust mohair, decaled tin eyes w/wire-rimmed glasses, velveteen pads, jointed, ca 1930, 13"......$275.00
Animal Toys Plus, brown plush Banker Bear, plastic eyes, removable vest & jacket, 1979, 16"........................$20.00
Berg, bright gold wool & cotton plush, plastic eyes, floss nose & mouth, Made in Austria tag, 1946 on, 5¾".$50.00
Clemens, white mohair w/self-fabric vest, unjointed, mohair pads, blue neck ribbon, 1960, 9"...........................$65.00
Eden Toys, thick gold plush, nylon fiber stuffing, velveteen pads, floss nose & felt mouth, eye missing, 1975, 14"...$20.00
German, gold prickly mohair, red neck ribbon, stationary head w/jointed limbs, straw stuffed, no pads, 1950-60, 5½"...$75.00
German, short gold mohair w/plastic hair, long snout, leather pads, gruff expression, loud growler, 1940s, 14", M...$195.00
Gund, brown mohair, 85th Anniversary, jointed, 8"..$125.00
Hermann, long tan mohair, swivel head, jointed, 1950s, 16", M...$400.00
Hermann, Zotty, long brown mohair, squeaks, jointed, 10", EX $195.00
Ideal, strawberry-blond mohair w/white mohair snout, glass eyes, molded plastic nose, 1950s, 12" $250.00
Japan, sparse gold mohair, straw stuffing, sm glass eyes, skinny limbs, squeaker, bow, wire-jointed, 11", NM..............$65.00
Knickerbocker, brown plush body w/pouting molded vinyl face & ears, soft stuffing, 1955, 15"........................$25.00
Knickerbocker, chocolate brown short mohair, straw-filled head, cotton-stuffed body, velveteen pads, jointed, 1940s, 24"..$65.00

Schuco, Bigo Bello, tan mohair w/googly eyes, wire arms & legs, felt pads, red plaid pants, 10", EX.................$75.00
Schuco, caramel mohair, w/tag marked West Germany, 2½", M...$250.00
Schuco, light gold mohair, sheared snout & pads, glass eyes, flat card soles, worn, 1930s, 14"...........................$150.00
Twyford, gold mohair, straw & kapok stuffing, red oilcloth pads, jointed, 1930s, 15½"....................................$225.00

Unknown manufacturer, black & white med pile mohair Panda, hard-stuffed cotton & straw, jointed, ca 1950, 18", EX, $150.00

Unknown manufacturer, champagne mohair, red neck ribbon, flannel pads, straw stuffing, jointed, early 1930s, 14"..$200.00
Unknown manufacturer, dark brown fur, straw filled, fully jointed, some wear to pads, 15", EX....................$175.00
Unknown manufacturer, golden blond fur, fully jointed, 1 eye missing, torn paws, fur wear, 19" $225.00
Unknown manufacturer, tan fur, humpback, dressed in lederhosen, some wear, 23" $150.00
Unknown manufacturer, yellow mohair, embroidered nose, excelsior & kapok stuffing, jointed, 1920s, 19", G.$165.00

Toy Soldiers

For a thoroughly definitive book on this subject, you must get a copy of Richard O'Brien's book, *Collecting Toy Soldiers*. It covers them all, from plastic dimestore soldiers to those he calls 'connoisseur category.' In our listings, values are given for Britains in excellent condition; all others are for mint condition examples. A soldier in only 'very good' shape is one that has obviously seen use, has signs of wear and aging, but retains most of its paint and has a generally good appearance. In this condition, it would be worth only half of mint value. Of course, there are grades in between, and they would be evaluated accordingly.

Auburn, bomb thrower	$24.00
Auburn, officer on horse	$36.00
Auburn, Red Cross doctor	$35.00
Auburn, signalman	$60.00
Auburn, US infantry officer	$14.00
Barclay, army doctor in brown, flat underbase	$18.00

Barclay, flagbearer, tin helmet, long stride, $25.00; bugler, tin helmet, short stride, $15.00

Barclay, drum major, short stride	$22.00
Barclay, Indian on horse	$35.00
Barclay, Indian w/bow & arrow	$10.00
Barclay, knight w/pennant	$15.00
Barclay, naval officer, long stride	$16.00
Barclay, nurse kneeling	$22.00
Barclay, officer on horse	$28.00
Barclay, officer reading orders	$20.00
Barclay, officer w/sword, tin helmet, long stride	$18.00
Barclay, parachutist landing	$20.00
Barclay, red cap w/bags	$13.00
Barclay, sailor in blue uniform, marching, short stride	$22.00
Barclay, sniper, kneeling & firing, short stride	$14.00
Barclay, soldier at attention, cast helmet	$19.00
Barclay, soldier bomb thrower	$15.00
Barclay, soldier charging, short stride	$15.00
Barclay, soldier charging w/machine gun	$14.00
Barclay, soldier crawling	$21.00
Barclay, soldier falling w/rifle, cast helmet	$32.00
Barclay, soldier marksman	$10.00
Barclay, soldier sentry	$15.00
Barclay, soldier stretcher bearer, open hand	$72.00
Barclay, soldier telephone operator	$15.00
Barclay, soldier w/AA gun, cast helmet	$18.00
Barclay, soldier w/gas mask, charging w/rifle	$16.00
Barclay, 2 soldiers on raft, cast helmets	$60.00
Britains, #115, lancer, 1st version	$54.00

Britains, #116, trooper, 2nd version, rectangular base	$35.00
Britains, #135, officer, 1st version	$110.00
Britains, #151, petty officer	$25.00
Britains, #177, Austro-Hungarian Infantry, trooper	$44.00
Britains, #193, Arabs of the Desert, Arab on camel	$65.00
Britains, #215, French Infantry Firing, machine gunner	$25.00
Britains, #229, US Cavalry, trooper	$18.00
Britains, #33, 1950 officer	$30.00
Britains, #33, 1950 trooper	$24.00
Britains, #36, Pre-War officer	$25.00
Britains, #46, bugler	$44.00
Britains, #99, trumpeter	$65.00
Britains, Belgian Cavalry, Pre-War officer	$40.00
Britains, Drum & Fife Band of Coldstream Guards w/Rank & File, 25-piece set, each	$40.00
Britains, Pre-War trooper	$20.00
Britains, Spanish Cavalry, Pre-War trooper	$85.00
Britains, Uruguayan Military School, cadet, later version	$30.00
Grey Iron, Foreign Legion machine gunner	$28.00
Grey Iron, Indian chief w/knife	$17.00
Grey Iron, Indian w/hatchet, early	$14.00
Grey Iron, Legion drummer	$15.00
Grey Iron, Red Cross nurse	$24.00
Grey Iron, US Doughboy w/bayonet	$22.00
Grey Iron, US naval officer in white	$13.00
Grey Iron, US sailor in blue	$15.00
Grey Iron, wounded soldier sitting	$96.00
Johillco, bugler, khaki	$10.00
Johillco, cowboy firing rifle	$5.00
Johillco, cowboy on foot w/gun	$5.00
Johillco, drummer, khaki	$8.00
Johillco, infantryman	$11.00
Johillco, Infantryman, prone, khaki	$8.00
Johillco, stretcher w/wounded soldier, 2-piece	$15.00

Manoil, cowboy w/gun pointed up, $20.00

Manoil, cowboy w/hands up $20.00
Manoil, doctor in khaki $32.00
Manoil, flag bearer, 3rd version $20.00
Manoil, Indian w/knives...$15.00
Manoil, machine gunner, prone, no aperture, pack on
    back $18.00
Manoil, marine, hollow base....................................$65.00
Manoil, motorcycle rider $40.00
Manoil, navy gunner...$23.00
Manoil, nurse..$16.00
Manoil, parachute jumper $20.00
Manoil, parade soldier, 5th version $16.00
Manoil, signal man, 2nd version...............................$36.00
Manoil, sniper kneeling, short thin rifle $18.00
Manoil, soldier charging w/gun $44.00
Manoil, soldier crouching w/hand grenade $60.00
Manoil, soldier w/barbed wire..................................$35.00
Manoil, stretcher carrier, no medical kit..................$16.00
Marx, Indian standing...$8.00
Marx, infantry private at attention.............................$6.00
Marx, navy signalman $8.00
Marx, parachute trooper $8.00
Marx, pilot w/papers $11.00
Marx, radio operator $9.00
Marx, Red Cross nurse $8.00
Marx, Russian infantryman $8.00
Marx, ski trooper on patrol $24.00
Marx, US cavalryman $10.00

Trains

Lionel is a name that is almost synonymous with toy trains. The Lionel company was the one that introduced the O guage to the public in 1915, and it became the industry's standard for years to come. Some of their best toys came from the period of 1923 to 1940, when in addition to their trains they also brought out an extensive line of special sets. They bought out their competitors, the Ives corporation, in 1928, and except for the years from 1929 until 1934, when the nation was crippled by financial collapse and during WWII, they remained a giant industry. Sales began to decline in the fiftes, but even today, Lionel trains are being made in limited numbers.

Some of the other toys companies whose trains you may encounter are American Flyer, Marx, Buddy L, Tootsietoy, Unique, and Manoil. All these companies are included in *American Premium Guide to Electric Trains* by Richard O'Brien.

American Flyer, #21105 engine & coal car, NM...........$45.00
American Flyer, #22077 Pig Palace stock car, S gauge,
    NM...$190.00
American Flyer, #2416 tank car, EX.............................$10.00
American Flyer, #3006 log car, VG+...........................$100.00
American Flyer, #648 service car, S gauge, VG+ $50.00
American Flyer, #977 caboose, S gauge, VG+ $30.00
Dorfan, #600 gondola, EX..$95.00
Dorfan, #605 hopper, VG+..$10.00

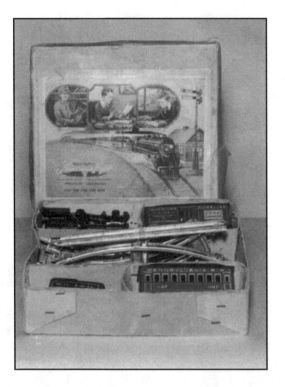

American Flyer, #10 locomotive, #120 tender, USRR express car & PRR passenger car, clockwork, complete set in box, M, $700.00

Ives, #130 combine, roof flaking, VG+........................$65.00
Ives, #17 locomotive w/tender, black & red cast iron w/gold
    trim, 4 boiler bands, clockwork, VG+ $100.00
Ives, #4 locomotive, black & red w/gold trim, clockwork,
    VG..$90.00
Ives, #67 caboose, VG+...$45.00
Ives, #70 caboose, red & peacock blue w/brass trim, transi-
    tional, 1 coupler missing, VG+.............................$60.00
Lionel, #12 gondola, gray w/pea-green trim, late coupler,
    standard gauge, EX...$50.00
Lionel, #18303 Amtrak GG1 locomotive, MIB...........$380.00
Lionel, #18601 Great Northern locomotive, MIB $98.00
Lionel, #18615 Grand Trunk West locomotive, MIB..$105.00
Lionel, #19309 Seaboard Quad hopper car, MIB.........$28.00
Lionel, #211 TX Special Alco AA locomotive, EX+....$150.00
Lionel, #212 Sante Fe dummy locomotive, red & silver,
    EX..$50.00
Lionel, #217 caboose, red & peacock blue, EX $125.00
Lionel, #249T tender, Pennsylvania, EX $25.00
Lionel, #2660 crane, plated, EX..................................$90.00
Lionel, #33000 Railscope locomotive, MIB................$225.00
Lionel, #3461 log dump flat car, EX...........................$35.00
Lionel, #50 locomotive, dark green & maroon, standard
    gauge, rewheeled, EX+..$170.00
Lionel, #6024 Shredded Wheat boxcar, EX $25.00
Lionel, #6356 New York City stock car, EX..................$65.00
Lionel, #6465 Sunoco tank car, original box, VG $12.00
Lionel, #6821 flat car w/crates, EX.............................$40.00
Lionel, #806 cattle car, EX...$45.00
Lionel, #8141 Pennsylvania steam locomotive w/tender,
    M...$55.00

Lionel, #8204 locomotive w/C&O tender, 4-4-2, EX....**$65.00**

Lionel, #8304 steam locomotive, 9½", EX, $110.00

Lionel, #87504, Union Pacific flat car, MIB **$30.00**
Lionel, #9805 Grand Trunk, O gauge, EX **$40.00**
Lionel, flat car w/no pipes, otherwise EX...................**$40.00**
Lionel, Livingston passenger car, silver, VG...............**$55.00**
Lionel, New York City gondola, VG **$55.00**
Lionel, Toys R Us boxcar, EX.....................................**$40.00**
Lionel, track cleaner, HO gauge, original box, VG **$55.00**
Lionel, US Navy Submarine Car, 10", EX.....................**$65.00**
Lionel, Western Pacific boxcar, silver, VG+ **$45.00**
Lionel #637 locomotive w/#773W tender, original box,
    EX+ **$170.00**
Marklin, Diesel DB CL #212 locomotive, NMIB.........**$140.00**
Marx, #6000 Southern Pacific locomotive, tin plate, orange
    w/silver stripe, powered unit w/dummy, EX........**$45.00**
Tyco, #327-14 Illinois Central Gulf caboose, HO gauge,
    NMIB..**$2.00**
Tyco, #339A Santa Fe boxcar, NM in EX box **$3.00**
Winner, #1035 locomotive w/#10116T tender, black
    w/orange frame, copper trim, standard gauge, EX.**$75.00**

Transformers

The first Transformers appeared on the toy shelves of American in 1984. Originally there were twenty-eight, eighteen of which were Autobots, cars that became heroic warriors who desperately tried to terminate the evil Decepticons (the other ten). These became so popular that the line was expanded to contain more than two hundred different figures. Hasbro discontinued the Transformers late in 1990, but today their fans continue to clamor for more, and recently a new, limited edition series has been produced.

Action Masters, Jazz, MOC **$8.00**
Action Masters, Wheeljack, Hasbro, 1989, MIP...........**$30.00**
Autobots, Aquablast, England, 1993, MIP **$22.00**
Autobots, Rotorstorm, England, 1992, MIP.................**$40.00**
Autobots, Tracks, England, 1991, MIP........................**$22.00**
Cars, Inferno, MIB..**$40.00**
Cars, Ironside, 1st series, 1984, MIB **$30.00**
Cars, Skids, MIB...**$55.00**
Constrictors, Blaster, MIB **$50.00**
Constrictors, Crane, MIB...**$20.00**
Constrictors, Scrapper, M...**$20.00**
Decepticons, Aquafed, England, 1993, MIP **$22.00**

Decepticons, Talon, England, 1992, MIP.....................**$25.00**
Dinobots, Swoop, Hasbro, MIB **$70.00**
Insections, Ransack, Hasbro, MIB...............................**$70.00**
Insections, Shrapnel, Hasbro, 1984, MIP **$15.00**
Jets, Ramjet, Hasbro, MIB...**$45.00**
Jets, Thundercracker, 1st series, Hasbro, MIB.............**$55.00**
Jumpstarters, Blitzwing, M...**$28.00**
Micromasters, Autobot Hothouse Station, Hasbro, 1988,
    MIP..**$10.00**
Micromasters, Autobot Off-Road Patrol, Hasbro, 1988, set of
    4, MIP...**$15.00**
Micromasters, Construction Patrol, MOC.......................**$8.00**
Micromasters, Race Track Patrol, MOC..........................**$8.00**
Mini-Car, Beachcomber, 1985, MIB **$20.00**
Mini-Car, Brawn, 2nd series, 1985, MIB **$35.00**
Mini-Car, Bumblebee, yellow, Hasbro, MIB................**$50.00**
Mini-Car, Powerglide, 1985, EX..................................**$8.00**
Pretender, Doubleheader, US issue, 1988, MOC.........**$15.00**
Quickswitch, Hasbro, NM **$38.00**
Sparkler Minibots, Cindersaur, Hasbro, 1987, MIP **$10.00**
Sparkler Minibots, Guzzle, Hasbro, 1987, MIP............**$10.00**
Stranglehold, US issue, 1988, MOC............................**$20.00**
Targetmaster, Landfill, Hasbro, 1987, MIP..................**$10.00**
Whirl, Hasbro, MIB...**$80.00**

Vehicles

These are the types of toys that are intensely dear to the heart of many a collector. Having a beautiful car is part of the American dream, and over the past eighty years, just about as many models, makes, and variations have been made as toys for children as the real vehicles for adults. Novices and advanced collectors alike are easily able to find something to suit their tastes as well as their budgets.

One area that is right now especially volatile covers those fifties and sixties tin scale-model autos by foreign manufacturers — Japan, U.S. Zone Germany, and English toy makers. Since these are relatively modern, you'll still be able to find some at yard sales and flea markets at reasonable prices.

Bandai, #333 Ford Custom Ranch Wagon, red w/black top, rubber wheels, friction, 11½", M in poor box, $225.00

Bandai, Buick Century Ambulance, white-painted tin, friction, ca 1958, 8", NMIB...**$35.00**

Bandai, late 1950s Cadillac Sedan, rubber wheels, friction, 11", EX.................................$250.00

Bandai, Rambler, blue w/white top, friction, VG+ in VG box..$125.00

Bandai, 1933 Cadillac Old Timer Convertible, tin w/black rubber tires, fold-down windshield, 8", EX+ in VG box..$85.00

Bandai, 1958 Chrysler Imperial Sedan, plastic windshields & steering wheel, 9½", NM in EX box....................$225.00

Beach Buggy, #227, yellow, EX+.................................$15.00

Brooklyn, Packard Light 8 Coupe, #6, beige & brown, MIB...$65.00

Brooklyn, Thunderbird Coupe, #13, die-cast metal, red, MIB...$65.00

Brooklyn, 1955 Crysler 300C, die-cast metal, red......$150.00

Brumm, Jaguar XK 120, #r105, die-cast metal, black, MIB...$35.00

Brumm, Mercedes 1837 Formula 1, #r070, W25, silver, MIB...$15.00

Cragston, Volkswagon Micro-Bus, painted tin, red & metallic gray, friction, original box, 8", EX+ $230.00

Dinky, Aston Martin, #153, silver & gray, no insert, MIB..$35.00

Dinky, Austin Atlantic, #106, blue w/blue seats, VG+.$30.00

Dinky, Berliet Gazelle Missile Truck, #816, EX...........$35.00

Dinky, Chevy Corvair, #552, pale blue, NM.................$85.00

Dinky, Chevy El Camino, #449, green & cream, EX+..$30.00

Dinky, Cuisine Marion, #823, MIB...............................$80.00

Dinky, Dragon Tractor, #162A, NM.............................$65.00

Dinky, Ford Cortina Rally Car, #212, white & black, MIB $125.00

Dinky, Holden Sedan, #196, turquoise, MIB..............$75.00

Dinky, Land Rover, #340 ....$55.00

Dinky, Leopard Anti-Aircraft Tank, #696, M.................$75.00

Dinky, Volvo 1800 S, #116, red, MIB..........................$30.00

Eligor, Bentley T Saloon, #1048, die-cast metal, navy, MIB $22.00

Eligor, Citroen Rosalie Sedan, #1005, med blue, MIB .$22.00

Eligor, Ford Tudor Ambulance, #1221, die-cast metal, white, MIB $25.00

Gama, Ford Taurus Coupe, #995, die-cast metal, orange & blue, M..$65.00

Gama, Opel Cadet Adac, die-cast metal, yellow, MIB.$25.00

Goodee, Ford Police Car, die-cast metal, blue w/black rubber tires, 1950s, 3", NM..$18.00

Goodee, Moving Van, die-cast metal, blue w/black rubber tires, 1950s, VG $12.00

Goodee, Truck, die-cast metal, red w/black rubber tires, 1950s, 3", EX+ $16.00

Hot Wheels, Airport Rescue, yellow w/black walls, 1981, NM...$6.00

Hot Wheels, American Victory, blue w/red line tires, 1975, M...$20.00

Hot Wheels, Army Funny Car, white w/black walls, 1982, NM $15.00

Hot Wheels, Corvette Stingray, silver w/black walls, 1978, NM+ $25.00

Hot Wheels, Dixie Challenger, orange w/black walls, 1981, NM...$6.00

Hot Wheels, Double Vision, dark blue w/red line tires, 1973, EX+ $55.00

Hot Wheels, Fire Chaser, red w/black walls, 1979, NM ..$5.00

Hot Wheels, GMC Motorhome, orange w/black walls, 1977, NM $12.00

Hot Wheels, Greased Gremlin, red w/black walls, 1979, VG+...$15.00

Hot Wheels, Greyhound Wheels, silver w/black walls, 1980, NM $12.00

Hot Wheels, Hot Heap, purple w/red line tires, NM...$20.00

Hot Wheels, Lowdown, gold w/red line tires, 1977, EX.$15.00

Hot Wheels, Mongoose, red w/decals, red line tires, 1970, EX...$25.00

Hot Wheels, Mustang Stocker, chrome, orange & magenta, red line tires, Ford/450 decals, NM.......................$50.00

Hot Wheels, Racebait, gold w/black walls, 1979, NM+.$20.00

Hot Wheels, Rockbuster, yellow w/red line tires, 1976, EX...$10.00

Hot Wheels, Side Kick, red w/red line tires, EX..........$35.00

Hot Wheels, Strip Teaser, flourescent green w/red line tires, Shell promotion, 1973, NM...................................$50.00

Hot Wheels, T-Totaler, black w/black walls, 1977, NM..$20.00

Hot Wheels, Torino Stocker, red w/red line tires, #23 decal, M...$25.00

Hot Wheels, Twinmill, light green w/red line tires, 1968, G+...$6.00

Hot Wheels, X-ploder, dark green w/red line tires, 1973, EX+ $75.00

Hubley, Sedan, #452, die-cast metal, blue w/rubber tires, ca 1940, 7", EX...$30.00

Kingsbury, Ladder Truck, steel & cast iron w/rubber tires, wood ladder, clockwork, working, 18½", G+ $80.00

Majorette, BMW, #229, die-cast metal, white, M in bubble package..$2.00

Majorette, Garbage Truck, #247, die-cast metal, Hippo emblem, green cab w/gray dumper, M in bubble package........$1.50

Majorette, Grand Prix Corvette 'ZR1,' #215, die-cast metal, red, M in bubble package..................................$1.50

Majorette, Ice-Cream Van, die-cast metal, metallic red w/yellow canopy, M in bubble package $3.00

Marx, Big Load Van Co, painted tin, 13" long, G, $225.00

Marx, Coal Truck, red body w/blue bed, Lumar Coal stamped on sides, black tires, red hubcaps, battery-operated, 11", G $40.00

Marx, Dump Truck, pressed steel, red w/green bed, plated grille, black wood wheels, clockwork, 5¼", G **$65.00**

Marx, Fire Pumper, pressed steel, red body w/black chassis & fenders, anodized gold boiler, celluloid window, 9" **$75.00**

Marx, Mustang Convertible, die-cast metal w/plastic wheels, metallic blue, 1960s, 2⅜", EX **$10.00**

Marx, Power Road Grader, pressed steel, 1950s, 7½", NM **$125.00**

Marx, Stake Truck, pressed steel, red, yellow & black, rubber wheels, w/plastic farm animals, 13½", EX+ **$90.00**

Marx, US Mail Truck, lithographed tin w/plastic wheels, red, white & blue w/gold trim, 12½", EX................**$120.00**

Matchbox (Regular Wheels), Caterpiller Tractor, yellow w/original green treads, EX+..................**$14.00**

Matchbox (Regular Wheels), Chevrolet Impala Taxi, black wheels, M **$11.00**

Matchbox (Regular Wheels), Fiat 1500 Sedan, green w/brown luggage rack, black wheels, M **$9.00**

Matchbox (Regular Wheels), Land Rover Series 2, black wheels, VG+..................................**$18.00**

Matchbox (Regular Wheels), London Bus, 'Longlife BP' decals, black wheels, NM **$12.50**

Matchbox (Regular Wheels), Mercedes Truck, orange canopy, black wheels, MIB **$12.50**

Matchbox (Regular Wheels), MG 1100 Sedan, black wheels, M **$12.50**

Matchbox (Regular Wheels), Pipe Truck, silver grille, w/7 original pipes, black wheels, NM...........................**$8.00**

Matchbox (Regular Wheels), Taylor Jumbo Crane, yellow, 1965, $18.00

Matchbox (Regular Wheels), VW 1600TL Fastback, racing stripe decals, black wheels, NM...........................**$10.00**

Matchbox (Superfast), Baja Dune Buggy, green, M in EX box **$7.50**

Matchbox (Superfast), Chevy Van, orange w/red & black stripes, M in NM Box **$7.50**

Matchbox (Superfast), Ford Cortina, green w/red interior, M in NM Box **$4.50**

Matchbox (Superfast), Lamborghini Miuri, gold w/white interior, M in NM box **$12.50**

Matchbox (Superfast), Mercedes 350SL, yellow, M in VG box **$7.50**

Matchbox (Superfast), Mod Rod, yellow w/black wheels, M in NM box.......................**$10.00**

Matchbox (Superfast), Red Rider Dodge Charger, Hong Kong, M in NM box.......................**$15.00**

Matchbox (Superfast), Rolls Royce Silver Shadow II, silver, M in EX box **$5.00**

Matchbox (Superfast), VW Bug Dragon Wheels Dragster, M **$10.00**

Matchbox (Yesteryear), 1910 Benz Limo, light green w/chartreuse roof, red seats, NM **$24.00**

Matchbox (Yesteryear), 1911 Ford Model T, red w/black hood, grille & seats, brass wheels, MIB...............**$29.00**

Matchbox (Yesteryear), 1911 Renault 2-Seater, green, NM **$19.00**

Matchbox (Yesteryear), 1912 Rolls Royce, silver w/dark red ribbed roof, brass wheels, M....................**$24.00**

Matchbox (Yesteryear), 1930 Duesenberg, red, M in NM box **$25.00**

Mattel, Tricky Trolley, red plastic w/yellow trim, tin lithographed passengers, early 1950s, 4½x7½", EX......**$85.00**

Midgetoy, Army Truck, die-cast metal, olive w/black rubber tires, ca 1950s, 4½", EX+...................**$150.00**

Midgetoy, Convertible, die-cast metal, blue w/black rubber tires, ca 1950s, 5⅜", EX+....................**$20.00**

Midgetoy, Jeep, die-cast metal, military green, crimped axles, ca 1950s, 1¾". NM **$5.00**

Nylint, Jungle Wagon Ford Econoline Truck, pressed steel, lime green, w/6 animals, 1960s, 11½", NM, $125.00

Nylint, Model T, 1960s, M in VG box **$35.00**

Nylint, Tractor-Trailer, Wix Filters Promotional, pressed steel, ca 1981, 21½", MIB......................**$70.00**

Schuco, Chevrolet Corvair, lithographed & painted tin, white, brown & blue, friction, original box, 9½", EX......**$140.00**

Schuco, Mercedes Race Car, 1970s, MIB.................**$110.00**

Steelcraft, Dairy Truck, Sheffield Farms, red w/Bakelite wheels, electric headlights, nickle-plated grille, 18⅞", G- **$220.00**

Steelcraft, Dump Truck, Mack series, red cab, bed & wheels, black fenders & chassis, lever-action dump, 26", VG...**$330.00**

Steelcraft, Steam Shovel, #172, black w/red roof, black extension shovel & boom, decal on boiler, 1935, 16½", M..**$140.00**

Structo, American Airlines Lift Truck, G.......................**$75.00**

Structo, Cadillac, red w/black rubber tires, ca 1953, 6¼", EX..**$24.00**

Structo, Fire Truck, red w/black fenders, dummy headlights, Bakelite wheels, decal on hood, fillable tank, 23½"...**$132.00**

Structo, International Scout, pressed steel, turquoise & white w/2 interchangable tops, ca 1965, NM...............**$125.00**

Structo, Steam Shovel, pressed steel, orange, light blue & black, 18½", VG..**$35.00**

Taiyo, Ford Highway Patrol Police Car, tin, ca 1960, 10½", NMIB...**$35.00**

Taiyo, Volkswagon Ice-Cream Van, lithographed tin, friction, 9", NM in VG box.......................................**$170.00**

TN, 1958 Ford Skyliner, roof slides out of trunk to convert to hardtop, friction, 7½", EX...............................**$185.00**

Tonka, camper, painted metal, 1973, MIB.................**$50.00**

Tonka, CAT Dumpster, yellow metal, M....................**$25.00**

Tonka, Dune Buggy, painted metal, 1970, VG............**$50.00**

Tonka, Fisherman Pickup, #110, 1960, 14", M..........**$150.00**

Tonka, Lumber Truck, #998, 1956, 18¾", M...............**$185.00**

Tonka, Military Jeep, #251, 1963, 10½", M.................**$65.00**

Tonka, Pumper Truck w/Turbine, painted metal, EX.**$100.00**

Tonka, Stake Truck, #56, painted metal, 1964, 9½", EX.**$65.00**

Tonka, Thunderbird Express Semi, painted metal, 1957, 24", G..**$125.00**

Tonka, Winnebego, 2-tone painted metal, 1973, M.....**$70.00**

Wyandotte, Ambulance, plastic, w/siren & stretcher, friction, early, 9", EX..**$125.00**

Wyandotte, bus, light blue w/plated grille, black wood wheels, stamped mark on left side, 5¼", VG......**$105.00**

Wyandotte, Delivery Truck, red & green w/plastic tires, rear door opens, 17", VG...**$50.00**

Wyandotte, Dump Truck, black rubber tires, 1930s, 6", G.**$35.00**

Wyandotte, Express Truck, red cab w/plate grille, apple green non-detachable trailer, black chassis & wheels, 17", VG+..**$105.00**

Wyandotte, Fire Chief Hook & Ladder Truck, NMIB...**$75.00**

Wyandotte, Gasoline Truck, orange w/plated grille & bumper, black rubber tires, tailgate opens, 10¾", EX............**$130.00**

Wyandotte, Sedan, light blue w/4 molded wheel covers, silver grille, black tires, 5¾", VG+............................**$85.00**

Wyandotte, Streamline Touring Sedan, blue w/gray front grille, plastic wheels, 6", VG+..............................**$35.00**

Wyandotte, Tow Truck, lithographed w/green & white pinstriping, red plastic wheels, tools missing, original box, 15", VG..**$160.00**

Yonezawa, Valiant Convertible, red tin body w/black rubber tires, working wipers, EX+ in VG+ box.............**$175.00**

Wind-Ups

Wind-up toys, especially comic character or personality-related, are greatly in demand by collectors today. Though most were made through the years of the thirties through the fifties, they carry their own weight against much earlier toys and are considered very worthwhile investments. Mechanisms vary, some are key wound while others depended on lever action to tighten the mainspring and release the action of the toy. Tin and celluloid were used in their manufacture, and although it is sometimes possible to repair a tin wind-up, experts advise against putting your money into a celluloid toy whose mechanism is not working, since the material is too fragile to tolerate the repair.

Alps, Cowboy Whirling lasso, lithographed tin, MIB ..**$265.00**

Alps, Sharp Shooter, celluloid soldier crawls, stops, fires & continues, 8", MIB...**$80.00**

B&R, Kid Special, lithographed tin, yellow, red & blue, rear string-wind, clockwork, 2 motions, working, 6½", VG...**$200.00**

Courtland, Rocking-R-Ranch See-Saw, lithographed tin, ca 1955-57, 6x18", M in VG box...............................**$215.00**

Cragston, Playland Roller Coaster Shoot the Shoots, yellow & red lithographed tin track w/cars, 11x22", EX+ in VG+ box...**$190.00**

Gilbert, Teddy Bear Bicycle Aerialist, lithographed tin, 7", EX...**$187.00**

Haji, Juke Box, tin, non-working, 4¾x4", $135.00

Ideal, Frankensycle (Scare Cycle series), EX in VG box..**$85.00**

Irwin, Children on Seesaw, 2 actions, ca 1955-56, 4½", EX..**$75.00**

Wyandotte, Soap Box Derby Racer #226, red, white & blue tin body w/red wooden wheels, 1940s-50s, 6½" long, EX, $165.00

Irwin, Dancing Cinderella & Prince, painted plastic figures, working, original box, 5", EX.............$110.00

Japan, Baby in Pony Jump Seat, plastic & tin, 6", NM, $75.00

Lindstrom, Sweeping Betty, tin, 1930s, 8", EX...........$195.00

Linemar, Begging Roll-Over Pluto, yellow plush, rubber tail & tin eyes, clockwork, original box, 6½", VG+ ..$130.00

Linemar, Boxer Dog, plush over tin, nodding head & tail, bell around neck, 6", NM in EX box......................$50.00

Linemar, Donald Duck w/Whirling Tail, lithographed tin, white w/red, yellow & blue, w/red paper umbrella, 5", VG.................$225.00

Linemar, Ferdinand the Bull, tail & head move, G....$175.00

Linemar, Hopping Cow, lithographed tin, EX..............$65.00

Linemar, Walking Pluto, yellow plush w/rubber tail & ears, lithographed tin eyes, clockwork, working, w/box, 5½", EX.................$95.00

Marx, Dancing Butler, lithographed tin, black, red & yellow, hand-operated rod & gear mechanism, working, 5½", VG+.................$170.00

Marx, George the Drummer Boy, moving-eye version, bass drum, working, 9", VG $155.00

Marx, Harold Lloyd Walker, expression changes, clockwork, working, replaced arms, 11", VG.........................$200.00

Marx, Hee-Haw, balky mule cart, lithographed tin, 10" long, EX.................$180.00

Marx, Hopping Calamity Clara, lithographed tin, yellow, red & blue, clockwork, working, original box, 3½", VG ..$120.00

Marx, Mickey Mouse, plastic, tail spins, 1950s, NM...$145.00

Mego, Buck Rogers' Walking Twiki, head turns as he walks, 1979, MIB $35.00

Occupied Japan, Moving Elephant, celluloid, nods head w/vibrating movements, tail spins, ears move, bell rings, 6", MIB.................$175.00

Occupied Japan, Teddy's Cycle, EX $125.00

Ohio Art, Circus Shooting Gallery, tin, working, 1950s, EX $65.00

Ohio Art, Injun Chief, crawling Indian w/tomahawk, 7½", NM $100.00

Schuco, Monkey Violinist, lithographed tin, cloth clothes, 4½", EX.................$175.00

Schuco, Pick-Pick Chicken, yellow mohair over metal, working, EX $95.00

Schuco, Pig Playing Violin (may be from The Three Little Pigs), felt over tin, 4½", EX+ $200.00

Suzuki, Crawling Baby, celluloid w/painted features, cloth outfit, 4½", NMIB.................$35.00

TN, Mr Dan Hot-Dog Eating Man, lithographed tin & vinyl, lifts hot dog to mouth, chews & wipes, 7", M in NM box $75.00

Linemar, Running Pluto w/Moving Tongue, yellow-painted tin, 4" long, MIB, $350.00

Linemar, Superman Turn-Over Tank, lithographed tin, green w/yellow & blue trim, clockwork, working, 3¾", VG .$300.00

Linemar, Tramp from Lady & the Tramp, fur-covered tin, tail spins, legs move, EX.................$100.00

TPS, Clown on Roller Skates, lithographed tin upper body w/blue cloth pants, working, 6", EX, $215.00

TPS, Suzy Bouncing Ball, lithographed tin w/vinyl head, bounces tin ball attached to wire, arms move, 5", EX in NM box...**$90.00**

Unique Art, Bombo Monk, w/water-damaged box, 9½", EX...**$120.00**

Unique Art, Gertie Goose, lithographed tin, goose bounces around while pecking the ground, 9", EX..........**$145.00**

Unique Art, GI Joe & His Bouncing Jeep, lithographed tin, clockwork, working, 6½", VG.............................**$110.00**

Wolverine, Drum Major, yellow & blue w/black highlights, working, 13½", G-..**$65.00**

Wyandotte, Humphrey Mobile, lithographed tin, clockwork, working, chimney missing, 8½", G.....................**$180.00**

Wyandotte, Pool Players, lithographed tin, 14", VG+..**$145.00**

Trading Cards

Modern collector cards are really just an extension of a hobby that began well before the turn of the century. Advertising cards put out by food and tobacco companies sometimes featured cute children and their pets, stage stars, battle scenes, presidential candidates, and so forth. Some cards were included with the products they advertised, and some were simply stacked on the grocer's counter for his customers to pick up when they visited his store. Collectors gathered them up and pasted them in scrapbooks. In the twentieth century, candy and bubble gum companies came to the forefront. Sports figures have become popular, so have fictional heroes, TV and movie stars, Disney characters, Barbie dolls, and country singers!

For more information, we recommend *Collector's Guide to Trading Cards* by Robert Reed.

Abbey, Magic Action, 1964, series of 24, each...............**$2.00**
Bowman, America Salutes the FBI, 1949, series of 36, each...**$20.00**
Bowman, Frontier Days, 1955, series of 128, each........**$3.50**
Bowman, TV & Radio Stars of NBC, 1953, series of 96, each..**$6.00**
Bowman, Wild West, 1949, series of 180, each.............**$5.00**
Burry's, Howdy Doody, 1950, series of 42, each..........**$4.00**
Calico, Endangered Species, 1990, series of 36, each......**$.40**
Calico, League of Nations, Series I, 1989, series of 18, each ....**$.20**
Cameron, Airplanes, 1940, series of 30, each...............**$6.00**
Comic Images, Art Adams, 1989, series of 45, each..........**$.35**
Comic Images, Art of Greg Hildebrandt, 1992, series of 90, each...**$.25**
Comic Images, Boris Vallejo, Series II, 1992, series of 90, each...**$.25**
Comic Images, Colossal Conflicts, 1988, series of 90, each ....**$.40**
Comic Images, Conan, 1988, series of 50, each...............**$.35**
Comic Images, First Covers, 1991, series of 60, each ......**$.25**
Comic Images, Flaming Carrot, 1988, series of 40, each .**$.35**
Comic Images, Ghost Rider I, 1990, series of 45, each....**$.30**
Comic Images, Honeymooners, 1988, series of 50, each...**$.40**
Comic Images, Incredible Hulk, 1991, series of 40, each ..**$.25**

Comic Images, Savage Dragon, 1990, series of 11, each.**$.15**
Comic Images, Spider Team Up, 1990, series of 45, each ..**$.45**
Comic Images, X-Men, 1991, series of 90, each.............**$.20**
Crown, Sky Force, 1991, series of 9, each....................**$.60**
Dart Flipcards, Vietnam Fact Cards, Volume I, 1988, series of 66, each..**$.45**
Diamond, My Little Pony, 1986, series of 200, each ....**$.20**
Donruss, Awesome All Stars, 1988, series of 127, each...**$.15**
Donruss, Bionic Woman, 1976, series of 44, each..........**$.45**
Donruss, CHIPS, 1977, series of 66, each.....................**$.25**
Donruss, Combat Series II, 1964, series of 66, each.....**$2.50**
Donruss, Dallas, 1981, series of 56, each.....................**$.25**
Donruss, Flying Nun, 1968, series of 66, each..............**$4.00**
Donruss, Kiss, Series I, 1978, series of 132, each...........**$.75**
Donruss, Monkees, 1967, series of 44, each..................**$1.50**
Donruss, Odd Rods, 1970, series of 44, each...............**$1.00**
Donruss, Voyage to the Bottom of the Sea, 1964, series of 66, each..**$2.50**
Dynamic, Believe It or Not, 1962, series of 35, each.....**$6.00**
Dynamic, Popeye, 1962, series of 35, each...................**$6.00**
Eclipse, Coup d'Etat, 1991, series of 36, each.................**$.40**
Eclipse, Drug Wars, 1991, series of 36, each.................**$.35**
Eclipse, Famous Comic Book Creator Cards, 1992, series of 110, each..**$.20**
Eclipse, Heroes of the Blues, 1992, series of 36, each.....**$.35**
Eclipse, Iran Contra (Scandal Special), 1988, series of 36, each...**$.30**
Eclipse, Rotten to the Core, 1989, series of 60, each.......**$.15**
Eclipse, Savings & Loan Scandal, 1991, series of 36, each..**$.30**
Eclipse, True Crime, 1992, series of 110, each..............**$.15**
Fleer, Casper, 1960, series of 66, each.......................**$5.00**
Fleer, Gomer Pyle, 1965, series of 66, each.................**$1.50**
Fleer, Here's Bo, 1981, series of 72 w/12 stickers, each..**$.15**
Fleer, Hogan's Heroes, 1966, series of 66, each, from $5 to...**$10.00**
Fleer, Ms Pac Man, 1981, series of 54 w/28 stickers, each .**$.25**
Fleer, Three Stooges, 1959, series of 96, each.............**$10.00**
Fleer, Tiny Toons, 1991, series of 77 w/22 stickers, each ..**$.25**
Fleer, Yule Laff, 1960, series of 66, each.....................**$1.50**
Goudey, Histories of Aviation, 1936, series of 10, each, from $35 to...**$65.00**
Historical Images, Defending Freedom, 1991, series of 144, each...**$.15**
Imagine, Grande Illusions, 1988, series of 60, each.........**$.15**
Imagine, Scream Queens II, 1990, series of 60, each ......**$.20**
Impel, GI Joe, 1991, series of 200, each ....**$.20**
Impel, Marvel Universe, Series III, 1992, series of 162, each...**$.20**
Impel, Minnie & Me, 1991, series of 160, each ....**$.20**
Impel, Nightmare on Elm Street, 1991, series of 120, each...**$.15**
Leaf, Foney Ads, 1960, series of 72, each....................**$1.25**
Lime Rock, Mad Magazine I, 1992, series of 55, each .:...**$.20**
Lime Rock, Pro Cheerleaders, 1992, series of 45, each....**$.25**
Manor, Star Trek, 1979, series of 33, each....................**$.40**
Monty, He-Man, 1986, series of 100, each....................**$.15**
Monty, James Bond, A View to a Kill, 1985, series of 100, each...**$.60**

Monty, Popeye & Friends, 1988, series of 100, each .... **$.40**
Monty, Sesame Street, 1986, series of 100, each .... **$.20**
Monty, Webster, 1985, series of 100, each .... **$.25**
Nu-Cards, Dinosaurs, 1961, series of 80, each **$3.50**
Nu-Cards, Horror Monsters, 1961, series of 66, each..... **$2.50**
Pacific, Andy Griffith, Series III, 1990, series of 110, each. **$.25**
Pacific, Bingo, 1991, series of 100, each .... **$.25**
Pacific, I Love Lucy, 1991, series of 110, each .... **$.50**
Pacific, Operation Desert Shield, 1991, series of 110, each . **$.25**
Pacific, Total Recall, 1990, series of 110, each .... **$.25**
Pacific, Where Are They?, 1992, series of 110, each .... **$.10**
Pacific, Wizard of Oz, 1990, series of 110, each .... **$.25**

Philadelphia Gum, Dark Shadows, Series II, 1968, series of 66, each, $7.50

Philadelphia Gum, Quentin, 1969, series of 16, each.... **$4.50**
Philadelphia Gum, War Bulletin, 1965, series of 88, each. **$2.50**
Piedmont, Terrorist Attack, 1987, series of 35, each .... **$.30**
Price, Krazy Kards, 1960, series of 66, each **$1.00**
Pro Set, Guinness Book of World Records, 1992, series of 100, each.. **$.15**
Pro Set, Little Mermaid, 1991, series of 90 w/37 stickers, each.. **$.25**
Pro Set, Rock Superstars, 1991, series of 260, each .... **$.25**
Pro Set, Super Stars Musicards, 1991, series of 260, each. **$.15**
Quaker, Dog Cards, 1949, series of 36, each **$4.00**
Quaker, Planes, 1957, series of 27, each **$4.00**
Rosan, Famous Monsters, 1963, series of 64, each **$2.50**
Rosan, John F Kennedy, 1964, series of 64, each .... **$.75**
Rosan, Midnight Madness, 1990, series of 72, each .... **$.40**
Spectra Star, Series I, 1991, series of 60, each .... **$.15**
Star Pics, Alien 3, 1992, series of 80, each..................... **$.20**
Star Pics, Twin Peaks, 1991, series of 76, each .... **$.15**
Sunbeam, DC Comic Heroes, 1978, series of 30, each.. **$1.25**
Top Pilot, Stealth Bomber, B-2 Edition, 1990, series of 7, each.. **$.45**

Topps, American Gladiators, 1992, series of 88, each ..... **$.20**
Topps, American Heroes Stamps, 1963, series of 88, each **$8.50**
Topps, Autos of 1977, series of 90 w/20 stickers, each... **$.35**
Topps, Batman the Movie, Series I, 1989, series of 132 w/22 stickers, each .... **$.15**
Topps, Beatles Diary, 1964, series of 60, each............... **$3.00**
Topps, Beverly Hillbillies, 1963, series of 66, each........ **$5.00**
Topps, Brady Bunch, 1970, series of 88, each............. **$15.00**
Topps, Bring 'Em Back Alive, 1950, series of 100, each.. **$7.50**
Topps, Charlie's Angels, 1977, series of 55 w/11 stickers, each.. **$.50**
Topps, Desert Storm Victory, 1991, series of 88 w/11 stickers, each... **$.25**
Topps, Disgusting Disguises, 1967, series of 24 w/36 stickers, ea... **$2.50**
Topps, ET, 1982, series of 87 w/12 stickers, each .... **$.35**
Topps, Flags of the World, 1956, series of 80, each...... **$2.00**
Topps, Fright Flicks, 1988, series of 90 w/11 stickers, each.. **$.30**
Topps, Funny Valentines, 1959, series of 66, each........ **$7.50**
Topps, Get Smart, 1966, series of 66, each **$4.00**
Topps, Ghostbusters II, 1989, series of 88 w/11 stickers, each.. **$.25**
Topps, Good Times, 1975, series of 55 w/21 stickers, each.. **$.50**
Topps, Gremlins, Series I, 1984, series of 82 w/11 stickers, each.. **$.20**

Topps, Isolation Booth, 1957, series of 88, each, $4.00

Topps, Land of the Giants, 1968, series of 55, each....**$10.00**
Topps, Man on the Moon II, 1969, series of 99, each ...**$1.50**
Topps, Mod Squad, 1969, series of 55, each.................**$2.50**
Topps, New Kids on the Block, 1990, series of 88 w/11 stickers, each .... **$.20**
Topps, Planet of the Apes, 1975, series of 66, each .... **$.35**

Topps, Raiders of the Lost Ark, 1981, series of 88, each .**$.25**
Topps, Rat Patrol, 1966, series of 66, each.....................**$2.50**
Topps, Return of the Jedi, Series I, 1983, series of 132 w/33 stickers, each ....**$.25**
Topps, Robin Hood, 1957, series of 60, each **$5.00**
Topps, Room 222, 1969, series of 44, each..................**$18.00**
Topps, Six Million-Dollar Man, 1975, series of 55, each..**$4.00**
Topps, Supergirl, 1984, series of 44, each ....**$.25**
Topps, Superman, 1966, series of 66, each **$4.00**
Topps, Superman the Movie, Series I, 1978, series of 77 w/12 stickers, each...**$.35**
Topps, Tarzan & the She-Devil, 1953, series of 60, each..**$5.00**
Topps, US Presidents, 1956, series of 36, each **$2.00**
Topps, Valentine Postcards, 1969, series of 33, each **$4.00**
Topps, Wacky Packages, 1991, series of 66, each ....**$.25**
Topps, Wacky Plaks, 1959, series of 88, each................**$2.00**
Topps, You'll Die Laughing, 1960, series of 66, each....**$1.50**
Tuff Stuff, Civil War, 1991, series of 100, each.................**$.20**
Tuff Stuff, Johnny Clem Diamond Edition, 1991, series of 10, each..**$.85**
Tuff Stuff, Peanuts, 1991, series of 33, each ....**$.50**
Tuff Stuff, Presidential Prospects, 1992, series of 9, each .**$1.50**
Tuff Stuff, World War II Propoganda, 1991, series of 120, each..**$.20**

Trolls

The legend of the Troll originated in Scandinavia. Ancient folklore has it that they were giant, supernatural beings, but in more modern times, they're portrayed as dwarfs or imps who live in underground caverns. During the seventies there was a TV cartoon special called *The Hobbit* and a movie, *The Lord of the Rings*, that caused them to become popular. As a result, books, puzzles, posters, and dolls of all types were available on the retail market. In the early eighties, Broom Hilda and Irwin Troll were featured in a series of books as well as Saturday morning cartoons, and today trolls are enjoying a strong comeback.

The three main manufacturers of the 'vintage' trolls are Dam Things (Royalty Des. of Florida), Uneeda (Wishnicks), and A/S Nyform of Norway. Some were made in Hong Kong and Japan as well, but generally these were molded of inferior plastic.

The larger trolls (approximately 12") are rare and very desirable to collectors, and the troll animals, such as the giraffe, horse, cow, donkey, and lion made by Dam, are bringing premium prices.

Baseball player, 1960s, 6", NM......................................**$40.00**
Batman, vinyl, stapled-on clothes, w/mask, Uneeda, 1966, 3", M...**$25.00**
Boy bank, white hair, green & red outfit, 6½"............**$35.00**
Bride-Nik, formal outfit, Dam, 1978, MIP....................**$15.00**
Brother Bear, vinyl w/jointed neck, inset glassine eyes, comes w/passport, Leprechaun Limited, 1970, M.**$80.00**
Caveman, marked Ughie, Ughie, 3"...............................**$15.00**
Cow, vinyl w/glassine eyes, 3", EX...............................**$50.00**

Elephant, black hair, Dam, sm, EX................................**$30.00**
Elephant w/drum, Dam, 1964, 3", NM...........................**$45.00**
Eskimo, green hair, pink & white outfit, Dam, 1964, 13", EX, minimum value **$100.00**
Frankenstein, Hong Kong, 3", NM................................**$28.00**
Hawaiian Troll, vinyl, marked 1964 on back, 3", M **$15.00**
Little Devil, Reisler of Denmark, 1965, M.....................**$45.00**
Little girl, original clothes, Dam, 1960s, 5", M.............**$30.00**
Lover Boy-Nik, vinyl w/mohair, original clothes & cap, Dam, M...**$15.00**
Lucky Shnook, white hair, blue body, 1960s, 3"..........**$20.00**
Monkey, vinyl w/jointed neck, original clothes, Shekter, marked on foot, 1966, M **$75.00**
No Goodniks, Wishnik series, 1970s, MOC..................**$10.00**
Pirate bank, Dam, 1960s, 6½", M, minimum value......**$40.00**
Santa, vinyl w/rooted hair & beard, painted inset eyes, suit & cap w/bell, 4½", M...**$60.00**
Sappy Claws, Dam, M..**$25.00**
Tartan Girl, no hair, original tag, 1964, 12", NM..........**$45.00**
Toronto Blue Jays, MOC..**$8.00**

Viking, molded helmet, blue cloth dress, Dam Things, 3½", EX, $135.00

Weird creature, real animal hair, 1960s, 3", MIP..........**$30.00**
Werewolf Monster, 1960s, 3"...**$40.00**

TV Guides

This publication goes back to the early 1950s, and granted, those early issues are very rare. But what an interesting, very visual way to chronicle the history of TV programming.

Values in our listings are for examples in fine to mint

condition. For insight into *TV Guide* collecting, we recommend *The TV Guide Catalog* by Jeff Kadet, the *TV Guide* Specialist.

1952, November 21, Howdy Doody, $125.00

1953, April 3, Lucy's $50,000,000 Baby **$550.00**
1953, July 24, Groucho...**$115.00**
1953, June 26, Dinah Shore...**$35.00**
1954, December 4, George Gobel **$12.00**
1954, February 12, Red Buttons **$18.00**
1954, May 14, Frank Sinatra **$45.00**

1955, April 30, Fess Parker as 'Davy Crockett,' $50.00

1955, January 22, Ed Sullivan......................................**$15.00**
1955, July 9, Patti Page **$10.00**
1955, September 3, Johnny & Jody Carson **$23.00**
1956, June 23, Steve Allen...**$14.00**
1956, March 17, Maurice Evans & Lilli Palmer **$8.00**
1956, September 8, Elvis Presley **$220.00**
1957, February 2, Jane Wyman **$8.00**
1957, June 8, Lassie...**$20.00**
1957, March 23, Ernie Ford **$10.00**

1958, March 22, Perry Como **$9.00**
1958, May 3, Shirley Temple **$20.00**
1958, September 13, Lennon Sisters..............................**$8.00**
1959, February 14, Alfred Hitchcock.............................**$9.00**
1959, May 30, Steve McQueen **$47.00**
1959, October 31, Fred Astaire **$12.00**
1960, June 25, Cast of 'Bonanza'.................................**$50.00**
1960, March 26, Donna Reed **$20.00**
1960, November 12, Fred MacMurray............................**$8.00**
1961, April 15, Mitch Miller **$6.00**
1961, February 4, Clint Eastwood **$50.00**
1961, October 14, Red Skelton **$9.00**
1962, February 17, Danny Thomas **$10.00**
1962, May 12, Don Knotts **$22.00**
1962, October 6, Cast of 'Hazel'...................................**$25.00**
1963, August 31, Richard Boone **$8.00**
1963, February 2, Jack Webb **$23.00**
1963, May 4, Cast of 'The Virginian' **$11.00**
1964, June 13, Fred Flintstone, only TV Guide w/a chiseled logo..**$92.00**
1964, March 28, Lawrence Welk **$9.00**
1964, September 26, Dan Blocker...............................**$21.00**
1965, February 6, Jackie Gleason **$9.00**
1965, July 3, Jimmy Dean **$5.00**
1965, October 23, Chuck Conners **$11.00**
1966, April 2, Dean Martin **$8.00**
1966, January 1, Carol Channing...................................**$6.00**
1966, October 1, Vietnam War **$7.00**
1967, December 16, Sebastian Cabot.............................**$9.00**
1967, June 10, Smothers Brothers **$16.00**
1967, September 23, The Monkees...............................**$34.00**
1968, April 13, Carl Betz..**$10.00**

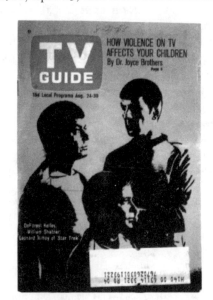

1968, August 24, Star Trek, $100.00

1968, March 24, Joey Bishop...**$4.00**
1968, September 21, Rowan & Martin **$8.00**
1969, April 26, Jack Parr..**$4.00**
1969, August 16, Merv Griffin.......................................**$4.00**
1969, February 22, Cast of 'Lancer' **$15.00**
1970, January 24, Tom Jones..**$8.00**
1970, June 27, Liza Minnelli..**$6.00**

1970, October 24, Don Knotts......................................$6.00
1971, January 23, Flip Wilson......................................$6.00
1971, June 26, Cast of 'Adam 12'...............................$4.00
1971, October 16, Mia Farrow....................................$6.00
1972, April 22, Don Rickles..$3.00
1972, January 29, David Janssen...............................$17.00
1972, November 4, John Wayne...................................$8.00
1973, February 24, Cast of 'M*A*S*H'.......................$15.00
1973, November 24, Cousteau Explores Antarctica $5.00
1973, September 8, Special Fall Preview Issue $19.00
1974, April 20, Peter Falk of 'Columbo'......................$6.00
1974, February 2, Dom Deluise of 'Lotsa Luck'.............$4.00
1974, July 13, Johnny Carson $3.00
1975, April 12, Cher...$7.00
1975, August 2, Mike Douglas....................................$3.00
1975, November 1, Lloyd Bridges as 'Joe Forrester' $4.00
1976, April 3, Baseball...$3.00
1976, June 26, Mary Tyler Moore................................$5.00
1976, September 11, Bob Dylan.................................$14.00
1977, August 6, The Muppets......................................$5.00
1977, February 12, Cast of 'Kojak'..............................$5.00
1977, June 11, Grizzly Adams......................................$3.00
1978, April 8, Cast of 'Alice' $5.00
1978, December 2, Benji..$3.00
1978, July 15, Robert Conrad of 'Black Sheep Squadron' ..$4.00
1979, March 3, Gary Coleman.....................................$3.00
1979, November 10, The Bee Gees $8.00
1979, September 1, Miss America.................................$3.00
1980, August 2, Real People.......................................$4.00
1980, December 20, Merry Christmas $3.00
1980, May 31, Cast of 'Vegas'.....................................$4.00
1981, April 25, Alan Alda by Hirshfield $5.00
1981, August 1, Miss Piggy...$4.00
1981, January 24, Super Bowl '81...............................$3.00
1982, July 10, cast of 'Facts of Life' $5.00
1982, March 27, Larry Hagman....................................$4.00
1982, October 2, Genie Francis....................................$4.00
1983, March 5, Valerie Bertinelli.................................$4.00
1983, May 21, Bob Hope...$3.00
1983, October 1, Gregory Harrison...............................$4.00
1984, March 17, Priscilla Presley.................................$7.00
1984, May 12, Crystal Gayle..$3.00
1984, October 27, Brooke Shields................................$4.00
1985, August 10, Madonna..$8.00
1985, March 2, Michael Landon...................................$8.00
1985, May 11, Cheryl Ladd..$5.00
1986, August 2, TV's Macho Man.................................$4.00
1986, December 20, Cast of 'Our House' $3.00
1986, March 22, Bill Cosby..$3.00
1987, Ann-Margret...$5.00
1987, August 15, Alf...$4.00
1987, May 2, Cast of 'Cheers'......................................$5.00
1988, January 9, Emma Samms....................................$4.00
1988, June 4, ABC Sports..$3.00
1988, September 17, Olympics......................................$4.00
1989, March 4, Vanna White $3.00
1989, May 6, TV is 50, collectors' issue $5.00
1989, September 16, Rosanne Barr & Bill Cosby ...$10.00

1990, February 17, Elvis...$4.00
1990, November 17, Muppets.......................................$3.00
1991, April 27, Dinosaurs $4.00
1991, November 23, Madonna.....................................$5.00
1992, May 9, Goodby-Y-Y-Y-Y-Y-E Johnny $3.00
1992, September 12, Special Fall Preview Issue...........$8.00
1993, August 21, Loni Anderson $3.00
1993, May 15, Closing Time at 'Cheers' $7.00

TV Shows and Movies

Since the early days of TV and the movies right up to the present time, hit shows have inspired numerous toys and memorabilia. If they were well established, manufacturers often cashed in on their popularity through the sale of more expensive items such as toys and dolls; but more often than not, those less established were promoted through paper goods such as books, games, and paper dolls, just in case their fame turned out to be short lived.

Already in some of the newsletters specializing in toys, you see dealers speculatively offering Roger Rabbit memorabilia for sale, and the same is true of Indiana Jones, The Equalizer, and Ninja Turtles. So with an eye to the future (possibly the *near* future), see if you can pick the shows that will generate the collectibles you need to be hanging on to.

See also Beatles Collectibles; Character and Promotional Drinking Glasses; Character Collectibles; Elvis Presley Memorabilia; Games; Halloween Costumes; Movie Stars; Paper Dolls; Puzzles; Shirley Temple; Star Trek; Star Wars; Toys; and Western Heroes.

A-Team, air freshener, Mr T figure, M $3.00
A-Team, Rub & Play Transfers, MIP.............................$5.00
Addams Family, bank, Thing figure, NM in VG+ box.$150.00
Addams Family, doll, Morticia, plastic w/soft plastic head,
    long black hair, Remco, 1964, 5", EX+ $150.00
Airwolf, wallet, action scene, NMOC...........................$7.00
Alf, kite, sealed, MIP..$4.00
All in the Family, record album, 33⅓ rpm, 1971, EX...$25.00
Alvin & the Chipmunks, record player, working, 1965,
    EX+ $50.00
Back to the Future, Delorian car, 6", MIB...................$20.00
Banana Splits, Kut-Up Kit, w/scissors & stencils, Laramie,
    1975, NMOC $24.00
Banana Splits, switch plate, 1960s, MIB $40.00
Banana Splits, tambourine, 1972, MIB........................$35.00
Batman, standee, cardboard movie display, 60", EX ...$70.00
Batman Returns, lobby card set, Zanart, M $12.00
Batman Returns, playing cards, 52 photo cards, complete,
    US Playing, 1992, EX..................................$4.00
Battlestar Galactica, tablecloth, paper, MIP $3.00
Ben Casey, diary, w/lock, 1962, NM...........................$15.00
Ben Hur, coloring book, Sampson Lowe, 1959, M......$45.00
Benji, doll, plush, original collar w/metal name tag & paper
    tag, 1978, EX $70.00
Beverly Hillbillies, coloring book, Whitman, 1964, EX..$30.00

Beverly Hillbillies, fan-club postcard, features cast & facsimile signatures, 1963, unused, 3x5", M.....................**$15.00**

Bewitched, activity book, 1965, EX+ **$25.00**

Big Valley, book, Whitman, hardcover, EX................**$10.00**

Black Hole, original movie soundtrack, M.................**$10.00**

Blues Brothers, poster, orignal, M **$65.00**

Bonanza, cup, metal lithographed w/Ponderosa ranch house & characters, NM..**$9.00**

Bonanza, tin cup, features Hoss, Ben & Little Joe, EX, $12.50

Bonanza, writing tablet, early, unused, M...................**$24.00**

Brady Bunch, soundtrack, Meet the Brady Bunch, 1972, EX...**$30.00**

Captain Kangaroo, coloring book, features Mr Greenjeans, 1959, NM **$25.00**

Captain Kangaroo, hand puppet, vinyl head w/cloth body, EX **$35.00**

Captain Kangaroo, magic slate, w/stylus, old store stock, EE Fairchild, 1960s, M **$8.00**

Car 54 Where Are You?, puppet, Muldoon, 1962, EX .**$10.00**

Charlie's Angels, stickers, 1st or 2nd series, Topps, 1977, M, ea **$2.50**

CHIPS, Colorforms, 1981, MIB **$15.00**

Close Encounters of the Third Kind, collector cards, 48 cards, complete, Crown, 1978, 3½x5"....................**$20.00**

Cosby Show, scrapbook, color photos, hard-bound, 80 pages, 5½x8", NM **$7.00**

Dark Shadows, poster, House of Dark Shadows, original, EX+ **$125.00**

Different Strokes, coloring book, 1983, VG **$4.00**

Dukes of Hazzard, bank, General Lee car w/decals, 1981, 4½x16", EX **$8.00**

Dukes of Hazzard, folder, 1981, 10x8", EX **$4.00**

ET, Colorforms, MIB **$25.00**

ET, key chain, 1982, M **$5.00**

ET, TV tray, steel w/fold-out legs, images of ET & Elliot, 1982, EX..**$15.00**

Fall Guy, activity book, 1982, EX.................................**$6.00**

Fame, coloring book, photo of 5 stars, 1983, EX..........**$5.00**

Family Affair, coloring book, Whitman, 1968, EX........**$20.00**

Flintstones, book, Take a Vacation, Durabook, 1974, EX...**$8.00**

Flying Nun, soundtrack, 1966, EX...............................**$30.00**

Ghostbusters, playing cards, sealed, Belgium, 1986, MIP **$5.00**

Gremlins, bendee, Stripe, 5", MOC.............................**$10.00**

Gunsmoke, badge, Texas Ranger Sheriff, 1963, MOC.**$20.00**

Happy Days, Fonzie's Paint Set, sealed, 1979, MIB.....**$15.00**

Hardcastle & McCormick, walkie-talkies, Jaru, 1983, NMOC...**$15.00**

Hawaii Five-O, book, Top Secret, Whitman, 1969, EX+.**$18.00**

High Chaparall, paperpack book, Coyote Gold, John & Victoria on cover, 1969, EX+ **$10.00**

Incredible Hulk, bank, figural, Remco, 1978, NMIB....**$10.00**

Incredible Hulk, iron-on transfer, sealed, 1980, 4", M ...**$2.00**

Indiana Jones & the Temple of Doom, patch, M...........**$5.00**

Jetsons, coloring book, Rand McNally, 1986, NM **$6.00**

Karate Kid, playset, sealed, Remco, 1987, MIB............**$15.00**

Knight Rider, bank, Kit the car, black plastic, M **$10.00**

Lassie, beach ball, 1950s, M **$45.00**

Laugh-In, notebook holder, pink vinyl, 1969, EX........**$20.00**

Lost in Space, note pad, 1960s, 8x10", M **$42.00**

M*A*S*H, beer can, empty, M.....................................**$17.00**

Magnum PI, gum cards, set of 66, Donruss, 1983, EX.**$10.00**

Man from UNCLE, book, Affair of the Gentle Saboteur, hardbound, Whitman, 1966, EX **$14.00**

Man from UNCLE, poster, Napoleon Solo, black & white, 1965, 24x36", shrink wrapped, M..........................**$25.00**

Mickey Mouse Club, poster, Back on the Air, 1971, 36x22", EX..**$75.00**

Mickey Mouse Club, projector w/screen, record & double-feature slides, Mattel, 9", NM in VG box, $125.00

Mistress of the Dark, poster, features Elvira, M **$12.00**

Mod Squad, book, Pyramid, Sock-It-To-Em Murders, paperback, #3 in series, 1968, EX+.................................**$4.00**

Mork & Mindy, book, The Mork & Mindy Story, paperback, 1979, EX..**$5.00**

Mork & Mindy, doll, Mork, w/talking space pack, MIB .**$25.00**

Mr Ed, hand puppet, plush body w/vinyl head, pull-string talker, Mattel, working, 1962, 13", VG **$55.00**

Mr Magoo, doll, vinyl head, Ideal, 1960s, NM **$65.00**

Munsters, book, The Last Resort, Whitman, 1966, NM .. **$35.00**

Munsters, doll, Herman, Remco, M **$200.00**

Munsters, hand puppet, Grandpa, Ideal, 1964, EX **$75.00**

Munsters, hand puppet, Herman, 1966, EX **$100.00**

Munsters, hand puppet, Lily, Ideal, 1965, NM **$95.00**

Munsters, magazine, #1, 1965, EX+ **$100.00**

Munsters, serving tray, features Herman, M **$12.00**

My Favorite Martian, coloring book, 128 pages, some pages colored, Whitman, 1964, EX **$22.00**

My Three Sons, coloring book, uncolored, Whitman, 1963, M **$25.00**

Old Yeller, soundtrack, 1964, sealed, M **$20.00**

Our Gang, coloring book, Saalfield, 1933, G+ **$40.00**

Our Gang, tablet, shows classroom, 8x10", EX **$10.00**

Partridge Family, magazine, Tiger Beat, David on cover, 66 pages, 1972, M **$12.00**

Pete's Dragon, gum cards, complete set, Panini, M **$35.00**

Petticoat Junction, coloring book, Whitman, 1964, 8x11", NM **$100.00**

Planet of the Apes, candy box, Phoenix Candy Co, photo of the Apes on front, portrait on back, 1967, 5x2½x1", NM .. **$25.00**

Planet of the Apes, cup, plastic w/pictures & logo, EX. **$5.00**

Planet of the Apes, press book, 20th Century Fox, ca 1974, 8½x14", NM **$8.00**

Rat Patrol, book, Desert Danger, paperback, EX **$15.00**

Real McCoys, Walter Brennan photo, black & white glossy, signed, 1961, NM **$25.00**

Shazam, coloring book, Whitman, 1967, M **$35.00**

Simon & Simon, walkie-talkies w/telescoping antennas, Gordy, 1983, MOC **$15.00**

Simpsons, frisbee, Bart Simpson w/Radical Dude, white plastic, EX **$3.00**

Six Million-Dollar Man, coloring & activity book, 1977, EX **$50.00**

Soupy Sales Show, fun & activity book, 1965, EX **$18.00**

Space 1999, Colorforms, MIB **$18.00**

Starsky & Hutch, viewer w/4 film strips, Fleetwood, 1976, M on EX card **$28.00**

Terminator 2, make-up kit, Imagineering, MIP **$20.00**

That Girl, coloring book, Saalfield, 1968, M **$35.00**

Three's Company, sticker set, 44 card-size stickers w/color photos from show, 1978, NM **$18.00**

Three Stooges, dolls, set of 3, 14", M **$65.00**

Time Tunnel, coloring book, uncolored, Saalfield, 1966, M **$75.00**

V, puffy stickers, set of 6, 1984, MIP **$5.00**

Welcome Back Kotter, Colorforms, complete w/booklet, 1976, EX **$9.00**

Willow, place mats, laminated, Kraft mail-in, set of 4, NM **$10.00**

Wizard of Oz, coloring book, abridged edition, 48 pages, Whitman, 1939, VG **$40.00**

Wizard of Oz, magazine article, Life, July 17, 1939, 2-page color tear-out sheets w/8 photos, NM **$35.00**

Wizard of Oz, Scarecrow jack-in-the-box, plays music, Mattel, 1967 .... **$45.00**

Wonder Woman, switch plate, 1977, MOC **$10.00**

Twin Winton

A California-based company founded by twins Ross and Don, the company called Twin Winton Ceramics had its beginnings in the mid-thirties. The men remained active in the ceramic industry until 1975, designing and producing animal figures, cookie jars and matching kitchenware items. One of their most successful lines was mugs, pitchers, bowls, lamps, ashtrays, and novelty items modeled after the mountain boys in Paul Webb's cartoon series.

If you'd like more information, read *The Collector's Encyclopedia of California Pottery* by Jack Chipman and *The Collector's Encyclopedia of Cookie Jars, Vol I and II,* by Joyce and Fred Roerig. See also Cookie Jars.

Ashtray, Hillbilly, Clem reclining on base **$45.00**

Bank, Dobbin, seated colt wearing hat, hand-painted flowers, marked, pr **$45.00**

Bowl, Cereal in script in bottom w/floral decoration, baby sitting on blue rim, marked Twin Winton Pasadena & W **$35.00**

Candy jar, turtle shape, bunny w/lollipop on back, wood-tone, marked **$50.00**

Canister, Ye Old Sugar Bucket, wood-tone brown, marked **$30.00**

Cigarette box w/match barrel, outhouse shape, marked TW Pasadena **$60.00**

Figurine, School Boy, in stride on round base **$35.00**

Ice buckets, Hillbilly figure draped over top of barrel, in-mold mark, $125.00; Bathing hillbilly scrubbing back in barrel of water marked Ice, 1962, $125.00

Mugs, Ma & Pa, circular profiles embossed on front w/wood-textured background, branch handles, white interiors, each **$45.00**

Napkin holder, Poodle, bright-eyed dog lying on pillow, Snyder................$30.00

Napkin holder, Ranger Bear, wood-tone finish w/lightly painted detailing, unmarked $35.00

Pitcher, Hillbilly, banded barrel shape w/spout & figural hillbilly handle $65.00

Planter, Squirrel, leaning on tree trunk $22.00

Pretzel bowl, Hillbilly, half barrel shape w/hillbilly head & feet emerging from ends $40.00

Salt & pepper shakers, Cop, portly figure saluting, Winton Calif on bottom, pr $35.00

Salt & pepper shakers, Cop, right hand to head, brown w/yellow star, black features, marked, pr............$35.00

Salt & pepper shakers, Friar Tuck, brown robe, marked, pr.......................$30.00

Salt & pepper shakers, Hillbilly, head emerging from keg, pr.......................$25.00

Salt & pepper shakers, Ranger Bear, wood-tone brown, no mark, pr.......................$30.00

Spoon rest, Lamb, Snyder.......................$20.00

Spoon rest, Sailor Elephant, in profile, wood-tone w/white spoon & hat, no mark.......................$25.00

Table lamp, Hillbilly, sleeping figure on moonshine keg, ca 1949 ....$125.00

Tankard, Hillbilly, straight sides, brown bands, hillbilly figural handle, marked.......................$40.00

Universal Dinnerware

This pottery incorporated in Cambridge, Ohio, in 1934, the outgrowth of several smaller companies in the area. They produced many lines of dinnerware and kitchenware items, most of which were marked. They're best known for their Ballerina dinnerware (simple modern shapes in a variety of solid colors) and Cat-tail (See Cat-tail Dinnerware). The company closed in 1960.

Ballerina, creamer.......................$12.00
Ballerina, cup $7.50
Ballerina, egg cup $20.00
Ballerina, gravy boat.......................$15.00
Ballerina, sugar bowl.......................$15.00
Calico Fruit, bowl, soup; tab handles $7.50
Calico Fruit, plate, 6".......................$5.00
Calico Fruit, platter, tab handles, 11½".......................$20.00
Calico Fruit, salt & pepper shakers, utility; pr.............$18.00
Circus, pie server.......................$20.00
Holland Rose, plate, Old Holland shape, sm.................$5.00
Iris, casserole.......................$24.00
Iris, jug, canteen.......................$20.00
Iris, stack set, w/lids, 3-piece $30.00
Largo, bowl, utility.......................$4.50
Largo, pie baker, 10".......................$12.00
Largo, plate, luncheon.......................$5.00
Largo, salt & pepper shakers, pr.......................$8.00
Rambler Rose, gravy boat.......................$10.00
Rambler Rose, pitcher, utility or milk $20.00

Rambler Rose, plate, 9".......................$8.00
Red Poppy, plate, sm.......................$4.00
Windmill, bowl, utility; w/lid $6.00
Windmill, salt & pepper shakers, pr.......................$14.00
Woodvine, creamer & sugar bowl.......................$20.00
Woodvine, cup & saucer.......................$8.00

Woodvine, platter, round w/tab handles, 13", $15.00; jug, 7¼", $18.00

Woodvine, plate, 9" $5.00

Valentines

Valentines that convey sentimental messages are just the type of thing that girls in love tuck away and keep. So it's not too hard to find examples of these that date back to the early part of the century. But there are other kinds of valentines that collectors search for too — those with Black themes and Disney characters, advertising and modes of transportation, 3-dimensionals, and mechanicals. Look for artist-signed cards; these are especially prized.

Airplane, mechanical, 1940s-50s, 3¼x4½", EX $8.00
Angel among flowers, 2-D, chromolithograph, Germany, 1900s, 3x4x2", NM.......................$25.00
Baseball player, mechanical, USA, 1940s, 5½x3", NM.$20.00
Batman & Robin, 1966, VG $10.00
Big-eyed child riding mechanical duck, 5½x7", VG $35.00
Black child eating watermelon, 3x2", VG.......................$10.00
Boy in winter clothing, mechanical, tab stand, Kautz, 7⅜", EX.......................$25.00
Boy playing violin, mechanical, 1930s, 10x4", NM......$15.00
Brownie & Cub Scout, USA, 1960s, 6x3¼", EX $15.00
Cowboy, mechanical, 6x4", NM.......................$5.00
Dog w/felt ears, Halls Bros, 1940s, 8½x6¾", VG.........$15.00
Elephant w/clown, USA, 1940s, 4½x3½", NM.............$10.00
Flintstones, 1950s, 4x3", VG $5.00

Minnie Mouse, Hallmark, 1936, EX..............................**$35.00**
Parrot, mechanical, 6x6", VG...**$6.00**
Pickaninny girl w/watermelon & baby w/bowl of hearts,
    heavy die-cut paper w/hinged parts, 1930-40, 7¼",
    EX **$40.00**
Pink Panther, 1960s, 3x3", NM **$5.00**

Pony pulling children in cart, 3-D, German, 10" long, $50.00

St Bernard, mechanical, 5x4", NM **$10.00**
Uncle Sam, Made in USA, 1943, 5x6", VG....................**$15.00**
Victorian children, 3-D, 4x2", VG.................................**$5.00**
Wizard of Oz, die-cut Cowardly Lion & the yellow brick
    road w/poppies, rare, ca 1940, 3x5", NM...........**$115.00**

Van Briggle

This pottery was founded in Colorado Springs around the turn of the century by Artus Van Briggle who had previously worked at Rookwood. After his death in 1904, his wife, Anna, took over the business which she controlled until it sold in 1913. The company has continued to operate up to the present time.

Because many of the original designs were repeated down through the years, it is often very difficult to determine when some pieces were produced. There are several factors to consider. Until late 1907, pieces were marked with the 'double A' logo, 'Van Briggle,' and the date. The 'double A' logo was in constant use until the mid-fifties, and a few marks still indicated the date. Others contained a design number. Many times 'Colorado Springs' was included as well. Earlier pieces had glazed bottoms, but from 1921 until 1930, the bottoms were left unglazed. From 1922 until 1929, U.S.A. was added to the Colorado Springs designation. Pieces made from 1955 to 1968 were usually marked 'Anna Van Briggle' with no 'double A' logo, but it does appear again on those made after '68.

Colors are another good indicator of age. Until 1930, colors were limited to turquoise, blue, maroon, brown, green, and yellow (in blended effects or in combination). In 1946, the mulberry was lightened, and the shade was named 'Persian Rose.' It was a popular until 1968. 'Mountain

Craig Brown,' used from about 1915 until the mid-thirties, was one of their most famous glazes. It was a warm brown color with a green overspray. (This effect has been reproduced in recent years.) 'Moonglow' (white matt) has been in constant production since 1950, and their turquoise matt was made from the very early years on. High-gloss colors of brown, blue, black, and green were introduced in the mid-fifties, though matt colors were still favored. Other colors have been made in addition to those we've mentioned.

Still another factor that can be helpful is the type of clay that was used. Dark clays (including terra cotta) indicate a pre-1930 origin. After that time, the body of the ware was white.

If you'd like more information, we recommend *The Collector's Encyclopedia of Van Briggle Art Pottery* by Josie Fania and Richard Sasicki, and *The Collector's Encyclopedia of Colorado Pottery* by Carol and Jim Carlton. *Lehner's Encyclopedia of U.S. Marks on Pottery, Porcelain, and Clay* by Lois Lehner is another good source.

Ashtray, back of headdress has stamped-in logo, 7½", $150.00

Bookends, reclining ram, blue, 1930s, pr..................**$175.00**
Bookends, squirrel w/nut, blue, 1950-60, pr **$125.00**
Bust of Sitting Bull, blue, limited edition, 1981 ....**$185.00**
Candle holders, acorn cups on leaf base, handles, 1940s-50s,
    pr..**$60.00**
Conch shell, mauve, late 1980s....................................**$25.00**
Figurine, elephant, trunk touching forehead, marked, mid-
    1940s to '50s **$50.00**
Figurine, Indian kneeling, holding large pot, late 1980s..**$65.00**
Figurine, owl on perch, blue, late 1980s.....................**$25.00**
Figurine, prancing stallion, blue, late 1980s...............**$40.00**
Lamp base, squirrel form, maroon, 1960s (no shade).**$100.00**
Night light, owl figure, blue, ca 1915 ....**$400.00**
Paperweight, crouching rabbit, marked, early 1980s...**$25.00**

Planter, swan embossed on side, flattened sides, footed, scalloped rim, 1930s-40s..$80.00
Tankard pitcher, green, angle handle, 1906..............$700.00
Vase, #310, Persian Rose, ca 1920, 3¼".........................$65.00
Vase, #654, blue/green, 1908-11, 4"..........................$195.00
Vase, #689, bowl shape, 1922-26................................$150.00
Vase, #774, amphora form w/handles, 1922-26.........$220.00
Vase, #798, blue, bulbous, marked, 1918..................$375.00
Vase, #822, brown tones, 1922-26..............................$150.00
Vase, #841, blue, 1920s..$85.00
Vase, 4 Indian head masks around top, Persian Rose, 12x5"..$325.00

Vandor

For more than thirty-five years, Vandor has operated out of Salt Lake City, Utah. They're not actually manufacturers, but distributors of novelty ceramic items made overseas. Some pieces will be marked 'Made in Korea,' while others are marked 'Sri Lanka,' 'Taiwan,' or 'Japan.' Many of their best things have been made in the last few years, and already collectors are finding them appealing — anyone would. They have a line of kitchenware designed around 'Cowmen Mooranda' (an obvious take off on Carmen), another called 'Crocagator' (a darling crocodile modeled as a teapot, a bank, salt and pepper shakers, etc.), character-related items (Betty Boop and Howdy Doody, among others), and some really wonderful cookie jars reminiscent of fifties radios and jukeboxes.

For more information, we recommend *The Collector's Encyclopedia of Cookie Jars, Vol II,* by Joyce and Fred Roerig. See also Cookie Jars

Bookends, Flintstones, ceramic, Fred & Wilma figures embossed on stone shapes, Made in Japan on paper label, 1989, pr, $45.00

Ashtray, Betty Boop, ceramic, figure of Betty Boop posed on black hollow baby-grand piano w/prominent key board, 1989...$30.00
Bank, Baseball, figure in batting pose atop baseball w/All-Star in script, paper label, Snyder, 1991...............$30.00

Bank, Flintstones, ceramic, Pebbles atop Dino resting on gray 4-footed base, Made in Japan on paper label, 1989 .$45.00
Bank, Mona Lisa, ceramic, bust figure in famous pose, Pelzman Designs, Made in Sri Lanka, 1992...................$25.00
Bank, Swee' Pea, ceramic, sitting w/hands clasped, 1980 .$100.00
Bowl, Howdy Doody, ceramic, straight-sided, decal in bottom, 1989..$10.00
Box, Howdy Doody, ceramic, features a waving Howdy on lid w/a pink convertible as base, paper label, 1989 .....$35.00
Boxes, Betty Boop, tin, set of 4 different sizes w/Betty Boop in various poses, 1989......................................$25.00
Clock, Howdy Doody Wristwatch, red plastic w/black numbers surrounding Howdy on white face, 55".........$40.00
Eyeglasses case, Betty Boop, cloth, features Betty's head on red heart-shaped glasses on yellow background, 1989....$10.00
Frame, Howdy Doody, ceramic, It's Howdy Doody Time in script over top w/figure of Howdy seated at bottom, 4x3"..$15.00
Mug, Flintstones, ceramic, shaped as Wilma's head, paper label, 1989..$20.00
Mug, Howdy Doody, ceramic, various decals.............$12.00
Mug, Jetsons, ceramic, features George playing baseball, paper label, 1990..$10.00
Music box, Howdy Doody, ceramic, features Howdy standing in front of microphone on round base, 1989 .$30.00
Plate, Betty Boop, ceramic, name lettered above Betty posed on movie-reel film w/Sixty Years in script below, 1989..$45.00
Salt & pepper shakers, Cowboy, ceramic, bust figure in hat w/drawstring, paper label, 1991, pr.......................$20.00
Salt & pepper shakers, Crocagator Shoes, ceramic, lady's green high heels w/blue bows atop smiling 'gator' faces, pr..$20.00
Salt & pepper shakers, Mona Lisa, marked 1992 Pelzman Designs, Made in Sri Lanka....................................$20.00
Salt & pepper shakers, Popeye & Olive Oyl figures, ceramic, marked Vandor 1980 KFS, pr..............................$50.00
Soap dish, Swamp, girl alligator in sunglasses on dish appearing to have head out of water, in-mold mark, Snyder..$20.00
Spoon rest, Howdy Doody, ceramic, shaped as Howdy's smiling face, Made in Japan on paper label..........$20.00
Teapot, Crocagator, green ceramic shaped like lady's purse w/alligator head & tail, gold trim, Made in Korea ..$35.00

Teapot, Mona Lisa, ceramic, Pelzman Designs, Made in Sri Lanka, 1992, $40.00

Vending Machines

Coin-operated machines that were used to sell peanuts, gumballs, stamps, even sandwiches, were already popular by the turn of the century. But they saw their heaviest use from the first decade of the 20th century until about 1940.

Values are determined in part by condition. Original paint and decals are certainly desirable, but because these machines were often repainted by operators while they were still in use, collectors often allow a well-done restoration. There are variations that bear on value as well, such as color, special features and design.

Dixie Cup vendor, Dixie-Vortex Co, 1¢ cups, tall glass dome on cast-iron base, 31x4", VG................................**$225.00**

Gum vendor, Adams Chewing Gum, A Flavor for Every Taste, 4-sided cast metal w/glass insert, 6 levers, 17½", VG+...**$70.00**

Gum vendor, Baby Grand 10¢ gumball machine, wood case w/painted cast-metal & plastic front, 13½", VG....**$60.00**

Gum vendor, Superior Mfg Co 5¢ machine w/4 name-brand gums, chrome-plated metal, rust on bottom, 19½", G **$60.00**

Gum vendor, Toy 'n Joy 1¢ King Size Gum, 4-sided red-painted steel w/glass front, 14½", VG **$60.00**

Gum vendor, Zeno 1¢ Chewing Gum, oak case w/embossed tin insert, Zeno lettered on base, 16½x10½x9¼", VG..**$600.00**

Gum vendor, 1¢ gumball w/4-sided glass top on red-painted cast-metal base, 16", G...............................**$40.00**

Gum vendor, 10¢ gumball machine, 4-sided plastic w/yellow steel top on yellow steel base, 17½", G+.......**$15.00**

Match vendor, Safety Matches 1¢ Box, glass dome on oak base w/cigar cutter attachment, 18x11x10", G....**$350.00**

Match vendor, Safety Matches 1¢ Box, glass dome on wooden base w/cigar cutter attachment, 18x11x10", G, $350.00

Pencil vendor, Parker Pencil Service & Everywhere Folks Write embossed on silver-painted metal, ca 1930, 10x9x5", VG, $50.00

Postage stamp vendor, painted cast metal w/glass insert, working, 12¾", G+...**$25.00**

Vernon Kilns

Founded in Vernon, California, in 1930, this company produced many lines of dinnerware, souvenir plates, decorative pottery, and figurines. They employed several well-known artists whose designs no doubt contributed substantially to their success. Among them were Rockwell Kent, Royal Hickman, and Don Blanding, all of whom were responsible for creating several of the lines most popular with collectors today.

In 1940, they signed a contract with Walt Disney to produce a line of figurines and several dinnerware patterns that were inspired by Disney's film *Fantasia*. The figurines were made for a short time only and are now expensive.

The company closed in 1958, but Metlox purchased the molds and continued to produce some of their best-selling dinnerware lines through a specially established 'Vernon Kiln' division.

Most of the ware is marked in some form or another with the company name and, in some cases, the name of the dinnerware pattern.

If you'd like to learn more, we recommend *The Collector's Encyclopedia of California Pottery* by Jack Chipman.

Barkwood, plate, 10" **$10.00**
Barkwood, platter, 13½" **$14.00**
Brown-Eyed Susan, chop plate, 12"...........................**$18.00**
Brown-Eyed Susan, teapot **$45.00**
Chatelaine, cup & saucer, jade....................................**$30.00**
Chatelaine, plate, dinner; 1-leaf, bronze.....................**$17.00**

Coral Reef, plate, blue, 10½" $45.00
Coral Reef, plate, maroon, Don Blanding, 9¾" $40.00
Early California, casserole, turquoise $35.00
Early California, egg cup $15.00
Early California, pitcher, 1-qt $30.00
Fantasia, plate, Nutcracker, 9" $150.00
Fantasia, salt & pepper shakers, Milk Weed, pr $75.00
Fantasia, salt & pepper shakers, mushroom, pr $125.00
Gingham, bowl, divided vegetable $22.00
Gingham, bowl, mixing; 9" $35.00
Gingham, bowl, vegetable; 9" $16.00
Gingham, cup & saucer $10.00
Gingham, pitcher, bulbous base, 7-pt, 7" $20.00
Gingham, pitcher, 2-qt $45.00
Gingham, plate, 6¼" $3.00
Gingham, plate, 9½" $9.00
Gingham, sugar bowl $12.00
Hawaiian Flowers, bowl, fruit $12.00
Hawaiian Flowers, plate, 9" $25.00
Heavenly Days, creamer $8.00
Heavenly Days, mug $15.00
Homespun, chop plate, 12" $18.00
Homespun, chop plate, 14" $25.00

Mayflower, sauce boat $45.00
Modern California, egg cup $20.00
Modern California, teapot, orchid $65.00
Monterey, bowl, chowder $12.00
Monterey, cup $12.00
Native California, chop plate, 14" $30.00
Native California, salt & pepper shakers, pr $16.00
Organdie, chop plate, 12" $15.00
Organdie, plate, 9½" $10.00
Organdie, platter, oval, 12" $15.00
Organdie, sauce boat $18.00
Organdie, tidbit tray, 1-tier, 7½" $15.00
Plate, souvenir; Hollywood $25.00

Plate, souvenir; Mission San Fernando Rey, $20.00

Plate, souvenir; Oklahoma map, blue $18.00
Plate, souvenir; San Francisco cable cars $20.00
Rhythmic, cup & saucer $45.00
Rhythmic, plate, 10½" $35.00
Salamina, cup & saucer $50.00
Salamina, plate, 9½" $95.00
Tam O'Shanter, bowl, divided vegetable $30.00
Tam O'Shanter, butter dish, ¼-lb $35.00
Tam O'Shanter, chop plate, 12" $35.00
Tam O'Shanter, coaster $18.00
Tam O'Shanter, platter, 11" $15.00
Tickled Pink, bowl, divided $25.00
Tickled Pink, relish dish, 3-section $22.00
Ultra California, bowl, Buttercup, 1-pt $20.00
Ultra California, cup & saucer, Ice Green $20.00
Ultra California, plate, luncheon; Aster $12.00
Ultra California, pot, demitasse $75.00

Homespun, coffee server, $35.00

Homespun, creamer & sugar bowl $25.00
Homespun, cup & saucer $12.00
Homespun, plate, 9½" $10.00
Homespun, platter, oval, 14¼" $20.00
Lei Lani, chop plate, 12" $95.00
Lei Lani, creamer, signed Blanding $35.00
Mayflower, creamer & sugar bowl $35.00
Mayflower, cup & saucer $18.00
Mayflower, plate, 6" $6.00
Mayflower, platter, oval, 14" $35.00
Mayflower, salt & pepper shakers, pr $18.00

View-Master Reels and Packets

William Gruber was the inventor who introduced the View-Master to the public at the New York World's Fair and the Golden Gate Exposition held in California in 1939.

Thousands of reels and packets have been made since that time on every aspect of animal life, places of interest, and entertainment.

Over the years the company has changed ownership five times. It was originally Sawyer's View-Master, G.A.F. (in the mid-sixties), View-Master International (1981), Ideal Toy, and most recently Tyco Toy Company. The latter three companies produced it strictly as a toy and issued only cartoons, making the earlier non-cartoon reels and the 3-reel packets very collectible.

Sawyer made two cameras so that the public could take their own photo reels in 3-D. They made a projector as well, so that the homemade reels could be viewed on a large screen. 'Personal' or 'Mark II' cameras with their cases usually range in value from $100.00 to $200.00; rare viewers such as the blue 'Model B' start at about $100.00, and the 'Stereo-Matic 500' projector is worth $175.00 to $200.00. Most single reels range from $1.00 to $5.00, but some early Sawyer's & G.A.F.'s may bring as much as $25.00 each, and character-related reels sometimes even more.

Blondie & Dagwood, 3-reel set, 1966, MIP **$25.00**
Brady Bunch, 3-reel set w/booklet, 1972, MIP **$15.00**
Buck Rogers, 3-reel cartoon version w/booklet, 1978, MIP **$10.00**
Captain Kangaroo, 3-reel set, 1957, MIP **$15.00**
Charlie Brown, It's Your First Kiss, 3-reel set, 1980s, MOC...**$8.50**
Close Encounters of the Third Kind, 3-reel set w/booklet, 1977, MIP **$16.00**
Daktari, 3-reel set w/booklet, NM **$20.00**
Death Valley, 3-reel set, MIP **$15.00**
Dennis the Menace, 3-reel set w/booklet, 1967, MIP **$8.50**
Dr Strange, 3-reel cartoon version w/booklet, 1979, MIP **$10.00**
Dukes of Hazzard, 3-reel set w/booklet, 1980, MIP **$12.50**
Eight Is Enough, 3-reel set w/booklet, 1980, MIP **$12.50**
Flash Gordon in the Planet Mongo, 3-reel set, 1976, MIP **$12.50**
Flipper, 3-reel set w/booklet, MIP **$10.00**
Frontierland, Disney World, 3-reel set, MIP **$8.00**
Goldilocks & the Three Bears, 3-reel set w/booklet, 1970s, MIP **$8.00**
Grand Canyon National Park, 3-reel set, MIP **$10.00**
Green Hornet, 3-reel set w/booklet, 1966, MIP **$75.00**
James Bond Live & Let Die, 3-reel set w/booklet, MIP .**$20.00**
James Bond Moonraker, 3-reel set w/booklet, 1979, MIP **$15.00**
Jetsons, 3-reel set w/booklet, 1981, MIP **$4.50**
Johnny Moccasin w/Jody McCrea, 3-reel set, 1956, MIP..**$20.00**
Land of the Giants, 3-reel set w/booklet, 1968, MIP ...**$65.00**
Lassie & Timmy, 3-reel set, MIP **$20.00**
Laverne & Shirley, 3-reel set, 1978, MIP **$12.50**
Little Yellow Dinosaur, 3-reel set, MIP **$10.00**
Lone Ranger, Mystery Rustler; 3-reel set, 1956, MIP **$25.00**
Lovebug, 3-reel set, MIP **$15.00**
Mary Poppins, 3-reel set, MIP **$10.00**
Michael Jackson's Thriller, 3-reel set, 1984, MOC........**$12.00**

Mickey Mouse, 3-reel set, talking, MIP **$12.00**
Mickey Mouse Club Mouseketeers, 3-reel set, 1956, MIP ..**$30.00**
Mighty Mouse, 3-reel set, 1970s, EX **$4.50**
Mission Impossible, 3-reel set, 1967, MIP....................**$20.00**
Mr Magoo, 3-reel set, 1977, MIP **$8.00**
Nanny & the Professor, 3-reel set w/booklet, 1970, MIP.**$25.00**
NASA'S Manned Spacecraft Center, 3-reel set w/16-page booklet, MIP **$16.50**
New York World's Fair, General Tour; 3-reel set, 1964, MIP **$25.00**
Partridge Family, 3-reel set, 1971, MIP **$30.00**
Pebbles & Bamm-Bamm, 3-reel set, MIP.....................**$10.00**
Princess of Power, 3-reel set, 1985, MOC......................**$8.00**
Rockefeller Center, 3-reel set, 1958, MIP.....................**$18.00**
San Francisco, 3-reel set, MIP **$12.00**
Six Million-Dollar Man, 3-reel set w/booklet, 1974, MIP .**$12.50**
Spiderman, 3-reel set, 1980s, MOC **$8.00**
Tarzan Rescues Cheeta, single reel w/booklet, 1950, NM **$4.50**
Time Tunnel, 3-reel set, 1966, MIP **$40.00**
Top Cat, 3-reel set w/booklet, 1962, MIP....................**$20.00**
US Spaceport, 3-reel set w/16-page booklet of JFK Space Center in Florida, 1965, MIP **$10.00**
Waltons, 3-reel set w/booklet, 1972, MIP....................**$15.00**
Weeki Wachee, Spring of Live Mermaids, 3-reel set, 1971, MIP **$20.00**
Who Framed Roger Rabbit, 3-reel set, 1988, MOC **$12.50**
Winnie the Pooh, 3-reel set w/booklet, 1979, MIP **$10.00**
Wonders of the Deep, 3-reel set w/booklet, 1950s, NM .**$10.00**
Yellowstone National Park, 3-reel set, 1948, MIP **$6.00**
Zorro, 3-reel set, MIP **$30.00**
101 Dalmations, 3-reel set, MIP **$15.00**

Vistosa Dinnerware

This was a solid color line of dinnerware made from 1938 until sometime in the middle forties in an effort to compete with the very successful Fiesta line by Homer Laughlin. Vistosa was produced by Taylor, Smith, and Taylor, who were also located in the famous East Liverpool/Newell, Ohio, pottery district. Though T.S. & T. duplicated several of Fiesta's popular early glazes (mango red, cobalt blue, light green, and deep yellow), they completely lost out on the design. Instead of the wonderful Art Deco shapes the public evidently favored in combination with the primary colors, Vistosa's evoked more country charm than sophistication because of the dainty 5-petal flower molded into the handles and lid finials.

Vistosa is relatively scarce, but collectors find the same features that spelled doom for the line in the early forties more appealing today, and its scarcity only adds fun to the hunt. Red is the most desirable color, and you may have to pay a little more to get it.

Bowl, salad; footed **$95.00**
Bowl, 5¾" **$8.00**
Bowl, 8½" **$24.00**

Chop plate, 11" **$15.00**
Chop plate, 13" **$18.00**
Chop plate, 15" **$35.00**
Creamer **$10.00**
Cup & saucer..**$15.00**
Egg cup...**$22.50**
Gravy boat..**$78.00**
Pitcher, cobalt **$75.00**
Pitcher, red **$75.00**
Plate, 7" **$7.50**
Plate, 9" **$10.00**
Salt & pepper shakers, pr..................................**$18.00**
Sugar bowl **$15.00**
Teapot..**$95.00**

W. S. George Dinnerware

From the turn of the century until the late 1950s, this East Palestine, Ohio, company produced many lines of dinnerware. Some were in solid colors, but the vast majority were decaled. Most of the lines were marked. If you'd like more information, we recommend *The Collector's Encyclopedia of American Dinnerware* by Jo Cunningham.

Bluebird, plate, Derwood shape, 6" **$14.00**
Breakfast Nook, plate, Rainbow shape, 9" **$10.00**

Floral, platter, 11½", $8.00

Iroquois Red, creamer, Ranchero shape......................**$12.00**
Iroquois Red, sugar bowl, Ranchero shape.................**$18.00**
Ivory, cream soup & liner, Lido shape **$16.00**
Petalware, bowl, 5½" **$6.00**
Petalware, plate, 9" **$10.00**
Petalware, saucer **$4.00**
Petit Point Rose, dinner plate, Fleurette shape, 10".....**$10.00**
Poppy, platter, Rainbow shape, 11½"...........................**$14.00**
Rainbow, bowl, deep, Rainbow shape, 5" **$10.00**
Rainbow, egg cup, Rainbow shape **$18.00**
Roses, gravy boat w/liner, side handles......................**$12.00**
Roses, soup bowl, Bolero shape, 8" **$8.00**

Rosita, creamer, Ranchero shape **$10.00**
Rust Floral, cup, Lido shape..**$8.00**
Sailing, creamer, Georgette shape **$10.00**
Sailing, saucer, Georgette shape **$4.00**
Sailing, serving bowl, Georgette shape **$18.00**
Sailing, sugar bowl, Georgette shape **$10.00**
Smart Flowers, plate, Lido shape, 8".............................**$8.00**
Tiny Roses, egg cup, Lido shape.................................**$14.00**
Wheat, coffe server, Ranchero shape **$40.00**

Wade Porcelain

If you've attended many flea markets, you're already very familiar with the tiny Wade figurines, most of which are 2" and under. Wade made several lines of them, but the most common were made as premiums for the Red Rose Tea Company. Most of these sell for $3.50 to $7.00 or so. Some of the animals are much larger and may sell for more than $100.00.

The Wade company dates to 1810. The original kiln was located near Chesterton in England. The tiny pottery merged with a second about 1900 and became known as the George Wade Pottery. They continued to grow and to absorb smaller nearby companies and eventually manufactured a wide range of products from industrial ceramics to Irish porcelain giftware. In 1990 Wade changed its name to Seagoe Ceramics Limited.

If you'd like to learn more, we recommend *The World of Wade* by Ian Warner and Mike Posgay.

Bank, Lady Hillary, Westminster Piggy Bank Family, 1983 to present, 7"...**$35.00**
Figurine, baby giraffe, Happy Families series, 1978-86, ⅝x1¼" **$5.00**
Figurine, Boy Blue, Nursery Favorites, set #3, 1974, 2⅞x1⅛" dia base **$25.00**
Figurine, cat, Happy Families series, 1978-86, 1⅞ **$12.00**
Figurine, corgi puppy, Dogs & Puppies series, set #2, 1979, 1⅝x1⅜"...**$6.00**
Figurine, foal, Horse Set #1, 1974-81, 1⅞".....................**$5.00**
Figurine, frog, Red Rose Tea promotion, 1967-73, ⅞x1⅛"..**$7.00**
Figurine, grizzly bear, Whimsies series, set #9 (North American Animals), 1958, 1⅞" **$40.00**
Figurine, hedgehog, Whoppas set #3, 1978, 1¼x1⅞"..**$18.00**
Figurine, leaping fawn, Whimsies series, set #1, 1953, 1⅞"...**$25.00**
Figurine, Little Miss Muffet, Red Rose Tea promotion, 1971-79, 1½" **$8.00**
Figurine, Madam Mim (hen) from the Sword & the Stone, Disney's Hat Box series, 1956-65 ....**$30.00**
Figurine, Old King Cole, Red Rose Tea promotion, 1971-79, 1½x1¼"...**$5.00**
Figurine, polar bear, Whoppas set #1, 1976, 1½x2¼" .**$20.00**
Figurine, rabbit, Red Rose Tea promotion, 1½" **$4.00**
Figurine, Scamp from Lady & the Tramp, Disney's (Blow-Ups), 1961-65, 4⅛x5"...**$150.00**
Figurine, Si from Lady & the Tramp, Disney's (Blow-Ups), 1961-65, 5½x5"...**$120.00**

Frame, heart shape w/embossed floral design, Romance Range series, 1983-85, 5½x5½" **$22.00**
Party Crackers, from $10 to **$20.00**
Pipe rest, Irish setter, 1973-81, 3¼" dia.......................**$25.00**
Spirit container, baby chick, ca 1961, 3⅜x2" dia base.**$35.00**
Tankard, Oldsmobile, amber, #10 from series 4, 1-pt .**$14.00**
Teapot, allover paisley design, rare, 6¾x8"................**$180.00**

Teapot, duck figure, ca 1938, $90.00

Teapot, stylized red poppy design on white, 6½x5½" .**$40.00**
Trinket box, egg shape w/embossed flowers on top, Romance Range series, 1983-1985, 2¾x1¾" **$15.00**

Wallace China

Although they made decaled lines and airbrush-stencil patterns as well, this California pottery (1931-1964) is most famous for their 'Westward Ho' package of housewares. There were three designs, 'Rodeo,' 'Boots and Saddle,' and 'Pioneer Trails,' all created by western artist Till Goodan.

Today, anything related to the West is highly collectible, and as a result, values have drastically accelerated on many items that only a few months ago tended to be sometimes overlooked on the secondary market. Any dinnerware line with a Western or Southwestern motif has become extremely popular.

Jack Chipman's book, *The Collector's Encyclopedia of California Pottery*, has a chapter on Wallace China.

Bowl, Chuck Wagon, restaurant china, dated 1955, 6¾", $20.00

Ashtray, Pioneer Trails, Sam Houston **$55.00**
Ashtray, Rodeo...**$55.00**
Bowl, chili; Rodeo, 5¾" **$65.00**
Bowl, Pioneer Trails, 3x9"..............................**$200.00**
Bowl, salad; Boots & Saddle, lg.........................**$350.00**
Bowl, vegetable; El Rancho, round, 10"....................**$150.00**
Chop plate, Pioneer Trails, 13" **$200.00**
Chop plate, Rodeo, 13" **$200.00**
Creamer, Rodeo **$125.00**
Creamer & sugar bowl, Pioneer Trails.....................**$225.00**
Plate, Boots & Saddle, 9"..................................**$125.00**
Plate, Rodeo, 7¼"..**$60.00**
Platter, El Rancho, oval, 13½".............................**$125.00**
Salt & pepper shakers, Rodeo, 5", pr **$150.00**

Wall Pockets

A few years ago there were only a handful of really avid wall pocket collectors, but today many are finding them intriguing. They were popular well before the turn of the century. Roseville and Weller included at least one and sometimes several in many of their successful lines of art pottery, and other American potteries made them as well. Many were imported from Germany, Czechoslovakia, China, and Japan. By the 1950s, they were passe.

Some of the most popular today are the figurals. Look for the more imaginative and buy the ones you like — these are light-hearted collectibles! If you're buying to resell, look for those designed around animals, large exotic birds, children, luscious fruits, or those that are especially eyecatching. Appeal is everything.

For more information, refer to *Collector's Guide to Wall Pockets, Affordable and Others*, by Marvin and Joy Gibson.

Angel, hand-painted porcelain, blue-draped nude w/yellow hair & white bow, gold trim, paper label marked Germany **$75.00**
Angel in front of cross praying, pink robe, glossy finish, unmarked Japan.....................................**$25.00**
Bamboo, yellow w/brown overspray, unmarked........**$12.00**
Bananas, 3 yellow bananas w/brown accents on 3 lg dark green leaves, unmarked **$20.00**
Basket, green w/multicolored design on bright yellow band at top, glossy finish, marked Made in Japan.........**$35.00**
Basket w/bird & flowers, multicolored w/glossy finish, marked Hand-Painted Tilso Japan 53/355.............**$20.00**
Bib overalls, glossy blue, unmarked............................**$15.00**
Bird motifs, lustre finish, 7", each **$40.00**
Bird on stump, multicolored bird on brown stump, marked Made in Czechoslovakia 5675-A **$50.00**
Bird on well, bird in shades of yellow, blue & brown, marked Made in Czechoslovakia 5676-A...............**$50.00**
Birdhouse, light blue, unmarked **$20.00**
Bowl & pitcher, white w/colorful fruit motif, gold handle, paper label marked Imports Enesco Japan, also marked E2365 ....**$15.00**

Boy playing violin, porcelain w/boy embossed on front of vertical rectangular pocket, lustre finish, marked Japan **$30.00**

Bunch of bananas, marked Made in Japan on paper label......................**$20.00**

Butterfly, ivory w/purple & mauve overspray, unmarked.**$10.00**

Canoe, vaseline glass w/Daisy & Button pattern, unmarked......................**$55.00**

Cherub on pink, marked Japan......................**$25.00**

Christmas carolers holding banner, A Merry Christmas to All!, multicolored w/gold trim, marked Japan.......**$15.00**

Cone shape, amethyst glass, unmarked **$50.00**

Cone shape, glass w/black matt finish, multicolored flowers hand-painted around top, unmarked **$40.00**

Cone shape, orange lustreware w/multicolored bird on branch of white blossoms, marked Made in Japan .**$40.00**

Cup & saucer, white w/pink flowers & gold trim, marked Fred Roberts Co China...Made in Japan on paper label....**$25.00**

Cup & saucer, white w/purple plum & leaf decor, blue trim, marked NS Co Clev O USA SP3 ....**$20.00**

Dust pan, white w/3 embossed strawberries, painted-on leaf & stem decor, mauve trim, unmarked......................**$25.00**

Dutch boy & girl, bust figures w/white skin & rosy cheeks, yellow hair w/blue hats & upper bodies, unmarked, pr......................**$32.00**

Dutch shoe, blue & white w/windmill motif, marked Elesva (Crown) Holland 015 ....**$10.00**

Dutch shoe, yellow w/embossed tulip, marked Oct-1948......................**$10.00**

Elf & flowers, multicolored, marked Hand-Painted Royal Sealy Japan......................**$20.00**

Floral motifs, glossy finish, 7¾" & 5¼", from $12 to....**$18.00**

Flower, ivory w/pink & green overspray, unmarked..**$25.00**

Grape cluster, clear glass, unmarked......................**$40.00**

Hat, white w/mauve trim & brown bow, unmarked...**$12.00**

Iron, mauve, unmarked......................**$15.00**

Japanese woman w/basket, multicolored w/glossy finish, marked Made in Japan **$55.00**

Juggler, colorful hand-painted porcelain w/lustre finish, marked G-DEP-16071 Germany......................**$110.00**

Kissing Dutch girl, white w/red dress & hat, unmarked ..**$20.00**

Lady in wreath, multicolored w/glossy finish, 7" dia, $20.00

Leaf, airbrushed brown, pale green & yellow w/overlapping brown stem, unmarked **$30.00**

Mexican man, bust in profile, dark-skinned w/yellow hat, blue scarf & orange shirt, marked Japan......................**$20.00**

New Mexico, brown rope-trimmed double hearts embossed w/longhorn steer, Indian chief & lettering, marked Made in Japan **$15.00**

Oriental couple, yellow & black bust images on white rectangular backgrounds w/black trim, L&F Ceramics, Calif, pr......................**$45.00**

Oriental dancers, black & white trimmed in gold, paper label marked Japan, pr......................**$80.00**

Oriental man & crane w/pink urn, 8", $14.00

Owl on limb, yellow, blue & brown w/glossy finish, marked Made in Japan **$55.00**

Parakeets, 2 blue bodies w/yellow heads perched on brown branch, no mark......................**$20.00**

Parrot on cluster of grapes, shades of yellow, brown, white & blue w/purple grapes, marked Made in Czechoslovakia **$50.00**

Peacock, shades of brown, unmarked **$20.00**

Pear, yellow w/lg green leaf, marked Made in Calif 303..**$15.00**

Rolling pin, ivy on white, unmarked......................**$15.00**

Scoop, brown w/embossed grape cluster & leaves, marked Kingwood Ceramics Made in America......................**$15.00**

Seashell, black & pink, unmarked **$15.00**

Ship motifs, lustre finish, 5¼", 7¼", from $20 to......................**$30.00**

Shoe w/Raggedy Ann & Andy, white w/multicolored image, marked Raggedy Ann & Andy...Japan **$25.00**

Skunk, marked 8204, De Lee Art hand-painted skunkette, Los Angeles, Calif, late 1940s **$35.00**

Sprinkler can, white w/yellow & brown chicken motif, mottled brown trim, marked Japan S727R......................**$12.00**

Straw hat, yellow w/brown airbrushing, marked Stewart G McCullock c Calif **$15.00**

Strawberry, red w/green leaves & stem, lg $20.00
Sunflower, lg yellow petals w/brown center, unmarked..$12.00
Vase w/flowers, pink flowers on white textured background, silver trim, marked Made in Japan..........$15.00
Violin, shades of blue w/gold trim, unmarked $20.00
Wishing well, pink, unmarked....................................$10.00

Watch Fobs

Strap-type watch fobs have been issued by the thousands by companies advertising farm machines, traps, guns, ammunition, heavy equipment, and products of many types. Some are relatively common and are worth only about $3.00 to $10.00, but others may go for $100.00 or more. To learn more about their values, we recommend *Collecting Watch Fobs* by John M. Kaduck.

Allis-Chalmers, bronze, frontal view of shape bulldozer, 1940s $40.00
Baseball batter, silver, round w/embossed figure, scalloped edge, 1925 ....$10.00
Bulldog, bronze, embossed figural head, 1908...........$12.00

CAT Track-type Tractor, Dean Machinery Co, silver or bronze, 1970s, $8.00

City of Troy 3000, silver badge shape, 1940s..............$15.00
Esco Construction Equipment, bronze, shows lg shovel, rectangular w/rounded corners...................................$10.00
Football, bronze, figural, 1925..$8.00
Gooch's Best Macaroni, silver figural man holding box of product, 1915 ....$50.00
GOP embossed on banner above strutting elephant, bronze, vertical, 1912 ....$15.00
Gray & Dudley Hardware Co, celluloid center w/G&D above portrait of George Washington w/leaf border, 1906 ....$35.00

Green Whiskey, silver, horseshoe shape w/Black man standing beside horse, She Was Bred In Old Kentucky, 1910 ....$20.00
Heinz, embossed metal, The Girl In The White Cap arched above girl holding bottle, One Of The 57 below, scalloped edge $40.00
Indiana 1861-1911 Semicentennial, bronze, boy w/ax in encircled landscape, Indiana lettered below, scalloped edge $12.00
Initial P, solid brass, 1925..$10.00
International Harvester, bronze HI logo above embossed die-cut image of heavy equipment, 1970s...............$8.00
Jamestown Tercentennial Exposition, White Furniture Co, Mebane NC, embossed figures encircled by lettering, 1½" dia...$40.00
Jersey Creme, The Perfect Drink..................................$50.00
Mack (Trucks), silver w/red enamel, bulldog shape, 1970s $10.00
Mermaid, bronze shield w/embossed mermaid encircled by leaf wreath, 1908.......................................$8.00
National Sportsman, bronze, antlered deer w/shotgun & lettered banner below, scalloped edge, 1920...........$20.00
New York Casualty Co, Safe Driver, scalloped edge, 1½" dia, NM $10.00
Northwest, silver, lg embossed crane above Northwest lettered at bottom, vertical rectangle w/rounded corners, 1960s $8.00
Old Dutch Cleanser, enameled $70.00
Order of Railroad Telegraphers, bronze, lettering around telegraph encircled by leaf wreath, round w/scalloped edge $22.00
Pabst Brewing, enameled..$125.00
Patriotic, bronze, sun rising behind eagle & flag, horizontal oval, rope border, 1917 ....$10.00
Patriotic, bronze shield shape w/stars & Salute The Flag on banner above waving flag, 1917 ....$10.00
Phil G Kelly Co Richmond VA, Jefferson Whiskey, Friend of Personal Liberty, embossed image of Jefferson, oval, 2x1½"...$40.00
Pierce's Golden Rio Coffee, bronze, shaped like vertical coffee bin, 1908...$25.00
Pingree Shoes, bronze, The Girl Of The Pingree Shoe arched over cameo image, scalloped edge $30.00
Shapleigh Hardware Co, diamond shape w/DE lettered in center, 1¼x2", EX..$20.00
Silver Moonshine Corn Whiskey, A Hatke & Co, Richmond VA, embossed moon face encircled by lettering, 1½" dia, EX $60.00
Taft & Sherman 1908 Washington engraved on shield, bronze..$25.00
Texaco, features the word Listen & 2 Scottie dogs w/heads cocked, EX $20.00
Thew Lorain, embossed lettering & construction scene on hexagonal shape, 1⅜", EX....................................$10.00
United Spanish War Veterans, bronze, Liberty Bell form, 1940 ....$10.00
Victory, embossed figure on irregular shape, 1½x1½", EX..$20.00

Wabco, bronze, Wabco lettered above embossed image of heavy equipment, horizontal rectangle, 1970s........**$8.00**
Western Live Stock Insurance Co, silver, oval w/lettering around image of horse, 1910 ....**$30.00**
Western saddle, silver, 1940 ....**$20.00**

Watt Pottery

The Watt Pottery operated in Crooksville, Ohio, from 1922 until sometime in 1935. The ware they produced is easily recognized and widely available today. It appeals to collectors of country antiques, since the body is yellowware and its decoration simple. Several pieces of Watt pottery were featured in *Country Living* magazine a few years ago, and it was this exposure that seemed to catapult it onto the collectibles market.

Several patterns were made: Apple, Autumn Foliage, Cherry, Dutch Tulip, Morning-Glory, Pansy, Rooster, Tear Drop, Starflower, and Tulip among them. All were executed in bold brush strokes of primary colors. Some items you'll find will also carry a stenciled advertising message, made for retail companies as premiums for their customers.

For further study, we recommend *Watt Pottery, An Identification and Price Guide,* by Sue and Dave Morris.

Apple, bowl, #24................**$225.00**
Apple, bowl, cereal/salad; 2x5½"................**$35.00**
Apple, bowl, individual spaghetti; 1½x8"................**$100.00**
Apple, bowl, mixing; #63 ....**$55.00**
Apple, bowl, mixing; #8 ....**$65.00**
Apple, bowl, oval, 2x5x6" **$100.00**
Apple, bowl, ribbed, w/lid, 4x5" **$145.00**
Apple, canister, straight-sided, dome lid, 9½"................**$500.00**
Apple, casserole, #601 ....**$165.00**
Apple, casserole, individual; French handle, #18 ......**$265.00**
Apple, casserole, individual; French handle, 4x8"......**$225.00**
Apple, cookie jar, bulbous, thick rim, 7½x7"................**$300.00**
Apple, creamer, #62................**$110.00**
Apple, creamer, 4¼"................**$75.00**
Apple, mug, #121................**$225.00**
Apple, mug, barrel shape, 4½"................**$225.00**
Apple, mug, straight-sided tapering to flat bottom, ring handle, 3¾"................**$200.00**
Apple, pie plate, #33 ....**$150.00**
Apple, pitcher, #15................**$85.00**
Apple, pitcher, 6½"................**$110.00**
Apple, platter, 12" **$275.00**
Apple, salt & pepper shakers, hourglass form, pr **$275.00**
Apple, sugar bowl, #98 ....**$425.00**
Apple (Double), bowl, mixing; ribbed, 2x4" **$110.00**
Apple (Double), casserole, #96................**$325.00**
Apple (Double), creamer, 4¼x4½"................**$125.00**
Autumn Foliage, bowl, mixing; #07 ....**$45.00**
Autumn Foliage, fondue, 3x9"................**$90.00**
Autumn Foliage, ice bucket, 7¼x7½"................**$130.00**
Autumn Foliage, mug, #121 ....**$225.00**
Autumn Foliage, pie plate, 1½x9"................**$80.00**

Autumn Foliage, platter, #31................**$150.00**
Autumn Foliage, salt & pepper shakers, hourglass form, pr................**$250.00**
Autumn Foliage, sugar bowl (open), #98................**$150.00**
Banded (Blue & White), pitcher, 7x7¾"................**$45.00**
Banded (Brown), sugar bowl (open) **$75.00**
Banded (White), bowl, 4½x6"................**$25.00**
Banded (White), casserole, 7x9"................**$65.00**
Brown Glaze, dog dish, #7................**$145.00**
Butterfly, ice bucket................**$185.00**
Cherry, bowl, cereal; #52................**$55.00**
Cherry, bowl, cereal/salad; 2½x6½" **$25.00**
Cherry, bowl, spaghetti; #39 ....**$175.00**
Cherry, bowl, spaghetti; 3x13"................**$100.00**
Cherry, pitcher, #15 ....**$125.00**
Cherry, pitcher, 5½"................**$45.00**
Dogwood, bowl, serving; 15" **$150.00**
Dutch Tulip, bean pot, tab handles, 6½x7"................**$225.00**
Dutch Tulip, bowl, #05................**$250.00**
Dutch Tulip, bowl, mixing; #7 ....**$125.00**
Dutch Tulip, bowl, mixing; plain rim, 5x7½"................**$75.00**
Dutch Tulip, bowl, salad; #73 ....**$250.00**
Dutch Tulip, cheese crock, 8x8½" **$400.00**
Dutch Tulip, pitcher, square shape, #69 ....**$600.00**
Dutch Tulip, serving set, covered bowl w/4 individual bowls, 6-piece set **$325.00**
Kitch-N-Queen, bowl, mixing; ribbed, #8 ....**$45.00**
Kitch-N-Queen, bowl, mixing; ribbed, 4½x8"................**$30.00**
Kitch-N-Queen, bowl, mixing; 8" **$30.00**
Kitch-N-Queen, ice bucket, w/lid, #9................**$125.00**
Kitch-N-Queen, pitcher, 8x8½"................**$100.00**
Kla-Ham'rd, pie plate, #43-13................**$35.00**
Moonflower, casserole, pink or green starflower, 8¾" .**$150.00**
Morning Glory, bowl, mixing; 8" **$50.00**
Morning Glory, pitcher, 8" **$300.00**
Morning Glory, sugar bowl (open), #98................**$250.00**
Pansy (Cut-Leaf), bowl, spaghetti; 3x13"................**$80.00**
Pansy (Cut-Leaf), bowls, mixing; thick rim, 7", 8" & 9", each **$35.00**
Pansy (Cut-Leaf), creamer & sugar bowl (open) **$100.00**

Pansy (Cut-Leaf), cup & saucer, $225.00

Pansy (Cut-Leaf), Dutch oven, 7x10½"................**$150.00**
Pansy (Cut-Leaf), platter, bull's-eye pattern **$100.00**
Pansy (Cut-Leaf), platter, 15"................**$100.00**

Pansy (Cut-Leaf), snack set, bull's-eye pattern w/red swirls, 11¾" **$125.00**
Pansy (Old), casserole, 4¼x7½" **$55.00**
Pansy (Old), pitcher, cross-hatch pattern, 7" **$150.00**
Pansy (Old), platter, 12" **$100.00**
Pansy (Raised), pitcher, 7x7¾" **$200.00**
Rio Rose, bowl, mixing; 8" **$65.00**
Rio Rose, bowl, spaghetti; 13" **$75.00**
Rio Rose, casserole, individual; stick handle **$125.00**
Rio Rose, cup & saucer...**$85.00**
Rooster, bean pot, tab handles, 6½" **$175.00**
Rooster, bowl, spaghetti; #39 ....**$375.00**
Rooster, bowl, w/lid, #67 ....**$225.00**
Rooster, bowl, 3¾x10½" **$90.00**
Rooster, creamer, 4¼" **$85.00**
Rooster, pitcher, refrigerator; 8" **$275.00**
Rooster, salt & pepper shakers, hourglass shape, 4½", pr...**$175.00**
Rooster, sugar bowl, w/lid, 4½" **$275.00**
Starflower, bean pot, tab handles, 6½x7½" **$90.00**
Starflower, bean server, individual; 2¼x3½" **$25.00**
Starflower, casserole, individual; tab handles, 4x5"...**$150.00**
Starflower, ice bucket, 7¼x7½" **$185.00**
Starflower, mug, sides curved inward, 4x3" **$195.00**
Starflower, pitcher, refrigerator; 8" **$250.00**
Starflower, pitcher, w/ice lip, 8" **$165.00**
Starflower, platter, 15" **$140.00**
Starflower (Green-on-Brown), casserole, tab handles, 4x5" **$125.00**
Starflower (Green-on-Brown), pitcher, 8" **$150.00**
Starflower (Green-on-Brown), tumbler, tapered sides, flat bottom, 4½" **$150.00**
Starflower (Pink-on-Black), bowl, 2½x11" **$125.00**
Starflower (Pink-on-Green), casserole, individual; stick handle, 3¾x7" **$125.00**
Starflower (Pink-on-Green), cup & saucer **$65.00**
Starflower (Pink-on-Green), plate, dinner; 10" **$100.00**
Tear Drop, bowl, mixing; plain rim, curved sides, 4¼x6½" **$35.00**
Tear Drop, bowl, mixing; ribbed, 3¾x7" **$40.00**
Tear Drop, bowl, mixing; thick rim, curved sides, 3½x6" **$35.00**
Tear Drop, casserole, square shape, rare, 6x8".........**$275.00**
Tear Drop, cheese crock, 8"..**$275.00**
Tear Drop, salt & pepper shakers, barrel shape, 4", pr.**$150.00**
Tulip, bowl, mixing; plain rim, 5x7½" **$70.00**
Tulip, bowl, plain rim, curved sides, 4x9½"..............**$100.00**
Tulip, cookie jar, tab handles, 8¼" **$300.00**
Tulip, pitcher, 5½" **$225.00**
White Daisy, casserole, individual; stick handle, 3¾x7½".**$125.00**
White Daisy, casserole, 5x8¾" **$165.00**
Woodgrain, bowl, w/lid, 7½x9" **$90.00**

Weil Ware

Though the Weil company made dinnerware and some kitchenware, their figural pieces are attracting the most collector interest. They were in business from the 1940s until the mid-fifties, another of the small but very successful California companies whose work has become so popular today. They dressed their 'girls' in beautiful gowns of vivid rose, light dusty pink, turquoise blue and other lovely colors enhanced with enameled 'lacework' and flowers, sgraffito, sometimes even with tiny applied blossoms. Both paper labels and ink stamps were used to mark them, but as you study their features, you'll soon learn to recognize even those that have lost their labels over the years. Four-number codes and decorators' initials are also common.

If you want to learn more, we recommend *The Collector's Encyclopedia of California Pottery* by Jack Chipman.

Ashtray, Bamboo, 5" **$8.00**
Bowl, Blossom, rectangular, 8¾" long............................**$16.50**
Bowl, Dogwood, white on gray, oval, 10" **$12.00**
Bowl, salad; Rose, sm **$5.00**
Bowl, shell form, pink w/pale green interior **$12.00**
Bowl, vegetable; Rose **$12.00**
Butter dish, Blossom, ¼-lb **$20.00**
Coffee server, Bamboo **$25.00**
Cup & saucer, Rose..**$6.00**
Dish, Dogwood, divided, square, 10½" **$8.00**
Figurine, boy w/wheelbarrow, #4005............................**$22.00**
Figurine, Buddy, boy figure, 7".....................................**$18.00**
Figurine, bust of lady w/fan, hand-painted flowers, 8".**$35.00**
Figurine, girl w/bowl, 11"..**$30.00**
Figurine, girl w/chin up, incised flowers on skirt, lg ..**$35.00**

Figurine, girl w/hand to hair & lifting skirt, 11", $40.00

Platter, Blossom, 13" **$18.00**
Shelf sitter, Oriental girl...**$25.00**
Vase, Ming Tree, #946, w/coralene, 6" **$20.00**
Vase, ribbed, mint green w/pink interior, 8" **$25.00**
Vase, sailor boy w/flowers next to white vase, 10¾"..**$35.00**
Wall pocket, Oriental girl, #4046 ....**$25.00**

Weller

Though the Weller Pottery has been closed since 1948, they were so prolific that you'll be sure to see several pieces anytime you're 'antiquing.' They were one of the largest of the art pottery giants that located in the Zanesville, Ohio, area, using locally dug clays to produce their wares. In the early years, they made hand-decorated vases, jardinieres, lamps, and other decorative items for the home, many of which were signed by notable artists such as Fredrick Rhead, John Lessell, Virginia Adams, Anthony Dunlavy, Dorothy England, Albert Haubrich, Hester Pillsbury, E.L. Pickens, and Jacques Sicard, to name only a few. Some of their early lines were First and Second Dickens, Eocean, Sicardo, Etna, Louwelsa, Turada, and Aurelian. Portraits of Indians, animals of all types, lady golfers, nudes, and scenes of Dickens stories were popular themes, and some items were overlaid with silver filigree. These lines are rather hard to find at this point in time, and prices are generally high; but there's plenty of their later production still around, and most pieces are relatively inexpensive.

If you'd like to learn more, we recommend *The Collector's Encyclopedia of Weller Pottery* by Sharon and Bob Huxford.

Alvin, vase, embossed apple motif on tree trunk, 8½" ..**$45.00**

Arcadia, fan vase, blue leaves flare out to form bowl on round base, 8x15" **$60.00**

Arcadia, vase, #A-4, embossed leaves wrap around to form bulbous body on short foot, points of leaves form rim, 5½" **$30.00**

Ardsley, corner vase, iris motif at 3 corners, footed, 7" .**$120.00**

Ardsley, double wall pocket, cattail motif, 11½" **$200.00**

Blue Drapery, bowl, embossed rose motif on deep blue 'drapery' background, 4" **$85.00**

Blue Drapery, planter, embossed rose motif on deep blue 'drapery' background, 4" **$75.00**

Bonito, bowl, freehand stylized floral & leaf design around rim, 3½" **$85.00**

Bonito, vase, freehand floral design on ivory footed trumpet shape w/sm scrolled tab handles, 6½" **$100.00**

Brighton, figurine, bluebird #5, looking up, 5½" **$275.00**

Cameo, basket, white floral design on green ball shape w/cut-out top, fancy irregular handle, 4-footed, 7½" **$45.00**

Cameo, planter, embossed white floral design on blue w/sides curving inward, plain rim, flat bottom, 4" .**$40.00**

Clarmont, bowl, brown w/floral & leaf design, beaded ear-shaped handles, short round foot, 3" **$45.00**

Clarmont, candlestick, brown w/embossed grape design on cup, horizontally ribbed neck, dome base w/grapes, 10", ...**$100.00**

Classic, bowl, green, cut-out design on flat rim, 11" dia **$50.00**

Classic, plate, white, looped cut-out design w/flowers around rim, 11½" **$45.00**

Claywood, candlestick, incised floral design on tall flared base, 5" **$65.00**

Claywood, mug, incised floral design, squared handle, 5" **$100.00**

Claywood, vase, incised spider-web design on cylinder shape, plain rim & flat bottom, 5½" **$85.00**

Coppertone, basket, embossed floral design on fan shape w/twig handle, 8½" **$200.00**

Coppertone, vase, trumpet shape w/bronze & green mottled effect, flared base, 6½" **$150.00**

Cornish, bowl, incised flower & leaf design on ball shape w/ribbed band, closed scrolled handles, footed, 4" .**$35.00**

Cornish, vase, incised flower & leaf design on cylinder flaring then tapering to flat bottom, knob handles, 10" **$40.00**

Creamware, match holder, rose & swag design, 6½" ..**$110.00**

Creamware, planter w/liner, profile cameo & swag motif, cut-out design around rim, 11½" wide **$85.00**

Darsie, flowerpot, ivory w/embossed swagged tassel design around scalloped rim, flat bottom, 5½" **$30.00**

Darsie, vase, embossed swagged tassel design on ivory cylinder w/flared scalloped rim, flat bottom, 7½".**$30.00**

Delsa, basket, colorful floral design on green textured background, ribbon & bow handle, 4-footed, 7".........**$50.00**

Delsa, ewer, colorful floral design on blue squatty bulbous shape w/textured background, 7"........................**$30.00**

Etna, mug, grape design on gray shading, plain flat rim & bottom, ear-shaped handle, 5½" **$125.00**

Etna, vase, embossed floral design on light gray shading to white, thick neck w/angled body, 6½", $125.00

Etna, vase, lg pink floral design on barrel shape w/lg curved handles coming from thick rim, flat bottom, 9" **$350.00**

Evergreen, console bowl, fluted w/flared rim, footed, 5".**$70.00**

Evergreen, triple candle holder, fluted cups on scrolled base, 7½" **$75.00**

Flemish, jardiniere, floral & leaf design around bottom of 3-footed bowl, 6" **$110.00**

Flemish, tub, embossed rose design on round basket, handled, flat bottom, 4½" **$110.00**

Fleron, bowl, #J-6, rose-colored folded-down ruffled rim over green horizontal ribbing tapering to flat bottom, 3" .**$65.00**

Florenzo, basket, fluted fan shape w/green shaded to white, embossed flowers line handle, round foot, 5½" ...**$95.00**

Florenzo, vase w/frog cover, fluted side flares to scalloped rim on green shaded to white, water lily frog, 4-footed, 7" **$120.00**

Floretta, ewer, embossed grape cluster on brown, flat bottom, 10½" **$135.00**

Floretta, ewer, orange floral design on brown bulbous shape, footed, 4½" **$75.00**

Floretta, vase, lg pink floral design on urn shape w/gray shaded to beige & rose, flared bottom, 19" **$600.00**

Floretta, vase, purple grape design on gray shaded to white on flared shape w/4 ball shapes below scalloped rim, 5½" **$100.00**

Forest, pitcher, high-gloss glaze, 5"............**$200.00**

Forest, tub planter, 4" **$100.00**

Gloria, bowl, #G-15, embossed blossom & branch design on green, ruffled rim, slightly scalloped base, 3½" **$35.00**

Gloria, vase, #G-12, embossed butterfly & floral design on tan 'acorn' shape w/ruffled rim, 3-footed, 5" **$40.00**

Hobart, flower frog, girl w/flowers, turquoise, no mark, 8½", $250.00

Hudson (Blue & Decorated), vase, cylinder shape w/band of flowers around plain rim, 8½"........................**$200.00**

Hudson (White & Decorated), vase, floral motif on paneled cylinder shape, flat bottom, 11" **$225.00**

Ivoris, jar, embossed monochrome floral design in ivory, w/lid, 5" **$55.00**

Ivoris, vase, ivory bulbous shape w/3 fancy feet, 5½" .**$45.00**

Ivory (Clinton Ivory), planter, square shape w/dragonfly design, footed, 4"..**$110.00**

Klyro, bowl, vining floral design on paneled bowl w/square cutouts around rim, 4-footed, 3½" **$60.00**

Klyro, fan vase, floral & berry motif on paneled vase w/square cutouts at rim, 4-footed, 8" **$50.00**

Lido, basket, pink shaded to deep rose, swirled design w/ruffled rim, 8½"..**$45.00**

Lido, candle holder, #15, green shaded to blue, 2-light, 2½", each **$45.00**

Lido, planter, white swirled leaf shape shaded to yellow, 2x9"..**$25.00**

Lorbeek, vase, 'folded' V-shape in high-gloss lavender on square base, 8" **$125.00**

Malverne, boat bowl, embossed floral & leaf design wraps around to form handles, footed, 5½x11".............**$60.00**

Malverne, circle vase, embossed floral & leaf design on textured background, 8" **$75.00**

Manhattan, vase, green vertical leaf design on lighter green cylinder w/flared foot, plain rim, 9" **$85.00**

Manhattan, vase, random green leaf design on lighter green urn shape w/curved handles, plain rim, flat bottom, 8" **$70.00**

Marbleized, bowl, 1½x5½" dia **$45.00**

Marbleized, vase, trumpet shape, 7½" **$75.00**

Marvo, bowl, allover embossed floral & leaf design, 5" .**$50.00**

Marvo, vase, allover embossed floral & leaf design on cylinder shape w/flat bottom, 8½"................................**$60.00**

Melrose, console bowl, embossed rose motif on ivory bowl w/deeply fluted rim, short base, twig handles, 5x8½" **$115.00**

Melrose, vase, embossed rose & branch design on bulbous shape w/indents, fluted rim, twig handles, short base, 5" **$85.00**

Muskota, figurine, fish & stump, 5" **$175.00**

Muskota, figurine, girl on stump, 8½" **$350.00**

Muskota, figurine, 3½" boy in 10½" boat **$525.00**

Noval, bowl, applied apples & berries on bowl w/ivory & black panels, black rim & base, 3½x9½"...............**$75.00**

Noval, comport, applied apples & berries as handles on ivory bowl w/tall pedestal foot, black banded rim & foot, 5½" **$75.00**

Panella, basket, yellow & green floral design on shaded tan 'egg-cup' shape w/pointed handle, 7"...................**$35.00**

Panella, cornucopia, yellow & green floral & leaf design on shaded green, 5½"...**$20.00**

Paragon, bowl, allover incised floral & leaf design on blue, 4½"..**$55.00**

Paragon, vase, allover incised floral & leaf design on honey color, lipped rim, short foot, 7½"..........................**$85.00**

Patricia, bowl, white w/embossed leaf design, 4 duck heads around rim, sm round foot, 3" **$40.00**

Patricia, bud vase, ivory squatty bulbous shape on short pedestal foot, embossed leaf design w/swan-head handles, 4" **$30.00**

Pearl, basket, rose motif w/pearl swags on cream, scalloped foot, 6½"..**$150.00**

Pearl, vase, bulbous shape w/swags of pearls & jewels on cream, black band around rim & bottom, 5" **$75.00**

Pumila, candle holder, water lily blossom on base, 3", each...**$70.00**

Pumila, wall pocket, embossed lily-pad design, scalloped rim, 7" **$90.00**

Roma, ashtray, band of roses & leaves above vertical ribbing, 4 rests, 2½"...**$60.00**

Roma, bud vase, roses & swag design on ivory cylinder, 5" **$65.00**

Roma, comport, lg decorated bowl on short handled base, 5" **$90.00**

Roma, console bowl w/liner, embossed grapes on ivory, footed, twig handles, 6½x18"..............$175.00

Roma, jardiniere, embossed rose & swag design on ivory bowl tapering to flat bottom, 5".............$70.00

Roma, square bowl w/swag & cut-out design on tall 4-sided base w/cut-out design, 9½"..............$175.00

Roma, vase, floral design on ivory w/cut-out circle design around scalloped & flared rim, flat bottom, 2½".$200.00

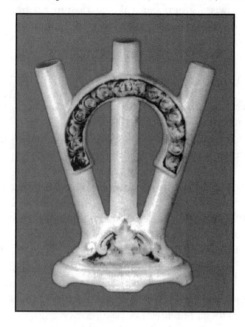

Roma, vase, triple bud; marked Weller (die impressed), $110.00

Roma, wall pocket, embossed spray of roses tied w/blue bow, ruffled rim, 7"..............$250.00

Rosemont, jardiniere, incised apple motif on black & cream lattice background, 5"..............$110.00

Rosemont, vase, incised blue bird on blossom branch, bulbous urn shape, footed, 10"..............$375.00

Rudlor, console bowl, blossom & branch design on boat shape, 4-bead handles, short foot, 4½x17½".........$50.00

Rudlor, vase, blossom & branch design on green slightly bulbous cylinder, footed, drooping handles, plain rim, 9"..............$45.00

Sabrinian, bud vase, upright swirled shell w/flared rim, 7"..............$120.00

Sabrinian, window box, fanned-out shell design, 3½x9"..............$200.00

Senic, vase, #S-2, embossed landscape on blue bulbous shape, short foot, plain rim, angled cut-out handles, 5½"..............$65.00

Senic, vase, #S-2, embossed palm-tree landscape on shaded gold, ruffled rim, footed, 6½"..............$35.00

Silvertone, candle holders, embossed blossom & branch design on base, 3", pr..............$100.00

Silvertone, fan basket, embossed grape design, twig handle, 13"..............$275.00

Sydonia, cornucopia bud vase, green mottled effect, 8".$50.00

Sydonia, vase, triple bud, 2-tone blue mottled effect, 8½"..............$70.00

Utility ware, cookie jar, embossed basket-weave design, 10"..............$70.00

Utility ware, teapot, pumpkin shape, 6"..............$110.00

Velva, vase, berry & leaf panel on brown bulbous shape w/upturned tab handles, short round foot, 9"......$70.00

Voile, fan vase, stylized embossed apple tree on tan background, 8"..............$75.00

Warwick, double bud vase, embossed bud & branch design on tree trunk, 8½"..............$75.00

Warwick, jardiniere, bud & branch design on bark background, 7"..............$150.00

Wild Rose, basket, floral design on tan ball shape w/cut-out top, twig handle, short round foot, 5½"..............$25.00

Wild Rose, vase, white floral design on green slightly bulbous shape, drooping handles, round foot, 6½"...$20.00

Woodcraft, bowl, embossed cherry & leaf design on bark-like background, plain rim, flat bottom, 3"..........$70.00

Woodcraft, planter, fox family in tree stump, 5½".....$275.00

Woodcraft, wall pocket, owl peeking out of hole in tree, 10"..............$250.00

Zona, compote, incised flower motif on bowl, thick pedestal foot, 5½"..............$60.00

Zona, pitcher, incised apple motif on ivory w/twig handle, flat bottom, 6"..............$50.00

Zona, pitcher, Kingfisher, 8", $200.00

Western Heroes

No friend was ever more true, no brother more faithful, no acquaintance more real to us than our favorite cowboys of radio, TV, and the silver screen. They were upright, strictly moral, extremely polite, and tireless in their pursuit of law and order in the American West. How unfortunate that such role models are practically extinct nowadays.

This is an area of strong collector interest right now, and prices are escalating. Some collectors prefer one cowboy hero over the others and concentrate their collections on that particular star. Some unlikely items are included in this specialized area — hair tonic bottles, cookie jars, wallets, and drinking mugs, for instance.

For more infomation and some wonderful pictures, we recommend *Toys, Antique and Collectible,* and *Character Toys and Collectibles, First and Second Series,* all by David Longest.

See also Big Little Books; Character Watches; Games; Puzzles; Paper Dolls; Pin-back Buttons; Premiums; Toys; Trading Cards.

Bat Masterson, book, hard-bound, Whitman, 1960, EX..**$16.00**

Bat Masterson, playsuit, vest, shirt & pants w/2-part cane, 1959, NMIB.........................**$50.00**

Buffalo Bill, gloves, w/original tags, sm, M.................**$40.00**

Cisco Kid, coloring book, 1963, NM...........................**$20.00**

Dale Evans, necklace, silver-tone horseshoe pendant w/sm stones & bow on card, Dale Evans Official..., 13" long, EX.........................**$20.00**

Daniel Boone, coloring book, features Fess Parker as Daniel Boone, Saalfield, 1964, 8x11", M.........................**$62.00**

Daniel Boone, figure, solid plastic w/lg rubber head, Fess Parker image w/real hair, powder horn & bag, 1964, 5", EX.........................**$25.00**

Davy Crockett, Auto Magic Picture Gun, MIB **$135.00**

Davy Crockett, candy box, Walt Disney, 1960s, VG....**$22.00**

Davy Crockett, charm bracelet, enameled, MOC.........**$65.00**

Davy Crockett, coloring book, EX............................**$20.00**

Davy Crockett, drinking glass, 1950s, 5", NM **$10.00**

Davy Crockett, guitar, MIP **$55.00**

Davy Crockett, gun, Frontier Fighter Cork Gun, Japan, tin & wood, cigarette flint mechanism at muzzle, 1950s, 21", NM **$65.00**

Davy Crockett, gun, Marx, plastic & metal flintlock pistol w/working trigger, 11", NM in EX box...............**$110.00**

Davy Crockett, gun, Wyandotte, litho tin clicker type, working, sm scratches, 1950s, 8", VG **$60.00**

Davy Crockett, jam jar, glass w/graphics of Davy & Alamo in green & white, EX **$12.00**

Davy Crockett, mug, brown & white, EX.....................**$10.00**

Davy Crockett, mug, white w/black graphics, Davy & Indians in canoes, ...Famous Frontiersman 1786-1836, EX..**$10.00**

Davy Crockett, outfit, #406, fur cap, gun, powder horn & belt, LM Eddy Manufacturing Co, complete, EX+, $165.00

Davy Crockett, pencil pouch, 1956, EX.......................**$35.00**

Davy Crockett, pocket knife, 2½", EX+ **$25.00**

Davy Crockett, powder horn, box features Fess Parker, Daisy, 1950s, MIB.........................**$95.00**

Davy Crockett, record album, 3 Adventures of Davy Crockett, Disneyland #1315, 33⅓ rpm, VG+ **$42.00**

Davy Crockett, shirt, features Fess Parker, Blue Bell, 1950s, NM+ **$75.00**

Davy Crockett, stamp book, complete w/all stamps applied, EX.........................**$30.00**

Davy Crockett, tie, brown w/jewelled leather slide, EX.**$35.00**

Davy Crockett, toy watch, MOC **$18.00**

Davy Crockett, wallet, plastic, shows Davy in real coon skin cap, w/original ID card, calendar & certificate, 5x4", MIB **$40.00**

Gene Autry, bandana, blue silk-like fabric with 10½x6½" corner portrait, early 1950s, EX.........................**$40.00**

Gene Autry, book, Gene Autry & Red Shirt, 8 chapters, Sandpiper, 1951, 5x8", M.........................**$25.00**

Gene Autry, book, Gene Autry & the Ghost Riders, by Lewis B Patten, hard-bound, Whitman, 1955, EX...........**$15.00**

Gene Autry, box label, Gene Autry Cowboy Boots, unused, 1950s, 4½x13", M **$10.00**

Gene Autry, coloring book, Champion, 40 pages, unused, Whitman #2953, 1957, EX.........................**$15.00**

Gene Autry, coloring book, 4 pages colored, 1949, EX .**$12.50**

Gene Autry, gun, Buzz Henry, gold-plated cast-iron cap pistol, 1950, 7½", M.........................**$115.00**

Gene Autry, gun, Kenton, dummy cap pistol, cast iron, white plastic grips w/90% signature, 1939, 8½", VG **$185.00**

Gene Autry, gun, Kenton, Junior Model cap gun, cast-iron w/simulated pearl insert handles, 1938, w/pin-back, NMIB.........................**$275.00**

Gene Autry, songbook, 1950s, VG **$35.00**

Gene Autry, wallet, vinyl, M4.........................**$20.00**

Gene Autry, 6-gun paper popper, advertises his TV show, 1950s, NM **$6.00**

Hopalong Cassidy, bank, plastic bust, NM...................**$45.00**

Hopalong Cassidy, barrette, silver-tone metal, embossed head & shoulder image of Hoppy flanked by engraved initials, M **$15.00**

Hopalong Cassidy, book, Hopalong Cassidy Makes New Friends, 1950, EX **$14.00**

Hopalong Cassidy, coloring book, Authorized Edition #216525, 10 colored pages, 1951, 11x8½", EX+, $28.00

Hopalong Cassidy, decals, 3 water-transfer decals featuring Hoppy & Topper, ca 1950, 2x1¾", EX..................**$20.00**

Hopalong Cassidy, dominoes set, w/images of Hoppy & Topper, 1x12x9" box, EX **$90.00**

Hopalong Cassidy, drinking glass, black graphics on milk glass, marked Dinner Milk on back, 1952, 3" dia, NM **$30.00**

Hopalong Cassidy, field glasses, EX in box, $295.00

Hopalong Cassidy, gun, Wyandotte, gold, fires caps, EX..**$250.00**

Hopalong Cassidy, gun & holster, Wyandotte, 8" die-cast repeater, studded holster w/embossed concho, 1950s, VG+..**$229.00**

Hopalong Cassidy, milk carton, waxed cardboard, Leigh Valley Dairy, Hoppy's Favorite Milk, early 1950s, 9x2¾", VG+..**$25.00**

Hopalong Cassidy, mug, milk glass w/blue Hopalong drawing his guns, cowboy roping steer, 1950s, NM **$32.00**

Hopalong Cassidy, note cards, white w/yellow border, Hopalong Cassidy Bar 20 Ranch, w/color images, set of 25, M..**$18.00**

Hopalong Cassidy, pennant, black felt w/Hoppy in white, 8x18", M..**$14.00**

Hopalong Cassidy, pocketknife, Hammer, VG **$50.00**

Hopalong Cassidy, pop-up book, Hopalong Cassidy Lends a Helping Hand, EX..**$80.00**

Hopalong Cassidy, punch-out book, unpunched, Whitman, 1951, EX **$130.00**

Hopalong Cassidy, single holster & belt, EX................**$80.00**

Hopalong Cassidy, sleeping bag, EX.......................**$225.00**

Hopalong Cassidy, sticker book, partially used, 12x10", EX+ **$30.00**

Hopalong Cassidy, tie tac, metal, embossed figure of Hoppy, ca 1950, M...**$14.00**

Lone Ranger, book bag, M.....................................**$125.00**

Lone Ranger, brush & comb set, 1938, NMIB...........**$125.00**

Lone Ranger, camera w/3 boxes of film, De-Lux Cine-Vue, 8x9" original M box, EX+ **$245.00**

Lone Ranger, gun, Kilgore, blue frame w/nickel-plated cast-iron hammer & trigger, white grips, 1940s, surface rust, VG...**$125.00**

Lone Ranger, hand puppet, cloth w/rubber head, 1955, scarce, 10", EX...**$65.00**

Lone Ranger, key chain, bullet w/figure of Lone Ranger inside, 1950s, EX...**$45.00**

Lone Ranger, Official First Aid Kit, tin w/hinged lid, dated 1938, 4x4", EX, $95.00; Figurine, plaster, Lone Ranger on rearing Silver w/name embossed on base, dated 1938, 4", EX, $40.00

Lone Ranger, paint book, unused, 1940, M **$45.00**

Lone Ranger, pencil box, brown cardboard, EX+........**$42.00**

Lone Ranger, pencil sharpener, facsimile signature on side, M...**$55.00**

Lone Ranger, pin, metal, head w/mask & scarf, worn & tarnished **$40.00**

Lone Ranger, pocketknife, red w/silver bullet, EX......**$18.00**

Lone Ranger, radio soundtrack, Adventures of the Lone Ranger, EX...**$15.00**

Lone Ranger, scrapbook, Lone Ranger on Silver shown on front & back, unused, Whitman, 1950s, 10x13½", EX **$20.00**

Lone Ranger, sticker fun book, some stickers used, Whitman, 1952, VG+ **$20.00**

Lone Ranger, target game, tin stand-up featuring Lone Ranger & Silver, Marx, 1938, original 9½x9½" box, NM **$175.00**

Lone Ranger, tie, brown w/silk-screened bust image of the Lone Ranger, 1940, EX...**$70.00**

Lone Ranger, toy watch & badge set, unopened bag w/die-cut perforated black mask at top, Gee Wiz, Japan, 1950s, M..**$15.00**

Lone Ranger, wallet, vinyl, M.................................**$50.00**

Matt Dillon, outfit w/chaps, beige & brown cotton, likeness of Matt Dillon on shirt, 1958, EX+ **$125.00**

Red Ryder, gun, Christmas Story BB gun, VG-EX........**$65.00**

Rin-Tin-Tin, canteen, VG...**$20.00**

Rin-Tin-Tin, coloring book, 1959, M..........................**$24.00**

Rin-Tin-Tin, paint-by-numbers set, 9 8x10" scenes, unused, complete, Transogram, 1956, EX+ **$65.00**

Rin-Tin-Tin, wallet, vinyl, M.....................................**$50.00**

Roy Rogers, ashtray, bronze-tone metal depicting Roy on rearing Trigger in center, EX................................**$25.00**

Roy Rogers, bank, china figure of Roy on Trigger, ca 1949-early 50s, 7½", EX...**$95.00**

Roy Rogers, binoculars, w/case, 1950s, VG+ **$85.00**

Roy Rogers, book, Favorite Western Stories, Whitman, 1956, EX in NM box................**$40.00**

Roy Rogers, cup, figural boot, M **$45.00**

Roy Rogers, guitar, Jefferson, MIB................**$200.00**

Roy Rogers, gun, Classy, Roy Rogers Shootin' Iron, embossed design of Roy on rearing Trigger, on illustrated card, EX **$152.00**

Roy Rogers, gun, Kilgore, gold cap pistol w/plastic inset hdls, 8", NMOC **$244.00**

Roy Rogers, gun, Leslie-Henry, die cast, break-to-front w/lever release, smoking action, unfired, 1950s, 9" NM................**$175.00**

Roy Rogers, gun, Marx, gray plastic carbine repeater, pull-down cap magazine, 1950s, 26", NM in worn box.**$135.00**

Roy Rogers, harmonica, 1950s, G+ **$45.00**

Roy Rogers, key chain, gold bullet, MIP **$15.00**

Roy Rogers, lamp base, plaster figures of Roy & Trigger, inscribed Many Happy Trails, Roy Rogers & Trigger, 12½", VG+ **$60.00**

Roy Rogers, lantern, lithographed tin, bail handle, 7¾", EX, $45.00

Roy Rogers, neckerchief, M................**$35.00**

Roy Rogers, paint book, unused, Whitman, 1944, 11x8¼", EX+ **$50.00**

Roy Rogers, paint-by-number set, complete w/2 picture panels, 12 oil colors, 2 brushes & cleaner, 1950s, EX................**$95.00**

Roy Rogers, pencil case, vinyl, EX+ **$25.00**

Roy Rogers, postcard, w/picture & facsimile signature, 1950s, NM................**$25.00**

Roy Rogers, ranch lantern, tin, Ohio Art, in original box, 1950s, 8", NM **$200.00**

Roy Rogers, record set, Pecos Bill (from movie Melody Time), sleeve shows Roy & Sons of the Pioneers, 78 rpm, 1940s, VG+ **$30.00**

Roy Rogers, rodeo playset, black graphics on brown cardboard box, complete, Marx #3690, 1950s, NM....**$270.00**

Roy Rogers, scarf, w/Trigger, EX................**$50.00**

Roy Rogers, wallet, w/Trigger, mid-1950s, EX.............**$40.00**

Roy Rogers, 7 35mm slides, Mark of the Big Cat, Give-A-Show Slide Strip, Kenner, 1962, NM................**$20.00**

Tom Mix, bracelet, EX+ **$40.00**

Tom Mix, patch, M................**$35.00**

Tom Mix, pocket mirror, black & white head portrait, 2" dia................**$40.00**

Tom Mix, toy wagon, Big Six Circus & Wild West, white wood w/red images of Tom & inscriptions on both sides, 1930s, G **$50.00**

Tonto, coloring book, cover has illustration of Tonto on horse, 18 of 40 pages colored, Whitman, 1957, 7½x6½", VG................**$10.00**

Tonto, coloring book, 1957, M................**$10.00**

Tonto, hand puppet, Ideal, 1966, EX................**$35.00**

Wild Bill Hickok, gun, Leslie-Henry, Young Buffalo Bill Cap Pistol, die cast, single shot, unfired, 1954, 7½", NM .**$45.00**

Wild Bill Hickok, gun, Leslie-Henry, 44 Cap Pistol, die cast, swing-out/side loading, cylinder revolves, 1950s, 11", M.......**$155.00**

Wyatt Earp, badge, 6-point metal star, Wyatt Earp Entertainment/20th Century, 1959, MOC **$15.00**

Wyatt Earp, color-by-number stencil set, NMIB...........**$28.00**

Wyatt Earp, coloring book, 1958, EX+ **$15.00**

Wyatt Earp, gun, Hubley, fires caps, 1950s, 10½" barrel, NM................**$100.00**

Wyatt Earp, wallet, 1957, EX................**$235.00**

Zorro, bowl, 1966, EX................**$15.00**

Zorro, cap gun, Lone Star, NMOC **$100.00**

Zorro, cap pistol, plastic, 1960s, EX................**$35.00**

Zorro, charm bracelet, 5 charms, EX **$40.00**

Zorro, coloring book, some coloring neatly done, Whitman, 1958, EX................**$25.00**

Zorro, gum cards, 82 of 88 multicolored photo cards, Topps, 1950s, EX+ **$230.00**

Zorro, hat, black w/white & black front label featuring title & Zorro on his horse, Benay-Albay, 1950s, EX.....**$30.00**

Zorro, hat & mask, felt, EX................**$75.00**

Zorro, mask, whip & lariat, 1960s, MOC................**$85.00**

Zorro, paint-by-number set, 4 10x14" scenes, 2 scenes partially painted, complete, Hasbro, 1958, EX+ **$70.00**

Zorro, pillowcase, sealed in illustrated package, 1958, M **$40.00**

Zorro, pencil holder & sharpener, ceramic figure, white with black accents & red cape, 1950s, 6", $65.00

Westmoreland Glass

Before the turn of the century, this company was known as the Specialty Glass Works and was located in East Liverpool, Ohio, where they produced tableware as well as utilitarian items. They moved to Grapeville, Pennsylvania, in 1890 and added many more decorative glassware items to their inventory. Carnival glass was their mainstay before the years of the twenties, but they're most famous today for their milk glass, black glass, and colored glass tableware patterns.

Early pieces carried paper labels, but by the 1960s, the mark was embossed in the glass itself. The superimposed 'WG' mark was the first of the embossed marks; the last was a circle containing 'Westmoreland' around the outside with a large 'W' in the center.

For more information, we recommend *Westmoreland Glass* by Philip J. Rosso, Jr., and Phil Rosso.

See also Animal Dishes; Carnival Glass.

Old Quilt, candy dish, milk glass, pedestal foot, square, 6½", $30.00

American Hobnail, cup & saucer, milk glass **$10.00**
Beaded Edge, tumbler, milk glass, footed **$10.00**
Beaded Grape, bowl, milk glass, footed, 9" **$45.00**
Beaded Grape, bowl, milk glass w/hand-painted roses, flat, square, w/lid **$65.00**
Beaded Grape, candle holders, milk glass, pr **$25.00**
Beaded Grape, candy dish, milk glass, pedestal base, 4" .**$20.00**
Beaded Grape, sugar bowl, milk glass **$15.00**
Beaded Grape, vase, milk glass, tall **$45.00**
Della Robbia, basket, color stain, 12" **$150.00**
Della Robbia, bowl, gold fruit, rolled rim, 13½" **$65.00**
Della Robbia, creamer & sugar bowl, milk glass **$22.00**
Della Robbia, plate, crystal, 10½" **$15.00**
Della Robbia, tumbler, crystal, footed, 4¾" **$15.00**
Dolphin, candlesticks, milk glass, 4", pr **$30.00**
English Hobnail, bowl, amber, 4⅜" **$15.00**

English Hobnail, bowl, crystal, 4¾" **$8.50**
English Hobnail, cocktail, amber **$15.00**
English Hobnail, compote, milk glass, handled, 8" **$35.00**
English Hobnail, creamer, crystal **$7.50**
English Hobnail, cruet, milk glass, sm **$18.00**
English Hobnail, sugar bowl, crystal **$12.50**
Fruit, cup, strawberry, milk glass **$12.00**
Fruit, saucer, grape, milk glass **$8.00**
National, plate, milk glass, 6" **$25.00**
Old Quilt, bowl, fruit; milk glass, footed, 9" **$45.00**
Old Quilt, box, milk glass, #41, square, w/lid **$35.00**
Old Quilt, cake salver, crystal **$45.00**
Old Quilt, creamer & sugar bowl, milk glass, lg **$28.00**
Old Quilt, pitcher, juice; milk glass **$35.00**
Old Quilt, tumbler, milk glass, 9-oz **$15.00**
Panelled Grape, bowl, milk glass, low foot, 9" **$45.00**
Panelled Grape, candlesticks, milk glass, 4", pr **$25.00**
Panelled Grape, candy dish, lacy **$20.00**
Panelled Grape, candy dish, low foot, 6½" **$22.00**
Panelled Grape, cup & saucer, milk glass **$20.00**
Panelled Grape, gravy boat, w/underplate, milk glass .**$65.00**
Panelled Grape, jardiniere, milk glass, footed, 5" **$25.00**
Panelled Grape, mayonnaise, w/underplate, milk glass ..**$30.00**

Panelled Grape, salt & pepper shakers, milk glass w/metal tops, footed, pr, $22.50

Panelled Grape, vase, bud; pastel fruit, 16" **$25.00**
Peacock, creamer & sugar bowl, milk glass **$40.00**
Princess Feather, bowl, crystal, 4½" **$12.00**
Princess Feather, plate, crystal, 8" **$15.00**
Princess Feather, salt & pepper shakers, crystal, pr **$24.00**
Ring & Petal, cake plate, milk glass **$37.50**
Roses & Bows, honey dish, milk glass, w/lid **$40.00**
Roses & Bows, vase, bud; milk glass, 10" **$30.00**
Thousand Eye, sherbet, crystal, 4¼" **$12.00**
Thousand Eye, sherbet, purple & marigold stain **$15.00**
Thousand Eye, wine, ruby, marigold & blue stain, 5" .**$18.50**

World's Fair Collectibles

Souvenir items have been issued since the mid-1800s for every world's fair and exposition. Few fairgoers have left the grounds without purchasing at least one. Some of the older items were often manufactured right on the fairgrounds by glass or pottery companies who erected working kilns and furnaces just for the duration of the fair. Of course, the older items are usually more valuable, but even souvenirs from the past fifty years are worth hanging onto.

St. Louis, 1904

Napkin ring, embossed fair building on metal, EX......**$35.00**
Paperweight, Central Cascades view in glass, 4x2¼" ..**$25.00**
Pitcher, ruby-stained glass, 4½"....................................**$45.00**

Picture, 'Cascade Gardens,' gold-tone tin frame, wire easel back, 8x9½", $40.00

Postcard, Palace of Transportation, NM.........................**$3.00**
Tray, metal, Education & Electrical Buildings, 5x3¼", EX.**$20.00**
Tumbler, milk glass, embossed buildings, 5"..............**$15.00**

Philadelphia, 1926

Book, Flags of America, John Wanamaker Store, 32 pages, 5½x8", EX...**$14.00**
Lamp, Liberty Bell, glass shade w/white metal posts, 5", EX.**$28.00**
Pamphlet, Sesquicentennial Daily Program & Guide, illustrated, 32 pages, 9x6", EX.......................................**$20.00**
Pencil case, Liberty Bell on leather, calendar inside, 3x8", EX...**$30.00**
Program, Ohio Day, 32 pages, 6x9", EX......................**$10.00**
View book, Philadelphia The Birthplace of Liberty, Sesquicentennial Exposition, illustrated, 32 pages, EX ...**$25.00**

Chicago, 1933

Bank, tin, can shape, American Can Co, various designs of fair buildings on sides, 1934 date, 3½x2" dia, EX+ .**$28.00**

Book of needles w/threader, A Century of Progress Field Museum & Carillion Towers, Hall of Science, 6½x4¾", EX..**$8.00**
Bracelet, buckle type, embossed w/vignettes of the fair & 1933 logo, EX...**$24.00**
Key, copper, Travel & Transport 1933 Key to the World World's Fair, Hall of Science Chicago...1933 on back, 8½", EX...**$20.00**
Key chain, medallion type, advertises Kelvinator, A Century of Progress..., view of fairgrounds, 1¼" dia, EX....**$12.00**
Napkin ring, metal, gold-tone outlined in red w/design of 3 different buildings, comet logo, 1¼x1½" dia, EX..**$15.00**
Plate, heavy copper, various scenes around rim, Buckingham Fountain shown in center, original box, 4¾" dia, EX+ **$20.00**
Ticket, A Souvenir of a Century of Progress International Exposition Chicago 1934, EX................................**$6.00**
Tip tray, Hall of Science..., 5x3⅞", EX **$5.00**

New York, 1939

Ashtray, brass, Trylon & Perisphere design, embossed lettering w/1939 date, 4½" dia, EX...............................**$25.00**
Bank, painted white metal, Trylon & Perisphere on stepped base, 8½"...**$170.00**
Bank, tin, Trylon & Perisphere on beveled rectangular base, may be Chein, 12¼", EX......................................**$250.00**
Coasters, metal, set of 6 w/various multicolored scenes, EX **$75.00**
Compact, fair logo & date on fabric-covered metal top, 2x1¾", EX..**$55.00**
Creamer, ceramic, George Washington figure, scarce, 5", EX **$30.00**
Mechanical pencil holder, celluloid, metal & cardboard, windmill w/pencil attached to dog by chain, NYWF decal, EX..**$35.00**
Pin-back button, celluloid, blue on white, GM Exhibit, 'I have seen the future,' 1", EX................................**$35.00**

San Francisco, 1939

Ice pick, 1939 World's Fair, Golden Gate International Exposition, San Francisco Cal, EX **$8.00**
Pennant, w/lg pencil, California World's Fair 1940 America!, Cavalcade of a Nation, 11" long.........................**$16.00**
Token, aluminum, Union Pacific — Golden Gate International Exposition 1939, Aluminum Co of America, EX **$4.00**

Seattle, 1962

Bowl, black lacquer, pictures various fair sights w/Century 21 Exposition logo, 7⅝" dia, EX.............................**$8.00**
Catalog, Masterpiece of Art — Seattle World's Fair..., exhibited in the Fine Arts Pavilion, softcover, 160 pages, EX...**$12.00**
Cuff links, gold lettering on blue background, shows fair views, MIB, pr **$8.00**

Saucer, white & blue, various scenes of Washington around rim, Century 21 logo in center, 5½" dia, EX............**$5.00**

Snow dome, Space Needle, lettering on base, 3⅜", M..**$6.00**

Tray, black lacquer, pictures various fair views, 10¾" dia, M **$12.00**

Bottle opener, gold-tone w/emblem & jewels, EX, $15.00

New York, 1964

Amusement coupon book, Visit the New York World's Fair 1964-65, complete w/coupons, unused, EX..........**$12.00**

Bank, Unisphere atop upright rocket on round inscribed base, painted white metal, mechanical, 10¾" **$90.00**

Candy dish, smoked glass, scalloped edge w/World's Fair images, Peace Through Understanding, Houze Art, 7" dia, NM **$25.00**

Pin tray, gold-tone metal, Unisphere in center, New York World's Fair 1964-65 lettered around rim, 5x3½", EX..**$6.00**

Plate, Unisphere shown in center, various fair vignettes around rim, 8" dia, EX..**$15.00**

Salt & pepper shakers w/tray, shaped like Unisphere, New York World's Fair 1964-65 embossed on tray, 4x4", 3-piece set **$12.00**

Spokane, 1974

Ashtray, ceramic, white w/gold trim, logo in center w/various fair vignettes around rim, unused, 4½", EX **$8.00**

Drinking glass, pedestal foot, Expo 74 logo, 5⅛" **$8.00**

Tray, metal, aerial view of fairgrounds in center, places of interest lettered around rim, 11½" dia, EX **$12.00**

Knoxville, 1982

Belt buckle, brass, red fair logo, 2x3", EX...................**$10.00**

Cookbook, Official Cookbook Expo 82, hardcover, EX.**$18.00**

Pocketknife, bronze finish, fair logo, EX......................**$10.00**

Writing tablet, fair scenes on each page, 9¼x5½", EX...**$4.00**

New Orleans, 1984

Coloring book, Color the Fair, 4 pages, colored, EX.....**$5.00**

Cup & saucer, gold trim, fair logo, 4⅝" dia, M, set........**$8.00**

Key chain, plastic, US Pavilion, M **$2.00**

Stein, glass w/pewter lid, fair logo, 2½", NM.................**$8.00**

Trinket box, porcelain, footed, logo on lid, M............**$10.00**

Auction Houses

Many of the auction galleries we've listed here have appraisal services. Some, though not all, are free of charge. We suggest you contact them first by phone to discuss fees and requirements.

A-1 Auction Service
P.O. Box 540672
Orlando, FL 32854
407-841-6681
Specializing in American antique sales

Alderfer Auction Company
501 Fairground Rd.
Hatfield, PA 19440
215-368-5477 or FAX 215-368-9055

America West Archives
Anderson, Warren
P.O. Box 100
Cedar City, UT 84721
801-586-9497
Quarterly 26-page illustrated catalog includes auction section of scarce and historical early western documents, letters, autographs, stock certificates, and other important ephemera. Subscription: $10 per year

Andre Ammelounx
The Stein Company
P.O. Box 136
Palatine, IL 60078
708-991-5927 or FAX 708-991-5947
Specializing in steins, catalogs available

Anthony J. Nard & Co.
US Rt. 220
Milan, PA 18831
717-888-9404 or FAX 717-888-7723

Arman Absentee Auctions
P.O. Box 174
Woodstock, CT 06281
203-928-5838
Specializing in American glass, Historical Staffordshire, English soft paste, paperweights

Autographs of America
Anderson, Tim
P.O. Box 461
Provo, UT 84603
Free sample catalog of hundreds of autographs for sale

Barrett Bertoia Auctions & Appraisals
1217 Glenwood Dr.
Vineland, NJ 18630
609-692-4092
Specializing in antique toys and collectibles

Berman's Auction Gallery
33 West Blackwell St.
Dover, NJ 07081
201-361-3110

Bider's
241 S Union St.
Lawrence, MA 01843
508-688-4347 or 508-683-3944
Antiques appraised, purchased, and sold on consignment

Bob Koty Professional Auctioneers
Koty, Bob & Clara
P.O. Box 625
Freehold, NJ 07728
908-780-1265

Brian Riba Auctions, Inc.
P.O. Box 53, Main St.
S Glastonbury, CT 06073
203-633-3076

Butterfield & Butterfield
7601 Sunset Blvd.
Los Angeles, CA 90046
213-850-7500

Butterfield & Butterfield
220 San Bruno Ave.
San Francisco, CA 94103
415-861-7500

C.E. Guarino
Box 49
Denmark, ME 04022

Castner Auction & Appraisal Service
Leon Castner, President
6 Wantage Ave.
Branchville, NJ 07826
201-948-3868

Charles E. Kirtley
P.O. Box 2273
Elizabeth City, NC 27096
919-335-1262
Specializing in World's Fair, Civil War, political, advertising, and other American collectibles

Chase Gilmore Art Galleries
724 W Washington
Chicago, IL 60606
312-648-1690

Cincinnati Art Gallery
635 Main St.
Cincinnati, OH 45202
513-381-2128
Specializing in American art pottery, American and European fine paintings, watercolors

Col. Doug Allard
P.O. Box 460
St. Ignatius, MT 59865

Collectors Auction Services
326 Seneca St.
Oil City, PA 16301
814-677-6070
Specializing in advertising, oil and gas, toys, rare museum and investment-quality antiques

Christie's
502 Park Ave.
New York, NY 10022
212-546-1000

David Rago
9 S Main St.
Lambertville, NJ 08530
609-397-9374
Gallery: 17 S Main St.
Lambertville, NJ 08530
Specializing in American art pottery and Arts & Crafts

Don Treadway Gallery
2128 Madison Rd.
Cincinnati, OH 45208
513-321-6742 or FAX 513-871-7722
Member: National Antique Dealers Association, American Art Pottery Association, International Society of Appraisers, and American Ceramic Arts Society

Douglas Auctioneers
Douglas B. Bilodeau
R.R. 5, S
Deerfield, MA 01373
413-665-3530 or FAX 413-665-2877
Year-round sales, specializing in antiques, estates, fine art, appraising

Doyle, Auctioneers & Appraisers
R.D. 3, Box 137, Osborne Hill Road
Fishkill, NY 12524
914-896-9492
Thousands of collectibles offered: call
for free calendar of upcoming events

Duane Merrill
32 Beacon St.
S Burlington, VT 05403
802-878-2625

Dynamite Auctions
Franklin Antique Mall & Auction Gallery
1280 Franklin Ave.
Franklin, PA 16323
814-432-8577 or 814-786-9211

Du Mouchelles
409 E Jefferson Ave.
Detroit, MI 48226
313-963-6255 or FAX 313-963-8199

Dunning's Auction Service, Inc.
755 Church Rd
Elgin, IL 60123
312-741-3483 or FAX 708-741-3589

Early Auction Co.
123 Main St.
Milford, OH 45150

F.B. Hubley & Co., Inc.
364 Broadway
Cambridge, MA 02139
617-876-2030

Fredericktowne Auction Gallery
Thom Pattie
5305 Jefferson Pike
Frederick, MD 21701
301-473-5566 or 800-962-1305

Freeman/Fine Arts of Philadelphia
Leslie Lynch, ASA
1808-10 Chestnut St.
Philadelphia, PA 19103
215-563-9275 or FAX 215-563-8236

Garth's Auctions, Inc.
2690 Stratford Rd., Box 369
Delaware, OH 43015
614-362-4771

Glass-Works Auctions
James Hagenbuch
102 Jefferson
East Greenville, PA 18041
215-679-5849
America's leading auction company in
early American bottles and glass

Greenberg Auctions
7566 Main St.
Sykesville, MD 21784
Specializing in trains: Lionel, American
Flyer, Ives, Marx, HO

Guernsey's
136 E 73rd St.
New York, NY 10021
212-794-2280
Specializing in carousel figures

Gunther's International Auction Gallery
P.O. Box 235, 24 S Virginia Ave.
Brunswick, MD 21716
301-834-7101 or 800-274-8779
Specializing in political, Oriental rugs,
art, bronzes, antiques, the unusual

Gustave White Auctioneers
P.O. Box 59
Newport, RI 02840
401-847-4250

Hake's Americana & Collectibles
Specializing in character and personal-
ity collectibles along with all artifacts
of popular culture for over 20 years.
To receive a catalog for their next
3,000-item mail/phone bid auction,
send $5 to:
Hake's Americana
P.O. Box 1444M
York, PA 17405

Hanzel Galleries, Inc.
1120 S Michigan Ave.
Chicago, IL 60605
312-922-6234

Harmer Rooke Galleries
3 E 57th St.
New York, NY 10022
212-751-1900 or FAX 212-758-1713

Harris Auction Galleries
8783-875 N Howard St.
Baltimore, MD 21201
301-728-7040

Iroquois Auction Gallery
Box 66
Port Henry, NY 12974
518-546-7003

Jack Sellner
Sellner Marketing of California
P.O. Box 308
Fremont, CA 94536
415-745-9463

James D. Julia
P.O. Box 210, Showhegan Rd.
Fairfield, ME 04937

James R. Bakker Antiques, Inc.
James R. Bakker
370 Broadway
Cambridge, MA 02139
617-864-7067
Specializing in American paintings,
prints, and decorative arts

Jim Depew Galleries
1860 Piedmont Rd., NE
Atlanta, GA 30324
404-874-2286

L.R. 'Les' Docks
Box 691035
San Antonio, TX 78269-1035
Providing occasional mail-order record
auctions, rarely consigned; the only
consignments considered are exceptionally scarce and unusual records

Leslie Hindman Auctions
215 W Ohio St.
Chicago, IL 60610
312-670-0010 or FAX 312-670-4248

Litchfield Auction Gallery
Clarence W. Pico
425 Bantam Rd., P.O. Box 1337
Litchfield, CT 06759
203-567-3126 or FAX 203-567-3266

Lloyd Ralston Toys
447 Stratford Rd.
Fairfield, CT 06432

Lubin Galleries, Inc.
Irwin Lubin
30 W 26th St.
New York, NY 10010
212-924-3777 or FAX 212-366-9190

Manion's International Auction House, Inc.
P.O. Box 12214
Kansas City, KS 66112

Mapes Auctioneers & Appraisers
David W. Mapes
1600 Vestal Parkway West
Vestal, NY 13850
607-754-9193 or FAX 607-786-3549

Maritime Auctions
R.R. 2, Box 45A
York, ME 03909
207-363-4247

Marvin Cohen Auctions
Box 425, Routes 20 & 22
New Lebanon, NY 12125
518-794-7477

Mid-Hudson Auction Galleries
One Idlewild Ave.
Cornwall-on-Hudson, NY 12520
914-534-7828 or FAX 914-534-4802

Milwaukee Auction Galleries, Ltd.
4747 W Bradley Rd.
Milwaukee, WI 53223
414-355-5054

Morton M. Goldberg Auction
   Galleries, Inc.
547 Baronne St.
New Orleans, LA 70113
504-592-2300 or FAX 504-592-2311

Noel Barrett Antiques & Auctions
P.O. Box 1001
Carversville, PA 18913
215-297-5109

Northeast Auctions
Ronald Bourgeault
694 Lafayette Rd.
Hampton, NH 03842
603-926-9800 or FAX 603-926-3545

Nostalgia Co.
21 S Lake Dr.
Hackensack, NJ 07601
201-488-4536

Nostalgia Galleries
657 Meacham Ave.
Elmont, NY 11003
516-326-9595
Auctioning items from almost every area
of the collectibles field, catalogs available

Parker's Knife Collector Service
P.O. Box 23522, 5950 'C' Shallowford Rd.
Chattanooga, TN 37422
615-892-0448 or 800-247-0599
FAX 615-892-4165

Paul McInnis
356 Exeter Rd.
Hampton Falls, NH 03844
603-778-8989

Pennypacker Auction Center
1540 New Holland Rd.
Reading, PA 19807

Phillips Fine Art & Auctioneers
406 E 79th St.
New York, NY 10021

Rex Stark Auctions
49 Wethersfield Rd.
Bellingham, MA 02019

Richard A. Bourne Co., Inc.
Estate Auctioneers & Appraisers
Box 141
Hyannis Port, MA 02647
617-775-0797

Richard W. Oliver, Inc.
Plaza One, Rt. 1
Kennebunk, ME 04043
207-985-3600 or FAX 207-985-7734
Outside Maine: 800-992-0047

Richard Opfer Auctioneering, Inc.
1919 Greenspring Dr.
Timonium, MD 21093
301-252-5035

Richard W. Withington, Inc.
R.D. 2, Box 440
Hillsboro, NH 03244
603-464-3232

Roan, Inc.
Box 118, R.D. 3
Cogan Station, PA 17728

Robert W. Skinner, Inc.
Auctioneers & Appraisers
Rt. 117, Bolton, MA 01740
617-779-5528

Sanders & Mock Associates, Inc.
Mark Hanson
P.O. Box 37, Tamworth, NH 03886
603-323-8749 or 603-323-8784

Sloan's
Ben Hastings
4920 Wyaconda Rd.
Rockville, MD 20852
301-468-4911

Smith House
P.O. Box 336
Eliot, ME, 03903
207-439-4614 or FAX 207-439-8554
Specializing in toys

South Bay Auctions, Inc.
485 Montauk Highway
E Moriches, NY 11940
516-878-2909 or FAX 516-878-1863

Sotheby Parke Bernet, Inc.
980 Madison Ave.
New York, NY 10021

Sotheby's Arcade Auction
1334 York Ave. at 72nd St.
New York, NY 10021
212-606-7409

TSACO (The Stein Auction Company) East
Ron Fox
416 Throop St.
N Babylon, NY 11704
Telephone and FAX 516-669-7232

Weschler's
Adam A. Weschler & Son
905 E St. NW
Washington, DC 20004

Willis Henry Auctions
22 Main St.
Marshfield, MA 02050

Winter Associates, Inc.
Regina Madigan
P.O. Box 823
Plainville, CT 06062
207-793-0288 or 800-962-2530

Wolf's Auctioneers
1239 W 6th St.
Cleveland, OH 44113
216-575-9653 or 800-526-1991
FAX 216-621-8011

Woody Auction Company
P.O. Box 618
Douglass, KS 67039
316-746-2694

Clubs and Newsletters

There are hundreds of clubs and newsletters available to collectors today, some are generalized and cover the entire realm of antiques and collectibles, while others are devoted to a specific interest such as toys, coin-operated machines, character collectibles, or railroadiana. You can obtain a copy of most newsletters simply by requesting one. If you'd like to try placing a 'for-sale' ad or a mail bid in one of them, see the introduction for suggestions on how your ad should be composed.

AAA Newsletter
American Lock Collectors Assn.
36076 Grennade
Livonia, MI 48154
313-522-0920
$16 per year, issued bi-monthly

AB Bookman's Weekly
P.O. Box AB
Clifton, NJ 07015
201-772-0020 or FAX 201-772-9281
$80 per year bulk mail USA ($75 per year Canada or Foreign). $125 per year 1st class mail (USA, Canada, and Mexico). Foreign Air Mail: Inquire. Sample copies: $10. AB Bookman's Yearbook: $20. All advertising and subscriptions subject to acceptance

Abingdon Pottery Collectors Newsletter
Abingdon Pottery Club
Penny Vaughan, President
212 S. Fourth
Monmouth, IL 61462
309-734-2337

Action Toys Newsletter
P.O. Box 31551
Billings, MT 59107
406-248-4121

The Akro Agate Gem
Akro Agate Art Association
Joseph Bourque
P.O. Box 758
Salem, NH 03079

The Aluminist
Aluminum Collectors
Dannie Woodard
P.O. Box 1347
Weatherford, TX 76086
817-594-4680

American Barb Wire Collectors Society
John Mantz
1023 Baldwin Rd.
Bakersfield, CA 93304
805-397-9572

American Carnival Glass News
Dennis Runk, Secretary
P.O. Box 235
Littlestown, PA 17340
717-359-7205

American Ceramic Circle Journal and Newsletter
American Ceramic Circle
Grand Central Station, P.O. Box 1495
New York, NY 10163

American Game Collectors Association
49 Brooks Ave.
Lewiston, ME 04240

American Lock Collectors Assoc. Newsletter
Charles Chandler
36076 Grennada
Livonia, MI 48154
313-522-0920

American Militaria Sourcebook and Directory
Terry Hannon
P.O. Box 245
Lyon Station, PA 19536-9986
800-446-0909 or FAX 215-682-1066

American Political Items Collectors
Tony Lee
P.O. Box 134
Monmouth Junction, NJ 08852

American Pottery Journal
P.O. Box 14255
Parkville, MO 64152
816-587-9179 or FAX 816-746-6924

American Quilter magazine
American Quilter's Society
P.O. Box 3290
Paducah, KY 42002-3290
$15 annual membership includes 4 issues.

The American STAR
American Scouting Traders Assn., Inc.
Dave Minnihan, President
P.O. Box 92
Kentfield, CA 94914-0092
415-665-2871

America West Archives
Warren Anderson
P.O. Box 100
Cedar City, UT 84721
26-page illustrated catalogs issued quarterly. Has both fixed-price and auction sections offering early western documents, letters, stock certificates, autograph, and other important ephemera. Subscription: $10 per year

American Willow Report
Lisa Kay Henze, Editor
P.O. Box 900
Oakridge, OR 97463
Bimonthly newsletter, subscription: $15 per year, out of country add $5 per year

Antique Advertising Association
P.O. Box 1121
Morton Grove, IL 60053
708-446-0904

Antique and Collectible News
P.O. Box 529
Anna, IL 62906
Monthly newspaper for auctions, antique shows, collectibles and flea markets for the Midwest USA. Subscription: $12 per year

Antique and Collectors Reproduction News
Mark Cherenka, Circulation Dept.
P.O. Box 71174
Des Moines, IA 50325
800-227-5531
Monthly newsletter showing differences between old originals and new reproductions. Subscription: $32 per year

Antique Bottle Club of Northern Illinois
P.O. Box 571
Lake Geneva, WI, 53417

Antique Gazette
6949 Charlotte Pk., #106
Nashville, TN 37209
Monthly publication covering the antique and collectibles market. Subscription: $16.95 per year

Antique Monthly magazine
Stephen C. Croft, Publisher
2100 Powers Ferry Rd.
Atlanta, GA 30339
404-955-5656 or FAX 404-952-0669
Subscription: $19.95 per year (11 issues)

Antique Press of Florida
12403 N Florida Ave., Tampa, FL 33612
Subscription: $12 (6 issues) per year

Antique Souvenir Collectors' News
Gary Leveille, Editor
P.O. Box 562
Great Barrington, MA 01230

The Antique Trader Weekly
P.O. Box 1050 CB
Dubuque, IA 52004
Subscription: $28 (52 issues) per year;
sample: 50¢

Antique Week
P.O. Box 90
Knightstown, IN 46148
Weekly newspaper for auctions,
antique shows, antiques, collectibles
and flea markets. Write for
subscription information.

Antiques and Collecting
1006 S Michigan Ave.
Chicago, IL 60605
Monthly magazine with a wide variety of
information and extensive classified section. Subscription: $24 per year; sample:
$2.95 (refundable with subscription order)

Antiques Americana
K.C. Owings, Jr.
P.O. Box 19
N Abington, MA 02351
617-857-1655
Specializing in paper collectibles

Appraisers Information Exchange
Art Deco Reflections
Chase Collectors Society
Barry L. Van Hook, Director
2149 W. Jibsail Loop
Mesa, AZ 85202-5524
602-838-6971

Arts and Crafts Quarterly
P.O. Box 3592, Station E
Trenton, NJ 08629
800-541-5787

Ashtray Journal
Chuck Thompson, Editor Publisher
Box 11652
Houston, TX 77293
Subscription $14.95 a year (6 issues),
sample $3.95

Auction Block newspaper
P.O. Box 337
Iola, WI 54945
715-445-5000
Subscription: $8 per year

Auction Opportunities, Inc.
Doyle Auctioneers and Appraisers
109 Osborne Hill Rd.
Fishkill, NY 12524
800-551-5161
Subscription: $25 per year

The Autograph Review
Bimonthly newsletter
Jeffrey Morey
305 Carlton Rd.
Syracuse, NY 13207
315-474-3516

Autographs and Memorabilia
P.O. Box 224
Coffeyville, KS 67337
316-251-5308
Six issues per year on movie and
sports memorabilia

Automobile License Plate Collectors
  Newsletter
Gary Brent Kincade
P.O. Box 712
Weston, WV 26452
304-842-3773

Autumn Leaf newsletter
Jim Steele, Treasurer
2415 Brookhaven
Canton, MI 48188
313-397-8169
Membership: $20 per year

Avon Times newsletter
℅ Dwight or Vera Young
P.O. Box 9868, Dept. P.
Kansas City, MO 64134
Inquires should be accompanied by
LSASE

Barbara Eden's Official Fan Club
P.O. Box 5556
Sherman Oaks, CA 91403
818-761-0267

Barber Shop Collectibles Newsletter
Penny Nader 320 S Glenwood St.
Allentown, PA 18104
215-437-2534

Barbie Bazaar magazine
5617 Sixth Ave., Dept NY593
Kenosha, WI 53140
414-658-1004 or FAX 414-658-0433
6 bimonthly issues for $25.95

Barbie Talks Some More!
Jacqueline Horning
7501 School Rd.
Cincinnati, OH 45249

The Baum Bugle
The International Wizard of Oz Club
Fred M. Meyer
220 N 11th St.
Escanaba, MI 49829

Beam Around the World
International Association of Jim Beam
Bottle and Specialties Club
Shirley Sumbles, Secretary
5013 Chase Ave.
Downers Grove, IL 60515
708-963-8980

Beer Can Collectors News
Beer Can Collectors of America
Don Hicks, President
747 Merus Court
Fenton, MO 63026
314-343-6486 or FAX 314-343-6486

The Bell Tower
American Bell Association
Charles Blake
P.O. Box 172
Shoreham, VT 05770

Berry-Bits
Strawberry Shortcake Collectors' Club
Peggy Jimenez
1409 72nd St.
N Bergen, NJ 07047

Beyond the Rainbow Collector's
  Exchange
P.O. Box 31672
St. Louis, MO 63131

Big Little Times
Big Little Book Collectors
  Club of America
Larry Lowery
P.O. Box 1242
Danville, CA 94526
415-837-2086

Blue and White Pottery Club Newsletter
224 12th St. NW
Cedar Rapids, IA 52405
319-362-8116

Bojo
P.O. Box 1203
Cranberry Township, PA 16033-2203
412-776-0621 (9 AM to 9 PM E.T.)
Issues fixed-price catalog containing
Beatles and Rock 'n Roll memorabilia.

Bookmark Collector
Joan L. Huegel
1002 W. 25th St.
Erie, PA 16502
Quarterly newsletter: $5.50 per year
($6.50 in Canada); sample copy: $1
plus stamp or LSASE

Books Are Everything
302 Martin Dr.
Richmond, KY 40475
Subscription: $25 (4 issues) per year in
USA; $7.50 for sample

Bossons Briefs
International Bossons Collectors
Dr. Robert E. Davis, Executive Director
21 John Maddox Dr.
Rome, GA 30161
404-232-1266

Bridal Collector's Roster
Ann C. Bergin
P.O. Box 105
Amherst, NH 03031
603-673-1885

Buckeye Marble Collectors Club
Betty Barnard
472 Meadowbrook Dr.
Newark, OH 43055
614-366-7002

Bulletin
Doll Collectors of America
14 Chestnut Rd.
Westford, MA 01886
617-692-8392

Bulletin of the NAWCC
National Assn. of Watch and Clock
Collectors, Inc.
Thomas J. Bartels, Executive Director
514 Poplar St.
Columbia, PA 17512-2130
717-684-8621 or FAX 717-684-0878

California Pottery Newsletter
℅ Verlangieri Gallery
816 Main St.
West Cambria, CA 93428
800-292-2153

The Cambridge Crystal Ball
National Cambridge Collectors, Inc.
P.O. Box 416
Cambridge, OH 43725-0416
Dues: $15 for individual member and
$3 for associate member of same
household

The Candlewick Collector Newsletter
Virginia R. Scott
275 Milledge Terrace
Athens, GA 30306
404-548-5966

The Candy Gram
Candy Container Collectors of America
Douglas Dezso
864 Paterson, Ave.
Maywood, NJ 07607
201-845-7707

The Cane Collector's Chronicle
Linda Beeman
15 2nd St. NE
Washington, D.C. 20002
$30 (4 issues) per year

Captain's Log magazine
World Airline Historical Society
Paul F. Collins, President
3381 Apple Tree Lane
Erlanger, KY 41018
606-342-9039

*CAS Collectors Assoc. (Ceramic Arts
Studio Collectors Newsletter)*
P.O. Box 46
Madison, WI 53701
608-241-9138

*Cast Iron Seat Collectors
Association Newsletter*
RFD #2, Box 40
Le Center, MN 56057
612-357-6142

Cat Collectors Club
33161 Wendy Dr.
Sterling Heights, MI 48310
Subscription: $18 per year (includes
bimonthly newsletter and catalogs);
sample package: $4

Cat Talk
Marilyn Dipboye
31311 Blair Dr.
Warren, MI 48092
313-264-0285

Century Limited
Toy Train Collectors Society
160 Dexter Terrace
Tonawanda, NY 14150
716-694-3771

Chain Gang Key Chain Collector
P.O. Box 9397
Phoenix, AZ 85068
602-942-0043

Chicagoland Antique Advertizing
Slot Machine and Jukebox Gazette
Ken Durham, Editor
P.O. Box 2426
Rockville, MD 20852
20-page newsletter published twice a
year. Subscription: 4 issues for $10;
sample: $5

Classic Amusements
Wordmarque Design Associates
12644 Chapel Rd., Suite 204, Box 315
Clifton, VA 22024
Subscription: $36 (6 issues) per year in
USA; $42 in Canada

Clear the Decks
52 Plus Joker
Bill Coomer, Secretary
1024 S. Benton
Cape Girardeau, MO 63701
For collectors of playing cards, unusual
and antique decks

Coca-Cola Collectors Club International
P.O. Box 49166
Atlanta, GA 30359
Annual dues: $25

Coin Machine Trader
Ted and Betty Salveson
569 Kansas SE, P.O. Box 602
Huron, SD 57350
605-352-3870

Coin-Op Newsletter
Ken Durham, Publisher
909 26th St., NW
Washington, DC 20037
Subscription (10 issues): $24;
sample: $5

Collecting Tips Newsletter
℅ Meredith Williams
P.O. Box 633
Joplin, MO 64802
417-781-3855 or 417-624-2518
12 issues per year focusing on Fast Food collectibles

The Collector
Box 158
Heyworth, IL 61745
309-473-2466
Newspaper published monthly

Collector Glass News
P.O. Box 308
Slippery Rock, PA 16057
412-946-8126 or 412-794-6420
For collectors of promotional and fast food glassware

Collectors' Classified
William Margolin
P.O. Box 347
Hollbrook, MA 02343-0347
617-961-1463
Covers collectibles in general; 4 issues: $1

Collector's Digest
P.O. Box 23
Banning, CA 92220
714-849-1064
Subscription: $11 (6 issues) per year

Collector's Mart magazine
P.O. Box 12830
Wichita, KS 67277
Subscription: $23.95 per year; Add $15 in Canada

Collectors of Findlay Glass
P.O. Box 256
Findlay, OH 45839

Cookbook Gossip
Cookbook Collectors Club of
   America, Inc.
Bob and Jo Ellen Allen
231 E James Blvd., P.O. Box 85
St. James, MO 65559
314-265-8296

Cookie Crumbs
Cookie Cutter Collectors Club
Ruth Capper
1167 Teal Rd. SW
Dellroy, OH 44620
216-735-2839 or 202-966-0869

The Cookie Jar Collector's Club News
Louise Messina Daking
595 Cross River Rd.
Katonah, NY 10536
914-232-0383 or FAX 914-232-0384

Cookie Jarrin' With Joyce:
   The Cookie Jar Newsletter
R.R. 2, Box 504
Walterboro, SC 29488

The Co-Op Connections
Sagebrush Treasures
963 Williams
Fallon, NV 89406
Subscription $15 per year for 12 issues

Coors Pottery Newsletter
Robert Schneider
3808 Carr Pl. N
Seattle, WA 98103-8126

Costume Society of America Newsletter
55 Edgewater Dr., P.O. Box 73
Earleville, MD 21919
301-275-2329 or FAX 301-275-8936

Crown Jewels of the Wire Insulator Collector
John McDougald
P.O. Box 1003
St. Charles, IL 60174-1003
708-513-1544

The Courier
2503 Delaware Ave.
Buffalo, NY 14216
716-873-2594
A Civil War collector newsletter published bimonthly

The Cutting Edge
Glass Knife Collectors' Club
Adrienne S. Escoe, Editor
P.O. Box 342
Los Alamitos, CA 90720
Subscription: $5/yr. (4 issues); sample: $1.25

Daguerreian Society, Inc.
John F. Graff, President
P.O. Box 2129
Green Bay, WI 53406-2129

Dark Shadows Collectibles Classified
Sue Ellen Wilson
6173 Iroquois Trail
Mentor, OH 44060
216-946-6348
For collectors of both old and new series

Decoy Hunter Magazine
901 North 9th St.
Clinton, IN 47842
Subscription: $12 per year for 6 issues

Decoy Magazine
Joe Engers
P.O. Box 277
Burtonsville, MD 20866
301-890-0262

Depression Glass Daze
Teri Steel, Editor/Publisher
Box 57
Otisville, MI 48463
313-631-4593
The nation's marketplace for glass, china, and pottery

Dept. 56 Collectors: *The Village Press*
Roger and Khristine Bain, Publishers
1625 Myott Ave.
Rockford, IL 61103
Subscription: $20 (8 issues) per year; free sample copy

Dionne Quint Collectors Club
Jimmy Rodolfos
P.O. Box 2527
Woburn, MA 01888

DISCoveries Magazine
Mark Phillips, Associate Editor
P.O. Box 255
Port Townsend, WA 98368-0255
Specializing in collectible records, international distribution

Doll Investment Newsletter
P.O. Box 1982
Centerville, MA 02632

Doll News
United Federation of Doll Clubs
P.O. Box 14146
Parkville, MO 64152

Doorstop Collectors of America
Doorstopper newsletter
Jeanie Bertoia
2413 Madison Ave.
Vineland, NJ 08630
609-692-4092
Membership: $20.00 per year, includes 2 newsletters and convention. Send 2-stamp SASE for sample

Dunbar's Gallery
76 Haven St.
Milford, MA 01757
508-634-8697 or FAX 508-634-8698
Specializing in quality advertising, Halloween, toys, coin-operated machines; holding cataloged auctions occasionally, lists available.

Early American Industries Association
J. Watson
P.O. Box 2128, Dept. PR
Empire State Plaza Station,
Albany, NY 12220
Providing information on early tools and trades

Eggcup Collectors' Corner
Joan George, Ed.D.
67 Stevens Ave.
Old Bridge, NJ 08857
Subscription: $18/year (4 issues); sample copies or back issues available at $5 each

Ephemera News
The Ephemera Society of America, Inc.
P.O. Box 37
Schoharie, NY 12157
518-295-7978

The Ertl Replica
Ertl Collectors Club
Mike Meyer, Editor
Highways 136 and 20
Dyersville, IA 52040
319-875-2000

Facets of Fostoria
Fostoria Glass Society of America
P.O. Box 826
Moundsville, WV 26041
Membership: $12.50 per year

Fair News
World's Fair Collectors' Society, Inc.
Michael R. Pender, Editor
P.O. Box 20806
Sarasota, FL 34238
Dues: $12 (12 issues) per year in USA; $13 in Canada; $20 for overseas members

Farm Antiques News
Gary Van Hoozer, Publisher/Editor
812 N Third St.
Tarkio, MO 64491
816-736-4528
Annual subscription: $14, includes a free classified ad

Favorite Westerns and Serial World magazine
Westerns and Serials Fan Club
C/o Norman Kietzer
R.R. 1, Box 103
Vernon Center, MN 56090

The Federation Glass Works
Federation of Historical Bottle Clubs
Barbara A. Harms
14521 Atlantic
Riverdale, IL 60627
312-841-4068

The Fenton Flyer
National Fenton Glass Society
P.O. Box 4008
Marietta, OH 45750

Fiesta Club of America
P.O. Box 1583
Loves Park, IL 61132-5383

Fiesta Collector's Quarterly
China Specialties, Inc.
19238 Dorchester Circle
Strongville, OH 44136
$12 (4 issues) per year

Figural Bottle Openers
Contact: Donna Kitzmiller
117 Basin Hill Road
Duncannon, PA 17020

Fire Collectors Club Newsletter
David Cerull
P.O. Box 992
Milwaukee, WI 53201

Flag Bulletin
Flag Research Center
P.O. Box 580
Winchester, MA 01890
617-729-9410

FLAKE, The Breakfast Nostalgia Magazine
P.O. Box 481
Cambridge, MA 02140
617-492-5004
Bimonthly illustrated issue devoted to one hot collecting area such as Disney, etc., with letters, discoveries, new releases, and ads. Single issue: $4 ($6 foreign); annual: $20 ($28 foreign); free 25-word ad with new subscription

Flashlight Collectors of America Newsletter
Bill Utley
P.O. Box 4095
Tustin, CA 92680
$12 (4 issues) per year, single copies and back issues $3 each

Flea Marketeer
P.O. Box 686
Southfield, MI 48037
313-351-9910 or FAX 313-351-9037

Folk Art Messenger
P.O. Box 17041
Richmond, VA 23226

Fox Hunt Newsletter
R. Atkinson Fox Society
Hugh Hetzer
209 Homevale Rd.
Reisterstown, MD 21136

Friends of Hoppy Club
Laura Bates
6310 Friendship Dr.
New Concord, OH 43762-9708
614-826-4850
Publishes newsletter

The Front Striker Bulletin
Bill Retskin
P.O. Box 18481
Asheville, NC 28814
704-254-4487 or FAX 704-254-1066
Quarterly newsletter for matchcover collectors, $17.50 per year for 1st class mailing + $2 for new member registration

Game Times
American Game Collectors Association
Joe Angiolillo, President
4628 Barlow Dr.
Bartlesville, OK 74006

Garfield Collectors Society Newsletter
C/o David L. Abrams, Editor
744 Foster Ridge Rd.
Germantown, TN 38138-7036
901-753-1026

Gaudy Collector's Society
Suzanne Troll
P.O. Box 274
Gates Mills, OH 44040
For enthusiasts of Gaudy Welsh, Gaudy Ironstone and Gaudy Dutch china

Gene Autry Star Telegram
Gene Autry Development Association
Chamber of Commerce
P.O. Box 158
Gene Autry, OK 73436

George Kamm Paperweights
24 Townsend Court
Lancaster, PA 17603
Specializing in paperweights; color
brochure published 4 to 5 times a year.
$5 (1-time charge)

Ginny Doll Club News
Jeanne Niswonger
305 W Beacon Rd.
Lakeland, FL 33803
813-687-8015

Glass Chatter
Midwest Antique Fruit Jar
  and Bottle Club
P.O. Box 38
Flat Rock, IN 47234

Glass Collector's Digest
P.O. Box 553
Marietta, OH 45750-9979
800-533-3433
Subscription: $19 (6 issues) per year;
add $5 for Canada and foreign

Glass Shards
The National Early American Glass Club
P.O. Box 8489
Silver Spring, MD 20907

Golf Club Collectors Association Newsletter
C/o Dick Moore
640 E Liberty St.
Girard, OH 44420-2308

Gonder Pottery Collectors' Newsletter
C/o John and Marilyn McCormick
P.O. Box 3174
Shawnee KS 66203

Gone With the Wind Collectors Club
Newsletter
8105 Woodview Rd.
Ellicot City, MD 21043
301-465-4632

Grandma's Trunk
P.O. Box 404
Northport, MI 49670
Subscription: $8 for 1st class or $5 for
bulk rate, per year

Hall China Collector Club Newsletter
P.O Box 360488
Cleveland, OH 44136

Haviland Collectors International
  Foundation
Jean Kendall
Iowa Memorial Union, Univ. of Iowa
Iowa City, IA 52242
319-335-3513

Headhunters Newsletter
  for head vase collectors
Maddy Gordon
P.O. Box 83H
Scarsdale, NY 10583
914-472-0200
Subscription: $16 (4 issues) per year

The Heisey News
Heisey Collectors of America
169 W Church St.
Newark, OH 43055
612-345-2932

Hello Again Old-Time Radio
  Show Collector
Jay A. Hickerson
P.O. Box 4321
Hamden, CT 06514
203-248-2887 or FAX 203-281-1322
Sample copy upon request with SASE

Hobby News
Bimonthly newsletter
J.L.C. Publications
Box 258
Ozone Park, NY 11416

Holly Hobbie Newsletter
Helen McCale
Route 3, Box 35
Butler, MO 64730

Hopalong Cassidy Newsletter
Hopalong Cassidy Fan Club
P.O. Box 1361
Boyes Hot Springs, CA 95416

Ice Screamer
C/o Ed Marks, Publisher
P.O. Box 5387
Lancaster, PA 17601
Published bimonthly, dues: $15
per year

The Illustrator Collector's News
Denis Jackson, Editor
P.O. Box 1958
Sequim, WA 98382
206-683-2559
Subscription: $17 per year

The Indian Trader
Martin Link
P.O. Box 1421
Scottsdale, AZ 85251

Inside Antiques monthly newsletter
Antique and Collectible News Service
Robert Reed, Editor
P.O. Box 204
Knightstown, IN 46148
317-345-7479

International Association of
  Dinnerware Matchers
P.O. Box 50125
Austin, TX 78763-0125
512-264-1054

International Brick Collectors Assoc. Journal
International Brick Collectors Assoc.
8357 Somerset Dr.
Prairie Village, KS 66207
913-341-8842

International Carnival Glass Association
Lee Markley, Secretary
R.R. 1, Box 14
Mentone, IN 46539
219-353-7678
Dues $15 per family per year; annual
convention held in July with displays,
seminars, auction and banquet.

International Club for Collectors of
  Hatpins & Hatpin Holders
Lillian Baker
15237 Chanera Ave.
Gardena, CA 90249
Enclose SASE for information

International Figure Kit Club
P.O. Box 201
Sharon Center, OH 44274-0201
216-239-1657 or FAX 216-239-2991

International Perfume and Scent Bottle
  Collectors Association
C/o Phyllis Dohanian
53 Marlborough St.
Boston, MA 02116-2099
617-266-4351

*International Pin Collectors Club
  Newsletter*
P.O. Box 430
Marcy, NY 13403
315-736-5651 or 315-736-4019

International Society of Antique
  Scale Collectors
Bob Stein, President
176 W. Adams St., Suite 1706
Chicago, IL 60603
312-263-7500
Publishes quarterly magazine

International Society of Appraisers
P.O. Box 726
Hoffman Estates, IL 60195
708-882-0706

Just for Openers Newsletter
John Stanley
3712 Sunningdale Way
Durham, NC 27707-5684
919-419-1546
Quarterly newsletter covers all types
of bottle openers and corkscrews

Kit Builders Magazine
Gordy's
P.O. Box 201
Sharon Center, OH 44274-0201
216-239-1657 or FAX 216-239-2991

*Kitchen Antiques and
  Collectibles News* Newsletter
KOOKS (Kollectors of Old Kitchen Stuff)
Dana and Darlene DeMore
4645 Laurel Ridge Dr.
Harrisburg, PA 17110
717-545-7320
Membership: $24 annually, includes 6
issues of *Kitchen Antiques & Col-
lectibles News*

Knife Rests of Yesteryear and Today
Beverly L. Ales
4046 Graham St.
Pleasanton, CA 94566-5619
Subscription: $20 per year for 6 issues

The Lace Collector newsletter
Elizabeth M. Kurella
P.O. Box 222
Plainwell, MI 49080
616-685-9792
A quarterly publication for the study of
old lace.

The Laughlin Eagle
C/o Richard Racheter
1270 63rd Terrace South
St. Petersburg, FL 33705
Published quarterly

Liddle Kiddle Klub
Laura Miller
3639 Fourth Ave.
La Crescenta, CA 91214

Light Revival
Restoration newsletter
Tom Barnard
35 W Elm Ave.
Quincy, MA 02170
617-773-3255

The Link
National Cuff Link Society
Eugene R. Klompus
P.O. Box 346
Prospect Heights, IL 60070
708-632-0561
For collectors of cuff links and related
accessories

The Lone Ranger Silver Bullet Newsletter
P.O. Box 553
Forks, WA 98331
206-327-3726
Subscription: $12 per year

Madame Alexander Fan Club Newsletter
Earl Meisinger
11 S 767 Book Rd.
Naperville, IL 60564

Maine Antique Digest
Monthly newspaper
Sam and Sally Pennington
P.O. Box 645
Waldoboro, ME 04572
207-832-7534

Majolica International Society Newsletter
Michael G. Strawser, President
Suite 103, 1275 First Ave.
New York, NY 10021

Marble Mania
Marble Collectors Society of America
Stanley Block
P.O. Box 222
Trumbull, CT 06611
203-261-3223

Martha's Kidlit Newsletter
Box 1488A
Ames, IA 50010
A bimonthly publication for children's
books collectors. Subscription: $25 per year

Matchbox USA
Charles Mack
62 Saw Mill Rd.
Durham, CT 06422
203-349-1655

Maytag Collectors Club
Nate Stroller
960 Reynolds Ave.
Ripon, CA 95366
209-599-5933

McCoy Publications
Kathy Lynch, Editor
P.O. Box 14255
Parkville, MO 64152
816-587-9179 or FAX 816-746-6924

McDonald's Collecting Tips
Meredith Williams
Box 633, Joplin, MO 64802
Send SASE for information

McDonald's Collector Club Newsletter
C/o Tenna Greenberg
5400 Waterbury Rd.
Des Moines, IA 50312
515-279-0741

McDonald's Collector's Club,
  SUNSHINE Chapter
C/o Bill and Pat Poe
220 Domica Cir. E
Niceville, FL 32578-4068
904-987-4163 or FAX 904-897-2606
Annual membership is $10 per individual
or $15 per family (includes 6 newsletters
and 2 McDonald's Only shows); send $3
(US delivery) for 70-page sale catalog of
fast food and character collectibles

Medical Collectors Association Newsletter
Dr. M. Donald Blaufox, MD
1300 Morris Park Ave.
Bronx, NY 10461

The Milk Route
National Assoc. of Milk Bottle Collectors, Inc.
Thomas Gallagher
4 Ox Bow Rd.
Westport CT 06880-2602
203-277-5244

Mini Thistle
Pairpoint Cup Plate Collectors
of America
Box 52
E Weymouth, MA 02189

The Miniature Bottle Collector
Briscoe Publications
P.O. Box 2161
Palos Verdes Peninsula, CA 90274

Miniature Piano Enthusiast Club
Janice E. Kelsh
5815 N. Sheridan Rd., Suite 202
Chicago, IL 60660
312-271-2970

Model and Toy Collector Magazine
137 Casterton Ave.
Akron, OH 44303
216-836-0668 or FAX 216-869-8668

Modern Doll Club Journal
Jeanne Niswonger
305 W Beacon Rd.
Lakeland, FL 33803

Morgantown Newscaster
Morgantown Collectors of America
Jerry Gallagher and Randy Supplee
420 1st Ave. NW
Plainview, MN 55964
Subscription: $15 per year. SASE
required for answers to queries

The Mouse Club East
(Disney collectors)
P.O. Box 3195
Wakefield, MA 01880
Family membership: $25 (includes
newsletters and 2 shows per year)

Movie Advertising Collector magazine
George Reed
P.O. Box 28587
Philadelphia, PA 19149

Mystic Lights of the Aladdin Knights
J.W. Courter
3935 Kelley Rd.
Kevil, KY 42053
Subscription: $20 (6 issues, postpaid
1st class) per year with current buy-
sell-trade information. Send SASE for
information about other publications

NAOLH Newsletter
National Association for Outlaw and
Lawman History
Hank Clark
P.O. Box 812
Waterford, CA 95386
209-874-2640

NAPAC Newsletter
National Association of Paper and
Advertising Collectors
P.O. Box 500
Mount Joy, PA 17552
717-653-4300

National Association of Breweriana
Advertising
℅ John Murray
475 Old Surrey Rd.
Hinsdale, IL 60521

National Blue Ridge Newsletter
Norma Lilly
144 Highland Dr.
Blountsville, TN 37617
Subscription: $12 (6 issues) per year

National Book Collector
National Book Collectors Society
65 High Ridge Rd., Suite 349
Stamford, CT 06095
Annual dues: $20 (includes 6 issues)
per year in USA; $25 in Canada and
foreign countries; sample copy: $2

National Button Bulletin
National Button Society
Lois Pool, Secretary
2733 Juno Place
Akron, OH 44333-4137
216-864-3296

National Early American Glass Club
P.O. Box 8489
Silver Spring, MD 20907

*National Ezra Brooks Bottle and
Specialty Club Newsletter*
420 W 1st St.
Kewanee, IL 61443

National Fantasy Fan Club
(for Disney collectors)
Dept. AC, Box 19212
Irvine, CA 92713
Membership: $20 per year, includes
newsletters, free ads, chapters, conventions, etc.

National Graniteware News
National Graniteware Society
P.O. Box 10013
Cedar Rapids, IA 52410-0013

*National Greentown Glass
Association Newsletter*
℅ Annette W. LaRowe,
Secretary/Treasurer
P.O. Box 107
Greentown, IN 46936

National Imperial Glass
Collectors' Society
P.O. Box 534
Bellaire, OH 43906
Dues: $12 per year (plus $1 for each
additional member in the same house-
hold), quarterly newsletter, convention
every June

*National Milk Glass Collectors'
Society and Quarterly Newsletter*
℅ Arlene Johnson, Treasurer
1113 Birchwood Dr.
Garland, TX 75043
Please include SASE

*National Reamer Collectors Association
Quarterly Review*
R.R. 3, Box 67
Frederic, WI 54837
715-327-4365

National Valentine Collectors Bulletin
Evalene Pulati
P.O. Box 1404
Santa Ana, CA 92702
714-547-1355

The Nelson McCoy Express
Jean Bushnell, Editor
3081 Rock Creek Dr.
Broomfield, CO 80020
303-469-8309

News and Views
The National Depression Glass
Association
Anita Wood
P.O. Box 69843
Odessa, TX 79769
915-337-1297

Newspaper Collectors Society of America
P.O. Box 19134
Lansing, MI 48901
517-887-1255 or FAX 517-887-2194

Night Light
(miniature lamp collectors)
℅ Bob Culver
38619 Wakefield Court
Northville, MI 48167
313-473-8575

Noritake News
David H. Spain
1237 Federal Ave. E
Seattle, WA 98102
206-323-8102

North America Torquay Society
Jerry and Gerry Kline, members
604 Orchard View Dr.
Maumee, OH 43537
Quarterly newsletter sent to members;
information and membership form
requires LSASE

Novelty Salt and Pepper Club
℅ Irene Thornburg,
Membership Coordinator
581 Joy Rd.
Battle Creek, MI 49017
Publishes quarterly newsletter & annual
roster. Annual dues: $20 in US, Canada,
& Mexico; $25 for all other countries

Old Ivory Newsletter
Pat Fitzwater
P.O. Box 1004
Wilsonville, OR 97070
SASE for sample copy

The Olympic Collectors Newsletter
Bill Nelson
P.O. Box 41630
Tucson, AZ 85717-1630

On the Lighter Side
Judith Sanders
Route 3, 136 Circle Dr.
Quitman, TX 75783
903-763-2795
Send SASE for information regarding
vintage lighters

Paper Collectors' Marketplace
470 Main St., P.O. Box 128
Scandinavia, WI 54977
715-467-2379
Subscription: $17.95 (12 issues) per
year in USA; Canada and Mexico add
$15 per year

Paper Doll News
Ema Terry
P.O. Box 807
Vivian, LA 71082

Paper Pile Quarterly
P.O. Box 337
San Anselmo, CA 94979-0337
415-454-5552
Subscription: $12.50 per year in USA
and Canada

Paperweight Collector's Bulletin
Paperweight Collector's Assoc., Inc.
150 Fulton Ave.
Garden City Park, NY 11040
516-741-3090 or FAX 506-741-3985

Peanut Papers
Planter's Peanuts Collectors Club
804 Hickory Grade Rd.
Bridgeville, PA 15017
412-221-7599

Peanuts Collector Club Newsletter
Peanuts Collector Club
Andrea C. Podley
P.O. Box 94
N Hollywood, CA 91603

The Pen and Quill
Universal Autograph Collectors Club
P.O. Box 6181
Washington, DC 20044-6181

The Pencil Collector
American Pencil Collectors Society
Robert J. Romey, President
2222 S Millwood
Wichita, KS 67213
316-263-8419

Pepsi-Cola Collectors Club Newsletter
Pepsi-Cola Collectors Club
Bob Stoddard
P.O. Box 1275
Covina, CA 91722
714-593-8750
Membership: $15

Perfume and Scent Bottle Collectors
Jeane Parris
2022 E Charleston Blvd.
Las Vegas, NV 89104
Membership: $15 USA or $30 foreign
(includes quarterly newsletter). Information requires SASE

Phillips Archives
Robert W. Phillips
1703 N Aster Place
Broken Arrow, OK 74012
918-254-8205 or FAX 918-252-9362
CompuServe: 73203,576
E-Mail: YUPM24A
Author and leading authority on western
genre and Roy Rogers. Current books
include *Western Comics Journal, Bob
Wills Journal* and *Singing Cowboy Stars*

Phoenix Bird Discoveries
Joan Oates
685 S Washington
Constantine, MI 49042
Membership: $10 per year. Includes
newsletter published 3 times a year

Picard Collectors Club
Alicia Miller
300 E. Grove St.
Bloomington, IL 61701
309-828-5533

Pie Birds Unlimited
Lillian M. Cole
14 Harmony School Rd.
Flemington, NJ 08822

*Plantation Galleries International
Newsletter*
6400 Davison Rd.
Burton, MI 48509
313-743-5258 or FAX 313-743-5791
Subscription: $24.95 per year

The Plastic Candy Dispenser Newsletter
Sue Sternfeld
90-60 Union Turnpike
Glendale, NY 11385
information on Pez containers

Plate-O-Holic
Plate Collector's Stock Exchange
478 Ward St. Extension
Wallingford, CT 06492
203-265-1711

*Playing Card Collectors Association
(PCCA) Bulletin*
P.O. Box 783
Bristol, WI, 53014
414-857-9334

Points newsletter and *Pictorial Journal*
International Club for Collectors of Hatpins and Hatpin Holders (ICC of H&HH)
Lillian Baker, Founder
15237 Chanera Ave.
Gardena, CA 90249

The Pokey Gazette
Steve Santi
19626 Ricardo Ave.
Hayward, CA 94541; 510-481-2586
A *Little Golden Book* collector newsletter

Police Collector News
Mike Bondarenko, Publisher
R.R. 1, Box 14
Baldwin, WI 54002

Positively PEZ
Crystal and Larry LaFoe
3851 Gable Lane Dr., Apt. 513
Indianapolis, IN 46208

Postcard History Society Bulletin
John H. McClintock, Director
P.O. Box 1765
Manassas, VA 22110
703-368-2757

Pottery Lovers Newsletter
Pottery Lovers Reunion
Pat Sallaz
4969 Hudson Dr.
Stow, OH 44224

Powder Puff
P.O. Box Letter S
Lynbrook, NY 11563
Subscription: $25 (4 issues, USA or Canada) per year

Precious Collectibles magazine for Precious Moments® figurine Collectors, *The Ornament Collector* magazine for Hallmark ornaments and other ornaments, and the *Collectors' Bulletin* magazine for all Limited Edition collectibles
Rosie Wells Enterprises, Inc.
R.R. 1
Canton, IL 61520
Rosie also has informational secondary market price guides for Lowell Davis collectors, Hallmark Ornament collectors, and Precious Moments® collectors

Quint News
Dionne Quint Collectors
P.O. Box 2527
Woburn, MA 01888
617-933-2219

Red Wing Collectors Newsletter
Red Wing Collectors Society, Inc.
David Newkirk
R.R. 3, Box 146
Monticello, MN 55362

Roseville's of the Past
Jack Bomm, Editor
P.O. Box 1018
Apopka, FL 32704-1018
Subscription: $19.95 per year for 6 to 12 newsletters

Roy Rogers-Dale Evans
    Collectors Association
Nancy Horsley
P.O. Box 1166
Portsmouth, OH 45662

Royal Bayreuth International
    Collectors' Society
Howard and Sara Wade
P.O. Box 325
Orrville, OH 44667

*Royal Doulton International Collectors
    Club Newsletter*
C/o Royal Doulton, Inc.
P.O. Box 1815
Somerset, NJ 08873
908-356-7929 or 800-582-2102

Schoenhut Newsletter
Schoenhut Collectors Club
Robert Zimmerman
45 Louis Ave.
W Seneca, NY 14224

Scoop News
Margaret Alves
84 Oak Ave.
Shelton, CT 06484
Issued bimonthly; send $1 for sample copy

Scottie Sampler and fellowship
    group Wee Scots
P.O. Box 1512
Columbus, IN 47202

Scouting Collectors Quarterly
National Scouting Collectors Society
806 E Scott St.
Tuscola, IL 61953

Scout Memorabilia
R.J. Sayers
P.O. Box 629
Brevard, NC 28712

*Sebastian Miniatures Collectors
    Society News*
Cyndi Gavin McNally
C/o Lance Corp., 321 Central St.
Hudson, MA 01749
508-568-1401 or FAX 508-568-8741

SFPCS Newsletter
Southern Folk Pottery Collectors
    Society
Roy Thompson
1828 N. Howard Mills Rd.
Robbins, NC 27325
910-464-3961

Shawnee Pottery Collectors' Club
P.O. Box 713
New Smyrna Beach, FL 32170-0713
Monthly nationwide newsletter. SASE (C/o Pamela Curran) required when requesting information. Optional: $3 for sample of current newsletter

The Shirley Temple Collectors News
8811 Colonial Rd.
Brooklyn, NY 11209
Dues: $20 per year; checks paybable to Rita Dubas

The Shot Glass Club of America
Mark Pickvet, Editor
P.O. Box 90404
Flint, MI 48509
Non-profit organization publishes 12 newsletters per year. Subscription: $6; sample: $1

The Silent Film Newsletter
Gene Vazzana
140 7th Ave.
New York, NY 10011
Subscription: $18; Send $2.50 for sample copy

The Silver Bullet newsletter
Jerry and Kay Klepey
P.O. Box 553
Forks, WA 98331
Subscription: $12 per year; sample copy available for $4; licensed mail order seller of memorabilia and appraiser

Singing Wires
Telephone Collectors International, Inc.
George W Howard
19 N Cherry Dr.
Oswego, IL 60543
708-554-8154

The Ski Country Collector Bottle Club
1224 Washington Ave.
Golden, CO 80401
Informational newsletter on decanters

Sleepy Eye Newsletter
Jim Martin
P.O. Box 12
Monmouth, IL 61462
309-734-4933 or 309-734-2703

Smurf Collectors Club
24ACH, Cabot Rd. W
Massapequa, NY 11758
Membership includes newsletters. LSASE for information

Snow Biz
℅ Nancy McMichael
P.O. Box 53262
Washington, D.C. 20009
Quarterly newsletter with information on snow domes (subscription: $10 per year); also collector's club

Society for the Advancement of Space Activities - SASA
Michael S. Mitchell
P.O. Box 192
Kents Hill, ME 04349-0192

Spoutings
Watt Pottery Collectors
Box 26067
Fairview Park, OH 44126
Supscription (4 issues): $10 per year

The Spur
National Bit, Spur and Saddle
   Collectors Association
P.O. Box 3098
Colorado Springs, CO 80934

The Stained Finger
The Society of Inkwell Collectors
Vince McGraw
5136 Thomas Ave. S
Minneapolis, MN 55410
612-922-2792

Statue of Liberty Collectors' Club
Iris November
P.O. Box 535
Chautauqua, NY 14722
216-831-2646

Steiff Life
Steiff Collectors Club
Beth Savino
℅ The Toy Store
7856 Hill Ave.
Holland, OH 43528
419-865-3899 or 800-862-8697

Stein Line
Thomas A. Heiza, Publisher
P.O. Box 48716
Chicago, IL 60648-0716
FAX 708-673-2634
Bimonthly newsletter concerning stein sales, auctions, values, etc.

Stretch Glass Society
P.O. Box 770643
Lakewood, OH 44107
Membership: $8; Quarterly newsletter, annual convention

Swatch Collectors
9595 Mt. Nebo Rd.
North Bend, OH 45052
513-941-5565

Table Topics
Table Toppers Club
1340 W Irving Park Rd.,
P.O. Box 161
Chicago 60613
312-769-3184
Membership: $18 (6 issues) per year. For those interested in table-top collectibles

Tea Leaf Reading
Tea Leaf Club International
P.O. Box 904
Mt. Prospect, IL 60056
Membership: $20 (single) or $25 (couple) per year

Tea Talk
Diana Rosen
419 N Larchmont Blvd. #225
Los Angeles, CA 90004
213-871-6901 or FAX 213-828-2444

Thimble Guild
Wynneth Mullins
P.O. Box 381807
Duncansville, TX 75138-1807

Tin Type
Tin Container Collectors Association
℅ Clark and Mary Beth Secrest
P.O. Box 4555
Denver, CO 80204

Tobacciana
Chuck Thompson and Associates
P.O. Box 11652
Houston, TX 77293
send SASE for free list of publications

Tobacco Jar Newsletter
Society of Tobacco Jar Collectors
Charlotte Tarses, Treasurer
3011 Fallstaff Road #307
Baltimore, MD 21209
Dues: $30 per year ($35 outside of U.S.)

Toothpick Bulletin
National Toothpick Holder
   Collectors' Society
Judy Knauer, Founder
1224 Spring Valley Lane
W Chester, PA 19380

*Torquay Pottery Collectors
   Society Newsletter*
Torquay Pottery Collectors Society
Beth Pulsipher
Box 373
Schoolcraft, MI 49087
616-679-4195

Toy Gun Collectors of America Newsletter
Jim Buskirk, Editor & Publisher
175 Cornell St.
Windsor CA 95492
707-837-9949
Published quarterly, covers both toy and BB guns. Dues: $15 per year

Toys and Prices magazine
700 E State St.
Iola, WI 54990-0001
715-445-2214 or FAX 715-445-4087
Subscription: $14.95 per year

The Trade Card Journal
Kit Barry
109 Main St.
Brattleboro, VT 05301
802-254-3634
A quarterly publication on the social
and historical use of trade cards

Trainmaster newsletter
P.O. Box 1499
Gainesville, FL 32602
904-377-7439 or 904-373-4908. FAX
904-374-6616

UHL Collectors' Society
Steve Brundage, President
80 Tidewater Rd.
Hagerstown, IN 47346
or Dale Blann, Vice President
R.R. 1, Box 136,
Wheatland, IN 47597
For membership and newsletter infor-
mation contact either of the above

The Upside Down World of an
   O.J.Collector
The Occupied Japan Club
C/o Florence Archambault
29 Freeborn St.
Newport, RI 02840
Published bimonthly. Information
requires SASE

Political Bandwagon
Larry L. Krug
18222 Flower Hill Way, #299
Gaithersburg, MD 20879
Published monthly. Free with $24
annual membership in American Politi-
cal Items Collectors (You also receive
The Keynoter magazine 3 times a year).

Vernon Views
P.O. Box 945
Scottsdale, AZ 85252
Published quarterly beginning with
spring issue, $6 per year

View-Master Reel Collector
Roger Nazeley
4921 Castor Ave
Philadelphia, PA 19124

Vintage Clothing Newsletter
Terry McCormick
P.O. Box 1422
Corvallis, OR 97339
503-752-7456

Vintage Fashion and Costume Jewelry
Newsletter/Club
P.O. Box 265
Glen Oaks, NY 11004
or call Davida Baron: 718-969-2320

Vintage Fashion Sourcebook
Kristina Harris
904 N 65th St.
Springfield, OR 97478-7021

Vintage Paperback Collecting Guide
Black Ace Books
1658 Griffith Park Blvd.
Los Angeles, CA 90026
213-661-5052
Information about terms, book fairs,
auctions, and references; available for
$2 postpaid

Walking Stick Notes
Cecil Curtis, Editor
4051 E Olive Rd.
Pensacola, FL 32514
Quarterly publication with limited dis-
tribution

Watt's News
C/o Susan Morris and Jan Seeck
P.O. Box 708
Mason City, IA 50401
Subscription: $10 per year

Wedgwood Collectors Society Newsletter
P.O. Box 14013
Newark, NJ 07198

Westmoreland Glass Society
Jim Fisher, President
513 5th Ave.
Coralville, IA 52241
319-354-5011

The Working Class Hero
   Beatles' Newsletter
3311 Niagara St.
Pittsburgh, PA 15213-4223
Published 3 times per year; send SASE
for information

The Wrapper
Bubble Gum and Candy Wrapper
   Collectors
P.O. Box 573
St. Charles, IL 60174
708-377-7921

Zane Grey's West Society
Carolyn Timmerman
708 Warwick Ave.
Fort Wayne, IN 46825
219-484-2904

Zeppelin Collector
Zeppelin Collectors Club
C/o Aerophilatelic Federation
P.O. Box 1239
Elgin, IL 60121-1239
708-888-1907

Interested Buyers of Miscellaneous Items

In this section of the book we
have listed hundreds of buyers who
are actively looking to buy items from
specific areas of interest. Don't expect
a response from them unless you
include an SASE (stamped self-
addressed envelope) with your letter.
Describe your merchandise thoroughly
and mention any marks. You can
sometimes do a pencil rubbing to
duplicate the mark exactly. Photographs are still worth a 'thousand
words,' and Xerox copies are especially good if you're selling paper
goods, patterned dinnerware, or even
smaller 3-dimensional items. Be sure to
read the Introduction for more suggestions about how to carry on a successful transaction by mail.

It's a good idea to include your
phone number when you write, since
many people would rather respond
with a call than a letter. And suggest-
ing that they call back collect might
very well be the courtesy that results in
a successful transaction. Whether
you're doing the buying or the selling,
though, always stop to consider the
local time on the other end of your
call. Someone who's dragged out of
bed in the middle of the night will very
likely *not* be receptive to doing business with you.

With the exception of the Character Collectibles section which we've
alphabetized by character, buyers are
listed alphabetically under bold topics.
A line in italics indicates only the specialized interests of the particular buyer
whose name immediately follows it.
Recommended reference guides not
available from the Nostalgia Publishing

Company may be purchased directly from the authors whose addresses are given in this section.

Advertising
Vendor jars and counter displays
Abalone Cove Antiques
7 Fruit Tree Rd.
Portuguese Bend, CA 90275
310-377-4609 or FAX 310-544-6792

Gasoline globes, pumps, signs
and promotional items
Author of book
Scott Benjamin
P.O. Box 611
Elyria, OH 44036
216-365-9534

Planters Peanuts
Marty Blank
2032 Central Dr. N
E Meadow, NY 11554
516-485-8071 (6:30 pm EST)

British figural biscuit tins
The Butler Did It!
Catherine Saunders-Watson
P.O. Box 302
Greenville, NH 03048-0302
phone or FAX 603-878-2171

Gas station items and promotional
salt and pepper shakers
Peter Capell
1838 W Grace St.
Chicago, IL 60613-2724

Items marked Fairbank Co.
Jim Fairbank
Rt. 4, Box 5428
Clodfelter Rd.
Kennewick, WA 99337
509-627-0933

Monarch Foods and Red Wing items
Bruce and Nada Ferris
3094 Oakes Dr.
Hayward, CA 94542
501-581-5285

Porcelain door push plates
Edward Foley
P.O. Box 572
Adamstown, PA 19501
717-484-4779

Reddy Kilowatt and Bordon's Elsie
Lee Garmon
1529 Whittier St.
Springfield, IL 62704

Henry F. Hain III Antiques and
 Collectibles
2623 N 2nd St.
Harrisburg, PA 17110

Signs, displays, tins, etc.
House of Stuart
P.O. Box 2063
Jensen Beach, FL 34958-2063

State Farm Insurance
Denny Kaufman
5918 S Columbia Ave.
Tulsa, OK 74105

African Art and Oceanic Art
Scott Nelson
Box 6081
Santa Fe, NM 87502
505-986-1176

Airline Memorabilia
Richard R. Wallin
Box 1784
Springfield, IL 62705

Alamo Pottery of San Antonio
Thomas Turnquist
Box 256
Englewood, CO 80151

Aluminum
Author of book
Dannie Woodard
P.O. Box 1346
Weatherford, TX 76086
817-594-4680

American Flags
Early, vintage
Robert Banks
18901 Gold Mine Ct.
Brookerville, MD 20833
301-774-7850

American Indian
Especially prehistoric artifacts
Author of book
Lar Hothem
P.O. Box 458
Lancaster, OH 43130
Also schoolhouse collectibles

ca before 1940
Fred L. Mitchell
835 Valencia
Walla Walla, WA 99362

Animal Dishes
Author of book
Everett Grist
6503 Slater Rd., Suite H
Chattanooga, TN 37412-3955
615-855-4032
Also aluminum, advertising playing cards, and marbles

Art Deco
Accent on Antiques
P.O. Box 4516
Boca Raton, FL 33428
407-368-6823

Mark Bassett
P.O. Box 771233
Lakewood, OH 44107
Also art glass and American art pottery (especially Cowan), Gustavsberg, Gouda

Art Glass, Contemporary
Especially Boyd, Summit, and Mosser
Chip and Dale Collectibles
3500 S Cooper
Arlington, TX 76015

Art Glass
American and European
Mirko Melis
4589 Longmoor Rd.
Mississauga, Ontario
Canada L5M 4H4
905-820-8066

Durand
Ed Meschi
R.R. 3, Box 550
Monroeville, NJ 08343
609-358-7293

Arts and Crafts
Mission, Stickley and Roycroft
Bruce Austin
40 Selborne Chase
Fairport, NY 14450
716-223-0711

Automobilia
Dulce Holt
504 Broadway
Chesterton, IN 46304
219-926-2838 or 219-926-4170

LMG Enterprises
2500 Newning
Schertz, TX 78154
phone or FAX 210-658-5207

Original paper ephemera
Original Literature
Box 23576
Mandarin, FL 32241-3576

Gearshift Knobs
Ed Sprankle
1768 Leimert Blvd.
Oakland, CA 94602-1930

Autumn Leaf
Edits newsletter
Gwynneth Harrison
P.O. Box 1
Mira Loma, CA 91752-0001
909-685-5434
Buys and appraises

Avon Collectibles
Author of book
Bud Hastin
P.O. Box 43690
Las Vegas, NE 89116

Tammy Rodrick
Stacey's Treasures
R.R. #2, Box 163
Sumner, IL 62466
Also character toys, glasses, cereal
boxes and premiums; beer steins, Blue
Willow, head vases, and trolls

Banks
*Those with keys (will accept examples
whose keys are missing)*
Doris Caloggero
2 Charles St.
P.O. Box 961
Methuen, MA 01844
Also trade cards featuring banks and
pre-1960 toys

Marked Ertl
Homestead Collectibles
P.O. Box 173
Mill Hall, PA 17751
Also decanters

Reynolds Toys
Charlie Reynolds
2836 Monroe St.
Falls Church, VA 22042
703-533-1322

Barb Wire
John Mantz
American Barb Wire Collectors Society
1023 Baldwin Rd.
Bakersfield, CA 93304

Barber Shop Collectibles
Burton Handelsman
18 Hotel Dr.
White Plains, NY 10605
914-428-4480

Barware
Specializing in vintage cocktail shakers
Stephen Visakay
P.O. Box 1517
W Caldwell, NJ 07707-1517

Battersea Boxes
John Harrigan
1900 Hennepin
Minneapolis, MN 55403
612-872-0226
Buy and sell

Bells
Unusual; no cow or school
Author of book
Dorothy Malone Anthony
802 S Eddy
Ft. Scott, KS 66701

Black Americana
Buy, sell and trade
Judy Posner
R.D. 1, Box 273
Effort, PA 18330
717-629-6583

Pre-1950s items
Jan Thalberg
23 Mountain View Dr.
Weston, CT 06883

Black Glass
Author of book
Marlena Toohey
703 S Pratt Pkwy.
Longmont, CO 80501
303-678-9726

Blade Banks
David Geise
1410 Aquia Dr.
Stafford, VA 22554

Stephen Skorupski
P.O. Box 572
Plainville, CT 06062
203-828-4097

Bobbin' Heads by Hartland
Patrick Flynn
Minne Memories
122 Shadywood Ave.
Mankato, MN 56001

Boch Freres or Keramis
John T. Coates
324 Woodland Dr.
Stevens Point, WI 5481
715-341-6113

Bohemian Glass
Tom Bradshaw
325 Carol Dr.
Ventura, CA 93303
805-653-2723 or 310-450-6486

Bookmarks
Joan L. Huegel
1002 W 25th St.
Erie, PA 16502

Books
Children's illustrated
Noreen Abbott Books
2666 44th Ave.
San Francisco, CA 94116

Hippie, beat & counter-culture paperbacks
Black Ace Books
1658 Griffith Park Blvd.
Los Angeles, CA 90026

Vintage paperbacks
Books Are Everything
R.C. and Elwanda Holland
302 Martin Dr.
Richmond, KY 40475

Buck Creek Books
838 Main St.
Lafayette, IN 47901

Paperback originals
For Collectors Only
2028B Ford Pkwy #136
St. Paul, MN 55116

American Indian archaeology
Lar Hothem
P.O. Box 458
Lancaster, OH 43130

Children's
My Bookhouse
27 S Sandusky St.
Tiffin, OH 44883
419-447-9842

Children's
Nerman's Books
410-63 Albert St.
Winnipeg, Manitoba
Canada R3B 1G4

Little Golden Books, Wonder and Elf
Author of book on Little Golden Books
Steve Santi
19626 Ricardo Ave.
Hayward, CA 94541

Bottles
Bitters, figurals, inks, barber, etc.
Steve Ketcham
P.O. Box 24114
Minneapolis, MN 55424
612-920-4205
Also advertising signs, trays, calendars, etc.

Dairy and milk
O.B. Lund
13009 S 42nd St.
Phoenix, AZ 85044

Painted-label soda
Author of book
Thomas Marsh
914 Franklin Ave.
Youngstown, OH 44502

Dairy and milk
Author of book
John Tutton
R.R. 4, Box 929
Front Royal, VA 22630
703-635-7058

Breweriana
DLK Nostalgia and Collectibles
P.O. Box 5112
Johnstown, PA 15904
Also Art Deco, novelty clocks, toys and football cards

Steve Gordon
G & G Pawnbrokers
1325 University Blvd. E
Langley Park, MD 20783
Also beer cans

British Royal Commemoratives
Audrey Zeder
6755 Coralite St. S
Long Beach, CA 90808

Brush McCoy Pottery
Authors of book
Steve and Martha Sanford
230 Harrison Ave.
Campbell, CA 95008
408-978-8408

Buggy Steps
John W. Waddell
P.O. Box 664
Mineral Wells, TX 76067

Button Hooks
All types
Richard Mathes
P.O. Box 1408
Springfield, OH 45501-1408
Has duplicates to sell or trade; single items or entire collections

Buttons
Tender Buttons
143 E 6th St.
New York, NY 10021
Also buckles

Melanie Kadair - Ivy Ridge Plantation
8534 Old Tunica Rd.
St. Francisville, LA 70775
504-655-4696 or 504-655-4646
Also trade beads

Calendar Plates
Dated before 1950
Elizabeth M. Stout
152 Hwy. F
Defiance, MO 63341

California Perfume Company
Not common; especially items marked
Goetting Co.
Dick Pardini
3107 N El Dorado St., Dept. G
Stockton, CA 95204-3412
Also Savoi Et Cie, Hinze Ambrosia, Gertrude Recordon, Marvel Electric Silver Cleaner, & Easy Day Automatic Clothes Washer

Cambridge Glassware
John and Peggy Scott
4640 S Leroy
Springfield, MO 65810
Also Florence figurines

Cameras
Wooden, detective and stereo
John A. Hess
P.O. Box 3062
Andover, MA 01810
Also old brass lenses

Harry Poster
P.O. Box 1883
S Hackensack, NJ 07606
201-410-7525
Also accessories and 3-D projectors

Candy Containers
Glass
Jeff Bradfield
90 Main St.
Dayton, VA 22821
703-879-9961
Also advertising, cast-iron and tin toys, postcards and Coca-Cola

Glass
Doug Dezso
864 Paterson Ave.
Maywood, NJ 07607
Also Tonka Toys, Shafford black cats, German bisque comic character nodders, Royal Bayreuth creamers, and Pep pins

Carnival Chalkware
Author of book
Thomas G. Morris
P.O. Box 8307
Medford, OR 97504
503-779-3164

Carnival Glass
Robert Greenwood
201 E Hatfield St.
Massena, NY 13662
315-769-8130

Cast Iron
Irons and pressing devices, salesman sample stoves, cookware, children's toys and cookware
D & R Farm Antiques
4545 Hwy. H
St. Charles, MO 63301
314-258-3790

Door knockers, sprinklers and figural paperweights
Craig Dinner
P.O. Box 4399
Sunnyside, NY 11104

Ronald Fitch
315 Market St.
Suite 2G
Portsmouth, OH 45662
614-353-6879

Especially marked cookware
David G. Smith
11918 2nd St.
Perrysburg, NY 14129

Cat Collectibles
Crystal figurines and limited edition plates
Glenna Moore
440 Lewers St. #205
Honolulu, HI 96815-2445
808-924-2226

Ceramic Arts Studio
Vera Skorupski
P.O. Box 572
Plainville, CT 06062
203-828-4097

Author of book
BA Wellman
88 State Rd. W, Homestead Farms #2
Westminster, MA 01473

Cereal Boxes and Premiums
Scott Bruce, Mr. Cereal Box
P.O. Box 481
Cambridge, MA 02140

Character Collectibles
Author of book
Bill Bruegman
Toy Scouts, Inc.
137 Casterton Ave.
Akron, OH 44303

Batman, Gumby and Marilyn Monroe
Colleen Garmon Barnes
114 E Locust
Chatham, IL 62629

Beatles
Bojo - Bob Gottuso
P.O. Box 1203
Cranberry Twp., PA 16033-2203
Phone or FAX 412-776-0621

Beatles
Michael and Deborah Summers
3258 Harrison
Paducah, KY 42001
502-443-9359

Betty Boop
Leo A. Mallette
2309 Santa Anita Ave.
Arcadia, CA 91006-5154

California Raisins
Larry De Angelo
516 King Arthur Dr.
Virginia Beach, VA 23464

Dark Shadows
Steve Hall
P.O. Box 960398
Riverside, GA 30296-0398

Dick Tracy
Larry Doucet
2351 Sultana Dr.
Yorktown Heights, NY 10598

Dionne Quint Collectors Club
Jimmy Rodolfos
P.O. Box 2527
Woburn, MA 10888

Disney, Western heroes, Gone with the Wind, character watches ca 1930s to mid-1950s, premiums and games
Ron Donnelly
P.O. Box 7047
Panama City Beach, FL 32413

Disney; buy, sell and trade
Judy Posner
R.D. 1, Box 273
Effort, PA 18330
717-629-6583

Dr. Seuss
Michael Gessel
P.O. Box 748
Arlington, VA 22216

Elvis Presley
Author of book
Rosalind Cranor
P.O. Box 859
Blacksburg, VA 24063

Elvis Presley
Lee Garmon
1529 Whittier St.
Springfield, IL 62704

Garfield, The Garfield Collector's Society
David L. Abrams
7744 Foster Ridge Rd.
Germantown, TN 38138-7036

Gone With the Wind
Author of book
Patrick McCarver
5453 N Rolling Oaks Dr.
Memphis, TN 38119

I Dream of Jeannie, Barbara Eden
Richard D. Barnes
389 W 100 S
Bountiful, UT 84010
801-295-5762

Lil' Abner
Kenn Norris
P.O. Box 4830
Sanderson, TX 79848-4830

The Lone Ranger
Terry and Kay Klepey
C/o The Silver Bullet Newsletter
P.O. Box 553
Forks, WA 98331

Peanuts and Schultz Collectibles
Author of book
Freddi Margolin
P.O. Box 512P
Bay Shore, NY 11706

Roy Rogers and Dale Evans
Author of book
Robert W. Phillips
1703 N Aster Pl.
Broken Arrow, OK 74012-1308

Shirley Temple
Gen Jones
294 Park St.
Medford, MA 02155

Star Trek and Star Wars
Craig Reid
P.O. Box 881
Post Falls, ID 83854
838-54-0881

The Three Stooges
Soitenly Stooges Inc.
Harry S. Ross
P.O. Box 72
Skokie, IL 60076

Tom Mix
Author of book
Merle 'Bud' Norris
1324 N Hague Ave.
Columbus, OH 43204-2108

Wizard of Oz
Lori Landgrebe
2331 E Main St.
Decatur, IL 62521

Norm Vigue
62 Barley St.
Stoughton, MA 02072
617-344-5441

Chase
Barry Van Hook
2149 W Jibsail Loop
Mesa, AZ 85202
602-838-6971
Also Frankart

Christmas
Jackie Chamberlain Antiques
P.O. Box 20842
Wickenburg, AZ 85358
602-684-2296

Aluminum trees (all colors), unusual color wheels and motorized stands
Ted Haun
2426 N 700 East
Kokomo, IN 46901-9343

Cigarette Lighters
Terry Cairo
C/o Lighters
P.O. Box 1054
Addison, IL 60101
708-543-9120

Bill Majors
P.O. Box 9351
Boise, ID 83707

Jack Seiderman
1631 NW 114 Ave.
Pembroke Pines, FL 33026-2539
Catalogs issued

Clarice Cliff Pottery
Louis and Susan Meisel
141 Prince St.
New York, NY 10012

Cleminson
Marilyn Whittingham
7290 Thunderbird Lane
Stanton, CA 90680

Clocks
All types
Bruce A. Austin
40 Selborne Chase
Fairport, NY 14450
716-223-0711

Comic character; also watches
Author of book
Howard S. Brenner
106 Woodgate Terrace
Rochester, NY 14625

The Clock Doctor
Steve Gabany, Ph.D.
585 Woodbine
Terre Haute, IN 47803-1759
Also cameras

Novelty animated and non-animated
Carole S. Kaifer
P.O. Box 232
Bethania, NC 27010

Clothing
Vintage; also accessories
Leah and Walt Bird
P.O. Box 4502
Medford, OR 97501

Vintage; also accessories
Rhonda Hasse
566 Oak Terrace Dr.
Farmington, MO 63640

Coca-Cola
Craig and Donna Stifter
P.O. Box 6514
Naperville, IL 60540
Other soda pop memorabilia as well

Cocktail Shakers
Arlene Lederman Antiques
150 Main St.
Nyack, NY 10960

Coin-Operated Vending Machines
Ken and Jackie Durham
909 26th St., NW
Washington, D.C. 20037

Colorado Pottery (Broadmoor)
Carol and Jim Carlton
8115 S Syracuse St.
Englewood, CO 80112
303-773-8616
Also Coors, Lonhuda, and Denver White

Comic Strip Art
David H. Begin
138 Lansberry Ct.
Los Gatos, CA 95032

Compacts
Jette Bellew
15243 Profit Ave.
Baton Rouge, LA 70817
504-756-4875

Author of book
Roselyn Gerson
P.O. Box Letter S
Lynbrook, NY 11563

Lori Landgrebe
2331 E Main St.
Decatur, IL 62521

Cookbooks
Author of book; also advertising leaflets
Col. Bob Allen
P.O. Box 85
St. James, MO 65559

Cookie Jars
Joe Devine
1411 3rd St.
Council Bluffs, IA 51503
712-232-5233 or 712-328-7305

Laurence Koon
1033 Lynn St.
Parkersburg, WV 26101
304-485-8636

Buy, sell and trade
Judy Posner
R.D. 1, Box 273
Effort, PA 18330
717-629-6583

Joyce Stratton
RFD #4, Box 550
Augusta, ME 04330
207-622-1001

Corkscrews
Antique and unusual
Paul P. Luchsinger
104 Deer Run
Williamsville, NY 14221

Cowan
Author of Book
Mark Bassett
P.O. Box 771233
Lakewood, OH 44107

Cracker Jack Items
Phil Helley
Old Kilbourn Antiques
629 Indiana Ave.
Wisconsin Dells, WI 53965
Also banks, radio premiums & wind-up toys

Wes Johnson, Sr.
106 Bauer Ave.
Louisville, KY 40207

Credit Cards and Related Items
Walt Thompson
Box 2541
Yakima, WA 98907-2541

Cuff Links
Also related items
National Cuff Link Society
Eugene R. Klompus
P.O. Box 346
Prospect Heights, IL 60070
708-632-0561

Currier and Ives Prints
Original only
Rudisill's Alt Print Haus
Barbara and John Rudisill
24305 Waterview Dr.
Worton, MD 21678
410-778-9290

Dakins
Suzan Hufferd
6625 Sunbury Dr.
Indianapolis, IN 46241
317-630-7180 or 317-487-6352
Also vinyl advertising figurals, fast-food collectibles

Decorative Arts
Turn of the century; lamps, windows, Tiffany, paintings, etc.
Carl Heck
Box 8416
Aspen, CO 81612
303-925-8011

Depression Glass
Elegant Glassware
John and Shirley Baker
673 W Township Rd. #118
Tiffin, OH 44883
Also Tiffin glassware

H.E. Gschwend
1421 Camden St.
Pekin, IL 61554
309-347-1679

John and Peggy Scott
4640 S Leroy
Springfield, MO 65810

Dan Tucker
Toledo, OH; 419-478-3815
Also Fiesta and Hall

Dinnerware
Russel Wright, Eva Zeisel, Homer Laughlin
Charles Alexander
221 E 34th St.
Indianapolis, IN 46205
317-924-9665

Cat-Tail
Ken and Barbara Brooks
4121 Gladstone Ln.
Charlotte, NC 28205
704-568-5716

Discontinued patterns, specializing in Castelton, Lenox, Spode, Syracuse
Classic Tableware
P.O. Box 4265
Stockton, CA 95204
209-956-4645
Also Fostoria, discontinued crystal patterns

Fiesta, Franciscan; Russel Wright, Lu Ray, and Metlox
Fiesta Plus
Mick and Lorna Chase
380 Hawkins Crawford Rd.
Cookeville, TN 38501
615-372-8333
Also other Homer Laughlin patterns

Franciscan
Franciscan Dinnerware Matching Service
323 E Matilija, Ste. 112
Ojai, CA 93023
Mail order only; buy and sell

Blue Willow, Fiesta, Franciscan, Hall, Royal, Staffordshire
The Glass Packrat
Bill and Pat Ogden
3050 Colorado Ave.
Grand Junction, CO 81504

English by T.G. Green and others
Deborah and James Golden
3182 Twin Pine Rd.
Grayling, MI 49738
517-348-2610

Mason's Ironstone
Susan and Larry Hirshman
540 Siskiyou Blvd.
Ashland, OR 97520

Homer Laughlin China, author of book
Darlene Nossaman
5419 Lake Charles
Waco, TX 76710

Matching service, specializing in English and American companies, Shelley, Haviland, Mikasa
Old China Patterns Ltd.
P.O. Box 290
Fineview, NY 13640
315-482-3829
Also matching service for discontinued crystal patterns

English with allover floral decoration
Bruce E. Thulin
P.O. Box 121
Ellsworth, ME 04605
207-667-5225

Dolls
Strawberry Shortcake
Geneva D. Addy
P.O. Box 124
Winterset, IA 50273

Raggedy Ann and related items
Gwen Daniel
18 Belleau Lake Ct.
O'Fallon, MO 63366
314-978-3190

Barbie and accessories
Irene Davis
27036 Withams Rd.
Oak Hall, VA 23416
804-824-5524

Barbie and modern
Mariam F. Donerian
P.O. Box 133, 42 Patsun Rd.
Somersville, CT 06072-0133

Cabbage Patch and Xavier Roberts limited editions
Mari Forquer
P.O. Box 714
Cleveland, GA 30528

Skookum
Barry Friedman
22725 Garzota Dr.
Valencia, CA 91355

Liddle Kiddles
Cindy Sabulis
3 Stowe Dr., #1S
Shelton, CT 06484

Betsy McCall and friends
Marci Van Ausdall
P.O. Box 946
Quincy, CA 95971

Dollhouse Furniture and Accessories
Marian Schmuhl
7 Revolutionary Ridge Rd.
Bedford, MA 10730

Egg Beaters
Author of Beat This: The Egg Beater Chronicles
Don Thornton
Off Beat Books
1345 Poplar Ave.
Sunnyvale, CA 94087

Egg Cups
Joan George, Editor
Eggcup Collectors Corner
67 Stevens Ave.
Old Bridge, NJ 08857

Egg Timers
Jeannie Greenfield
310 Parker Rd.
Stoneboro, PA 16153

Farm Collectibles
Farm Antique News
Gary Van Hoozer
812 N Third St.
Tarkio, MO 64491-0812

Fast-Food Collectibles
Author of book
Ken Clee
Box 1142
Philadelphia, PA 19111
215-722-1979

Authors of book
Joyce and Terry Losonsky
7506 Summer Leave Lane
Columbia, MD 21046-2455

POE-Pourri
Bill and Pat Poe
220 Dominica Cir. E
Niceville, FL 32578-4068
904-897-4163 or FAX 904-897-2606
Also cartoon and character glasses, PEZ, Smurfs and California Raisins; send $3 (US delivery) for 70-page catalog

Figural Ceramics
Teapots, shakers, kitchen items, etc.
Richard and Carol Silagyi
CS Antiques and Jewelry
P.O. Box 151
Wyckoff, NJ 07430

Fire-King
Author of book
April M. Tvorak
HCR #34, Box 25B
Warren, PA 18851
Also kitchen glassware, Pyrex, Corningware, etc.

Fireworks and 4th of July
Dennis C. Manochio
4th of July Americana and Fireworks Museum
P.O. Box 2010
Saratoga, CA 95070

Fishing Collectibles
Dave Hoover
1023 Skyview Dr.
New Albany, IN 47150
Also miniature boats and motors; publishes fixed price catalog

Flashlights
Editor of newsletter
Bill Utley
P.O. Box 4094
Tustin, CA 92680

Florence Ceramics
John and Peggy Scott
4640 S Leroy
Springfield, MO 65810

Fountain Pens
Cliff and Judy Lawrence
1169 Overcash Dr.
Dunedin, FL 34698
Catalogs issued

Frank Lloyd Wright & Prairie School
Richard A. Haussmann
25 Hampton Rd.
Montgomery, IL 60538-2321
708-896-8287

Frankoma
Authors of Frankoma Treasures
Phyllis and Tom Bess
14535 E 13th St.
Tulsa, OK 74108

Author of book
Susan N. Cox
Main Street Antique Mall
237 East Main Street
El Cajon, CA 92020
619-447-0800
Also unsharpened advertising pencils, complete matchbooks, Horlick's advertising, women's magazines from 1900 to 1950

Masonic and Shriner
David Smies
Box 522
Manhattan, KS 66502
913-776-1433

Odd Fellows
Greg Speiss
230 E Washington
Joliet, IL 60433
815-722-5639

Fruit Jars
Especially old, odd or colored jars
John Hathaway
Rte. 2, Box 220
Bryant Pond, ME 04219
Also old jar lids and closures

Fry Glass
Ron Damaska
738 9th Ave.
New Brighton, PA 15066
412-843-1393
Also cut glass

Fulper
Douglass White
P.O. Box 5400672
Orlando, FL 32854
407-841-6681

Gambling and Gambling-Related Items
Robert Eisenstadt
P.O. Box 020767
Brooklyn, NY 11202-0017

Games
Billiard pool cues, racks and chairs
Edward Blumenthal
Rt. 2, Box 2365A
Grayling, MI 49738

Paul Fink's Fun and Games
P.O. Box 488
59 S Kent Rd.
Kent, CT 06757
203-927-4001

Geisha Girl Porcelain
Author of book
Elyce Litts
P.O. Box 394
Morris Plains, NJ 07950
Also ladies' compacts

Glass Animals
Author of book
Lee Garmon
1529 Whittier St.
Springfield, IL 62704

Glass Knives
Editor of newsletter
Adrienne Escoe
P.O. Box 342
Los Alamitos, CA 90720
310-430-6479

Glass Shoes
Author of book
The Shoe Lady
Libby Yalom
P.O. Box 7146
Adelphi, MD 20783

Glidden Pottery
David Pierce
27544 Black Rd.
P.O. Box 248
Danville, OH 43014
614-599-6394

Goebel
Friar Tuck and Cardinals
Carol and Jim Carlton
8115 S Syracuse St.
Englewood, CO 80112
303-773-8616

Goofus Glass
Rare or unusual
Dan Gandolfo
3 S 577 Elizabeth Ave.
Warrenville, IL 60555
708-393-9115

Graniteware
Helen Greguire
716-392-2704
Also carnival glass and toasters

Griswold
Author of book
Denise Harned
P.O. Box 330373
Elmwood, CT 06133-0373

Hall
H.E. Gschwend
1421 Camden St.
Pekin, IL 61554
309-347-1679

Hallmark Ornaments
Susan K. Holland
6151 Main St.
Springfield, OR 97478

Author of book
Rosie Wells Enterprises, Inc.
R.R. #1
Canton, IL 61520

Halloween
Jackie Chamberlain Antiques
P.O. Box 20842
Wickenburg, AZ 85358
602-684-2296
Also ice cream molds

Specializing in costumes
Craig Reid
P.O. Box 881
Post Falls, ID 838-54-0881

Chris Russell and The Halloween Queen
4 Lawrance St., Rt. 10
Winchester, NH 54559
Also other holidays and postcards

Hatpins and Hatpin Holders
Author of book
Lillian Baker
15237 Chanera Ave.
Gardena, CA 90249

Holly Hobbie Collectibles
Holly Hobbie Club of America
Helen McCale
R.R. 3, Box 35
Butler, MO 64730

David Kolodgie
Holly Hobbie Collections
5860 N Courtenay Pkwy.
Merritt Island, FL 32953
407-452-3863

Homer Laughlin China
Dreamland and Holland
Aletha Barlow
Rte. #1, Box 8
Clearmont, MO 64431
816-729-4688

Hull
Mirror Brown
Bill and Connie Sloan
Rte. 32, Box 629
Pt. Pleasant, PA 18950

Illustrator Art
Louis Wain cats
Jackie Durham
909 26th St. NW
Washington, D.C. 20037

Icart etchings and Maxfield Parrish prints
Ed Meschi
R.R. 3, Box 550
Monroeville, NJ 08343
609-358-7293
Also American oil paintings

Imperial Glass
Lee Garmon
1529 Whittier St.
Springfield, IL 62704
Also Fenton plum opalescent

Imperial Porcelain
Geneva D. Addy
P.O. Box 124
Winterset, IA 50273

Paul Webb series
Carol and Jim Carlton
8115 S Syracust St.
Englewood, CO 80112
303-773-8616

Insulators
Mike Bruner
6980 Walnut Lake Rd.
W Bloomfield, MI 48323
313-661-8241
Also porcelain signs, light-up advertising clocks, exit globes, lightening rod balls and target balls

Len Linscott
3557 Nicklaus Dr.
Tutusville, FL 32780

Irish Belleek
Richard K. Degenhardt
Sugar Hollow Farm
124 Cypress Point
Henderson, NC 28739
704-696-9750

Jewelry
Rhinestone ca 1920 to 1960
Ronald Fitch
315 Market St.
Suite 2B
Portsmouth, OH 45662
614-353-6879

Mexican silver
Richard Haigh
P.O. Box 29888
Richmond, VA 23242

Antique and estate
Mirko Melis
4589 Longmoor Rd.
Mississauga, Ontario
Canada L5M 4H4
905-820-8066

Pamela Wiggins
6025 Sunnycrest St.
Houston, TX 77087
713-649-6603

Josef Originals
Eclectic Antiques
Jim and Kaye Whitaker
P.O. Box 475, Dept. GS
Lynwood, WA 98046
206-774-6910

Kay Finch
Doris Frizzell
5687 Oakdale Dr.
Springfield, IL 62707

Kentucky Derby and Horse Racing
B.L. Hornback
707 Sunrise Lane
Elizabethtown, KY 42701

Knives
Author of book
Jim Sargent
Books Americana, Inc.
Florence, AL 35630

Dennis Stapp
7037 Haynes Rd.
Georgetown, IN 47122

Lace
The Lace Merchant Newsletter
Elizabeth M. Kurella
P.O. Box 222
Plainwell, MI 49080

Labels
Cigar Labels and Boxes
David M. Beach
Paper Americana
P.O. Box 2026
Goldenrod, FL 32733

Cerebro
P.O. Box 1221
Lancaster, PA 17603
1-800-695-2235

Lalique
John R. Danis
11028 Raleigh Ct.
Rockford, IL 61111
815-963-0757 or FAX 815-877-6042

Lamps
Specializing in Aladdin
Author of books
J.W. Courter
3935 Kelley Rd.
Kevil, KY 42053
502-488-2116

Motion Lamps
Eclectic Antiques
Jim and Kaye Whitaker
P.O. Box 475, Dept. GS
Lynwood, WA 98046
206-774-8571

William Durham and William Galaway
615 S State St.
Belvidere, IL 61008
815-544-0577
Specializing in parts and restoration

Law Enforcement, Crime-Related Memorabilia
Antiques of Law and Order
Tony Perrin
H.C. 7, Box 53A
Mena, AR 71953

Locks, safes and keys
Charles Chandler, MI
36076 Grennada
Livonia, MI 48154

Especially restraints, badges and photos
Gene Matzke
2345 S 28th St.
Milwaukee, WI 53215-2925
414-383-8995

Handcuffs and leg irons
David Pierce
27544 Black Rd.
P.O. Box 248
Danville, OH 43104
614-599-6394

Restraints
Joseph M. Tanner
3024 E 35th St.
Spokane, WA 99223
509-448-8457
Buy, sell, and trade
Especially restraints, badges and photos

Lefton
Author of book
Loretta De Lozier
1101 Polk St.
Bedford, IA 50833

License Plate Attachments
Edward Foley
P.O. Box 572
Adamstown, PA 19501
717-484-4779

License Plates
Richard Diehl
5965 W Colgate Pl.
Denver, CO 80227

Magic and Escape Art
Especially Houdini-related items
Joseph M. Tanner
3024 E 35th St.
Spokane, WA 99223
509-448-8457
Buy, sell and trade

Magazines
Monster from 1950s-'70s, from movies (not comics)
Steve Dolnick
P.O. Box 69
E Meadow, NY 11554
516-486-5085

Mad and related collectibles
Jim McClane
232 Butternut Dr.
Wayne, NJ 07470

National Geographic
Author of book
Don Smith's National
  Geographic Magazines
3930 Rankin St.
Louisville, KY 40214
502-366-7504

Majolica
Laura L. Walker
3907 North Blvd.
Tampa, FL 33603
813-229-6332

Marbles
Daria Canino
HC 73 Box 991
Locust Grove, VA 22508
703-972-1525

Author of book
Everett Grist
6503 Slater Rd., Suite H
Chattanooga, TN 37412-3955
615-855-4032

Pre-1940
Yvonne Marie Holmsberg
7229 Pine Island Dr., NE
Comstock Park, MI 49321-9534
616-784-1715

Matchcovers
Bill Retskin
P.O. Box 18481
Asheville, NC 22814

Match Safes
George Sparacio
P.O. Box 791
Malaga, NJ 08328
609-694-4167

Militaria
Especially US Navy
Ron M. Willis
2110 Fox Ave.
Moore, OK 73160

Moorcroft
John Harrigan
1900 Hennepin
Minneapolis, MN 55403
612-872-0226
Buy and sell

Morgantown
Literature, catalogs and glass
Editor of newsletter
Jerry Gallagher
420 1st Ave. NW
Plainview, MN 55964
507-534-3511

Mourning Collectibles
Postmortem, memorial, photography and ephemera
Steve DeGenaro
P.O. Box 5662
Youngstown, OH 44504
216-759-7737

Mouse Traps
Boyd Nedry
728 Buth Dr.
Comstock Park, MI 49321

Music Boxes
Mechantiques
26 Barton Hill
E Hampton, CT 06424
203-267-8682
Also anything related to antique mechanical music; monkey organs, musical clocks and watches, band organs, coin pianos, orchestrions, player organs, mechanical birds, automata, and phonographs with horns.

Non-Sports Cards
Newspaper Collector Society
Rick Brown
P.O. Box 19134
Lansing, MI 19134

Nutcrackers
Earl MacSorley
823 Indian Hill Rd.
Orange, CT 06477

Obsolete Postal Artifacts
Especially postmarking handstamps, badges, mail locks, street letterboxes, mail route schedules, postal hand guns
Frank R. Scheer
12 E Rosemont Ave.
Alexandria, VA 22301-2325
703-KI 9-4095; FAX 703-TE 6-1955
No stamps, postmarked envelopes or recent postique collectibles; send SASE for illustrated want list with prices paid

Occupied Japan
The Occupied Japan Club
  and Newsletter
℅ Florence Archambault
29 Freeborn St.
Newport, RI 02840
401-846-9024

Old MacDonald's Farm
Rick Spencer
3953 S Renault Cir.
W Valley, UT 84119

Oil Company Collectibles
Author of book
Scott Benjamin
P.O. Box 611
Elyria, OH 44036
216-365-9534

Orientalia and Dragonware
Susie Hibbard
2570 Walnut Blvd. #20
Walnut Creek, CA 94596

Paperweights
19th-century glass
Tom Bradshaw
325 Carol Dr.
Ventura, CA 93303
805-653-2723 or 310-450-6486

Antique and modern; leading artist and Baccarat
George Kamm
24 Townsend Ct.
Lancaster, PA 17603
717-872-7858

Specifically Blue Bell
Author of book
Jackie Linscott
3557 Nicklaus Dr.
Tutusville, FL 32780

Contemporary and antique
The Paperweight Shop
Betty Schwab
2507 Newport Dr.
Bloomington, IL 61704
309 662-1956

Pen Delfin Rabbit Figurines
George Sparacio
R.D. #2, Box 139C
Newfield, NJ 08344

Pencil Sharpeners
Martha Hughes
4128 Ingalls St.
San Diego, CA 92103

Pennsbury
BA Wellman
88 State Rd. W, Homestead Farms #2
Westminster, MA 01473

Joe Devine
1411 3rd St.
Council Bluffs, IA 51503
712-232-5322 or 712-328-7305

Pepsi
Craig and Donna Stifter
P.O. Box 6514
Naperville, IL 60540
Other soda pop memorabilia as well

Perfume Bottles
Especially commercial, Czechoslova-kian, Lalique, Baccarat, Victorian, crown top, factices, miniatures
Monsen and Baer
Box 529
Vienna, VA 22183
703-938-2129
Buy, sell and accept consignments for auctions

Pewter
Oveda Mauer Antiques
34 Greenfield Ave.
San Anselmo, CA 94960
415-454-6439
Also hearthware and lamps

Pez
Sue Sternfeld
90-60 Union Turnpike
Glendale, NY 11385

Pfaltzgraff
Gourmet, Gourmet Royal
Bill and Connie Sloan
4965 Valley Park Rd.
Doylestown, PA 18901

Phoenix and Consolidated
Author of book; editor of newsletter
Jack D. Wilson
P.O. Box 81974
Chicago, IL 60681-0974

Phoenix Bird Chinaware
Buy and sell; newsletter available
Joan Oates
685 S Washington
Constantine, MI 49042
616-435-8353
Also Erich Stauffer figurines

Phonographs
Parts and Accessories
Hart Wessman
600 N 800 W
West Bountiful, UT 84087
801-298-3499

Photographica
Any pre-1900
John A. Hess
P.O. Box 3062
Andover, MA 01810

Tammy Rodrick
R.R.2, Box 163
Sumner, IL 62466

Pie Birds
Also funnels
Lillian M. Cole
14 Harmony School Rd.
Flemington, NJ 08822
908-782-3198
Also old ice cream scoops

Pink Pigs
Also Pink-Paw Bears
Geneva Addy
P.O. Box 124
Winterset, IA 50273

Pin-Up Art
Original art only
Louis and Susan Meisel
141 Prince St.
New York, NY 10012

Playing Cards
Ray Hartz
P.O. Box 1002
Westerville, OH 43081
614-891-6296

Pocket Calculators
*International Association of
    Calculator Collectors*
Guy D. Ball
14561 Livingston St.
Tustin, CA 92680-2618
714-759-2116 or FAX 714-730-6140

Political
Before 1960
Michael Engel
29 Groveland St.
Easthampton, MA 01027

Pins, banners, ribbons, etc.
Paul Longo Americana
Box 490
Chatham Rd., South Orleans
Cape Cod, MA 02662
508-255-5482

The Political Bandwagon Newspaper
P.O. Box 348
Leola, PA 17540

Pond Sailboats
English and American; 1890-1950s
Louis and Susan Meisel
141 Prince St.
New York, NY 10012

Postcards
Author of book
Margaret Kaduck
P.O. Box 26076
Cleveland, OH 44126

*Post office views, any others
    related to postal service*
Frank R. Scheer
12 E Rosemont Ave.
Alexandria, VA 22301-2325
703-KI 9-4095; FAX 73-TE 6-1955

Pottery

Niloak, Camark, Ouachita, Ozark, Hy-Long, Marie, Mussel Shoals; buys damaged marked items
Arkansas Pottery Co.
Marshall F. Brennan
217 Feathervale Dr.
Oroville, CA 95966

Damaged fine pottery; repair service
The Finders Shoppe, Inc.
1076 York Way
Port Orange, FL 32119
800-211-9177

John Harrigan
1900 Hennepin
Minneapolis, MN 55403

American companies
The Shop
1344 Broadwell Mill Rd.
Jacksonville, AL 36265

Especially Fulper, Newcomb, Teco, Grueby, Marblehead
Douglass White
P.O. Box 540672
Orlando, FL 32854
407-841-6681

Powder Jars
John and Peggy Scott
4640 S Leroy
Springfield, MO 65810

Precious Moments®
Author of book
Rosie Wells Enterprises, Inc.
R.R. #1
Canton, IL 61520

Primitives and Country Collectibles
Lana Henry
1147 Terrace Ave.
Jasper, IN 47546
812-634-9819

Purinton Pottery
Susan Morris
P.O. Box 708
Mason City, IA 50401

Purses
Veronica Trainer
P.O. Box 40443
Cleveland, OH 44140

ca 1930s and earlier
Victorian Touch
P.O. Box 4
Micanopy, FL 32667
904-466-4022

Puzzles
Mechanical, dexterity types
Thomas M. Rogers Jr.
1466 W Wesley Rd.
Atlanta, GA 30327

Quilts
Artisons
Rte. 1, Box 20-C
Mentone, AL 35984
205-634-4037

Radio Premiums
Doug Moore
57 Hickory Ridge Cir.
Cicero, IN 46034
317-877-1741

Radios
Antique Radio Labs
James Fred
Rte. 1, Box 41
Cutler, IN 46920
Buy, sell and trade; repairs radio equipment using vaccuum tubes

Author of book
Harry Poster
P.O. Box 1883
S Hackensack, NJ 07606
201-410-7525
Also tvs, advertising items, old tubes, cameras, 3-D viewers & projectors, View-Master & Tru-View reels & accessories

Transister, novelty and character
Mickey Starr
2722 340th St.
Keokuk, IA 52632
319-524-1601

Railroadiana
Globe lantern frames and globes
Bill Cunningham
Plano, TX 75023
214-596-9646

Any item; especially china and silver
Grandpa White
1616 17th St., #267
Denver, CO 80202
303-892-1177

Lisa Nieland
1228 W Main St.
Red Wing, MN 55066
612-388-4027
Also steamship and other transportation memorabilia

Fred and Lila Shrader
Shrader Antiques
2025 Hwy. 199
Crescent City, CA 95531
707-458-3525
Also Buffalo, Shelley, Niloak and Hummels

Records
Especially 78s
L.R. 'Les' Docks
Box 691035
San Antonio, TX 78269-1035
Write for want list

Red Wing
Stoneware
Keith and Kevin Boline
BCC Enterprises
7811- 35th Ave. NE
Salem, OR 97303
503-393-0321
Also American gray graniteware, advertising tin lithographed pot scrapers

Lisa Nieland
1228 W Main St.
Red Wing, MN 55066
612-388-4027

Tom Tangen
2860 80th Ave.
Woodville, WI 45208
715-772-3205

Regal China
Van Tellingen, Bendel, Old MacDonald's Farm
Rick Spencer
3953 S Renault Cir.
West Valley, UT 84119
801-973-0805

Road Maps
Oil company or states
Noel Levy
P.O. Box 595699
Dallas, TX 75359-5699

Roselane Sparklers

Lee Garmon
1529 Whittier St.
Springfield, IL 62704

Rosemeade

NDSU research specialist
Bryce Farnsworth
1334 14½ St. S
Fargo, ND 58103
701-237-3597

Rowland and Marsellus

David Ringering
Salem, OR 97301
503-585-8253
Also other souvenir and historical china with scenes of tourist attractions from 1890 through the 1930s

Royal China

BA Wellman
88 State Rd. W, Homestead Farms #2
Westminster, MA 01473

Royal Copley

Author of book
Joe Devine
1411 3rd St.
Council Bluffs, IA 51503
712-323-5233 or 712-328-7305
Buy, sell or trade; also pie birds

Royal Doulton Tobies

John Harrigan
1900 Hennepin
Minneapolis, MN 55403
612-872-0226
Buy and sell

Royal Haeger and Royal Hickman

Author of book
Lee Garmon
1529 Whittier St.
Springfield, IL 62704

Ruby Glass

Author of book
Naomi L. Over
8909 Sharon Lane
Arvada, CO 80002
303-424-5922

Russel Wright

Author of book
Ann Kerr
P.O. Box 437
Sidney, OH 45365

Saloon Memorabilia

Author of book
Richard M. Bueschel
414 N Prospect Manor Ave.
Mt. Prospect, IL 60056
Phone or FAX 708-253-0791
Also trade stimulators and coin-op machines

Backbars
Greg Speiss
230 E Washington
Joliet, IL 60433
815-722-5639
Also fireplace mantels

Salt and Pepper Shakers

Joe Devine
1411 3rd St.
Council Bluffs, IA 51503
712-232-5233 or 712-328-7305

Pattern glass
Authors of book
Mildred and Ralph Lechner
P.O. Box 554
Mechanicsville, VA 23111

Figural or novelty; buy, sell and trade
Judy Posner
R.D. 1, Box 273
Effort, PA 18330
717-629-6583

Rick Spencer
3953 S Renault Cir.
West Valley, Utah 84119
801-973-0805

Schoolhouse Collectibles

Kenn Norris
P.O. Box 4830
Sanderson, TX 79848-4830

Scouting Collectibles

Author of book
R.J. Sayers
P.O. Box 629
Brevard, NC 28712

Sebastians

Blossom Shop Collectibles
112 N Main St.
Farmer City, IL 61842
800-842-2593

Sewing Collectibles

Leah and Walt Bird
P.O. Box 4502
Medford, OR 97501

Sewing Machines

Toy only; authors of book
Darryl and Roxana Matter
P.O. Box 65
Portis, KS 67474-0065

Shaving Mugs

John J. Bellew
15243 Profit Ave.
Baton Rouge, LA 70817
504-756-4875

David Giese
1410 Aquia Dr.
Stafford, VA 22554

Occupational
Burton Handelsman
18 Hotel Dr.
White Plains, NY 10605
914-428-4480

Occupational
Ed Meschi
R.R. 3, Box 550
Monroeville, NJ 08343
609-358-7293

Shawnee

John Hathaway
Rt. 2, Box 220
Bryant Pond, ME 04219

Rick Spencer
3953 S Renault Cir.
West Valley, UT 84119
801-973-0805

Shot Glasses

Author of book
Mark Pickvet
P.O. Box 90404
Flint, MI 48509

Silhouette Pictures (20th Century)

Author of book
Shirley Mace, Shadow Enterprises
P.O. Box 61
Cedar, MN 55011-066

Silver Plate
Rick Spencer
3953 S Renault Cir.
West Valley, UT 84119
801-973-0805

Snow Babies
Linda Vines
P.O. Box 721
Upper Montclair, NJ 07043
201-746-5206
Also candy containers, Steiff, Christmas, Halloween and other holiday items

Snow Domes
Author of book
Nancy McMichael, Editor
P.O. Box 53262
Washington, DC 20009

Chloe Ross
7553 W Norton Ave. #4
Los Angeles, CA 90046
213-874-3044

Soakies
Sue Sternfeld
90-60 Union Turnpike
Glendale, NY 11385

Soda Fountain Collectibles
Harold and Joyce Screen
2804 Munster Rd.
Baltimore, MD 21234
410-661-6765

Space-Related Memorabilia
Michael Mitchell
P.O. Box 192
Kents Hill, ME 04349-0192
207-897-6855

Sports Collectibles
Paul Longo Americana
Box 490, Chatham Rd., South Orleans
Cape Cod, MA 02662
508-255-5482
Also stocks and bonds

Robert Edward Auctions
P.O. Box 1923
Hoboken, NJ 07030
201-792-9324 or FAX 201-792-2469
Catalogs available

Sports Cards
Sally S. Carver
179 South St.
Chestnut Hill, MA 02167

Sports Pins
Tony George
22431-B160 Antonio Parkway #252
Rancho Santa Margarita, CA 92688
714-589-6075

Stangl
Birds, dinnerware, artware
Popkorn Antiques
Bob Perzel
P.O. Box 1057, 4 Mine St.
Flemington, NJ 08822
908-782-9631

Statue of Liberty
Mike Brooks
7335 Skyline
Oakland, CA 94611

Stauffer (Erich) Figures
Joan Oates
685 S. Washington
Constantine, MI 49042

Stereocards
Hollywood, Old Movie Theatres, World's Fairs, anything movie related
Chris Perry
306 Logenita Dr.
Palm Springs, CA 92264
619-325-4530

Sterling Silver
Also silverplate and souvenir spoons
Margaret Alves
84 Oak Ave.
Shelton, CT 06484

String Holders
Al Little
P.O. Box 288
Antioch, IL 60002

Swanky Swigs
M. Fountain
201 Alvena
Wichita, KS 67203
316-943-1925

Tea Leaf Ironstone
William Durham and William Galaway
615 S State St.
Belvidere, IL 61008
815-544-0577

Teapots and Tea-Related Items
Tina Carter
882 S Mollison
El Cajon, CA 92020

Telephones
Antique to modern; also parts
Phoneco
207 E Mill Rd., P.O. Box 70
Galesville, WI 54630

Tire Ashtrays
Jeff McVey
1810 W State St., #427
Boise, ID 83702

Tobacco Collectibles
Any related items
Chuck Thompson
P.O. Box 11652
Houston, TX 77293

Toothpick Holders
Antique, souvenir
Judy Knauer
1224 Spring Valley Lane
W Chester, PA 19380
601-431-3477

Torquay Pottery
Jerry and Gerry Kline
604 Orchard View Dr.
Maumee, OH 43539
419-893-1226

Toys
Aurora model kits, and especially toys from 1948-1972
Author of book
Bill Bruegman
137 Casterton Dr.
Akron, OH 44303

Model kits other than Aurora
Gordy Dutt
Box 201
Sharon Center, OH 42274-0201

Especially die-cast vehicles
Mark Giles
P.O. Box 821
Ogallala, NE 69153-0821

Lionel, American Flyer, Marx and other makes of trains; author of books
Bruce Greenberg
Greenberg Publishing Company, Inc.
Sykesville, MD 21784
410-795-4749

Tin litho, paper on wood, comic character, penny and Schoenhut
Wes Johnson, Sr.
106 Bauer Ave.
Louisville, KY 40207

Especially transformers and robots
David Kolodny-Nagy
3701 Connecticut Ave. NW #500
Washington, DC 20008
202-364-8753

Advertising, Hartland, Breyer, lunchboxes and character
Terri Mardis-Ivers
1104 Shirlee
Ponca City, OK 74601

Phil McEntee
Where the Toys Are
45 W Pike St.
Canonsburg, PA 15317
Also games

Doug Moore
57 Hickory Ridge Cir.
Cicero, IN 46034
317-877-1741

Slot race cars from 1960s-70s
Gary T. Pollastro
4156 Beach Dr. SW
Seattle, WA 98116

Charlie Reynolds
Reynolds Toys
2836 Monroe St.
Falls Church, VA 22042
703-533-1322

Especially from 1950s-60s
Rick Rowe, Jr.
Childhood, The Sequel
HC 1, Box 788
Saxon, WI 54559

Walkers, ramp-walkers, and wind-ups
Randy Welch
1100 Hambrooks Blvd.
Cambridge, MD 21613

Trade Cards
Rudisill's Alt Print Haus
Barbara and John Rudisill
24305 Waterview Dr.
Worton, MD 21678
410-778-9290

Trade Catalogs
An Antique Store
1450 W Webster
Chicago, IL 60614
312-935-6060 or FAX 312-871-6660

Author of book
Richard M. Bueschel
414 N Prospect Manor Ave.
Mt. Prospect, IL 60065
708-253-0791

Architectural related
Greg Speiss
230 E Washington
Joliet, IL 60433
815-722-5639

Tramp Art
Artisons
Rte. 1, Box 20-C
Mentone, AL 35984
205-634-4037
Also folk carvings and primitive arts

Trolls
Roger Inouye
2622 Valewood Ave.
Carlsbad, CA 92008-7925

TV Guides
TV Guide Specialists
Jeff Kadet
P.O. Box 20
Macomb, IL 61455

Twin Winton
Joe Devine
1411 3rd St.
Council Bluffs, IA 51503
712-232-5233 or 712-328-7305

Typewriter Ribbon Tins
Hobart D. Van Deusen
28 the Green
Watertown, CT 06795
203-945-3456

Typewriters
Jerry Propst
P.O. Box 45
Janesville, WI 53547-0045

Valentines
Katherine Kreider
Kingsbury Productions
4555 N Pershing Ave., Ste. 33-138
Stockton, CA 95207
209-467-8438

Van Briggle
Dated examples, author of book
Scott H. Nelson
Box 6081
Santa Fe, NM 87502
505-986-1176
Also UND (University of North Dakota), other American potteries

Vaseline Glass
Terry Fedosky
Rte. 1, Box 118
Symsonia, KY 42082

Vernon Kilns
Maxine Nelson
873 Marigold Ct.
Carlsbad, CA 92009

View-Master and Tru-View
Roger Nazeley
4921 Castor Ave.
Philadelphia, PA 19124

Reels, filmstrips, 3-D slides & equipment
Chris Perry
306 Logenita Dr.
Palm Springs, CA 92264
619-325-4530

Harry Poster
P.O. Box 1883
S Hackensack, NJ 07606
201-410-7525

Walter Sigg
3-D Entertainment
P.O Box 208
Smartswood, NJ 07877

W.J. Gordy or Georgia Art Pottery
Rudy Ferguson
Resaca Mall Antiques
3050 Hwy. 41 N
Resaca, GA 30735-0517
706-629-0035

Wade
Author of book
Ian Warner
P.O. Box 93022
Brampton, Ontario
Canada L6Y 4V8

Warwick
Any item or research materials; authors of book
Pat and Don Hoffman Sr.
1291 N Elmwood Dr.
Aurora, IL 60506
708-859-3435

Walking Sticks and Canes
Bruce Thalberg
23 Mountain View Dr.
Weston, CT 06883

Watch Fobs
Author of book
Margaret Kaduck
P.O. Box 260764
Cleveland, OH 44126

Watches
Character & personality; author of book
Howard S. Brenner
106 Woodgate Terrace
Rochester, NY 14625

All brands and character
James Lindon
5267 W Cholla St.
Glendale, AZ 85304
602-878-2409

Swatch
W.B.S. Marketing
P.O. Box 3280
Visalia, CA 93278

Watt Pottery
Author of book
Susan Morris
P.O. Box 708
Mason City, IA 50401

Rick Spencer
3953 S Renault Cir.
W Valley, UT 84119

Tom Tangen
2860 80th Ave.
Woodville, WI 54028
715-772-3205
Also Red Wing

Western Americana
Author of book
Warren R. Anderson
American West Archives
P.O. Box 100
Cedar City, UT 84720
801-586-9497
Also documents, autographs, stocks and bonds, and other ephemera

Documents
David M. Beach
Paper Americana
P.O. Box 2026
Goldenrod, FL 32733

Barry Friedman
22725 Garzota Dr.
Valencia, CA 91355

Especially Civil War items
K.C. Owings, Jr.
P.O. Box 19
N Abington, MA 02351
Also autographs, paper items

Gordon Totty
Scarce Paper Americana
347 Shady Lake Pkwy.
Baton Rouge, LA 70810
504-766-8625

Westmoreland
Westmoreland Glass Society Inc.
Jim Fisher
513 5th Ave.
Coralville, IA 52241

World's Fairs and Expositions
D.D. Woollard, Jr.
11614 Old St. Charles Rd.
Bridgeton, MO 63044
314-739-4662

Yard Long Prints
Also Long Ladies; author of book
William Keagy
P.O. Box 106
Bloomfield, IN 47424
812-384-3471

Authors of Book
Charles and Joan Rhoden
605 N Main
Georgetown, IL 61846
217-662-8046

Yellow Ware
Author of book
John and Barbara Michel
Americana Blue
200 E 78th St., 18E
New York City, NY 10021
212-861-6094
Also spongeware; architectural items and shooting gallery targets

Index